Augustus Schade, Rudolf Rocholl

The philosophy of history

Augustus Schade, Rudolf Rocholl

The philosophy of history

ISBN/EAN: 9783743322806

Hergestellt in Europa, USA, Kanada, Australien, Japan

Cover: Foto ©Suzi / pixelio.de

Manufactured and distributed by brebook publishing software
(www.brebook.com)

Augustus Schade, Rudolf Rocholl

The philosophy of history

THE
PHILOSOPHY OF HISTORY

BY

REV. A. SCHADE, PH. D.

BASED UPON THE WORKS OF
DR. R. ROCHOLL.

With rights obtained from the Author and Publisher of
the German Original.

1899.
A. SCHADE, Publisher.
1134–1138 Pearl St., Cleveland, O.

SYNOPTICAL INDEX.

CONTENTS.

SECOND DIVISION (I. B.) Operative Mode of History.

Powers dormant in nature-bound races—"Fluxion" of **Newton**—Life: process of self renewal—Import of rest, *i. e,* latent motion, as applied to ethnical movements: **Zoellner.**—Peoples with arrested cultures rest, preparatory to future activity, perhaps for purposes of reviving others—Contrast of expansive strain and condensive pressure; energy and apathy forming the tension of polarity; a synthetic formula, perhaps for the cognitions time and space. **Bowne.**

58　22.　Tranquil progress propelled by alternating counteractions in the undercurrents of hist.—Ethnical movements of this kind indicated by layers of languages—Physico-historic progress, straight line; cultural advance, wave-line—Circular movement tantamount to a standstill. **Culture advances in spiral-helically corresponding curves** wherein freedom comes to its right—Hist. not calculable from statistical figures—Materialistic concept of hist. without analogy in the laws of mechanics. **Lotze**—Free will as against blind "fate"—Under aspect of "dynamics" hist. remains incomprehensible, because man is not the product of the elements.

60　**IV Ch.　Means of Historic Development.　Mind's Interaction.—**

23.　Distinguishing movement from development, which only pertains to organic life—Evolution limited by decadence and decomposition—Ascent and descent in organic life: **arch-line**—Permanent disposition (national temperament, etc.) in the ethnical world: **horizontal lines**—These lines are of partly natural inclinations and partly real mind life intersected by **vertical line:** men excelling in energy and ingenuity—**Guizot's** definition of civilisation—Natural and historical evolution analogous—**La Place's** theory: detachment, departure towards self hood—Tendency of the purpose unfolding itself—Differentiation caused by division of labor among specially adapted organs—In the tendency to selfhood the character of membership is never lost, not even in the highest developed organism.

62　24.　In the social differentiation the organism becomes an organisation—Genesis of nationalities—Three periods of physico-psychical development—First: colonial life; folk-lore—Cultural degree of the future nations depends upon higher or mean recognition 'of the deity, to which every detail of existence is related—Second: Traditions distorted, symbols of primitive truths and of subsequent picture-thinking misunderstood, will cause 1, idolatry; 2, mythology—Relative good in nature made a surrogate for the Supreme Good—Perversion of inner remnants of religiousness finally renders most abject depravity religious—Reminiscences of human unity applied in founding world-empires—Third: Authority questioned—Thoughtful people withdraw from the masses—Subjectivism; Class-hatred—Invention of an indifferent deity—Differentiation outruns itself—The purpose safe with certain barbarians—**Limit of natural, cultural development,** analogous to plant-life, which includes decline—**The line drawn where the deepest** but empiric relations to the world of "formal unity" begin—New series of development, pertaining to religious life, the most personal matter—Attention to be chiefly engaged with the results of the interaction betw. physico-historical and purely personal development.

65　**V Ch.　Plan of History.**

25.　Reason in hist ; sense to be adduced from without—Plan not to be discovered by analysing co-efficients, but by way of logics, *i. e.* by establishing their relations—Illustr : Architect, plan, building, and beholder—Motif and plan (design) inherent in plant-life—So in hist. plan partly inherent, self-developing; partly exterior objective guidance—1 Part of the plan inherent; provided there is one typical man conveying within him the type and design of hist. which is but man unfolded; provided, possibilities of abnormal development—2 Part of the plan in thought, objective; "Fore-thought" the postulate of reason.

BOOK SECOND.

71　Syllabus.

II. A.　Turano-Malayans, Ugro-Tatars.　II. B.　Aryans: Hindo-Iranians, Graeco-Romans, Indo-Germans.　II. C.　Mediterranean Basin; Cushito-Semites; Hebrews.　II. D.　Concentric Middle.　Theme of Hist. appears at the Divide of the Times.　Solution of all problems.　Pivot-point of History.　II. E.　Roman orbit: pervaded by Christianity.　II. F.　Indo-Europeans, transformed under strains of orient-occidental forms of consciousness.　II. G.　Age of celerity and of Missions.　Æra of organising the realm of unity, perpetuity and perfection.

The plan evinced through history indicates this arrangement of the hist. material.

FIRST DIVISION. (II. A.) Great Pre-Historic Substructure of History. Polarities.

First Circle of Nations: Turanians.

74　**I Ch.　Scenery: 1. Celestial Background.**

26.　Man related to the celestial as well as to terrestrial worlds; issue of both and center of the universe—Illustr: Pyramid—Mind, history, heaven—Sidereal conditions directly bearing upon human interests—Man with his story and the visible universe committed to each other—His central position not fortified by the illusory idea of inhabitable stars; neither weakened by quantitative insignificance—Thought more than equivalent to the vastness of dimensions—Man the microcosm as contemplated by the natural philosophy of by-gone times: Zodiac, Kabala—Experiments leading **Kepler** to the "equation of the center."

75　27.　Cosmos, the reflex of the higher world of true reality, a system of substantialised thought—**Kant's** categories, the regulative and eternal laws of thinking imprinted into the cosmos—The precipitate of thought—The universe, despite its nascency, consists of mere stuff in dead motion—Spectral analysis, the "chemistry of the heavens:" "world of material unity"—Unprofitable hypothesis of the inhabitability of the stars not harmless—A better hypothesis—Earth man's own universe, belonging to him—The blossom of creation and its crown—Human body is the scion of heaven and earth, hence both influence history.

II Ch. Stage-scenery: Terrestrial Back-ground.   77

28. La Place's hypothesis: continual detachment; differentiation the fixed tendency of nature—Formation of the globe; Werner—The earth's history repeats itself in history proper, but no further than human biography is involved in nature's nascency.

29. The globe firm, its surface still changing; Lyell—History interested in the articulate   78 formation of the earth's surface, to a certain extent—Teleological view upon the geographical differentiation—Ritter's overzealous teleology—Formation of Asia and Africa—Riddles of anthropography.

30. Remarkable instances of symmetry—African-Asiatic axis—The two Americas—This   79 symmetry has no significant bearing upon hist.—Axis of the Asiatic-European system of mountains and African-Asiatic chain of deserts—Common axis poising upon Bolor-Tagh—System of oceans—Articulation of coast-line—Three Mediterranean gulfs.

III Ch. Remnants of Pre-historic Man. Locality of his Origin.   81

31. Chinese apperception as to the universe—Astral, mundane, historic sphereoids—"Fossil man." Lyell—Man's existence in the tertiary period not established—Darwinistic "Descent of man" refuted; J. Ranke. Virchow—Better to meditate upon "destiny of man"—Lake-dwellers. Keller—Stone, bronze, iron ages—Definite chronology irrelevant.

32. Region most favorable to evolution—Untenable suppositions—One common origin—   82 Pure fountain-head. Racial changes—"Lemuria" affirms the scientific postulate of one common home.

33. Humanity a connection not a collection—Our method in the search after the "Syn- 83 thesis;" Illustr. lock and key—Unity of the race axiomatic conclusion from induction—Full knowledge possible, despite Hamilton.

IV Ch. Original man. One common Source. Language, Right, Religion.   84

34. Proofs of unity of the human family—One original language—After nature had assumed its present form, development continued solely in the invisible world of mind-life. Identity of American Indians with Asiatics proves unity of humanity—"Meander crosses"—Common mental endowments insufficient to explain prefixes, suffixes, etc.—Import of Sanskrit: M. Muller on Pentecost—Import of missionary work upon philology: Klaproth—One universal language to be anticipated—Idea of right possessed by all men—Universality of religiousness bespeaks the oneness of humanity—M. Mueller on "Origin of Religion"—Imagination (source of religion ?) never surpasses the compass of perception—Want creates no consciousness of the Divine, but reminiscence of the Good does—Self-made religion."Dog-philosophy" Kingsley (Hypatia)—Religion the basis of every culture.

35. Hypothetical: "God is"-Origin of religion in a positive thought-Ontogeneity—Found- 87 ed in empiricism—Not a matter of mere intellect—God keeps on speaking terms with man—Conscientious promptings not of natural growth, not from centrifugal tendency which they oppose—Conscience not in the first place the religious, but moral phase of consciousness—Re-cognition of the "image"—Religion revealed from the central source; natural religion starts from the circumference—False premises of evolution as to religion—It makes its way through hist. as a principle of personality, in the direction of concentric intensification—Postulate of one typical person—Illustr: Key-stone bearing all the strain of the cross-vault.

V Ch. A First Man. The Hieroglyph of History.—   89

36. Alone in him may solution of life's problems be found—Bridge between two worlds—Key to history,"the web in which necessity forms the warp and freedom the woof"—One first man as feasible as the proto-plasm in the interest of natural science; the postulate not an unscientific demand in the interest of humanism—Symbolic presentation of the postulate at the entrance of various nations into history.

37. The spiritual constituent of the first man must be the microcosm of the spiritual world—Mind: 90 illustr. by the dim light in a treasury vault; Fortlage—Zschokke's "Central Vision"—The "soul" is more than what we are conscious of—Duality of mind's relations causes two forms of consciousness: "Reflecting" and "unreflected" (or sub-) consciousness—Both sides generically different—Illustr: two adjoining rooms—Head; heart; the place of contact with the spiritual world—Anthropology of Fichte.

38. Phenomena of abnormal condition of nerves—Man passive under mysterious powers, 93 a patient—"Rudimentary" faculties dormant in human nature: visionary flash; ecstatic grasp—"Telepathy"—Development pledged, short only of absolute perfection—In what sense man is created perfect—The gifts delineate the ethical process, prescribe man's ethical task. (Gaben-Aufgaben)--Man to elevate nature—Engaged in setting free nature's potentialities, man's own are set free.

39. Practicing at the apparatus in co-operation and concurrence with the divine plan 95 overt in nature—Man to deliver confined life to his own advantage—Task and significance of true culture—The goal of complete transformation—The calamity of the fall not to be blamed upon the duality of the mind—Polarity betw. nature and spirit works beneficently after the fall—Polarity betw. masculine and feminine principles latent in first man—Man less perfect and more natural than what Lotze imagined—Questions not to be solved unless full self-knowledge has been gained, which begins with the consciousness of the effects of the fall, and becomes complete when the issues of the conflict appear—Instead of unity and quality we are confronted by a multiplicity in conflict—Full recognition of man's wretchedness only possible at a point where depravity becomes undeniable and inexcusable.

VI Ch. The Great Calamity and the Catastrophes.

96

40. Nature of the bad—Confined life of nature-bound people—**Bastian**—Preparation for the answer which lies in that which "ought not to be:"(**Schelling**)—Matter not the cause of the trouble—Immanency of thought in substance thrown out of balance—Nature insubordinate to man—Rent through the human soul extends throughout nature—Conditions in nature and nations defying every idea of purposeness—Gloomy moods of mind echo the reproachful sighings of the creature—Mysterious phenomena of darkness—**Cazotte's** predictions—Human sacrifices not explicable from natural grounds—Droysen on sin—The lie—The Bad living off the good proves its reality—Refutations of false tenets concerning the bad, which is not the foil rendering the Good the more brilliant—**Leibnitz**—**Schelling**.

99

41. Origin of the Bad—"**Anxious suspense**"; **Lotze**—Pseudo-culture attempts to neutralise the reproaches of conscience—Denial makes sin more dangerous, aggravates guilt—Conscience is but manifesting the right of the Good to reclaim man for participating in the enjoyment of its reality, but demands expiation—Physical origin of the Bad—**Buckle; Droysen.**—Referring it to the moral realm; **Rothe**—Indestructibility of moral elements—**Materialism** attempts to destroy ideals, to supplant other regulatives; failing therein it serves the firmer to establish **the Good, the Beautiful and the True**—What the Bad is not—It is a will—What the Good is—Features of the perverse will; investigation as to its origin postponed—Depravity of human nature is alien to its essence; belongs not to its type—Great rupture a historical fact, which must have occured in the spiritual, not the sensuous part of existence; in consciousness prior to the confusion of languages—**Schelling**—Spiritual relation torn asunder—God-consciousness utterly corrupted—Humanity fell into the sphere where detachment is the order of things—The catastrophe which must have preceded the dispersion—The old way of explaining heathenism: **Burnouf**—**Brugsh**—**Ebrard**—**Cushing**—**Prescott**—**W. v. Humboldt**—Savagery not the primitive state.

102

42. Indications of the great **calamity**—Remnants of original God-consciousness; overshadowed by world-consciousness gained in the diversions of worldly culture—Weakened remnants, yet strongly remind man of returning from centrifugal diversions to center; they alone warrant a reunion of the human family—**Apostasy** originated in the spiritual side—Its consequences: losses—"**Con-tent-ment**" gone—Rent through man's inner nature extends to nature's totality—**Deification of the secondary good—Polytheism:** exertions in self-salvation—Traditions, "family-heirlooms," etc. mixed into self-made religions—Heathendom ancient and modern—Genesis of **pantheism**—Gnosticism the transitory step betw. polytheism and pantheism, which attempts to restore the lost union by natural generalness—Confessions of humanity in its sacred writings.

104

43. Empiric proofs of centrifugal and downward inclinations—Visible things seem nearer and more necessary—Secondary good not at fault in the disappointments—**Certain frightful shadows arise** from the demoralised duality of the inner nature—Idols inadvertently established as "**centers of cohesion;**" hence polytheism instrumental in self-preservation—Remembrances of original unity, of dominion, of "something better;" of immortality—After objectivising all possible idiosyncracies the **state and its representative is deified**—Personality lost with the knowledge of one personal God—The apostasy neither physical nor rational, but moral, outward evils resulting not bad but salutary, as disciplinary measures—Religious undercurrents determine the shape of every age and nation—Environments assist in molding character—Man under the law of natural necessity—Influences from transeunt worlds of light and darkness—Necessary to discriminate betw. the influential factors.

105

VII Ch. Genesis of Mythological Religiousness.

44. In refutation of "evolved" religion—Natural science illicitly appropriates principles alien to it—Conditions of formulating theories on mythology; **Adrian**—Perverted traditions, ruins of primitive revelations **mixed** with fear of ghosts, with misconceived inner remnants of God-consciousness and corrupted external traditions—Religious cravings to be satisfied by acts, not ideas—Remnants of truth always separable from superstitious perversions—Discrepancies betw. life and thought call forth reflections upon them—Esoteric theories to keep the masses in subjection—**Religio-historic** memory awakens, rendering nations historical; **only then are myths formulated**—All forms of life arranged in conformity with the conception of the deity—Historic nations alone have myths with distinctive ingredients—**Myths not parental to religion**—As truths are interspersed with superstitions, so superstition always clings to advanced culture which is never able to abolish it.

107

45. Fear produces no deities but demons—Genesis of Shamanism: in comparison with the sorcery, fetishism and most debased form of ancestor-worship mythical religion is far in advance—Fear not the parent of faith! Feeling of an unknown God called forth fear—**Shintoism**, the primitive form of ancestor-worship; witnessing to original knowledge of immortality—Shamanism, corruption of the former, spreads as demonolatry and snake-worship, infects all subsequent mythology—Fetishism, snake-worship in India; **Schlagintweit**; in America: **Peet**; Necromancy—"**Feidicos**" of the Portugese; **M. Mueller**—Hob-goblins—Fetishism in the church not of biblical, but of Hamito-Semitic origin—**Instances of such travesties** upon ecclesiastical religiousness: **Motley; M. Mueller; Ranke**—Snake-worship brought to America by black, red, yellow and white men—No human being below salvation despite such aberrations.

110

46. Materialistic monism, deifies force-substance, disparages and depreciates personal life—Malthusian theory and Darwinism: related to feticism and feticide—**Virchow and Tyndall** discountenance socialism as the practical attempt to supplant Christianity by its dogmatistical world-theory—Evolutionism, superstitious in itself, is not qualified to displace superstition—Intellectualism utilized in, and hated for its class-rule—Psychical and traditional elements in the quasi-religion of fear: night, death, the serpent—Myths are but attempts at

—Mind surrenders in despair to fear of death and ghosts— Tradition of sacrifice turned into dreadful rites; tradition about the serpent turned into demonolatry of Shamanism —Vestiges of monotheism in sacred traditions and inner reminiscences preserve cultural aspirations, create historic sense—Traces of truth in traditional religiousness and their subversions—**Speculative heathenism brings forth pantheism, the systematised compromise with polytheism**— The object of applied pantheism—Hieratic rule in Hlassa; **Prschewalsky.**

133   56. Resume: Mongolian world-consciousness in art—Mechanical activity—Æsthetical products excite abhorrence—Patriarchal authority perverted into despotism–Rousseau, Guizot. Drilling by state-machinery—**State-theocracies**—Abject servility, enuring nations to endure oppression—Lessons drawn from Chinese culture—Misanthropy-**Dangers of identifying religion with cold intellectualism**--Man treated as a natural force causes anarchistic explosions—Fundamental error in any pantheistic world-theory—Clannishness—Substratum of West-Aryan culture.

SECOND DIVISION, (II B.) Second Circle of Nations. Aryans.

136
Syllabus.
   Nations reared upon the natural basis of the first circle—Pamir regions—Controversies as to the home of the Aryans—Yenissei-inscriptions, pre-Mongolian?—**Iwanowsky's** similar inscriptions south of the Altai—**Richthofen and Jadrinzew** meet the objections as to climatic conditions of the Pamir.

137   **I Ch. Orient, Right Wing. Southern Part: 1. Hindoos.**
   57. Separation from Iranians—Rig-veda—Brahmins —Kapila philosophises—Priests forbid warriors to approach the gods without their intercession—Mahabharada—Sanskrit literature—Aryan life born under pains of religious misunderstandings—Four periods: 1. **Varuna,** monotheistic—Guilt vividly felt—Knowledge of man's dual nature— 2. **Indra:** esoteric, polytheistic—Phases of nature personified, ancestor-worship—Reading of scriptures forbidden— Liturgical rites—Pantheism-compromise betw. esoteric theology and philosophy— 3. **Brahma.** Atma-Choda: world soul—Religion rationalised, intellectualism—Identity-philosophy: Choda-Nirwana—Pantheism invites oppression—Mysticism associates with scepticism to oppose priestly arrogance—Ethics of the Bhagavad-Gita—Subjectivism— 4. **Sutra**—Sectarianism, vulgar polytheism—Three chief systems: 1. Yoga— 2. Njaja: **Buddhism:** Kanada, atomistic; Vedanta, monistic— 3. Sankhyia, dualistic; Prakriti: metempsychosis, from which Nirwana is deemed the salvation; Purranas—Hindooism not the stage of awakening God-consciousness, but the stage of its expiring—Mental-spiritual activity mistaken for spirituality and religion—God the substance from which the universe emanates, matter the substance from which the mind evolves—Felicity of agnosticism.

142   58. **Buddhism Dismantled.** Buddha: St. Jehoshaphat—Burnouf—Lassen—"Light of Asia" Arnold—Pessimism—**Orientalism disseminated**—Heartlessness of nature-bound men—Scene on the Ganges—Human life thrown away to deified crocodiles: for conscience's sake—Hindu-mind analysed; destitute of historic sense—Products of phantasy—Even mathematical sciences in the garb of poetry—A fancy-world—Phantasmagories represented in baroque style of pagodas— Weird phenomena rise from the occult substratum—Intellectualism unable to cope with superstition, of which the educated partake—Anthropophagy of Fakirs in Benares—Phenomena not explicable on natural grounds—Criterion of ethical value and ethnical temperament of a nation given in its religion—Indestructible remnants of original religiousness—Recapitula-
146 tion: **Incarnation.**

   II Ch. Aryans of the Orient, Right Wing. Northern Part: 2. Persians.
   59. Iran—Friends of Varuna-Indra separate from those of Mithra—Remnants of common traditions—Religious cause of estrangement: Hindoos:deva, deus—Persians: dews, devils— Characters at variance—Ahuramazda, monotheistic—Resistance of the bad—Indra and Hindoos more to Greek taste; Mithra and Persians akin to Roman trend of mind—Universal humanism propagated: Zend-Avesta (**Spiegel**) in contrast with Hindooish all-the-sameness—Dualism: To fight Angromaingus, ideal of warfare—Truthful and chaste—Cause of cultural collapse: significance of the bad minimised, by objectivizing it—Moral strictness gives way to extravagance and effeminacy—Centralisation of power changes national character—**Cyrus going to worship**—His retinue to picture the **Heavenly Kingdom**—Absence of temple ruins—The spiritually transcendental; conceived as immanent in historic reality—Susa-Sardes—Zoroästers religion corrupted —Parsism—**Nestorians influential**—Ormuzd revived—Merits of Persian culture—No brooding over the chasm betw. matter and mind, but fighting the bad—Summary: Inductive data from East-Aryan life—Anticipation of the Divine as condescending to dwell in this sinful world,
149 which Asia views from points of **Transcendentalism.**

   III Ch. Occident, Left Wing of Aryans. I. Greeks.
   60. Wardens of remnants of universal revelation. Hamito-Semitic wedge driven in betw. Aryans. **Wasks** –Lake dwellers–**Celts** (in Ægypt under Marmaiu ?)—**Slaves** (Vandals) Folk-lore—Land in common possession. **Germans:**—Teutons, Goths, Franks, Saxons, Norsemen. Southern Europeans:—**Pelasgian** legends divulge fear of inraids from Asia—**Hellenes** fit their central position, appropriating, systematising, distributing the issues of ancient cultures. Rites transplanted from Babylon to Dodona. Trade with Britons—Colonies. First encounter with Punic avidity: Syracuse.—**Civil liberty a new phenomenon.** Centralisation of government resented. Constitutional rights. Confederacies.

153   61. Free position of man, whom scientific thought delivers from a belief in astral decrees of fate—Ionic School—Analysis of personal life —Mythology. Self-projections of the agile mind. **Symbols of deities to represent the reality of ideals**—Centers of cohesion, symbolising the differentiation of world-consciousness.

vit made to Augustus' apotheosis—Ægypt in him celebrates the "Redeeming" god. Emperor-mania. Pliny—Imitation of Persia; Plato's "ideal state" idolised; whereby the occidental mind is permanently imbued with orientalism—Man-god preferable to the contemporaneous beast-god—To save humanity from falling into fetishism, man fell rather back upon self-adoration, rediscovering the postulate of oneness.

175   79. History tends to carry out the principle of unification—Human nature gravitates to large national organisms which warrant social order and security of customary existence—Also to carry out the idea of dominion—Perverse nations disqualified to continue—Wrong apperceptions of dominion and liberty miscarry—Uniformity the leading idea of Roman polity—Ancient monarchies fail to establish this unity.

II Ch. Disintegration of State-Theocracy.

176   80. Genesis of subjectivism and cosmopolitanism—Intellect at work in Alexandria—Rome the apparatus for setting free the components of the ethnical compound—Hellenism to conduct the isolation—Greek thought furnishes the "Word"—Neither sinister cults nor higher culture, nor annihilating national peculiarities of the vanquished would avail as a solvent power to disintegrate the lumps of theocratic affinities—Gods and "Courts of Heaven" being abolished, state unity fell asunder—Personality gained was overstrained—Subjectivism Futile attempts to reconstruct society from Plato to Alexandrian doctrinarians—Theorists propose cosmopolitanism as a solace for lost nationality—Dissatisfaction no bad sign of times. State once built into the frame of religion: now theory of a mental cosmos built into the ruins of the state—Hellenism spreads comopolitanism—Alexandrian book-trade—International learnedness observable for the first time.

179   81. Thoughtfully and filled with doubts the Graeco-Roman world goes down—Buddhism and scepticism—Causes of decay—Platonism the conductor of the oriental views of life to Rome—Analysis of Stoicism. It affects contempt of earthly conditions, evaporates personality into generalness, lauds in Hindu pessimism. When sympathy for suffering fellow-citizens is appealed to, it is convenient to act the cosmopolitan—Stoicism powerful through state-officials throughout the Roman world-orbit—Cicero—Areios. Import of Alexandria: Serapeion—Ray of light watched falling upon the lips of the idol—Philo, the Hebrew—Sum and substance of Aryan progress.

III. Ch. Cushito—Semitic Nations.

180   82. Necessity of merging oriental transcendentalism with occidental immanency. Extremes met but would not mingle in the Roman crucible—Semitic predisposition for intermediating—Semites and Cushites located, and to be discriminated—Hommel.

181   83. Substratum, a people of Uralo—Altaic descent. Cave-dwellers—Akkado-Sumerian fetishism—Lenormant.—Babylonian antiquities vary from Assyrian, bear marks of Cushite origin—Elam—Susania—Discoveries at Kuyundshik—Layard. Akkadian culture corroborates biblical records—Pre-Semitic Shamanistic substratum, source of conjury—Kings of Ur—Psalms of contrition—Formula of exorcism—Sumero-Akkadian rites brought from Mongolian regions to Mesopotamia, Schrader.

182   84. Monotheism preceded Cushitic rites: Chaldean culture—Man's dual nature recognized—The fall—The flood—Divine ancestors fighting the "dragon"—Delitzsch—Yearning for forgiveness of sins—Assyro-Babylonian art—Templar architecture in Babylon, palatial in Ninive—Art not idolatrous—Letters to Tel el Amarna.

182   85. Ægypt's culture of Mesopotamian extraction—Nature determining the history of the Ægyptians—Ritter—Climate, temples and tombs preservatory to relics of Ægyptian thought and life—A mixture of races—Bunsen, Brugsch, J. G. Miller—Cushites form the substratum—Nahasu-Amu, the Celtes?—Faidherbes.

183   86. Monotheism of Ægyptian esoterics—"Book of the Dead."—V. v. Strauss—The enneat—Paut-Thot-the Thought—Brugsch—Trias of Maspero, Champilion—Disk-heresy of the Amenophises—"Judgment of the Dead"—Keeps consciousness of guilt, and cognition of responsibility and immortality vivid—Resume: High merit of this culture—The crop raised from the wild seed in the subsoil—Scene in the Serapeion—Clemens Alexandrinus—Snake-worship—Apis-tombs—Combination of two religions represented in human figures with beast's heads—Human figure free from pillar, but wall still attached.

184   87. Art never excels the cult underlying it—Death personified everywhere, mirrors the stability of theocratic rule—Character and inner life of man better understood than in Greek art—Overbeck—Even death under orders of deified royalty—Tirhaka's picture at Medinet Abu, Roscellini—Names of unpopular rulers erased—Attempts at reforms by Amenophis IV: Pharao of the Exodus; Wilkinson—Tablets of Tel el Amarna—Domestic life described in pictures—Brugsch-Marietta—Present Ægypt under the same geographical conditions.

186   88. Phenician Semites acting as dissolvents upon Aegyptian culture—Came from Sumer-Akkad to the coast; transmitted the most pronounced and worst traits of Cushite elements; adopt Melkart cult from Ægypt—Obscenity of templar rites—Bal, Kamosh, Moloch; Ashera-Lucian—Movers—Mylitta—Abomination spreads—Phenician adapted to worldly intercourse, to act the dissolvent—Overreach the Aryans in mercantile traffic, which they monopolise upon small strips of sea coasts—Finally vanquished mentally through Greek thought, and by main force of the Romans—Retribution upon "Punic faith," Moloch and Mammon.

187   89. Chaldeans: Primeval monotheism—Ur:Mugheir—Maspero—Larsa, sanctuary of the sun-god—Most ancient seat of learning.

IV Ch. The Hebrew Community.

187   90. Representing the centralising and solvent power—Despised because of their peculiar-

ities—Polity of all nations hinges upon the sociology of the twelve tribes—Situation of the Holy Land,a foothold upon earth for this household—The only nation in the Roman basin not completely crushed—Their pride of pedigree;clannishness—This nation and its book which is not "the product of the national spirit"—Covenant under conditions—Sin and Grace—Special revelation.

91. Historic-natural basis of Mosaic legislation, Egyptian externals —Sychronology— 189 Discovery of Monotheism—Israel a small group of the decaying Semites, surviving disasters all around—Its hope and sobriety—No extolling of heroes.   Niebuhr—Unique position of "Prophecy"—Revealed as against mythical cosmogonies. Steinthal.

92. Absence of plastic art—Qualified only to receive and to keep, "the Secret" Contrast 190 with other nations concerning the past and future—Not intoxicated by naturalistic progress, because cognisant of the historic future.   Lotze—Disciplinary purpose of the "decalogue"—Trust in divine promises—Israel pardoned and burdened—Proclamation of conciliation of real exist-ence with final destiny—Prophecy in the negative work against erroneous expectations of the kingdom; positive task in fore-casting the figure of the "Servant of God". Inspiration.

93. Resume of Semitic culture (Renan) in comparison with the Aryan—Grill on Hebrew 192 etymology—Old Testament catholicity, understood by very few intensely pious minds—Jews in the diaspora impress the gentile world with their hope—The Rabbi of Alexandria bent upon a compromise.

FOURTH DIVISION. (II. D.) The Divide of the Times.

Syllabus.

94. Postulate of the "Synthesis" 1. Logic of hist. not a theory but a fact—Synthesis is 194 not a syllogism but a person. 2. Death postulates a cosmical Mediator—Sacrifice in the nations upon the periphery and in that of the center—Founding a new humanity.

I Ch. Intermediation Logically Postulated. The Historical Synthesis.

95. Survey of educational factors in the Roman basin. Greek thought (Alexandria the 195 observatory) and Roman law. Hellenism tinctured with Hindooism. Goal: to bridge the chasm betw. the finite and the infinite. Historic postulate from empirics.

96. Remnants of original God-consciousness in emotion and intellect (anxious sus- 196 pense) utilised to cultivate receptivity for "something better."   Cultural development con-sonant with the nature of the national cults—Intellectualism unable to uproot superstition— Higher classes prove to degrade religiously. The lowly people not always of mean character.

97. Incessant polar strain betw. east and west—Buddhism an ingredient in the crucible 197 Heracleitos' pessimism—Juvenal—Systematised agnosticism demands two impossibilities— Stoa —A theory tends to embody itself in an organisation.

98. Philosophy of despair as to all reality is unable to invent a God present in the 200 world—Pantheistic generalness and political oppression. Only a false conception of either Buddhism or Christianity could once have taken Platonism and Stoicism as transitory approach-es to Christianity. Idea of incarnation not so much a logical postulate as an emotional antici-pation—Two aberrations: "Sorrow of this world" or "abandonment to carnal pleasure." Facts foreshadowing the Incarnation. The shape which the force of human longings took in Greek mythology.

99. Comparison betw. Hellenistic and Hindoo anticipations: Hindoo mind in nature's 201 embrace, materializes the gods and evaporates the world; Greek embraces nature, humanises it and the gods are objectivised men—Divinations as to the unification betw. God and the world in Rome as compared with those of Greece—Man to become divine—Extremes of Benares and Rome meet—Decree of the universal census—Balancing accounts in the Roman clearing-house.

100. Semitic ingredient as to incarnation—Monotheistic law and Jewish tradition— 203 Philo's compromise betw. revelation and gnostic ecclecticism—Heinze, Keferstein.—Philo endeavors to render Judaism acceptable to everybody; whereby its catholicity becomes con-spicuous for the first time.

101. Oriental and occidental postulates of the incarnation dove-tailed, the terminus of 204 reasoning in this respect—Discrepancies in Plato's and Philo's theorisings: impure matter ill adapted to become the vehicle of personified holiness—Philo's merit. Plan and purpose in unison throughout physical life, whilst in personal life each person has the purpose in itself and the design becomes destiny remaining outside the person—Plan in hist. in general, pur-pose individualising as the task, to work out the common destiny.

102. Review of empiric, inductive data in proof of the correctness of deductive syllogising. 205 —Equation of contrasts and strains betw.the antitheses of oriental idealism and occidental real-ism the historic necessity—Theoretical conclusions that the combination of the theses may prove the key spoken of. This conclusion is drawn and forms the postulate of pre-Christian history—Mode in which alone the Synthesis can realise itself.

103. Logic of hist. demands the solution of the problems through a fact, a person. Plato 207 demonstrates the necessity of the effects of personal incarnation to become universal—Philo's and Plato's postulates combined include a third one: perfect union betw. Deity and humanity in one real man. This mode of the Logos' entering the world under historical conditions is the stumbling block of gnosticism—Refutation of modern attempts at solving the problem in worse than ancient style.

II. Ch. Intermediation Postulated Physically. The Sacrifice.

104. The Infinite to take the initiative in assuming finite forms of existence at a certain 208 time and proper locality—Preparation for, and appreciation of the Advent—Social misery—

2

Unavailing devices on the score of reforms. Attempts at self-salvation render matters worse —The delusion that the state is the Supreme Good in the last resort vanishes—Ancient culture collapses—The nativity.

209   105. The singular ordinance of Prophecy a fact as well as a miracle, not interpretable from pragmatic inferences—Unparalleled hist. of the chosen people: clearly designed to remain typical for every human heart: under pressure—Disclosures upon Golgatha—Solution of all problems, affirmation of all suppositions here made—Synthesis locked—Parusia and judgment according to terms here stipulated—Zend Avesta, Seyfarth. Voices from heathendom not necessary in proof of the everlasting significance of this Self-Sacrifice. Its bearings upon the cosmos—Necessity of the redeemer's death—Wailings reverberating through all nations because of death.

210   106. Guilt to be propitiated, demanded by the universal order of things. Absolute justice of retribution universally acknowledged in the promptings to offer sacrifices—Sacrifices expiatory under conditions—Vicarious atonement. Effective for those only who submit to the reasonable, simple conditions of the New Covenant—Man judged or acquitted according to the attitude taken towards the atoning sacrifice. Evidences of guilt and the necessity of expiation —Juvenal, Movers, Preller. Cosmical conditionalities remain in full force wherever redemption is rejected.

212   107. The great atonement foreshadowed in many perversions of the idea of sacrifice— Solidarity of human sin and guilt -Dorner—Human sacrifices. Voluntary self denials for the welfare of others—Sophocles. Victims of calumny—Animal sacrifices—Lassaulx.

213   108. Sacrifice means:"Man's being in earnest about religion"--Wuttke—All sacrifices but foreshadowings of the divinely appointed sacrifices of the Old Testament, which in turn were typical of this one sacrifice in which the typical ones are abated. The "Son of Man" the central figure of the entire cosmos—Incarnation and atonement in their significance for mankind--The Crucifixion. Appropriation of the saving effects to transpire upon the historic lines demarcated by the Testator—Historical, but transeunt—by faith alone. Understanding the process of renovation escapes scientific demonstration but not personal experience. The reason of this secrecy. As unnecessary for mental schematising as it is impossible and un-necessary for finite beings to become absolute.

215   109. Retrospect from the position "under the Cross"--Knowledge of the Triune God and of creation restored—God the Father of men solely with reference to salvation—True self-knowledge--Paradise; apostasy—God's purpose being challenged the universe was to keep its course to preserve the purpose and act as its means as against human arbitrariness, aberra-tions and satanic mystifications--"Sicut deum eritis"—Total subversion of original God-consciousness—The"gods"were projections of anguish: because ghostly phantoms haunt the fratricide —Cause of the bad not revealed: it betrays itself—Causality of sin in a world of spirits--Sinner not a devil himself; else man would be irredeemable. His nobility still the essence of his being.

218   110. Traditional knowledge of the deplorable calamity neither mythical nor superstitious —Evidences of deep and dark undercurrent otherwise inexplicable—Satan's fury at becoming exposed--Prince of darkness betrays himself in his imitating God and mystifying revelation —Word of God and his preachings verified by the manner in which the lie and the bad are provoked—Taking sides with Satan—Demonology not to be skipped over--Dorner.

219   111. Aid of metaphysics indispensable—Language witnesses against evolution from depravity upwards—Abstract parts of speech fixed first." O. Miller—Languages weakening —Burnouf—"Products of degeneracy"—Martius. Lepsius. Von Loehen.

220   112. A glance afforded into the background of the hist. drama, from whence the effects of the bad issue and become observable. The bad is in the plan of hist—Dorner—The Savior's method of relieving humanity of the effects of Satan's workings—Death in its empiric form— Effects of the apostasy upon nature —Man's dual nature—Possibility of death—First principle from which alone the cognition of objective and authoritative duty can be derived--Dorner—Necessity of the ethical process of healing the break betw. spirit and body by means of the soul.

222   113. Principal constituents of human nature in conflict signifying severance of the two spheres of existence to the extent of abnormal relations—Chasm betw. cosmical life and the sphere of "essential unity" goes through human nature in the first place and means--death. Man stretched out as upon a cross: above and below, right and left. (Reflecting and unre-flecting consciousness described and defined.) Hence cosmical significance of the atonement— Gregory of Nyssa.

223   114. Ethical significance of the atonement. Two main lines of cultural development: Sethites, cults, central. Cainites, culture, peripheral--Universal revelation.—World-empire and its culture the aim—center of cohesion. Self-salvation through self-culture—Birth of paganism: organised—General Revelation: covenant with Noah, universe included. Special revelation: covenant with Abraham, paganism excluded; still catholic as to humanity—Intensi-fied religion, under pressure of heathendom.

224   115. Four imprints perpetuating the plan of universal hist. I "Genealogical Table." J. v. Miller —Unity of humanity, uniqueness of God—Other nations claim to be emanated from particular deities—Lenormant. 2. Babylonian tablets: Disclosing confusion and dispersion— Apostasy dares to organise, after the parole "sicut" etc. Asiatic despotism subsequent to subversion of the proper motives of progress—For the first time boast of higher culture with anarchism at bottom—Folly of misdirected aspiration and vain glory demonstrated—3 Image of the "Monarchies." Erroneous interpretations. Danger-signal as to false progress. Whenever culture displaces cultus national disaster is imminent—4. Pentecost. Its bearings on the unity

of humanity and "the" civilisation issuing—The dispersed to be gathered into God's household. **M. Mueller**—New covenant not to perpetuate any part of the decayed matter of the old world—Fulfillment of the promises save one—**Genesis of the Church,** the type of the ultimate rehabilitation of the coming Kingdom in contrast with Babel—Jewish theocracy the typical vehicle of universal civilisation, *i. e.,* Christianised culture. Its "secret" made public to the gentiles—Final fulfillment not without certain death-struggles.

III Ch. Intermediation in its Ethical and Æsthetical Bearings.

116. **Effects of the Resurrection**—A nucleus of a regenerated household to work as a leaven **227** in the dough of humanity—Process of disseminating in ever widening circles analogous to, but not identical with, the developments in natural spheres—Scale of progress in general from the inorganic to the celestial kingdom—Transition by five graduations with a hiatus betw. each, to be bridged from the higher stage in degrees of diminishing distinctness but increasing intensity—Christ alone imparts the life eternal and indissoluble in historic ways of organically connected ordinances—Adaptability of the physical world to become spiritualised—"Second Adam," scion from above, grafted into the ethically prepared humanity of the first, as its natural crown—New in history: **Personality conceived in its ideality and eternal value.** **229**

117. All constituent parts of humanity, as far as they partake of the Holy Spirit recognise each other as a unity of common origin and with a common destiny—The question of unity of language raised for the first time and answered at the same instant. **J. Grimm**—**The Church**—Its binding ties as to Head and membership in a mystical body are **brotherly love** and compassion in response to the Great Sacrifice—Another novelty: **general love** to fellow-men—Sum of the effects of Christ's resurrection is "humanism" for which not even Socrates and Plato had a word. **M. Mueller**—The **type of humanity in its totality and in every detail.** Individual renewal under conditions—Life and death of the God-man typical as to all historic eventualities up to final consummation—Valuable in history is only that which approaches to conformity with, and reflects the model-life of, the "Image"—Virtue in the main: **humaneness,** including the most abandoned specimen of human degeneracy as well as Christ Jesus.   "**Bild**ung" (conformance to the "Image") is education in the proper sense.   **231**

118. Resurrection and æsthetics—In the cognition of final transfiguration into the **State of Glory** lies the criterion of the Beautiful—The resurrection discloses the plan, the goal and the mysterious mode of development—Heterogeneity of matter and mind is virtually overcome—Contrast betw. pagan and Christian ethics as æsthetically expressed at Benares, (**Oldenberg**) at Athens, and at Jerusalem—Adornment of "the House of God" a matter entirely unknown to surrounding nations—The **"Magnificat".**   **232**

119. History but the expansion of man in all of his incipiencies—**Asceticism** inclined to hold the secondary good in contempt; to make abnegation meritorious and criterion of piety, to make the temple of the spirit a penitentiary—Whilst **worldliness** is disqualified to judge things pertaining to the realm of glory—Hence either false enthusiasm or wild fanaticism—Optimism and pessimism conciliated in Christianity—"With the gospel progress proper is initiated. **Lenormant**—Aryan activity and Turanian lethargy contrasted—**Compact masses to be broken up in order to set personality free**—Christianity the solvent force—Polarity betw. "Church" and "society", dogmatism and free thought.   **234**

120. Resume: "The man towards whom heathendom tangents, through whom alone history can be interpreted." **Droysen**—**St. Paul in Europe:** making public the plan of social reconstruction—Program of universal history before the Areopagus.

FIFTH DIVISION (II E.) Third Circle of Nations. Rome's Post-Augustean Period.
Syllabus: **235**

121. The three concentrating circles to be re-examined in reverse order—Three distinct stages of Christianizing cultures with a view to universal civilisation—Judaism, the alloy mixed into Church-life, together with the other orientalism (§81) causes serious perturbations.   **236**

I Ch. Rome and the Church.

122. Roman **rule** made to **serve** Christianity: preparing nations to accept the Gospel, and channels for its distribution—Curse of bureaucracy—Effeminating extravagance—The "Barbarians"—Syncretism and indifference—Christianity tolerated if it would serve political ends —Disappointment as to the state being the Supreme Good.   **237**

123. **Plato's ideal** naturalised in Rome, utilised in securing ecclestical permanency by **Augustin**—State-absolutism encounters the Christian conscience —Attempts to rescue statetheocracy cause persecutions—"The most heroic emancipation." **L. v. Ranke**—Obedient to even a Neronian government, the martyrs could not be disloyal to their Lord—Christians excommunicated from humanity.—Illustr.:   Well at Antioch—No danger of becoming worldly—Roman forms of organisation adopted without guile—Danger lurked in theocratic tendencies— Worship in catacombs—Pictorial badges as confessions of faith against hostile espionage— **Christian antique (Martigny—De Rossi)** represents the consistency of esteeming the secondary good without detriment to the heavenly realities.   **238**

124. Paganism warded off in doctrine was allowed to intrude in practice—Contempt of the world transferred by Persian fugitives into the Thebais and the Church—Origin of monastic communism—**Augustin's "De civitate Dei" copied from Plato** to fortify the Church—Oriental Aryanism separated from the occidental through the Semitic wedge of **Mohammedanism**—Semitic encroachments perpetuate the strain of old polarities in aggravated forms—Hilarius' army of monks—Gregory called **pope**—Pantheon a relic-market—Degeneracy of the church conspicuous—Rome rehabilitated in the church-state. "A decaying corpse on one side, rejuvenating on the other:" **Gregorovius.**

II Ch. Deformation: The Byzantine Church.

239   125. East-Roman empire—Partheuon a church of "the Mother of God"—Abissynian Church, mummified—Armenian Church: "Prester John"—Constantine's statue emblem of Byzantinism. His city the archive of Hellenistic souvenirs. Asiatic court-life imitated. Ecclesiasticism supreme. Antioch eulogized for its relics, by Chrysostom—Art emblematic of national character, which is determined by religious tenets and cults. Art under cesaro-papal surveillance—Copy-book of the Saints' portraits at Mt. Athos—Byzantine pictures mirroring the adulterated thought of humanity.

241   126. Cause of the decline, Gibbon—Intestine outbreaks of fanaticism—Barbarian inraids diminish the territorial extent. Defenseless border-lines—Court-theology and cruelties; palace-revolutions—Diocletian's further introduction of orientalism: "Persian tiara." Pompousness and impotency—Barbarians made body-guards—Mischief of the Augustinian theory manifest; amalgamating "throne and altar."

242   127. Sum and substance of first phase of Christianized culture. German element modifying—Justinian's figure emblematic: prerogative of state made subordinate and subservient to the priest-state, Hergenroether—Heraclius carrying the "Holy Cross" from Persia to Jerusalem; receives letter from Muhamed on the way—Constantinople the depository for the remnants of classic culture; Painting in the cloister of Iviron (Mt. Athos) foreshadowing the reunion of the old and true element of Aryanism with evangelical catholicity.

III Ch. The Church and the Talmud.

243   128. Comparison of Jewish with Aryan propensities: Aryans speculate, Jews calculate. Semites forced into Mohammedanism and Talmudism. Talmud and Koran to stir up Christendom. Church under obligation to Jewish effrontery.

245   129. Rise of Talmudism, i. e., systematised pharisæism. Retaliation upon Jerusalem—Succession of the synhedrion. Babylonian origin of the Talmud is ominous. Hatred of the "cross" made the sole center of cohesion—Kabala—Babylonian substitute for the Alexandrian synthesis of Philo—Source of Jewish arrogance, of casuistry and probabilism: Statutes of elders.

246   130. Biblical element in Judaism amalgamates not with Talmudism. Allegorical exegesis —Influence upon the church in the time of Maimonides, Albertus magnus, Thomas Aquina—Magic art, the filth of Babylon catalogued, practiced and peddled out—Sample cited from "Tract Sanhedrin"—Cause of riots in the Middle ages—Intimacy betw. Jew and Moslem; Graetz—Metatron's prediction.

IV Ch. The Church and Islam

247   131. Jews of Arabia; sanctuary at Mecca—Self-sufficiency, requiring no religious conviction, only political subjection and external conformance—Rise of the Crescent—Koran on the calling of Muhamed, who does not argue—Sum and substance of his world-theory. Import of Saracenic translations upon Mediæval Europe—Sciences transmitted to Cordova and Zaragossa—Samarkand, Asia's university—Arab culture not self-productive—A. v. Humboldt— As a religion Islam is but plagiarism; Koran the type of Mohammedan culture—Idea of "immaculate conception" derived from Islam: St. Bernard. Fra Paolo—Moorish style of architecture copied from India—Arabesque in lieu of forbidden images.

250   132. "Lions court in the Alhambra symbolises that Islam culture can never come to an understanding with occidental culture. Polygamy the curse of Turano-Semitic culture and national life—Harem-life makes reform impossible—Islam-Semitic culture a parasite upon decaying ethnical matter—Onslaughts of Asiatics repulsed by the two Karls as before by the two Catos—Comparison of principles in Christian and Islam cultures—Order of life under determinism—Iman, conscience by proxy.

251   133. Retrospect and prospect: Pope of Rome and caliph of Mecca at the close of that cyclical period—Mandates of both essentially diagonal tho converging—Collections of legal customs. The real Middle-age bisected by the year of the Nativity. The Word and the Cross.

SIXTH DIVISION (II F.) Second Circle of Nations Indo-Germans. Middle-ages.

252   Syllabus. Struggles for supremacy betw. emperors and popes. Rome under the bans of the Semitic ideal of a world-theocracy.

I Ch. German Characteristics. Karl the Great.

253   134. Liberty of the Germans: Tacitus—Trade betw. Getes (Goths) and Assyro-Babylon— Their territory from the Tweed to Mt. Atlas; Ranke—Rome's end; Germans enter—Soil upturned, new principles planted.

254   135. Semites, calculus; Greeks, intellect; Romans, will; Germans, sentiment; requisite for thorough "Bildung." Traits common to Persians, Greeks and Germans—Tradition of the world's destruction and transmutation: Edda-myths—The world-embracing One to come. Thor's temple at Upsala. Adam of Bremen—Traces of snake-cult. Human sacrifices—Acceptance of the "Good-spell." The "King akin to all the kinsfolks " German sincerity meets the cordiality of the Gospel half-way: Culdean and Anglo-Saxon missionaries.

256   136. German paganism never entirely abolished; Roman method of accomodation and symbolism—Scene of worship of German converts. "Heliand" the single idea upon which German tribes agree—Qualities of doubtful nature, but conducive to develop a rich culture— Love for the fatherland and the mother-tongue—Belt of colonies from Cape North to Carthage preserved individualism against concentrated power—Scene in Italy, illustr. period of transition: German culture roots in agriculture. Civil government passes into the hands of clergy. Petty states forming under laws of their own. Imperialism vanishes. Theodoric and Ulfilas, the great Ostra-goths. Bible in Gothic-German.

137. Hist.!educates nations towards unity. Karl's coronation crowns the nation's desire **258** for ideal and authoritative representation—Karl's cardinal idea: succession upon Constantin's throne—Patronises Latin science and German literature—Scene at the palatinate of Aachen— Fondness for Byzantine nimbus—Constantinople the bridge for orientalism; **Herder**—Nobility and antiquity—Karl's three emblematic silver tables. "Holy Roman Empire of the German Nation"—Commences its career by fighting off oriental invasions but admitting portentous influences. Byzantine court-etiquette; meaning of the "dalmatica"—Sycophancy—Conception of the Savior Byzantinized—Karl not adverse to court-theology, cautioning the hierarchy to beware against imperial infringements.

II. Ch. Principles Developing European Civilisation.

138. Specific German ideas concerning personal freedom and rights of possession; (not **259** those barbarians as misrepresented by **Robinson** and **Guizot**)—Two sets of legalistic ethics enjoined; **Dorner**—History to grope its way of progress, especially in matters of ethics. **Culdean Gospel-preaching. Boniface's** counteraction. Later consequences of Thuringian aversion to being Romanized. Subjective piety—France rash to accept objective ecclesiasticism. Germans to sustain reciprocity with Rome until a definite settlement could be reached. Tension salutary against separatistic subjectivism—Slaves Byzantinized, no tension, no improvement.

139. Fidelity of retainers to their princes, who are wardens of rights under oath. **Genesis 261 of constitutional, representative government.** Heliand not after Byzant. pattern. Elective kingship based upon love of freedom, parole of honor, vow of fidelity. Priestly caste-rule could not establish itself—Middle-High-Germans never completely Romanised despite **Boniface's** diplomacy; relationship to Culdean Christianity never obliterated. **"Muspilli"** designates the end of mythical religiousness, whilst simultaneously the **"Heliand"** opens the æra of civilisation proper —Bearing of cultus upon culture in a new light: **Agriculture** the first domain to profit from the reinstatement of ethical principles—Right of possession and "marks" regulating it, develops another form of **jurisprudence.**

140. Fundamental cognitions of **German rights conditioned by discharge of duties. German 264 "rights"** conflict with **Roman** (canonic) **law**—Serfdom, humane treatment of subjects. Country nobility upsets the simple honest methods of justice; Sword-law; Ecclesiatical vassalage; Free peasantry, especially in France, disappears. Vassals make their fealties hereditary: **Feudalism—Anarchism** of upper ranks, changes functional departments of state—Transition to modern monarchism: **freedom of cities** against eastern invaders and feuds of the nobility.

141. City life; affects royal prerogatives. Municipal and episcopal immunities granted **266** by embarrassed kings—Feudal sociology in process of changing. City-leagues; Swiss confederacy—Three epochs of German civic polity: 1. Imperial banner floating over free cities. 2. Rediscovery of Pandects: Council of Peace to settle combatant interests by "right and reason." ameliorating the anomalies of canonic law at variance with German rights; legal cognitions prevail over judgment from sentiment by sentences, proverbs etc—3. Bearing of the victory of Roman jurisprudence upon agrarian interests. Value of a person measured by his capacity for taxation. "Allodials" now parcelled and salable. Changing conditions of husbandry cause corresponding changes in "National Economics," especially since **ecclesiastical functionaries** ("**Canonics**") **manage marriages and inheritances.**

142. Saxon emperors curb the secular aspirations of the clergy. Reign of Otto the Great **268** resembles that of Karl the Great. Providential arrangement in **amalgamating German subjectiveness with Roman objectivism.** Reappearance of those forces of the first circle furnishing the pressure necessary to unite the Germans—Tho barred out on the German side orientalism succeeds in encroaching the Roman. Henceforth Mongolians exert influences upon the history of the orient.

III. Ch. Church and State.

143. Old polar tension betw. east and west reinforced. Militant forces in array upon **269** European arena—Humanism tested to maintain itself. Germans compelled to unite; necessity of union felt but unwilling to relinquish personal selfhood and honorable loyalty; admiring Roman organisatory talent, but unwilling to swerve from a natural unity of national growth under internal adjustment. Not disinclined to follow the demand of history, but contriving to form a state after their own ideal—Religious instinct made German union desirable, but not for the subjection of either church or state. Persistency in antagonistic ideas caused national split but salutary in the end.

144. Profound interest taken in religious matters. Influence of German sincerity upon **270** Middle-ages. Ecclesiastical self government among Goths and Franks. Chlodwig pocketing an insult at his baptism. Henry, the Saxon's independence of Rome—Charles the Bald, painted by monks, memorialises what French royalty owed the hierarchy—**Plato-Augustinian concept works mischief.** Contrast betw. the beginning and end of Middle-ages. Emperors too weak to wear crowns, popes strong enough to transfer them—German idea of **service** of the crown in protecting the church taken advantage of by the popes to become **rulers;** the more the emperor takes his office in a religious sense, the more does the pope run politics-"Sacred orders" revived to form a standing army of political agitators. "Investiture" conflict—Excommunication of Henry V—Laity led by priests against princes—Offence given causes people to side with popery and power—Henry Plantagenet— Emperor holds pope's stirrup—"Saxenspiegel" amended—Princes deemed servants of the "vice-gods"—**Hauck**—Feudalism applied against recreant kings, their vassals; nations receive dispensation from their oaths of allegiance. **272**

145. Parallels of oriental and occidental development during the cyclical epoch at A. D. 1200. Emperor and pope, sultan and caliph: Scene at Bagdad: reception of Togrul Beg—

Crusades utilized by the "Holy See." **Results of the crusades.** Nations benefitted—Widened horizon, impulse to commerce; awakening of national consciousness; militant orders—Other results as yet occult—Idea of theocratic rule resented. **Frederick II.**

IV. Ch.　Church State and Lamaism.

274　　146. Ideas to work themselves through difficulties—Dawn of enlightenment. **But German consciousness remodeled by introducing oriental legends** and folk-lore; by way of Persia, Arabia, Spain. **Waitz—Benfey**—Magic night covers the countries of the setting sun—Ecclesiastical miracles based upon Hindoo phantasms of metamorphoses. Buddha canonized—Picture of the world as refracted in monkish brains of 13th century.

276　　147. Chasm betw. real existence and human destiny reappears, practically a relapse into Hindooism—Abhorrence. of mundane conditions—Platonic reality. Flight from the world means fight against the state. State to abandon itself to "God's vicar"—Enrichment of the "mortmain"—Coenobial communism. Buddha—Platonism fulfledged.

277　　148. Semitic legalism added to Hindoo contempt of nature. ·"Compel them to come in"- The kind of Church-extension demanded of the state, the necessary evil—**Aquinas.** Tolerance is cruelty. **Augustine.** Gregory VII completes ecclestical supremacy. Crusades against heretics— Merits of mediæval church—Import of Montecasino.

279　　149. Causes and effects the same under the pope as under the Dalai Lama—Scene in modern Tibet—Demonstrative pilgrimages etc. the same in Potala as in Poland—Scene in modern Rome—Redeeming feature: mysticism of Meister Eckhard—Art frees itself from Byzantinism.

SEVENTH DIVISION (II G) First and Largest Circle of Nations: Turano-Mongolians.

280　　**Syllabus.** Mongolian as bearing upon European culture. Invasions instrumental in establishing trans-oceanic relations and international intercourse. Mediterranean communication passes over to oceanic dimensions.

I Ch.　Turano-Mongolian Bearings upon European Civilization.

281　　150. Organism of the church's inner life encysted by pagan elements—**Structural** part of the system: Graeco-Roman; **functional** parts: Semito-Buddhistic elements; **mediums transmitting them**—Two sets of ethics for two grades of Romanized humanity—Aggressiveness of Asiatics the indirect means of dispelling the confounded and distracted views of life—Fall of Athens— Turcomans in sight—Ambassadors (monks) to Mongol. courts—Poetical legends revive the dread of Mongol. invasion (**Raumer**)—Dgengis in Southern Asia, Batu khan in Eastern Europe. Just in time when papal power is in its prime and the German empire is demoralised; simultaneous with the investiture of the Asiatic pope—Culture of Korakorum, Bagdad etc—Byzantine emperor sends tribute to Timur—Suliman leading a group of fugitive Turks—**Fall of Constantinople**—Fugitives of A. D. 1453 incite Italy to study the classics; "humanistics"—Historic task of Constantinople transferred to Russia; "Eastern question" in the foreground—Sycop hant funeral eulogy at Byzantium.

284　　151. "Renaissance:" Not because of the arrival of St. Andrew's alleged head to the successor of his brother—Italy's receptivity for the more valuable bequest, the humanistic thought of Hellas—Self-reliance and self-government of citizens—Cosimo Medici, Petrarca and the novelty of "an infidel" in Florence—Humanistics scandalized.

285　　152. Renaissance at the French court—**Benvenuto—Tizian**—"Gargantua" of **·Rabelais;** burlesque compromise betw. libertinism and absolutism; Hutten and German enthusiasts— New formations of social life—Cause of womanhood better served than by chivalry— Econo mics founded upon statistics—Architecture—This transitory period cannot be fairly judged unless by the contrast betw. antique-mediæval culture and the evangelical world -theo ry— Failings of the "Gospel of Nature" obvious under meditation of the secondary good as appreciated by the "Gospel of free Grace"—Direct effects of Turano-Mongol. commotions : diffusion of the humanistic thought causes.the **regeneration of occidental world-consciousness**— This renders the conciliation of real life with human destiny intelligible and sets the mind free to criticise Semitic legalism and formalism, to emancipate itself from Buddhistic pessimism.

287　　**II Ch.　Widening of the Horizon: Æra of Discoveries.**

153. Sudden advance upon the whole line. Man having discovered himself makes for the discovery of his world—Cyprus and Sicily depositories for remnants of every culture in the Mediterranean basin. **Cesnola**—Genesis of modern commerce and trans-oceanic intercourse, as connected with Mongolo-Turanian commotions—Moors blockade the Venetian routes of traffic—Corsairs became the direct cause of new marine enterprises. **Columbus** commissioned by Ferdinand at the Alhambra coincident with expulsion of Arabic rule from Spain.

288　　154. Vasco de Gama doubles Cape of Good Hope—Christians draw anchor at Calicut— The earth taken in full possession—Albuquerque trades with China—Cortez conquers Mexico: a prelude to the storming of Pekin—Toltecian culture in Peru—Inca and China compared— Europe's surprise, news of Mongol. culture arrives simultaneously from east and west—Changes wrought by the discoveries—Dawn of the grandest era since the divide of the times.

289　　155. Geography proper begins with discovery of Brazil. **Copernicus**—Humanity exploring at the same time the oceans and the heavens—New cognitions slowly forming as to space and time—**Luther's** remarks as to the reconstruction of astronomy—Roman inability to judge what was going on in Germany—Liberating effects of the discovery—Back to the spiritual center—New standard of superiority: spiritual quality instead of physical quantity—New views upon the spiritual world—Both forms of existence as congruent entities in living interrelations without eliminating the aseity of either—Superstitions as to astral determinism abandoned.

where it reigned at pleasure.   Romanism popular, nevertheless—The typical figure of the counter-reformation; in contrast to Laurentius, his patron-saint.

V Ch.   Absolutism,   Enlightenment, deranging the Thought of Humanism.

309   167.   Full extent of this cognition—Spirit of inquiry awakened; the **Bible and God-con**-sciousness the criterion set up by the Reformation—Emancipated minds fearing another popery take world-consciousness for their sole criterion. Cursory attempt to set up the conception of that humanism which had been outraged by ecclesiasticism —The reformation, single-handed, had established the true and full meaning of humanism: 1. relative to man's destiny for the higher world: order of **salvation;** 2, relative to present conditions of existence: **self-culture**— This dual position of man now given up, either part to be cultivated at the expense of the other—Precept and project of evangelical Christianity, proper blending of sacred with secular concerns—Onesided theories caricature either religion or ethics—Sum and substance of the thought as formulated by the reformation.

311`   168.   **Distortions of this thought—Radicalism** restricted by the Church, which protects the freedom once procured—Enmity to Christian thought not to be foiled by force—Romanism had not been able to crush free thought upon its own territories.   **Strossmayer**—Christine, daughter of Gustave Adolphus ridiculing the popes—Results of Philip's   broodings to force the inquisition upon Holland: Calvinistic nations become maritime powers; **Hugo Grotius** writes on "International Law;" **Water-beggars found New York**—A **Dutch soldier muses about his "ego"**— Man as the major premise put in central position—Significance of **Descartes** speculation: "Aufklaerung" in its scientific beginnings.

312   169.   Saxon element with its propensity for subjectivism—Calvinistic synods and repre-sentative government—Queen Elizabeth—**Shakespeare** is for the people what Descartes was to the scholars, pointing out the way in which philosophy of hist. is to proceed—**Hume** considers humanism under the low aspect of naturalism—**Rousseau** shows how little religion man needs to be happy—English deism translated into French sensualism by **Voltaire**—Results of this enlightenment of the "Encyclopedists" summed up by **Carlyle**.   Encyclopedia proscribed by the French government; its authors feted by Frederick the Great.

314   170.   State absolutism and pantheistical indifference nourish one another (**Hegel**)— Enlightened despotism tolerates all except the Christian cognition of humanism: A state-church with an enlightened "Landesvater" as bishop ex-officio keeps the religious side of the thought of humanity in bondage—Cabals of cabinets disregard not only the idea of personality but also the principle of nationality—Reaction of enlightened subjectivism against enlightened absolutism.

315   171.   Right of private judgment abused in onesided inquiry as to humanistic problems— Denial of the mind's duality aggravates the confusion, leaves a world-theory and all forms of civilised life without a center of cohesion—Nations disintegrate under a humanism which disparages theism—Effects thereof upon jurisprudence—Humanism to supplant rationalism in religion (**Herder**) The church cannot fill the place of the true center of humanity (**Schleiermacher, Kaftan**) This to enlightened thinking had become obsolete—**State ceases to be Christian to the great satisfaction of papists.**

VI Ch.   Civilisation rendered Trans-oceanic and the Thought of Humanism Cosmopolitan.

317   172.   State-churchism paralysed—A reaction—Turn of the tide bearing upon its enlarging wave-circles, the neglected religious side of humanism—New era created not by **intellect**-ualism, but by extending trans-marine relations which require the energy of the **free will**— Contact with Mongolians rendered permanent through a new kind of colonisation—**Revival of missionary impulses**—Latin nations, controlling the seas, take the initiative—Scene at Rome: **Asia paying homage to the pope**—Patriarchal authority not transferable to the extent of a world-empire.

318   173.   Germanic nations make different use of trans-oceanic connections—Signal success of the water-beggars—Roman marines assigned to secondary import—Fate of the **Hindoos** since the isolation through Islam—**English investments** in India for mutual benefit.   **Heeren**—Higher than mercenary profits: Revival of missionary zeal invigorates religious life at home—Anglo-Saxons to divide the bequest made by the Testator with eastern relatives.

320   174.   Benefits accruing to Europe from the American reaction against corrupted concep-tions of the humanistic thought—**The Pilgrims on board of the "Mayflower"**—The human right to live independently.The grand document of modern civilisation—Norman traits discarded, Anglo-Saxon fostered—Career of David Crockett; Illustr.   North-American pioneer life and specific national character—Labor for common interests procures the true level of human and dignified equality—Antiquated conventionalities abated—Experimental test whether the Good or the Bad is more attractive and gives better satisfaction.

321   175.   Retrospect upon European precedents which condition the success of the above experiment—Thirty years war a necessity to preserve freedom—Contest of intrigues ended "without an ideal." **Hegel** —Europe exhausted; Germany, its battle field, empoverished, paralysed except in mental activity—Cause of freedom negatively furthered by Jesuitism, taken up positively by the great jurists **Hoppes, Grotius, Pufendorf,** etc.—Small beginnings of representative government in Rhode Island—**Why England escaped the craze of the French Revo-lution?**   (**Lecky**) Wesleyan (Zinzendorf) revivalism—Genuine religiousness alone assures national freedom and prosperity—The entire world ready for the first time to be imbued with higher influences—Universal history proper begins—Oceans bear messages: also from spheres above to spheres abroad—The thought of humanism in its fulness acknowledged as "the" cardinal factor of civilisation"

VII Ch. Cognition of Humanity in its Distortions.

176. Grand prospects in view—All potentialities latent in human nature assume tangible 323 shapes—Abyss yawning in close proximity to the summit—Effects of the French Revolution threatening repetition on larger scope. Evils as means of preservation: To keep man susceptible to something better—Influence of obscure nations, incite sympathy and missionary activity—, Correctness of interpreting signs of better days is conditioned by the way the golden rule is applied.

177. Aim of history, tho plainly revealed yet shrouded in mystery—Mode of restoring 325 the "image"—Cause of humanity distortioned now in the church, then by the world: Genesis of revolutions: Chateaubriand—En lish revolution as compared with the French, Cromwells army.

178. Cause of the French revolution—Opportunities of normal development neglected. 326 Gerson—Beza in Poissy. Huguenots not bent upon social overthrow—Suppression of the religious reform—First symptoms of morbidity in French literature—Parallel with the age of Boethius—Legitimists, "Mortmain" exempt from taxation—Privacy of the cabinets—Class-privileges—Masquerade of Kloots' representatives of the human race—The humanity required for reconstruction not at hand—Reaction under Napoleon, despising such humanity—His program ready for erecting a universal theocracy previous to the Russian campaign.

179. Lessons derived from the experiments to establish humanism without and in spite 329 of God—Rousseau's threadbare theory put to a practical test jeopardised humanism. DeMaistre —Responsibility of the hierarchy and of the real instigators—Epidemic nature of such paroxisms—Advantages after stormy times, in which history unmakes that which seems to make history—Overthrows administer wholesome humiliation to artificial culture.

VIII Ch. Cosmopolitan World-Theories. European System of States.

180. Germany once more encounters false humanism, now that of freethinking worldli- 331 ness—National boundaries broken down for a few decades by anarchy and despotism; profound reforms were procured and rendered permanent—Klopstock shows in Milton's strain the idea of humanity in his "Messias"—Literary reaction against infidelity initiated by Hamann—Religious realism. Oettinger—German antique and Tauler's mysticism revered—but captivated by Romanticism—Relapse into national narrow-mindedness, clannishness—Conspiracy against liberalism, meaning Protestantism—Jesuitism applies the power of the press—Papal infallibility advised by DeMaistre, as a basis for social order and the reconstruction of Europe—Haller's intrigues—Metternich's intrigues—Revolutions hatched in Romanized countries.

181. Examination of the persistant tendency to repristinate oriental views upon Europe- 333 an forms of government, aiming at the establishment of a world-empire—Catholicism and the task assigned to it, in counter-position to Protestantism—Romanism will not acknowledge the necessity of being providentially complemented by Protestantism; persists in the wrong course —Flexibility of principles renders it an unreliable custodian of the thought of humanism— Possibility of modifying Catholicism is forestalled by "papal infallibility."

182. Reaction against Roman orientalism by way of modern "national economics."—Ger- 335 man cognition of rights is adverse to absolutism of one person—Oriental ideas as to state-power imposed upon Germans—Genesis of the "system of states"—Conformity of political arrangements and international rights founded upon common assent; system the stronger for the want of written instruments—Secrecy of cabinets obnoxious but necessary to maintain the "Balance of Power"—Machiavellian devices headed off by William II of Orange— Mercantile transactions demand reconstruction of financial methods—Militarism—Organism of modern government, differentiated departments.

183. Christianity charged to carry out the thought of organized humanity—Rome fell 337 back on "theocracy"—Westphalian peace did not dismember Germany; but Austria's preponderance curtailed—Germany to poise national polarities, to cultivate interstate relationship and international culture; resists the rearing of a Roman world power upon oriental premises —"Congress of Vienna"—"Holy Alliance"—Not the pope but the princes advance fraternal relations. Treischke—Monarchies as yet indispensable in Europe in the face of the rapidly growing power of money—Corrupting influences of capital—Making and unmaking legislatures, provoking social upheavals—Dutiful monarchs as safe-guards against radicalism and factitious contests which render social standing insecure—Nervosity of public life most unpleasant feature of modern republics.

184. Reactionary alloy in the "Holy Alliance"—It is perverted to prolong cabinet-rule— 339 Corporate representation of the people frustrated—Royal promises eclipsed by advisers of the crowns: Metternich, Gentz, Beust—Austrian hegemony in German diet becomes unendurable; academic youth demands unity of the nation—Their patriotic zeal compared to national games of Greece—"Regeneration of the fatherland"—Necessities of the time but vaguely comprehended—Arndt—Decline of middle-classes.

IX Ch. The Thought of Humanism philosophically conceived and socially applied.

185. Formal reinstatement of man to be traced to its essential source, the reformation 341 —Renaissance, void of evangelical Godconsciousness, was rendered profane under sway of enlightenment—Contents of the thought to be realised in every particular; this revelation not to be forcibly restrained—Romanticism calls forth the "philosophy of identity" which is to obtain a monistic view of life—All orientalism combined in Spinoza—His "substance" but Hindooism pure and simple in the Semitic version; he is in a clandestine way the father of Hegel's pantheism which is ever fostered by political absolutism—Man represents the cosmos (Schelling) at the apex of creation—Illustr. pyramid is the microcosm. Lotze—He is the completion of an infinite past, turning-point of an unlimited presence; concealed starting-point of an infinite future.

XI Ch.   Ethnical Chaos resulting from the corrupted Cognition of Humanity.

197.   Resume of the dangers to which the cause of humanism is exposed upon its course 361 of extension—Final issue of progress: will reveal what use man had made of his endowments and opportunities—Humanity as reinstated by the glorified Redeemer in order that by it the world may be spiritualised.   Deformations and reformations of this thought; its Jewish and gentile adumbrations—False spirituality—asceticism ; natural side emphasised : worldliness of the renaissance—Identity-philosophy: religious side entirely discarded —Temporal prosperity jeopardized: materialism claims first rank for its world-theory—Homogeneity of unrestricted egoism—Humanity made a mechanical "**association of production and consume**"—Misgivings as to such a fabric, (**Lemontry, Perthes,**) poorly qualified to unite men into the great brotherhood —Changes incident to city and industrial life, and in economics--No progress toward general welfare—**Marx, Sismondi, Cherbuliez.**

198.   Dangers not in overpopulation or scarcity of food. **Malthus**—Valuation of individual 364 life, a sign of advanced civilisation; its reverse side the "labor market" which cheapens life-- Danger not in the wars of the future, but in the **moral decadence**—Loss of liberty in the associa- tion of productions and consume—Materialistic sociology (**Schaeffle**) worse than old Roman state authority—Social body resembling a protoplasmic mass—Highly differentiated organism liable to sudden collapse—The dark shadow of modern civilization—Possibility of averting disastrous experiments.   Rational methods of adjustment and reconstruction—Confederacy of European free states would not avert the dangers to which humanity stands exposed.

199.   Danger located.   Man's condition not bettered through mere culture.   Vice of past 366 ages cast into new molds—Depravity emboldened, despises to borrow respectability from hypocrisy—Growing indifference as to resisting wickedness.   Old age prudent to avoid such annoyances, as connected with combating the bad (**Lasaulx**)—Decrease of ethical decisiveness —Less vagueness of allowances and expediencies—Parallel betw former and present forms of social life—"Phantasy evaporating, reason gaining strength" **Darwin.   Herein the danger: Decline of sentiment and piety not to be repaired by rationalism**—Virtue at random in cosmopolitanism —Materialistic phantasm of a "European Republic."

200.   Arch-type of perverted Humanity as to unity and dominion: Babylon --Tendency 367 perpetuated: "Fasces" of Rome; Byzanz-Aachen; Rome-Moscow; is to culminate in an antitype —Figure now assuming shape corresponds with the daring attitude of the Babel emblem— **Christian thought in single-handed contest**, because unsupported by nations—Mixed nations agitat- ed by antispiritual forces (**Ratzel**) **North America**—Semitic blood diffused in Christian nations works more than ever disintegration, under the label of cosmopolitanism—Deference to **Droyson's** conclusion—Forerunners of the final appearance of the personified bad arising—No **state will risk to commit and endanger itself by contracting the odium of defending the Christian thought** which encounters a trio of old enmity.

201.   Combinations of infidelity and superstition at the times of Christ to be repeated— 369 Stoic superciliousness and superstitious frenzy—Spinocism; Pantheism a "crazy-quilt of Indian patches stitched together by German needles": **A. Guenther**— Schopenhauer's **pessimism**— Spiritism akin to Shamanism (**Wundt.) Buddhistic "theosophy"**—Never did infidelity displace superstition **Kant. Swedenborg** — Sinister phenomona—Man to appear in the completion of all his known and hidden potentialities-Catastrophe not to set in without preceeding counter- action against the perils of the latter days.

202.   Separation of the contesting powers,aggressive persecution versus enduring resigna- 870 tion—Contents of the "Sicut deus"— Final result of godless culture and godly aspiration— Outline of the figure consolidates, which represents all that is base and bad.   The bearers of the"image"—Abhorrence of godlessness equal to the degree of love to Christ—Beastly features of the Bad all in one lump. Man as a unit laid bare to the root of his being, before the deep roots of the Bad back of him come to view—The evil-one debarred from becoming incarnate, his final representative, the "man of sin"—The ideals preserved by the classic world.   The ideal of humanity could not then be attacked.   Undermining the basis of human ideals causes the degradation to brutality—The umbel fully developed—Metamorphoses of the forms assumed by the antagonism to Christianity—"Beast risen out of the sea." Miracles mocking the mockers.

203.   Postulate of History: Man in both repects, love to God and hatred against Him and 873 His, to be fully revealed in person—Expectation of the Church—Instinctively the world, i. e. organised enmity against God, is waiting for its leader—Seductive influence of, and intimida- tion through, the representative of the irredeemable part of the human race—Adherents of true humanity put to the last test in the crucible of suffering —**Christianity to partake of all the phases of the life of Christ**—Complete vindication of the truth in the "sicut deus" as separated from the lie—Reappearance of the God-man upon the earthly scenes of action.   Separating effects thereof: the "crisis" or last **judgment** - Execution of verdicts rendered long ago—Dark spirits expelled from the world of men—**But for this final manifestation, hist. would be natural history pure and simple.**

XII Ch.   Consummation of the World's History.

204.   Part of hist. is natural history.   The earth continually dying, i. e. transmutating, 875 partakes of the "fate of man"—Physicists only differ as to a fiery (**Tyndall**) or frigid (**Dubois-Raymond**)mode.   They make man's destiny dependent upon the fate of his temporary domicile, are of the opinion that nature, not mind, determines the closing act of history—Absurdness of a will in the abstract—The crisis not merely tellurian but cosmical—Decomposition of the broad cosmical basis alone warrants man's unique position above all creatures—What, "ought not to be" remains irredeemable.

377   205. Real progress to complete unfolding must include abolition of the opposites into which man's dual nature is distracted—Polarities to cease—Reconciliation of faith and science —The sudden transmutation into that form of reality which is nature in essence—True aims of art and science, as means to realise the ideal—Character of miracles : Substance fashioned into instrumentalities of thought—Reference to the cosmical significance of the resurrection— Visible things changed from being concealing garbs of reality into luminous environment of the new humanity—Glory of "man made perfect"—Former incognito of the Lord—Crisis at the great day. by the discharge of an electric flux into a chemical compound—Completion of the reductive process begun when the "Word" was discharged into the composition in the Roman crucible.

379   206. Communication of strength to Christ's adherents; illustr: Action of the magnet upon elements of affinity—A higher imponderable force suspending the law of gravity— Christians are agents of the attractive power—Humanity proper is to the universe what the spirit-soul is to the body —Transition from nature to spiritualisation goes through man's personal life—All arrested life bound up in matter is virtually liberated by Christ, under conditions of the ethical process prescribed by the order of things and the order of salvation— "Corporeality the end of all of God's ways." History complete and at rest only after this consummation—Human nature to reach perfection in a multiplicity exhibiting the gifts as fully developed; and the tasks accomplished in all directions and every.relation—All potentialities free and at man's disposal—The fruit, the reproduction of the seed—The universe exists for the maturition of its secret : the new humanity. Origen—Amidst the scenes of his deeds, witnessing his failures and successes, man is judged according to the manner in which he adjusted himself to the center and the periphery.

BOOK THIRD: DILEMMA OF HISTORICS.

385   Syllabus. References to items postponed. General topics: 1. Enigmata of hist. as to its finality. 2. Progress after a plan. Investigation of degrees of development.

FIRST DIVISION. (III A.) Enigmata of History.

History no further elucidated then we have knowledge of ourselves. Government of the world.

I Ch. Nature-bound Peoples. Mummified Nations.

386   207. "Children of nature" and cultural relapses—"Products of degeneracy"—Causes of arrested development—Instead of missing factors, polarisation and "pressure," much is found which "ought not to be"—Civilisation means death to barbarism—Conditions bordering on embryonic life—Children of civilised nations pass through all the stages of cultural development betw. childhood and adult age.

387   208. Wolf as to the idea of "arrested" life—Account given of arrested logic—Isolation.— Wolf's exception does not deny downward progress—"Products of degeneracy"—Argyll,Martius D'Arbigny—Esquimaux Acca, etc.,all show traces of primeval culture—Mummifying effects of conquering upon vanquished peoples:Mongolians upon Mohammedans,Islam upon Christians.

388   209. Purpose of prolonging existence of withering nations—Conscious life inconceivable as the product of inanimate being. (Lotze)—All men participate of inner life, reflect the light of life fixed as conscience—Value of existence not to be estimated by degrees of pleasure or grades of refinement. Waitz—Potentialities latent in the soul designed to be universally recognized (Leo)—Insignificant threads in a piece of tapestry indispensable,if the effect of the whole is to be procured.

II Ch. Paroxysms of National Life.

390   210. Places where hist. seems on a rush, others where it seems to be at rest—Tranquil times compared to recuperation during sleep—Labor deserves more attention than philosophy has given it—Prosperity not to be measured by means to gratify appetites—Parasites upon social body—Laws of reciprocal interaction to be fixed and taught—"Catastrophism" in Geology—Historic law of pressure—National differentiation demands continual adjustment— Custom-bound people, each bears physiognomy of its social body, of the clan, which is but a vehicle of the life of its genus.

392   211. Genesis of distinct national character—Natural law governs history to the extent in which man is part of nature—Volcanoes and social eruptions—Stages in the history of revolutions—Commotions resembling "law-suits" are historical necessities. Paroxysmal fits explode the euphonisms calculated to extol man in his "unregenerated" state. Kant —Seduction to false world-theories always ends in destruction of dignity and freedom.

393   212. Insane destruction of human life—Mysterious phenomena receiving some new light—Human nature open to infernal infusion—Hypnotism, mimicry in Java. Bastian.—Propensity for insanity lies close beneath the tender surface of the intellect in every man: Illustr. by double set of lenses in the meniscus; the least displacement in dual consciousness sets in rapport with either part of the spirited world, disturbs at least the focus in viewing life.

III Ch. Undulations in Ethnical Life.

394   213 Oscillations, like Rhythmical occurrences, must be reducible to peculiarities of the human soul—Emotions and passions alternatively determine the views men take of life—New views to undergo the ordeal of conflicts—One great descent, one great ascent: Sinking began with the break of human unity; ascent begins when this unity is manifested anew—Rotation upon the center (the cross) conspicuous enough—Simultaneous commotions: Lasaulx—Nations

pendulating betw. poles of energy and lassitude—Selfishness punished by interspersion of aliens—Semitic element, the dissolvent upon decaying masses, to teach nations appreciation, of that, whereof they have become indifferent, and to spurn mam monism, sham and effrontery.

214. Undulations in the conception of humanity betw. cosmopolitan "generalness" and **396** national self-complacency, are in keeping with two fluctuating modes of thinking which ever attempt to embody themselves in social transformations: Universalistic and subjectivistic forms of world-consciousness—Alternations in the concept of authoritative rule—Will in the abstract sense of generalness—People exist for the sake of the state: Individual rights subordinate to the will of the organisation: advocated by **Guizot, Hegel**—Subjectivism reacts: State the product of individual wills, a contract on terms, separable at pleasure of parties: There the ancient, here the modern state—Alternations of public opinion—Seasons of fashions—Oscillations of æthetics—Both, universalistic or communistic and subjectivistic forms of world-consciousness to poise the erroneous views in their attempts to rule true humanism out of order.

IV Ch. Hero-Worship. Genius and Talent. The Press.

215. Who are the "Great?"—Regulators of the oscillating world-theories: **Carlyle**—Concept of the world's government rendered profane if attributed to popular favorites: (**Niebuhr**)— **399** Genesis of leading minds—What great men owe to the totality of their respective nations. Language—Influence of mental and moral atmosphere—Receptivity to be cultivated first and foremost—Duties of society to individuals, punishment of their neglect—In what the wealth of a nation consists.

216. "Spirit of the time," Nations have no souls—Definition of "national spirit"; great **400** minds not developed regardless thereof. Yet personality is not the result of circumstances— Apparatus of environments not to be disregarded—**Not even the greatest of minds claimed his glory as due to himself.** Crystalline structure of excellent characters—**Talent**, virtuosity of receptivity, skill in self-adjustment to externals—**Genius** hidden in the texture of the inner life. It partakes of the nature of the conscience (**Kæhler**)—At this point the "**finger" procures the changes** in the directions which human affairs are to take—Genius a failure if not receptive— No quantity of talent can supplant ingenuity—Vividness of imagination, the creative power of mind. "Intuitive grasp"—Arrangement of given matters into new combinations by appropriate methods.

217. Masses now claim their part of the glory, because they participate in making or un- **403** doing heroes—Tyranny of the press. Facility to defame and ostracise the best at the pleasure of the vilest—Press a tool of schemers—Shortlived renown obtained by demagoguery—True heroes not recognized until their weaknesses are forgotten—Hero-cult but a sign of the search after the mind which manages human affairs through human instrumentalities—The radiance of great minds grows dim, because they were but surrogates for the light from heaven.

V Ch. Government of the Universe.

218. Divine Guidance not to be inspected whilst at work in minor details of history. **404** (**Lacordaire**)—Purpose and plan underlying, partly transcending hist., as disclosed by the Mediator. Pure induction could have discovered it—Axiom that man possesses "Vernunft," intellect—Materialistic definition of this faculty: **Schaeffle**. **Fichte's** concept of divine rulings criticised.

219. Problem: How to conceive of the inframundane relation of the Absolute Mind to **406** history—Development of history not under laws of **natural necessity**, but under laws of its own, under **ethical necessity**—Limit of self-development—"Free will" under "Divine rule."—No forensic determinism—"**Immutability" of God** misleading, not to be misconstrued as in dead deism —**Divine interaction** testifies to the incompleteness of things—If scepticism had been rendered impossible, freedom would have been nullified—The Supreme Will rather works in limits of self-limitation and incognito.

220. Providential interactions—In migratory movements: To generate new forces to **408** guide to new ethnical constellations, to benefit subjugated nations by pressure—**Indestructibility of cultural effects: a historic dogma**— Day of Judgment: the prerogative of the world's constitutional government, presided over by God in person—God's condescention is not to be understood by reason alone.

221. **Recapitulation:** Issue of hist. incalcuable—**Schelling**—Difficulties of understanding **410** originate in the interference of the bad, mystifying matters—Freedom is kept safe only within the invisible organisation framed into the visible organism of humanity—Interrelations betw. the two represented by binding threads running horizontally, interwoven with binding vertical lines—Three interlocked spheroids: natural universe, human world, Kingdom of Heaven upon earth—Happenings under auspices of blind fate exist not—Small affairs furnish the apparatus to exercise patience, prudence and trust—Everything hinges upon the relation to the Redeemer.

SECOND DIVISION: (III B.) Result of History.   413

Inquiry as to real progress on the line of human happiness—Pessimism as to cultural achievements. Helio-spiral and circular motion of progress. Civilisation must have a specific and definite goal. Taken under aspects of economic, rational, æsthetical advance and ethical improvement.

I Ch. Progress under the Aspect of acquired Dominion over Nature.

222. No law of progress since history is no mechanism—Evolution as individualisation **414** by detachment, valid—Differentiation and organisation—Nomade-life—Primitive agriculture— Rational agriculture—Emancipation from the clod—Rise in the value of labor.

223. Third stage of progress marked by preponderance of the money power—Parcellation **415**

of family-tenures—Abolition of serfdom and slavery, only indirectly caused by Christianity, directly by capitalistic interestedness —New economical conditions conducive to the welfare of laboring classes, owing much to increasing density of population—Liberty to a large extent the fruit of heightened productiveness of the soil and of "ploughing" the ocean—Contrast illustr.—Labor in German and Latin nations.

417   224. Conquering distances of space and time—History of means of intercourse—Age of speed—Pacific less extensive than Mediterranean was in St. Paul's time—Globe subjected to man's mind—Long course of developing present iron-industry—Lively interaction of all sub-divisions of culture, all claiming title of civilisation; thereby the esteem due Christianity on account of its results–Do the results of economic progress benefit the cause of true humanism?

II Ch.   Intellectual Advantages gained.

418   225. Survey of the field of research, to ascertain the modes of thinking. Schubert—Thinking called forth by promptings to understand nature; mind attracted by the starry worlds in the first place—Temple-wisdom consisted in arranging knowledge of nature—Genesis of science in astrology—Ancient science never emancipated from priestly tutelage—Greek historiography in vindication of oracles. Curtius—Church took "worldly wisdom" under its care, tho teaching the laity to renounce it—Antique ideas allowed to adhere to theology, marring the clearness of Christian world-consciousness—"Philosophia humana". Bacon —Freedom of inquiry. Descartes—Auxiliary branches become specific sciences—Spencer's definition of scientific progress.

419   226. Man nowhere finds the affinity confirmed which exists betw. necessities in things and in reason—To displace imagination (Buckle) is impossible —Spencer's ideas cannot be carried out. There is unity of purpose in all scientific quarters to carry on the humanitarian cause.

III Ch.   Progress in Æsthetics.

420   227. Each form of world-consciousness mirrored, each conform to religious tenets—Art of transcendentalism vilifies human form, maltreats the body in monasteries and torture-chambers –No realistic background,no perspective in pictures—Art representing sentiment,rapport with nature in landscapes. Raphael.

422   228. Music elevated to express ideal sentiments: Slowly like other arts emancipating itself from temple-rituals and funeral-rites—Stringed instruments—Triumph of the most abstract of the fine arts—Independent world-theories: Art represents them even in their conflicts—Arts' criterion:that it makes itself universally understood—Diversity of nations approaching to unity.

IV Ch.   Advance in Religio-Ethical Matters.

423   229. Cultures of yore destroyed, because sciences were fettered, upon which technical progress depends,mention of Dubois Raymond's" disregard of the moral factor" —Social ethics —Public opinion—Ecclesiastical ethics—Legalism –Christian ethics—History the realisation of true manliness—Progress of legalistic morality. Ethics roots in religion.

424   230. Progress in religiousness? Religious side of civilisation cannot be said to develop—"Man is apt to be restored to true humanity by a kind of regeneration"—A moral community, "a people under rule of divine law," which is secure against arbitrary changes and above human sanction. Kant —Man's renewal illustrated: crystallisation of precious stones –Utilitarian moralism void of religion, compared to dazzling, cold jewels. Culture owes every thing to benign influences of Christianity—New life from above, outlined in the changes it procures. —In experimental religion man finds himself, assured of realising his destiny.

426   231. Reasons for the fact that "religious progress" is on the decline—Appearance of representing continual defeat - Spatial extent of the dominion of true God-consciousness always diminishes at the rate in which politico-moral culture under the name of civilization spreads out—Intensiveness—Ignorance as to the inner difference of the moral and religious sense causes the neglect to harmonise piety and morality, God-and world-consciousness, which are finally to merge—Theocracies attempted to force this unification, whilst in the nature of things religious and political (ethical) institutions are to be kept separate—The "invisible church" as compared to the corrosion of natrium—"Image of the monarchies."

V Ch.   The World in the State of Perfection.

428   232. The world's entering the state of glory is frustrated by the bad—Phenomena of demoniac nature. Satan's hiding place: that which ought not to be, doomed to destruction—Aim of hist. as projected in man, is to be realised through him—Sublimity of man not fully exhibited until the entire universe is recognised as belonging to him—Totality of creation bound to become conformed to life resurrected—In the transit to perfection the celestial is included which also administered to his best interests. Else the termination of the fight for the possession of the world would not be assured.

429   233. Visible world but the symbol of the world of true reality and permanency—What ought not to be must have issued from immaterial principles. Renouvier—Fechner—Lotze—Mind must be able to affect physical matter in the same mode as imponderable matter affects the ponderable. Illustr. sand transmuted to glass—Nature ceases to be merely the semblance, but continues to be the most adequate expression of the sublime without further impossibilty of degradation—Reappearance of the Mediator– Body's temporary form inadequate to mind's nature –Consequences of the transmutation of the cosmos—True theocracy –Closing scene of history—Completion of the Church—Scaffolds vanish—Dedication solemnised –Anthems of praise—Full appearance of the Beautiful—Inheritance of God's children, includes sum and substance of all cultural achievements.

Conclusion.

PROSPECTIVE REMARKS.

Philosophising upon Universal History began with arranging historical matter in such a manner as might be rendered suitable in affirming or assailing either religious tenets or world-theories. Because of such inferential use or abuse of evidences the necessity of much preliminary work soon became apparent. The data of history were to be sifted critically, sources to be compared and verified. The undercurrent ideas needed cautious discernment in order to understand the events arising from them, and to test the correctness of judgments formed respecting them at the time of their occurrence as well as by the posterity of the actors. Thus the records of human activity during fifty centuries, at the least, had to be examined by our science, now scarcely one century old. Herder's "Ideas about the education of the children of men," up to the time when he published his humanitarian aspect of civilisation, were taken up for practical purposes by Von Stein, Bismarck's forerunner in the work of reconstructing the German empire. He organised the first society for historic investigation, and he encouraged Perthes to venture into the gigantic enterprise of publishing the "Heeren and Uckert History in Monographs". Thus the zeal for the study of history was stirred up in the Napoleonic period.

Shortly after a college of experts, such as Chateaubriand, Joh. von Miller, Tennemann, Neander, Niebuhr and others created the study of "Sources." With the "Rosetta-stone" found and deciphered, the world of scholars became as interested in discussions of Ægyptian archives as in German chronicles and French memoirs, or in the results of excavating expeditions. But owing to many modified interpretations of history as those of Schlegel, Hegel, Guizot etc., each trying to support his preconceived view of church and state, the public lost faith in historical evidences. A sceptical attitude as to the reliability of the new science was the result. Consequently objective exposition was demanded. Even the arduous labors of Schlosser, Weber, Leo, etc., to meet the demand, did not afford general satisfaction. One would find them either tinctured with deism or too orthodox; the tinge was too monarchical or too democratic, whilst others again would have the historical facts and figures strung up in such a neutral, nugatory manner, that nobody would care to study them.

The "Philosophy of History," published by Dr. Rocholl in 1892, found it necessary to start, twenty-five years ago, with clearing the ground in which to plant this "young upstart" of systematic knowledge. Still more difficult it is to cultivate in this country. In our system of education a place must first be secured for this philosophic discipline. Our college-curricula are so overburdened as to leave little time for this all-comprehensive study. Annexes to universities and historical seminaries and post-graduate courses prove the fact that historic instruction had been crowded out, but at the same time shows the growing necessity of its pursuit. In order to make the revelations of history applicable to Ethics, Sociology and Political Economy its contents must be digested by philosophical treatment. This is an indispensable requisite for the journalist and statesman, yea for every voting member of a nation of "sovereigns" with forms of self-government; especially at the present time, when public welfare and the perpetuance of our national institutions are expected from law and legislation, rather than from the Gospel and its application; and when Ethics seem to supersede Dogmatics.

Where, then, is the chair of history to be placed? Is this science with its outgrowth, the Philosophy of History, to be classified with the Natural Sciences, where a certain Sociology offered a back-seat to Clio? Or with Metaphysics, by means of which

Hegel made his "Idea" to develop into phantasmagorial realisation? The first chapters are to prove, that neither physical nor metaphysical dispositions can do justice to history, since as the regulator of world-theories, it must stand above suspicion of partiality. History, we claim, is not a cloud of effervescences emanating from above, nor evolving from below. History like man himself, the traces of whose character it bears, belongs to both spheres. But insomuch as science as well as society, whose theories history embraces, becomes the more differentiated, the nearer the organism of civilisation approaches the period of bloom and fruit bearing; and inasmuch as all vital relations become more sensitive, the more the functions are strained under increasing intricacy, we find that relations are to be adjusted, and labor must be divided. The fields of science are to be parcelled out, and special cultivation of each department is to be entrusted to qualified workers who know enough of the kindred sciences as to be entitled to co-operation. Each has to take cognisance of the other's labor and progress. For it is obvious, that science forms a co-partnership, and no particular branch ought to act as tho it held the monopoly of explaining the universe. Each is to serve with joy and without envy as an auxiliary to all the rest. Thus by mutual furtherance the sciences enrich not only themselves and their contemporaries, but also future generations. True civilisation is an inheritance to be improved and to be left again to such heirs as are trained to appreciate and to augment, instead of squandering, the wealth acquired by the sweat of the brow, and preserved by the shedding of much ancestral blood.

Hence we trust that "The Philosophy of History" with its claim to admittance will not be unwelcome to the American circle of systematic thinkers. The application for an introduction ought of course to be accompanied by credentials, demonstrating its possibility and utility; by a proof of method, a statement of topics, and a sample-production of its laboratory. The synoptical statements of the Philosophy of History, drawn from empiric data shall be legitimately obtained, and made testproof by the judicious application of critical principles, so as to secure conclusions untainted by harrangue, mystifications and illusive deductions. A consistent interpretation of historical facts will then bring to view that original plan, according to which the material is reared heavenward into a sublime structure. The design of the ethical cosmos will then stand out in bold relief, enabling us to contemplate it as that edifice, for which the nations, scattered through the ages and over the whole globe, furnish the pillars, the girders and decorations.

As to the method of construction let it be confessed, that the investigation and interpretation of undisputed data of history are not to be carried on "without prepossessed ideas". As often as such disinterestedness was simulated, it was unmasked as a scheme to beguile the unwary. Any assertion in the premises of "neutral objectivity" ought to be met with distrust. But at the same time permit the declaration, that no such preconception shall influence our search after the meaning of history, as that which vitiated, for instance, the Hegelian and similar world-theories. In them witnesses were put to the torture in behalf of the "Idea," until their utterances suited the purpose of the inquisitor; or they were spirited away, when it was known, that instead of yielding to the "Idea", they would confound and disprove it. Such procedure does not deserve the adjective honest, nor can it claim the distinction of being scientific. Abuse of a predetermined tendency, however, does not prove that prepossessed convictions always invalidate philosophic deductions. It is possible that interpreters may arise, who, endowed with the gift of discerning the spirits, like Dr. Rocholl, need not engage in dialectic subtleties; who interpret facts conscientiously, just because of their pronounced view of life.

It is to be expected of the historian, that his studies have filled him with a decided aversion to everything vicious, because he continually has before him illustrations of influences, which prove destructive to the sacred interests of humanity. He ascends to the pinnacle of the philosophical observatory into the clearest atmosphere possible, with confidence in the availability of, and insight into, the fundamental plan of divinely-human designs.

The historian, furthermore, from dealing with examples of heroism continually, may be expected to possess the courage of his convictions. Is he, then, to conceal the

Christian standpoint? to avoid the use of religious terms, the exclusion of which from philosophical discussions seems to have become the fashion? and to be ashamed of the Christ, lest he would run the risk of ridicule? The historian, no more than history, needs to be ashamed of Christian piety, to say nothing about the incomprehensibility of history without Christ. Faith does not obscure reason nor obstruct the light of science; faith has no more cause to shun its glare, (which it throws, perhaps, upon some weird caricatures of Christianity) than the Bible has excuse for the failings of its saints.

Equipped, then, with hatred of the Bad, and with love for, and unwavering confidence in, the True and the Good, let us take up our study. And not without reason, for who wants to find reason in things must bring reason with him. We do not intend to appeal to credulity. Solely the cognition of the Absolute Good and its necessity, as represented and manifested in the human conscience, free and unreserved acknowledgment is asked for in the premises. This necessity itself insists upon the freedom of thought.

The method shall be chiefly inductive. History is "THE" empiric science; it speaks from rich experience. Advance in knowledge is possible only on solid ground; facts, critically sifted, prescribe the line of procedure; their import must be carefully weighed, before taken into account. Essentials must be grouped in proper connection, where they appear to be most effective in yielding a sound comprehension. Small beginnings are not to be despised. So called accidentals are relegated to the category of every-day occurrences, without being depreciated. Nothing is to be ignored from fear lest the beauty of the system would be marred. Rather deny ourselves the satisfaction which might be derived from a nicely constructed system. Whenever the principles, underlying a catena of facts, the nexus between cause and effect is believed to have been discovered, then exceptional cases shall not be ignored. A conclusion shall not be announced unless the objections have been cautiously dealt with and recorded for eventual re-examination. More scientific circumspection can hardly be required.

Mere analysis and rearrangement of data, according to parallel periods or their semblance, could be no more satisfactory to us than it was to Bacon. Like him we dare not epitomise generalisations to form practicable syllogisms. We thereby shall find ourselves compelled to ascend, in search for the key of explanation, into the realm of metaphysics, if senses, and intuition, and all indications unmistakably point in that direction.

Alexander von Humboldt, in such emergencies, used to say: "It does not agree with true progressiveness to despise every attempt at deeper insight into the intricacies of things by way of analogy and upon the basis of induction, as tho the conclusions thus drawn had no more validity than a guess. Nor does it behoove us to condemn the noble endowments of the mind—now reason, aspiring to knowledge under speculative exertions, and then again imagination, that vivid energy of representation, which is often indispensable where discovery is to be made, or where shape is to be given to lofty conceptions."

If Humboldt's acknowledgment, and similar sentences of Goethe, hold good for comprehending the physical world, how much more must it be the case respecting the moral cosmos. We adopt the advice as our apology, as often as we are compelled to fall back upon intuition; and also whenever we have to refute that presumption, which boasts of the ability to explain riddles of empirical phenomena merely through the mediums of dissecting knife and retort.

The mind of the artist, whose fancy enables him, chisel in hand, to breathe life, as it were, into the marble, is filled with enthusiasm at the moment of conceiving his ideal delineated before his mind, as projected by his imagination. In giving external expression to it, he is of course, bound to the most minute observance of given outlines; imaginative contemplation does not furnish him the technicalities. But on the other hand, neither does the sculptor work out his ideal by mere external measurement. He must identify his own idea with the object, and must study the inner character to be represented by the image, i. e. the marks of physical life to be imitated by the chisel. The same subjective-objective identification is required for an intelligible reproduction of historic movements in space and time. Unless the historian can transfer himself to the stages of a nation's physical development, the real meaning of ethnographical characteristics will remain a mystery. The solution is to be found nowhere but in sympathy, in the inner act of recognition.

This would lead us to what is now called Ethnological Psychology, the consideration of which will be taken up in due time. In the first book no other notice can be taken of it, but what bears upon the problem before us and the method of its treatment.

Scientists assume that all human affairs can be explained by materialistic atomism; while most all historians maintain, that history cannot be understood, unless viewed from the position of Theism. Upon one conclusion general agreement reigns, viz: that history exhibits a development of humanity, an onward march, a continual advance toward higher civilization.

The question, however, arises: What is this civilisation, which moves on, seeming interruptions notwithstanding? Does it consist in the skillful adjustment of conduct to environments by way of prudent expediency? Or in the concentration of governmental power according to the survival of the fittest? Or in the lowering of personal' superiority to a common level of generalness under pretense of liberty, equality, and fraternity? Is not the prolongation of life the greatest desideratum, so that the barometer of civilization ought to be hung up in the health-office or in the statistical bureau? Reasoning thus, naturalistic Sociology gains popularity and wins an advantage over the Philosophy of History and its metaphysicians, because they can not make civilisation so simple and pleasant a task. For they, and we among them, hold that the *aim of civilisation is such cultivation of character, which, because of the objective necessity of the Absolute Good, endeavors to bring reason, feeling, and will under the control of a free agent, into equilibrium and proper mutual co-operation.* In other words civilisation is to us that culture of body and mind, which is based upon the cheerful exercise of the endowments and obligations, that is, upon the proper conduct of a person practicing the duties, which grow out of his relation to God, fellow-men and nature.

We claim that nothing less will answer the demands upon our science of civilisation but the inductive analysis combined with experimenting upon the contents of our dogma. By this method our science will be made as nearly as possible to correspond with the laboratory work of the scientist, from which praise and prayer to the Author of the universe and Ruler of kings need not necessarily be excluded.

All learned men now agree upon the division of the labors of investigation. They also agree that no branch can succeed, if it feigns indifference to the philosophy of the moral process. Even Spencer saw the necessity of vindicating the evolutionary world-theory by a sort of rehashed Hedonism. There must be a moral philosophy concerning man's inner constitution and life's purpose. In the realm of morals any world-theory is to be tested; from this source doctrines react upon history.

Materialistic moral brought forth the branch-study of ethnographic psychology, in order to show the germs of culture as sprouting in natural soil.

Nationality, however, is merely personality extended. The true understanding of neither can be derived from onesided investigation. Psychology must be inquired into to explain, for instance, the problem of languages, where it must fail again and again, unless it adopts a hypothetical premise to assist in its induction. This illustrates once for all, how natural science is directed for advice to a higher council, to metaphysics.

At once we stand upon the threshold of another world. It is impossible to evade questions like these: Can not the empirical field of history be explored without taking recourse to Heaven? Is it probable, that solutions may be obtained by referring to another world, since nothing on earth can explain certain divergencies and disturbances of cosmical, mental, and sensuous life?

This will suggest to us whither our inductive method may, yea must lead to. Whenever we are obliged to set foot upon the domain of metaphysics, or to make a balloon-ascension, as it were, into the heights of speculation, we shall—in keeping with the postulates, and in order to keep up communication with the solid ground, and in order to keep open the line of retreat—try the relevancy of a hypothetical fact. We shall then be in the same situation as that for which the Paris astronomer is renowned. Le Verrier's calculation is said to have been disproved by Peirce's equally daring confidence in mathematical analysis on the occasion of the discovery of the planet Neptune.

But Le Verrier's success of intuitive reasoning none the less proves as much as Peirce's corrective computations, the value of the hypothetical and intuitive calculation; both prove the legitimacy of applying a hypothetical fact. Methods of conjecturing like these, have more than once been sanctioned by success. We may be allowed to refer to the similar venture upon a hypothesis in the mind of Columbus. Analysis always either requires or prophesies a synthesis from which, as from a coherent whole, a special case implied finally receives its confirmation. The method of taking a hypothesis into service is obviously closely related to that of the mathematical sciences, and yields similar evidences: resting on physical grounds, it reaches up, at the same time, into the metaphysical spheres. Mathematics is to space, what history and ethics are to time, and what all three in the abstract are to real existence.

The right to propose a hypothesis is vindicated, because it forms the justifiable, if not the only legitimate connection between inductive and deductive syllogising. Nothing can hinder the mind from calling upon hypotheses for assistance, in order to discover an approximately correct view of human life, of its original design, and its final consummation. The result must justify the method, when all parts are comprehended in one synthesis that binds together the whole. From this unified conception, if correct, the parts receive their light and reason, according to our axiom, that the single can not be explained unless viewed from the aspect of the whole, and that the higher can not be understood by the lower.

At every stage of our procedure striking parallels may suggest instructive lessons and elicit comparisons between conditions of the human family in former ages and the present phases of history as to the woe or weal of humanity. Our philosophy thus applied can not but act the part of a philanthropist and patriot, warning against evil tendencies, so as to avoid, if possible, such recurrencies as would, by means of modern contrivances, prove more disastrous than any catastrophe on record.

BOOK FIRST.

Historics,

Prolegomena of the Philosophy of History.

A.—COEFFICIENT FACTORS IN HISTORY.
B.—OPERATIVE MODE OF HISTORY.

A. FIRST DIVISION.

CO-EFFICIENT FACTORS IN HISTORY.

SYLLABUS.

A person in the development of his life passes through three stages. Life given begins and continues for a certain length of time under physical conditions—man is passive.

Then intellectual discrimination dawns; he asserts himself, and learns to adjust his being to the objective world, in which he finds himself—he becomes receptive.

The age of maturity places before him the task of mastering and appropriating the external world, along with the practice of selfpossession and selfcontrol, so as to fit him for cooperation in elevating the natural into the spiritual—man is active.

These three topics first ventilated by Lessing and Herder, were utilised in Hegel's elaborate interpretation of history.

To his speculation on the development of mind individually, and of mind generally throughout history, he had been led by Fichte, who deduced all being from the "ego " by way of "thesis, antithesis, and synthesis." Hegel started his deduction from the "absolute idea," after the formula "subject, object (projection), and subject-object"—position, opposition, and composure—or "being in itself as unconscious; being in the act of becoming or reflected in the form of something else; and being in and for itself; selfconscious." '

Scharling divested such triads of their vagaries, where the sovereign mind is imagined as undergoing a physical metamorphosis, while at the same time nature is maintained as the opposite of mind pure and simple. By such extravagant inconsistencies thought is made to reveal itself in history, while at the same time the continual apostacy of history from its very idea renders both nature and history standing contradictions to the "IDEA," instead of its exposition.

Scharling in " Humanism and Christianity " reduces the true elements of the traditional tripartition to a very practical division of the ethico-historical process, viz,: Man as determined by nature, by his own, and by the Divine mind. Dorner, in throwing the light of Ethics upon determination, selfdetermination and predetermination, very convincingly describes the moral progress of man (1.) from the state under the law to (2.) the state under the gospel and (3.) to the kingdom of God's realised purposes.

So much has been made evident by the labors of all preceding masters, that the historic-empiric world is to be recognised as natural. moral, and divinely human—not in the order of time, as tho it had begun with Hindooism and wound up with Hegel's great decades, but in coincident stages of progress.

This brief sketch may have suggested, what physical and metaphysical matters and methods are to be considered in this first division. For, since natural and spiritual life condition each other, so the sciences of either province must over-lap where both elements approach their union in man.

Proceeding from physics through logic to ethics, we shall find the truth contained in the Greek phrase, that "man is the measure of all things," representing, as he does, in his constitution the whole universe as a microcosm. We shall behold man as the theme of history, and as its key. We shall discern, that man in every respect represents more than the mere material for the construction of a scientific evolution-theory.

CH. 1. RELATIONS OF THE PHILOSOPHY OF HISTORY TO NATURAL SCIENCES.

§1. Man is indeed the connecting link between two worlds. This happy figure of speech, first suggested by Herder, who had also initiated that tripartition of human life mentioned above, includes at once the necessary background and apparatus for the theatre of history and the actors upon its stage. It intimates at the same time that two worlds are contending for the possession of his heart, since he is designed for both, the possession of the earth, and the inheritance of Heaven. We shall not be in danger of trespassing our limits by stating, that man is of greater significance even than representing the apex of that structure, whose foundation consists in nothing less than the cosmical universe. For man's dual being is rooted also in the world of spirits. Hence Herder took man as the child of two creations.

Philosophy of late, however, in its endeavor to reduce all dualistic modes of consciousness into the one concrete entity of materialistic Monism, has allowed the impression to spread, that human existence was to be consigned to the globe alone. The intellectual trend of the time was more than favorable to the degradation of the Philosophy of History into a branch of Natural science.

Buckle in 1853 wrote to Lord Kington: "I confess that long ago I was convinced of the fact, that the development of a people is regulated by principles, called laws, which work with the exactness of those in the physical world."

The great geographer Ritter wrote to the celebrated historian Ranke: "The moral process runs in the curves of natural laws."

The emphasis laid upon the study of structural geography in connection with the study of history, in a treatise read before the Association of Colleges (Swarthmore near Philadelphia A. D.1892), is a significant sign of the pressure, which the atmosphere of the time exerts upon the modern author and instructor.

Bleek made mere natural causes account for the fall of Rome.

The antiquated notions of Herakleitos and Lucretius were revived by the German "Identity-Philosophy." In consequence of it, the origin and development of man and of history once more were deduced from such pseudo-syllogisms as "Natural Selection," etc.

Spinoza had reasoned out, that thought and extension were modified states or attributes of the same "Substance." Schelling, following this trend of speculation, almost identified the spirit with nature, leaning toward physical Monism. Hegel improved upon both by substituting the "Idea," as abstracted from the world of physical phenomena, for "Substance."

For some time the world was made to believe that history was but the hypostatisation of that abstraction. Hegelianism thus dissolved the essential value of historical facts also into mere phenomena, (Schein). This explains, why Hegel for the largest part of his Philosophy of History meditates upon the Hindoos and Chinese, of whom he makes the most in support of his theory. He loves these "dreaming Asiatics," in whom, according to him, the Deity was asleep as yet in order to come to itself in the consciousness of Jesus and the Hegelian school.

The weapons for the defence of outspoken Pantheism were forged from Buddhism. Much of this philosophy reflects its rays in Arnold's poem "Light of Asia". Under the proud title of "Theosophists" some spoiled philosophers now try to displace the Cross by the Lotus.

How far our century has become contaminated with such phraseology is illustrated by the popularisation of the "Christ-Idea" in Miss Evans' (George Eliot's) novels which still enchant some literary amateurs. Her "ethics" are deemed by a great many the most refined essence of religion, because it relieves one from accepting the truth of the historical records about the Crucified One. This evaporated gospel is the result of applying Hegelian Philosophy to the biblical facts of salvation. Everywhere we observe, how from that colorless spectre "generalness" the particulars are deduced and contorted into semblance with certain pet notions; how from a void vagueness the apparation of a copious reality rises up—a fata morgana. And this furnished the apparatus in which sacred history was to be distilled into intoxicants to the religious taste of everybody, into stimulants which, under the guise of science, were to give strength for scoffing at faith. Not a few of those claiming "education" delighted to move in such a world of delusions, aping that quasi-religious attitude of self-adoration. Thus were the earthly and heavenly things, the natural and spiritual worlds, brought to the level of indifference; and the compromise was hung low enough for selfcomplacent minds to see religious things under that perspective.

Schelling and Hegel, by force of their dialectics, had commanded matter and mind to lie down quiet in that indifferent identity, that chaotic Pan into which they had been thrown. Strauss ridiculed that philosophy of identity and unconcern. He defined materialism to be nothing but idealism set upon its head, but now turned upside down, so as to stand upon its feet again. As the precipitate of ambiguous speculation, modern materialism comes under our observation among the residue of other sublunar freaks of history. It is necessary to become fully acquainted with its roots and ramifications, its lineage being quite natural, and its seasons of growth recurring not without purpose, nor without cause. As a reaction against impudent theories, it was not the first time that materialism meted out to them what they deserved.

When the lingering clouds of idealism had been scattered by the storms of '48, the earth was taken into consideration Ritter raised geography to the rank of a science. He brought the globe to the notice of men, reminding the Germans at last, that they had something solid under their feet which was preferable to the cloudy realm above their heads. He showed how the various formations of the earth's surface exert their direct influences upon the natural dispositions or temperaments of men. The shapes of continents, direction of mountain-chains and watersheds, the extensions of plains or coast-lines, or river-bottoms, the wave-lines of the isotherms and the latitudes—all were asked to contribute toward the differentiation of the race with regard to languages, customs, cultures. A period of praiseworthy emulation was inaugurated by savants like Ritter and the Humboldts. Ether and ocean, strata of antediluvian and pre-glacial rocks and forests, the tellurian relations to the galaxy and the sun's spots, all yielded their share to enrich not only the storehouse of knowledge, but also to increase the conveniencies of life. The investigations of ocean-bottoms and of mountain-slopes not only caused the eye to have visions of vegetable and animal biology, but also resulted in direct and more practical advantages—perhaps the laying of a cable or the erection of a smeltery.

No wonder that some heads were turned by exalting the utilisation of scientific research. It is true, that this culture caused a decline of cultus, yet the industrial triumphs of human sagacity need not to be frowned at; for, the increasing worldliness and profanation of life is as much, perhaps, to be blamed upon theological stagnation; while on the other hand, the progressiveness of worldly culture in its conquest of space and time and masses, celebrated in a series of world-expositions, bears a marked feature of ethical import. The prosperity we owe to technical inventions and the triumphs alluded to, are so many evidences of the superiority of mind over matter; of the superiority, too, of the Teutonic part of Christian civilisation.

Decline of cultus not to be blamed upon culture alone.

Prosperity in Christiandom, especially on the Evangelical side proves the superiority of mind over matter.

Still no biology nor electricity will afford sufficient explanation for the differentiation and development of the social or any other organism. Only as an ethical personality can man render nature intelligible and serviceable, he alone being the rational agent with power to be a cause himself, on account of whom and because of whom every thing exists.

In man alone is to be found the explanation of the great successes of modern times, because he alone possesses consciousness which fits him for universal and perpetual aspirations. Without memory, that is without experiences traditionally accumulated, it would be impossible to improve upon, and utilise the prior acquisitions made by the mind and through its culture.

Now history is to humanity, to man collectively, what memory is to the individual. Without this manifestation of self-consciousness, persisting through all ages, all changes of localities and opportunities, the previous approaches toward our final acme of culture would have been of no avail to us. The boast of our high attainments might even be toned down a little, if that memory were duly refreshed. For considering our inherited facilities and comparing with them our present state of affairs, which to a great extent justifies the complaints of pessimism, we may as well confess, that with the means at hand a still higher civilisation and more beneficial results ought to have been obtained by this time.

History is to humanity what memory is in man Sec. 47.

Boasting of culture to be toned down.

The solution for which many problems are still waiting is to be expected from man's inner constitution alone, and certainly not found in geognostic conjectures. As yet by far the largest part of man's own self is hidden to systematic knowledge, and the largest part of the human race as yet stands on the low grade of arrested development, and belongs to the lowest strata of personal life. Were it otherwise we would as gladly give our cordial assent to the great geographer, as we thank him for being enabled to enter upon a new line of argument, where the physico-monistic view may hesitate to follow suit.

A new line of argument. Sec. 2, 21, 27.

Evolutionism and anthropo-geography, being entangled in environments, and posing upon soil and climate, try to evolve from them what never was embodied in them. The earnest labors of geographers and geologists might have been utilised to greater advantages, than has been done by Darwinism.

Influences of environment undeniable: to a certain extent.

According to the latter, climate, coast-lines, food, or any conglomeration of atoms constitute the principal motors and factors of human activity. It is true, surroundings exert strong influences upon the inhabitants.

But not always, not with the same effects, not at all exclusively. Let us examine.

Asia is the continent of the most varying contrasts, preeminently adapted to produce the greatest variety of human characteristics. Deserts reach down from high plateaus to the shores of gulfs and rivers. Jungles, prairies, forests, regions of veritable garden-lands, the highest mountains and the largest peninsulas change off everywhere. But man forgot to profit by the changes. He remained a child of nature, which he could not learn to understand; instead of making it serviceable he deified that nature below him.

Criticism of anthropo geography.

Geographical and ethnical characteristics of Asia. Sec. 29, 33.

Peschel's suppositions on culture do not hold good.

Haeckel and Renan: reductio ad absurdum.

If environments affect man, then man is no less to be credited with power to transform nature.

Terrestrial conditions affect human development:

not beyond a certain limit. Sec. 5, 10, 44, 45, 101, 219.

T. G. Mueller's argument fails.

Rivers create no cultures.

Buckle: led ad absurd. by

Goldwin Smith and Peschel.

There, through all ages, we find mixed masses of nomades and mariners, farmers and hunters, traders and robbers, moguls and beggars, crowding each other, fighting and migrating. Such "friction and mixture," according to Peschel, "are the main conditions for future culture." Friction and mixing he takes for the cause of Asiatic culture, while Hegel imputes Chinese stagnancy and Hindoo melancholy and inertia to the same localities.

Wide, waste regions may create robbers; the Sahara swarms with Tuaregs; the Gobi with Tu-kiu; but so do certain quarters of certain large cities swarm with people not less rapacious and not "down town" only. Nature fortified the people along the upper Danube against the unwelcome guests from the Volga by a pass, called the "Iron Gate", while the Chinese had to build their wall against the incessant intruders. Now why were the peaceable people in the regions adjacent and just as waste, not robbers also? Comanches and Apaches squirm through the barren steppes of sage and cactus in Mexico and Arizona, but the Gauchoes are none the better for their green pampas. Did the rovers of these deserts ever ascribe their savage life to their environments when justice forced them to abandon their favorite occupation of scalping? Would they have asked to be excused for their savagery, on account of the wild canyons of the Colorado, if Herr Haeckel had met them there on their trails? They all have not the slightest idea of the relation between their zones and themselves. But all their countries assume a quite different aspect, as soon as people from civilised nations even their refuse, take possession of, and irrigate such regions and plant orange groves. Since soil and climate and food have been considered as determining coefficients of history in forming human character, why may not rather man form, even transform the character of the country? As a part of nature he has at least the same privileges. We see the theory of evolution from environments is alluring only where it binds man to nature—but it proves too much. The beautiful regions around Nazareth did not produce the model character of the carpenter's son, as Renan strongly insinuated; else why could Nazareth, proverbial for its unproductiveness of any thing good, also produce those citizens who tried to dispatch their rabbi? "Evolution" would forbid the conclusion that expansive regions contract the horizon of reason, whereas it is simply because man continues on the plane of the natural, that he never rises to understand, much less to dominate over nature.

Granted, that the shape of the coasts and mountains of Europe was favorable to a manifold culture, while the tribes of Africa and Australia were deprived of such advantages by the compactness of their continents and by the straightness of their ocean-coasts. The monotony of scenery tells on the people in their lack of phantasy, in the melancholy and monotony of their physiognomies and lingual forms of expression.

Yet all of these terrestrial conditions do not affect human beings beyond a fixed limit.

In most cases they do not suffice to account for glaring differences which leave the scientist in a dilemma, despite the natural "conditions being equal," as Spencer's magic formula has it.

J. G. Mueller, for instance, asserts, that the torrid zones produce sun-worship, and frigid latitudes a superstitious belief in ghosts, Shamanism. According to that theory it should be very cold in the Congo state. It has been often repeated that the great river-valleys bring forth civilised states, since the Nile figures as the creator of Aegypt, the Ganges for the mother of Buddhism. But why does father Nile not continue to provide for the poor Fellahs of the present time?

The three streams of Africa put together do not convey such water-power, nor afford such great opportunities as the Amazon river alone. How shall we explain the fact, that the children of the former fell behind, and the neighbors of the latter stayed behind? On the contrary, as against the river-bottom theory we might argue in favor of high plateaus; think of the states and cultures of the Toltecs, Aztecs and Inkas in Mexico, Yucatan, Quito and Peru. Why were the Chinese, why the Arabs at times so expanding, whilst the neighboring Aegyptians were always stationary? Not because of too many or not enough geographical barriers; for we have seen the Indians of Alaska coming down a thousand miles in their canoes to pick hops around Seattle, while the Amazon is not used by the Brazilian Indians to cross to the nearer Antilles, much less to New York.

As a general rule, mountains, lakes and steppes did not so much separate people as rather increase their migratory inclinations. Yet the Mississippi, Amazon and Orinoco did not accomplish that with which the Nile, Euphrates and Ganges are accredited. This shows that rivers become assisting factors of culture only, where advanced people dwell; to abandoned people they become distinct boundary lines, as the Senegal became for Berbers and negroes.

Buckle, "most severe upon the extravagancies of the race-theory," himself falls into absurdities. He connects the religious character of the Spaniards with imaginary volcanoes and earth-quakes, whereas it palpably had its origin in the long struggles with the Moors. He in like manner connects the theological tendencies of Scottish thought with the thunder storms, which he wrongly imagined to be very frequent in the high-lands; whereas "theology and religious tenets almost identical with those of the Scotch were generally formed in the low-lands and among the Teutons, not among the Celts" says Goldwin Smith.

Buckle was very assiduous in making man's religion the product of his birth-place and nothing more. Peschel in his Ethnology refers to Mexico in rebuttal of this argument. This is a land of sun-shine and serenity; but behold into what dark souls the Aztecs must have evolved, when we read of a collection of 170,000 skulls, the relics of human sacrifices, built up into pyramids in Montezuma's cosy court-yard. Such exceedingly unnatural depravity, where the conditions were so conducive to refinement! And is the depravity less, or are the conditions more unfavorable to civilisation in some street not a mile from the Tuilleries or from Wall street? *[Mexican ethnography disproves anthropogeographical allegation.]*

In our expectations, roused by propositions like those of Buckle, we were disappointed. He importuned us to believe his promise of a full account of historic development through terrestrial causes, but he did not keep it. We may name a man after his native home, but originally the countries were named after their inhabitants and by them. This goes far to prove, that man ever had the feeling of what we formulate into this axiom: **The key of nature lies in man**, and not vice versa. *[Originally countries were named after their inhabitants.]*

The proposition, that terrestrial circumstances were shaping ethnical characteristics aggravated the dilemma in which the scientific expounders of historical development were caught. We on our part now propose a higher causality of determining influences. Let us try the astral hypothesis, that line of argument, to which previously allusion has been made. It once sufficed the Chaldeans who invented the zodiac for the very purpose of disclosing man and his mysterious history. *[Another hypothesis: Astral influences. Sec. 1, 5.]*

History knows of more than one Napoleon who followed his lucky star.

"Pope Paul III, according to Mendoza (as quoted by Ranke) held no important session of the consistory, nor made he a journey, without first having consulted the stars on the choice of fitting days. *[Superstitious application of astral influences: Pope Paul III. Mendoza—Ranke.]*

Newspapers, abetting the views and opinions of the "creme" of society, contain columns of advertisements for the benefit of such of their patrons as frequent the star-readers. One certain Sachse ("the Law of Numbers in the Excitability of Nations") with all seriousness deals once more in astrology, demonstrating nervous sensitiveness by tabulated wave-lines, wherein ascending curves correspond with the increasing number of sun-spots. This is "Ethnographical Psychology" and automatic evolution with a vengeance. *[Sidereal relations exist, Sec. 1, 5, 21, 27,]*

Now, as the choice of our hypothesis indicates, we are far from denying a very direct action of the whole sun-system on our bodies, not so much through the physical elements of our corporeal parts, as by way of our planet. These sidereal relations do exist. We shall even recur to them and make extended use of them, noticing how the sun connects millennia, at the least, of natural with modern universal history. *[and point to a world above.]*

The allusion to these sidereal influences, however, has no other object but to show, that we are pointed to a world above where, perhaps, we may find causes not divulged by terrestrial grounds. By the way we may take the liberty to show also the futility of that abortive attempt to degrade man, humanity and history to a mere issue of the play of matter and motion. We grant a world full of natural influences upon human nature. But as against the view of "dynamics," we stand by our axiom, which will be rendered more and more lucid, that **the laws of natural development do not affect the human being beyond a certain limit.** *[but as against "dynamic development" the axiom is reiterated: not beyond a certain limit. Sec. 1, 101, 219.]*

We shall keep in mind, that the deep chasm between the inorganic, organic, and psychical parts of nature on the one hand, and the psycho-spiritual and pneumatical sides of our nature on the other, can not be bridged by any superficial subterfuge of a certain scientific leger-de-main. Functions can not be explained by structures, Spencer notwithstanding. Intrinsically as the workings of the highest differentiated organisms may interact, (read the old article on "Logic" in the Britanica) life can not result therefrom. Life precedes and supersedes the cells, the protoplasm. *[Spencer refuted: functions inexplicable by structure.]*

Goethe's homunculus was a travesty upon the presumption of man to figure as a creator. Liebig wrote: "Chemistry in all its laboratories can never succeed in manufacturing a single cell or a nerve or the like, which would be fit for a conductor of the vital power much less a vital germ itself." Virchow and Dubois-Reymond have endorsed this statement. *[Goethe's travesty: Homunculus. Limits of natural science: Liebig, Virchow.]*

The latter enumerated these seven riddles of the world; "(1.) substance of matter and force; (2.) origin of motion and life; (3.) conformity to a purpose apparently preconceived altho seeming unintentional; (4.) the rise of a simple sensation; (5.) of a thought; (6.) of consciousness; (7.) of free will. *[Dubois-Reymond: Seven riddles.]*

Why, then, continue to amuse the uninitiated with the dire myths of "spontaneous generation" and the like?

Our axiom, that despite the much popularised and believed dogma of automatic, or dynamic evolution, natural selfdevelopment can never transcend a certain limit—is certainly vindicated, even by many concessions of Tyndall himself, altho evasive. He condemns the erection of a world-theory upon so frail a basis and so fraught with error. *[Tyndall: No world-theory to be built on a basis so frail.]*

We are therefore most assuredly justified to search for the vital and life-connecting principle in the world above. Is that what the naturalists are so much afraid of? Why? The presumption of founding a world-theory upon spontaneous generation and natural selection certainly has no right to interdict our search higher up. We are not to blame for seeking explanation in the metaphysical realm. Why should we not suppose the postulate to which all indications point: that human activity is determined by causes beyond nature as we know it? Why not risk an experiment? We on our part have no reason to fear the loss of our good senses thereby, much less since we have sure historical experiences by which to go as pledges of success!

Result: Human activity determined by causes beyond known nature.

Suppose then, we set aside the unprofitable and unavailing hypothesis of mechanical lawfulness and natural necessity ruling history, and place ourselves on the lookout for liberty. In case we should fail in an intelligible manner to prove real influences from a higher sphere of life or a supernatural source, setting things in motion and manifesting sway in history, it would be no disgrace to retreat.

Research passing over into the metaphysical realm.

In Mexico and India and all around us, wherever mankind is as yet shackled by nature, and lives in that stage of arrested life, which results from natural development alone, we find human progress at an end. The limits of ascent being reached with that point where for instance the Chinaman contents himself to dwell, naturalism leaves humanity in a lamentable condition. Even astrological fortune-telling, altho betraying the consciousness of better things along with that mysterious longing of which we shall take notice as a historical fact, only aggravates the situation. Hence natural science is not competent to fill, and should not attempt to usurp, the chair of history. To philosophise upon history means to view life from an aspect higher than a kitchen, to look upon the world from transcendental grounds, from the supernatural, if it pleases better to call it so, or as we here and there may say, from spheres transeunt, which need not be ruled out of order as being unnatural.

Natural science incompetent to fill the chair of history.

Surely, such a standpoint can not disqualify philosophy, nor can it be forbidden her. Nor ought it to be ridiculed, if she ascends one step higher, above baffling mystifications and terminologies so as to gain a free position and the most comprehensive range of vision possible. Philosophy is pressed to rise above mere empiricism, which labors under its own present predicaments, not to speak of the difficulty of finding itself out of the labyrinths of those sixty or seventy centuries full of the enigmas of human affairs which are not as yet irrelevant to us. The Philosophy of History does not need to sever her connection with the world and its nature for all that; nor to infringe on foreign grounds. If naturalism prefers deduction from below, from material premises, to cover or account for even mathematical transcendentals, by borrowing from metaphysical a prioris and results, then we, too, may claim the right to use the path of deduction and to call upon intuition for assistance, without jeopardising what was gained by induction. By applying both deduction and intuition, we will test the legitimacy of postulates gleaned by induction, and so doubly test the truth of our conclusions. If we should be arraigned for the announcement of a purpose, for advocating the aim, for speaking of a teleological intent, we beg to differ from Materialism simply in that we seek the very end, which dynamic evolutionism puts into things, so that they may have something to swing around in their circles. In that which secures the **goal of moral development**, we hope to find the one thing necessary which, concerning personal life, we regard as "the" necessity to the exclusion of any other, in the necessity of the real, the Absolute Good of humanity, i. e. the necessity of its realisation.

Philosophy claims to reason inductively from empirics with as much right as science assumes to account for "mathematical transcendentals" by borrowing "universals".   Sec. 14.

Teleological intent vindicated.

The sole presumption: Necessity of the "Absolute Good."

The aim for which we look, is nothing less than the glorious perfection of creation. We could not satisfy reason nor comfort the heart with the reiterated dogma of materialism according to which human happiness and blessedness should depend on environments and be jeopardised by outward circumstances. We have advanced too far since the age of Stoicism, as to fall behind even that. We mean to preserve the dignity of history and humanity, and not to suffer them both to be consigned to the metempsychosis of water-bubbles, as it were, nor the cosmos to a pyro-technical fiasco. Not until the naturalistic scientists have adduced demonstrative proof of their insinuations to that effect, will the Philosophy of History hand in her resignation.

The dogma of a naturalism which falls behind Stoicism.

CH. II.   RELATION OF THE PHILOSOPHY OF HISTORY TO METAPHYSICS.

§3. Because Naturalism conceives matter moving under "laws" of inherent necessity, as the ultimate cause of all, even spiritual activity, and because it is apt to ignore phenomena which it cannot explain nor deny by these laws—it gets entangled in nature instead of getting emancipated from it. *Presumptuousness of Naturalism.* *Law of necessity inherent in matter explains neither nature nor emancipates man.*

Philosophy of History in the interest of humanity refuses, as humanity itself does, to be made the victim of such drudgery and treadmill business under mechanical "laws." She is getting herself ready for the rescue of personality and the liberty of thought. Even tho the attitude she takes, may to Materialism look like pugnacity, she nevertheless cultivates friendship with the Natural Sciences.

On the other hand, however, our science must also settle a few items with Metaphysics. This has always shown a tendency to deprive the natural world of free movement, to decry its relative independence, to depreciate its value as the secondary good, to calumniate it as the seat and source of sin, to despise its aesthetical import. From such wrongs nature must be exonerated; it is to be set aright as the mirror of celestial splendor and harmony. It is to be shown how and why nature is able to retain and to display these reflections, notwithstanding its changes, its deficiencies and vicissitudes. *Philos. cultivates friendship with natural sciences* *and must, on the other hand, settle a few items with Metaphysics.*

A false spirituality had tainted the judgment as to the relations between mind and matter. It could see nothing in nature but contemptible cosmic stuff, void of any formative principle. It therefore still acts as though it must take away from nature the capability of preparing itself for the reception of new scions to be engrafted upon it as tho the capacity for a cooperative process of unfolding itself must be denied to nature. That false spirituality thinks it necessary to wipe out the gradation of the ascending scale of formations by unduly emphasising. Leibnitz's law of "continuity." False spirituality considers the minutest details in nature as immediate creative acts, as tho the Creator himself were pushing every blade of grass and were throwing millions of blossoms into waste. *Misconception of nature by a false spirituality.*

In order to spare philosophy such absurdities of a mechanical omnipotence, Malebranche composed his system of the "Occasional Cause," improving, as he supposed, upon Descartes. Suggestive and plausible as this system seemed, yet nature and mind were so far alienated as to represent two distinctly separate entities running, without any parity or community of being between them, alongside of each other without ever coming to united action, not even in the human person. Body and soul are treated as heterogeneous quantities; yoked together, they never even incite each other to simultaneous action. *"Occasionalism": MALEBRANCHE. Sec. 15, 17, 19.* *Mechanical conception of the relation between mind and matter.*

According to that theory it is no proof that the foot is moved by the mind, tho the mind be conscious of the motion. Neither are any corporeal mutations, affecting the moods of the psychical part of human nature, nor any facts proving that the body affects the mind, considered as proofs by this theory. *Impressions from without, impulses from within, LOCKE.*

Physical motions and mental emotions, impressions from without and impulses from within, incitements of subjective thought by objects, were dimly distinguished by Locke, and were made, or rather described, as fitting each other by Leibnitz in his attempt to correct "Occasionalism" by "Preestablished Harmony." Thus it only appears to us as if the body was actuated by the mind or vice versa. For, "the monads of Leibnitz have no windows," through which any external agency, foreign to them, could enter or go out so as to affect their internal condition. *LEIBNITZ's attempt to improve upon Malebranche's theory.*

This view, begging the question of having any view at all, illustrates the absurdity of the other side. One can scarcely distinguish this mechanical spiritism from dynamic mechanism. *"Mechanics" of spiritism, "dynamics" of materialism.*

The old paths must be abandoned and new roads built, whereupon to arrive at the solution of the problem, viz: upon what ultimate principle is the formal construction of the natural world to be based? Herbert Spencer,—detaining us a little longer at dynamic-mechanism—in the interest of materialistic monism, answers: Upon motion! And motion, under the subtle proviso of "all things being equal," always moves in the direction of the least obstruction; it everywhere follows the presupposed requisites of centrifugal and centripetal gravitation. Every branch of a tree, the atti- *Is motion the constructive principle in nature? SPENCER.*

tude of every flower proves this truth, says Spencer. The whole fabric of blood-circulation substantiates the theory of "least resistance." Science at once is made very simple. Ziehen has told us that the whole story of man's being can be explained from the structural and functionary components of man himself. We do not wish to find fault with this mode of generalizing vegetable, animal and personal movement as equivalent phenomena, under rubrics of mechanical energies, which in higher organisms become only more differentiated and intricate. In its limits and its place we do not dispute the truths brought out by evolutionism, if understood as the unfolding of created life. Evolution in the progress of its affiliation or thought-filtration and with dexterously manipulated wordings may conclude, that everything organic is a mechanism. This is not what compels my organism to the reverse nerve-action of raising an objection. We enter protest for the simple reason, that taking such a view the cognitions of type and design, i. e., teleology, are condemned without trial.

The doctrine of the purpose is not thus, on the sly, to be replaced by that of motion; we do not allow this manner of killing the purpose by silence, or forcing it brevi manu out of recognition.

The purpose has a claim as yet upon admittance to the discussion. Many investigators find a purpose inherent in every thing, not for itself alone, but for every thing besides. I surmise a purpose in Spencerian theories even, if they possess any value whatever. According to them the development of the species is to be understood as caused solely by external conditions. Possibly organic life may be rendered equal to mechanical force. Yet this could not force us to relinquish our conviction, that the **first protoplasm must have been endowed with an immanent impulse, indicating some design and prompting the unfolding of that protoplasm in an appointed direction.** We would not offer the least obstruction to motion as the constructive principle on that score.

But Spencer's theory, in order to maintain itself and its consistency, must deny both impulse and direction. Spencer admits nothing but a selfconstituted organic mechanism, evolution pure and simple, externally conditioned by environments which, of course, he finds ready made for no purpose. This is the long and short of it. This forbids the supposition of any higher or deeper cause outside of things as being not only superfluous but also confounding. Immanent design, the reason of things in themselves equal with their ultimate causes outside of them, and concomitant with their causal bearings upon other things, is denied for no other reason that I could think of, but to get along without the "Unknowable" and the "Hereafter." But on this line of cheap denial, with argument inferred from silence, and in this cowardly manner of dodging the question at issue, science turns into nescience.

By "design" the followers of Spencer and Haeckel understand "the emancipaton of the highest differentiated organism" from the necessity of the "Supreme Good." That a new set of rules of "conduct," misnamed ethics, had to be promulgated, so as to escort Materialism into respectable company, or to fortify it with pilfered material, is a tacit admission of—the purpose for which the system was designed. By such ethics, evolved from the mollusk, spiritual truths were to be rendered indifferent — and of no purpose. It was to hide the strategem, by which the loss of the Good was to be kept out of view, by which the attention was to be diverted from the manipulation of spiriting away the "Supreme Good."

Will ethics of the evolutionary brand ever be able to produce, out of matter-motion combined with sociological statistics, any substitute for what is thus treated with silent contempt in the interest of " the emancipation of the flesh " ? Not even a counterfeit semblance to it, if one knows that genuine Ethics means more than rules for conventional conduct.

Some people seem to think that, because of the conclusions jumped at by socialists, materialism had lost its prestige and danger. This optimism, however, looking a little like spiritual affinity and sympathy with agnosticism, might take advice to be cautious. Since we see even defenders of the Christian world-theory, staunch opposers of Darwin, Spencer and Haeckel, cooperating with them unawares, in that they propagate a mechanical view of nature themselves, we must engage somewhat in the exposure of the errors of wrong spirituality.

§4. In order to maintain the dignity of man, the idealists, siding with asceticism, take the soul out of nature. They leave as little free movement to vegetation, and as few of the psychical attributes as possible to the animal kingdom. Thus a wide sphere of organic life is withheld from nature, in which from an impetus given to it, nature spontaneously may ascend the ladder of rich development and variation. The first cause is continually required for the direct production of creative effects. The almighty power of the Creator is deteriorated into a sort of world-soul. When it comes ^{Profanation of the miracles.} to the definition of miracles, the observation that they never are without a natural basis, one and all, is rendered suspicious of rationalistic heresy by that school. In other respects a special manifestation of the divine will is alleged for every particular and simple phenomenon, so that every movement in nature becomes a miracle; hence the significance of the miracle itself is lowered to an every-day affair, is made a mere natural fact.

Weiss, for instance, warms up occasionalism in his mechanical presentation of providence which flagrantly profanes the miracles and Him of whom they are to testify. A doctrine is preferred of vital force being infused continually from outside instead of attributing so much of vitality to matter, as is necessary to make it serve henceforth as the vehicle of that imparted principle, which is to resuscitate the dormant or arrested life. These ever repeated life-infusions are not quite the same as the "elementary (fire, water, air, and earth) spirits" of mediæval speculatists. The "spirits" were kept apart from the elements whilst the elementary substance was looked down upon as something not only lifeless but opposed to life. Even their susceptibility for becoming vitalised is ignored, their adaptability for glorification denied. Matter then remains to be regarded as that which— **not only in the state of final glorification, but also in the present state of existence, ought not to be.** Matter is taken for irrational stuff, for a sedimentary refuse without any meaning, as being of no use, nor of any account whatever, which therefore can not and need not be understood. The latter sophism—corresponding with the denial of the spirit by nescience, in the way extremes generally meet,—is made the excuse for dropping the stubborn thing as unworthy of further consideration.

Now all this caution to ascribe as little as possible to nature in majorem gloriam dei; this injunction as to the relative independence of nature by which it is attempted to restrain force to play around matter like a flame around a wick; this reluctance to grant animation to nature, which nevertheless continues ascending upward in the physico-psychical constituency of the human body, results from misconceptions of the human soul and of divine omnipotence. It forms the rightful opposition of conservative theology against pantheism and materialism, both denying the personal, living God. But it betrays, at the same time, a poor opinion and narrow view of, and little faith in, Divine Providence, as tho the power of the creature would detract part of the authority and honor of God, as tho nature might become too much for Providence, if man and things had a real soul in common; or as tho man's immortality would suffer under nature's participating in the soul. This fear of irreverence, or of curtailing the almighty power, or of giving room to pantheistic inferences and imputations, this super-cautiousness is, what caused our friends to meet with the opposite extreme in the mechanical conception of the moving and formative or constructive principle in nature and history. The **dynamic-mechanical** view cannot, and pretends that it needs not, to know the "Unknowable." To that view things spiritual are of no purpose! The **pneumatic-mechanical** view profanes the miraculous and direct interventions, and the purely **spiritual** manifestations of divine condescension in the manner shown. It cannot understand the good-for-nothing **matter** for which at bottom there is no use —which is of no purpose!

Materialism and Pantheism attribute divinity to nature; erring idealism, a **pseudo-spiritualism or asceticism divests nature of a life of its own, that is, of the capacity for divine immanency!**

It is plain; both modes of speculation,—the dynamic and the pneumatic mechanical, the one in the interest of matter, the other for the sake of mind—create each a different conception of history peculiar to itself. The views obtained from such preoccupied standpoints bear not only upon the philosophical interpretation of history, and upon all its auxiliary sciences, but also upon every-day life.

Dynamic contemplation of nature makes things purposes in themselves (gold for
4

Side notes:
- Weiss: Christ's miracles and "Occasionalism."
- Mediæval "Elementary spirits."
- Capability of nature to become matter identified with that which "ought not to be." Sec. 40, 204, 232.
- Misconception of the human soul and of divine providence,
- caused by super-cautiousness where the extremes meet in the mechanical views of nature.
- MATTER OF NO PURPOSE.
- Materialism and pantheism deify nature. Pseudo-spiritualism and asceticism divest nature of its capacity for divine immanency.

" Dynamics " posits the purpose into purpose. Gold. Pneumatic " Mechanics " keeps it entirely apart from nature.

instance or the state;) i e. it drops the purpose. On the part of the mechanics of Occasionalism facts and things are underrated as nothing in themselves but mere manifestations of pre-established harmony, or rather as direct results of divine intervention in the most trivial occurrences.

(NOTE: Further discussion of the topics of this chapter in 1. A. ch. 5. and on purpose 1. B. ch. 1.)

CH. III.   PERSONAL AS DISTINGUISHED FROM NATURAL LIFE.

Life the constructive principle of nature.

§ 5. For reasons given, our discussion of the constructive principle in nature must begin with determining the meaning of the word "life." The major premise which we take for granted is, that life is the totality of the manifold (tho no monas).

Goethe's suggestion.

" Mechanical atomism " —individualisation— as well as the cognition " personality " and " Ethnographic Psychology " are outgrowths of Meister Eckhard's, Leibnitz' and Herbart's theories.

Unity of the human race rescued by Herbart in "creationism," and by Leibnitz in " pre-established harmony ". both transcending their postulates.

Goethe already in the "Morphology of plants" saw the bearing of this cognition. This suggestion may enable us to conciliate the results of former attempts, such as those of Malebranche and Leibniz, without a lapse into onesidedness or committing us to ambiguity. If we are not mistaken, both sides call for an adjustment of the truth which each seeks to establish. It is peculiar that mechanical atomism—grown out of Meister Eckhard's and Leibnitz's " individualisation," to which also Herbart's mode of thought gravitates, and to which we are indebted for the fixing of the idea of personality—has advanced to be formulated into " Ethnographical Psychology." This is a very welcome, new auxiliary to our science; and the cultivation of this new specialty is indeed of singular significance. From the atomistic concept of the soul as an individualised entity the idea of a "national character," of a "spirit of the times," much less the cognition of the unity of the whole human family could scarcely have been expected. That the latter especially was maintained, we owe to the precaution which made both, the "monad-theory" of Leibnitz as well as the "creationism" of Herbart, transcend their postulates, the one in "pre-established harmony," the other in "ethnographical psychology."

Speaking of created life, we know of but two manifestations—natural and personal life.

Two manifestations of created life: natural and personal.

Meaning of the term " arrested-life."

Entering the domain of nature we are ready to meet the objection, that the basal ground in which mind is planted, is not to be regarded as a substance with immanent vital qualities, but as destitute of life, as dead matter.

Of course, since we are accustomed to have movement implied in the notion "life," analogous to living creatures, inorganic life can not be called alive. Yet since motion is the most conspicuous symptom of life, we can not help calling the compositions and combinations of cosmical dust latent life—life bound up as it were, confined, compressed, retarded, or (as we will use this term henceforth in this sense) arrested life.

All organic life is but life latent in matter disengaged.

Storage-batteries of motion participate in the " anima mundi " in its dormant state.

Organic life is merely the life latent in matter disengaged, life set free—as we use the phrase in chemistry—life delivered from its confinement. For all these rocky masses, forming the framework of the globe, all the different strata, sediments, alluvial deposits and deluvian driftings are the store-rooms for all organic life spreading over their surface. More than that, all these massive storage-batteries of motion act as coefficient factors in all historic events. The whole process of "becoming" or "coming to" life, and "to live," is conditioned by them. In these dormant powers the "Anima Mundi" is lying asleep, as it were. If we speak of spontaneous growth of animate nature; if natural phenomena are personified in paganism, and if ideals are hypostatised by Plato and Hegel, then more than scientific figures of speech, more than random poetical phrases are expressed.

To take life in this wider sense is altogether appropriate. For, looking upon these seeming "lifeless" masses, we find them in sympathy and in contact even with the planetary system. We have terrestrial life partaking of the astral. Sidereal life, not as blind force but in well-articulated pulsations, pervades, animates and agitates

Well articulated pulsations, magnetic fluxes and chemical polarities of sidereal life pervade the terrestrial. Sec. 2, 21, 27.

The essence which renders nature a unitary and nascent entity.

the crust of our globe. Magnetic fluxes and chemical polarisations vibrate through the earth, causing it to quake and men to tremble. Hence in this sense no part of the universe can be imagined as void of life, else it would represent a nonsense; it would remain unintelligible, irrational and purposeless. But as soon as the material components are conceived as confined, repressed or arrested life, life bound up like lightning prior to its discharge, the cosmos becomes intelligible, becomes an individual, as it were. Whether its fundamental principle may then be called force, world-soul, law of becoming (Werde-gesetz) as Ebrard termed the anima mundi, or what you please, it is a potential energy, a latent potency; it is the nascency of nature; it is present and alive. It is the essence that makes nature a unitary nascent entity. It has caused many a portentuous change in the world—not in nature alone, but in the chain of personal life, in history. Where, for instance, would our coal be gotten from if it had not been for the death-struggles in which an eon of existing organic life expired? And what would civilisation be without coal?

The choice of our designation "arrested life" will vindicate itself throughout our discussion, if it is kept in mind, that in this deceased, dead matter the very nascency lies dormant, those potentialities which make the plants grow, just as it awoke when the plants were called forth by the command given to the earth. This "dead" matter conveys the very potentialities which restore health to patients, which help to build up the animal body, and from which—**the human soul arises.** Remember always that this world of mere elements, of dormant life and objectivised (Bowen would say hypostatised) thought, is to be set free incessantly from the form of a mere aggregate (nebeneinander); and is to be led up from the state of detachment and opposition (auseinander) into the state of pneumatic immanency (ineinander). It was on the suggestion of this truth that the notion of "Consubstantiation" was discerned to have once been rendered emblematic in the Eucharist.

Nature is to be delivered from her confinement or arrested state, so as to enable her to receive new impartations, and to produce, under harmonious cooperation, a condition in which the created but nascent life latent within her can prosper, preparatory to a next higher form of existence. Step by step the same process of deliverance—after cooperative preparation for receiving the impetus for the next higher unfolding of life—is repeated, life in general always remaining intimately connected in all its interrelations, even with the lower stages passed, in whatever shapes the higher formations assume; so that even astral life remains identical with the stars of our flora. Thus developing life differs in the degree of its metamorphoses but not in essence, so that upon each higher notch on the scale of ascendency each individualised or differentiated part of general life, in connection and cooperation with the whole, may become the receptacle of the higher life that is to come. This is the truth of evolution as far as it goes, and several times already we have conceded this with certain reservations. This is the truth underlying the inter-relation between natural development and ethical selfculture, between religious sanctification and resurrection. In every stage the individual entity is to keep up the connection with all the preceeding lower stages of life, so that even the earth is obliged to cooperate in that preparation, by which the reception of, and transition into, the highest forms of the final state of glorified existence is conditioned.

In emphasising the identity of all created life, we are well aware of the purport of the statement. We do not discriminate between the animation of the crystal, the lily, or the ruby-topas humming-bird, or the brain of man even—with the proviso of course, that this connection of the intensified natural life in the human soul with life in general does not include the human spirit, because that does not belong to the realm of nature.

But the natural world in its various stages of delivery of formative life, from the dust in the street up to the intensified, individualised life in the soul of man at the zenith of natural animation, this whole royal road of modification and elevation, including the galaxy of fixed stars and the crown of queen Victoria—we deliberately consider as a oneness in substance and essence.

Nature is life in its entirety, a subsisting reality, manifesting itself in countless selfdeveloping formations,—images,—which represent the alphabet of God's imprinted manifesto.

We termed the one, the inorganic part of the visible world, compressed, "arrested" life. And now we assume the right of designating the whole animate world, from the crystal to the human soul inclusive, as such "arrested" or retarded life, which from stage to stage is to be delivered from the confinement, awaiting its elevation to its next higher sphere. This allegation may seem audacious, extremely paradoxical, but we warrant due explanation and are confident of general consent.

It must suffice for the present to be only reminded of the other great enigma which hovers about all physical and ethical phenomena in this world, which is unintelligible to minds as yet in the lower state and which become intelligible only to those having passed into the sphere of pure God-consciousness.

The "irrational something" reaching from another world into this.

And need we be reminded of that irrational something, which from the "spirit-land," called the other world, reaches into the kingdom of the human mind, ever instigating turbulence which as yet will give us much to think of?—and which will remain unintelligible until it comes in contact with embodied holiness.

Sphere of personal life:

§ 6. At this instant we enter the new sphere previously hinted at, the world of the human mind—personal life. We enter at that moment where the acme of evolution and ripeness, demonstrating the oneness of natural life, is reached in the human soul.

Natural self-development reaches its acme in the human soul, then ceases. Sec. 9.—It is arrested on account of man, whose task it becomes to redeem the confined life of nature.

At this stage nature ceases its conditional selfdevelopment. Natural life is arrested. Man has to take up the task of influencing nature and of elevating its life, that is, redeeming that natural life which became arrested on his account.

We speak now of the human soul as mind, in which we meet the personal spirit, coming as a new endowment from above, long before Pentecost. This spirit takes possession of that soul which evolved from below, coexisting and consubstantial with the body.

That soul had become the inner, the liberated and intensified life of nature, separable, but as yet not disengaged, from material life. This soul is still confined life but now in that form of natural existence, wherein nature accomplished her preparation for entertaining the spirit. This intensified and individualised unit of natural life, the humanised soul is coessential if not consubstantial with the body. Separable from it, yet without severing its connection with the totality of physical existence, this soul is subjoined to the new, the other oneness or totality of the spirit. The monas "Nature," by its representative, by proxy as it were, through its highest or most intensified essence, the human soul, enters with the "Spirit into an indissoluble" union in man.

Soul separable from the body but inseparably subjoined to the spirit—in their union constituting THE MIND.

Unification between spirit and soul indissoluble, tho the soul is to perpetuate its nexus with nature.

At the moment of the impartation of this higher life the natural part is in the passive or receptive mood, the spirit alone being active.

The natural part, the soul now becomes mind, or rather to say: personal life, in contrast to the monas or unit of natural life in its generalness with which it is to perpetuate its nexus, nevertheless. We now observe a spiritual nature sui generis. With "human mind" we have the cognition of a world of embodied spirits, a very substantial and concrete spiritual world. We have, in fact, aside and above and within the complex of the natural cosmos another well organised system, the embodiment of an ethical cosmos.

"Ethical cosmos" Immanent in the physical. Each a unit per se.

But this latter is an entirely different, a unique world in itself. It is the world of history proper, the world of permanency.

Yonder the ocean, metaphorically speaking, where the single waves are nothing but emerging and submerging transient appearances, always part of the whole, never becoming something in or for themselves. For in the world of transiency in that world below, including personal life, nothing had a purpose in itself; everything was intended for something else; the final purpose of all was man alone.

In the world of transiency—sphere below personal life—nothing has a purpose in itself: the final purpose of all was man.

In the personal world, now, each unit has a purpose in itself. Here we are in the sphere where each spiritual unit is qualified to assert itself, where it is relatively independent inasmuch as everybody is an individual which may possess or—lose itself; may appropriate the universe to its mind, or may give itself up to nature and become absorbed by it. Every one is somebody in himself, who, regardless of something else or of the whole, possesses a value on his own account.

In the world of personality and permanency—history proper—each unit has a purpose in himself.

In the lower sphere we had an essential, material unit, wherein the single entities are but formally different. In the world of personal life we find a formal unity in which the individuals maintain material selfhood. Hence in the natural world material unity under formal diversity; while the spiritual world of personal life consists of formal unity under material diversity.

Nature is the world of "Material Unity under formal diversity."

There a world under sway of necessity and generalness; here personality asserts itself and freedom reigns,—two worlds essentially different

History deals with the world of "Formal Unity under material diversity." There necessity, here freedom.

Thus a blending of dualistic existence is achieved, a fact which we substantiate by empirics. It only remains for us now to observe what kind of phenomena become manifest in both worlds. Each has a great deal in common with the other on account of their unification in personal life—a few things they cannot have in common according to the nature of the spheres to which these phenomena severally belong.

§ 7. What are such analogous forms, the so called "physical analogies," in which the utterances of both worlds are alike? Both, natural and personal life are ruled by the same principles of polarity, as for instance sympathy and antipathy, manifesting themselves in the affinities of minds, just as much as in the affinities of chemicals. Upon the theatre of either world the powerful laws of attraction and repulsion, of adhesion and expansion are enacted. We speak of accumulation and concentration, of assimilation, digestion, circulation and decay in a mental as well as in the physical sense. We speak of exhaustion, restoration and propagation, of losses and gains in the same way,—each the reflection of analogous and congruous processes in the world opposite to, yet immanent in either one, each with reference to the ethical purport of the procedure. It is just along the line of these analogies in which that preparation of the lower part of personal life is to be accomplished, which conditions the reception of higher life-infusions, and the transition of natural into spiritual forms of existence. In the transactions of personal life natural circumstances find their final purposes furnishing in the meanwhile the material for building up the ethical ascent. ·

In both worlds, the natural and the moral, we have the same laws of growth with its refinement, thrift and improvement; or of obstruction, retardation and death—according to the use or abuse of faculties, according to the attention paid to opportunities or their neglect. In both the same effects of repeated actions upon formations, developments and deformities of habits, opinions, fashions, characters. In both the same demand for either freedom from embarrassment or for the necessity of compulsion; the demand of system, of discipline; the same perils of becoming crippled; the same sufferings of separation and deprivation, and the same participations in merits or reverses, because of the solidarity of interests or default of mutual obligations. In both spheres the energies are either augmented or become inert under almost the same conditions. As it frequently occurs in nature that homogeneous masses consolidating gain force with dimensions or intensity, so thought increases to become an idea of overwhelming and almost irresistible power in proportion to the enlistment of new enthusiasts. On the other hand, we find in both spheres increasing indolence and inefficiency from neglecting or suspending or suppressing the exercise of organs or faculties; from lack of concentrated and determined effort; or from deficient encouragement, cooperation or discipline. It is astonishing to find the same causes of diminishing vitality to the point of exhaustion, whenever the delivery from conditions and laws occurs prematurely, when restraint is removed or support withdrawn, or when accustomed relations are abruptly changed.

To an observer there is nothing new in all this; only we seldom apply such congruities to sociological problems. While posing on conservatism, we make a virtue of laziness and show apathy to progressiveness by doing all to obstruct it, or else abuse it in heedless or dangerous experiments. Rise and decline of states, eruptions and subjections among peoples, owe their effects to the same polarities which regulate tension and equipoise in nations as well as in nature.

In this connection of nature and spirit by virtue of personal life we see the reciprocity between natural and moral laws, and their validity and objective authority revealed.

Recognizing the union of nature and spirit in this light elicits the much debated cognition of "duty." This union of body and mind in man implies that both have to take care of each other under the penalty of separation, called death. Solely from this task of maintaining and cultivating the unification, Ethics can deduce the first principle of duty.

It was upon this plain axiom that Dorner at last succeeded in demonstrating the objectivity of duty and in establishing its obligatory character beyond controversy. We here see how natural law executes retribution in order to maintain the authority of the moral laws, in order to keep up the conditions under which alone higher life can be received. We see how and why all law is one, and why the physical and ethical manifestations of the same are harmonious in their intention to stimulate susceptibility for the higher gifts, to create the desire for the Absolute Good, and to set the will free to acquiesce in the necessity of that good.

Sidenotes:
"Physical analogies"; phenomena of both world's; each reflecting processes analogous to such as are going on in the opposite world; each procedure bearing an ethical import.

In the transactions of personal life the natural circumstances have their final purposes.

Examples of the congruity of both worlds.

Effects regulated by laws valid in both spheres. Sec. 5, 9, 20, 23, 35, 39, 100, 116, 117.

Participation in deserts or reverses.

Inefficiency from neglected or suppressed exercise of faculties. Diminishing vitality under premature delivery from laws and conditions.

Insight into such congruities too seldom applied to sociological problems.

Reciprocity, and objective authority of natural and moral law.

Objective and obligatory character of "duty," deducible only from the unifying process between spirit and matter in the human soul. Dorner.

Physical and ethical manifestations of the one law harmonize in stimulating the receptivity for "the Good." Drummond, Schelling, Schleiermacher.

Drummond for the first time called public attention to this congruity of the natural law with—he ought not to have said "in"—the spiritual world. But Butler had long before him shown the way. Schleiermacher and Schelling had glimpses of this great concurrence, so that now the ground for a more systematic exhibition of its interaction is explorable.

Altho (for reasons just given) we insist upon the essential difference between the two worlds of created life, natural and spiritual, as focused in man; yet in reference to the circumstances conditioning all earthly life, those facts occur, which offer such striking resemblances as are enumerated above, and prove the mutual adaptability, the interactive reciprocity and prospective unification of the two worlds; but which are also apt to make nature and spirit to appear identical.

Here a wide field invites explorers: here lie the secrets and stand the puzzles of statistics. In view of the duality and the analogies ensuing, the meaning of philosophical terms must be cleared and fixed, where so many definitions need to be revised, From this, our dualistic standpoint, the truths in the systems of Kant, Fichte, Schelling and Hegel can easily be appreciated, sifted from their errors, and reconstructed.

Here also the independency of the spiritual world in its unity can be proved as against natural generalness.

For, a few phenomena distinctly belong to the superior world alone, such as decidedly refuse to be mixed with nature, and offer no natural analogy.

The similarities arising from the analogous processes going on in the combination of matter and mind within the personal soul on the scope of ethical designs, become **more distinct** in a measure as the faculties and functions of the spiritual side of personal life—being of specific spiritual quality—alone come into play and act free from physical encumbrances. The analogies **diminish** in proportion as those processes, in which the union of higher forms of rational with natural life, and also the union of moral and religious ingredients, approach completion.

The analogies **disappear** altogether, where the distinctions between natural and spiritual functions are perfectly overt, or where the natural functions are entirely under the control of consciousness—that is under control of feeling, intellect and will in their harmonious cooperation—so that both, mind and matter, embrace each other in normal exchange of liberty and in mutual appreciation, nature being consecrated and the spirit predominant. This consummated, complete unification may be illustrated by the relation between the instrument, its player and the symphony touching other minds.

Such purely spiritual manifestations are those which concern the "world of formal unity under material multiplicity" exclusively.

As examples of such entities we may mention thought, intuition and language, conscience and obedience, faith and character, genius and honor, justice and grace— in short all such factors which require the ethical cultivation of each individual for itself. Associations do not possess them in such a way as to answer for their constituent members.

Hence we must not be disappointed at finding out, for instance, that a "trust" or company of consolidated interests can have no conscience, no love. Neither must such be expected of the empiric Church. Of love and liberty in the Christian sense nature scarcely possesses the faintest foreshadowing. Whatever semblances thereof may be adduced are so faint that reason of itself was not able to gather them into coherent concepts. Unspiritual people mistake meekness for weakness. The masses can do no thinking; to this task man individually was assigned and is to accomodate himself.

The pious mother can not leave her virtue to her children by way of heritage. The pastor can not create faith nor convert his hearers, neither can he rent out his conscience to his parishoners in order to afford relief or excuse to the consciences of his flock.

Art, science, liberty, honor, right, friendship are such of the good things in which similarities between natural and spiritual interactions are yet to be found in a measure, because in them the unification is as yet in the process of becoming accomplished—they being intended to become individual property. The mind must appropriate them to itself in the process of spiritualising nature by way of performing its ethical task. Hence provision was made that these mixed goods with their natural and spiritual aptitudes for each other could not be bought and sold as long as the article is genuine. Here the equality of all men has its limits. Here also lies the cause why religion can not be disparaged and allowed to become a matter of state or any government, it being intended for the service of God alone in spirit and in truth.

§8. Personal life, i. e., **soul and spirit** representing each its particular world in their union, must remain, however, in contact with all earthly relations, in which alone the ethical task can be performed.

For the sake of their common ethical purposes their existence is separably but intimately conjoined to, and conditioned by, the natural world. Hence the congruity of laws and developments spoken of. From the rejection of this dualism in our existence—from the prejudices of a monistic world-theory, attempting at all hazards to argue away the reality of either matter or mind—all that confusion has sprung up which impairs insight and judgment with regard to true selfknowledge, God—and world-consciousness.

Ethical task to be accomplished only by the spirit and mind in their union, i. e. in personal life
MIND
remaining in contact with all earthly relations.
Sec. 9, 39, 41, 117, 159.
Hence the analogies.

From want of discretion of what is to be kept separate in theorising, and what is to be applicable as common to both worlds—or as we will rather say now in this sense, to both spheres—many blunders committed, many pseudo-syllogisms are occasioned and paralogisms perpetuated.

Indiscrimination regarding them is the cause of many mischievous paralogisms.
Sec. 10. 11, 70.

We need not wonder that, in the American phraseology the shades of meaning between the words "culture" and "civilisation" are as yet controversial. We deem it necessary to use "culture" in the European sense which implies agriculture, that is, elevation of nature, improving the environments; and to use "civilisation" in the sense of advanced humanitarianism, i. e. Christianised culture on the basis of Ethics, which in turn signifies a higher than "moral" philosophy. We take Montezuma's empire for a state of high CULTURE, but without civilised citizenship which can not be cultivated upon any other basis than that of the CHRISTIAN CULTUS. A similar discretion should abandon the promiscuous use of the term "liberty." This noun indicates the more natural or politico-social condition of personal life in distinction from "freedom," which applies to the purely spiritual mode of being, entirely above the sphere of natural necessity—in the way we distinguish the "liberty" of the press from the "freedom" of conscience. In like manner the word "intuition" ought to be left at variance no longer. "Intuition" certainly conveys the idea of immediate comprehension by the spiritual side of consciousness, the counterpart to that which we understand by "instinct" in purely natural beings; hence intuition should not be used where reflection upon sense-perceptions is implied as the chief source of knowing.

Examples of terms promiscuously used:
Sec. 35, 62, 79, 136, 139 182'
Culture—civilisation,

Liberty—freedom:
Sec. 230.

Intuition—the spiritual extreme opposite to natural "instinct;"
Sec. 15.

It is for such a mixed mode of conceiving and reasoning concerning the relations between the natural and spiritual functions of the mind, that the differences between "soul", "mind" and "spirit" are so little understood; only thus can it be explained, that the English language has no adequate term for "Vernunft", which neither of the terms mind nor reason (Verstand) will cover. Since reason must be ascribed to animals, it is vitiating to translate Kant's "Vernunft" with "reason." VERSTAND i. e. reasoning or COMPARING INTELLECT, understanding, pertains to the natural—VERNUNFT, i. e. INTUITIVE INTELLECT to the ethico-spiritual sphere of personal life alone. Mind would perhaps come nearest to Vernunft, if this word were not so vaguely used, not only when we speak of intellectual but also of emotional and imaginative phenomena of our inner life. To the word mind we have assigned a definite cognition already, since we use the term to convey the very same synthetical thought expressed in the phrase "personal life."

Soul, mind, reason.

Vernunft is not reason—which is Verstand—but INTELLECT.

Our use of the term MIND given in the margin above.

On similar grounds we need not become confused in regard to religion, when one is said to have become insane from religion, as the heavenly influence—for other dare not be recognised as being religious,—had any thing to do with the derangement of an unfortunate soul: notwithstanding the "religious insanity," of which some scientists are pleased to speak. We need not wonder that some withdraw from the "world," in order to lead a spiritual life, and are usually none the less conquered by worldliness. Such religious separatists and orders, pretending to conform their conduct to celestial patterns, are not aware, that "conduct" means just that execution of our obligations to both of the spheres to which we are related, and that this conduct becomes impossible unless we remain in proper contact and concurrence with the world of tasks and duties. Dogmaticians, in more than one system have sacrificed the freedom of the will entirely to the natural component of man to the point of denying it altogether. As yet the doctrines about conscience, about its independency, its unreliability or its infallibility, whether it is an original capability, or merely a psychical mood, are in such entanglement that Bestmann found forty-three, often widely diverging definitions of conscience—just because of the indiscriminated or misapprehended relations under discussion. The confusion and difficulties in discerning these relations was taken advantage of by Spencer in the upbuilding of his ethics upon the basis of, and from data in, mollusk-life. Such discrepancies will always be at the bottom, where, as we say, "extremes meet."

Blunders from misapprehending the relations between soul and spirit.
Religious insanity.

World in the sense of hyper-asceticism.

Freedom of the will.

Conscience.

extremes meet
Sec. 4, 8, 10, 11, 17, 87, 88.

All this certainly demonstrates the necessity of clear discernment with respect to the relations between soul and spirit in the functions of the mind, and with respect to the relations of each on its part to either the physical world or the spiritual. The distinction is easy as soon as it becomes manifest, which side preponderates in this concurrent interaction.

It is true, matter and mind, when it comes to practical life, are so intrinsically interwoven, and, when it comes to theorising, the confusion seems so inextricable that

Discrimination so difficult as to lead many to the denial of the spirit.

our conception of the matter may seem a delusion to some, while to many others the nonexistence of the spirit is a forgone conclusion.

In controversies of this kind an additional fact, fraught with still greater difficulties, was overlooked, if not frequently intentionally misrepresented, viz: that the essence and the effects of personal life are never to be made fully intelligible scientifically from what one perceives of it.

Still greater difficulties on account of the mysteries of the world of formal unity

Spiritistic deceptions.

Forfeiture of the right to argue against the spiritual realities.

There are mysterious phenomena coming forth from the spiritual world—to which every human soul stands connected by virtue of its spiritual component that inseparably belongs to the sphere of "formal unity"—which are often willfully ignored or trifled with. Spiritism went to great lengths in making these mysteries ignominious. Only the deceptions of spiritism are at fault for disbelieving the reality and objectivity of such occurrences It is in the nature of things that life stupifies man from becoming acquainted with them, thus, of course, forfeiting the right to argue against their reality, as in the case of music, justice, love, truth, beauty—Heaven.

Dual relationship of the spirit; only one side involved in earthly conditions.

Many psychical phenomena, not to be ascertained scientifically, but neither to be explained away, give evidence that the spiritual side of our being is involved in the earthly conditions only so far, as it must, through its connection with the soul, partake of the mode of planetary existence.

Soul of our soul is the side of the spirit which by embracing the soul participates in planetary life.

This is that innermost part of our mind, the soul of our soul, through which the mind becomes conscious of itself, upon which only thus we are able to reflect, which we are apt to identify with the physical nature of our soul.

The other purely spiritual side remains in direct contact with its native realm; while in touch with the mind also announces its presence in feeling;

transcends earthly confines; is not subject to accidentals of the natural part of personal life;

The other, probably the principal part, keeping up the connection with the spiritual realm of unity, is not directly exposed to the rough handling of an epistemological vivisection, because it should not be jeopardised to a complete spoliation.

This part is that primary and pure spirituality, which controls, we might say possesses us by force of the feeling peculiar to it; which announces its presence within the soul, whilst at the same time it remains in touch and communication with the world of permanency and reality; and which by far transcends all the earthly confines into which it did not, but conditionally wants to, enter entirely. It is not subject to nature nor to the accidentals of the natural part of personal life.

not even that side of which we are conscious is subject to space and time.

Thus the unit or "oneness" of our innermost mind, the human spirit, consists of two sides. We can not call them parts, because this section of the world of unity is inseparable; and because one side only as far as influenced by the soul, is in relation with, but not even in this relation subject to, space and time.

The one side is purely spiritual, let us say pneumatic: the other psychico-spiritual. Only the latter is in contact with the lower world, whilst the former alone is in touch with the spiritual world, of which otherwise we would not have the faintest idea—both sides nevertheless continuing their inseparable unity, rapport and sympathy. And only by the tension of this polarity, agitating the two sides of the human

Polar tension, caused by the duality of the spirit's relations, renders spiritual things perceptible of which otherwise we could have no idea.
Fichte Jr.; Dorner.

soul, this divine substance or essence of our being—of which we become clearly conscious on rare occasions—becomes more or less perceptible.

After Fichte Jr. in his "Anthropology" Dorner has also in his "Ethics" conclusively shown the correctness of this binary concept of the human spirit. A consistent method then, of explaining the duplex relativity of personal life has been gained by metaphysical deductions and inferences, despite their rejection as untrustworthy by many empiricists. Now since we can compare the cognitions thus derived with **psychical experiences,** which could be understood in no other way,—we make the existence of this spirit axiomatic in our world-theory. This spirit added to the physico-psychical soul—called psyche, inasmuch as a part of natural life in general, is now embraced, penetrated, and animated by the spirit—makes man a "living soul"; both united constitute the individual, i. e. indivisible mind, and are focused in the "heart."

Integral relations of the component parts of personal life focused in the HEART.

Thus personal life, in one respect, sustains close inter-relations with all earthly conditions; in the other it excels the visible world by virtue of its native dignity, freedom and continuity.

Existence of the spirit our axiom. Empiric proof for those indications of duality in the human spirit to be gathered in. Sec. 9, 10, 109.

How this human mind can maintain or lose this position may be made approximately-certain from many indications which have to be gathered up as we proceed.

At this point and for the present the statement must suffice, that the freedom of the will, the touch of conscience preceding a wrong act and the facts of divination could not be made intelligible, but for this supposition of the spiritual partner of the soul, and of its binary existence. To simply push aside these and many other manifestations of "unreflected or sub-consciousness," explicable in no other way, or worse yet, to store them into the lumberroom of hallucinations, could certainly not be considered a scientific operation.

Understanding of subconsciousness depends on this proof. Sec. 15, 97, 111, 113, 221.

Furthermore, under this proposition alone are we justified to discriminate between personal and natural, psychical and pneumatical life, between matter and mind; only under this proposition can we account for the similarity of physical and moral advances and relapses spoken of in §7.

So much depends on the acceptance and proof of our as yet hypothetical proposition the dualistic aspect of the human mind and of the binary mode of existence of the spirit—that only thus we are enabled to form a correct idea of that polarity, which yields the only probability of escaping erroneous views of either Monism or Dualism. Upon the force of this argument alone can we account for the wealth and corresponding responsibilities of real life; can we reason about and meditate upon the profundity, the sources and the prospects of spiritual and future life, concerning which we experience so many indications.

Only probability to escape false Monism and erroneous Dualism.

Unless the investigator is given concession to set up this premise in the form of a probability at least, science has no right to dispute our right of emphasising that polarity by which the world is urged on in the aspiration to ethical value. But if our axiomatic proposition proves correct, then that polarity stands confirmed, which is the main support of the identity of moral and natural law, and of the natural counteraction against moral abnormities; then that polarity, resting on a dual form of existence must be acknowledged as the cardinal principle of all cosmical existence, which finds its final counterpoise in man.

The polarity between natural and spiritual life.

Owing to which polarity the natural law executes the verdicts of the moral law;

The existence of the spirit we have announced as an axiom; we feel justified to render its dual mode of existence axiomatic too, under promise, that due affirmations shall be adduced presently, so that of this legitimate position we may take full possession.

It is the cardinal principle of all cosmical existence.

The duality of the world in our sense, as manifested in the historical union of personal life, will enable us to comprehend and to delineate the biology, as it were, of universal history.

Dual mode of existence of the spirit made axiomatic; if recognized the biology of history is delineated.

The affirmations drawn from empirics of what Ethics deducts logically, namely of the objectivity and congruity of physical and ethical law, make our position impregnable.

RETROSPECT

Our inductive introspect will become the more useful as it throws light upon our retrospect. It affords new illustrations of the truth that life as such enters from on high at every transitory stage of advancing development. In the ideal concept of man's composition we found the reason for the formation of nature as it is. In man the whole of creation reached its purpose. The world is made for his sake, intended to become his possession, designed as the place where—for reasons of the necessity of the Supreme Good and its attainability—the ethical task is to be worked out. Man is the mediator of creation, the selfdevelopment of which stopped on his account. The arrested life of which he therefore has to redeem. His superiority was projected in, and foreshadowed through, and postulated by nature, its successive grades of development prophesying his advent. The creature is formed, so to speak, after the image of man (analogous to the creation of man in and for the image of God.) Thus nature does neither emanate out of God, nor does life evolve from below. It is handed down.

Ideal conception of MAN.

Sec. 56. In him nature reaches its purpose.

Man the mediator and redeemer of nature.

Creatures below man made after and for his image. Sec. 13, 15, 115, 118, 120, 131.

Mineral does not spontaneously create organic life; the "word" called it forth after it had been "thought" of. The earth—in accord with the thought which it conveyed, that is, the purpose for which it was conceived and which is contained in it, and in accord with the preparations made by it,— was enabled to receive the word, and to answer its command.

Genesis of higher grades in natural life, in stages marked by miracles.

The result of this impartation of the word was the generation of a new form of life; spermiation of organic life. The concept being communicated to nature became the generative conception. The birth of the first life-germ, set free from the life confined in inorganic matter or the address—is a miracle.

Generation of organic life from inorganic by communication of THE THOUGHT.

The organic world in its turn does not in its passage to mental life, of itself ramify and multiply in an entirely fortuitous manner.

The inbreathing of life into the first man was more than the utterance of the word: "Let there be!" Man's creation was the result of a special consultation, with which an act was connected. The instantaneous impartation of supernatural life resulted in a new species of generic life It was an animation far different from any former elevation in the prior department of organic nature, of arrested life. Out of mere natural organic life,—altho it furnishes the organic matter upon which the new creature's life is to subsist,—rational life can not be expounded. The first manifestation of personal in contrast to animal life answering an act- is a miracle.

Spiritual, i. e. mental, personal life denotes a new departure, conditioned by the lower stage where life had become endowed with the capability to prepare itself for becoming engrafted with a higher animation. Personal nature, having inherited all the accomplishments of the former stages together with the results of their cooperation, and having been equipped with new endowments in addition, is now to use all of these acquirements in preparing itself for a next higher communication. Man has, at the least, to preserve his susceptibility for it, if he does not improve his receptivity for the impartation of the higher gift.

Receptivity, cooperation, and selfpreparation in the lower stages are always required for receiving the impartation of higher principles. This is the rule in all natural and all historical development. The impartation of higher endowments at each essential notch in the scale of ascending gradation is a miracle, intelligible only after man himself has graduated from the lower classes of natural life to the High school of a new spirituality. Unless the lessons of universal revelation ensuing from creation receive due attention, man can not pass to the class where special revelation is to be comprehended.

With rational life moral development begins, based on the endowment of divine gifts. This further development originates under the rule and command of the only, but supreme necessity by which potential, elective volition is set free; it proceeds under the educational discipline of warning by which potential conscience is set free, the feeling and judgment of value; it proceeds under encouraging promises—given to strengthen human nature against the allurements of wrong valuation and of a bribed judgment trying to fill the heart with rank desires, and tempt it to neglect the obtainment of the Supreme Good through which independence from nature and responsibility are set free.

Thus, encouraged to determine himself for the good, and amply provided with discouragement to do wrong, man is guided on to selfculture. We recognise the outfit for a still higher attainment under condition of preserving all this freedom and selfhood, by which condition personality is dignified and set free.

The apparatus given for the moral task is well adapted for assisting in spiritual advance—gratia praeveniens.

Now the selfcultivation of harmonious development and control of nature (man's own nature in the first place) is to be persevered in and accomplished. The moral task, then, consists in man's proper conduct toward creation and the Creator. The endowments, the capacities and gifts, come from God: the opportunities for their proper appliance are given in the world. The gifts internally and the chances externally, constitute the moral apparatus, set up to practice thereon the salutary work of selfculture. In the system of this assigned task and in the method of working the apparatus we see the conditions for development in the previous state, i. e. in the natural world,—we see the natural law, the one law aiming at the preservation of the Supreme Good for the benefit of all men, the law which pervades the whole fabric of development still in force.

For, altho we are now in the sphere of freedom, the final attainment, namely partaking of the highest good—is not and never was intended to be, unconditional.

§9. We repeat the reasonable conditions governing the moral as well as all natural development, of the means and results of which nothing is abandoned on entering a higher state. The conditions now are as ever: cooperation; preparation; selfpreservation; conduct with creatures and the Creator; that is preserving at least, if not promoting, the capability of receiving something better. In the endeavor to fulfill the conditions, men will be engaged in cultivating the susceptibility for that guidance which, by way of chances or opportunities opened in the world, leads up to the grand reception. These are the requisites for the next higher state, for which development is to be set free from its nature-bound state. Man is called to rise above mere natural-moral culture, where he, perhaps, busies himself with the improvement of environments, whilst neglecting his own—into civilisation, where a new spiritual relationship and religious selfconsciousness are to become his recreation, his comfort and delight.

from life confined in inorganic matter to organic life by the womb, and to personal life through an act.

Attainability of the Highest Good pledged

The **pledge** assuring the obtainability of the best gift and highest good, quickening a hoping and trusting susceptibility; and the test at the same time, proving whether the quality of the Supreme Good is appreciated, and whether the receptivity for it has been preserved, is—inspiration, with which the cultivation of **religion** proper, i. e., the development of civilisation, begins. This mode of communication is evidently chosen on account of the nature and disciplinary intent of the Supreme Good, which thus alone could be shielded against deterioration and profanation, and preserved for the benefit of all men. Hence such communication by the **word** first (analogous to the first and **universal revelation in creation**) can be granted to those only who have properly practiced on the apparatus set up for natural culture, that is to such as have seized those opportunities brought forth, and have cultivated the mental and moral faculties set free from their potential state through the command: "Thou shalt!"

and receptivity for it tested by the miracle of inspiration.

Man to preserve susceptibility for appreciation of, and to cultivate receptivity for the Supreme Good by moral self-culture in the state under the natural law.

Communication of the WORD first, analogous to universal revelation at the creation of organic life.

"Thou shalt" sets free volition, feeling of value, and selfhood.

To such only the gift of higher impulses is to be extended, who acknowledge themselves under the **dispensation of the Law!**

Genesis of higher grades of moral development into religiousness marked by another set of miracles.

The preparation thus inaugurated for religio-ethical advance is just as reasonable as that required for the prior state of mere physico-moral culture. The new condition enjoined rather corresponds to, than that it should be found at variance with, the rule of natural law of selfdevelopment in evolution. Still, participation in this **special revelation**—although well founded in the nature of all concerned, in the whole system of obtaining the best life imaginable, as well as in the nature of the desideratum itself, and altho an act not without an empiric basis—is to natural-minded men shunning the preparatory task—**a miracle.**

Dispensation of the LAW.

Special revelation.

By those who participate in inspiration it is easily comprehended. But smaller grows the circle of those who remain under the discipline that sharpens receptivity, preparatory to a still higher communication and impartation. This circumstance, rather hastens and prepares, than prevents the great advent in the fulness of time. Religiousness, i. e., receptivity for the impartation of divine life in substance (**analogous to the first creation of man by an act,** not by a mere command as in the case of the lower creatures) ripens under pressure of misery! It becomes intensified. It lives on promises, lives in the **dispensation of the Gospel.** It comprehends, embraces the fact. For at that instant the world's attention is called to **"the"** man: "Ecce Homo!"

Definition of religiousness.

Impartation of divine life by an act analogous to the creation of the first man, the miracle of incarnation. Receptivity under pressure. Sec. 98, 115, 142, 210.

Dispensation of the GOSPEL.

"ECCE HOMO!"

His appearance was not unexpected, not unconditional, not without the natural substratum, and with no ostentation. He merely made known how the human being is really constituted, and what his moral task is, showing it by example, and simplifying the apparatus. Still,—**the miracle.**

Last stage of development. The ultimate goal.

One more manifestation of, and elevation into, a higher state is to be experienced and does not surprise those who have perceived "man" as having ascended into it already.

Method of accomplishing the moral task simplified; hence shirking obligations so much the less excusable,

But easy and sweet as the moral task has been made, and freely as the means and opportunities for its accomplishment have been vouchsafed: those can not believe themselves included who worked obstructively and helped to scatter by merely standing idle, instead of keeping the natural law of cooperation; who, instead of preparing themselves by practicing on the apparatus, turn their backs to it with contempt; who inadvertently, perhaps, are in sympathy with those who cried: "Crucify!"

and selfabandonment to perdition by joining those crying "CRUCIFY!" the more amazing.

Least of all can the highest state be entered into unconditionally. The laws of all the preceding spheres are still valid; the apparatus, altho simplified, still stands on the plane of preparation for the last transition.

The star, the stable, lily and sparrow, the storm-tossed ship and the great calm, the fish and the fishermen, oil and wine, barley-bread and farmer, shepherd and warrior, Caesar and carpenter, weaver and lawyer, banker and beggar, leper and Lazarus are parts of the apparatus; temple and rampart, sword and dice, manger and tombstone, sweat and blood and prayer, and " the tree," are all rendered instrumental and significant in the development toward the final glorification thus inaugurated.

The cross, standing for the ethical apparatus, symbolises
Sec. 98, 142, 210.

But this will not ensue well for such as show disdain or indifference to the meaning which the apparatus bears on redemption, who treat the offer with feigned innocence or unconcern, If they do not reject it with rank hatred—miraculous, such a monstrosity of perverseness.

the pressure necessary to intensify religiousness

The spheres of a happy completion can not be reached by trying to evade the cross, that is, not without the sorrows caused by the tension between the flesh and spirit in which piety is tested and the entire person purified—or else rendered obdurate; not without that pressure which ever intensifies religiousness. This concentration, to which all history tends, as we shall verify, is the point from which spiritual-mindedness will expand again toward the periphery of humanity in general, toward that transition to glory which includes the globe if not the sun. Until then we stand under the tension of the polarity of the two worlds which is said to continue between a redeemed and a—lost world.

and for the development to the state of glory.

Tension betw. flesh and spirit to continue between a redeemed and a lost world.

The duality of life upon which we are agreed, finds its synthesis in man. Him we could not understand unless taken as the intermediate agent between the material and the spiritual world, as the focus of natural and spiritual life. Natural life can only be understood under the aspect of its intrinsic connection within man.

Resume:

Duality of life finds its synthesis in man.

We accept the conclusion obtained by our introspective analysis, that man belongs to two worlds, and that the appropriation and elevation of the lower by the higher will prevail in a glorious realisation of all purposes. The movements of the formative or constructive and of the material coefficients meet in man. The lines of observation converge in the human being, bringing to view the combination in his being along with the apparatus and the task performed by which the goal of his true life is obtained.

Only following the old advice " know thyself " will solve the sevenfold riddle.

Science nevertheless has to confess its inability to fathom man's dual constitution in its whole depth. Before natural knowledge as yet stands the old, old advice: "Know Thyself!"—stands the man as the sevenfold compound riddle.

Reconstruct Anthropology on ethical grounds.

There is no other help but revision of our Anthropology, or rather a reconstruction of it on ethical grounds. A monistic analysis of the nerves and their ends will not discover the bridge between matter and mind. Nor will monastic contempt of nature bridge the chasm by tearing down the spans already sprung on both sides. The indefatigableness, however, with which science nevertheless endeavored to construct the bridge, testifies to and admits of the certainty, that the bridge is to be found in man. It is only necessary to go one step further and take man in the broad compass with all that really belongs to him.

Neither monistic nor monastic views of life can bridge the chasm between matter and mind.

CH. 4.—MAN THE SYNTHESIS OF MATTER AND MIND.

§ 10. Physical science, claiming to embrace the sum total of the knowledge of nature, can not but yield a materialistic world-theory, unless it takes in the whole man and relinquishes the aversion against the supernatural. We find that it hesitates to do this. We have intimated why we judge physical science to be not natural enough. Metaphysics, pretending to furnish a thorough cognition of life, did not pay sufficient attention to mind as a whole, being chiefly concerned with the intellect alone, and has only formulated a multifarious and shadowy monistic idealism.

Natural science in regard to human nature not natural enough.

Metaphysics formerly treated of scarcely anything but the mental faculties.

Ethics was compelled to be in earnest with the dualistic condition outlined in the preceding sections. It comprises both, nature and spirit, under the aspect of human destiny; it conciliates the binary sides of dualism and shows to anthropology, how the bridge over the chasm is to be founded not upon mere thinking but upon doing, and that it is built in the real person of the ideal man.

Ethics grapples with the dualistic problem.

Philology alone adduces empiric data, the utterances of both worlds.

But after all, it is Philology, which possesses the empirical data in the utterances of both worlds. Language signalises the fact that man is the scion of both worlds; his language hoards up the results of their potential unification which in and through him is to be consummated. Here, in language, must be sought, and will alone be found, the key for disclosing the problems involved.

"Is not the trial of man, for reasons of his own constituency, that is, because of his conscience and of his retentive and reproductive memory, to be conducted upon the open forum of history?" Lazarus, thus formulating the problem at our hands, is certainly correct. Before this, the only competent tribunal, issue is actually joined and the taking of testimony, examination and crossexamination of witnesses in trial of the cause of humanity upon its merits is going on as before a court. This consists of the judge duly authorised and of the jury properly impaneled. To them the case is given and between them the trial is continued when all the evidence is in as to empirical facts and perceptible data. This corresponds with our inductive part of the investigation, which has now to stand the test of deduction or vice versa. Upon the analytical follows the synthetical treatment of the points at issue, wherein neither the law arising from the facts and applied in the judge's charge, nor the facts belonging to the jury must be lost sight of. Thus all the pleadings and proofs undergo a twofold review, so that upon **inductive** grounds the verdict is to be found by the deliberation of the jurors as directed by the **deductive** information of the judge. That is, induction and deduction harmonised are to establish truth and right, and to vindicate the justness of the judgment. Nothing less must be the rule under which the suit is to proceed in the Philosophy of History; else her claims upon the recognition of her legitimacy would have to be quashed. Law abstracted from facts, and evidence weighed in the scales of equity must decide even her case. Man's being is rooted in the elementary world. Vigorous yet most tender organs tie him to the world of sensuous perception; but his crown lies in the transcendental, invisible world. In a straight line, like a flame, his life rises out of mysterious depths, and differentiates itself into a multiplicity of rational and moral relations which increase as civilisation advances.

With reference to his cosmical conditions, man (in the words of Steffens) represents the truths contained in nature. The individualisations of nature delineate and prophesy him, aspiring to meet and to culminate in him. With the personal life of man the goal and purpose of nature is reached; nature here in the human mind, solemnises her nuptials with the spirit, her sabbath-day. Up to that point nature was man potential, man had not come to himself as yet. Nature was the natural "ego" in its preexistence, as it were; it is the altruistic state of the ego, which is tantamount to the "non-ego" of Fichte. This was the truth of "Pan-anthropism," as it might be called, which hovered about the mind of Hegel.

In the human soul we behold the totality of cosmical nature mirrored because it is the epitome of the universe; but in this revelation of the universal homogeneity, in the physical correspondency between type and antitypes, the spiritual part of man is not included. We emphatically maintain our essential proposition of the independency of the spirit as the representative of that oneness in the other form of existence, the world on high. The spirit in contrast to nature and to the soul, nature's contrast, is independent from nature, is above space and time, is selfexistent.

Philosophy owes the establishment of this truth to Herbart, viz: that the spirit is an ontogenous entity, that is, not a manifestation of being in its general form (which is the soul)—but formal, i. e. personal being. Spirit is an entity sui generis, is not the manifestation or hypostatisation, not the mere gradually modified qualification, of the developed soul of Rothe. But this spirit takes the soul into partnership as in sacred wedlock in order to elevate it to its own sphere, thus generating the physical incipiencies, peculiar to the human mind. Natural man is thereby enabled to occupy the intermediating position assigned him by his relations to both units, the physical and the psycho-spiritual orb. On the part of nature man is to become the net result, the flower and crown of nature, to represent all its essence as displayed in the psychical aptitudes. On the part of the spirit, establishing its union with the soul of nature as individualised in man, he is to act (as the representative of both the great spiritual and the material units of Heaven, and the physical world,) in the upbuilding of an ethical within this natural cosmos.

Henceforth, we can but occasionally take cognizance of Anthropology as regards man's individual make-up (Physiology, Psychology) or the social organism (Ethnology, Sociology). The scope of our science does ,not yet allow the interlacing of Anthropology with our system in consecutive order or parallel progression. Such symmetrical exhibition of the congruity of, and systematic reciprocity between, physical and ethical science must be left to a future Philosophy of History.

The repository and synopsis of all the sciences just now referred to, is language. In a striking manner it reveals the fact, that spirit and matter were designed for each other from the beginning. Language at the same time forms the great divide and the juncture of both worlds. It means communication,and furnishes the means for it. The word is the conductor and symbol of thought uttered in the world of space and time. It is the symbol of the concinnity and conjunction of body and mind, of the sensuous and the mental-moral concomitants, of Heaven and earth. The material factor and formal part of speech is sound, derived from a specific set of organs, not so wonderful for their delicacy as in their arrangement—while personal thought and emotion constitute the essential substance and formative principles.

Schelling and W. v. Humboldt accredited too much to language, when they esteemed it as the creative principle of national peculiarities, as tho language were propagating mind. We claim that national characteristics are rather creating the languages. They merely bring to consciousness those distinctive features of native or naturally innate propensities which coexist with, but are excelled by, language. For the gift of speech, as we shall prove, can only be taken as a descendant of the spiritual world, and hence as the capability of the mind to work upon the line of the inceptive, we might almost say, nascency of the mind.

Languages therefore are to be considered rather as tongues, offsprings of the vernacular of particular groups of people ; but language as a function of the spirit, speech as the vehicle communicating thought, existed before such clusters of people became nations and races.

The notion that language was of human invention, and began with mere imitation of natural sounds, is given up by every person, even tho slightly educated, since that crude idea could not prevent the rise of Philology to the rank of systematic knowledge and to philosophical importance. The other notion of language having been instilled by the Creator ready made, went the same way.

National consciousness was at first molded in the forms of the mythological mode of picture-thinking, and moves on by way of tradition. It loses the feature of immediateness in conceiving the relation of things.

Concepts were fixed to stereotyped signs, and the past was reproduced without being understood. Whenever language had assumed this symbolic shape and had become mere repetition in expressing fixed parabolic idiosyncracies, then it became diversified. Each branch again molded and stereotyped sectional peculiarities in keeping with changing religious apperceptions and their symbols, in times when everything was deemed closely related to the deity. This becomes very evident from M. Mueller's teachings of lingual affiliations, and from Brugsch's ingenious interpretations of the Aegyptian picture-language.

Language proves its spiritual descent by becoming—according to its nature in the physical sphere—a unifying factor, by virtue of which it outlives the fates of nations. Hence language may with all propriety be designated as embodied spirit. In this capacity it combines separated tribes into generic units. It becomes the elaborate vessel, wherein the remembrances of the childhood and home of each set of people are handed down to successive generations; conveying the most tender sentiments and the noblest inheritance: becoming a mother-language. Thus even the diversity of languages, once separating people, is rendered a means of reuniting humanity again, since now in its old age the remembrances of its childhood return with that mysterious vivacity of the memory in second childhood. Translatable as languages are, dead but immortal, they communicate to us, what our antipodal Aryan cousins kept sacred ever since our ancestors separated from them four thousand years ago.

W. v. Humboldt said: " I am convinced that language is to be regarded as a potentiality given to man in his early childhood, since its origin and essence can not be explained as a mere product of understanding or mature consciousness. The supposition that thousands upon thousands of years must be taken into account, will be of no avail in proving its evolution. Such an invented contrivance can not be thought of, unless a proto-type, present to the mind, is presupposed.

Here we stand upon the great divide, before the mysterious hiatus—no evolution without proto-type; no word without the thought that was reflected from the meaning of things, in their interrelations, and in their relation to man as their issue and purpose, even before his world-consciousness had matured. A re-ligere (according to Webster a re-viewing of things of which a cognizance is present in the mind's idea) takes place; and an unconscious, intuitive remembrance of the truth, that objects were created after and for the image of the subject in whom they find their purpose, re-curs to the mind (Herbart's discovery). Language is born. Man named things according to their import upon himself; manifesting his right to be their master, he takes possession of what was delineated within him and assigned to him. With the first utterance of thought the first revelation of the spirit is given. In language the spirit announces his appropriation of the natural world. And up to date there is the instinctive feeling in man, as McCosh remarks, that unsophisticated language comes nearer to the truth than most of our artfully twisted diction—the terminology of diplomacy which, according to Talleyrand, uses language rather to conceal, than to reveal the real meaning of a thought.

Language is innate in man. This we can prove by deduction at least, while materialistic monism can not disprove it, either by intuition, induction or deduction. Man ever possessed language in the same way, as now consciousness lies dormant in the mind. Both consciousness and language were born within man in exactly the same manner as he is born now, that is, unconscious of their possession. Now as ever internal impressions from above are received in that silent camera upon the sensitive plate as it were, by way of instantaneous instinctive feeling as from a "voice," as well as from sense-perception by way of the sensorium. Now as ever does the impression awaken the adequate expression reverberating the incurring "voice" from the diaphragm of the mind.

Max Mueller corroborates this truth in noticing that "the language of children, because of its originality is more regular in its declension and conjugation." This shows reconstructive ability in the unconscious recesses of consciousness where the mind carries its formative principle. It reveals that competency for making intuitive valuation and comparison, and for drawing logical conclusions—the inexplicable a priori categories of Kant and Aristotle,—that ability which is not always and never all at once present to reason in its engaged state.

Language does not result from so called progressive and inheritable evolution. Its height of symmetrical perfection is not even to be accounted for by empirical education and scientific culture. Rhetoric partakes too much of the nature of virtue as that it could be put on from outside to every person by any training. As the eye and the light preceded ophthalmology, so language precedes grammar; it contains its types of beauty, its parabolic nomenclature in the back-ground of the psycho-spiritual part of the mind, along with which those types were given to man. In this reserved recess the potency of language is working with the same exactness with which the many-colored crystals shoot together in the dark cavities of the rocks. It works with the simplicity of the heptachord governing the sounds, and with the precision of the bee, building its hexagons with the greatest possible saving of time and the least expenditure of wax.

The ability to express relationship, and to communicate the essence of personality is always present as a unit in conformity with the nature of the spiritual realm of unity from whence it was spoken into, and is again called forth from, the human soul. Mind within creates and constructs its expressions in its own way, in precise answer to the external occasion. This is the meaning of speaking the truth. Lying is contemptible just for the reason, that thereby language is abused in representing man and things to be what they are not, thus corrupting the whole sum of personal relations. The special arrangement of the organs of speech in direct connection with the organ of thought has also been taken notice of as indicating and illustrating the distinction, directness, and, to some extent, the independence of speech from the lower functions of our organism. As speech is certainly the most spiritual function of the person in its entirety, this special physical adaptedness indicates its spiritual significance, especially in the offering of prayer. These unique phenomena of spiritual life prove, in every respect, that language does not evolve from below.

Prototypes the prerequisites

re-ligere, re-cognising, re-currence of the thought reflected in things. Herbart.

With giving names to things as to their relations, language is born.

With the first utterance man proclaims his right of appropriating nature.

Abuse of language: Talleyrand.
Sec. 183.

We prove by deduction what materialism can not disprove.

Language innate in the spirit along with consciousness originated in man as he is born now, in an unconscious state.

Not the result of reflection.

Language precedes grammar.

A priori categories of Kant.
Sec. 27

Correctness of the child's speech. M. Mueller, McCosh.

Language always a unit corresponding with the relation of the spirit to the opposite unit of measure.

Gift of speech is akin to the spirit; is its "voice" spoken into the soul; proved by its retaining "formal unity under material diversity."

Conveys the essence of personality.

Speaking the TRUTH, telling a LIE.

Offering PRAYER! the most spiritual function of the person in its entirety.

The objection has been raised, that the monosyllable languages doubtless belong to the age of man's childhood, only arrested in their development, and were still waiting to be made perfect. This circumstance was alleged as proof against the character of unity and spirituality of language, because the Chinese had become isolated on that account. But the inference is futile. That erroneous view could only have been taken when comparative philology was in its childhood, that is, when we were not yet acquainted with the immense copiousness of Chinese literature.

No. The assault against the truth that man as a person excels the natural world, could derive no succor from language. For language scorned an alliance with all that went in denial of the spirit; it became our ally. If ever the truth of the spirit's aseity could have been shaken, language would have revealed what is in man,—as the physican reads the stomach's condition from the tongue.

Language renders man conscious of the fact, that a spirit lives within his soul, which by virtue of this union stands in direct communication with the spiritual world. This demonstrates personal man as being the medium between the two spheres of his existence. Thus again man's position is verified, his spiritual excellency substantiated, his freedom assured. This latter assertion is now to be proven by still more convincing evidence.

§ 11. Man's moral task requires of his corporeal constitution to obey the necessities of nature in the order preordained, as mirrored in grammatical rules and a priori categories, and without severing the connection with the preceding development in the lower stage. This conclusion has been found already as the starting point of duty. But the task—originally the pleasurable cultivation and preservation of his person and of paradise—consists in the very contest with nature to obtain or regain full dominion over it. Man began his task with the proclamation of taking possession of nature by the "invoice" made of the creature at the birth of language.

One may call this a clever allegory of things which man is supposed to have formed in his child-like beginning. But granted that the description of the fact was childish talk, it would only corroborate what M. Mueller says of the original freshness and correct directness of the child's language. The discovery and understanding at so late a date, of the truth of the fact under discussion having been narrated at such an early time and in language so unsophisticated, speaks promptly against an invention of either the language or the story.

All lasting results of endeavors made to master the situation, of the endeavors in which the "word" always took the principal part, were retained in language. Monuments intended to proclaim victories of the mind over physical stubborness, were in turn destroyed by mute or brute force. But the thoughts symbolised in words took wings and lived forever, testifying to their own spiritual nature and indestructibility, witnessing their victory over ruined matter and over physical power after all.

Thus the word, not to be fettered or killed, proclaims the freedom of man as against the subjection under natural necessity; it proclaims relative independence from nature upon moral grounds. The word maintains the liberty of man in his dominion over nature as inherited from his spiritual side exclusively, where alone he can preserve it. Free movement, rational and free choice, does not cover all that we mean by freedom; these civil liberties are the natural analogies merely of freedom in the higher and causal sense. It is the energy of the mind, felt as the will, which Gretchen insisted upon, when she would not follow Faust from the dungeon into liberty, that is, freedom in the natural sphere,—is the parent of liberty.

We define will as the spirit's feeling of its own energy, as thought in action. Hence freedom is an attribute of the will inasmuch as it is heaven-born. Hence language is akin to freedom of the will as it initiates the dominion over nature.

Perhaps language could speak more clearly of the union of the natural and spiritual in man, and of will and freedom in particular, were it not for the difficulty of discerning physical from ethical motives, and for the paralogisms perpetrated on that account. It is for this reason, that the concepts of freedom and liberty—just as that of conscience for the same reasons—are liable to be mixed up and taken amiss. Liberty suffers as much abuse as language, wherein we find another proof of their spirituality and for the ontogeny of the spirit itself. For, it is the common fate of the highest blessings, when brought into intercourse with natural life, to be turned into curses.

Freedom is often entirely identified with liberty, and thus lowered to the class of these analogies between physical and spiritual life, which become so natural to us, that we forget to distinguish mental, corporeal, if not carnal, incitements, events, and results, from spiritual motives, events, and effects. Such a mistake was made by Leibnitz, when, for an illustration of the difference between necessity and liberty, he made the magnetic needle speak to other needles about choosing another direction. He sadly failed, of course, to show his point. Notwithstanding the blunder, he illustrated the kindredship of both, language and liberty, because of their common, purely spiritual source. Leibnitz's disparagement of them was merely one of those cases alluded to, where "extremes meet." The caution, desirable for a definite concept of liberty, that is, of freedom in the NATURAL moral sphere, is to be exercised especially where a true and clear picture is to be drawn of the correlations between liberty and necessity. Hence we shall always use the term liberty in distinction from freedom, its spiritual source.

With reference to necessity in nature— human nature, i. e. the physical part of the mind always included—we find in nature appropriation and deprivation, distribution, and assimilation, and excretion of the refuse in the processes of both, bodily and mental nutrition. We know our existence to depend on the normal course of these processes. Of the imponderable influences, impressions and oppressions of the physical and mental atmospheres, as to their healthy or nefarious conditions, we receive very decided convictions, usually without much reflection. Altho we are dependent upon or oppressed by these things, yet in spite or perhaps in consequence of compulsion or want, we feel free, we take the liberty, to form our judgment about them. Notwithstanding the resigned attitude we are forced to assume against inevitables we maintain—our liberty? no—our freedom. Gretchen told Faust; "Ich will nicht!" This illustrates that by our reflecting upon these necessities and the conflict with them, we affirm our consciousness of the higher life which wants to deliver us from the restraints of natural confinement. This feeling and thinking over the matter proves our innate freedom. Otherwise it would prove that we would not care to preserve our freedom and did not deserve liberty. We may choose to deny ourselves of it, but this again would prove that the deliberation and the decision are in our own hands, that even in foregoing liberty we are at liberty to do so. Thus we affirm the freedom of the will even under serious constraint.

We are agreed that if it comes to the moral sphere, the idea of freedom must not be suffered to remain a mere capricious notion, but must be disentangled from the accustomed analogies and from a promiscuous use of language.

Let us here ask: Do liberty and necessity always exclude each other? We hesitate to hastily adopt such a conclusion. There is a natural necessity to which we voluntarily submit. Now what prompts our volition to do it? In the first place there is a feeling that it will be better for us to choose against our inclination, because of an advantage to be gained in this direction or a damage to be avoided in that—or out of regard to an obligation higher than both, higher than Utilitarianism would prescribe, or Eudemonism would care for. This feeling may be very faint, generally it is more so, the more reflecting thought is turned upon it. It is a potent faculty of the mind, which must be developed under cultivation along with the other faculties and in harmony with them.

However feeble this feeling, it infallibly indicates (i. e. speaks into) what is better for us and what is worthy of us or not. We may be conscious of the advice at once, and in this case have an immediate judgment; or we may refer the indication to reason for disquisition and adjustment. In the usual cooperation of both, feeling and reason, the latter will preponderate in the verdict; and this, in most cases, will endanger the verdict. For there are sundry grounds to suspect reason of unreliability and partiality; there are suggestions and motives felt to rise from another kind of feeling, from sensuous sentiency, which have an interest to bribe reason so as to decide in favor of a misrepresented value, under the influence of the will, which then will make the mistake.

"Mind" will argue in favor of something preferable for certain "reasons", while the inward feeling, our moral sentiency has a fine sense for the "Absolute Good." It is conscience pure and simple, which feels the sole necessity of this Good and recognises nothing besides. It is most certain of the Supreme Good as having all value and virtue in itself. It acts as the plenipotentiary of the realm where freedom and

5

Judgment and reason unreliable: under motives arising from the sensuous feelings.

Conscience the pleni-potentiary of the sovereignty of the "Absolute Good."

love reign supreme by necessity of the spiritual nature in its "formal unity under material diversity." It represents the sovereign Good which alone is necessary but not to be forced upon persons lest its value would be lowered. Hence the free conscience whilst insisting upon the solitary necessity, at the same time respects and preserves personal freedom, liberty included. That fine feeling, even retreating, yet ever continuing to remain in immediate touch with the Absolute Good, and very distinct from "reflective consciousness," if decided against by deliberate reason—i. e. judgment in conjuncture with sensuous motives, that is, "willfulness"—withdraws because of its esteem of freedom, not however without holding the person under durance of responsibility and thus upholding man's dignity.

Now reason by its preponderance has formed a wrong judgment. It has willfully, perhaps, mistaken the arbitrariness of volition for freedom of the will, and has led the whole person into error as to the real value, as to that "which might be better;" mistaking it for the highest and alone necessary, i.e. the Absolute Good. It has

Guardian of freedom and personal dignity;

suing free will to agree with the conditions of the solitary necessity

Craving for "something better." is an affirmation of our

destiny for the "Good" which is designed for us.

misapplied the secondary good in nature, if not something worse. Still the subterfuge of having erred from ignorance is no excuse, since that yielding to the imagined something better, wanted by the will, implies the affirmation and acknowledgment of the higher destiny which determines what is really serving the best interests all around and is truly in our favor and for our own benefit.

We feel "the best" to be destined for us, and ourselves destined for it. Now the cultivation of harmony within ourselves, that is making our faculties and their functions to agree with our destiny, the cultivation of harmony between the natural and spiritual worlds as being blended in our being, is the very task to be performed for reaching perfect communion with the world of unity. It is the necessity of this order in the nature of the Absolute Good which sues free will by warnings to consent to, and to voluntarily determine itself for, this union. For, notwithstanding this necessity, will is to remain as free as the Good held out to it, is free inasmuch as it is not to be forced upon our acceptance. Freedom is to be maintained under all circumstances for reasons of love and because of the whole constitution and nature of the spiritual world. Only in this sphere and under consent to this inner necessity the freedom of the will can prosper!

The task to be worked out in freedom.

Task of cultivating harmony among our faculties and desires.

Subsequent to wrong preference of the secondary good.

Corrupt concept of independence leads into servitude.

Whenever reason and volition—in their capacity of free choice—(both obliged to cooperate by virtue of their spiritual kinship, since the principal character of the spiritual sphere is unity, and since the apparatus contains the condition : interrelated connection and cooperative interaction of all spheres of development) whenever reason and volition give way to false valuation of the preferable, mistaking the secondary relative good in nature for the Supreme Good and misapplying it, and ignoring the spiritual interest under the spell of selfdelusion, then personal life becomes estranged from its source and native home. The transgressor becomes sensual in proportion to the practice of habitual arbitrariness. In the confusion ensuing he takes perverseness and obstinacy for consistency of character, especially when laboring to turn relative independence and dominion into emancipation from the authority of the spiritual, and—into corresponding servitude to the lower world.

Incorruptibility of the "still small voice."

Kinship between conscience and language.

Part of personal life, however, always individual and resisting absorption into the generalness of the sphere of "formal diversity under material unity," is not thus to be seduced and adulterated. It is the language of the spirit-land, the "still small voice." It is the universally understood expression of the feeling which can not be intimidated to leave its post as representative of the Absolute Good and as witness for its necessity ; which can not be alienated from keeping communication with God. It remains on speaking terms with the Good. It alone perpetuates the connection and contact with the indissoluble spiritual side of personal life, of which we know that it transcends selfconsciousness It surpasses that part of our being which is confined to the form of existence limited by space and time.

Conscience keeps up communication with the world of "formal unity" but, for reasons of preserving itself and man's dignity, withdraws into the privacy of subconsciousness.

This feeling, in order to maintain its independence, its incorruptibility and freedom, retires into the innermost recesses of the mind (the psycho-spiritual life), where, out of reach of peripheral turmoil, the purely spiritual constituents of personal life are bound together by their nature of unity, where the person is kept in durance of responsibility, so that the dignity of man is at the same time preserved in the privacy of retired conscientiousness.

In the meanwhile other feelings usurp the function of deciding what is necessary, belying the ego as to the necessity of the secondary good, by denying it to be the highest good. The whole mind gets confused and disturbed and unbalanced. The appetites, cutting loose from the authority of the spiritual principle of unity, become dissolute ; and they dominate, altho losing themselves into the sphere of the manifold. They oppose and reject the control of the spirit in order to reign under assumed liberty, notwithstanding the reproachful feeling of the misery of serfdom under natural necessity. This painful split is the empirical state of personal life, aggravated by the unceasing conflict between " the spirit and the flesh." Serfdom is humiliatingly felt, it is mortifying. Free will is lost, and the rest of the will-energy by degrees will also be lost entirely, because the natural part, when severed from the spiritual union, falls under the natural law of disintegration and cannot live.

Holding its own, it holds man under durance of responsibility.   Sec 41.

Freedom of feeling preserved while freedom of will is lost.

The answer to the question: "How may the loss be retrieved?" is to be obtained from the science of the purely spiritual Good. We can here only give the assurance, from what we know of its selfesteem, that amends will not be forced upon man at this hour of the world without the asking.

Thus the equipoise of the two worlds virtually is balanced in man who belongs to both. Under this aspect alone he and his history may be understood. That equipoise is indicated by the tongue of the scales of righteousness as held up here beneath by conscience weak and alone. And thus solely and truly the equation between the paradoxical relations of necessity and freedom in either sphere is demonstrable. It will even stand the test of experiment!

Equipoise of nature and spirit indicated by the tongue of the scales of righteousness, held up by conscience, weak and alone.

The features of mutual adaptability of nature and spirit to each other, and the features of kinship among the spiritual entities of language, conscience, and freedom are also demonstrable and empirical in every relation of love. Its spiritual nature intimately unites love with the feeling of value and the freedom of the will.

Necessity and love.

Nobody will deny that love, like conscience, is a personal matter.

Again it is the promiscuous use of the term caused by the misleading analogous processes spoken of, which transfer love to things. We can only love persons, not even ideas, were they ever so holy. The doctrine of this unique energy and entity "Love" belongs to Ethics, altho the autonomic, we may say mechanical-autonomic Moral-philosophy of the Kantian school, (Calderwood closely following,) utterly ignored it. Kant mentioned love only as a poetical luxury.

Kinship of the spiritual entities; language, conscience and freedom in love, the bond of perfection.

Kant slurs Calderwood slights love, the cardinal principle in ethics.

Considering then the relation of love to freedom, nobody will deny that it is in the power of any person to accept or reject, to renounce it, or to deny oneself of the person loved, or to make one's self even a sacrifice out of love, and in the interest of the person loved. All who understand the strong hold it takes and by which it draws; who can the more appreciate its necessity for life because of the very separation from its object: all such will testify that in this highest and most intense power of "the bond of perfection," freedom and necessity are intrinsically interwoven. The grief of separation demonstrates anew the indestuctibility, indissolubility and unifying power of the spiritual essence, and also the interrelations of those coefficients of human nature, which we know already by their family-likeness. As language and conscience, feeling and willing or volition and valuation, judgment and adjustment, are recognisable as twin-pairs, as it were, so freedom and necessity permeating and balancing them all, seek to escape from being paradoxically misconceived, and they seek to find their conciliation in the human heart. At any rate the conciliation between necessity and freedom is wrought by love.

Love personal like conscience.

Unifying power of love like language.

Here the indiscretion, identifying spiritual functions and purposes, and blending them indiscriminately with the correlative processes of natural life, works most disastrously. Think of the comparisons made between the "love of a tigress" toward her cubs and the love of a mother. The necessity as well as the freedom of love come, of course, under the class of analogous processes in which, on account of the union between the psyche and the spirit, both modi of necessity, along with love itself, penetrate most deeply into the physical part of human nature. Hence the tangle and wrong application of the "communicatio idiomatum" as it were, becomes peculiarly mischievous in incidents of this kind. More so, since emotional differ from rational phenomena in that they belong to the sphere of passiveness, and are therefore prone to split and to burst out in passions. Here clearness about attributes and functions, motives and purposes is of highest importance for history whenever it is to announce judgment.

Caution against identifying the freedom and necessity of love with their physical analogies is of high ethical import.   Sec. 7, 8.

The blending of necessity and freedom with love,and the blending of love with the whole fabric of the human being is exceedingly important to morality. Hence it is especially desirable in this instance, that the lines between spiritual emotion and natural sentiment, and between that set of sentiencies and the rational energics must not be obliterated.

For the sake of humanism the cognitions of these psychological items should be allowed no longer to become corrupted and misconstrued through the pseudo-conclusions alluded to upon the naturalistic basis. For, severed from their spiritual source love and freedom must pine away!

There are theories, popular and easily propagated because pandering to the low predilections of growing sensualism, which teach to apply love along with liberty in the mere natural sense. Both are equivocally attributed to physico-psychical life, after the psyche has been purged of every vestige of spirituality. This is evidently done to humor the masses, who mistake the spiritual for the religious life, which per se, and in the sense here propounded, it is not.

It is evident that in such a muddle of affairs the understanding of man and his history in the most sacred and solemn concerns is not only impossible, but that then wild world-theories are promulgated, and wrong views of life prevail which can not but be pregnant with very serious consequences. On the other hand, it is evident that with the proper achievement of the unification of spirit and nature in man, and through their proper permeation in the rational-moral sphere, that is, under methods of applying Ethics to actual life : truth, conscience, necessity and freedom and love will all fully and forever stand by each other in personal relationship. These entities, if such we may call these cardinal factors, will by virtue of their purely spiritual nature, render the union inseparable and will form a partnership of coefficients for still higher purposes.

Meanwhile love's emblem, representing the union of the necessity of the good with freedom and with love, is—sacrifice.

§ 12. Let us frame the results of the inductive analysis so far found into a syllogism. Max Mueller once said : "Language stands one foot in the realm of nature and the other in that of the spirit." This corroborates our axiom and the result of our investigation, that language reveals what is in man. For this reason the mere "scientific" way, if one-sided analysis dares to assume the name, will not lead to our discoveries.

Neither comparative craniognomy nor the hap-hazard measurements of physiological and experimental psychology will by themselves be able to disclose the generic constituency of a single person and his grand significance, much less that of the race as a whole.

Neither will the philosophical disciplines by themselves accomplish this, altho Des Cartes already opined that out of his "cogito" and his "sum" he could explain everything, in doubts of which he had begun his inquiry   Comparative philosophy of religion attempted to explain the formations of national characters and to account for forms of governments, revolutions, dissolutions—but at its best it treated only one side of life, discarding the other.

As previously mentioned, more might have been expected of moral philosophy. But it was rarely made a rule that a moral philosopher should know as much of history as of metaphysics, and that for a genuine anthropology all historical material as well as the whole of nature should be ransacked. It is not generally conceived that universal history and ethnography must be to ethics what natural history is to physiology, and what both are to the medical science. Had ethics been aware of its relation to history and physiological psychology, it could have pondered over a little more material ; it could have availed itself of a few more auxiliaries and coefficients than Plato and Spinoza had at hand. Still it lacked the ethnological and the philological data, contributed only since the quiet, empirical work of missionaries had begun to command the respect of the philosophers. It also lacked the discoveries, archæological and philological, made by a score of daring explorers. It is only recently that ethics, like Dorner's system, seems to become a qualified coworker with philosophy of history for the most correct interpretation possible, of man, humanity, and history, so as not to leave out of sight the final goal of historic progress. We found that so far the most conclusive arguments for the union of the spiritual and natural worlds in man, have been furnished by comparative philology. By the study of tongues, and of families of languages, the truth of real life can be discerned approximately correctly, because it deals with disclosures from both worlds; and because in its documentary proofs it possesses a firm basis of historical realities and the evidence of disinterested eye and ear witnesses. Altho a great many are mutilated and some are mere fragments, yet others are found which supplement the meager suggestions of the first, and when all are deciphered and speak, one set will restore the full sense otherwise missing, whilst an other will correct erroneous interpretations of former times along the whole line.

While races mingle, states break up, and nations perish, their languages com memorate their fame or their fate, and dead stones become living witnesses above suspicion. Languages may be called dead, but in their tombs we find more than retarded or arrested, we find resurrected, life. They possess that character by virtue of their higher substantiality, which never becomes subject to the natural law of decomposition, but which on account of the unity holding sway in the spiritual realm, can ever be resuscitated by translation. They are like sighs for deliverance, uttered by that creature which forms a part of our own being, notwithstanding our being unconscious of it. Hence philology alone is competent to show beyond controversy the true import of history and nature associated. It learns man's inner condition not without due consideration of the material part that serves as the substantial conductor of the spiritual elements, nor without criticism, and not without handling—some solid stuff in excavating. *The essentials in the sphere of consciousness, cohesion and continuity.*

Philology exhibits the proofs of the dual character of personal life—of human nature we will say henceforth,—as her triumphs. From the proofs we posit as the essentials of the sphere of "formal unity in personal diversity": cohesion, continuity and unity of consciousness. *The sum and substance of the inductive survey and the prospects for our deductions.*

Unless we are sure of these three manifestations of the spiritual in this material world, we can have no knowledge of what we mean by humanity, and what may be the purpose of its life. We could know as little of this, as we could be sure of our own selves, if our lives were not held together, under all bodily changes, by our selfconsciousness. The tripartition of conscious life, alluded to in the beginning, and the triad with which we conclude our first glance at man, is to be materialised in the "cogito" of the person who is sure of his "sum." Without recognising his consciousness, all the "formal diversity of the world of material unity" remains a dire riddle, the most portentous of all enigmata.

Now let us examine, whether our ascent from the manifold to that unity to be perfected in the One, did not mislead us; or whether the One is superfluous, so that the secret hidden in diversity, might be discerned regardless of unity.

In the first germ of plant life, (exact science states), the prototype of the genus must be—anticipated, imagined. Were we able to introspect that type, and to interpret its design, we would be able also to delineate or construct in our mind the peculiarities of a plant from germ to crown. We might further be able to explain the significance it bears upon its whole genus, yea upon the whole economy of nature. The first germ containing the type, then, would represent the character of its generic totality. Such conjecturing is legitimate,and evolution constantly works upon this proposition which gave birth to the young science of biology. It is legitimate because the totality of nature does not consist of a collection or an agglomerated mass, but is an organised unity, be it ever so finely differentiated and widely variegated. *Germinal type contains the essentials of the genus. Proto-type to be anticipated—imagined. Sec. 13.*

In a much higher sense does the theme of universal history rest in man—as its type. The whole fabric of its continual and progressive development is implied in him. He is the key to it. Man's being as a person is bound up with the region below him,—circumscribed only by the limits of the material unit of nature in general, —on account of his intrinsic connection not only with articulated organic life, but also with inorganic, compressed, confined life. On the other side man is just as intrinsically connected with the spiritual unit of personal diversity. He has thus be- *The postulate, derived from man's development, presents him as the prototype of historical development.*

Man's dual rela-
tion to inorganic
life even, and to
the spiritual unit
as an
individualised
member.

come individualised as a member of the spirit-world, a natural—spiritual entity, a specimen of a higher genus, a person. His development, as such a personality—by way of selfcultivation in the moral process, that is, in his advancing appropriation of nature in order to lead it upward in and with himself—makes it necessary for him to remain a member of the lower genus also. This, for the present, is his vocation and position. He, and nature (forever belonging to him) with him, is in a state of transition to the spiritual, unified mode of existence.

Altho a member
of the higher
genus, yet
necessary to
remain one of
the lower also;
so as to elevate along
with himself the whole
of nature belonging to
him.

If this dual membership of human nature, implying connection inter se as a genus; if this formation of one unit called humanity, conjoining in itself the polar units above and below, is established by the science of languages, then we possess in language a focus true and sure, from which universal history may be looked into. Through this object-lens its whole significance and all its conjunctures must be observable.

Humanity a unit;
conjoining in
itself the two
units of the
worlds above
and below.

All history is then conceived as one entire whole, from the connections of which the single items can be examined as to their merits or demerits, their value or their faults; we can then trace out the interchanging causes and effects of oppressions, insurrections, progresses, relapses, failures: we can locate depravity and its consequences. Not without this reference to the whole are we able to judge of what is worthy to be imitated, or what is to be avoided as dangerous. The good results obtained in the happy realisation of the true and the good and the beautiful, are thus sorted out and exhibited, treasured up and made applicable. Such a practical and beneficial service of the Philosophy of History, is vouched for by analogous services of other applied sciences, and by precedents in the past. We thus become encouraged in the attainment of the good, and in the resistance of the bad. For, notwithstanding all earthly distress, and all obstacles, the good is within reach of all. With due attention and circumspection false steps may be avoided, if errors are laid open.

Language the focus
from which to view the
unit of universal history;

History not intelligible
unless considered as a
totality.

MORAL COSMOS.

Humanity considered as man developing, and history as the macrocosm of man—so that man is conceived as the microcosm of both, the natural and the ideal (ethical) cosmos—will deliver into our hands the key to both worlds in the human person. Man's personal character will then reflect from his surroundings, from improvements made, from the way his environment are cultivated or influenced by him, instead of the environments determining his fortune. The shaping of man's private and civil affairs is laid into his own hands. The elevation of nature, by pressing it into his service, that is, by making nature cooperative in her own elevation, will then be beautifully illustrated. Wildernesses become transformed into festive grounds of world's exhibitions, or into ideal resorts of idyl life: into the imitations of paradise, called parks after it; into orchards with choice fruits to sweeten life, and flower gardens to adorn it.

History's teachings
made applicable in a
sound world-theory,
founded upon the
duality of human
nature.

The Good in
reach of all.
The Bad
avoidable and to
be resisted.

Man the microcosm of
the natural and moral
cosmos combined;
Humanity considered as
man developing,
History as the
macrocosm of man.

Historic importance of
every individual.

Man's esthetics become refined with his ethics, but of course, not vice versa. His ethics will be purified by the true aspect, appreciation, and acceptance of the Supreme Good, until civilisation in its noblest sense becomes his habit, his second nature, individually and collectively. Hence the singular importance of every individual member of humanity. For not only the day is given to him or her, but also the opportunity for higher attainments, which selfinterest should teach him to use properly for the good of others also. Not only does he exert some influence for good or evil, which spreads (the latter more rapidly according to a mysterious, subnatural law) in smaller or larger undulations, but he also, in great part, helps to mold the weal or woe of coming generations. The development of potentialities in the human person is repeated in all directions throughout human history, hence history must be conceivable as man unfolded, explicated, explained, extended, (the truth in Spinozism). The initiative required for new steps of progress is to be taken from a sense of personal duty.

Man, not the
environment,
shapes his weal or woe.

Moral and mental
progress initiated
by personal and
national life
issues from the
spiritual sphere
of personality,
not from that of
natural
generalness.
Sec. 6.

This explains why true advance of a nation under abolition of inhumane practices, why social reforms etc. can not be expected from the masses. That is the duty of those to whom the principles of the higher life were transmitted most felicitously; in whom the continuity and unity of consciousness have become crystalised, as it were, so as to form the vital part of their being; while the masses will resist laws restrictive to selfish and natural inclinations, and will vote for laws for others to obey. It is the tendency toward generalness which schemes at class-legislation.

Stages of advance must proceed, not from the oneness or generalness of nature, but from the oneness of the spiritual world of which individuality is a characteristic attribute by way of—the deliverance of each personality from the natural-state. Christianity was planted and is to be propagated only in this way. Take the development of a person. In the first years of life natural propensities predominate, altho *Personality developing in a measure as the faculties are liberated from natural generalness.* little by little traces of moral and mental potentialities, of the union of soul and spirit, that is, of mind, become apparent. Special features of future combinations of temperament and character assert themselves, even sparks of genius. Appetites gov- *Relative purity of childhood.* ern the will until judgment gets the upper hand. Physical obstruction, restraint, or compulsion sets the will free; the word sets reason free; conscience emancipates itself *External incitements of inner development* from reason, while the moral sense is yet more vivid than the mental capacities; con- *under practice on the natural apparatus. Import of the latter* science becomes distinct from other sentiencies or emotions, and in case of contradic- *upon Ethics and upon the* tion, it indignantly withdraws. For it is questionable whether love and conscience in *genesis of consciousness.* their orignality and relative purity are ever more undefiled and vivid than in early *Sec. 9, 39, 117, 159.* childhood. At first the natural predispositions and spiritual capabilities are not yet differentiated. Incitements from the outside world under the discipline of attention, imitation, education, must aid in setting the faculties free, according to the ethical condition of cooperation of the lower state in its being guided on to the higher.

This is the significance of the natural apparatus not only with respect to the ethic- *Influences from the higher sphere conditioned.* al task, but also in respect to the genesis of consciousness and to moral deportment. But task and apparatus do not alone procure the deliverence of the mind. The dif- *Harmonious development under cultivation of inner endowments is rare.* ferentiation of the faculties goes on also under the other condition,—to which the dis- cipline at the apparatus is only preparatory and mediative,—of receiving and accept- ing influences from the higher sphere of permanence and unity. Thus the manifesta- tions of selfconsciousness ripen into internal character and external adaptness and conduct. The more harmonious the endowments of the mind are disciplined to bal- ance each other, and the more habitually the moral and mental activities are regulat- *Civilisation is but inner personal and normal development extended.* ed by the spiritual concomitants,   the better will a person be fitted to overcome the obstacles and adverse circumstances arising from the natural sphere; and the more *Sec. 23.* virtuously, serenely   will the person fill his place in the cooperative order of so- cial life. To be sure, such normal, proportionate development is rare, very rare. The combined process of it, called civilisation, advances slowly, under difficulties increas- ing with differentiation growing more complicated, intricate and subtile. Thus, one- sided cultures are generated in which, as a matter of course, nations participate.

Reason and discipline cultivated at the expense of feeling, produced the Roman char- acter and the Kantian frame of mind. Aesthetics and imagination cultivated at the expense of ethics, produces Greeks, Frenchmen, and Goethe. Speculation and resignation at the *Examples of* expense of the will, are the stamp of the Hindoos and Schoperhauer; legal sense at the *one-sided culture.* *Reason at the expense* expense of love, produces Pharisees, Moors and fanatics. Emphasising faith without love, *of feeling—Roman.* deadens a church; love without fidelity, ruins the family, the hearthstone of the state. *Esthetics at the expense* Being busy with the whole world from selfish interests will sharpen the calculative trend of *of ethics—Greek.* Carthage and Venice. Much urbanity but no patriotism, developes to only that sort of public-mindedness which has its eye upon a golden upper crust. Abandonment of mind and heart for the sake of the stomach, will create a populace crying for "bread and circuses " at all times; brutes who will overthrow law and order, crush authority and superiority, and demol- ish what they cannot rebuild, as they have done in yonder city once in a while. For we had barbarians not so much in the Hercynian forest as in that town which used to march at the head of civilisation, prescribing "refined" fashions to the world for centuries. And even in some great towns nearer home, we find lower and upper strata of arrested life, under the influence of mean spirits.

For this reason of defective, onesided culture we cannot philosophise about history upon *Philosophy of History* crutches of calendar-schedules and social statistics. Higher topics and larger categories *must avoid one-sidedness.* must be systematised, instead of cutting up history into centuries, localities, anecdotes and details. History digested, is not to build screens of generalness for the individual to hide *Questionable education.* himself, but to bring out the truth of individual culture, which is more than the training or good breeding now called "education." History moving in cycles, measured out in heaven, and concentric with eternity, must not be considered in a one-sided and narrow manner.

In expanse, the civilisation of the Twentieth Century for which we must get ready, will, Deo volente, surpass that of any previous period. But whether it will make human happiness more general without increasing misery in extensive pro- portions also ; whether it will intensify civilisation on the line of true ethical per- *Progress of culture at the expense of the cultus renders civilisation problematical.* sonal culture, and not at the expense of genuine culture—these are the problems. Their solution depends on the deliverance of personal life from the generalness of the natural sphere, depends on the practice of personal excellency which will have to be qualified for encountering the baseness of that sphere, which is, for the sake of generality and from its nature, inimical to excellency. Philosophy of History has to find out the onesided tendency of culture, and to give warning.

Personal excellency tested by encountering the enmity of the sphere of generalness.

It must, therefore, guard itself against onesidedness and dead dogmatism. Honest and sober and circumspect, it must qualify itself for pointing out the way to prosperity, and the goal of progress ; it must throw light upon it from above, and gain the confidence due an experienced guide. It must be critical, **theoretical**, and realistic in the study, in order to build up a consistent world-theory and thus enable itself to give **practical** hints to the schools, and to Houses of Parliaments.

§ 13. History has brought to light what is in men. The natural grounds, occupied by all men in common, afford every possible opportunity which develop formations as various and innumerable as those of the oceans and the atmosphere. As one tree,

Futility of arranging a system by which humanity in general could be comprehended from typical specimens of times and nations.

in aspiring to the light, spreads its top more than another, while at the same time its ramifications spread in the ground and go deeper for nourishment, still resembles other trees whose common mother is the earth, just so mankind multiply their relations and wants, invent contrivances to satisfy them, diversify their aspirations and occupations, and yet always bear the same stamp. Theoretically, nothing would be in the way to exhibit the stages of development by a specimen of each nation, and to combine, as Carlyle would have it, such types into a system or a scheme of universal progress.

This was Lavater's idea when he collected his pictures of typical physiognomies. He attempted to show to some contemporaries what time it was in the world, whether 1794 A. D. or 1894 B. C.; but Lavater and phrenology would by such means show it as little as a clock

CARLYLE,　Sec. 215.
LAVATER,
JOH. V. MILLER.

can do it. Such a construction would lead to the same result which Joh. v. Miller arrived at, after he had summoned the manes of heroes and rulers, of thinkers and speakers, for examination. "And now Ye giants with beasts in your escutcheons, Ye of old pedigree, looking up to us from cathedral-crypts and down upon us from ruined castle-portals; Ye conquerers from Memleben and Westminster; Thou enchanted Hohenstauffen in Thy Kyffhaeuser; Ye holy eminencies from Peter's tomb; Caesars and barbarians with stiff necks; Kings with your once many-crowned skulls under your once mighty arms; Ye councilors of popes, and Ye beauties once ruling them and ruining their countries; Ye scholars with laurels upon your high foreheads and with august frowns; all Ye majesties in fields of sciences; all Ye leaders in bloody

All earthly fame would not suffice to fashion a satisfactory pattern of true humanity.

battle-fields stand up! Who were Ye? Human beings of high qualities? Rarely. Noblest of characters? A dozen at best out of your thousand names. Were Ye the disposers of the fates of billions of people, avengers of wrong and vanquishers of the bad, protectors of the weak— or were Ye mere drivers of men?—O lie down again! Tools Ye were, with the maddest of passions some of you! Wheels Ye were, nothing more, wheels in the great clock-work of time, just like others far more numerous than Ye, only less notorious here beneath, through whose interactions the Ancient One on High moved the hands of the clock of the world. It does not yet show time to adjourn for final judgment. We must wait as Ye must, and we must lie low down like Ye ! Lie down again !"

A construction of history of this sort, as we will find again with Carlyle, may yield poetical satisfaction ; but humanity as a body, if contemplated as such a me-

Proto-type of humanity.
Sec. 9, 12, 35, 92, 105, 117, 120, 233.

chanical unity, is torn asunder in a manner as to freeze out its heart. In putting it together again, we need to be careful to save the dignity, freedom, and personality of humanity.

Without much art it has been demonstrated as the object of history to unfold the whole of man's nature to full view, and hence as the task of our science to summarise the meaning of all the contents thus revealed, and to reduce it to a unitary personality. Our curiosity has been aroused for a comprehensive glance at such a per-

The seer's vision.
Sec. 115.

son by reviewing "personal life" in the inductive method and the deductive. The first philosopher of history who received such a vision saw the contents of human development represented in the figure of a person made of metals. At the proper time we shall introduce that seer and his vision.

But since that visionary figure can not be recognised as the typical man, who can be the one who would completely answer the image? Who is so perfectly fitted to represent the ideal of each of us as to be recognised at once and by all? How is

Impossibility to compose the proto-type or ideal man by reason or imagination.
ROUSSEAU.　Sec. 12.

the picture to be composed as to light and shade and tone of color? Considering the thousand-fold caricatures and mutilations to which the human frame and mind are subject, when not even an Apollo or a Venus would suit everybody as a model—how is the typical and ideal image to be conceived? From whence would the standard and normal measure have to be taken? Whence the rule, to begin with, for singling out and putting together the main features only of all that is worthy and sublime enough to answer your ideal and mine, and to be respected universally, into a mere mosaic—to say nothing of the adaptability of a person, thus theoretically composed, and if actually realisable, for this rough life? Rousseau said, the one who could invent such a picture, even if merely wrought out in the shape of a simple biography, would need be deemed God himself.

And where, if that ideal image of man was really discovered and exhibited, where would the standpoint have to be chosen for its admiration? What would be the criterion required for duly appreciating it without bias and without wild reverie?

At a more suitable occasion we shall take up these questions. But since there must have existed one primitive man, carrying within him the type of the human race (so far as we are allowed to go back according to our agreement in Sec. 12 without provoking the suspicion of reasoning in favor of a foregone conclusion), then there was latent in this truly human person the whole project, the image and theme of human history.

To listen to the accords and discords of this theme, to the music in the spheres of the eons, through many variations, but ever with a harmonious solution like the most sublime symphony—this is our conception of the Philosophy of History.

CH. 5.—THE PHILOSOPHY OF HISTORY versus UNSATISFACTORY INTER-PRETATIONS OF HISTORY.

NOTE.—With reference to the position of our science we are obliged to solicit patience for a few moments. It is necessary to dwell a little longer on that position, so as to gain the epistemological aspect under which to enter the system proper. The present remarks stand connected with those in the first and second chapters, which had to be postponed until the disquisition with the sciences on physics and metaphysics might clear up the wrangle, so as to confront us with the real object of the contention, We thereby were furnished with the material or coefficients to be considered. We like to take from the fullness thereof and let the conclusion follow as the natural result.

§ 14. The question next in order, therefore, is : How is philosophy to be rendered applicable in subservience to a comprehensive interpretation of history?

Each empiric science, of either nature, or law, or language, deals with a specific object of which we can have subjective experience. Experience alone entitles a theoretical construction of the particular subject to a claim of objective weight and significance. The establishment of the objective truth is the reason for, and the purpose of, theorising ; it is the privilege of science and its vocation.

But the empiric sciences, notwithstanding the experiences, have to build upon first principles universally granted, altho, perhaps, not empirically explicable, such as the immutability of space, the continuity of time, or the universality of right, etc. Natural sciences, for instance, take it for granted, that there exists, apart from the mind, an objective, corporeal, visible, and tangible world. Without such presuppositions the sciences stand in the air ; they are hanging in the wind—especially that of jurisprudence—of current opinions swaying the times. Likewise does historic science presuppose that at some time this or that happened, whether we were present or not, and regardless of our opinion about it. But neither of these sciences is able to substantiate its allegations relative to any first cause or, as the case may be, to any secondary effect, or to time, or to substance, etc.,—conditions which are irrelevant to the theory erected into the framework of first principles.

Other empirical sciences which could prove or disprove doctrines by facts, we have none ; provided we are allowed to classify Mathematics with Metaphysics on the same grounds that we claim language as belonging to the historics. We therefore state : each science in demanding objective and authoritative validity for its theory, must concede a partial disability to acquire or to adduce full proof of the reality of its knowledge. Each contains something of the nature of " nescience ", of the " posse nescire "; each is confined to a more or less limited domain of knowledge, each suffering from incompleteness, or from breaks, or some hiatus on account of some deficiency or other, not to be supplemented from its own resources. Hence each stands in need of a certain "transcendental equation ", as it were, of what the astronomers call the "equation of the center." None of these sciences can vindicate its presuppositions unless it overreaches the terminals and terminology of its own domain and thereby ceases to be that "exact science." It certainly, to say the least, forfeits the right to dogmatise on a world-theory.

The complement required by each is to be afforded by another, whereby a general and comparative science is achieved whose duty it is to find reasons, to make "abstracts," as it were, warranting the sacredness of the terminals, and the clearness of the title, stating the encumbrances pending and the derivation of principles from other sciences; and sanctioning the legitimacy of their application—lest one theory may steal a march on the other. This science, defining the cognitions underlying each, and proving their true relationship with impartiality, is Philosophy,—the umpire.

There is a certain aversion noticeable to such superintendency and surveillance on the part of Metaphysics; the "Sciences" seem agreed to set up "Epistemology" of late, in order to put it in the place which Logic since Locke's time occupied, and which is now said to be vacated because of the mixed-up condition of antiquated Logics. Epistemology is to show that philosophy, too, is superfluous on the strength of the self-sufficiency of Physiological Psychology. The Logics of old thus modified may suit well enough to supplant the name of "Mental Philosophy;" but all of that is not what we mean by the Philosophy of Sciences—Wissenschafts-lehre.

Says Murray of Montreal: "Philosophy is precisely 'the' endeavor to bring our knowledge to complete unification. And while it must oppose any attempt to reach this end by hasty generalisations, it can not rest satisfied with a recognition of principles in such complete independence, as to bar the way against their being brought under some superior principle which comprises them all."

Such independence however is forestalled by the experience made in the intuitionalistic schools of Germany. Philosophy depends upon the two empirical sciences which it deems neither inferior nor superior, the natural and the historical. The function of philosophy is not as Bowne thinks, to "make laws." It is not "obvious that, because philosophy cannot borrow its principles from the other sciences, it must impose its own principles upon them." On the other hand, philosophy is not simply to engage in surveying the government's lands, as it were, to map out the sections and the roads by which the harvest is to be gathered in, or to locate the mills where the grain is to be garnered and ground. That is to say, philosophy is not so much to describe nor to prescribe, the brain-work in the derivation of first principles upon which agreements are facilitated, but rather to explain the origin of ideas held in common and their subsequent application in either causing on interpreting facts and phenomena of spiritual as well as physical life.

Of course, exception here may be taken again on the part of some savants against our combining the physical with the spiritual under the standing protest that the latter was "Unknowable." This incessant assertion may be renunciated with the remark that Materialism is welcome to act as tho it had nothing to do with it. Whether it honestly ignores the spiritual altogether and can get along without it, is no concern of ours. We think naturalism per se has enough already of what it does not know, let alone the spiritual world and our experiences of it. But this cannot induce us to waive our right and freedom of inquiry.

Philosophy congratulates Science in its endeavor to establish monistic naturalism or natural monism, provided it does not promulgate immature results as an all-sufficient view of life and as "the" correct world-theory. The Philosophy of History only asks in return, whether it is to be blamed for taking cognizance of matters which have been the talk of men throughout at least forty centuries? A standing and sneering protest against the "Unknowable" is, in its fidgetiness, a sympton of the weakness, indigency and willful nescience of materialistic evolutionism; it is an admission of that one-sidedness which not only refuses to listen to honest advances of conciliatory correspondence, but which ever generates intolerance and fanaticism.

We do not rebuke naturalistic monism for its incompleteness and deficiencies, but we condemn the arrogance with which, in spite of this concession, it decrees to the public, that its dogmas are incontrovertable truths, that they prove all spiritual corollaries and co-efficients to be at least insignificant and therefore nugatory, if not dangerous. Feuerbach for one drew these conclusions with great force and fervor, and he now has scores of disciples misrepresenting the German nation in its Reichstag. Such popularity shows the secret of the impudence with which the public is imposed upon, which is in keeping with the poverty of that kind of thought defined as mere phosphorescence of brain matter. It shows the dishonesty of Agnostics for reasons well known to themselves, reasons which do not like to get an airing and to be unmasked. But this justifies our reproach, previously expressed in the statement that they have forfeited their claim upon science and their title of being scientific, since real science can not pose in a simulated attitude of unconcern and leisure, as long as not all is rendered intelligible that is present in history as an efficient or an effect. Our attitude, in withdrawing scientific courtesy from materialistic monism, is justified by none less than Tyndall himself, since, in his settlement of the controversy with Virchow, he discountenances the agitation of unqualified journalists, who, to the chagrin of the great searcher after truth, prejudice science as being an ally to social-democracy. *(Materialistic Sociology disavowed by Tyndall and Virchow.)*

Empiricism may certainly have its reasons for its animosity toward the spiritual. We need not cast this up to it as an imputation. But, if it denies philosophy the right of umpire, and the acknowledgment of being a science, then we can only make allowance and account for its clamor to exclude Metaphysics by averring that empiricism prefers scepticism to certainty! In the meanwhile, Philosophy is not thus cheaply to be ruled out. As yet it is included in the college of sciences. And it need not be ashamed of taking full cognizance of the spiritual world, where after all, and nowhere else, the synthesis of true monism is to be found. But on account of its very relationship and inner nature it forces itself upon nobody, merely rising in defence of certainty and of freedom. *(Empirics preferring scepticism to certitude.) (True Monism to be found in the spiritual synthesis.)*

Philosophy already is, and has been for a long time, engaged with the postulates and premises of the common truth, namely, that the particulars require the universals—the primum cognitum Leibnitz would say—for their explanation. Of this general comprehensiveness and scientific consistency it is the criterion and discipline. It aspires to bring all knowledge to a unity in which contradiction is silenced. It defends the comprehensibility of everything connected with personal life (i. e., with natural spiritual life), with human nature, as we shall say henceforth, emphasising the adjective human. It also defends the ability of the mind (i. e. the synthesis of soul and spirit, not merely that of the intellectual or mental faculties), to understand its position and to comprehend spiritual manifestations. *(Philos. the criterion and discipline of true apprehension)*

Now, whenever a particular branch of science shall assume that it may dodge such discipline and still appropriate principles not belonging to it, philosophy will detect the smugglery and will denounce the false use of the filched property. The particular science thus exposed will then, of course, hate philosophy and cry thief, so as to divert the outsider's attention. But the unreasonable hatred alone should throw suspicion on such presumptuous empiricism, and should cancel its claim of being unbiased, truthful, and trustworthy. For, if any science stealthily deals with wrongfully acquired propositions, whereby it tacitly admits their value as general principles, without being able to give an account for their possession—how can we be sure that such science, tearing the general and true principles out of their proper connections, made proper use of them in its conclusions? That the misapplied principle is true in the premises certainly does not prove the truth of the conclusions thus erroneously, if not surreptitiously, obtained for deceptive purposes. *(defends the comprehensibility of all which concerns "human nature"; defends the mind in its endeavor to understand its position. Empiricism appropriating principles alien to its value proves their value. Sec. 2.)*

It has come to the knowledge of history, that such tricks have been practiced. It is therefore to the interest of all the sciences, that they should not lose their credit on account of a case of embezzlement or forgery having been exposed in one or another quarter of the domain of systematised knowledge. Any branch of true science therefore, will certainly lend its support to a responsible auditor who examines the vouchers. For, philosophy in itself has a more dignified office than the occasional detective-work alluded to. It aims at the correctness of all knowledge as a whole, so that out of its conservatory of synthetic rehearsals the particulars of a special branch-science may receive new light or additional confirmation from other than its own sources; so that for each part of knowledge it can be decided, satisfactorily all around, which inferences are admissible; so that each in the concert can have its vouchers and collaterals sanctioned as testproof. *(The credit of true science maintained. Veracity of philosophical judgments to be ascertained by the concert of the empirical sciences.)*

In turn the veracity of philosophy can thus be ascertained likewise. If any general axiom does not cover all facts brought to notice by any experience or new discovery, does not suffice to account for all the phenomena observed and reported by qualified witnesses; or if any principle, hitherto held as an axiom, is plainly and successfully contradicted: then that conception is erroneous and needs to be adjusted or must be abandoned.

Erroneous axioms to be abandoned.

The umpire an expert.

This occasionally occurs; but philosophy as a whole is not overthrown on that account. Not all its judgments are void because some verdict or law had to be repealed after better information. On the contrary, philosophy thus corrected is rendered the more reliable. Enriched through experience it is the better enabled to give cautious advice, judicious assistance, and just decisions. The umpire thereby becomes an expert.

Contempt of empiricism by the idealists avenged by Darwinism. Sec. 15

When and why does philosophy once in a while get off the track? Perhaps empirical sciences did not furnish correct, perhaps even entirely mistaken data. This is not impossible. For it must be kept in mind, that philosophy can not be expected to leave her own observatory or court-room in order to find out particulars which within her own domain she can not find. If this were possible, then philosophy would be the only science, the others mere auxiliaries, drummers and errand-boys; then empirical science, aside from it, would not be necessary. Proud Kantianism and Hegelianism acted in that manner toward the scientific schools. Darwinism with its saucy Spencers, Feuerbachs, and Huxleys caused a revision by avenging the errors of the former.

Philosophy is to the sciences what the clearing house is to the financial world.

Thanks to the dual tension of rational life the usefulness and necessity of philosophy is endorsed so much the stronger, and it is fully restored through the recent detections of its fallacies. It could not have made the blunders if it had not either confided too much in the facts as represented by scientists, or if it had not despised the reality of things beyond the horizon of reason purged of those things between "Heaven and earth" with which Goethe upbraided them. That some of the conclusions from defective premises were found wrong, not purposely counterfeited, and were set aright, or were marked spurious and set out of value and circulation, is to be accredited to the **philosophical clearing-house**.

Science unable to prove the congruity of knowledge.

Just as impossible as philosophy could go out in search of the material of knowledge and just as much as it has to confide in the empiric reality of this material, trusting the love of truth and keen observations of scientific experts,—just as little can empiricism find, describe and prove from its own sources the general congruity of knowledge thus contributed and accumulating. Both have to work together, to take notice of and advice from each other. Confidence must strengthen this union despite some unavoidable controversial altercations; and the good fellowship must not be allowed to turn into antagonism by the occasional boisterousness of a colleague. Thus "the contest of the faculties" for preeminence, of which Schiller spoke a century ago, may be compromised; and the good understanding will not be shaken but strengthened when inconsistencies are announced immediately.

"Contest of the faculties." Schiller.

All sciences to be co-ordinate.

It is not so much the sum total of collected experiences and evidences (regardless, perhaps, of their intrinsic value) that is to be compared and booked; but it is rather the equilibrium established, the consistency of the insight gained, which elucidates the truth from corroborative evidences brought along by each special science, under the double (inductive and deductive) trial.

Phil. not to be dictatorial;

On this line the negotiations are to be carried on to the exclusion of all dictatorial dogmatic assertiveness. Otherwise philosophy could, in one case, yield but lifeless and unprofitable abstractions of doubtful quality, and would merely be tolerated for amusement, perhaps, or as a curiosity-shop. In the other case philosophy would render herself obnoxious once more. If history, for instance, should be construed from the thought-affiliations of Spinoza-Hegel, then its conception would run out as theirs did, namely, with the infallibility and omnipotence (that is, rather, with the preposterousness and impudence) of the "idea." It behooves philosophy to be modest. Her modesty will bear the test in that she is not oversensitive to criticism; she virtually will court it and even criticise herself, so as to maintain her competency, lest she be pushed aside again as before.

not to be sensitive to criticism,

Both empiric sciences, the natural and the historical, needing and complementing each other, make philosophy indispensable, and rehabilitate her prestige just at present, when the empirics split up more and more into special branches and often overload the system. Philosophy for this very reason has no inclination to monopolise science; it stands against the formation of esoteric rings; it can not abuse the influence of its necessary control and connecting power. It rejoices over every advance, discovery, and successful experiment of the empirics, because it thereby becomes more enriched in itself and ever better equipped to serve as the beacon-light at the harbor where the nations communicate and exchange their goods; to serve also as a candle-holder, occasionally, for some who dig in dark shafts to bring out the material that affords warmth and light. is the less dispensable the more sciences split up into specialties.

Philosophy is encouraged again by the feeling of satisfaction from being appreciated. Her offices are certainly worthy of esteem at the present time, when the differentiation of the social organism necessitates not only "division of labor" but also "organised labor;" and when a rank subjectivism necessitates the laying of deeper foundations for the reverence due to mental and moral pre-eminence and authority. Else that peril of disintegration would befall society of which Goethe already gave warning to theorists: Philosophy worthy of esteem when "division of labor" calls for "organised labor."

> Die Theile habt Ihr in der Hand;
> Nur fehlt Euch leider das geistige Band.

Physics, Psychology and Epistemology along with these sciences, which are in need of metaphysical axioms, have a natural inclination to encroach on forbidden ground; and they do this under pretense of manufacturing each its own principles by its own logics. They are multiplying and treat each other as tho each had the ninety-nine-years lease of the whole field of knowledge for itself; as tho each stood for the whole organism of systematic knowledge.

Pride and jealousy on that score are pardonable as the natural outgrowths of the enthusiasm each must have for his discipline and of the pedantry which is almost unavoidable in the schoolmasters' life. But the stiff, apodictic contradictions protruding into public life in our age of hurry and brittle paper, of inexperienced reporters and satiated or perplexed readers, make the literary clearing-house a necessity, where the circulation is watched and value is made legal tender. Whenever shallowness or error is most noisy and busy in making proselytes, then it is time that largeness and profundity of learning, that soundness of private judgment and adroitness of system are more than ever to be insisted upon in all public institutions and especially in those of mental and moral training.

It is proper to predicate of the animal organism that it contains systems of nerves and muscles, of circulation, digestion, etc. In order to understand either one of them, even the medical specialist is obliged to bear in mind that the various systems work together for the organism, else they severally collapse. Their functions can be observed in the vital state alone, that is, in their connection among themselves by means of the whole. So must the WISSENSCHAFTS-LEHRE be more than a schematic presentation of the contents of universal knowledge, for schemata are not systems, much less organisms of interactive systems. Precisely in the same manner as our bodily and psychical organisms are constituted and interwoven, does philosophy represent the living organism of harmonised knowledge with its many systematised sciences. It keeps up the connection and preserves the health and vitality of the two complicated sciences of personal life as manifested in nature and history. The relation of philosophy to the empiric sciences dealing with men, is analogous to that between the various systems in the human body among each other.

In philosophy the observatory is established from which the movements of both, nature and history, can be properly and distinctly espied. Out of our laboratories with their apparatus, efficients, and agencies, we have ascended to this observatory. It is not so crowded as that we might not entertain the hope of being understood, when we enlarged upon the necessity of the Philosophy of History as being the philosophy of human nature in action. Sciences as laboratories, philosophy as the observatory. Phil. of Hist. is the philos of "human nature in action." See. 16.

The sequel may demonstrate the propriety of its pretensions, where it requires less selfdefence and selfpraise in the measure of its value and truth becoming more obvious. Our apology for the selfrecommendation—which was deemed necessary while stating the position and project of our work—is based upon the facts that idealistic philosophy did not only distort history, but was also calumniated and ostracised. Phil. fell with the false phil. of hist.

§ 15. Together with the idealistic construction of history in the forepart of our century, philosophy itself was overthrown, blown down by the storms of '48. The excesses of speculation had caused a general derision against the studies of things of the mind. The disregard of experimental sciences was paid back with more than silent contempt. The reaction against the "Identity-Philosophy" was one of those recurrent oscillations in history whose nature we will have a chance to discuss later on. Men let go of the a prioris. Scientific problems were to be worked out without prejudgments. This was well enough. But that the scientists of natural, and, considered of course as the vastly more practical, knowledge pretended the necessity of Cause of unpopularity of spiritual things.

Guizot's "government of religion." Intellectualism identified with religion. Sec. 11, 56, 66.

emancipating their investigation from the "oppression" of spirituality (because this was suspected as being identical with religion, as being ecclesiastical authority in disguise," the government of religion," upon which Guizot enlarged)—that was the result of jumping from false premises to wrong conclusions. The fact is, that soul-life was mistaken for religion, since religion had been misrepresented by rationalism as a matter of mere intellect. Hence all mental superiority was identified with the government of state-churchism, wherein religion had been identified with reason

Intellectual superiority together with all which came from above was deemed oppressive. Sec 11, 56, 58, 66, 72, 95, 98.

and a cultivation of sentimentality. Without sufficient cause all "intellectualism" had become unpopular ; whatever came from "above" was regarded as an impugnment on the freedom of thought. And every thought had to be flattened out, and all

Leveling and flattening of thoughts.

science put to such a level, that even ignorance and mental inertia might grasp it. There was a time when German burghers organised "Bildungs-Vereine" in which "Bildung" was made a pretext for vulgarity.

And we also have experimented to democratise learnedness. We have arrived at practical times with a largely increased number of special studies, in the enumeration of which college catalogues vie to excel each other; with which the students are overburdened and inflated. Analytical studies are the fashion—unaware as yet of the truth, that analytical methods, indispensable in the realm of natural sciences, are vitiating all those studies which from the nature of the spiritual sphere require synthetical treatment, for instance languages.'

Criticism of the pretentiousness of colleges under pressure of the analytical method of studying.

Studies requiring a lifetime are put up, cut and dried, in abridged manuals, which are rushed through by reading and reciting so many pages on the part of the students. It is not the custom with us, as in Europe, that the student goes to hear Prof.—. In our country the professor goes to hear the class. It takes a lifetime to study experimental psychology or similar specialities, so as to master them, and to become able to experiment, and to keep abreast with the times. Yet schools promise to imbue students with them in a "nutshell" in a term or two. If one glances at the books, which most of the students return to the second-hand book-stores after the close of the term. he will see the essential, and of course, more difficult chapters marked: "omit." In the latter parts of these books he scarcely discovers a finger-mark; the book was not "read;" the term was too short.

Surely, the world has arrived at the pinnacle of this glorious century in a fin-de-siecle spirit, which calls for the restoration of philosophy, that is, for the rehabilitation of the mind. Less "belle-letters," more profound ability to form true, judgment and a noble character are now in demand. It is said that even the better medical

Return to the "Humanistics."

schools again recognise Metaphysics. Perhaps Anthropology, too, will soon be rehabilitated in its former place from which physiological psychology pushed it aside, so that man becomes better acquainted with himself, i. e. comes to himself again, and that a true sociology may result therefrom. A pressure from below threatens more danger to freedom, to love of fellow-men, to the administration of justice, in short to civilisation, than any oppression from above ever did. The collision, if not collapse, must be prevented if possible by removing the cause, viz.: inhumaneness.

Settling accounts with modern "Epistemology." cf. Sec. 14.

Note:—We touched on Epistemology, and on Sociology and much of the present academic practice not with the intention to offend. The discussion on the genesis and formation of thought, and about the organism of knowledge perhaps, might have been carried through to the conclusion when in the preceding chapter the relation of our science to Metaphysics was ventilated. But the few sections intervening had to intercede in order to show what stand we take in regard to Epistemology. This part of the anthropological investigation, presently to be resumed, will organically lead over to the following division.

"Musing and thinking."

Musing and thinking are different phases of mental activity, tho at the root they are one. We may call that root immediate conception, intuition, inspiration, imagi-

Genesis of self-consciousness and comprehension.'

nation, divination, vision, presentiment, if not "pure reason" itself:—it is always a peculiar flashing-up from the occult recesses of man's being of which he is unconscious. The Germans call this deep source in the mind "Nachtseite des Seelenlebens."

"Nachtseite des Seelenlebens." "Sub-consciousness."

We termed it "Sub-consciousness." But just as in the case of the promiscuous use of the term "intuition"—which even Bowne often identifies with reflection upon sense-perceptions, whilst it ought to be distinguished as a phenomenon of the purely spiritual

Term intuition ought not to be applied to reflective function of the mind. Bowne. Sec. 8, 10.

side of the mind, despite its character of being analogous to what in the purely natural part of the soul we call "instinct," its radical opposite—so we must have some more definite term for this obscure recess of the mind. We therefore, and for reasons becoming apparent later on, will denominate it: "unreflected consciousness."

"Unreflected consciousness." Sec. 8, 87, 115, 221.

By its undeniable presence man's being is perceptibly proven to be in contact and touch with the really existing world of higher, of unconfined life, with the world of spirits.

Evidently it is necessary to clear up our opinion on this subject. The phenomena of that sphere must be brought forth again from the lumber room of hallucinations where they were stowed away out of sight. They need be separated, also, from the alloys of sprites, of mere imagery, and phantoms ; and they need be defended against aspersions wherein they were identified with the latter.

If we succeed in the discriminations repeatedly referred to, as we should, then the way is open for correcting the definitions of intuition and its kindred phenomena, and for their distinction from other states and modes of mental activity ; then the wellspring of intellectual functions will become observable and the genesis of our thoughts and cognitions, and their relations to inspiration and divinations, also, will be better understood and appreciated. Then epistemology, now prone to interpret thought as the simple result of the molecular motion of nervesubstance, will see its way clear to pass over the "threshold" that separates the sensational from the emotional and spiritual sphere. It is correct, that we must watch the catena in which the series of conceptions is gathered in, stored up, and arranged, from sense perceptions up to compound thought-combinations, ratiocinations, and transeunt cognitions. *Perceptibly proves the reality of the spirit and its contact with the world of spirits.* *Vicissitudes to which the formation of ratiocinative cognitions is exposed.* *Sec. 3* *Loces.*

The work of discussing correlative or analogous phenomena, of critical siftings, of comparing notes, of giving reasons for approval or disapproval ; or of showing causes of misconceptions and misapprehensions and pseudo-deductions ; or giving account of the ways in which disturbances of sound judgment are possible—all must be settled before we may logically proceed toward not only plausible but cogent and consistent conclusions, compatible with unsophisticated facts.

But it is not correct to denounce all this work as being in vain, and to drop the work before all this is accomplished under pretense of the unavailibility of the truth —just because of ignoring the source or root alluded to. The investigation of it brings us face to face with delicate points which require special and penetrating studies on dangerous ground. It is an operation in which the observations are sometimes subject to justifiable doubts, if one from that root, which ramifies even into planetary life, would cut loose under the illusion that pure reason itself would answer the purposes for which intuition must serve, or that pure reason alone could explain intuition and its kindred phenomena. *The primary source of thoughts not to be ignored in the process of proving what intuition, thought, truth, etc., is, or is not.*

We must repeat that the particulars can not be understood unless explained under consideration of all their bearings upon the whole and of the bearings of the whole upon the particulars, that is—from the aspect of unity. *General cognitions obtainable only from the aspect of unity.*

No such an all-embracing cognition, no synthetical comprehension is ever obtainable by way of pure logics, nor by methods of everlastingly sceptical criticism and dialectic sophistry ; it can never be conceived without the cooperation of some other, if not all the endowments of the well-balanced mind. All the faculties are in unceasing reciprocal interaction when one is engaged, altho the one may preponderate according to its or their momentary activity. This point was first and well taken in Herder's Metacriticism of Kant's "Kritik." *All coexisting faculties and their cooperative functions to be considered in explaining the process of thinking and its products. Herder.*

Is it not the same with the functions of the physical part of human nature? Do not the bodily organs sympathise in their functions and cooperate without our consciousness being aware of it? And do they not cooperate in acts of purest thought? That they do this, is so emphatically admitted, that many claim to be convinced of the origin of their consciousness from these very bodily interactions alone. We see that the difficulty of conceiving this general and complete reciprocity is not a whit greater than to comprehend the cognition— "sensuous perception." *Bodily functions cooperative in forming thoughts etc., so that this fact is made an argument against the reality of spiritual things.*

We may be able to overlook a whole sphere with all its radii, as we stand in the center, or imagine our point of view to be there and "take in" the whole compass by look or thought in successive order or even all at once—in the same manner as we never can see all over the surface of a globe and yet comprehend it.

It is not our purpose to argue for omniscience, altho for a view that shall come very near to it. All we desire to maintain is but the right to acknowledge imagination as taking part in the transaction of comprehending, in forming what may be called a compound apperception, analogous to the taking of an instantaneous photograph. *The concept of complete reciprocity of the mental faculties as well as that of sense perceptions is intuitive.*

Comprehension means more than a chain of conclusions gained by consecutive reflection upon causes and effects, by a relative or negative mode of thinking, or by deductive or inductive abstraction, in all of which intuition also plays its role. Perception does not advance to the grade of a comprehensive cognition, and comprehension is not realised, unless our intellectual faculties, imagination included, cooperate in harmony with the feeling of valuation and with the energy of decision, that is, under the discipline of mutual control. Full and true comprehension, of course not in the absolute sense, is obtainable; but not without the untrammeled use of that introspective capability manifest in the depths of our being, not without that quick flash of in-tell-igence which outruns thought as fast as the glance of the eye outruns our slowly following feet.

Of phantoms and the like we need not be afraid if we agree with this assertion. On the contrary, never was a grand system of rearranged ideas conceived and projected from any mind without the genius that influenced a Copernicus or Columbus, a Newton or Haydn. It is the genius which always first discovers the full original import of old but rearranged ideas under a spell of an infusion, as it were, as tho the discovery or invention had been suggested to his mind by some outside mind other than himself. The form of such a more than ingenious idea is analogous to yonder event, when the greatest legislative organiser beheld on the mount the archetype of the new creation.

The difference between musing and thinking may be illustrated by the two philosophers of Koenigsberg and Frauenburg; the one, pen in hand and bent over books—the other leaning at the window in the silent dark of midnight and pensively looking into realms above.

Malebranche has proved, and Bowne reiterates, that "vision" is actually independent of light. That architectonic power of the phantasy, so frequently spoken of with disdain, that apprehensive imagination, has the plant and design of the structure complete before the mind at one stroke, long before the "hands" slowly go to work.

Intuition nevertheless, does not spare us the labor sequent to its revelation. Genius does not release us from the task of methodical thinking. Each single instance or inference must properly be put to its place as indicated by the design of the whole. In order to do this work swift enough, before the vision of a beautiful and clear combination of thoughts withdraws from consciousness, many a writer puts writing utensils in near reach of his place of repose. Every one of us has repeatedly become aware of the fact that the most desirable insights, so plainly before his mind, vanish from him beyond reproduction, as soon as reason begins to reflect upon them. Other conceptions of similar rank are only retainable if immediately fixed. This proves that intuitive cognitions are compelled to undergo the process of reflective reasoning in order to become recognised as knowledge.

Hence science does not only not suffer from, but becomes enhanced by such competition of the intuitional with the usual rational conceptions of thoughts. Science may be obliged to open her eyes more widely at some or the other occasion, and to extend her borders; or perhaps, to revise a theory here and there that before seemed so nicely to fit everywhere, in order to embrace the whole. Does it hurt, if the truth of any, even be it theological, system or interpretation, or of any construction of opinions is challenged and put to the test by new discoveries? or if experiences from real life demand a reconsideration?

No. We have more faith in the truth, in its attainability and indestructibility, than to fear damage from any source. New discoveries or experiences will never cause more than a revision, perhaps, or a rearrangement, sometimes a restoration, of formerly rejected elements. For it will never be possible in the world as it is to demolish entirely whatsoever took its origin in personal life—not even a falsehood much less a truth; neither will it ever be possible to create or invent new conditions for the existence or the exercise of personal life. And not only was there always a ray of life and light in any rational concept brought forth, as in a crystal that may deserve a resetting: but even when the time of its significance was spent, it retained a certain value in collections. Such tokens then still serve as object lessons, instructive at least as to the place once occupied by them in the fabric of the whole;—yea, of which, as illustrating certain truths, we often need thus to be reminded.

Deduction consists in the efforts to comprehend and to formulate the general effect resulting from single or combined activities from which to show the effectual bearings of the whole upon the constituent particulars. We may as well name it speculation. For, this whole, this totality of compound apperceptions and synthetical judgments as to man's standing before the court of history, must stand before our view as a world in itself, as a synthesis or rather as an organic system of various, of all syntheses, as one compatible and consistent, tho at the same time adjustable, body of complex conceptions. This is virtually the goal toward which all thinking inadvertently aspires; it is the presentiment of that which is felt must be true, and the comprehension of which must be within our reach.

The proto-type of knowledge on which speculative thought is ever inadvertently bent.

The body of these compound syntheses may well be compared to a unanimous resolution of the "House and Senate in joint session," representing the thoughts and wills and all the combatant interests of forty-five well organised states containing about seventy millions of intelligent people. And in addition, to a resolution carried similarly by an international congress, which would bear on the common interests of humanity in general. The name for such an all-comprising synthesis of organised knowledge can be no other but—Truth. And the key to its inner combination can be nothing else but Faith.

An organism of adjustable syntheses illustrated.

Faith.

This compound cognition is not a mere imaginary world, altho our conception of it be like a negative partly prepared in a dark enclosure of our being. It contains the universe as it really is; for the soul has forwarded, focused, and concentrated in itself all the essential contents and mysteries gathered up on its way of development through all spheres and stages of nature, besides those mysteries, which are the innate inheritance of the spiritual constituent, and in which the soul by virtue of its union with the spirit participates.

Presentimental contents of the obscure recesses of the mind i. e. the compound of incipient cognition from which general concepts, i. e. the "universals," are developed under the sun-light of reason.

Hence, the mind contains, under the name of "universals", (Kant's "Categories"), not only the frame for the reality of the universe, but also the feeling of what the universe ideally even should be. This true perspective image is reflected there, and there waits to be developed, that is, to be recognised under the sunlight of the reflecting mind: to be awakened—"occasioned" said Malebranche,—by incitements from outside, by suggestions from the spiritual as well as from the natural spheres. The latent reflexes are to be lifted up into, to be appropriated and comprehended by, consciousness. This is the work of the speculative activity of the mind on its spiritual part. The "image" is thus made intelligible, and may then be shown to those, who can now understand what they themselves felt before, without knowing the process of developing, i. e., obtaining it. The world thus reflected has made its first step toward its realisation and transfiguration into the spiritual form of existence. Upon that scope of speculative comprehension of true reality Schelling, Oken and Hamilton found their object-lens for looking at things in their realistic theorems of nature at the very period when Daguerre experimented with the camera obscura—a singular coincidence, illustrating the correctness of Dr. Reid's Scottish realism.

Kant's categories. Sec. 5,10,17, 18, 27, 37, 38. The "image" of nature is man. Sec. 9, 10, 13, 115, 131.

Daguerre.

Scottish realism of Reid.

From inductive retrospects we have now gathered sufficient indications to show that man alone offers the focus for philosophical reflection. We found the human being to embody that whole, which is the requisite for understanding the single factors and events. Man is the world in miniature. The image after which nature is developed lies in man. In personal life, as we use this term, we found the theme of history, after nature in her way and on his account had celebrated her wedding with the spirit, and had begun to commemorate the festive occasion in her serene sabbaths.

Schelling, Oken, Hamilton.

Indications gathered by the retrospect.

In man, nature and history, matter and mind, are present in their mutual adaptability. Their relations are felt to be reflected upon the background of consciousness so as to be formulated into a unitary concept of concrete, altho hyper-phenomenal and transeunt, reality. All historic truth must be explicable by deduction from this compact synthetical cognition.

Image of nature as reflected in man. Sec. 9, 10, 13, 115, 131.

§ 16. We understood how history is the unfolding of man with all his gifts, potentialities, predispositions, faculties, and opportunities. We now add: History unfolds man in his fallen state; as having lost the vivid consciousness of his destination by which he ought to have allowed himself to be constantly inspired; but as "coming to" again by way of feeling his loss.

Man the microcosm and at the same time the theme of history. the focus for philosophical reflection upon nature and history.

The vista of the typical man of our expectancy, mirrored in creation, becomes blurred on that account. Its presentation and proof is made a great deal more difficult. Still the craving for a general concept remains as a sign of the real presence

Man's unfolding furnishes history its material. Sec. 9, 10, 13, 18.

6

of the image—i. e. of the integrity of the archetype—remains only so much the stronger. And in our search for the synthesis of syntheses we grapple with the various topics of historical development in order to explain them even in their vexatious tangle with the other problem just now hinted at. Human life must be followed out in all its details as it actually is ; human nature must be comprehended in every respect and under all circumstances. But most all philosophers have failed in this. In Hegel's otherwise clever exposition, for instance, all the derangements caused by the losses were left out of view—a sad defect.

In generalising these conditions and relations the following topics would result:

Man's PHYSICAL condition, now passive and dependent, offers to our consideration the history of the development of his physical endowments; those gifts, common to all and to be put in use by all; capabilities which assert themselves in the earliest beginnings of culture. With them these effects were worked out which would come under headings of gratification of appetites, propagation of the race, maintainance of existence by means of food, cover, defences. This comprises the results of activity in agricultural husbandry, in architecture, mannfacture, traffic, war. Objects of observation on this line would be cities, tools, weapons.

The investigation of the PSYCHICAL self leads to the problems of languages and knowledge; to man's scientific search, within himself and without, after means for extending dominion over physical forces; it leads to the refinement of emotional and intellectual faculties and optional energies. The results consist in geometry, astrology, arts, literature, æsthetics: of which we find the traces in temples and tombs.

With regard to the MORAL sense we observe man speculating upon the authority and objectivity of rights, laws, duties, retributions. The coercive and corrective executions of the moral law within and of the natural law without in their cooperation keep him from utter degeneracy; they urge him on to improve his condition, and to better and free himself.

The faint manifestations of the sole necessity of the Good within him secure his aptitude for the elevation of character under selfculture, and his susceptibility to the influences from above which draw him upward;—secure his dignity and his freedom. Man learns to respect rights and duties, liberties and restrictions for the sake of reason and for reasons of state. Man organises, sets up sacred land marks delineating possession. He deliberates upon legislation, judges conduct, modifies government. He also loses himself in the lusts and despairings of sensual dissipation; he feels how the natural and the spiritual constituents of his inner being react upon and resist each other. The results of these activities we observe in the founding of states, in the rise of philosophers and legislators, of despots and liberators; in civil institutions; in the formation of ranks, castes, dynasties.

Then, and not least of all, because representing the cardinal principle of culture, we would have to philosophise upon the phenomena of man's RELIGIOUS sense. The movements in this sphere are most numerous and most distinctly pronounced. There is the sacredness of tradition, transmitted in the internal remnants of primeval God-consciousness; and there are the external and ruined symbols and tokens of original universal religiousness. There is the universality of worship in which offerings of prayers and sacrifices ever predominate. There are to be compared the cosmogenies, myths, rites, theologies; the various forms of religious deformations and reformations, of hieratic doctrines and institutions. The molding influences of scepticism upon society and private life morally and mentally—its causes, effects, and its cures, too, would here have to be looked into. We would have to demonstrate a primitive and universal, then a general, then a special revelation, culminating in the intensified and saving religion; and finally the consummate blending of the moral and religious aspirations. We would have to trace depravity to its deepest, and meditate upon salvation in its highest manifestations. We would have to follow all this through traditions, symbolic figures and rites, sacred writings and holy writ; through religion intensified under pressure, expanding again into the periphery of universal humanity—all these movements under the captions of Cultus, Church, Missions.

A Philosophy of History certainly would embrace all these revelations of human life; and the outline drawn would be the proper arrangement in groups—representing indeed the cyclopedia of all the sciences. Do we need to give reasons for declining a method of such analytical treatment?

To draw parallels like musical scales upon which to copy the signs of a symphony, scales picturing the ascending and descending stages, rests, and arrests of progress, symbolising the music thus written; and to set under these musical scales as a text or theme all the interactions, perhaps, of all the coefficients, of each part of culture in its reciprocity—is not our design at present. That fine attempt of Spencer's "Sociological Tables" may some day come to completion, but can nature bottle up the spirit? And what materialist would have enough interest left for buying the highpriced books with their reiterating rubrics of structural and functional evolution, in order to possess that sort of a key to human affairs? For after all, the best arrangement of the immense amount of material would not much simplify the survey. It would be so analytical as to impair the desired result, namely, the focusing of human nature and its development in one universal and comprehensive synthesis. It would but resemble the natural history of man as given in a report of his post mortem examination, filled out upon a statistical blank.

In this work we shall not endeavor to arrange the explanatory arguments of man and history according to such schemata. We would get no more than a series of special monographs on languages, governments, arts, letters, etc., each by itself, and would get no further than where we are now. Such books we have; they are of little avail in comprehending the leading principles underlying human affairs. *since reason aims at comprehensive synthetical world-theory from a few cardinal principles.*

To understand man is all that is necessary in order to render the books of nature and history legible. Know the human type or typical man, and life past and present becomes as lucid and cursive reading, as this imprint—from a score of graphite types, made of the lead that rested in a mountain far away and prepared by a hundred hands—now conveys these thoughts to the readers mind. In a similar manner is man the type, as it were, communicating to us the fundamental principles of history, the essence of whose unfolded fulness he is. After the essence is extracted and the sense understood, that is, when man's contents are epitomised, then the matter is exhausted and the remaining bulk becomes irrelevant. The character of an African forest may be correctly presented to the mind from the description of a few characteristic trees, without inspecting all the forests extant there by actual exploration. *The natural and spiritual elements of man life mirrored in history; history the biography and mirror of man.*

In History all constituent elements point to man; for in him implicitly lies their cause and purpose and resolvent. Whosoever undertakes to write or read his biography has easy proof of the truth at hand. He has himself for an object lesson, his inner and exterior life is a sample and epitome of the whole. The **Philosophy of History as we take it, is the harmonious consultation with humanity on the subjects of self-possession.** Thus our science makes man acquainted with himself, for history is personal matter unfolded, extended, revealed. Hence personal man himself (not in the abstract of human nature) furnishes the material for the Philosophy of History as well as History furnishes the material for the mirror in which man sees himself. In his ascending grades and perpetual succession he solves the problems assigned to him in every respect, from compressed, arrested, confined life up to glorification. *Definition of the Philosophy of History as the harmonious consultation with humanity on the subjects of self-consciousness and selfpossession.　Sec. 14.*

Indeed, up to perfection. For man is not only the type and theme of that historic development which precedes the transition into the state of final realisations; but also the type of the ultimate goal and continuing state of consummate perfection which surpasses and supersedes all present realities. At present the ideal of that world of absolute reality is reflected in him by refracted rays only, at its best. This ideal we will try to show later on, when in due course of our observations we shall pass the meridian where it shines forth from human nature in full orb. *Man also the type and theme of the world of absolute reality. The ideal at present refracted by broken rays, but will shine forth in full orb.*

B.　SECOND DIVISION.
OPERATIVE MODE OF HISTORY.

SYLLABUS.

Having surveyed the coefficients of history, and to some extent inquired into the methods of their treatment by the sciences, we now address ourselves to the modes in which, and the means by which, history itself works with the material, making time and space the repository of the effects of its activity. *Means with which history works.*

In a general way we might think of those means which are at man's disposal, namely, the instincts of preservation and propagation. The one will act in the manner of contraction, seeking to protect life better and better against increasing insecurities; the other will work in the direction of expansion, inciting effects of dominion, teaching organisation, or urging on to migrations. *Such as are at the disposal of man.*

Furthermore such other means would have to be noticed by which historic movements are conditioned, as for example the influences exerted by climes and localities. But about all of these things, not much need be added to what was quoted from Ritter to Buckle. The time is past for such broad and yet cursory discussion as Eith, the engineer, and as Spencer used to carry on about environments. *Localities and climes, Etм. disposed of in Sec. I.*

The present state of knowledge requires of us to stand face to face with more complicated problems. Questions are now brought up which demand a settlement, during the deliberations of which the position of our science with reference to history proper will be determined, outlined, and illustrated at once. We are confronted with the terms, purpose, movement, development, and plan of history.

Problems which require more profound disquisition.

CH. I. THE AIM OR INTENT OF HISTORY.

§ 17. The concept of purpose implies, in the first place, a complex proposition. Some agency intends, that is, wills to operate upon some object, in order to accomplish—a certain end.

Purpose. Sec. 3, 4, 101.

How all this is to be explained, or whether it is possible and necessary to find an explanation at the outset, has been a matter of much controversy. It was just this question which was ventilated in "Occasionalism", that mechanical view fixed upon the "Occasional Cause" which was unable to account for the notions of cause and effect, and unable to connect motion and aim in their mutual adaptability.

Theory of the "Occasional Cause" foundered at demonstrating the adaptation of motive to its aim.

In the animated world the **purpose** comes in for realisation; the end is reached in such a way, that the means become purposive themselves. The human soul, being the aim of nature, is nature's purpose realised in man. Besides this end nature had no other purpose. The purpose is now man himself, having a purpose in himself. His organs are his means serving the higher end of his soul. A living whole is presented, in which each organ serves as a means and has, by virtue of membership therein, a purpose in itself for the sake of other purposes. Things have no other meaning but that they are means to realise a purpose. We stand before the purpose which lies in the objects themselves.

Human soul is the purpose of nature realised. Sec. 5, 6, 15, 18

Things have a meaning as far as they are means for other things.

When reasoning about any circumstance we evidently bring the idea of purpose along with our minds and constantly apply it. This is explicit whenever we find it necessary to ask, whether things are of any account. We claim the right to ask, for instance, for a reasonable account of the notion time, or space, or substance, etc. If any value is claimed for them, proof is to be given for their possessing specific attributes.

but have no purpose in themselves. Sec. 6.

Reason seeks a reason in things; they must reveal what their object is in order to be recognised as objects. Unless we find a meaning in, and a reason for them, we can not understand them. Their reason or meaning we find in their rational order. In order to ascribe any fitness to them, we expect of them that, besides their being put into a proper arrangement, they possess certain qualifications. Whenever their import is discerned thereby, the cognition of the purpose is established; what achievement results from their purport is the purpose of the object. The thought of purpose governs history down to the scene of action, to the earthly circumstances, environments, and concomitant factors of the event.

Meaning of things lies in their rational order.

Purpose only to be found by considering the whole.

Let this be illustrated by a machine. Certainly, anything unusual in the line of these contrivances attracts our attention. This is the truth contained in Occasionalism. We expect the expression of some clever thought in it, just as the Niagara Falls suggest grand conceptions and emotions, speaking to us, as the poets say with deep truth, in the immediate childlanguage of the mind. The first idea called forth by the strange thing is the question as to its adaptability for a certain performance. Unless that much interest is awakened we treat the machine with unconcern; we deem it nonsensical. But the arrangement of its parts strikes us; it attracts the attention of the beholder who brings a sense for the indicated fitness with him; yet not the fitness is asked for, but the "finality" of the purpose. If the intent is pointed out, thought becomes satisfied; and then every detail of the mechanism is found worthy of closer inspection, since it is seen to partake of the purpose of the whole. As soon as any detail becomes irrelevant, that is, if the purpose can be realised without it, then that part is thrown out as an encumbrance. The machine is simplified because its aim is to economise. Hence it is more to the purpose to take out the encumbrance, so that an improvement, perhaps, may be put in its place.

Illustrated by a machine: Truth in Occasionalism. Sec. 2, 3, 4, 15, 19.

We now venture to assert that there is no entity thinkable per se, which would lack all relation to a higher aim than what it has in itself. Even the random heap of sand, the most indefinite formation imaginable, is more than mere being, because not intended for itself alone. That sand is of more import than at first appears; we shall yet see how it exceeds its actual reality. For all real being exists with regard to something else, which determines its value according to its being subservient to that something else. This relation to its purpose is what renders any object valuable. The purpose is the reason for any entity.

Genesis of the concept of purpose.

The relation of any entity to others determines its value.

"Dead matter" and its agglomerations would be unmeaning. The existence of an irrational thing we cannot conceive. If anything is nothing to us, that, of course, does not say that it is nothing to the whole. The thought of nothing is therefore, as Descartes said, not demonstrable. It has been found by Max Mueller that there is something, yea a great deal, even in the Nirwana. The thought of a purposeless life is akin to suicide, and even this can not be perceived without raising the question " why?" For these reasons we see some sense in the great sand-deserts if viewed from their historical relations, from the aspect of their unity with the whole.

A "nothing" is inconceivable. Descartes.

Nirwana is the fancied state wherein all relations are neutralised.

We have the genesis of the concept of purpose in that everything real exists in order to conform to an equivalent value. The attribute of quality assigned to it postulates its purpose, whilst purpose in turn stipulates its value. Thus we derive the cognition of a world full of purposes. The world as a whole with all its component parts receives its significance from this all-controlling concept of a realisation of final purposes.

The tendency of life is the realisation of purposes.

Following out this line of thought, we arrive at the great antithesis apparent in the world around us, viz: the contrast between thought and matter. Analysing the mode of existence in the world of life as it is given, that is, considering it from the aspect of interacting causes and effects, we find the complex workings of life determined by thought, underlying it all. We find that world of life to be nothing else but thought in the process of substantiating itself, aspiring to embody and thus to express itself in the extending objectivity of the world. This is the Idea which hovered before Spinoza, Fichte, and Hegel In order to do this, thought needs energy, substances, means. Thought makes them subservient to itself by way of appropriating them in order to subject them as means for this end, hence the objective self-projection of thought.

Antithesis of thought and matter.

Matter is thought in the process of substantiating itself

is the means which serve the end of the selfobjectifying power of thought.

A glance at plant-life may illustrate this. The construction of the vegetable world is evidently based upon design, determined by a formative principle. Obviously the design is implanted, inwrought with the peculiarities each plant possesses, independent of external conditions. The influences from without upon its typical principle may cause abnormal formations, even artificial improvement; but they can not alter the ground plan. The influence ceasing, the plant will return to its generic type. Much less can such influences supplant the ground plan by types at variance with the primitive and inwrought character. For this is not to be reduced to chemical processes, or to a number of moving atoms, or to a hap-hazard combination of molecules.

Design in plant-life can not be altered or supplanted by any other type.

The naturalist will maintain that the coherence of homogeneous particles, forming ever more differentiated species of organic structures, depends on those higher grades of arrangement in the vegetable structure which are regulated by the characteristics appearing in the more perfect species. Very well; this particular norm-prescribing principle, hereditary in the ascending scale of vegetable life is the ground plan we speak of, the devised scheme, the engrafted project, the vital force which makes plant-life what it is in contrast to crystal life. In accord with, and through this principle the purpose reveals itself. We desist as yet from showing that purpose, for which matter is thus prepared and guided up to the formation of higher organic life, for which it makes, to which it aspires.

Vegetable life is not reducible to chemical processes nor to the electro-magnetism of Tyndall.

Development reveals the purpose.   Sec. 21.

Bossuet found the same inherent design in relation to purpose and described it thus: All that shows order, proportions well chosen and means fit to produce certain effects, shows also an express end, consequently a formed design, a regulated intelligence and a perfect art. What Janet syllogises as to the catena between final cause and ultimate effect also corresponds very well with our line of thought—giving even the reason for the adage that history throws its shadows ahead: "When a complex combination of heterogeneous phenomena is found to agree with the possibility of a future, and which was not contained beforehand in any of these phenomena in particular, then this agreement, being comprehensible to the human mind only by supposing a kind of preexistence of the future act itself in an ideal form, transforms the fact at the instant of its realisation from a result into an end—then we have a final cause."

Inherent design. Bossuet, Janet.

Finality underlies the unit of the organism.

An inner purport is necessarily to be ascribed and attributed to every object of organic life, an intention for development by means of a more and more articulated organism. This purport, characterising organic life, does not acquire the organs from outside as something alien to the organism, not in a mechanical manner. But as many as are needed are produced by the organic life itself under the norm-giving and constructive principle, for the sake of and in conformity with the whole organism in which all the developed organs or adapted structures have their significance and unity. The many are for the sake of the one whole organism, and that whole conveys

Agreement with natural science as to the norm-giving principle.

its purport which also, on the other hand, is not acquired since or through the development from without. The organism, as a whole is, moreover, held together by its purpose, so that it may become a means for a greater purpose in wider relations beyond its own sphere. The purport or tendency to carry out finality is what gives unity to the whole combination in subservience to the general purpose. This purpose is the thought which interlinks the chain of changes through causes and effects.

§ 18. Purpose is thought in the act of objectivising itself; thought projected is matter, is the means for the selfrealisation of the purpose. Suppose now, we denominate this unit of the purpose "**the soul**"; Ebrard called it the "Law of Becoming;" and Hegel too, for that matter. It surely is the thought inherent in things, the meaning or sense which we found in them. This granted, then the variety of means wrought out by the living organism which conditions their entity and unity—outside of which those means can have neither purpose nor being—would constitute "**the body**".

Purport, then, is purpose in its process of becoming realised; it is thought, substantiating itself—by projecting the means in behalf of the unitary purpose—in the organism, that is, developing the organism as a means for realising itself, for its own sake. Thus purpose becomes the soul as a unit, while the means in their connection and oneness of purpose become its body, which consists in the variety of means and exists merely for the sake of the purpose, i. e. for the sake of its soul.

The means, the single organs in their connection, receive their adaptness and significance, i. e. their purport, from their relation to the common purpose managing the whole-from their relation to the soul. The body possesses its ideal and its unity in the apprehension of, and adaptation for, the purpose. The organism is substantiated purpose in which the antithesis of body and soul finds its synthesis, its identical individuality. Mechanical interaction, the chemical process of the alteration of matter is reduced to mere instrumental and secondary purport, relating alone to the body in which nature's purpose ends. The physical processes have no further import for, or relation to, a higher purpose—no immediate purport with regard to the purpose of the soul. After functional life ceases, the chemical inorganic life continues its mere formal purpose of disintegrating the material elements, because they are intended solely for the cycling life of the lower sphere.

The unit of purposes, on the other hand, the soul continues to convey the thought of purpose to higher forms of life or modes of existence serving the spiritual purpose, where the purpose and value of matter exhausts itself or ceases. Hence the soul is separable from matter. The multiplicity of elementary or secondary purposes has been exalted to the sphere of qualitative unity, from which, by the substantiation of thought, they had become differentiated, and for the sake of which they had been embraced and used as means by the thought of design.

In order to render the gradual revelation of this thought of design in the substantiated purpose more explicit, we state the chain of our syllogising thus:

The physico-psychical organism was intended to lead up to rational existence that very matter, which before—in its irrelative and detached mode of existence, multiplying by the differentiation of means—seemed rather indifferent to the purpose. And that very same material substance, which—prior to its elevation into the sphere of, and consequent participation in, rational life—appeared to be of no purpose, proved itself fit for the purpose in the form of select material, and served its part in the graduation of the purpose.

For it is the issue of the natural order of things, it is the end for which the natural world exists, to serve the spirit in its unity as a means for its objectivation and expression—as its polarity. For this end spiritual essence substantiated itself as the thought of purpose in the concrete, and to this end, in order to be materialised, the individual purpose entered the transitory unifying stage in the organism of personal life. It is here where the intensified purpose-the soul-where the ends and issues of the natural and instrumental purports in their concentration are realised; where the very soul and quintessence of nature appears—individualised in the highest differentiated organism; where on the scope of personal life the soul is embraced by the spirit, and its unique purpose becomes evident.

Here the process of mutual appropriation and permeating penetration tran-spires. Here the qualification or fitness for the still higher aims of the purpose is measured by the moral standard.

The soul's purpose to be the medium of unification between matter and the spiritual essence in personal life;

Through the ethical process—this is the true element in Rothe's system—the natural world is designed to be appropriated, we may say sublimated, and elevated by the spirit which is engrafted into it. Nature, in the form of the rationalised, personified soul, obtains in mind its permanent value, finds its rest and ultimate purpose. The mind—the combination of individualised natural soul-life with the personifying and unifying spiritual essence—being intended for the most sublime mode of real existence, finds its purpose in the consummation of its personal union with the spiritual world of equipoise or perfect equanimity in yonder world of real-ised purposes, absolute reality and perfection.

where fitness is measured by the moral standard; and nature obtains its permanent value. True element in Rothe's system.

We spoke of the natural world as being predisposed or designed to convey matter i. e. substantiated and willing thought of purpose, up to the sphere of moral quality in human nature.

In equal manner is history designed to conciliate sovereign thought with its object, i. e. with confined or arrested life, with unrevealed purpose—its raw material, as it were, to be prepared and to be led up to better conditions, to an existence worthy to live. It is the intent or object of history to win over the raw material of nature-bound, or arrested, or unredeemed human life to the established purpose. History works to win life from all ethnological circles, and persists in urging them on to higher attainments. Just as we saw the copiousness of living creatures in progressive degrees of development, so we may expect a variety of historic material in stages of development and degrees of value, being worked out through rounds of ages and made subservient to higher purposes. In the moral cosmos we clearly dis-cern that progress in which the thought of humanity, its destiny and its life, is re-vealed more and more, and is sheltered from endangering situations, so that human-ism may unfold and philanthropy fully realise itself, so that mind may gain the control over the mere physical force-substance.

Immanency of the purpose in history; i. e. in the moral cosmos analogous to that in the natural cosmos.

Mind finds its purpose in introducing the world of transiency to the world of true reality.

Purpose of history is the revelation and preservation of the thought of personality, of humanity and philanthropy.

This, speaking in a general way, is the purpose of history. It mirrors that which,in a very abstract but,we trust, in a correct way, we tried to formulate in the preceding section.

Bacon blamed the sterility of the sciences up to his time, upon the false deductive method of seeking explanations of matters known but not understood from purposes —instead of seeking their explanation by induction from efficient causes. He gave a loud warning against the abuse under which a true view of nature is mutilated, on account of which nature is treated with contempt, and through which it is degraded to serve hollow, not holy opinions.

Bacon's censure of " methods," viz: deduction from pur-poses instead of induc-tion from efficient causes;

This is still to be deplored in cases where the purpose is conceived as existing apart from the objects, where it is only brought to bear upon things in a mechanical way from outside, instead of demonstrating the reason of things, whereby alone they can become objects and obtain their value.

is still in order.

Not only the natural sciences were thrown into confusion by the false methods. More than they, was history made to suffer from distortion, misconstruction, and ar-bitrary application of its manifestations and teachings. All sorts of purposes were interpolated, in order to derive such principles from it, which were to serve corrups purposes. History was made to serve as witness to falsehoods imputed to it, which were entirely foreign to its real course.

Wrong purposes imputed to history.

The whole aspect changes, however, as soon as the immanency of the purpose is understood and this truth is established. Then purport gradually reveals itself as " the final purpose ", purpose per se,—Selbst-Zweck.

Purpose per se: Selbst-Zweck, in history.

Droysen in his "Historics" corroborates our exposition, saying: "The secret of all motion is the purpose." This discovery came just in time to confirm what we were trying to demonstrate. In these few words the dawn is signalised of the revolu-tionising import of those pregnant paragraphs 17 and 18.

Droysen's corroboration of this pregnant Sec. 18.

The course of history, incessantly moving toward the mysterious future, would be as meaningless as the nonsensical machine, if it did not reveal the thought of its purpose in rising degrees; if we could conceive no true and valuable object in it; if

Movement in history must have a goal. § 3.

there were no higher ends in view for humanity, no goal where higher purposes will be realised. History would be utterly nugatory if we could not draw on a sum of clear and beneficial profits; if its value could materialise nothing in the interest of true philanthropy.

Is there any other purpose than that immanent in history ? Sec. 101, 218.

Taken for granted that actors and actions have a value or a purpose, then there is a reason in history. The single question remaining open is, whether the purpose immanent in history is the only one. The answer will appear when the plan of history comes to be discussed.

CH. II. THE LAW OF HISTORICAL DEVELOPMENT.

§19. In order to reach a certain end, means must be employed. And if they are expected to do proper work, more than mere probability must be presupposed of

The order in which means are employed to reach the ends.

them. They must not only be suitable for a definite purpose, but also stand ready for service at the place and time needed. We have no use for fortuitiveness, disorder, probability, nor for occasional accomodation and gradual adaptability. Each agent is demanded to be at the post of his service so as to be relied upon in the great combination of life's emergencies. If the order of means were insecure or deranged, the rationality of the purpose would be thrown back into doubt. The means, then, must

Lawfulness not from mere natural necessity; but arising in thought, to adjust and perpetuate "the "purpose" to "finality."

appear in spatial and temporal order, where their fitness will be affirmed by their ensuing effects. They will, moreover, enter into operation under conditions which make their occurrence a prognosticable certainty. The regularity and unerring certitude of their effects—conditioned, of course, by the noninterference of restraining counteractions, and by persistent competency—awakens a feeling not only of security and of the fitness of things, but also of **appropriateness under the sway of judicious laws.**

The best proof for the constant energy and effectiveness of these laws lies in the unquestioned dignity ascribed to them, whenever natural necessity is even made the pattern, instead of the analogy or corollary, of those moral laws, which govern human affairs in the sphere of personal life above the natural. Those scientists who unwittingly furnish this proof elevate the lawfulness under discussion so high as to declare the moral law superfluous and as being supplanted by "natural necessity."

In fact we all are used to attribute so much rationality to the chain of actions, that our reason attaches the rule of the law, i. e. the thought of adjustment, as specific laws, **to the occurrences themselves.** We cannot help doing this, because

Reason applies the idea of regulative rules to warrant the competency of reason itself.

reason not only demands for its satisfaction the thought of the final purpose, but it also applies the idea of a regulative rule in order to understand the fitness of things, and to be sure of the soundness of reason itself. In no other way can the consistency and competency of reason be warranted.

Notwithstanding the truth of this axiom, some may rejoin, that nowhere in nature had they found laws, which certain phenomena were bound to obey. It may be enlarged upon that it only seems to us as if nature was penetrated by lawfulness, because our sensibility is affected by such conjunctions of concurrences, which happen in the same ways and under equal conditions.

In order to secure the explanation of lawfulness in the universe against all misleading premises or irrelevant inferences, it may be added that nothing demands our attention save these concurrences, and that every consideration not pertaining to their respective chains of phenomena must be ruled out of order—whilst every assured recurrence of certain changes, following the same given impulses, must be taken into account.

Despite these exceptions taken in the pleading for natural necessity, we feel inclined to make use of our liberty to try a hypothesis and to bring forth our evidences

"Fitness of things" is the law inherent to occurrences : i. e. their adaptness to their effectuality; it is their "motif."

in its support. We posit the supposition, that the "fitness of things" is inherent in the occurrences and is not a mere fitness of things in a transcendental order or in forensic motives. We need this supposition in order to reason correctly, that is, consistently with the reason of things and in accord with the laws of logic.

Truths of Mechanical Occasionalism and of dynamic mechanism apt to be harmonised. Sec. 4, 15, 17.

We suppose, then, that the adaptability to the ruling principle, the law, lies in the very motive energy itself. (If this can be substantiated, then the error of "Mechanical Occasionalism" is corrected, and the truth which, as it seems, "dynamic" mechanism wants to establish, is admitted and utilised.)

Wherever a force stirs, moves, works—there it follows an inner method, and owes its direction to its own law. Force can not be described nor systematised in any other way. Force only becomes apparent in the order of phenomenal series, hence we are accustomed to call law what is nothing else but our conception abstracted from what we observe, and imagine to know, about the nexus of recurring appearances. Law, in fact, is the power of thought as exercised upon matters and facts, in order to express, in this manner, its right of controlling them ; thus regulating their mutual relations and subsequently their qualitative attributes ; also manifesting that right of thought in making matters the means of announcing itself, and making them to adhere to the thoughtful arrangement for their own sakes.

Law is the power of thought over matter and facts; the declaration of the right of reason to control them.

In what, then, does the authority of this individualised, or, if you please, hypostatised law consist? We answer, in the fitness of things ; in the appointed direction of force, and in the selection of what substance is to move toward a certain result ; in the regular arrangement of means to a certain end. This arrangement, selection, adjustment, and direction of means to explicit purposes, is exactly the same formative reality in natural life, as that which in the sphere of personal—physico-psychico-spiritual—life is called mind. (The appellation rationality or reason would be inadequate and insufficient.) It is the reason of things—i. e. that part of the purpose inwrought into them—which ordains and directs forces, and contrives at means, and arranges and disposes of masses ; which conducts the movements, effectuates events, and acts, so as to realise its end. Law is the manifestation of the soul's right to live in union with the spirit, that is, to realise itself as the purpose. This is our conception of the reality of the natural law.

It is the manifestation of the soul's right to live in union with the spirit.

Wherever we find the fitness of arrangement under an apparent guidance as referred to, there we recognise reason in the conformity of facts to law, or, if to some another word would sound better—we find homogeneity. If we ourselves make such arrangements, we want them to be consistent with the fitness of things in general ; we require of them to be reasonable theoretically and practically ; we expect of them as proof thereof, that they answer a certain chief purpose. The motives, as we call the differentials between the law and its direction toward the purpose, these motives are adjustable, since the natural law is in unison, and at bottom one, with the moral law. The authority and power of all law lie in its being a continuously operating unit which, as the manifestation of thought, knows how to adjust circumstances and to direct relations very strictly—on the whole. There is no contradiction in this all-embracing lawfulness ; here is the sphere where right is might.

Natural law in unison with moral law. §7,9.

Right is might wherever matters and facts conform with unity of purpose.

It is very significant that we had to enlarge upon this explanation. Whoever is initiated into the intricacies of sophistry about natural and divine rights, needs not to be informed that we occupy contested ground. Before we can procure our title of legitimate occupancy —to the examination of which the fifth chapter shall be dedicated—we must first determine the province of law.

The domain of lawfulness.

Renouvier (Les Principes de la Nature), in his suggestive, altho unsatisfactory manner, entertains a similar view of force being identical with law. Taking the offensive against dynamo-mechanical evolutionism, he brings out arguments which corroborate our synthetical conclusion. He looks upon common matter as the vehicle of a radiant energy of force. In the formation of living things the physical and chemical laws seem to work as "under plastic guidance". When his "monads" of a superior "order" appear, then the phenomena ensuing need new laws to exhibit them. "Living matter must be "the space-corollary" of a form of psychic existence superior to that of which dead matter is the adequate embodiment. The connection of our soul with the body in the "synthesis known as a person" involves new modes of conduct in the bodily materials themselves, which out of that connection would not be found moving as they now do, namely "in the service of mentally determined ends." Our imaginations, our passions never occur without the cooperation of all our faculties and acts from degree to degree, from the highest organs to the lowest atoms, being modified according to the law. Each of these acts, while existing inwardly for itself, is a "force" in relation to other correlative forces. The effects of these forces constitute a phenomenon of harmony beyond which we can not penetrate, and which is one with existence itself; for there is no existence except by relations and communications."

French—monistic— philosophy goes far to corroborate our line of argumentation. RENOUVIER.   Sec. 233

Each manifestation of any human faculty represents a force in relation to other forces.

Existence inconceivable without such relativity. Sec. 17, 2L

That that which has no purpose is unreasonable, Renouvier does not deny. The pity is, that he from this idea could not find his way open to accept our "thought" in place of his "monads"; it would be so easy, natural, and rational. It is barely this

Prejudice against the sovereignty of thought; Monads put in its place.

prejudice against the sovereignty of the thought, that hinders him and others from seeing the way clear to accede to our world of absolute unity, continuity and freedom. He transcends the materialistic monism of the evolution theory in admitting that the congruous concept of law and purpose indicates that there is something in the world

Something in the world really wrong.

really "wrong." And he comes near the assertion, of an original and entirely animated world, from which this partially dead world has fallen and is to be restored by redemption.—"**This is congruent,** (William James said in the Philosophical Monthly,

New biological hypothesis "an originally entirely animated world." W. James.

May '93) **moreover, with a biological hypothesis, of which we seem likely to hear more: the notion that dead matter has evolved from the living, rather than living matter from the dead.**"

From this excursive illustration of our thesis it is to be seen how much caution is

Caution needed in fixing laws for the natural world.

advisable in finding and fixing the laws of the natural world. Frequently natural phenomena are determined by coincidences of various causes, which may mutually support or neutralise their effects. In a case of such intricate happenings it is by no means easy to find the special law for each. One not familiar with the difficulties does not hesitate to jump to a conclusion.

On the strength of some conjecture a seeming law is readily postulated. The expert will be careful in rendering judgment. He will take into account many agencies, especially in fixing the law of history.

§ 20. In establishing rules for judging historic events care and modesty should

Modesty to be exercised in establishing rules for judging historic events.

certainly be exercised; for they are the laws whereby descendants judge those ancestors at the bar of history, who in their day and generation did much earnest labor and suffered no less privation for the benefit of posterity. With caution, then, we proceed to find the laws.

History results from the reciprocal interaction of the correlative factors: liberty

Activity of history partly under natural necessity but partly in freedom.

and necessity. It is man unfolded, thought realised, the purpose differentiated into a countless variety of purposes; and it tends, under the practical forms of every-day life, toward the complete union of the two worlds in the human mind. The natural part of man, to which, as we have seen, the whole of nature contributes and belongs, is subject to natural lawfulness. But exempt from the dependency of this realm where necessity holds sway, is that side of personal life, which remains intimately connected with the "world of formal unity", and which is not necessarily and never

The limit of evolution. Natural determinations well definable.

directly influenced by natural life. Hence, altho laws can be abstracted from historical data which actually rule the temporal life of man individually and collectively, yet nations as well as persons are subject to them only to a certain extent, under conditions and circumstances well definable.

Human destiny affected by climes, etc.

To this category belong the laws by which climate affects human destiny. Owing to them the Southern Aryans, inhabiting the low-lands of the Ganges, are characterised by that gloomy, brooding mood of the mind, which dulls all energy and

Examples:

kills personality. It is a melancholy sight to see a nation of several hundred millions of people held in check by a few thousand foreign conquerors; whilst other climatic influences, have assisted the Germanic nations, their kinsfolks, to become an industrious, hardy, liberty-loving people—the standard-bearers of civilisation.

Hindoos in contrast to Germans.

Let us here, once for all, state that wherever we speak of the Germans in these pages, we mean what is explained in §45. In addition we trace German blood even in the Hidalgos and in the savants of the Paris of today. All three Romanised (the Latin) nations contain as much German, as Roman or Celtic elements. The tribes with   scarcely any mixture are those between the Alps, Rhine and Elbe, and the Scandinavians, from whom the Normans set forth about a thousand years ago. Hence the Anglo-Saxon Americans are always included with first honors.

Geographical situation has much to do with nutriment, tho the temperament of a nation is never entirely depending thereupon, and laziness is not to be reduced to the absence of cold. Modes of character may, more than we think, depend upon

Javanese. Moleschott.

modes of life and victuals, so that Moleschott, on that score, was not so much out of the way, when he said, that the Javanese and the negroes of Suriname will remain in subjection to the Dutch, as long as they feed upon rice and banana. Yet all this can not discourage our hope that something can be made out of these nature-bound people notwithstanding their poor food.

To environments belong the effects caused by the law of motion. This Historical course under law of motion. in a special manner modifies human development. We shall have to say a great deal about polar tension, a strain by which the great family-opposites act and react upon each other. Ethnic polarity works in such depths as to be scarcely noticeable, yet not less distinctly, persistently, and beneficial as the system of gulf-streams or of the electro-magnetic fluxes. There are the mysteries of the centripetal and centrifugal power, drawing and binding great masses, affecting thereby individual life without the individuals becoming conscious of it. Occult law of ethnical polarities.

These occult influences cause those differentiations of the masses by which all life continues to aspire to higher formations. The laws underlying these processes work effects in history similar to those of natural fissuration, segmentation, cell-division, etc., upon which the propagation and growth of plants and animals depend. These laws operate in migration and colonisation, in the excretion of defunct matter, in the precipitation of unfit material. They may be observed wherever nations suddenly rise, or gradually become stagnant in their public life ; where people wilt and wither after periods of prime and bloom without yielding fruits of any account ; where people finally disappear with the forests they cut down or burned, after their welfare had run down in proportion as their springs disappeared. Physical analogies in history, sequent to the rule of natural laws, and according to the degree in which people remain in, or relapse into bondage of natural necessity. Centripetal and centrifugal gravity;

The natural laws prevail in proportion to mental and moral neglect and they recede according to the advance of true civilisation. They largely direct the alter, nate stratification of "lower" classes and "upper crusts", of castes and outcasts ; and they frequently help to shape political oppositions, breaking through the strata from below in answer to the percolations of licentiousness or to the aggravating pressure from above. They are active where polarity sharpens the social contrasts into class-hatred, and where nations are split into parties ready to extirpate each other. Upon all such movements these laws throw their imponderable weight. Beside the law of first germinal articulation pointed to the fact of stratification. The formation of more or less hereditary and castelike classes acts analogous to Volta's pile, if our figurative speech is not pressed too far. By that stratified condition of certain people a tension is established, which is necessary to incite retarded life to action ; or to arouse the thwarted dignity of selfhood. Manliness, abandoned before, so as to allow nature to rule and to degrade human beings into mere things, will then no longer allow men to be spoken of as "labor on the market." Thus caste acts upon caste,either stimulating and exciting, or conservatively and as a sedative. Each claims the strength and service of the other, both balancing each other in the limits of their functions. Thus the social ranks may be compared to electro-magnetic batteries in that they contain at the same time the energy of apathies and sympathies ; discharging currents which now paralyse, now enthuse and electrify the masses; now with clannish jealousies and then again with a kind of involuntary public-mindedness. Here we meet laws which become demonstrable even in the cystic incrustations and agglomerative affinities of our own surroundings. It seems to be a historic law, that only such races and families improve by "crossing", which stand related by neither a too close nor a too remote kindredship. In the proper degree the infusion of new blood affords not only a transient incentive but creates even nobler species. If the distance of relationship is abnormal, then malformations ensue from such unions, and the weaker element becomes defunct. germinal articulation; stratification; National differentiation under pulsations of polarity similar to electro-magnetic fluxes. Sec. 2L Cross-breeding: "Natural selection." Reaction of classes upon classes;

It seems to be a law that the periodical assaults of rude nations, possessing youthful vigor, generally stimulate people or dynasties, which labor under superannuated culture, to new exertions of defense at least : and that by the amalgamation of the conquered with the conquerors dynasties and nations are rejuvenated, which were almost exhausted by over-refinement and effeminacy. of nations upon nations.

It seems to be indispensable that nomade tribes break in at critical turningpoints. of history, in order to supplant imbecile dynasties by elevating their leaders from the saddle to their shields and to the thrones they have declared vacant. Some nations, it seems, needed repeated invasions to keep them awake and alive, and that on their account regions became exhausted, or others were deluged by sands or waters, or rendered uninhabitable by the drying up of extensive lakes, whereby peoples were coerced to wander and to push themselves into the territories of those who needed to be aroused. Indications of providential interference, by which nature is brought to bear upon history.

Rhythm in epochal
recurrences.

Most of the European aggregations and many of Asia were thus compelled to cease their internal feuds and to organise states and political state-systems. This for instance, was the apparent reason for the Germans being harassed by the visitations of Attila's, Dgengis-khan's and Soliman's Hungary-Polish and Tatary-Turkish hordes, in the years A. D. 444, 888, 1214, and 1688.

Polarity balancing
fashions.

And most probably—to take another illustration of the balancing power of polarity—the fluctuations of public tastes or ruling fashions also must be reduced to nervous relaxation and reaction, or an analogous physical law. There arises a pleasure in contemplating a foreign ceremonial, or an admiration of ancient art. The fancy becomes more than satiated by a craze for Rococo style or for Chinese decoration until the taste for each of them in turn suddenly slackens. We have a symptom of fatigue; reaction sets in; Queen-Anne style or some other fad agitates the factories and the bazars. The polarity and the tension move, repulse, and attract, so that the display of forces, thus disengaged and generated and transferred, makes commotion perpetual and not altogether disadvantageous.

We are children of our
times.

Trifling as the caprices of fashion and custom are—yet even such of us have to obey the laws of their removal or revival, as think ourselves above its tyranny. There is truth in the phrase, that we are children of our time. While meditating upon ruling laws of desire and satiety and discontent in their reversed order of sequels, we are unable ourselves to escape the power of a catch-word, or the enchantment and effect of a ruling idea—or the whims of our tailor.

Spontaneity of ideas.

There is a sway of natural lawfulness propelling the contagious and spreading power of ideas which often has assumed the form of an epidemic; exciting the masses and rushing them along into the vortex of wild enthusiasm. It generates that infectious fear, which instinctively stuns everybody, and instigates the frantic ragings of heedless crowds, of the unbridled rabble.

with respect to the
changes of anarchism
into despotism.

Natural law, furthermore, shows its signs of changing polarity in the interactions between the progressiveness of emancipating tendencies and the hesitancy of conservatism. What a ponderous problem for ethnological psychology is presented in the regularity with which anarchy ever turns into despotism, easily altho not entirely explicable as it seems by giving fatigue as a reason. In the excitability of political hopes and fears we see the regard for the law of obstructive and promotive forces in the processes of life—the very forces which are in the purposes of the "forethought." As laws of polarity they are in close relation with the laws of gravitation—tho the oscillations of the pendulum regulating this sphere are beyond calculation. There is a rhythm of epochal recurrences, tho their causes may remain inexplicable and their intervals can not be measured.

Above all, there are many more signs of the dominant position of natural necessity as regards personal life, to which we must submit, without being able to account for them by any hypothesis. Natural laws are the prerequisites for the growth of a multitude of empirical sciences and for technical adroitness. Through all kinds of
Reflex nerve-action, i. e.
fatigue with respect to
progressiveness and
conservatism;
inherited qualities and acquirements, and in all sorts of accomodations to surroundings; and in the mechanism of "reflex action" from repeated sense-perception, they exert their silent influences. They manifest themselves as the all-embracing and modifying power of usages and habits. The inquiry into the laws of the rise and spread of ideas in any age, and their exhaustion after their force is spent, leads to in-
Inquiry into certain
laws leads to heights
inaccessible to scientific
investigation.
explorable realms. Those laws of historic expansion and contraction, exaltation and depression, and the order in which they alternate—all point toward the height of half-embodied spirit-life, that height which is inaccessible to scientific investigation. Our not understanding them, however, does not necessarily prevent us from seeing lawfulness in what proceeds from thence.

The limit of
physical
conditions
bearing on history is
precisely delineable
where the influences of
the spiritual side of the
mind become manifest.
Sec. 1, 5, 19, 24, 57, 101,
219.

Yet all that lawfulness is powerless after a certain limit is reached. The effects upon history caused by nature differ from those caused by spiritual influences in a degree similar to effects of waves of light or sound upon those receptacles of sense-perceptions—the sensitised keyboard of the sensorium, as it were—in their contrast to the conceptions of the work of art formed by the ontogenetic, creative consciousness.

There will always be minds rising above the level of mere law-regulations; always a few, who do not submit to prejudices, false tendencies, and capricious public opinions; who care little for the praise or disdain of the world. There always will be great characters, who outgrow the law of growth and maintain their superiority as regards the law of relapse and retrogression. For here we have approached the sphere of mind-life proper, where the genius reigns.

Influence of men of genius upon historic progress.

The origin, growth, and effect of a school of painters may serve as an illustration. In ascending degrees the followers of a particular master may improve in correctness of drawing, in technique of colors, etc. This, of course, altho the result of practice and experience is the mere formal, nonessential part of the art. The essential part is the ingenuity of the master and founder of the school. He is celebrated and held in highest esteem, until a still greater artist arises, who sets aside the whole sum of previous achievements, and digresses from the trodden path of a traditional rule of aesthetics. Independent of the drawing-master and of former theories of color, he will render another set of techniques suitable to his ideals, enhancing thereby, perhaps, the general state of the culture of his age.

Manifestations of the spirit in men who excel mere lawfulness.

Recall to mind how prominent explorers in the fields of astronomy and chemistry, for instance, had the courage to break the fetters of time-honored doctrines and biasing views, and were successful despite the derision of their contemporaries. Think of the religious reformers of all zones, how they animated large strata of retarded life, elevating whole races to a better consciousness and more profound convictions, by bursting the incrustations of distorted traditions and heinous usages, wide-spread, hoary with age, and seemingly inseparable from the lives of the nations.

Explorers:
Reformers.

Reforms consist in abolishing such customs as result from mere natural development and which in that lower sphere have become still more base, abnormal and corrupt. Or they counteract the poison oozing from the corpses of national bodies which died of their abominations, the poison which is ever carried along by a certain historic undercurrent.

Corruption counteracted. Sec. 67.

In the spheres of the True, the Good and the Beautiful, we everywhere see mental life endeavoring to preserve or to regain its proper freedom. The cardinal inquiry concerning these spheres, therefore, is not about that which stirs up, provokes and challenges the laws ruling in history, but that which seeks the law and abides by it, submits to its rule, thus coinciding with the plan in history. Before we proceed to investigate that problem, however, sundry preliminaries may be necessary, which are obtainable in the best way by looking at the great movements of history at large.

Inquiry chiefly concerned with that which coincides with the plan of history, not with that which provokes and challenges the laws ruling in history.

CH. III. HISTORIC MOVEMENT. NATURAL COROLLARIES.

§21. Motion and development are to be strictly discriminated. The terms convey distinctly different conceptions. The cognition of motion does not include the momenta of progress or of purposes which are contained in the term development. Motion as such is aimless and merely serves the latter. To the mineral kingdom development is not attributed. We speak of it only where motion serves to unfold, only in the activity of the organic world. The term motion takes in the wider scope.

"Motion" does not imply aim; "Development" implies the direction to a goal or final purpose.

In the astral world we have the great circuitous movements of revolving masses. In this purely mechanical concurrence they serve in measuring the distance of time and space, and in perpetuating certain commotions going on upon our planet. In our world the ponderous masses of stone are conductors of incomputable motion and polarity; our whole earth, oceans included, receives impulses and irritations from the movements going on in the firmament, movements so rapid as to appear to us as the emblems of absolute rest, of solemn silence, yea, devotional quietude. True, we are as yet unable to fix the causes of the regularity in the rotation of planetary solids and fluids. But if by conjecture we can ascertain how motion all around us becomes apparent and measurable, so that we can reason backward and apply the measure found to the divisions of astral measurement which prove correct to the second—then we may in like manner conjecture the effects of sidereal motion upon the knowledge gained from experience. Why should our inferential conclusion not also claim an approximate correctness?

Movement comprises the inorganic world; development takes place in the organic alone. Sec 23.
"Firmament" dead matter, disengaging force.

The moving star plays its part in revealing the relationship between matter and motion. By the movements of matter nothing but the fact is rendered explicable that elements change places. But what power they are possessed of is only brought to view by observing the phenomena of attraction and repulsion. Hence we hold

Bearing of sidereal movements upon history. Sec. 1, 2, 5, 27.

that force is the characteristic feature of motion.- Without this motive principle
neither the motion of masses nor of their parts would be thinkable. The mutual
tendency of finding itself or fleeing from itself is inseparable from matter. Hence
force and, ultimately, motion can not be subtracted from matter. Dead matter is an
impossible idiosyncrasy, since force can never be observed as accessory to matter—
but is always demonstrable as its essential attribute. Perhaps matter is found to be
the substance subsisting upon force, which becomes force in the concrete whilst it is
moving.

Force in motion becomes substance in the concrete.

The purport of forces set free in the living organism aims at the embodiment of its principle ; through assimilation it embodies itself to increasing thickness and surrounds itself with means. The consequence of this increasing selfin-
crustation, or of this accumulating encasement, or of this selfassertion of life, substantiating itself according to the thought of purpose by virtue of its indwelling energy, is the generation of new forces. Thus we have now concurrent motion, commotion. Affinity and accumulative assimilation are the first phenomena of induced
motion, i. e. disengaged or liberated force—as soon as the latent force is aroused
by breaking the lifeless bulk of consolidated matter.

Force in motion is the self-assertion of life, substantiating itself by virtue of the purpose, to establish the relation of existence.   Sec. 43.

The purpose indicates forces as the means for its self-incrustation or embodiment, for materialising itself.   Sec. 17.

In the social organism the very same series of generations will be found. Take
the promiscuous mass of an uncultured people in which the powers of historic movements lie dormant. More than we see upon the surface of individual life is force active in attraction and repulsion. More and more the adjustment of affairs causes
modifying changes. Tribal groups represent the first accumulations. The immediate effects are marked by a general pushing and shifting in the crowded locality.
Additional force is generated ; more warmth is set free by friction and expansion ;
migration is the result. In such a permanent state of internal commotion from
latent heat and growth, we actually find the bulk of uncultured masses, altho
history in general becomes scarcely aware of it, as long as the motive principles of
that latent force are not called forth by other powers and set free to expand for
higher purposes.

Generation of force in the social development.

Nowhere in nature is rest or inertia to be found. "The particles of those bodies
even are in permanent motion toward each other (says Kirchhoff) which seem to us
hard and immovable." "Not a particle of all that exists is dead or motionless,"
Lotze corroborates. Nothing can be perceived as being, unless being related to something. But without motion there is no relation. Take relation away, and existence
is inconceivable. (This thought of Dr. Rocholl was in print before Renouvier's similar
conclusion had been published.)

The power dormant in nature-bound races. Permanent motion of bodies toward each other. Kirchhoff, Lotze.   Sec. 22.

It is the purport of motion to give expression to the purpose in its establishing relation-ships.   Sec. 19.

And this relationship upon the premises of motion and force (the rudimentary
element of all created life) includes the idea of purpose. In that sense the sand of
the dunes and the block of granite are but force bound up, motion in the concrete,
motion substantiated, life compressed, like that which is presented to the mind by
the term: firmament! Affinity penetrates the universe and all therein, and adhesion
holds together and keeps up the secret connection among all the things related to
each other—by means of the incommensurable "fluxion" of Newton.

Motion in the concrete. The firmament emblem of absolute rest.

"Fluxion" of Newton.   Sec. 20.

Analogous to this seeming inertia of nature is the life of the hordes upon the
steppes, or of those people who must be assigned to the lowest notch in the scale of
historic life. They are moved by as great a variety of compulsive and repulsive incitements, by pleasure and pain, etc. as any high-wrought human being, tho their
commotion influences or reflects upon history no more than the compressed life and
the oppressive silence of the Rocky Mountains. Such people were ever full of life, as
they still are, just as the mountains contain the powers which make them the backbone of a hemisphere. Forming, as these people do, and as we shall see, the basal
substratum of the human race, their movements cannot be morally indifferent; even
they possess qualifications which contribute a certain value to history, whereby they
become objects of great import. Were it otherwise, their emotions and the commotions ensuing would not fit into the order of things. But since the idea that there
ever existed a people void of any trace of culture is unwarranted and since a mere
supposition of that sort would be absurd—they are rather people of consequence, the
purpose of whose existence will evince itself throughout all history.

Motion at rest as applied to people unnoticed in history, but yet of consequence.

In motion history originates; motion sets it in operation; but rest also, being latent motion, plays a very significant part in, and does much for, the activity of mankind.

Importance of rest, i. e. latent motion.

Life is a process of renewing itself out of itself. At regular periods, at certain points of ascent and decadence, rest supersedes motion. These periods of rest are the opportunities for recreation and concentration, that is, for gathering renewed force. Going to sleep means to the human body the restoration of nerve-tension; not only the saving of the given, but also the accumulation of new strength. The same is true of the large bodies of nations with whom the change bears the character of a natural necessity, in proportion as their intellectual life is less apt to recover part of the required strength from a different source. It is to them necessary for the same physical reasons that childhood, first and second, needs more sleep than the mentally vigorous and well supported organism.

Life a process of renewal

under tension of polarities.

The import of our conclusion becomes obvious. Zoellner says: "During sleep the organism is busy to refresh and replenish forces and faculties for the active thinking and doing of the coming day. In like manner are these epochs of intellectual standstill or retrograding culture times of recuperation for the moral instincts." Such is the fact, only that we would prefer the word sentiency to instinct.

Sleep the opposite from inactivity; applied to ethnical life. ZOELLNER.

In sleep the "machine" seems to stand still, because the incessant working of the physical organs and of the soul, going on in the unconscious state and in the lower departments of natural life, are less esteemed. We generally deem them as unessential, because the governor of all, for which, as a matter of course, reason is taken, has retired. We forget what work is going on in the various inner departments for his sake. We lose sight of that motion by which new vitality is contracted and those energies are stored up, which are in demand for future mental and corporeal activities. We are apt to neglect the truth, that behind the screen of seeming inertia the nourishing of the several systems and their hundreds of sub-divisions, the indispensable changes of physical stuff, the secretions of vital saps, and the excretion of the noxious refuse, are taking place undisturbed. In no more salutary manner than in sound slumber can the forces spent be recruited and the reenforcements be marshalled again into rank and file, and the means be put in proper state of readiness according to the needs of consciousness when returning to its day's work.

Physical activity during sleep undervalued,

because reason, deemed the governor of activity has retired.

No less needful are those periods in the lives of nations, during which every sign of mental progress has disappeared, periods which, nevertheless, are times of invigoration and preparation for some great event in the future, when, perhaps, even to them shall be assigned an important role in the reconstruction of humanity.

People with arrested culture in their rest preparatory to future activity—perhaps a reformation.

Of a movement of history as a whole —advancing as it does after a method of rhythmical, or rather fugue-like arranged, synchronisms and anachronisms—we can only speak in metaphors. All we can do is to classify or systematise specific series of similar situations by severing the historic motions from their contemporaneous connection, and then to arrange the grades of advance into series of dates according to the consecutive order of time. Notwithstanding the cumbersomeness of the procedure the following results are gathered together.

History on the whole moves like a fugue—like an arranged system of anachronisms and synchronisms.

The uninterrupted current of history never runs smooth like a pleasure trip down the river of time: it rather runs through and across the ocean with its cycles of rising and submerging billows. This is as necessary to the world of nations as it is to nature. Tides stopping would mean general stagnancy and would cause putrefaction in every domain of organic life.

Tidal motion as necessary to history as to nature.

The motion in the moral sphere, to be sure, differs from that in the natural. Motion provides the natural sphere with the equilibrium of gravity. Movement in the moral sphere must serve to balance between predispositions for either inertia and restiveness, or insomnia and restlessness.

Nobody may compute, where the rush and push of energy will exhaust itself, or where and when the reaction of apathy will begin to resist even normal progress. So much is sure: no energy can be lost. And so much we may venture to state, that the tendencies of motion in space with their contrasts of expansive strain and concentric pressure, are always under the tension of this polarity. By serving each other they obtain their force to maintain themselves.

By serving each other the forces maintain themselves.

Motion—relation: æon, Bowne.

By and by we will probably find that the vexatious categories of time and space will find their synthesis in, and be reduced to, the same formula. Borden T. Bowne in his Introduction to PsychologicalTheory settles this problem with Mill, Part I. Chapter 4.

Continuity of every energy.

Power and æon (Zeit-raum) remain, at any rate, the prerequisites for every progressive and retrogressive movement. Beneath the surface of the scenes of action, there is always moving the undercurrent of that noiseless progress which becomes recognisable only post eventum. It is there, where an equalisation and amelioration a transmission and transition of ideas is going on, no less, if not more formidable, than the revolutions and their counteractions alternate upon the broad plane of

Undercurrent of noiseless progress.

history. Motion and rest, exertion and exhaustion propel the historical movements. With regard to their continuance and intervening stops we dare not omit to consider a few more items.

Definition of "POLAR TENSION."

§ 22. Geology and history throw light upon each other in certain respects as to their silent but powerful movements under the law of "polar tension," that is, in their common subordination under the relationship between purpose and force in the concrete.

Tensions of polarities propelling the movements: conditioning motion and rest, exertion and exhaustion.

Looking over the history of the crust of our earth, we seldom notice any other but those energies in action, which silently and steadily produce the most portentuous changes. Sudden catastrophes are usually of a mere local character. Gradual washings, scourings of rocks, and glacial driftings of the moraines, sediment from slowly moving elevations and submersions have wrought changes of no less import than eruptions and floods.

Sudden catastrophes less important.

There lies a granite block which broke from a mountain hundreds of miles away, carried that distance by a slowly moving glacier which on its way down smoothed off rocks, carved out long and broad valleys, and formed narrow passes, all on the same journey.

Analogies of silent but powerful movements from geology.

Yonder rocky layers covering hundreds of square miles, were produced by the still and steady work of almost invisible creatures of the animal kingdom, and by their death. The faded shells of the seamussel, brought to light by miners who worked a mile or two above sea level; the luminous crystal, deeply imbedded in the primeval granite; the round pebble, ground and smoothed by currents of water during centuries before time was measured, and now found below thick and alternating strata of alluvium, shifted down upon them from the mountain slopes—to all of these it once happened, that they were put in their places and were given their shapes by the formidable, quiet movements of natural forces.

Steady and tranquil movements in history analogous to those in nature.

In an analogous manner the silent work of history transpired. Unavoidable eruptions, sudden overthrowings, invasions, and conquests are not the rule, but in most cases local affairs. As a general thing we observe the weightier transactions, the migrations and colonisations, to be the lasting effects of slow and unobserved, so-called prehistoric movements.

Since we are now enabled to trace out the shiftings and driftings of the rhythmical masses, let us do so. The raging torrents of sudden start, and the lasting occupations of territories in consequence of them, were rare events. The settlement of new countries usually proceeds less turbulently, as illustrated in that of North America. The pressure in the rear was caused, perhaps, by the gradual change of

E. g. the settlement of America.

fields of pasture into arid sand-steppes. The shifting movement of the people, thus becoming nomades, goes in the direction of more favorable regions. First the high plateau was preferred on account of a feared inundation. Then the rivers were followed down to their fertile bottom-lands.

Ethnical strata as indicated by languages

Thus the stratifying material is sliding down layer upon layer. We notice this process in the formation of languages, where one supersedes the other. At the base we have e. g. a layer of Turanians ; an Accado-Sumerian layer shifts in upon it ; and

e. g. the sequence of Turnian, Accado-Sumerian, and Semitic layers.

upon that again an Assyrian, the Semitic layer. The partial amalgamation thus traceable signifies the gradual and long enduring movement. We need not always

Movement in history partly natural but none such as that of a mechanical perpetuum mobile.

imagine bloody upheavals and conquests for an explanation of lingual changes. We may as well, and rather, take it for granted, that a quiet force moved in the direction of least obstruction and formed ethnic sediments and strata.

Mere movement represented by a straight line— the course of which is not calculable in advance. Van Hoeven.

Suppose then, we represent a succession of such movements of history in general— because from the aspect of the whole alone can we understand the parts and in this case the plan—by an unbroken straight line. The advance of political organisation among the alternating ethnical augmentations would then have to be imagined as another line of culture, running along with the first as to time. But the line of advancement must not be drawn straight as that of movement, because the culture. line, denoting ascents and descents, that is, representing the rise and decline of nations and of whole epochs of culture, would have to be a **wave line**. *Cultural advance represented by a wave-line.*

But does this pictorial parallel of **cultural advance** afford an explanation as to **historic motion**?

Movement through space is **natural**; cultural advance through time is to its largest part mental and **spiritual**. Those who would make history a thing evolved from nature pure and simple, will show by statistical figures that movements of history may be figured out like the distances of the firmament. They take movement and development for the same thing. The consequence must be, that culture would be the same at all times a thing of mere natural concern.

So did Van Hoeven lately deny that culture makes any progress. He said, we are no further advanced than the Ægyptians of old, and that mankind turns in circles, only to return to former conditions. Very well—instead of parallel wave lines take the figure of the snake biting its tail, that is, a circular movement of culture like those going on in the firmament· And in that case we would, after all the hurly-burly, be compelled to reckon culture as remaining at a standstill. Sometimes it seems so. It is a sad spectacle for the humane observer to see that civilisation in the side streets of Paris or Washington is not a bit advanced from that of Babylon or Carthage. We actually have "street Arabs." But we must postpone the melancholy theme for future consideration, until we shall have understood more of the whole. *Culture moves not in a circle § 221.*

Only so much may now be stated in regard to this parallel between cultural advance and physico-historical motion, that the latter, as movement, keeps on straight in its natural line, whilst culture goes on in circles. *but in spiral, helically corresponding curves; wherein freedom comes to its right.*

By a mechanical conception of history advancing toward its purpose, the moral creator of history, i. e. human free will, is debarred from its influence. Would not free will under this aspect have to be taken as a mere extension or succession of geological motion, resembling at best the hand on the dial plate, merely pointing to the place in the circle of the movement? In that case Spencerianism would be justified in reverting universal to natural history. Then, of course, history must be calculable by a system of statistics and numbers, which point out the gradual prolongation of natural life as the highest Good and most ethical purpose of modern, progressive humanitarianism.

Be it conceded, for argument's sake, that under the scientific sheen, under this mechanical aspect, life's movements and human destiny could be figured out, and the horoscope could be set, after the movements of the firmament—then materialistic evolutionism would likewise have to admit that such calculations are futile. We on our part can see no other purpose in those experiments than to amuse ignorant infidels for a while. In the affected scientific agility we surmise the hidden tendency to prove meditation upon the spiritual world as superfluous if not ridiculous, or at least as stupidly unscientific. *Technical, i. e. materialistic concept of history has no analogy in the laws of mechanics.*

But the derision will fall back upon the horoscoping and tabulating of "dynamism." For, says Lotze, "nowhere, not even in the transmission or simple mechanical motion is to be noticed a complete equation between the causal impetus and the produced effect. The result of the pressure urging on is rather determined by the efficiency of every agency participating in the movement. The resulting motion is the summary of both, the force urging, the object reacting. On the part of the object to be moved, cooperation is the more necessary, the more complicated its constituency. Hence there will be observable in any combination of agencies, and in proportion to their variety and mode of cooperation, a system of reciprocal interaction, in which the counter efficients determine the final effect." *Motion resulting from pressure is determined by the force urging and the object reacting. Lotze.   Sec. 2L.*

Under these circumstances nothing would be gained for the computability of historical movements by substituting any impersonal principle in the place of free will. The blind power supposed to move history under the classic name of "fate", would still hover like a dark cloud beyond calculation, to be vanquished by thought no more than by superstition. The idea of history would remain obscure, and any regularity of its course would be only the more incomprehensible, if man were imagined as a complex system of natural elements and as their mere playground. *Free will versus blind "fate," which latter is vanquishable neither by thought, nor by superstition. § 58, 96. Under the aspect of "Dynamics" history must remain incomprehensible, since it takes man as merely a system of physical elements and their play-ground.*

Fate directing historic movements upon tracks ever so even and straight means death to all thinking. Culture advances in circuitous movements indeed, but it

7

tends upward and moves in spiral, helically corresponding curves, the curves of the nuts, representing, as it were, the grooves of natural necessity, and the threads of the screw representing personal will. And in these uplifting circles not only human thought but also human freedom comes to its right.

CH. IV. HISTORIC DEVELOPMENT—MIND'S INTERACTION.

§ 23. The error to be avoided in speaking of historic progress consists in identifying movements with developments, progress with advance. What is the difference, and what is to be understood by development?

Since **motion** does not explain the course of history—whose purpose can be nothing short of humanity in its full and true sense, and whose goal is not reached by mere indefinite "progress"—we take it for granted, that history moves, at least, in the line of **development.** In order to see what that means, we proceed in our usual manner. We first define the principle of development by way of induction, setting out with the investigation of empirical facts in natural life. We are determined to secure a firm hold and a clear conception.

The idea of development is borrowed from the province of organised life, outside of which the process is not found. Development means the unfolding of the inner wealth of thought, purpose, life. At present we confine ourselves to the unfolding of physical organisms without mixing in any speculation upon relations.

On that score development is that mode of motion which, after having arrived at its acme of individualised being, ceases to convey a definite thought. Vegetable life develops in upward movements until the bud unfolds into bloom. The purport of the plant is then exhibited; development in the proper sense is exhausted and terminates. The processes and interactions of the system have reduced the manifold elements of being to the oneness of intensified life in the individualised seed-germ. Plant-life has returned to its generic type. All that follows the blossom can only be considered as the decline of plant-life, ending in decomposition. This descent, this devolution which is no longer evolution, does not deserve the name of, nor ought it to be considered as pertaining to, development. For, its declining stages with increasing clearness represent mere being, not life. To merely vegetate is not to exist. It is, therefore, development in a wider sense, if the line of ascent and descent, describing a semi-circle, is considered as comprising the sum of life in an organic entity.

With this geometrical figure as an emblem of a compound cognition we shall operate to good advantage, since in the life of nations we deal with more than mere botanical specimens.

The law of necessity under which nature labors, and nations too, as far as their consciousness is to be described as nature-bound—is surpassed in man, nevertheless, by the liberty which is derived from the sphere of spiritual freedom. In the life of nations we see not only the aggregate of individualised souls, blossoms of nature as they are, but we discriminate also a sphere of voluntary and individual activity moving above the natural inclinations. In a people as a whole always exists a permanent disposition of which all personal activity partakes and by which the latter is largely conditioned. That public spirit, this fixed national temperament, we may well represent by a **horizontal line.** But then we see how this is everywhere intersected by **vertical lines** denoting more or less independent personal life. Only thus the fact can be explained, why a nation (determined by their nature, as Scharling has it, who for this reason failed to explain their having rulers), may contain excellent minds of highest aspirations, altho having outlived itself and plainly bearing the marks of decadence. We would greatly err in taking the conspicuous minds of Plato and Aristotle as representing the mental condition of their time and generation in general. Isaiah, Neander stood in direct opposition to the simultaneous decline of their respective nations.

Keeping in mind this phase of our subject, we may speak the more appropriately of the development of the human race as a whole. For, altho diversified into self-existent parts, and presenting a picture of a manifold articulated, simultaneous and consecutive activity of interchanging effects in the frame-work of space and time— yet we have before us the unitary process of a general progress under a series of

---

Marginal notes (left column):

Discrimination between movement and development. §21.

Development pertains to organic life only,

but ceases after its acme of individualised being is reached.

Manifold elements of being reduced to the oneness of intensified life in the seed-germ.

Natural development limited by decadence and decomposition.

Ascent and descent of organic life—as below personal—represented by an arch-line.

The permanent disposition, the national temperament of a people, consisting partly of inclinations toward natural generalness, partly of manifestations of real mind-life, represented by horizontal lines,

which are intersected by vertical lines representing men of energy and excellent minds, overlooked by Scharling.

Development of the race as a whole.

A general progress under various orders of levelopment,

developments. These arise from the mysterious depths of the species homo; they reveal and may bring to the consciousness of the individual a wealth of inner potentialities, of which, whether becoming conscious of the possession or not, each partakes. It is owing to these various degrees and series of special developments, that those potencies within each human individual are called forth, so as to be recognised by the ego in order to be cultivated under the increasing support of the whole. But altho this individual cultivation may partake of the collective facilities, it is yet a thing of the free will and not of any compulsion. Individual selfculture may help, on its part, to further elevate common interests, but no earthly force can coerce a person to assist in the improvement of the social condition. *calling forth individual capabilities which are to be cultivated under the increasing support of the whole.*

If now this process, thus progressing under the reciprocity of willingness, is steadily going on, as on the whole it really does, underneath and in spite of all the turmoil—then **civilisation advances into what Guizot defined as that state of human affairs, where society takes care of the best interests of the individual and is ready to appreciate his good services in return.** *and under reciprocity of individual willingness.* *Civilisation defined. see page 36 preface. Guizot.*

All of that which pertains to such unfolding of relations, to those augmentative attainments, and to this continuance of changing and enriched formations of cultured life, we aptly design as development. *Truth in evolutionism.*

Let us consider the **means by which this sort of evolution** is brought about. We think of La Place's theory. Parts sever themselves from an original astral mass of condensing gases. By the rotation of the main body they are carried along in their motion, being attracted by the regulating forces of gravity. Each part moves centripetally towards a concentrating nucleus of its own, and centrifugally towards the solidifying main body. The whole solar system, along with every phase of natural evolution as far as the sun reigns, can be explained by this more than a clever supposition, namely under the originally intuitive now inductive aspect of severance and departure toward selfhood. These two, aperture and detachment, are the first principles of, and the means for, development. Applied to organic life we call it differentiation. The first cell tends to unfold itself: for, movement in organised life immediately shows a tendency to realise its purpose, to express the typical thought it represents. It is the tendency towards individualisation in the midst of a complexus of combinations which seem unfavorable to that tendency; whilst all, nevertheless, further its best interests by way of higher differentiations. *La Place's theory.* *First principles of development:* *detachment and departure toward selfhood.* *called differentiation in organic life;* *tending to unfold the purpose, i. e. the inherent typical thought.*

Unfolding goes on in repeated extension of roots, stems, branches, augmentations, blooming, and ripening of new germs of intensified life for the renewal and multiplication of the species. A moner has been discovered in the Atlantic Ocean, named Protomyxa Aurantiaca, which shows no trace of differentiation. It is simply a gelatinous, animated plasma. It contracts its nourishment by antennae-like protruding, slimy protuberances. Then the tiny ball contracts itself, excretes a cyst, and, after a cleavage, the fold or furrow of fissi-gemmation becomes visible. It separates into a number of small globules, which again grew to the shape of the parental body. The same mode of development which La Place adopted for explaining the formation of the telescopic worlds in the firmament, we recognise in the microscopic world in a drop of water. We may elucidate this mode by another example.

Observing the vital movements of the egg-cell we notice fecundation, fissuration, segmentation, detachments and augmentations, in short, the unfolding of organs. This is the evolution of the animal body: a progressive fission into parts, i. e. differentiation.—The puny, round, filmy and moving pellicle, this jelly-like, jerking substance, called Amoeba, has neither mouth nor digestive organ, neither muscular nor nervous structure, no organ for motion nor respiration. All these services are rendered by a viscous mucus through which nourishment enters at every point, while it moves by the oscillations of its fluxional structure, as an entity propagated by self-detachment. *Protomyxa Aurantiaca, the moner without a trace of differentiation.*

Analogous to this latter example are all the functions of the members of a developed organism involved in the undifferentiated structure, in the form of latent potencies. Progressive division of labor causes the constructive development of the animal organism. As it increases, the functional energy forms its particular structural instruments. All the functions of assimilation and propagation, for which the finest systematised body correspondingly needs the most diversified and adapted organs, are found to be bound up together or undifferentiated in the wonderful capabilities of animated matter in its most primitive and simple form. *Amoeba illustrates the compound unit of latent potentialities.*

The higher stages of development are conducted upon the simple principle of division of labor. The energy, originally resting in every part of the bodily substance, *Division of labor the chief principle of higher development, i. e. differentiation.*

undivided and identical, is, in the course of evolution, set free to assume the diverse shapes which the functions require, until it finally appears inherent in a system of distinct groups of structural members or special interacting agencies. The perfection of the animal-body is reached. It consists in its fitness of construction for the most complicated functions, in the aptitude of particular organs for their own special work and for that of the organism as a whole. Differentiation and all permeating motion in ever increasing selfhood, mark the progress of development; but in such a manner that the character of membership is never abandoned.

§ 24. As the means by which development pursues its progressive tendency and nascency we found: spontaneous detachment, unfolding articulation, and distribution of functions.

Now we apply these factors to the social body, the bearer of history. Here the diversity of functions renders the organism into an organisation, wherein the social formations continue to differentiate themselves into families, into various kindred tribes, social grades, and international connections.

Every real growth of any social organism is conditioned by the possibility of unfolding, and by the multiplying and variegated selfassertions of its constituent parts. Industrial enterprises, governmental functions etc. will, in course of progressing organisation, branch out into so many special departments, each requiring its own book-keeping and consequently the multiplication of offices. So each business sets up its own factories, requiring the aptness of each factor in its place. And whenever superabundant energy obstructs the selfassertion of ambitious persons, and crowds out individual aspiration, then colonial nuclei detach themselves from the nation, only to transplant the same process into other quarters in behalf of a new nation.

This affords a picture of historic movement, development included; it is for the sake of the latter that the natural, bee-hive-like commotion continues. In the first period of existence a nation is embarrassed by natural necessities, and is scarcely dreaming of its future political possibilities, being engaged only with itself. The spirit of the new settlement works noiselessly and attracts little outside attention. The aggregation of neighboring households seeks mutual concord and succor. The incipient nationality disengages, however, from its embryonic condition. It forms, under modifying circumstances, its own vernacular.

As in folklore mysterious structures and sceneries arise by moonlight, so society in its primitive stages shapes its thought-pictures into fanciful poetry, until language outgrows this youthful condition and becomes the wonderful depository from which the wealth of characteristic propensities shines forth, which originally were lying dormant deep in the soul of the new-born nation.

As such, that stage of society is to be imagined (and really is wherever new prairie is "broken") which immediately precedes the appearance of a nation upon the theatre of history. The "national spirit" is generating, in accord with the higher or more degraded cognisance of the deity, with which every fact pertaining to life is thought to stand in connection. Whether God-consciousness bears a higher or lower character does not depend on the culture of the intellect, but culture rests upon it and will stand higher in proportion to the purity and unsophisticated feeling of dependence, responsibility, and relationship. This height is to be measured by the degree in which the originally inborn susceptibility has not succumbed below its level of the adulterated original and universal traditions. The national spirit will stand high in proportion to its retaining the unity and genuineness of the God-consciousness which manifests itself at the awakening, and marks the beginning of the selfconscious personality.

The second period of the development of any nation is indicated by the display of phantasy, the awakening imagination, the creative function of the mind. Now the national peculiarities are brought out. Natural forces are personified and the dead are deified; soon after attempts are made to pacify evil spirits, or to represent ideal relations and conceptions; the idols are shaped which populate heaven and earth, in consequence of picture-thinking and picture-language. Whatever excites consciousness most profoundly, or arouses fretful apprehension most seriously, whatever influences the emotions and sentiments of a people, call it fear, hope, devotion, tradition, religious instinct—anything but love; for of the relation of love between man and the invisible, no language in that stage has a term—all this is represented by a confusion of ideals, and finds its expression in corresponding idols, images, rites, temples, and tombs. Tradition is the more firmly clung to and kept sacred, the less it is understood.

*Traditions and the symbols of picture-thinking misunderstood causes   Sec. 20.
1. Idolatry,
2. Mythology.*

Wherever the eye, since man has forgotten to look to heaven, did not lose itself in earthly things and beasts ; and wherever, therefore, a better sense had made persons ideals and deified ancestors and heroes of the past : there myths of the gods spring up. They keep a powerful sway, and are nourished by the faint echoes of the inner life and by narratives of a hazy past. The mountains, the forests and waters of the distant home are immortalised by immersing them in the resplendent "morning dawn of the gods", in the dim recollections of an intercourse of God with man upon earth. The tree and the spring are fancied to be inhabited by ghostly beings—the inner anxieties objectivised. The sphere of the relative good is identified with that of the Absolute Good. Nature in its entirety is taken for the deity. The raptures of sensuality are taken for the highest blessings. The disgust with, and contempt of, life are the next steps where abandonment to the most abject depravity is made religion.

Relative good in nature made the surrogate for the "Supreme Good."

Perversion of the religious elements, until a most abject depravity is made religious.

Now all these distracted, and finally completely subverted notions react powerfully upon the formation of the people. In the meantime the unavoidable differentiation of national life proceeds, ever more threatening to desintegrate and scatter the people, unless the idea of a world-empire, or the reality of a powerful dynasty—the perverted reminiscence of human unity—keeps that cultural nation together. Progress notwithstanding its being thus arrested in one place, goes on differentiating and forming varieties, in another. Here goes on, however unnoticed, division of labor, selfassertion of functionaries, assertion of might ("survival of the fittest" some term it, wherein we however, find the perverted idea of dominion and personality). There we see the growth of population; but the activity in every direction, the irritations, provoked by combating interests, rights, and liberties, lead to wars. Or the increase of friction and transmission of heat spread inflammation of the passions through the body politic, shaking it as with fever and causing civic upheavals and revolutions. Then again the accumulation of capital, and of landed estates, and the emulative endeavor of the wealthy to drain the physical world and the personal of its proceeds; and, above all, the great polar tension balancing all the intricacies of relations multiplying thousandfold—all must serve in differentiating, cultivating, developing society.

Reminiscence of the unity of the human family applied in founding world-empires.

Progress, arrested in one nation, advances in an other.

Reminiscences of man's original dignity and dominion over nature perverted into tyranny and "survival of the fittest."

Multiplication of relations must serve to develop society.

The third period of national development generally approaches the critical point Take Rome for example, or its modern parallel—our own culture. The wealth of emotional life and moral sentiment recedes in proportion as the preponderance of cold reason and practical calculation increases. Conduct is governed by considerations of utility and by selfishness. The diplomacy of expediency takes the place of acting upon principle. Urbanity is simulated to take the place of humaneness and cordiality. Thinking is misused to set aside the necessity of the objective good and the obligations resultant, as well as the authority of the common good with its rights and duties and its discipline. Reasoning turns to "the knowledge of words and their uses," dialectics, rhetoric, and sophistry ; and in the form of scepticism it decomposes the roots, annihilates the fundamental conditions for normal progress and common welfare. Patriotism pines away. From the oneness of national aspirations an abstract, philosophical morality detaches itself like the bark from a sick tree. The ascent of the vital sap in the core and the bast of the trunk ceases While the core turns black and moldy, the naked wood assumes a selfsufficient attitude, and under its smoothness hides the inner hollowness and dry rot.

Third period of national development: symptoms corresponding with those described by the semicircle of rise and decline in plant-life.   Sec. 28.

Authority questioned;

thought withdraws from the masses;

Scepticism causes decomposition of the roots of progress and welfare.

It is symptomatic of this state of affairs, that intellectual and moral thought withdraws from the masses and from public life, and an occasional warning remains unheeded. Summing up of experiences and observations for critical analysis signalises the period preceding the wreckage of a ship of state, the moral bankruptcy of an overestimated "culture."

Differentiation, as in the case of the deeper cell-cleavage preceding fissuration, begins development. But it becomes disintegration, whenever it continues to split up the activity of the developed organisation to the point of dissolving membership. The crisis sets in when the mutual recognition of **personality changes into subjectivism or egoism.** "Our age declines," the contemporaries then say. The break between the intellect and the moral sense, and the detachment of both from public life, ends in a general collapse.

A remote and transcendental, an indefinite and indifferent deity, which nobody needs to revere and nobody can love (because we can only love a personality), unites minds no better, not even as well as the nearer relationship of being fellow-citizens could do. Finally nothing binds people together but egoism and class hatred. Subjectivism, the caricature of the grand cognition of personality, which was the best boon that posterity derived from the fights and thoughts of the dark ages—becomes the prevailing principle, the basis of scepticism; subjectivism emancipates itself, subject only to the "mysteries" of orders and to scantily covered passions. It is that principle which estranges the individual from philanthropy; which, at the expense of all that is holy, is declared fashionable and deemed aristocratic; it renders "society" reserved, dignified and stiff—until it dies. Differentiation has outrun itself. Hence the seeds of such a culture, too, severed from a personal God and falling from the husks of a deistical world-theory, have to undergo the process of death.

Remember, reference was made to Rome as the example.

Nevertheless, the purpose was as safe as it ever will be. For at the period of Rome's decline, within a people which seemed dead material, there lay the promise of higher advance. Rome—"Mistress of the World"—thus furnishes an object lesson of the semicircle of development (§ 23) diverging with the basal line of its diameter at its descending end, at the moment of her death.

The purpose lay dormant, but safe—as we shall see—with certain "barbarians." We have arrived at a point of development, where it is very sensitive to anything sharp. We shall return to it with something that heals.

So far we have treated of development as procured by, and derived from, nature. This evolution as applied to national life fortunately has its limits; not all that is to be developed is going that way. The line is drawn, above which the laws of "inheritance" and of "accomodation" lose their efficiency. The genius of art is not heritable, much less religiousness. All which pertains to the world of formal unity, perpetuity and freedom, is above natural necessity. And if it were above reason, it is only because it was not intended to be visible from a point below reason.

The deepest, most vivid and empiric relations of each single individual to the spiritual and supernatural world can develop in no other but personal mode—but as such personal matter they can bear experimenting.

These experiences can not be put on by training, nor handed down by tradition; they can not be indoctrinated nor acquired by culture—least of all by onesided cultivation. In this sphere we make experiences each one for himself alone. I must follow the dictates of my own conscience. The conscience of another has no claim upon mine. This was the point which Kant intended to demonstrate; if he failed it was not the fault of his theme. We know that societies have no conscience; and now we add that not even the Church can vicariously make these experiences for its members. This kind of empirics can only in a modified sense, that is, as to their effects, become a common good—inasmuch namely, as the results of the inner life of the "religionist"

may affect the inner life of others by way of a certain rapport, which, tho never without strict adherence to the principle of personality undefiled, unites the spiritual world.

In this sense civilisation possesses a treasure which is inheritable from generation to generation and transferable from nation to nation. Nevertheless it is only the sum total of theoretical empiricism concerning spiritual matters, and is, after all, limited to mere exhibitory technicalities. Whatever immortal elements are parts of this treasure can not be verified as issuing from natural development. Hence the development of the mind in its full sense and in every direction is not to be expected from history. The so-called religious progress is simply the perpetuity of fixed methods to facilitate personal development. Whatever natural elements are contained therein,—as referred to in the description of its progress through times and nations and from the globigerinæ upward to the issues of psychico-moral life inclusive —constitutes but the natural basis for just so much of development as is sufficient to unite mankind, because of its psychical grandeur, into a natural unity, a genus. So-called religious progress is simply the perpetuity of a fixed method of personal development approaching perfection.

But the development of the mind as a personality does not stop here. And from this onward only that effect of the naturally developed basis upon the inner, that is, the personal, or psychico-pneumatic life comes under consideration, which reacts against the spiritual influences. In the course of further development we have to pay attention simply to the interactions of both, the natural basis and the spiritual influences, and to investigate the residuum and the results of this interaction and reaction. Henceforth the reaction of physico-historical against purely personal development chiefly demands our observation. One more notice is to be given, however, before we go to this work, viz: that this interaction and reaction is observable only to such persons as for themselves have some personal experience thereof. All preceding development is but its natural substratum. Observable only to such as have some personal experience of those interactive relations.

CH. V. PLAN OF HISTORY.

§ 25. The surview of the coefficients of history in the first division led to the conclusion that man is the type and theme of history. In order to reach the conclusion of the second, which treats of the operative mode, it remains to discover the plan of history. Is there such a thing as a preconceived destiny, a plan determining the movement of history? For the present, and for the sake of closer connection with the foregoing, let us take up the question stated in § 17, ff.: Is there reason in history? Connective with Sec. 17ff

Looking again at the monotonous heap of loose sand upon the seashore we see no reason in it. The first impression we receive is one of nonsense, of the unintelligible. Why? Because there appears to be no order, no ruling principle ; we see no fitness of the parts for a definite purpose ; the thing has no value, so that we miss even the excuse for its preservation ; the mere thought of it is annoying. We have the involuntary feeling that every idea of consistency is lacking, or rather, we forget even that disorder reigns. The sight of it becomes utterly indifferent to us, because it reveals no thought, nor does it suggest one within us. We miss all reason in or for the sand-heap. Do we? Then perhaps the thoughtlessness is on our side. For we must remember that the particular cannot be understood unless considered in its relation to the general. We can think no parts without the "universals." If thought shall be educed, we at once ask: why? If there is any sense to be found in the parts, it must be attributed to them from without. Things mechanically incite reason to make a comparison, that is, to imagine the relationship. In the things themselves we must not expect to find a plan ; we would not even be able to see things per se, unless we observe their relations. The concept "plan" we solely gain through the method in which the laws of logic, operate within us. We recognise a purpose, and this cognition is based upon a conclusion. This conclusion is derived from repeated events, from events subsequent to incidents of similar import, which we have noticed before and now compare. The conclusion is the synthetical apperception of various generalisations, which are consistent among each other, and all of which can be accounted for by reason. Hence the prerequisites for forming a conclusion can not be gotten out of an analysis of things taken by themselves. In the aggregations of sand particles there is no suggestion for our mind which would awaken the idea of a purpose, or, as we now say, of a plan. The reason in historic movements, i. e. the purpose in any event.

We may analyse things as much as we please, as infinitesimal as possible, a reason for them we do not find in themselves. We come to a judgment about them only by observing their interrelations. Remember the machine and its parts. In equal manner the thought of purpose immediately strikes us, when we "take in" a panorama of a city, a theatre, or a church. What "matters" us, is the mechanical incitement of thought by things, to form a comparison, i. e. to imagine their relationship.

In any structure we see a plan realised. Order and system prevail about the whole. Thoughtfulness, yea forethought is expressed in every detail. By utilising minds and materials, and by preparing and arranging either of them, according to

Plan of movements is not to be discovered by any analysis of the coefficients, but by way of logic, that is, by establishing their relations. §22,24.

Illustration: The architect and his plan in relation to the building, and to the aspect of the beholder.

their adaptness, a specific idea is carried out. We imagine motion, i. e. differentiation, etc., to have taken place in the execution of the plan, whereby thought found its articulate expression. In our contemplative absorption we even became surprised, perhaps, at finding our own thought engaged in criticising and judging, that is, in comparing the apparent plan of the builder with our own idea of practicability, with what the plan ought to have been. Every part stands for reason, hence the reason of the architect calls forth our own. His design is made identical with his person; he is even made responsible, not only for the appropriateness, but also for the execution of the plans and specifications.

In the plant motives and plan are inherent.

The plan underlying the construction of a plant is innate in the plant; all its motives are inherited.

But the design of the cathedral of Cologne stands in an external relation to it.

In history the plan but partly inherent.

The plan which outlines the upbuilding of history is partly inherent in its development; but it, at the same time, controls the historic movement to a considerable extent from the outside, that is in so far, as the plan remains objective.

I. Part of the plan which is in history.

With regard to the objective guidance of the historic development, the thought which animates the latter, also distributes its formative principle among the great nations of culture. And among them, on the other hand, that part of the plan becomes evident, which points out the course and task of history from its own natural conditions. Just as the plan is identical with the plant, that is, with the matter of which it consists and which at bottom is substantiated purpose, or life, its soul —so is the plan of historic development inherent in history, making it selfdeveloping in accordance with the nature of its material.

First proviso: One original typical man carries within him the type and design of history which is but man unfolded.

His endowments constitute the material of history; since the unfolding of his potentialities causes the outgrowth of relations and opportunities. Sec. 10, 12, 16, 88, 117, 119, 168, 176, 185, 197, 201, 206, 232.

And the material of history is man. In his nature he carries the type of history. Now, if there is one original, typical man—which in the meanwhile we take for granted, as we took for granted one first amoeba—then he will contain within him the plan of all the formations into which human affairs may shape themselves, since he represents the common root of the entire, wide-branching genus. History is but man unfolded. Hence the project must be delineated in him. Then the structure of history is but the explanatory unfolding of that with which his inner life is endowed. Thus history is to be considered as the unfolding of all human potentialities and all the opportunities growing out of their realisations: as the unfolding, furthermore, of all the relations existing among these potentialities themselves, and between them and the opportunities growing out of these relations to the world without.

History is at man's disposal, and does not consist of mere possibilities.

History is the actualisation of that for which man is destined; and this is deeply implanted into his entire being and disposition. His development will prescribe the formation of history. It will be what he makes of it, for it is at his disposal. He causes his own felicity and fatalities. History merely consists of this expansion of all the copiousness of possibilities lying within him in form of his own incipient potencies. Hence the unfolding of his capabilities does not only consist in indefinite possibilities and notions, but will enter into relations, will realise itself, will take place, will become facts. It will form the synthesis of pure formal being and formative existence. In other words: Man comprises all the material which—with reference to the development of the historic process and its completion—is formative principle and plan at the same time. That is, man is not only the type and theme, but even the creator of history.

Man shaping his own felicities and fatalities; is the creator of history.

All this is correct, provided there is one historical, typical, original man.

At this instant we as yet desist from considering the possibility of abnormal movements, and from considering the fact of man's activity being restricted in many ways. Disregarding all these circumstances as most all philosophers have done, we might very well perceive in this historic development the vision of an ideal unfolding according to the plan which originally was designed in his own person. But we dare not lose sight of these circumstances because others have done it.

Second proviso: That possibilities of abnormal development are not taken in consideration.

II. Part of the plan has objective existence in "thought,"

Hence we are referred to that part of the plan which, on the other hand, is not encompassed by man alone, but which in the "thought" has also objective existence and stands outside of man and history, ever contriving to procure his welfare.

The design and plan, i. e. as far as it is imparted and has entered into the combination of the human constitution, does not make history alone. If this were the case the historic development would be in jeopardy. It would be exposed to irreparable malformations and monstrosities. Misunderstandings, as those of the analogies between the natural and the spiritual, misapplied liberty, for instance, without a regulating, rescuing control of fore-thought, upholding the original design, would bring the best intentions of pure thought to naught. Development would be reverted to the worst entanglement. There could be found no standard by which to adjust development worthy of, and in harmony with, personal life. The ideal, original plan would be marred beyond recognition. The true theme of the great symphony, composed for the worlds "concert", would be drowned in the noisy turmoil and by the boisterous conduct of such disposers of history as were heard of at the "fin de siecle" a hundred years ago—and by the clashing of their plans.

In order that the purpose, i. e. communication of the Supreme Good—be not jeopardised.

The symphony composed for the world's "concert" would be drowned without the rescuing control of the forethought,

We close our several lines of argument with this statement : as the sum and substance of our observations we find that the plan controlling the development of history lies partly in it as the motive potency, and partly outside of it in an overruling Providence.

without the rule of "Providence."

We have not hesitated to hint at the place where the plan may be looked into, which stands aloof, and apart from, earthly commotion; how it is to be perceived and to be put to the test. Whether it can be handled as the necessary rule and measure, can be demonstrated by its effects. A closer inspection we reserve for the proper occasion. It must suffice that we have shown, why this plan is a postulate of reason, and that its correctness must be demonstrable. Unless we are agreed in this, we must despair of ever becoming able to give reason the satisfaction, that man can account for matters and facts. Despite such a negative result, the reason within us would insist upon its claim for an answer to its postulate. This postulate of reason can not point us all into an empty void which is unthinkable—since matters and facts press upon us with incitements to think, and since reason itself continues to challenge reasons.

The place where the plan is preserved aloof and apart from earthly commotion.

The plan a postulate of reason; its correctness must therefore be demonstrable.

BOOK SECOND.

The

Philosophy of History.

SYLLABUS.

Having become acquainted somewhat with historics, the fundamental principles of our philosophy we are prepared to consider the construction of history as exhibiting these principles.

The first of the seven divisions, into which the data of the second book arrange themselves will be given to a survey of those regions in which, according to the ethnographic material found there, history had its beginnings.

As soon as the race-enters upon its stage of action, the first indications of a universal polarity, agitating it, become noticeable and are to be scrutinised. This will at once put us in the position from which we may view the first of our three concentric circles of nations.

We look upon the scenery where history performed her first great feats with least ostentation. Here the broad ground-works of future complications come in sight ; for out of the obscurity of prehistoric eons in which time and eternity seem to be mixed up in the dense vapors of a Tohu Vabohu there protrudes, distinct enough, the fundamental masonry of the structure. Its Cyclopean massiveness is to a great extent impenetrable to scientific research. Yet this much becomes apparent, that the race then already was subject to the law of polarity. The systematic workings of this law are intimated by the curves and courses of the substructure. The same strained condition, we may say "polar tension", is observable which henceforth always exists and produces the contrasts between the Oriental and Occidental nations.

Under "polar tension" that historic strain may be denoted, which is caused by such contrasts of matter and mind previously referred to, or by such characteristic opposites as the one here pointed out.

(1.) Taking our position upon the great divide which the Asiatics up to date call "the Roof of the World", we distinguish between Turano-Mongolo-Malayan nations of the East, and the Ugro-Tatarians of the West. The right wing consists of the aborigines of China, Tibet, and the coasts of the Pacific, America included. The left reaches across Siberia, out to the Finns and Lapps of Europe. Their common center is the high plateau of Central Asia. Africa is irrelevant as yet to history, only serving as a dumping-ground, as it were, for fragments of different peoples, the scattered elements of which occasionally react across the northern and eastern borders.

This outlines the widest compass of ethnological propædeutics.

The eastern part of the first great circle of our race leads but a vegetating existence, so to say; its natural temperament represents feminine passiveness, whilst in the western part virile characteristics of personal and energetic aggressiveness prevail. All these nations lead a nature-bound life, bearing the impress of their physical environments more marked than the few features of spiritual qualifications.

The use of the word "nature-bound" may be permissive for conditions of human life, where, through neglect of cultivating the mind, man allowed himself to remain under the bondage of natural necessity, instead of entering upon his career of spiritual development, so that this side of personal life became arrested.

(2.) An equal ethno-psychical contrast determines also the next smaller circle. The people constituting it progressively enter upon a most promising career. This second circle comprises the Indo-Germanic people—the Aryans. With them again we have a right and a left wing, which are each subdivided into northern and southern counterparts. To the right wing belong the inhabitants of Iran, and those of the Indus and Ganges regions ; to the left the Germanic nations and those of Græco-Roman culture. In the reciprocal irritation, reaction, and augmentation of energies, the strain of opposition, i, e. the ethnical polarity, here again produces those distinct features of history, which we associate with the presentations of Oriental and Occidental life.

(3.) Then follows the third and innermost of the concentric circles under Roman dominion It represents a basin in which all the ethnical elements of the ancient times flow together, and where the ever agitating polar forces are discharged into the bulk, so as to prepare a new order of human affairs.

(4.) The fourth division will then demonstrate that the course of events arrived at the turning-point of history. The opposing principles now cross, pervade, penetrate, and neutralise each other. We find ourselves in the midst of contrasts—upon the historic height of many disclosures where the hidden theme assumes plastic form. The key is given which opens the reality of things anticipated. Light is thrown upon the retrospect and upon the prospect of the ultimate issues. After looking up from physical life and looking back from personal life fully realised, reviewing the postulates and forebodings of the mind in all directions, and seeing the union of spirit and matter completed, we will become convinced that the solution of all problems is found, and that our axioms are affirmed.

A new factor now enters into the life of mankind. It is the pneumatic principle which henceforth works through history, aiming at the realisation of human destiny. This new efficient is imparted from the higher sphere. It had been typified by surprising phenomena at every new stage of development, even in the evolution of the natural world. In ascending lines and cycles this principle of personality and perpetuity affects the human masses one by one, attracting, influencing, uniting them and all their further relations.

(5.) In the fifth division the gradual permeation of humanity with the new power, proceeding from the center, begins to work toward the periphery of the three concentric circles. This gradual expansion corresponds in reverse order to the former narrowing down of the cultural progress. This newly engrafted energy, this life proper, had appeared concentrated and intensified in the One in whom the realm of unity and perpetuity centers. From His immediate surroundings a unique influence now expands over the entire mass mixed together in the Roman basin.

(6.) The sixth division again reviews the second of our concentric circles as brought under the transforming activity of the new leaven. Again we meet those kindred people who in the remote past already sustained that polar tension between the oriental and the occidental modes of thought. The leaven now works throughout the whole lump, until every branch of the Indo-Germanic race is enlisted in the movement and therein recognises its special task and destiny. By virtue of the new life the cultivation, not only of the natural forms of existence, but also of the spiritual side of life, in the special sense, aspires to higher attainments. Man becomes conscious of the full value of a person and begins to prepare himself and nature for a still higher form of existence.

(7.) With personality enfranchised, the task of humanity is fully understood. Man as co-worker with God spreads the new life to the countries of the largest circle and penetrates the broad, massive substratum of arrested human life. This, the seventh division will show as the work to be executed in the present age. The thought realised upon yonder highland in that year, which is the pivot-point of the times, in deep condescension, in the form of history condensed,—this thought now manifests the most expansive power; it becomes world-embracing, world-transforming.

Human life in its most sacred relations is now unfolding, whilst the sharp contrasts of dark shadows also extend. The organisation of the realm of consistent unity, harmonious continuity, and spiritual personality is initiated. The goal before us is the consummation of the Good, the True, and the Beautiful in the final process of transfiguration to perfection and glory. This will be the theme of the closing part.

The original intent to elevate and deliver confined life penetrates into the same life universal, from which we saw history emerge in the first division. When the end aproaches the purpose again surpasses the sphere of empirical investigation: it transcends scientific research. As it was at the beginnings of history that prophetic vision alone could see the dim, prehistoric past of which the mind had retained only faint recollections,—so the ideas about the future, floating in the mind, as yet scarcely more than intuitive presentiments and anticipations, can only be conjectured from analogies in nature and history. For, tho this mysterious future transcends our present understanding, yet it does not entirely lie beyond our ideal apprehension. In the seventh division we merely present the fact that these ideas of origin and destiny are ever present in human life, as proofs of the fact that history actually ever moves at the threshold of that grand consummation of all purposes, which is indicated by all analytic and synthetic thought. The new energy of the spiritual stimulus, transmitted to, and taken up by, the masses of people in the widest circle pushes onward until it encompasses the periphery in an unbroken line. This activity seizing nature-bound people and delivering them from the long confinement of arrested life makes it evident, that they now joyfully partake thereof; this activity, which thus signalises the approaching completion of the purpose of history:—is nothing but the extension and multiplication of that solvent power of affinity which rests in the centre.

In a brief resume let us review this development with reference to the Histories in Book First. Let us take a glance over the plan of our arrangement which we judge to be clearly indicated by the data actually at hand.

Three orders of self-culture in a concentric progress of preparation rotate around the center. The most distant circle and most obscure culture extends farthest into the dim horizon. The uniary and unique center, the great point of gravity, comes to view as the apex of the broad substructures, and as the synthetical oneness of all preceding centripetal movements. This unit proves itself to be the climax of true life intensified, and as the purpose in the concrete.

IIc is the life of humanity personified, the project of human destiny substantiated, consecrating himself to the satisfactory solution of all truly human problems. He is fully able to ameliorate all earthly conditions, consequently qualified to impart the new principle, i. e. the thought and will from above. This perfect personal life thus becomes the well-spring of the new issue. It seizes the narrow, nearest circle in its preparatory state of culture, in order to lead from thence upward. Gradually spreading, the forces augment while permeating and influencing the second circle. Personality develops in due relation to its arche-type, until the idea of a new, and universal humanity prevails.

The members of this truly human family in concurrence and cooperation with the central unit of the world of "formal unity" assume the work of freeing those nature-bound remainders of humanity from their arrested state of life, which constitute the largest, heaviest, most distant and dead-like orbit. All along the lines of advance the new principle becomes acknowledged as the radiant center; as the One substantialised in a generic new race; as the One who always had been the hidden proto-type and is now the sum and substance of all truth and all life, i. e. of reality itself.

The following exposition must justify our arrangement of the historic contents. It must appear, whether the disposition of the material is made to order for the sake of some invented plan and then artificially imputed to history; or whether history actually moved in these concentric, upward and downward cycles, in which each human being is carried along, tho revolving upon its own axis and in its own course. It must become evident, whether history is here constructed to suit an erratic, private orbit, or whether history itself brought along the reason, the material and the method.

The plan is so lucid, that it may easily be shown, whether such interpretation of history's revelations is forced or fanciful; or which of the data, adduced as empirical testimony, witnessing the truth, would have to be challenged, or be thrown out as an interpolation.

A. FIRST DIVISION.—SUBSTRUCTURE OF HISTORY.

FIRST CIRCLE: TURANO-MONGOLO-MALAYAN NATIONS.

May the comparison of history to a theatre, where the drama of the world is given and repeated, hold good once more. First in order, then, will be an inspection of the foundations of the building itself. After this the construction of the stage in its natural sequence will be described. The wide firmament will form the back-ground, our globe the solid play-ground. Here the natural conditions will be outlined. Then humanity in general, as a unit, is to be comprehended. The great enigma of history, the bad, must not be overlooked. The diversity of the human race is to be rendered intelligible. This multiplicity of nations will at the same time bring us face to face **Polar tension. Sec. 22.** with the law of polarity. The "polar tension" displays its power in the array and contrast of those peculiarities, by which fractional parts of the race either regulate or outbalance each other, conditioning thereby in a great measure all future activity, and directing the march of progress.

Upon the basis here indicated we must pursue the investigation to the point where the broad stratum of the Turano-Mongolian peoples assumes a definite shape. **Importance of this** We have to take better notice of all this, than has been done heretofore, because the **mass of peoples not** substratum in its wide range bears strong relations at every point to the historic **sufficiently considered by science heretofore.** structure built upon it.

CH. I. DESCRIPTION OF THE SCENERY ; CELESTIAL BACKGROUND.

§ 26. Entering the proscenium upon which the human race is to act its first role, we find the curtain down. Nevertheless, we may examine the external equipments, and even endeavor to search into the hidden scene. What we metaphorically call the opera-house is the place for the people who were actors without knowing it, and at the same time spectators without understanding what was going on. What we call the structure of the great edifice includes those manifold conditions in the midst of which our earth is situated. In order, therefore, to understand the mighty preparations, we have to consider a series of influences, which are as yet almost incommensurable, which however interweave themselves with the civilisation of the entire world.

Humanity as well as man individually forms the apex, as it were, of a pyramid resting below in broad extent upon earth, and at the same time reclining, as seen from every side, against the starry sky. Or rather: Man in his earthly appearance is the center and partly the result of the enormous periphery of the whole universe.

We are in the same perplexity as the Ægyptologist, who, unless he brings the constellations of the heavenly world into relation with those funeral piles upon the borders of the desert, is unable to interpret the full meaning of these monuments. In other words: We must look at man and his history not only with reference to his earthly transient situation, but also with respect to his position in, and relation to, two worlds.

Says Walter Scott:" Do not Christians and Heathens, Jews and Gentiles, poets and philosophers unite in allowing the starry influences?"

Without emphasising the fact admitted on every side, that the world is appropriated by the human mind wherever the cosmos is reflected in reason; and without laying much stress on the fact that man, the microcosm, is a combination of all elementary components of the universe; and not deeming it necessary to refer to a third fact of the influence exerted by the skies upon history, in handing down from heaven the measure of space and time, and in conditioning the distribution and development of our race:—there yet remains another view to be taken of human life. There are problems concerning the relations between personal life and the physical skies which reach far beyond the facts mentioned. But our present surview compels us to postpone the consideration of that aspect,which takes account of those cosmical relations of our planet whereby our lives are but indirectly influenced.

The effects of sun and moon upon the electric currents, encircling and affecting the globe, are established beyond doubt; so are the interferences of forces from both of these bodies with the tremendous convulsions going on within the thin crust of our earth.

The billows of lava belching forth from subterranean depths, and the undulations of the atmospheric shell, depend as much upon the cyclical return of astral perturbations as the tidal waves. In occurrences of this kind, in volcanic eruptions, the mechanism of the laws and the regularity of their effects are apparent, altho hidden by the variety of the phenomena and by their sudden changes and incomputable intervals.

All this, however, does not cover what we understand by the central position of man in the universe. It all merely shows, how man with his history and the visible universe are committed to one another and mutually related.

When Krause lectured on the Philosophy of History, he, in his pensive manner, spoke of our human race as being merely a "part of humanity." Mankind on earth, our empiric humanity, did not satisfy him. He held, that Universal History necessarily transcends mundane existence. To him it resembled a turning wheel. The starry world formed the rim; and the stars he imagined to be inhabited by human beings in various stages of perfection. A grand apperception; a pity only, that it is an idea with no more probability of realisation, than the idea of establishing communication with the man in the moon.

Dismissing the claim upon a star for a man's future dominion may seem unfavorable to his central position; it seems to become weakened more yet under the impression, of which we can not rid ourselves altogether, that between the enormity of the solar and astral systems and the insignificance of our diminutive world, there exists such a contrast in quantity, as to render the role we play upon our scene of action a paltry affair. This is one of the incitements of thought to arise and show itself equal to the occasion; to exercise its power in the mastery of physical magnitudes and in manifesting itself as more than their equivalent; to outbalance the vast-ness of bulk and dimension so oppressive to our feelings.

Thus our problem reaches farther than the cosmical conditions alluded to. The "Natural Philosophy" of former times took its ease in contemplating man as the "Microcosm". He was estimated as being the heart and center of the visible universe, the entire macrocosm in miniature.   The radii of the stellar orbits concentrate in him; the planet moves and forms its constellations in his behalf; it fondles and feeds him.   Resting upon alchemy and soaring up to astrology this science of nature from its heights of attainment looked down upon the compound of the elements as upon one grand, unitary and animated body.   With the glittering stars on high as well as with the sparkling crystals, and with the brilliant, precious metals deep in the bosom of the rocks man converses and stands connected as by magic.   Innumerable junctures and ominous cycles, represented in the Zodiac and Kabbala symbols, and secret forces seeking and fleeing each other: all form a mys-terious nervus rerum which is imagined to connect that one animated and resounding body.   Such were the endeavors of thought to find the total differential and counter-poise in the interest of burdened feelings.

Man and the universe as contemplated by the "natural philosophy" of by-gone times.

Resume of the ancient oriental conjectures about man as being really the Microcosm. PARACELSUS, AGRIPPA VON NETTESHEIM, FLUD. JACOB BOEHME, KEPLER.   Sec. 130.

It was no mean superstition that made the Magi of old follow the star of Bethlehem. And if those were superstitious notions to which Paracelsus, Agrippa von Nettesheim, and Robert Flud were addicted, when in simplicity of heart and integrity of purpose they searched for the "philosopher's stone," they ought to be praised, rather than upbraided. This trio simply drew the sum total of oriental intuitions, when they outlined cosmical life by geo-metrical figures or kabbalistic buffoonery. The rays of the stars were forced down to man to focus in him; and man made the best possible use, under the circumstances, of these scanty lines of light in order to reach up into the stars—by force of magic, if not by virtue of thought. People conversant with the art in which Jacob Boehme excelled, set up the figure of man in the midst of the zodiac belt; and then—by lines drawn from the signs and constel-lations wherein each planet stood toward each corresponding organ and mood in the human body—they would establish connections with the feelings and fates of a poor little heart. In this manner Kepler set the horoscope for Wallenstein, and figured out the emperor's "nativity."

Kabbala Zodiac.

These attempts, upon the whole, were made to solve a great problem, indiscrim-inately formulated but vividly felt. They were philosophical experiments of a high order and of real merit. Using the incompetent means then at hand, these thinkers tried to bridge the awful abyss between astronomical expanse and human predica-ments in "close quarters." It was the unintentional and unconscious activity of the intellect to liberate feeling from the pressure of overwhelming immensities and dis-tances, and to assert the right of substituting qualities and values in the place of quantities. The weight of man was put into the scale opposite the gigantic masses and their embarrassing order, their stiff, chilling method.

Man's royal highness was to be exalted over the universe spinning through space. In a word, it was the search for the true position of man in contrast with mere nature ; the search, too, for freedom from an ecclesiastical providence which made man's dignity its game. Aspirations like these assuredly desire to be appreci-ated rather than to be derided. It is significant that by these very efforts more sci-entific gains were procured than some seem to imagine. Kepler, for instance, dis-covered the real transcendental equation, now known as the "Equation of the Center." The leading idea of all these speculations—more and more cleared of erroneous inci-dentals during the process—about the value of the mind in contrast to the bulk of matter, will maintain its right as long as science itself exists as the proof of this truth.

Attempts of the mind to gain its true position above nature. Philosophical experi-ments whereby Kepler discovered the "Equation of the Center."   Sec. 14, 42.

§ 27.   The cosmos presents itself as an admirable arrangement and systematic distribution of masses, moving in orbits of geometrical exactness, and concealing their perfect harmony under an artistic carelessness as to symmetrical order, whereby mechanical monotony is avoided. To admire and magnify it as reflecting the glory of the higher world, as the parabolical resemblance of the true altho transeunt reality is certainly not improper.   We take it, at any rate, as a system of substantialised thoughts sublime.

The cosmos as the reflex of the higher world of true reality, as a system of substan-tialised thought.

There are eternal laws of life at work (regulating the polarity of potential energies along with the relations procured thereby) known as the "Universals", or as the a priori cognitions tabulated in Kant's categories which determine our thinking, and which are innate in mind: eternal laws which operate with mathematical precision and with logical necessity, and which are imprinted also upon the cosmos in the forms of proportionate measures and weights, chemical affinities, animal instincts, etc.

Kant's categories regulative and eternal laws of life imprinted upon the cosmos.   Sec. 10, 15.

8

That is to say no more, however, than that this precipitate of thought into which we can see, is nothing but matter in dead motion. It is blind nature tied up to necessity, altho reflecting the mind outside and above it. The universe as the product of the nascency of nature is not a creation of unrestricted life, but of the strained contrasts which cause the phenomena of polar tensions. This explains why the contemplation of the masses above, if stripped of their poetical lustre of being glorified worlds of light, fills man with awe and consternation. Pondering over that sway of domineering legality, stringent order, and blind necessity, man at first becomes dizzy and confused. Looking into the distance of space, discovering ever new worlds in boundless expanse, he arrives at a point, where the understanding comes to a standstill. This incomprehensible realm seems continually to reproduce itself out of the nascency of the world-ether.

Yet we insist upon the fact that this totality of nature is in itself but elementary stuff in dead motion; it is proved to consist everywhere of the same substance. The galaxy as well as the most distant asteroids and nebulae shining through the galaxy from the farthest depths of space, are all composed of the same materials as the street we are passing. Spectroscopic analysis has established this beyond controversy, since it initiated the "chemistry of the heavens."

* The atmosphere of the sun has been proven to contain zinc and copper; that of the fixed star Adebaran, quicksilver and tellurium. The spectroscope has revealed the fact that nebulae, which were a standing puzzle up to present times are nothing but masses of burning gaseous substances. This visible universe thus presents itself as a fabric of incessant formation. There is no void in space; everywhere things are generating and passing away; passing into transition and reproduction, compactness and explosion, concentration and combustion. The history of the cosmos with all its splendor comes under the heading of dead motion. And this commotion of masses in space remains to us as incomprehensible as space itself. And a star is to all appearances a lonely deserted portion of space, not to say a gloomy waste, evidently not a suitable dwelling-place for angels.

But will not such an assertion have to be taken as a reproach against the eternal wisdom of God, if life in the common-sense use of the term, if animation is denied to the multitudes of stars? if they have to be conceived as purposeless? The emptiness of such a universe in the vast expanse of which our earth should whirl around without neighbors fit for companionship may become oppressive indeed. It seems harmless and preferable to imagine, that, if not goddesses, at least creatures inhabit these worlds: now astral ghosts, now angelic beings. But these suppositions were not quite so harmless in times past; and a certain amount of danger is still lurking in such fancies.

The error of such imaginary reasoning originates in the poor, mechanical presupposition that this visible universe, our cosmos, was all that had been created. A part was taken for the whole. May it not be possible, even probable, that the universe, including the most distant star-heaps, is to be conceived as a fraction only, a diminuitive world, as compared with worlds beyond? The averment that our visible universe is unlimited and the single one, is to be taken for what it is worth: as an arbitrary and gratuitous supposition by which to prop another unprofitable hypothesis. For, scientific bearing it has none. Against the truth that this world is ours, no objection on the ground of its being the only and limited world, could stand the test. If raised it could in no manner shake our dogma, viz: that man is the blossom and crown of creation; and that for his sake the earth, altho not as to its quantity and astronomical position, yet with respect to its purposive significance is really the center of all created worlds, of the entire universe.

We take it for granted and sufficient for all practical purposes, that this visible world is that of man, that it belongs to him; that around him and his secret the cosmos revolves. A transient cloud-picture in the clear firmament is as nothing compared with the extended blue background. Just as insignificant may this visible universe be, when compared with the impenetrable invisible world.

If we may venture to suppose the possibility, at least, of a similar difference between the cosmos and the invisible world then the solitude of our little earth will be less awful, tho this small planet alone be inhabited by rational beings.

If from a certain fear of loneliness we would reject this hypothesis, then we would be moved to awe none the less by the sands of the Sahara, each grain of which forms an unintel-

The cosmos as the precipitate of thought: in itself but matter in dead motion.

The entire universe, despite its awful vastness and glory and nascency, consists of mere stuff in dead motion.

Spectroscopic analysis proves it to be the world of "material unity."

Samples of the "chemistry of the heavens."

The hypothesis of inhabitability of the stars not harmless.

The hypothesis of a limitless, unitary, and inhabitable universe unprofitable.

The visible finite world a small part of the invisible; yet the center of the created universe, which is limited by the invisible.

The earth is man's own, as the universe belongs to him.

The invisible world influences the visible in equal manner as creation influences man.

ligible and to all appearances purposeless particle. Amazement at each armor-scaled infusorium of the genus foraminifera of which the chalk formation in the cretaceous strata consists; or at the compressed ferns and other cryptogams of the primeval world, which form layers like the lignite-bearing beds on the Pacific coast, and like the Appalachian coal-fields of 50000 and 60000 square-miles respectively-would be just as justifiable, as our astonishment at an empty, useless star.

Immensity is a mere relative conception. The hugeness of the heavenly bodies can no more be compared with the smallness of our earth, than the Himalayas with a human brain. In order to make comparisons, we need a standard measure for magnitudes; we ought to agree, first, upon what is to be called magnificent. A microscopic object may cause admiration as profound as another, discovered through the telescope. Perhaps the standard of greatness wanted is hidden in the lens through which we look, after all. The splendor of starlight above our heads glittering through incommensurable distances, and the unlimited throng of luminous jelly-fishes (medusae lucernuridae) glistening upon the briny deep below our keel, will make it difficult to decide, whether the greater or more astonishing facts of natural science are found above or below.

Yet both these worlds, the starry sky full of brilliancy and mysteries, and the wonderful deposit of organic life, reduced to an inorganic world, are made of the same structure, an entity of homogeneous elements.

For the sake of argument we might enlarge upon a notion of Hegel, corroborating our view. He was of the opinion that the earth is the most concrete, and in its kind the most exalted member of the cosmical organism, of this visible universe. But since this opinion, if pushed to a conclusion, would fall in with the cosmogonies of ancient traditions, we will not commit ourselves to it.

Upon the earth, small as it is, mighty commotions have been and are still going on, in which the entire universe cooperates as the concomitant,   to which it renders the background. More than that. The whole periphery and background with all their spheres are engaged in the upbuilding of the human body. This is formed under influences from very distant environments not less than from the terrestrial world around us. Thus heaven and earth assist in the formation of universal history. The cosmos furnishes the stage, and portions out the duration of seasons, periods, eons. This universe being that of man, makes his story universal history indeed. It is this which requires our attention; hence we hasten to get away from yonder expanse, where poetic fancy loves to roam, but thought declines to follow.

CH. II. THE STAGE SCENERY OF HISTORY—TERRESTRIAL BACKGROUND.

§ 28. If we have not succeeded in bringing out the invisible celestial world as the corollary of the visible universe; if we dare not flatter ourselves to have demonstrated the excellency and importance of our planet as its center, purpose and issue, for whose sake all the astronomical constellations take place in order to serve as chronometers and to disclose the first principles of mathematics—we may yet entertain the hope of having secured a greater esteem for, and to have excited some higher expectations with reference to, our little planet and its marginal average, as compared with the immensity of the astral display.

We will for a moment present to our minds that gigantic nebular ball which arose in La Place's imagination.

From that gaseous globe, by force of its rotation, one part after another became detached and was thrown out into space. Each of these projectiles continues to whirl around, condensing and rounding itself, under the law of gravity. Each in order to concur in the rhythmical dance of the spheres, is kept in perpetual eliptical motion by reciprocal attraction, proportional to the quantity of matter and the squares of distances. Their interdependence does not forbid ensuing subdivisions.

Thus the solar system is,—owing to Herschel's affirmations and to the proofs of the spectroscope—despite the exceptions taken by Ross,—generally acknowledged to have originated, under such separations, and the differentiation to have been thus animated, of which the multiplicity of nature's formations are the copies and final results. Hence the "material unity under formal diversity."

Concerning our earth, which now alone interests us, we adopt, for argument's sake, this theory of its gaseous origin. Heat diminishes, some elements enter new combinations, new conditions multiply. Complex portions become solid and separate

Fixed tendency of nature to develop from unity into the manifold.

or protrude from the gaseous mass according to their more liquid or more solid shapes. The first heterogeneity signifies the beginning of the formative process, that is, of differentiation. It becomes the fixed tendency of nature to develop out of the oneness into the manifold.

Gases moving into new relations generate what now is discovered to be "liquid air." The fluids, being heavier, gravitate to the center of the spheroid. The gaseous remainder escapes from the nucleus, which cools off and contracts. Chemical affinities are on the increase. Sidereal changes occasion upheavals, ruptures; and torrents of the liquids rush to

Formation of our globe.
Werner.

and fro, especially when mountains rise and immense areas of oceanic bottoms suddenly sink. Such are the rudimentary premises of the generally accepted or, at least, most popular geogonic interpretations. From this stage of geognosy let us follow the course of Werner's

A. v. Humboldt,
L. v. Buch.

arguments, which were but little modified by those of A. v. Humboldt and Leop. v. Buch. It describes a mode of slower formation.

Genesis of the globe.

At the bottom of the liquid which covers the nucleus, the promiscuous mass of a stony precipitate stretches forth. New driftings form upper strata whose pressure upon the lower causes them to harden into crystalline stratifications. The flowing waters carry together homogeneous matter. The elements find and bind, flee and free, and amalgamate with, each other.

Intermingled matter is gradually transformed into solid combinations. A kind of fermentation agitates the masses. Pressure, then counterpressure is exerted. The granite crust warps, it bursts. Furrows open, folds double up. Mountain ridges are lifted up, whilst below the labor of stretching and rising continues. Transverse folds ensue so that the backs of mountains are broken and cross-ridges, passes, and gorges, and valleys are formed thereby. The steepest peaks and wildest ravines alternate where the most primeval layers are lifted highest and do not furnish loose material enough to fill up the gaps.

The gases and waters also continue their transitions. Rains and floods wash out watercourses. For many centuries glaciers convey and deposit moraines, which are now high plateaus. The mountain chains stretch away from east to west on the eastern, and from north to south on the western hemisphere. The austere "Rockies" and the Alpine systems, owe their origin to the mechanical and subtile movements of crystalline formation; while the rugged Cascades owe theirs to sudden and more recent eruptions.

The fact is, that water and ice had more to do with the formation of the present surface of the earth than subterranean fires; that the expansion and warping of the crust was a more indirect result; and that sudden volcanic eruptions are not the rule, being as a general thing of rather local occurrence, as, for instance, those convulsions which must have taken place around the Pacific Ocean.

The earth's history repeats itself in history proper; but no further than what human biology is involved in the nasceney of nature.

Thus we see the ground coming forth into daylight, preparatory to higher and ever more selfdifferentiating forms of being. We refrain, however, from tracing out the formation of human history as if it were analogous to that of the structural universe. The earth's history repeats itself no further in history proper, than human biology is involved in the nascency of nature.

Such construction has been tried and history trifled with. Here and there we shall not hesitate to allude to the analogies, whenever the process of natural development bears upon both nature and history, with sufficient importance or real congruity as to justify their being noted.

§ 29. The foundation of the theatre of history is laid deep and stands firm. The great partitions, those mountain ranges between which the life of the nations is to move, the coulisses from which the actors enter, are erected.

The globe firm, its surface still changing.
Ritter, Lyell.

But the earth is, to say with Carl Ritter, "a cosmic individual designed for progressive development." Hence we, too, proceed. After the main formations were completed and the continents delineated, a series of finishing touches are discernible.

Lyell (taking Europe alone into consideration!) speaks of a "First Continental Period" when the mainlands were higher and extended farther into the seas. A period of general sinking seems demonstrable in which many islands were separated from continents. The depression was, however, more general than Lyell thought; and it must have taken place even at the ocean bottoms. The very large basins of greatest depth must have sunk so abruptly as to suddenly drain the continents by roaring floods and thus considerably tear them up.

This must have happened before the "Glacial period," i. e. Lyell's "Second Continental Period," set in. New elevations cause the reunion of some islands with their mainlands. Isthmuses emerge from the floods and connect continents. Glaciers spread themselves here and recede there; one-half of what are now the United States is buried under moving ice-fields.

Changes of even the surface in the second and through the fourth or Glacial period up to the "stone age."

It seems strange, but it has been ascertained even in America, that the traces of the elephant and the hippopotamus, and even man, are to be assigned to this period. Up to the fourth period various detachments of islands, climatic changes, etc., are caused by the sea-currents being changed, the sea-bottoms subsiding and the sea-coasts being submerged. Tranquil and slow as such changes continue, and little as the present condition differs from that of the lake dwellers in the pile-villages—who are said to have had their time in the "stone age," at least five thousand years ago—the quiet procedure of similar changes is still observable.

Let those whom it pleases not seek other explanations for paleontological or paleonto-
graphical and geographical problems. Let the question be discussed whether water or fire
took the most important part in preparing our scenery. Answers to these inquiries are of
little consequence to the problem now before us.

All that we are concerned with is a definite cognition of the labor of progressive
differentiation. If we may compare the body of the earth, as it surmounts the level
of the ocean covering two-thirds of the surface and articulating the continents, with
the organism of the human body, then we are justified to speak of continents as
members and organs by means of which the earth-body performs its part in the task
of universal history.

The labor of progressive differentiation.

History is interested in the formation and articulation of the earth's surface, so far only as conditions of human life are determined thereby.

The formative or constructive principle, i. e. the thought underlying our corporeal structure, can not be understood, unless we learn for what purpose and functions the parts or organs are intended. So the thought which underlies the formation
of our globe becomes intelligible as soon as we learn to appreciate the historical
significance which the continents bear by virtue of their position and natural characteristics.

Geographical articulation of the earth's surface is, like that of our body, only explicable from their historical importance.

Hence we now contemplate the teleological significance of our terrestrial scene
of action.

Teleological view upon the geographical differentiation of the earth's surface.

According to Ritter, again, the course of history is prescribed by the given situations and relations to geographically divided space. He undertook to prove "the possibility of predicting the progress of every nation as modified by the region it in-
habits." "Only upon the appointed soil is that welfare obtainable which fate, eternal
and just, has put in store for every loyal people". So much for the teleology
of the geographer. The fallacy of such sanctimonious effusion results from a
lack of insight. The fact is overlooked, that the natural grounds of national development are nowhere and no longer the original and normal conditions. And it is just
this difference between original and present geographical conditions which we ought
to consider, for it is indicated on every side. Teleological contemplation is valuable
only in proportion to the modesty of its expectations. Thought (and the wish fathering it) must not undertake to prove too much.

Ritter's overzealous teleology; not considering the changes of the geographical conditions.

Asia at one time extended a great distance farther east, and was also more closely contiguous to Malayan India than at present; for the South Sea of China seems to be a more recent depression. A series of open questions startles us at the very beginning of our inquiry
for original conditions. We see that we must reckon with, at the least, variable quantities,
tho we thought the basis of the earth's history to stand so firm.

Original shape of Asia.

Capeland was by Hooker recognised as a primeval and independent island, annexed to
Africa only by the subsequent alluvions which made the continent grow toward the south.
We have, on the other hand, a number of main-lands, the greater Antilles for instance, which
become islands by the subsiding and receding coast of their continent, the very coast which
previously had been the interior country of South America. The Po and the Adigo have, in
almost imperceptible manner transformed the old sound between the Alps and Apennines into
very fertile lowlands. So have Volga, Nile and Mississippi created large plains for pastoral
tribes and for organised and powerful nations. The coasts of the Scandinavian peninsula are
perceptibly rising whilst the opposite Prussian low-lands are sinking into the Baltic. The
symmetrical arrangement of circles of volcanic islands under the very remarkable circumstance, that most of the volcanoes are situated in rows which often exactly correspond to the
curves of eruptive quakes; the Cordillera-like chains of atolls; and many other phenomena
indicating method in their occurrence, present perplexing conundrums to a teleological view
of geography.

Hooker on formation of Africa.

Conundrums of teleological geography.

§ 30. Teleology thus stands with us before an incessant restlessness and transformation. It is selfevident that symmetrical shape in the articulation of continents
attracts the attention and incites speculation as to the import upon the life of their
inhabitants. Let us look upon some of the most striking features of this kind.

Instances of remarkable symmetry in geographical data which must not be pressed teleologically.

A diagonal line drawn through the Isthmus of Suez across the middle of both
the African and Asiatic continents, forms a very suggestive axis for both of these
grand parts of the world, which, because of their connection by the narrow strip
between the two great gulfs, may well be considered as one continent like the two
Americas. And a line cutting the latter lengthways will show a similar division
into equal parts of area on both sides.

African-Asiatic axis.

Similar division of the two Americas.

Now both of these lines may have a bearing upon the condition of the inhabitants; but their significance does not lie in their symmetry.

Historical significance not in the geographical symmetry.

What in these geographical profiles we fancy to find as being symmetrical, we rather ought to conceive as such ingenious strokes which we notice in the sketch of an artist, who does not care for details, but is certain of thus representing the character of the whole, and who is sure of his success in expressing the ideal conception which stands out plastic before his mind.

Under this proviso we admit that geographical import is unquestionable, especially with that other axis formed by the portentous Asiatic-European mountain-system from the Biscayan gulf to the Amoor river separating the countries north and south. Posterior events render this axis of so great significance as to convey the idea, that it had been predestined as a means for very definite ends.

To the north of this mountain-axis there camps and wanders in the east, up to recent times in the west, too, a great variety of peoples, of barbarians, which history has passed by nearly unnoticed. To the south we clearly observe from the earliest times organical differentiations of one civilised people after an other. In the several well articulated countries on this side we admire now the ancient Asiatic culture, and then the all-controlling civilisation in the Mediterranean basin. And both of these have not ceased as yet to partake of the very perceptible polar tension, which seems to poise in this axis and which makes the heirs of these cultures divide among themselves the task of enlightening the world.

Equally important is that row of almost contiguous deserts, which stretches from the western coast of Africa far into China, running, in the main, south of, and parallel with, these mountains which cut the world in two. Bolor Tagh, the "Roof of the World", intersects that catena of deserts, which begins at Cape Blanco and extends to the steppes of the Obi, through the Gobi desert as far as the Amoor. Those deserts lie under zones of distinct and regular atmospheric currents. From the barren slopes of the gigantic partition-wall drifts of sand were carried away by the prevailing north-eastern trade-winds. Thus the plains were changed into desolate wastes, impressing their sterile nature upon the character of the people who also had drifted thither.

These natural conditions, caused by the wall and the winds, gave rise to those migrations, which like tornadoes, more than once, in a mad rush devastated countries and buried cultures under ruins.

The lofty crests and windy sand-oceans are of greater importance than merely to serve in dividing and differentiating nations or to form "dead" ethnical substrata. Such mountain heights possess a power of exerting not only direct influences, but also to cause and to control far-reaching effects.

The clefts into which they are torn, the storms and rains which they attract and curb, the waters which they send down in specific river-systems—all must help to create nations, to locate cities, to found or destroy empires, to stimulate national prosperity, to propel history. As in the case of mountains and deserts, so it is with the oceans. It will be advisable to adopt a division of the world's waters into three great basins with their annexes of seas, gulfs, and sounds, viz: the Atlantic, the Pacific, and the South Sea, each maintaining its more or less peculiar character. The other adjoining or surrounding waters are but inlets of these oceans. The Mediterranean for instance is an inlet of the Atlantic; nothing else is its other, the American Mediterranean, as Buffon named the Gulf of Mexico. With equal propriety may the third one, between Asia and Australia, be considered as a part of the South Sea. Each of these gulfs separates the main-lands of its vicinity in such a manner, that these countries severally seem to have been necessary as ethnographic mediums for both differentiations and connections.

There are reasons, indeed, to believe, that with the changes wrought upon the earth's surface, with the formation of coastlines, and with the increase of local modifications, there went on, simultaneously, the variegation of the fauna and the flora, together with the formation of the ethnical peculiarities of the inhabitants. The more historic coefficients, bound up in confined life, were set free, the more was this increasing variety enabled to further the independent development of specific nationalities, and to afford them bases and places for operation.

At this stage of the formation of the surface, when it is finally fixed so that the map of the earth presents its modern geographical accuracy, the geologist started in with his investigations.

To the historian the task begins when, upon the fundamental substructure for the theatre of history, the first man enters the scene. The further work, the rearing up of the historical superstructure, is given into his charge.

CH. III. REMNANTS OF PREHISTORIC MAN—LOCALITY OF HIS ORIGIN.

§ 31. Preceding considerations of the theme of history induced us to symbolise our synopsis of man's natural appearance by the figure of a pyramid resting with its base broadly upon the earth and its apex leaning against the sky. Equally descriptive will be the hollow, carved ivory ball of the Chinese which contains a number of other involuted spheroid shells, and by which they symbolise their conception of the universe and all that is going on in it. We may for once adopt the metaphor of three hollow, concentric or rather involuted spheroids of which the largest represents the astral, the narrower the mundane world, whilst the third and innermost represents man as the essence and center of both ; or, what is equivalent to it, the historic world, which is man unfolded, forms the third spheroid. We averred that man is the final and visible issue of both our external spheroids, under the proviso that his spiritual essence belongs to still another world, which, invisibly, and from an innermost and central source, pervades, transcends, and embraces all our spheroids.

For the present, however, we descend from these heights of ideal apperception and lay aside the crutches of metaphoric representation in order to resume the inductive method of viewing man as he really appears.

Geology presents us with fossil man. Here history finds the starting point.

As early (or as late) as 1863 Lyell made an index of the remnants of men found in the deluvian driftings.

They lie in the caves of Languedoc, firmly imbedded among the bones of hyenas and rhinocerotidæ. They lie in the caverns of Liege together with the remains of various extinct species of the fauna. Parts of the skeletons of seventy men are found in the cave of Aurignac together with flint-knives and tools made of bones of the cave-bear and the reindeer. All these and other circumstances indicate an exceedingly remote antiquity. The fact is corroborated, that man lived in Europe and perhaps in North America, too, contemporaneously with the elephant and rhinoceros, animals extinct long ago in those parts of the world.

There was a time, when the Vosges, the Peaks and Grampian groups were covered with glaciers. "Fossil man," so Fahlroth designated the find in the Neander-glen, may then have lived in proximity to these glaciers. Nobody can decide for or against this. But so much is certain that despite these late discoveries the search after the "connecting link" was in vain. It only became the more evident thereby that scientists made a poor show with the labored proofs deduced, rather inferred from cephalic measurements. That skull of Cannstadt, so much "monkeyed" with, has become valueless as regards the desiderata of extreme evolutionists, since it was sent from Stuttgart to Paris. The renowned "Neander skull" has been demonstrated by Virchow to be a malformation, an object of pathology of the same sort as the Shipka jaw-bone. On that score the investigators have good reason to coincide with Schottky: "Man's origin remains an unsolved riddle. Yea, the further we follow the earliest trace of the existence of our race, the less can the veil be lifted which obscures our view as to the descent of man."

Joh. Ranke affirms: "Among all the known parts of humanity of present times not one tribe, not an individual even, exists which, zoologically considered, could fairly be designated as the mean between man and monkey." If some would deem a witness like Virchow more authoritative, he too, may be quoted: "Man's existence looms up at the beginning of the quaternary (diluvial) period—for his existence in the tertiary (glacial) is not yet established. The oldest skulls extant show features of men, who, taking the lowest estimate, were in that stage of development in which we find the Papua or the Peshara upon Tierra delFuego. But however brutal the propensities of these lowest of our species, man is still man and never becomes an ape"—which according to the law of relapse into the original type of a genus would have to be the case.—All seeming transitory formations, those interesting digressions inside of the human type, are easily accounted for by science. They are either individual variations, or results of interbreeding" (of "natural selection ").

With concessions like these we may content ourselves. They will remain in force altho the man of the glacial or tertiary era should be unearthed, whereby self-knowledge would be neither advanced nor thrown back. For the whole argument proceeds from the unproved supposition that man gradually evolved in a rather subnatural than supernatural way from below; otherwise the controversy has no meaning. No other science would have dared to jump at such conclusions from a basis of evidence so meagre.

It is now denounced as an act of scientific violence, if a few utterly mutilated pieces are made to prove such a portentous assumption as the transition from ape to man, in exhibiting his descent.

Upon the whole, would it not be better to become interested in the **destiny of man** rather than thus to argue upon that sort of a **"descent of man?"**

Marginal notes:

Man based upon earth, leaning towards heaven.

Pyramid. Sec. 1, 23, 185, 204.

Emblematical representation of the Chinese conception of the universe.

Three spheroids representing the astral, the mundane, and the historic worlds. Sec. 221, 234.

Inductive investigation of man.

"Fossil man." Fahlroth.

Index of the remains found; made by Lyell.

Remote starting-point of history.

Schottky, J. Ranke, Virchow on "descent of man."

Man's existence in the tertiary period not established.

Rather think of destiny than thus argue about the descent of man.

The results of paleontological investigations become more marked as we approach the "lake-dwellers." It is known that the first discovery of this kind of evidence was made in Zuerich in the spring of '54. Seven years later Keller described the Celtic "pile-villages." Shortly after similar remnants were found everywhere; the "stone-age had been hit upon."

Stone weapons and utensils were, however, found only in the deepest layers "kjoekken-moedding." Above them bronze objects, and in the last layer on top of all iron tools were found.

It was a little preposterous to classify all culture in these three successive periods; but for central and northern Europe its prehistoric significance was clearly shown. The Danish explorers divided that age into pine, oak, and birch periods, as the layers seemed thus to concur with the stone, bronze and iron discoveries. Of course all of this systematising does not take away the difficulty of reconstructing distinct eras of universal culture with such spurious material as the kitchen-offal of the lake dwellers.

The one fact seems to be established by these discoveries that the lake dwellers were emigrants who imported ornamental objects from Asia. If we are allowed to utilise this, then we are justified in asserting that the mud-covered layers of the "kitten-mittens" of about ten feet of thickness originated in Abraham's time, and that at that time already commercial relations had been established between Ur on the Euphrates and the markets on the Thames and Clyde. There is no special ethnological reason why we should desire a definite era for the age of our race upon earth. It is scarcely worth while to mention that some scientists, for some reason or other, have very gratuitously thrown in millennia with liberal hands, where there was no demand for them. Unwittingly enough they imitated the childlike naiveté of the ancients in pretending to be very, very old.

When the durations of Ægyptian dynasties were to be ascertained, we had occasion to find out how chronologists blundered in putting contemporaneous reigns into successive instead of parallel series. We expect some more sobering up of chronological calculations.

Taking all facts together we will not be to blame for our satisfaction with the impartial judgment of E. v. Baer, who greatly limits the prehistoric age.

§ 32. Of far weightier import than chronological computations is the settlement of another question. A very limited space of time is at our disposal from which to determine the earliest history of mankind. The localities first occupied by the Oriental nations are almost unexplored as yet; so are the countries inhabited before the age and culture of the Aztecs.

Let us suppose that thousands of human skulls should be found at a thousand different places all over the earth; suppose that in a thousand other localities lake-dwellings should be discovered. What would it avail? Would it follow that many periods of cultural development independent of each other must be fixed? Would it follow that they corroborate the supposition, that the origin of man took place wherever the most favorable conditions existed, necessary for a very gradual evolution of animate life to such a degree? We can not understand the necessity of such an induction. At least we cannot see, that such a length of time and precisely such circumstances as the present, and such evolving as is inferred, are found in the nature of the case. Nor does this view explain a number of circumstances, as for instance, that we find people nearly void of any culture just where the most favorable conditions possible would lead us to expect the highest grade.

A much simpler explanation of the conditions and circumstances of man's origin would be obtained by inverting the case.

We would then propose, for argument's sake, instead of one thousand localities of such discoveries, or instead of five—one single fountain-head for the whole flow of human existence. From this single point we may, perhaps, be enabled easily to trace the courses, by which companies of people started out into the rounds of the earth. The elements take their rise from a single, clear source, then flow off and branch out in every direction; and each on its way, we are at liberty to think, partakes of so much of the peculiarities of the soil as to assume various tempers, various qualities and tastes, and even to change its color—all in accord with the various channels, basins and pools in which they run, appearing quite different from what each was at or near the pure, common fountain head. The problem of man's origin virtually stands as thus indicated, especially with reference to his first home. Altho much disfigured and decried, and in spite of all the learned efforts to discredit this aspect of the problem, it still stands in the midst of all the search for the data of the unity of humanity.

The main-land of "Lemuria", situated on the imaginary line from Madagascar to Sumatra, seems to have once been invented merely for the purpose of substantiating the hypothesis, that the primitive home of the Lemuridæ (those "ghost-like moving" semi-monkeys) may come handy to be utilised for the original home of man. Hence the Dravida, Papua, and African dwarfs were enlarged upon as being the lowest creatures in the human scale. By a turn of the hand the dexterous manipulator then patches together a fraternity of Lemurs, gorillas and men. It need not be demonstrated, that mental efforts like these are nothing but plays of fancy, which never ought to have been taken in earnest, and cannot be ranked with scientific hypotheses. This phantasm inadvertently reveals the feeling (and but for this reason we took notice of it) that a common center would be very welcome, from which the variety of species could be established, if such a center could be gotten up with some scientific decorum.

Place of origin.

"Lemuria" and descent from Lemurs.

One central common home a scientific postulate.

Th. Waitz.

At a conclusion much like ours did Waitz arrive, when in his "Anthropology of Nature-bound Nations" he speculated on the generic unity of all human races. He admits that a proposition like ours of one single fountain-head "presents less difficulties and has a greater inner consistency in its favor, than the opposite view of different originals".

Such corroboration is not necessary, however. We only need to follow the natural impulse of the human mind, which subordinates single facts in order to correctly understand them, to the concept of the whole, and whenever through this method inconsistencies are discovered, the mind is in doubt at once as to the truth of inferential judgments. The results of experience, moreover, do not offer any serious objection to our premise. We are confirmed in the truth that humanity is an oneness.

Humanity a connection not a collection.

§ 33. The next question is: How can humanity be reduced to a unit? If one should answer: from below, by way of several evolutions; or by creations, either successive at different places, or simultaneous; then we would have a mere collection instead of an organic connection—and this view would throw us back to the time before the guess at the abode of the Lemuridæ was made. Under this aspect an Ægyptian's idea of an Israelite being kindred to unclean beasts could scarcely be taken as an insult.

The oneness of our race, which humanitarianism needs as its first postulate, can not be maintained unless we answer: from above!

Sprung from a common center.

The unit is warranted solely, if humanity is conceived as having sprung from a common source of a generic vitality, altho this central starting point may have to be sought for. Until it is found we accept humanity as originally connected with such a center. In doing this we have, notwithstanding the various modifications of human nature, that unity in diversity which explains them all.

This proposition necessary for humanitarianism and for the explanation of unity in diversity.

Our very method of induction compels us to proceed by drawing inferences from definite empiric results. Combined correctly they place before us the secret of the locked synthesis. Thus we may be sure to have found the right key to the problem at the same time, as lock and key ever belong together. If by way of analysis and syllogising we arrive at the correct conclusion, then this conclusion will fit the keyhole. The lock, which contains the simple but ingenious and hidden lockwork of the full synthesis, and to which our key—i.e. the correct conclusion formed from the analytical judgments—belongs, will then easily open. The conclusion will prove the right key—that is, it will prove whether analysis and syllogism were correctly executed—if a slight touch of the key—i. e. a legitimate application of the conclusion—will disclose the secret of the locked synthesis. Whoever has come to know the combination, to him the synthesis proves to be the treasury contained in the safe which is found when disclosed to be filled with wealth and wisdom in which he is to share.

To restate the relation between induction and deduction, between analytical and synthetical syllogising in our philosophy without metaphor, we repeat: All the analytical data properly combined or generalised, either affirm or disprove the consistency of arguments and judgments derived from the special findings. Their true interpretation depends upon rendering their proper correlative bearing upon each other, and upon the general conclusion so cogent, that each judgment explicitly and without any contradiction yields a clear understanding of the adduced phenomena and incidents. The proof of their correctness lies in their common agreement with the synthesis, i. e. the formula and figure implying the ideality and reality of the facts and truths under consideration. This synthesis in turn yields adequate explanation and proves the soundness of the theory.

Digression on our method in the search for THE SYNTHESIS, Sec. 15, 77, 102, 105.

Unless we can thus reduce facts and reasons to plain unsophisticated and practical knowledge, enabling us to engage in making the experiments and tests, our final conclusion is wrong, and the syllogising needs a revision along the whole line of phenomenal empirics and logical comprehension.

As the legitimate conclusion derived from all the premises we posited the unity of the race. The binding force of this conclusion awakens the anticipation that it will also serve as a resolvent. Our conclusion will show how it unites the results of analysis and induction into a round synthesis which under the process of resolving analysis by way of deduction will stand the test. In order to become assured of the unchangeable truth and demonstrative force of our syllogisation we must be sure of its correct method. Then our science stands fortified, and the truth for which it contends will be proved both ways. To say that such comprehensive knowledge and convincing exposition of the subject under discussion were impossible—as Hamilton might be understood to advocate such affected modesty—betrays a desire to keep certain phenomena out of sight, or else an inclination to mental inertia. In the knowledge of what man is, all other knowledge is at stake. He is the key to history. Hence our zeal to arrive at a full understanding of man, which amounts to nothing more than true selfknowledge. The disclosure of history by the use of this key, i. e. the knowledge of man unfolded, means nothing less than the correct comprehension of the times in which we live. And such comprehension is the requisite for obtaining the proper world-consciousness, and for the adjustment of conduct accordingly, that is, for future wisdom, for "Applied Ethics."

CH. IV. ORIGINAL MAN. ONE COMMON SOURCE OF LANGUAGE, RIGHT, RELIGION.

§ 34. Our method compels us to found our reasoning upon the basis of assured empiric results. Aside from the previous consideration of the common origin, we are driven to the same conclusion of the unity of the race by some other premises and postulates which analysis furnishes. For as soon as we leave the field of paleontological discoveries we meet with new facts commanding our attention. The progressive development, attained when the present form of the earth was completed, now continues solely in the inner life of man. All development is now transferred to the invisible world of consciousness.

It is not within the range of our disquisition to prove language to be the dividing line between the brute world and the human. What is necessary concerning this, has been mentioned in histories. We now take language under the aspect of its cardinal importance to the history of mankind. Leibnitz was the first to call attention to this importance. It was thought that the classification of all languages into isolating, agglutinating, and flexible groups would explain the different descent of

the three races, the white, the yellow and the black. But it became evident that the peculiarities of the three chief families of languages indicated more than different degrees of mental training. A.v. Humboldt had already remarked, that the grammatical

aptitudes for construction are signs of certain stages of culture rather than of kinship. Right here we may insert what lies near and what A. v. Humboldt mentioned: "As incomplete as (isolated) languages at first glance seem to be when cut off from

outside influences, or as odd and capricious their structure may appear, they have certain analogies in common, nevertheless. These characteristics will be seen more clearly as philosophical insight and comparative philology approach perfection." Thus it was formally pointed out which way philological investigation is directed and, associated with competent philosophical scholarship, is bound to go.

In the latter part of our century Max Mueller's studies of the isolating languages followed in this direction and widely opened the way for the future labor in the field of comparative philology. In one of his Cambridge Lectures on the shifting relations of languages, after adducing examples of the softening of consonants, he emphasises the fact: "In proportion as we appreciate such changes of words we will become more competent to judge, whether we shall hereafter have a greater mass of testimony for the common origin of language."

We on our part are convinced of this common origin by force of the monosyllabic languages from which the others evolved, of these very isolating languages which only lately become known to us after they had attained their high state of inflections. Hence we are of the opinion that we only stand at the threshold of this new field of exploration.

"In order to understand language, says G. v. d. Gabelentz, in all its wealth of possible formations, we must take into the scope of our observation phonetic, metamorphologic and syntactic factors of all languages, besides the relation of each to the logical and psychological requisites of the mind in general."

Jaquet thinks as we do, that "the tendency toward concluding the unity of the race marks the present really philosophical method of ethnology." Ratzel ("Anthropo-geographie, Stuttgart '93,) says: "Every consideration again and again returns to the sapiens homo," and adds:

"If we succeed in proving the identity of the American Indians with the Asiatics, then the question of the unity or diversity of humanity is solved in favor of unity." This is now well nigh accomplished.

With reference to the requisites of the mind which Gabelentz alluded to, Hein lately spoke (in Vienna '91) about "Mœander crosses." Senf, in his review of the discourse, acknowledges their concurrence in all nations as shown for instance in the sun-signs and especially in the symbols of "life-giving,"—the Ankh in Rawlinson's Ægypt,—and he concludes: "The sameness of symbolism in all those nations of earliest culture is founded in the unity of the human race". We add that their common sense of symmetry points the same way. From the fact that the same mode of forming new words by prefixes, suffixes and affixes appears in all groups of languages, Prof. Fisk reasons, that such lingual idiomacy points to an essential oneness of the original language which is not explained by the mere participation of all men in the common mental endowments.

It concerns us to comprehend the various expressions of the one faculty of speech. This will not be possible before all the typical and most important languages have been fully indexed or "invoiced" as it were, and grammatically compared. Then only may we fix to a certainty that unitary original language into which the nine hundred languages enumerated by M. Mueller seem to be reducible. But here as everywhere formative thought is swifter than the analytical treatment of the necessary material. Thought runs ahead of a piece-meal collection of the material to be investigated. With the certitude which from the sum of two ascertained angles determines the adjacent third, do we from the ascertained empirical data anticipate a common and central source of languages.

It has been stated that the "rediscovery of Sanskrit had a resuscitating effect." As one electric discharge may isolate, combine or crystalise a chemical composition, so did the knowledge of Sanskrit bind its twenty-nine derivative languages together. Sanskrit became the center of affinity and the standard for systematising the meaning of roots; and was the thread which led out of the labyrinth.

With the deciphering of Sanskrit that composite synthesis was completed to which many antecedent facts had pointed as upon the binding key-stone. Because of this fact we feel justified to syllogise still further and to postulate that central mean of communication upon which the understanding of the chorus of lingual expressions depends. We anticipate a re-union meeting at a common source in which all misunderstandings and harsh dissonances shall be solved. We expect to hear some day, how all the discordant tones shall unite into a final harmonious accord. Then all the differentiations shall be reduced to the seven notes of the scale and the few letters of the alphabet, as it were, that is, to the simplified unity of the spiritual mode of converse. As from the composite thought of the synthesis we can interpret the particulars, so all languages receive their due significance as units of the lingual oneness, altho the latter is concealed as yet. M. Mueller somewhere dates the birth of the true idea of humanism together with the birth of philosophy as a science from Pentecost, where the ruptures began to heal, which the confusion of tongues had occasioned.

Since that time comparative philology, largely assisted by the Missionaries whose zeal was ridiculed only a hundred years ago, and along with missionary activity in general, made such strides, that Klaproth can now declare: "Universal kinship of languages is set in such clear light that we are compelled to accept their common source as an approved axiom."

The feeling of right is, no less than language, the common possession of all men, and a witness for our right to take humanity as a oneness, notwithstanding the fact that justice in the concrete nowhere exists ; at least nowhere does it appear as a unitary whole. Like language and unlike mathematics, justice never could embody itself so as to stand above the liability to err. Altho the idea of right has assumed the shape of a "practice", and realises itself everywhere in tangible and very empiric forms, yet it is not found anywhere, not even in an abstract form, as of worldwide and equally recognised authority. Forms of speech and tribunals of justice have both grown and become differentiated to a nicety in organisms of tribes, castes and states and in the midst of emerging and submerging events.

Right in the concrete exists nowhere on earth, yet it is present in the most diverse and modified constructions of the law everywhere as the same definite reality.

Religion will be found of equal weight with language and justice upon the problem of the unity of our race. We are not intent upon establishing a dogma as to the origin of religion, tho M. Mueller once thought he had a call to do something in that direction. It behooves history simply to reckon with the fact of its existence

According to all indications every detail in the life of the ancients was bound up in religion no less than parts of the life of modern nations. To explain its origin in this connection is only possible by venturing upon the way of hypothetical reasoning. Should we enter into the merits of the problem we would soon become convinced of the insufficiency of a theory which lets religion evolve from a defective intellect and from natural wants or fears, for the gratification or pacification of which "primitive" man should have conjectured higher beings or projected them from his own self. It is repeated (as if mere repetition were needed to strengthen the assertion) that man created the deity in the abstract out of his concrete gods, as if this were a matter too well settled and too antiquated as to go to the bottom of it. The matter was represented in such a manner, as that man thus overreached himself, outwitted himself, dreamt of a world of poetry and phantasy, and, if he did not lose himself in more abject superstition, gradually transferred the concept of his multiplying relations from the sensuous into the supernatural sphere. This is easily said and may all sound very rational. But a religion grown or built up in that way must be a frail thing, and would surely have disappeared entirely as soon as people had outgrown their childish notions ; it would have vanished with the very stage of culture which produced it.

It is rather questionable, moreover, whether childlikeness, if it ever existed in the quality required by the argument, would have created gods. Heman is right when he says : "Childlike it is of the negroes to shoot arrows against the eclipsed sun. But they do this not in order to please any higher powers, but to drive off the snake which, according to their phantasy, is trying to devour the sun". This, rather, is childlike.

To call upon the artist phantasy for assistance in explaining the origin of religion would be of little avail. Imagination can put together only such things of which it knows something beforehand. Imagination never surpasses the compass of perception. This goes no further than the visible world from which alone phantasy can draw the material for the patterns it weaves into its projections.

To aver that destitution was the cause of creating gods, would sadly reverse matters. The effect would be taken as the cause. Absence of resources of itself does not lead to any consciousness of the divine. On the contrary, it is simply the reminiscence of plenty which connects the idea of the Good with the giver, hence the thought of the Good must have preceded the need. Destitution does not create consciousness and what is contained therein. Thirst in itself does not create the fata morgana. But because a deity is present to consciousness, it is the most natural thing to take refuge there.

Indigence teaches to call for help, that is, to pray.

If the Roman soldier was in extreme distress he would forget the command to pray with face turned Rome-ward, but involuntarily would wring his hands above his head.

No. Religion is not the product of ignorance, fear, want or selfishness. This phenomenon so unique and universal, which alone escapes the "dog-philosophy" of old which Kingsley pictured in "Hypatia"; this grandest of all ideas, confounding natural explanation, can not be made to depend upon childishness in any respect; nor upon imaginary or perhaps peevish and capricious desires; nor upon the inability to endure the calamities of life in silent grief. The ideal of "pure reason" can not be a selfmade collective conception; the idea of that which is necessary can not be reasoned out of a heap of negatives, or of fatal accidents and circumstances; neither can it be reasoned away. What breaks forth from the depths of the human mind everywhere and irresistibly must rest in the mind as its most indestructible element.

This being a fundamental fact, let us be induced to exercise some such profound thinking wherein the Germans delight, in keeping with their habit "den Dingen auf den Grund zu sehen," altho some of them find as many religions at the bottom as they put in themselves. The subject deserves a thorough consideration—for the religious thought has ever been the most powerful undercurrent in the stream of history, the chief factor in every culture, and the cardinal principle of our own civilisation. Let us try, as we have done in other instances, to work up the problem by reversing the customary mode of its treatment.

Marginal notes:

Refutations of a few errors as to its origin.

Heman on childlikeness as origin of religiousness.

Phantasy never surpasses the compass of perception.   Sec. 15

Want does not create consciousness of the divine.

Reminiscence of the Good.

Prayer in earnest.

Religion not the product of want, ignorance, fear or selfishness.

Selfmade religions.

"Dog-philosophy" in "Hypatia" of Kingsley. Sec. 95.

Religion the fundamental basis of every culture and our own civilisation. Sec. 43, 54, 56, 58, 59, 71, 78, 95.

§ 35. Let us modestly state the first premise of our disquisition in the form of the hypothesis that—God is.

If so, He planted at the creation a consciousness of Himself into the human creature—and not only into the small part of the intellect. This imparted thought of God reveals itself in the expectation of the creature to receive something from its Creator, and in feeling itself drawn to Him in all circumstances, so as to open itself for Him and to remain susceptible of Him. The Creator sees in this human creature the reflection of His own image, and man, the creature, feels that he is thought of and looked upon. All this, at the least, is understood by the term God-consciousness. Thus the "Idea of God," as the creature circumscribes its concept of the thought-representation of Him, is the ingrained part of man's potential consciousness, framed into the mind at that center where all its relations are focused. It is man's most direct recollection and reminder, because it is his innermost and most essential capability of intimate converse and communion with the Creator. If in some way the development of this consciousness becomes disturbed or arrested, the "Name of God" is forgotten. Under this estrangement the thought of Him becomes the opposite of intimate. But tho the distinct feeling of God's friendship recedes and becomes obtuse and indescribable, yet a reminiscence of former beatitude is felt to assert itself. It reappears to awaken man's consciousness, because it remains the insoluble ingredient of his being. God—by way of this lasting endowment implanted into the frame of the mind in its entirety and not only, we emphasise it, into the small intellectual spot—ever keeps in touch with man; and at every manifestation of this fact which often seems to occur in a very indirect manner, the consciousness of this fact becomes vividly revived. This is all very empiric. The human mind is ever ready to meet the thought of God, and even to seek Him. It possesses within itself an instinctive, almost determining presentiment of being created for the sake of that thought.

To be sure, this feeling, this "voice so weak and still" within us, seems to be caused by external impressions. Even the internal impulses seem to come from without, often in spite of our attempts to avoid them, and against man's natural will. This feeling of the divine touch announces itself as distinctly separate from, altho along with, or before, or after those other impressions and sensations which the environments call forth in the mind. Usually it is felt just because of its conflict with the world and selfconsciousness. It wants to tell us that God is still our speaking terms with man. This feeling intercedes in this manner, because of our living in a world with which we are so intrinsically connected, as tho we were entirely bound up with it. The mind indeed would be suffocated in the coils of worldliness, if it were not for this gift, through which it remains in immediate connection with its purely spiritual sphere. It awakens one in such manner, because thereby alone man begins to emancipate himself from this mere natural intricacy to become a real selfconscious ego. Altho we find ourselves as if lost, at the moment when the touch from above on the one side, and the contact with the diverting world on the other, sets our faculties free one after and with the other: yet only thus do we learn by degrees to adjust ourselves to obligations, to cause other conditions and circumstances, and try to control them. We then and thus feel ourselves as subjects, and it generally takes some time until many of us can understand ourselves as being subject-objects. And even then we have not learned to know ourselves thoroughly, because we can not understand the single object apart from the sum of its relations to the whole. We have to learn for instance, that conscience, i. e. the knowledge that we are known, is not ' the" religious, but in the first place the moral sense, since it forbids man to retire to a private orbit of his own from his duties to nature and fellow-men. We cannot come to a clear definition of what conscience is, unless we see that it is not congruous with the religious sense, but that both must discriminately be kept asunder in our reflection as long as God-and world-consciousness are not ethically harmonised and consummated within us.

Morally we really and solely find ourselves, if, under the process of emancipation from natural necessity, we "come to" again from the moral stun of the fall. Religiously we find ourselves in higher connections and sacred relations, if we recognise the "image" within us, altho with sorrow for its being so distorted. The recognition must once have been a cognition. This finding, now the result and goal of a retrospective way of reflecting—a re-ligere, as the Romans inadvertently coined the word for us,—is a re-collection. This is awakened by the very same incitements from without, from the sphere in which consciousness had diverted and scattered its thoughts. In this mood the mind remembers its relations, that is, reconstructs them into a state of unity and permanency. Under reminding conditions the attention returns to and gathers around the central starting point. The mind gets to be converted. Such is the origin, the sum and substance of incipient religion under our supposition.

Hypothetical assumption: God is. cf. Sec. 100.

Seeing in man his own image. § 46, 116, 134, 176.

The origin of religion a form of a positive thought being felt of the ontogeneity of God.

Founded on empirics.

Religion not a matter of mere intellect.

Conscientious promptings not an outgrowth of nature, but opposing its centrifugal tendency (§ 11) in man.

God keeps on "speaking terms" with man.

Man's awakening to a sense of moral duty, to emancipation from nature.

Conscience not the religious but, in the first place, the moral phase of consciousness.

Moral restitution. Religious conversion.

Religion the recognition of the "image." § 5, 9, 10. 13, 15, 115, 131.

Selfknowledge possible only by being reminded of all relations to the One.

Whilst revealed religion starts from a central source the other starts from the circumference.

We found the essence of all religion in the tendency of man's consciousness toward the central starting point, the reunion with God. We only reversed the order of that theory which starts from the circumference into which the ego,—after detaching itself from the center and after having become eccentric in its natural inclinations,—had scattered its thoughts and desires.

Difference between evolved or natural and given religion.

The course by which man is conducted from the uncouth circumference of Fetishism up to the mental postulate of Monism, and further up to the consciousness of Monotheism, leads into the most perplexing difficulties. Wherever this method is used, it seems to be done for the purpose of ignoring some inconvenient, yea annoying empirical facts which defy explanation by any natural process. That method of demonstrating the origin of religion from frenzy and fetishism explains nothing but a greater, because more conscious, estrangement from the Creator ; reveals nothing but aggravated guilt of selfincurred, selfcontracted incapacity to obtain selfknowledge ; and a more contemptible moral dissipation, if not willful aversion to the one thing necessary—the Supreme Good. The perversion of the true relation of God to man by way of a selfconstituted religion gets entangled into insolvable difficulties.

Facts defying naturalistic explanation. § 40, 58, 110, 112, 302, 212.

Selfmade religion reveals but aversion to the one thing necessary.

False premises of the religion of evolutionism, and its lack of results.

Theoretically such a course can only be chosen under a onesided conception and false definition of "personality" or from its denial. If a person is taken for a mere blank of an ego, the latter route may be taken. If this blank is filling out according to the spontaneity by which physical development evolves, and by which the inner life of man is imagined to become mind by way of secretion, reflex nerve action and the like, passing from the lower sphere of pictorial thinking to the higher of associated ideas and purged conceptions, going on in reason alone and ignoring the feeling of qualitative value: then the way may be passable, but not without denying the ultimate purpose of all that. The "telos" must be either ignored or denied before religion can be said to originate like any other natural product, to be used for certain purposes like other products—nobody knowing where it will end or how. Then religion is levelled indeed to that kind of misconstrued evolution which works itself out of the food furnished by climate and the soil.

Religion made a means for certain irreligious purposes.

If on the contrary, mind is conceived as a wealth of originally innate and latent potentialities, then the opposite direction is indicated. We then arrive not at a religion from below, issuing from the diversity of radii which originate upon the periphery and converge toward a center ; not at a religion derived from atoms, mythical nomads and erratic parts ; not at a religion growing up wild and haphazard in order to become a socially stipulated but unbinding contract. But we come to "the" religion from above, from that central source which above arbitrariness and not submitted to human sanction. It lies there, where mind and God-consciousness are simply given. They are given for the purpose of a more or less free, ethical selfdevelopment ; that is, given in order to make its way through history aside from and independent of natural necessity. True religion is protected against being rendered subject to either arbitrary inventiveness or physical growth and decline.

True religious organisation above an unbinding social contract.

It conveys the purpose in itself for certain ends.

Religion to make its way through history upon the principle of independence from natural development

For this reason we reversed, by way of a new departure, the method of treating this subject (end of § 13) and did not begin our explanation of religion on the periphery. Every attempt at reducing religion to eccentricities must raise the suspicion of being an abortive effort to explain its purpose away. Hence our starting point is the center of unity, and our procedure of demonstrating its true import passes on in the direction of concentric intensification. The English, or rather Latin prefix, re, the same as er in German, in such words as re-ligion, re-minding, re-cognition, re-collection, re-velation, re-generation, re-demption, is thus reduced to its intelligible meaning and to the religious bearing upon the inner life.

In the direction of concentric intensification.

Humanity an ethnical organism, a connection not collection.

We set out from the proposition, implying all which we thus far wanted to demonstrate, that humanity is not a collection. Considering all its connections we take it as a unity, as an ethical organism, as a oneness ("Einheit").

Postulate of one typical person as the center of human unity.

Forms of speech, of laws and religion lie dispersed throughout the length and breadth of the earth like broken relics. In their dismembered condition they are inexplicable.

Illustration: Key-stone bearing all the strain of the cross-arch.

The problem which they present to us may be illustrated by the construction of a crossvault, a double arch. The hewn stones lying around on the ground are known to the architect alone who values them on account of the purpose they are to serve, with regard to their destiny which he has in mind. He determined their different angles according to his plan of the building for which they are intended, and in which they are to occupy unostentatious but very important positions. Our understanding of their shapes clears up as soon as we see them joined in their order, resting upon the centering frame as the arch is sprung from both sides. The entire structure, however, the significance of all the converging angles is not fully appreciated until the keystone is inserted. This gives the equipoise to the whole by taking upon itself all the strain, so that the bearing tension of the whole is bound up in it. Then the parts as one whole depend upon and lean against it. The whole is rendered selfsupporting since the keystone carries all, explains the intent of the builder, explains the import of the cross-arch to the building and the value of each single stone. *Explains the value of each part in its relation to the whole.*

Oppert needed such a binding insertion in order to demonstrate the existence of a primitive Turanian stock. He had studied the Mongolians, the Finns, Tatars, Turks, and Hungarians in all their bearings upon his science. The essential characteristics common to them all, underlying all their differences, were pronounced enough, still the cause of their similitude seemed inexplicable. They severally presented many definite circumstances, each demanding special explanation. This could not be made by supposing a probable analogous development going on contemporaneously in different localities. Nothing would answer but the supposition of an original primitive stock of Turanians. Original unity became more than hypothetical, it became a demand, an absolute postulate. *Oppert on unit of Turanian languages. Illustration: the scientific right of the postulate of the unity of humanity.*

In this very manner do we insist upon the scientific demand of the unity of the human family. We take it for granted, that with a first man as a proto-type there is given such an original unit of central potentiality as represents the nucleus of true humanism and affords equilibrium to all the strains under which our race writhes. If mankind is not only a whole, constituted of agglomerated parts, not a mere mechanical collection but an ethical connection and interrelated unity, then the mind is constrained to find the center of tension which bears the strain of the polarity between the two worlds, even if it is to be looked for in depths far beyond the efforts of deliberating reason. This center, or fountain-head, or proto-type must be the starting point as well as the final focus of all the indicative rays which in direct lines not only radiate through the spheres, but also penetrate the spheroids of natural and spiritual life in all directions. This center must be what we demanded when speaking of the key and knowledge of the secret to unlock the combination; it must be what the keystone is to the cross-vault. The formula pressing this axiomatic problem is: Homogeneity in the concrete, that is, the organic unity of the human race, must lie in a first man. *One First Man, the proto-type. § 12, 13, 82, 33, 37. 92, 105, 117, 120, 232. He is to be what the "locked synthesis" meant and the keystone in the cross-vault. Conclusion from induction to be proved.*

CH. V. A FIRST MAN. THE HIEROGLYPH OF HISTORY.

§ 36. By correct analysis, we trust, based upon, and guided by, historic facts, we have ascended to our conclusion. The facts became propositions from which, by the necessity of logic, we had to start in search of the composite synthesis, and to carry on our disjunctive and conditional syllogising. *Proposition: Humanity a oneness, represented by its proto-type,*

After extending the lines of thought consistent with the data, in the direction to which the proper inferences pointed, and where the lines converged, we came to the conclusion that the human race forms a oneness. And as the result of combined syllogisms, we anticipated a figure which alone can save us from the dilemma, we posited the postulate of a primary representative person. *standing out from celestial spheres in contrast to the realm where natural necessity holds sway,*

If our conclusion can be substantiated, it promises to prove humanity a unity and to render its doings an intelligible fabric. The figure will represent that comprehensive whole, which will answer all the requirements demanded for the explanation and interpretation of history. For only when taken as a whole does "human nature" stand out prominent and lucid from the background where the mere natural forces hold their sway, and where, in contrast to the realm of light, love and freedom, the tendency toward diversity and dissolution is ever manifest. In no other way is it possible to understand humanity, and to make it the object of an ingeniously projected and intentionally perpetuated history. Here man is mirrored so that he can observe his own life as truly reflected. In no other way is it possible to study history to any real advantage, than by conceiving in it that grand web to which history has been so fitly compared, in which necessity forms the warp and freedom the woof. *and the tendency to dissolution is ever manifest. In him alone the solution of life's problems; the bridge between the two worlds. Necessity and feasibility of one first man. § 10, 12, 13, 16. In the interest of nature science lies a perfect right to postulate*

For a successful pursuance of this study the original man is postulated. He bears within him the theme of the opera and carries through the fundamental note, the motif of the grand fugue. He is the keystone in the arch of the bridge connecting both the worlds to which he belongs. The solution of the problems of history and human life can lie only in one person. For only oneness can be organic, can be an idea, can furnish the systematic knowledge of the organism of history. That organism needs but the typical germ from which to sprout, and into which, analogous to plant-life, to concentrate again in order to bloom, to bear fruit and seed. History needs *one single protoplasm. § 26, 52. In the interest of history the postulate of one first man is not unreasonable, not an unscientific demand. § 12, 13, 15, 16.*

only this one man, in order to become intelligible throughout just as science needs but one protoplasm which potentially comprises the whole fabric of development rooted therein.

Scientists have always been very willing to derive the whole living world—not excepting a single thing, because that would have opened the door for a miracle—from a single primary protoplasm, Why, then, with so flagrant prejudice and a very suspicious aversion do they persistently rebuke the much nearer proposition of one first man for explaining language, history, etc. ? But such are the inconsistencies of human nature, materialistically speaking, that one denies privileges to others, which he claims for himself. Or may it be an inconsistency like that according to which the motion of brain matter within my skull has brought about the conviction that materialism is a poor subterfuge for a certain simulation of willful ignorance? It is at this point that the difficulty of the matter lies. But discrepancies of this sort need be cleared up with tender care.

The question brought up in the first book of this Philosophy, must now be faced viz: How shall we conceive the all-sufficient, all-embracing, all-explaining mind, which so delineates this real first man as to be easily understood by all.

In the countries of the rising as in those of the setting sun, history meets with evidences everywhere that man possesses intuitive knowledge of his microcosmical significance, of his cosmical position.

Chinese myths have it, that out of chaos man emerged as the ghost of earth and as the Pure One in Heaven in the same person. His head became the mountain; the sun and moon were his eyes, rivulets his arteries and veins, the trees his hair. Thus the members of man stretch forth in the universe. The primitive man of the Japanese creates the waters, standing upon the rainbow. Weeping for his broken lance, the splinters of which became islands, the tears out of his left eye became the sun, those out of the right eye the moon —both his daughters.

The deity Yama, the first man of the Rig-veda is the first who died and showed his descendants the way to the place of the spirits.

The German god-legends, according to Grimm, are full of such stories in which man's corporeal parts are conceived as a miniature world.

The body is the center in which the image of the whole universe is reflected [and recognises itself. The flesh is made of loam; the drops of perspiration are his share of the dews of heaven. The blood was taken out of the sea; the arteries from the herbs of the woods and the fields, the hair from the grass. Man's eye, so much like the sun, originated in that orb. Thus heaven and earth, flowing through man, bloom forth and sparkle through him, their child. Mythology contributes hundreds of similar reflections of nature in the mind. We see in them more than childish fancies, for which some have only the smile of superiority.

In these poetical expressions there is clearly to be seen the intuitive insight of these natural peoples into the connection of things, as into the living organism which everywhere reflects, conceals, and reveals the whole in all its parts. The entire universe is concentrated in man, who is its quintessence. A standing conundrum is this figure of man as he appears in every nation at the entrance-gate of its history —much like the sphinx, keeping watch over desert and tomb and temple, taciturn. In that figure the world's riddle is symbolised, whose hidden ends run out in the meaning of man. This sphinx seems to have been given to history for interpretation as the object lesson of its development. Its symbolism includes our postulate even, which from time immemorial everywhere stood before the human mind.

§ 37 Man as he stands upon the earth, is the allegory of the visible world, symbolically containing all its truth and virtually all its reality. With his head erect toward the starry heavens, his figure intermediates between the highest and lowest formations; whilst spiritually he surpasses all. Transcending the visible he reaches into the invisible world As the representative of the visible he, in a microcosmical

manner as it were, unites within himself at the same time also the invisible world. Here however we come to a halt. We are not allowed to penetrate even thus far unless accompanied by facts. We will not proceed any further until we have adduced them so as to carry our credentials with us. But from this point on, we have to draw on the psychical life of the race for such facts as are at hand and well authenticated. Let us find, then, and consider such data:

Fortlage paints this impressive picture: "Our soul is like unto the vaults of a national treasury. In its guarded recesses a flickering flame lightens up a small portion of the numberless treasures—small in contrast to the enormous wealth covered by the ghostly shadows of the subterranean storage-rooms." The meaning is this: The greatest component part of our mind is asleep, even in our waking state. What is awake within us is never the ego in its entirety; it is but that small part of it which is brought to our consciousness by the concentrating function of the mind, called attention. It is this attention which suggested the analogy of the lamp in the cellar vaults. We are told of states of the soul in exultation, after the use of opium for instance, in which the intoxicated victims have panorama-views as of landscapes under sunshine.

The writer knows from his own experience of the rather trance-like "central" vision which has been described by many others, whose souls in extreme perils were at the brink of separation from the body and had before them all they had ever experienced, done or seen, except the bad; whatever sceneries they had beheld or things they had known. It is a moment of beatitude; a condition of youth and ideality. In delirium tremens quite different pictures, but on the same grounds, unfold to the pitiable sufferer. *[margin: Illustration: The unreflected part of the mind;]*

We leave these pictures to rest on their own merits, altho we know of very well authenticated facts of similar nature in large number, not sequent to intoxication but always to an abnormal condition of the organism in dangerous situations, where sudden death seemed unavoidable. Experiences were had and are on record, upon which the hallucination theory can cast no suspicion as being illusive because physiological psychology can offer no explanation therefor.—"The state of our psychical being which we call awake is never awake in the full sense; it is rather a permanent daze. Still more humiliating is the fact, that under the condition of things this half-sleep must regularly change off with full sleep, when the dim light in the treasury becomes almost extinct." *[margin: hidden because it is beyond observation of reflecting reason.]*

Fortlage's view is corroborated by many such psychologists as Fichte, Jr., Kerner, Kreyher, Erdmann, etc., and why should we not mention Shakespeare and Goethe along with them? These views are further supported by hosts of witnesses who were, and are, competent to judge scientifically of their own experiences. *[margin: Psychologists taking subconsciousness into account.]*

Zschokke, the extreme rationalist, tells us in his "Contemplations upon Myself" about his gift of the "central vision". He could read the inner life of such as were strangers to him at the first occasion of coming in contact with them. Face and voice of such a one addressing him, would make scarcely any impression upon him; externals he perceived very indistinctly. But the mind of a stranger he saw clearly before him, often to the greatest surprise of those who were witnesses, and always to his own annoyance. Such facts are amazing only to those, who pay no attention to phases of the mind or moods of the soul. Even among psychologists some feign to ignore the facts. Altho such phenomena may not be explicable, and can not be housed with certain pet theories, they are undeniable; they may be troublesome but can not be evaded. *[margin: Zschokke's mind-reading "central" vision.]*

Reason builds systematic knowledge in the conscious state of the mind upon the basis of facts. But this does not say that judgments are reliable in all cases, nor does it deny that a great deal of wisdom was received independent of reason. We dare not lightly ignore such data of psychical life, neither do we need to despair of their explicability. Much more important than the precocious construction of a system into which these unknown quantities will fit, is to us the weighing and considering of phenomena which ever and anon intrude upon our theories. Attempts to put them to derision are unbecoming to serious science.

The conclusion drawn from the observation of these facts under this topic may be presented safely in this axiom: The soul in its entirety contains more than we are aware of. *[margin: Conclusion: The soul is more than what we know thereof.]*

Since the largest and perhaps chief portion of our life is concealed as by a veil in the innermost and almost impenetrable recesses of the soul, then this sphere of intensified life must be the workshop of the mysterious phenomena alluded to.

We have already noticed the duality of the human soul. *[margin: Duality of the mind. § 6, 8, 9, 15, 113.]*

A misty veil, as it were, not to say a hiatus or break, divides consciousness into two departments, one of which comes under control of the mind, whilst the other we can only catch an occasional glimpse. *[margin: causes two forms of consciousness.]*

Every one of us has perceived some of the latter's very energetic manifestations. Only in Hegel's daughter, as far as has come to the notice of history, these manifestations seem to have become abashed after her father had peremptorily told her: "Es wird von jetzt an nicht mehr geträumt," I do not want you to dream any more!

"Day-consciousness" and "Night-consciousness" (Tag-und Nachtseite des Seelenlebens") the Germans denominated these two sides of the spiritual constituent of our mind, whilst now the better terms "reflecting" and "unreflected' or "sub-consciousness" have come into use. *[margin: "Day" and "night"—side of mind-life,]*

"Reflecting" describes that part of the soul in which the mind deliberates upon its own acts and perceptions; reflecting also in the other sense, insomuch as the mind in this state reflects its impressions and compound cognitions upon the deeper background of memory for future attention and reproduction, where they stay, whether called up before the conscious state or not. *[margin: "Reflecting" and "unreflected" consciousness defined. § 8, 15, 37, 111, 113, 221.]*

9

"Unreflected" consciousness on the other hand, denotes that phase of the inner life where the mental capabilities of the mind can not consciously deliberate upon acts, impressions and promptings; hence have no control over them. Many manifestations of the unconscious activity from that side flash up before the conscious part, but they are not retainable as a general thing and seldom reproducible on the part of ordinary reasoning, remembering and consciousness.

These two phenomenal spheres, for reasons given, must not be considered as mere moods of the soul, but pertain chiefly to either one of the purely spiritual or the physico-psychical constituents of the mind. Discrimination between them might be more distinct, if it were not for the fact that the physico-psychical part of the mind largely contributed and deposited its reminiscences of its preexistence also in the "unreflected," or "subconscious," department of the mind.

One who comes to himself from a state of ecstasy or from hypnotic sleep can not remember anything he thought or did in this condition. In a succeeding repetition, however, the soul is able to recall the doings in the previous hypnotic state. "A duality of formal existence like two adjoining rooms with different contents" was what Gillers de la Touresse demonstrated in 1889 for Medical Jurisprudence.

Nothing but this duality of reflecting and unreflected consciousness in the mind —i. e. soul and spirit in their combination—explains the discrepancies between "faith and science", between immediate, intuitive cognition and deliberate reasoning, between intuition and instinct, between genius and talent, musing and thinking, between the "head and the heart."

Both these latter appellations are not philosophical. But inasmuch as McCosh says, that common sense possesses the truth before the thinkers arrange it scientifically, we must make the best of both of them.

The heart, in this empirical sense, is understood to be the central seat of personal life, of mind and emotional sentiency (Gemuethsleben).

In the head this life becomes apparent by way of the reflecting functions of the mental faculties in the form of awakened thought. This is the reason why the intellect is prone to claim consciousness and discursive thought only for itself; and that we grant the claim, unaware of the fact that all the other faculties and even the physical conditions in their quiet way cooperate with "pure reason."

The head is the acknowledged seat of mediated or secondary, of discursive and reflecting thought—the opposite of "central vision." It is generally occupied by the multiplicity of things on the circumference; is often bribed by base promptings, gets easily confused and sometimes altogether prepossessed by the world of glitter and sham. In the heart (of course not in the mere physiological sense) we see not only the core of all physical, that is, unconscious soul-life, but also, and primarily, the center and focus of the psychico-spiritual life. It bears along all spiritual and ethical movements, all sentiments. And not only this emotional activity as caused by man himself pertains to it, but it represents moreover, the sphere where finite life is stimulated by the infinite.

With reference to the physico-psychical side Schubert and Beck pointed out years ago, the necessity of considering the blood in conjunction with the nerves in explanation of psychological experiences. When this is done our statements will be acknowledged as more than feasible. So much is certain, that, the dry, i. e. onesided psychology with its nerve-fluids notwithstanding, the heart does not cease to show "cordial" feelings, to believe, to love, and—to "break," is not simply a thing of poetry altho it is true even in this respect that "the heart speaks most when the lips move not."

Here is the seat of conscience, independent of will, reason and sense-perceptions, but with its direct influences upon the circulation of the blood. Hence the heart is said to possess immediate knowledge and certainty and is deemed the medium through which the Absolute Good is represented, and its reality and presence announced. Here is the form where the right and the value of the Good is manifested and vindicated.

Here the verdict of what is worthy is rendered, and the feeling of appreciation of the one thing necessary is preserved. Here intuition, divination, faith, vision, contrition and consolation stand connected with all those virtues which are the flavor of genuine religion, historically known as the "fruits of the spirit."

Here is to be located—not, however, in a spatial sense, since all that pertains to the spiritual part of the mind lies above space and time—the deep-lying seat of "unreflected" or subconsciousness, the point of contact and intercourse with the allsurpassing and allcomprising order of a higher world—and with the "underworld," too.

Neither of these chief constituents of personal life should unduly preponderate over, or be cultivated at the expense of, the other, and ethical culture alone can tend to the happy mean. Whatever may be accepted or rejected of these statements, so much is certain, that physiological psychology will not overthrow their truth in order to replace them by materialistic or agnostic dogmas. "Natural science (especially as far as it is materialistic) treats of the conditions of world consciousness.

But if it seeks to forestall spiritual truths which stand equal to empiric facts, then," says Zoellner, "as is known to everybody today, it will not succeed" (not even with its present apparatus of forty odd classified nerves, each under so much pressure per inch, we add)—"in demonstrating pain and pleasure as the first principles of consciousness or of ethics."

Nobody will successfully object to these words of the great scientist. But neither will we succeed in explaining the "unreflected" consciousness in a scientific and unchallengeable manner. We simply wanted to call the attention to the need of recognising and investigating such phenomena as deserve it. We will spare ourselves the effort to find the connections between them and to classify them, for reasons which will appear later on.

Before leaving this fascinating subject for the present, notwithstanding our incomplete view of it, we can not refrain from pointing to the "Anthropologie" of the "younger" Fichte. A few thoughts suggested by this keen observer and clear thinker may be profitably added when this whole matter will receive more light, when we behold the figure of the first man.

§ 38. There exists a horrid magic art, through which uncultured hordes influence the animal world. Among them we find occult powers at work, which need not be, and have not been, acquired by studies in sorcery, but which have broken forth from the depths of "unreflected" consciousness.

"In the performances of sorcery, spiritism, mesmerism, etc., the amount of demonstrated fraud is so great as to cast suspicion over the whole. In general there is a very strong presumption against any alleged fact which stands apart from the established order of life. The uttermost care must be taken in determining the facts before placing any faith in them; a certain lukewarmness is highly to be recommended." This advice of Bordon Bowne is appropriate: but may not lukewarmness in religious matters take umbrage and justify itself on the same grounds ? To omit the mention of these facts does not remove them from history.

He insists upon the necessity that such psychological phenomena and occurrences receive their due share of observation and that they be subjected to the most rigid examination as the facts of hypnotism have been. Then things may be made plain and innocuous which heretofore were pushed aside as uncanny mysteries and upon which, nevertheless, superstition was feeding. Those psychological phenomena have exerted decided influences in epochal events; and in general, their historical import has not received that attention which it demands.

We keep in mind that they are to be designated as abnormal with reference to the ordinary course of things, as symptoms of an unhealthy condition under the power of which man is passive, is a patient!

The effects of these powers, and the wily, mystifying and baffling manner in which they assert themselves, lead us to surmise an organ or a potentiality in the nature of man which in the normal state lies dormant. This "rudimentary" and facultative organ, coming nearer to the surface in proportion of more or less debility of the nervous system, shows its susceptibility in the sphere of central vision as well as in that of reflex nerve action.

It shows itself now at an occasion of a visionary flash, and then as an ecstatic grasp. The capability of perceiving such a flash or glance is perceptible in the milder and nearer forms of forebodings: it rises to the state of second sight, to the ecstacy of a trance, to mind-reading, and up to the eccentricities of clairvoyant visions into immeasurable distances of space and time. Manifestations of this kind indicate a faculty of central vision, a potentiality which everybody carries within himself.

The capability of the grasp touches, in spite of distances, other souls and bodies, in a depth and by means which to us are sealed up. Of course we have a scientific name for it: Telepathy. But what becomes of its diagnosis ? Surmise magnetism ? Too clumsy; perhaps there is some power analogous to it at the bottom. Certain it is, that it is there and at work. We can notice it in the way that people passing on the street will simultaneously turn and look at each other. Nobody will deny that such a rapport exists, and has revealed itself by instantaneous monitions in cases of extreme peril between friends, notwithstanding the oceans between them.

We were reminded of the rudimentary organs as analogous to what we suppose to be dormant capabilities of the inner life. Perhaps we may find more in them than mere illustrations. A whale's skeleton, they say, plainly shows excrescences in the place where the organs of locomotion grow on quadrupeds. The horse carries in its hoofs the crippled bones of five toes. Such retarded growths we recognise as remnants of original adaptabilities. If the animals had relapsed from a higher state, then these undeveloped members would have to be explained as checked growths, since the organism of the animal adapted itself to environments and modes of life, where the member was not brought into exercise and its growth stopped.

Or we notice on the other hand the hidden probabilities which could have obtained their full development only in a higher sphere, where the use of such incipient organs will tend to their unfolding. The metamorphosis of the butterfly will serve most adequately in illustrating this. From whatever side we look at this matter, we will agree that such physical predispositions can not be understood from the present condition of the species showing such rudimentary organs. Alone by comparison with, and in reference to, other species can we comprehend these peculiarities.

We may consider them purposeless ; whilst in fact we have hidden organs before us which were not used, or will come to be used. Would it be unreasonable, then, to conjecture upon the presence of similar rudimentary faculties in man? In the combination of his nature we have observed aptitudes which we think to be intended for use in another form of existence. Being not in use for the present, they are taken out of his hands : at the proper occasion we expect to see them developed, and to be restored for free use.

They may indicate, too, how many potentialities, generally hidden from view, may have been in possession of the first man. We shall find some more facts to strengthen such a supposition.

Should this supposition be proven by other and palpable indications, then the first man stood like a king, having powers at his command which we can only guess at from what is left ; then he possessed within himself the pledges for a development short only of absolute perfection. And in this first man the theme of history is enwrapped. History is but the development of the wealth of potentialities wherewith the representative of mankind is endowed. In him are deposited in concentrated form the means with which history works. In him lie the contrasts or antithetical principles in an undifferentiated, promiscuous bundle of possibilities and dispositions which, after having been set free and applied, will mold individual and social life under tensions and equations.

The opposites united in man run in the direction of two strongly antagonistic

principles which by their conflict stimulate and restrain each other.

In the first place man, owing to the finiteness of personal life, finds himself a dependent entity which once was not, but has become such. Hence finite man has himself not entirely in his own power; he does not control his beginning and cannot penetrate into the depths of his own nature. Altho the first man doubtless did, probably

involuntarily to some extent, apply the wealth of gifts in a manner of which we can have no experience. Notwithstanding his relative perfection, there must have been incipient in him even the duality of consciousness. For he ever represented the unity of the natural and the spiritual world, combining both in the form of his existence, while not even the depths of his natural parts, consisting of an epitome of the

universe, were altogether comprehended with conscious intelligence. Man had to learn to know the world and his relations to it by the use of his incipient faculties which he thus had to develop himself. What he possessed were gifts, bestowed upon

him in such a manner as to render their application and elaboration his duty, to serve him as the outline of what he had to learn. Seine Gaben wurden seine Aufgaben.

Next to the task of selfculture, that is of developing and adjusting, balancing and controlling the harmonious interactions of the faculties themselves in order to fit him for the work appointed to him by the opportunities which the world affords him, was the improvement of his estate, the elevation of his world.

This task, concurrent with the first duty of keeping up the union between body

and soul, consists in cultivating the natural world which, at his appearance, ceased to develop. It became man's duty to elevate nature to his own exalted state, to define,

direct, and rule over its unceasing movements. In doing this, he was to begin with his nearest environment—his own body in its then simplest relation. Nature's forces

through him were to be set free for his own benefit, just as the faculties of his own mind were to be set free, subject to the condition of their proper exercise at the apparatus, and their engagement in due order. This is the part of obligation assigned to him—to cultivate himself by cultivating nature. To be thus engaged is to his own advantage; his fortune is given entirely into his hands. In pursuance of this work his own dispositions and potentialities are to be set free by way of selfdetermination, since the process of man's development can only be ethical. It can only prosper as it concurs with the plan of glorification and personal communication—in freedom and love. *This conditions man's moral and intellectual progress, since only thus engaged man's own potentialities are set free.*

§ 39.   Man's faculties are set free under condition of applying them in proper cooperation, hence they become differentiated under the progressive division of labor, whereby all development is to proceed harmoniously. Especially his own gifts are to develop according to the "image" within himself and in concert with nature. Toil, woe, and strife are not necessary for development under these conditions. Necessary is nothing but the voluntary, joyful concurrence with the Absolute Good which reigns supreme, and which has its representative in man for his own good, securing its own value and preserving man's dignity under all circumstances. The entire creation is arranged to this end. Man from his own resources is to liberate the possibilities latent in things and in persons. He is to redeem the retarded life of nature, which became arrested life on his account, in order that this work of liberation should become his task for his own advantage and progress; to deliver the life confined in nature so as to elevate it to his own level and lead it up with himself to spiritual perpetuity and reality. This is the ethical task and significance of true culture. Man is to keep himself ahead, abreast at least, in this line of advance, and to conduct all in harmony with himself, and himself in harmony with all, to the goal of a glorious and complete transformation. This must be the procedure of civilisation, and nothing short of it. It is the method according to which history follows its course. *Exercise at the apparatus. § 5, 9, 36, 41, 117. Cooperation with the divine plan and concurrence with the order of things. § 5, 7, 9, 19, 116, 220. Differentiation of man's faculties under division of labor. Man to deliver confined life for his own advantage. The ethical goal.*

The duality and consequent polarity of human nature was adapted to the normal exercise of man's spiritual and natural obligations ; the tension and duality were intended to bring about a complete and happy union in perfect conformity with the supreme purpose—if it had not been for a certain great calamity. That it occurred was not, however, the fault of the necessary and beneficial polarity and duality. But after the event had happened, advance not only stopped abruptly, it is even made almost impossible. Advance would have been rendered altogether impossible had it not been for the polarity which keeps up its work in full force. *Duality of human nature is adapted to the method in which history pursues its course. The calamity of the fall not to be blamed upon this duality. The polarity between nature and the spirit works the more beneficially.*

For notwithstanding the calamity, nature and history kept their course, as delineated in the first man once and forever.

One more coincidence in the polarisation of human nature must not be lost sight of. It is an essential part of finite personal life to become effective under the polarity of the masculine and feminine principles, under the polarity of activity and receptivity. *Polarity of the masculine and feminine principles latent in the First Man.*

As a potentiality at least, the tension of this polarity must have been latent in the first man already, tho concealed and undifferentiated as yet. This principle of a peculiar strain is growing the more intense, and is balanced the better, too, the more forces are differentiated and come into play. We believe we have found the secret of this emulative principle expressed in both the reflecting and unreflected forms of consciousness.

Thus alone the deep problems, high aspirations and sad failures in the lives of individuals and nations may be understood. Unless the occult powers pervading and agitating human life receive due consideration, history remains unintelligible. The tension caused by this duality of human nature as now pointed out, the polarity manifesting itself between the active and passive tempers, continues even to predominate through the entire course of history. It lies at the root of that all-pervading and portentous strain between the oriental and occidental parts of humanity. It is just this strain which furnishes history most of its means and instrumentalities. *Polarity of active and receptive (passive) natural development furnishes history the means for realising its ends.*

Such is man, standing before us at the beginning of history as its prophesying figure. He is not quite that "embellished initial" of a mediæval manuscript, which Lotze's philosophy would make him. He is more natural and less perfect, and less sophisticated. It was not the "strive for existence" in accord with the law of the "survival of the fittest, which forced him to assume his erect posture," as Dierks wrote as late as A. D. 1881. *Man less perfect and more natural than Lotze imagined.*

On the contrary. It was his inner value, the incognito majesty of his spirit which exalted man; because this alone does not come from below. But how came this hieroglyphic figure to stand at the gate of history containing the theme of it and also the means for it in himself? And how does it correspond with all the dark designs substantiating themselves in the miseries of real life? These questions have scarcely been touched upon as yet. If it seemed as tho the deciphering of the hieroglyph should be evaded in this work as was done in others of its kind, then it is time to correct the impression. But we can not begin to answer these questions, until we have the phenomena before us in all their bearings. In the phantom-like appearance of the first man as he stands before our expectations, all contrasts are compounded and equalised in the simple concurrence of motion, mere emotion in his case—because the tensions are all as yet under the regulating pendulum of the God-consciousness pure and simple.

It is only when man becomes aware that this is disturbed, when by the break of the order of duality connections are severed, when the contrasts become conflicts, and the natural strains alone have their sway; when the God-consciousness expires, as it were, under the prevailing symptoms of rupture, detachment, departure, dispersion, dissolution—that the sinking and precipitous descent begins to be conceivable—not until then. It is after man has lost the best part of his life, after the true and vital core of consciousness, namely love and peace have receded, that he, collectively as well as individually, becomes conscious of his selfhood, is concerned about, and engaged with, himself. Unless he becomes aware of these sad facts, he does not become known to himself. It is thus that man as a person or as a nation may find himself in an impoverished condition and feel his great losses; under the vicissitudes which arise from the multiplicity, where unity ought to be maintained; which originate in quantites sinking by their own weight, where quality should preponderate. A multiplicity in conflict—this is the distress of consciousness with which new knowledge is to begin, under which the mind is to be awakened. Not before this consciousness of sinking into the abyss of selfabandonment is recognised, can we begin to understand the first man. We are unable to realise the decadence with all its wretchedness; we are too much disabled to endure a single glance into the chasm yawning between destiny and reality; and if we could, our seeing would be of no avail, for we would become completely terrorised, until the cause of the misery and the consequences of the fall appear in their whole compass.

CH. VI.   THE GREAT CALAMITY AND THE CATASTROPHES.

§ 40.   The proofs adduced for the quality and high position of the ideal man (notwithstanding the questionable and unsatisfactory "achievements", that is, notwithstanding the ideal which man would improvise on the spur of his lamentable condition, his present reality) and the vouchers for the permanent significance of the first real man justifying our position: bring us face to face with the most vexatious of all problems.

"In the dreamy existence of nature-bound, uncultured people, the night side of human life (our unreflected consciousness) constantly reaches up, or is extended into their day's work" (Bastian, Volks-und Menschenkunde, Berlin, 1888.) This is an important observation. For what is meant by "dream-life?" In the preceding chapter we had to utilise such proofs as are found in man's actual condition. In the realities of life surrounding us, we met something irrational which marred the understanding of the first man. Burdened with incomprehensibilities we stand before the great question.

Looking upon the sum and substance of the world's doings as unbiased as possible, we find to our dismay at every step what Schelling called "das Nicht-sein-sollende," that which ought not to be. Does that cause all this trouble?

We have endeavored to show, how even in the so-called dead geological mass there are imponderable forces interrelated and at work, and how they on their part are instrumental to, and in all their movements cooperative with, the historic purpose. But this was saying very little as regards matter itself. We merely hinted at the idea that matter may be taken for substantiated power and purpose, as compressed, arrested life, perhaps. This we did under the conviction that there is a life of a higher nature, the principles or elements of which interact

---

Marginal notes:

Questions which cannot be solved unless full self-knowledge has been gained.

This begins with the consciousness of the effects of the fall and becomes complete when the issues of the conflict become apparent. I. A. Ch. 12. II. D. Ch. 2.

Conditions of self-knowledge:

Acknowledgement of the Bad, desire for restitution of the losses.

Instead of unity and quality a multiplicity in conflict;

Quantities sinking by their own weight.

Full recognition of man's wretchedness only possible when it appears in its own whole compass. § 40, 41, 58, 109, 112, 115.

Bastian on confined life of nature-bound people.

Preparation for the answer, which lies in that which "ought not to be." Schelling. § 4, 51, 202, 204, 223.

with that of the lower order in free motion, substantiating themselves and complementing each other in form of opposites, without limit and without conflict, We only refer to the "Monads" of Leibnitz in their blind confusion, despite their "pre-established harmony," altho they have been put up again in array against our axiom of the invisible reality of the spiritual world.

Whatever theory is set up does not forbid us to see forces in what is called matter, which, (under the auspices of a thought, combining them in systematic and mutual equation as complements to each other)—substantiated themselves and moved in perfect equilibrium and serenity. Hence we can not charge either force or its substance with being the cause of the troubles under discussion.

Matter not the cause of the trouble.

It was from some other cause that the gladsome and harmonious immanency of thought, or of life, or force in matter became severed. The intimate relation sustained a rupture, it broke into separable relations. Force-substance realised the possibility of standing outside of, and opposite to each other. Elements became loosened, detached themselves, asserted independence, and pushed on in setting up separate relations of existence of their own.

Immanency of thought in substance thrown out of balance.

Nature insubordinate to man.

This insubordinate attitude of the forces in nature is due to the unbridled propensities and distorted inclinations and dissipated appetites of the human soul, so impotent and yet so arrogant. For the human soul is the focus of all principles and forces and elements in the life of nature. Hence the loss of equilibrium in the human soul must of necessity affect all natural life.

The rend through the human soul extends through nature,

Many speculatists have tried to describe nature as thoroughly purposive in all its formations. Doubts about it were taken for ignorance. Never can we be convinced that all the destruction going on in nature and history is necessary for any natural or moral purpose.

which on this account is not thoroughly purposive.

If billions of tender and harmless molluscs are thrown by a single wave upon the hot sands to perish, it will always be difficult to establish any purpose in their death. Likewise will it be in vain to reduce the sensations of abborrence or disgust, caused by monstrosities or nauseous objects, to the variety of taste or to the lack of information, as to their necessity for a purpose. And as it is in regard to nature, so it is with respect to nations. There too, the waste of forces is appalling. How incomprehensible is the contrast between exertions and successes. With all the impetuosity of propagation how few of the products are well qualified specimens and fit for the world. What swarms of people crowd some poor quarters of the globe, whilst finer regions are not appreciated by the few occupants. Beside the proportionally narrow strip of the northern temperate zone, not many other parts of the globe's surface seem adapted for raising that superior quality of human beings which is of value to the cultural life of the rest of the world.

Conditions in nature and

In nations defying every idea of purposeness.

A feeling of gloom seizes one at reading of the uncouth peoples which roam over the dreary steppes, or swarm in the thickly settled portions of Asia. The wretchedness of humanity there is so disheartening as to make the value of man almost vanish. It is similar to the awe oppressing the mind at the sight of the wild vegetation of swamps, or the barren monotony of such vast tracts of "bad lands" as those of the Dakotas. It bewilders us to behold such environments, because we can not comprehend why there is so much of the distressing and the crude around us, ever reproducing itself so rapidly, whilst the good and that which is noble is augmenting so slowly. There seems no system nor even picturesqueness in such dreary vastnesses which defy any idea of plan or purpose. And besides, such views fill us with gloom because there is something within ourselves which inadvertently finds the inner condition of the mind reflected in nature. Our gloomy moods are generally the echo of selfreproach which nature calls forth by its physical analogies.

Gloomy mood of mind: the echo of the reproachful sighing of the creatures.

In addition to the sighs of the creature within NATURE inexplicable and occult phenomena have to be considered of which HISTORY speaks, in order to understand the melancholy mood of the mind. The Greeks and Romans —notwithstanding their natural hilarity, their bravery and their frivolous attitude to their religion—felt a chill of horror in the imaginary presence of embuses and lamiae at the mysteries of Thessalian, Colchian, and Assyrian black arts. Equally stultified by a ghastly dismay was that illustrious company of Paris in 1788, those scurrilous merry-makers assembled with Malesherbes, Condorcet, Bailly, Grammont—La Harpe, etc., to whom Cazotte predicted their fate of 1793.

Occult phenomena. Cazotte's prediction.

The witchcraft of the Middle Ages, of which Solden gives full report in his History, demonstrates the terrors of old pagan rites and their continuance under cover of Christian culture. Hidden depths of sinister and powerful influences are opening and give vent to an overflow of abominations. The combination of lust and bloodthirst is inexplicable from any order of things or other natural sources. The orgiastic revelries of the Mylitta cult, the frantic ecstasies of Shamanism among the Jacutes is more than unnatural. When they become "mergretch," Wundt classifies them with the hypnotised. But what is Hypnotism? The Hametzians of Vancouver in their mad dances tear pieces out of the bodies of the spectators with their teeth, presenting, according to Jacobson and Bastian, "the most horrible spectacle imaginable." Bishop Zumarraga computed the number of human sacrifices among the Aztecs

Moral darkness; Orgies of "mysteries"; witchcraft. Sodden.

Hypnotism. Bastian, Wundt. § 54.

Human sacrifices etc.
Zumarraga, Waitz,
Prescott.

at about twenty thousand annually. Montezuma, it seems, set a horrible example. In his city of Tlascala alone 800 victims were actually butchered at one particular feast every year. Waitz has ascertained that the dedicatory ceremonies of the main temple at Tenochtitlon required 34,000 victims. In the court-yard of the Mexican temple stood a pyramid of 136,000 human skulls, according to Prescott.

The Bad in history. §106, 110.

Withal that the "Bad" has scarcely been mentioned as yet.

not explicable from natural grounds.

How are these mysterious phenomena of the dark sides of life to be accounted for? Facts challenge thought which defy explanation from natural grounds.

Droysen on sin.

According to Droysen the "excretions" of the Bad are to be expected as natural consequences of civilisation. He takes the Bad, like Schiller, poetically ; as the unavoidable appendage of the finite mind ; as the "shadow of the mind's transciency, indispensable for the appearance of the Good," as that which by virtue of the nature of things is destined to annihilate itself and to disappear.

Cultural advance and infernal depravity keeping pace.

Whenever artificial refinement is taken for civilisation, so that under this self-delusion of a period with high literary culture, perhaps, social abnormities are palliated until the smooth surface bursts, it will always be found to have concealed a more than brutal, an infernal depravity. And this, we claim, is really on the increase, rather than showing a tendency to diminish.

Refutation of false ideas concerning the Bad.

Inspecting even the praiseworthy institutions of modern humanitarianism, all the different asylums, or the long chain of prisons filled with fallen men in numbers increasing, we find something more than simply delinquencies of human nature: or when looking over all the misery which these houses contain, besides that which they do not contain and which in most cases is selfinflicted, we find something worse than the mere reverse side or the foil of the Good. In the face of all these dreadful, dismal phenomena, does it still seem harsh to go

The Bad will not disappear of its own accord.

to the bottom of the matter and call the deficiency by its right name? Or are those men to blame and to be gibed, who in their way counteract the dark powers which will not disappear of their own accord? Are we to be rebuked if we find something infernal working underneath history, which we denounce and hate, and with which, because of the havoc wrought by it, to compromise in any form we indignantly decline?

The single true phase of such philosophy as that of Droysen is the fact that the Bad lives by its opposition to the Good. The Bad is something which is ever ready to annihilate anything else in order to save itself. It tries at least to maintain itself by blackening what is noble, if it can imitate it no longer; or by palliating its own obnoxiousness in order to justify its clamor for tolerance. It is the practice of those who countenance the Bad, to calumniate the Good under the hypocritical garb of moral indignation or intellectual seriousness: it is the strategy of the Bad thus to

strategy.

mystify the unwary and inexperienced, and to intimidate and scoff at those who will not make "allowances" for it. There is always that shrewdness connected with the

The lie (§38) is the pliable instrument of the Bad;

Bad, which calls superstitious what is really good and sacred, and calls those hypocrites who combat it. Thus the lie is the pliable instrument of the Bad, made strong by intermixing some truth so as to assume to itself the appearance of the Good. The Bad

lives off the Good, proving thereby its own reality as well as that of its opposite .

lives by sapping out the Good, acting as tho it were not in opposition to, but in unison and sympathy with it. Now when we recognise that the Bad is a parasite, which maintains itself at the expense of the Good by sapping, falsifying, mystifying, calumniating and denying the Good—then we acknowledge the reality and heterogeneity of

The shelter under which nothing but the Bad can prosper. §110.

both principles. In other words the Bad thereby proves what it intends to deny, namely, its own existence and at the same time the reality and life of its opposite and superior.

Doctrine from Plato to Schleiermacher.
§ 39, 41, 109.

Let us summarise. From Plato to Schleiermacher it has been taught that the Bad was something which had no reality, a nonentity: or something which is merely not good as yet. It was regarded as something which would disappear as soon as a

contriving at another than Christian cultus;

new form of culture, other than the Christian, were once established, as Socialism makes its adherents believe.

The Bad an "non-ens." (?)

If this were the case the Bad would be innocent enough to be left alone, and allowances might be made for it. Then it would be wise and convenient indeed, to become reconciled to the Bad. Then the partisan of the Bad might be excused without the asking; he would be jus-

Theories making light of the Bad;

tified in following his own inclinations, under the pretense that such was his religion; and the Christian moralist would be the most contemptible fanatic; Christianity, in fact, would be superfluous; to provoke the revenge of the Bad would not only be folly, but a downright sin—and thus, they claim, all the depths of which we speak would be shut up. The energy of the Bad would then be only imaginary, a theoretical nuisance; it would lose its terror by the spreading of intelligence; illumining progress and progressive prosperity would be the natural result. It was a French philosopher who was allowed to expound this philosophy before Frederic the Great. "Old Fritz" merely answered: "You do not know the 'canaille,'" and the philosophy of the advocates of the Bad soon after was realised in a place near Versailles with a vengeance. Again it revives under the fostering care of such as overestimate popularity and who certainly must have an interest in covering up rather than unmasking the Bad, or of such as utilise it by dishing it out in spicy and sensational reading matter. To all such sophistry we simply give the lie.

Others argue that the Bad originates in the finiteness or sensuality of the human being as such. Then it would have to be considered as something essentially necessary for every individual being, because everything continues to be finite. Or should the Bad be identical with the sensual appetites? It then would be as necessary as in the other case, since man continues to be a corporeal being. Under both of these suppositions the Bad would have to be recognised as a necessary momentum in the order of the physical and ethical cosmos. It would have to be explained as a means designed for the good purpose ; as the principle by which forces, through opposition, are to be incited to higher development, that is, it would have to be thought identical with the great natural polarity, and would be "THE" motive, the corresponding pole of the Good! But the polar tension necessary to realise progress is not thinkable as something contradictory or refractory. The stigmatic mark of the Bad is not simply a derogatory negation ; neither does the concept of the sensuous or of the finite indicate anything bad on account of its limitation. In contrast to finiteness it is one of the chief characteristics of the Bad that it maintains the most stubborn persistence. It ever tends to detriment, destruction, annihilation. It never "does any good." Hence we repudiate the schemes which dare to render the Bad the mere reverse side of the Good, or the foil which is to give the Good its brilliancy. We denounce the allegory which is to represent the Bad as merely the shadow of the painting, necessary for making the figures appear plastic ; for if the painting of history, that is to say, its true reality, would depend upon the Bad, then this would have to be taken for the plastic principle of personality also. Then the monstrosities and caricatures, in their particular instances, would have to be adopted as the good products of the Bad, to which the normal formations were owing their significance. Abnormities would be prerequisites of history, and essential premises for its explanation.

marginal note: ascribed to man's sensuous, or to his finite nature,

marginal note: described as belonging to the order of things.

marginal note: The Bad not to be coordinated with the physical polarities;

marginal note: is not the foil by which the Good is rendered brilliant;

marginal note: not the shadow to bring out, by way of contrast, the characteristic features of history.

Leibnitz made use of all that shadow-philosophy, absurd as it seems, in the construction of his "best of all the worlds." He needed that mixture to a degree almost of identifying the Good with the Bad, insomuch as the discords are needed in the composition of musical colors—as much as Rothe needed it for the definition of morality.

marginal note: The use which Leibnitz made of the foil and shadow theory.

It is odd, when after all, one becomes almost persuaded even by Schopenhauer, that the Bad is founded in the order of yonder world, just as Schelling made it ascend from the obscure chasm which yawns in the nature of the deity!

marginal note: Origin of the Bad in the Deity (?) Schelling, Schopenhauer

§ 41. The Bad is now acknowledged as that which detached itself from universal order and which, in opposition to it, hides and seeks to maintain itself. Despite its subterfuges it stands convicted as something very real. It is unmasked as a power which unfolds itself and had no need of being especially revealed because it reveals, or rather betrays, itself in the sphere of personal life, and in the form of evils throws its shadows also upon nature. Its shadows are darkest in that portion of nature and of history which is nearest to its light and crown. It is a power which presses so hard upon consciousness, and which leaves traces upon it and all pertaining to it so deep, that it can not be laughed or sung away, nor stifled by ignoring it.

marginal note: It needs no revelation; reveals itself.

That "anxious suspense resulting from the Bad, Lotze observes, is rendered the more distinct, the more the consciousness disowns guilt under excuse of natural deficiencies. Denial oppresses so much the worse, because man becomes the more vividly conscious that the excuse is not true, since mere deficiency can be overcome through the superiority of the mental part by education and selfculture, whilst guilt and fear can only be taken away by a higher liberation of the mind". This emancipation will have to proceed in accord with the truth, and on the strength of the spirit's reaction against the suspense by ceasing to submit to selfdeception, by ceasing to identify wickedness with weakness, and by earnestly seeking that which sets consciousness at peace. Thus the proper discrimination is formulated which must be made between natural deficiencies and the tendencies of pseudo-culture.

marginal note: "Anxious suspense." Lotze.

marginal note: Pseudo-Culture, attempts to stifle the selfreproach by conscience, but only brings out the more sharply the difference between weakness and wickedness.

It is chiefly through the latter that the power of the Bad endeavors, and at great lengths succeeds, to maintain itself by establishing subterfuges of its being necessary, or convenient, or indifferent, or insignificant; if it does not even with an affected naivete insist upon its utility. But the lie is nailed fast tho it ever more tightly encoils the very person who seeks the false excuse, or who tries to shift the fault upon something or somebody else, or who would screen himself behind ignorance. Such attempts only betray the culprit's consciousness of the fact, that the guilt becomes the clearer to him the more he dodges the inner reproach, or rejects the verdict which holds him responsible for his clinging to the Bad.

Denial
makes sin the more
flagrant and aggravates
guilt.   § 11, 12, 109.

Innocence or excusable ignorance become the more distinguishable from guilt, and refuse to be mixed up with it, or to serve as screens, the more emphatically the denial of the wrong manifests its wickedness.

If now an "emancipated mind", which describes conscience as a coward, would call that "anxious suspense" of Lotze imaginary, or a thing with which superstitious ignorance alone troubles itself—then the questions arise: Who or what is it, that coerces consciousness to institute an inspection of those misgivings? What is it that, in spite of philosophical selfabsolution, conducts an objective, undaunted, investigation? Who is that incorruptible prosecuting attorney, whose truthful evidences avails with the culprit to own his guilt? That anxious suspense, this despondency of the mind, can not for ever be tyrannised by simulated courage of dissembling knownothingism. It is such a counterforce as seems to affect man antagonistically, whilst ultimately it only manifests the right of the Good to reclaim man for participating in the enjoyment of its reality.

**Conscience is but
manifesting the
right of the Good
to reclaim man
for the enjoy-
ment of its
reality.**

Whenever this witness of the Good reappears from the realm of unreflected consciousness to testify against the Bad, it stirs up dreaming souls to such awakenings, that as empiric facts millions of bloody sacrifices are made in answer to the crying demands of expiation!

It arises from unreflect-
ed consciousness,
awakens the sleeping
soul, reclaims man for
the pursuit of his
destiny, demands
expiation.   § 11.
Wuttke.   § 109, 157.

If Droysen's assertion were correct that with cultural rearrangement, or Buckle's, that with proper food, the bad would disappear from history, then we would have to lay aside the Good as the standard rule for measuring historic value; and as with the Good, so it would be with the right and the beautiful, both implied therein. If these are really ideal and not mere PHYSICAL qualities, then the Bad, too, must be referred to the department of MORAL concepts, where it is to help us, by the comparison of the contrast, to define the boundaries of morality. This was the true element, and most probably the meaning in Rothe's exposition of the Bad as something moral.

Droysen and Buckle on
physical origin
of the Bad: Rothe's
referring it to the moral
realm.

Into whatever fashion humanity may develop, never will it come to pass, that a tendency will gain the victory, which would despoil those moral qualities of the Good, the True, and the Beautiful of their ideal contents.

**Indestructibility
of the moral
element.**

Materialism in this as in every other respect, signifies no more than an intervening episode, recurring in order to remind the human mind of the difficulty of approaching its ideals. Never can materialism for any length of time discourage the mind in its aspirations toward realising them. Ill-tempered about the difficulty, man may for a time become so exasperated as to undertake the destruction of these ideals. But soon he sobers down again, and in turn begins anew to reconstruct the fabric of the ideal world, the image of which is profoundly imprinted into his entire being. After each of such general smash-ups he searches for a broader, deeper and more solid foundation, and for less destructible material to complete the edifice of social welfare, and to secure its future safety. The structure becomes more firmly joined together in proportion as the ideals of moral excellency are more generally appreciated and taken hold of, and as the ever threatening dangers become known the better.

Materialistic
attempts to
destroy the ideals
and to supplant
them by other
regulatives, only
serve the firmer
to establish
the Good, the
True and the
Beautiful.

The Bad is to be apprehended as more than the not-yet-being of the Good; as more than a shadow; as more than a discord; as worse than a deficiency. It is more than a "negative principle." It is a positive reality. **The Bad is a will.**

What the Bad is
not.

It is a will.

And it is an act of the will, a manifestation of its freedom, if one has the courage of his conviction, not to shield this arbitrariness of the will by frivolously misconstruing the reality or sublimating the essence of the Bad. Of course, it takes a strength greater than the headstrong perverseness of the human empiric will to unmask the Bad and to face it, instead of yielding to, or compromising with it.

Ethical conduct can not be based upon intellectualism; it must be based upon the will.

Ethical conduct not to
be based on mere
intellectualism.

The Good, on the other hand, can not be reduced to a fortuitous coincidence of happy circumstances at the beginning, and to subsequent hereditary transmission. This would amount to no more than an external correctness without any per-

What the Good is.

sonal merit. Morality put on from the outside is but a caricature of the "mos" of the Romans which even they conceived as containing an inner motive. Morality as well as its opposite has its source and seat in the innermost depths of personal nature in a pristine will. It can only be determined upon by a converted, that is by a freed will: and its contents, the Good, can only be maintained and preserved by resisting, and conquering the Bad.

The perverse will betrays itself by the unwillingness to engage in this combat. It is prone to do the Bad, or at least to secretly adhere to it, to sympathise with it, or to negotiate with it, that is, to try the realisation of the lie. The explanation of its origin and the demonstration of its malicious intent must be postponed, until we have found the actual confirmation of that, which at the present stage of the investigation could only be conjectured. We must first gather up the facts issuing from the bad will. In the mean time each may look within himself for the proofs of our presumed axiom concerning the will and its entanglement with the Bad.

From what has been demonstrated so far, we stand, to all appearances, before a great depression, before a deplorable descension, a steep incline—before a veritable sink.

Of the proclivity toward moral baseness, which pervades the combination of human nature, abundant proof is extant ; the deterioration of the whole world of nations depicts the depravity of human nature sadly enough. The entanglement of the evils with the bad ever manifests itself in one way or another. We hear complaints about it as of a conflict, a discord, a turbulence, a passion affecting all human relation at every stage of culture and in every age. But the complaints also divulge the truth that the Bad is alien to human nature, that it belongs not to its type.

Somewhere, at some time, a rupture must have happened that caused a general upsetting, a complete ruination. There alone can we seek for the origin of all the dilemmas encumbering our problem. Only from such an occasion is it possible to derive the disfigurement of all ideals, to account for the perversion of all blessings destined for man, and to explain that incessant detachment and estrangement which tends to utter dissoluteness. So humiliating is this degradation that, a few serious thinkers excepted, men would not even touch upon this open sore of humanity.

How this sinking could have commenced, and why it should have occurred in the spiritual sphere of existence, from whence we become conscious of it in the feeling of guilt, has been previously alluded to and will be ascertained more explicitly further on, when profound selfknowledge shall have been rendered possible.

Schelling, with reference to this problem and with deep insight came to the conclusion that "the human race could not as yet have left the stage of its nearest family or tribal relations prior to the exceedingly more developed national relations, when it underwent that crisis." It was a break so portentous, and there ensued changes so thorough-going, that we can place the disaster nowhere else but at that point of the consciousness from whence all the faculties emanate as their common focus. The reason for this statement we derive from the fact that the differences of nations cannot be thought of without different languages; and language is something spiritual.

A confusion of languages cannot be thought of unless considered as an internal event ; hence a distraction of consciousness must be acknowledged as preceding the break of human unity, the fractured condition of the race. What preceded the estrangement of the human family and its separation must have been a violent upsetting of the fundamental parts and vital principles of which human nature consists.

A historical catastrophe must have occurred; a manifestation of preternatural depravity. A rebellion, a scandal, a crime must have been the cause of the shock which deranged consciousness to its very foundations, and benumbed the feelings to their very core, to that center which was to maintain the union of mankind. The spiritual relationship was torn asunder. The God-consciousness left after the first great calamity must have been utterly corrupt ere the sense of shame could have become lost so far as not to be able any longer to restrain man from the base deed, and ere the feeling of guilt could thus have been trifled with. No other but this hypothesis explains the situation. After tearing up happy relations and falling away from a glorious destiny, departure after departure was taken. Man fell back under the law of inferior nature where detachment is the order. Faint recollections of a lost state of blissfulness, and faint conceptions of a glorious destiny, now receded into a dim distance. This the fugitives took along with them, together with a few symbolic ordinances as old and sacred but fading family-heirlooms. Entirely misconceiving their original destiny, they pursued the goal of blessedness in a wrong direction. At their birth the nations started down the steep incline. The sphere of sinking expanded, the falling away into deeper demoralisation accelerated at the rate of geometrical progression.

Since for good reasons we made the fractured portions of humanity analogous to geological strata and conglomerates, we are justified to suppose the cause at bottom of that sunken condition as being analogous to a previous eruption.

During the last thirty years the idea of a downward tendency of religious cognitions, instead of evolving Monotheism from Fetishism, has evidently gained ground. Since Burnouf recommended to fall back upon the old way of explaining heathenism (in the Revue du deux mondes, 1864), many have found it passable. Ebrard's demonstration of the truth of religious degradation from original purity (1874) stands unchallenged, despite M. Mueller's attempt to theologise upon the "Origin of Religion."

Brugsch some years ago established original Monotheism from Ægyptology; and subsequently v. Langegg brought out the original Monotheism of the Chinese. We hardly need refer to the history of the Church in the fourth century as the most striking example of the quick deformation of religion pure and simple. And another instance of later date has been averred by Cushing. His investigation warrants the supposition that the Zuni-Indians, showing traces of Monotheism, are descendants of that highly cultured Toltec-Aztecian nation which used to rule from Chile to the Salt Lake regions. Prescott already was of the opinion that their human sacrifices commenced not earlier than about two centuries before the conquest of Mexico. It is now established as a fact, that previous to this period the Mexicans offered flowers. The fact of original Monotheism might be corroborated by hundreds of weighty quotations but the time draws near when any such defence of our axiom will be antiquated.

Savagery was not the pristine state of the human family. Quite the contrary is true. "It is," so we say with W. v. Humboldt, "the state of a fast extinguishing society, resulting from a disastrous subversion of things in general. This must have been preceded by a deplorable catastrophe which broke up the race and caused it to weaken and to wander."

In what way could this portentous and ruinous accident, preceding the disaster, have been wrought?

§ 42. Primitive God-consciousness must have been the same in every person, uniting them all. It was a unit in itself, paramount to the unit of the first man whom we consider as the common root of the race because of its common God-consciousness. It must have consisted in a deep immediate cognition, a vision-like and pure conception of God, and it was a gift.

In primitive Monotheism (Ur-Monotheismus) which the Germans deem established through archæology, comparative philology, and the philosophy of religions, man found himself enwrapped, as it were, in the enjoyment of the tasks enjoined upon him together with these gifts. That form of consciousness must of necessity vanish like a sun-set as soon as man's central vision is changed to different views, to relative blindness. Darkening is the sight of the would-be-God, when for the first time he observes his condition and finds himself much like an animal, creeping out of sight. Sequent to doubt and disobedience his cordiality to his partner, part of himself, turns to brutality, because of his being held responsible for what is going on in the family. And with the suavity of family affections his whole existence becomes disruptured.

Of the primitive God-consciousness, every man carries a remnant within himself as his conscience, as the point of connection where union may be re-established. It is personal, but it holds equal sway over all, because it partakes of the nature of the spiritual world whose character we found to consist in formal unity under material diversity, that is, personal multiplicity. This great preservative gift remained with man throughout all the vicissitudes of his progressing degeneracy. When mankind entered into the diverse and complicated relations multiplying with the descending stages of worldly life, world-consciousness began to compress the remnant of God-consciousness to the hardness and stuntedness of a "rudimentary organ."

Yet that weak remnant, on the strength of its belonging to the realm of indissolubility, proves ever strong enough to take care of man's interest which he neglected. It thus remains his reminder (die Er-inne-rung), the witness of original and universal revelation, and shows to him in the darkness the way back to clearer God-consciousness. One remembrance after another reviving, a cognition of reconciliation brightens up, until by way of intensifying religiousness (Ver-inne-rung) the mind is gradually led to return from the manifold to the One.

In God-consciousness, what there is left of it, the unity of mankind is warranted. Even the weak remnant of it prompts man to return from diversion upon the periphery toward the center, so that instead of losing himself into the manifold, the reunion with the One, consequently with all men, may be established.

Herein the history of the religions of mankind consists, provided our proposition is correct—which we still hold to be hypothetical—that the "I Am" is.

In order to fully appreciate the reconstructive efforts as prompted by conscience, we must enlarge somewhat on the consequences of the apostasy. The communion with the center of the divine coherency being rent asunder, affects not only man's inner nature: For from him as the apex of nature, the disrupture extends to all that externally belongs to him. Nature, in keeping its true course, seems to revolt against him, because it does not, on account of man's eccentricity, cease to revolve around its great center, the Creator. Man, appointed to be the lord of nature, becomes its dependent and serf. Rebellion is retaliated by rebellion. It is now felt to be a great loss what a great lie had promised to be a great gain. Man is now conscious of being left to his own self, of being deprived of his contentment (the root of which word means "to hold together") deprived of harmony within himself and of communication with the deity. This deprivation as now held forth to consciousness proves the most mortifying of all its loneliness and its losses. Man feels himself lost in an oppressive silence, in solitude with that still small voice for his nearest companion, which now is going to take care of him in a peculiar way; he finds himself alone under the pangs of selfreproach for being at variance with his destiny.

What is left of original God-consciousness alone warrants the reunion of the human race.

Contentment. § 43.

The losses.

Henceforth man's selfconsciousness sustains gradual changes. The eye of humanity, open for unity as long as it was not entirely abnormal, stares away into an empty distance as under an epileptic spasm. It opens to meet the multiplicity in conflict and to seek diversion therein, in order to pacify the mind. And the mind became absorbed, indeed, by the beautiful things of the realm of the secondary Good; man works hard for his momentary enjoyment, regardless of the unsatisfactory pleasures they yield; he goes to the eccentricity of deifying these things.

Selfreproach.

Consciousness diverted in the multiplicity.

Thus Polytheism is created, wherein man instinctively attempts to make up for godliness in his own ways. To make up for union lost, he will create a world-empire. To make up for lost dominion over nature and for his loss of possessing the world, he sets himself to either rule or ruin, and to gain the world in spite of Heaven, trying, at the same time, to claim Heaven his own as a matter of right.

Deification of parts of the Secondary Good.

Polytheism.

The main feature of selfmade religion then becomes apparent:—the mixture of true elements of the religious sense with phantastic outgrowths of a frightened imagination and of superstitious ignorance.

Exertions in selfsalvation.

Memories of a once blissful state are mingled with wrong aspirations to happiness, the loss of which man tries to retrieve by satisfying sensual appetites and wild passions. The sacred traditions, rites and symbols, recognised as the old family-heirloom altho their meaning being lost, are mixed in with those "different views" which perceive God as being in bad humor and needing to be made good; to which religion seems to be all wrong and man all right; on strength of which man attempts to justify and to save himself by blaming something else with being at fault.

The family-heirloom: tradition, rites, etc. mixed into a selfmade religion instrumental in selfpreservation. § 26, 40, 61, 74.

Such is the history of heathendom, ancient and modern.

Man, stunned by the fall, wanders as in a daze into exile. Selfconsciousness succumbs to worldliness and man becomes bewildered like a sheep lost in a desert.

Heathendom ancient and modern. Religious mixture.

Gnosticism of old witnesses how the various forms of idolatry were intermixed by minds, which had allowed themselves to become inveigled and put in the fetters of carnal propensities from which they were now trying to extricate themselves. The result was a compound of polytheistic naturalism and Pantheism.

Genesis of Pantheism. § 54.

Of the precipitate of a sunken consciousness; of the diversion of the mind into externals; of the departure from the center of life toward the indistinct and hazy periphery; of inner estrangement followed by exterior dissolution and dismemberment, dissipation and derangement; Pantheism, even in the garb of its aristocratic and dissembling indifference, will ever be the refined sublimate and final product.

Gnosticism: transitory stage between Polytheism and Pantheism.

Pantheism: attempt at restoring the lost union,

Pantheism, always in keeping with its precedents, is to be defined as the ever reiterated attempt to restore the lost union under the form of natural generalness, that is, in the sphere of "material unity with mere formal diversity."

in the form of natural generalness.

This is the selfconfession of humanity before the bar of history as confided to its most sacred records.

Confession of humanity at the bar of history.

§ 43. Our own life affords plentiful empirical evidence to prove the truth of our inferential judgment. From the earliest awakenings of our own consciousness—hedged in by juvenile trustfulness, and enchanted by continual surprise and amazement—as soon as the incipient intellect is set free and thought becomes intensified, we may observe a posteriori how we ourselves take the downward course, and how we follow the centrifugal tendency in proportion to our consciousness becoming distracted by the multitude of outside impressions. With the increase of selfmade wants, and in spite of their gratification, dissatisfaction grows. The mind yearns for things pleasing, for contentment, bliss and rest, ever striving after something better. Seeking the Good in the wrong direction, seeking happiness in outward circumstances, we find fault with the temporal and sensuous objects; tho being good in themselves, our disappointments are charged against them. Whilst man becomes aware of his dependency upon the lower world, he begins to feel his relationship to the higher. Yet he imagines the visible things nearer to him, and they seem to him more necessary. He tries to court the favor of his "good luck" and to cultivate more favorable circumstances. From creation he selects surrogates for the almost forgotten and distant "higher being". He allows himself to become inflated on account of "his" gifts and ceases to be thankful to the giver. He symbolises the qualities of created things and then addresses his worship to the symbols. Devoting himself to the service of what was intended to serve him as the ethical apparatus, he allows himself to become subject to superstition. Stricken with paralysis, as it were, he is almost unable to use the apparatus, and becomes not only nature-bound, but finds himself under the bondage of strong appetites, of wrong passions and of demoniac fears in addition. Man then becomes frightened, moreover, by certain shadows arising from the unknown depths of his dual, and now also dissolute, nature. Seeking in error, getting confused, terrified by inimical powers, he attempts to conciliate or to bribe them. Polytheism thus runs out into demonolatry. And yet man's inner nature, tho entirely out of joint, never ceases to reach out for something above. Not knowing the meaning of all that haunts him on one side and entices him on the other, he is kept from sinking below the degree of recovery.

Polytheism, embodying pantheistical misconceptions of the ideal in symbols and finally in idols, is to be understood in every case as that phase of the dilemma, when people, in their discomfiture dreaming and trembling, establish idols involuntarily as centers of coherency, so as not to become lost entirely in the perpetuating and widening secession.

For they all have remembrances of original unity, of dominion over nature, of the objective existence of the Supreme Good, and of immortality. Guided as the human mind is as yet by dim ideas and faint feelings of these truths, necessity induces men to united efforts for selfprotection and dominion.

It is in that stage of natural development that state-organisations are mistaken for the Supreme Good, and the representative of the state is made the deity. Erratic vestiges of the religious sentiment and its erroneous apperceptions are objectivised in sacrificial and funeral rites, in temple and tomb, in the capitol of the world-monarchy. · The gods are identified with the world in its multiplicity of phenomena, first with heavenly bodies, then with the generative forces, then with the destructive powers below, with beasts and demons, with guilt objectivised, then with ancestors and rulers, revered as deliverers with beasts in their escutcheons. · ʾ

Every act and event is brought into relation with the idols, whilst together with God-consciousness the cognition of personality is lost. The traditional and inherent truths are no longer understood; mutilated they are mixed in with a medley of distorted but personified idiosyncrasies, as to exterior relations and inner promptings, personified in lieu of the lost human personality.

Thus the conglomerate mass of superstition even must serve, for the time being, as a means not to save, but to preserve humanity from sinking below its nature and below the beasts. It must serve as a means of selfculture by which man is to keep himself above the line of irretrievable perdition, just as a shipwrecked person will

---

Marginal notes:

Empiric proof of the centrifugal downward tendency.

Secondary Good not at fault in our disappointments·

God-consciousness being deranged, man becomes inveigled in world-consciousness.

Visible things seem nearer to men and more necessary

Certain frightful shadows arise from the dissolute duality of the inner man. § 49, 54, 55, 109.

Demonolatry.

Idols inadvertantly established as centers of cohesion. § 26, 46, 61, 74, 75, 79, 114, 183, 177.

Polytheism instrumental in selfpreservation. ¶61.

Reminiscences of original unity, dominion, of the Supreme Good, of immortality. § 47, 55.

Deification of the state and its representative. § 78.

Cognition of personality lost with the consciousness of one personal God

whilst all possible idiosyncrasies are personified. § 45.

Superstition must for the time being serve as a preservative.

cling to a chance piece of timber. In or rather behind the idols the mind searches after the center of unity which was lost with the God-consciousness, because that loss is most acutely felt and least comprehensible or describable.

The severance of self-consciousness from God-consciousness can only have ensued from a deliberate act of the mind. After this rupture disintegration went on not only in humanity as a whole, whereby the race crumbled to pieces, but also and primarily in the faculties of the individual mind. The ego became distracted. Wrong inclinations and arbitrariness, fear and perverseness turn into wild fancies, insubordinate appetites, passionate temper and utter dissipation. The blessings of life are turned into curses. The promises of luck and lusts turn into the loss of energy, of dignity, of property, liberty and life.

Severance of the race lies in the departure from God-consciousness.

Origin of the calamity in the individual mind;

The calamity was at first not of a physical nor an intellectual nature—it was an ethical apostasy. And the outward evils resulting were not bad in themselves. On the contrary, they were turned to good purpose by inducing man to turn from his tendency toward the periphery of things and their diversion, and to return to the center of unity. The laws of nature, working in unison with the moral law and purpose, inflict punishment in the way of educational discipline. The rupture could be brought to the recognition of man in no other way than by its consequences. The sudden, and steep, and general sinking, the collapse of his applied gifts and the heartrending distress of the soul, could at first be perceived in no other manner, but in the feelings. It was only afterward, that the rupture was perceived physically, in the miseries of privation and that it was conceived intellectually by reflecting upon the turmoil of national differences, sequent to the disturbances of social relations.

is neither physical nor mental but moral—an apostasy.

Outward evils resulting are not bad; serve as disciplinary measures.
§ 61, 74.

CH. VII.   THE MYTHOLOGICAL PROCESS.

§ 44. The series of ascending improvements of consciousness, passing through mythological phases, as "evolution" was trying to demonstrate with reference to the cultured nations, does not exist.

Evolution of religion refuted.

The spurious inferences, upon which the logics of Physiological Psychology attempted to build its conjectures, can not be generalised and explained by materialistic monism. Comparative philosophy of religion, now investigating this matter, finds it not so easy to construct God-consciousness from fetishism and base it upon cloud-pictures of poetry. The diverse strata forming the historic substructure must be unearthed, before the cardinal principles in the formation of consciousness can be rendered intelligible.

Such a procedure as filling out gaps by borrowing philosophical premises, or by the mechanical mode of interpretation engaged in by those, who put evolution in the place of the manifestation of the spiritual world, can not claim that recognition which is granted to empirical science. The natural mind, insisting upon its liberty, acts, in the first place, not simply by way of accidents, not mechanically. Much less will sound reason persist in dishonesty, if it erroneously appropriated metaphysical arguments for the sake of building a consistent world-theory irrespective of theology.

Example of illicit appropriation of principles alien to natural science.   § 14.

Natural knowledge honest enough to discountenance illicit use of metaphysical arguments in explaining religious problems.

Comparative mythology must consider three principles, says Adrian (in Bastian and Ranke, Archives of Anthropology, Oct., 1891, page 260.) viz: the faculties and endowments of the mind common to all men, and its propensities in general; the antecedent traditions; and the derivative intermixtures, interpolations, and interpretations indiscriminately construed from both in subsequent times and nations.

In the course of uninterrupted development and transmission of progress these lines of discrimination often vanish entirely, because of the chaotic state of blending idiosyncrasies. Hence it is in many cases very difficult to analyse the meanings of personifications; for the derivation of traditional rites and symbolised ideas is not always so demonstrable as in Greek and Roman mythology. Golther even despaired of the disentanglement of ethnical and mythological compounds.

Conditions of formulating theories of Mythology. Adrian, Golther.

It is clear, that Philosophy of History rendered its work as questionable as the Natural Philosophy of Hegelianism had become, when it built upon Schelling's premises of "identity."

By mythical religiousness commonly that phase of consciousness is understood, in which all impressions of the natural life are as yet promiscuously flowing together with the remnants of primeval intuitive God-consciousness. But such a muddle, such an aggregate of disconnected ideas has not as yet been discovered in the myths of any nation. This lack has slipped the attention of investigators.

Mythical religiousness never a compound of sense-perceptions and mental intuitions.

Stratification of
differently symbolised
Ideas and traditions
variously interpolated
and modified.

The fact is that national life in the stage of promiscuous or indefinite forms of religiousness always rested on distinct layers of different forms of religious consciousness according to differently symbolised ideas and variously interpolated or modified traditions, which in turns strove for ascendency and shifted one above the other.

Wars generally sprung
from religious motives.

The wars of those periods were generally caused by the religious eruptions sequent to the inability to discriminate between or to harmonise conflicting ideas, in matters of tradition and symbolism whenever one layer broke through the other. The broken remnants, however, were hardly ever thrown away by either the conquerors or the conquered, notwithstanding the anomalies arising from their intermixture.

Examples of .
perverted
traditions.
Further proof of the
calamity will be
adduced.
§ 41, 46, 107, 108, 110.

They thus became still more antagonistic, confused and perverted. For instance, what had been the deva, common to both the Sanskrit and Zend speaking people, became, after their estrangement, the dews of the Iranians, and the dev-ils of our vernacular, whilst the Greeks utilized the word in Zeus, and the Latin nations in deus.

Genesis of
mythological
religiousness.

That calamity, which befell the consciousness of union with God, we presupposed under condition of adducing proof. No other proposition will account for the subsequent catastrophe, for the break of the unity of humanity in which the parts were flung to all directions. At this stage of clearing up the problem, this proposition also yields a preliminary account for the abyss into which, religiously in the first place, humanity fell at some historic moment.

Ruins of primitive
revelation.   § 55.

As fractures and confounded elements of religious consciousness we recognised the psychological state of dissatisfaction with the secondary Good which was mistaken for the Supreme Good, a dissatisfaction always accompanied by the desire for something better, of which conscience has the standard measure of value in charge.

Fear of ghosts.
Shamanism.

As the first historic result of the deranged religious sentiency we observe Shamanism with its fear of ghosts, its ancestor-and snake-worship. The source of these perturbations, as it appears to us, lies in the false interpretation of the feeling of de-

Mixture of misconceived
external tradition with
inner remnants of
God-consciousness.

pendency and obligation. Mixed with the inner remnants of original God-consciousness and with corrupted external traditions these misconceptions gather strength in their downward course. In the confusion ensuing the mind becomes overwhelmed and stupefied. This explains the phenomenal attempts to satisfy the religious cravings of

Religious cravings of
the mind to be
satisfied by acts,
not ideas.

the mind by perverted rites and superstitious contrivances, that is, through acts and not with ideas or theories. The ruins of primitive revelation (which we shall gather up as we go along) no longer understood and twisted into corrupted idiosyncrasies, were transmitted and carried along with the external and ritual performances now

Remnants of
truth separable
from
superstitions.
§ 43, 55.

conceived as being religiously effective in themselves. These externals served as vehicles, in such a manner, however, as to be always easily distinguished and even to be instantly separated from the remnants of primitive, universal revelation.

Whenever nations advanced somewhat in culture, but never before, a layer of higher intellectuality formed itself above the lower stratum of superstitious ignorance. That a nation rids itself of the wild vagaries of the demoralized consciousness is

Discrepancies between
life and thought call
forth reflections upon
them.   § 55.

owing to the meditation upon these very idiosyncrasies perplexing them. They challenge reflection to disentangle the discrepancies between internal remnants of the original religious consciousness and the external traditionary fragments. For

Superstitious
acts
of homage superseded
by theories and
symbolism.

the mind ever involuntarily craves after centers of coherency. The creation of symbols and framing of theories is the result of these reflections attempting the emancipation of the mind, and the reinstatement into its birth-right.

In esoterics religion is
made the means to keep
the masses in
subjection.

Whilst in the lower stratum fear (that "anxious suspense") and ignorance are not dispelled, in order to keep the masses, as the weaker portion of the nation, in dire superstition and subjection,—thought in the layer above builds up esoteric systems and exoteric symbolism which are handed down by priestly castes in the forms of oracles and mysteries.

Religio-historic
memory awakens,
rendering
nations
historical.   § 1.

When "memory", that is the historical sense, awakens, when the idea of cohesion and continuity of human affairs dawns upon consciousness, then, and never before, a nation becomes historical. It is then that thoughts and deeds are deemed to be of

All forms of life
arranged in
conformity to
the conception
of the deity.
§ 42, 54, 71, 86, etc.

religious import, and that the whole of life is arranged under aspects of religious obligations and is brought into relation to the deity in every particular. It is only then that, under the auspices of historic memory, the formation of myths begins, which is explicable in no other way. None but historic nations form myths with distinctive features. It is the awakening of religio-historic consciousness, the translation, as it were, of the inner, religious promptings into thought which supersedes superstitious acts. The religio-historic consciousness fastens these thoughts to symbols and establishes fixed theories and systems from which the myths ensue. **Hence, we assert, that myths are not the parental source of religion—but that religio-historic memory is the source of the myths.** Historic nations alone have myths with distinct ingredients. Myths not the source of religion.

§ 45. Correctly, we trust, the genesis of mythology has thus been set forth from actual phases of religious selfculture, and from the phenomena of religious motives or incitements.

It is only after the problem has thus been cleared up that we have a right to speak of religious development and advance, which is greatly at variance with the ideas alledged by, and involved in, evolutionism. The first stage is utter degeneracy and perplexity, caused by the acute feeling of a great loss and the faint reminiscence of something better. Then follow attempts to reduce them to order around **reconstructed centers of cohesion;** then follows the displacement of superstitious acts by invented theories, and their embodiment into religio-historic legends. Now we may observe the further process of religious formations, deformities, and reforms. First degeneracy, perplexity, then attempts to form centers of cohesion. § 42, 46, 61, 74. and explanatory theories, then myths, then either development or relapse.

Just as we witnessed the rapid disintegration of man's consciousness after the great disruption, with some religious truth ever shining through, just so we find the nature of the lowest stratum of prehistoric and distorted tradition, mixed with superstitious anguish, always betraying itself by breaking through the advanced layers above. In the lower strata we find elements of truth ever present in superstition. In the upper classes there is a higher mental culture always tainted with the basest remnants of heathenism. For, the higher ideas in computed theories of natural religion were never able to abolish old superstitions. Hence we emphasise, that such an account of the character of mythology as given here, and such alone, is congruous with the empiric facts. As truths are intermixed with superstition, so superstition always clings to advanced ideas in natural religion. Advanced ideas never able to abolish superstition.

The Gods, in fact, are not creatures of fear: fear projects demons. Fear produces no deities but demons.

It is sickness with its perplexing incidents and its appalling end in death from which ancestor-worship, in the first place, originated.

The daunted mind contrived to appease the souls of deceased relatives or to ward off the dreaded designs of dead foes and haunting demons by means of conjury, magic art and sorcery. These became the religious usages predominant with the Mongolians of the Gobi regions, and developed into the witchcraft of the Akkadians who came from thence. Among the former the occult substratum may be observed in all its baseness to this day as the only form of consciousness; while the higher, a historic-mythical form of thought has gradually covered the nethermost layer to some extent. And a similar process is demonstrable in all nations, our own not excepted. Genesis of Shamanism, sorcery and Fetishism. Most debased form of ancestor-worhip, § 54. Mythical religiousness preserved original ideals much better. § 61.

They all know of an antecedent history beginning in times immemorial since which in some nations peculiar shades of religious consciousness have solidified and hardened into myths, whilst in other nations specific imaginings took their shapes in ways similar to the oozing of black fluids from subterranean cavities or gathering in swampy morasses or cheerless heaths. But none of the phantasmagories of the latter sort bears a higher relation to regular mythology, monumental or documentary, than shifting slang or capricious dialects bear to the literary wealth of a well-constructed, highly articulated language.

Once for all we take exception to the argument which implies that faith is the bastard of fear, to the inference that fear invented the idols of gods. We refute the conclusion by the fact, that it is the feeling of disobeyed obligations in the true religious sense which calls forth fear. This feeling of duty is a priori inherent in man in such a manner that he tries in vain to rid himself thereof. Fear not the source of religion, not the parent of faith.

Hence we review the course of religious deterioration in the following order. At first we observe the feeling of an indescribable loneliness and loss, rising from amongst the ruins of corrupted God-consciousness. Then the distracted and perplexed ideas, by thinking in pictures, mold the traditional and misapprehended rites into correspondingly grotesque symbols and unavailing idols; and finally, sequent to the utter loss of their meaning, into fetishes. Resume:

Religion was not produced by fear. On the contrary: fear is the buoy, the floating mark, signalising the submerged wreck of religion. **The feeling of the unknown God caused the fear.** Fear did not make the gods, did not bring forth speculative ideas of probable deities, but it caused consciousness to fall back upon superstitious acts of probable propitiation. Course of religious deterioration. The feeling of an unknown God called forth fear.

10

Shintoism
the nobler form of
ancestor-worship
testifies to the knowledge
of immortality.

Shamanism,
derived from it, its
corrupted form;

spreads as snake-cult
and
demonolatry;
infects all subsequent
mythology.
Hence devolution of
Fetishism.
ACHELIS.

Fear is the concomitant of death and darkness. There lies its natural genesis. Our conclusions as to its rise from religious grounds will be vindicated, none the less, if we present to our minds that form of Shintoism, which lies bare upon the surface in Central-Asia, where we can fathom the deepest depression of superstitious consciousness, and from whence, mixed with the fear of ghosts and with sorcery and Shamanistic demonolatry, it spread everywhere. Originally it consisted of subverted notions based upon such true elements as had been obtained from the knowledge of immortality. The stultified mind in its almost unconscious state, grasps at any apprehensible object and attributes supernatural forces to it. Fetishism is the result, and the beginning, at the same time, of heathenism proper—the modern and home-made forms included. In this sense Achelis's evolutionism is to be understood.

This is the offshoot of
necromancy
the world over.
TRENDELENBURG, BASTIAN,
SCHLAGINTWEIT, PEET.

Abhorrence of death, and being afraid of the night and of sprites, lie at the bottom of Chinese and Japanese idolatry. This is the main feature of ancestor-worship, kept up among them despite their seeming indifference to religiousness, and combined with the dragon-worship to which all Turanians are addicted. Equally universal among them is the reverence paid to skulls (or scalps in lieu of them) and the practices of conjury and necromancy. These elements of Shamanism have, as by contagion, spread even into the Persian system. So was Hindoo culture tinctured with Mongolian idolatry and snake-worship by way of the primeval population of India. Schlagintweit has proved this for the whole extent of India as dating from the time of pre-Aryan occupation. Peet has done the same with reference to all the primitive inhabitants of North and Central America in his "Serpent-Symbolism" 1887.

Neither is snake-worship and anthropophagy ever missing with the West Aryans. The Greeks were addicted to it as well as the Druids. At both terminal points, Peking and Rome, exactly the same spiritism prevails. Intercourse with the dead by means of mediums, prisms etc., is nowhere more firmly established than in China—only paid better in Paris or New York. The rites associated with spiritism have been enumerated by Bastian. The proofs

Means of protection
from evil spirits.

for this custom in Rome have been gathered long ago. For, under cover of the official worship of the gods, the fear of phantoms held even the heroic Romans in awe. It was in consequence of wild spiritism that more than one emperor butchered children in order to obtain magic charms from their intestines.

In the old Pelasgian culture, and in later times at the construction of bridges, we notice what Trendelenburg described as the "worship of infernal demons so intrinsically connected with necromancy." Owing to the same circumstances the capitol in Rome received its name from a dead head. With the Siberian Wotjaks the same custom is in vogue up to date. According to von Steinen's conjecture their house-spirits are the spirits of ancestors.

The souls of the dead are as prominent in the life and consciousness of the Micronesians and Melanesians, as in the world-theory of the Chinese and Japanese. Upon the island of Mangaia the dead are imagined to walk about the most desolate regions of the seashore. They consist of a ghostly network, wearing herbs as their garments, and red creepers around their heads. Moaning they flit about their former homesteads until, gathered by a leader, they are conducted in droves to the dark place. The religions of the Papua and the Palauans seem to be made up entirely of such imagined relations to the realm of spectres. Among the Austral-negroes the superstition prevails, that departed souls sit wailing under the trees; ever on the alert they fill the woods, and see without being seen. At night demons are supposed to fly through the air, causing man to be in trepidation all the time, and to be on the defensive, so that for his protection he is ever in need of magic bones, of the fat of kidneys of the deceased, of innumerable talismans of that sort. Much of the same beliefs and customs prevail among all the Micronesians and Melanesians. With the Dajjaks the skulls of ancestors

Skulls of Dajjaks

Mirrors in Japan.

are venerated just as they are in Japan. Before the mirror once used by ancestors or before their images, the Japanese make oaths just as the Romans, who imagined their city to be crowded with penates and lares, solemnised theirs. And how many little hobgoblins of pagan origin have been handed down to our juvenile world, as for instance the Irish customs on the Hallow Eve of All-souls-day, especially in homes where Christian literature is despised.

Everywhere we find the same thralldom of rank fearfulness, or the enchanting belief in mischievous fairies, or in frightful manifestations of souls doomed to restlessness.

The Australian aborigines believe that not only departed souls but even the sorcerers, called "mediums" with us, ride through the air and are carried hither and hither by spirits—just as it was held with regard to Wodan's wild chase to the Brocken, and with regard to the horse-shoe lost on such occasions.

Horseshoe of Wodan.

In Leipzig everybody knows the beer-cellar from which Dr. Faust rode up in the air upon a cask: and every Erfurtian knows the small alley through which he drove —much more since Goethe wrote about him; and we must not think that the "lower classes" who fairly believe this, are not "enlightened," for they read the daily paper and have outgrown going to Church.

Roots of necromancy in
the Himalayas.

The belief in witchcraft, sorcery, necromancy, and soothsaying pervades all nations, the "upper crust" nowhere excepted. It is that very profusion of roots from the Himalayas, which ramifies below the surface throughout all parts of humanity, sending new shoots into the open air not only among the savages, but wherever we meet black arts, talismans, amulets good luck horse-shoes —fetishes.

Upon the Gold-coast of Guinea the office of the fetish-priest is highly revered. But such alone, as are specially endowed can obtain its honors, those who are experts in frantic dancing and raving mania, just as it is in Asia where Fakirs and Brahmins have learned to make it their specialty. Fetishpriests in Guinea.
Fakirs in Asia. Libations.

In that part of Africa mentioned as in other parts, nobody would neglect to make amends to the fetishes mornings and evenings. At every meal the fetish receives homage; libation is made at every drink. Before any enterprise is undertaken the fetishes must be bribed to favor it; after every success thank-offering is the first duty. If expectation is disappointed, then of course it is so much the worse for the fetish. Thus the fetish may be anything and is good for everything. It renders the conjugal state prolific and protects family life; it serves as a lightning rod for the burst of ill humor, or a pretext for caricaturing and rejecting even Christianity.

Now what tainted the church is of a far opposite nature and entirely alien to it, as the sequel shall prove. Fetishism is not of religious, much less biblical origin; neither is biblical religion in any way related to it, nor can it by any means be brought into relation with it. Whatever infidelity may pick out of the biblical contents to illustrate its derivation from Asiatic paganism, can not deteriorate the things sacred to the faith in revealed religion. Fetishism in church is of Hamito-Semetic not Christian origin. § 201

True, I know of a family who gave "holy water" of a good old age to a sick hog in order to prolong its life, whilst, when the daughter became sick and died, there was great lamentation, because the application of the elixir had been forgotten in her case. In another house the father suffered with tooth-ache. The son was sent to the neighbors after midnight for their large "Mother of God" which stood behind the door in the "Putz—Stube," because "our own, being so small, is of no avail". In the year A. D., 1853 on the festivities of the chief relics in the Bamberg cathedral we read on the large placard hung up at the main entrance: "O holy Nail, ora pro nobis!" Instances of such caricatures: "Holy nail" at Bamberg.

But such travesties upon religion, such tolerance and fostering of superstition in the Church even, must not be imputed to Christianity. Such cases can as readily be proven to have been allowed to encroach upon it from Hamito-Semitic sources, as those which the Old Testament history repudiated in such an awful manner.

What does all this fetishism denote? We answer that human consciousness has an idea of some power above that represented by the fetish. In the protecting charms, a horse-shoe, perhaps, or an owl nailed to the barn door— in consecrated fluids, in rituals, æthetically embellished, in sacrifices working ex opere operatum, etc., people believe that some one may possess the means for gaining power over the fetish, if only the right, that is, the stronger fetish were hit upon.

Examples of that sort have been described at length by Waltz, from the details of daily life, private and public. He related, how the filling of the fishing-nets, the ripening of the grain produce, the stoppage of pestilence, the making of rain-showers, etc., are ascribed to the fetishes. Crocodiles and sharks are not to be slighted when the different offerings upon the list of sacrifices are to be complied with. In these observances, we detect the cause of, and the mode in which, the Ægyptian Paut (of Champillon) or the Enneade (of Brugsch) had become corrupted. And we can not, in this connection forget what Motley gathered from the Dutch archives concerning the fetishes found with the assassin of William the Silent, fetishes which the Jesuits had given him to make him invisible after the deed. Nor can we forget what Max Mueller says with reference to the "feidicos" of the Portuguese which reminded the Africans of their own magic charms, so they adopted even the Christian name for them. Magic bones were not only bought up by the Elector Frederick the Wise for his new chapel in Wittenberg to the number of 5005 (L. v. Ranke, Reformation I, page 163.) but also the Mongolians are fond of them, and the Ojibway Indians embellish them with their rarest feathers. Ulterior significance of Fetishism. Waltz.

Fetishes found with the assassin of William the Silent. Motley.

Derivation of the word from the feidicos of the Portuguese. Max Mueller.

Relics of Frederick the Wise. Ranke.

This leads us to our own country. The favorite practice of scalping is nothing but modified skull-or ancestor-worship. Shamanism, the corruption of the latter, held sway over the Maya-Aztecs and their comrades throughout the whole continent between the Nittinahts of Vancouver to the Potowatomies of New Jersey. The snake as well as the bear was held to be divine from the Ural east to the Appalachian mountains. Skulls appear as ornaments of the long cornices of Mexican pyramids and around the kraals of Dahomey. "Frequently we find the cult of the dead as being affiliated with snake-worship" says Ratzel "The Kaffirs attribute luck and distress to the departed souls, especially those of their chiefs, whose spirits are called Ozituta and are supposed to dwell in snakes." Scalping is modified ancestor-worship. §54.

Kaffirs believe their departed chiefs to dwell in snakes. Ratzel.

This snake-worship requires special attention.

It is known that in Abomey the most is made of the boa constrictor. Its cult, tho not as conspicuous as fetishism, stands the higher in the esteem of the populace. The tree-fetish must be strong enough to bear a hundred corpses hung up for the vultures to pick off the flesh from the dangling skeletons; the walls of the domiciles of the aristocrats are beset with skulls; human skulls and bones are used as ornaments to every gate. Yet the snake, in company with the leopard and the shark, is the principal deity of Dahomey. The snake-cult in the kingdom of Ardra was discussed in an article of the Revue de deux mondes. The rites consist of weird dances ending with convulsions and mantic ecstacies. We were apprised of the presence of these very rites among the negroes of St. Domingo, and we are surprised to hear that "Hoodoo" has not been forgotten as yet, even in Georgia and Alabama. Thus the black man imports snake-worship from Africa to the east, while the red man propagates it in the west, Snake-worship affiliated to ancestor-worship

Principal deity of Dahomey.

Remnants of snake-cult in every nation.

Imported to the United States by way of Peking-Rome, by the red man, the yellow, the black and the white man.

There the yellow man also pets his dragon brought along from Peking, whilst the white man in Baltimore, according to Roman, but originally Mongolian ritual, perfumes with incense the statue of St. Michael and the dragon under his feet.

Genesis of snake-cult to be discussed. § 54, 56.

No man below redemption despite such deterioration.

We close the exhibition of the mixture of traditional legends, ill-understood symbolism and inner remnants of religiousness. The roots of this oldest and wildest growth will be further discussed when we stand face to face again with the stupor of an irreligious, frightened and benighted consciousness. We have looked into the substratum of human degradation, and there have observed an occult undercurrent of history up to the present. No tribe has been found void of all religious sentiment, and none is below the capability of being redeemed from its dreadful abnormities.

Acca-boys in Verona. SCHWEINFURT.

Schweinfurt on his return from Africa found two boys of the Akka people, a nation of dwarfs which he had visited. These boys had been brought to Verona in order to be educated. In a comparatively short time they learned to play the piano pretty well.

Natural religion. Monism of the materialists (Mammonism) unable to destroy superstition.

Deifying force-substance and disparaging personal life.

§ 46. Now, is it not the laudable aim of Natural Science to destroy all such superstition and fetishism, and to make room for a natural and rational religion? We rejoin that evolutionism can no more annihilate superstition than Brahmanism and Buddhism could abolish snake-worship in Asia. For, materialistic monism is but another form of deifying natural objects. As far as a world-theory has been founded upon this monism, it is tantamount to mammonism, cultivated by labor as much as by capital alike in that each in its way deifies natural goods, makes gold its fetish, depreciates personality.

Science demoralised: feticism and feticide.

Malthus and Darwinism. § 198

The laborer is treated as a market commodity; the soul of the fetus as the property of which the parent may dispose ad libitum. Capital does not want to be disturbed in its accumulation by being divided among too many heirs, so that one of the practical results of this materialistic view of life has been "the" growing "social evil." It is an open secret, that Darwin was led to his theory by that of Malthus, who thought overpopulation was all that impoverished his country. It can not be denied, that the Darwinian theory was made a screen for carrying out the Malthusian.

Naturalistic dogmatism VIRCHOW as applied to socialism. TYNDALL.

We repeat: The noxious world-theory founded upon the immature scientific dogmatism which abets depreciation of personal life and deification of matter-force, is to be charged to evolutionism as far as it is identical with materialistic monism. Virchow had good reason to make it responsible for the ways in which the dogmatism of the Tyndalls was applied by Socialism in the assault upon the Christian world-theory.

Their world-theory superstitious in itself, is unable to displace superstition.

Evolutionism can not even claim the honor of having weakened superstition, despite its attempts to supplant the faith of Christianity by a belief in its own authority—an act superstitious enough in itself.

Inferential theories of natural religion never manifest force sufficient to clean out superstitution. As far as the cultured nations of ancient times are concerned, there was always spread out a layer of higher, that is mythical form of religiousness above the crude form and residue of depraved Shamanism, circumscribed by birth and death, entrance into and exit out of life on earth.

Genesis of systematised natural religion; Theorising upon the discrepancy between thought and life, reality and destiny.

Advanced intellectualism utilised in the interest of Class-rule. § 54, 57.

The awakening of reflection upon the often enumerated discrepancies, and the corresponding religious advance, become first manifest in the higher classes of these nations. They improve their chances and enhance their world-consciousness by new observations made in trade, travel, and rule. Ranks are forming in which intellectual superiority gains power and the means for further mental improvements, through which again power and lordship become the more able to establish themselves the firmer.

Tombs to perpetuate security of existence, against the chief foe. Possession organised.

Mixture of inner remnants of original religion with symbols of forgotten meaning and mutilated traditions. BASTIAN.

Old nobility and anachronistic religiousness. § 67, 73, 78, 137

More ideal views of life are gradually obtained thereby, outmarshalling those of the rude, materialistic mind, which takes its own view of life as the only true and real. Under rules of organised and legalised possession, security develops by way of architectural constructions in defense against external foes; it develops by erecting tombs to secure the prolongation of existence against the foe most dreaded—against death. Thus the religio-philosophical elements arrange themselves to perpetuate security and—class-rule. **In systems thus ensuing, the incoherent remnants of primitive consciousness, and the enigmatical fragments of original symbols, and the mutilated traditions —all of these petrified souvenirs of the original unity of the race and of religion, are patched together regardless of their heterogeneity. The less understood, the higher they are esteemed; the older they grow, the more are they held sacred,** especially in the circles of the old nobility. In this sense Bastian's conclusion is correct, that "the worship of ancestors, and the deification of things associated with their memory, became the first principles of religion"—after heathendom had to some lengths gone its own way.

With this portion of inheritance man went to housekeeping for himself: this explains why we meet the same religious traits and family features in the most widely separated regions. It reminds one of the religious kinship existing "between the worship upon the most isolated islands and all other religions."

The religious appereptions totally governing a people in remote isolation vary from those with widening relations simply in that the former are more retarded and sink deeper. Natural religion can only rely upon its own diminishing resources; and there is nothing in its background but fright—fear of ghosts and the night, unless there be a still deeper background into which the eye of reason can not, and the eye of faith need not, penetrate; in the search of which the hand gropes along the wall in the dark, because of the dimness of the "light in the treasury vault." *Psychical and traditional elements of the religions of fear: night, death, the serpent. § 43, 48, 54, 55, 109.*

Doubtless a few traditions with reference to the first death and the snake were never forgotten. And these did not, nor were they intended to, lessen that fear. As a symptom of the conflict between consciousness and perverted selfhood that fear was utilized to establish "man a law unto himself." *Fear utilised as a salutary measure of discipline.*

It is fear that makes the mind grasp after those "first principles" just spoken of, which are indestructibly imbedded in consciousness, innate in the mind, never entirely dropped from tradition, and always separable from corrosive ingredients. It is trouble alone which thoroughly reminds man of those "first principles" and makes him grasp at them, as a shipwrecked mariner struggles for a hold upon a broken piece of timber. The "anxious suspense" causes him to observe, and, in the process of reflection upon historic recurrences, to gather the disjointed vestiges together in order to construct such a temporary makeshift as may suit the emergency—a pseudo-religious view of life. **What are called religious systems, are in fact but mental attempts at formulating a somewhat reasonable world-consciousness; they are rudiments of scientific generalisation in the search for the center of cohesion.** *Mythologies but attempts at formulating world-consciousness. § 55, 61.* *The salutary results of the mental exertions § 61, 74, to gain a hold upon (centers of cohesion).* *Difficulties in the attempt to arrange an evolutionary methodology of mythical religiousness.*

Wrong conceptions symbolised and mixed with fragments of truth; natural forces of mental moods personified and mixed with absolute selfdelusions constitute that world-consciousness. The less man understands the meaning of the component elements, the more anxious will he hold fast to their mere symbols. The being engaged in this exercise is very beneficial nevertheless. In the search for a hold, man is unknowingly seized by higher longings and drawn away from the abyss of positive demonolatry. These hapless exertions, however, show also the reason why in all self-invented religious methods the pristine stratum reappears, like a water spot strikes through the plastering, and shines through the lacquer of mere outward culture.

It seems to have been sufficiently shown why we are unable to accredit much value to such religio-rationalistic schematising or methodising of religious obligations and gravings into schedules of continually advancing and well defined stages.

Modern attempts to arrange the course of mythical religion, in the way as botany was systematised by Linne, Couvier, etc., either arise from selfconceit or produce it. Dialectics is carried into religious history; wish becomes father to the thought; and the history of religion, intricate enough already, is rendered the more confused. Man in his less experienced stage of life usually goes by impulses and inclinations; he is sensuous merely, like the child in the first years of its growth; whilst in his maturity he is apt to disregard the feelings, and to become onesided on the part of reason. We have had occasion to observe, in what an eccentric and erratic, in what a capricious and often selfworshiping manner fancy either wanders or becomes a fixed idea. We have seen and shall see still more, how the most faint and incongruous recollections are yoked together. Sometimes even written and official forms of cultured consciousness suddenly change and get mixed up, just as languages do. We have contemporaneous parallels in which the changes, wanderings, and leapings of religious notions and rites will baffle any attempt to construct a theory of natural religion. Nobody will ever succeed to derive one from spontaneous generation. Michelet made a clear breast of the matter in his scientific confession, illustrating a felicitous return from confusion to logic. Where he framed a formula for that phase of consciousness which unconsciously labors under the prejudice of lingual and mythological evolution, he described individual man at that stage of development as being enraptured by the immediate view of the objects around and the discoveries within himself, *Nature-bound man swayed now by emotion, then by reason. Michelet.* *Wandering, shifting notions, and fixed ideas in self-made religions.*

Religious under-
current deter-
mine the shape
of every age and
nation.
§ 24, 43, 52, 54, 56, 98.

wrapped up, in an atmosphere of mere instinctive feelings. No description more cogent and terse could have been given of that condition of man which we term "nature-bound", notwithstanding the amount of rational virtuosity he may possess.

Do the facts bear us out in this conception of heathenism, when history is made to test out theory?

Character molded not
from within alone.

The specific character of a people is the result not only of external but rather of internal conditions. Humanity in each of its parts, in every one of its ages and countries, will without exception shape itself in conformity with the religious undercurrent. This determining influence never dares to be ignored by our Philosophy.

Under influence of
environment after
relapse under natural
necessity.

But notwithstanding the individual or national propensities and the selfdetermination required for the formation of character from within, we find every person conditioned also by environments. Much of life's course depends upon inherited temperament, and is limited by the nature of its surroundings, especially since the relapse under natural necessity and in proportion to the extent of the relapse. In addition life's course depends on the work engaged in, and upon influences exerted by one nation upon the other. Above all, man's life is affected and almost governed by a transcendental world, either of light or of darkness, for the influences of which

Influences from the
transcendental worlds
of light and of
darkness.

man is accessible, of which scientifically, however, we possess a knowledge so limited that science, judging the matter after its purely inductive methods, denies the possibility of knowing anything at all about it.

Hereditary transmission, modification and adaptation produce further changes and give rise to ever new conditions and perplexities. With reference to this morphology it will become evident why it is very necessary to discriminate between direct and intermediate adaptedness and accomodation.

Necessary to discrimi-
nate between the factors
influencing the forma-
tion of national
character.

By direct accommodation we mean adaptness to such modifying circumstances as food, climate, involuntary habituation to national customs and usages, etc., which rule the particular social organism during the time in which the frame of mind in a person, or the character of a nation, begins to take shape. Inasmuch as such influences are not plainly observable, they must not be considered without scrutiny.

By indirect or intermediate adaptation we mean adaptness to such hereditary modifications as show themselves in the descendants of individual personages.

Proper discretion after that method renders the knowledge of the mode of sociological differentiation with reference to the division of labor, the origin of castes, the formation of class-lines, etc., more distinct and preventive of serious mistakes. Much the more is it necessary to classify the molding influences and to distinguish between the differentiating principles, since we are now put to the task of discerning national origins from among a chaos of races.

CH. VIII.   CLASSIFICATION OF THE ETHNICAL MATERIAL.

Chaos of
prehistoric races.

§ 47. Surveying the ethnical mass, not singling out any particular nation, irrespective even of our "first circle", let us look at the chaos as we would look upon a geological stratification. To begin with, we draw a line from the mouth of the Obi to Cape Comorin, thus dividing the great proscenium upon which prehistoric history was enacted. This line intersects the Himalayas and part of the Tibetian plateau, crosses the Alps of the Tian-Shan, the steppes of the Kirgheeze; and the Siberian lowlands.

The region to which the
separation of peoples
is traceable. § 51, 57.

The smaller half, Europe included, lies to the left of our line. To the right we have the immense regions of the Gobi desert, of China and Farther India. This line we will have to study more closely in the sequel. Its middle part passes over the great crest and watershed of Ethnography, the "Roof of the World" as the western boundary line of the Pamir plateau is called, and the Tarim basin sloping down toward the great "Sand Sea" of the Gobi in the east. This sea-bed of the old Asiatic Mediterranean is a mixed variety of steppes; they present depressions in which most of the streams flowing down from surrounding clay bluffs either run dry, or form salty marshes encircled by poplars and willows.

The ethnographical
watershed:
Central Asia.

The most abandoned part of the globe, closed in by enormous mountains covers a broad belt of Asia, extending through twenty degrees of latitude. The length of the Russian mail line from Kiuchtu to Kalgan is nearly 1000 miles, whilst the distance of the whole series of contiguous deserts, rarely interspersed with an onsis, measures a little more than that between New York and San Francisco. The name of the largest and treeless portion is Han-hai, where not even Chinese squatters are eager to settle. *Gobi, the "Land Sea," once a lake.*

Colonel Prschewalsky was the last so far, excepting a few Chinese traders, who roamed through that part of the Gobi. It took him two weeks of hurried travel over the Mushum strip. He could report   no other discovery but that of coarse, red sand; sand and spots strewn with sharp stones and skeletons. The thermometer went up to 119, and the heat of the ground was 185 degrees Fahrenheit. *Prschewalsky.*

The supposition that the whole Aralo-Caspian low-lands also were covered by waters to a considerable depth until long after the Gobi had absorbed the brine of the great Asiatic inland lake, is sustained on palpable grounds. If this were the case, then the northern and eastern slopes of the Thian-Shan systems must have offered very inviting abodes, full of springs and verdure to early settlers. In the Tarim, and about the Gobi even, the climate must have been well suited for forests and pastures. But the situation totally changed when the waters of the ocean and the Caspian basin receded from each other, when the contracting waves left dry sands and salty steppes, when shifting dunes enlarged the barren area. *Aralo-Caspian depression also once covered by water.*

By the change of climate thus ensuing, the interior of Asia became too sterile to produce enough food for the inhabitants, who also receded. *Change of climate.*

The nomade tribes roaming in the lake regions now high and dry knew of but two outlets in the ring-walls of their high mountains, of only two gates from which to descend into geographically better articulated countries nearer to the sea coasts. Remusat   has   found important hints in Chinese legends confirming such conjectures. *People left the Pamir and Tarim regions § 51, 57. Remusat.*

One of these passes opens toward the east, where in one valley a tributary to the Hoang-ho is forming. The hordes following this furrow descended into that region which now forms one of the most fertile parts of the Chinese empire. *through only two mountain passes.*

The other pass, leading westward, opens upon the Pelu terraces. From Lake Sairam-nor the road leads through the pass in the Talki range toward Kuldja. The large Dsungarian depression is connected with these western terraces and offers the wanderers-facilities for pushing on their descending journey. More than once countless hordes have poured down from these outlets upon the people of the West, their precursors. The Scythian low-lands especially were overrun by great numbers, when in the third century B. C. the overflow toward the east was checked by the Chinese wall and was made to recoil with augmented force toward the west through the Dsungarian outlet. But many centuries before that time already the Scythians had made formidable invasions into Mesopotamia and Ægypt, bidding defiance even to the superior tactics of Cyrus, Darius, and Alexander. *Spread of the Turanians. Mongolian raids in pre-Christian era.*

From these ethnical fountain-heads of Bolor, Tagh or Pamir, and the barren basin of the Tarim the torrents of the Turanian floods spread everywhere. They occupied those countries of enormous expanse which henceforth were held by the Turanian tribes of the Ugro-Tatars. From the highlands of Central Asia the first emigration radiated through a wide, fan-shaped semi-circle, stretching from Lapland through Siberia to America down to Peru, encompassing even the island-groups of the Pacific. *Western Mongolians. Ugro-Tatars or Scythians*

All Mongolian nations are of Turanian origin. By many common characteristics they are as easily generalised as those nations which belong to the basin of the European Mediterranean, the Caucasians. *Eastern Mongolians.*

The   four main branches are: (1.) the Northern Asiatics, the Mongolians proper; (2.) the Chinese and Siamese· (3.) the Koreans and Japanese; (4.) the Malayans. Subdivisions of them are the Tungusians, East-Jaklans Kamptshatkians, Korjaekans, Tshukchians, Esquimaux, Aleutians, and the American aborigines, north and south. *American Indians*

The western Mongolians are still more diversified. Some of them have returned to the eastern parts where they form erratic clusters. As Ugro-Tatarian fragments, casting their lot with the Caucasians we enumerate: the Khirgeeze, Huns, Avars, and Turks; many tribes of Russia mixed with Slavonic elements as for instance the Mordvinians along the Volga, the Watjakians along the Dwina and up the Ural; the Esthnians, Finns, and Lapps around the Baltic; the Tatars of Kasan and the Krimea, including Bashkeers and Jacutes; also the Samojedes camping north and east of the Behring straits. *are Mongolians.*

The Aleutian islands furnished the bridge for the most energetic roamers bound for Alaska. For Alex. v. Humboldt's supposition is verified, that the Indians are decidedly of Mongolian descent. *Alex. v. Humboldt.*

Ebrard has demonstrated and corroborated what Rougemont and Bradford had advanced, when he speaks of the Malayan and Ugro-Finnish cultures in America. Ratzel's pictures of the feather-masks of Hawaii plainly show the same type as the figures from Palanke. The

ESSARO, ROUGEMONT, BRADPORT, RATZEL, MOTHE, PESCHEL.

same is the case with his pictures of idols discovered upon the Easter-Islands. Mothe's illustrated work shows stone figures of Farther India, the physiognomies of which are exactly like those of Aztecian sculptures. Pruner Bey and Peschel observed long ago, that the heads of the Botokudes of Brazil differ not much from those of the Chinese. The heads of people of Toltecian descent have almost the very shape of those of the Javanese Malayans. Especially striking is the similarity of the red man of America with the New-Zealander.

Botokudes are Chinese.

Mongolo-Malayans of the Pacific Ocean.

The Mongolo-Malayans of the Pacific require special attention. Their characteristics are decidedly Turanian. They proceeded from their original seats in Central Asia in a south-western direction and passed across the Indian archipelago. We can still trace their route to Buru, an island of the Moluccian group, then to Samoa and Tonga. From these centers they populated one group of islands after another. In contrast to the Melanesians of negro origin they are called Polynesians. They extend to the Caroline Islands. This is upheld by Fr. Mueller against Keane, who among others argued against the kindredship of Malayans and Polynesians, taking the latter for a degenerated branch of the Maoris. On this subject further information and results of investigation are to be waited for.

FR. MUELLER and KEANE on difference between Melanesians and Polynesians.

Another stream of emigration must have started from New Guinea. It is the Papua branch, which came to the islands southwest of New Guinea to Australia and its surroundings, in the earliest times.

The Papua: SCHLEINITZ, VIRCHOW.

Traces of the existence of these first occupants have been found elsewhere, so that Wallace counted them as a separate family from the Malayans and Polynesians. To the Papua probably belong the Negritos which are found as far north as the Philippine Islands. Types very similar to them are found in the interior of Borneo and Sumatra, even upon Malacca. Peschel denominates them "Asiatic Papua". If we count them all in as Virchow, Semper and Fr. Mueller do, then a large playground is conceded to the Papua, reaching from Andamanes and Malacca across Borneo over to the Solomon Islands, to New Caledonia and New Guinea; it would also take in the Charlotte Islands and the New Hebrides. Even all Melanesians we may then consider as fractions of the Papua race because with reference to language they stand between the Polynesians and Malayans.

Turanians of the South-Sea remnants of most ancient Malayans

All these nations, spread over the islands of the South-Sea, are without any history; that dark race, which v. Schleinitz has introduced to us as being the conquerors of all the others, least of all—for it seems to have existed only in his hypothesis. We

are becoming people of consequence.

have taken a survey of the wide semi-circle of the Turanian peoples. It embraces the north of the eastern and the whole of the western hemispheres, solidifying into the most antique culture of unrivaled permanency. The survey may have seemed tedious and unprofitable. But before long all these people will become historical,

Mongolo and Negrito-Malayans unhistorical.

so that we shall meet them again and again. We may just as well accustom ourselves to the study of their nomenclature, because we shall, henceforth, hear more and more of them, in the "Dailies" perhaps as much as in Missionary Magazines. At present history is interested in them only in so far as they form the nethermost stratum of our substructure. Upon these ethnic layers, this Turanian basis, other types reared their structures, as for instance the young nation of the United States.

Hamito-Cushites spread over the South. Asiatic origin. LEPSIUS.

§ 48. The Hamito-Semitic nations, according to Lepsius, also descended from Central-Asia. The Hamite family is represented in history by its main branch, the Cushites. As such the most ancient occupants of Southern Arabia, Æthiopia, Habesh (Abissynia) and Nubia are recognised. The Doms and Kohls in India, upon the Sunda Islands and the Philippines are considered as Hamites; we find them as Melanesians, Negritoes, as Alfurus, and perhaps as the Papua. Everywhere these races seem to have been forced into the mountains by Mongolians, or down to the lowest caste by other nations. Everywhere they are of slender stature with black skin and woolly hair. Here and there, as in the case of the Kohls especially, we find tribal legends of highest antiquity. In the first place they spread from the Ganges to the Nile. In the regions around the Persian Gulf they were the first settlers, from whence they crossed to the eastern shore of Africa; they interlinked the movements between that and Ceylon, so that Lepsius calls them the Phenicians of those times. In fact, their ancestral blood ran in the veins of the Philistines and Punians, since they reappeared in Mesopotamia and there mixed with Turanians, and later on with the Semites.

Legends of the Kohls.

Semito-Cushites.

Sumero-Akkadians.

The Cushites yielded the material from which the Chaldean empires were constructed; for if we follow Maspero, the Susanian people became agglomerated into the Elamite empire. On the other, the western side of the Tigris, the Sumerians and Akkadians intermingling afforded the first elements of culture to the Chaldeans.

Phenicians form the basis of Chaldean culture. MASPERO.

The question, who were the Chaldeans, has, ever since Heeren pondered over it, remained "one of the knotty problems of history." We regard them as the aborigines of Arabia and denominate them Southern Semites. At an early period they pressed northward into Syria and Mesopotamia and became Northern Semites with Babylonia as their center. They branched out into Babylonians, Assyrians, Aramæans, Canaanites and Israelites. That part

Chaldeans. HEEREN.

Semites.

of them known as Hittites will prove, most likely, to have been the first bearers of culture to Greece. The recent excavations in Hamath (on the Orontes) and in Sindshirli, corroborating the Cyprian discoveries, strongly indicate this. Blend the views of Maspero and Schrader and the proof is established that the ancestors of both the Cushite and Semite families descended from Central-Asia. Schrader formerly derived them from Arabia; but of late he has shown more of an inclination to admit that their northern home was in the vicinity of the Aryans. *(margin: Hittites, the bearers of culture to Greece.)* *(margin: Views of Maspero and Schrader blended prove the descent of Cushites and Semites.)*

When the Schlagintweit brothers (vol. IV. of their "Travels") had been so fortunate as to surmount yonder eastern pass in the Kuen-Lun range, and arrived at the northern slope, they were astonished to meet Aryans pure and simple. These good people, who were shepherds and had never heard of nor seen any European, pastured their flocks in the far expanding plains of Khokan and Jarkand. People of "splendid physique, beautiful normal shape" they are, and well provided, surprisingly so, with all the necessaries of life. Thus the old supposition became confirmed, that here is the primitive home of the Indo-Germans. From here, for the first time, they started "westward"! Some of them betook themselves to the South. The one stream went through the passes of the Caucasus into the Sarmatian plains of Europe; the other found room and the welcome of a mild climate in the Punjab and in Hindoostan. But the latter also found the best parts preoccupied by Turano-Mongolian as well as by Hamito-Semitic tribes, forming the Drawidian substratum. The Mahabbharadha describes the conflict with them. *(margin: Remnants of the Aryan stock in Central-Asia. Schlagintweit.)* *(margin: Primitive home of Indo-Germans.)* *(margin: "Westward" for the first time.)*

Looking upon these SOUTHERN ARYANS we notice a lively variety of Sanskrit speaking people: Brahmine Hindoos, Benghali, Nipali, Kashmeers, Pandjabi, Hindi, Marhali, and Bilha (Gipsies). To the north of them all the Zend speaking people of Iran: the Pehlewi, Kurdes, Armenians, Phrygians, Albanese, Cappadocians, Beloodshistans, Afghans; and the tribes of Khiva, Bokhara, and Khokan. *(margin: Eastern Aryans: South—Sanskrit; North—Zend-people.)*

With the WESTERN ARYANS, the European branch, we are familiar. They comprise all Northern Europeans, (except the Ugro-Tatarians) namely, the Lithunian (Prussians) and Slavonic peoples (Slovenians, Croates, Serbians, Wallachians, Vandals, Poles, Czechs, and Basks). They also comprise the Southern Europeans, viz; the ancient Gauls (or Celts), the Galish (or Walish) the ancient Etrurio-Pelasgians, and the Græco-Romans; and finally the Germanic nations, viz: the Goths (or Getes, Scandinavians and Icelanders) the Teutons, Cymri, Friesians, and Anglo-Saxons. *(margin: Western Aryans: South—Græco-Romans; North—Germans.)*

The mere mention of these names indicates an ascending scale toward the highest approach to civilisation, the task obviously assigned to the Aryans in the order given.

Up to this eleventh hour of history there remained to our own time and race the duty to explore the dark continent, and to call its ethnical chaos to order. There the Teuto-Germans meet their extreme contraries, and yet their compeers, their fellowmen at any rate. *(margin: Ethnical chaos of Africa.)*

From the zenith of the times and of culture the Germanic nations now look back upon the beginnings of history; they look after the masses of long abandoned and less fortunate nations as if searching for lost brethren. The five hundred millions of Christendom become interested in the thousand millions outside of it. The dark continent is said to contain two hundred millions of the latter. *(margin: Advanced nations seek the abandoned.)*

Ascending the terraces from the Nile and the Red Sea, Abyssinia was rediscovered, the Habesh of old with its ancient culture, which once competed with that of Ægypt. The empire of queen Candace, in its remnants of obelisks, tombs and rock-temples, shows how the Ethiopians were qualified to appreciate the culture of the Mizrim, their cousins in Ægypt. Like sandstone lying upon beds of granite, so we find the fixed and massive substratum of earliest inhabitants below the loose fragments of Arab emigration. The remnants of this later Arabian overflow cover the primitive culture of Hamito-Semitic natives in Æthiopia and Nubia just as we found it on the lower Nile and on the Euphrates. *(margin: Æthiopians followed by the Arabic immigrants into the Mizrim.)*

Lepsius believed it to be indubitable that the African races formed a unit. He tried to prove an original unity of languages, necessary for this supposition. The multiplicity of them he took for the result of historical accidents. Very well; then we would have an original unity, followed by conflict, rupture, dispersion and degeneration of nations, tongues and minds. But whence would the essential unity have to be derived? Obviously from the first migrations across the isthmus of Suez. *(margin: Africans supposed to have formed a national unit. Lepsius.)* *(margin: This supposition would prove the unity of humanity.)* *(margin: Kaffirs surmised to be of Hebrew descent.)*

At the foot of the Blue Mount, upon the vast Kaffrarian hunting grounds, which swarm with giraffes, antelopes, and buffaloes, certain Kaffir tribes wander about who can not deny their Hebrew features, altho absolute proof of such relationship can not be adduced. A traveler who started from the Babiroa writes however: "It is undeniable that the Kaffirs not only resemble, but are blood-relatives of, the Jews. They vividly relate the story of the great *(margin: System of African ethnology. Lepsius.)*

flood, and even know something of Noah's ark. Mount Ararat, (madi-ma-tbe) is the point, they say, from whence they came, The laws of stoning, of the preparation of food, not to mention circumcision, come so near the Jewish ceremonials as to astonish one."

Middle zone of African languages. STEINTHAL.

In his Nubian grammar Lepsius laid down the ethnological system of the African nations. South of the equator the Bantu languages prevail, except with the Hottentots and Bushmen; so that the unity of languages there can be established without difficulty. In a distinct line north of the equator the other main branch spreads out, comprising the Ægyptian, Libyan, and Berber languages. These are Hamitic idioms of unquestioned Asiatic origin. Even the Cushite sister-languages spoken by the Bega, Soho, Donkali, Somali, and by the Galla from the Kilima-Njaro to Babelmandeb, belong to that northern group.

Illustr. the first confusion of languages, and subsequent national decline.

Now all these distinct branches of each of the two main stems of languages intermingle in a broad middle ground of negro dialects, and form puzzling combinations. Between the Sahara and the equator languages are mixed as indiscriminately as the loose rubble around Mount Sinai. Fr. Mueller took pains to catalogue the most typical and to classify as many as possible. With comparatively little trouble the mixture in these regions may be accounted for; but to disentangle them is another thing. The mixture is not to be taken as "the product of a quiet, vegetable sort of development of national life", as Steinthal thinks. It must have originated, rather, in persistent and hot contests, in violent clashes of tribes against each other. Perhaps "one nation was crushed, and its fragments were scattered beyond hope of being fitted together again."

In short, we have before us the phenomenon of a confusion of languages. The subsequent decline of nations we see illustrated in the fate of the Haussa.

Second inundation of Africa: Hottentots.

This is, as Lepsius thought, Libyan people, "degenerated into negroes". In the Hottentotian he recognises an essentially Hamitic language, "taking its origin from the Cushite branch of it." He traces the Hottentots as coming from the northeast and as having been pushed south. This emigration —which in keeping with the original movement of all nations over from Asia, we may call the second inundation of Africa—was a Cushite wave covering the eastern shore. Let us dwell a few moments longer upon the picture of an African turmoil; we will have no occasion to return to it.

Identity of the Shagga, Wazimba and Galla.

The African commotion repeated itself, when from the interior regions near the sources of the Congo and the Zambezi the Shaggas (Wazimbas) pressed down upon Bantu negroes, throwing themselves upon the Congo valley. It was then and there that the Portuguese checked these cannibals whose leader had his yard paved with human skulls and bones. Being held in check, the Wazimbas recoiled upon the Arabs, from whom they wrested Kiloa, eating the garrison of 3000 men. Merensky ascertained the date of their settlement opposite the island of Mombas to have taken place A. D. 1585. After that they disappear, or rather, what seems probable, they reappear as the Galla. Since this people took their present quarters north of the Kilima-Njaro just at the period of these great commotions, our inference can not be termed preposterous.

Their present quarters since A. D. 1585. MERENSKY.

Movements of the Fellatah, Hottentots, Tuaregs.

With the moving of the Galla stands connected, at any rate, that of the Fellatah, who then invaded Bornu for the first time. And with theirs the migration of the Mandingo is connected, who, pressing on from east to west, pushed aside the Kaffirs, Basutos and Betshuanes, who in turn pushed before them the Hottentots—whilst into the Fellatah the Tuaregs from the north wedged themselves. This Berber tribe from its city of Timbuctoo ever since continued to be the most formidable foe of the Fellatah on the Senegal, who ceded the middle section of the Niger to the Tuaregs, retaining for themselves the regions of the headwaters and the mouth of that river.

Besides the illustration of the confusion of languages and the disrupture and degeneracy of nations sequent to it, we see in these African movements also the example of the slow drifting of people; and we become aware of the difficulty of classifying such a medley of ethnical fragments.

Somali rather Caucasian. BURTON.

The Somali especially offer a baffling riddle. Being neither negroes, nor Gallas, nor Kaffrarian Jews, nor Hottentots, they show many Caucasian ingredients. In their country, the rocky highlands of the north-eastern corner of South-Africa, north of the German possessions, Burton found them rendering homage to stones and sacred trees—the substratum of ancient paganism under the thin garb of Islam.

Scene at Kartoom.

VIRCHOW's brachy-cephaly.

In the filthy streets of Kartoom Arabs and Berbers meet with Abyssinians, and with the negroes of Darfoor and from the lakes of the Nile. They bring to market the ivory of the White Nile, ostrich feathers, gold-dust, rubber from Kordofan, and slaves from everywhere. But distinct as their national characters and customs are, nobody is able to define the antecedents of all these people selling and being sold. Altho the measurements of 40 Wei-and

Kru-negroes were made under Virchow's directions, no light was shed upon the pedigree of the West-African tribes and their eastern neighbors by brachy-cephaly. Ethnologically the African portion of humanity seems to be dried up like a mummy on the one side, and to be "a product of degradation" in its most heinous forms on the other. As such it is known. But who can realise African every-day life, especially since these savages handle the rifle as the first gift from European civilisation? Slave-trade. Livingstone, Vogel.

Kartoom and Zanzibar until recent times have both been the emporium of "the black ivory." Livingston was told by the English consul at Zanzibar, that the regions of Lake Niassa alone furnished 19000 slaves annually. He tells us: "The innumerable skeletons which we saw in the woods and among the rocks, along the rivers and trails of the wilderness witness the terrible sacrifices made to that infernal traffic." Vogel describing the Tibu as remnants of the black aborigines of the desert, yet being neither negroes nor Berbers, said that slave trade is their sole occupation. "Along the road from Tegerri to Bilma there lie the bleached bones of thousands of human beings upon the sand; and among them corpses dried up like mummies in the very positions in which these poor blacks were released by a merciful death from their suffering. When Schweinfurth came to the Niam-Niam, who sparingly populate a region of about 3000 square-miles, he witnessed the most sickening spectacle in front of Munsa's residence. The lower half of a mule corpse, was being handled by a woman flaying it with the expertness of a butcher, in the process of preparation for supper.

Vogel wrote to Ehrenberg, that "the Tangalese on the Benue river eat all their enemies captured or killed in battle. The breast belongs to the sultan; the heads are given to the women; the tender parts are dried in the sun, then pulverised and mingled with the porridge." Anthropophagy, the darkest riddle not explicable by natural science. § 35, 38, 39, 40, 54.

The darkest of all riddles, inexplicable from premises of natural science, here hovers before us. Time may bring to light many dark interiors; but the darkness of interior Africa is solid as yet and covers unspeakable horrors. We shall not return to its nauseating story. It behooved us to take a glance into this abyss of abomination; to penetrate to the bottom of it no eye could endure.

Before dismissing the subject, however, we must not leave unnoticed one more scene from this huge continent. The large mangrove-forests of river bottoms like that of the Niger for instance, stretch out away in the distance under an oppressive monotony. Perpetual darkness reigns, and a solid spot is a rarity below the evergreen roof of leaves. The giant trees upon their grotesque root-stocks rise up from deep morasses. The rice-bird flits away, the golden eagle perches upon a death bough, but a human being is rarely met with. Whenever one appears, his whole behavior reminds one of the spectres he dreads. With him all things revolve around ancestor-worship and upon fetishes. His bleared imagination takes anything for a fetish, but prefers the most abstruse object, be it the head of a snake, or a dried lizard in lieu of it. Is connected with snake and ancestor-worship. § 42, 43.

§ 49. Our survey of the races, our investigation of the ethnic material, forming the substratum of history, requires one more glance upon the dying Indian nations of the "new world." Our retrospect here makes more sure of certain connections alluded to with the Mongolo-Malayans. American aborigines. Mongolo-Malayans.

In several large droves they migrated to the Pacific coast of America. The present inhabitants do not say that they are living "in the west", but "on the coast". To them there is no west any more; there is an involuntary feeling that the Pacific rather belongs to the East. The meteorologic conditions of the state of Washington particularly, have that peculiar equilibrium and affect the nerves similar to those of Japan and Korea.

But when the Mongolian came over and went south, he found natives there already, with some nativistic pretensions, too, altho they had been nothing but emigrants themselves, of Cushitic extraction, most likely, from Polynesia. By the new comers, the Indians, they seem to have been treated the same as the Dravida were by the Hindoos. Native Americans before the immigration of Toltecs and Aztecs.

The little we know about the first emigrants will forever, perhaps, remain as problematic as it is now, on the whole, rather contradictory. The cave-dwellers and "cliff-builders" in Utah, New Mexico, and Arizona—called Pueblos by Holmes, seem not to be as ancient as the "mound-builders" of Oregon, Ohio, and Wisconsin. Only so much is sure, that the most antique culture in America moved in the course from north to south. Mound-builders prior to the Cliff-dwellers. Holmes.

All those tribes which, between the 7th. and 14th. century took their war path across the Mexican plateau to certain parts of Central-America, Desire Charney calls Nahuas. The first comers during this second period of immigration were the TOLTECS, much earlier than the Aztecs. They were tall men with white beards, offering flowers, their sacred place, Tlaloc. Their structures at Tula show technical skill, and like that at Teotihoankan, indicate energy and eminent industriousness. Oppressed but emancipating themselves, their empire broke up, nevertheless, and they went south. There the Toltecs exhibited the same kind of monumental culture as in Tabasco, Yucatan, Guatemala, etc. Having mingled with vanquished preoccupants, and in turn subjugated by the Incas following (ca. 1000 A. D., since the 11th Inca reign dates 1453) the Toltecs must have formed the substratum of their empire. It has been conjectured, that Toltecian-Polynesian remnants fled from their oppressors toward the South, in order to account for the inhabitation of the dreary cliffs of Terra del Fuego. Nahua of Charnay. Toltecs made flower-offerings. Aztecs introduced human sacrifices. First immigrants pushed south as far as Terra del Fuego.

The flower offering men in Central-America were Mongolians, and, to all appearances, Japanese. The settlers flooding upon them from China founded the AZTEC empire upon the Toltecian ruins, and introduced human sacrifices on Mexican soil. Further north the Tshuktchis left their traces in crossing the Aleutes. And not only the Californian Mona are of explicit Finno-Tataric origin, but also the Delawares and Susquehannas and Wyomings from the neighborhood of Washington, D. C. and all the seventy tribes of North—and the thirty tribes of South America.

R. Brown said long ago: "The Esquimo on the American and the Tshuktchis on the Asiatic side perfectly understand each other." Equally affirmative of our conclusions do the traditions of the Indians, who once roamed about the "eastern shore", fully agree with those upon the western plains.—Tschudy directed the attention to the marvelous similarity of the Botokudes of Brazil with the Chinese as mentioned before. And if it is an image of Buddha, which was found in Yucatan, as it is supposed to be, it would seem too rare a case as to afford the final proof for an early Chinese influx. Yet it tells much in favor of such a supposition.

Morton, who took the Indians as a product of the soil and "spontaneous generation", has long ago been refuted by Pritchard who coincided with this view of Martius: "The nations of the new world were not in a state of primitive barbarism, nor living in a state of the original simplicity of an uncultivated mind. On the contrary. They represent the last remains (about

half a million in North-America) of a people once high on the scale of culture and mental attainments, now almost worn out and perishing, sunk to the lowest point of dismay and degradation." In all this we perceive an unambiguous example of that degeneracy into a state of savagery, which repudiates the theory of evolution, with its claim of a far more remote beginning of chronological computations than our seven or eight thousand years of human existence, with their sufficiency to account for the changing modes of development and decline.

We must not close our retrospect of the forsaken families of the human race without a notice of the main stock of the Australians—the Tasmanians. Like the Papua of New Guinea and upon the Solomon and Fiji Islands, like the Drawida in India, they present a peculiar phenomenon by themselves.

Curr's work on Australia with its description of 239 tribes (London 1886) has contributed much to the completion of the ethnological index. But the enunciations made therein, have not weakened the force of our axiom which is endorsed by Bonwick, namely, that the fundamental layers of all these tribes gradually shifted over from Asia, either in waves, or by terrace-like driftings, and that they are all of Mongolian descent.

A very condensed sketch only of the ethnological chart could be outlined upon these pages, since our aim was simply to show the ethnic strata in their driftings and depositions of prehistoric people. It represents the gist of such conclusions as drawn by authorities like Waitz, Bastian, Peschel, Pritchard, Ranke, Ratzel. The perusal of a few ethnographical periodicals will afford more satisfactory information on this subject.

We started out from the Mongolian body of nations, all speaking the monosyllabic Turanian languages. We went along with the Hamito-Cushite-Semitic people and with the Aryans upon their wanderings. Having thus made the rounds of the earth, we again met the Mongolians, scattered broadcast and lost so long, in worlds but recently discovered.

Is not past and contemporaneous history taking the same course? Just think of the meetings which took place amongst these old races with Guetzlaff, Gordon, Stanley, Livingstone, Dr. Schnitzler (or Emin Bey) ; with Haddington and Merensky. And keep in mind that a host of missionaries, represented by the four enumerated, were the pioneer philanthropists in the endeavor to regain forlorn men for their high destiny.

Think what old memories will revive, when the Danube problem shall unroll the "Eastern question." Think of the legislation in the United States against the smuggling in of coolies and opium, and of the recent Russian transactions with China. Think of the 310th. translation of the "Scripture" now nearly complete upon the isle of Efat near Erromanga in the group of the New Hebrides, where now the sons of the murderer who killed John Williams sixty years ago teach theology ! It all means that history returns to the places from whence it started. Both ends of the historic movement are on the approach to perfect the cyclical course.

CH. IX. DIFFERENTIATION OF THE ETHNICAL MASS.

§ 50. As yet we are confronted by the ethnical bulk covering the wide earth. What principle shall guide us in discerning a point from which to unravel the entangled mass in order to arrange it under proper topics?

An illustration may give us light.

Before a solitary bluff of Eastern Asia stands an explorer.　Loose stones cover both the hill before him and the vast waste around him; his thoughts, however, are not engaged with the region, tho it be of interest to him on account of the life once animating it.　As yet his attention follows another direction.　But suddenly it is drawn to a bunch of ordinary weeds surrounding a few solitary stones, and then to some others on a pile.　Creepers run over them, giving the scene a mitigating, an inviting aspect. *and also the value of parts which seem irrelevant*

To the astonishment of his servants and of the guard, sent along by the pasha, camp is to be formed upon this insignificant spot; the tents are pitched.　Strange as it seems to the attendants, the keen scientist has his reason for it.　Among the rubbish of the desert a stone is found with a few peculiar scratches, which he knows to be an ancient inscription.　Some other pieces show traces of a sculptor's chisel.　They seem to fit; they form the cap of a pillar —since some imagination guides the attempt to reconstruct it from the fragments.　Finally a slab is found which, cleaned from moss, exhibits the outlines of a figure in relief, which is nobly conceived and artistically executed.　Diggings are commanded, the hole deepens into an excavation; curiosity is stimulated by large hewn stones, by a row of them, by a well preserved plastic figure, by an ornamental base of a pillar, by a doorsill.　A flight of regular staircases is unearthed.　Not the smallest fragment is thrown aside unexamined.　Figures are found repeatedly, resembling each other; they mean something, of course, they are symbolic; inscriptions multiply, are photographed and sent home.　The papers of the civilised world describe them in detail.　Philologists work with closest attention, compare, wait for more material in order to correctly decipher and interpret the great discovery.　The historians revise old traditions, and bring the results into connection with other traces of similar kind. At last it becomes evident that those stones speak of facts by which erroneous theories are corrected, and knowledge long discredited is now confirmed. *Illustrated by the procedure of excavating in historic discovery.*

Thus we become acquainted with the thoughts, works and troubles of peoples of four and five thousand years ago.　This is the result of the journey, the toil, and the risk.　The work is carried on under such encouragement at a dozen different localities with results corroborating and amending each other.　The chaos becomes intelligible; former perplexities disappear; many a controversy is settled.　Every fragment becomes important, so that a single sign even may serve as a key for disclosing both causes and circumstances of the catastrophe which once befell that locality, revealing the form and the purpose of the whole. *Antiquities best preserved by their long rest in deep graves.* *Utility of historic discoveries.*

The searcher now finds various traces of the activity of the human mind, but he soon learns to distinguish the characteristics of two principal orders of antiquities.　Among the meaningless rubbish, strewn over the wilderness by a people almost void of any culture, he finds remnants of a nobler sort.　To him they testify of the thoughtful master's works, whilst the rubbish silently speaks of the destroyer.　Ornamental parts once joined with mathematical exactness, divulge their interesting story when reduced again to their well definable original relations.　In most cases such remnants are found best preserved by their long rest and deep grave, as they are covered by the layers of, and intermingled with, the crude material of their native home.

Nevertheless the friends on the other hand ask: Of what practical purpose is all this? We can only say, that such discoveries help us to understand our own world, and our own soul, and to understand the more thoroughly and correctly the drift of our own time and of its undercurrent.

Another conclusion can not be drawn by an observer of the remnants and their messages; messages which come over to us from dispersed and extinct nations, with whom we are connected by a direct chain of only a hundred odd links.

The question presented by our problem is, whether the ethnologist will be able in a similar manner to demonstrate the kinship of people constituting a nation, the oneness of the uncultured debris with, and its difference from, the cultured part. For, the offal of the material, the ethnical nondescript from which the purposive principle in history selected the constructive or formative elements of society, may well be considered as belonging to the same race, especially if it has been ascertained that the essential homogeneity is upheld by a general similitude of monumental style, written characters, and sculptured symbolism, notwithstanding their many variations and modifications in particular cases.　Whenever the indications favoring identity increase, we are justified in acknowledging it as more than probable that lingual and religious kinship existed between the cultured and the retarded parts of a national unity. *Principles of disseminating marks of primitive culture.* *Kinship between cultured and retarded parts of a race.*

Such indications of ethnical identity may be found scattered here and there among the forms of more or less contemporaneous culture.　Even in such cases, tho other signs of historical connection were missing, their semblances may legitimately be taken for family features.　True, certain samples of culture may appear similar and yet belong to another race, because the mental faculties common to all men may produce similar expressions of the mind at different times and in different peoples; but such cases are too rare to confute our general principle of classification.　More, *Indications of oneness in language and religion.*

however, than proof of national consanguinity is implied in our premises. Peculiar phenomena present themselves, for explanation of which the investigator must have cause to suppose a definite culture in that locality and at the time, tho that presumed culture may point to no more than original unity of language. Previous assertions concerning the oneness of the human race are thus brought to view again under a new light, so that we now become interested in the matter from a new aspect.

We are compelled in the first place, to divide each ethnical and identical mass into cultured and retarded people, so that the latter may receive due attention. The importance of the uncultured parts once being acknowledged, will render the diversity more distinct and aid us in conceiving the unity the more clearly.

In short, we desire to establish the truth, that the promiscuous loose debris of the lowest stratum is as worthy of our consideration as the parts hewn out thereof. For history teaches that unhistoric people are of no less consequence, than the historical nations. In the premises we acknowledged them all as the manifold parts of one generic whole, in which they severally are to be assigned to their different places. From their relation to their corrollaries their condition is to be made intelligible, inasmuch as the whole derives its significance from the analysis of the various constituents just as much as the particulars are only explicable from the whole. Whichever course is taken the problem demands discrimination between people of culture and such as stayed behind.

Still another criterion is to be sought for, when we come to distinguish nations and classify races evidently belonging together tho they may seem alien to each other. This new principle of classification lies in the great polarity pervading the entire visible universe determining the motion and propagation of life: we mean the sexual contrast. There are spheres in the domain of our investigation, where the sexual opposites are irrecognisable, and where, for this reason, perhaps, this principle was overlooked by former investigators.

In the large genera of sponges and mushrooms, of ferns and seaweeds, of mosses and heathers, bisexual difference is hidden. There is a world of cryptogamic life remaining, not to speak of that which submerged in prehistoric æons. May we not say, by way of analogy, that there are cryptogama among national organisms also? They present masses often entirely unaffected by the progressiveness of cultural advance. But since we do not inquire into natural but personal life, we remember that nations are molded by circumstances under which they may step forth into conceivable historic activity, as well as relapse into comparative inertia.

We restricted the analogy of a neutral state of sexual polarity and cryptogamic life in nature to the indistinctness of the activity in ethnical life where it appears as being more or less conceivable or eclipsed; for we remember that life nowhere is entirely inactive. As the wide orbits of nature ultimately help to mold the history of the earth and its inhabitants, so does every horde and tribe of seemingly forsaken portions of humanity, its arrested development notwithstanding, take its part in the complicated workings of history. That part may be compared to the drudgery in the work of constructing a foundation where the unskilled journeymen carry stones and mortar, or fill up uneven places, whilst the master-builders and masons hew the stones and join them in their proper order.

The real work of history is always in the hands of comparatively very few; it is given into care of those nations in which the forms of life have become differentiated and the polar contrasts developed·

A tree in bloom may show the meaning of this assertion. Of the blossoms the smallest part only will yield fruit; in most of them the sexual difference remains indifferent, so that they fade and drop without having fulfilled their purpose. The many simply remain in the condition of formal appendance whilst few attain to the realisation of their inner potentialities. This analogy sufficiently delineates our conception of the significance of uncultured people.

Among the nations we find a limited number, and in each of the latter again a very few persons only, with whom the great and determining contrasts of life are appreciated and become effective. There are very few nations among whom the contrasts of natural and personal life become harmonized and equalized under the conflicts which must benefit the whole.

In few people that clear consciousness becomes explicitly mature, which reflects a true view of life and of the world. The great mass of people live and try to enjoy life unconscious of the fact, that they labor in the interest of the whole, and that they, in addition must share the tribulations of the whole along with the blessings. Altho they show little concern in all that, yet they fulfill some purpose, even tho their existence seems to serve merely as a fertilising element. They are utilised by the few who rise above the common level of that feigned activity and officiousness which after all may be but inertia, because the many will try to avoid anything which disturbs their laissez-fair consuetude of life. *A few select nations have among them comparatively very few select workers conscious of their obligations to the whole.*

Still less grows the number of those who, with reasonable selfreliance, face the conflict for the sake of the common good, and spurn the very notoriety for which they are envied; who do not engage in a laudable risk for reasons of vain glory. It will be almost impossible to pick out one tenth of the few thousand renowned names in all history like that nameless Spartan who was glad that his country possessed three hundred men better than himself. Comparatively few would pass as types of their times and generations, in whom the true character of a nation and the real progress of an age are concentrated; whose life work might be deemed representative of the task which their respective nations had to work out for the benefit of humanity; whose names deserve to be enlisted as emblems of general advancement; the teachings of whose exemplary lives goes further than the influence of books. *Measure of full value of usefulness.* *Petri's race-division: Negroes, Mongolians and Europeans.*

With reference to the particular destiny and value of peoples in their periods, Petri's classification of humanity into Negroes, Mongolians and Europeans would seem the most natural among the many unsatisfactory race-divisions. Around these "central masses" the peripherical would group themselves well enough. But this method of classifying would not relieve us of the difficulty to appreciate the historic purport and value of specific nations, when the positive and characteristic significance of each group is to be determined. To define, which are to be taken as belonging to a sinking nation of culture, or only to a retarded grade of culture, would remain just as vexatious a job as under any other abandoned method. *This classification as unsatisfactory as others.*

§ 51. In judging the cultural condition of a nation, either succumbed or merely arrested, discretion is essential. For, of a nation fallen away from a high state of culture we generally can expect no more usefulness for history; whilst of those nations which only go to sleep, a future period of bloom and fruit bearing may yet be predicted. It will be difficult to deny any conglomerate group of tribes the capability for entering a progressive career, however fast asleep it may be. Compare for instance the nations along the Danube with the Arabs and Moors of Morocco. *Perished cultural nations.* *People of retarded culture fast asleep.*

On the whole it must be conceded that certain portions of mankind resemble the debris lying about a new edifice. There is the offal of mortar, there lie the fragments of sculpturing, and there are the tracings of scaffolding, once indispensable then useless and torn down long ago. Yet all this building rubbish of history lying around on the ground, figuratively speaking—as for instance the Jews, is rendered highly instructive as soon as our supposition of the oneness of original culture is brought to bear on our problem. Then the effort to exhibit the significance of the fragments, even of the human "alluvial humus" becomes justified. True to our maxim, according to which we assign each loose part to the proper place which it formerly held, and its relation to the whole, we will discover that the rubbish even bears interest. *Ethnical debris still interesting.*

Let it be illustrated: what is meant by the lost position and the relation of a discomfited nation to the whole of human history? *Illustrated by the connection of the Cordilleras with the Coral islands.*

The coral islands of the Pacific in their situation parallel with the chain of the Cordilleras point the geologist to the supposition, that the latter were once united with the islands, and still have a deep connection with their base. The westward extension of South America must have been lying between them. The largest part of that continent sank and was submerged so that only the peaks of a parallel mountain range now reach up nearly to the level of the sea and afford the coral builders their foundation.

In a similar way we suppose submersions of peoples who sank in order to serve as a substratum for historic people to rise upon. They went down, but their existence furnished the basis upon which conquerors reared organised states. Even in historic times oppressed and disappearing people, inclusive of such as are now far behind in culture if not destitute of it, are still bearers of original and elementary forces.

Such peoples arrested in their historic development serve to keep declining nations under the polar strain by which they are either to be stimulated, rejuvenated and aroused to emulation, or else to be pushed aside in order to clear the way for new departures in the line of advance. Others resemble depositories in which those antiquities were stored up through which we are now enabled to study the ancients. Their relics fill the museums in which succeeding nations to their astonishment, find preserved the monuments and documents of their history, of their own preexistence. *Analytic proofs for the import of studying nations with retarded culture.*

Upon the Island of Madeira, Oscar Heer found plants of most antiquated formations, far in arrear of the flora of the main-lands in the vicinity. They have been called "animated petrefactions." We have such among mankind. The aborigines of the South Seas and of Australia decaying as soon as brought into contact with European culture may, with all propriety, be compared to such relics of primeval ages, for they retain forms of retarded or arrested life which, after severance from continental progress, partook more and more of the character of mere vegetation.

Concerning the preservation of philological remnants the uncultured people are, at any rate, more important than what they are ethnologically.

The old language of Gothic Scandinavia has been preserved in Iceland. In some parts of England we hear, how the Gaelic language of prehistoric Britany was pronounced; in the dialects of the peasantry in some secluded districts of Thuringia or Siebenburgen we hear how the old Anglo-Saxon sounded. W. v. Humboldt could learn the old Kawi language of Java only upon the island of Madura, which long ago had become severed from its main-land. De Lacouperie tells us, that the prehistoric language of China is recognised solely upon the island of Formosa. The "Sibir" only ten years ago reported, that there exists a remnant of the aborigines, called the Karagassians, of whom could be learned how they once spoke in the regions of the Irkutsk.

Remnants of most ancient cultures we thus see protruding from the dimness of the past like apparitions from mythical realms.

Our conclusion, that any uncultured mass of people, scattered over the whole surface of the earth as by an explosion is correlevant as yet to the whole of humanity, seems to be sufficiently proven by empirical facts.

The chaos, now to be analysed in accord with the rules laid down, forms the first of those circles, wherein the selfculture of natural man advances in narrowing concentration. The widely extending connection of nationalities and race of prehistoric age in this first circle represents the quarry from which history hauls its material, or forms, if you please, the solid foundation upon which history rears its edifice. This chaotic circle of nations is to the world of the henceforth differentiating personal life equally important as the geological crust of our planet is to the physical world. Its importance, either as a whole or in its seeming insignificant parts, remains the same, whether the nations form massive strata, or whether they appear as scattered fragments; or whether they are to be compared to small nuclei of future nations found imbedded here and there, nestwise, like crystals in granite.

When we arrive at our third part we will better understand the necessity of the principles laid down in this ninth chapter. At present we desist from further details.

In the ethnical rubble now before us elementary forces and rudimentary forms predominate. As the rocks represent the inorganic part of nature supporting a countless variety of organic life, so this bulk of prehistoric humanity in its state of confined life, now compressed in strata, now shifting over such strata in drifts, now breaking into fractions and scattering, forms at this stage of our inquiry, the foundation-wall for the theater of history. It resembles at the same time, the lowest but fundamental note in the music of the opera. As in visible nature, so we find at the base of this promiscuous rude material of the historical world, that which, according to Schelling "ought not to be."

As we found that in the inorganic world, as reduced to its fundamental principles, there is no "dead matter," so is this substratum of history all alive—unless a selfsufficient party of us late-comers would or could sever all connection with the past, detach themselves from the current of history, and disdainfully look upon ancestry and upon the past as being nonsensical and of no purpose whatever.

We have thus far made a survey of all the raw material of history from that point of view which presented to us the oneness of humanity, ethnologically and philologically. As a whole, however, the bulk is not as yet articulated, nor did we succeed with its classification. For the theoretical division into cultured and uncultured people is insufficient after all.

Think of the shades of such differences as present themselves in our own nation, in any single city. The essence of human nature does not warrant such rubrics. A division on the line of relative superiority of culture amounts to no more than a generalisation which would have to be altered whenever the unstableness of historical movements changes the conditions.

External circumstances and the commotions going on at all points of the world and in all relations of social life, continuing through every stage of individual development in every period of history, ever causes the dividing line between the two sets of cultured and uncultured people to shift in such a manner, as to render classification of mankind under the two topics of pre-eminence and destitution untenable.

Since the constructive principle of history lies in man individually

A division on the score of culture would be of no avail in the search for the constructive principles of history, lying in each man individually. However conspicuous a few noble persons stand out, and, maintaining their position, may command the admiration of their fellowmen ; yet in each group of people, if classified merely according to their degree of culture, the ebbings and flowings of the tide of development —which tends either to elevation or degradation, and to brutality as much, if not stronger as to civilisation—will be found as equally effective and equally hazardous in every mortal.

not in external, shifting conditions,

We have so far (and not we alone, but the philosophy of civilisation has hitherto) represented the nations, and judged their standing, under aspects of specific periods with distinctly marked changes, and definite grades of general progress. No wonder, that the concepts of humanity, as drawn from such cursory views of history, were subjective, capricious and contradictory—hence of little scientific value, subject to fruitless disputes, and apt to work mischief under false and misapplied deductions.

not in grades, changes and definable periods of general progress.

It is time then, to search for those principles of differentiation, and to arrange the topics of historic movements in accord with that original predisposition of human nature, which alone enable men to build up that organic system of causes and effects, which we call history.

A classification of humanity on the score of culture may turn out rather mischievously,

CH. X. THE TENSION OF POLARITY DIFFERENTIATING THE FIRST CIRCLE OF NATIONS.

§ 52. Once more we must present to our minds that ethnical nondescript which covered the earth as from an overflowing reservoir. Let us imagine this fluent mass as analogous to a chemical compound solution, resembling in history what mother-lye, I think it is termed, is to chemistry.

Primitive society compared to a chemical compound.

In precisely the same manner as electrosis resolves such a composition to its original ingredients as soon as the wires charge the fluid with the mysterious force, the acids isolating themselves at the positive, the bases at the negative pole;so the ethnical mixture before us undergoes an analogous process, except that the isolating power is of a different nature.

Electrosis of a chemical composition illustrating polarity.

In other words : Only the terminal points of a magnetized bar demonstrate the principles of adhesion and repulsion most decisively ; the nearer to the middle, the weaker is the "force." At the center all tension ceases. Where the polar difference poises all opposition is rendered neutral, the integral forces balance and rest in the central energy where they seem to have turned into inertia. These very phenomena are reiterated in the way of physical analogies in the history of the individual, of a nation, of all mankind.

Polarity in the magnetic bar.

The great polarity which determines the course of history rests in man himself as a latent potentiality. We shall try to show the effectiveness and functions of this coherent and corresponding contrariety under the pendulum of consciousness. But ere we are warranted to succeed in the attempt we must fetch up one thing omitted when we indexed man's estate. We were convinced that the natural world and the spiritual are blended in man. But at the same time and by reason of this union the spheres of activity and passiveness also interlap in his constitution.

Natural and spiritual world blend in man.

The natural world is consigned to the bans of circumferential and circumstantial generalness ; its formal variety notwithstanding it, forms a material unity and moves under the sway of necessity. It consists of that which is to remain under determining influences, which is designed to be acted upon, which must sustain the supremacy of the other realm ; which is doomed to passiveness.

Nature—subordinate, and passive.

The spiritual world of personality, on the other hand, is that which influences, animates and determines, is the sphere in which activity in freedom is the order of existence. This is true, and, we trust, has been made clear.

Spirit supremacy, active and exerting influences

But as yet the problem, as to how both of these worlds claim a part of man's being, whereby its disintegration is rendered possible, has been scarcely touched upon.

Death rendered possible

Whenever man takes an introspect into his life, he finds himself subject to both the constituent factors under discussion. He is to decide for himself, choice being determined as much or as little, and being forced into his course of action no further, than he is determining himself.

Polarity founded in man's combination of matter and mind.

11

With a will he endeavors to accomplish the obligations of his vocation; with energy he ventures upon difficulties to be surmounted. Filled with zeal he will persist to conquer opposition and will not yield to oppression; conscious of his courage and selfhood he will assert the right and prerogatives of human life and personal choice. The internal tensions of his nerves and muscles fit him to surmount external obstacles, whilst exercise and engagement requite the gladsome consciousness of strength. This all continues until—reaction sets in.

Man representing the union of matter and mind, is thereby caused to move in freedom under necessity after a method of ethical ends, designed for the very purpose of realising the unification enjoined upon him by his own constitution. Personal life, asserting its energy and liberty at one moment, becomes exhausted and recedes behind the natural form of life at the next. Passiveness and suffering from prostration take the place of buoyant agility. There man steps forth as a free agent,

here he retires a patient. Now he feels himself a being which can play with nature in serene carelessness, and then again he finds himself in a despondent mood, subject to his own frailness, an object for nature to trifle with as when the waves of the

ocean play football with his ship. As the transient waves submerge into the whole, so despondency drags down personal life, hiding itself behind the drapery of worldly sorrow, of unfavorable or unavoidable circumstances.

The transition from one mode of consciousness to the other generally signifies almost as much as a change in the mode of thought along the whole front. Manifesting itself mostly in the method of persuading the will, his change seems to take place

in accord with a necessity equal to that which causes the exchange of forces between natural poles. On closer examination, however, this duality of an active and passive phase of consciousness, either voluntarily or naturally determined, simply shows that man is a combination of nature and spirit. Hence the forms of thought and of imagination will assume their bend in proportion to the preponderance of either the natural

part or the spiritual side. The same dualism, becoming distinctly manifest in the miniature world of man individually, also conditions the advance or relapse of humanity as a whole. In the totality of human affairs the two great antitheses become apparent

under the same rule of predominance of either spiritual or natural temper. The difference may be fittingly compared to the more feminine or masculine features of each of the two sets of temperaments. Concerning our problem of cultural development, the one part of our race will be found more active and influential, the other

more passive and receptive. Thus the great universal contrast is outlined. We are comfronted by the great polar tension which stimulates and molds the variety of subordinate differences. And this mutual strain, balancing the whole, pervades all circles and all radii of progressive culture, and in a succession of concentric cycles and regulates the problems, and directs the final issues of developing humanity.

Upon the first and widest of these circles coming forth from the misty dawn of prehistoric ages, and hence showing very few and very indistinct features of differentiation, we shall now meditate.

It is the Turano-Mongolian circle, the lowest and broadest stratum of the human race.

But in order to look over its wide compass we will first take a firm position, and then observe that circle parting into two semi-circles.

Our point of view is the enormous partition-wall of the Himalayas, from the snow-capped ranges of which more than eighty peaks rise up to heights of twenty thousand and more feet. This backbone of the world forms an axis from which mountain spurs run out to the north and brace up the large Pamir plateau which further north is sheltered again by the Alaichain. Toward the west this expansive plateau leans against that mountain stock which forms the ethnographical divide.

At the southern seam of the Tarim basin—in the western regions of the Gobi between Kashgar and Kotan, if not upon the large plateau of Pamir itself—the native home of the Chinese is indicated. There these Turanians dwelt in the vicinity of the Aryans or Indo-Germans, on the shores of their "Dragon Lake" (Kara-kul). From thence the Chinese migrated eastward, whilst the Aryans "went west." What, ethnologically, they both have in common is owing to that ancient neighborhood.

According to Richthofen it was as late as 2300 B. C. that the Chinese performed governmental functions over the region of the Bulungir. And as late as three thousand years after that time the similarity of the inhabitants of Khotan with the Chinese was deemed remarkable enough to be noted down in the official annals of China.

The large steppes of the very expansive plateau of Central-Asia, lying more than 10000 feet above sea level, really form the natural Chinese wall, by which the IRANIANS were protected against the TURANIANS, and by which Mongolian culture became separated from that of Western Asia and of Europe.

From the great, terrace-like slopes of the plateau these first main divisions of the nations possessing the ambition requisite for higher culture glided down in opposite directions. Their cultures thus grew up in antagonism toward each other, and in their polarity became the foundations of the grand superstructures which both, up to present date, recline against these eastern and western declivities. Despite this local proximity, however, the relations between the Chinese-Malayan world and the Western-Asiatic and European cultures became so distinct, that for four thousand years they remained obscure, since the nations of both these semi-circles lost sight of each other. The few marks of cultural progress standing out in full historic light are insufficient to render discernible the ways and means of communication, if the people kept up any at all. On the whole, they seem to have lost all knowledge of each other

(margin: Long period of seclusion of Eastern Asiatics.)

Our full attention was to be directed toward the eastern and western poles of the ethnographical axis with its fulcrum on the Pamir. For to this axis we henceforth assign many demonstrable effects of a strong strain, of a polar tension which is perceptible throughout all historical movements, under which the two chief ethnical factors of universal history were always laboring. We also venture to distinguish the occupants of the two semi-circles under the strain caused by their masculine and feminine characteristics, the one with a preeminently active, and the other under a pronounced passive, tendency. These three principles: the polarities between spirit and physical nature, between Mongolians and Aryans as conditioned by the ethnographical situation, and between the active and passive forms of world-consciousness —mete out to universal history by their action and reaction, its modes and its motions.   •

(margin: Pamir the axis of another polarity.)

(margin: Three kind of polar tension.)

CH. XI. FIRST CIRCLE OF NATIONS.—TURANO-MONGOLIAN CULTURE.— AN EASTERN SEMICIRCLE.

§ 53. Turning to the east from the great Central-Asiatic divide, we observe, in the first place, how the culture and history of the eastern Asiatics was built not so much upon geographically outlined conditions, as upon the cultus and form of consciousness which wrought the national character of these Turanians.

When Oppert wrote his review of Lenormant's studies of cuneiform inscription, he asked: "What, after all, do we know about the primeval history of mankind, of the mental development of prehistoric tribes? Nothing, absolutely nothing!" We, too. set out with this declaration. At each step of our investigation we shall be reminded thereof.

(margin: Oppert on primeval history.)

Concerning Northern Asia we have to suppose an underlying stratum of most ancient inhabitants, who left no remnants from which to conjecture their peculiarities, except the Yenisei-inscriptions which must be taken into account as such. Abel Remusat directed that attention to these inscriptions which ought to have been paid to them, seventy years ago. They shall receive further mention in the next chapter, when the western wing of the Mongolians comes under consideration.

(margin: Yenisei-inscriptions Remusat. § 57.)

We now attempt to reconnoiter the right wing with the culture of China and what pertains to it. Of course, we can touch only upon the most salient points.

(margin: Mongolian migrations to America, to the South Sea and Africa. Oppert.)

Our present range of vision comprises the "Empire of the Middle", Mongolia, Tibet, the Amoor countries and Japan. It extends across the islands of the Pacific to America. The pristine cultures of Mexico and Peru are products of these Turanians, which were destroyed by other Mongolians following the first immigrants much later and spreading themselves over North- and Central-America.

The Mongolian migrations toward the south and to Africa seem to correspond with those to America.

Since Hirth of late has given us the translation of the Tshu-fen-tshi which he made in Shanghai, it has become evident, that in very early times a lively traffic was carried on between China and East Africa, namely with Dshunguli or Somali-land, with Sofala, and with old Berbera at the straits of Babelmandeb. From Berbera the Chinese hauled storax, myrrh, and tortoise shells. Their revenue records very accurately describe the articles of commerce. The porcelain vessels from China, found in the pyramids, also receive their explanation from Hirth's labors.

(margin: Traffic with Berbers. Hirth.)

(margin: China porcelain in the pyramids.)

The beginning of Chinese literature is dated six thousand years back by Von der Gabelentz in his lecture given in the aula, Leipzig, 1879. Some chronologists no doubt declare this an exaggeration, but we can see no sufficient grounds to coincide with them. The songs of the Shu-king were composed, according to Von Strauss's computations, before the year 2160 B. C. On all sides the fact is corroborated, that the culture of China is the most ancient known. This we take for granted, for nothing equals the copiousness and variety of that literature. Where else is to be found such a splendid edition of the principal works of a nation, in 1000.

(margin: Age of Chinese literature Gabelentz.)

Its wealth.
Von Strauss.

volumes, as the one which the British government bought in the year A. D. 1877? We know but few of the literary productions of China "and of them how little" as Gabelentz complains. Yet what little we know of them is sufficient to dispel the old prejudice that the Chinese were to be dealt with as a petrified nation. There is a world of mental activity disclosed upon most any subject and up to date. An enormous number of monographs, besides the

Yet Chinese culture reveals only forms of arrested life.

hundreds of volumes of circumstantial and monotonous state-annals, contain descriptive treatises on sociology even, and on modern civic economics. They divulge the movement and growth of feudal, independent, and anarchical conditions of the realm, through times of sword-law and all possible social formations of private and public life, up to the state-craft of the united empire. An astonishing zeal and any amount of scholarship was spent upon the construction of that redundant language. A collection of belles lettres in 1800 volumes mirrors the life of the nation in all its detailed features. And yet there is, as we shall see, nothing but the cultivation of a confined life, an arrested culture.

Poverty of the Chinese mind.
Richthofen.

    "The scientific capacity of the Chinaman is rather broad, not deep," says Richthofen. Knowledge does not tend to new improvements, but spreads out upon methods of application which were in use from times most remote. In the fall season Chinese phantasy still transforms the quails into moles in order to let them become quails again in springtime. Such scientific ignorance is held almost sacred because of its age. Reverence for that which is ancient is the most characteristic trait of this whole culture.

The Chinese have no science for the purpose of arriving at the truth. They possess dexterity and imagine that they know everything better, but being disqualified for comprehending anything abstract, they are unable to formulate a theory or to make an

Causes of the unfitness for abstract reasoning.

invention. It does not occur to the mind of Chinamen to reason from phenomena to causes. And we have reason to believe that this peculiarity is not merely to be accounted for by the seclusion and proud selfsufficiency of this culture. For not even the influence of foreign and acknowledged superiority can incite a Chinese mind toward profundity. And whenever this is missing, consciousness will enlarge on things as they appear side by side, and will thereby always become flattened. Profound thought and formation of judgment will always receive the opposite of encouragement, where, under pretense of paternal government, despotism regulates and disciplines the most minute movement of thought and action—or rather imitation. Whilst on the other hand the mind, under neglect of mental penetrativeness, becomes too lazy to become   dissatisfied, and invites despotic rule.

Paternal government.
Child's fear of ghosts.

Deeply imbued is the consciousness of that race with nothing but ancestry-worship, and with the fear of the ghosts imagined to reign in the regions of their native homes. Old as the Chinese are, they remain children who see a spectre in every dark corner.

Imperial Shintoism.

The emperor is the highest representative of the realm of the dead, and even its ruler. Deceased mandarines are promoted by him to the celestial court, or deposed by him from their high position, as the case may be. At any rate, and without a doubt being uttered by any Chinaman, the emperor's will is done in heaven as it is upon earth. Undoubted is his ability and sole authority to dispatch money and clothing to the departed.

It is known what careful attention is paid to this, the imperial form of Shintoism ("ghost" worship,) and what complicated means of intercourse with the other world this ancestor-worship produces : each being made an affair of state and diplomacy.

Over the total darkness of ancient Shamanism there is spread out a layer of Sabism, a somewhat embellished copy of the former.

"There existed a being, perfect and incomprehensible; before heaven and earth came into being. It was so silent, so supernatural. It alone remains unchangeable. It can go through anything without getting hurt. It may be considered as the world-mother. I know not its name. If I want to designate it, I name it TAO."

Taoism, mixture of primitive tradition with astral Shamanism (Sabism.)
V. von Strauss.

So we read in V. v. Strauss's translation of the Tao-te-king. Tao is the mental presentation of the unity of all, an uncorporeal, apparition-like spirit. This is enough for the practical sense of the Chinaman.

Attempt to form a center of unity and continuity.

In this apperception we recognise that form of consciousness which seizes upon those most ancient and primitive traditions, whose meaning is entirely forgotten, construing them into some center of cohesive continuity.

Cause of Chinese tolerance.

Phantasy, as a general thing, has no access to the institutions of social or political life. It is not historically inclined ; least of all the phantasy of the average Chinaman, whose religious sense has become absorbed by other weird phantasms. The Chinese let the state attend to thought and religion, this being considered as the business of government exclusively. Hence that peculiar tolerance, or rather indifference in religious matters, with which the Chinese are accredited ; a tolerence easily to be reduced to the utter lack of imagination, of all intuition. Such a kind of formalism and unmitigated, dull superstition never creates fanaticism. *Total lack of the creative power of the mind and of intuition.*

In the art of China the ancient nomade life as yet shines through the thin cover of lacquer culture. The architectural style is a reminiscence of the tent in the steppes at migration times. The gable end of the roof, bent upwards, and the flimsy ornamentations represent the hangings of the temporary habitations as they floated in the winds of the wilderness. *Reminiscences of Nomade life in architectural style.*

The dogmas of political economy also date from the times of patriarchal nomade life. Parental authority, applied to the organisation of the family, the tribe, and the state, is the whole secret of China's peculiarities. *Secret of Chinese peculiarities.*

Under the cultivation of these traits the minds had become so enured to fixed rules that, when the people came in contact with foreigners whose customs were considered inferior, as a matter of course, alien culture found no weak spot where to intrude. *Results of Chinese training*

The seclusion, haughtiness and selfsufficiency, the narrowmindedness, sullenness and shrewdness of the Chinese character, the finish and conservatism of the political machinery, the circumstantiality and ceremoniousness, the unconcern or its dissemblance in matters of conviction, the permanency of social habits, are all explained by the submissive attitude to a government of patronage. With this an authoritative tutelage and management of all the affairs of life is established, which deprives the obedient individual of all freedom even in the details of everyday life. Every thought is restricted to conformance. and coined into a performance which is prescribed as with a stencil pattern, and controlled by common habit. The least digression is ostracised, the nation of children is kept in leading strings. *the same as in any clannish community. § 56.*

The cardinal virtue is loyalty, to which any effort of promulgating a different opinion is offensive, is rendered useless if not dangerous, and is deemed a sacrilege, as it is the case in any clannish community. The more ancient and leveling a custom, the more binding it is. Incorporated into governmental law, custom is utilised in keeping the people in the bounds of fear and good behavior. Thought or private judgment is not wanted in such a mechanism of citizenship. If the individual should see fit to exercise a little selfhood, it only remains to him to be tricky. Thus obedient children are trained, who necessarily become dull and tedious, if not sullen. They do not threaten, do not object or gainsay, are not rude and naughty—but neither are they affectionate or sympathizing, despite the thousands of conventional phrases of feigned cordiality. *Good behavior.*

"Here in Sikkim and Nepal as in Tibet", H. v. Schlagintweit relates, "abusive nicknames, in which the conversation of the Hindoos and lower Moslims in India abound, are not heard at all. Such good mannerism is the result of Chinese training or rather drill, but it is of too questionable an inner quality as to be counted with civilsation. The same in almost every respect may be said of the Japanese. From beneath the shallow refinement of formal conventionalism the barbarian traits of savagery and original steppe-life occasionally break forth again. Wild nature is not broken if it is only subduded; it may be polished by patriarchal rule, turned to gilded despotism, and it may be repressed by the tyranny of custom, but it can not be inwardly abolished." *Schlagintweit,* *Lacquer of refinement. Inner barbarism.*

China resembles a man, who after a premature old age has become very pedantic, grave and sedate. The vast empire was an upshot of rapid growth, rough and ready made. At present boyish traits look at us out of a wrinkled face with a dismal squint. Such is the physiognomy of that nation, such its characters: "A mixture of cunning craftiness and studied naivete, of pride and dissembled unconcern, of artful conventionalism and passive endurance." *Resume of the Chinese characteristics.*

The traits of character, here as in every other nation, reflect even from their architecture, their æsthetics. According to Semper "the elements of Chinese arts are not organically connected, but mechanically set side by side, held together by nothing like a leading idea. A Chinaman can not abstract a single principle, to modify any of his maxims which are riveted into the details of daily life and do not allow the least change, lest the whole fabric of Chinese necessity should collapse." This is descriptive enough, and, since it contains no misrepresentation of the Chinese mind, proves our estimate of its calibre. *Æsthetics lack of any leading idea* *Semper.* *§ 55.*

With reference to the ritualistic exhibition of the mixture of God and world-consciousness that is, reviewing the cultus, from which this national character has grown, as it is the case in every other nation, we are, for the first time, confronted by an imperial religion. *Cultus always the source of national character. § 54.*

A space as large as the city of Paris, fenced in by high walls, a garden full of shrubbery, lakes, cottages, and kiosks of exquisite splendor—such is Yuen-Min-Yuen, the imperial residence at Pekin, the seat of deified lords of the "Empire of the Middle", surrounded by a superabundance of oriental vainglory. In the center of the park stands the celestial pagoda enshrining the colossal statue of Buddha, decked with gold and jewels.

When in 1860 the French and British broke into that solitude and frighted the celestial lord from his lair, they found the halls yet filled with stupefying incense. The ampulla-lamps threw their gloomy flickering light upon the grotesque statuettes of semi-deities, of monsters and beasts. This interior illustrates what we meant by the religious mixture of an upper layer with the fragments thrown up through the frail broken cover, as by an eruption from the substratum beneath.

§ 54. Before we further speak of Buddhism and its shifting a layer of speculative religiousness over the substratum of Taoism and Shamanism, we turn to Japan, where Buddhism flourishes galore.

Anterior to the period in which Nipon was inundated by Buddhism, it had always had its Mikado, the "Son of Heaven."

In his person as in the Chinese emperor, the regal and sacerdotal offices are united. And the dominant classes wrought the remnants of a monotheistic heritage into a multiform mechanism of polytheism. Old Shintoism knew of three pristine, personified powers, which presided over the affairs of the whole world. But from the bath of Zsanagi's purification so many deities arose, that at one time, when evil spirits squirmed in the air, not less then eight millions could be mustered   for defense.

Under this heaven full of good and evil ghosts a grand literature grew up. The nursery of national learning was the old capitol of Nara. Here the Ko-ji-ki, the "book of old traditions", was compiled and published, the oldest source of the historic knowledge of the Japanese. At Nara the old imperial city the governors of the provinces had to report the topographical, physical and political condition of their parts of the realm. Then the priests of Buddha from Siam, India and China made an inroad into the old town of the Mikado, the monumental city of Great Nipon with its wealth of historic material. Buddhism knew how to advertise itself at this place by founding a large library of Buddhistic, especially Chinese literature.

Underneath that conglomerate of Shinto-Buddhism lies the formidable stratum of ancestor-worship and spooks. This appears especially in the cult of the Kami, the apotheosised national heroes.

Many families of the nobility claim a Kami as their ancestor. Thirteen thousand and seven hundred of them are enumerated, of whom three thousand and seven hundred have temples dedicated to them. Their worship continues to send its roots into the deep old substratum underlying Buddhism thus draining off below the surface the vital saps of the official religion. For the Japanese find it more congenial to their ideas, to conjure departed souls by the tinkling of bells and by rappings, and to attract them and accomodate them by pieces of paper strung up between the posts of the temple-gates, than to undergo the selfcastignations required by the Buddhistic hierarchy. Hence almost every family in Japan keeps and venerates the miraculous shinto mirror in private, besides the official Buddhistic altar, either in a

screened closet or in a tiny pocket-case. Beside the image of Buddha tiny boards are put up, with the names of the departed members of the family written upon them. Concerning the double-shrine it gives human nature a satisfaction to worship one's own ancestors and children. Concerning the tables we find the same usage from the same source in some parts of Europe this day, where the boards upon which the dead are laid out are inscribed with some epithets, a few crosses painted on, and set up at bridges and crossroads so that whoever passes by may say a "prayer for the dead."

As the puckered jumble of the written characters of the Turanians look to us most awkward, so Eastern Asiatic art reveals idiosyncrasies which have nothing at all in common with occidental conceptions. That bold, pouchy realism, that mechanical copying of nature without an idea of perspective and without a standpoint,

notwithstanding the realism, is accompanied by a mania for picturing ghosts with most absurd grimaces and distorted corporeal shapes. The monstrosities of the decorative arts of the Turanians surpass all that ever could be invented by Europeans in the line of caricature representing freaks of the brain. The conceptions which these drawings reveal, awaken a sort of surprise, whether the variegated categories of thought may not have affected the structure even of the painter's brains.

Ingrained as these dark superstitions are into consciousness and life, yet such darkness is alien to human nature, is not essential to it. The good traits and elements of truth contained in every syncretism, are always separable from superstitious

incrustations. The Japanese at least are quick to distinguish the genuine truth from fictitious religiousness. Naturalism can not satisfy even those Mongolians, tho

It has become embodied in every tissue of their lives. This is the reason why the "great East-Asiatic reformation" caused by the "Light of Asia", as Arnold chose to call and to solemnise the father of Buddhism, was so successful after all.

What Buddhism is, we only learned since Bohlen and Remusat discussed it. What we then knew of it heightened our esteem, with regard, at least, to the good will in the Kantian sense. It can not be expected of us, to enlarge upon that world of gods with their groups of triads, etc. Prof. Panzer in Peking has of late suffi- ciently dwelt upon "the Lamaistic Pantheon", to justify us in taking the name of Tibet as emblematic for that "reform" by which Asia is said to have been felicitated. For that church-state, as it might be called, represents today the fountain-head of shamanistic eclecticism, and governs the large domain of Buddhistic hierarchism.

In its seclusion, accessible only by mountain passes at the height of our highest mountains like Mt. Blanc or Mount Renier, Tibet is the stronghold of the Buddhism of modern times. The Dalai-Lama with his hierarchy and his 30000 cloisters is a vassal of China, but his rule is more penetrant, than that of his suzerain, the son of heaven, himself. Those hundred large volumes of the Kandshur with the commandments of Buddha tend to that formalism of which in the days of our childhood we read in the description of prayer-mills.

The worship of images and relics is diversified and made impressive by the heat of wax candles and by clouds of incense. We find this culture from the Caspian Sea down to Ceylon and up to the Altai range.

We presume on the reader's acquaintance with the Central-Asiatic doctrines of incarnation, and with the fact that Lamaism is not only a mixture of Shamanism with Buddhism, but also with Christianity. Buddha taught to refrain from all symbolism and dogmatism and for this reason tried to prevent written formulas. Thus his teachings remained unwritten for six centuries. Symbolism was engrafted upon Buddhism when the Nestorians, driven from Persia, preached their most corrupt form of Christianity all over India and eastern Asia between A. D. 636 and 731, as the inscriptions of Siganfu prove. Kosmas Indicopleustes testifies that even as early as A. D. 540 Nestorianism had been successfully preached to the Huns and Bactrians. Hence the many similarities of Buddhism with Roman Catholic rites.

Bastian restored an old picture of "Buddha becoming incarnate at Mavadewi in the form of a white elephant, descending from the Tushita heaven surrounded by a jubilee-choir of gods." This illustrates the Asiatic mixtures and tolerance. Gautama afterwards once more left his abode of Tueshid in order to enter the motherly womb of queen Maha Maja in the form of a light of five colors.

The restlessness of these transmutations and this religious eclecticism continues in every man, until rest is found in his dissolution into Nirwana. This is the final accomplishment of the "divine" Gautama. The effects of this speculation upon public life we shall show in the sequel. Yet nothing has been held forth as more praiseworthy than Buddhistic toleration, which in reality is nothing but an inertia, only of late arousing itself to a degree of aggressiveness in its death struggle. A Japanese picture shows Lao-tse, Buddha and Konfu-tse, each in full figure. The three "founders of religion" taste of a porridge out of the same pot. Each finds the taste different: sour, sweet, bitter. This is a piece of Asiatic toleration, indifference and arbitrary subjectivism. Such toleration did never disturb any of the layers drifting alternately one over the other, all covering the preceding ancestor-worship; the latest layer least of all. The "religions" were all amalgamated into the porridge of Shamanism, the worst form of ancestor-worship. When later on Nestorianism and Mohamedanism were added to the great "Reform"-Buddhism, Brahmanism, Taoism, and Shintoism, the demons of the lowest stratum held their sway none the less over the inhabitants of the Gobi, than over those under the palm-trees along the shores of the Irawaddi. The adherents of the "great reformation" in their satiety with the porridge of the imperial religion, keep aloof in the heights of all-the-sameness.

This attitude alone is suited to the pantheistic inclination of the oriental world. The individual is to Nirwana no more than what the drop is to the ocean. Man is but the transient appearance of that which is mere being in general. It will become evident, however, that pantheistic philosophy was not confined to the Orientals. It is always favored by statesmen as a mean to accommodate all shades of religious opinion and as a preventive against questioning the authority of the ruler who represents the natural generalness of a state in which personality is suppressed. The lowest form of pantheism is abetted, since ignorance and fear of the bad are the most convenient

Dissatisfaction with superstition made the introduction of Buddhism possible.

"Great Asiatic Reform" § 53.

Character of Buddhism § 58

Bohlen-Remusat; Arnold.

Panzer Lamaism in Tibet.

Dalai Lama, Pope of the Mongolians.

Kandshur. Prayer-mills.

Lamaism tinctured with Christianity.

Nestorians furnished symbolism. § 58, 59, 124, 149.

Siganfu inscriptions. Kosmas Indicopleustes.

Pantheon of Tibet. Mixture of Shamanism, Shintoism, Taoism, Nestorianism, Buddhism Mohamedanism. § 55, 145, 149.

Bastian's discovery of a Buddha-picture with Lao-tse and Konfu-tse eating porridge from the same pot. § 56, 58.

Secret of tolerance rather indifference.

Explaining the easy accommodation of governments to religious changes—as pantheism always does—and of subjects, so long as the lowest stratum is left untouched. § 55, 56, 57, 78.

Pantheistic mode of thinking favored by rulers. (§ 55, 56, 57, 78, because it nullifies personality. § 27, 86, 65, 72, 89, 97, 170, 185

Pantheism a compromise between philosophic indifference, arbitrary legislation and abject supersition. § 42

Advantages accruing to political absolutism from imperial pantheon and court-theology. Deongls Augustus. § 55, 56, 77.

means to keep people in subjection, to preserve the unity of an empire under centralised power, and to compromise between philosophic indifference, arbitrary legislation, and abject superstition.

Hence also the abuse of language, multiform and adjustable as it is, in all the diplomacy, ambiguity, and sophistry issuing from such religious views. From that source imperial theology and syncretism derives its advantages. By right of Buddhism the state can say with Napoleon; "I am fate, to me the person is nothing." By right of ghost-cult the subject can
say: "I worship myself." Thus both are suited, and all must now be preserved in accord with that theory of existence in order to avoid trouble. Hence the sullen servility in matters of politics, and stupidity in things concerning the mind.

Chinese-Japanese influences are diffused over the large fan-shaped area of which Farther-India represents the handle. They are spread over the Malayan Sunda Islands, over Polynesia and the Maori, over Micronesia and Australia, all lying in the mean between the farthest corners of the fan. They hold sway over the inhabitants of the entire Pacific basin, all being of the same Mongolian stock. Viewed from the distance these islanders all show equal conditions of life, the same monotonous ex- pression in their physiognomy, all sullen and servile on a common level. On a closer examination we notice that in many places the lowest stratum with its fear of ghosts is covered by a growth of runners from Southern Asiatic culture. On the eastern wing especially the uniformity dissolves into as great a variety of formations as the flora of these regions. We have there what we designated a rubble or debris of nationalities, difficult to classify, tho distinct enough ; for in one respect they are all
alike ; everywhere we discern that state of consciousness, which, besides the fear of ghosts, is subject to snake-worship.

Let us see, whether we are better enabled now to understand, what, concerning this matter, was slightly touched upon in § 45, 49. We return to a somewhat closer investigation of the old immigrants of America.

What we know of the prehistoric "mounds" found throughout the United States and Mexico, is sufficient to draw conclusions tantamount to circumstantial evidence. Heaps of buffalo bones surrounding these mounds, split open to obtain the marrow, lead us to infer that entire nations must have held their wakes upon these burial-
grounds. These mounds date back to a period of culture whose traces long ago have been overgrown by old forests, just as the sands of the Gobi have swallowed up the traces of that culture in its old native home. The outlines of these mounds resemble the figures of panthers, leopards, buffaloes and stags, as Peet has described even those of Wisconsin where they are more numerous than in Ohio and Oregon. Others have the lineaments of snakes. The snake-shaped outlines of mounds and buildings in
Mexico and adjacent countries, and the snake images found in them, remind us once more of the conclusions of Humboldt as to the relations of the Mexicans with Ægyptian and Phenician culture. They still more vividly remind us of the dragon, the emblem of the Chinese, and of their emphatic dragon-worship of old. What the dragon was to China, the rattlesnake was to Mexico, the escutcheon of the nation. The scant but very interesting remnants of the rich culture and literature of the Aztecs which have escaped the vandalism of the Spaniards, are still said to be enig-matic. The writings upon deerskins and agave fibres do not afford much proof of any historic sense in these people ; hence they afford a meagre knowledge of their
history. But so much is divulged by all the monuments, that a combination of ancestor-and snake-worship under awe of death was in vogue, and demanded incredible hecatombs of victims for human sacrifices. A numerous caste of priests, worthy of comparison with the Lama church-state of Tibet, had knitted the meshes of the most weird superstition. Witness the masks worn at their solstistic dances !

Nowhere, perhaps, is the God of death more terribly pictured, than in the hiero-glyph Maya manuscript at Dresden, which represents him with the flesh torn off the back. And the cults among the Central American tribes seem ever to have corres-ponded with those illustrations. Schelhas quotes Diego de Lando where he says that the Maya were "possessed of an excessive fear of death." The natives of Yucatan
are possessed thereof to the present time.

It was in 1889 that A. J. Mueller found the ruins of a prehistoric Indian city in Honduras, ruins which compare well with the monuments of Peru and Mexico.

They appeared to him like objects of a fairy tale in the midst of the primeval forest, nothing having ever been heard of them.

Now let us suppose that the Toltecs, of unquestioned Eastern Asiatic origin, once peopled the regions of Central America ; and that one of their tribes, pushed by the following Aztecs, went south as far as Peru—then we can but expect another center of culture of that very same character, which really existed. For whatever objects of art have so far been found and investigated anywhere in those regions, bear the sign of the toad and the serpent.

The Inka empire extended from the Sierra of the temperate zone, from Rio Maule in Chili to the boundaries of Ecuador. Many small tribes of their predecessors disappeared or took shelter in the folded valleys of the mountain-bound empire.

The consciousness of the Inka must be admitted to have comprised wrecks of a Monotheism which they had brought along with them. For **of Monotheism the sun-service is always the emblematic reminder**, and the Inkas had a fine liturgy of that character. As the emperor of China, son of heaven, plows a furrow once a year, so did the ruler of Peru who was likewise, in his own estimation and in that of his subjects, —a son of the sun.

But the sun-service was broken into fragments under the overwhelming massiveness of stark fear of night and terror of death, fuming up from the lowest stratum. Along the whole line from Peru to Utah the same dismal aspect. All those illustrations which Humboldt copied as early as 1816, and those which Squire of late published from Pensacola and Masaya, show the same repulsive combination of animal and demon. They indicate also the origin of anthropophagism in worshiping that which is most terrible and loathsome.

When Seler visited the Toltecian ruins of Xochicalco in Mexico at the close of 1887 he found a free-standing stone figure of a decapitated man with the breast cut open and the ribs laid bare. It represents the symbol of human sacrifices, a skinned victim. The custom of scalping among the Indians here finds its explanation: and perhaps, that of anthropophagism. With this we close the analysis of the first part of the first circle of nations which comprises the great Mongolo-Malayan group.

CH. XII. TURANO-MONGOLIAN WORLD: B. WESTERN WING.

§ 55. From the earth's ramparts in Central-Asia our glance followed those emigrants starting from the regions of the Dragon lake over the wastes of the Gobi and over the waters of the Pacific. We are now going to look up those Mongolians who went westward. We here also strike those fundamental layers upon which the edifice of history is being reared.

Toward the north and thence to the west the Ugro-Altaic, Ugro-Tataric, and Finnish tribes spread out. Previously we called them Western Mongolians of whom some as yet speak the Turanian, and which we now enumerate as East-Jakians, Wogulians, Hungarians (of Magyar descent) and Turks, coming from Central Asia. They were followed by the Shamanic nomades, the Jakians from Tobolsk and Toms. Supplementary to the notice taken of them we annex the mention of a few facts which, in their proper connection, may serve to verify our explanation. Into the masses of Ugrian tribes Permians and Wotjakians pushed themselves, and even some Samojedes pressed on to the west.

In Num, the supreme deity of the Samojedes, there is most probably a remnant retained of the primitive monotheistic tradition. According to B. v. Struve there sits near every hut of the Samojedes a bird idol with spread wings, a rough sample of wood carving, upon a high pole. The bird is imagined to take wings and communicate matters to the highest god.

Priklonsky in a lecture given in 1885 informs us that the Jakutes will seldom rest in the shade of a tree, but hurriedly try to get around, being afraid of the ghost that might dwell upon it. Their frame of consciousness precisely equals that of the Australian negro of today.

The Shamanist, raging before the fire in his narrow jurte filled with dense smoke, is imagined to be possessed of evil spirits. He is then "merjætsh" as they call it, in the same condition which the South Sea Islanders designate as "lata", or the learned white people as "hypnotized." Those nature-bound people do not understand what the white people pretend to know about this condition; whoever becomes merjætsh is thought to be bewitched, or under control of a strong spirit governing his grimaces and his speech.

Around the Caspian Sea, on the Tobol and Yenisei, at the foot of the Caucasian mountains, and in the Crimean peninsula, the Tatars made themselves at home. In their broad steppes Shamanism took its most advanced forms. There the spectres, the souls of the departed, dwell in the clefts of the rocks, or roam about the steppes and snow-fields; to prevent them from doing mischief is the all important question, a thing of indefatigable efforts and permanent anxiety. The conjurer called for appears in a leather cassock hung with bells, eagles' talons, fur rugs, and—dead snakes. Dancing in the moonlight or in the weird glare of

Toltecs ; pushed to the south. Peru. Emblems: Toads and snakes.

Inka empire,

Of original Monotheism sun-service, always the remainder. Mikado—son of Heaven.

"Son of the Sun." Peru's and China's emperor.

Plowing a furrow in honor of the Sun-God by Inka rulers, equal to the Chinese custom.

Indications that snake-worship and human sacrifices from fear of death must be traced to the same source. Humboldt.

Squire,

Origin of anthropophagism or cannibalism.

A skinned victim—Stone figure found 1887, indicates the rise of the custom of "scalping." Seler.

Western Mongolians.

Remnant of monotheistic tradition among Samojedes : Num, a bird upon a high pole. B. v. Struve.

Superstitious fear of death among Yacutes the same as with Australian negroes. Priklonsky.

Hypnotism among Shamanists; "merjætsh."

§ 40

Shamanism of Tatars.

Paraphernalia of conjurers—dead snakes—who fight off the souls of the departed.

torchlights to the beat of a drum until he falls into a mad stupor, his members become distorted, he foams out of his mouth; he hears the ghost and goes into a trance. Now his soul wanders, and frights off the souls of the dead, transformed into a beast, as the poor dupes believe.

More of the hordes from the Asiatic table lands push toward the west. Bulgarian people, Tshermissians and Mordwinians, wander round about the Caucasus, while the Esthonians, Livonians, Finns and Lapps move to the Baltic lowlands where they form the last drifts of the Mongolian left wing.

The Lapps, reindeer-nomades, were distinctively fetish worshipers. The hundreds of small idols, which Nordenskioeld gathered upon Waigatsh Island in 1882, were nothing else but fetishes. They were wooden sticks and splinters stuck close together into the ground around the spot where sacrifices used to be made. Near the upper end of the splinters at equal height,

crudely carved faces can be distinguished, eyes and mouths at least being marked. And the marks of the mouths were bedaubed with blood at the sacrificial meals.

The Finns in their Jumala and Taara also preserved the idea of the one God. Their other gods are, like those of the Ægyptians, merely the forms of his appearance. So, at least, we are told by those who have been there. Thus, all these people who originally started from the high plateaus of Central Asia and, following the waters, moved on to Cape North, to Iceland and Greenland, dropping a tribe occasionally, which went with other hordes to the south-west, as for instance the Baskes—appearing like storm dashed waves, enduring hardships, rather than to be left behind and alone.

Not a few, Carl Ritter among them, have associated the great inundation of the west by the swarms from Asia, ceasing at the time of the Hunnish invasion, with the building of the Chinese wall. This occurred when the far west was sufficiently organized to ward off the savages by the powers of mental superiority.

The turbulent elements throwing themselves upon Western Asia and Europe, caused those commotions, by which Europe was populated. Harrassing again and again the horrified nations between the Euphrates and the Rhine, they were instrumental in breaking down the Roman empire and in making the Germans that nation, which henceforth was destined to repel oriental onslaughts and to regulate the balance of power this side the Himalayas.

Through the passes of the black Yrtish, across the Tsungarian plains the Huns sallied forth, the same savages which were recorded as the "Hunjo" in Chinese annals as early as 2000 B. C. They came down like a tornado, vanquished the Alanes and the Goths and settled down between the Volga and the Danube. There Attila sat in his wooden castle; and whenever he took to the saddle, Europe trembled from the Ural to the Pyrenees. If not on

horseback he sat upon his wooden throne and drank from wooden cups, whilst out of doors day by day were waiting for an audience the ambassadors of Goths and Gepides, princes of Tatars from the regions of the Volga and the Dniepr, keorls of the Burgundians and from the downs of the Baltic, emissaries from Geiseric in Africa, from Theodosius' sons in Byzantium and from Ricimer in Rome. Ushered in finally to the presence of "the avenger of God" as he proudly calls himself, they drink to his good luck, out of golden chalices and dine off the silver plates of Attila. Under the glittering splendor of gold and jewels they listen to the singers from Moguntia (now Mayence) and are now amused by the puns of a Scythian buffoon

and then again by the torch-dance of Caucasian mountaineers. Motionless and austere in crude plain jacket and leather pants, sits Attila, eyeing his surroundings. He eats his raw meat, softened under the saddle, from a wooden saucer, selfcomplacent in the consciousness that thrones shake when he will mount the horse, because an empress refused his hand or a princess was denied him by her brother. Was he less civilised than a certain Napoleon ?

Much like the turmoil of the Huns that of the Seldjukkians sallies forth under Togrul Beg. They push on from the Oxus (Sihon) through Iran and Syria down to Ægypt. They set up and upset throne after throne, and are imitated by the Turks following close at their heels, mere bands of adventurers, all of Mongolian descent. Every child knows how their move-

ments, in western Asia brought the knights of Europe upon their feet once more.

And once more the Moguls rush their hosts down from the Central-Asiatic fountain-head of nations toward the south-west. Soon an empire is founded, reaching from Japan to Prussia and to the Persian gulf. The Dsengis Khan held sway over an area of quicksand which many a czar has coveted ever since. He bridled the wild and fluctuating masses; but he could not make them all adopt Mongolian culture. His nephew Batu whirled along with his

throngs other swarms over 90 degrees of longitude, until the Turks were flung way out to the Wahlstatt on the Katzbach. Such progress, working destruction only, could not induce the remnant of the vanquished to enure themselves to Mongolian culture, neither could fear paralyse them for a great length of time, altho nine sacks and the ears of the slain Germans. Two centuries later from China to Greece, from the Indus to the Volga

the earth again groaned under the hoofs of Mongolian millions, called "the golden hord." Timur, the grandson of the great Khan, made Samarkand his residence, from thence to conquer Bagdad and Damascus, whither he dragged learned men and libraries. Samarkand became for the dominion of the Moguls what Nara of old had been to Nipon.

Dsengis' policy to unite the world under the religion of "ONE GOD AND THE LAMA" seemed to become realised, for the Mongolians upon their travels and exploits must have become conscious of the fact, that the mind alone, and not millions of swords in the fists of savages, will ever be able to subdue the world.

At Samarkand—once built by Alexander, under a similar adaptation of court theology to politics—among phantastic monuments of mixed religions, Timur's tomb is shown, the resting place of the ninth descendant of an "immaculate conception." It lies in the mosque of Turbeti facing toward Mecca.   It was immaterial to the advanced Mongolians that the Lama had to recede in their esteem, in exchange for "ISLAM AND ALLAH"—if only the idea of being a son of "the" god prevailed. Vambery found the tomb covered with a green slab, cracked through the middle. More than one Mongolian empire burst   likewise; and many another kingdom for that matter. But few had obtained to such large proportions in so short periods and caused such wide-spread commotions.

§ 56.   Now we are ready for a retrospect upon that large circle of cultured nations stretching fan-like from the Asiatic crest-line of the globe eastward to Peru and the Delaware--westward to Cape North and the Vistula.

As the basis of the uncultural life of these nations we found a very ancient sunworship, carrying along with it the remnants of original Monotheism. Its rays reflect a broken light, broken in the colored prism of Heli-olatry; or it goes side by side with it, down even into lower forms. The remnants we found with the Finns, the Samojedes, and the Inkas as well as in China.

As the product and final outcome of religious degradation we here found, as we will find everywhere, impotency of personal life wherever its spiritual side tries to manifest itself, and the relapse into, if not below, common natural life. Wuttke justly observed, that "the sum and substance of Chinese consciousness, in consequence of its tradition, may be formulated into this judgment: "Only that type of life is perpetuated, which bears the stamp of natural generalness, whilst individuality and personality completely submerge and vanish."

Confu-tse proclaimed: "If I should say, that the dead were conscious of anything, pious sons would squander their property with funeral obsequies." We agree with M. Mueller in that the issue of Buddhism, despite all the ado made as to its reformatory effects, amounts to "entire extinction." Hence the feeling of guilt vanishes first from personal consciousness, and what faint knowledge of the bad is indelibly imprinted upon the mind is objectivised and fastened to something outside. The only principle warranting a hope of recovery succumbs into the terror of outside powers which are held to be the evil-doers. Scarcely a faultiness common to all is perceived much less acknowledged; the presence of sin and guilt and their consequences is only indicated by being changed into common dismay and sad resignation. Hence a person's suffering does not come under consideration of sympathy. Within the Mongolian form of consciousness or character there is no more sympathy than that a young brother shows to his little crying sister. The sufferings of earthly life in general are only here and there slightly spoken of in a theory. These intoxicant, misty pantheistical theorisings are extremely confounding to popular understanding; but we will always find them to suit despotism and to aggravate the condition of the lower classes brooding apathy and seeking solace in superstition. Hence, despite the ignoring of personal sin and guilt, we find no trace of real felicity in the whole Mongolian circle. But everywhere we find the mind as having surrendered to habitual dejection under the permanent fear of death, under the fright of ancestral ghosts as tho they were the foes of the living, to be either pacified or fought.

This is the secret of the permanent abomination of wild Shamanism; it turns one more element of tradition, the truth represented in sacrifices, into the dreadful rites of scalping and anthropophagy. In its further degradation Shamanism, with its arts of conjury and necromancy, turns to fetishism, where still another remnant of traditional truth is perverted to snake-worship. This latter most emphatically exhibits the fear of the evil spirit, and is, as we had occasion to observe, the earliest and basest form of corrupted God-consciousness, into which we found humanity to have fallen, and by which it was dragged into abject fear of the night and the anguish of

Dsengis Khan's diplomacy in regard to religion; acknowledgment of the advantages which Monotheism yields. One God and Lama.
(§145 Frederick II.)

Adaptation of courttheology to politics. Pantheism and oppression. (§ 15, 24, 49, 54—56, 58 etc.

Timur's tomb fronts toward Mecca.

Allah annexed to Lama. Vambery.

Retrospect upon the Mongolian world.

Sun-worship the most ancient.
(§ 54.)

Consequence of Paganism: Man's forgetting God's personality causes loss of his own personality, which relapses into the life of the genus.

In Chinese culture only that type of life perpetuates, which bears the stamp of natural generalness. Wuttke.
(§ 53.)

Reason for denial of consciousness in the state of immortality: fear of the dead, causes extravagance in obsequies. Confu-tse.

Issue of Buddhism, despite the ado made of its reformation, amounts to "entire extinction." M. Mueller.

The bad is objectivised; guilt fastened upon something external.
(§ 24, 59, 109.)

Common dismay, leaving no room for one's sympathy with others. (§ 15, 65, 68, 72.)

Pantheistical theorisings suit despotism and aggravate the condition of the lower classes. (§ 15, 20, 24, 54, 55, 56, 57.)

Despite the denial of sin and guilt no trace of enjoyment of life.

Mind surrendered to sullen resignation, to the fear of death and of ancestral ghosts, who are supposed to be the foes of the living and must be fought or appeased. §109.

Abomination of wild Shamanism turns one more element of true tradition—sacrifices—into the dreadful rites of scalping and anthropophagy.

Turns the tradition about the serpent, into snake-cult and fetishism.

from fear of the night and of the dead.

Vestiges of Monotheism create a historical sense, incite discussion, and aid in preserving culture through Sun-Worship, THE BETTER PAST OF PAGANISM.
(§ 41, 54, 55; § 44 Mythology.)

death—after the great calamity. It was only where the vestiges of Monotheism were, to some extent, preserved in traditions and in the sacred reminiscences of the mind, that a historical sense was created by which memory was revived and by which society was cultivated and organised. On the basis of tradition, however, these vestiges became distorted in myths and under rituals and symbols no longer understood. Owing to them it was, that reminiscences perpetuated the elements of pristine truths to be discussed by better situated people of leisure—that these disjoined remnants were even by the Turano-Mongolians combined and established as sun-service and similar rites of higher paganism.

Traces of truth in traditional religiousness; and their subversions.
(§ 24, 41, 47, 48, 53.)
Demonolatry, Bad objectivised,

On the score of traditional religiousness we thus far collected the traces of the following viz: one God above, in Heaven; man's personality notwithstanding the unity of humanity; his dominion over nature, and his immortality; his consciousness of guilt and of the necessity of expiation through sacrifices; his strong recollections about the arch-enemy. We saw them all, however, subverted into necromancy, cannibalism and fetishism on the one side, and into pantheism, despotism and nihilism on the other. In the worst forms of demonolatry we observe the "bad" conscience objectivised in snakes, dragons, demons; in fearful foes haunting "bad lands" as nights, which the terrified pagans are only too anxious to conciliate.

Speculative heathenism brings forth PANTHEISM, THE SYSTEMATISED COMPROMISE WITH POLYTHEISM.

The object of applied Pantheism.

Speculative paganism finally takes shape in pantheism, which is but the systematised compromise with polytheism, by means of which the knowing ones take the advantage of the lower class; for we will find again and again that religion is thus corrupted, or rather such scheming eclecticism aims at nothing with more insidiousness than to keep the raw, great bulk of uncultured people in political subjection and in ignorance, and in the mistrust and fear anent to it.

Hierarchy in Hlassa.

(§ 54, 149.)
PRSCHEWALSKY.
Parallel with Bagdad 145
Parallel with Rome 144
173.

Parallel with the theocratic despotism of China
(§ 54·

In the Mongolian quarters of the city of Urga, where the "chair of the Kutucha" is disposed of by the rulers in Hlassa, Prschewalsky found most of the people to belong to the priestly caste, to the rank of Lama. He ascertained, that one-third, at least, of all the inhabitants of Mongolia belong to that class. The Higenes in the temples of that country are self-conceited enough to esteem themselves as corporeal gods, whilst of still higher rank in the hierarchical scale they deem their spiritual brother in Bogdokuren before whom they all prostrate themselves on the ground. This hierarchy of Higenes and Lamas drains the sap of the country and the marrow, as it were, out of the oppressed subjects. They are the parasites who live high at the expense of the rest of the people, and use all the prerogatives of birthright to hinder the poor mass of their nation from obtaining any knowledge and from escaping the benighted and paralysing superstitions in which they spend their lives and are thus purposely kept. We remember what, in the same method, the paternal system of imperial theology has done for the despot in Peking and for his stupefied people.

Arts of the Mongolian world: give expression to mental and æsthetical culture, and political mechanism; all rooting in religion.
(§ 43, 54.)

With reference to arts, as far as they always most explicitly and inadvertently reveal the moods of an age and a nation, there hovers over the whole Mongolian world the solitary tendency to keep the whole beehive in mechanical activity. With regard to mental culture—which on the whole, is neither more nor less tinctured with religion than any other concern of life, inasmuch as every phase of it must be officiously religious—everything and everybody is kept on a conservative level, which the government well understands how to regulate by its political mechanism.

Mental progress stifled by governmental, i. e. official—religious prescriptions.
§ 43, 64.

With regard to æsthetics one taste only is allowed to be fashionable, but one absolutely weird, odious, and horrible style is fostered. Any digression from the customary forms of representative art would betray a disloyal tendency which would throw the state machinery out of gear and is, therefore, ostracised by the common and silent consent of public opinion, if not by legal action.

Mongol. world-consciousness in æsthetics, exciting abhorrence. Merciless subjects.

All the idols of the Incas, Aztecs, and Japanese, down to those of the Esquimaux and Laplanders excite the same abhorrence, conveying the impression not only of what can ever be imagined in the line of the brutish and the repulsive, but of that which is frightful and satanic in the line of monstrosities.

Absolute despotism wields the machinery of the state
(§ 11, 15, 49, 54, 55, 58, 68, 72.
Perverted patriarchism.
§ 53. 70, 172.

All social and political matters of the Mongolians must thus remain under the sway of the individual willfulness and unquestionable authority of an absolute despot. A perverted patriarchal government rules over masses void of any will of their own, merely drilled into a most abject servility and endurance by pressure. Merciless castes by right of birth domineer over, and abuse stupid inferiors who bear no sympathy toward each other, and who do not see any wrong with all their suffering. What originally was patriarchal control became a governmental mechanism of tutelage far from paternal care, over intimidated masses of intellectual minors.

Drill in abject servility, endurance of pressure, and loss of all feeling of sympathy with others.
§ 55, 58, 68, 72.

Such rule is always observable in states of East-Mongolian origin, in the empires of the Chinese and the Aztecs, for instance; but also among the West-Mongolian hordes which once covered, or still populate, or at least temporarily inundated, the largest part of Europe. And on another occasion we shall find the judgment corroborated, that the patriarchal conditions, once lauded by Rousseau and Herder, that a paternal rule with a system of patronage as recently advocated by Guizot may conduct the training of good-mannered children and political dependents, but will always turn into despotism— of which the modern "bossism" in politics is not always just a mild form, under whose party whip, even in republics, the spirit of freedom is as much in jeopardy as it is killed by the Russian "knute."

Dangers of patriarchal government, as one of "patronage" and tutelage, once extolled by Herder Rousseau, and Guizot. (§ 53, 70 Romans, 172 Popery.)

Despotism then, in its Asiatic as well as occidental forms, ever shows its fundamental peculiarities in two always recurring characteristics. A state built upon filial devotedness and loyal obedience will abuse that good-naturedness and apply the iron rod in order to retain its senile children in a state of pliability, external subordination and good behavior. But such a condition of public affairs and such voidness of private character is possible only, when a pantheistic world-theory holds sway over the mind, a view of life which prefers natural generalness to any assertion of personality and to the ideas of human dignity and liberty. Hence it ·is that despotism will always favor pantheism. The consequence of such all-the-sameness is that indifference and tolerance prevailing in China, which on that account is extolled by modern agnostics.

State Theocracy.

Pantheism and despotism.

Lessons drawn from Chinese culture.

It is there as in every other case, wherever religion is deemed identical with, and in fact secularised as, the official state-religion for the purpose of holding the empire together; wherever a **system of intellectualism** far above the mental horizon of the "unprivileged" classes is operated to the end of keeping them in superstitious fear, ignorance and subjection, that both, religion and **intellectual prominence will be identified and hated as means of oppression. Such state-churchism may make it easy for the ruler and his courtiers to keep the subjects from disturbing the rounds of high life, and it may spare the** subjects the annoyances connected with fighting the bad, so that the lower, unthinking classes may become reconciled to their condition on that account, and subject to the cold, heartless rationalism regulating their social relations. **The poor will, nevertheless, feel the oppression and surmise that the "educated" operate religion so methodically, just in order to deprive them of every chance of becoming educated,** to withhold from them the means of elevating and emancipating themselves.

Religion rendered into mere intellectualism, indifferent deity created, as means for political ends;

§ 54.

becomes odious to the lower classes as means of their oppression. § 15, 24, 34, 43, 58, 66, 72.

The fruits of a culture as that of China become apparent wherever the religion is allowed to become a tool of such as thirst for power over the minds of the masses. They consist in a simulated submissiveness and calculating politeness, and a sullen servility. No sympathy all around, no cordiality, but knavish trickery and petty intrigues everywhere. Thus the poor, oppressed and stultified, nevertheless, imitate the rich in holding religious and intellectual repose for the same thing; and because this is fashionable, the poor learn from the example of those "successful in life", to treat religion with equal indifference, with that unconcern, which the pantheistical all-the-sameness deserves. This stoic callousness is made a great national virtue, is held up even by some Europeans as the pattern of tolerance. It suits everybody, since under it everybody may pretend to have religion, whilst in fact nobody needs to have any as a mark of good standing. Nobody bothers himself about religion or intellectualism, for everybody dislikes to be molested by the obligation to resist the bad. Rather endure the loss of liberty, but let us have peace, peace by all means—for **it is very dangerous to provoke the bad.**

Fruits of a lacquer-culture, dissimulation.

Heartlessness.

Aping intellectualism,

Religious callousness.

Loss of manliness; afraid to provoke the Bad.

Thus cowardice and absence of manliness is considered wise and virtuous. To act upon principle is foolish where one may accomodate himself to the diplomacy of expediency.

Policy of expediency instead of action upon principles.

China is worldly wise indeed: No talk about sin, no mention of depravity—but plenty of tolerance, and allowances, and endurance, and an abundance of modes and ways to adjust oneself to circumstances with studied circumstantiality and evasiveness.

No talk about sin and repentence.

If such a dry rot befalls a nation, which under the rounds of everyday conventionalities is still pursuaded to believe itself a free nation, notwithstanding the sufferings of the largest part, then that part will not for ever remain in sullen endurance; not even among the Mongolians. The oppressed part will, as the first thing, throw religion aside, because it is held to be identical with mere smartness in the use of God as a means of oppression, which such a religion really is. The lower class will hate the prominent, the people of the higher class, because of their refinement, education, and mental superiority—and it will hate religion in the bargain. For, after the fashion of the "prominent" who made intellectualism and rationalism identical with religion, all have forgotten to discriminate the ingredients of that ."porridge"

Dangers of identifying intellectualism with religion. § 8, 10, 11, 15, 40, 57, 66, 72, 79.

Lower classes will hate religion along with all that causes mental superiority. § 15, 24, 44, 49, 54, 55, 57, 66, 72, 79.

of Confu-tse, or have lost the standard for valuing the ring of "Nathan the Wise." Thus pantheistical despotism, treating a large part of a nation as mere natural force, so as to render sympathy an unnecessary luxury, must expect this natural force to explode at some time without mercy. It did so repeatedly in China, where anarchy and despotism change off at regular intervals.

The fundamental and fatal error in Mongolian or any other pantheism is that it does not own up to the bad. Prerequisite to a true view of, and honest walk in, life is the decisive breaking with affected childish naivete, and with a boyish view of the world and of self. This is brought about in no other way but by confession of sin, which not as yet has been accomplished in the sphere of pantheism. To be sure, sacrifices are made there as everywhere; but they generally originate in fear; in rare cases they are made from sympathy, and never from the motive really required.

The deep ethnico-religious substratum of arrested culture and confined life with its clannishness, narrow-mindedness and selfconceit, notwithstanding its age, its wealth, and its sway—lies now open before us. It is precisely analogous to the low stratum of compressed life in geology. Above and beyond it there developed a layer of more concentric and more personal, altho less consolidated national life from which a less expansive but clearly definable history grew up, which shall be examined in the second circle of nations.

In the old nations of eastern and northern Asia that substratum is lying bare upon the surface to this day. Without any culture to speak of, almost in its prehistoric condition, it covers a wide expanse upon the surface of the globe. Only now and then did terrible forces from this substratum break through the second layer of historical nations affecting humanity like a discharge of an electric current. They broke forth like the basalts belched forth from subterranean caldrons, devastated cultivated regions, and left no traces but of destruction.

B. SECOND DIVISION.

THE SECOND CIRCLE OF NATIONS: ARYANS (INDO GERMANS.)

SYLLABUS.

We approach to historic times and a rich display of polarities. The fan-shaped territory over which Mongolian life had ramified, is still present in our minds: handle in Malayan Oceania; east-wing embracing Peru, Mexico, Alaska, Japan, Tibet; west-wing the steppes from the Altai to the Baltic. The foundation being outlined ethnologically we are now privileged to look at the superstructure of a new and closed circle of nations reared upon the natural basis of the first. Returning home to our own, the Aryan family, relieves us of contemplating the melancholy scenes of Mongolian life.

Standing again, with Schlagintweit, upon the heights of their old home, our eyes follow the movements of our blue-eyed and blond ancestors, through the western gate of the Pamir, down the venturous inclines. For we have become ever more convinced of our supposition being a fact, that the native home of the Indo-Germans is the Pamir region.

Altho Pamir is a Turco-Tataric term signifying a wilderness, we take the name in its wider meaning, as that plateau about as high above sea level as Mt. Shasta, and about as large as the states of New York, Pennsylvania and Ohio put together, with New Jersey and Delaware thrown in. We take the name as ascribed to that territory which forms the head-water district of the rivers of Tatary (the two Turkestans). The only eastern river spoken of by the classic ancients (who well knew the western—the Oxus and Yaxartes) is the Oecharies or Imaum extra. All that was known was that this river flowed through the Cassia region, from whence Kephrit and other fine things were gotten, and where the "silk road" used to be frequented in the times of Tacitus. Our maps include the "great Karakul" or Dragon-Lake in the north, and the small Karakul in the south with this Pamir region, of which Biddulph said: "A cloud of mystery has, from time immemorial hung over this region which, vaguely enough, we call Central Asia". This highest of all highlands was, after Marco Polo's visit and Ritter's description, visited and partly described by a dozen of explorers as the center from which radiate the greatest rivers and hugest mountains.

Of late a certain school has tried to antiquate our axiom that this locality once inclosed the fountain-head of all the streams of migration; but the latest investigations on the spot abundantly vindicate it. As late as fifteen years ago Latham, Bonfrey, and Otto Schrader disputed the immigration of the Aryans from Asia. Justi and Penka attempted to prove that Scandinavia was their native home. The latter's only trouble was that he could give no reason for his hypothesis of the change in the color of the skin by the ozone in the atmosphere. John Schmidt lectured 1890 in Berlin on the problem from the aspect of comparative philology. He "joined with the generally adopted opinion altho it lacked sufficient scientific proof." In 1891 Fick wrote to Rocholl that he had been successful in his researches, to some extent, west of Scandinavia and in the regions of the southern Ural in order to "ascertain the earliest seats of the Germans.""New proofs have since been discovered which point to the upper regions of the Oxus and Yaxartes, the modern Ami-darja and Syr-darja. He admits that"under this supposition the problem of the distribution of the races receives the approximately most correct solution, since there, up to the present time, the yellow and the white races live as nearest neighbors; and since many of the Western Asiatics bear a negro type strongly reminding us of Herodot's Æthiopians of the east."

Tomashek holds the Galtsha, the ancient inhabitants of the Pamir, to be Iranians beyond a doubt. They are the most degraded of all the peoples with blond hair. The Galtsha about the Zerafshan glacier are taken for Persian relatives of comparatively lowest culture by Mushketoff. And Prschewalsky takes the aborigines around the Lob-nor river for Aryans. He was, after Marco Polo, the first European who visited and described them.

The latest proofs however, for the Central-Asiatic descendency of the Indo-Germans have been furnished by the Yenisei inscriptions. As early as 1835 Abel Remusat gave a report of their discovery, and found the characters--so Tychsen remarks--much like those which the "old inhabitants of Prussia" used as their marks. Donner as late as four years ago presented the Congress of Orientalists with 33 inscriptions, all from the upper Yenisei regions, explored by him and Krohn, which he declared to be of pre-Mongolian origin. The "Zeitschrift fuer Ethnologie", Berlin 1889, is of the opinion that these inscriptions were made by people with Turkish language, but that they were to be considered as of Indo-German stock. Above all, however, Iwanowsky found similar inscriptions near the lake Issik-Kul, south of the Altai, so that Richthofen avers it to be a plain fact, that in Central-Asia the Iranians and Turanians lived in close proximity. The question, whether the high and dry steppes could possibly be the fatherland of those people, he solves by proving the decline of water in the Arabic-Caspian lowlands. Jadrinzew demonstrates that there since 1786 no less than 300 lakes have dried up.

Wheresoever the origin of the Aryans may be located, it suffices that they are here, and are recognised on all sides as a very distinguished and select branch of the human family. We once more muster the several members.

From the Ganges to the Boyne we find descendants of a people who once spoke the same language—Sanskrit, demanding our consideration first as the language of the Veda. Then there are the Iranians, speaking the Zend in which Zoroasterians wrote the Avesta, and in which the old Elamite cuneiform inscriptions of Turanian origin again speak to us. Next in importance are the Scythians, the Slavs, Baltic and Levantic tribes ; Albanese, Phrygians, Armenians ; then the Graeco-Italians ;Humbrians, Sabines, Latins ; the Celts ; Ibernians, Gauls, Britons, Culdeans ; and finally the Germans with their many sub-divisions, including the Goths, Vandals, Anglo-Saxons, and Normans—the ancestors of Spain's Hidalgo nobility.

Fick's new Indo-German dictionary enumerates twelve main stems of lingual relationship. This is sufficient for our purpose.

As we found the Mongolo-Malayan groups of the Turanian family in two distinct camps, so, looking down from the old Paramabiso, we find the Aryans divided into southern and northern parties. Without any artificial construction the nature of our second circle is given by the separation between the Iranians and Hindoos. For, in accordance with the age and importance of their culture, we have to deal with them first, following up and closing the ranks with the Greeks and Romans, (in the next division). The first pair form now the right, the latter the left wing, The basis of operation for the interior parties of the two pairs is Bactra-Marathon; for the extreme pairs Benares-Rome.

CH. I. ORIENTAL ARYANS: RIGHT WING; I. SOUTHERN PART—HINDOO.

§ 57. Much speaks in favor of the supposition that the stream of the Aryan migration, soon after the departure from Central Asia, split in two branches on striking the western walls of the plateau of Iran. After some stay, which is definitely indicated and may have lasted for centuries, perhaps, religious animosities caused one branch to pull stake at once, and to take the course of the Indus valley to the south, whilst the other branch gradually flowed off westward to the Caucasus and to Europe.

Controversies about the descent of the Aryans. LATHAM, BONFREY, SCHRADER. Justi, Penka.

JOH. SCHMIDT.

FICK.

REMUSAT. Yenisei-inscriptions. §53

TYCHSEN; DONNER; KROHN; 32 other inscriptions south of the Alai, Pre-Mongolian. IWANOWSKY, RICHTHOFEN, JADRINZEW, meet the objection as to climate condition of the Pamir.

Members of the Aryan family: HINDOO-ELAMITE (PERSIAN-GREEKS) AXIS BACTRA-MARATHON and GRAECO-ROMAN upon the axis Benares-Rome.

FICK's Indo-German dictionary: 12 main stems of lingual relationship.

Aryans separate;
Hindoos from Iranians.
↑ 9.

Rig-veda

Worship
in free air.

With a high degree of certainty it may be computed that it was about Abraham's time (ca. 2200 B. C.) when the East-Aryans separated from their kindred who partly remained in Iran and partly followed the others, by way of Kabul, down to the Punjab. In their youthful vigor, ingenuousand impulsive, inspired by their new and pleasant surroundings, they sang those hymns under the free canopy of heaven which were centuries later collected in the Rig-Veda. Shortly after the time of Moses (ca. 1500 B.C.) swarms of them pushed on and fought their way toward the Ganges, accomplishing such exploits, as in their national epic were composed into the myths of hero-worship. They found the south occupied by settlers who had already exchanged merchandise with Egypt in queen Hatasu's time, the Dravida, who were driven aside or made to serve. In a comparatively short period the large peninsula was in their possession, and by them cultivated with their "ar" or plough,—for these "Ar"-yans were agriculturists par excellence, as the root of their name implies. As such they depended upon the kind heavens, and became a pensive and peaceful people. The thrifty, sultry climate of the tropics, however, on the one hand, and the want of communication with other nations on the other, caused the Hindoos to sink into that dreamy lethargy, which paralyzed their energy, and made the simple-hearted and goodnatured peasants submit to the craftiness of the priests with their thirst for power.

Pre-occupants of India.
Hero-worship:
mythology.

Ar, the plough: Aryans.

Process of degradation.

Kapila philosophises.

Brahmins forbid the
warriors to approach the
Gods directly, without
priestly intercession.

Liturgical form of wor-
ship.

The decadence began at the time when the priests argued that warriors did not dare to approach the gods; when Kapila philosophised upon the superfluousness of priestly intercession and liturgies; when the Brahmins forbade the reading of the Rig-veda; and when the stupefied nation permitted their sense of liberty to be stifled and their idea of personality to be filched. Given to idealistic yearnings and meditation in the embrace of blissful surroundings, they came, besides being under the rule of the priestly caste, also under the seducing influences of a rich nature and into the dangers of wealth. Through neglect of normal exercise, so essential in the recuperation of strength, the body becomes languid and the mind lulled into a state of phantastic phlegm, a form of soul-life which we chose to call nature-bound. The soul is cradled into placid sleep, rocked as in a boat that leisurely drifts upon the waves of natural things—among the lotus in stagnant waters. The soft breeze swaying the boat of life lulls the mind into ease and passiveness, into that faint-heartedness, which is ever afraid of coming to grief or into trouble. In that semi-consciousness of a doze, the mode of thought becomes habitually natural instead of personal. As upon an external touch or sound a series of kaleidoscopic images is called forth in the drowsy soul as it continues for a while in involuntary oscillations—so it happened, that nature spontaneously worked itself into possession of the spirit of the Hindoo nation. Its thought and poetry is the effect of the phantastic play of an imagery enchanted by nature. Such are always the effects of a pantheistic view of the world—absorption of the personality by generalness, a nebulous dissolving of both, spiritual oneness and physical manifold, into each other. Thus the strength of any nation will necessarily fail and finally vanish. Such rock- and stone-temples as of old, the Hindoos no longer were able to build; such feats of valour, as are praised in the war stories of the Mahabharadha could be no longer accomplished by people so effeminate. This decline is not caused by the contrast of classes and castes, but by the loss of personality and freedom. Castes are but the result of abandoning the idea of personality in exchange for a mystical, hazy transcendentalism. "The idea of liberty", says Oldenberg in concluding his observations, "with its either reviving or destroying tendencies has never been recognised in India. If one even had thought and told of it, the stupefied mass could not have been made to understand it." The peculiarities of the Hindoo-character and the causes leading to it, can be portrayed no better than has been done by Hegel and M. Mueller. With Hegel the preference for their mode of thought took even the shape of personal partiality on account of the similitude of Hindoo philosophy with his own. With M. Mueller it was an act of humaneness to tell the British "what India can teach us", namely, that their new subjects are not only human, but very amiable beings.

Hindoo form of consci-
ousness and its effects.

Personality absorbed by
generalness of natural
life.

No longer the Heroism of
the times of the Mahab-
haradha.

On Hindoo character:
Oldenberg,
Hegel,
M. Mueller.

Sanskrit literature re-
veals 15 centuries of life
born under pains of re-
ligious misunderstand-
ings.
§ 59.

Sanskrit literature reveals a history of fifteen centuries of Aryan national life To all appearances this national life was born under the pains of religious misunderstandings, and the three turns which it took in its unbroken course, are also to be ascribed to religious differentiations. During the first period, beginning about 1830 B. C. the religion of the Vedas is degenerating from traditional teaching to symbolism and ritualism. As yet the deities or deva are called eternal. They see the Good and the Bad.

Four periods of Hindoo
national life·

They are the creators, the greatest of the gods; Varuna, Indra, Mitra, among others are conceived as under suzerainty of the Being One, the king of heaven. This coordination without a trace of priority or descendancy has led to the opinion, that the trimurti was but the name for the identity of the gods, that is, for the monotheistic recollections which stood back of it. In a passage quoted from one of the oldest hymns of the first rig this cognition seems to be expressed with sufficient clearness, when it is said that "they call Him Indra, Mitra,

Varuna, Agni". On the strength of such plain indications we are justified in taking the pristine monotheism of the Hindoos as a historical fact. They only gave different names to the same personal spirit according to different localities or to variable manifestations of his power—in a manner much like that which Brugsch explained as the esoteric theology of the Ægyptians.

1. Period:
Rig-veda,
  Varuna, Heaven;
  Devas eternal.
  Monotheistic.
Original monotheism of the Hindoos a historical fact.

Of more importance than the monotheistic background in Hindooism is to us at present, the undeniable fact that at this period an earnest acknowledgment of sin is manifest, of which we remarked, that it is silently passed over by every pantheistic theory. In the prayers to Varuna (Uranus) we hear supplications like these: "Judge us as being acquitted from the sins of our fathers and of those committed by ourselves with our own bodies". To be sure, the petitioner makes an addition in which we detect an expression of something more true than a mere self-absolution or a shifting of responsibity, even more than an acknowledgment of the necessity of expiation. We find somewhat of the remembrance that the human being consists of more than a physical organism, when they add: "It was not our own doing, it happened involuntarily. It was a venomous draught, it was a passion, it was fate."

Earnest acknowledgment of sin and of the necessity of expiation.
  § 83, 91.
Recollections of man's dual nature—not only a physical part.
Rigs quoted.

Then the second period is entered as demarcated in M. Mueller's description of it: the Indra-period, beginning at about 1400 B. C. Varuna is now less esteemed than Indra. Composition of hymns slackens; personal deity subsides; free prayer is no longer made; Brahmins assume the office of mediators between the deity and the sinner; religion and sacred writings become formulated and are prescribed; worship turns into ritualism with its symbolic performances; and the doctrines become esoteric.

2. Period:
Indra:
Free prayer comes out of use.
Priestly intercession.
Deity rendered polytheistic.
Doctrines esoteric.
Distortion of original religiousness.
  § 105, 109, 115.

The gods, the "shining ones" are conceived as apart from each other. They are also severed from the world, notwithstanding their being considered as essential personifications of natural elements and forces. The divine attributes are dragged into that form of consciousness which is diverted by the manifold in nature. From below ancestor-worship strikes through; the religion of the Veda becomes infected with the polluted traditions of darkness and superstitious dread.

Phases of natural life personified.
Ancestor-worship rises from the substratum.

The mixture of both suits the Brahmins because it facilitates the establishment of hierarchical supremacy. The lower and weaker people are to be kept in ignorance; and in order to curb their aspirations toward humane forms of existence, and to check the promulgation of such views of life as the theistic Yoka and the ethico-mystical Baghavad-Gita teach, THEY ARE FORBIDDEN TO READ THE SCRIPTURES. Priests separate themselves from warriors, castes are in their incipiency; society begins to desintegrate in keeping with the doctrines, which desintegrate the nature of the deity and separate the gods. Under the oppression thus ensuing the spiritual wants are felt the more keenly, and an anti-hierarchal tendency manifests itself in mysticism, which teaches direct communication with the gods without the interference of the intermeddling priests. The religious sense is quickened and becomes intensified; the mind strives for liberation. Everybody learns to read, whereby the people break away from priestly rule. In the meanwhile the theologians, in order to head off the danger of disestablishment of the religious organisation, by what they scurrilously call the "mystical innovation," accommodate their doctrine to it nevertheless, and conclude a truce by making a compromise with philosophy. They invent a method of communion with their abstract godhead in which the deity needs to be naturalised and nature deified.

Yoka reform:
Mystico-theistical.
Bhagavad-Gita;
Ethical.
Reading the scriptures prohibited.
Theologians, unable to stifle ethical thinking,
construct theoretical pantheism
compromise with philosophy.

With M. Mueller as a guide we proceed into this third period of Brahmanism as ushered in by the caste of divines at the time when Solomon built the temple. about 1000 B. C. Brahama is the name for the materialised world-soul Atma, or Purusha, or Choda; and his religion is taken care of by his life guard, so to say. The concept of the Brahma is so ingeniously framed as to yield all possible explanations of the one as well as the manifold, of the union between life and matter, of the fusion of the good and the bad. All is called good that conforms with the code of rituals, that the Brahmin sanctions, that furthers his interest. Nothing is considered as a crime but the neglect of, or a mistake in, the rituals. And these ceremonials are for the lower classes who cannot and dare not participate in philosophising with the "shining ones". In Brahma God is no longer conceived as supermundane. It is only expected that by the service of Brahma, instituted with this intent, the multiform worship of the manifold in natural objects may be held in check. And thus, instead of men serving God, He, under appellations other than Brahma even, is made a tool to serve this or that end. And in the meantime the degradation of religion into crude polytheism goes on rapidly among the lower classes, whilst the growth of barbarism is connived at by the higher.

3. Period:
Brahma—
the materialised world-soul Atma or Choda.
Brahma invented to check coarse polytheism.
Deity made a means to serve the ends of the priest-caste;
  § 82.

The Brahmin Identity-Philosophy sets up Brahma as the thought; that is, thought in its reaction against polytheistical absurdities, in order —not to relieve the harrassed soul, but—to justify intellectualism in its compromise with these absurdities. It is the attempt of thought to unite the totality of the natural element into a somewhat consistent concept; to personify philosophical abstractions; to explain the immanency of nature in God. Any idea going beyond and above this apperception of an immanent infinity, anything incompatible with the elaborately wrought figure of a world-god, is Choda at one pole and Nirwana on the other. This all-surpassing mode of being is obtainable for such a mind only which abandons itself to an all-absorptive brooding; to any other it remains completely hidden and unknowable. Annihilation is thus made the highest stage and aim of agnosticism, which may be defined as the compromise between knowing nothing and that indifference to which no designation seems to be more appropriate than our term: all-the-sameness.

To the Brahmin the personality of the deity or the reality of his abstraction becomes irrelevant, and the idea of human personality is blurred if not altogether lost along with that of God. The priest wants the people to become indifferent to all else beside him and to waive the exercise of their own wills to the authority of his drill, under which they are enured to be led like a flock of sheep. The people must be turned into noughts, so that the priest, the figure put before them, may count the more. Hence he does not want the people to obtain any certitude as to their inner life, for this would arouse scepticism as to his authority. Yet scepticism and opposition could not be evaded despite the compromise. Philosophical reflection was imitated in the measure as the intensity of absorptive meditation and forced thoughtlessness lost the charms of a reverie in self-forgetfulness. An ethical tendency, once awakened by the Yoka and Sankhja philosophy, works its way within a few minds; for a stray conscience here and there craves consolation. Some take recourse to the Vedic form of God-consciousness and keep alive the piety of the Baghavad-Gita, while others, for the sake of sheer opposition, construct materialistic systems upon identity premises. The result is sectarian distraction; subjectivism unsettles the social habitude throughout the whole nation.

The state of affairs characterising the **fourth or Sutra-period**, is plainly reducible to religious **subjectivism**, sectarian separatism, and unscrupulous opposition to priestly arrogancy. The reading of holy writs having been forbidden, and the priests having supplanted the monotheistic realism of the Veda by the merely intellectual and sophisticated dogmatics of the Samaveda: mysticism, to the increasing bewilderment of the ignorant masses, had undermined hierarchal formalism, dogmatism, and legalism. In their indifference as to intellectualism and deistical and pantheistical terminologies, the Hindoos now try, on the one hand, to find solace for the religious sentiencies in either moralism, or anomism, or in asceticism; whilst symbolism, on the other hand; i. e. the misdirected traditions with reference to the mind's forebodings of immortality—make people embrace the old ancestor-worship which forces itself through from below into hearts void of any religious truth. Thus, in spite, if not in consequence of, pantheism the submergence into vulgar polytheism becomes complete.

The Sutra period presents at least six theories of philosophic eclecticism, from which to choose the material for a selfmade religion; any person was left at liberty if he had a mind to construct one for himself. Countless sects availed themselves of the opportunity to make selections. The old Yoga system of the theistic-mystic-ethical Bhagvad Gita alone could gain no popularity, altho it revived in prince Gautama-Buddha. This dissoluteness of all religious life began about 600 B. C. It is one of the most remarkable coincidents, that Gautama's, the Sankhjamuni's great "reform" brought the Brahministic dough to the Buddhistic fermentation at the very period, when the religion of Israel was by force carried deeper into Asia and seemed to be doomed to succumb in the captivity.

While speculative Buddhism could not succeed for two centuries in having its doctrines canonised and whilst it was persecuted until king Asoka made it his state religion and built the 8,000 topes or pagodas; speculative gnosticism attempted to explain material and spiritual life by the empiric method of renouncing natural conditions of life. Gautama's Nyaja-system wanted to discern laws of reason upon which to found his moralism—just like Kautianism of late—whilst Kanada engaged himself with atomism. The Vendanta system wanted to demonstrate a monism in the supposed oneness of the world's soul Brahma-Atma with the human soul. Choda alone with its realized end of Nirwana really exists, everything else is but phenomenon, phantom, delusion—is Maja. The Sankhya-system in opposition to the Vedanta, defended a dualistic view of life, or rather of nature. The infinite and eternal oneness of nature is imagined to comprise a manifold of souls under the categories of the Prakriti. The soul migrates through a series of metamorphoses until it becomes conscious of being a part of nature no longer, when, of course, the necessity of the metempsychosis ceases.

In the confusion ensuing morality was, like religion, transformed into a mere external conformity to maxims, prescribed by the medley of teachings. This legalism seems to have been well adapted to the lower classes who had taken refuge in tangible idolatry. With a few ritualistic performances they were enabled to acquit themselves of the duties demanded by their superiors, who did not care to disturb the subjects in their idolatry, lest the schools would lose their popularity and adherents. At this stage of sectarianism in competition it becomes impossible for any sect to carry out discipline. *The world's soul; Atma. Phenomena of real life only delusions—Maja. Disgust of life:*

Thus the nation was seized with disgust in matters of doctrine and with despair of ever learning the truth. The external world, first taken as the source of happiness, was now looked upon with apathy as the cause of all misery. Dull brooding ended in a philosophy of world-soreness and hopelessness. Annihilation was made desirable, for it saved men from the dreaded transmigration of the soul, from the Brahminic metempsychosis. *Nirwana as a salvation from the metempsychosis of the priests.*

When Alexander the Great came in contact with India the Brahmins had just accommodated themselves to the scholasticism of the Purannas to check the religious dissolution. But India was benumbed already by being indoctrinated with sense-delusion, and dreamt under its heavy incubus of Maja. Of personality nothing was left but a shadowy apparition. Ascetic selfrenunciation was the highest virtue. Neither snakes nor tigers were killed any longer, and no meat eaten; the Hindoos henceforth only vegetated as a nation of vegetarians. Hope and the future were waning away into Nirwana and Nihilism. Thought had been outraged and liberty smothered—now conscience, too, receded and went to sleep. *Purannas-eclecticism. § 77. Resume of the concomitant causes of Hindoo frame of mind.*

Evidently this period was not one of revival of letters or of awakening of thought, as Hegel tried to make us believe. It was not the first stage of the development of the "idea" into God-consciousness, but the arrival of a once God-praising and wide-awake nation of warriors, thinkers and farmers at the stage of spiritual death and dire abandonment to natural necessity. The philosophical evolution from Brahma to Nirwana in all its conflicting statements and stages again proves, that religion and culture decline together wherever the friends of idealistic speculation, and then those of materialistic reasoning under the name of science, busy themselves with religion. The results show that whenever anything concerning the mind is identified with religion, at first by the educated and then by the masses of the lower classes, then the latter begin to hold religious and spiritual, mental and moral life for the same thing, until finally they take as religious all which they do not understand, and all that is above them. *Hindooism not the stage of the awakening God-idea as Hegel thought; but the dying away of God-consciousness. An evolution detrimental to religion and cultural progress, from Brahma to Nihilism. Mental (spiritual) activity of the mind mistaken for spirituality and religion; oppressed masses averse to both. §§ 11, 15, 16, 22, 47, 54, 55, 56, 66, 68, 72, 95, 97, 98, 179, 185.*

The Vedanta, the encyclopedia of Indian knowledge in a bulk, prides'itself on having detected that the deity is the substance rather than the source of the world; that the deity is even the matter out of which the universe emanated, while the mind, in turn, is conceived as evolving out of this hardened effusion. But how could a world of consciousness proceed out of an unconscious god or vice versa? Nothing simpler than that, Hindoo induction rejoins, forecasting Hegel's idealism and Hall's substantialism. Hairs and nails of the animal body are void of sensibility, tho they grow from sentient being. Is this not analogous enough to prove plainly that God is the substance from which nature emanates and that matter is the substance from which the mind evolves? Hence, remarks Baumann with all the gravity of Hindoo reason, "hence it is that multiplicity and corporeality are but delusions. In truth there exists one being only, the most supreme all-world's soul, an indistinguishable and indifferentiated entity". Eureka! The great monistic philosophy is established, rendering any further trouble of research superfluous. It is more desirable not to be at all, or not to know the real world, than to bother with dualism or even science, for that matter. Science may go to sleep as it did in India long, long ago. Give us poetry, cries a satiated age, give us the world of novels to dream away the silent worry over higher obligations. *Vedanta-materialistic monism. God the substance from which the universe emanates; matter the substance from which mind evolves. Hegel's idealism and Hall's substantialism nothing new. BAUMANN. Felicity of agnosticism; imaginary world. § 58, 146.*

Buddhism sustained a complete overhauling, and when Buddha's (in China Fohi) teeth and toes were made relics and worshiped, all the philosophical starch of ideality was taken out of it. Idealism could scarcely be ascribed to the offerings of a rich devotee who, in the 15th century, brought 6,480,320 flowers before the shrine of the tooth in Ceylon, a piece of ivory as long as the little finger.

This pantheistical trend in the minds of all Indo-Germanic people shows itself in its practical consequences only in so far, as it seems the peculiarity of the Aryan character to bring to reason that deep-mindedness which wavers between feeling and phantasy. In Buddhism it was brought to the surface and grew at random. *Relic worship. §§ 48, 58, 124, 125, 127, 151.*

In the world of the western learning the Pantheism of Buddhism and its fruits have come to their true estimate very gradually since 1820, when Hodgson sent the result of his studies in Sanskrit literature from Nepal to Paris—those works which Burnouf perused and

Buddhism dismantled.
§ 58, 81, 97, 185, 188.

Hodgson, Burnouf, Lassen.
"Light of Asia."
Arnold. § 1.

Buddha canonised·
St. Jehoshaphat. § 46.

examined, and which incited Lassen to further investigations. Nearly at the time of Hodgson's labors Koeroes travelled in Tibet, Wassilgew in China, Schmidt in Mongolia, and Turnour collected Pali-inscriptions in Ceylon. Thus we have finally obtained the clear picture of that "Buddhistic" reformation in Asia, of which we spoke in connection with the Lamaism of the Dalai, the pope of Asia. None but Arnold, following Hegel in the praise of the "Light of Asia" was kept in the dark about it; and so must that pope of the thirteenth century have been, who —after the return of his emmisaries to the powerful moguls—canonised Buddha under the name of St. Jehoshaphat. (It is only since 1850 that this saint has disappeared from the Roman calender.)

Issues of Buddha's "pain and pleasure" theory.

§ 58. All that this reformation did was to render Brahmanism pessimistic. The inextricable and painful sufferings in such a world of vanity as that of Hindoo-consciousness is, where man, in punishment for the least mistake made at a sacrificial ceremony, is again driven through the process of becoming by a tedious and disheartening repetition of return and annihilation: such an everlasting anguish prompts in the soul the desire to escape into the all-god, who alone is free from sorrows. The Hindoo knows that men cannot approach by way of meritorious works, may they be imagined as ever so holy. But human thoughts may obtain access to him by way of concentrated contemplation, by renouncing this evil world, by patient suffering. By dy-

Renouncing the bad world.
Throwing away the ego.

ing, by fleeing into nothingness one may attain the stage of being dissolved into divinity. A nation drilled to such resignation is more than half way to its final doom.

Salvation by indoctrination.

The idea of freedom once lost, a salvation in mere doctrine is soon despaired of. The mind then scorns life and covets death.

Such are the views which made Buddhistic priests, dissembling a profound worldsoreness, to grow fat under their garb of poverty, piety and sublime wisdom. And that wisdom turned up again and again, rooting its seeds now in the Thebaid conveyed

Pessimism.
Piety of mendicants.

thither by Persian refugees, and then in the determinism of the Islam, from whence, it encysted in the dry seeds of asceticism and obedience to "mendicant" orders, it was disseminated across the deserts and over the Alps.

Dissemination of this orientalism; partly over the Thebaid to the Occident.
§ 54, 55, 59, 67, 78, 81, 87, 97, 122, 125, 131, 136, 142, 144-150, 185.

Buddhistic pessimism was propagated among other nations on the whole extent from Japan to Spain—the result of it we find in the beggar-monks of both these countries. In India it was at last overwhelmed by a restoration of pristine Brahmanism in a sort of counter-reformation. But pessimism was retained, and beggary, too, because the priests deemed it very convenient. The pessimistic world-theory combined with the pantheo-polytheistic compromise made caste-rule impregnable.

A new Brahmanism, compromise between pantheism, polytheism and pessimism;

The present Hindoo-philosophy sums up the findings of its preceding stages in the chief dogma: "To be is but to perish, being is transient and unsubstantial; it is nothing but an everlasting becoming, y natura nasceans. All appearance is hollow and empty, vanity is the essence of all that is. Everything is subject to change, sorrow, and misery, and is void of substantiality. The very life itself is an evil, the greatest

makes caste-despotism invincible.

of all evils, marked by tears at its entrance and its exit, made up entirely of griefs, sickness and death." To all these moans of despair Schopenhauer as spokesman of

Schopenhauer.

the modernised Hindooism of the Occident has fully agreed, adding that "life is a business not covering expenses."

This is the doleful end of all that serious and gloomy view of life which assumes the dignified mien of practical wisdom or the garb of monastical piety, but which is merely the fruit of unmitigated "natural" religion when merged into the great name of monistic science or Identity-Philosophy. Its orthodoxy consists in calumniating nature. Exchange the sceptre for the alms-box; give up the luxury of dressing ac-

Air-line to Nirwana preferable to metempsychosis.

cording to your own taste which stands as an emblem of personality and distinction; throw away your own suit of clothes and don the yellow rags of the hermit, then you are on the air-line to Nirwana.

So long as England winks at the excrescences of such a philosophy, the 90,000 British souls are safe in ruling 255 millions of miserable subjects. It cannot be denied that in India the thought divine is recognised in the lowest Paria, but not less

Results obvious in social life.

is it in a louse. What once had been crushed by Brahmanism was tenderly lifted up by Buddhism. The right of the individual was recognised once more; the reform bore some fruit for the benefit of social economy and religious tolerance. Nevertheless we must adhere to our former opinion expressed with regard to the Buddhistic "reformation," since in furtherance of human practices it is void of any real merit. For, the

Buddhistical cognizance of individual rights does not enjoin a positive manifestation of personal duty and regard for a fellow-man's welfare: **it does not arouse sympathy for another in his sufferings.** The excuse is made easy, that he belongs to another caste, is not pious, not orthodox, else he would not need to suffer; hence the individual practically amounts to nothing after all. Things in general only are considered of some value; and a person is used as a thing to serve ones own interest. These principles are brought to bear upon social relations under all circumstances—in India. Complete renunciation,withdrawal from bothersome practical life, anachoretic abstinence, contemplative and penitential exercises are considered the highest virtues and as meritorious. Laziness and selftorture are admired. The Hindoo grade of world-consciousness calumniates the realm of secondary good in nature, yet deifies it to the extent of throwing away personal life in the worship of nature's meanest objects. Whenever such principles lead any Hindoo to the disavowal of all human feelings, even of parental and filial love, the higher does he stand in public esteem. For, such utter regardlessness is taken as the strongest proof of obedience to the precepts of religion, as for instance when a mother throws her baby alive into the Ganges to feed the sacred crocodiles.

Natural religion causes human emotions to perish. Man a tool not deserving sympathy.

The Ganges pilgrims of Gangotri arrive naked, covered with ashes and filth, a rope around their waists. The long hairs, twisted into snake-like strains, hang down over the shoulders upon the skeleton-like trunk,and thus appearing as figures which resemble apparitions from the graves rather than human beings. They impress the holder with the idea that the fervor of fanaticism has dried out the muscles and sapped the marrow from their languid bones.

A scene on the Ganges.

Human life abandoned to the deified river and the deified crocodiles;

It is in this frightful manner that nature-bound personal life is thrown away to a deified Ganges with its swarms of sacred crocodiles. Indeed, all this asceticism, carried out in dead earnest, knowing nothing of the theoretical compromise between pantheism and crocodiles divine, all these appalling practices of selftorment, those selfmutilations of which the mere reading makes one's blood curdle—are considered as the acme of ethics and are endured in order **to gain the remission of sins,** because the "bad" conscience of the poor Hindoo is not objectivised in demons as in the case of Shamanism. Here lies the great and characteristic mark of distinction between Shamanistic selfabandonment to the bad and the Aryan's yearning for the better. We call attention to this circumstance as of vital importance in order to resume its discussion further on.

All for conscience's sake to obtain forgiveness of sins.

Analysis of the Hindoo mind as to its God- and world-consciousness.

To be resumed:
§ 73, 81, 97, 149, 150, 185, 188.

No feature distinguishes the Hindoo frame of mind more definitely in contrast to that of the Chinese than the lack of historical sense. Of course, memory can be of no value to such views of life. If the world is a delusion of the senses and life a burden, then the past is not worth minding and history but a folly.

Destitute of historic sense.

Save the few myths derived from the times of heroism, Hindoo literature contains no narrative of facts, despite the superabundance of whatever imagination may be apt to construe. Products of the phantasy burden the Sanskrit writings to such an extent that even algebra, medicine, and law are dressed in poetry. Hence a fairy world of soft features and high colors floats around the horizon of Hindoo fancy, and spreads a mystic hue as of an evening dawn over things visible and over the pictures of abstraction. Even when the favorite children of fiction, the drama, the epic, the fairy tale step upon the scene, the figures seldom rise above the tendency to effectuate enchantment. Like narcotic flowers and tenacious creepers, twisted into garlands and wreaths, so the plays and songs do not conceal the purpose of decorating life with something sweet and harmless. Notwithstanding their heavy laden hearts these guileless children of nature have a fairy-land left to them, whenever they are among themselves; for they do not like the stranger to pry into their private life and their world of sacred ideals. Their fairy-tales are like significant dreams, rich in childlike anticipations, full of evidences of deep-mindedness and uprightness. And these very fairy-tales have found their way from the banana-palms of India to the pine forests of Norway and through Anderson's appreciation into our own literature. They grew up under high shade-trees, and like the voices of merry youth, full of touching sentiments, they reverberate through the whole Germanic world. Wherever boyish heedlessness needs to be kept out of mischief and the unwary girl is to be cautioned; where ambitious youthfulness is wanted to sit spellbound so as to direct adventurous thoughts to inward enthusiasm; or where the mind is bent to dreamy indecision, resembling the combat between the morning fog and the rays of the rising sun: there the old fairy-tales ever find an echo.

Products of phantasy.

Algebra, law, medicine—in the garb of poetry.

A fancy-world of fairies. § 57, 144

Even the great epics of India suffer under the drowsiness of its climate. The figures drawn in them reveal a fulness of soul and touch, but like the Lotus-flowers and the "pious gazelles" they appear extremely hazy and are, like king Vismavitra, exceedingly fictitious.

Climatic influences.

The obtuse phantasmagories of inverted Hindoo-thinking, attempting to represent unthinkable abstractions, are embodied most tangibly in the architectural style of the huge pagodas which rise high up from the mango groves—to say nothing of the idols set up therein.

Terrace-shaped,these towers consist of a confounding mass of stories and cupolas, and strikingly represent the structure of Buddhistic dogmatics with its thousand subtleties and contradictions which are forced to fit the system, and which to unravel takes the 72 a priori categories of a Brahmin's brain and their subdivisions—all stereotyped in terra cotta. And an impossible tooth or a gigantic footprint of a Buddha (for there are over twenty of his incarnations) is after all that deep-minded mysticism,the holy of holies, within all these abstruse embellishments.

Recall to mind the picture of the Mahu-stupa, the Buddhistic monastery resting upon 1600 pillars which a Zingalesian king built upon the island of Ceylon. Looking at such a baroque, bombastic monster-edifice, one is not only oppressed by its senselessness and absolute ugliness, but also confused as by the best emblem imaginable of a perfect chaos. So much of India in its official decorum, or public deportment, the India of Sanskrit and Systems. Different, however, it appears when we look into the depths of consciousness, which out of the masses of human beings in general inadvertantly reveals itself.

Of snake-worship, flourishing in spite of dogmatic and philosphical scholasticism, because of Buddhistic-pantheistical indifference to truth—we need not say much. But to observe demon-worship ruling in India just as much as we cared to see of it in Mongolia—this is surprising. Its chief seat was Tinnevelly. Long before the Brahmins rose to pre-eminence the demons were predominant throughout India down to Ceylon. Demon-worship was the religion of the Dravida, it is said, and, we

add, was a part of the religious peculiarity which is common to all the Aryans. For, these demons, the existence of which was believed by the former occupants of India who formed the substructure of Hindoo culture, were never driven out altogether by the poetical, religious, and metaphysical systems elaborated by the well-to-do classes. Among the latter we met the rational pole of human understanding in its endeavor to bring religious feelings and traditions before consciousness, that is, into intelligible order and clear comprehension. At the same time and on the very same spot we find the other, the superstitious pole agitating the "lower" classes, to which some of the "educated" must ever be reckoned, so long as they can look on with indifference to the very queer practices below, without a motion to rescue those under durance of the powers of darkness.

They give divine adoration to a "virgin cow", rendering their doorsills and dishes sacred and inviolable against the influences of the demons,or of the "evil eye" by besmearing and besprinkling them with the excrements of that cow.

We descend further down to where our poor Aryan cousins forego one meal after the other rather than risk that the evil eye of the stranger, or of one from a lower caste, may glance at his victuals whereby they would be defiled so as to make the consumer unclean.

Further down to where the poor maiden drinks with deep veneration the water in which the Brahmin beggar has washed his feet, whereby she hopes to obtain a higher state of purity within herself, and to imbibe an affluence of his divinity.

The fakirs, sitting around the gates of Benares in dirty nudeness, carry a skull in their hands, on occasions which are not so very rare, either, of which skull they have just eaten off the flesh, the eyes, and the brain.

Facts like these point to more than a degeneracy from a higher form of religion and culture. They point downward to a wild, spurious and thick undergrowth; to elements of an infernal nature breaking through the upper stratum from underneath. From premises of natural science the indelible phenomena of demonolatry and anthropophagy cannot be explained.

In the talks about incarnations into a fish, or a bear, or a tiger: everywhere the former ancestor-worship and beast-service into which the fallen race had been enthralled comes to the surface again.

In one of the 1454 Hindoo temples of Benares more than a thousand monkeys are cared for and enjoy even the freedom of the city. A golden ape stands in the sanctuary. "Surely", Montegazza exclaimed on viewing this spectacle—"sound common sense has embodied a great truth in the belief of the devil." So unspeakably obnoxious and mad did this perversion and depravity of reason appear to him.

Into that deep degeneracy and hideous mixture of fears and hopes men have dragged down with themselves also the indestructible remnants of original and traditional religion, namely : the consciousness of a God above ; the cognition of unity of the human race by common descent ; the reminiscence of a better and a higher good.

for the possession of which man is destined : the idea of dominion over nature ; and *Criterion of cultural value of a nation always given in the expressions of its religious consciousness.* §§ 24, 34, 43, 47, 54, 56, 71, 84, 86, 93, 96, 125, 126, 131, 132, 137, 139, 156, 175, 190.
the recollection of the necessity of an expiation by way of a sacrifice without
hierarchal interference. And all these remnants are as clearly indicated in the
inner and exterior life of the Hindoos as with us ; only that among Indian surroundings they prove their incorruptibleness so much the stronger.   Thus the standard by
which the ethical character of a nation and the value of its culture is to be measured, is always given in the expression of the religious consciousness ; that is, in the
way people speak of, or in the manner in which they aesthetically represent their *Most knarled branch of the human family.*
idea of, the deity. And as we never find the remnants entirely absent, so do we not
miss the measure alluded to in this most knarled branch of the Aryan family.

Vishnu with his four arms rides upon a symbolic figure, partly man and partly bird. *Vishnu-Siva. Ganesha-Kali.*
Siva with his three eyes sits nude upon his ox, wearing a chain of skulls around his neck.
Millions of devotees pay homage to either one of those deities thus represented. Other millions favor the elephant-headed Ganesha, sitting upon a rat. Kali, with her hair disheveled,
like a fury, the chain of human skulls around her bust, her bloody tongue bulging far out of
her mouth, is conducted in solemn procession through the principal streets of Calcutta.

All this divulges black secrets protruding from a sphere more corrupt than de- *Secrets of a sphere more corrupt than deranged nature protrude from a superhuman intelligence energy and persistency.*
ranged nature itself, by its spiritual denizens who must be endowed with supernatu-
ral energy, superhuman intelligence and indefatigable persistency. The effects of
the agility in this sphere, upon human life in prehistoric culture, become stratified as
demon-service and beast-cult, which out of this lowest stratum has ever and anon *Phenomenal usages contradictory to reason.*
broken forth, and which in India gradually was mixed into the Veda-religion of the
Rig-period, in proportion as the latter was allowed to become formalistic and to
petrify.

Buddhism was not able to suppress this wild growth from below. Not even neg- *Intellectualism unable to extirpate the roots ramified in the substratum.* §§ 22, 27, 47, 65, 72, 73, 96, 97.
atively could it accomplish the reformation promised by it and ascribed to it. The
Mongolian from Urga to the Kuku-noor lets the wild beasts devour the remains of departed friends, whilst he will not kill an animal, but spares the life of the vermin
upon his own body. The Indo-Aryan, on the other hand, the soft, melancholy Hindoo
with the same considerateness for vermin, throws children alive into the stream, because the Ganges is sacred. Hindoo burial-places are the most horrible looking localities imaginable. But to the same Hindoo his European cousin is the uncleanest
thing, just because he uses a water-closet and does not step aside like the Hindoo with
a small shovel in his hand.

Let us recapitulate. Aryan culture we find to be of a decidedly higher grade. *Recapitulation: data for induction in Hindoo characters.*
As compared with the Mongolian we find the Hindoo possessing the consciousness of
a rupture, acknowledging that which ought not to be, being disgusted with the bad. *Consciencious-ness of sin kept alive; but sin attributed to nature.* § 4, 25, 83, 92.
In his disgust he takes creation, in which man is but a transient phenomenon, for
sin itself, and yearns to be delivered from both. Yet so deep is the feeling of the
moral deficiency within the Hindoo, that man appears to him even worse than nature,
worse than all his fellow creatures, so that he esteems them as superior to himself, *Personality (the standard of valuation) abandoned, since the cognition of a personal God is obliterated.*
even as holy in comparison with himself. This shows that the Hindoo has lost the
standard of valuation. The worth of a person goes to naught wherever the belief in
the personal God is abandoned.

The bewilderment of the mind increasing, the capability to understand and to explain
the mysteries of nature decreases; and by asceticism the Hindoo tries to get rid of nature
instead of ridding himself from the wrong conceptions which he holds the more sacred in
proportion to their absurdity and unmercifulness. Under such circumstances speculation
fails in its purpose to master the situation, the practice of endurance and selftorture notwith- *Still persevering to solve the riddle at the entrance into history.* § 87 Yama.
standing. The Hindoo, nevertheless, perseveres in his labor to solve as much of the riddle of
his existence, which stood at the entrance of his history as he can recollect of it.

The enigmatical fact of sorrow and sin is the pivot upon which all Indian search
and sacrifice hinges. During this perplexing search thought broods over the deep *Upon sorrow and sin hinges Indian search and sacrifice.*
abyss—over the antithesis of nature and spirit. The Hindoo's mind attempts to bridge *Search for the bridge over the chasm between spirit and nature.*
this abyss, that is, to close the synthesis, at the expense of the reality of present life.
For, the polar tension between the two, matter and mind, as manifest in human
nature or personal life, causes, as he thinks, all the trouble and torment.

The intense desire to have the deeply felt wants of the present life filled with *Natural presentiment of the incarnation.*
real contents, and to be liberated from grief and gloom causes the remarkable phe-
nomenon of the Hindoo—

INCARNATIONS.

CH. II. ORIENTAL ARYANS: ORIENT—RIGHT WING.
2. NORTHERN PART: PERSIANS.

§ 59. Iran is, like the Pamir region, a highland of large dimensions. The distance from Balch (the Bactra of old) to Teheran almost equals that between New York and Chicago, and the district forms a large square with equal extensions of its boundary lines.

Country of Iran.

This plateau expands from the steep mountain walls of the Hindukush,—the southern spurs of which separate Iran from India,—to the Kurdic Alps in the west and the Armenian parts of the Caucasus in the north-west. Its height above sea-level averages about three thousand feet, containing great salty marshes and steppes, and a number of broad, dry water courses where former rivers have been swallowed up by the sands of the deserts. Whilst draughts of cold air move across the heights, tropical heat makes the long deep valleys and their southern slopes hot-beds of sweet scenting vegetation, clothing the regions with a pleasing variation of verdure in high forests and in pasture lands. To imagine, however, the empire full of the fragrance of the province of Shiras, would cause a wrong apperception about Persia. For, in the most parts of its area glowing winds from the Southern Ocean heap up moving dunes of drift sands in and around the deserts.

Separation of the Hindoos from the Iranians.

When the eastern Aryans set out from the heights beyond the Himalayas, toward the regions where now Kandahar in Afghanistan is located ; when the friends of Varunna then separated and took their route down the Indus inclines : the other branch stayed—as we have seen—to occupy this henceforth Iranian country. The indications are that down to about 2000 B. C. the religions of the sister nations were identical, just as in regard to language the original unity is demonstrated by one glance over a table of words from the Sanskrit and Zend languages. The figures of Mithras, the God of light, that of the tree of life, and of Manu, the common ancestor after the flood, the same names and rites in numerous instances, prove this axiom of kinship to have outgrown the nature of a hypothesis. The unity of the Indo-European family up to 2000 B. C. is an incontrovertible fact. And that the cause of the separation was a religious difference is more than problematic, as illustrated by the misunderstanding in the matter of the Hindoo devas and the Persian dews, and as indicated by many other circumstances.

of the friends of VarunasIndra from those of Mithra.
§ 57.
Remnants of pristine traditions held in common:
§ 42, 55, 58, 59, 74, 95, 109, 115.

Unity of Sanskrit and Zend-people.

Religious cause of the detachment:
Hindoo devas: devs;
Persian dews: devils.

In yonder period before the separation, Varuna, corresponding to the old Persian Ahuramazda, seems to have possessed the dignity of the sole, or at least the predominant, deity. To this period of unity and common experience is due the vivid impression of the power of the bad. On account of the contests in which the Iranians were continually engaged, they had more occasion to revive this impression, and learned more and more to understand the duty of resisting the bad; whilst with the Indo-Aryans that cognition became obliterated by the quiet life in a most happily situated country during a long period of peace.

Genesis of differences in character of Hindoos and Persians.
Resisting the bad, kept up by conflicts and religious symbolism. § 56.

Besides the dualism, developing from the concept of the reality of the Bad, the theology of Iran became far more differently formulated in the highlands from what Hindoo-philosophy had made out of the ancient traditions. Geiger has shown the genesis of the doctrinal differences in question. The Indra of India is plastic, is a poetical, yet a life-like figure of a god with whom the Hindoos were as familiar as the Greeks with their deities. The Mithra of Persia is abstract, is deistically conceived, and is treated with the same stiff, cold and distant respect, which the Romans paid to Jupiter in an emergency. The fresh and natural Indra is, of course, preferable to Geiger. According to him Ahuramazda is altogether too transcendental, a mere mirage of priestly designs. For reasons given (§ 24, 41.) natural-mindedness with its proneness to carnal-mindedness always renders the fact of sin a mere point of doctrine and controversy: because taken as a fact it would lead to certain consequences which, as postulates of salvation, are offensive to naturalism. Hence the objections to, and the dislike of, the good Ahuramazda.

Ahuramazda:
originally monotheistic.

Indra and Hindoos akin to Greek bond of mind. Mithra and Persians move like the Romans. Geiger.

Subsequently the fact of sin is taken simply as a matter of doctrine.

Upon investigating, whether the Vedic gods—as Geiger believes, and as Schiller looked upon the gods of Greece—were really considered by the Hindoos as figures of "flesh and blood" we do not enter; we simply reject the supposition.

Another cause of the difference is to be found in the practical sense of the Persians who could neither put so much phantasy into their conception of the divine as the Hindoos did, nor give themselves up to such intense contemplation as the Hindoos did. Upon the basis of their more active life the Iranians discriminated more resolutely between thought and deed, making poetry a seperate thing. Hence the Persians did not swerve from traditional universalism, while the Hindoos only returned to this idea after they had taken the round-about way through Buddhistic speculation and abstractness, whereby the idea of the original oneness of the human family had lost the freshness of reality, and had become dissolved into an indifferent and nebulous all-the-sameness. Persian universalism stands higher morally, than the Hindoo with his satiety, senility and misanthropy, with his disgust of a life worn out in the times of levity.

Iranians less fervent, but also less immoral.

Iranian universalism in contrast with Hindooish all-the-sameness.

The Zend religion knows of a divine will, which embraces the destinies of all men in a future life. Spiegel in his "Holy Writs of the Persians" quotes a striking declaration. The question, whether there might exist people who were pure without being followers of Zoroaster is answered in the affirmative: "Surely there are such, everywhere, have been created pure by Ormuzd and have kept themselves as pure as possible, having lived in accord with the good law without knowing it." This universalism becomes complete in an apocatastasis of all things. According to passages gathered and adduced from Persian sources, there was taught a final restitution of the bad spirits even. *(Analysis of the national character of the Iranians. Cognition of universality of humanity in Zend-Avesta. Spiegel.)*

The wide area, and the contact with many people assisted the Iranians in becoming broad-minded. They have not that silly pride which calls its own language "the perfect" and calls people who do not speak it mlekka i. e. "dumb people." Thus they became that sturdy, intelligent and truthloving nation, which created Medo-Persian culture, and created a state which checked Roman impetuousness. Upon their highlands they lived in a healthy atmosphere, not soft and effeminating, but always brisk and invigorating, among environments which favored energy for work and for war; which favored the sentiments of freedom and independence. The sense of honor and duty was cultivated; manliness and bravery became proverbial. A peculiar constitutionality of clans and districts encouraged selfconscious merit, individual excellency, and tribal emulation. Every man had a value and bore a dignity in partaking of the management of general affairs by his council and his courage. *(Influence of physical environments. Freedom grows on highlands. Energy for work and for war stimulated. Selfconscious of merits.)*

Upon the field occupied the Iranians had to be ever ready and swift on horse-back in its defense on all sides. At an early date the challenge of the Turanian nation of Akkadis had to be accepted. And when they, on the whole, were defeated and driven westward into the plains of the Tigris and the Euphrates, the victors had gained more than a free country of their own; they had become accustomed to selfreliance, to vigilance and other ennobling traits. *(Tribal emulation challenged by Accadians.)*

As the Hindoo idols mirror the lethargy and disgust with real life, so the clear cut character of the Iranians is reflected from the forms which objectivised their religious tenets, and which reflect their God-consciousness. In fact, their readiness for the fight was only the reflection of that struggle between light and night, which intonates the key-note of the concert of world-and God-consciousness in the history of the Iranians, yea of the Indo-Germans.

Ahuramazda stands out conspicuously as the personification of the good, opposed by Angromayngus, the leader of the bad gods and the evil spirits. That opponent, however, is not conceived as being a rebel, but as possessing independence, tho less powerful and in a sense subordinate—as dwelling in hell. His shape is that of a snake. Under that form he corrupted the purity of a nature, which in spite of him and as a partition wall against him, had been created by Ahuramazda. About that bulwark of separation the war ensued and is waged on both sides under many vicissitudes through all the ages of history. At the end of it the hosts of spirits will be drawn up in array of battle and the decision will be fought out. Then the well organised band of the resurrected will overwhelm the throngs of the prince of darkness. *(Dualism: Ahuramazda (Ormuzd) Angromayngus (Ahriman) prince of darkness—representing the bad in the shape of the snake. Ideal of warfare.)*

Upon this principle of the reality of the bad, and upon the definite distinction between the good and the bad, the construction of the straightforward morality was possible which by far excels that of the Hindoo, and of the Greeks. *(Strict distinction between the good and the bad,)*

Truthfulness and chasteness are more highly estimated than even the fortitude of the warrior. Since propitiation can not be circumvented, it is held that absolute and honest deeds can repudiate sin. So far the Persians are in earnest. But here begins the corruption of the moral sense. *(Truthful and chaste.)*

The means for paying the religious debt are arranged in such a manner as to resemble a stipulated set-off; expiation assumes the nature of an external business transaction. The equivalent for guilt is put down to the lowest terms possible, and may even under such cheapening of sin be set up as a counterclaim. With that lowering of rates, the moral unconcern and negligence were instigated through which the ideal meaning of life's combat was lost; the duty of resisting wickedness was mechanically balanced without putting the performer under much inconvenience. Henceforth the spirit of pugnacity was stimulated merely in the interest of aggrandisement and imperious extravagance, as we find Persia when outwardly it had its zenith in the night of Belshazzar. When the ideal of the religious warfare against sin had become oblivious, then was not heroism on the wane, but the old-fashioned morality disappeared. The downward course began with objectivising the bad, with laying the fault to outward circumstances or upon other persons. It will end in the depreciation of the good, or in heaping calumny and ridicule upon it. Under holocausts of relatively innocent victims the culture of Persia went up in smoke. *(Lowering the significance of the bad. Extravagance and effeminacy displaces morality. The guilt located outside of self—sin objectivised. § 24, 55, 109. Culture collapses.)*

In the classic times when Persia was at its prime everything was thought and done under aspects of combative forces. From the struggles with the Chaldeans and afterwards with the Roman eagles, the Persians profited, at the least, a spirit of chivalry similar to that which a thousand years later made "the Franks" respected in the east. There existed a noble knighthood, arrayed in splendid coats of mail and with helmets decorated as fine as ever a crusader wore. Chosroes Parviz in his accoutrement, majestically sitting upon his charger, looked exactly like one of the good swordsmen of Richard the Lionhearted, or of Barbarossa when he entered the lists at a tournament or mounted the warhorse for the long ride against the Saracens.

Of a decisive influence upon the formation of the peculiarities of the Persian character was the combination of the Iranian tribes into one nation under a thoroughly centralised government. But when the dominion was thus rendered compact, the oppressive administrations of satraps, organised after the pattern of the iron despotism further east, became the signals of disaster, of the collapse of Persian glory.

When Cyrus arose from his seat under the canopy of his throne in order to go to worship he was forbidden by law to walk further than to the portals of the Great Hall of State at the foot of the broad stairway. There his team waited and 6000 body-guards presented arms; also

four heifers stood ready, decorated for his sacrifice to Ahuramazda and his subaltern gods. Then the horses dedicated to the sun-god were led to the front, and the wagon of the god, to which a special team of four white horses was hitched, drove up; then the bearers of the sacred flame followed, and now the king took his place beside the driver of his chariot; the procession started. Crowned with the tiara and wearing a loose purple tunic with a white stripe from the neck down to the hem, he was greeted by the populace in solemn silence; dexterously the four thousand guards in front and two thousand in the rear of his chariot fell in line, whilst three hundred lancers rode alongside the royal car; then the kings horses of noblest pedigre, decked with gold-embroidered equipments and striped shabracks are led along the broad, paved avenue; then follow two thousand spearmen afoot in the parade, and another army of ten thousand cavalry in squadrons of hundred each, under the commands of Chrysantes, Hystaspes, Datamas and Gadatas. Finally a numerous retinue of Median, Armenian, Hyrkanian and Scythian nobles under the command of Arbaces make up the rearguard of the enormous cavalcade.

This magnific despotism was not the product of southern drowsiness. It represents the issue of an eventful history since those days when Bactra was as yet the seat of Iranian piety and culture. This Persian world-monarchy was welded together by wars. When the monarch rides to the simple altar, the splendor of the other world is to be reflected by this demonstrative display of sovereignty. The throne surrounded by the princes of the proud empire becomes a picture of the Heavenly kingdom. It was Persian conservatism in regard to the spirituality of religion which kept the Persians from imitating the Babylonian forms of lowest paganism. Hence, also, the absence of such gorgeous temple ruins on Persian soil, wherefore we are spared meeting with the lowest of religious subversions practiced in the same localities in pre-eranian times.

The buildings of Persia were, on the whole, mere copies of Assyrian architecture, as shown by the winged bulls with human heads which support the portal pillars of the Grand Hall upon the terraces of Persepolis. The doors, however, mark development in a different direction. The pillars are taller, and the heads of animals which in Ninive support the arches above, are here lowered to the base of the columns. And those Persian pillars with double-headed capitals show the combination of masonry with woodwork in the loftier, higher, and lighter, and more expanded ceilings. Those horse-heads supporting the upper joists remind one of the swifter movement in war as well as in nomadic freedom; the swift retribution of justice in the dominions of Cyrus. They were about as expanded as the territory of the United States. Yet it took no more than a hundred hours to deliver a message from Susu in Sardes with 1400 miles between.

As Buddhism sprang from Brahmanism, so is Parsism the parasite which feeds upon Zoroaster's teachings. The Hindoo-"reform" traveled to the north-east, the innovation of the Parsees remained in its native home of western Asia. The former celebrates silent triumphs upon the islands of Farther India, the latter becomes stale in its stability in the old Iranian home, with the exception of the short interval in which the Sassanides reacted against Nestorianism, when those unfortunate and much persecuted heretics undertook to make Christianity a means of subjection on their part. It was these movements which caused a new proclamation of the wisdom of Zoroaster, or rather the goodness of Ormuzd. Otherwise the Persians shunned to make proselytes to their religion of universality. It was not from indifference, but because they held their faith too pure as to be made a means of conquest after the fashion of Alexander and the Romans. For purposes of conquest they remained honest enough to apply more appropriate measures. Religion not to be made the means of conquest.

We have discovered in what we henceforth call the Orient, a decided progress being obvious. Admitting that the eastern Aryans in the Persian empire did not attain to a higher culture than which they enjoyed at the commencement of their career, it is to be deemed commendable nevertheless, that they were the first nation which did not sink below their starting point. After they had signalised so much of an advance toward European progress, it was not the doctrine of fighting the bad which stopped it. Retrospect: upon Persian culture. Merit of Persian culture: individual worth (§ 72) in contrast to Roman.

Not to be undervalued is the development of manliness and of the idea of individual worthiness in the interest of which the current of Persian life and history ran so favorably, at least up to Xerxes time. Especially worth remembering is the other circumstance that the Persians were more deeply convicted of personal sinfulness, even if—in remarkable contrast to the fear of other nations who had lost that cognition—the feeling and acknowledgment of this source of all misery was taken with surprising ease. Sin, as viewed by the Persian, is not the torment of existence; it is to him but that complication of affairs which causes the lusty fight between light and darkness, from which to shrink would be a shame. The Persian discountenances a whimsical behavior and dismal mood, and that unavailing, tho ever so desperate attempt at selfsalvation. He avoids bothering himself with still more disheartening, enfeebling and useless theorising and brooding over the problem. To the matter-of-fact Persian the trouble is not with the problem of the deep chasm between nature and the spirit. This is, in the opinion of the Zend-Avesta, not to be solved intellectually, or to be bridged over by throwing existence into it, as the Hindoo tries to do, making suffering under the attempt the chief virtue. It is the fight against the bad, cherished by the Persian, on account of which the sound of the bugle fills him with pleasure. Deep conviction of personal sinfulness. Not to be brooded over as in Hindooism, but sin to be fought down.

The resume of eastern Aryan culture was presented neither to show the tensions, nor for the purpose of drawing parallels. Our object was simply to glean out the one synoptical thesis, that the Persian comprehension of the realities of this world was the proper complement to Indian idealism. In summing up the characteristics of the Asiatic Aryans we find that singular and most important of all peculiarities: **A sincere longing for incarnations, the intuitive anticipation of divine condescension toward the mundane realities, and the confidence originating therefrom, that the good will finally lead off triumphantly.** Resume of the inductive data from East-Aryan culture. Sanskrit-Zend thought. Anticipation of the divine condescension into the reality of the sinful world.

In India lie the roots of the twelve chief languages of Europe; hence there as yet stand the old molds in which our mode of thinking was cast; for the Sanskrit of our ancestors, who lived there only a few hundred and odd generations ago, still represents their wealth of speculative thought, of which the Europeans recently became the chief explorers and gainers. To India we owe our bent of mind more than we are aware. Our form of consciousness, which shows so great a contrast to, and yet so much affinity for, East-Aryan traits, does not connect us any closer with Abraham's children than with the hymns of the Rig-veda. All the difference is, that the one furnished the universal receptacle into which the peculiar contents of the other were to be emptied. Germanic traits connect with Rig-veda cognitions as much as with the revelation in the Book of Genesis.

If we want to reduce into a formula that characteristic trend of Oriental thought which the Occident was only to bring under the normative control of reason, then its sum and substance will be comprised and expressed in: Eastern Aryans the wardens of the remnants of primitive truths. § 24, 41, 42, 47, 48, 53, 55, 57, 58, 59, 74, 95, 115, 158.

TRANSCENDENTALISM.

CH. III. INDO-GERMANS. OCCIDENT. LEFT WING OF WESTERN ARYANS:
I. THE GREEKS.

§ 60. In the observation of the Oriental branch of Aryan culture we spent two chapters. The eastern Aryans preserved better than the Turanians nearly all of what was left of primitive truth. No less will we take care of the good thus inherited. We now turn our attention to the west as the Aryans ever did, to the countries into which great numbers quietly migrated and had become settled, so that by this time they formed a prosperous branch line of the old noble house.

Contemplation of the
Hamito-Semitic wedge
between Eastern and
Western Aryans to be
postponed. § 81, 90, 192.
In order to avoid the erroneous practice of too much analysing and to avoid the danger of getting lost therein, let us from the start and once for all take that under general topics which belongs together. In the eyes of those who insist upon mere pragmatic connections in the series of political transactions or geographical causes and effects, we will be held liable to censure. We expect this in the present instance for intentionally passing over, or rather postponing, the observation to be made upon the Semito-Hamitic culture, which to us appears as a wedge driven in between the two halves of the Indo-Germanic family circle. As long as that family is not rent asunder so as to split even its very name, we will proceed upon the given line of thought. Following up its continuations we step over upon European soil.

Europe, using Peschel's expression, is the Alpine peninsula of the Asiatic mainland. Its articulate formation, so exceedingly favorable to the development of a specific culture, is its own; but the capital with which the new plant of culture was started, Europe owes to the Asistic mother-country.

Favorable situation of
Europe for diversified
culture.
The amount of coast-lines and the direction of the mountain ranges, which divide Europe into a northern and a southern part and thus provide it with a considerable force of polarity, are especially conducive to the most delicate differentiation of the social organism: to the division of labor as well as to a healthy community of interests, to cooperation.

The European partition wall is shaped in such a manner, that numerous valleys and watercourses facilitate the intercourse of the diverse territories in all directions. And Europe owes it to its isothermic situation that its northern part falls into the zone of rainy winter seasons.

From the almost mysterious highlands of the east these prolific Aryans immigrated into, and enjoyed the lovely and animating sceneries of, the "wild west" with its variable but moderate climate.

Wasks. (Basks-Viscaya.)
The first in motion along the Caucasus, through the puchtas of Russia, and toward the upper Danube seem to have been the Wasks. In black clothes, the legs enwrapped in long strips of a texture roughly woven from goats hair, they rested there from their wanderings at the time when glaciers as yet extended down to the lake of Constance. At war with the mammoth, with hyenas, cave-bears and—lions, they settled around the many lakes in the first place. It was not very long, however, after they had sought refuge from the beasts upon pilings in the lakes, that they also reared up cyclopean walls for their protection. They used stone-weapons, effective enough to hunt the elenndeer and auer-ox; but after a short time they manufactured

Phenicians (bronze.)
§ 81.
iron weapons and tools, and traded even articles of bronze from the Phenician caravans which through wilderness and forests, had found their way to these lake-dwellers.

Lake-dwellers.
—Pushed by the Celts following them, they left their name to the Vosges mountains and the Wasgau, through which now runs the very sensitive line dividing the modern

Biscayan Gulf.
children of the Gauls and Teutons. They took new abodes at the foot of the Pyrenees where the Biscayan gulf is named after them, and where their descendants have dwelt up to present times. They have kept up their special nationality so that many

Californian Basques.
of the prominent early emigrants of Mexico and California today take pride in their national antiquity.

Celts:
Caledonians,
Gauls, (Druids.)
The Celts, so we suppose, had followed the Wasks. Their druids and bards served a variety of gods and made the blood of multitudes of captives flow in their behalf. They took their seats, many of them only temporarily in Gaul, went over to the Hibernian Isles which were to become Great Britain, and settled in Ireland and Caledomia for good. Some of them went south and took homesteads in Iberia, which

Invasion of Greece.
afterwards became Spain, or in northern Italy, Illyria and Serbia, from whence they

Founding of Galata.
invaded Greece, demolishing Delphi, and proceeded to the conquest of Galata. Long years before this a reflux of Aryan masses had preceded the Celtic reflux through the passes of the Danube. In short, as a nation the Celts broke up or were dispersed again and again by the heavy bulk of Slavonians or by some German tribe, if it was

Improbable that
Slavonians pushed the
Celts.
not their mobile and quarrelsome temper that kept them roving about. For, as to encounters between Celts and Slavonians, the latter seem not to have ever been much addicted to warfare or exploits in smaller parties. Those Celts who remained together on French and English territory were mere remnants of the original bands of immigrants. And since history meets them everywhere, besides their present

Hibernians
countries, it is most likely that some of them, living in Spain at the time, were

under Marmaiu,
invading Ægypt. § 85.
among these enigmatical forty thousand who, under Marmaiu, broke into Ægypt when Mernephtah was Pharaoh—a century or two before the Trojan war and a century after Moses.

After the Celts came the Slavs.   Under the names of Sarmatians, Sorbes, Wenes or Wends (Vandals), those "excellent fellows" spread over eastern Europe simply to keep it, and to stay there.   Comparative investigation of the myths has ascertained that concerning folk-lore the place of honor next to the Vedas is to be ascribed to the Slavs.   After many wanderings hither and thither crowds of them pressed onward and became masters of Bosnia, Serbia, Dalmatia, and Bulgaria.   They wrested eastern Germany and large parcels of western Russia from the Sorbes.   They made the Wends move to (V-)Andalusia; and the proudest of them called themselves Poles and Tszechs in their new homes.   The largest part of Russia had been theirs already—we would say, was their property, if it had not been for their being communists and, anticipating Henry George, were opposed to the private possession of real estate.   With the neighboring Mongolians they did not mingle; altho they accepted from them the name of Bog for their deity.

[margin: Slavs over Eastern Europe, simply to stay there and keep it.]
[margin: Their folk-love second only to that of pristine Hindooism.   § 171.]
[margin: Russia. § 126, 150, 189.]
[margin: Wendes, Vandals, Andalusia.]
[margin: Communists as to private possession of land.   Henry George.]

In the mean time the Germans had made their appearance.   They contented themselves with the interior and secluded parts of Europe, taking possession of its heart, as it were.   Their settlement extended from the Vistula to the Vosges mountains and from the Baltic and the North Sea to the Danube, until the Slavonians crowded upon them and pushed them even deeper into the forests of Germany beyond the Elbe river.   They populated the low-lands of the Rhine and, exchanging the oar for the plough, they "ploughed" the sea for the first time, roaming over to Scandinavia or landing in England.   As Kimbri, Teutons, Goths and Franks, as Saxons and Longobards, Thuringians and Kattes, Allemanes—after whom the French named the Germans—and Marcomani, Hermundurians and Herulians, Cheruskians and Sigambrians, as Swedes and Swiss, they again and again swept down upon their southern neighbors in a most provoking manner.   All these people will in due time come under our consideration as "the" historic nation.   At present we limit ourselves to the south-western Aryans in Greece and Rome, just as in Asia the southerners came first into historic significance.

[margin: Germans]
[margin: pushed for the first time to exchange the oar for the plough—they ploughed even the seas.]
[margin: Normans.]
[margin: Their chief tribes.]
[margin: " The " historic nation.]

Parts of southern Europe had been covered by streams of earlier immigrants : by the various Greek tribes, the Albanese, Etruscans, and Italics.   These at any rate emerge earlier than any other Europeans of whom we know from the mist of prehistoric ages.   Naturally the Balkan peninsula, being nearest to Asia, came first to the notice of history.

[margin: Southern Europeans.]

The earliest settlers spoken of in Greece were the Pelasgians and, tho of less consequence, the Lelegians.   It seems that a constant dread of barbaric invasions had become almost hereditary with these old residents, who were somewhat advanced and lived in comfortable circumstances.

[margin: Pelasgians.]

Only recently De Gœje has shown this habitual worry and anticipation of danger, arranging clusters of legends relating to the times of migratory movements.   As it is generally the case with tell-tales that the elements of truth contained in them are mixed with fiction, so the analysis of De Gœje proved the fact that the legends had mixed up Alexander's expeditions with the much later reports about the building of the Chinese wall.   It was believed that the Great Macedonian had closed the inroads of further invasions from Central-Asia by raising iron gates on the Yaxartes against the hordes of the Gobi.   The nuclei of truth handed down in those legends have a bearing on the supposition that there had always been connected with the faint memory of the Alpine regions of Pamir not only a certain anxiety as to dangers threatening from thence, but also a melancholy, retrospective yearning after the scenes of childhood in the far distant old home.

[margin: Fear of Asiatic raids, extracted from legends by De Gœje.]
[margin: Hearsay of the Chinese wall.   § 14, 55, 150.]

In the time, however, at which we now arrive, that Pelasgian period of fretfulness was far behind, in which the pioneers had built the cyclopian bulwarks against the rough and obtrusive mountaineers of the north.   The hilarious people with whom we now come to converse knew no longer any fear of which their forefathers had been afraid.

It would have been impossible to put a nation better fitted than the congenial Hellenes for the various forms of intercourse into the center of the world's traffic.   Soon after they had colonised the nearer islands they became intrepid navigators and ingenious organisers of self-governing districts and towns.   Strong and clever, liberty-loving and law-abiding, endowed with a rich mind, and entrusted with one of the prettiest spots on the face of earth, they could not help becoming one of the most amiable, bouyant, wellbalanced, and susceptible races known to history.   Keen

[margin: Hellenes fit for the central position of the worlds traffic.]

Talent of the Greeks: for appropriating systematizing, and distributing the experiences and thoughts of ancient cultures.

observers, they gathered and appropriated to themselves the most valuable substance of the wealth which, under strife and labor, under bitter deprivations and a thousand hard earned experiences, had been accumulated by all the old nations around them. And the Hellenes enriched, condensed, and comprehensively arranged these treasures and in turn communicated them to those nations with whom their teachers or their writings ever came in contact.

Their "antique" of so recent times as to be almost our own.

Ancient history, as hitherto it has been called, is comparatively modern; it is, we may say, almost our own. Yet what we know of it we only can deduce from fragments and ruins.

Excavations near Thebes.

Recently the old sanctuary of the Kabiries, mentioned by Pausanias, was discovered near Thebes and excavated. On the spot where in Macedonian times the temple area had been extended by filling in earth and dumpings, a heap of rubbish was struck upon, which contained numerous objects of bronze, lead, and terra cotta. They were mutilated and hence had been thrown away. They now become highly appreciated as souvenirs of great value, because useful as object lessons in the study of the history of culture. In such a manner the relics of ancient handicraft, once thrown away as useless by building and destroying nations and sunk to the bottom of the river of time, become now in their most minute details elevated to the rank of documentary evidence. Thanks to them we are enabled to reconstruct phases of public and private life and forms of cultures which have perished long ago—and to read off them the signs of moral decline, perhaps, which caused the collapse of these cultures. Ours is the age of gathering up the vestiges, especially in old Greece. When properly arranged they will tell true tales carrying along with them their own interpretations.

Oriental basis of Hellenic culture.

Hellas was hemmed in, and of course influenced, too, by Phenician and Ægyptian culture. The many objects brought out of the tombs behind the lion-gate at Mykenæ, ornaments of the Assyro-Babylonian style as well as the idols made of burned clay, have once been imported there through the agencies of the Phenicians or of the Hittites. Things of the same kind have been unearthed upon the coasts of Greece as well as upon the Ægean islands, upon Rhodes, Crete, and Cyprus. The Tyrian Melkart had his altars not only in the colonies of the "Philistines" in Gades

Cult of Melcart-Heracles.

near the "pillars of Hercules," on the Guadalquivir, upon Madeira and the Canary Islands, but the cult of that Melkart had also been introduced in Greece, where he became the favorite of the nation under the name of Heracles.

Hittite culture. Von Luschau.

Von Luschau has made the Hittite antiquities accessible, enabling us at last to form a tolerable satisfactory conception of the great empire of the Keta, the chief enemies of the Pharaohs. They undoubtedly wielded a decisive influence upon Hellenic culture. The Keta

Rites transplanted from Babylon to Dodona.

transplanted old Assyrian culture upon classic soil, and together with the fashions transmitted religious rites from Babylon to Dodona.

The Greeks, rather friends than rivals of the Philistines, imitated them by dotting many parts of the Mediterranean shore with their colonies. The Ægeans were the first to take a foothold in southern Italy. After they had experimented with organising petty but vigorous

Colonies: Great Greece—Pæstum.

states in Kroton and Sybaris, they spread out into the confederacy of "Great Greece" with its center in the pillared temple at Pæstum. On the northern coast of Africa a band of Greek adventurers nestled into the crevices of the gulf of Bomba, and soon the fort of Cyrenæ became the headquarter for Hellenic culture in Africa. Sprouts of that colony took root in the interior of Libya even, took tribute from the sons of the desert, and as in recompense to such tribute checked for ever the annual raids made by the Ægyptians into these parts in order to catch slaves.

Cyrenæ in Africa stopping Ægyptian slave-hunting.

In Gaul, at the mouth of the Rhone and further up the river, the Phocæans founded staple-places of merchandise and built roads through France by which to reach the North-Sea

Trade with Britons. § 76.

and to visit the Britons. They spread over northern Italy and over Spain. Syracuse, founded by Corinthian traders, had over a million inhabitants already, when Rome in Cincinnatus' time was as yet struggling to hold its own as a mere town. This Greek Republic was then already powerful enough to enter into leagues with Hamilcar and with Xerxes. And from Syracuse, the free state when Rome as yet was ruled by mythical petty kings, Greek ideas and

Syracuse; first encounter with Punic avidity.

tastes were disseminated. Syracuse was first in defying Punic avidity, in showing Athens its independence and Rome its skill in diplomacy.

Greek daring not only bound together the people dwelling upon the Mediterranean shores, and defended their liberty, or liberated minor nations round about; but also pushed forward from Taurus the Krimean peninsula) up the Don river into Scythia and to the

Civil liberty a new phenomenon

regions of the Volga. From Kolchis upward to the Caucasian valleys the Greeks made gold-washing Scythians their subjects.

We have marked out the compass of Greek influence as far as colonial politics are concerned. In the mean time civil liberty developed in the mother-country, which to history, up to that time, is an entirely new phenomenon. This liberty grew up from the old Hellenic institutions, which were of a more religious than political nature. Slavery, however, as a measure of humanitarianism mixed with principles

aside of slavery.

of utility, seemed to Greeks, of course, not inconsistent with their idea of freedom. To uphold this liberty they simply discountenanced a centralised power of government—that very centralisation which, after Guizot, has been considered for a long time even as the acme of civilisation. The Greek idea of liberty would permit of no more consolidation of political power than the formation of confederacies by cities and, what we would call, counties. Sometimes members of such associations succeeded in establishing hegemonies whenever the circumstances demanded that a city, enjoying the greatest amount of prestige, should take the lead and the responsibility in the management of   common affairs on land and water. On other occasions communities with private interests in common would unite to form states on a small scale, with well defined constitutional rights, however, and with a regular system of taxation and a common treasury. *Centralisation of governmental power discountenanced.*

Constitutional rights of individual states in the confederacy.

§ 61. By the rational method of civic and specific organisation (appropriate to the particular quarters of each clan, and yet adjustable to an occasional confederation), the idea of liberty became realised in a degree unthought of before. It was appreciated, cultivated, watchfully guarded, and held the more precious in the measure as the arbitrary and random management of public affairs under "tyrannois" and oligarchies threatened to become a standing menace to peace and prosperity. But as to the genesis of this new form of social progress, it can be shown, how it was simply the result of thought delivering the mind from the bondage of nature. It was Eudoxus who broke the fetters by which the stars had been imagined to enchain human existence. Man and his fate were freed from planetary powers by his demonstrative reasonings. Upon Eudoxus' premises Greece did not gradually obtain freedom as such; but to begin with, it was sufficient that, man's position in the visible universe being established, a free position was also gained for him in the state, in his social rights and duties. *Scientific thought delivers the mind from its nature-bound state. Eudoxus.*

Free position of man; no longer under "planetary rule."

Ever since the Ionic school began to investigate the nature of things, the Greek mind endeavored to find, and by degrees did arrive at, the apprehension of a reason in things. That mind commences to philosophise even upon its own functions, that is, it superintends the process in which, and the conditions under which, rational concepts and logical conclusions are wrought within. It learns to discriminate between an idea and a substance. In those free commonwealths, where no monarch could make religion the means of holding masses in subjection, and shaping doctrines to suit his designs; where religion was free and a matter of personal right and sentiment, of reason and private judgment—the thinkers, reluctantly at first, began to meditate upon the intuitionally and traditionally inherited reminiscences of God-consciousness. They speculated upon the transcendental axioms, which surpass naturebound consciousness. In a thorough manner they searched the innermost mysteries of human nature or personal life, which, tho beyond space and time, are yet indelibly engraven into the mind and ever manifest themselves as realities in every human being alike. It was found that these mysteries of the inner life are realities, because, as thus early it was argued, they manifest themselves in such a manner that the very attempts of psychological anatomists to render them unreal and ridiculous proved to be selfevident. *Ionic school seeks after the reason in things.*

Beginnings of epistemology.

Attempt to analyse the mysterious functions of the mind.

The Hellenes upon their long coasting expeditions or at home in the stone castles of their Pelasgian ancestors amused themselves with trying their hand at metaphysics, that is, with construing the old traditions and intuitional reminiscences spoken of, into pleasant deities. Dev, the shining one, is translated into Dius-pater; he is imagined as identical with el, bel, helios, that is with the light-bearing, or the bright-shining god—and with the father of the bright, namely with the father of the Hellenes. Thus Zeus is before the mind; something innate to it is objectivised; it is blended with sense-impressions, and—the personification of Zeus as well as of Jupiter is complete. He is a reflection of consciousness, formed without asking epistemology for its consent. *Origin and growth of Greek mythology. § 47, 49.*

Zeus, a selfprojection of the mind.

Then Pallas, the blue sky, was made coordinate with Zeus. In the story about Apollo killing the dragon, as well as in those of giants fought and subdued, we hear the dim distant echo of that war between the light and the night which pervades the legends of Iran, and which is at the bottom of almost all the ancient stories illustrating life's conflicts, ever since the brothers Iran and Turan hated each other enough to separate. *Apollo killing the "dragon" reminiscence of the old Iranian fight between light and darkness.*

Certainly, the inadvertent, unsophisticated selfprojection of the mind in the attempt to understand itself and to explain its contents to some degree of satisfaction, was prettier and more human-like, than the objectivisations of the Bad by way of an artless excuse or a sort of selfabsolution; more worthy of the mind itself, than the method of rendering the feeling of guilt into a fear of demons, and then the very dread into a cult to pacify the demons with the devilish devices found at the bottom of Mongolian consciousness.

Be it remembered, that the Greeks on the whole never identified the symbols of these reflections with the ideas themselves. All they wanted was thus to express in some adequate manner their conviction as to the reality of their ideals. Not until thought had become materialistic, sequent to the perversion of moral sentiment into sensualism, did one part of the Hellenic nation become idolators and the other scoffers. *Symbols of deities to represent the reality of ideals.*

At those times of incipient mythology the conflicts were all taken as very real, religiously as well as politically; for religion and politics were held to be identical to such an extent that a temple was in the ancient art of warfare of the same significance which we used to ascribe to a fortified city. The worldly relations were then

Gods symbolise differentiation of world-consciousness, arrangment of relations and reflections under groups of generalisation.

not considered quite as profane and as sharply excluded from religious tenets as in later periods. What was thought and done was considered worthy of being done in real good earnest. As relations and reflections became more complicated and increased differentiations, they were attached to particular gods so as to guard these growing complications against baneful confusion. Thus the gods multiplied. Their growth in number was unavoidable, as each additional deity represented a new group of abstracted generalisations in the concrete. For under such circumstances the mind becomes ever more depressed with the necessity to preserve the unity of cogni-

Centers of cohesion: § 42, 44, 74, 75, 79. 114, 133, 171. which consciousness cannot give up without abandoning itself.

tion with the reality underlying the recognitions, which consciousness cannot abandon without giving up itself. To save itself from complete derangement the mind could take no other hold upon the principles of social existence than by classifying real things under general topics. We have agreed before that the mind needs centers of cohesion since it refuses to altogether lose itself into the distractions of the manifold.

During the time in which the composition of Greek mythology from intuitions and traditions, from folk-lore and fiction proceeded among the Pelasgians, they had become Hellenes. Further on particular clans secured more or less selfhood whereby the creative process of mythical religiousness underwent modifications adequate to the demand of the particular tribes for the recognition of their favorite gods. The old custom of each nation having its own national god caused an analysis of the imagination as to the deities so far in authority.

1. Center: Olympian Pantheon the ideal house of representatives.

Their attributes were rearranged and exchanged. Thus the court upon the Olympus, which in fact may be considered as an ideal house of representatives, increased in proportion to the splits of the nation into proud little states.

This high college of particular gods for the diverse national sections was to represent the individuality and versatility of the Greek mind as well as to foster the unity of the nation and the sacredness, objectivity and authority of social duties. It was unavoidable and can not be denied, that the Olympian pantheon assumed a polytheistical character. But this occured a

Homer and Hesiod no longer understood.

long time after Homer and Hesiod, when the deep truths and fine sentiments embodied in their quasi-system were understood no longer by a nation which suddenly, we may say, became superficial, conventional, pleasure-seeking and pain-avoiding, sensual in practice and materialistic in theory. It was only then that the gods were either taken as coarsely material or made fun of.

Under such circumstances it was but natural that the apperceptions of divine severity should be remodeled. Religion, people ever say, must be upheld. But if this upholding is

Religion popularised but lowered by materialism.

made a matter of expediency in order to retain popularity, then people say, religion must come down to the level of the intellectual capacity of the public, it must be popularised.

Hence it occurred in Greece, that æsthetics and religion became merged, and that sensualism, once made æsthetical, came to be esteemed such a substitute for religion as would "draw the masses." The higher realities, the old fashioned devoutness were thus accommodated to lower views of life, and to levity. The gods were shaped after the image of man, first of an ideal man, now of sunken men. And they were believed to have come down to the level of public opinion accordingly. Man could not help but feel a little bigger since he stood on terms

Element of the truth that fear in religion is unprofitable.

so familiar with the gods. The true element in the feeling of the Greek mind was, that fearing the gods would improve neither piety, ethics, nor æsthetics. That feeling was the more true, since nobody can love a subjective abstraction, much less fear a selfmade ideal with a few weaker spots than the maker admits of himself.

Reforms contemporaneous with Buddhism and revival of Zoroastrian cognitions. § 64.

§ 62. The Greek innovations in the line of God-consciousness transpired contemporaneously with those attempts made in India to reinstate the Vedic religion in popularity; contemporaneously also with the new applications made of Zoroaster's old Iranic tradition. It was about 600 B. C. that under Dorian influences this awakening of a profound interest in religion took place in Greece. Delphi, by silent consent,

2. Center of cohesion. Delphi, the central sanctuary:

became the center and main-stay of conservative faith. Solon's legislation, which

Solon.

brought about a beneficient reorganisation in Athens, would have been impossible, had it not been for this general movement in the religious world. As it was, not even Attica could escape the acknowledgement of the gods as ethical powers. The oscillations of this revival continued to the time when Ægyptian influences where allowed to creep into the Greek combination of ideas.

Herodot.

Some sophists blamed Herodot for thus aiding the corruption of Greek mythology. But from all indications we are inclined to think that the ethical tendency continued to prevail over a stiff allegiance to particular gods until Hesiod was calumniated for composing

his physico-philosophical poetry. He was accused of intentionally having made the Greeks Hesiod's views put to
ridicule.
believe that the gods were corporeal persons.　Such raw opinions of their own the dema-
gogues of that time imputed to Hesiod's "theogony", in order to decry theosophy as a set of
old superstitions.　The sincerity of ancestral piety once undermined by such misrepresenta-
tions, it was an easy matter for moralising materialists as Protagoras and Heracleitos to boast Undermining religion.
§ 66.
of having sought the god in vain, despite the proper experimenting and anatomising,　so
that finally they could glory in the overthrow of the puppets of their own invention.

True as it is that Hesiod's political and parabolic religion was a harmonistic and subjectivistic playing with the gods, equally true is it that the popular apperceptions of the gods,
the intelligent as well as the vulgar mind-presentations of the divine, were not disturbed
thereby.　It was only after misconstrued conceptions of those "centers of cohesion" were
made the themes of plays and songs, that scepticism and licentiousness missed no chance to
treat everything sacred with contemptuous sneers.

Like forest trees in their primitive home, had the god-ideals prospered in ancestral times.　It was a pleasure to be religious in idyllic life.　A poetical contentment
could be drawn from the ideals when the sky above was serene, and when certain
inner longings of each could be gratified just as it suited him.　Thus Hesiod had
succeeded in deepening the interest of the Hellenes in their world of deities.　With
the help of foreign and native legends he had generalised and internally connected
the ideals so as to represent truths by intelligible personifications.　This is to be un- Merits of his
"Theogony."
derstood by "the theogony" of Hesiod.　It was a profound exegesis of ethical ideals;
and their harmonising with intuitional and traditional facts and truths in forms of
human analogies, was certainly the most appropriate method of presenting them.
Viewed from this standpoint the writings of the thinkers in the earlier times designate an improvement, which to a large extent the Greeks owed to Hesiod.

As a most remarkable circumstance—the other coincident of Greek with Asiatic Epochal cycle of
600 B. C.
life may be emphasised, that this elevation of the gods from mere emblems of the § 57, 76, 124, 127, 133,
145.
phases of nature to personifications of ethical concepts caused a decided advance along
the whole line of Greek life.　For concerning religious thought as well as secular
events Asia was deeply affected by a similar and simultaneous epochal commotion,
indicated by the names of Daniel, Gautama, Nebucadnezar, Cyrus, etc.

Herodot said, that "Hesiod as much as Homer prompted the Greeks by the theogony
of their personified gods to respect their dignity and to appreciate THEIR SERVICES."　This
by the way, is all that Herodot meant, instead of having said, as he is often quoted, that
those old sages had created the Gods.

Speaking of Hesiod, we beg leave to bring out a feature of his teachings, which has not Farming especi-
ally honorable.
received the appreciation it deserves.　We refer to his wisdom in praising labor as honorable, § 136, 139, 222.
especially field labor—which has ever been a cardinal point of merit with the Aryans in
general.

Hesiod thus addresses his brother: "Without sweat, O Perses, no quality, no distinction is Hesiod's
to be obtained.　Work is pleasing to the gods, and none needs be ashamed of it.　Only honest "Works and days."
gain secures prosperity."

In the "Days and Works" of Hesiod the idea is put forth everywhere that "it is by will "Order" of labor
of the gods that seasons were so arranged, as to have a special time assigned for each kind of conditioning blessings.
labor and to bless each in this order."

Cheiron, seated in his grotto on mount Pelion, instructed Achilles from a work which is
lost, in wise deeds and proper service, upon a basis of similar maxims. The German Middle-age
seems to have understood what the Greeks had hinted at.　The Germans praised them for
principles combining "service with nobility" (noblesse oblige), and incorporated those sentiments in their "Ritter spiegel" i. e., in the rules of chivalry.

Another merit is due to the Greek mind.　We admire its progress of inner assimi- Merits of
Greek thought:
lation.　At first, the many Gods were taken as concrete entities, really subsisting in
the world, altho described as transcendental powers.　Subsequently they were transformed into idealities but anthropomorphised, so as to render their immanency in the
world real and conceivable.　We may well accredit to the Greek mind not only the It retains Hindoo
transcen-
　　　dentalism
but combines it
with realistic
immanency.
preservation of the true element in Hindoo-transcendentalism, but also their combin-
ing this idealism with that true realism which the Hindoos had sacrificed.　Avoiding
this error the Greeks rescued personality from being dissolved into natural generalness or pantheistical all-the-sameness.

§ 63.　The gods were conceived as immanent in the world, real and alive.　The What Greek art reveals:
serenity of the Greek consciousness, expressing itself in the unique and august Divine immanency in
nature.
creations of art, was the result of this habit of thinking.　This serenity consists in
the complete satisfaction which nature affords to all reasonable desires in proportion

13

to the measure limiting each. It is in this sphere that calm contentment is enjoyed, where, in the assurance of reaching or having reached its moderate goal, ambition comes to rest. Hence passion has no right to disturb the composure. There is no room for envy; there must not be the fidgetiness of a weak cause or a bad conscience. It is the harmoniousness of life at which Greek culture aims, the beauty of a character which we try to present to our cognition under the very appropriate term equanimity.

Search after equanimity. § 37, 42, 43.

The Greek, the educated Greek knows of guilt only from what he has seen in the drama; of a personal guilt of his own, he seems to be as entirely ignorant as if he ere perfectly innocent. He only thinks of an evil coming to him from without, of a misfortune into which the foot becomes entangled. A trait of the Persian temper is noticeable therein. The cultivation of fearlessness was to counteract that habitual anguish which had become master of the Mongolian. This artificial deportment, as if free from guilt, was a symptom of the intuitive certainty that man consists of two natures and that the bad as such does not belong to the human being. Neither was there much bad in the gods. Hence a culture of the mind was held possible, which would bring all desires and appetites under its control. To avoid the evil, nothing else was deemed necessary but harmony of the soul, harmonious cooperation of the faculties, and their proper exercise for their mutual improvement. **Wisdom in adjusting conduct to circumstances was the acme of the Greek ethics.**

Artificial appeasement of guilt:

Persian trait in Greek character.

Dual nature of man, wherein the bad is not an essential constituent element.

Wisdom in adjusting conduct to circumstances is the gist of Greek ethics.

Of course the bad and the drama, or rather tragedy, is not abated withal the drapery; only that the Greek reduces either of them to fate or accident. It is admitted that the Bad, silently and darkly hovers about persons and things, but inner composure and guilelessness need not be disturbed thereby, because the passions of an insulted deity dare not enter, nor can they agitate, the realm of fate; because fate itself holds the scales which balance and adjust all things, the gods included; hence nobody needs be afraid even of fate. The inner composure, the calmness of mind thus gained is shown in the single-heartedness of purpose, in the simplicity of recitations and all artistic representations. All exciting elements are mitigated or palliated whenever they break forth to baffle the rules of æsthetics. It is for such reasons that the group of Laocoon and his sons is so enigmatical to critics—because it does not comply with the maxim under discussion. To Greek thought and refinement it was offensive to provoke passion by teasing, or envy by exaggeration; it was frowned down as vulgar to nourish excitability by sensational alarmings, by officiousness, obtrusiveness, or by sensual allurements. Harmony and its cultivation in mind, in deportment, and in the social relations was deemed worthy of being religiously observed.

Unconcern as to the bad, lest equanimity be disturbed.

Fate holds the scales, is therefore not to be feared.

Laokoon an exceptional specimen of Greek art.

Hellenic selfpossession, complacency, and calmness, is the art of the mind to appear without evil design and without harboring suspicion against another. This may be understood more precisely and appreciated the better, by comparing its artistic representations with those of the Romantic art.

In the Romantic school of art existence and destiny are kept separate; the attention is directed to life's imperfections. The soul's expressions must be painted in colors of sadness, and must call forth a sigh of dismay from the beholder ere a piece of art can find approval. Look at the contrast between Greek taste and the ostentatious sanctimoniousness, the artful hiding and even chiding of reality, the affected unnaturalness, and the studied, stiff posture for the sake of appearing perfectly indifferent, as exhibited in the Roman style of the Middleages. It reminds me of a photographic picture of herself, which a pious old maiden had presented to one of my friends. It represented her in the attitude of fervent prayer, kneeling and eyes closed. Now compare such hypocrisy with the tasteful and chaste, the amiable and yet dignified naturalness of early Greece. Its refreshing efficiency has outlasted thousands of years down to the time of the renaissance in which the study of its mere vestiges was sufficient to cause the revival of letters and arts.

Comparison between Hellenistic and Romantic art. § 180.

Artful unnaturalness, against

unaffected single-heartedness, harmonious union of spirit and nature in real life.

Greek art is unsophisticated, because unconscious of a difference between actual existence and the dissembling tendency to deny realism. It exhibits as a matter of course both real existence and a natural tendency toward perfection as being immanent in, and reconciled to, one another. This is the secret of the artistic representations of Greece : unaffected simplicity, and **harmonious union of spirit and nature in real life, whereby the problem of destiny is solved through immanency of joy, purity, and peace.**

Real existence and final destiny conciliated. § 64, 91, 123, 139, 147, 152, 158.

The situation of the country greatly favored the development of these Greek characteristics. Every island, every change of scenery, made a pleasing impression, had a soothing effect. Everything concerning his native land, so congenial to his own nature, was conducive to his satisfaction and contentment. And the Greek made it his principal study, to establish unison between himself and his surroundings. His ethics aimed simply at the adjustment of the inner to external life. This ethics was at the same time his applicable religion and any form of application must be æsthetical. The terrors of the Asiatic deserts were things of the

Geographical influences upon the temperament of the nation.

past; altho not so entirely forgotten, as that present security would not be the better appreciated. The wild hordes of the steppes could no longer disturb the enjoyment of the beautiful moment. The Greeks thought it the main symptom of foolishness to borrow trouble from the future. Under a laughing sky harmless hilarity became habitual. By art a tangible gospel of earthly happiness was proclaimed which was as easily understood, as the examples through which children are susceptible to educational influence. An unconscious selfdelusion concealed from them the strange things in the world and its shrill discords. Upon the richly colored surface and under the the appearance of happiness a national temperament took shape, which, easy going and unpretentious, found satisfaction in things as they are, or at least persuaded itself to make the best of them.

§ 64. Considering the trend of mind peculiar to the Greeks the deity could scarcely be expected to be revered as a supernatural mystery. It became a habit with them to ignore and forget unpleasant reminiscences; thus they imagined themselves on such intimate terms with the gods as to persuade themselves that they had condescended to hold intercourse with mankind. The divine beings were conceived as having accommodated themselves to ways and manners quite human, as having assumed historic reality, and as promoting men of merit who had been active in the cause of general welfare, to divine dignity and honors. The human form is, of course, best adapted for this highest manifestation of the divine; humanity had become gloriously divine by these changes in mundane conditions. The cultural hulls of Semito-Hamitic growth, once conveying the beginnings of cultural transformation and elevation into the islands, had thus become refuse. For an art based upon the aesthetics of Ægypt and Babylon the Greeks had no further use.

Overbeck in his "History of Greek plastic art" testifies to this independence and originality of the Greeks as against Semites who had become a barrier of obstruction in their intercourse with, and of more complete separation from, the Eastern Aryans. Ægyptian art had taken its start in the architecture of huge dead-chambers. It fastens to the column even the human form stiff and dead; for, from its own knowledge Ægypt knew nothing of a free standpoint. Its flat and geometrical uniformity was rejected by Greece immediately and exchanged for a free and upright body with active organic members, of which not even the Ægyptian paintings reveal any idea. In this as in almost any other respect Greece excels Ægypt as an organism surpasses a mechanism.

This soon enabled the Greeks to render their ideal of beauty divine and human into the most adequate and perfect shape possible in statues of marble. In an equally befitting manner is the immanency of the divine in the natural sphere exhibited and fostered by Greek architecture. Majestic simplicity seems to have been intended to make the ideal feel itself at home in this world of ours. Even the cognition of the formal unity, which we attribute to the spiritual sphere of being, is inadvertently, perhaps, but unmistakably expressed by the similitude of the temples as they stand surrounded by the diversity of earthly forms. They are always situated in solemn and serene localities, in the midst of scenery which impresses the mind with its solitude and silence.

There, indeed, the ideal is made to feel itself at home under the charm, of properly toned and composed colors as well as musical airs, so as to enchant the mind with the corresponding apperceptions of consonancy and conciliation. Every detail is calculated to form a totality impressing the mind with feeling and immediate understanding of the fact, that human existence and human destiny are not only not rent asunder, but inherent in, and prearranged for, each other.

The reports of the German Archeological Institute of Athens show, how ingeniously the Greeks handled their art in giving expression to a gleeful enjoyment of earthly happiness, as illustrated in the tints of those paintings which decorated the Acropolis, dating back to the epochal century spoken of. They are painted in deep and pure, yet chaste and sombre shades, and pertain to the pre-Persian style of drapery.

Hellenic art exhibits the harmony between real existence and ideal destiny, the immanency of the deity in nature and in man, nature's prototype. No infinite extension of space, no craving for a misty distance can rob the Greek of his contentment with the present which alone he considers his own. No infinite duration of the time in which gods may have existed or may not, embarrasses him so as to bother himself about a past or a future limiting his existence. No brooding about the emptiness before the beginning, or the void after the end, shall cheat him out of the enjoyment of the moment or the improvement of the opportunities at hand. In short, his world-theory culminates in a gospel of nature; the sum and substance of his cultus is the harmonious consistency of natural life with the fates of final humanity.

Margin notes:

Gospel of earthly happiness.
§ 64, 152.

Educational influence of plastic object-lessons.

Greek as against Ægyptian sculpture. Overbeck.   § 87.

Greek art in contrast to that of Ægypt and India.

Conception of the Divine by the Greek mind—if unsophisticated—under the aspect of the purely Human.

Harmony and glory. Heroes-demigods.   § 67.

Temple architecture breathes august simplicity and "formal unity."

Tones and colors.

Conciliation of real existence with human destiny, which Hindooism could not find.
§ (58, end) (62, end) 63, 91, 123, 147, 153, 158.

Condescension of the Deity alone elevates man.

Paintings from the acropolis 6th century B. C.   § 61.

Realism of Greek art represents the world-theory which culminates in the Gospel of nature.   § 152.

Hellenistic aesthetics as compared with Hindoo tastes.

Against nonsensical monstrosities, symbolising agonies under an incubus.

Greeks make the symmetrical development of mental and corporeal excellencies of man their study,

they nevertheless did not learn to understand the human head.   § 87.

Criticism of Greek art: Ruskin, Thausing.

The great deficiency of Greek culture:

permanent smile of sculptured faces.

Greeks not quite as natural as they affected to be.

Inwardness of the Greek mind scrutinised:

Moralism disparages religion.

Scepticism the fashion since the short "golden age" of Pericles.

Popular and unpopular teachers.

Misunderstood symbolism is given the place of religion, in order to caricature religion.

Mythology only remembers golden times in the past, has no hope for the future, no prophecy.

The esoterics of the mysteries. Pindar.

Even the gods are not held to be eternal, since they are conceived as being too intimately involved in the affairs of this world as to be apprehended in the abstract.

The oldest works of Hellenic art of which we know are the two tympanums or gable-frontispieces from the temple of Hercules found A. D. 1885 in the Acropolis. The time of their origin is computed to fall in with the period of Draco and Solon. They represent Hercules fighting the many headed hydra. This work indicates that the struggle with the monstrosities of oriental tastes had then not been overcome as yet. In contrast with the attempts to picture the impossible—that is, with the intricacies and colossal abnormities of Hindoo art, the Hellenes aspire to cultivate a symmetrical development of the mental and corporeal excellencies of the human person. For the sake of this idealistic realism every allusion to stupefying magnitudes was rejected in the political as well as in the artistic formations. The code of arts prescribed definiteness, that is, a thought must be rendered completely intelligible at first sight. And in this ability to understand and to represent the realities around itself the Greek mind took pride. This means a great deal.

But one exception is to be taken.

The Hellenes understood those parts of man which pertain to his lower, physical nature: the finely shaped and well-knitted body in its free mobility; the head of man they did not understand. Herein lies what Ruskin finds fault with, too: that in representing psychical life they did not succeed. Artistic representations of emotions as expressed in the human face, the art of delineating particular traits of individuality,—so Thausing judges when speaking of Duerer's school of art—remained "insignificant and nugatory as yet, the stereotyped smile notwithstanding."

This absence of marks of character denoting the various temperaments or moods of the mind, and the way of hiding the deficiency by this permanent smile of feigned superiority, shows the habit of the Greeks to help themselves with levity over difficulties by ignoring them as far beneath their recognition. These facts become significant when the inner nature of the Greek mind comes to be scrutinised. Then we detect that the Hellenes were not quite as unsophisticated as they simulated, after all. The naivete of their later years was studied; much of their hilarity affected. Prone to superficialness, if not to say frivolous shallowness in viewing life, they could not solve its grave problems. Theoretically the difficulties may be ignored for a time, as it is natural to boyhood; whilst as facts they are stubborn and will test the assiduity and perseverance of mature age. Mirthful Greece neither stood this test, nor could it evade the settlement of the unliquidated damages, which had resulted from undervaluing the vicissitudes of life. And when finally the account had to be squared, it happened under such appalling concurrencies, that in the three or four similar disasters mentioned in history the nexus between profligacy and collapse was not brought out more flagrantly than in the destruction of Corinth, simultaneously with that of Carthage.

§ 65. Greek art had caused religion to be disparaged by moralism. By degrees morality was rendered into something which was mistaken for being able to stand upon its own dignity, because of having its value in itself; as something useful, if expedient. In corresponding degrees the imaginary apperceptions of concrete gods were left to the uneducated masses, who could not understand the Elysian and other "mysteries". They were not initiated, they were profane. After the golden age of Pericles scepticism was fashionable among those who wanted to be considered as "liberally educated". To an Athenian nothing was sacred any longer.

Socrates stood forth in his solitary grandeur, stared at as an odd, ugly fellow, with all his "genius". Solitary stands Plato with his "idea," now exile and slave, now aristocrat. Aristotle, however, is popular. If one wanted to be counted with the intelligent class, it was necessary to agree with Aristotle. Aristotle was authority. The secret of his popularity was that he left the invisible world alone, saying it was unknowable and need not be cared for. Still more popular became Aristophanes despite his merciless satires, through which he cut the world of the clouds into pieces, making comedies of the cuttings.

One element of the mystic games must not be left unnoticed. Looking backward the Hellenes mused and versified that Kronos, lord of THE WORLD IN ITS GOLDEN TIME, and father of Zeus, had ruled upon the islands of Okeanos over a world of peace and bliss. Altho his son had liberated the chained Titanes, he had become reconciled to Zeus. The tormenting powers have their sway, but—allowances are to be made for that.

Pindar praises the realms of bliss; but they lie FAR AWAY IN THE DISTANT PAST. Of prophesics of a blessed future neither the ancient nations so far reviewed, nor the classic nations had any idea. To some select people only, to such as were "in it", as the proletarians have it in their vernacular, to such, who as the "respectable" people were accepted into the secret societies of the "mysteries",—some sort of a glance into a peaceful future was granted.

So Pindar sings: "Blessed is he, who has had a vision of them before his descent into the hollows of the earth. He knows the end of life and the god-given beginning." The truth is that there must be a knowledge equal to the life eternal; but this means a state of consciousness above mere reflection and more than visionary. We hear the old mistake that to know is all that is required for blessedness, as if ignorance were not bliss.

The Elysian mysteries were accompanied by the annual festivities, celebrating the return of Persephone, Demeter's daughter, from the realms of the shadows to the upper world. In them a palingenesy of some elect men at least was promised. But it was a resurrection in secrecy, for the knowning ones alone.

The Pagan festivities never show the character of any historical commemoration, but are always celebrating natural phenomena, and represent the deification of the various phases of nature. *Pagan festivals celebrate natural changes, not historic memorials.*

Some one may remind us of the Orphic games. But what was really going on therein was withheld from the public. The Orphic games served only as embellishments to and advertisements of the Bacchanal orgies. Under a set of liturgical rites the steer of Dionysius was torn to pieces and its raw meat eaten at the sacrificial meal. Never would a participant henceforth even touch another meal made of anything which had been alive. Like the Ægyptian ascetics they would strut about in their white linen, without being of any benefit whatever to society. Why, then, should anyone care for their mysteries? It may here be pointed out, that those ceremonials were the opposite of philosophical symbolism. Virtually all those games were no more than conservatories of the occult remnants of Shamanism, bubbling and gurgling up from the dark substratum.

We have now on the one hand that Pantheism again which invites suppression, with the only difference that here in Greece the pressure comes from below. What causes political dissatisfaction and the harangue against moral restrictions, is at bottom the unpopularity of the logic of Pantheism. Teachers and restrictive authorities are treated as old fogies and ridiculed as a disgrace to illumined times. We have the precedent and pretense of a science being advanced too far to retain any religious faith. On the other hand we have two kinds of superstition: the adherents of a more subtile superstition join the mysteries of the select few, whilst the humble classes believe in the reality of the nature-gods. Circumstances like these furnished the opportunity to the sophists of Greece to accomplish the same work which in France the Cyclopedists performed a hundred years ago. Intoxicated by the plausibilities of platitudinarianism, that is by the foam-like thought produced with the aid of fiery stimulants, sceptics turn demagogues. The molds of common weal or public welfare, the modes of thinking, are burst; and the destruction of the social fabric must follow. *Intellectualism in lieu of religion; "philosophy" in the hire of superstition. § 11, 15, 22, 23, 24, 46, 47, 57, 58, 66, 68, 72, 73, 81, 85, 89, 96, 97, 98, 170, 185.* *Parallel; French infidelity of the 18th century.*

§ 66. The history of Greece furnishes an ample illustration of the genesis and growth of infidelity. The first stage is a simulated indifference to piety with the smile of superiority over the poor dupes. As yet however respect for religious convictions is dissembled in order to secure toleration of free thought. As a next step tolerance is insisted upon, not only in the interest of free thought but for the ridicule of religion. At the expense of sacred truths they are made responsible for the fault of hierarchical formations or religious misapprehensions, and occasions are watched to put religion as such to hatred and contempt by enlarging upon its caricatures. Finally the plea of tolerance changes into the fanaticism of infidelity which finds an easy prey in a hated and defamed victim like Socrates. The tendency comes to the surface which began with modifying the formulated religious tenets, and then made the demand of their abolition a pretense for the overthrow of the institutions protecting them. *Genesis and growth of infidelity; Feigned indifference. Plea for tolerance, not for free thought but for ridicule of religion. Scoffing at religious misapprehensions and deformations. Fanatical intolerance defames men like Socrates and then demands the abolition of their hatred.*

It then appears that all the efforts of enlightenment had but the one aim: not so much to shield the hatred against tottering and antiquated doctrines and deformations, but to accomplish the "emancipation of the flesh." Nothing else had been the object of purging the nation of its religious faith. *Surreptitious workings of scepticism: Modification and then abolition of dogmas, Overthrow of the institutions protecting them.   § 57, 62.*

Under guise of investigating problems of moral philosophy libertinism agitates revenge for the repression sustained so long, for the restraint of the lusts which the old fashioned teachings used to enjoin. Moral criteria are undermined in the first place, until "public opinion" sneers at their regulative rulers, and soon sets them aside. By this method the re-ligio-ethical cash is thrown into the crucible of demagogical analysis in order to be dissolved, adulterated, and coined over. By virtue of the new ingredients of a scepticism which is no less dogmatical and even more tyrannical, all moral maxims decompose. A Socrates foresaw the coming disaster as the necessary result of perverting the idea of personality into the arbitrariness of subjectivism. As a mere natural result it always turns out, that disregard of moral authority throws a nation into the agonies of despotic anarchy and terrorism. *Scepticism no less dogmatical but more tyrannical than hierarchical demagoguery.*

Parallel:
Socrates' and Kant's
time.

Socrates endeavored to counteract the wanton spirit of the time by the recon-struction of a moral standard upon the basis of a deeper consciousness. By way of argumentation he attempted the same reform which a hundred years ago was under-taken by Kant with pure reason.

But see what arguing and proving the existence of God, for instance, will accomplish. It will cause the masses to listen to sophists, onologists and demagogues. The struggle be-tween wary conservatism and conspiring radicalism generally assumes the title of scientific progressiveness. At the next stage we hear intentional scepticism giving out the parole : We can't believe this and that, until in the end materialism and mental laziness shield infi-delity under the foregone conclusion: We can't know this! Thus faith and science are severed. By silent consent   leading minds aim at the detachment of religion from its institutions, and the masses catch on to the idea that morality stands independent of religion, declaring the latter superfluous. Henceforth the masses hold intelligence and religion identical, and take psychical and spiritual matters for the same thing. And since mental superiority will always take the lead and religious intelligence is ever antagonistic to vulgarity, the masses, unable to distinguish between a hieratic and an aristocratic state, will take all that is above them as being connected with rule and oppression. Pantheism indeed always being such, ren-ders religion and its externals the more unpopular. Whenever religion is diluted into in-tellectualism, then both are suspected as means of deceiving the uneducated and as cheating them of their liberties. Hence all that excels common generalness becomes opprobrious; all that is surmised as coming from above is to be leveled to the grade of popularity, if not vulgarity. Nothing must tend upwards, least of all a church-steeple. Society severs; class-hatred animates the majority.

Religion
identified with
intellectual
culture, both
hated as means
of oppression.
§ 11, 15, 56, 58, 65,
72, 87, 96, 98, 170,
185.

Plato on Ægyptian and
Greek peculiarities.

Plato, the aristocrat, speaking of the state, remarked that the Ægyptians and Phenicians were to be credited with their mercenary, the Greeks to be congratulated for their inquisitive, trend of mind. He defined the difference of character as dis-tinctly in sense as terse in the sentence : "The occidental mind is bent upon search-ing and intellectually assimilating the real world." The Greeks have furnished that mind with the instrument best adapted for its task, namely their language, "the word." The Hellenes also spared the occidental mind the relapse into oriental phan-tasms and gloom, inasmuch as they saved it from the indescribable abstruseness of the Hindoo brain and its products.

What Europe owes to
Greece.

But what is still more, the Hellenes rescued the history of human affairs in gen-eral from being pressed into the oriental mold. On the memorable line from the Bosporus, recently yoked at Byzantium, across Marathon and Salamis and passing over to Syracuse, the Hellenes broke the tools of enslavement which were in the hands of the Persians and Punians, leagued for the purpose of subjugating Europe.

The day of
Salamis and
Himera.
Hamito-Semetic assaults
beaten off.
§ 71, 98, 132, 137, 142.

It was on the day of Salamis that the Hamito-Semitic assault was repelled; the day on which Xerxes was forced to beat a hasty retreat with the fragments of his innumerable hosts of Semites. And it was on the very same day that the Punians were vanquished at Himera. The combined onslaughts being thus beaten off, Europe was preserved to remain as the place of refuge, where the mind   might develop in freedom.

Greece under a different
aspect.

§ 67. Let us look down, however, from this altitude of Greek attainments in order to observe also what was going on in this nation beside the liberation of person-ality and below the free development of the intellect.

The crop raised from
certain wild seeds.

Besides the remnants of spiritual gifts and sacred keep-sakes of original relig-ious tradition there, as everywhere else, lay dormant those seeds of perverted God-consciousness, whose broken rays ever refract even from the occult depths of the lowest layer of culture.

In the period of epic poetry already Hellenic heroism had flourished, because great enterprises were then carried out. Undaunted mariners had made discoveries, had forced landings, and formed colonies. Like the Normans in later times they took cities and brought home booty. The legendary remembrance of the daring sea-kings, like Jason, was stored up in folk-lore as equal to the fame of the Trojan warriors. In the uneventful home-circle gossip made them heroes, favorites of the gods, demigods. Achilles was taken for the son of Thetis; the Atrides, for children of Zeus. Real men they were, Greeks at that, in behalf of whom the deities were wrought into a mytho-logical system. With the personified symbols of natural phenomena and national notions (which the deities were in the first place), those pets of the people were asso-ciated and finally idolised as real gods.

From folk-lore to
idolatry.

Pelasgian beginnings
of mythology—
ancestral reminiscences.
§ 61.

The zeal for glorifying veteran patriots was not prompted by pride alone. Another circumstance favored the growth of myths. For the more ancestors some Hellenic tribes counted in their lineage, the more susceptible were the descendants to oriental propensities. The colonists in Asia minor especially intercommunicated such influences for which the old nobility at home possessed so much predilection, and with whom old remembrances and affinities were the easier revived, the further back they would trace their pedigree. "Blood will tell" says Thackeray.

Hero-worship: demi-gods. § 64.

Repristination of oriental ideas, despite the repulsion of oriental armies. § 78, 81, 97, 123, 146, 149, 185.

Alexander's expedition was not intercepted from thirst of revenge, nor for the purpose of diverting attention from civil rivalries and contentions; not so much for the sake of conquest as for the satisfaction of curiosity. The trip to the oasis of Ammon, that sanctuary most renowned for its antiquity, ended with the title of divinity being conferred upon the Hellenised Macedonian. Lysander was honored by the cousins of the old world with altars dedicated to him. Phillip of Macedonia was received with divine honors at Amphipolis, whilst his illustrious son, young as he was, was made a god in his lifetime like a native king. To Eumenes, his successor, sacrifices were brought at Pergamon. Immediately after Alexander's time Greek art plainly shows the importation of corrupt motives from the old country. And with this change another is closely connected. O. Rossbach points to the fact, that the art of this epoch shows a great fondness for making the abject homage paid to rulers its chief theme and study. It was art with an eye to profit, which began to flatter the vanity of the men in power and their subjects. Among their satellites and sycophants the kings appear upon the paintings "made conspicuous by the use of the most costly material."

Old nobility preserving old traditions. THACKERAY. § 73,78,137.

Corrupting principles imported. § 20, 62, 78, 81, 97, 122, 123, 146, 147, 150, 185.

Phillip, Alexander and Eumenes allow their own deification. *Prostitution of art.*

Sycophancy. ROSSBACH. § 76, 125, 126, 137, 139, 150.

What of foreign culture is imported by a nation as yet laboring to acquire a definite character of its own usually amounts to a spreading of the poison from the corpses of decomposing nations who died of hyper-culture. Robust and ill-advised parvenues are eager to imitate artistic refinement, that which has caused general discussion, and to introduce outlandish notions and luxuries under the label of higher education and advanced views. And in proportion to this infection a decadence of heroism and patriotism, of virtuosity and morality is always to be deplored.

Fondness for outlandish thoughts and tastes.

Poison of decomposing cultures. § 20.

Retrogression of heroism and patriotism.

So it was in Greece which took to the Assyro-Syriac poison; so in Rome imitating the fashions of Corinth; so with the courts of Europe, when they became the lickspittles of Paris or of the pontiff's slipper.

§ 68. Athens, permitting the old virtues to be ridiculed, took the leading part in shaking the pillars of Hellenic strength and fame. The Attic sneers signalised the end of Greece.

With the same unconcern which marked his "modern" æsthetics, the Greek turned his attention away from ethical problems, lest they might annoy or perplex him. Who would listen to such morose old croakers as Diogenes or Democritos? Who cared for the opera of Æschylos or Sophocles with their exposure of guilt? The acknowledgement of guilt would have forced upon a Greek the recognition of sin, which recognition,—æsthetics taught,—was to be abhorred. It certainly was not shirked because of delicacy, but because courage was lacking to face sin, to hate it, and to fight it. With the same self-complacency and supreme indifference in which the later Greeks chided the memory of Æschylos and Sophocles, the Greek would look over his shoulders at a fellow-man from an adjacent district. To him a stranger was simply a barbarian; towards a foreigner he did not feel himself under any moral obligation whatever. Concerning humane feelings the Greek was no more cordial at home than in his behavior toward a member of another clan.

Disregard for ethics in theory and in the opera.

Disregard for human rights in others. Barbarians.

"The mutual relations of the Greek states or tribes—Hermann observes—rested upon the idea that a man had no rights outside of his native place. This is reason enough for a condition of constant belligerency of every one against all." Hence it was not necessary in Greece to go very far in order to be treated as a foreigner. If a stranger took his abode anywhere he was put upon his good behavior, he was to feel that he was merely tolerated. If he contracted the displeasure of any native he found himself an outlaw. This was an explicit doctrine of Aristotle even. The duties toward a barbarian, if there were any to be observed, were simply classified with those to animals.

Aristotle on rights of strangers. HERMANN.

The same was the case with the domestics, the slaves. It is in the nature of husbandry that they be made use of; inasmuch as there are tools required, inanimate or living, and a tool is the property of him who uses it, and as human service necessarily belongs to a complete outfit, such human tools are, therefore, the property of the master of the manor.

No human sympathy. § 55, 58, 72.

Hence with all the analytical theorising about the nature of things, and about the personality, liberty and divine dignity of a Greek, pantheism had invested the state with power as absolute over the individual citizens, as the master wielded over his slave. **The recognition of personality had not as yet been extended to the cognition of humanity.**

"There is something
holy over which the
state has no power."
Antigone. Sophocles
In the tragedies of Sophocles Greece surpassed itself, not only as regards its gods and its fate; but by virtue of these tragedies Greece became impressed with a kind of premonition. It had a foreboding of a collapse of its own social fabric. Sophocles makes Antigone utter the bold declaration, that "there is something holy over which the state can exercise no power!"

Other protests against
the absorption of
individual rights by
the state.
Socrates, Euripides,
Protagoras, Cynics.
The meritorious attempts of Socrates and Euripides to defend individual rights are not to be depreciated. The part which the Greeks took in the improvement of the race in general, secures their due recognition forever. Even the Cynics in their quaint way assisted in solving the problem of exempting the individual from the capricious "reasons of state". A few others, like Protagoras who was banished for those very reasons of state, stood by the maxim that "man is the measure of all things". But, after all, these protestants stood alone, comparatively speaking. In the state of Plato individual rights are not as much as alluded to with one single word. In all pagan nations it was taken for granted that man existed for the sake of the state. The state was held to be the center of cohesion in which the indigent idea of human unity found an approximate realisation. **The state was even deemed to be the Supreme Good.**

Inhumaneness of
Plato.

Communistic practices:
Family-life not recog-
nised as the hearth-
stone of state.
(§ 71. Romans)
The state disposes even of the children. Before they have outgrown their tender age, they are to be delivered at the public institutions for being drilled into citizenship. Provision is made to avert their acquaintance with their parents even. Their future occupation is prescribed by law. Individual property is prohibited; even the females are possessed in common.

Children to be given up
to the state.
So much for concentrated power of state, of communism in force. With nature-bound humanity the center of gravity lies always in the direction of material unity and generalness under formal diversity.

Wrong measures to
secure moral progress.
In matters of ethical elevation nothing can nor should be ever expected of any state, much less of the political wisdom of the people in classic times. It proves always a serious blunder in national economy to think, that, with the increase of political weight, or with the growth of the wealth of a nation, or with æsthetical refinement and advance in the arts, or with the increasing number of law students, the progress of morality were paramount, and distribution of happiness in equal measure would go hand in hand. Far from it. Ethics, and the commensurate spread of prosperity rising from or falling with, it lies in the sphere of "essential unity under personal diversity".

Ethics and prosperity
lie in the sphere of
"essential unity under
personal diversity."
§ 8, 113, 159.
Culture in
Homer's time
compared with that of
the
The happy times of Greece were those of Homer, when republican simplicity and frugality had not yet been corrupted by putting on external distinctions, by luxury and its attendants: snobbishness, envy, sensualism, and effeminacy. In those times chaste manners took first honors as illustrated by a Telemachos and a Nausikaa.

Periclean age:
external prime;
internal rottenness.
Compare now the age of happiness and heroism with the Periclean period and its very transient glory. What had become of the moral condition of Athens despite its refinement, wisdom and wealth? Of the domestic contentment and comfort and virtue of Telemachos' time scarcely a trace is left. In a repulsive manner slavery and "hetairism" defile the ideal beauty as exhibited by the circle of Pericles' companions. Vice is cloaked by graceful drapery, vice of the most unnatural sorts. Connubial relations, the hearth-stone of the state and keystone of morality, are more than undermined. The main-stays of the state-edifice are rapidly decaying with dry rot from basement to pinnacle. Polybios, surviewing the general situation exclaims: "Not even those of the Greeks who have been entrusted with the management of the affairs of state are able to remain honest; and no more than one talent may be entrusted to them, even if put under the caution of ten countersignatures, of as many seals, and twice as many witnesses."

Judgment of this
period. Polybios.

Venality of magistrates;
corruptibility of judges.
Extravagance, lasciviousness and indolence explain the venality of magistrates, and the corruptibility of judges, always the first and surest omen of either despotism or the downfall of a state, generally of both. And are not always the lower classes, instead of being upbraided for the degeneracy, rather to be excused for imitating the example of "the better classes"? With ethics vanishing, the æsthetics turn to vulgarity.

Good taste changed to
uttermost ugliness.
The swiftness of the transition, of the change of good tastes into uttermost ugliness is illustrated by the phylakes painted upon the common pottery, and upon the costly vases of Great Greece as well. Nothing can surpass the obscenity of these pictures; no figure of speech would answer in describing the impudency and utter abandonment revealed in the drawings of these buffoons with their phalloses. One stands amazed at the sight and understands Mommsen's judgment upon the low, crafty 'groggery business combined with the most shameless brotheldom of Athens."

§ 69. Greece has received full credit at the hands of   historians for the high es- Greece's fast course downward. Noskkxx. teem in which the dignity of man was held, and to what high degree human beauty was valued; and for the fact that the thought of freedom had first dawned in Greece. Merits of Hellenism. Justly are the Hellenes praised for being one of the most illustrious nations, far above comparison with the hapless masses under Indian and Persian despotism.

And yet the benefit gained from Greek culture for the cause of humanity is very questionable. Considering the seriousness of life's duties and the anxieties and miseries of mankind, in comparison with the laughing and the fun with which the frolicsome nation skipped the dark problems   penetrating   into deep secrets below the surface and extend into realms above the skies: then that nation's world-consci- ousness must be adjudged as abandoned to unmitigated frivolousness. It was at any Greek levity. rate, unbecoming a nation of philosophers; or it was wrong at least that the world became accustomed to esteem the Hellenes as such. For neither ignoring nor laugh- ing will dispose of the persistently recurring questions of sin, guilt, and fate; nor as- suage the mind laboring under the dismal problems. These realities do not die off by Laugh away sin, guilt, fate, but they will not let man alone. being left to take care of themselves. The policy of leaving them unmentioned will be of no avail so long as they will not let man alone. Scurrilousness will only give them chances to augment forces and to gain area for   multiplication and·for ag- gravating the predicaments of the race. Ignoring evils does not diminish them; neither does dare-deviltry frighten them off.

Fate, guilt, and sin never cease to announce their presence. Either one of them or all of them at once will show up in the mystic circle, the guarded entrance notwithstanding — will show up even in the sanctuaries. That portentous trio causes the anxiety upon which Sin, guilt, fate—portentous trio. the tragedy hinges in the theatre, in the acts of sacrifices, in oracles, sorceries; the anxious suspense ever lurking close beneath the thin cover of taste, education, or culture. Wherever that trio grows in the darkness, where its monstrosity cannot be seen and the sleeping victim is not alarmed, there the anxiety rises and knocks at man's inner door. Answering the knock Anxious suspense, the unsolved problem. § 39, 41, 56, 59, 71, 72. he finds it to be—our open question, unsolved. In the depth of the soul it sighs from love for the victim in his peril,—and is treated like a prisoner in return. Aroused, however, by the persistency of this strange anxiety, man perceives a whole inner world opening with its won- . derful relations to a higher world. Man now perceives that both of these worlds remained shrouded mysteries only because his faculties had been allowed by his own default to become absorbed in the mere transient appearance as in a dream. Man now recognises, too. that the interrelations of both worlds are for his sake and that his own self is deeply concerned in them—and that these relations had suffered a great deal during his sleep. Man finds both of these worlds to be as real as the interrelations, in behalf of which the anxiety gave utterance.

If man should prefer to ignore the knocking, and turns in continuance of his sleep and his dream, the anxiety, growing more anxious tho less pronounced, may retire too. With it vanishes the revelation—from consciousness, but not out of reality.

This process of reminding the thought, Greece experienced in the same way as Forebodings of disaster. every thoughtful mind experiences it, namely, through facts never to be forgotten, nor to be laughed away. It was the fault of the Greek mind that it did not want to sober Sudden collapse of Greek culture. up and to meditate upon that of which it had been admonished by way of premonitory presentiments.

All at once CORINTH WAS SET ON FIRE at twenty places, under the hilarious sounds of Corinth in flames ! trumpets. Bethink ye now of the irony of fate! The BLAZE ILLUMINATES THE COLLAPSE OF GLEEFUL GREECE. The main emporium of European commerce, grown wealthy by the gold of Asiatic   monarchs once sent as offerings to Aphrodite, and by the purchase moneys for articles of luxury and art bought from its markets—Corinth went down to ruin and ashes. The black dust of its palaces covered the whole of the devastated Peloponnesus.

Alexander had taken the notion to set himself up as the pioneer missionary of Greek culture on the barbarous East. The result in that direction had been stagna- tion and entire cessation of Greek influence. To gain the world over to better life by conforming oneself to it and adopting its ways, was the wrong method for the great Macedonian to pursue. Above human error human destiny determined to spread this influence further west instead of going back to Asia, and there to make it last under Greek influence assigned to the west. a wonderful·preservation up to this day. For, Greek thought and Greek patterns of beauty are things not only of the lower realms but pertain to the spiritual sphere of idealities, and cannot, therefore, be doomed to annihilation. Both of these relative Things imperishable. II. § 41, 234. goods have pervaded the civilisation of Europe, which resulted from their blending with German characteristics and with Christian culture.

CH. IV. INDO-GERMANS. OCCIDENTAL: RIGHT WING OF WESTERN ARYANS: 2. THE ROMANS.

**Polar axis.
Benares-Rome.**

§ 70. Led on by ideas and events we further trace the line of progress among the Aryans. It moves westward until it reaches from Benares to Rome. What rendered the characteristics of India and Persia at variance, also distinguishes Hellas and Rome. Rome represents the other pole of the tension between India and Italy.

Similitude and yet strained relation between the four Aryan branches.

Between them Persia and Greece form the inward now neutralised conductors. Under the strain between Persepolis and Phillipopolis the wires became crossed, as it were, at Marathon. The Persians on the right wing of the eastern Aryans take a rest, whilst the Greeks withdraw from the left wing of the western Aryans and give room to the Romans, their successors in operating at the ethical apparatus. The Greeks had many traits of character in common with the Persian-Hindoos, whilst in swift energy and practical sense, for a length of time also in discipline and uprightness, the Romans resemble the Persians. Despite the affinities between India and

Rome. Philipo- Benares. polis. Marathon. Persepolis. martial

Hellas the polarities plying between Greece and the East are transmitted to Rome in order to spread their full force in the West rather than to resume those relations which Alexander had planned.

Latins. Persians. Greeks. Hindoos.

speculative.

Niebuhr has assigned to Rome its true position in our science. Besides Japygian and Etruscan elements we find one specifically Italic. As such are to be counted all the people

Situation of Rome.

who spoke dialects of the Latin idiom; Umbrians, Marses, Volscians, and Samnites. Those Italians came into the peninsula from the north. The trail of the Umbric-Sabellian tribe is, according to Mommsen, still traceable from north-east to south-west across the central crest of the Apennines.

Nations of Latin idiom. Niebuhr.

From the Umbrian, Sabellian, and Oscian tongues the language of Latium arose into that prominence which nobody dreamt of in those days of small beginnings. It became the vernacular of that set of people which was destined to fix the cardinal principles of jurisprudence and of constitutional government. This language and these people were remarkably well adapted for political supremacy by virtue of their organisatory talents; altho the first legislative movements of the Latins were incited by the Greeks.

Rome directed its entire energy to the definite purpose of becoming the leading town of the adjacent districts and thus became the stronghold of Latium.

Roman purposeness, united efforts, discipline.

Bent upon this single issue its citizens soon made their influence tell. Determined to obtain the end in view they lost no opportunity and spared no effort to realise the object of their ambition. With every step forward they exercised purposeness and public-mindedness, and practiced progressiveness and aggressiveness under the discipline of unity. Clannish pride, based upon strict observation of customs agreed upon, was the motor nerve of Roman discipline.

Patriarchal elements Mommsen. (§ 83, 56, Guizot.) (§ 172 Pope.)

Others have verified what Mommsen expounded: "What may be called the patriarchal element in the primitive organisation of this state has become permanently effective; it consisted above all in the maintenance of the moral and honorable state of matrimony. Man was compelled to live in monogamy; and a case of connubial infidelity on the part of a wife

Nudity in Greece. Toga emblematic of Rome.

was terribly punished." The difference between Roman and Greek deportment is delineated in this observation: "Among the Hellenes the gymnastics of nude boys; among the Roman's chaste enwrapping of the body. The toga thus became emblematic. Rome made the family-hearth the corner-stone of the state."

On many occasions and among all ranks this principle proved its strength. When a Lucretia is disgraced, or a Virginia insulted, the citizens arise as one man; and the national scorn is hurled upon a libertine regardless of his prominency or his wealth. Chastity is a power tho jealousy may be its chief motive. And these sentiments remained in force up to those later times in which a Frenchman, taking liberties with a lady, provoked the outbreak of the "Sicilian Vesper."

Purity of conjugal life demands strictness of justice.

The sacredness of matrimony demanded strict justice. Upon that basis the talent for legislation and organisation of the state as a household at large became developed. The ingenuity for adjusting grievances became apparent when those of whom advantage had been taken called for equity and insisted upon a written enactment of the simple code of laws upon the twelve tablets at about Solon's time; whilst the rigidity of national tradition and custom were allowed to remain unwritten for

Genesis of Roman jurisprudence.

the time being. Obedience to them was considered more practical than engraving them upon stone or bronze. It was only in consequence of the increasing and ever more complicated relations with cliental, confederate and conquered states, that these costumary laws had to be modified. Negotiations to that effect were rendered consistent and organical by plebiscita and senatorial resolutions, by edicts of magistrates, consular treaties and imperial constitutions. Once agreed upon, these were equally binding for everybody, and their authority was never questioned. All judicial instruments reflect Roman sagacity for reasons of domestic economy.

For centuries the Roman senate gave the noblest decisions expressing the national will. Its wisdom and consistency, its unanimity and patriotism, its courage, integrity and judicious use of power make the Roman senate the most exemplary assemblage of which history knows. Its reliability in the dealings with allies or clients was the secret of political successes throughout a long period of prosperity. Even the Numandians were conciliated by the allowance to use the Punic language on official occasions when the government might have been justified in insisting upon their Latin.

Besides that "bench of kings" the venerable "college of the Vestal Virgins" deserves honorable mention. Never shall history cease to keep sacred their memory also. Into their custody the domestic hearth-fire of the state was given, symbolising the high esteem, in which family life was held by the nation, because of its fundamental importance for the state. They alone ranked equal with the august senate. Many times they may have acted "the power behind the throne", but may not the influence have been the more beneficial for the unostentatious and benign manner in which it was exerted? Throughout the whole period of their existence as a state-institution, down to the time of Stilicho their integrity stands almost without blemish, whilst everywhere else female influence in public affairs, with comparatively rare exceptions, causes Clio to blush. *[marginal: Senate and Vestal virgins. The Vestal hearth-fire emblem of the sacredness of matrimonial life and its import upon the state. (§ 68 Greeks in contrast.)]*

§ 71. Rome soon became conscious of her advantages ; but rely on empty fame for being respected she would not. It was to be the right that should clothe her with might. And history could not but give the impartial verdict, that it was the cause of right which triumphed, when Rome accomplished her greatest feat in punishing the Punians by exterminating Carthage. *[marginal: Rome's right to wipe out Carthage. § 60, 66, 88, 132, 142]*

Great thoughts were not altogether absent in the mercantile city; Hannibal had a few of them. But that state was destitute of any discipline whatever, until it was too late to bring some system into the municipal management. Rich Carthage was lacking in what Rome possessed, not credit but trust in her treaties. With this lack another was combined. The city of commercial travellers and without any regard to conjugal life, and consequently without sufficient manliness left to restrain that heat of sexual excess which as a general thing goes together with cold cruelty, owes it to the Semitic Moloch-cult, that it is branded with the imfamy of cultivating this combination of carnal lewdness and blood-thirst. *[marginal: Plato on mercenary traits of Carthage. § 66.]*

Of the deeper roots of Roman morality and legalism we soon become aware from what the Greek Polybios shows: "It seems to me that the main cause of Rome's supremacy lies in the high opinions of the Romans in general about their gods. What other nations have vituperated as being a fault appears to be the tie which binds their state together. I refer to their reverence for the deity. For in exalting the gods and at the same time conceiving them as so intrinsically interwoven with private and public life, the Romans excel other peoples in a degree which makes a higher grade of devoutness impossible". *[marginal: Religion the foundation of Roman greatness § 24, 34, 43, 47, 54, 56, 58, 59, 71, 84, 87, 93, 96, 125, 126, 131, 132, 137, 139, 156, 175, 190. Reverence to the gods. Polybios.]*

The system of the Roman deities never received that finish which Hesiod gave to Greek mythology, or which the Greek accredited to the Romans. Their confederate cities adopted gods without finish, if they only could be taken into practicable service by the state. The Romans never became so enthusiastic about, or so familiar with, the gods as the Greeks had been. Fearing the gods made the union firm, and preserved and protected domestic life; much more was not required of them. *[marginal: Religion made the means for political ends. Gods taken into the service of the state. § 57, 62, 73.]*

Under these circumstances it was found expedient to utilise the reverential spirit by promoting polytheism to the rank of the imperial religion. *[marginal: Polytheism promoted to the rank of imperial religion.]*

But beneath the official cult, under cover of public service to the official gods, or rather the service of the gods to the state, we again perceive the occult prepossessions, hidden in the old substratum, manifesting their eruptive force by breaking through the surface even of the established state-religion.

This basal mixture of tradition and superstition had grown up from Sabino-Latin, Tusclan, and Etrurian seeds, notwithstanding the reforms of Numa, which however were also ascribed to Pythagoras. Under this aspect alone it becomes clear how the worship of the Manes crept in, and whence the little house idols, bandaged in dog's skins, came from. *[marginal: Religious notions derived from the substratum. § 42, 45, 48, 51, 55, 57, 58, 65, 66, 72, 73, 78, 83, 86, 109, 135.]*

Etrurians, Sabines and Marses were known for their snake-worship in early times: their vampirism is expressly set forth by Ovid as very ancient. With the fear of the Lamies was *[marginal: Etrurian snake-worship. Ovid.]*

blended the fear of the Striges and of the throngs of wandering Larvae—the souls of the departed. It would not have been necessary to introduce the Thessalian and Kolchian arts of sorcery since the preparation of magic drinks and the manufacture of protective charms had been practiced in Italy a long time previous to Numa's innovation.

Roman character legible from its architecture.

Architecture, such as Rome had on hand worthy of that name, had at first been left under the direction of Greek masters. Gradually Rome developed this art in its own way, being bent upon producing effect, upon commanding respect. Hellenic beauty, posing on selfconscious elegance and ease, or in majestic simplicity, had to

Not the temple should monopolise the attention

recede; first in the details, and soon after also in general composition. The Romans would not allow the temples to monopolise their attention. The state demanded a representation of its power and pomp. A spoiled populace had to be pleased, which

Display of power and pomp in order to command universal respect of the state.

could only be done by the hugeness of the theatres, the banquet halls, and baths. The well-proportioned Greek pillar, corresponding with the style and use of a building, was put upon a solid, stern-looking stone cubit. What had been gained in grace and delicacy during the short Periclean period, became in the Augustean age changed into selfconscious pride and grave dignity, in accord with the greatness and the splendor of the monarchy. In the silver-age of Latin literature that originality and large-mindedness begins to sink together with thoughtfulness, decaying under the "study of words" and rhetorical dilettanteism.

Wealth without education corrupts aesthetics.

Art prostitutes itself.
§ 67, 123, 126, 137, 139,
§ 150, 190.

Seasons of political intrigue and rule of the money-bag are not conducive to art. It fails under temptation and prostitutes itself by making money out of uncultured and pretentious but stingy parvenues. Buildings are overladen with ornaments. The colosseum must unite every style of Greek taste with Roman gravity, now consisting of quantitative heaviness. What of the noble forms of Hellas had been preserved became by Roman contractors disseminated throughout the whole empire. We find Roman masonry on the tombs of Petra near Mt. Sinai, and in Treves beyond the Rhine; from the Atlas to the bridge of Nismes, and from the wall of the Picts to the towers along the lower Danube. This brings us to the limits of the thought to which Rome owes its greatness.

Limits of power.
Lecky.

§ 72. Saying with Lecky that "the limits of the Roman empire went not much further than its moral feelings" may be taken as rather exaggerated; but it contains the substance of a correct syllogism. Officially appointed slave-hunts kept up

Slave hunts in Syria.
Plautus.

slavery. The Syrians—that sort of people which Plautus thought the most suitable material—were dragged from their homes by revenue collectors, and brought to

Parallel to present "Social Problem."

market in large droves by the traders of Cilicia and Crete. And the trade grew in proportion to the accumulation of wealth in the hands of a few land monopolists.

Labor and Capital.
Mommsen.

The oppression of labor by capital caused the Gracchian disturbances, inasmuch as labor had been cheapened through the slave-trade. "Formerly the small farmer had been made a dependant by ready advances of money-loans at usurious rates of interest, rendering him the tenant of a lord who exacted exorbitant ground rents. But now he was driven to extremes

Slave labor; accumulation of real estate; foreclosed mortgages; middle class subsiding.

by the competition of cheap grain, raised upon transmarine latifundia by slave labor. Mommsen could form this conclusion without much strain of reason; but at the time the consequences to which matters drifted, could scarcely have been foreseen. Yet some seem to have anticipated that the impoverishment of the agricultural middle class would mean the ruin of the free state.

Agrarian legislation.
Tib. Gracchus,
L. v. Ranke.

Tiberius Gracchus on a journey through Etruria—according to a remark by Plutarch which L. v. Ranke has brought to our notice—observed to his dismay what danger threatened the state from the growth of a population living under the slave-like condition in which he found the descendants of prisoners of war. His proposed bills, aiming at the preservation of a middle class by granting freedom to country people and civil rights to the plebeians were

Curse of slavery.

the issues of this conviction. Where the curse of slavery is lurking, from thence the friend of the people and of the state sees the public peril ensuing. In the face of this fact the fortunes of the Roman state were not to be repaired by enjoining laws upon conquered nations, whilst "the city" reserved to itself all legislative, judiciary and military prerogatives. It must

Citizens deprived of rights and liberty for reasons of state.

accrue to the contrary of welfare to invent measures enabling the rich the more to press down poor citizens at home; or to grant a few provincial, but actually mere municipal, privileges which only burdened the grantees.

Limit of ancient ethics: Inhumaneness.

Here lay the perilous breakers. Along this line ran the limit of all ancient ethics: presumptive arrogance, domineering selfishness—inhumanity! Principles of utilitarianism were to veil the inhuman ownership of human beings as tools. Since slaves are outlaws and means of enrichment, it was in the interest of the rich to reduce as many as possible to a condition of slavish dependency. When men allow themselves to become inured to the idea that right is a matter of mere privilege, depending on the favors of a few who have power to ruin any one, then liberty can no longer be assigned as the common inheritance of man as such; then none but those may lay claim to liberty who have a share in power and influence. Liberty in the Roman republic soon became a delusion, a mere name taken for the emblem of freedom which in reality meant nothing but class-rule. No emperor nor law could change the course of affairs which Gracchus had thought to be avoidable in the beginning.

Stoicism may be considered as the culmination of ancient ethics. But even the admirer of that school of philosophy must concede, that it contains two sets of moral laws: one for the illiterate people, the other for practicing dialecticians. The latter hold, that to suffer is equivalent to being foolish. Suffering is the outgrowth of ignorance. But neither suffering nor ignorance is held as standing connected with sin. The custom to judge people by their success makes something else the criterion of badness. Concerning this essential matter stoic sophistry takes the following jumps toward its conclusion: "The poor are ignorant, but the 'vitium' consists in the poverty, hence the fault lies in being poor;—poverty is the sin." This was the gist of the aristocratic set of morals in the Stoa: "If you would accept of our wisdom you would become rich and be virtuous. For, to be virtuous is tantamount to being wise. To be wise consists in avoiding unpleasantness and in joining the Stoa. Whoever neglects to do that has to blame himself for his troubles; he is justly to be blamed by others for the vice of being poor, and has no right to expect the sympathy of the wise people." Everybody understands this to be virtually the chief maxim of the Stoa: at bottom nothing but a cheap excuse for heartlessness. Its assumed attitude of resignation, its voidness of feeling, its unconcern about the world and feigned contempt of it, its cosmopolitan talk of humanism were only so many pharisæical affectations to conceal the contradictions of the pretentious theory.

Well then, the unsophisticated poor Roman, disqualified for reaching up to Stoicism, needs to follow only the common kind of morality. He will obey the prescriptions of the law and fulfill the customary performances expected of a good standing citizen. The only trouble with this moralism is that such performances and conventionalities are detached from thinking and willing personal life. Of the significance of this prerequisite of morality nobody in classic times had an idea. Good behavior is a mere mechanical habit and as such not to be considered as an expression of the mind and not entitling man to the value of a character of his own. Minding the law is thereby rendered the mere product of external circumstances. No wonder that under such repudiation of personal honor the services go scarcely as far as the servant is pushed and kept under surveillance. Of course, detached from personal consciousness and cheerfulness, such "dead works of the law" have no ethical value. If works are "dead" then their value can only lie in themselves, in their utility. Then a deed conveys no personal merit, consequently man cannot but be taken as a mere utensil.

As a further result of this theory of legalism the state has appropriated all human rights to itself; and the state being conceived as identical with government it follows that none but the representatives of rule have rights. Hence the unbearable overbearance of a bureaucracy. But since, at the same time, the works of a law-abiding people are not done in a cheerful compliance with duty, or from unselfishness, it follows that man merely gets his deserts, i. e. that which a thing deserves. He is worth what he earns; his esteem rises with the taxes he pays to the state; otherwise he has no merit worth the person.

The ethical results of Stoicism are therefore easily summarised: the stoic will nurse his apathy and rid himself of all earthly ambitions. He will dismiss all mundane interests from his mind. Since he finds it to be a futile attempt to elevate them to his ideal of universality he considers the furtherance of common welfare a matter not worth his attention, a thankless job. Ethics is virtually given up. And what that implies becomes obvious when it is remembered that ethics was the private religion of the schools. Thus by its legalistic morality Stoicism forfeited by default the last consolation which cheerful performance of duty in the interest of personal improvement affords. The default consisted in allowing personal merit to become ignored, and advocating the substitution of a general state-morality in its place—a morality with the motto: "every body's business is nobody's."

§ 73. It would have been worse than unnecessary to dwell upon Stoic ethics, had there not been something else connected with it. The Greek, it has been said, appropriated and assimilated external matters in the mind, whilst the Romans rendered formal and forensic even the most spiritual things of the world of thought, the most intrinsic concerns of personal life. There was no action, no sacrificial celebration in which a portentous omen might not occur, or mistake be made, necessitating a literal repetition of the ritual. Words and symbolic rites were thought to work in such magical and legal punctiliousness as that the efficacy of the whole act was rendered doubtful by the least error or mishap.

We find consciousness under a stress of legalism and formalism which needs another explanation than that obtained by a circulus in probando. For this would be all that Stoicism would amount to, if we would rest with having explained Roman legalism and formalism by the abstractions "Law" and "State."

True enough. Rituals and cultus were the official expressions of civil polity as formulated by the state. Being affairs of government they finally may have transformed individual consciousness and private life to the stamp of their tentative bearings, analogous to the influence of custom or the "spirit of the times." In this respect Mommsen's word has much weight: "Morality with the Jews and the Romans was a catechism or index of deeds either allowable or unforbidden." Yet there is more than an habitual legalism at the root of the ceremonial punctiliousness alluded to.

We can not fail to observe that the "mysterious anxiety" has a great deal to do with the painful uncertainty of ceremonious devotion, even with the Romans. Their heroism, decisiveness and assurance of final success notwithstanding, the Roman consciousness is as much afraid as we found that of the Greeks, despite their hilarity and familiarity with the gods; in spite of their boast of fearing neither fate nor the styx.

Why did the "portenta" i. e. the ominous signs which the haruspex or the augur pretended to find at the "auspices", why did they wield such a power over Roman consciousness? The belief in both, omens and auspices, again indicates the presence of that darkness solidified in the substratum. In precarious situations consciousness, in the ratio of its darkening, feels compelled to either ward off, or conciliate, or bribe the powers of evil by scrutinous observances, by the use of magic formulas and rituals and charms, or, on the other hand, people contrive, by means of odd usages and "sympathetic" applications, to attract good spirits for succor; in short, to use either power for selfish ends. All this goes to prove that the mind, even in its natural bondage and inverted foreboding of its rescue, becomes conscious of its innate destiny to become selfdetermined and to master the situation.

This ominous suspense, assisting man's promptings to rise above himself, belongs none the less to that form of wretchedness, in which we found enthralled the nature-bound people of Inner-Africa and Oceania even up to the mouth of the Obi river. Here in Rome we find that anxious suspense covered up, not very deeply at that, by a layer of higher religious culture wrought into every form of cultural life; covered by a growth of religious offshoots which had crept hither from foreign fields, but were now thoroughly Romanised. Here as well as in Greece the lower layer shines through the upper crust, just as the Christian inscription around the cupolo of St. Sophia strikes through the Moslim plastering fortunately in reverse order. The same old priestcraft of sorcery again protrudes in the various manipulations, whenever the intestines of this or that fowl are examined, under sanctimonious mock-solemnity, as to their indications of the human fate.

With these superstitious practices that old Roman ancestor-worship stands connected, for which old nobility has the more predilection the older (and of course nobler in the esteem of insipid folks) it becomes. Of the high and brilliant umbel crowning the poisonous flower-stalk of this plant we shall see more anon.

The family altar of the Romans with its Penates is essentially what the mirror is to the Japanese; with this difference however, that, what appears childish and weird in Asia became, by the occidental and by the Roman mind most conspicuously, transformed into heroworship—which also will turn up again before our view.

Upon the whole it will always have to be admitted, that the man of the antique climbed the highest notch of his scale in Italy. Earnest in action, honoring age and parentage, respectful to womanhood, loving his country, and fearing the gods, are qualities of the Roman which by far excel all those of the other ancient nations combined.

Those Romans were a matter-of-fact people, just the opposite from what the Hindoos are, that nation of contemplation. The Romans made history and wrote it, in polar contrast to the Hindoo cousins who doze and dream. The epic is common to both on account of their Aryan descent, but a sense of history, besides the Greeks, only the Romans possessed. Rome in the prime of its manhood is the best type of the Aryan stock down to the time of its decline.

The three stories of the theatre of Marcellus symbolise the three epochs of Roman culture. The Doric colums below remind one of the Spartan firmness and simplicity in the time of the rise of the republic. In the second story the Ionian column, symbolising a free horizon, shows how the Roman character had become tempered during the time of the constitutional struggles and intestine conflicts. It was then that the Roman seized the world and the city made herself ready to become its mistress. The third story column, the Corinthian, pictures the artful coquetry, the levity and luxury of the imperial period, and—the collapse of the colosseum. We do not now enlarge upon the latter period. We wait for the results to be summed up, when the whole realm of the Mediterranean basin in the golden Augustean age has become Romanised to the full extent.

Marcellus' theatre in its architecture represents three periods of culture.
Doric: Firmness and republican simplicity.
Ionic: Widening horizon, constitutional struggles.
Corinthian: Coquetry, levity, luxury —and collapse.

§ 74. Closing the review of Greece and Rome, of the Aryan Occident, as far as it then had become historic, we square our accounts with them as we did with India and Persia. We are thereby still more confirmed of the importance of our discovery that among the four branch lines crosswise correlations and interrelations existed. These were not construed to suit our system. In arranging them, we simply followed the order in which they actually resulted from their interorganic connection by force of polarities, as the natural outgrowth of history in its working after a plan and for a purpose. Evidently there is method in the onward and westward movement of culture and improvement of the race. The feature of feminine passiveness, selfdevotion, yea selfabnegation predominant in the eastern branch, we find to have become superseded by manly selfassertion and activity in the West. There thought in the process of sublimating, here action determined to cause further activity.

ARYAN polarities in their CROSS-WISE INTER-RELATIONS.
INCARNATIONS.
TRANSCEN-   IMMA-
INDIA (feminine)
THOUGHT. (inner   PERSIA conductors)
GREECE   ACTION (virile)   ROME.
BENT.   DENTALISM.
APOTHEOSES.

What fruits then did the four branches of Aryan culture yield? In the first place we recognised the wrinkled features of the "image", in other words, the faded remnants of a monotheistic consciousness deep in the background of the human being, which, howsoever deranged, is found innate within every member of the family. We found monotheistic traditions embodied in symbolical acts, never understood but ever venerated as family-heirlooms, reminders of the common home and the happy days of childhood. We found them a fragment here and a vestige there strewn over the entire area, lying about on top of the lower layers as a confusing mixture.

Resume of the cultural advance among all the Aryans:

The innate remnants were faintly felt; altho misunderstood because of their mutilated condition, they were always discernable from among the bundle of anxieties and abominations, and separable from the superstitions about ghost and demon, snake and fetish. . We found the latter to be subversions and objectivications of those inner remnants or of external symbols and traditional family-heirlooms. Some phenomena we found to be inexplicable from natural causes. Subverted truths, by force of their innateness, and occult phenomena of infernal origin break through the upper stratum in places where superstition would have been least expected. Again and again the better cultivated Aryans were attracted by the conundrums of the inner life, working out systems and being benefitted by the work in mental elevation. They arranged interrelated groups of higher and minor deities around a common center in the dim distance of a golden time—without finding a name for it. They never could rid themselves of the idea of unity and were ever possessed by a craving for centers of coherency. They knew of myths about a calamity, a confusion, a dispersion. We saw their attempts at remembering and systematising facts and fictions, ideas and phantasies, symbolising them and idolising the symbols. We saw them personifying nature and objectivising cognitions, which, tho vividly present, they could neither account for nor get rid of. We could not but conclude that such attempts were practiced by vigorous minds ripe with experience, and forming upper grades in the social differentiation.

Remnants of primitive religiousness; § 42, 47, 48, 53, 55, 57, 58, 59.
easily to be distinguished from anxieties, from fear of demons, snakes, fetishes.
External traditions (family-heirlooms) with inner reminders of an anxious suspense.
In trying to solve these riddles, Aryans became elevated through selfculture. § 57, 61, 74, 78, 176.
Idea of unity sought after in centers of cohesion. § 42, 48, 61, 75, 79, 132.

Not dispersed so far nor sunk so deep, as the Turanians, these Aryans, on the whole, preserved and improved their faculties and advanced thereby, of course not without leaving behind some of their race who abandoned themselves to apathy and sheer despair. No large part of the Aryans thus became such decidedly superior nations, as to gain the upper hand over the inferior. Spreading over the territories of subjugated preoccupants, each progressing in a somewhat different course, they planted better, specific cultures in the fallow soil—until they in turn would relapse into the wild nature of the uncultivated subsoil.

Personifying nature, idolising ideas.
Grades of social differentiation. Advancement.
Relapses Abandonment to lethargy.

Besides those religious relics and cognitions, the Aryans had peculiar gifts in common, which, however, did not cure them of their proneness to adopt some other pecularities, lower than their own, and to blend them with their own. The Aryan mettle, nevertheless, maintained its quality sufficiently genuine to preserve the higher gifts and true intuitions plainly distinguishable from the alloy of perverted consciousness and from poor imitations.

Higher gifts and true intuitions preserved; plainly distinguishable from bad alloy.

The four component parts of the Aryan family turned upon a significant axis. Imagine this axis as a bipolar magnetic bar whose forces grow the more neutral the nearer they approach the middle. Upon that rather indifferent part of the axis, half way between the poles, Persian and Greek cultures turned, both qualified for intermediating the polar fluxes merely to serve as good conductors. Their intercommunications in trade and in war show their equalising effects as distributive agencies, as tho they had agreed upon the execution of their historical tasks, and had understood their reciprocity as having been prearranged.

Greeks and Persians qualified for transmitting the effects of the polarity between Benares and Rome.

But at the opposite ends of the axis the full force of the polar tension recuperates itself. The outer poles lie in Benares and Rome, where the extremes each take their definite shape. Yet they are nothing but contrasts under strain; hence the extremes may meet, the tension may spend itself without a discharge, and may, under a neutralisation of forces, come to its equipoise.

Feminine pole: selfabnegation.   Ganges.

If we may take the yearning of the passive mind,—addicting itself to nature and retiring, plant-like, to sleep—as the feminine pole, then this ceases to be effective

Virile pole: selfassertion.   Tiber.

and becomes fixed on the Ganges; whilst the opposite pole of virile exertion, determined to master the world, spent its energy on the Tiber. Yonder the reality of earth-

World-soreness: transcendentalism.

ly things is reduced to mere illusory apperception, despised and averted and avoided under the groans of world-soreness, on account of an ideal world. Here a real value is ascribed to the environments, founding that view of life which sees a moral destiny and persists in the activity of realising the purposes of real life. But just as in India blessedness is sought in dropping the ethical problems of actual life, so Rome stands

Worldliness: Immanency.

in peril of worldliness at the expense of Heaven.

Orient: incarnations.

In the Orient a patient longing for incarnations, an intense desire to have the gods dwelling with man. In the Occident an impatient impetuousness in reverse manner,

Occident: apotheoses.

tending to heroism and apotheoses, extolling man to rank with the gods.

Yonder the idea of condescension of infinity divine to human nature in its generalness; there the ascension of personal man to an indistinct deity.

Thesis: Transcendentalism.

When we formulated the mode and common characteristics of eastern thought into a comprehensive synopsis, we termed it: TRANSCENDENTALISM.

Anti-thesis: Immanency.

Likewise we formulate that of the west as: IMMANENCY.

C. THIRD DIVISION.

THIRD CIRCLE. THE NATIONS AROUND THE MEDITERRANEAN BASIN.

SYLLABUS.

Analysis of the ethnical compound in the Roman crucible.

§ 75. Thus far our object has been to present to our minds the Aryan culture in the shape of an edifice, with wings opposite one another upon a substructure of compressed life. This building is reared upon a hardened and raw subsoil of Turano-Mongolian beginnings, which at this stage of historic development as yet surrounds it in an extensive compass.

We now proceed in outlining the third circle as the narrowest and innermost compass of the three. It encircles the basin into which, figuratively speaking, all elements of ancient history empty themselves. At a certain season the solution appears as if it were neutralised and at a standstill, the boisterous commotions going on notwithstanding. Then that powerful center of coherency is perceived to come

Composition seems to stand neutralised in the Mediterranean basin until the "center of cohesion" appears.
§ 42, 47, 61, 74, 133.

forth, around which all the ascendant cycles of the ancient world had been rotating. In the center of the chaotic mass we observe the formation of a nucleus, around which the elements of a new organism may silently concentrate as by a law analogous to that of natural affinity ; and from which subsequently it will permeate the entire mixture flown together in the basin.

Comparing the Roman orb with a basin will prove a very appropriate metaphor. The Syllabus.
component elements of the chaos gathering therein, the ingredients of the compound mixture Contents of the chapters.
have to be isolated in order to set some of them free.   There is, in the first place, the leading
influence of the "urbs" itself.   As the rivers tend to the ocean, so the host of idols and the
treasures of all the nations are emptied, almost in their entirety, into the lap of the "Mistress I. Rome's leading influence.
of the World".   The Olympus is extended into the Pantheon.   All deities to be found through- Olympos–Pantheon.
out the whole monarchy are summoned to assemble and to pay homage to the god of govern- Emperor–God.
ment. Political forces.

Then the Hellenic influence is to be taken into account.   Together with that, all the II. Greek influence.
diverse grades of culture, the sum of all the accomplishments acquired, including mytholog- Mental powers.
ical piety and moral philosophy, came flowing along.   The states corroding in the general General dissolution under cosmopolitanism.
dissoluteness, both cultus and culture are set free, and the mental forces, like escaping gases,
spread and disinfect the historical atmosphere.   As soon as, for instance, the idea of a cosmopolitan citizenship is sublimated from the mass, it prevails.

Another chapter, the third in this third division, at last leads us to investigate the third III. Hamito-Semetic culture upon Cushite substratum.
and most concentric circle of humanity, and to analyse the peculiarities of the Semites.

What had been contrived in the Roman basin, what attempts at unification had been Chaldeans.
made by Aryan forces, was to be brought into a tangible form by Semitic coefficients. These Egyptians.
factors we study in the cultures of Mesopotamia and Ægypt where they rest upon their Idea of universality.
Cushitic substratum, until we see how among the Phenicians the Hamito-Semitic talent
brings out the idea of universality.

The fourth chapter then will acquaint us with the enigmatical nation of the Jews.   Its
peculiar destiny, its particular position in the world, and its predisposition of characteristics
from the beginning, its conservatism and progress despite its reserved attitude, its persistency and preservation in the midst of decaying nations, its triumphant outlook into the
future whilst all other nations deplore only the sunny past,—and its remarkable, final catas-
trophe, will constrain us to concede to them an exceptional significance in universal history. IV. Contribution of the Hebrews.
In all this, and more, too, a natural development of national predispositions is manifest, pre- The great advent.
paratory to the entrance of an entirely new factor. For, in that seemingly insignificant people the true "center of coherency," the center of equation," figuratively speaking, comes to
view, around which, unbeknown, all former attempts to harmonise thoughts, to unify sentiments, and to satisfy the soul's cravings, all premonitions, and all aspirations to excellency
had been oscillating.

CH. I. THE ETHNICAL COMPOSITION IN THE ROMAN BASIN.

§ 76.   "Roman history overshadows the whole world.   The wide compass of its Rome's significance.
import embraces all other events, engulfs the history of all other nations."   This is the Niebuhr.
bearing upon history which Niebuhr assigns to Rome.   We shall see how far, altho Cyclical epoch 600 B. C.
§ 20, 24, 62, 124, 127, 133, 145, 213.
not deep enough, he saw.

That wonderful religious movement—reformatory to a certain extent   and thrilling No unity among the people; only conglomerate of conquered nations,
Asia at about the time of the destruction of Solomon's temple,—vibrated through the then
known world even to Japan from the Ganges to the Tiber.   Appearance of Buddhism, reform
of Confu-tse, Zoroastrian reformation, Israel's captivity, Hesiod's theogony in Hellas, Pytha-
gorean mysticism in Great-Greece, the circumnavigation of Africa, the fall of Jerusalem,
Ninive, and Babylon: these are the wave-crests of the universal commotion.   The altitudes of
Aryan cultures at about 600 B. C. are marked by the names of Gautama, Hesiod and Numa.

With the organisatory success of Numa the fundamental principles were laid
down which Rome never lost sight of up to present times.   In the program of
Roman life thus promulgated, the genius is embodied which may figure as the mold
by which the cast of the empire was determined.   In vain, however, heaves the
world-monarchy under its efforts to represent a complete unity.   It remains but a
conglomerate of conquered states, which were to smooth off each other by grinding,
analogous to that which polished the granite blocks of the moraines.   During the
operation the nations of imperial Rome became tired of wars and lay   down to rest,
as if waiting for peace.   In a sense the empire had the aspect of an enormous ex- waiting for peace.
panse over which a conflagration had raged "where only here and there—as Curtius (Curtius)
says—the sparks of smothered passions rekindled the flames."

From the latest ruins of Carthage and Corinth columns of dense smoke as yet rolled up
and flames licked through.   The extension of the northern boundaries meant death to the
Illyrian and Thrakian tribes, who withered and vanished at the approach of a culture to or perishing.
which, like the Indians in the United States, they would not conform themselves.

On the other hand strong peoples were called to the front for historical cooperation.   Their territories being drawn into national intercourse they helped, in the first
place, to enlarge the world's market.

14

India along with Southern Arabia was seized by the movement, whereby both received new stimuli for the prolongation of their historic existences. The ruins lately discovered upon the coast of the Somali country corroborate this allegation. The Euphrates countries were prevailed upon to exchange their goods by way of the Mediterranean ports. Even the Hercynian forest regions in Germany yielded contributions to the traffic now connecting the marshes of the Vistula with the oasis of the Sahara and with the Soudan. The extensive system of overland-routes was frequented by the "currus publicus." The connections of travel and trade over land and by water were regulated by time-schedules. Even with China correspondence was opened: the "silk-road" to the Sererians went towards the rising sun along the northern slope of the Kuen-lun. A Roman by-way led to the Lob-nor through steppes in which the situations of numerous towns have been discovered, but which are now avoided because of the oppressive solitude reigning there. Previously, as we have seen, Greece had established itself as a medium of lucrative international traffic. Its colonies and factories dotted the interior of Scythia up to the Ural, and the Mediterranean shores to the pillars of Hercules and up the Rhone. Regular roads led across Gaul in the direction of Thule. Intercourse with the Hindoos was reopened by the Greeks. In Persia they stood high at the court of Cyrus. Carthage had done its equal share to facilitate commercial intercourse. Its ships continued hauling umber from the Baltic; and its caravans communicated with the people on the Niger river and around the Tshad-lake. The West-African coast had been explored beyond the Green Promontory. It was a Phenician whom Necho had fitted out to double Cape of Good Hope for the first time.

In short, nation after nation was drawn into relations of reciprocal interests. The Roman Basin had become a general exchange on a large scale. The importance of this newly created solidarity of interests and of these commercial relations, which in addition brought about new political negotiations, is not to be undervalued.

This may be illustrated by the support sent to the Rhodians, when an earthquake had not only caused their colossus to tumble down, but had demolished their city. Polybios enumerates the amounts of aid-moneys sent from everywhere to relieve the distress. Hiero of Syracuse, Ptolemy of Ægypt, Antigonus of Macedonia, Prusias of Bitthynia, and even Mithridates contributed benevolent gifts for the sufferers— A NOVEL PHENOMENON.

The most distateful feature of the medley in the basin was the conflux of the ideas which the overwhelmed nations entertained about their gods, and of all the cults pertaining thereto. A veritable pandemonium was the result.

The Phrygian highlanders presented Rome with the Syrian goddess, with her black stone. The Serapis service of Alexandria with the processions of Isis, which earned so great renown in Corinth, and were described by Apulejus—became exceedingly popular throughout the realm. The devotees of Bacchus, who devoured the bleeding meat of kids, and who had themselves entwined with snakes, celebrated their games and exhibited their performances in many cities, in connection with the "Mysteries of the Hekates," the primitive deities of Latium. From Phrygia the Zabasios-service with its nocturnal debaucheries was introduced. From thence also came those Tauobolies, in which the initiatory services consisted of purifications with ox-blood at the midnight hour in the pit. They took quarters upon the Vatican hill.

Diverse emperors took pains to augment the collection or rather to swell the conflux. We need but to mention Nero and Heliogabal. The different rituals were all thrown into the strange potpourri, in which not even blood was spared, in order to obtain warm human entrails for the haruspex.

Beside the hall of the Quirites the temple of the Persian sun-god was erected, so that Mithras, the Siva of India, reigned from the Araxes and the Ganges to Tauris, being influential in Delphi and at the Capitol, as he had been at home and in Dodona. Since this idolatry had become naturalised in Rome it marched on with the legions to become dominant as far as Ratisbona and Mayence. The sun-service finally became a digest, indeed, of Indian, Persian, Phrygian and Græco-Roman mythologies, in which the whole promiscuous mixture of godheads thickened and amalgamated like the diverse ores in a smelter or the metals in a crucible.

It looked as tho the oriental sun should dawn upon the occident. Under different names he became the most prominent idol. To Rome he was Apollo. So much was made of him, that a later writer in a satirical strain made the sun utter the following complaint:

"Some drown me in the Nile; others darken and then bewail me; some again pierce my smashed parts with seven spears, whilst others cook me in a pot. Deplore me Liber, mourn for Proserpina, mourn about Osiris and bemoan Attys! All right. Only be careful, that I may not suffer indignities. Ye must not drag me through every ditch!"

§ 77. If we glance over the whole situation as the sun does, we find ascending or elevating tendencies nowhere. But we observe stuntedness, and behold cripplings of a fidgity phantasy everywhere.

Strange to say that such eclecticism should have been mistaken for enlightenment, when in fact it is a sure symptom of the mind becoming eclipsed. It does not impress us with an idea of mere incompleteness of knowledge. Neither does it resemble the night with its fertilising and recuperative effects; not night as the time in which strength is recruited for resuming work after a short and sound rest. That sun which smiled on the empire, once a sure symptom of original monotheism, or rather that night which changed off with him, represents the most noxious perversions of religion.

This is a night in which the inflamed brain suffers insomnia approximating madness ; a night in which manly energy is consumed by random and wantou agility, or in which, worse yet, the vital forces are debauched.

This night of eclectic syncretism was like a phantom shadow ,thrown upon a chilly and thick fog. The shadows then lengthen according to the degree in which the real sun of the mind, that hidden center of the invisible heavens, sinks towards or below the horizon of consciousness.

For, a sort of a presentiment respecting the veiled presence of that central sun of suns in the background of the heavens —whose rays reflect even from in the wondrous mirror of pristine traditions, and innate cognitions, which mythology had attempted to bring to a focus, or to reduce to a synthesis, or to reconstruct by way of esoteric systems and symbolic rites —man is known to have ever experienced. Ever and anon there arose one as a solid mountain-cone rises above the plain of flattened or levelled ideas. The shadow of this apex then covered the surroundings with so much denser darkness as the sun sank deeper and as finally, only the brow of the mountain reflected the last rays of the glowing light, before it suddenly and completely vanished.

Thus, under the suspense of a magic dusk, the outlines of personal and natural objects, of human and divine matters, of this world and the spiritual, flowed together like the dissolving views from two magic lanterns. All grades of consciousness, and all phantoms of fear had subsided into a chaos which, in a certain sense, resembled that, which preceded the first day. And in such a mental and moral chaos development is no longer to be sought for. Dissolution takes the place of evolution; instead of development confusion reigns and human affairs lie in a hopelessly perplexing en- tanglement, which no human reason nor natural force can unravel. Least of all the emperor who was hailed as the rescuer just at the moment when all the guy-ropes of human existence had become twisted into a tight knot. It did not take long until the people became aware of their disappointment seeing that the emperor merely played a figure, instead of being "the" figure expected. He was not so much as a mere sign of a new dawn; he was only presiding over the pandemonium. Sure enough, the world lay at his feet, no longer by reason of right, but on grounds of might, since opposing fortitude was exhausted. Among pygmies, comparatively speaking, he was announced pontifex maximus, the state incarnate.

The people had become disgusted with the multiform humbuggery of proselyting idolaters outcrying one another. In preference to this rabble, and in lieu of their lost faith, these people substituted the representative of their highest idea, their "Supreme Good", the state. For man ever must have some kind of faith, being always in need of something tangible upon which to lay hold. `No part of humanity can ever shift for more than the length of a life time without some "center of cohesion."

Sixteen pillars of granite with Corinthian capitals of white marble supported the vesti- bule of the Pantheon. The roof consisted of glittering tiles of bronze, and rested on iron, gold-plated rafters. The lofty and spacious hall under the dome was beset with a row of sculptured figures standing in a circle, noblest pieces of art. They were to represent the several gods of all subjected nations, whilst the true object of the assemblage was the glorification of the triumphant victor, the state. They had to serve as foil to the glory of Augustus, whose statue they surrounded as if waiting upon THE EMPEROR—GOD.

§ 78. We stand here before a phenomenon of supreme significance to history. "The Roman religion on the whole assumed the shape of a specifically imperial cultus", Preller avers. It was nothing but policy, this official religion. God was noth- ing to the Roman if not the embodiment of his highest idea, the state for ever. To him God can be but politics personified. Preller concludes his mythology with the emperor-cult.

Old nobility not averse
to old superstitions.
§ 17, 67, 73, 187

Ancestor-worship (and demon-service, its caricature) has always outlasted the better conceptions of the chief deities. But so energetically promulgated and so perfectly systematised as in Rome it was not even in China. Nowhere, not even in Ægypt, was old nobility more inclined to stretch its legendary lineage on the score of respectability, than the Roman aristocracy at this period. Hero-worship always commands a large retinue; but never had an entire conglomorate of nations so readily acquiesced in such a novel modification of it, as that of divine adoration of dead cæsars. We have noticed already, how the Orient assisted in this innovation. When Rome put

Ancestor-
worship modi-
fied into
deification of
dead cesars.

its foot upon the neck of the ennervated Asiatics, their cities and states were eager to pay homage to the Roman sort of religiousness in order to secure easier terms. In this manner Rome became the patron deity of Smyrna; it is not so certain whether of Pergamon also. But it was never heard of, that a Roman would have denied his re-

Roman
steadfastness
in its religious
traditions,

ligion, that is, his loyalty to the state; or that for reasons of diplomacy he should, (as Alexander and Napoleon had learned in the Orient) accommodate himself to the re-ligion of those he wanted to rule. Hence Rome became ever more successful in making religions bow to her.

overcome by
copying oriental
practices.
§ 20, 54, 57, 62. 67,
81, 97, 122, 123, 146,
147, 149, 150, 185.

In the end Rome, nevertheless, allowed Oriental ideas to enter by another way, and in that round about way was conquered by them. For we must not forget that Roman Cesarism was, after all, but a copy of the Asiatic pattern. In theory it was the same Pantheism, ever favoring despotism, which we found in China, and India, and Macedonia. Since Rome had virtually taken possession of the heritage of Alex-ander's estate, the occupants of the Roman throne saw fit to utilise the secret of the

Pantheism
courting
despotism.
§ 54, 55, 56. 57. 66, 68,
72, 78, 97, 89, 170,
185.

eastern monarchies with their dynastic successions. The newly discovered secret of taming barbarians or refractory aliens, of firmly establishing large empires and con-tinuing powerful enough to rule them and to maintain authority of state, seemed to depend on the deification of royalty. The transfer of government to Byzantium was no

Secret of the success of
Oriental dynasties
utilised in the
emperor's deification.

more than the realisation of the long nourished desire to take the place and continue the glory of the ancient dynasties. Rome thought of taking   advantage of the Asiatic custom by making it subservient to its own interests. But once captivated

Rome captivated
by the oriental
thought,
could never rid herself
of it.

by the oriental thought, she could never again free herself from it.

After the impirium, i. e. a world orbit, had become a fact in the Occident a common central idea was to be procured by which the mixed compound could be rendered cohesive. It was found in the august majesty of the most popular man. "Urbs" and "Orbs" cringed before him. Greek thought with its fancy for hero-worship employed its mode of religion in apotheo-

Augustus' apotheosis.

sising the emperor. In Athens, Corinth and Sparta altars were erected in honor of Augustus and formally dedicated to him. Rome did not lag behind. It had made the public games ovations to Octavian Augustus before his apotheosis. Cities counted their new era from the date at which on his journeys he had passed through. Soon after his death the senator Nume-

Affidavit of
Numerius
          Atticus.

rius Atticus declared under oath that he had seen the emperor ascend to heaven. As fast as the report could be spread, temples were built everywhere. Priests were installed, and kids

Sueton.

and calves were sacrificed, to the new god in heaven. In solemn procession, so Sueton relates, his statue was carried about upon a vehicle expressly built for the occasion, and drawn by elephants. In due form the new state-god was added to the old gods, the whole empire unhesitatingly swearing allegiance to him.

At Lyons and Cologne we know of this new rendition of allegiance to have been observed by the numerous princes, dukes and representatives of the Gauls and by some Germans.

At the confluence of the Rhone and Saone an altar was dedicated to, and the smoke of in-cense rose in honor of, the statue, the attending priest being one of the tribe of the Æduans, Near this altar stood a temple for this pet of the nations as a sign of their eagerness just then to serve a real god. The people of Narbo like many others had reared temples for his wor-ship when he was still living; the temple upon the Spanish Tarraco was built immediately

Egypt worships
Augustus as the
"REDEEMING"
GOD.

after his death. But Greece, because nearer to Oriental usages and ideas had outdone all others already in order of time as well as in the degree of fervency. Ægypt celebrated the memory of Augustus as the "Redeeming" god.

The mania of the
emperor cult;
Pliny.   § 104.

The judges throughout the empire from the Euphrates to the Atlantic had no sooner made people swear by the name of Augustus, than that the streets leading up to the capitol became too narrow for the herds of animals driven thither to be sacrificed. "They were driven up there in order to adore the mean image of the wicked despot with as much blood of beasts as he was used to spill human blood. This is what Pliny thought of the latest fashion in idolatry, of the effects of the "emperor-god-mania". Firmitius Maternus formulated this

which was formulated
into a dogma by
Firmitius Maternus.

into the dogma, that the emperors were gods of that class upon whom the stars, being of so much lower order, could exert no influence. The fate of the emperors, for this reason can no more be read from the stars than that of the gods or the demons.

Cyrus after his elevation to the gods, is pictured with four angelic wings, according to the copy of his monumental representation in Lenormant's work. This shows that Rome, notwithstanding its philosophy and its cultural accomplishments, adopted the Persian form of idolatry together with the much lower forms which break through the surface of the best established culture from the stratum beneath.

Persia imitated.
§ 59, 126.

This last repristination of mythical cultus was, however of very transient glory.

Astonishing is this close of ancient history. No sooner had the Occidental consciousness deviated from its destination and become imbued with the old Oriental ideas, than its defeat became obvious. Rome for once untrue to itself, had in this indirect manner allowed itself to be conquered by an idea most thread-worn of all ideas. The principal element of hero-worship is a compound of selfadoration and selfconceit. But considering the circumstances, what better could the Romans have done than making this inadvertent attempt at selfsalvation? Perceiving the peril of falling below the line of human dignity, it was certainly more rational to idolise the state than to fondle fetishes.

Occidental consciousness imbued with Orientalism.
§ 20, 62, 67, 51, 97, 123, 124, 130, 146, 147, 149, 150, 185.

Deification of man preferable to fondling fetishes; as nirwana was preferable to metempsychosis.

That state had already absorbed the privileges, which by right of their innateness ought to be kept inalienable by every possessor. Had not Plato invested the state with the attributes of being man collective, the personification of the ideal man, the synthesis of the metaphysical good of infinite value?' When therefore the state had been interpreted as the Supreme Good it could not be inconsistent with highest intellectualism to deify its representative. Of Orientalism, as transmitted through Platonism to the orient, the man-god was the natural result.

Plato's ideal state idolised;

a compound of self-conceit, selfsalvation and selfadoration.
§ 122, 124, 126, 144.

He was the result, too, of the unperishable, altho corruptible cognition of personal immortality. As an attempt of unaided reason at the realisation of this thought, the man-god signifies an advance. For, another and far more precipitous line of human logic had abruptly run out, as we shall see elsewhere, in the beast-god.

personified in the man-god
§ 145-150.

still preferable to the beast-god.   § 86.

By the contrivance of state-deification humanity, entangled in crude superstitions, had, in a rather nervous haste, tried to save itself from still another predicament of the mind. Relations growing more complicated had sharpened the attention. The more extensive the range of observation became, and the more intelligence was exercised, the more vivid grew, under the danger of getting lost in physical diversity, the presentiment that refuge could be found in a metaphysical oneness alone. Either one man had in reality to become God, or one personal God had to become man. Simply this alternative remained at the remarkable conclusion of ancient history.

To save humanity from fetishism, men fell back on selfadoration and rediscovered the postulate of oneness.

In that part of the world where the idea of personality had been rescued, in that part of humanity which, upon that basis, had risen to the highest degree of self-culture—in the west, man chose the first of the two postulates. The world-orbit prayed before the man-god.

Wholesome incitements by erroneous religiousness.
§ 58, 61, 74, 176.

§ 79. History incessantly persists upon equation. It aspires to bring the nations into communication and to guide them to unity. It keeps them in balance, ever seeking their equilibrium by means of that polarity which retains them inside the sphere of the invisible center of attraction. The growth of the ancient monarchies evinces this, where a great variety of ethical coefficients had to obey a mysterious instinct. This instinct made nations submit to the rule of equity and render even the discipline of social order attractive. A promiscuous manifold is to be reduced to a unit by being cast into the mold of a new pattern. Preparatory to this transformation the great national bodies assume their definite shapes as units with specific characteristics, destined to consummate a final organised union. This is the tendency of history because the promptings towards this goal are inherent in human nature.

History gravitates to carrying out the principle of unity.

Nations gravitate to social order which is warranted only by great national organisations.

During the process of national consolidations the irresistible inclination to dominate asserts itself in behalf of history's finality, tho in seeming antagonism to the principle of freedom. Ethnical units never stop to deliberate on harmonising the corollaries of dominion and liberty. Under the hostility in which these factors appear, the confounded units put themselves in array against each other for the ensuing conflict. Some become too proud to obey the historic traction towards unity; other parts are too obstinate to join the whole. Those unfit for freedom are then routed by the hostile forces who indulge the maddening lust of destruction.

History also tends to carry out the principle of dominion.

Perverse nations doomed to extinction. These conflicts will not cease until it is universally understood, that both liberty and dominion are to serve the same law of unification. With those refractory parts which persist in remaining detached from the center of union, and labor under false apperceptions as to the true form of either unity or liberty, all human contrivances employed to obtain the unification miscarry.

Wrong apperceptions of dominion and liberty miscarry. § 8, 10, 11, 35, 56, 62, 136, 139, 182. This again is one of the instances of confused physical analogies mentioned in § 7. Here the indiscrimination about originally true phases of consciousness with respect to dominion, liberty and unity comes in and works mischief.

Inversions of true contents of consciousness, § 42, 47, 55, 56, 58, 59, 74, 115. The restlessness of earthly conditions and man's own nature and disposition rival in urging upon him the obligation to establish tranquility. From his anxieties he longs to be freed, and against dangers he wishes to be protected. To counterpoise the diverging tendencies of the manifold towards dissolution, personal life instinctively seeks a center of cohesion, a general bond of connection. All of these desiderata are necessary to enjoy and to improve earthly conditions. From union alone the powerless individual can expect protection and freedom. It was upon these principles that, as if under silent agreement, the Roman state amalgamated the many heterogenous parts constituting the empire.

Search for the center of cohesion. § 43, 47, 61, 74, 75, 114, 133, 171. In ages past and among nations gone the adjustment of these principles had been attempted again and again. Each of the ancient monarchies represents a mode of realising the unity, in which each unit sought to possess the freedom and to preserve its dignity, the unity which guarantees personal security and rational dominion. But in forming such a unity —in which selfcontrol (individually) that is true dominion, and self-government (collectively), that is true form of civil liberty, may be cultivated —the old monarchies utterly failed.

Unification the leading idea of Roman polity.

Ancient monarchies failed in establishing unity and liberty.

Hellenism failed. History then took Aryan material to bring about the unification of humanity. The Greek mode of thought devised a new method for the preservation of individuality. Personality is indeed set free, and the persons brought forth are kept together as a nicely organised community—in theory. Something new is preparing on the score of real advance towards dignity, liberty, and unity. The Hellenes failed, nevertheless. Their aversion to authority subverted personality into subjectiveness, and liberty into libertinism.

Rome fails.

Subjectivism and Cosmopolitanism. At the end of our period history forms the Roman monas, apparently surpassing all former results. Under the rigorous discipline of Rome, the separate groups of nations are now released from the restrictions of their limited spheres. Being drawn into mutual contact and a solidarity of interests, their mental horizons widen. They meet to exchange their thoughts along with their goods, mutually benefitting each other. Here forces are bound, there others are set free. Everything works practical in the uniform of the Roman straight-jacket. Yet Rome fails, too. Liberty is a make-believe and unity is vested in the despot alone: ere long not even with him. When the time comes that the state is unable to protect, each of its citizens will try to protect himself as best he can. Authority then is lost and the state falls asunder.

Nevertheless, the truths, worked out in ways preparatory to their realisation, will live henceforth, until the unity, dignity, and liberty of humanity eventually take their historical shapes.

CH. II. DISINTEGRATION OF STATE-THEOCRACY.

Intellectual work in Alexandria. § 80. Rome simply completed the preparation for the new æra. It had to serve as the immense crucible, figuratively speaking, into which the fragments of bursted nations were thrown to be dissolved. There was in this large Mediterranean basin one place above all where intellect was at work, trying to solve the problem for which Roman power could find no answer. That place was Alexandria.

The Romans with their disregard for ideas wrought out the cramp-irons and chains which kept the joints together by force of state and law; whilst the Greeks furnished the binding cement. What brittle material the Roman discipline had thrown into the smelter of state-absolutism was rendered pliable by the alloy of the Greek language then pervading the medley composition. History evidently assigned this function to the Greeks as their portion in carrying out its purpose of civilising humanity. By the acumen of the Greek mind for receiving, molding and distributing ideas and by their position in the world's emporium of literature, the Greeks were well fitted to perform their part. Rome, then, furnished the apparatus for the experiment of concentrating the affairs of the entire world; but Greek thought had to preside over the experiment and to conduct the analysis and reduction of the component radicals to the figure of the synthesis.

Rome the apparatus for setting free the ethnical compound.
Hellenism to conduct the experiment.
Greek thought furnished the "word."

Greek thought had to find the "word" which would set the elements free, and make humanity understand and appreciate that nucleus of affinity, of which it might avail itself as of a hold in its sinking condition. All this had been floating before Greek idealism ; and the truth universally felt to be contained in Greek philosophy gave it such prestige, that together with Roman discipline of the body politic, this Hellenism continued to engage the minds in the discipline of selfculture. Hence it may be said that the "mind," after all, controlled the inner springs of historical movements upon Roman territory ; and it would prove profitable to remember, that institutions of learning ought to be to their nations what Hellenism was to Rome.

Nations rendered pliable.
Roman consistency could not break the barbarians of their stubborn adherency to their religious usages.
State-absolutism never able to answer the ideal of unity;
the annihilating the nationality of vanquished peoples.
From huge masses latent forces to be set free. § 19, 23, 119, 196.

The most powerful states of the East knew nothing of the secret of reducing ethnical particles to civic units. The monarchies conquered nations and crushed their gods and their customs ; yet the most cruel oppressions never succeeded in abolishing them so entirely but that some always had to be tolerated. Scarcely ever did absolutism prove able to infuse higher culture into subjected people, since as a general thing these ethnical elements remained unmitigatingly stubborn. The vanquished, for a while, would seek solace the more fervently in their own formalism and symbolism, and the more stubbornly adhered to them, the more it became manifest that the state did not answer the ideal of unity.

As a dissolvant of theocratic world-empires § 80, 119, 196. (to which class the Mosaic Theocracy does not belong)
neither higher culture nor occult cults could serve
in the necessary process of disintegration

The victors, on the other hand, held it below their dignity to mitigate and to adjust ; and, hardening correspondingly, they saw fit to annihilate the forms in order to exterminate the nationality. Thus neither obscure cults nor higher culture could serve as a solvent. All that the state-theocratic fusion of religions and politics in the Roman basin could achieve was, to bring the obstinate exclusiveness of the ancient nations to an end. And in the end the religio-political, i. e. the theocratic state had also to be disintegrated, if the formative elements of civilisation were to be rendered soluble and communicable. The process of this disintegration is plainly observable among the Greeks. Their gods, in undergoing the poetical sublimation, fade away and are practically used up. They are gradually shown to be nothing but artificially arranged reflectors of prosaic every-day life. In the light of philosophy these phantoms disappeared, and under scientific analysis the mirage of the other world as represented, for instance, by "the ceremonials of Cyrus" court, vanished, and the old notion of state-unity was discarded.

of celestial courts on earth.
Celestial empire of China. § 55, 56. Incl. Hlassa and Bagdad 199, 191.
Babel: § 115.
Cyrus 59. Olymp 61.
Pantheon 78.
Oriental dynasties copied 78. Pontif. max.
Oriental ideas perpetuated:
Constans I. 125 Dioclet. 126. Justin 127.
Byzantinism: King and priest in one 126.
Talmud. Koran.
Karl I. 137. Otto I. 142.
Frederick II. 145.
Gregory VII. Innocent etc. 144-150.
Dgengis 150. Batu 191.
Maximilian I. 165.
Napoleon I. 178.
Czar 191.

Scarcely is the idea of personality gained, however, until it, also, is overstrained at the expense of unity. Instead of being extended to the cognition of humanity, it relapses into mere individualism, where independence is sought in subjectivism, and authority disavowed. Willful arbitrariness rushes to anarchism wherein "humanism" becomes mad and commits suicide. This course the problem took in Greece at least, where once the state had been built into the framework of a deism in the concrete.

Personality gained but overstrained.
Authority disavowed.
Subjectivism.
State built into the framework of religion. § 24, 34, 43, 47, 54, 56, 57, 58, 71, 84, 86, 93, 96, 125, 128, 132, 137, 139, 156, 175, 190.

The hieratic thirst for power, abusing the fear of the gods, is, under circumstances like those of Greece, the first incitement for a community to emancipate itself from priestly predominance. Energetic efforts are made to cultivate selfhood and communism side by side, whereby the advantages gained become subverted into so much damage. Clannish interests and envy detach themselves, now from the preponderance of a hegemony, and then from the tyranny of communism. Man becomes conscious of being a person with rights equal to those of other persons of his nationality. He claims the right, for instance of being his own and of possessing property of his own. Rights felt to be inborn are defended against the abuse of might and of authority with the simple truth, that man does not exist for the sake of the state, but vice versa. The ulterior result and last phase of the state's disintegration is sophisticated legislation which begets radicalism and demagoguery.

Hieratic abuse of influence.
Greek clannishness.

In this manner successively the old world of the gods symbolising unity and authority then the old state and the old foundations of society, crumble to pieces, since all civic affairs become unsettled and soon upset. Such is the natural history of a culture which takes man as a natural force, or as an atom of a state founded upon the basis of natural generalness. Greek thought and art had liberated the person from being conceived as a tool for the purposes of an almighty state, Sophocles, through Antigone, reminded the state power of this fact. The mind follows the direction of similar reflections, until antiquity as such is no longer considered sacred, until the customs and the forms of social life and the traditions of former times are dropped without reluctance. This, in itself, would be no bad sign; but when it is found, that accompanying this, respect for old age and for authority is being changed into profanity, then wise men become alarmed and advocate the employment of conservative means. A Platonic citizenship or an Aristotelian cognition begins to counteract the error of liberty without unity. Society is to be reorganised; theories spring up, which demand reforms throughout the commonwealth in accordance with the advices volunteered; thought applies measure after measure, forms a body politic, advises leagues, warns to depend upon them. All these contrivances did the Greek mind (and does public opinion in any nation, for that matter) put together from its own resources, upon grounds abstracted from experience and observation; for everybody had become aware of the results derived from the contact with wider spheres, and of the changing conditions sequent thereto. The contrivances seemed to be of little avail. "Constitutions did not march," said Carlyle, of a process similar to that of Greece here analysed.

Nevertheless, exertions like these, made by wise men, are not in vain. A world of knowledge ensues; an ideal cosmos is the product. To this cosmos one may belong independent of, even detached from, his particular nation. Philosophy has found solace for the loss of national existence. MAN BECOMES A COSMOPOLITAN. Yet neither the individual nor society advances far enough as to succeed in the practical application of the cardinal principles of human welfare and true humanitarianism, namely: freedom, dignity and unity. The uncertainty of the experiment seizes the experimenter. The cravings for something strange, something mysterious are accounted for by the causes and signs of general dissatisfaction and mistrust. It is to be seen precisely of what the intelligent class was in search, when, in repristinating the old mysteries of Isis and Mithras, it was tried whether the mantic practices and the old astrology of the Chaldeans might not be made serviceable as props of society once more. Even the unthinking but ever aspiring masses invent new usages to assuage their discontent, which at such a time is the most hopeful sign of recovery. Thus Hellenistic learning, thought enfranchised from hieratic theories upon mythical grounds, calls forth thought everywhere, and demands a freedom never dreamt of before,

The mental cosmos had been erected upon the ruins of the Greek monarchy, an edifice reared by philosophy, science, and art, in which even the state of the Pharaohs found comfortable rooms for exhibiting the results of international relationship. For it was by way of Ægypt that oriental thought passed into Platonism and over to Europe. Alexander's visit to the then crumbling diadochate was no part of his plan of conquest. The object of his expedition was to experiment upon an instinctive cosmopolitanism. For this reason he not only caused the writings of Sophocles, Æschylos and Euripides to be sent after him to India, but also encumbered his train with fakes and performers of all sorts. His generals and satraps no less than himself found pleasure in such diversions and in making show of them as cultural factors in accord with his conception of his mission. According to Plutarch the children of Persians, Susanians, and Gedrosians sang the choruses of the Greek tragedies. Even the far off Indians were influenced by Greek mathematics, astronomy, and medicine. In exchange for spreading Greek culture researches were made in the East with respect to literature, philology, history and grammar—not only by Greek scholars and traders, but even by manufacturers and military hirelings.

Along with the noisy traffic carried on with Alexandria by the barges of all neighboring countries and by the vessels of every sea-port, the more silent intercourse of literary exchange took place. The book-trade was in its prime even in Rome, where book-stores occupied entire street-fronts. The poems of Martial, dictated simultaneously to a hundred copyists, were comparatively cheaper than the products of our electric presses; and the branch-houses at St. Remy and Lyons delivered books as cheap as the store in Rome. Cicero was read in every school; and with the scholars and students, no less than in the boxes of merchandise, the products of the mind traveled from city to city.

The result of such mingling of minds and nationalities was an international learnedness and universal mental progress which history then witnessed for the first time. This became evident in the great libraries of Alexandria and Pergamon. In the objects of art both at Rhodes and Pargamon the ideals recede and historic realism prevails. Personality, relieved of the constraints which an abstract construction of the state and objectivised deities had imposed upon it, becomes conscious of its value. War as a means of gratifying individual ambition is silenced. Events of historical import seldom occur, so that it seems as if men could no longer make history for future generations to reflect upon and to be by them described and admired. But the uneventful season is conducive to progress of some kind, nevertheless. Over the ruins of the Mediteranean states the high dome of international and cosmopolitan culture expands, in which tolerated cults, arts and sciences may find lodgement.

§ 81. Thoughtfully and filled with doubts the Græco-Roman world went down. It died of scepticism which alleges that all finite things are mere illusions, that the reality of the infinite is not credible, maligning all that exists by questioning if not denying its truth. Such scepticism ultimately is equivalent to a relapse into that oriental Pantheism which values nothing but a promiscuous all-the-sameness, into which every transient form of being subsides. The imaginary apperception of a Hellenic heaven, filled with gods ad libitum; the notion of an ideal state, and a hard-earned world-theory, are all considered mere phantoms—under that Buddhistic influence, of course, which later on will have to be discussed once more.

Græco-Roman world went down thoughtfully and full of doubts.

Scepticism as derived from Buddhistic pantheism.
§ 62, 67, 78, 97, 148, 149.

Such was the mood of Græco-Roman culture during its short period of decay. The Greeks had brought this mood to method and mannerism. Philosophy had put the confession of this gloom into systems.

Buddhism again to be discussed.
§ 67, 95, 99, 201.

Socrates, according to Cicero's saying, had attracted Philosophy to come down from Heaven. In the shape of Platonism it became exposed to contagion with oriental thought. Something new, indeed, is pointed out by the postulates of both these sages. Both have presentiments of revealed truth, whilst from Plato's combination of Greek and Oriental thought the Stoic school took its rise. Cypros and Cilicia, Rhodes and Seleucia on the Tigris were the centers of Asiatic cultures and furnished the realm its teachers.

Causes of decay.
§ 71, 78, 88.

Henceforth the wise men of the Stoa recommend freedom from passion, quietism, and apathy as to—the "one thing necessary," for which the state was taken.

Platonism the conductor of Oriental thought into the Occident.
§ 20, 62, 67, 78, 97, 122, 123, 124, 130, 146, 147, 149, 150, 135,

If such dogmas were to the taste of the strong-minded, much more did insipid people perfectly agree with them. Far above pleasure and pain the wise man soars, in fact above all feeling, sympathy and love included. Matrimony is gibed at. Service to the state and public life are matters of supreme unconcern. The value of an action depends entirely on its reasonability, that is, upon how one can make its avoidance plausible to himself. Hence to the wise man praise and blame are indifferent. Prostitution, incest, pederasty, etc., are considered as unobjectionable in themselves. They do not amount to anything, since they cannot stain the soul of the wise man; his selfsufficiency renders them all innoxious to his superiority. Hence that aristocratic superciliousness toward all matters beneath the notice of stoicism. Hence his contempt of the vulgar masses, of the poor, of the state. The stoic's virtue is cheap; because as a professional cosmopolitan he can easily settle with the wide world; to his neighbor he owes nothing but good will. The wide world he blesses with the maxim: "The greatest good for the largest number", or: "Act so that your maxim may be fit to become universal law!" For these maxims the world is now indebted to him.

Analysis of Stoicism.
Selfsufficiency.
Apathy.
Character of a cosmopolitan stoic; §72.
affects contempt of earthly conditions.
Stoicism evaporates personality into natural generalness.

Such is the stoic as a citizen of the world; dealing in universalities he avenges the inversion of personality into subjectivism by his generalisation of individual pretentiousness. Upon such a concept of humanity, as being a collection instead of a connection, the Stoa prided itself. By the "Middle-Stoa" that deity was expounded which, by means of the world's ether, diffuses itself into the entire universe. It is conceived as an indefinite generality to which the soul of man, as its specialty, stands in such a relation, that according to Panætios, it has no right to exist and hence must vanish. There is evidence ad nauseam to show, how cheap human life was to the stoic. Whenever a claim upon his sympathy was proffered by an unfortunate fellow-man, he simply acted the cosmopolitan.

It lands in Hindoo-pantheism.
Individual soul should vanish. Panætios.
When sympathy is appealed to, it is convenient to act the cosmopolitan.
§ 11, 15, 49, 54, 55, 58, 68, 72.

The stoic has brought us back to the Pantheism with which we became acquainted in the Orient. Through the Stoa it became the common acquisition of the Occident. It became THE mental power since the learned men and especially the state officials were addicted to it. Cicero moderately but effectively extols that mode of world-consciousness. In his "Officiis" he acquainted the enlightened with the maxims of the Stoa in the way Panætios had expounded them. The works of this stoic were held in high esteem by Augustus; and Areios of Alexandria was so highly appreciated by this emperor, that on his account he spared the conquered city its doom.

Power of stoic world-theory throughout the empire.
Cicero.
Panætios.
Areios.
Import of Alexandria.
§ 80.

Thus we meet again with the importance of Alexandria.

In almost every respect it is that place of the empire where the determinate step was taken to solve the big problem of equalising and harmonising the oriental and occidental forms of consciousness. Here stands the stronghold of the then modern Ægyptian wisdom in the midst of modern folly.

How to harmonise the oriental with the occidental form of consciousness.

Priests in white tunics, very officious personages; relic shrines with images of beast-gods; a dark, half-naked populace crowding the place of worship—may outline the chief features of Ægyptian culture. Everybody rushes up the broad stairs leading to the spacious temple-area a hundred steps higher above the pavement of the public square, where the great cupola, borne by four massive pillars, forms the entrance into the enormous Serapeion. Its interior is very dark, and in the central hall, darkest of all, between walls covered with gold and

Serapeion.   § 88.
Ray of light made
to fall upon the
lips of the idol.
§ 90.

bronze, the figure of the god towers up. From a hidden opening in the ceiling a ray of light falls UPON ITS LIPS! Overwhelmed the worshipers fall prostrate upon the floor. Do they really long for a word of divine utterance? In the immediate vicinity Greek philosophy has set up its chairs, in close proximity, also, to the renowned lecturers residing in the populous Jewish quarters. Among them, at this time, one especially excels his contemporaries. Deep in thought he endeavors to harmonise two antitheses, to solve the problem of problems by one all-embracing, all explaining conclusion. He is a Semite.

Philo,
the Hebrew.
§ 39.

It is Philo, one of the Hebrews.

Here we must stop, however, in order to resume what seemingly had been skipped. We are in arrear with many things yet to be considered, before the problem can be understood upon which Philo ponders. Peculiar circumstances present themselves by which the problems are rendered still more ponderous, and by which at the same time the preparation for the historical solution was completed.

Sum and
substance of the
cultural progress
of the Aryans.
§ 74.

In the Aryan world progress has been made up to the cosmopolitan view of human affairs, up to a universal participation of knowledge. Man has arrived at a state of consciousness where it is conceded that there are feelings and rights which all men have in common. A sense of freedom and union is cultivated, and a few other postulates of reason are set forth, of which thus far no man had ever thought. Yet not even to moderate expectations can promise be made of any satisfactory theory after which (least from the fragments of an ancient world, now cooling off without being welded in the Roman caldron) a new world might be constructed wherein men could live.

CH. III. SEMITIC NATIONS.

Resumption of the
postponed history of
the wedge driven in
between eastern and
western Aryans.   § 60.

§ 82. The catena of Aryan cultures—Hindoo, Persian, Greek, and Roman— of wide compass, is distinctly arranged in such manner, that the two inner links represent the lesser contrasts. At the extreme poles, in Italy and India, the opposite modes of thinking as to transcendentalism and immanency have become conspicuously historical in every respect, in all relations and formations of private and public life. Equally universal is the feeling of the necessity of an intermediation

Necessity of
merging oriental
transcen-
      dentalism
and oriental
immanency.
§ 48, 74.

between the two opposites, which in irreconcilable antagonism disastrously react upon each other so long as the conciliatory factor is not found. Hitherto history had not succeeded in adjusting the wide divergency. The extremes could not be alleviated

The extremes
met but would
not mingle in the
Roman crucible.

so as to recognise their common derivation and center or their merely antithetical relation, altho we saw them meet as equals in the Roman caldron and mingle on a level with the rest of the saturated solution.

The reason is to be found, why both modes of thought act so antagonistic, whilst virtually they are but the two hemisphere of the same spheroid. Transcendentalism and immanency, the two essential products of Aryan mind-culture, we observed floating in that chaotic mixture as the most heterogeneous radicals; and we alluded to the new experimenter who ostensibly searches after the mediating ingredient, the solvent factor, the binding principle of affinity.

The wedge driven
in between the
Aryans.   § 60.

Now there was a certain ethnical concomitant destined to serve in such an intermediating capacity. It consisted of those nations which formed the wedge driven in between the two wings of the Aryans. We then already had the Semites in view, when alluding to that

Semites predisposed to
intermediate.

race of divisors and intermeddlers.

The Aryans had their best talents employed to solve the problem of combining the talents floating before their worried minds. But we saw them advance no further than that stage which human development, even at its most sublime culmination, cannot surpass.

Some people we saw watching the lips of the deity for an utterance.

Ethnographically the Semites form that drifting unit which we call the third circle of nations, and which extends from the Tigris to the Sahara, from the northern

Semites and Cushites
located; Hommel.

coast of Syria to the southern coast of Arabia. Under the term of Semites we subsume (with Hommel) the Babylonians, Canaanites, Arabs, and Sabeans. Under the

and to be discriminated.

designation of Hamito-Semites we add the Phenicians, Ægyptians. and Libyans of northern Africa.

This drift of nations was vertically driven into the lateral line of Aryans, bisecting it in the middle.

As we found the polar axis of the Aryans lying between Benares and Rome, so the basis of the Semitic family rests upon the coasts of Malabar and Libya. Nile and Euphrates form the side-borders of the territory, upon which the fulcrum-points of their mutual leverages are fixed.

§ 83. Beneath that drift lay a stratum of dark color and of Uralo-Altaic descent. In the first place, therefore, the preceding culture of the Cushites interlinked the connection between Æthiopia, Arabia, and India. To them the enigmatic cave-dwellings are to be ascribed which, whether found in Æthiopia, India, or Kurdistan, bear the mark of common lineage.

Substratum of a people of Uralo-Altaic descent.

Cave-dwellers.

With reference to the original homes of the Cushites we can only compute, that they were also settled between the Libyan desert and the coast of Malabar. The supposition that the Cushites of prehistoric times belonged to the Turanian or Altaic substratum, is now an almost established fact, since even stronger inferences can be drawn in its support than those derived from the appellations Kurdistan and Hindookush. As early as 1864 Lenormant averred that the Akkado-Sumerian basis of Mesopotamian fetishism greatly differed from the Semitic system of religion; and that the old naturalism of the Cushites—from whom the Akkadians copied their talismans and conjurative formulas,—was that of the Tatars, Finns, and Turks, those European nations kindred with Cush. Poole in 1880 published the portrait of an Elamite—i. e. Cushite—king found upon a vase in Susa. This is black and distinctly shows the Cushitic features, Whilst Assyrian antiquities are always of the Semitic type, the Babylonian never deviate from the Cushitic. Whenever the latter type—tantamount to the Æthiopian—appears upon Assyrian monuments, it is expressed as unmistakably as the Jewish type, which is always distinguishable from the Arabic.

Hamito-Cushites.

Akkado-Sumerian fetishism. LENORMANT.

Vase discovered in Susa. POOLE.

Babylonian antiquities vary from Assyrian; bear marks of Cushite nature.

There is sufficient proof extant to vindicate the proposition, now generally acknowledged, that the Cushites came into the country of the two rivers from the south. Around the Mesopotamian region they founded two empires, viz: east of the Tigris a Susanian kingdom, that of Elam; west of it the people of Sumer-Akkad soon amalgamated with the inhabitants of the first Chaldean empire. In Mesopotamia the Cushites are identified beyond a doubt. We may as well call them Hamites at once.

Elam-Susania.

Hamites in Mesopatamia.

The valley is about 500 miles in length, running a great way along the Arabian desert and up to the highland of Aram. In the north the Taurus mountains shield the valley, whilst the Persian Gulf makes it accessible from the south.

The fact is well known how in the spring of 1874 George Smiths discovered the libraries of Sennacherib under the heaps of rubbish at Kujundshik. Layard had excavated a rather small set of tablets; Smiths found 8000 of them, counting in the fragments. Dr. Hilprecht is now translating more than 20,000 tablets brought to Philadelphia, only last year (1898). Sufficient material, therefore, is at hand to evince the culture of a date more ancient than any other.

Discoveries at Kuyundshik. LAYARD, GEO. SMITHS.

That culture is named Akkadian from the biblical town of Akkad. Its discovery most affirmatively disclosed the Cushitic character of the dark deep substratum.

Culture of Akkad. Discoveries corroborate biblical notices.

The interpretation here accepted was, as late as 1890, held to be an untenable conjecture, altho the kings of Erech and Elam have come forth from what was called mythical darkness, as persons of historical reality equal to that of Cyrus. An extremely old system of writing, a reckoning by sexinals, and, according to Lenormant and Hommel, a belief in ghosts similar to Shamanism has been uncovered as the imperishable substructure of Semitic culture in succession to the Cushitic layer which had drifted over the lowest substratum.

Erech-Elam.

Shamanistic substratum underneath Semitic culture.

LENORMANT, HOMMEL.

In the regions of the lower Euphrates many a glazed tile of exquisite workmanship speaks of "Urukh, king of Ur," and of "Dungi, king of the Sumers and of Akkad" —and reveals a ghost-cult, too, which goes far to verify our conviction as to the dark abyss into which evidently human consciousness once had sunk.

Kings of Ur.

The Akkadian cultus mixes demons of water, earth, air, and storm in most frightful manner. It is more than probable that here we stand before the source of all the formulas of the black arts in general, which later on were transplanted into Europe.

Source of conjury.

There, already, are monstrous sprites, which "came from the bowels of the earth to kick down the estuaries built to ward off the ocean," according to Hommel's translation. Other ghosts, according to Maspero (Ægypt and Assyria 1891) are meant by "the big worms sent down by heaven—the horrible ones, whose howling overspreads the city, who fall down with the water from heaven."

Akkadian cults of demons and snakes.

Thus, what Lenormant suggested, long before we received the latest evidences, has been proved: that they are Uralo-Altaic reminiscences without doubt or mistake. Hommel as yet refuses to acknowledge traces of hymns to the gods in the cultus of the Sumerians. Further north, however, such traces appear in the "psalms of contrition" written in the Akkadian dialect. In them we hear heart-rending bemoanings of "deeds of iniquity". Only that the intensity of mortification is almost outbalanced by the terrible dread of witchcraft. Take for instance the formula of exorcising the earth-ghosts which trampled down the walls of the ocean:

Sprites and spectres to be outmarshalled. HOMMEL, MASPERO.

Pre-Semitic Shamanism. LENORMANT.

In the northern part: Psalms of contrition. § 57, 84, 92.

> They are seven, seven of them,
> Seven down in deepest waters;
> Luring on the roads to kill us,
> Heaven's destroyers which they are.
> They are bad, too bad they are.
> Heaven's spirits please to conjure.
> O, ye spirits conjure them !

Formula of exorcism. E. SCHRADER.

Sumero-Akkadian rites brought to Mesopotamia from Mongolian regions.

"The hostile utuk, the hostile alu, the hostile gihim"—so the incantations continue under repetitions which depict a most intense anguish. E. Schrader (Sammlung von Babylon. und Assyr. Texten, 1889) coincides with our supposition that Sumero-Akkadian demon-rites were brought from the present regions of Shamanism, where since then they have become more fully developed.

Monotheism preceding Cushitic rites.

§ 84. Preceding this demon-cult, however, the traces of the worship of one God are found, of the sun, too, and of a knowledge of the starry skies. In hymns and psalms, as stated above, the consciousness of human weakness and sinfulness is expressed so deep and sincere, that complaints more touching and pure are found in no other nation save one.

Chaldeo-Babylonian and Assyrian cultures are Semitic but tinctured with Cushitic elements.

It is beyond the scope of the present induction to show, how that drift of Semitic origin alluviated on top of the Cushitic stratum. Most likely the shifting of the Semitic layer was caused by the Aryans pressing upon them from the north. Pushed to the south the Semites there fixed their abodes and founded their monarchies. That the Chaldea-Babylonians took possession of those regions is unquestioned. With that a mixture of cultures ensued which wrought products of Semitic material with Cushitic alloys. Hommel just recently (Ausland 1892, § 7.) adduced proofs, that Chaldean astronomy with its lunar and planetary constellations has many features in common with Arabian, i. e. Semitic, but none with Hindoo or Chinese astronomy.

Tales of the fall and the flood.

Concerning religion it is simply to be stated that the dualistic view of life is plainly indicated among the Assyro-Babylonians. The renowned traditional tale of the flood—found by Smiths upon the now partly restored clay tablet, written in very ancient cuneiform characters—and also the Babylonian version of the fall in unison with many other documentary remnants similar in kind, know of the fight between the divine ancestors and the dragon.

Divine ancestors fighting the "dragon." Delitzsch.

In this dualism we again recognise, that, as Delitzsch said, even this nation possessed a vivid feeling and consciousness of guilt, and made confession of it in doleful utterances of contrition, since in every trouble and vicissitude they perceived the well-deserved punishment of the gods. Their psalms of repentance bemoan the com-

Cognition of man's dual nature in Assyro-Babylon. Smith.

missions of sins in a thrilling manner, and express a deep yearning after forgiveness of sins, expiation of guilt, and cleansing from wickedness. All this is going on under the high pressure of a most massive despotism, which the works of art bring to view.

Yearning for the forgiveness of sins. § 57, 83, 92.

This art is entirely ornamental, pertaining exclusively to architecture. For religious purposes art was no further applied than in the Babylonian temples, whilst the architecture of Ninive remained largely palatial. The bas-reliefs were intended to simply adorn stairways, entrances, pillars, etc., since for shaping plastic figures of idols there was no occasion. The winged lions and the few statues are calculated to break the monotony of spaces.

Temple architecture of Babylon; palatial of Ninive.

Assyro-Babylonian art.

Every artistic design evinces the stiff deportment of courtly mannerism. Even in the nude or in drapery, realism pure and simple is avoided. The manes of horses are laid into elaborately twisted plaits as well as the hair and beards of human heads.

Assyro-Babylonians not idolatrous,

Every figure is represented as either posing or cringing under pompous conventionalism; every arrangement is ceremonious and commanded; each detail must impress the beholder with awe for the unapproachable dignity of the monarch who has taken the place of the patriarch. All must move by steps measured and prescribed, and dress in the garments

but shows culture under despotism.

which austere court-etiquette demands. As Ægyptian art is dedicated to the gods, so that of Assyro-Babylon celebrates the kings. And what a set of rulers they were. Look at Assarhaddon in festive attire. Bound with the rope, which he holds in his hands, are a Syrian king and a vanquished Pharaoh; the rope goes through the lips of the captives.

Letters from Babylon to Tel el Amarna. § 87.
Lehmann.

It is no mean strip of land which produced this art. From the tiles discovered at Tel el Amarna (which by the way, reveal a correspondence between contemporaneous kings of Ægypt and Babylon), we glean the fact, that Babylonian language and writing were in vogue at Joseph's time as the means of communication "throughout eastern Asia down to Ægypt."

Ægyptian culture of Mesopotamian extraction Hommel.

§ 85. This leads us to the Mizraim, the two Ægypts of the Nile-valley. The old controversy as to the origin of its culture has been decided in favor of the two-river-valley, i. e. of Mesopotamia.

"As far as history discloses the past we know of no nation dwelling by the side of a great river, where the culture, the inner character and external relations are so entirely conditioned by nature and geographical situation, as that of Ægypt. This seems to be the reason why the Ægyptians alone in all history contracted such pronounced peculiarities as their arts show forth."

In the case of Ægypt this observation of Ritter contains much truth. Bound up in nature the consciousness of this nation is largely determined by the torpidity of the waste surroundings. *Nature determining Ægyptian history. Ritter.*

Our almost complete knowledge of Ægyptian life and mind, we owe to the preservation of monumental and documentary relics, and this is due no less to the unique climatic conditions, than to their religion which furnished the temples and tombs as archive-chambers. *To climate we owe the preservation of relics as much as to temples and tombs; i. e. to the religious life of the Ægyptians.*

Concerning the national character, however, Ritter's assertion is to be modified; in a race thus mixed it can be true but to a certain extent.

J. G. Mueller has emphasised this in his work on the relations of the Semites to the Hamites and Japhetites. It was also emphasised by Bunsen. Brugsch Bey, too, in his "History of Ægypt under the Pharaohs" accepts our axiom of Cushite negro tribes having formed the substructure for the high culture of this nation. Those very Cushites were "the ancestors of the negro tribes of today". They were the Nahasu of the hieroglyphs, dark brown and black. Beside them the yellowish brown Anu appear; and later on blue-eyed Libyans (most probably Celts, who had immigrated from Europe) are, according to Faidherbes, plainly delineated in the paintings. *A mixture of races. T. G. Mueller, Bunsen, Brugsch. Cushite negroes the substratum of Ægyptian culture. Nahasu-Anu. Celts. § 60 Faidherbes.*

Viewed irrespective even of the later Asiatic immigrations, the principal features of the Ægyptian nationality are very singular. Their earlier legends contain many incidents concerning their arrival from interior parts of Africa. As early as 1806, before these legends were known, Seezen intimated to Hammer-Purgstall his supposition as to such an origin. He had been led to this inference by observing that the teeth of mummies had been trimmed with files, which is the custom of all Africans. Hammer quotes Seezen's letter (Fundgruben I, 64.) as worthy of being noticed. Hence two alternate strata of culture are obvious. There are the traces, first, of the lowest and primitive Cushitic substratum. Then came a large wave of the Semitic inundation from the east across the isthmus of Suez, which had been set in motion by the starting of the Aryans from their homes in Central Asia. This Aryan invasion of Iran caused the propulsion of the northern Semites to Mesopotamia, consequently that of the southern Semites to the Nile. *Immigrants from interior Africa: prior to Asiatics; inferred from filed teeth of mummies. Seezen. Conjecture to explain the complex culture. 1. Cushite substratum. 2. Immigrating into southern territories—sequent to Aryan invasion of Eran. Gobineau, Courtet.*

The latter spreading over Cushitic territory formed a layer over their culture. This conjecture alone explains the whole situation, explains the conundrum of the duplex character of the culture of Ægypt, that "Hieroglyph of History." Gobineau also, and Courtet too, arrived at this conclusion.

§ 86. Testimony more definite and complete than in the case of Assyria is procured from Ægyptian literature of an original Monotheism, purer even than that of the Rig-Veda. In the "Book of the Dead", now in Turin, the departed soul is heard to muse: "I take possession of the two worlds and restore order in the name of Nut who provided (things) in the beginning, who saw what is right before it was put in shape, before even the gods in divine council managed the affairs." *Monotheism of Ægyptian Esoterics.*

From numerous passages of similar tenor this one, quoted by V. Strauss, is sufficient to convince us of the fact, that the Ægyptians prior to any mythological systematising of their local modifications of the divine attributes, were conscious of the unity of God. Brugsch in his latest work on the "Mythology of the Ægyptians" has established the "Eneate" of "Thot", the "Thought", beyond further dispute. He states: "The religious movements clearly testify that the bearers of the hieratic gnosis were well acquainted with the unity of one supreme Deity. They well understood to use the abundance and well arranged variety of forms, representing the Deity, as more availing than that originally pure doctrine, which subsequently was transmitted to the mystic orders as their secret and wisdom." *"Book of the Dead" quoted by V. v. Strauss. The "eneat" (Pout) of Thot, the thought. Brugsch.*

"To priests initiated into the esoteric grades the doctrine of one eternal God was expounded".

Following on the track of Champillon's "Trias", Maspero had arrived at the same conclusion. Paul Pierrot judges the old Ægyptians as monotheists under guise of polytheism. The reform of the two Amenophises at about 1500 B. C. consisted in simply giving the secret to the people, in order to curtail the power of the priests; hence the "disk heresy", the rebellion, and the exodus. *Trias of Champillon, Maspero, Pierrot. Disk heresy of the Amenophises. § 84, 87, 91.*

Add to these proofs of Ægyptian Monotheism the gravity of their "judgment of the dead". *Judgment of the dead.*

There Horos stands, designated by the head of the sparrow-hawk. Toth with writing utensils sits in the midst of the parties concerned. If the soul in the scales is found wanting in quality, it is doomed to depart to the inferno of the nether world. A deep moral earnestness must underlie this conception and these solemn obsequies. And tho perpetuated by mere stiff formalities and ostentatious usages, yet that earnestness, thus exhibited and manifested, prevented the idea of personal responsibility and the consciousness of guilt from becoming obsolete. That these moral principles were retained so vividly as to remain in full force through long periods of religious corruption is due most probably to nothing else but these very funeral services of which they made so much. Not less significantly do these obsequies express the indestructible belief in the immortality of the human being. *Consciousness of guilt and responsibilities kept vivid; also of immortality.*

Resume;
High merit of
Ægyptian culture.

The crop raised from
wild seeds of the
substratum.

Scene in the
Serapeion.
§ 88. § 81.

Clemens Alexand.
Snake-worship.
v. 43, 45, 48, 49, 54, 55,
109, 135.

Looking over the signs of a tolerably well preserved original culture; and taking into account the plenitude of moral tenets, which to preserve for posterity the Ægyptians were so careful, and which were so noble as to evoke even our admiration; considering also the remnants of the unity of "Pout" as cultivated by hieratic theology—there yet remains one circumstance to be reviewed which to science will be a standing puzzle forever. Do we refer to the meaning contained in the sphinx, in those colossal pylones, or those gigantic buildings and huge funeral piles? No, only witness the surprise of Clemens·of Alexandria and his surmise, when he looked at the priest who drew back the heavy, gold-embroidered curtains. A glance was granted to him into the innermost sanctuary,and behold—upon purple cushions a snake uncoils! Such, then, is the loathsome and wretched secret of all these monstrous labyrinthian halls. "See here Ægypt," exclaims Clemens, "behold your gods!" Such, amidst the splendor of the Serapeion, was the cause and is the result of the stiffening rule of fear.

Tombs of Apis.

Light in tombs:
exceptional
phenomenon.

Sacred crocodiles.
Mummified cats.

There are the caves containing the marvellous tombs of Apis. In the chambers or rather excavated crypts to the right and left stand the sarcophagi of the sacred bullocks. At one time a holy lamp was burning above each of these niches, throwing a dim light upon the cells and the middle corridor:—an exceptional and inexplicable phenomenon in the history of religions. Just as incomprehensible are the swarms of sacred crocodiles once fed and feted in pools adjoining the temples; to say nothing about the magnificent funeral rites of mummified cats, the remains of which are now exported by shiploads as fertilizer.

Combination of
religions; represented in
human figures
with heads of
beasts.

The mystery of Ægypt lies in this sharp contrast of the two different cultures, at the bottom of which we see the worship of brutes common to all African negroes. Above that a culture of a much higher nature with noble maxims of an highly ethical character, and with the judgment of the dead. Stages of culture at such variance are nevertheless, generally blended, as we found it in Mesopotamia and as they always mingle where Semites inundate an area previously occupied by Cushites. And whenever the old, rude element of the massive substratum was heaved up and became victorious, then the beast predominated; then even the human figure was made sacred by putting the head of a beast upon it. Beast-worship is characteristic of the lower element ever since the time of the sad calamity.

Ægyptian stability:
Art never excels
the cult underlying it.
§ 54, 55, 56, 80, 128.

Human figure
in sculpture,
set free from the
pillar
but was still attached to
the back.

Death personified
everywhere.

§ 87. Ægyptian art no more than any other was ever able to surpass the character of its underlying cultus. The Ægyptian representations of the human being have their significance solely in architecture. The stiff figures are fastened with their backs to the walls or the pillars. True, later on the human figure is set free ; but altho taken off the pillar, the wall is still attached to the back of the sitting statue. The human being seems to exist chiefly for serving architecture and for the sake of being entombed. Hence art, enchanted by the all-dominating conservatism and the charm of sacred antiquity,can,throughout its existence for a score of centuries, do nothing but picture absolute rest. It shows no sign of an idea as to organic functions of members and actions of the body, so that the works of Ægyptian art seem to personify death everywhere. Being but caskets of petrified life these works are unfit to represent anything but stability. The sculpture of muscles indicates languor, on the one hand, and the indifference of art to real life ; whilst on the other it shows faithful adherence to methodical and monotonous regularity of present and future existence.

Character and inner life
better understood
than in Greek art.
§ 64 Overbeck.

In one respect Ægyptian art, however, is remarkably in advance even of the Greeks. The human physiognomy is conceived more in the order of grandeur, and the inner value expressed with admirable precision and ingenuity. Character seems to have been more appreciated than graceful appearance, and to have been studied with delicate criterion.

Overbeck in his observations on that score declared, that more freedom in general at that stage of development would have signified decay of art and culture rather than progress.

Stability of theocratic
rule.

Divine honors to rulers.

The same rigid stability reigned in the hieratic form of government. The Pharaohs, according to the myths, were considered as the successors of a series of divine dynasties, as the heirs of Horus, the child of Osiris. From time immemorial such descent and exalted position had been attributed to the kings, but still more were they extolled after the expulsion of the Hyksos. Subsequent to this event the king is looked up to as standing in direct communication with the gods. For this reason it was nothing very extraordinary that divinity was conferred upon Alexander by the priests of Amon. Even Ptolemy Epiphanes schemed to accept the appellations "son of Ptah, son of the sun, giver of life for evermore !"

Upon that basis the kings were supposed to reign over the realm of death even.

On one side of the propylees of Medinet Abu is painted the life-size picture of Tirhaka (according to Roscellini) with his right arm raised as in the act of striking with his maze. In his left hand he holds the fetters of a bundle of captives ready to be dispatched by him.

Death even under royal control: Painting of Tirhaka in Medinet Abu. Roscellini.

It is on account of these priest-kingly dynasties, that any historic progress is forestalled. Nevertheless, there is plenty of movement going on beneath the measured surface. And such commotions are indicated once in a while by chiseling out the names of unpopular rulers, or by intermittent suspension of the customary inscriptive records. The most flagrant instances of this kind are those which bear upon the memories of Hatasu, Thotmes' sister, who reigned during his minority, and of Amenophis IV, now by Wilkinson acknowledged as the Pharaoh of the Exodus.

Names of unpopular kings erased.

He felt an outspoken aversion to the gods of the Mizraim, which, of course, was very unconstitutional; especially to the predominant Amon, their chief. Following the example of his father, or perhaps induced by his affectionate queen, a southern lady like his mother and grandmother, he prays to the god of light, his favorite Aten. He goes further and sets himself up as a reformer, making himself supreme pontiff. Worse yet,—in the eyes of the priests—he has the audacity to build a new capitol midway between both the ancient capitols of the empire. For his sacred surname he assumes the title "Friend of the Solar Disk." Obviously he is an enemy of the state, a rebel against the old constitution which had been strengthened by a certain Joseph. Autonomously Amenophis IV rules, specifically stubborn in his relation to Moses; rules among his granite palaces and the works of a renaissance accumulating in his new city. All at once he disappears from his happy domestic board, and his name is hastily chiseled out of the monuments. We only know that between him and the great-grandfather of the great Ramses an interval of palace intrigues and riots gaps in the monumental records. The period is known as the "Disk-Heresy." This was the doom of an attempt to break Ægypt from its conservatism. The city mentioned is now a field of ruins with a sprinkling of huts between, called Tel el Amarna, the same place to which the Babylonian letters had been addressed by the Assyrian court. The tables covered with cuneiform characters are now in the museum of Berlin. But Amenophis' mummy has not as yet been hit upon, neither his tomb.

Attempt to a religious reform by Amenophis IV Pharaoh of the Exodus: §§84, 86, 91, Wilkinson.

Tablets of Tel el Amarna.   § 84.

From the literature pictured upon the walls a complete aspect of public and private life, as was presented by Brugsch, may easily be reconstructed. Under such an aspect we have to admit that the rigor of Ægyptian principles did not at all prevent the enjoyment of the day in frolicsome social amusement, not marred by the anxious care of tomorrow. Fun and travesty are sketched in comparative preponderance.

Imagine those relief pictures at Sakkhara below which Marietta had struck his tent amidst the ruins of the desert. Think of the mausoleum of Ti, a private citizen altho a courtier. Under the gleam of a torchlight the flat reliefs upon its inside walls are shown, from which we read how an Ægyptian of yore conducted his household. You see the master with his servants hunting the hyppopotamos; you see depicted the every-day life of a man of leisure. Here sheep are driven out to pasture, there a heifer is being butchered. Upon one square of the wall you notice women engaged with their wash; on the opposite field mowers swing their scythes through the ripe rye or wheat. Here a drove of fine cattle are led to their watering place; yonder youths are playing at tennis or throwing the disk. On one side an overseer punishes a slave, on the other a servant milks a cow, while a third feeds the calf. Frequently such sketches are accompanied by the repartees or burlesques exchanged by the persons, or by explanations of their ridiculous attitudes. Thus, looking a little deeper into the social and domestic life of Ægypt we find quite the contrary to a torpid and melancholy existence. This contrasts so strongly with what we expected as to suggest thoughts worthy to meditate upon. In the same country, with the same climate, where once a tolerably well balanced people lived, where some solid comfort reigned unshaken by such insecurities and sudden disappointments as modern civilization is entailed with, there present Ægypt under the same geographical conditions has, by the defaults of man, become proverbial for its stupor and poverty.

Painting descriptive of domestic life. Brugsch. Marietta.

Present situations of Ægyptians under the same geographical conditions.

The monuments of the victorious exploits of the Pharaohs reach northward to Colchis. The edges of the Mediterranean were dotted with the large white sails of the Ægyptian barges. But withal this there was no progress, because the empire had the opinion of itself to be complete in itself. Its humiliation, then an intermediation between the secluded selfsufficiency of sedate Ægypt with young upstarts of nations, and finally its unavoidable entrance into connection with them became historical necessities.

§ 88. The solvent ingredients mixing themselves with Ægyptian culture were none other but the very same Semitic elements which had acted with the same effect on the banks of the Euphrates. The role of go-betweens with the Ægyptians was taken, in the first place, by the subtile and crafty Phenicians.

Phenician Semites.

After the separation from their Semitic fellow-tribes in Sumer and Akkad the Phenicians left the two-river-country for the West. As it is always the case that the bad likes the Bad and takes to it much easier than to the Good, so these Semites from natural proneness to, and affinity for, the meaner quality, appropriated some of the worst Cushitic features of sensuality, whereby they became well adapted to take possession of the sea-front, to take the advantage of their inferiors in shrewdness, and became above all, most perfectly qualified to intermeddle with the affairs of the rich and inert nation with Hamito-Semitic propensities, so much like their own.

Acting as the dissolvent of Ægyptian life. §§ 87, 78, 90, 128.

Came from Sumer-Akkad to the coast;

The Phenicians bear a pronounced Cushitic stamp throughout. Brugsch in his: "Stone-Inscriptions and Biblical Word" (1891) drew the parallel between the Hamito-Semitic Phenicians and the Cushite aborigines of Ægypt:

and transmitted the most pronounced and worst traits of the Cushite elements.

"The probability is, that, from dwelling in the Pelusian plains and the Kasian countries, the Phenicians became tinctured with some of the higher elements of Ægyytian culture, which crystalised in their Melkart and Adonis cults. Their Baal, however, is specifically Babylonian." Bel is the sun-god, correlative to Baltis or Ashera (also Ashtaroth or Astarte), the goddess of the starry heavens and of nocturnal, lunar fructification. Her worship chiefly consisted in sacrificing virginity or womanly chasteness to her honor, according to rites of Babylonian invention.

But the special and chief god of the Phenician nation is the Melkart of Tyre, identical with Heracles, whom we found upon all the isles this side and beyond Gades. The lewd service, imitating the propagative functions of nature, degenerated into absolute obscenity. Side by side with the rudest indulgence in lasciviousness there are described selfmutilations of the priests and the gangs of Kinades to such an extent as to border on suicides en masse. Holocausts of children which were made burnt-offerings to Baal-Chammon or Moloch, accompanied the debaucheries going on in the groves and tabernacles of Ashera. Phenician wickedness beggars even the descriptions of Lucian in his "Syrian goddess", or those of Movers of recent date.

Adopted the Melkart-cult of Ægypt.

Melkart-Heracles.

Baal-Camos-Moloch.
Ashera.
LUCIAN, MOVERS.

In the temple of Hierapolis, peopled by swarms of Galla eunuchs, the exercises partly consisted of sacrificing young children which, according to Lucian, were sewed up in bags and thrown down from the terrace-heights of the temple. This raging against their own offspring, the Phenicians practiced wherever their own settlements grew up along the coasts. Virgins and married women gloried in abandoning themselves to   anybody in temples and under the trees of high places, under guise of religion. At Paphos and Carthage the templar rites were conducted the same as those of Ascalon and Babylon. In the service of the Taurian and Ephesian Diana, the Cybele of the Phrygians, the same filthiness prevails, as in that of the Mesopotamian Astarte. The repulsive modes of worship, polluting the Phenician soil and from thence spreading everywhere, rendered under the name of the Paphonian Venus, were not less wild and orgiastic than the Babylonian form of prostitution. Phallos service was always celebrated with selfmutilations of a most unnatural sort in the frantic and boisterous revelry of the Corybants. Toward the close of the orgies this "cult" out-raged itself in the mad frenzy of dances in which the last sparks of carnal lust and shame cannot but have been so completely exhausted as to become entirely extinct. In the face of such facts we reiterate the statement that this Semito-Hamitic tribe was better adapted than any other race could have been to manage worldly intercourse.

Mylitta—Cypele—Diana—Venus.

Obscenity of Phenician temple rites.

Abominations spread everywhere. §§ 71, 78, 81.

The international commerce, created by these kinsmen of the two-river-countries and the two Ægypts, was also sustained and monopolised by them. This was the meaning when the Semites were described as the wedge driven in between the two branches of the Aryan family, and were called a dissolvent, at the same time serving as the link of connection, as the intermediating factotum.

Phenicians adapted to worldly intercourse.

Semitic element intermeddling, dissolvent. §§ 67, 75, 128, 200, 213.

The Philistines carried on the traffic between Asia and Spain, hauling tin even from Wales, and bringing copper from Cyprus. Connoisseurs of valuables from among the Jews picked up the precious stones and jewelry which Alexander's soldiers had taken along from the sack of the Persian palaces and thrown away on their march through the southern deserts. From the coasts of Greece and the shores of the Lake of Constance their peddlars went into the interior countries, with small notions and decorative articles. After the Hellenes had cleansed themselves from the Phenician curses on the day of Salamis, repelling their influence together with that of Ægyptian culture, these traders proved the obduracy and impertinency of their Semitic natures by hunting up new fields of operation in the border countries, as the Semites are doing up to date in every zone.

Overreaching the Aryans § 93, 128.

These Phenicians were indefatigable in indemnifying themselves. Pushing on, they founded colonies among the goldminers on the Black Sea, or in the Libyan desert, always underhandedly overreaching the Aryans, ever encircling them in the wide compass of the border-lines. From thence they brought Scythian metals as well as ostrich feathers and ivory, and the leopard skins which the Ægyptian priests needed as part of their ritual paraphernalia.

Trade their specialty.

The Philistines (with scarcely any landed possessions except a few strips thickly studded with commercial cities, pseudo-republics at that), had managed to control the traffic of the entire known world from the Sierra Leone to the Indus and the Thames. *(margin: Small possessions of land. Traffic monopolised, through colonial outposts.)*

As Greece had repulsed the Phenicians mentally, so did the Romans route them with their short sword. With the Roman grabbling-hook their marine power was destroyed for ever. To maintain it Hannibal had made sacrifice of three thousand Hymenæan victims to Mammon Moloch—in vain; the proverbial "Punic faith" had to suffer its consequences. The much lamented cruelties of the Israelites against those very people, the final destruction of Tyre by Alexander, and the extirpation of Carthage, deplored by Scipio, may seem harsh means of weeding out the Cushito-Semites. But therein consisted the necessary retribution of history for their persistent propagation and dissemination of the most abominable vices. *(margin: Phenicians first mentally vanquished by the Greeks, finally exterminated through main force by the Romans. Retribution upon "Punic faith," Moloch and Mammon. § 60, 66, 71, 110.)*

"Punica Fides" ever since stands for that Mammon service which, by means of shrewdness, deceitful strategy, and cunning extorsiveness, commits the most cruel exactions. Any company of traders, any commercial republic like Carthage or Venice, may, in lieu of Moloch, fall victim to Mammonism; and it is Mammonism, more noxious even than carnal indulgence, which produces that vile, cringing crookedness of mind, which ever remained the heritage of that people with typical noses and without a native country—the Punian Semites.

§ 89. We stand at the brink of another kind of a downward grade.

Recently there arose from deep excavations the foundation walls of a temple once dedicated to the moon-goddess in the country of Sumer, city of Ur (now Mugheir) in the extreme south of Mesopotamia. It is almost certain that these immense brick mounds were built into our substratum of history at least sixty centuries ago in honor of "Sin" who now witnesses Monotheism to have existed first in Chaldea. As late as 560 B. C., on the fatal night, perhaps, when Semitism sustained its first disaster, Nabun-aid, king of Babylon, directed his prayer to Sin. *(margin: Chaldeans. Primeval Monotheism.)*

Not far from Ur old Larsa was located, the sanctuary of the sun-god and the most ancient seat of learning, according to Hommel. North of Ur and Larsa comes Urukh to light, the Erech of the Bible. There lately the extreme ends of human knowledge, (as to the order of time,) celebrated a reunion: the inventors of the first symbols of speech, and the explorers of the "Babylonian Exploration Fund" (Philadelphia). *(margin: Mugheir—Ur. Hommel. Larsa, sanctuary of the Sun-god, most ancient seat of learning. Maspero. At Erech extremes of most ancient and latest modern scholarship meet.)*

All this means that, as Maspero has it: "Back of all the Chushitic dissolution and subversions of religious consciousness we find again—One God who is both an unique and differentiated Being, ("ein einziger, aber kein einfacher Gott").

———000———

We have glanced over the Semitic nations. The Semitic type appears not to its advantage, because not in its purity, since it became mixed with the Hamito-Cushitic residue. Through the Semitic surcharge always shines the canny substratum. In relative purity it was preserved in the interior portions of Arabia, where original Semitism was protected against the encroachment of alien elements by the surrounding desert. In its full purity that type appears in the nation where it was not only preserved, because protected by special guidance,—but also cultivated with scrupulous care. Under the emphatic condition of such cultivation the strong arm of a powerful ally was pledged to this nation. *(margin: So far we dealt with Semitism in its utter impurity.)*

Have we now a few spare hours to devote to the study of that very peculiar nation?

CH. IV. THE HEBREW COMMUNITY.

§ 90. While engaged in analysing the composition, which had flown together in the Roman crucible, the Semitic ingredients arrested our attention. It was an element of a particular consistency, and yet of a peculiar affinity—hundreds of thousands of Roman subjects had turned atheists on its account. The ubiquitous Jew represents both the attractive as well as the solvent force. Notwithstanding the smallness and political insignificance of the country, with its single city worthy the attention of the ruling powers, it was the domicile of the grandest and most important of all ancient nations —provided one can appreciate that of which they are the bearers. It actually seems as tho the politics of all adjacent nations revolved about these twelve tribes. And now they contribute that principle of which the whole compound in the basin was destitute as yet : the Hebrew element, universally despised and rejected, yet ever intermeddling and decomposing putrid masses. *(margin: The people representing the attractive and solvent power. Despised for reasons of their peculiarities.)*

15

Polarity of all nations revolving upon the twelve tribes.   § 158, 221.
Last move in times of earliest migrations.   § 84.

Later than any other movement in migratory times one family without a son, descendants of a house in high standing in Mesopotamia, went west, not directly through the desert, but by the northern route. When these new immigrants arrived in the Jordan district they found the land occupied by Hamito-Semitic precursors. By them they were nicknamed as those coming from "beyond the river," where the more civilised, the high-toned people studied the arts. Treated as strangers the

"From yonder' over of the river, where a better class of people used to live.

A foothold upon earth for this household.

"Hebrews" led a nomadic life. Altho this country, where the patriarch set up an altar and struck his family tent, had been portioned out by destiny to him and his posterity : they yet had to wander from place to place. Altho mere sojourners, the household should here gain as much, at least, as a foothold on earth.

Situation of the holy land.

Equipoise between northern and southern Semites.

The geographical situation of that country is peculiarly adapted to the position which this family is to occupy in history. At even distance between the metropolitan cities of the Semitic world, Thebes and Babylon, this central region of the ancient world forms the equipoise between the two opposites of northern and southern Semitism in their polar strain. It is a peculiar parallel thus formed between the rivers of the old cultural countries with the small Jordan in the mean.

Second Circle.

ARYANS.

BA-BYLON.

JERU-SALEM.

MECCA.

CADIZ   CAPE COMORIN

SEMITES.

Third Circle.

The most definite and concentric circle of humanity with the most intensified religiousness
The only nation not completely crushed by Rome.
Clannish; proud of pedigree.
This nation and its book.
Israels singularities
Bible not product of "national spirit," which it surpasses in every respect.

And it is no less a weighty center for the circle of the Aryans. Let us draw in our minds a line from Cadiz to Cape Comorin, then strike a semi-circle , one point of the compass resting upon Palestine the other striking to the north from end to end of the diameter, and the whole area covered by the Aryan races is exactly bounded, with Palestine as the center. Fan-shaped the Aryans, the second of our three circles of humanity, branch out in all directions from—yes, let us say: Jerusalem.

The Hebrews form the third circle proper, the most concentric of human history —with the most intensified religion. It had become intensified under pressure; first in Ægypt, then between the two mill-stones of Babylon and Ægypt, now under Rome. And it was the solitary nation in the basin whose existence had not been completely crushed.

In this "Holy land" the sojourning family becomes a nation, the best organised body politic; severely exclusive; a puzzle even to kindred nations. Altho fond of association, they are a most obdurate and clannish folk, nevertheless; intensely proud of their pedigree, of their organic law, and their institutions.

This nation possesses, cultivates, and perpetuates above anything else an almost antiquated, yet ever progressive and singular literature. For, the more we compare both, the nation and the book, and these again with the contemporaneous nations and books, the more decisive will be the conclusion, that this nation is entirely inadequate to its literature. Its books are rather given to, than grown out of, this nation. To be sure, that literature bears the physiognomy of this nationality, but only as if to veil its deep pensiveness, and as if to protect itself from profanation. That literature came out of this nation, yet it is not its spontaneous product, being related to the nation like a child to its mother, bearing her marks, but being begotten by the father.

The nation is impregnated with its literature in a manner, that altho comprising its essentials and holding forth its history, the nation yet assumes its character only desultory, while in every sense the book surpasses the national spirit.

According to that literature God laid the foundation of that history in a miraculous method. God sets aside a patriarch by detaching him from his native soil. The patriarch trusts and, without seeing his God, obeys Him. Upon the principle of this faithful obedience, altho realised in a very unsatisfactory manner, and under a discipline which tends to wean the children of the household from things seen, that is from things diverting the mind—a nation is educated and built up.

Covenants under conditions.

Upon God's conditions it enters a covenant with Him, and is henceforth guided and protected by the almighty arm of its unseen and holy "Lord". The nation, nevertheless, disavows its faith and is left in the hands of those on whose account it broke the covenant, in order to be chastised by them, until it lies low and, looking up, cries for mercy and owns its guilt. Thus a sacred and unparalleled history ensues, a record of confidential intercourse and personal union between God and His own.

Sin and Grace.

Notwithstanding their sins Grace always takes the initiative in lifting up and encouraging the penitent without abandoning the least detail of the covenant stipulations. The institutions are thereby kept inviolable and intact. They continue to symbolise the facts bearing on both sides of the case, and reassure the frightened law-breakers of the Lord's forbearance in still owning them. Thus, tho punished, humiliated, and being made the most impotent of all nations, God is with them so ostensibly, that the gentiles become apprised of the fact. Thus the "Children of Israel", through holy discipline, are preserved and molded

The historical task and discipline of Israel.

into a vessel which is to bear to the world the secret of God's intentions. God speaks with them   "Special Revelation."
through "His word", by means of the Shechinah i. e., the reflection of His glory, through His   § 114.
representative, "the Angel of His Countenance."

§ 91. This nation is a marvel to all other nations, yet because of certain natural   Refutation of "higher criticism" attempting to decry Old Testament religion as a product of the national spirit," in order to undermine the religious institution § 55, 66, 91, 128, 168.
propensities, becoming peculiarly modified by their juncture with matters purely
divine, its features are often seen so distorted as to appear most revolting. For, in
itself it is a vessel with very much mean clay in its make-up. It is in no way better
than kindred nations northeast and southwest, in many things of a much inferior
caliber. But nevertheless it remains the nation to which are entrusted the promises;   The vessel mean and impure yet appointed warden of the promises.
which is to be the warden of the Supreme Good, and to continue, even under suffer-
ings, the witness of God's intentions with man and history.

The reality and attainability of the Supreme Good, and the truth of the divine
purposes are plainly discernible in the very facts through which they were manifested historically; in the methods of discipline, guidance and preservation; in the
manner in which the highest gift was bestowed.

These benefits were all of a moral character, pledged and bestowed in accordance
with conditions agreed upon, needless of much explanation.

It does not matter at all, what is thought of the elements carried along by this nation at   Historic basis of Ægyptian externals in the Mosaic legislation.
their deliverance from the bondage endured upon the flats of the Nile. Its sense of dignity
had become stupefied under task-masters, but it was there that the necessary awakening of
its national consciousness took place, since only there the great contrast between their religious traditions and those of the gentiles could have become fully apparent. Israel's convictions simply rested upon the authority of the fathers; but this authority was sufficient to
prevent the intermixture of corruptive elements from the substratum. MOREOVER BY THE
LAWS SUBJECTING EVEN THE MOST SACRED EXTERNALS AND SYMBOLS TO REPEATED PURIFICA-
TIONS A DEIFICATION OF THE INSTITUTIONAL PART OF RELIGION WAS FORESTALLED.

Moses may have been trained under the tuition of Pentaour, the renowned epic writer
at Ramses' court (as Lenormant thought, altho he would now certainly accept Wilkinson's   Moses in synchronology. LENORMANT, WILKINSON. § 84, 86, 87.
synchronology agreeing with ours as to the correctness of the biblical date, which sets Moses'
apprenticeship in Ægyptian wisdom 170 years farther back); or Moses may have been adopted
by Hatasu, the sister of Thotmes III, under whom Ægypt attained the zenith of its power. The
fact is, that neither the time nor the incidents of this or that reign alter these principles of the
unique covenant with the patriarch which ever stand in direct opposition and distinct contrast to paganism.

What makes the work of Moses so extraordinary is as little explained by the Ægyptian
externals in the Mosaic legislation, as the mental capacities of a scholar can be demonstrated
from the lecture notes of his teacher. The alleged "predisposition of the Semites for Monotheism" is nothing else but what ingenuity is in human nature.

Every man might be a genius—at any rate as regards receptivity.   Israelites rather receptive than inventive
The Israelitic mind was nothing if not receptive, and what had been bequeathed
to it was Monotheism as—a gift. There was nothing meritorious or inventive about   Monotheism given.
it. Moses merely received some new views simultaneously with certain rediscoveries.

The original receptivity had been exercised by the patriarchal father, of the now
grown family, when the personal God, the God of his fathers had made Himself
known to him. Abraham's Monotheism can be considered as a new religion in so far   Discovery of this special Monotheism.
only, as it was that personal communication by which the father of the people had
become affiliated with God, by which a friendly relation was established and kept up,
and which, by way of family tradition, had been handed down to posterity through,
at the least, five centuries. The rediscovery of Moses occurred when God chose to   Moses rediscovery in due historic form and order.
enter the historic situation in person for the purpose of liberating the children adopt-
ed on account of their father, and in fulfillment of the promise given to him. In due
form and without any inconsistency at all God intervened for the sake of humanity
whose cause was included in the covenant. Not at variance with any of the principles of natural propaedeutics God disclosed His further purposes to Moses, because
th's man like the nation itself had undergone special preparations necessary for
being entrusted with such high commissions. For the time being it was for the pur-
pose of making the first step towards special revelation; and therein consisted the   Traditional (FAMILY) covenant rendered a NATIONAL institution.
single secret of the Mosaic rediscovery and the whole of the Mosaic innovation: that
the federal relation should henceforth become the national institution.

Such of our modern "AUTHORITIES" (copying Celsus) as impute a Monotheistic "instinct"
to Israel, or others who describe the process how that instinct developed in Moses so far as to
impose upon the world a religion manufactured from Ægyptian esoterics—in short, who are
contriving to empty revelation of its objective AUTHORITY, and to explain away the miraculous
part of it;—such labor under a lack of information.

They wish to prove that this nation had arrived at worshiping the One, invisible God in the most natural and simple way possible, not being aware that such gratuitous proof is doomed to remain not only futile, but to recoil even on evolutionism. They overlook the fact

that the very Semitic group, of which Israel was but a small part, had degenerated into complete religio-cultural corruption long before this tribe arose —recovered, we might say from its infection with heathenism—by virtue of the discovery. They did not pause to inquire how it was possible, that such a stupefied nation could, amidst universal waywardness and decay, not only stand firm enough to hold its own by strict separation, but also, what is still more singular and significant, how in spite of terrible internal and international disasters it could gain that inner sublimity which alone enabled it to formulate its grand cognitions. What natural cause could be adduced for Israel's ability to rise repeatedly above ruination and to look triumphantly into the future? What other nation looked forward with such an assured hope to the future? All the contemporaries could but look back upon a glorious past that offered nothing but discouragement.

Israel's hope, a function of the spirit of a quality unknown to all the rest of mankind, was perfectly clear and sure and calm. Like a sober person among a staggering crowd of drunkards this nation stands by its religion, altho they learned to fully appreciate it only after many signs of divine displeasure. Such steadfastness would be desecrated by the mere comparison with the orgies of all the surrounding idolaters.

Furthermore, the historiography of all surrounding, yea, of all ancient nations, is more or less boastful. In every other instance the national chronicles exaggerate the deeds and admire the sins of their heroes, in order to magnify their own grandeur —or selfconceit. "The Old Testament alone—Niebuhr remarked—is an exception

to patriotic untruthfulness. Never is the sin of any of its heroes covered up; never hidden under silence is a humiliating chastisement of that nation whose history 'the book of the nations' puts upon record. Such honesty must be acknowledged

as the highest virtue of the historiographer, even by one who does not believe in divine inspiration."

Niebuhr was competent to judge. While investigating the sources of Assyro-Babylonian history, he is justified in calling it "old-fashioned and insipid mannerism, when some scholars betray the weakness of their cause by their hesitancy to adopt and to employ the pre-christian literature of the Jews as reliable sources."

The central position of their historiography is occupied by the prophets. They practice a relentless self-criticism never biased by any patriotic partiality, tho they

proved to be the staunchest of patriots.

The series of prophets is a succession of miracles through many centuries. None of them can be understood or interpreted merely from historical coincidents or from the spirit of their times. There is no accommodation to the spirit of the times with them. "Those men did criticise with an unequalled power and in utter disregard to

popularity. Lightning splitting an oak is as nothing compared with the short parallel sentences which dash to pieces forever one system of imaginary cosmogony

after another. Where are these systems now in the face of the word spoken to Isaiah: ' I form the light and create darkness. I make peace and create evil. I the Lord do all these things".(Steinthal).

§ 92. Such an aspect of the Jewish nation presents itself, as it stands there, a stranger in its solitariness, not understood and stared at by the nations. It stands reserved, looking careworn and harassed like a man who is anxiously concerned to keep a great and portentous secret, altho that care consumes his own vitality.

Hence this nation does not possess the buoyancy of ancient art, not the bubbling productiveness of its hilarious nonchalance. Israel is intensely religious and merely receptive. Its whole superiority simply consists in the qualification for receiving and —keeping the secret, until it is in order to circulate it. For, the thoughts and prom-

ises confided to this nation do not concern it alone; notwithstanding their reservedness they have great bearing upon the welfare of the whole world. Without a national literature (in the usual sense of the phrase) of spontaneous growth from seeds below, that nation is singled out to receive the "Word" from above, and to preserve this sacred, written covenant as its most precious inheritance in perfect integrity.

The children of Israel alone remained without an epic, without that class of poetry in which during the process of becoming conscious of themselves, the nations used to objectivise their innermost mind by contemplating its heroes and its caricatures. It is all the historic memory such nations possess. On that score Israel could afford to be without a national epic, since from its books the nation was well aware of the fact that every thing which happened was preserved in the memory of the Lord. Hence Israel alone had a real history, a true mirror for selfrecognition without flattery. *Israel in contrast to other nations concerning the past and the future.*

And yet this nation had been reared in the expectation of nothing less than the realisation of a truth stranger than fiction, of the divine condescension whereof others had dreamt. It had been made desirous and was in good earnest to meet its national hero from above. Upon the coming One all hopes were concentrated, whilst the nations of profane history without exception look backward upon a golden age in the past, upon an æra of peace and rest, of paradise and intercourse with the gods, an æra of demi-gods, of liberating giants and of helpful elves.— This nation alone looks upward for its liberator, looks ahead for its rest and its reunion with the fathers in times to come. Also in this respect Israel stands sober among the intoxicated, as it is well put by Lotze: "The Hebrews were not seized by the giddiness of an eternal rotation of nature, because they knew themselves to be involved in the prospects of a progressive history." In another and special sense this nation deserves the attribute of sobriety. It considers as "sin" what others lightly took for pain, passion, ills of life, or common weakness. From the time God called Abraham to sever earthly connections and to leave his native home, He always loosened the chosen nation from the soil, whenever its natural proneness toward ramifying into the soil and even the sub-soil would thrive in the growth of wild vines or water-shoots. *Not intoxicated by naturalistic progress, because cognisant of its historical prospects. Lotze.*

For this reason Israel was released from the Ægyptian bondage just in time to save the last spark of selfrespect, when it began to become so stupid as to enure itself to the basest indignities. God took the people aside to teach them reliance upon Him and resistance to enemies. He educated the children of Israel by historical experience, by symbolic acts, but especially by the gift of His commandments. These "Words" were to urge on each of them, in his way of duty as a member of the community, and at the same time as being amenable, directly to God, his sole ruler. These are the cardinal principles upon which the national existence of Israel is founded. But body and soul fail the Israelite, when, in sequence to these simple conditions, he lies prostrate under the mortifying consciousness of having sinned in the very face of God—and when, nevertheless, his spirit thirsts after God, after the living God. In this outcry the feeling of the rupture is expressed and confessed, by which the creature is severed from its Creator.

To other nations the abyss caused by this rupture seems to be irrelevant; a mere metaphor for denoting a metaphysical difficulty, in which man finds himself at sea and, perhaps, not altogether without fault—in case he cannot blame metaphysics for it. But Israel does not deceive itself. Instead of palliating guilt or shifting it upon other persons or circumstances, Israel daily confesses its iniquities as a personal, a very serious, and most pressing matter. No nation had come to such deep recognition of the chasm as the **religio-ethical source** of all trouble. *Sobriety in its cognition of sin and its consequences. Methods of Israel's preparatory education.*

Hence, here alone the contrite mind is heard to remorsefully complain: "Against Thee, Thee only have I sinned and done this evil in Thy sight!" Not one of the Akkadian psalms reaches so low, nor touches that height of conscientiousness. Notwithstanding the many attempts in Israel to smooth it off, the sin is under all circumstances branded as disloyalty and faithlessness against the faithful, the holy, and known God of the Covenant. But the trustworthiness of the divine promise of forgiveness with its just conditions is also known, and thanks to it guilt need not drive any sinner to despair; for, ALTHO SIN IS NEVER CONCEALABLE, GUILT IS NEVER IRRECONCILABLE. *Disciplinary purpose in the Decalogue: contrition of heart; confidence in restitution. Israel's consciousness of Holiness as compared with the levity of other nations.*

In keeping with the deep and never-to-be lulled consciousness of guilt and its actual confession, the all-pervading idea of sacrifice is here preserved in its purity, and prominently set forth, and cleared up. To this end the significance of sacrifice is specified in the ordinances of sin- and peace-offerings with their subdivisions. In the same light under which the fact of creation is revealed in this literature, so the true thought of salvation also becomes distinct by degrees conditioned simply by the presence of the honest desire for it. *Guilt not palliated; sin not trifled with. § 57, 63. Trust in God's promises. Integrity of the idea of sacrifice. Revelation of salvation by degrees— analogous to that in creation.*

Not merely the presence of God among the people, but His gracious, sin-forgiving presence among His own and pardon on His own terms is being vouchsafed. With the mysterious dwelling of God among His people, with the pledges of conciliatory reunion, final incarnation and ultimate full communion, this nation is highly privileged, indeed, but it is, at the same time, put under correspondingly great responsibilities. It is both, PARDONED AND BURDENED: being conditioned day by day, and bound over to a permanent probation, altho with reference to the world, this nation is to be the most free and independent. *God condescends to be present with His people. Israel pardoned and burdened, in its separatism.*

The nation to serve
others in the character
of a prophet.

To be and remain independent from the world was of most essential necessity to Israel, conditioning the possibility to fulfill its vocation and to accomplish its prophetical functions. For, the nation as a whole was charged with the duty of being a standing witness for, and thus to prophesy to the whole world, the conciliation of real existence with ultimate destiny. In order to be of any benefit to the world, the prophet must maintain his freedom from becoming implicated in its ungodly purposes, and must be wary not to commit himself, as if he were in league with it, or even its servant. Tho a servant of God, his function in the world implies a certain sovereignty.

Prophets proclaim
conciliation of real
existence with ideal
destiny.
§ 39, 63, 64, 122, 139, 147,
152, 158.

Sovereignty of
the prophets
in their independence

from the "world,"
in their
negative work
as to false messianic
expectations;

In two lines thought develops that sovereign policy of prophecy throughout the history of this race.

The one is to proceed on the negative, inasmuch as the people in general expect a popular ruler, a national king. In accord with a large measure of selfadmiration the imagination of the people attributes all possible glory with a large portion of illusive vain-glory added, to its Prince. It is expected of Him, that He coerce all nations of the earth to submit to their liberating rule. The prophets partook of their hope and were conscious of the value of the nation. But what they declared concerning this value, was made ambiguous by public opinion, and perverted into belief fathered by the common desire. The expectation dominates the vulgar understanding, that the coming king would force the entire world under the dominion of the chosen people. This very particular and selfcomplacent Jewish nation persuaded itself, that, caste-wise, it would put its feet upon the necks of the rest of mankind.

since the Messiah was
subtly conceived as
a means
to satisfy worldly
aspirations.

Jewish selfcomplacency.

Parallel to modern
errors of chiliastic
dreams.

2. Positive task of
prophecy:

The other is the positive line of prophetic thought. Erroneous expectations are corrected. Prophets predict that the clamor for a messianic kingdom, raised by demagogues under the subterfuge that public opinion with its pretensions demanded it so, will be crushed out of the political religionists. In this way the wrong opinions and selfish desires came to be exposed in the Bible. The prophets had many opportunities to preach the fallacy of the vainglorious ideas and to give warning lest the reliance upon worldly power should prove the extinction of their existence as a state. In contrast to the picture of the triumphant worldly king they present the figure of a suffering and despised one. Opposite the imaginary Lord is placed the forecast of the Servant of God. He is likened unto a tender branch sprouting from the root of Jesse, sprouting up from dry ground, from the withering stock of that nation. By numerous analogies the contrast is exhibited between the natural depravity of this select nation and the supernatural influences enjoyed by it. These influences are designated as infusions into the nation. The Servant of God is announced to enter history as "The Seed," the "Eternal Word," as the scion engrafted from on high, in order to take upon Himself the sins of the nation and of mankind in its entirety.

to present the true
figure of the
"Messiah" the
"Servant" of God.
§ 13, 36, 105, 117, 120,
223.

Natural depravity and
inspiration.

Resume:
of the results of Semitic
culture.

§ 93. What, concerning Israel, the world anticipated or despised, cannot be understood, much less properly esteemed, unless we first take our usual retrospect of the Semitic race as a whole.

The ancient seats of culture on the Euphrates and the Nile had wrought various and valuable improvements which, by way of Phenician inter-relations, had been communicated and distributed, and thus became common property of all the people around the Mediterranean.

Assyrian contribution to
universal culture.

Division of time.

The tribe of Asshur contributed to the progress of culture the partition of space by the zodiac, and the division of time into weeks of seven days, and into days of twenty four hours, and many other things irrelevant to our present investigation. For we are here only engaged in observing how the life of humanity in general was influenced by the Semitic form of consciousness, by the psychical phenomena manifest in this race.

Monotony of deserts
does not create
Monotheism, as alleged
by Renan.   § 1.

When Renan chose the line of argument, that Monotheism was the product of the stern and still desert, he must have admitted in his mind that for which we contend, namely that culture of any nation is conditioned by its God-consciousness, except that as to the form of Semitic religiousness the argument is futile once more. The desert does not create Monotheism. The truth in the matter is simply this. Whenever the mind, engrossed with reflections over its God-consciousness, at the same time allows itself to become nature-bound, as in this instance under the perpetual impress of the waste plains, then the abstractness of the empty and monotonous surroundings may mislead the imagination to form, much to the detriment of Monotheism, an obstinate, fanatical, and fatalistic monism.

but fatalistic monomania.

The ARYAN amidst the variety of changing scenes may on the one hand become enured to waive resistence, and to give himself up to enticing charms or the overwhelming dreads of the sensuous world. With the eastern Aryan the result is a profound apathy against a life so transient. Or these variations, on the other hand, urge man to overcome the annoying changes and charms and threatenings by bringing the manifold of phenomena under the control of the unity of consciousness. This took place in the Aryan occident. In both instances thought remains dissatisfied, because unable to arrive under such prejudices at a settlement of matters between itself and the diverse things of the environments. Aryan thought can not cease to compose, to arrange and adjust, in short, to reduce the diversity of things to the unity of comprehension in accordance with the nature of the mind. *as compared with the Aryan mind, which engages itself with reducing things to rational comprehension. § 86, 128.*

With that kind of harmonising meditation, inner assimilation, and conciliation the SEMITE rarely worries himself. Things may be single entities and may appear detached from unity—strange phenomena, or they may be forms which represent unity and bring their inter-relations to view—these things and their relations do not attract the interest of the Semite. *The Semite does not mind things which might worry him*

The Semite pure and simple is eminently selfish. He will adjust matters in his way as suits his advantage, or else not at all, and close himself up. *because of his unmitigated selfishness.*

This trend of mind became plain to Grill, when the relations of Indo-Germanic and Semitic roots of words were discussed. The comparison revealed the difference of mind and mode of thinking in a striking manner; "Indo-Germanic activity of the mind proves its talent by a wealth of inflective forms and derivations of words; while the Semitic mind is destitute of such comprehensiveness and taste for etymological forms expressing relations of things among each other; it prefers to recede into the essential substance of the thing per se, regardless of its relations." This is saying a great deal. *Trend of the Semitic mind revealed in the language: the etymology of which is, as compared with Aryan languages, not adapted to express relations. Gsll.*

The ARYAN evinces a liking for mythological conceptions, feeling his way through a multitude of ideas and idols. *Comparison between Aryan and Semitic mind.*

The SEMITE adheres to one fixed apperception resulting in his abstract and one-sided Monotheism. It is the same with respect to metaphysical matters, where the figure one is sufficient; it settles all, persisting only in getting before as many ciphers as possible. *S. uncompromising singleness of purpose; A. considerateness and sentimentality. § 128, 134, 142.*

The ARYAN frame of mind gives room to a marked considerateness. It pays attention to the cosmic diversity. Its extremely emotional nature either avoids being impressed, or responds to its impulsiveness, faces the question, takes up the task. Hence the Aryan is ever equalising, and thereby cultivates judgment and sentiment.

In the mean while the SEMITE looks at the variety of earthly interests with an air of disdain, if not his facial muscles will betray that much of regard for them; in matters of human concern in general he is sure to act the blase. Inclined to an abstract oneness, for the realisation of which he stakes his whole vehemency, regardless of all the rest, he loves to monopolise. *S. feigned unconcern of matters unpropitious to selfinterest.* *S. loves to monopolise.*

The ARYANS are given to philosophical speculation. The SEMITES assert, premeditate, and cultivate their talent of calculation. The SEMITIC nations one after another became subjects of Rome, whose eagles glistened on the Euphrates and Nile, in Tyre and Carthage, and finally on Mount Moriah. All their states were extirpated on account of their stubborn, unmitigated particularism. *A. speculative, S. calculating.* *S. particularism.*

Around about Jerusalem alone a few retired people under the rule of the gentile master kept their peace, remaining steadfast in their trust and hope.

They preserved their balance of mind amidst all the fanatical, factious riots into which pride upon Jewish particularism embroiled their fellow citizens. Not that they partook of the unconcerned blase of the aristocrats, but because they were inculcated with the most magnanimous kind of Old Testament catholicity. *A few minds understand Old Testament universalism or catholicity.*

They are awaiting the Advent of Him, for whom their contrition yearns, around whom their thoughts center in matters of conciliation, consolation, and peace. They wait for the appearance of their Redeemer, looking for Him with their faces covered, patient under unparalleled afflictions; tho sitting upon the ruins of their own earthly hopes, wandering in exile, yet sympathising with a lost world full of lost sinners. There are Jewish colonies in every town of Syria, throughout the Pelopone- *Faithful and patient waiting for the Redeemer.*

Jews in the diaspora
impress the gentiles.

sus, upon Cyprus and Crete, in Thessaly, all around the Black Sea. In Rome and in Spain Jews are at home ; Toledo is a new Jerusalem. These Jews in "the diaspora" exert as telling an influence as ever upon the gentiles, upon gentiles who are also —waiting. Think of the thirty thousand images and names upon altars at Athens. Yet they had to have one more for fear one God would feel insulted by being slighted.

The rabbi of
Alexandria
§ 81.

bent upon the
compromise

between the gentile
forms of consciousness
and Jewish hopes.

But the most numerous band of the Jews had flocked together in Alexandria. There, in the center of scholastic Hellenism, absorbed in deep thoughts, a rich, philosophical rabbi sits. Greek wisdom had been impressed upon him. He is an exceptional man, brooding over the secret of his nation, and how it might be made homogeneous to the general mixture. How could the coming One be amalgamated with such a world of thoughts as agitated and filled the large Roman crucible ?

The man thus contriving at a compromise is Philo.

D. FOURTH DIVISON.—THE DIVIDE OF THE TIMES.

SYLLABUS.

Postulate of the
synthesis of all that is
true in thought and
desire.

§ 12, 13, 83, 100, 102, 106.

History has now been traced to the pivot whereupon it hinges. We stand upon the divide of the time: behind us, its propædeutics, right before us, its completion. It is the time when, from the aspect of earthly development the ingredient is to be added . to the heterogeneous composition, standing stagnant in the Roman basin, the solvent ingredient which will set free the few useful elements contained in the mixture, and isolate them from the refuse. Whatever is truly human in all the ideas, desires and religions contributed by the nations and their cultures, is now to be reduced to one grand, all-embracing, all-explaining synthesis.

This could be accomplished only by a man recognised as impartial, reliable, and of universal authority; by a Mediator able to satisfy all reasonable expectations, and to restore human thought, heart, and will each in proportion to their normal state. The preparatory stage, in which the Mediator was promised and the fulfillment of the promise pledged, has come to its end. There are now held, what is called in school life, the "commencement exercises."

Chapt. 1. Logic of
history not a theory but
a fact,

The synthesis not a
syllogism but a person.

The first chapter of this division will serve notice upon Logics to appear as witness before the judgment-seat of history. It had charge of the work to combine the contradictory postulates of consciousness concerning God and the world. The premises now press for the conclusion which will justify the expectations in unlocking all the problems which have accumulated. And the solution will be given to humanity, historically given. For, the synthesis does not enter history in the form of a newly invented compound, not as a confounding or adjustable theory, howsoever ingeniously wrought in order to force itself upon every intellect. No. The synthesis appears as a fact, embodied in the person of the Mediator.

Chapt. 2. Death.
Postulate of a cosmical
Mediator.

In the next place we meditate upon the cosmical significance of the Mediator. His psychical suffering and the necessity of His death make it obvious how sin, being of SPIRITUAL origin, had completed its course PHYSICALLY. Both His passion and death explain what has become of this our cosmos and what was the cause of this present unsatisfactory condition. Being referred to the problem of death once more, we now learn to appreciate death not only as the necessary fate, rather as the destiny of this VISIBLE world, but also as the first step to, and the prerequisite for, its renewal in substance. We here learn, that death pertains to the metamorphical restoration and is but the transitory step to glorification. Meanwhile we shall have gathered additional insight into depths and heights of the INVISIBLE world found in close proximity to earthly history. In all of this we find postulates affirmed and reason satisfied; we find the realisation of hopes which so far had been pledged from above by realities which now become unveiled.

Chapt. 3. Genesis of a
renewed human family.

Finally we seek after the results of this death of the God-man. We look for it in the founding and developing of an ethico-historical, that is, organised realm of humanity. In the Christian consciousness we find the means given to attain freedom and to advance on the line of progressive civilisation. Of the theme and plan underlying all real development, which virtually always had been embodied in the person of the Mediator—we thus become cognisant.

CH. I. INTERMEDIATION POSTULATED LOGICALLY.—THE HISTORIC SYNTHESIS.

§ 95. When the learned, Hellenising Jews of Alexandria, Philo prominent among them, took a survey of the educational factors, which itinerated through the empire from east to west and back again —factors interchanging, if not amalgamating the rational, moral and practical elements of the Good, the True, and the Beautiful —then the following summary resulted: Survey of the educational factors in the Roman crucible.

At Alexandria, the point of observation, and to the right of it (if looking from the upper terrace of the Serapeion towards the harbor), the net gain of Semitic culture had accumulated, whilst to the left there extends the hemisphere of Aryan culture under discipline of Greek thought and Roman law.

This discipline had not hindered the Oriental element, which had been inoculated to Hellenism long ago, from being imposed upon the Occidentals. Plato's academy was absorbed in Asiatic wisdom just as much as the Stoa of Zeno affiliated itself to Hindoo-principles. Both of these schools were dominant in Alexandria, here the Platonics, there the New-Pythagoræans. Recapitulation of cultural results.
Alexandria the observatory.

In the vicinity of Alexandria the situation is this: Yonder in Hellas the customary rule of measure, moderation, and harmony in practice as well as theory. In Ægypt the customary stiffness: art not yet emancipated from the control of temple-rituals; cultus buried, out of sight and out of public life into the lightless Adyton. Only remember the twenty-two dark rooms secluding the Holy of Holies in Denderah. Monotony of Ægyptian culture.
Philosophic patchwork breaking down.

Here now, in Alexandria, in the university of Greek scholasticism, the platform of harmony and monotony broke down with a crash, like the rotten floor of an old assembly hall covered with mosaics. And from long covered depths below broke forth a phantastic enthusiasm and a turmoil of vociferous intuitions and sentiments, playing havoc with the forms and opinions of many centuries.   Revolous enthusiasm assumed the nature of an overheated frenzy. The dregs of the composition in the Roman crucible were stirred up. From the muddy solution emerged, crystallised as it were, the mystic systems of the New-Platonics and of the Gnostics. That is to say, the demand was formally stated that the chasm between this and the higher world must be bridged by any means: be it through illumination on the part of subjective cognition, or through revelation on the part of objective divinity. Sum and substance of Semitic and Aryan culture under propædeutics of Greek thought and Roman law.

Hellenism tinctured with Hindooism.

New Platonics.

New Pythagoræans: Stoa.
§ 54, 55, 58, 59, 62, 67,78, 81, 87, 97, 103, 122, 123, 124, 125, 130, 136, 137, 142, 144, 146, 147, 149, 150, 185.

Then already that mood of mind was in process of fixing itself, which Kingsley portrayed with masterly hand in "Hypatia". The issue is before us, the postulate is definitely formulated by historical incidents, and actual wants.

We proceed in gathering and connecting the results of our inductive inquiry into the mythological details. We thereby shall see whether our interpretation of the incidents is vindicated; whether the truth of our synthetical conclusion is confirmed and the propositions may sustain the test of deductive proof.

§ 96. Everywhere, at the bottom of the ethnical medley we found a deep stratum, a sediment of turbid and dismal superstitions, the fumes of which always tend to rise to the surface. This condition indicates the deep water-mark of religious consciousness. It shows the tremor of man after having torn loose from the enjoyment of the original central-vision into things eternal. It shows the fitful jerkings of the nature-bound mind in its abysmal depth sequent to the apostasy and aggravated by the anguish of becoming entirely lost after all. As presumptive facts, never entirely forgotten, we stated: the apostasy, the ensuing disrupture, and the dispersion; and either of them or all combined we took as the problematic cause of this fear and trembling, of the "anxious suspense." It stands to reason that by force of the fall the communion with God changed into fear of, and flight from, Him, and brought the mind into conflict with itself. The latter circumstance we took for proof of the fact that all intercourse was not broken off. An ineradicable religious sense was retained in the emotional touch perceived by the feeling of value, through which the possibility of a reunion is enunciated. The goal ever floating before thought was, to bridge the chasm between the finite and the invisible worlds.

Last attempts of Paganism to reconstruct its mixture of God- and world-consciousness HYPATIA, KINGSLEY. § 34.

With respect to the intellect the immediateness and oneness of a view into things eternal was blurred; only a glimmering as from the scattered rays of a distant star in a cold night continued its oscillations; only a faint memory as of childhood and home remained as an incipiency of visionary recollection.

The historic postulate of mediation as derived from empires.

Remnants of original God-consciousness in emotion and intellect. § 24, 41, 42, 47, 46, 53, 55, 57, 58, 59, 74, 95, 109, 115, 156.

Remnants of original religion: External traditions.

Anxious suspense. § 39, 41, 56, 59, 69, 71, 73, 96, 109, 113.

Internally: recovery to primitive religiousness. Remnants utilised to cultivate receptivity for "something better,"

to remain as an alarming reminder.

By forgetting the giver, and by the neglect of thanksgiving, the blessings in the realm of the secondary good were corrupted, and by being deified were turned into curses and plagues. But even these subversions were made serviceable in the reinstation of man to his share of the Supreme Good; for just because of the Relative Good affording no satisfaction, it sharpened the desire at least for something better. Notwithstanding this eventual utilisation of the remnants of original religiousness, consciousness ebbed so low that it was liable to become paralysed from horror. These fears, especially when they were misplaced and objectivised, became evident as the actual cause of man's pitiful condition. This condition was intended to become aggravated by the misapplication, abuse, or neglect of those indestructible fragments of religious incipiencies common to, and inherent in all men. The intention was that in these confused and obtuse remnants of primitive consciousness each human soul should possess so much at least as an alarming reminder.

In this forlorn condition we found all peoples—in an abject state of deathly pallor from fright. But that remainder of primitive religion which all possess, served as an incitement to selfpreservation and selfculture and kept them above the line of perdition.

Now two modes of departure towards cultural development ensued:

Two forms of civic development:

Layers of higher culture incite selfcultivation of the lower.

In the first place aggressive peoples separating themselves from advanced clans in quest of new homes, appear to have drifted over territories inhabited by preoccupants of an inferior caliber, thus forming a layer of higher culture above the stratum of crude aborigines. Their superiority resulted from their better use of the psychical faculties in the way of mental and moral selfculture. Such nations thus kept themselves above the line of unnatural degeneracy, kept themselves fit to receive restorative gifts. Their selfculture consisted in the rational exercise of the natural instincts of selfpreservation and dominion over nature. Taking up and pursuing this occupation with more or less united effort, they prepared themselves for progressive enrichment of the mind. After the subjugations of inferior groups, accomplished either slowly through migrations or by sudden conquests, the victors formed ranks above the timid and arrested life in the ethnic substratum,

Causes of arrested progress,

Development of nations according to the nature of their cultus. § 24, 34, 43, 44, 54, 56, 58, 71, 80, 84, 86, 87, 93, 125, 126, 128, 131, 132, 137, 139, 156, 175, 190.

Higher intellectual culture identified with religion and regarded as means of oppression.

Intellectualism unable to uproot superstition. § 11, 15, 22, 24, 27, 46, 53, 65, 72, 73, 95, 97.

In such cases a new world of culture arose above the pre-mythical order of existence with its distorted traditions and deranged notions. In proportion to the degree of their cultus the superiors then became a historical race. By composing myths and epics, objectivising inner troubles and deifying natural objects in order to bring impressions and abstractions to rational coherency, the systems of religious symbolism are constructed as witnessed in temples and tombs, however primitive art may appear in their ruins. There are always cliques of mentally or physically improved persons who urge on progressive development. The next stage toward the historic goal discloses the fact that, upon the basis of family or clan in patriarchal ways of associating, the better situated classes in command of means and leisure, form esoteric coteries, priestly castes, courts and states. In pursuance of such differentiation of social relations, rights and duties are fixed to hold society together. Conspiring rings in secret orders, screened behind mysterious usages, create and overthrow governments, whereby efforts to stop the wheels of progress only assist in its furtherance.

Oppressed cling to their religious symbols as emblems of opposition. § 11, 15, 22, 46, 48, 54, 58, 66, 68, 72, 78, 89, 95, 97, 98, 170, 197.

The higher culture resulting now dominates and changes the face of the country. The educated classes represent the nation, the low masses included. But tho the higher class in exceptional cases attempts to abolish the crude forms of life in the lower strata and to elevate the uncultured in the interest of the whole, it never succeeds. On the contrary, the subjected people look at culture as the cause of their oppression and misery of which they scarcely would have become aware, had it not been for the contrast. The less they are cared for by the "aristocrats," or the more attempts are made to force them into better habits, the firmer will they stick to their prejudices and low religious tenets. The more the neglected smart under contempt or oppression of the privileged, the more fanatical will they cling to their symbolism and ancestral usages. The ruling classes will try to break such symptoms of sullen withdrawal, now looked upon as conspiracy, and to train the ignorant to obedience and servitude. They do not succeed. The mass, always too ponderous to be lifted up, will consolidate in class-hatred. It will arise in fury.

Nobility prone to relapse into lower religiousness. § 48, 67, 73, 78, 137, 170, 197.

When thus the culture of a nation begins to shake, the higher classes, because of their dominion being threatened, will find it good policy rather to compromise on the base of popular ideas, to which they have a natural proneness any way, because their ancestors once held them in common with the forefathers of those now retarded. We have noticed this inclination on the part of the upper grades of the ancient nobility. A flagrant illustration of this fact is furnished by the British aristocracy of the present time. England counts thirty-one Catholic Peers, sixteen Lords, also Peers of the realm, fifty-five baronets, nineteen members of the privy-council, all Catholic. Ireland is represented with sixty-nine members in the House of Commons. This predilection of "old nobility" manifests itself with increasing force in the measure as their physical, moral, and intellectual ability to resist declines. Thus the old ideas of the lower strata gain the upper hand after all.

This process of a higher culture, sinking to the level of the subjected nationality, instead of elevating the retarded, or liberating the confined life of the substratum, we met with in India and Ægypt, less distinct in Mesopotamia, and more or less distinct among the southern Aryans of the Occident. In these nations the higher, immigrated tribes always found some elements even in the lower stratum which they could utilise in their construction of a higher culture. Sometimes it was language, in other instances the original tradition of the unity of the race. The higher race brought along with them recollections of the unity of God, an intuitive and relatively pure understanding of a created nature, or an intuitive insight into divine rule and human destiny. Such traditional heirlooms. dispersed throughout the entire human family, were not altogether unknown to the lower races. They always formed the principles upon which some amalgamation was possible. These innate higher truths, however faint, lay dormant even in the lower strata. at least in the form of dreams about childhood and home. They lay dormant until awakened by pressure. External heirlooms were the ritual forms and symbolic representations of religious import, especially sacrificial performances, always adulterated but never missing. All these aboriginal ideas, faint recollections, and misunderstood keepsakes, were generally used in the construction of an enhanced symbolism and mythological system, regardless of their fitting into each other. Such blending and eclecticism must of necessity have been detrimental to selfconsciousness, when the external exhibition of both, the internal and external or traditional remnants of religious truths became distorted into heinous caricatures of cultus.

Side note: Higher ranks more prone to relapse than lower are disabled from becoming ennobled. § 47, 65, 67, 73, 81. 85, 137, 170, 197.

Now, just as much as the lower sphere possessed some traces of truth similar to those of the higher, so did the higher partake of the natural proclivity to degenerate. Hence the higher classes were even more apt to relapse into superstitious practices and crudities of the lower, than the people of the lower strata were disabled from adopting the ennobling influences from above.

Side note: Nations in which the dark substratum is less observable.

Side note: Higher ranks sink to vulgarity.

Side note: The poor not always low in character. § 69.

Another kind of cultural development, however, has also been observed.

Some nations were destined to build up cultures without going to war or suffering invasion, without being inundated or suppressed by a race of superiors. Yet the same differentiation ensued, resulting in higher and lower ranks of the same age and generation. Family coteries are contracted. The common inheritance of elevating elements, the traditions of highest value, embodied for sacred preservation into symbols and legends, are misunderstood by some, and adulterated by others. The truths symbolised, if not idolised, are enlarged upon by prominent people who group themselves into classes, priesthoods, estates. whilst the truths, traditions and paraphrases are elaborated into a literature.

In such examples of social growth we have to deal with a well defined culture. The universal depravity of human nature, however, always tends downward, and it does not take many generations, until the sinking classes develop the lowest grades of superstition and sensualism. Now, since it is not the class of the poor people alone who thus become low-natured, a nation accelerates its treacherous downward course in the measure as the outward shell of culture is embellished, and the cultured nation poses in the refinement of its manners.

The nation then, in its entirety stands like a mountain with its broad base enveloped by heavy fogs, whilst its brow reflects the sun and sends refreshing breezes down through the valleys at its foot. In national mythologies, like the German, we shall behold the aspirations of mind as it draws upon powers above. In them the metaphysical world is taken hold of as a means of preservation, security and solace. In them the cleft between the higher and lower worlds is perceived, and the gaping wound of human nature is felt and its healing attempted. The dark abyss between the world of spirits and the visible world is felt to be unnatural.

In whatever direction this departure of natural culture develops, it is always impinged upon by that anxious solicitude which is not fretfulness, which turns into superstition, and of which ignorance is not the primitive cause.

We met that anxious suspense with the intelligent and hilarious Greeks as well as with the rational, practical, and heroic Romans. It is the same dreadful chasm, which Mongolian as well as Aryan paganism wanted to bridge by the same means of magic arts, sorcery, conjury, necromancy, selftorture, bribes, and even through expiation with human sacrifices. Whatever mode of construction was applied, the bridge was contrived in order to have powers of the other world present, to make use of the deity or of demons for either succor or success. Powers from above or below are to be attracted by all means: in orgiastic frenzy with selfmutilation, in ecstasies and trances; through illumination under mysterious ceremonies; or the help is expected from—revelation.

Side note: Paganism attempts to bridge the chasm between two worlds,

Side note: makes use of mental projections of the mind to get over the anxious suspence by all means,

Remember that suggestive ray of light which, piercing the Ægyptian darkness, fell upon the lips of the idol.

§ 97. By way of connecting the general retrospect which amounts to a universal census taken of the results of pre-Christian culture, with the prospects of the coming æra a few additional remarks are necessary, concerning the incessant strain ever conspicuous among the Indo-Aryans. From this polar tension between the Orient and the Occident specific issues have resulted. In a measure all forms of thought are reducible to these two hemispheres. The play between religious sentiment and phantasy, so agile at composing myths, is explicable alone from the contrariety under discussion.

Side note: Human initiative failing, revelation is expected. § 81.

The Turano-Mongolian substratum need not be reviewed in the present discussion, since it is possible for mankind in general to sink into the same baseness of consciousness which has been described to the point of tedium.

Intending to examine Buddhism as to its influence upon European thought, we abstract from its Turano-Mongolian substratum over which it was spread, lacquerlike, from Ceylon to Java. Of incomparable greater significance was Buddhism to

that part of the Indo-Aryan world, which was waiting for the solvent of the compound mixture in the Roman crucible and of which Buddhism also was an ingredient. When trying to analyse the compound, we observed that ominous commotion in the spiritual sphere, which in so remarkable a manner agitated both branches of the Aryan family and even the Semitic circle from the Ganges to the Rubicon.

Buddhism is in essence a philosophical attempt at formulating a world-theory

devoid of God-consciousness.

This granted, we may, considering its preceding phases of speculation, call it the methodology of scepticism which finally revels in sophistry, poses in indifference, or busies itself with eclecticism.

Buddhism as affiliated with Brahmanism reasons thus:

Existence which men find themselves thrust upon, or surrounded with, involves all in a continual flux of rise and decay. Existence is a state, a condition, it is not constituted of real entities, it is nothing but pain and passiveness. The cause of this misery is that we can not know the real essence of things. This ignorance insists upon agnosticism, which is but feigned nescience with regard to the bond of unity between ones own self, the ego, and the source of all selfhood.

Agnosticism is the knowledge merely of being so, i. e., the knowledge of not

knowing. But since not to know is the source of all suffering it follows that existence is misery pure and simple, that existence consists in nothing but endurance. Now, having this knowledge of mere being, that is, suffering without knowing, hence possessing nothing but agnosticism—what, then, constitutes knowledge? The agnostic science of being miserable is, at the same time, knowledge of the fact that upon earth there is, in reality, nothing. All that is real is nothing but perpetual undulation between being and being nothing, and back again. Hence becoming alone is really something. This "becoming" alone furnishes the world its contents; hence "becoming" alone is what the contents consist of, it is the essence of existence, namely of suffering, that is, of enduring. Life is to be taken as passiveness, that's all.

The acknowledgment of sin and guilt is evaded, and this is all that Buddhism cares for, all it signifies as—a religion.

According to this sophistry absolute restlessness, the fluctuating change of all things, alone creates suffering (was "Leiden schafft" said Oldenberg) and renders existence an unceasing suffering under passiveness. The trouble is that people who are fond of such knowledge would not be able to say: I suffer, or you suffer, because I and you would be mere apparitions, each an absolute selfdelusion in the concrete.

As a thing of certainty there would remain nothing but a state of sufferance, because this would be all that existence consists of; in reality it would have nothing on which to subsist.

Under any such distortive and abortive ratiocination such premises can yield no other knowledge, but that suffering happens to be the result of the process of becoming and vanishing. Evidently the science of agnosticism prefers to sublimate existence and to invent a theory of annihilation in order to dodge a confession of sin: rather than to acknowledge the real cause of misery. Still, for the time being Buddhism undefiled may be excused on account of real ignorance.

But how could this Asiatic world-theory encroach upon West-Aryan thought? For, with this formulation of nescience, with this systematised scepticism of the senile Orient—which dissolves everything into blue ether, as repeated by Hume, precisely corresponds the contemporaneous scepticism of the juvenile West as promulgated by Heracleitos and his followers. Listen to his famous reasoning, and see if it is not palmed off as the latest news by some writers of the Asiatic type:

"Not the being (the ens) is anything, neither is not-to-be. The vital transition of being into not-being, and of not-being into being, this becoming alone is really something. Everything else has no subsistence, all is of no value, all vanishes, all is in vain, because all is in a state of flux. We are bound up into an empty circuit of becoming, coming and going." *Systematised agnosticism. Formulated nescience; scepticism after a method.*

If Juvenal and Ælian speak of Heracleitos' continual weeping over the wickedness of the people, then they must not have understood him. His views of life, in keeping with his mode of thinking, make it evident, that his tears were shed over the delinquencies and the badness of the world as a whole, because nothing in it remains, all changes and vanishes. Penitential tears in confession of sinfulness they were certainly not. *Heracleitos' continual weeping was contemporaneous and corresponding with Hindoo-Pessimism. Misunderstood by Juvenal. Ælian.*

This condition of selfinflicted ignorance as to the cause of world-soreness affords the best insight into the origin and transmission of that mode of thinking which gives itself up to indifference, real or feigned, to that all-the-sameness which has abandoned every hold, every hope. Such a philosophy of despair, if consistent, would signalise the death of all science, of course. *Philosophy of despair.*

But agnosticism repudiates itself, because it is as impossible to give up the search after the bridge between the ens and the entity, the existing and the subsisting, as it is to cease thinking. Hence it is plain that nihilism does not expect of us to follow suit in selfcontradiction and selfannihilation, else it would not demand two impossibilities at once: to form a conception of nothing and then to stop thinking. *Nihilism demands two impossibilities at once: To form a conception of nothingness and to stop thinking.*

This aberration of the mind originated in yonder period when excitement went high and Babylon went down. For at that time culture had risen to one of these heights, where people are seized with dizziness, where Pantheism begins to level religious thought, that is, where the ruling classes try to palliate idolatry by applying speculative thought, by personifying pantheistic ideas in the same manner, as natural phenomena are personified and fears objectivised. It is now perceptible how all of the Aryans came to participate in every modification and mutilation of consciousness. The routes by which Buddhistic ideas were disseminated are marked by the gradual retreat of the spirit of reverence and devotion, until at the central point of time the Stoa extolled the wisdom of resignation, of suicide, of "all-one-ness." *Buddhistic pessimism levels the heights of culture through Pantheism, (i. e. compromise between speculation and superstition.) Transferred to the Occident. § 78, 81, 95, 123, 147, 148, 149, 185. Stoa and suicide.*

Intellectually, by the logic of facts, the heights of culture are thus all levelled now. In the East and in the West the ways are prepared for "the Advent". Still before we can begin to fully understand its great significance, a few more preliminaries need yet to be considered.

We understood Buddhism to be essentially a philosophical attempt. It must be added that it attempted something more practical, and succeeded. Asoka wanted to make use of it for governmental purposes. Hence it did no longer remain a mere theoretical scheme to be indoctrinated, but became a society incorporate. It ever propagated as a sort of an order; it now became an organism, until at about A. D. 1400, it assumed the form of a theocracy in Tibet. Without such an embodiment Buddhism would not have been able to start a series of "reformers", to the ranks of which the selfconstituted selfsalvationists from Benares to Kroton and Lhassa have been raised. Doctrines can not be perpetuated as mere theories; they must become embodied in teachers; then they become parts of the "Logic of facts." *Buddhism not merely a theory becomes an organism; § 54, 57, 58, 143, 185, 186. embodied in teachers and an institution through Asoka.*

Moreover, Buddhism was aggressive, and its success demonstrates the emptiness of the receptacle, ready for refilling. Thus it became an organising factor in the history of the mind, and equally so its counterpart, the almost monastic Pythagoræanism in Great-Greece and Sicily. Both of these influential organised societies east and west were in passiveness bound upon the great wheel of transmigration. They were well aware that the necessary conclusion from their premises must be metempsychosis, incarnation, palingenesis. It was that which set the brains all in a whirl. As memorials of ancient ancestor-worship these orders exerted such a reviving influence as to assist largely in bringing that old cult to its zenith in the apotheosis of the emperor-god. In that capacity both Buddhism and Pythagoræanism, its pendant, represent the prophecy of nature which carries in itself so many premonitions of the all-surpassing event in the garden of Joseph, the Arimathian. And as theocratical organisations they appear in line with, at least as foreshadowing the prevenient prototype of that community, which in the Middle-ages was to grow up among the European Aryans. *Buddhism and Pythagoræanism Premonitions of "the" incarnation; precedents of a new society. Buddhism the NATURAL prophecy of the Church. § 81, 95, 97, 123, 133, 145, 148, 147, 148, 149, 150, 186, 188, 191.*

Postulates of the divine presence to communicate with.

Thought despairing of all reality is unable to invent a God present in the world.

Neither can thought rest until it gets even with the chasm between Creator and creation.

Panthetstic generalness and oppression.
§ 54, 58, 66, 72, 89, 95, 96, 170, 185, 195.

resisted by the Greeks,

revived in the Stoa.

Only a false conception of either Buddhism or Christianity could once hold Platonism and the Stoa to be transitory stages toward Christianity.

The element of truth in mythological intuition.

Idea of Incarnation is not so much a logical postulate as it is an emotional anticipation.

§ 98. Nothing prevents us from passing now to the conclusive disquisition. The inciting principle, which unbeknown and inadvertently worked out the mythical and pantheistical development, was virtually the involuntary and unconscious longing of the heart for communication with a present deity. The mind craves after the assurance of friendship with, and the favor of, the divine being. The emotional part yearns after that satisfaction which can be enjoyed only in the intimate relation to God. Of this the mind became conscious by degrees. But how was thought to combine this personal presence with its necessary ubiquitousness in the world? Moreover, how could that form of thought, which judges the whole visible world and all that comes into man through sense-perception as that which is to be escaped from—how could that form of thought, which allows itself to be deceived by something which is nothing, comprehend and much less invent a real presence of God among men? Certainly, thought, totally perplexed and despairing of all reality, can not be expected to have invented an idea of a god worthy of being present in the historical world.

It is not necessary to enlarge any further upon the contradictions in the reasoning of Buddhism and its affiliations. Both Buddhism and Pythagoræanism (with Stoicism, its pendant) saw the difficulty. Of the chasm they had knowledge. Call it passion, misery, call it becoming, name it nothing—the names were given to hide the difficulty and to deny the chasm, since thought had ventured to look into it and would not admit that it could not bridge it. Why not take the chasm for what it really is, namely the crushing feeling of reproach and guilt, sequent to sin,—since denial is of no avail, and since the chasm of necessity remains to be bridged?

This necessity became an acknowledged postulate as soon as oppression awakened the oriental spirit from its speculative dreams about mind and soul, during which human consciousness floated away into the vapors of a most abstract and abstruse generalness. It became evident, how generalness is ever absorbing the dignity and liberty, the right of, and the sympathy due to, personal life; especially in a period of distress and despair like the one just closed, in which the totality of the human race was out of joint. Greece emancipated herself from that generalness which devours all aspiration, all thought, all personality, as Saturn devours his own children. For this, in the Greek vernacular, is the empiric fruit of the Buddha-Stoa.

In the face of this fact that culture which made even selfdestruction a religious duty rather than confess the sin and acknowledge the necessity of a Saviour; in the face of that culture, issuing from the old wisdom and talking about transmigration and preservation of forces, yet refusing faith in personal immortality, the Stoa and Platonism ought never to have been taken as links in the "evolution" of Christianity.

Or else that sort of Christianity needs to be branded as counterfeit which obviously has more in common with Tibet than with Galilee. Such Christian "religion" can not be estimated as more than barren intellectualism, or as more than a new and impoverished edition of Buddhism, which prefers a denial of the chasm to an acknowledgment of the necessity of the bridge.

After Greek naturalism had analysed the absurdity of Hindoo wisdom; after the demand was formally stated that "Pan" must be conceivable as something palpable or else withdraw his claim on consideration; when the deity again was conceived as being objectively differentiated, and definite attributes were assigned to it; then thought came nearer home to truth and hastened to draw the bridge of—incarnation. The conception of this idea by natural reason is its acknowledgment, that the chasm is to be bridged, and that this can be expected only—from above.

The idea of an incarnation, as repristinated even upon Buddhism under pressure of Brahmanism, was not so much a logical as an emotional postulate. The idea of incarnation arose from the wish fathering the thought, and the desire arose from the faculties of valuation and volition combined. As a postulate, tho only a demand of the emotion, the idea of incarnation simply anticipated the logic of facts, which is the logic of history.

In order to discern this genesis of the historical postulate, no more is required than to consider the true religious elements reflecting from the glowing mountain tops of retired minds, who stood alone with their serious thoughts, before the night of sceptical sophistry broke in. We understand the trend of mythological incarnations as the last attempt to hold to the deity as a present being. None but a definite God in history can be trusted as a rest and refuge in the wild rush, which on all sides, not alone in Benares and Rome, tears up existence with almost irresistible rage.

Meditate upon the empiric feelings of the human heart.

On the one hand, man is drawn to abandon himself to his grief in seclusion, when earthly expectations fail and turn to bitter disappointment. Snatched from his customary associates, or thrown out of position, the isolated person stands without hold and without hope in the wide solitude between the One up yonder and the unavailing plenitude below, distressed without any solace. In a dazed selfconsciousness, in brooding and dulling despondency, torturing himself whilst nursing his grief and his worldly sorrow, the unfortunate one covets to throw himself into the "all-One", who seems to open His arms above his head, in order to relieve him from all his trouble, and to receive and reward him for letting the world alone, by way of—selfannihilation. The subtile forms of that mood of a sick consciousness are quietism, asceticism, pessimism.

On the other hand man seeks to spare himself such melancholy. Something incites and prompts him to divert his mind in paroxysms of dissipation and sensuality. He strives to overcome tribulations by forgetting them on the bosom of mother nature. He hankers after, and throws himself away into, the pleasures of the world which bloom at his feet. The change from hedonism to pessimism in the Cyrenæan school once for all illustrates this double form of apathy as a selfsalvation from the woes of earth and of sin.

Is it put too strong if the statement is made, that there is not a single sane person who has not had the experience of this polar strain within his own consciousness? The suffering soul, harassed hither and thither, needs the mean and seeks a rest. Hence the willingness to listen to the solicitations of intuitive emotion; hence the attempts to construct them into incarnations in order to gain the presence of the divine being in human form and natural reality. Hence the expectation of God descending to become man. This impulsive longing after a perceptible presence of the infinite in the finite, so conspicuous in the oriental systems of religion, is reflected in the history of philosophy from the Vedas down to the gnostics with their emanations, and the agnostics with their "evolution." Everywhere the idea underlies, that if the immanency of the transcendental form of life were realised, all the problems of life would find their solution upon the grounds of the higher world. For never can man forget this higher world.

The desire was father of the thought, but the desire is perfectly reasonable—for man ever wants a something better to which he feels himself entitled. The thought was, of course, not thus concisely formulated; it is veiled inasmuch as the people uttering their longings were not clear about what was needed. It was the thought, nevertheless, which inadvertently divined what was going to happen, and which thought, tho unconscious of the logic of matters and facts, found that logic and those facts foreshadowed in itself, thus meeting its materialisation half way, so to speak. What other conclusion could be drawn from the "æons", from the 'middle-beings", the "wisdom', from "THE LOGOS"?

All the endeavors successively alternating in Asia Anterior, have only one end in view: to conceive the deity as entering into historical existence in order to become confirmed in their belief of the presence of God from above. The theme from all the various imploring invocations is the historical postulate: A God can, and is apt to become man.

§ 99. At the point of time under discussion the Asiatic anticipations of the Godman were reiterated by the gnostics, and the occidental countersign, as given in Greek mythology, was heard in the Orient.

It is clear at first glance that the Græco-Roman mode of anticipating the incarnation varies from that of the Hindoos.

This comparatively youthful culture had the advantage of being untrammeled by that ultra-conservatism which poses in its antiquity. Whilst the sedate Hindoo had been held in nature's soft but cruel embrace, the hilarious Hellene easily freed himself from its hypnotising charm. Instead of dozing under an incubus, he leaped forth to action. In Greece every circumstance would have allured the mind to sink into the embrace of nature, to encourage and elevate it so as to express thoughts beautifully. Serene Hellas was dear to her sons, for she responded to their ideas in

[marginal notes:]
Promptings of the heart are empirical.

Either selfdelivery into arms above the head

("Sorrow of this world")

or abandonment to the pleasures blooming at the feet of man. (Sensualism)

Human longings, actual and in earnest, convey the force of the historic postulate of "THE" incarnation. § 42, 44, 47, 54, 100.

Incidents expressing anticipations, and facts foreshadowing the incarnation. § 53, 77, 78, 81, 91, 96, 101, 103, 105, 120, 135, 157.

The shape which these anticipations took in Greek mythology.

her murmuring springs, meandering streams, and idyllic mountain dales. Yet it was no dream-land. The crude power of India had spent itself in the engagement with monstrous phantasms. In Greek memory still lingers the mirage of Titanic violence, but it is soon effaced, and is thrown down and out. Measured and composed the figure of man stands forth. With this the standard of value is given; man is the measure of all things, they shall not master him; ugly dreams and uncouth god-images are condemned; the gods are represented as ideal men.

Since nature is humanised, man alone is fit to personify deities; one more step and man is deified. It is no longer held, as it was in Asia, that the gods are naturalised and nature is doomed to evaporate. And the diverging course of Greek mythology proceeds, we might say, under the eyes of the people. They are wide awake, almost conscious of the procedure, and intensely interested in what they are doing concerning the matter.

The taste for adjusting and harmonising seemed greatly to assist in the attempt to close up the cleft yawning between the gods and the world. The Greek is conscious of his position as a mediator between them, hence, with a light heart, he covers the cleft by simply treating it with silent contempt. He himself puts the cleft away,

He is not sure of the accomplishment. But he is satisfied of this truth, at any rate that it is not necessary for man to annihilate himself. Rather annihilate the cleft. Hellenic consciousness has such high opinion of its thought and taste, as to feel itself above the cleft,—until it sees the futility of its experiment. Somewhat superficially framed, the Greek mind thinks to have found the divine man, and to have overcome the portentous difficulty. To have found man a divine being and his guest a hero of highest honors, canonised at the Olympian court: these are ideas so beautiful as to make Schiller and Goethe desirous of their revival and of their realisation becoming manifest.

Yet the cleft was merely deferred, covered with comforts taken from beneath. The material for the covering was mixed with the pre-mythical ingrain of ancestor-worship from the deep substratum. This made the selfdelusion the more severe. Man as he is, exercising his natural endowments so as to keep them in working order, cultivating their proper cooperation with other minds, so as to keep himself susceptible of higher gifts, and to prepare himself for their reception,—increases his capability of approaching the divine presence. For, he carries the idea of God within himself and thinks of Him, altho he cannot produce out of himself the Good, much

less during the process of selfabandonment. The Greek is indefatigable at his task. He thinks and toils to represent the presence of the divine in the realities of present life. He works all he can,—but the one little fault of levity spoils it all.

The Romans worked out their lesson not less assiduously and, in respect to earnestness, excelled the Greeks. Whatever divination the Romans observed to impress itself upon their minds, was not allowed to be marred by arbitrariness. Possessing more will-power, they kept the mind under discipline. The state personified, and—after the innovation of the apotheoses—even deified, afforded objective restraint against subjectivism. The idea of civic unity as symbolised in the "fasces", the emblem of authority, prevented subjectivism from dismembering the state. The Roman version of man's destiny to become like unto God is involuntarily rendered in the emperor-god. Just as the period of republicanism closed with Octavian, and just as the world looked up to the summit of its glory, where Augustus stood, so the gods of the ancient world were closed up in the "Pantheon."

The historic coefficients with combined energies moved in the direction of the necessity of a man becoming God. The principal modifications of the thought of a God incarnate, progressing toward the equation of the great antithesis, and toward amalgamation in a synthesis throughout the universal history of the old world, finally meet and mingle in the Roman basin. Here the contradiction seems to disappear. When the extremes of Rome and Benares meet, the process of anticipating comes to its climax and end.

Where the complex life of the old world with all its cultures and treasures is summed up in the inventory made by the emperor-god which revealed the bankruptcy of worldly culture, in the first year of universal peace; there also the strain caused by the duplex problem of oriental and occidental religious thought, may be expected to come to its equipoise.

For centuries this had not been possible. The young nations of the Occident could simply look at the oriental contrast, upon the reverse side of their own prevailing idea, as upon something very strange, or as something altogether unsuitable for their new conditions, as upon religions which had outlived themselves long ago.

The young nations with their pride of being "selfmade men" having selfmade gods, had first to grow old and sedate. And these young nations, living in much faster style, became old soon enough.

Now then, the balance sheets of the great Roman clearing-house were to be compared, and differences settled. The liquidations were carried out then and there, in those days when the command of the great census, to be taken, was sent into the provinces of the "world-orbit".

Decree of the universal census.

§ 100. But could any transaction at the exchange ever be accomplished without Semitic interference? Just recently the stiff orthodox Monotheism of the Semites had been forced into the medley crowd.

Balancing of accounts of cultural assets. Roman clearing-house.

This is now to be counted upon, too.

We have examined the quality of this ingredient to some extent. It is that outline of Monotheism which by force of its form excludes any idea of adjustment or compromise. Hard and intolerant it subordinates every relation of life to one dominant idea, which none but the Jews possess. Every thought and deed they render subject to law, and, to what is held even more sacred, their traditions.

The Semitic ingredient as to incarnation, § 89-93, 128, and false expectations. § 144, 200, 213.

This Monism, now overrun by wild, poisonous creepers upon the banks of the Nile and the Euphrates, had once in the best parts of the Semites, been made the keepsake of a family for a period of six hundred years, and then had been made the charter of the peoples grown out of that household. As a nation they formed the most insignificant branch of the race; but that in which Monotheism was preserved pure, was cultivated and protected in miraculous ways by a superhuman arm. The God of this small community, with its almost childlike fear and faith, was the God of their fathers, the God of revelation.

Monotheistic law and Jewish tradition. § 129, 300, 213.

Monotheism preserved in its purity in miraculous ways.

To Philo's philosophy this revelation afforded the criterion according to which a counterpoise between revelation and speculation was to be fixed. With this as his fundamental principle he labored to find points of similitude in Hellenic thought to which his own might be accommodated. With an eye to Jewish advantage and with national ambition, Philo undertook to bring about a compromise.

Philo's compromise between revelation and gnostic eclecticism.

Another light among the Hellenised Jews in Alexandria was Aristobul. With unscrupulous insolence he assigned Jewish ideas to Greek poets, and with unconcerned ambiguity distorted Jewish truths. He was the forerunner of Philo, showing him how to handle the problem, just as Philo may be said to have set the example to modern rabbis in making gentile philosophy agree with rabbinical doctrine.

Tho not the inventor, Philo was the manipulator of the levelling contrivance. He endeavored to show, that, what is meant by the Greek term of "Logos", was to be understood as "mind personified", and was identical with that which, in the Jewish sense of the "word", created and rules the world. In order to join the Greek sense to his artificial exegesis, he simply twisted Plato's meaning of the "eternal ideas" a little, and then intertwined them with the emanations from the deity which were supposed to spread themselves throughout the universe. Taking these emanations into play, surely pliable enough to be made suitable to any construction, Philo has those forces at hand which he needed for his idiosyncracy. So nimbly did he manipulate his device that the potencies ascribed to the deity under gnostic terms were managed to signify divine "thoughts and attributes" as well as "God's servants," God's ambassador, or the "Angel of His countenance."

Interpretation of the gnostic "middle beings" to construct the doctrine of the "logos." HEINZE, KEFERSTEIN, WENDLAND, ARISTOBOL.

Heinze, who made it a specialty to investigate the origin and growth of the Greek idea of the "logos" said: "It is Philo whose whole speculation centered in these very "middle-beings." Keferstein came to the same conclusion. Wendland, in 1890 pointed out the stoic streakings which Philo made use of.

The emanated forces furnished the material which dexterous Philo needed to put his logos together—his mediator. He harmonised biblical truth with everything which in any way may be twisted into use for building the bridge between the natural world and the spiritual.

Philo makes "forces" and "ideas" attributes and also "angels" of God.

16

Quotations from
Philo.

To forestall the injunction as tho prejudice had misrepresented the great syncretist
—for history can not rank him with the original thinkers—the floor shall be ceded to him as
spokesman of his age and generation. The logos PER SE, the "middle" and "metropolis" of the
ideas, incessantly invokes the Unchangeable for the protection of the troubled souls. As the
Mediator he proclaims to men: "I stand between the Lord and you. I am not created, I am
as God is; nor generated like you are, but the mediator between the extremes." This logos
of Philo governs all. "For like a shepherd and a king God rules and leads his flock, earth
and water, air and fire, according to righteousness. All that lives in these elements, plants
and beasts, what is mortal and what is divine, the organism of the heavens, the courses of sun,
moon and stars, He directs, inasmuch as He has set the logos, His first born son over them.
The logos has charge of this holy throng like the governor receiving his commission from
the king."

"Logos endiathetos"
at the same time
"logos prophorikos."

This logos is "endiathetos", the collective term of all the ideas indwelling with God, as
Greek philosophy expressed it. But then he is also "logos prophorikos" the "word" as Jewish
theology wants to have it understood, going forth from God to create and to support the universe. This is the way in which Philo takes in and arranges the whole matter. But in every
phase of his interpretation and construction he either moves away from, or approaches
nearer to, a Mediator of the world. It is his heart's desire to demonstrate the relation of the

Philo's endeavor to
make Judaism
acceptable to everybody.

whole world to Judaism and its sanctuary; to widen and to smooth, and to render acceptable
to everybody, the prerogatives and peculiarities of his nation and his religion.

Allegoric interpretation
of the high priest's
vestments.

In his life of Moses he speaks of the highpriest, whose pontifical vestments are
made allegories of the whole universe. "The long coat with the ornaments around its hem is
emblematic of the three elements air, water, and earth, out of and within which all mortal and
changeable creatures have their life." The outer garb of the high-priest is the symbol of
Heaven. In this apparel the priest enters the Holy of Holies to bring sacrifices; "hence when

Judaism
rendered
universalistic.

he enters, the whole universe, which he carries about himself, enters with him." Thus Judaism
was rendered universalistic by Philo.

§ 101. Contriving to bridge the chasm from above, the eastern Aryan form of
consciousness elaborated a way of descent, whilst those of the West thought it more
reasonable to reach this end by way of works and apotheoses, through an ascendancy

Oriental and
Occidental
postulates of
incarnation
dovetailed by PHILO.

of some sort. Now both of these endeavors of human thought were rather dove-tailed
than blended by Philo: the longing desire on the one hand, that a god might become
man; and the necessity, on the other, that man must become divine. Both were taken
by Philo, as two twigs from different stocks, and then intertwined into his theory of the

Theoretical
forecast of the
Mediator.

logos. As the keystone of the arch, rising upon the center-frames of oriental and
occidental anticipations, Philo introduces the mediator as standing between God and
the world. He did as well as the national mind could accomplish it.

The limit of
reason:
it can only
formulate the
demand of an
incarnation.

The ancient world had been led to its theoretical attempts to overcome the strain
between the opposite views seemingly so much at variance, by, let us say, intuitive
presentment, and by reflection upon the ultimate principles underlying each view
respectively. The bridging of the opposites by one adventurous span was brought to
the climax of a scientific postulate. And therein all the merits of Philo consist that

It is Philo's merit to
have theoretically
formulated the
postulate.

he explicitly formulated it.

This was all the logic of which natural reason is capable; further no Buddha, no
Plato, no Philo could get. Such earnest search of the mind always gleans some truth

Discrepancies of Philo's
and Plato's postulates.

from its own contents. But also some discrepancy comes in, some error is always
detected, when an equation is to be effected between different results of the speculating mind. It could not be otherwise between Plato and Philo.

To Plato the body appeared an encumbrance, a fetter of the spirit. Matter as

Plato's impure
matter ill
adapted for
being the vehicle
of Holiness
personified.

contemplated by Plato is impurity itself. How could Plato from such premises syllogise conclusions for a basis of his system? He could not make impure matter a vehicle
of holiness personified. For this reason Philo could not establish a completely locked
synthesis. He failed to demonstrate the secret of the combination. Scientifically he
could attribute no concrete reality to the conjectured picture of his "logos".

Hence the tension was not overcome nor the chasm bridged for all that. The
postulate underlying the difficulty could neither be argued away, nor was it intended
to be solved by any intellectualism or any theory, because such is not the logic of history.

The tension not -
however to be removed
except by a solvent act.

History proceeds by way of facts. The long existing tension—straining all relations
of life, (not only those of the Aryans), now formulated into a definite acknowledgment, then again demonstrated as the common postulate of both human reason and
universal history—was now, at the center of space and in the middle of time, to be removed by a solvent act.

But again we are brought to an abrupt stop. Ere we proceed any further, suspicion is to be headed off, that we were trying to shirk a difficulty which has been a standing conundrum to philosophers of history.

The question requires an answer: Is the logic of history revealed in the apportionment of various tasks to the diverse nations of culture according to their different predispositions? *What is the Logic of History ?*

Provided it be granted that in the correlative and concurrent procedures of mind and nature from which history ensues, purpose is an inherent factor:—then we assert that history works after a plan. *The plan in history. §§ 6, 17, 18, 218.*

In the natural sphere purpose works itself out spontaneously in the routine of necessity. In the sphere of the secondary good, purpose or intent manifests a relative independence. *Common destiny of natural and ethnical development.*

In organic life purpose divides the work into a variety of specially adapted members, which are definitely appointed to work together for the realisation of the general purpose. This purpose, governing all things and common to all, lies not within them, man being the purpose for which they are intended. What is in accord with the forensic purpose designed within the organism, is the plan which specifies the purport of things. A purpose of their own natural objects have none. *General purpose of nature in man.*

On the part of personal life however, the purpose is prevented from working in a general way, regardless of individuality. In the world of history the realisation of the purpose is limited to the constituents of the realm of "essential unity and material diversity". Here the purpose itself, but not the design or general destiny, is committed to persons and events themselves. Each possesses the dignity of being not merely for the purpose of something else. It is to be understood that in the sphere of personal life plan and purpose change places. The purpose, individualised in man, must concur and agree with the plan; it cannot effect its end regardless of the plan, and the plan stands objectively outside. And as we call the plan in nature design, so we call it destiny in history. For, in history a higher, the sovereign will cooperates in order to stimulate the activity of the subordinate wills. Hence in the realm of history the tasks for the accomplishment of the ultimate general purpose or destiny are prescribed and appointed to the proper participants. They carry their destiny within themselves only in so far as they are members of an organism, either personal, national, or universal. *In ALL NATURAL life plan and purport in unison. But tho the PLAN is in things, a PURPOSE of their own they have not.* *In PERSONAL life purpose and plan separated—each person having a purpose in itself; but the plan remains outside as designed by the sovereign will.* *In history the design is purpose individualised as a task;*

The thought of a definite purpose is imparted to the world of personal life where it becomes individualised as a thoughtful will in action for the benefit of humanity in its parts and as a whole; it is a purpose to be accomplished by innumerable interacting coefficients, concomitant agencies, cooperative organisms. This imparted thought cannot be but rational and practical. From its effects the logical conclusion is to be drawn; the purpose becomes revealed upon which we do well to reflect. Empiric data we reduce to premises; the given facts demonstrate that there is a reason present in them, by and according to which events happen and history is guided on to its finality. Thought may be concealed, and individual purpose may not conform itself to general destiny on account of many seeming or real malformations, or by fault of misconceptions, or by limits of the understanding. Notwithstanding this concealment and these misconceptions we draw practical conclusions from the premises, just as we adjust ourselves every day to the general course of human affairs, whereby we acknowledge that reason conducts them. Man cannot cease to reflect upon this reason in history, until he fully comprehends, that is, becomes clearly conscious of, the purpose in his own behalf, concerning his own destiny. *according to the Plan of working out the common destiny.* *Premises from which correct conclusion may be deduced as to the revelation of the purpose and plan of history.*

Hence we, too, review the data for the premises from which we endeavor to form the conclusion, i. e. to find—the purpose and object of ancient history in general. We want to be right and sure in our way of interpreting history. If the syllogising is correct, then our conclusion ought to show that we participate in the knowledge of the secret of the purpose. For the true conclusion easily opens the combinations and explains the truth hidden in history on its way to become—revelation. *Review of the empiric inductive data in proof of the correctness of our deductive syllogising.*

§ 102. From the domains on the right wing of the Aryan group, from the ancient Orientals, we gleaned that thesis concerning world-consciousness, according to which man conceives himself as an individual, dependent being, as finite in contrast to the Infinite. Man conceives the finite world himself included, as a mere apparition, of the Infinite. Compared with the Infinite the finite stands in the same relation to it, as a special phenomenon is related to nature in general. This notion of the finite which renders all that exists in reality into abstractions, and is accompanied and influenced by the notion that creation had emanated from God,—describes man as a finite, modified being, personified for a transient period of passive suffering, and relates him to the infinite exactly as a drop of water is related to the ocean. Thus the finite being is nothing in itself; it is something so far only, as it is a particle of an indefinite generalness.

From the fields of the West we gleaned the Occidental antithesis. Here the whole method of reasoning is less contemplative and produces a widely contrasting reflection of the world in the mind. Here the finite stands as a concrete reality; independently it steps forth, determined to act as a determining agency. Through art, science and voluntary formations of society and of states, mind despite its finiteness

manifests itself in such a resolute persistency as that the infinite seems to exist in a state of comparative dependency, as something almost irrelevant. According to that realistic world-consciousness nature has evolved itself in a multiplicity of finite en-

tities. These entities are objectivised as personalities. These finite personifications detach themselves from the infinite and even depose the same to such a relation to themselves as to make it appear that its recognition depended upon their good humor.

The infinite is composed of the objectivications derived from personified nature. In the Orient the infinite embraces the finite as a part of itself. Here in the Occident the finite, making the infinite a means for its own practical ends, conceives the infinite

as part of itself. Outside of that which is divine in man the Gods are nothing. No wonder that the nations could not come to an understanding under the strain between such a thesis and its antithesis.

The process of thought could not stop there. Each party developed one side of the synthesis, but the tension remained between the natural and the spiritual world up to this day, wherever onesidedness closed itself against finding the synthesis. The

strain is as real and affects every-day life as incisively as the polarity between Heaven and earth. It manifests itself in the most sensitive parts of the human being. Were it not so, nobody would feel obliged to concern himself about the problems. Ethical and intellectual activity would be folly. Thesis and antithesis were so cogently and succinctly fixed, were each sticking fast, unable to retract or advance, whilst thought in the mean time could not rest unless the synthesis were found.

Whoever knows a little of the history and of the excitement of philosophical syncretism since Plato, and then adds the search after truth, peace and solace by the New-Platonics, will understand how all political casualties and exigencies of those times hinged upon the cardinal points under discussion.

Whoever is able to comprehend this will agree with our statement that never did people in general take such a feverish interest in the solution of the problem in question. The future was felt to depend upon the result of the search after the synthesis. All the labor of that agitated age with its many gropings along dark paths of science toiled and moiled about this problem as around a hidden secret. So close an approach to the desired synthesis from all sides certainly gives to the finding of it the significance of a historical necessity. If we would take the antithetical postulates as matters of logical reasoning, then all that would be

required would be a theoretical solution. A formula like that of Philo might combine the antitheses into such a conclusion as would resemble the key of which we spoke, disclosing all the contents hidden in the locked synthesis. It would be the intelligible and communicable expression which answers all wants, all objections; which gives consistent explanation of the seeming contradictions; which proves or disproves all those hypotheses which, pending the solution, were utilised in the dilemma.

The antitheses,—as we take them after Philo's futile attempt, to which the data of cultural life were practically reduced, and which now demand equation,—state

the different cognitions of the interrelations between the finite and the infinite forms of existence and their contents. These opposites are to be conciliated and brought to a unity in such a manner that the truth in either premise receives due recognition, that neither is prejudiced and neither magnified at the expense of the other.

And this formula could only be the sentence: Somehow the infinites must be also the finite and vice versa. This conclusion is incontrovertible. But it does not harmonise the contrasts. It is simply a conclusion stated in the shape of a new postulate.

Considering the mode of harmonising the antitheses, the answer, that a mere abstract identification of the infinite with the finite form of existence might essentially realise itself by entering into the multiplicity of finite persons, is after the failures of precedent experiments also out of the question.

David Strauss intimated that "the idea loves to outpour itself into the manifold of the genus and thus to disclose itself to it". This "winged word" which Strauss offered is virtually but a substitute of another postulate in lieu of our conclusion just stated, and is obviously rather behind time. Buddhism would remind us that this solution had been tried without avail in its alleged incarnations, or rather impostures and delusions. In India the infinite had been dragged down to the finite, into the multitude of phenomena. In Italy the finite had been exalted to the infinite through a multiplicity of phenomena. The Greeks and Romans would marvel at our ignoring their gods of personified nature and their apotheosised emperor-gods. In all these attempts thought sunk down into the subnatural, we might almost say, exhausted by the random experiments to substantiate the anticipated appearance of God in the world. It is not necessary that such a universal fainting spell should repeat itself in the "idea" emptying itself into generaluess.

Mode in which alone the SYNTHESIS § 86, 77, 94, 100, 105, is to be realised.
Abstract identification of the Infinite and the finite would fall back behind the preambles.

§ 103. The correct logical form of the synthesis must be found in a fact as real as the phenomenal facts demanding it—because the logic of history works that way. And the fact must be the consummation of a union between the infinite and the finite in personal unification. It must come about in a synthesis as possible and as real as, and analogous to, the union of the soul with the spirit in human nature. The synthesis must come forth as a historical act in the concrete form of a real person. That person will be actually "the Mediator" between the two modes of human consciousness as well as between both the infinite, absolute and personal Being on one side, and the realm of finite but real entities on the other, each to continue its existence as a oneness in itself, neither neutralising or sublimating the other.

Logic of History demands a solution of the problems—unification of the modes of thought and union of the Infinite with the finite, each as a oneness in itself—through a fact, a person.

At this very stage of maturity the thought of the old world had arrived. It had penetrated into the problem of unification between God and the world far enough to come to the conclusion that mankind must look for a mediator to accomplish it in person.

Plato's synthesis had demonstrated not only the individual yearning and destiny, which made the universal effect of the union necessary but also at the same time the consistency of the unification with the unity of humanity and the sighing of the creature.

Necessity of the universal effect of the personal incarnation demonstrated by Plato.

Philo's compromise formulated the empirical postulates into the logical conclusion. His theoretical combination of the synthesis was, on the whole, correct. It remains only to be shown that in Plato's and Philo's combined postulates another was implied, altho quite obscure as yet, which timidly demands the perfect union of God with humanity in one real man. The one totality of the finite, in juxtaposition to the infinite as the other oneness, had not been held distinctly apart, so as to maintain the integrity of each. Nevertheless, it had inadvertently been presumed, it was implied in the postulated premises, that the unification of God with the universe was to be wrought by a person. Thus in theory even the individuality of the Logos and the universality of his function had been provided for.

Plato's and Philo's postulates include an other postulates.
Theoretically the individuality of the Logos and the universality of his function was thinkable.

But whilst the philosophers composed the theoretical compromise, another weighty momentum had entirely escaped the attention of these searchers in their eagerness to find the answer which head and heart demanded. The possibility had not been thought of nor accounted for: how this Mediator could appear in the reality of visible and definite substance, in this impure matter. This is not at all irrelevant in the matter of relieving and abolishing the strain. It was just this riddle which a little later became a stumbling-block to the gnostics. How real human appearance of God in equally real human but not docetic existence is possible, becomes a new and inevadable problem. All speculating and compromising is in vain, after all, if logic overlooks this condition of true incarnation. For, whatever is, must not remain being in the general, abstract sense. In order to be something, it must become a real something. This must be more so the case in personal life, where the something must become somebody. Personal being is just as much above being in general as fact stands above fiction. The Logos can not be conceived as the real unity of the contrasting forms of consciousness in which the truths of transcendency and immanency of the deity are mirrored, UNLESS THE LOGOS BECOMES A HISTORICAL FACT, A PERSON. In this manner alone the Logos proves to be the completion of the synthesis of idealism, individuality and universalism. Nothing short of that unification will pacify either reason or faith. Here lies the truth for which both Monism and Dualism contend in their vociferous debatings.

Theorising had only overlooked the difficulty of uniting the Infinite with impure matter. § 101.
Mode of the entrance of the Logos into the world and into history.
Stumbling-block of gnosticism.
Appearance of God in person, in real human form of existence.

The truth for which both Monism and Dualism contend—in which true monism is realised.

Not one of the seeming contradictions in the isms mentioned, from which the conflicts originated, and which ever excited the processes of thinking from two different aspects, can ever be solved or decided by the evolution theory. Neither progress of thought nor spread of mental culture, nor any theory, nor any form of intellectualism (for instance indoctrination of dogmas, idealisation of the "Christ-idea," etc.), can reconcile the heterogeneity of the antitheses. The true element contained in each of these isms can alone be accomplished through the real incarnation by force of the fact. The renewed efforts in these modern times to abstract from the "fact" in extolling the "idea" in a worse than ancient style can not screen itself behind Philo. Reason, imparted to history and underlying the course of its development, leads man up to the "LOGOS." That much reason can do—if guided by the Logic of History, but no more.

Refutation of modern attempts of solving the problem in worse than ancient style.

CH. II.   INTERMEDIATION POSTULATED PHYSICALLY.   THE SACRIFICE.

Import of facts more formidable than that of thoughts.

§ 104.   A deed proves more than a theory; in its influence fact goes further than thought.   An act continues to call forth thought, so that it may be thought over and over again.   An act leads from appearances into the essence of things; it sets persons to reflect thereupon.   Facts return to persons, because they belong to them.

If the apparent dilemma of logic with regard to our present life and to a better, higher life—if the conflict concerning the conceptions "finite" and infinite, if the contrariety between the absolute and the conditioned, is ever to be solved and pacified indeed,—then the Ínfinite had to take the initiative in realising the union and conciliation.   It had to enter into the finite (eingehen.)   But it could not suffer to become

The Infinite to take the initiative in assuming finite forms of existence;

absorbed by it (darin aufgehen); and it can not become inconsistent to itself (von sich abgehen).   The Infinite could enter only in such a manner, as to take the finite upon and into Himself, to appropriate and assimilate it to Himself as His own.

at a certain time and a proper locality.

Moreover, the Infinite had to appear not only somehow, but also somewhere.   The Infinite would be expected to appear, where, after the preparatory concentration of

Mode of the Infinite in entering nature and history.

the two ideas, the most channels, ways, and means possible were at hand for the progressive course of the finite to become affianced to the Infinite.   Such a place, affording the best facilities for spreading the assimilating and at the same time isolating influence, must be located where the means of communication offered the proper

The place

opportunities not only concerning commercial and political, but also literary, and ethical matters.   For, the historical current ever runs through human coefficients or agencies; and we have seen why, naturally and ethically, this course alone could be taken.

and the

Through the many expediencies and concomitant factors, by pre-arranged routes the news of the fact, the "word" as uttered into this world, could make itself universally understood by being communicated in appropriate manner.

After the word was taken to heart and appropriated by mindful persons, the glad tidings could be disseminated in every respect and in every direction.   In order that the spreading of the kindred fire, purifying, enlightening, and warming up

historic moment

humanity in general, be not   frightening but   glad tidings, the Infinite would appear at that historic moment, when all laboring and thinking was exposed in its incompetency, baseness and bankruptcy to such a degree, that it could not be denied or palliated.   The Infinite One, by virtue of His nature, neither could nor would

to be prepared for, and the appreciation of, the advent.

force Himself upon the world.   The world needed first to feel the necessity, so as to appreciate the "Advent."

Of the degeneracy of cults and culture we are convinced from what we have noticed. So was statesmanship at its wits end. All relations of life shared in the total eclipse. The nations were trodden down; their ancient institutions, old and only strongholds of existence which their symbols and customs were, had lost their significance.   Who would have ambition enough left to care for the public welfare?   The spirit of freedom and patriotism had given way to disgust and rascality.   The peoples under the feet of the ruling power and the fists of

Social miseries.

not less tyranical rioters, found protection neither in law nor in arms.   "The knights had turned bankers, the optimates were hanging around the exchange and the games.   The farmer was ruined by slavery, land-monopolies, and mortgages."

Unavailing devices on the score of reforms.

The more all sorts of reform had been experimented upon; the oftener the hopes for a revival of public-mindedness and of interest in public affairs, the hopes for help from ballot and legislation had been disappointed—the more had attempts at selfsalvation complicated matters for the worse.

When the decay of the state began to phosphoresce, even the wierd flickering of crazy cults, spreading over the whole empire and pretending to bring the panacea for all sores, soon lost its attractiveness.   People began to be as listless as they had before been superstitious.

Men were not so credulous any longer as to be duped by any soothsayer, and to be mocked in their dismay. From under the thin cover of gloss and splendor the running sores of pollution trickled down corruption, from every organ of the gigantic body politic now in full state of decomposition. The surface of public life showed stagnation, satiety, and vulgarity. The scum of brutal pugilists and pugnacious dialecticians or sneaking sycophants was on top, as the saying is.

The Roman crucible had become a witch's kettle, in which delapidated fragments of recent glory and dominion, of booties and triumphs swam around, that is, changed hands at random,and evaporated deadly gases. The nations and their cultures and treasures were now rapidly eaten up inwardly and outwardly by the very cultures which once had attracted them. And it is the poor effigy and cheap copy of that very culture which is even now bragged up so much under the caption "classic culture." All attempts at affecting reforms through finances and magic art had been made, all means had been applied and were used up. The state itself, so recently conceived as the Supreme Good, the last delusion tried in cementing the leaking basin, was fast becoming an impossibility.

Attempts to selfsalvation render matters worse.

The delusion of the state being the Supreme Good had vanished. § 42, 78.

The ancient world at the acme of the pride which it took in culture suddenly suc-cumbed from—overexertion? One may as well speak it right out, that it was from subtilised refinement. The higher classes, the money-aristocracy, worst of aristoc-racies, would not be reminded of the misery; they would not step down to dirty their feet by getting into contact with the lowly people, tho it was about Christmas time. The Mediator must appear. Many, then called "atheists" because they had dropped self-made gods, said so themselves. But where? Men like Philo were scarce; few were so fortunate as to possess wealth and leisure without feeling the loneliness incumbent on idealistic minds. Whilst Philo was on his chair in the hall between the Serapeion and the temple of Leontopolis, lecturing upon the Mediator to eager crowds of students, talking about the "first-born," the "Angel of the Lord," and of the "Word of God,"—that, on which his mind was fixed in sincere concentration, that became in his native land close by—a fact.

Ancient culture succumbed from over-refinement.

The nativity.

§ 105. Over there in Philo's country the great "advent" had been announced many times and ever more pointedly during the last thousand years through a series of prophets, a series which had reached down to four hundred years ago. Is your chronology correct there, Philo? your idea, then, is nothing new?

The prophets cannot be interpreted from incidents of, let us say, mere secular history. In its rise and long continuance prophecy is a miracle as well as a fact. Its uniqueness ought to be sufficient evidence that it is ordained from above. Toward the lower sphere it exercises, in its criticism, an authority which stands unequalled. Its period of prime falls in the Asiatic hexameron of spiritual re-creation, yet it seems to work rather destructively. It renders itself unpopular, rather than compro-mise with error or evade the displeasure of the vulgar. In matters of ethico-relig-ious concern the prophets punished regardless of fear or favor; and they used very solacing and encouraging language, too. With reference to intelligence they split into splinters one cosmogony after another, no matter how ancient and how proud of them the nations severally were, without forbearance.

The singular ordinance of prophecy, a miracle as well as a fact, not interpretable from mere historic inferences.

Here in close quarters, lying prostrate under oppression most of the time, the peo-ple had been prepared for the appearance of the Mediator through a history of vicis-situdes without a parallel. Evidently this history had been devised for the purpose of being typical, and of lasting import to all other nations.

Unparalleled history of the chosen people: clearly designed to be typical for every human heart— under pressure. §§ 9, 10, 13,117, 210, 228.

Here the meaning of the guidance by a higher hand was made demonstrable even to blinded minds. Here, in the heart of every one, the sufferings of all humanity had been ex-perienced and sympathy came to its right. Here in full view of all the world that tragedy was to be enacted which a line of prophets had predicted long ago; for 600 years is a long period even for universal history.

With the tragedy was given, wheresoever referred to by the prophets, a perspective view of a final parousia and of the transfiguration of the universe into the state of glory.

Henceforth there is no antithesis to this locked synthesis—for no opposite is left unsolved in this awfully "finished" conclusion neutralising all tension and breaking all chains of bondage. All nations witnessing the event are addressed as partici-pants, all being involved therein by reason of humanity as outlined in the "Table of Nations" put on record and published nowhere else but in this place.

Unity of the human race in the table of nations. § 115.

All are called to witness the appalling scene which centers in the sacrificial act; all are invited to ponder over the exhibit of the contrasts: not merely to look at, but to realise the most infernal cruelty manifesting itself beside the consummation of the adorable and profound love—a love unheard of before, and embracing all—once and forever!

On the strength of this fact each has his date appointed, when he or she is to be brought to trial or to terms for their part in perpetrating deeds which wound this love. Those acquitted shall be called up by their new names, henceforth to partake also of the great commemoration of the sacrifice and feast of communion. All of this is to continue to the end of the world, in the order as the veilings are drawn aside and the hulls drop down. All shall become fully aware of the fact, not in reason and emotion alone, but in both with faith added, that here and now their own case is brought up in order to be decided upon. For the actual crisis of each member of the human family is implied in yonder mode of solution.

At times there were voices heard coming out of the nations, which uttered divinations of this appearance of the Infinite, and of some of the proceedings connected therewith. "Zendavesta already has it"—says Seyffarth in his studies of the Turin-papyrus,—"that the son of the pure virgin once would hold judgment."

We waive the testimony of the voices of these people. In the face of the great fact it is irrelevant whether the "Sibylline oracles" and some Roman classics are reliable or worthless as witnesses. We deem it unnecessary, as you will have noticed, to adduce those intimations in regard to the Mediator, as ingraven in mythology, in traditions and documents, sprinkled over the whole globe. They lie around far and near where from their wide periphery the radii all point to the spot where we stand. Unless the rays of light fall upon these radii from the center, they are unintelligible and may be construed to suit any line of argument. In making judicious use of the "voices of the people" properly understood and applied in appropriate manner, some sages skilled in apologetics have often succeeded. Oftener some others, deficient in critical ability, have not. We on our part are rather loath to "apologise" for our belief in the facts, and for our clinging to the cross.

The Mediator of all is born into this cosmos. The infinite divine being, who embraces the entire universe, enters into this world of finiteness at a certain point; at an "infinitesimal" point, even, bearing the marks of Paternal and maternal descent.

He blends and completely unites His nature with the nature of man, thus becoming "the" man Himself. We see the Infinite and the finite united in One. Finite human nature is adopted by the Infinite (not indefinite) nature of God; it is pervaded and permeated by the divine nature, and elevated into the beautiful purity which had been its original form as the "image" of the Father, and as the prototype of man before the beginning.

The finite part of this new personality reaches this destiny of man in daily self-denial and selfconsecration. And the destiny of man is this, that the human personality in its entirety shall voluntarily become the organ of the Infinite without compulsion.

So the Mediator, the Christ, teaches by word and example.

He, in whom humanity as an organic unit recognises its head, speaking, acting, and suffering reveals the will of Him who sent Him in uniting His consciousness and will, His head and heart and soul and body with Him, in childlike faith and consecration, tho with perfect manliness.

Suffering, too.—For this Mediator stood upon this material planet in the realm of the visible, palpable cosmos, bearing its substance as His body. Hence He is Mediator even in regard to the universe, and because of that—He must die.

To assume our body He inanitiated deity, that is, limited His mode of being, by submitting to the heavy massiveness and crudeness of terrestrial conditions. The mass of the macrocosm from which our corporeal body is taken He substantially and formally appropriated and assimilated to Himself when essentially he united Himself with our finite nature. He did this in order to lead that earthly form of subsistence which is doomed to resolve or perish—as we call the disengagement or transition of elements, into new relations with and through Himself up again to the spiritual, eternal form of existence. And because the Mediator unreservedly consented to this, He must die.

Because He is agreed to deliver and to rescue humanity, ethically, by all means, He must and will die.

§ 106. There goes about among the nations a dismal moan, even through the most hilarious of them.

The mirthful vineyards of Hellas re-echoed the wailing for Linos. Raised among shepherds, the divine youth had been torn up by dogs; others sing how his beauty had wilted like the delight of the spring season under the torrid rays of the summer sun;

others deplore him, because Heracles had slain him with the cithara, when he desired to be taught music. The plaintive elegies of the Ionian lyrics reverberated from Syria through all nations, over the centuries, over fields of battle and among ruins. The melancholy chords always bemoan an only son, singled out from among the living and snatched away in the prime of life by a horrible death.

What causes these woeful sounds to haunt the solitudes of all nations?

Whether Phrygian corybants accompany the lamentations with wild bugle-blasts, or the soft tones of the flutes played by women with dishevelled hair, weeping for Attys—the outcries of agony from many voices, the selftortures, and the sacrifices: all arise on account of death. They arise from an anguish which is half conscious of the mysterious relations between innocence and guilt, sin and death.

Hence we can no longer defer the investigation concerning the cause of innate anxiety. The exclamations of anguish ever crying to Heaven demand satisfactory explanation. *Reference to the outlines of the paragr. 41, 47.*

Will the reader please to extend the lines of thought thus indicated back to their terminal points where they outline a certain figure? For, what in the former part of our expository course had to be postponed, is now to be taken up and to be considered under the proper aspect, since the veilings are now drawn aside, and all problems solved.

The animal and human sacrifices found at all times and everywhere on the face of the earth, are not traceable to any other cause than to the feeling of the necessity of a propitiation. Ever since the sad rupture of family unity mankind has had a remembrance of a detachment from the Heavenly powers, and of a disruption among the earthly relatives. *Sacrifices: guilt to be propitiated.*

An inner restlessness was to be appeased, a heavy burden to be lifted off from the innermost soul. It was in keeping with the nature of the relations existing between all parties concerned that retribution of guilt be made, that guilt challenges revenge. For a life torn out of the ground in which it is rooted, for a life doomed to death, only a life can be an equivalent. The justice of this doom being present in the nature of all things assumes in man the form and feeling of guilt, the demand of satisfaction uttered by the outraged constitution and order of the universe, whose representative and warden man himself was to be. In other words: Guilt is the demand of conformity to absolute justice, made upon the responsible person. By virtue of the feeling thus ingrained into human nature, guilt universally manifests itself in the offering of sacrifices. *Expiation demanded by the order of the universe.* *Justice of the penalty and relief from it.* *Significance of the feeling of guilt.*

The refuge taken at sacrificial altars testifies to the truth that involuntary feelings and promptings of shame and fear are left to the sinner, in order to keep him redeemable. The altar as an asylum witnesses sacrifice to be an established and given institution, the pledge of conciliation, declaring that under certain conditions the intervention of atonement and release is admissible. The significance of the feeling of guilt is that it acknowledges the justice of the death-sentence, and the refuge which the guilty one takes in sacrifice, signifies the faint recognition of the conditional pardon offered. The conditions thus assented to consist in the satisfaction of justice by payment of the penalty. The sinner's despondency at this stage is alleviated by the feeling, that he is not alone or not altogether responsible for the portentous consequences. The propensity, therefore, to put the blame upon something or somebody else, contains an element of truth. The truth is that, on account of the voluntary sacrifice of a consecrated and innocent life in lieu of the doomed life of the culprit, release is granted and restitution warranted him. For the time being he is put on his good behavior, kept under probation, and under surety of his bail. *Absolute justice of retribution is acknowledged in the universality of sacrifice.* *Sacrifice expiatory under conditions.* *Vicarious atonement.*

In its deepest sense sacrifice is the type for that vicarious atonement which alone fully answers the conditions. And hence it was truth contained in all expiatory sacrifices that blood alone, as the seat of life, can serve the purpose of propitiation.

The wrath of the deity is to be conceived and acknowledged as the just resistance against, and resentment of, the destructive violence of the bad. The anger of God is the reaction of the saving and rescuing purpose against that which annihilates, in order to save itself from annihilation. This just and holy indignation thirsts not for blood from vindictiveness, but requires life as a pledge for the maintainance of equity in behalf of the best interests of humanity as a whole. God accepts vicarious blood as a substitute for the life of the guilty one; as a memorial showing forth that God is ever so WILLING TO FORGIVE, PROVIDED THAT GOD HIMSELF AND NOT THE SINNER IS ENTITLED TO FIX THE TERMS OF PARDON. *Death, the penalty to be paid, or bail to be given.* *Anger of God the reverse side of rescuing love.　§ 40.*

Sacrifice as an institution, ranking with the first and fundamental ordinances of historical import, is a gift of God, held out as a pledge of reconciliation. Whilst man by virtue of this symbolic act is held under bond, God pledges Himself to suspend the verdict of death until the bondsman shall consecrate His life as a ransom to redeem the sinner's life from final condemnation, and for the present to free him from the disheartening fear of death. Salvation is thus made possible for all, whilst, of course, it becomes effective only with those, who accept of their redemption on the ground of the love and life laid down in the atonement: i. e. who submit to the conditions. *Sacrifice as an institution is a gift, pledging suspense of the death-penalty.* *Culprits held under bond.*

Atonement made for all; effective only for those who submit to the reasonable simple conditions.

Man judged or acquitted according to the attitude taken toward the atonement.

Intent of sacrifice subverted.

Evidences of guilt and of the necessity of propitiation. § 108, 157.

Cosmical condition of atonement remains in full force wherever the redemption be rejected. § 9, 36, 116, 117.

Scenes of frenzy in visionary abnegations. APULEJUS, MOSERS.

Instances from Roman life. JUVENAL, PRELLER.

Many victims for the fault of one,

or one to be sacrificed for the baseness of the many.

All being now fulfilled by the representative of humanity in the great sacrifice, man henceforth, is either judged or acquitted according to the attitude taken toward this one sacrifice.

In the consternation sequent to the great calamity, the leniency, the mercy of God was forgotten; as yet every deed and thought was related to supernatural power. But God-consciousness being sadly distracted, God was conceived as revengeful. It was the origin of heathenism when man took to the idea, that it was incumbent upon him to restore God to goodness. The evil consequences of godlessness were imputed to unseen beings, with whom the bad feelings were associated to the extent of objectivising guilt into bad spirits. It was then only a small step on the steep incline, that the idea of vicarious atonement,—altho engraven so deep into the human mind that man offers selfjustification in excuse of guilt by blaming it on others, if he does not take revenge for the sake of selfsatisfaction—was corrupted into bribes to conciliate demons or to make gods the means for his own purposes. Feeling of guilt associated with the thought of sacrifice remains so effective, nevertheless, as that many a criminal was prompted to give himself up to justice in satisfaction of natural justice, testifying thereby to the objective validity and perpetuity of its claim. The unwillingness to offer sacrifices in propitiation of wrongs in the proper and prescribed order ever caused man to rage against himself, at least.

Sacrifices withheld or arbitrary corruptions of the ordinance go to enhance the harvest of the evil one every time. Under this aspect come all the sacrifices of wars in which neglect of the Christian order of propitiation is horribly avenged. For, if Christ's bloody atonement would be held sacred in the full sense, man would not need to make involuntary sacrifices in destroying his own deranged existence. Think of Jerusalem in the year A. D. 70. **The law of sacrificial retribution remains in full force as a cosmical condition, wherever the universally valid sacrifice of the Redeemer is rejected.**

We hear an uninterrupted series of cries in hymns of contrition and psalms of repentance. They came from different motives and are, therefore, of different ethical quality, altho never without religious purport.

Those cries from Sumer, and Akkad and Babylon, from Ninive and along the whole Mediterranean coast preceded selfannihilation in orgiastic frenzy and demon-service. When in the performances of the Syrian Mylitta cult the gangs of the Kinædes wandered about, as Apulejus depicts them, with yellow turbans, half naked, waving hatchets, swords, and scourges in their mad dances,—then selfmutilations were practiced in which blood was spilled unsparingly, until one of the crowd, as Movers describes, would charge himself with the sins of all and chastise himself for them.

We let the curtain drop to hide the spectacle of carnage and blood-shedding on festive occasions in honor of Baal-Moloch at Tyre and Carthage. Such unnatural, may we not say, subnatural cults spent their fury even before the throne of the deified emperor. There one could see a frantic woman at the head of the procession of the Cappadocian highpriestesses, lacerating her arm with a double-edged adze, whilst the priests with flowing hair in dark clothes and caps of shaggy furs were jumping around her and the altar, brandishing their sharp blades. The blood running from the gashes in their bodies was caught up by the hands of admiring worshippers and sipped with eagerness, for it was believed to possess expiatory virtues. "Nowhere was the desire for absolution and reconciliation more seriously felt and more sincerely expressed, than in the religious usages of this society," says Preller in his "Roman Mythology." Juvenal alludes, "that long ago the Syrian Orontes had emptied itself into the Tiber."

And so we might observe how the extremes meet in the Haragiri of the Japanese and the codes of honor among our duelists. The modern descriptions of criminal cases speak of many instances where perpetrators of hidden crimes could find no rest until they unburdened their consciences by delivering themselves to the courts of justice, and confessing their deeds.

There are cases on record, that convicts begged to be executed in order to get rid of the tantalising reproaches of murdered souls. Many a case of suicide belongs to this category. All this shows the urgency of the compensation for guilt: it shows the mastery which the anxious suspense wields over man.

§ 107. The next stage of the craving for propitiation, common to all parts of the race under all zones, is that, where instead of the guilty person another receives the death-stroke or swallows the poisoned cup who partook not of the crime. There is no nation on the face of the globe whose history would not demonstrate efforts to satisfy the cosmical law of propitiation by vicarious atonement in smoking streams of blood.

At this stage the aberrations of the religious consciousness rest upon the intuitive thought and the too much neglected truth of the solidarity of human sin and guilt in general. Hundreds are sacrificed through the negligence of one, or the wickedness of another. Or on the other hand, one person of relative innocence must suffer for many or suffer with the rest.

None has better elucidated this difficult problem of the sufferings to be endured by Innocents, and of the indirect participation of each in the guilt of others, or of the responsibility incumbent upon all for the guilt of one, than Dorner in his dogmatics. We on our part can only give facts, in explanation of vicarious suffering on the principle of the solidarity of the race by the logic of history. This logic does not investigate the greater measure of guilt, or the lesser degree of innocence, but passes on to the order of the day since the sacrifice of the Mediator has solved also this problem. Solidarity of human sin and guilt. DORNER.

Innocence suffering for the faults of others.

It is, perhaps, not generally known, that human sacrifices were made when cities were founded or bridges were built among the Germans and Scottish as well as among the Greeks and Romans. Alexander sacrificed a virgin when he founded Alexandria. The same did Tiberius at the laying of the corner-stone of the grand theatre in Antioch. The Germans and Persians equally with the Slavonians kept up the usage of burying alive or butchering captives, before or after a battle. Upon the isle of Leucas the Greeks annually threw a man from the cliff down into the sea for an expiation of the sins of the populace in general. Upon Rhodes, opposite the temple of Artemisia at the annual festival of Kronos one was hung for the expiation of the common guilt. From Athens we hear, that once two men were killed instead of the one who was required for the benefit of the community at the annual feast of the Targelies. Sophocles makes Oedipus say, "A pure-minded soul has he, who dies voluntarily, being well qualified to serve as a ransom, and to obtain immunity from penalty for thousands." The Greek legends are full of such selfconsecrations since Codros chose death for the sake of the liberty of the state. Human sacrifices.
§ 41, 54, 110, 135.

Voluntary selfdenials for the benefit of others SOPHOCLES.

People ever held the idea that one can sacrifice his comfort, even his life for another. Up to date people act as tho the honor of one sacrificed to shield the baseness of another did not amount to much, tho life itself has no value without honor. It seems that victims of calumny find less sympathy, because the sacrifice of their honor is accomplished more easily than murder. Society winks at it, making calumny rather accrue to the prestige of the libeler. Victims of slander.

However this may be, human nature reveals the fact that one may be sacrificed, or deny and sacrifice himself voluntarily, in behalf of another.

In the next higher stage the idea and necessity of expiation is exhibited in animal sacrifices, taking the place of the human. This is the repristination upon the true symbolic and typical act, the institution of which was originally given as a memorial and a pledge.

According to E. Lassaulx a seal was branded upon the consecrated animals. The seal—most remarkable—represented the figure of a man, kneeling, with hands bound upon his back, the edge of a sword set to his throat, the bystanders striking their breasts with their hands. Here we see, that, as also the Indian rituals prescribe it, the sacrifice of an animal was made the substitute and ransom for the doomed life of the sinner. Animal sacrifices.
LASSAULX.

Meaning of sacrifice in general

§ 108. Summing up the gains of our analytic investigation as a basis for further conclusions, we find the result to corroborate the terse statement of Wuttke: "In the bloody sacrifices of men and animals, man shows that he is in earnest about religion." "shows man's being in earnest about religion."
WUTTKE. § 157.

Most assuredly. Here at last we stand before the seriousness of the situation. The blood of these victims cries to Heaven.

In the basest subversions of the original intent of sacrifice there is still discernible the typical purport underlying them all. The "anxious suspense" wants to secure a suspension of the verdict, an amelioration of evils.

Thus every offering is a shadow, more or less dark or distinct, of the grave solemnity of the moment, when the Highpriest in the capacity of a Mediator entered into the presence of the Unseen, interceding with the blood of the innocent soul. Purport of the ordained typical sacrifices, of which all others are adumbrations.

The sprinkling of the blood in the central sanctuary on the Day of Atonement signified reconciliation in behalf of the chosen nation, and ultimately in the interest of the whole world.

The sacrifices of the nations were shadows of this typical atonement, inasmuch as they virtually refract true elements of the fundamental thought in the originally ordained sacrifice. In the measure as the nations recede from the center toward the wide periphery and their religious sentiments darken, the sacrificial acts, in which the religious tenets always center, are corrupted correspondingly. But notwithstanding their corruptions they perpetuate remnants of pristine or universal revelation.

It is by virtue of special revelation that the celebration of the typical sacrifice in the Old Testament forshadows the real Atonement, without being in any way part of the same or adequate to it, because it chiefly rests upon externals and upon command.

The typical atonement

In the order of worship of the concentric nation the true import of the allegorical type of "The Sacrifice" proper was to be protected against all arbitrary changes and perversions. To this end God had stipulated the conditions of reconciliation according to His will and wisdom and ways in this impressive, instructive, and disciplinary ordinance down to its minutest details. But since the Great Sacrifice is now accomplished in every particular, and in perfect obedience to the sovereign will, the hulls fall and the type is abolished. It is the sacrifice upon Calvary, which ever had been divined, to which all offerings pointed, upon which all other sacrifices of the periphery revolved, in which religion is intensified, and revelation and religion are rendered identical. Nothing is to be added, no other merit can supersede it.

abolished.

Sufficiency of the Great Sacrifice which no meritorious act can amend, or render more effective, or supersede.

Everywhere we found affliction, agony and want of spiritual solace causing intense altho unconscious desire for the appearance of the Mediator and for his real atonement. Everywhere the conviction that life is the gift of God but forfeited on account of the disrupture; and that man therefore is justly condemned to die, is the confession implied in each sacrificial act. Everywhere, furthermore, it is before consciousness that guilt may be put upon somebody else, and that a life of an innocent one voluntarily consecrated to this end may intercede for, and suspend the doom of, the guilty ones, may save the lives of all. These premises in the problem had at last been comprehended well enough. It was in the groping search after the Innocent One where the error occurred. In the usual line of events and among men as they are, no sacrifice could give full satisfaction and answer the conditions.

The "Son of Man"

Now the Innocent One steps forth from the midst of men. He announces Himself to be the Mediator, "THE SON OF MAN." We are sure of having correctly understood Him, when we took Him for the real issue of humanity in the fullest sense, for the Ideal Man. As such He is the central personification of the macrocosmos, and we

the central figure of the macrocosmos. § 11, 13, 36.

have seen what that means, when speaking of the position of man as the medium of two worlds. As the Ideal Man, the perfect man in true reality, He is "the" representative of universal humanity, and He is the center of the universe.

The personality in the mean of the Triune God.

As the personality in the middle of the living and therefore Triune Deity which is unapproachable on the part of the world, Jesus came more than near to man; when he took his part, he identified himself with him. He actually became the perfect man so as to be capable of sympathising with every one who will let Him approach to his heart as a friend.

This God-man gave Himself for us. He was crucified.

———ooo———

Incarnation and Atonement in their significance for man.

Jesus the Christ bridged the chasm between the worlds spiritual and natural. By His intercession on high He equipoised all strains here below. By descending into the abyss He shut it up. Unifying human nature with the Divine through His person, He becomes not only one of us, but the head of all humanity and one with it. As the central person, as head and representative of the race He bears humanity not only upon, but also within Himself, in the very manner in which He carries the macrocosmos physically within Himself, and in which man is the crown and epitome of the physical universe.

In this capacity He obediently and voluntarily submits to bear all sin and shame of the race, all its suffering collectively, and the death of each individually. He takes upon Himself death as our punishment, and to full satisfaction pays the accumulated debts as our bondsman. He does it all, bears it all. But under forms of law, here overdoing itself in human administration by actually murdering Him,—

Crucifixion.

He sinks down under the burden.

Imputation of all forms and effects of the Bad to the One altogether righteous.

The Pure One identifies Himself with a wretched humanity. As its solitary healthy member, as its heart even, He is part of the organism of humanity, a body sick unto death. The poison and leprosy of the whole body throws its destructive force unitedly upon this single pure heart. It breaks.

But the plague also spends its force. Out-raging itself in raging against the Innocent One, the power of the Bad is broken.

Hence the possibility is in reach of each and all, to be healed and freed from sin and its effects. The cure is to be realised in the natural order of organic unification. There is a simple way of becoming embodied in the wonderful organism in which each is to prove a living member, by partaking of the vitalising forces circulating through it: the Blood and the Spirit.

As the incarnation and the sacrifice must of necessity be historic, so the participation in the new life is to proceed upon historical lines, marked out by the Savior for good reasons, in His testamentary bequest. *Appropriation of the fruits of the Atonement to transpire upon the historic lines marked out by the Testator.*

The cardinal facts—not mere doctrines—of this communion consist in these experiences, namely: Sins forgiven by virtue of the blood and death of Jesus Christ; new life given by the impartation of the Holy Spirit sent through Him. The synthesis lies in the compass of history, but here transcends it to be comprehended by—faith alone! *Appropriation of the principles of salvation, the transcendental, proceeds historically—by faith alone.*

The solemn orations delivered by the fathers of the Greek church, the pensive hymns of the Middle-Ages, the intellectual strivings of scholasticism, and of philosophy up to this day, could but revolve around the mystery of this death, from which proceeds the life of a new world, that is, a Christianised culture, (CIVILISATION) unknown before. They all could do nothing but feel their way around the mystery underlying the process of this renovation by way of regeneration and growth, thus initiated to continue to the end of the world and of the times. They could not do even this much, unless they remained in tender touch with the head and heart of humanity, not by mere intellectual assent, but by personal friendship.

Never will we be able to formulate in words the secret of the vicarious death objectively, or the imputation of righteousness to the petitioner for pardon subjectively, because these elements of reconciliation are involved in the principles of, and in the order of their effects upon, the living organism. The secret was not intended to be abstracted and to be bottled up for occasional use, as it were, so as to make superfluous the continuous touch and contact with the source of life by faith, superfluous the unbroken circulation of divine influences and the connection with the organism by love. The secret, for this reason, should become uncovered no more than can be found out about life pure and simple. It shall not be found out and applied in the way of scientific demonstration, because—so it seems to us—it would be misfortune in the extreme, if the finite being should obtain the full power over itself. It is as unnecessary as it is impossible for the creature to become absolute. *Understanding of the process of renovation escapes scientific demonstration but not personal experience. The reason for this secrecy. It is as unnecessary as it is impossible for finite beings to become absolute.*

To revolve upon the central fact, truth and person, means, nevertheless, to understand the necessity by which man is attracted to it. To understand the mystery of the fact or person itself would mean to stand above it, and to play the master with the mode and the combinations under which the consummation of the whole process of renovation is to be perfected. This can safely be trusted to the management of the Absolute One.

§ 109. Arrived at the middle of our observations in universal history we stand before its central figure, under the cross. Taking history under the aspect of its movements, we stand under its meridian. Taking it as the science of explaining human affairs, we stand at its base, below which an attempt at explanation dares not venture. Already a heap of material has accumulated waiting for decipherment. Presuppositions, for which at several stages of the disquisition we had to beg the question, must now present their vouchers and find their affirmation. *Retrospect from the position "under the cross."*

The observer of the suffering Innocent One here receives new light with reference to previous conjectures. Not before could he appreciate the graveness of the situation. The crucifixion deepens the interest. The earnestness of this death discloses the solemnity of history; no event save this could so keenly impress itself upon it. As the "Word" is the light of the world so is the cross the key to human history. We feel as tho we had so far only looked at its exterior. But since the glance can pierce behind the rent curtain into the invisible world, from the depth of which phenomena of historic reality arose; since the coverings are withdrawn from drowsy sleepers, beneath which many things concerning the visible world used to be hidden: matters become plain and distinct which before seemed fathomless. *Previous conjectures affirmed and elucidated.*

In this death and resurrection all is disclosed now; and that is affirmed which the heralds of the forthcoming Ruler of all nations proclaimed by virtue of His commission and according to His instructions. We see why, for the time being, it all had been enclosed in the peculiar wrappings of what we may call a sectarian nationality. Nowhere else but here are we made acquainted with the personal God perfectly independent of the world; a Triune God, because possessing an organic nature of His own. Being the very life in itself, blessed in Himself, His existence is in no way affected by His relations to the world, the creation of His will and wisdom. With these few self-evident truths—which are quite rational and so plain as to be estima- *Prophecies affirmed. Proclamation of the facts provided for. Knowledge of God restored. Trinity.*

ted as mere truisms, as to lose their majesty since they have become so familiar to us, tho they once had to be specially revealed,—all the weird phantoms and theognostic dreams of paganism are pushed into the rubbish.

Knowledge of creation.

Evidently the universe is not an emanation of divine radiancy, nor the reflection of such. Natural life aside from personal life contains not a particle of divine substance, by which it could be perceived as part of the divine essence. God exists not because of nature, nor does He exist for being made the means of its explanation.   God does not owe any of His dignity to creation; and He is not to be made the means for any earthly purpose whatever, neither He nor His name.

God is father to men solely with reference to the reconciliation, is

With respect to creation God is Lord and Ruler, Father He is solely and purely in regard to salvation. MAN HAS REASON TO RETURN THANKS TO HIM.

Standing under the cross we discern God especially as the regent of the world. We recognise His hand in creation, we feel His heart in salvation, but the ways and means of His Providence we cannot foresee, and it is a sign of the state of grace if one learns to perceive and acquiesce in them post eventum,—because to act the part of providence could be entrusted to no other but the Saviour's hands. We perceive

Sovereign Ruler of the universe and of historic movements.   § 218ff.

the interaction of His sovereign rule in that His free will persists in the realisation of His purpose for man's true benefit, whilst He does not force His saving love upon anybody. Thus God guides, provides, prevents and admits, adjusts and judges movements and men, and even causes new beginnings in history on the basis of the existing order of things, through human agencies. It is godly not to judge by external appearance and successes, or by reverses—and it is rational, in suffering, to trust Him.

Hypothetical argumentation justified.   § 35.

All this we laid down in the form of an hypothesis. We are now vindicated in declaring the existence of God as the most verified of all empirical facts.

True self-knowledge § 36, 37, 39, 40, 41, 56, 109, 115, 129, 169, 170, 185.

And we become here acquainted with ourselves: for we behold "the first man." He is on speaking terms with God. He is the root of the whole plant of humanity. He lives in the beatitudes of that paradise of which all children of man have faint

Paradise.

recollections as of the home of their own childhood. We see man as he then was, endowed with all the faculties necessary for cultivating his possessions joyfully, and for preserving himself worthy of his trust, preparatory to higher trusts.   From his mediatory position between God and the world the intention is indicated, that, in gladsome occupation and development, and in continuous intercourse with the Father, a happy progeny should spread over the earth, their dominion.

The apostasy.

But mistrust, doubt, and disobedience ensued, changing it all. The contrasts would not have become so palpable if they had not become so lamentable in the relations between the Perfect Man and his surroundings. It was not simply finiteness, nor the

God's purpose being challenged, the universe kept its course § 9, 106.

abuse of liberty or of the secondary good, it was rebellion of the creature, which resulted in rupture upon rupture, and subversion, and derangement everywhere. The purpose of God was questioned, was challenged.   To save it, as against human aberra-

to preserve it against human aberrations and satanic mystifications.

tions and satanic mystifications the universe had to keep its course, reacting against man, its intended lord, now an apostate. Sin was paid home according to the nature of things with its own product—with rebellion. Man's own nature most unnaturally turned against him, and severest of all losses was the loss of selfcontrol and freedom. Man fell back from his ambition to become as God, into a comparatively wretched state of dependence upon nature. In order to sustain his earthly existence man was condemned to hard labor, the earth, his paradise, changed into a penitentiary.   That act of tearing away from the Father, from the source of life into selfhood, was answered by his son slaying his son.

The worst of all subversions: God conceived to be bad, is to be conciliated.

It was a rapid progress downward and in waywardness. Ever more fatal became the estrangement, and fright increased at the rate in which the Bad assumed tremendous proportions. Man, judging God by himself, thought that He was bad,—the worst of all subversions. This objectivication or projection of the Bad in the wrong direction widened the breach into the deep abyss of which all of us know only too much. Man took sides with the calumniator of the Good, and went into league with his seducer, sharing his enmity against holiness, until the inner representative of the Holy One withdrew almost entirely.   In the loneliness and benightedness in which man thus was left, the "anxious suspense" seized him. And it is an open secret that in quandaries of wickedness men will not shrink from perjury to extricate themselves by making God an accomplice of their dark designs.

The pseudo-promise had come true in a measure as truth had been mixed with it: "Ye shall be as gods, knowing good and evil". To be sure, man now entertained different views, of the Bad he had plenty. Concerning himself man was ashamed to see much of the animal in himself, which disabled him from recognising the image of God. His own mate, nearest and recently dearest to him, he could treat with disdain and brutality. To man such misery in addition to his views was more than mockery, he could not rid himself of the recollection of his losses, of forfeited happiness; for he always knew of something better which now caused him acute remorse. *"Eritis Sicut Dii." The promise of knowing "the evil" was kept.*

It was just this recollection which aggravated his dejected mood; and it was in just this dejection in which, to his utter bewilderment, from the dark abyss the word flashed up again with a pallid gleam: "As gods shall ye be!" Was the abyss then the abode, perhaps, of the spirits tantalising him? Were not the ghosts of those he had maltreated, if not murdered, the gods who now persecute him with dreadful reproaches, yea, haunt him with their revenge? **The gods their ghosts!** so his frightened phantasy pressed the satanic promise home to him. Man could not rid his consciousness of the reality of the state of immortality, tho humane feelings, and the befriending idea of a human unity were rent to shreds. The thrilling recital of the event is not intended to reveal the depths of the Bad. This took every occasion to betray itself, as it did in an abundantly horrible manner at the crucifixion. *Total subversion of remnants of original God-consciousness. § 24, 41, 42, 47, 48, 49, 54, 55, 57, 59, 74, 83, 95, 115, 156. THE "GODS"—anguish objectivised. Source of the Bad not revealed, it betrays itself.*

If the whole had been told before, man would have been overwhelmed by terror; what was said was ultimately intended for encouragement and solace. Man should be set aright as to the origin of all the blood-curdling deeds which soil every page of history, and turn every blessing into a curse, by being apprised of the wild seeds sprouting from beneath the "bruised head." The uncanny light in which those dark phenomena appear glows from a hearth of which men formerly had not been aware. Now the cause of original sin in a world of spirits is here shown to mankind. *Ghostly phantoms haunting the fratricide. § 45, 49, 54, 55, 57, 58, 65, 67, 69, 71, 72, 73, 78, 83, 86, 95, 96, 113.*

We see at a single glance how sin was palmed off upon man by one who is at the head of this nether world of glow and darkness. We see how the noblest creature of God opened himself to his seductive promise through misuse of the fine gift of speech in a peculiarly religious conversation, under abuse of confiding guilelessness. Sin entered the world through man's spiritual nature by way of a lie. *Causality of sin in a world of spirits. Sin entered by way of man's spiritual part.*

We saw how man fell; how nature entrusted to his care, fell with him; since the rent through his nature extended to the universe belonging to it. The first murder was the issue of envy sequent to the first perversion of the sacrificial act. This last and strangely legalised murder in which "sin" culminated, by the perpetration of which the situation became cleared up in a way that darkened the sun, exposed the instigator and his plans beyond the possibility of an excuse for sin in any of its manifestations, Yet we are also apprised of the truth that, notwithstanding the impudence of the Bad, we need shudder no more. To look into the depth of the enigma which embarrasses the science of human affairs, we occupy a safe standpoint. Facing the fact from under the cross we gain courage and hope—because we discern that man is not the producer of the Bad.

Human nature is not bad in essence, not bad per se. Sin was reared in spheres transeunt and introduced as their product ready made. It had been kindled in the cold, remorseless passions of envy and hatred. It came in stealthily from that infected, rebellious part of the angelic spirit-world which kept its dominion, but was thrown down into darkness together with its principalities.

Without the knowledge of the real existence of this dark underworld, history in many places could not be understood, unless we would sacrifice human nature to the realms of darkness, and would acquiesce in the imputation, that man as a sinner was a very devil himself. The historian and the philanthropist are glad, that the word of truth uttered by authority of the mouth of truth never intimated a basis for such teaching. *The sinner not a devil himself.*

Humanity in itself, then, is not the source of infernal machinations. If sin were so essential to humanity as to originate from it, humanity, like the dominion of Satan would be lost beyond redemption.

As it is, and bad enough it is that on the one side man allows himself to be seduced, yet he is, by virtue of at least equal right, constantly reclaimed on the other. The nobility he possesses as by birthright, and which still constitutes his essential part, has been spared for him and put into safe keeping, so that it can be restored to him. Altho the "image" within him is henceforth so stained by sin and disgrace as to be scarcely recognisable from what he was before, he is still redeemable. And tho his descendants are so estranged in godlessness, and lost in the wide world, as to flee from holiness over the face of the earth, yet God does not lose sight of them. *Man's noble descent still constitutes his essential part; he is redeemable because not himself the source of the bad.*

Traditional knowledge
of the
great calamity
neither mythical nor
superstitious.   § 11,12.

Inferences correctly
drawn.

§ 110. Only thus and now are we enabled to understand the traditions relative to the great calamity, which previous to the Day of Atonement we could only propose as probable helps to explanation. We find the fall into an abyss an affirmed fact. The inferences drawn from traditional knowledge were correct: these traditions proved to be neither merely mythical, nor altogether superstitious.

Consciousness, severed from the Good, developed into a rich knowledge of the world with its diversions. But as to its normal progress it is now more than arrested. It now becomes filled with the fright of the great night in which the mind finds itself alone, without God in the midst of spectres of dreadful adversaries. Con-

Evidences of a deep and
dark undercurrent,
otherwise inexplicable,
when history meets its
cataracts and whirlpools.

sciousness, maimed from the stunning it sustained, was taken captive by cosmical powers and superhuman intellects. The traces of the ravishments, together with innumerable misfortunes we found in the wild, distorted features of character and in the hideous offspring of man's imagination. We found them in the debris of humanity and in the lowest substratum from whence they broke forth ever and again. At the time we were unable to account for them.

Unless we adopt this view with respect to the power of the Bad, we cannot understand the utter degeneracy and increasing depravity subsequent to another catastrophe, a worse departure, and a worldwide dispersion. Neither could we begin to interpret the ominous signs of an undercurrent not human, not brutal, but diabolical, which gushes forth into daylight whenever the course of history meets with its whirlpools and cataracts.

Holocausts of Carthage.
§ 41, 54, 107.

Human Sacrifices.
Hannibal,   § 71, 88.

When Carthage, for instance, makes a holocaust of three hundred of its finest youths of noble birth; and if such a rage seizes one country after another, then we cannot simply blame the carnage upon human error or superstition; but in the interest of reason, we are compelled to trace out the symptoms of an occult disease to the regions, evaporating such maddening fumes.

In sight of the "cursed tree" we find that strange fanatical fervor beneath a cover of culture and under guise of religion. All these thousands of years it has caused similar eruptions without ceasing, and that imitation of religion branded with the lust of dominion and persecution is to all appearances as yet aglow beneath the cover even of Christian culture. In explanation of this horrible persistency we can conceive of no other but the infernal source.

Fanatical madness at
sight of the cross—
cannot be conceived
but as of infernal origin.

Reducible only to
Satan's fury whenever
exposed.

Explicit reasons for facts of such premeditated wickedness as that which became manifest at the crucifixion are reducible solely to Satan's furious envy whenever he is exposed, revealing itself at the mere sight of anything that pertains to the Holy One. He is not merely a principle, neither a convenient scape-goat to be laughingly blamed with deviltries. He is the personal chief of a realm still lower than fallen nature and a deranged world. This realm continues under the management of an intelligent, personal will, of the Evil One.

"Prince of
darkness" not
belonging to the
sphere or the
means of
revelation,
betrays himself
in order to ape
and to
MYSTIFY
REVELATION.

Word of God and its
preaching approved by
the manner in which
the lie and father of
lies are provoked.

It ought to be better known, that this "Prince of Darkness" does not belong to the sphere in which, and to the means by which, God revealed Himself; but that he betrayed himself by obtruding with his wily counteractions upon the sphere of revelation, in order to instigate confusion and mystification, in order to caricature religion where he cannot corrupt it. The recognition of this fact demands discrimination in biblical matters, when the question is raised whether every word written in the Bible was spoken by God. It became historically manifest what negative part Satan attempted to play in the sphere of revealed religion, especially at the occasion of the great sacrifice. There the revealed word is explicitly vindicated by the manner in which it triumphed, when the truth of history and even the law were cramped and misapplied. The word of God was approved by the manner in which the lie and the father of lies became provoked; by the way he was exposed and his power paralysed when he fought to the bitter end for the maintenance of his cause and position. The test of the strength of the word will ever be repeated, and its truth evince itself by the way in which the Bad takes up the issue against it, by the manner in which the preaching of the word calls forth faith in spite of Satan's methodical contrivances to destroy its effects, by creating love for Jesus and a correspondingly decided hatred against His enemy. Defence or excuse of things

Taking side with Satan.
§ 40, 41.

clearly belonging to the dominion of Satan is a symptom of incipient enmity against the Savior and what pertains to Him. We would not drag this matter into the discussion, if the tendencies either for or against did not affect history at the most decisive turning points.

One event at any rate preceded others known to history as facts. We surmised a sudden catastrophe, a general rupture of all bonds of human affection and sympathy, causing that enmity among fellow-men which otherwise is inexplicable. Facts of extreme cruelty advised us to conjecture such an event as an historic postulate. And

Supposition of the
break of the unity of
humanity proves
correct.   § 41, 47.

now the one historical fact upon which we meditate affirms this cardinal supposition to be correct: namely, that the unity of humanity is not a mere doctrine founded on speculation. For outside of revelation we would never have come to the knowledge of this fundamental fact. Only under the cross we find the affirmation of what regarding this unity we at first presumed as a mere hypothesis. *Demonology to be revised. Dorner.*

The death of the One for all solves the problem.

In order to appreciate salvation to its full extent, it is necessary that, as Dorner states, demonology is to be fundamentally revised and reconstructed as consistent with facts, instead of slighting it altogether. As it is, Satan and depravity are rather denied or extenuated than the "word of the cross" recognised, tho it is evident, that depravity is growing in proportion as salvation is ignored.

But if it is admitted that salvation is the Christianising factor sine qua non, yea the most necessary factor of history in its chief efforts to break every fetter of bondage, then the first question demanding an answer is: "From what are we saved?"

Our age seems rather inclined to shirk the unpleasant controversy about the conflict of conflicts, that of Satan vs. The Saviour. Evidently it accrues not to popularity, if for instance, evolution of theology in its alleged anti-dogmatism is contradicted. By this evolutionism it is held to be more adequate to refined Christianity to understand it as the outgrowth of intellectual improvement on the basis of superstitious fright, than to believe what we, on the basis of bottom-facts, maintained, namely: that humanity suffered a great fall from a higher state of consciousness under a deception wrought by the arch-fiend of our race—and THAT THE RESTORATION TO TRUE RELIGION WAS IMPOSSIBLE FROM BELOW, SINCE ALL THE NATIONS DOWN TO THE TIME AT WHICH WE ARRIVED UNDER THE CROSS, PROGRESSED ONLY IN A DOWNWARD DEVOLUTION. Facts testified to by archœological discoveries constrain us to acknowledge this as the incontrovertible truth.

§ 111. From the outset we ascribed great importance to comparative philology as a guide in our researches. In order to see human depravity as the facts ostensibly show it, we are compelled to call upon metaphysics for assistance, just as we needed it for the investigation of the enigmatical origin and nature of the Bad. Metaphysics from above confirm the inference formed from what analytically we gathered below. *Aid of metaphysics indispensible.*

Inquiry into the states of degeneracy under cover of culture starting from mere anticipations has now, with the help of language, made the points of controversy perfectly clear. For the metaphysical coefficient in history is language; and this need not be allowed to be pressed only in the service of the lie. *Language the metaphysical coefficient of history.*

Languages have not built themselves up from imitations of natural sounds to such a height as we find in the earliest cultures. It ought to have been remembered what Otfried Mueller once said: "One certainly knows, that, on the contrary, just the most abstract parts of speech became fixed first." He meant such words which least of all could be designated as expressing impressions from without, or as products from reflex-action of the nerves by way of exclamations. All languages of our own lingual family prove the priority of abstract words which rise from internal sources. The fact is, that such words show their common roots most plainly. Hence we take them as pointing to a time before human relations had grown complicated and dictionaries had to be enlarged correspondingly. *Language witnesses against evolution from depravity upwards. § 10, 12, 34, 41.* *"Abstract parts of speech were fixed first." O. Mueller. § 10, 34.*

In illustration of this Mueller refers to the verb "to be", the conjugations of which in Sanscrit, Lithunian, and Greek are strikingly similar. The wealth of grammatical forms was produced in the earliest times. Since then, as far back as languages afford opportunity to observe their further formations, the number of their cases, modes, and tenses decreases. The history of derived languages, such as Latin and the Germanic languages, down to the conglomerate of the English, furnishes a remarkable object-lesson of the modifications through which the organism of a language—once powerful and rich in its capability to express the finest tints of emotion, relations, and actions—becomes gradually weakened, stiffened and impoverished, until of the original flexions the least possible traces are left." *Example: the verb "to be." Original wealth of grammatical forms. Languages weakening. Delicacy of thinking and expressing in primeval human family.*

All this speaks in favor of a "delicacy of thinking and speaking in primeval humanity," when languages were pliant, not despite but because of their strong sinews, by virtue of their muscles. They were well rounded, symmetrical, and musical in their cadences, whilst the modern languages with their intermelding of vowels, silencing of consonants, and dropping of forms, shrink, figuratively speaking, into comparative skeletons. *Degeneracy of speech indicates a retrogressive tendency at least in regard to an essential part of culture.*

In the face of such results of philological research it would have been proper long ago, to table that materialistic dogma, which, for the sake of denying the spirit, disparages language by setting up an ascending ladder of speech upon the base of a most beggarly primer. *Ethnology concedes such a decline subsequent to a dispersion. Burnouf. § 136.*

We mentioned Burnouf's return to the proposition of the degeneracy of nations subsequent to their dispersion into conflicting varieties. We then added, that ethnology, altho hesitatingly, concedes such a decline on the part of some nations. Martius, for instance, accepts it as a fact, that the Botokudes of Brazil are degenerated Chinamen. Lepsius admits that the Libyans "have sunk into negroes;" and Von Loeben judges that the inhabitants of the Canary Islands represent a similar case. *"Products of degeneracy." Martius, Lepsius, Von Loeben. § 41.*

17

Now, since ethnology enlarges upon "products of degeneracy," or, if the occasion requires, upon "relapses into the original state,"—why not be consistent and adopt the fall to begin with, since the probability is actually admitted. We are by all indications forced to stand by the axiom of the originally high position and unity of humanity, and a subsequent historical apostasy, because otherwise it is not so simple as evolutionism imagines, to comprehend humanity as a whole in such a condition, as it was found at the time of the fulfillment—one large lump of degen-

eracy! As such humanity can be fully conceived only in contrast with "the true man," whose crucifixion shows a depravity below the moral zero.

§ 112. Yonder crowd of national representatives, gathered around the cross raised in their midst, exhibits a sample of the product of degeneracy concealed under a thin cover of high culture. Now and here alone are we enabled to scrutinise the nature of what we call the substratum ; here alone can we look into that unearthly background of the historical drama and observe the effects of the Bad in its intensity and to its full extent.

The scene enacted upon the shaky floor of the stage brings to view the plot and the plans according to which the shifting is worked by contrivances all around, behind the wings, below the drops, above the bridges, moved by powers in Heaven on high and in the pit below.

There is no longer an excuse admissible as was made in Thyatira, that the depths of Satan were not known. '

The agility to which the actors are instigated from below, affords au introspect into the fathomless abyss and into incomparable mysteries (provided that these heights and depths are not imagined as spatial quantities).

We reiterate that history is rendered comprehensible no further than we recognise the unseen and incalculable concomitant factors. And their interaction never came to the surface more boldly than under the "cross." In that which the cross discloses we see no frustration of the preconceived plan of history ; on the contrary, every word and act had to aid history in accomplishing its objects. Of so much we gain indubitable certainty, that the Holy Will and Wisdom maintains His absolute

rule ; that the rancor burning with impotent hostility and flaming up from below is only admitted for a definite purpose. Providence employed the prince of darkness as executioner of the divine verdicts, as the most befitting manner in which the evil one himself should divulge to the world the infernal wickedness of his own schemes and at the same time destroy his successes.

That the perfect wisdom of the plan may be questioned is not excluded, since to Satan

certain powers were still left, and since his advocates work additional mischief for similar ends, but subject to the overruling Providence. The question is answered, however, most cogently by Dorner in his "Ethics", where reasons are given, why this plan of history does not exclude the possibility of the Bad, but requires it without making it a shadow, or reverse side, or foil of the Good. '

The practical gain of our introspect is that we are enabled to discern the separation of the elements, to watch the reduction of the radicals in that great compound, that medley—"product of degeneracy" which perpetuates the old "sicut dii."

To that ethnical body fallen among murderers, lying prostrate upon the desert in agonies of death, the great Healer of nations at the divide of the times stoops down and attends to the bleeding gashes with oil and wine. He puts Himself in its place and lifts it up to His own. For, notwithstanding the rescue from sin and the ransom of deliverance, the final issue of the degradation is death. The entire visible universe writhes under the convulsions of its approach. The possibility of explaining empirical death is given nowhere but in the premise of an abnormity within this world. The corporeal body of man is taken from its substance, and since this

could no longer remain in its nascent state, the human body cannot. A discord has been struck which is perceptible, as we heard Leibnitz say, in the perplexed condition of the "monads" ; or as we now say: the discord is to be conceived as the subversion of the pure mode of natural existence with its capacities for free and undis-

turbed evolution. The physical form of being became repressed life with incalculably complicated involutions.

From the moment that the roots of human nature had been torn from the ground of its life, the totality of nature was rendered subject to conflicting processes. As far as the eye can perceive, it became bound up into the form of materialised stuff under laws of dissolution. Pardon the repetition: Man's external being in his matter-bound state is rendered transient under conditions of time and space. Substantially the unification of matter and mind is achieved in his personality; and altho separable, this union was intended to become also essential. With the fall the inversion ensued and disintegration set in. Body and mind had to be put on their good behavior toward each other. *(margin: Man's dual nature. § 6, 7, 8. Possibility of death.)*

Since the spiritual part took the psychical to itself in an indissoluble blending, in a mode which precluded the materialisation of the spirit, the union between matter and mind was rendered separable. Thus the union of matter and spirit by means of the soul was placed under probation. It was made obligatory to body and mind to take good care one of the other; this was the condition in attaining to the state of glory without a painful rend, whilst default in harmonious concurrency with this rule was put under penalty of death. Upon this truth rests the first principle of obligation, the objectivity of duty and authority. *(margin: Reason for the separability of body and soul. The first principle for a theory of obligatory duty and its objective authority. DORNER.)*

Mind and body were placed under obligation to care for each other for the purpose of obtaining the "Supreme Good" by way of the ethical process. This was the single necessity enjoined upon man, because nothing but the Supreme Good is necessary. This necessity, however, by reason of its inner nature, does not force itself upon man's freedom. It waits to be reverently esteemed and lovingly accepted, in the order of ethical procedures. Against an aberration from this course the human mind had been forewarned under penalty of dissolution. The necessity of the Supreme Good was unnecessarily misconceived and misapplied, nevertheless, and a necessity of the Secondary Good in nature was substituted. Through the forewarning in form of a simple admonition the will was set free to actuate itself in option, in selfdetermination as against nature, and in becoming a cause of its own. But allowing itself to be influenced by inexperienced reason, the wrong direction was chosen from the start and the will lost its freedom which can only prosper in the sphere of the Supreme Good. Allured into a false desire for independency, into a wrong direction of the impulse towards perfection, and venturing to save selfhood from the obligations to the only and true necessity,—in an arbitrary assertion of the dominion over, and independency from, nature—the will became subject to natural necessity, at the same time domineering over reason to the detriment of both. The voluntary cooperation of body and mind was thrown out of balance, and the faculties of the mind into discord, whereby the ethical progress became abruptly arrested. With the digression from the ethical course into the natural , the break took place, simply because the Supreme Good was not "minded." Mind succumbed to a large extent and became entangled in sensuality. *(margin: Necessity of the ethical process of unification between spirit and body by means of the soul. § 6, 15, 17, 18. False application of necessity and liberty' with reference to the Supreme Good and the secondary good in nature. LEIBNITZ. § 8, 9, 10, 39, 43, 44, 46, 54, 56, 57, 79, 96, 97, 98. Voluntary cooperation of body and mind thrown out of gear and into discord. Digression from the ethical course into the natural.)*

The immediate consequence of inverting the relations between necessity and freedom was the great calamity, fraught with separation upon separation, and detachment after detachment. Both body and mind had to suffer under it. The body, addicted to matters of diversity, must partake of the inverse tendency of repressed life, of the changes of the material forms. As to the soul it is impossible to conform its individuality to this world of changes. For since it is kept in the embrace of the spiritual part of the mind, it has become a member of that oneness of the spiritual world, which stands opposite the totality of natural entities in their generalness, and can not be affected by these changes. *(margin: Death the inevitable consequence of sin; and its bearing upon nature in general. Soul and spirit inseparably united. § 6, 7, 8, 18.)*

The soul, after once being assimilated by the spirit to constitute a human mind, can no longer consubstantiate itself with matter, tho on account of its intimate correlation to the body it is continuously induced to gravitate towards the material world. The soul, thus made the medium ground for the connection of spirit and matter, is "discontent" in the literal sense of the term: it feels as if it could not "hold together". It is under the strain of its two poles. Two worlds contend for the soul: the one for its materialisation, so as to keep it in the state which we called naturebound; the other for its liberation from confinement, in order to elevate it to complete spirituality. *(margin: Severance between two worlds goes through human nature.)*

Principal constituents of human nature in conflict and in abnormal relations.

Thus the principal constituents of human nature live in conflict under the dread lest distraction may terminate in complete ruin so long as the essential **unification** under the obligation of ethical assimilation is not consummated. This is the full and true explanation of that state of the human mind which Lotze designated the "anxious suspense" wherein man languishes. This is what we meant by the chasm between the physical universe—constituting the oneness of earthly life and belonging to man as part of his being—and the invisible world, the sphere of "formal unity." The break between the worlds above and below is manifest in man, the representative and child of both, and is caused by his departure from the path of duty, to his own **mortification.** The great rupture goes through his being in the first place —it means death!

"Anxious suspense." Lotze.

Chasm between the oneness of cosmical life and the sphere of "essential unity." § 6.

This rupture goes through man in the first place. It means—death.

The poor sinner sold his life too cheaply when he thought lightly of the "Supreme Good". Now he becomes aware of the deception, of the seduction, and of his own apostasy. He becomes perceptibly aware of the fatal step, when he traces the conflict back to the "warring of the law in his members against the law of the spirit." He appears to himself as if stretched out upon a cross of strained relations between matter and mind.

Stretched as upon a cross of strained relations between "above" and "below."

§ 113. This exposition, resting on empirical data well known to everybody, in-involves and also explains another still deeper strain in the relation of man himself to his "innermost soul." Once before we spoke of this under the caption "reflecting and unreflected consciousness." Now we come to understand a little more of it. The polarity of our being with reference to the deeper and inner phenomena of our duplex nature is just as intense and real, as the tension between mind and matter, altho we feel it less acutely. We described the first set of polar strain between (1.) matter and mind as playing between **above and below.** Now, provided that spatial adverbs used in the attempt at fixing phenomena in their theoretical order are not pressed too hard, we locate this second manifestation of polarity playing between (2.) the dual form of consciousness itself to the **right and left!** The arrangement will not conflict with the findings of our friends in the Medical profession, who seem to be persuaded, that sub- (our unreflected) consciousness is to be localised in the right lobe of the brain.

Strain between "right and left," ("reflecting" and "unreflected" consciousness.") § 8, 15, 37, 111, 121.

Subconsciousness (unreflected) located in the right lobe of the brain.

At any rate, the most distinct of interrelations between the two sets of strain justify our allegorising man's inner distractions with the symbol of the crucifixion.

Inner distractions allegorised by the emblem of the reconciliation.

Considering the poles of tension just alluded to, we must refer to the dual mode in which consciousness manifests itself, as "reflecting" and "unreflected" (or sub-) consciousness, in its day-side and night-side as the Germans used to denote the clever distinction.

Definition of the two forms of consciousness. § 8, 15, 87, 111, 221.

We have chosen the term "unreflected" because (tho this side of consciousness in its peculiar way can think, remember and recognise and even reveals itself) its functions are very rarely, and the process of them never, reflected in our usual frame of mind.

Consciousness in its incipient state was essentially a unit, altho dualistically disposed, (angesetzt) in keeping with man's double relationship. By force of the fall this tender cord of the unity of consciousness (in which two worlds were focussed) broke (zersetzt) so that now man is placed under the affliction of a very mysterious, but very real polar tension, or inter-psychico-spiritual strain.

Polarity of an inter-psychico-spiritual strain.

The difference between this and the former polarity consists first in this, that the poles causing the strained interrelations of consciousness—the most intense and purely spiritual—are lying entirely inside of man, in his "innermost soul."

Differences between the two sets of strained relations in human nature.

This inner life does not depend upon sense-perceptions from the outside or physical world for its contents, and is therefore out of peril from physical abnormities.

We here gain an aspect of great significance: Not only the tension between above and below, matter and mind, but also this newly discovered tension between right and left in the inner life, as pertaining to the forms of consciousness, goes through man, through and through.

(2) This condition renders another difference, between the two pairs of opposite poles conspicuous.

Opposites of "flesh and spirit."

By the break between above and below the body, now seat of the "flesh", militates against the spirit. This causes the ETHICAL strain, pertaining to the WILL, to ACTIVE earthly life; whilst the other break, manifest in consciousness and independent of externalities, concerns only personal life in its relations to the spiritual worlds. Hence this break lies not in the domain of the will and is out of its reach. It pertains to the fundamental part of personal life, to the essence of human nature; it belongs to the purely psychico-spiritual life, to the sphere of the EMOTION, and its form is PASSIVENESS. This strain has no ethical but a pronounced RELIGIO-INTELLECTUAL bearing. All these phases of the inner life vary in their manifestations, inasmuch as each side of consciousness acts differently through the day and during health, from what it does through the night, during sleep or sickness.

Now all these tensions affect the cosmos in an analogus manner, because it is the periphery of man, its center, to whom it belongs. Both, man as the world in miniature, as the epitome or extract of the great visible universe,—and the cosmos with its history (which is the macrocosmos of man, or man unfolded) stand in the relation of solidarity, of reciprocal sympathy; they stand in a peculiar rapport with each other.

Tensions through man transmitted to the cosmos as to his periphery. § 26, 27.

Personal and cosmical life mutually partake of each others disturbances and vicissitudes. Man on the part of his body, born from the physical elements—with whom his own propensity involved him deeper than their nourishing him made it necessary—also dies of them, and sinks back into them. His death predicts the ultimate fate of the universe; for it partakes also of this inevitable consequence of the separation.

Here the universal, the cosmical significance of the Mediator's representative death comes to full view.

"The cross with its four extensions marking out four extremes which stretch forth from the center where they meet at right angles—this cross teaches us that He, who had consecrated Himself to die at the time when He was stretched out upon it, is the very same who holds the universe bound up within Himself. Harmoniously He connects all within Himself, uniting the different natures of things into one well arranged whole. Since the entire creation looks upon Him, surrounds Him, and has its connections in Him; since that above and that below, and that on both sides is all related each to another through Him: it does not suffice that we are led to the knowledge of God only through the sense of hearing, but vision also should become a teacher of those sublime cognitions.

Tensions: MIND. (spirit) Consciousness: EXTERNAL. "reflecting" spiritual. Receptive. EMOTI- ...

With this expostulation Gregory of Nyssa expresses the truth that, and tries to explain why, the physical death of the visible form in the center of all things was to be taken as a typical occurrence, prototypical of the fate and destiny of the peripheral cosmos.

Cosmical significance of the Atonement.

By entering this world, our house of mourning, by assuming our body, this vehicle of death, by suffering death Himself, the Crucified One adjudged and condemned death itself as that which ought not to be. He overcomes and abolishes death in allowing it to exhaust its rage against Him, upon whom it had no claim; because of His purity and uninterrupted connection with God, with men, and with nature.

Quotation: Gregory of Nyssa.

What, therefore, Christ accomplished while suffering death, bears as much of a physical as of a religious significance, since thereby also a physical transformation is initiated. Of still greater cosmical import is His resurrection, inasmuch as the glorification eradiating from the body of the Redeemer and His saved ones, extends through the whole cosmos, which is but the periphery of that central body. From this exalted view into the realms of the eternal reality of glory and beatitude we now return to trace out other premises for further conclusions with reference to the redeeming virtue of the sacrifice in the middle of the times and of the nations, where the historical macrocosmos centers, together with the natural cosmos.

Death of the Mediator prototypical of the demise of the universe.

Transition from the cosmo-universal to the ethical significance of the atoning death.

§ 114. The word: "Ye shall be as gods" affords a deep insight. Ever since its first utterance attempts have never ceased to make that promise good and true. In pursuance of the attempted fulfillment an array of hostile camps deploys before our view, which in its well drilled lines and frequently renewed attacks represents history as one continuous warfare, and the world as the battle field.

The two chief branches of the human family.

A pious race, that of Seth, bearer of the cult and of pure traditional religion and religious recollections, stands opposite the Cainite race given to worldly culture. The latter starts out with a selfmade, more convenient religion, substituting an unbloody offering, and sacrificing to its own envy a very bloody one. The one race is centripetal and centrally inclined, whilst the other is peripheral and centrifugal—and falls asunder.

Sethites: cults; central. Cainites: culture; peripherical.

Through the central race the peripherally inclined race should have been kept together, guided by, and in keeping with, the advices given in the common family tradition. But a periphery anon disengages itself, taking its own way of realising the inherited ideas of dominion, freedom, and propagation. The complications begin, the knot becomes tightened. Memorable traditions of the parental home follow the exiles; they are haunted by the reproaches of the murdered son and brother associated with those memories. Against the ghastly horror of strict retribution, against the fear of getting lost, and in imitation of the ingrained necessity of unity, a kingdom of the world is organised. Despite the broken union with God and kin-folks, the intent to retain dominion over the earth and in Heaven is proclaimed with undaunted impertinency. Thus paganism is perfected. Paganism is determined to save itself.

By this time, after about two thousand years of conscious resistance, the world of the periphery has not forgotten, but viciously subverted what was UNIVERSALLY known to be the relation of man to God. Another two thousand years of scoffing and godlessness pass away, not faster than now, and not less filled with progress, commotion, decay; only with this difference, that original vitality and talents weaken. We alluded to the time when GENERAL REVELATION, given in the line of Seth, began with the covenant with Noah and ended with that of Abraham. During this period religious consciousness was protected in a narrowing circle, while continual apostasies toward the dark, deep, and solid substratum of paganism persisted in preparing one religious nation after another, always shaping culture in keeping with the character of the cult. AND THE RELIGION OF THE NARROWING CIRCLE WAS PERPETUATED IN THE VISIONARY, SYMBOLICAL AND HISTORICAL WAY, WITHOUT A BIBLE, without another cult but offering sacrifices and prayers, keeping sacred the family-palladium of the promises, obeying and confessing God, that is, PREACHING HIS NAME.

On the periphery the valuable remnants of traditionary and symbolic religiousness became formal, solidified and materialistic.

In the narrow circle religion became intensified, and kept the mind prepared and susceptible for the reception of SPECIAL REVELATION. This began in Abraham's household, and was documentarily fixed through Moses. In order to set free the ethical potencies, the law was added to the promise, and the word was added to the few symbolic signs. Humanity in general was included for whose benefit this special revelation was thus to be preserved until its necessity should have become palpable to the world of the periphery. Different stages in the circle of revelation are plainly marked, as for instance the development of the cultus on the score of hieratic, ethico-prophetical, and royal preponderance. On the score of ritualistic and formalistic deformation, interchanging with reformations, the keeping up the cultural life depends upon the exercise of discipline and giving solace. Under pressure of the pagan world, incurred as punishment for sympathising and mixing with it, revealed religion becomes intensified, and is spiritually and ethically applied, preparatory to receiving the highest gift from the Most High. Then the "Word" appears— to a very small circle of souls with pure religiousness and exceptional spirituality.

§ 115. Inside of this closed, concentric, and strictly secluded circle of special revelation we meet with four inscriptions of universal purport.

These four inscriptions were to preserve the plan of the historic movement. With this object in view, the plan was deposited for safe keeping in the book of the nations—entrusted to the most separatistic of all nations.

These four inscriptions deserve more attention than is generally paid to them. Viewed now —from our position at the feet of the Son of Man lifted up on the cross with outstretched arms,—their meaning can be fully comprehended. They are instructive. They contain the germinal type of the philosophy of universal history. Let us read them, one by one.

In the first place there is raised the ethnological or genealogical table, the most remarkable historical document extant, "in which—as Joh. von Miller observed— history has its beginning, and of which the present condition of the ethnical world is as yet the commentary."

As yet we are not enabled to substantiate which of the ethnographical boundary lines are clearly mapped out, and in what manner all nations upon the face of the earth are represented in this genealogy. We are justified, however, in supposing that this historical survey, dividing the substance of humanity into the ternate of Hamites, Semites, and Japhetites, affords the foundation as well as the ground plan for the scientific construction of history. Here indeed lies the first great land-record open before us, showing the possessor's titles and the nationality of the permanent settlers. No nation possesses such an index of humanity, and such a land-record of nations. Where anything similar is met, it does not surpass the impartiality of this document without a sign of any national prejudice whatever.

Here we have a truly international pedigree which is prescribed and handed down from above. Here in plain words are the terms fixed according to which history begins and ends. We are shown the race as dispersed after the great flood, but still as branches of one family.

"The Genealogical Tables" in a comprehensive manner reveal the magnanimity of the sacred books of Israel as compared with those of other ancient nations. The best philosophers do not reach that height, whenever they have to deal with the reciprocal relations of the diverse parts of humanity." Lenormant, in his "Origines de 'l histoire. II, bases this opinion upon the correct inference, that the centrifugal parts of humanity ascribe their national pre-eminence to the fact of being emanations of particular gods; whilst in this nation of the center they are all recognised as the children of One.

Here the oneness of the root, from which all are said to have been sprouted, was to be affirmed by the unique blossom that should appear in due season to the joy of all, for the benefit of all, and intercession for all. To that crown the line points, which, like a vein of precious metal running through the wild mountain chain, runs through the ethnical mass here reduced to generic order. Catholicity of revealed religion.
Unity of humanity.
Uniqueness of God.

We pass on to the second inscription which narrates the very fact which from a thousand indications of our own experience we could not help to propose by way of conjecture. Ethnological analysis forced the very items upon our conviction, which we now find as the contents of the second table, answering our postulate of an opposition and a dispersion. Under date of Babel, which the book of nations alone has preserved in proper connection, we find the crisis described which we supposed to have taken place. We read of the disrupture of human unity. A new and deeper fall ensues. A new evolution begins with a preconcerted revolution, which proved a mad devolution, a disastrous retrogression. We read of a judgment so effective as to confuse the conspirators in their attempt to systematise "emancipation of the flesh", and to organise heathenism, the apparatus of selfsalvation. II. Babylonian tablet.
Emblem of godless culture.
Disclosing the cause of confusion and dispersion.　§ 41
World-Monarchy and organised apostasy.
Under date of Babel.

The building of the high tower, emblem of godless culture, brings the curse down which scatters the culturists themselves into building' debris. They form the pellmell of nations which is so difficult to be brought into any order again. The curse came down in answer to the rebellious parole given out, which at the beginning had been thrown into the human heart. **It is the lie, that man, out of his own resources, through mere intellectual and worldly culture could attain to the nature of a god.** Parol formulated after the old motto: "Eritis sicut dii."

Previously we endeavored to show the end for which the formation, or the verocious annexations, or rather the weldings of states into colossal world-monarchies might have been undertaken. Here we detect the motives which inadvertently prompt and favor such conglomerations. The necessity was felt that in protection, against the common foes, and for the sake of co-operation, unity must be kept up. Another motive was the inherent remembrance of the duty to cultivate, possess, and rule over the earth. Still another was the legitimate maintenance of independence, selfculture and selfgovernment. Motives like these were proper and even obligatory in the ethical process. Now, in their distortions, they only augment mischief and misery. The undertaking seems to bear the noble features of normal aspiration to unity and security in a world of change, and struggle, and enmity. It demonstrates the necessity of a center for meeting in reunion, of a center of cohesion in the well founded fear of getting lost in the wide world to be established as a home amidst the shattered condition of things. But the erection of the emblem of haughty defiance, the **founding of a counter-religion with a "name," of the organised defiance prototypical of the AntiChrist,** the scheme to gain Heaven, while at the same time retaining a world of wickedness in spite of God —became the occasion for open insurrection, and for a dispersion so much the worse, in penalty of wilfully subverting all the motives of ethical advance. Proper motives of progress subverted.　§ 78, 79.
United defence to secure what had been gained by cooperative improvement.
Dominion over nature.
Self-culture, self-government.
Necessity for people to hold together in fear of getting lost in the wide world of diversity.

In this beginning of premeditated worldliness we find the basis exposed upon which the great Asiatic empires were founded, where patriarchal authority changed into tyrannical despotism. It is marked by that haughtiness which dares to set God aside. Man, under plea of independence, in compliance with the first instigation of the "sicut dii", aspires at selfadoration and selfdeification. His wordly culture is calculated to secure him the honor of having improved upon the first creation. One collapse after the other notwithstanding, the attempt is repeated to such an extent that even the Mediator was met by a temptation of that nature. But each of these monster empires, shedding streams of blood, in pursuance of dominion under pretense of seeking human welfare, will only have to serve either one of the spiritual spheres. Whether willingly or not, knowingly or not, this thirst of power must ultimately serve the purpose and further the interest of the spiritual kingdom of deliverance. At Babel for the first time we hear the boast of high civilisation with riot and anarchism at the bottom. The humiliating chastisement is designed to demonstrate forever the utter folly of misdirected aspirations to vainglory. The terrible event was intended to be a warning for all time to come; as such it so far has remained proverbial. Open insurrection; deliberate defiance.
Patriarchal authority subverted into Asiatic despotism.　§ 56, 172.
Self-deification; deification of culture.
Despite the exemplary visitation equal attempts were repeated.
For the first time: boast of high "civilisation" with anarchism at the bottom.
Folly of misdirected aspirations and of vain-glory demonstrated.

Further on the **third monument** presents its object-lessons: the **"Image of the Monarchies"**, so called. Historic study, whatever there was of it in the Middle-Ages, was divided as to the number of Daniel's world-monarchies. They were thought to include the world of nations in general. We do not find that much in the vision, or perhaps more. Of the substructure —consisting of the Turano-Mongolians, then almost sunk out of sight into the night of solidified darkness,—the picture which Daniel saw and described shows no trace. It also ignores the ethnological structure of the cultivated nations in general. **In fact, this hieroglyph refers to that province of worldly culture pure and simple, which keeps up special relations with the people of God, without adopting, in exchange, the promises deposited in the intermediating organisation, and which even turns the heads of the chosen people to adopt the worldliness of God's outspoken enemies.** The rejection of the divine goodness for the sake of worldly alliances causes the ruin of their own culture.

If these coincidences are taken into consideration, then the third table reveals more than the first. **It reveals the condemnation of that kind of culture which detracts man from God and leads into the historic declivity.** The value of the earthly components diminishing from gold to clay is to warn those initiated into divine secrets against the growing tendency to overestimate, admire, and to ape, perhaps, a culture which has been compared to a cheap polish, daubed upon a smooth surface as a means of deception.

It is a fatal error to mistake cultural progress for what the book of the nations terms the glory of God. Worldly culture has its value as an embellishment or in its usefulness; in its place it is good as belonging to the domain of the relative goods of creation. But to slight the Supreme Good, in preference of things lying upon the periphery, causes that pride which precedes the crash every time. When a nation is in its prime, on the height of so called refinement, when culture takes the place of cultus, then the catastrophe is always fast approaching. At the time and place of which our figure speaks, the inverted scale of valuation had arrived at its lowest degree, where the cleft appears in its awful steepness; where the abyss is not screened in the least, whilst the "advent" is near. The cleft rendered obvious by the contrast lies between that culture which on the one side, struts out to the extremest periphery, and the other which cultivates the concentrative dispositions of the mind. The one pervades the whole plain and in its rapid progressiveness flattens out into all directions and details of training, money-making and luxuriousness, and soon exhausts itself; the other measures all thoughts and acts according to their nearness to God, the center of all relations and of all matters historical.

In proportion to the spread and growth of worldly culture, symbolised in the abundance of the base minerals in the image, the better class of culture had diminished; the gold of fidelity to the God once honored and known, had become as scarce as outward prosperity. Under the fostering care of the benign hand on high, something had grown, nevertheless. It was the intense desire, animating some lowly and oppressed, yet patriotic and pious people, that the promise might be fulfilled. This is the sort of cultivation which prepares for the reception of exceedingly greater things than could ever have been expected or imagined. It was the outstretched hand of faith which is sure to have its petition granted. This experience of the truth of revelation, in the fulfillment of promises comes only in answer to such prayer, tho it may be offered most unostentatiously by a poor relative of ancient nobility, tho of a house not so pure as not to contain some gentile blood.

And now we arrive at the **fourth record**, one of specific interest to philologists. We are better than ever prepared to appreciate its contents. This document corresponds with the first record of nations. It treats of a new brotherhood, praying in unison for fulfillment. See how the desire is granted.

Confusion of language and dispersion of nations are going to be ameliorated. Those once dispersed are gathered in the **house of God**. The heartrending discord is solved by the harmony of new tongues aflame with divine fervency, testifying to the truth and grace of the Mediator, and also signifying the resurrection of the unity of the human family once buried under the **ruins of Babel**.

The occasion on which the gift of this new coefficient of history miraculously came down in flames, conveys also a typical import. It throws light upon each member of this family of a new blood-relationship in a double sense. The event celebrates the birthday of new-born children of God and their gathering into the unity of a regenerated humanity. The occasion furnishes the pledge from on high that for those thus united the great chasm is bridged. The arches of the bridge are to be sprung the world over from both shores of the ocean of time. Full and intimate communion of both worlds is established and is to remain.

The main object of Pentecost was not to restore original language, the lost center of all languages. A fancy for Pentecost on that score would but indicate the recurring tendency toward the peripheral culture. Max Mueller tried to find the lost center there, since he believed, that the "Aryan, Semitic, and Turanian evidently show a convergence toward a common source." Burnouf thought that "hidden but real relations exist between the Semitic languages and Sanskrit." This, however, is all irrelevant.

Main object not restoration of original language—not in the interest of peripheral culture; M. MUELLER, BURNOUF, etc.

When the Spirit from above kindled the lights; when the secrets of the human family were disclosed in their depths, and were expressed in ardent praises going heavenward in the fire of spiritual offerings of first fruit,—it was not the resurrection of something old, but it was the enactment of the new covenant. The new hymn intonated on earth in answer to the gift, as understood by all the listeners around the witnesses and heralds of the King of Kings, gave thanks for more than ever had been hoped for on earth. What was given was received as the fulfillment of promises given in ages past; but it equally was the pledge and type of an ideal yet to be realised, of the only promise left to be fulfilled in the future at the goal of a new process of development thus begun. In its typical import the event initiates and illumins the new æon of the universal transfiguration. For the new structure in which,—just as in the old nation and covenant alone revelation was received and preserved,—the plan and the goal of destiny and the new order of the world are to be preserved and realised: for this new structure the foundation is laid. Then the new ontogenetic factor silently retires from the noise of the builders, from the noise of the incoming and outgoing nations, into the "Holy of Holies", the innermost recesses of a comparatively few sanctified souls.

New Covenant not to perpetuate anything of pagan modes of life.

Genesis of a new humanity. Founding of the Church. Fulfillment of all the promises, save one.

As a new and last promise: Type of the ultimate transfiguration.

Thus upon four powerful pillars: the Genealogical Memorial Tables; the Tower of Babel (with the confusion of tongues); the Image of "Humanistics"; and the Church (with the unification of languages) are based the further movements and the goal of history. Any conjectures formed to supersede this prophecy under the vandalistic attempts to overthrow these old pillars of humanism will be doomed to no less bitter disappointment than that of the builders of Babel. This prophecy, at the same time, announces that a higher hand has designed place, time, and task for the individual nations, as they are dismissed with the benediction and go to their work.

Church typical of the Kingdom to come.

In contrast to the tower and Kingdom of Babel.

Prophecy of an universal Kingdom to become an organism visible on earth.

It became the special charge of the Apostle to the heathens to explain this more explicitly. The secret, which had been preserved in the vessel of the Jewish Theocracy, he was now specially commissioned to preach to the gentiles directly, since the meridian dividing the times and the nations had been crossed.

Jewish theocracy the vessel of universal salvation and civilisation; now the secret communicated to the gentiles.

We cannot follow him just now. As yet we have to remain a little longer with the great sacrifice. It must be left to theology to formulate how the union of the human and the divine natures in the person of the Mediator, and their relation to the sacrificial death, ought to be conceived. True advance in this respect was signalised by Dr. Weidner of Chicago, in several passages of his "Ethics", to the effect that the ethical study of Scripture "will bring to light matters which a mere doctrinal" (dogmatical) "consideration would not take into account. This is especially the case in regard to the central point in Holy Scripture —the person of Christ."

Ethics and Christology. WEIDNER.

For our present purpose it must suffice to see in His death a necessity which throws light upon man, his history and this visible world belonging to him. This necessity will be rendered the more intelligible as the realised effects of this death shall stand out in history which now takes a new start.

For, with this death the accounts of history with the ancient nations are closed and the result of the settlement is enunciated. At the same time a distant view is opened upon the closing scenes of history in general from the scope of the empty sepulchre. The King of Nations outlined how much of these scenes may be anticipated, thereby enabling us to discern the last act, even the transformation of the stage. This transit of the cosmos, however, into the state of glorification is not to be expected without some things being pulled down, not without a great deal of destruction, not without the death-struggle.

Final fulfillment of promises and prophecies

not without certain death struggles.

CH. III. THE INTERMEDIATION IN ITS ETHICAL BEARINGS.

§ 116. The advent and immanency of the Savior is demonstrated as a logical necessity, so that, as we hope, the exhibition of the physical data did not weaken the strength of the reason of things. Now the ethical import of the Mediator's life and death remains to be discussed. Dying He drew all into His death in order that living He may draw all after Him into His life.

Effects of the resurrection.

The Redeemer's cross is our key which discloses and closes the history of the ancient world. Its culture resulted in a mass of degradations and unsolved questions which accumulated with increasing rapidity. Its season of prime brought to bloom a mass of involutions and subversions becoming ever more complicated, in which the plan and task of history seemed to disappear—sealed up in the sepulchre of the God-Man.

With His resurrection we plainly see the rise of the history of a new world, the history of one regenerated family as a leaven worked into the dough of humanity. By the working forces newly imparted, working in cooperation and standing in communication with the realm of divine influences: the veiled purpose of history becomes now gradually disclosed to ever widening circles through a process analogous to, and on the basis of, but not identical with, former developments.

Speaking of development, we are prompted to digress from our discussion a few moments for a summary review of the matter. The ethical necessity of the Mediation needs to be brought out from a synopsis of data preceding and succeeding the mediatory intercession. For the reiteration of these data the interruption will be excusable, because of the ethical import of the matter.

In the domain of the INORGANIC world, nothing is able to overstep its bounds at any point, or to transcend from itself into the organic. A hiatus yawns between these two parts of creation. Nowhere is spontaneous generation produced from Force-Substance. The gap is bridged only when life-germs enter this lower sphere, after it has prepared itself for receiving them from the sphere above. Then inorganic matter, impregnated with organic life, is appropriated, assimilated, and conducted by it to the next higher class of entities. This process continues through the entire scale of organic formations, even of social organisations, always conditioned by receptivity and reciprocal interaction or cooperation of the lower elements, preparatory to the reception of new impartations from the higher sphere.

In the ORGANIC world the hiatus between vegetable and animal life does not appear to be so wide, the formative elements not being so heterogeneous. Still it is not bridged unless a specifically different, generic life is added. At this step it is animal life which assumes and assimilates the force-substance of both the lower spheres, lending them up to personal life.

Again a hiatus, now between animal and PERSONAL life. Outwardly it seems to have disappeared, so that many deny any essential difference. But that hiatus between animal and human life is the more intense.

As a matter of course the creatures of the lower sphere can in no case understand the difference, altho the animal sees it. The difference lies in the psychical sphere and is profound, because the spiritual substance has entered the soul of man.

Again, in the sphere of personal life, a hiatus, scarcely perceptible at all from the outside. The absolute difference here cannot be understood by the inferior mind, altho a child can see it. And a child is very receptive for spiritual influences from superior minds, by whom its own is to be cultivated and developed under the condition of cooperation, always under the proper maintenance of the interrelation with the concomitant lower spheres. By way of preparation for receiving the divine, the PNEUMATIC infusion, the mind must be disentangled from the preponderance of the physical principles. Thus personal life may be guided up and elevated into the highest sphere of the life DIVINE-HUMAN.

It is always the factor from above entering the lower sphere, which unites the PREPARED lower elements to itself, in order to lead them along with itself up to new and higher forms of life. Here, in new connections and interactions, preparatory to the coming elevation, the transition into the next higher sphere upon the same terms takes place. The lower is always taken up by the higher, in order to serve as a coefficient in this stage of development to a still higher. The lower is always to be set free from the encumbrances of the lower on entering the higher sphere. And the higher can never be understood by the lower, unless it has obtained its position in the higher sphere, where the purpose of the development has become manifest, and where the difference becomes conspicuous.

To this end and for this very work the Christ entered the world and re-entered Heaven, namely: to impart to minds prepared under the law the necessary pneumatic life from on high. Otherwise, or apart from this, even spiritual life cannot understand nor enter the sphere of blessedness ultimately designed for man. The chasm between fallen man and his destiny, made still more inaccessible through man's own fault, is now bridged by the Savior. Through His assuming human life the truly real life, life eternal is revealed and imparted to human nature by its Mediator, the Liberator of the world.

The life appearing through, and imparted by Him is indissoluble. Being supernatural and eternal, this life is nowhere else to be found in the spheres of finite existence but in organic connection with the spiritual world through Christ embraced by faith. Outside of this organism, no other but soluble combinations are found here below. However great the difference is between physico-psychico-finite and spiritual pneumatico-eternal life, and necessary as it is to discriminate between them, the difficulty is, even at the points of gradation to distinguish the subtile demarkations because of their blending of the psychico-spiritual nature.

The eternal life descends in order to embrace earthly life, and to unshackle it from its confining conditions; to set it free from bases and gases, as it were. Unless life eternal by virtue of its association with temporal life prepares the temporal and elevates it to the grade of spiritual reality, and unless this life temporal allows itself to be taken into this treatment, it cannot be led back to the ideal life, i. e. to its source, to life in its real and adequate form of existence. Equal to the processes in nature,—which simply foreshadow the grade of highest development, where organic life takes up and assimilates inorganic forces thus leading the material world up to the possibility of being spiritualised,—does eternal life lead the highest earthly organism, the human world, up to the highest organisation. Eternal life —embracing the human world one by one, according to its principle of personal diversity —thus transforms the temporal or arrested life of the human world, by conducting it to the state of the only normal and real life.

Possibility of the spiritual world to become spiritualised.

This truth comes to light in the resurrection of the Liberator, the Redeemer. Unless bodily risen from death as the glorified, yet corporeal Mediator —in whom the spiritualisation of nature is complete for the first time —He could not have been credited with being the Head, the First-born, the life-germ, prototype and progenitor of a new family, a regenerated humanity. As such, however, He showed Himself. He appeared only to the disciples, prepared by Himself for the reunion in the higher sphere of true life. For, unless ethically prepared, the humanity of the mere natural and therefore lower grade, does not see, much less comprehend or receive, the higher life, the life divine.

Unless ethically prepared humanity of the mere natural grade cannot receive, much less conceive of the life divine.

Whosoever becomes, in this order, a member of true discipleship, to him it is manifest, to a degree of unshakable certitude, that the Lord of Glory, whom their hands had touched, is the very same One in whom the thought of the world was conceived, by whom and for whose sake the world was called into being, and who came in the fulness of time to seek and lift up persons lost and under bondage, and to guide them back to the Father.

Whosoever became a member of discipleship according to the order of salvation, to him concomitant facts and truths are intelligible.

This being clear to the followers, they became at once conscious of the truths connected with these facts; of the significance, for instance, of a first man of the race as its root and common parent, and of the significance of the "second Adam," the Son of Man and God: man, as the natural crown of humanity in one respect, and as the scion grafted into humanity in another. Thereby the disciples, in increasing numbers, recognised as never man had before the human being in its ideality and eternal value.

"Second Adam": the natural crown of humanity, the scion from above pruned into it.

This is something entirely new in human history. It is a revelation. It is not the discovery of advanced evolutionism, which posits an ideal quite different.

New in history: Personality conceived in its ideality and eternal value.

§ 117. It was then, that men began to see, not only subjectively their dignity and true origin, but also their objective oneness. After the divine nature had taken possession of the friends of Jesus, after the Risen Lord had poured out the Holy Spirit into their minds, humanity comprehended itself—despite the diversity of languages, etc. —as a unity in respect to both origin and destiny. "It may be surprising," said Jacob Grimm,"that it never came into the mind of Greek or Hindoo to raise,much less to attempt to solve, the question as to the variety of human speech and its origin."

Constituent parts of humanity as far as they partake of the HOLY SPIRIT, recognise each other as a unity with common origin and destiny.

Not the highest of gentile learning ever raised the question as to the variety of human speech and as to the original unity of humanity—

The question of languages and human unity had been lying open before all nations, and was silently passed over in all ages. It had been asked with astonishment at the single instance, after the reunion had become a fact, when even the dumb spoke. Then and there the answer was given.

until it was asked and answered at Pentecost. J. Grimm.   § 116.

There are lying dormant in man, or bound up within him, certain incipiencies (comparable to the so called "rudimentary organs") which are now awakened and set free by metaphysical assistance. Man "came to" himself, and was enabled to see himself with surprise as in a deep "central vision". The speaking with tongues is a supernatural gift—but after all: what speaking is not?

Human incipiencies and potentialities set free;—"rudimentary organs"— Central vision of personal import: speaking with tongues.

Through the word and breath the disciples had been perceptibly touched by their master now their glorified Head; and they knew themselves to be now in more immediate touch with Him, than when they held regular conversation with Him on their journeys. In this intimate connection with the Lord, and through Him also peculiarly united among themselves, they formed a nucleus of a new "humanity." All their new experiences were analogous to first creation; they knew themselves to be new creatures. It was not a reform—it was a renovation. A fire quickening, purifying, and light-giving is kindled as the Son of Man had desired that it should be. This new life in the similitude of fire shall henceforth, by mere praying and preaching and without any ostentation, seize nation after nation, and form history and transform the world.

Unity in spirit covers diversity in language.

THE CHURCH.
Analogous to first creation.
Nucleus of a new humanity.
Not a reform, but a renovation.

Christianity
means
not a new human
genus created, but a
new organisation.

Preaching of the
Gospel

The ties binding the
Head and members
into a mystical body
are brotherly love and
compassion, in
response to the
Great Sacrifice.

Love in general to
fellow man.

Another novelty in
history.

Sum of the
effects of Christ's
resurrection:
"Humanity"
a concept for which
not even Socrates or
Plato had as much
as a word.
M. MÜLLER.

There was created not an other human organism, but we emphasise it—a new organisation, that is, the organic connection of renewed personalities into one body or socially organised community. The college of the diciples and all who joined them and were embodied with the Head of the organisation, found and felt themselves without much reflection under this Head as members of one body. And without much reflection, but not without a new way of specific guidance, they made it their sweetest task, to spread the glad news. From this local center the world of nations was to be invited to partake of the membership in the mystical body, under this Head. The means of this gathering and binding are: Love and compassion by virtue of the great sacrifice.

It was an unheard-of story which spread like fire in ever increasing circles from the Orient to the Occident. The world's history had been crying to Heaven. Love answered with abundant proofs of mercy from Heaven. The call of this undiminishing but enriching love is to resound to the world's ends, and behold—it connects them so, that there be no end in the circulation of love.

It is proclaimed, that divine value and destiny is to be respected even in the most abandoned person; and that no man shall esteem another less than himself, except he were god-forsaken and to be pitied the more. And even then it is worth the while, that in order to rescue him from the awful doom of perdition, one may exercise love and compassion even unto death.

Now, whatever has been enunciated as an effect of Christ's resurrection is contained in the term "Humanism"! It is well expressed in that word, which, as M. Mueller said, "never passed the lips of either Socrates, Plato, or Aristotle."

Through the accomplishment of the plan of salvation by the Mediator up to this point, the ethical necessity of His entrance and intercession is proven.

The natural world from geological substances up to the highest of its formations cannot be explained out of itself. But as soon as man is taken into consideration the method of nature's workings becomes apparent, and system is demonstrable throughout, because he is the synopsis of nature, and because the part cannot be understood

Humanity to cooperate
in the spiritualisation
of the world.

unless viewed in its relations to the whole. The same is the case with the human world. In spite of all possible attempts to interpret it by itself, it remains an enigma unless the God-man is taken into consideration. Then it becomes explicable to those who accept Him as the real synthesis of this world of humanity, as the synopsis of all the true elements contained in every theory, as the source of all life and light.

In order to understand the loose variety of nations representing figures in the play of history, we needed a typical figure to make the success of their several peculiarities and the laws conditioning the variations intelligible. This must be a type in

Type of humanity
in its totality
and solidarity;
answering the
requirements of each in
the diversity of all
earthly situations.
§ 13, 35, 36, 92, 105, 120,
145, 191, 197, 201, 206,
232, 233.

which each finds himself projected, in whose life every individual person may trace his own, on whom he may call for succor, whose life mirrors his own case in every condition of the mind in every affair of daily life. Since we cannot help noticing that the affairs of man collectively, i. e, as history, follow the lines of an accurately planned combination, we discover the theme of this history to be actually and plainly revealed, in the life of the God-man. He is demonstrable as the very Son of Man; as the type and ideal of the whole race; after whom it unconsciously yearns; through whom and for whom it is fashioned; by whom each one individually shall become renewed under easy phy-

Typical figure
in whom all conditions
of life are mirrored,
to whose life every
person can trace and
conform his own.
§ 13, 30, 37, 105, 233.

sically and ethically fixed conditions.

Now humanity for the first time was made acquainted with the significance of the Mediator with reference to these things. Only in the fellowship of His disciples, and subsequently in His organised community was humanity perceptibly, however imperfectly in outward appearance, reinstated to its dignity and freedom.

The questions ever forcing themselves upon the mind of man as to his position among the complex environments, as to the wealth of potentialities and opportunities which he as the binding tie of two forms of existence holds in himself; as to the depths from which his consciousness looms up:—these questions are satisfactorily answered, and the implied discrepancies most consistently and naturally solved, only in the person and through the mouth of the God-man.

The life and death of
the God-man typical
of the movements,
issu s and final
consummation of
history.

Alone through Him mankind receives light as to its own high importance and deep significance; in Him the race is elevated to its ideal dominion over nature. What is ethically required of man, his task on earth, preparatory to the consummate reunion and blessedness in the higher life : humanity must determine by the measure of his exemplary excellency. Whatever is valuable in history since it entered the æra of a new development, consists in definitely reflecting and assiduously copying this model life, "The Image."

It is noteworthy, that with the study of the character and "Life of Christ" in our century the study of history in general received new impulses and deeper insight.

It must be one of the chief aims of humanity and its historic progress, to apprehend humanity in its entirety, its most abandoned specimens included, since each and every one of them participates in our high and common origin from the image "after Our likeness". And "the" main virtue ultimately consists in practicing humaneness, in accordance with the maxims drawn from the fact of this fellowship, Christ Jesus not excluded. The final goal of human development and the normal course of history is the liberation from mere natural conditions, and (of course under provisos) the subsequent elevation into glorious perfection. As the recognition of unity in "the Image" was obtained only from above, so the aspiration for union and the acquisition of real education necessarily ascend to where education ("Bild"-ung) is alone obtainable: in the direction towards "that which is above."

§ 118. Standing thus at the focus of the ethical principles, we find, closely related to Ethics, the principles of Aesthetics. They also lie infolded in the Mediator, the central man, in His harmonious deportment, in His doctrine and rhetoric, in His passion and resurrection. Well aware of the objections ready against so bold an assertion, we emphasise the truth, that the glorified corporeality of Jesus makes Him the First-Born of a new humanity, which with Him as the head, is to be made perfect in the transfiguration of the body into the state of glory. From no other source can ultimately the idea of the Beautiful be derived.

In the most majestic, tho meekest of men, we see, since His resurrection, our corporeal figure, which He wears, gloriously spiritualised. For, this corporeality as now transformed into the form of spiritual existence does not dissolve into the flood of ether.

The Hellenes boastfully but superficially talked about harmony, because of sin they thought so wantonly as to connive at it. Plato took sin into account to the extent of rendering the body sin itself. Hence he could not see the harmony by which his countrymen contrived to hide sin.

With Christ harmony is more than a contemplative conception; in Him it is realised and exhibited to perfection. In Him we have the ideal unification of the spirit with its body, the body expressing this ideal of harmony in consummate reality. The normal equilibrum is obtained in the most natural, i. e. unaffected and artless manner, so that every abnormity, especially that of affectation, the most abject of all, is abolished. The ideal thought deposited in human nature is fully realised. In the Risen One we see the norm, plan, and aim of historic truth fully uncovered in beautiful lines and tints, inasmuch as His life moves in curves of equanimity and perfect harmoniousness. We see man in his genuine, unassuming dignity, tho merely foreshadowed at present, yet warranted to become apparent and distinctly visible to all the world in all its glory. Virtually the heterogeneity between mind and body is overcome. The hateful soul in elegant forms of studied attractiveness, or selfishness in the garb of sanctimoniousness and similar matters of outward appearance must cease to deceive and to corrupt the judgment of men. Misleading contrasts, such, for instance, as may prejudice a noble character on account of a rough appearance, or a "beautiful soul" in a homely body, are reconciled, not through absurd mortification in a false spirituality with its contempt of the body, but by the spirit pervading the body as his temple and adorning it with the "fruits of the spirit."

Hence the extreme contrasts at variance with Christian aesthetics, especially strong between the eastern and western Aryans, become eliminated in widening circles after the corporeal appearance of the glorified Risen One to His believers.

Buddhism considers corporeal substance as a mere docetic apparition, as a spectre of reality. There the only good lies in unconsciousness, by which one imagines to escape the misery of this phantom existence. This is what presses the stamp of absurdness upon Hindoo aesthetics.

Marginal notes:

Human beings to be renewed individually under conditions. § 9, 12, 18, 23, 24, 35, 36, 39, 41, 54, 109, 115, 120, 134. 159, 177, 220.

Mediator in His relation to the Church.

Man's unique position externally and dual nature internally explained in the person of the Risen One.

Valuable in history is only what reflects the model life of the "Image." § 9, 35, 134, 176.

Virtue in the main !

Humaneness, which requires the conception of humanity as a oneness including even the most abandoned specimen of human degeneracy. § 176.

"BILD (i. e. Image)UNG" is education in its proper sense. § 9, 35, 48, 135, 176. (Selfconceit: § 15, 58.)

Closely related to ethics is æsthetics.

Bearing of the Risen One upon æsthetics.

Alone in the cognition of final transfiguration into the state of Glory lies the criterion and measure of the Beautiful.

Corporeality does not dissolve into ether.

Deficiency of the Greek ideals of harmony.

Affectation of equanimity and external abnormities abated.

The resurrection of Christ discloses the plan, the goal, and the mysterious mode of development. § 177.

Virtually the heterogeneity of matter and mind is overcome. § 205.

Contrasts of Hindoo and Hellenistic tastes according to their views of life.

In Hellenism the phenomenal world is divine. What is good, meaning that which is pleasant and agreeable, Greek phantasy shaped into idealistic conformity. The Greek enjoys his products of illusion with rapture, conscious of the fact, that it was his art with intent to produce that satisfaction or contentment in the beholder which makes him forget the indigencies of worldly life. But, even if unconscious of the intent to silence the reminders demanding of him a perfect life, there yet remains just that artifice, pendulating between tendenciousness and naivete, which stamps upon Greek sculpture the mark of untruthfulness.

This illustrates the close connection between ethics and aesthetics, consequently the difference between pagan morality and Christian Ethics.

"The society of Buddha, says Oldenberg, is a congregation of monks and nuns, It is what it styles itself—a "society of beggars." Prince Vassantra, the Buddha in the second last of his incarnations, will not kill a beast; and in order that not a worm shall die on his account he will not wear any silken garments. His benign tenderness does not allow it. But this same benignity does not forbid him to give away his wife and children. This benevolence turns to selfcomplacency which discards all sense of duty. One plunges himself in quietistic revelry so as to escape all molesting cares, and then enlarges upon his righteousness and strict religiousness.

The Hellenes on the other side, dodged the combat under indulgence of carnal desires, not finding it necessary to deny themselves the pleasures and diversions of the moment. Their onesidedness led them to make even religion consist of sensual enjoyment. They had completely forgotten, it seems, that the things in the realm of the secondary good are entrusted only to be made good use of in consecrating them to higher accounts. Having lost the idea of the Supreme Good as the standard measure for valuing the secondary good; having no sense for that which is holy, but merely for what is prudent in regard to a fill of pleasure, the Greeks mistook the world and the lusts thereof for the one thing worth living for, not-withstanding their pessimistic misgivings that such a life is a business which does not cover

the costs. At Benares earthly things are considered bad; because of generating distress, they are to be thrown away. At Athens life is a frolic, full of good things, to enjoy which man throws himself away.

According to Christian tenets the visible goods convey either pain or pleasure, in response to the manner in which, and the purpose for which they are used; but as signs of kindness and gifts of God they are estimated in either case. The secondary good must be worked for, nevertheless; and such well earned goods are to be appreciated, cultivated, idealised, spiritualised, that is, they must be husbanded and employed with reference to the giver and his purposes.

To these goods belongs corporeality, one of man's essential parts. The Humanists have done well to emphasise this truth, to insist upon its restitution and proper application. The humanitarian idea could have originated nowhere else but in Christianity, that is, after the new principles had been adopted and had become prevalent.

In yonder temple, honored with silent reverence by Greeks and Romans, to which Augustus had dedicated golden chalices, in which sacrifices were offered down to the time of emperor Vitellius,—there the Trishagion is chanted: "Holy is OUR God, holy is our GOD, HOLY is our God, the Lord Zabaoth", the worshipers knowing themselves to be a holy people. The prayers offered there as if under observances of sacerdotal duties include all other nations. Still more important it is that there alone was perceived, what the word holy signifies, whilst to the nations east and west of that temple the idea was entirely unknown. Here, in consequence of the cognition of Holiness, unadulterated purity of soul and body is kept up in the usages of every-day life, whilst not one single form of paganism knew of holy gods. Among the Jews alone, the grave and sober nation among the staggering, hearts and lips were touched and sanctified as by burning coals from the altar. Here alone, by means of a holy law, a flame from above (not selfkindled fire) had singed the flesh, and had cultivated that chastity

which finally could intonate the triumphant "Magnificat," so unique in all the literature of the world. In the Messiah of the nations that pious sentiment received its tangible object.

§ 119. The conviction of the historic reality of the God-man involves the premise that He also is the "Image" of all that is magnificent; and the conclusion, that also His kingdom is to be acknowledged as the realm of noblest humanitarianism, as the repository of all that is truly humane, and "herr"-lich at the same time. Here the

truth comes to bring forth its practical results, that history is but the exposition of man in all his incipiencies and dispositions. "There the image and likeness" appears resplendent from the God-man. Resurrected He appears as the model after,

and the end for, which man is to be "educated", to be "led out of" all that gravitates to ugliness and to the sphere of the vulgar, and to be conducted upward to purely humane and truly civilised forms of culture, to habits of genuine refinement.

Whenever at the expense of the present life, and in favor of another, perhaps a romantic world, the body (and nature as part of it) is simply treated as that which is to be mortified, or is taken for a penitentiary of the spirit instead of being its temple, then the education (the "Bild"-ung) of which we speak is out of the question.

Neither will the truth of the normal development and transmutation of the natural part of man—his universe always included—into the state of glorious perpetuity and perfection dawn upon those minds, who, on the contrary, with feigned indifference cover up the anxieties aroused in most serious predicaments, or who extol only the beauty of nature, or deify somebody, or sacrifice labor and life to mere earthly pleasure at the expense of the life to come. For such minds are nature-bound of whatever grade their educational standing may be; and, being arrested in proper development, cannot judge things of the higher sphere. *Worldliness disqualified to judge things pertaining to the sphere of glory.*

In either case the onesidedness either rises to false enthusiasm, if not wild fanaticism, or sinks to fatalistic apathy. *False enthusiasm or wild fanaticism.*

In both cases nothing propagates except either the Hindoo mood of dejection, or Greek vainglory—whilst the shrill discords between ideals and reality remain. *Hindoo dejection; Greek vain-glory.*

Now the glorified Redeemer in the mean between the dire extremes has wrought the solution also in this respect. Because in Him this life and the next, deity and humanity, nature and spirit, mind and matter are intrinsically united in pure and perfect beauty, a blessed state of peace and harmony is ever present. In Him the truth is substantiated, that we are the "offspring of God." Hence to His freed congregation the contradictions pertaining to present life and future destiny are reconciled. By the true cognition of what the world is made of and what for, the chasm between Heaven and earth is practically arched over, as typified by the rainbow, this beautiful symbol of the universal covenant. *Contradictory views as to present reality and future destiny are harmonised in Christianity. § 63, 64, 92, 126, 139, 147, 152, 168.* *Rainbow, the beautiful emblem of the bridge over the chasm.*

Hence it is written "all things are yours, whether Cephas or the world, things present or things to come, all are yours—and ye are Christ's." These cognitions, however, thrown into the contest of the ethno-cultural elements, seem to disappear for centuries: here they will be distorted by asceticism, there abused by libertines. But by the Risen One they are established in the permanency of such institutions as for instance the "Lord's day," ever commemorating Easter-morning with its sorrows and sympathies, and Easter-evening with its solace and gladness. By the simple, yet grand order of life, regulated through these ordinances, bliss or misery will ensue according to their proper celebration or their desecration. The Sabbath must be held as sacred as matrimony, its only compeer of paradisial origin. Deprive the sanctuary of the "Sunday," and not only the chief factor of education, (of Bildung after the "image," "das Bild") is curbed, but national welfare set at stake. Henceforth the labor for the true understanding and practical handling of these subjects forms no mean part of our sacred theme, the history of humanity. *"Lord's Day," sunny side of life.*

The names given to the opposite world-theories under the strain of oriental and occidental characteristics have received notoriety of late. It has been stated that Christianity combines darkest pessimism with brightest optimism. This is true. For nowhere has the inclination of men to carnal baseness, and the consequent malformation of the affairs of life, been more keenly felt and more sincerely deplored than among the Christians. Nowhere, on the other hand, has the original and sublime destiny of man and what belongs to him been magnified more gladly at the same time. Pessimism and optimism meet in their common endeavor to seek man from among the ruins, to counteract the work of devastation in which depravity is engaged, to rescue man from vulgarity, and elevate him to nobleness. It is one of the cardinal principles of Christianity to persist in making manifest the eternal value of the person. It puts man's personality on a grade so high, that no sage nor school outside the pale of Christianity ever ventured to think of placing him in so august a position. *Contrast between optimism and pessimism conciliated in Christianity.* *Personal value of man.*

Says Teichmueller, an authority on Greek philosophy; "The idea, that any definite individual belongs into the system of the world for ever, was not even dreamt of by either Plato or Aristotle." But with this thought another is connected: that the value of this newly discovered personality with eternal rights depends upon cheerful dedication to duty, and consists in personal responsibility, that is—in freedom. *"Any definite individual for ever belongs to the system of the world." TEICHMUELLER.*

In the terse remark, that the "Cross is the first (we would say, the ONLY) Tree of Liberty" a great truth is expressed. What we mean by this "liberty" is warranted by what we call "progress." Lenormant observed, that "only with the Gospel progress proper was initiated." *Right, duty, freedom.* *"Cross," the first "tree of liberty."* *"With the Gospel progress proper is initiated." LENORMANT.*

Why did the Mongolian states so obstinately remain in a cultural condition which Marco Polo already had praised, which had excited the admiration of the Franciscan emissaries more than five centuries ago? Because they think they have all they need; above that they know of no further aspirations. Everything is calculated to be preserved, nothing to be improved upon. These people have become totally destitute of originality and inventive thinking. The inner impulse for scientific research, for the amelioration of toil in manufacture, for developing artistic taste, is stupefied. That freedom is missing which alone makes progress possible. Of late they have become acquainted with the fruits of advance in civilised nations; but their skill in imitating can never take the place of personal ambition and international emulation, both of which alone secure ever new and selfproduced prosperity. *Contrast between Aryan agility and Turanian stagnancy.* *Masses without freedom become inert in mind.* *Compact masses are unprogressive.* *Must be broken up in order to develop personal ambition. § 18, 21, 80, 196.*

The despotic states of yore, tho graded class-wise, were like the compact masses which show motion only on their surface. Ere such solid stuff can be made to flame up, it needs to be broken up and thrown into heating motion, like a meteor or a lump of coal. Unless parts or atoms are set free and transported into the higher sphere of mobility, that warmth and efficacy of which they are capable cannot be developed.

Now such deliverance into the free motion of personal activity is given in Christianity alone. In producing that effect consists its most conspicuous proof of being a new factor, of being rendered the most beneficent agency in every respect. Wherever it is added as a solvent, it works fermentation; it attracts homogeneous elements and rejects the repulsive; it calls forth the crisis which is to isolate the Bad, and urges man on to a decision. It requires of the individual to act upon its own responsibilities in the interest of the whole. This is the new mode of operation which Christianity established for the benefit of history and humanity.

"If there is a law of regular progress upon a helic line", we say with Conrad Herrmann, "then it must imply no less than the gradual elevation of man to true freedom and his training in its proper use." Amended as follows we affirm this: **The thought of humanity in freedom cannot be preserved in its efficiency and purity, unless securely sheltered in the organism which is upheld by its exalted Head.** Herder did not follow this thought deep enough, which oversight was, however, made good by Schleiermacher.

Henceforth we shall observe this thought of freedom working itself out in the ensuing history under a polar strain. The poles lie in the antitheses "Church" and "Society"; one as the place of revelation, the other the sphere of reflexes. There the definite "dogma", here the current opinion under the title and style of "free thought", that is, thought unwilling to surrender its right of endeavor to formulate in its own way the contents of dogmatics. This free thought will be provoked especially when orthodoxism feels itself bound to conserve its understanding and its mode of interpreting the truth according to "faith", which sounds like mere intellectualism; or by legalistic observances and, perhaps, by the abuse of ecclesiastical privileges in addition. Whenever the church suffers at times, it is because the preceding age carried on things religious as tho the church held a mortgage upon the world. Whenever the church assumes more of a ruling than serving attitude, and imitates the state in that it prescribes prohibitory rules to the realm of thought, rules according to which it is to be decided which persons are to be treated considerately, or which are to be ostracised —then the tension becomes perceptible. Then public opinion or free thought will assert its right in protecting the humanistic idea, and will insist upon an estimate of man regardless of his standing in church or class.   .

Purposely we have signalised right here the course which the thought of humanism and personality—once imparted to an organisation at the center of the times—will follow in history; and what corruptions this thought, on account of old repristinated misconceptions, will have to sustain.

§ 120. Under a rather protracted discussion we lingered upon that summit where in the person of the Mediator we found "that man, toward whom,'to speak with Droysen,'all ancient heathendom verged, through whom alone its history can be interpreted."

This convergence we called the Logic of History, which demanded the Mediator and proved Him as fully answering the postulates. For in Him we found even the natural focus of both, the physical cosmos and the spiritual realm. And finally we discussed the plan after which the thought of humanity is to be realised ethically and organically in the readjustment of human affairs. We saw this thought to cover the whole range of social relations, and that mankind, solely through its realisation, may come to its own, preserve it, and arrive at its destiny. It is worth while to study the chief outlines of the plan for the reconstruction of humanity as expounded by the great Apostle.

St. Paul crosses over the Achæan Sea to Europe.

Standing before the Areopagus on Mars Hill opposite the pillars of the Acropolis, in the face of the thousands of god-ideals in marble, and in the face of the wisdom of this world as elaborated by the most intellectual nation of antiquity — he unfolds the predesigned purpose of the Lord whose messenger he is. He proclaims what his

Lord has deposited in the nation selected for the very purpose and in the same manner as a testament is kept safe and sacred until it is to be opened to the heirs after the death of the testator.

The Apostle, according to his instructions, takes the sealed secret from the combination-safe of the Jewish theocracy, and explains those clauses in which the audience is particularly interested, because pertaining to the development of history. He publicly announces his Lord's order, according to which "He hath made of one blood all nations of men for to dwell on all the face of the earth, and hath determined the times before appointed, and the bounds of their habitation; that they should seek the Lord, if haply they might feel after Him and find Him, tho He be not far from every one of us." Paul makes it known, that "God hath appointed a day, in which He will judge the world in righteousness by that man whom He hath ordained". So he unrolls the grand panorama in a Central Vision —whether the Athenians want to understand or ignore it—the program for every philosophy of history, a philosophy which demands for this history a major premise as a starting point, a syllogical middle and a satisfactory conclusion. For, unless human thought has set before it a well arranged and comprehensive whole, it cannot find its way through the difficulties which beset life's journey. And just that plan of the whole, not without the clearly defined final purpose and its complete execution, the Apostle has spread out before the Europeans and the nations on the surface of the globe in the solemn proclamation: all of one blood, subject to one Lord alone, all meeting at one date before the same court.

First stage of the spreath of Christianity.

The program of the world's history as opened before the world. Paul and the Areopagus.

E. FIFTH DIVISION.—THE THIRD CIRCLE OF NATIONS.
ROME IN THE POST-AUGUSTEAN PERIOD.

SYLLABUS.

Down three offsets, through three grand circles of nations we were led to that intensified central unit which unfolded to us history in its totality. Now we shall have to ascend the steps again, starting out from our Center.

The three concentrating circles before the middle of the time,

The steps were represented by strata of ethnical driftings upon the substratum. This latter, the lowest, most massive, and most extensive Turano-Mongolian layer lies bare as yet, away out on the periphery, forming a nebulous horizon. The narrower circle consisted of the four Aryan groups, As the third circle we designated the disintegrating Semitic element of the composition in the Roman crucible, wherein the nations were mixed and made ready for the separating or reducing element, for the addition of the solvent ingredient. The "Leaven" was added to the "dough" which now stands over night in order to rise. In proportion to the progress in which circle after circle of the human race is seized by the fermentation, we shall observe its pervading and elevating action, and follow its spreading through three different stages of civilising culture. We refer to the remarks introductory to division B., and simply give notice here, that we are now going to watch the effects of the Christian thought in the Roman basin. Division F, the sixth, will outline history under the sway of this thought in the Aryan world exclusively; while the seventh and last division of Book II must notice the prospects of the Mongolian nations on the circumference, as seized by the cyclical movements of history.

to be observed in reverse order, beginning with the innermost, extending towards the nations upon the periphery.

Three different stages of Christianising culture with a view to universal civilisation. Div. E. in the Roman basin; Div. F. among the Aryans; Div. G. in the world of the Mongolians.

In the first place, then, we will look at the Roman empire again from the aspects gained since we left it to concentrate our attention upon intensified religion. We shall see the new life from above setting the Mediterranean culture in motion, separating it by its isolating effects, affiliating elements from the decomposing mass, and neutralising certain infectives. The Semitic element becomes obvious as an alloy mixing itself into the church, causing ruptures which up to present times have defied the healing. So long as that Judaising intermeddling is not rejected the chances are, that the irritation thus generated, tho beneficial in negative ways, may on the slightest occasion turn into annoying inflammation. The old element, generally speaking, obtrudes upon Christianity chiefly by means of the Semites, notorious for their skill in negotiating transfers. Semitism tries to push itself into that again which so long had been enclosed by it, had proceeded from it, and is continually rejected by it.

Semitic element an alloy in church-life, cause of many and serious disturbances.

18

CH. I. ROME AND THE CHURCH.

§ 122. It had been Rome's part in history to prepare the nations by the discipline of her laws for receiving the great gift of salvation. He, whom taxgatherers and fishermen worshiped and preached—had come and gone. The message came from the most troublesome corner of the empire; Roman dominion was now to serve the progress of Christianity, as previously we saw the intellectual preponderance of Hellenism prepare at least the form of speech for the preachers. Rome served in building the highways for the spread of the glad tidings, until finally its ponderous portals opened, in order to afford Christianity its fixed domicile and headquarters. The first duty enjoined upon the church was to disentangle people from the forms of

thought and of cults circulating through the realm. The church was to be judicious and discreet in her administrations. Whatever could be utilised for the intelligible exposition of her truth was to be taken into service, and what proved a spurious or adventitious element was to be kept outside. The legal forms were to be applied for the protection of her organisation in order to maintain the establishment for times and nations to come.

The Roman State was then like a fortified city, defending itself against the attacks of the barbarians along the whole line from the Firth of Forth to the Tigris. They dashed over the boundaries like the floods of the ocean in a storm over the moles. For centuries they had been repulsed again and again, until at last they became irresistible in the measure as the besieged became effeminate. The bulwarks had become rotten and the hirelings upon the ramparts fraternised with the outsiders, especially when the insiders withheld their payments.

The barbarians crowd into Asia-Minor, force the military camps along the Danube, and swarm over devastated Greece. In Italy their hordes land; from Spain and Gaul their warcry is heard, mingling with the noise of battle-ax and hurl-but. Through the crevices of the crumbling palace-walls gleam the eager eyes of the Germans and espy that inside of them intrigue reigns and impotent despotism.

The despotism of the Roman emperors had ravaged the lovely spots of retired Greek culture. The springs of patriotism, of sciences and arts dried up under the sands drifting in with the tornadoes. Cities and magistrates sank into abject servility or cowardly fright. The nations became like herds of timid sheep, submitting to the disdainful treatment of the innumerable host of officious and greedy subordinates of the government.

After the Romans had transformed cultured regions into one vast desolate waste history emptied the swarms of barbarians into the dismal, dead country. History directed the barbarians hitherwards; barbarians whom Robinson classed with the savages, but who fortunately were sufficiently civilised not only to change the wastes into gardens but even to manage the affairs of the sinking ship of state, and to save humanity from the fate of oriental apathy and despotism. For a while the lease of life of that despotic power was prolonged. Inured to tyrannic dominion the people took the emperor for their providence and their god. And the despots knew how to keep up prestige and appearances.

The annual income of Roscius, the actor to the court, amounted to about 35,000 dollars; and the dancing belle of Rome, Dionysia, could afford to spend not less than 30 dollars every day. The means for such extravagance had been exacted and gained as booty from all the oriental courts, where treasures of gold and precious stones had accumulated through twenty centuries. The temple of Tolosa had been mulcted as well as that of Jerusalem.

Commodus, in real oriental fashion kept a seraglio of three hundred women and as many minions. At the Bacchanals of the palace the plebs was amused in free circuses. Karinus at one time had a park of trees planted in the theatre; then ostriches, deer, moose, and elens were put in, a thousand of each, it is said. To these were added two hundred lions and two hundred leopards arriving the day following for the grand hunt in the arena.

In the private chapel of Alexander Severus stood the statues of Abraham, Orpheus, Apollonius of Thyana, and—Christ. The eye met the imperial statue everywhere side by side with the figures of heroes and gods, with the Hellenic mysteries, and the New-Platonic teacher. As such the public opinion of the educated class esteemed—the wonderful man.

The Savior, as the hero of the spirit, was honored with a place in the Pantheon. His surroundings symbolised the dissoluteness of the New-Platonic compromise which contrived to furnish the world a religion to suit every body, from which any god could be chosen at pleasure since the worship of any one was indifferent to all. To such a mixture even the Christians were welcome, as we have seen, provided they would show themselves pliable enough to be made use of. For the state took anything into service, the gods even: else they were of no use. The religion of the Romans was the official religion of the state for definite political ends.

Christianity tolerated if it submits to serve political ends.

Varro, as Massen pointed out, described the antiquities of the state first, and then he added a few paragraphs with reference to religion as one of them. This indicates that the state, still considered as the Supreme Good ranks first, men and gods being recognised as existing merely for the sake of the state.

State the Supreme Good. Maassen.

§ 123. Under these circumstances the church was in danger of serving the public welfare in ways not pointed out to her. It was a great temptation to secure tolerance on the ambiguous terms of expediency; but the Church did not then fall under this temptation. No Christian would deny his King and Savior by offering a grain of incense to a piece of idolised art, nor to the deified emblem of worldly power, because Christ had shown how to triumph over this temptation. As it was, religion could only come in to take care of the perpetuity of the state and the welfare of the rulers. All revolved upon the Platonic ideal of unity in a centralised government to the extent of absolute power.

The Church in danger to follow a policy of expediency,

triumphs at first over this temptation.

Plato's ideal naturalised in Rome. § 62, 57, 68, 78.

We see here the ideal of Plato translated into Latin. His idea is now Romanised —and will remain so when once state-religion is changed into a church-state. When this change comes, Augustin, in the "State of God", will carry out the Platonic-Jewish polity of theocratic rule, and will contaminate Christianity with this fundamental and fatal error for a thousand years and more.

The Supreme Good of Platonism utilised for the benefit of the ecclesiastical theocracy through Augustin. § 62, 78, 81, 87, 97, 124, 126, 131, 137, 144, 148.

But at the period of which we speak, when imperial Rome fretted under forebodings of the overthrow by "barbarians", a new event occurred. Soon a phenomenon was noticed which alarmed the almighty state: its concentrated power suddenly met with the opposition of the Christian conscience. The Christians will do homage to no gods, much less to the emperor-god. There had been numberless Atheists, but never had they risked defiance like this. "I honor the emperor," Tertullian preached, "and I wish his welfare and that of the state. But I do not call the emperor god, because I can not tell a lie."

Opposition of the Christian conscience against State-absolutism.

Cause of the persecutions. Tertullian.

The answer was given through blood, fire, and lions. For this kind of settlement was considered expedient for upholding the religion needed to uphold the state. The Christians knew that and—suffered.

Efforts to rescue the old idea of "state."

"Crucify," Tertullian cries out, "torture, crush us; your injustice proves our innocence. The oftener you mow, the stronger we grow!" The struggle began between a maddened giant and the reconciled conscience of the weak church.

Was not this conscientiousness mad obstinacy? Who would have imagined that it could gain the victory? There lay the ancient errors coiled up in one big lump. Ready were the beasts to spring upon and devour the defenseless herd of the good shepherd which encountered the hostile onslaughts with no other protection but prayer for divine aid in the maintainance of dignity and freedom, and an assured hope for the future. Ranke was perfectly right in saying that "the Christian prohibition of offering incense to the emperors implied the most heroic declaration of independence."

"Refusal to offer incense to the Emperors involved the most heroic emancipation." Ranke.

For the first time since the world stood, history noticed a separation of those halves which theocratic state-rule had chained together. The same Church which enjoined obedience to even a Neronean form of government would not waver from the maxim: "We must obey God rather than men!".

The long series of persecutions against those who were to outlive the hatred of the world, were thought to be a dutiful measure for the rescue of the old idea of state.

Obedient to even a Neronian government, the MARTYRS could not be made disloyal to their Lord.

Upon the public square of Antioch a well was dug and an alter erected in front of it. The fountain was dedicated to all the gods. None dared to sell food unless it was sprinkled with that water. You surmise the purpose. The Christians should get nothing to eat or drink. They could not buy anything without partaking of, and burdening their consciences with, idolatry. In a manner so studied and profound the Christians were excluded from humanity and—shielded from worldliness. If the state were to prevail, the Christians could neither eat nor drink, simply die! The Church found herself assigned to Heaven alone. It was made easier for her to die to

Public well at Antioch.

Christians excommunicated from humanity,

whereby they were shielded against becoming worldly.

the "world", tho she was kept alive. Her way of thinking and educating entered, "even across rivers of blood", the house of the giant. Without guile nor fear she clothed herself with the accustomed forms of art and of organisation as she found them.

The apses of the basilicas of the empire contained the Augusteum with the statue of the emperor-God. The apsis seemed convenient for putting in a crucifix: and of course, along with the apsis the basilica was made appropriate for public services—became a house of God. Deemed as equally well adapted to embody the world-theory of the Christian faith, and as suitable vehicles of its organising principles were the Roman constitutional forms and political institutions. Thus the contents of Christianity were brought under shelter, and such housing was a necessity. No corrupting of the Church was to be feared on that account, as long as the spiritual life of the Church was in the state of primitive soundness, and the edification of heart and mind was the chief object. The externals were not deemed essential, in worshiping the Savior. All belonged to that faithful Church, be it Cephas or the world.

As long as the Church remained conscious of belonging to Christ, the forms were indeed innoxious.

But—of the church, standing definitely centralised and sharply outlined above the ruins in the dim distance, equipped with means of protection, and venerated by the nations, it has been said, that she had "crawled into the coat of mail of ancient Rome." With reference to ecclesiastical organisation this saying is not improper. But neither is there any impropriety in a stringent organisation, which in the times of the migration was certainly a necessity. Its harmlessness would have continued had the Church been cautious against Judaising ideas of dominion and theocracy, and against uniformity in lieu of unity.

As with the constitution, so it was held with art. Development in history never pursues its aim with firm steps; it feels its way along. Since new ideas are always contested, they walk and work in borrowed apparel. Until custom is persuaded to adopt progressive ideas they generally cloth themselves with the attire of a culture which is on the wane. Reforms must step forth cautiously under such shielding cover against unpopularity, until they can stand on their own merits, and fashion their own forms. Hence the Church held her services in the catacombs, because the sleeping-chambers of the dead were protected by law against all spying intruders. Her symbolism originated in the tufstone of subterranean corridors and baptisteries, where a picture, not understood by enemies, stood for a confession of the faith.

The allegorical figures impress us with the pensive mood expressed in them; they speak to us of the endearing sentiments, sacred memories and joyful hopes conveyed by them. There appears the good shepherd, the harp, the cock, the palmleaf, the dove, the fish, the ship, etc., representing truths in which the departed Christians had gone to their rest, for which they had died. The good shepherd upon that lamp of the apostolic period is, according to Martigny and De Rossi, worked out no worse than the finest specimen of classic art. In the sense of the apostolic sentence quoted, young Christianity with unsophisticated singleheartedness appropriated the arts ready made. With reference to old Christian frescoing and mosaics Otto Pohl lately demonstrated this fact in a thorough manner from the paintings in the catacomb of Domitilla. We find a variety of antique forms, but no sign of a rigid, ascetic contempt of the natural. Serene genii appear alongside of the Good Shepherd and Daniel.

In the imperial tomb of Placidia we yet admire the Christian antique as it was before Byzantinism demoralised art under mandatory rules. There emperor Honorius is entombed in a ponderous sarcophagus, and behind the altar his sister Galla Placidia, daughter of the great Theodosius. Their corpses in imperial attire were yet seen as late as three hundred years ago. Not far from them lies Constantin III. In the mosaics of this grand family-crypt the Savior is pictured in the classic forms of Hellenic art. In youthful beauty He sits resting upon a flowery hill. In the left hand He holds the cross as a sceptre. On the opposite side He is conceived as in riper years, with manly features and dark beard, looking beautiful and triumphant. Walls around and cupola above glitter in richly gilded ornamentation to set off the pictures of the Apostles. We have dwelt a little longer on Christian art in order to vindicate the conclusion to which the art of this period leads; namely that the Christian thought then was as yet able really to conciliate, not only to compromise between, earthly and heavenly life. But Christendom did not hold this exalted position for a great length of time.

§ 124. New-Platonism had begun its diverse philosophical attempts in order to unite Greek paganism with the religion of the cross. Long and earnestly the Church wrestled with that syncretism, until in the formulations of confessions it was barred out and the purity of doctrine preserved. What was true of the rather Oriental apperception of an emanation was inserted at the right place in the doctrine of the Trinity, and is contained in the going forth of the Son from the Father, and of that of the Holy Spirit from both. In this dogma the old cognition was enveloped and secured against heterodox misinterpretation.

But facts are stronger than—dogma. The persecutions had given the first impulses to renounce "the world". The Occidental Platonists, especially since Augustin, had some reason to fall in line with the oriental contempt of life, but there existed no necessity to import and to practice Hindoo asceticism, with its demand to mortify the body as the seat of sin and cause of all trouble, as that which ought not to be. *[margin: Warding off paganism in theory, adopting it in practice; § 20, 54, 57, 62, 67, 78, 81, 87, 97, 122, 123, 124, 125, 130, 131, 137, 139, 144, 146, 149, 150.]*

We have alluded to Agustin's importation of Plato's "Highest Good" with intent to fortify the Church. It was at the time when the persecutions in the East sent many orientals nearer Rome. Fugitives from Persia, Syria, and Arabia turned hermits in Hindoo fashion, and thickly populated the devastated region of the Thebais. They became monks, became inflamed with a wild fanaticism against the culture of the world, and the realities of natural life. Works of art appeared to these ecclesiastical zealots as demoniacal, as identical with pagan idolatry in general. It was not the way St. Paul on Mars hill had proclaimed the divinity of human nature in the words of the Greek poet. *[margin: In the denunciation of the world and contempt of life, sequent to the persecutions in Persia. § 54, 58. 59, 149.]*

The corruption of the church originated with the relapse of the new thought of humanism into the onesidedness of the oriental form of consciousness. It became almost complete at the time when Persia expelled the last of the Nestorians, shortly before Muhamed separated Buddhism so far from occidental Aryanism as to prevent further communication with Europe. More than was conducive to the normal development of humanism had Europe imbibed already of that fanatical onesidedness which now contaminated Christian territory for the first time. When the sharp opposition of the Semitic spirit turns against occidental Christian culture with intensified acrimony, and reestablishes that very same historic strain which Rome seemed to have neutralised and Islam to have intercepted, then more may be seen of the deplorable relapse. For the present it may suffice to observe the two thousand monks following Hilarion through the Ægyptian wildernesses on his inspecting tour through the monastic colonies. And the ten thousand monks around Serapion in his cell on the shore of the Dead Sea, are descriptive enough to cause alarm as to what the cause of humanism shall have to encounter. Such numbers are suggestive. They formed a cloud foreboding the coming storms in a graphic manner. Ephesus in A. D. 449 witnessed one of them. *[margin: Origin of monastic communities. § 68, 147, 160. Augustin's doctrine on the "State of God," copied from Plato, utilised in order to fortify the permanency of the church. § 62, 78, 81, 87, 97, 122, 123, 137. Hermitages in the Thebais. 54, 56, 59, 146, 147, 149, 160. Monkery originated in Ægypt. Christianity not adverse to art.]*

The cloud arose in the desert, grew dark over Rome, and spread over the whole empire. Rome, recently the Pantheon of all the gods, became now, under its bishops and its first pope, Gregory I—when the chronometer stood at A. D. 600 (!)—the chief relic-market of the world, the necropolis of all sorts of saintly bones and of mummified martyrs. *[margin: Oriental remainders in the church after the expulsion of Oriental Arianism—and after their separation through Muhamed A. D. 600.]*

From Rome the bones, hairs, splinters, etc. were distributed throughout the pope's great diocese. Large quantities of the filings off the chains of St. Peter became a ready selling article; they soon were "all the rage," to be worn upon the bosom in small lockets, formed into the symbolic keys. New inventions followed. The filings of the grate upon which Laurentius had been roasted, fetched as high a price, as the oil of lamps which had stood burning before the graves of the martyrs. Little cotton balls soaked in this oil were put up in capsules, shipped, and worn like other "charms" as preventative of almost any kind of bodily ailment. Cicero jokes about the brazen image of Hercules in the temple of Agrigentum, the many kisses of the worshipers had smoothed off the chin. Now the very same picture under another name was exhibited. In the atrium of the basilica of St. Peter stood a bronze statue of the "Prince of the Apostles." "The foot was smoothed off by the kisses of the superstitious of all nations." *[margin: Semitic encroachments perpetuate the strain of old polarities in aggravated forms. Hilarion's army of monks. Gregory I. Pope. A. D. 600. Pantheon now the RELIC-market of the western world.]*

"Rome on one side of its organism decomposed as a corpse (we quote Gregorovius) whilst rejuvenating itself on the other." For Rome, in the mean time had become a church-state inadvertantly inclining to Hindoo pessimism, to Roman deification of the living body, and adoration of dead ones. This was the mode of splitting human existence from heavenly life, and then trying to mend the split. Rome is a sinister creature whose phenomenal duplicity henceforth stands out unique in history. *[margin: From deification of dead cesars to veneration of dead saints. § 15, 54, 59, 125, 151. Holy nail 35, Buddha 58, 95 Chrysostom, 127 Holy cross, 151 Andrew's head, 137 Dalmatica dead bones, instead of dead cesars. Degeneracy of the church conspicuous. "Rome a decaying corpse on one side, rejuvenating on the other." Gregorovius.]*

CH. II. DEFORMATION OF THE CHURCH. BYZANTINISM.

[margin: Old Rome fully rehabilitated in the Church-state.]

§ 125. The exposition of the ecclesiastical deformity of Christianity in the Roman basin would be incomplete without a special survey of the eastern part of the empire.

From the solitude of depopulated Hellas—for Greece deserves a brief review, necessary to understand Byzantium—the Parthenon sighs up to Heaven, allegorically speaking. The Athenian Parthenon had been transformed into a temple of the "Mother of God". *[margin: Survey of the eastern part of the Roman empire.]*

The image of the goddess, Phidias' masterpiece, had disappeared. In the temple of Pallas Athene the eternal lamp spread a flickering sheen. The high edifices looked down on a dilapidated town, from which the last treasures had taken wings to Byzantium. *[margin: Parthenon, a church of the "Mother of God."]*

Before we follow thither we cast a side-glance at the northern and southern part of the eastern Church. The ABISSYNIAN CHURCH founded upon the Nicæan Symbolum has remained upon that foundation under a heavy surcharge of Ægypto-Koptic plaster-work. Pushed out of reach of the ecclesiastical turmoil, the history of that section of Christendom is instructive. We see our religion petrified in antique style, streaked with Judaistic elements, lost under rituals scarcely understood.

The liturgical performances are meritorious works. The thought of grace and salvation is not entirely extinct under the rind of this dried-up side-branch of the Church despite her hierarchy, her 180 feast-days, and 300 days of fasting. That ecclesiastical body represents a mummification unequaled; because of Judaism not there meeting the opposition of the Aryan mind, being left undisturbed to amplify its influence, that section of Christendom became disqualified for civilisation.

North of Derbend on the slopes of the Caucasian mountains toward the steppes of the Volga and the Don regions we find an old Christian "Kingdom of the Golden Throne." This throne stood at Sevir; Persia had once presented it to the Sassanides. In these regions, according to Jerome, the Apostle Andrew had spread the gospel. From thence to the Phasis river stretches "Inner or Pontic Aethiopia." Here dark-colored men arrived with the precious stones. Here it is, as Ritter thinks, that the "Prester" John reigned, whose renown in legendary lustre extended deep into the Occident through all the Middle-Ages. Subtracting the mythical elements, we need not doubt that a Christian state existed there. What Islam made of it is shown by the ruins around the Black Sea, if we consider them as remnants of that state rather than offshoots of the ARMENIAN CHURCH.

And now we proceed to Byzantium whose dominion includes both of these parts from Pontus to Habesh. By viewing the whole we shall understand and, perhaps, appreciate them a little better in their present significance. In the capital of East-Rome stood Constantine's figure upon a pillar in stylite fashion. At his feet burned lamps, attended to by praying people. This characterises the whole empire.

Along with the captive virgins of Greece, the sacred things of old Hellas had to be delivered at Constantine's city. The ivory Parthenos of Phidias, taken down from the once proud pedestal, stood now before the palace of the senate, stared at by the populace. In the imperial palace the muses of Helicon were set up. The Pythian Apollos with the gilt tripod decorated the Hippodrome. Finally the images of Zeus, Aphrodite, and Artemisia reappeared in the Church of St. Sophia. Not less noteworthy were the heaps of manuscripts rescued from Hellas and sheltered in the libraries of the emperor and the patriarch.

In the building of St. Sophia's Church pillars from Ephesus were rendered useful; so were those pillars of porphyry which Aurelian once had dedicated to the sun-temple. Works of art from Asia Minor stood by the side of pieces of booty from Hellas. Byzantium really seems to have been designated as the museum and conservatory of a subsided culture.

The dogmas of the church governed the empire. Adjoining the church of Mary, in somber seclusion, stood the parsonage of the patriarch. Whoever passed his gate, crossed the arms upon the breast and made a deep bow. From this imitation of the "High Portes" of the Orient numerous messages were expedited daily over a considerable part of the globe. This patriarch's diocese extended from the neighborhood of the Baltic Sea to the cataracts of the Nile. The ancient gentile thought had been restored to power; at the time when Chrysostomos congratulated the Antiochians on their city being fortified by relics all around. For we must know, that land and sea were filled with them. Shrines of relics, and the pictures of the "Mother of God" fastened to the masts of the Byzantine ships, crossed the waters everywhere.

The art of the empire, here as ever emblematic of the national character, became stationary, stiff, conventional.

The Second Nicæan Council already saw fit to decree as an utterance of the Holy Spirit, that artistic representations should not be left to the fancy of an artist, but should keep in strict compliance with the traditions of the church. The copy-book of Kyrillos of Chios, containing all the pictures of the saints, was henceforth made obligatory, strictly to be followed by the painters, and the monastery upon Mt. Athos had charge of the rigid surveillance of art. Personality, ingenuity and talent were under bans, monotonous technique alone remained. Not until we have looked at a picture of the infant Krishna upon his mother's lap, the heads of both surrounded by radiant haloes, and only after we have seen Isis with Horus on her lap, are we prepared to understand the stiff and repulsive forms of the Byzantine Mary, the theotokos with the child.

By degrees the pictures of the Redeemer become more lank, bony, shocking. From them He can no longer be recognised as the Liberator and Friend of man. The religion of the world had been rendered so worldly as to usurp the worse than worldly throne. This explains why Christ from that period on appears in the awful majesty of the stern imperial judge amidst a courtly suite of apostolic and saintly attendants with the addition of an angelic retinue.

Deformity of Christian cognition of humanity as mirrored in the pictures of the Savior. § 137, 139, 180.

To correspond with the pompous splendor of the court and to adorn the interiors of the palaces those figures were framed into mosaics of sparkling jewels set in colored glasses. With the sixth century that golden background begins to be indispensable, upon which the figures appear as heartless as possible. To inspire the devotees with awe, they are made to stare equally fierce and selfish. These pictures show not a sign of life or action; only serious and ceremonious sanctimoniousness is idealised, if a picture of absolute pharisæism can idealise any such frame of mind.

Art reveals the state of culture and the character of cultus controlling public life and tastes.

Such dreadful looking ideals menace the people through centuries from Ravenna to Erzerum, supplanting the preceding Christian art everywhere, so that no trace of it would have been left, had it not been for the sleeping-chambers of the early Christians.

§ 125, 131, 132, 179, 156, 175, 199.

§ 126. Think of it: repulsive pictures of the Christ expressly made to represent nothing but the fanaticism of intolerance. For so far the thought of humanism and the love to fellow-men had been diminished in this kind of Christianity, that it seemed to have outlived persecution and to have conquered only to indulge in retaliative persecution itself.

The situation did not change when the country lay open, a prey to hordes of savages. "The empire received its last and most deadly wounds," says Gibbon, "during the minority of the sons and grandsons of Theodosius. When these incapable princes seemed to have arrived at the age of puberty, they relinquished the empire to the eunuchs, the Church to the bishops, and the provinces to the barbarians."

Cause of the decline of Byzantium. Gibbon.

Byzantine pharisæism disqualified the rulers for government.

This in essence continued to be the case when at home the rulers fought out dogmatic subtleties even at the races and the games in the hippodrome, where on more than one occasion the blood of citizens was poured out in floods. This continued whilst on the borders Huns and Bulgarians made their raids unchecked, drawing nearer and nearer until they arrived before the portcullies of the capital.

Intestine outbreaks of fanaticism,

whilst hordes of invading barbarians narrow down the territorial extent of the empire,

They sneered at the long, strong walls, parapeted and studded with towers, extending from the city up to Salymbria, and down to the Black Sea; the walls notwithstanding, they ravaged the empire up to the Termophylees. It is an assured fact, that the court and the populace of Byzantium allowed themselves to become vulgarised by coming in contact with those crude peoples. Piercing out eyes, cutting off noses, ears, &c. was carried on by wholesale. Even Samuel, the prince of the Bojares, fainted away from horror at the sight of fifteen thousand of his warriors, which the emperor had returned to him with their eyes pierced out. But the blinded ones were called the "barbarians", and our school-books still copy the slander.

and serve retaliation upon

cruelties perpetrated

by princes under the influences of court-theology,

and under dread of palace-revolutions,

Employing measures like these the emperors thought to shield their persons against palace-revolutions, and their provinces against the invasions of "savages." The possessions reached much too far, however, for such a method of defense. Just remember the permanent struggles with Parthia and with the Persian kingdom of the Sassanides.

Byzantium now divided with Rome the old honor of being the seat of the central power, that reached from the Thames to the Indus, that ruled over Treves and Petra. What a stretch of border line was there to be defended.

It is instructive to observe, first, the long contest between Rome and Parthia, then the wars with the Sassanides. There in Rome and Byzantium the centers of a power dominating the western world from Athens and Alexandria to the Rhone and the Thames, here a romance of Persian knighthood in rows from Tyre to the Indus. What a line between these terminals! The spirit of chivalry had not as yet died out in the regions between the Leontes, Indus and Volga. But see how the lines are forced by Huns, and Goths, and Bulgarians. From the South the Saracens even are in sight, falling in line with the skirmishing sons of Ishmael and Esau. Thus the emperors, ever trembling for their lives, could scarcely avoid becoming unapproachable cowards and blood-thirsty despots. The eastern emperors were even more menaced than their associates in the West. For here monkish fanaticism and contempt of life had wrought a sturdy race of subjects into foes more fierce and aggressive than any which history thus far had met.

Borders defenseless.

Goths.
Bulgarians.
Saracens.

Diocletian already, who had pressed forward beyond the Tigris, had adopted the court-etiquette of Xerxes for his household. "His sacred deity, the emperor" was to be addressed on bended knees. His golden diadem was an imitation of the Persian tiara which Cyrus wore.

Diocletian introduced new features of Orientalism. "His sacred majesty, the emperor;" Persian tiara. § 73.

The doggish sycophancy in officious ovations of despotism knew no bounds. Manliness had disappeared as well as feminine decency. "Servile oratory" lasted as long as the empire with its abject prostration before emperors of whom the greater number were monsters of cruelty and effeminacy. This abuse of the Greek language had been commenced by the two Eusebiuses, the father of Church-history as well as the Nicomedian. The oriental ceremonials were kept up for appearance sake until the boundaries of the empire had melted away to the limits of the capital and pomp became ridiculous.

Sycophancy. (Eusebius). § 71, 125, 137, 150.

and effeminacy.

A strange contrast that, between the despicable fright and impotentency—and the dress; robes heavy with gold embroidery, purple buskins, a high silken cap decked with pearls and jewels, surmounted by the Persian tiara tapering out in a globe and a cross. Helpless were now these proud cesars, had it not been for the support of the wild Warægians rushing in for martial employment and for payment in gold or land-districts. These foreigners were made body-guards, since they could best be trusted with the protection of the emperor's life when he went to church.

Surrounding the emperor, with double-edged battle-axes upon their broad shoulders, they marched with him to the senate or to the hippodrome. In their keeping were the keys to the treasury, to the purple state-hall, and to the sleeping-room of their master.

Such was the embodiment of the Plato-Augustinian idea of "the State of God" in the Byzantine dominion, New-Rome and New-Jerusalem combined.

History in this case again and forever has demonstrated that this Augustinian idea is mischievous; that servitude is inevitable where king or priest in the same person usurps either office.

There will be plenty of cheap imperial benedictions; every soldier may have a piece of paper soaked with "holy" oil as a charm and talisman in war. No wonder that the pious soldiers clamor for three emperors instead of one. They insist upon an imperial trinity upon earth as the symbol of the Trinity in Heaven.

The end of it all was a general torpidness in formalism and hypocrjcy, a perpetual intrigue for getting into the dangerous position of power—and homicide.

§ 127. Ready to depart from old style Romanism and Byzantinism in the Mediterranean basin, it is befitting to sum up the results of the first phases of Christian culture.

We mentioned that the extension of the old empire, in its Greek capital at least, was the museum of classic antiquities. The inheritance of which Rome took possession when the empire was divided, was differently influenced and managed in Rome and Ravenna from the way it was in Constantinople. Here oriental stability as re-

pristinated upon government; whilst the conditions in the western part were somewhat modified by the Germanic element. When western Rome had become exhausted, simultaneously with oriental effeminacy and dissimulation in eastern Rome, where the walls were built to be manned by hired men from the North; then that sanctimonious langour and diplomatic wickedness became the fixed character of the East, which ever since goes by the name of Byzantinism.

For five centuries ancient Romanism had controlled the culture of the world. Now Constantinople took the lead from Edessa to Venice—for a short period.

One gift which the Latin part later on got back from the East, we will not slight, altho it has received more praise than its merits account for, viz: Roman Jurisprudence. Justinian's finely executed picture shows him as he points to his code of Roman laws with one hand, and to the church of St. Sophia with the other. It means a great deal. For a great accomplishment, and a peculiar product of history, is the completion of a Christian priest-state, to which state-rights are subordinated and made subservient.

In the memorable year 622 A. D. the church of St. Sophia supported more than eighty clerical officers, of which fact Hergenroether made a memorandum. This was the number remaining after an express reduction by Justinian. But in addition to the eighty priests, there were one hundred and fifty deacons, seventy subdeacons, and one hundred and sixty readers in attendance.

The army officers and curates connected with the other 25 new churches, if averaging in this ratio, must have been large enough to maintain that controversial fervency which cost thirty thousand lives in the few days of the Nica riot.

Collecting and condensing the laws—which however this emperor learned from the Germans in Spain and Burgundy—did evidently not at all accrue to the elevation of morality. It is a portentous mistake to expect civilisation from either priestly or royal legislation.

Emperor Heraclius entrusted the patriarch and "the Mother of God" with the regency when he went against the Persians. He wrenched the "Holy Cross" from them in order that he might, walking barefooted at the head of his soldiers, carry it back through the gates of Jerusalem.

Nobody had any idea that the letter he had received on the way from a certain crank by the name of Muhamed would cause such reverses to him, and such a tension in history. Like the cloud of a tornado Islam arose in the same year, in the year of the Hegira.

This, then, is the significance of Byzantium: It was to be the place of retirement for ancient Greek culture. In due time it should become the bridge also, across which these fragments would be carried by fugitives to an asylum in the West. Byzantium was well adapted to conserve the classic products of the Aryan mind. It was the better fit for such safe-keeping, as it was too stupid and selfconceited to appreciate the treasures. Had it been otherwise the "classics" would in all probability have been destroyed.

Roman law and Cesaro-papism were to be the vehicle for carrying, at the proper time, the mixture of Greek culture and Christianity—such as it was—to the Occident where Cesaro-papism prepared the peoples for the transition from bondage under the law to gospel-freedom. This then prevailing form of government was similar to that of the East, in that this alone was able to throw the raw material of Persian, Slavonian and Saracen hordes, gnostics and monks, too, into the smelter.

The mission of the Byzantine dominion to serve as a safety vault and as a bridge for Hellenic culture is typified in an old picture on one of the ceilings of the great old cloister at Iviron upon Mt. Athos. Represented is the Holy Virgin upon the throne, surrounded by angels, prophets, and apostles; but Plato, Aristotle, Sophocles, Thucydides are also present. Is it not like a prophetic vision of a future in which should be understood again:—the real sublimity and catholicity of the evangelical thought?

CH. III.   THE CHURCH AND THE TALMUD.

§ 128. In the Third Division we introduced a group of the Semites as a necessary element and coefficient energy in the task assigned to the Mediterranean culture. The Hebrews were especially important as the vessel into which the solvent ingredient had been poured out from above, and as being instrumental in distributing the remedy among the nations for their recovery. True to the Semitic temper in general the Jews with an eye to their own interest gave prescriptions but did not take the remedy themselves. Well adapted tho they were to intermeddle and to diffuse, they seemed utterly disqualified to accept the thought of Isaiah to "buy without money and without price." They did not take if not allowed to domineer. Hence in keeping with their natural disposition to hold their own, and not seeing in their headstrong perverseness that they threw away the seed kernel grown in the hull of their own externalism; they thought it meritorious to reject what seemed alien to their nature and their traditions, and in their obduracy turned their full animosity against the new movement, making the animosity their religion and single force of coherency.

Let us recapitulate what we gleaned after the reapers in the field of Sem. We appreciated the receptivity of the Semites. They took a firm hold of the one transcendental deity, which compels man to absolute dependence. This dependence was perceived, however, as an onerous servitude which renders earthly life colorless, and produces an habitual affectation of ennui.

The Semitic frame of mind may best be seen in its contrast to the Aryan. The Aryan manifests versatility and is inclined to divert his mind in the manifold of nature. In his fondness for analysing he becomes so attached to nature's beauties as to let his diverted mind run to dissipation. Because not so intensely interested in the externals of religion, the Aryan shows more considerateness for the personal sentiments of others, and more tolerance. Because of his idealistic anticipations being disappointed so often, he gives himself up to scepticism, grows melancholy, and loves to brood and to speculate.

The temper of the Semite, as a general thing, is quite the opposite. Above all he is inflated with a great amount of selfesteem; for altho cringing towards the powers that be, he is, whenever selfishness requires, oppressive to those he thinks below him. Concealing under a studied gravity of deportment every sign of his inner emotions, he is naturally prone to deceitfulness, and to count upon external appearance. We admire his faculty for concentration which makes the dispersion of his nation the only calamity which causes him real grief. He adheres to rigid dogmatism, and his fanatical vindictiveness for being baulked in justifying and carrying out his wrong world-theory is more dangerous than his making proselytes.

The Semite's view of the world and mode of life tends not to nature or agriculture; it centers in God and in himself as number one. In regard to the world he calculates, is ever full of prospects, and an expert in the art of financiering. Hence credit is due to Semitic development: with reference to religion and ethics for everything; concerning the part it took in aiding cultural progress on the scope of practical life: for commerce, distributing products, for traffic and financiering; in science for something, namely astronomy, measures and ciphers; in arts, nothing.

Aryan qualified for art, science, philosophy; a born agriculturist.

Semite a nomade; aversion to handicraft is not disavowed; a born trader; poor warrior— cosmopolitan;

seeks popularity, puts up with indignities, affects patriotism, ideality and fidelity to principles.

Predilection for judicial positions.

Affecting philanthropy.

Utilising other peoples' secrets and embarrassments.

Making gossip a business, eminently qualifying him for journalism.

But the Semite must be understood from another aspect. If the Aryan is a Christian, he is best qualified for art, science, and philosophy. At any rate he is the champion of freedom, resists the Bad, and is an agriculturist to "the manor born." He loves the soil of his "Heimath," and may become homesick for his native village. Now the Semite can never deny the stamp of that national character which was impressed upon the House of Israel during the first period of the exceptional position to which it had been appointed. Raised upon a narrow strip of the earth's surface, most of which was a wilderness, the Semite is a nomade. Hence love for the soil is lacking entirely, agricultural pursuits are avoided, and aversion to handicraft is not disavowed.

As a born trader the Semite loves city life, and, being spoiled for patriotism, is a poor warrior. As a cosmopolitan he takes no pleasure in the idyllic, possesses no principles and takes no interest in ideals. But he likes to affect all this, for the sake of the popularity which he needs in order to become a power behind the throne. He can put up with indignities as far as he sees a chance of turning them to his account and of coming out triumphant in the end. In law he is well versed so as to keep himself out of its meshes and to get others in. He then knows how to get them out again and to play off philanthropist under certain stipulations. He knows how to pry into, and to utilise other people's secrets and predicaments. Making gossip a business he is quick to swing himself into the saddle of journalism; watching the failings of others, which he may render opportune for improving his own chances, he can in this latter sphere most profitably unfold his talent of intermeddling.

What the Semite lacks of talent for organising states—despite his good qualities for domestic life—he makes up in talent for organising finances. Through concentrated enterprise he will occupy and try to monopolise the domain of commerce.

For the Jew the best mode of preserving and utilising his talents for the world in a legitimate way, of enriching these talents for his own true benefit, would have been to step forth from the clannish narrowness of Semitism and to ennoble the natural inheritance through Christian cultivation of the mind.

Inasmuch as the Ishmaelites and Israelites did not enter Christianity, they were sidetracked. It will be of no avail to the latter to obtrude themselves upon Christian civilisation, or try to sneak in on their own conditions in order to disintegrate in their cunning manner from within, what they could not demolish in open combat.

For in spite of affecting philanthropy after the very pattern of Judas the Iscariotite, in spite of acting persecuted innocence, Semitism cannot conceal its merciless, hateful and fanatical particularism.

Semitism forced into Mohammedanism.

Talmud

and

Koran

instrumental in stirring up Christendom.

Semitic assaults had to unite Christian nations.

The appellation Anti-Semitic may cause inquiry as to what Anti-Christian means.

The "higher criticism" in sympathy with Talmudism called forth wholesome counteraction. § 19. 168.

Church under obligation to Jewish effrontery.

Reasons for our indifference as to Anti-Semitic agitation.

Encroachments of Judaism to be retrenched. § 200

Semitism was forced partly into Mohammedanism, partly into Talmudism. To the latter the Jew is chained, altho he may boast of his unconcern as to any religion; tho he may simulate indignation over any symptom of inhumaneness; tho he may avail himself of pretended agnosticism in order to make friends among nominal Christians and fraternise with them: the modern adherents of posthumous Talmudism are the deadly foes of Aryan Christian culture. The well-spring of this antagonism is the Talmud. Its acquaintance must be made together with its companion and contemporary, the Koran. Both these foes of Christ's religion seem to have been designed by history to irritate and stimulate the culture issuing therefrom.

The pernicious methods by which the weakness, the failings, and embarrassments of the Christians are espied and taken advantage of, should remind Christendom of the duty of self-criticism and circumspection. By repeated assaults the Christians are reminded, that internal dissensions must give place to a united defense against the foe without. Constantinople and Jerusalem witness to the advantage which Semitism takes of the weakness of Christendom to this day. Hence the latter as yet needs a spur to its flanks and a prick to its heels to urge it onward, and to awaken it to the consciousness of the contrast, and of its task to preserve the essentials of European civilisation against the encroachments of Semitic moneypower. Since in our own days the word Anti-Semite has a jarring sound it would be well to inquire what Anti-Christian means. Perhaps the investigation will be called up shortly, just as the rich literature on the "Life of Christ" in recent years was called forth by the disparaging books written in sympathy with Talmudism, and as the publication of this book was stimulated by a certain anonymous "History of Civilisation of the World" in four volumes, in sympathy with the adherents of Talmudism. The Church might have succumbed under factional strife and intellectual inertia. It was the scientific research after proofs for the authenticity of the Pentateuch and of Isaiah which led to the discovery of the witnessing stones of Mugheir and Tel el Amarna. These are our reasons for being indifferent as to Anti-Semitism and for acknowledging ourselves under obligation to Semitism. But since it is undeniable that the ancient element, chiefly in the shape of Judaism, seek ways to assail and to undermine the Christian cognition of Theo-Humanism, we emphatically insist upon our right to arrange affairs of Christianity and criticism, to settle points of the Christian world-theory in our own way, and desire to be ignored by Semitism.

The fact, that occidental history up to modern times seems to have been destined to move between the Semitic and the Aryo-Christian frames of mind as between two poles, we have to admit. Before we get through we may have become aware, that the irritating effects of the polarity reach remarkably far and deep.

§ 129. Let us prove this polarity first from direct encroachments of Talmudism. *Effects of Talmudism upon civilisation.*

As soon as that "way and truth" had been banished from Jerusalem, for which the Jewish race had served as a vessel and vehicle until it had emptied itself and was left to itself, its ominous unsympathetical nature became conspicuous. In the first books of the Talmudistic collections already it betrayed its nature, where it poses upon the bizarre mystifications of the rabbis, and gives vent to its surreptitious fanaticism.

Assuming an attitude of self-sufficiency for the sake of effect the Talmud composes the Jewish traditions into a system of Phariseeism which renders the most trifling observances, void of any intellectual or ethical value whatever—into law. *Systematised phariseeism*

Its own exclusiveness notwithstanding, Judaism in its usual effrontery outwitted the Roman law in obtaining chartered franchises for its own. Thus Talmudism became legalised in organising itself against all the world, and against Roman state-unity in particular.

The Jews ever since have deported themselves as born lawyers, as experts in making out their cases through casuistry. Judaism took a liking to Rome in proportion to the growth of Rome's hatred against the Crucified. And Rome was only too well pleased to return a little liking since Judaism would stoop to serve the gentile state, at least in slandering and denunciating Christians. *"Lawyers" and pharisees" procure a state charter to legalise their own traditional laws.*

Gladiatorial shows, circuses and theatres were the things most popular; beauties ranked highest at court and the Jews espied every opportunity to utilise these things in the gain of popularity and influence, and to profit some cash besides. They could now endure all these things in the Holy City. Even the Hellenic-Roman courts of the Herods were tolerated in the City of David, if only Christ's memory was impugned.

Jerusalem was given into the hands of the gentiles in return for the victim of hatred whom the Jews had delivered to Pilate. They knew how to keep clear of the reproach of the legalised murder. The "Lamb of God" was sacrificed by the highpriest under forms of custom, of sacred tradition, and civil law combined, so as to prove Jewish innocence. Semi-tism indignantly will deny the murder, but cannot deny the retaliation. Jerusalem fell. The last of all the states of ancient culture was vanquished as the first nation which received exemplary punishment in the new æra. *Retaliation upon Jerusalem.*

Rabbi Jochanan was Nasi. He flew from the besieged city and transferred the seat of the Sanhedrin to Jamne, where the aristocratic Jews had taken quarters. Thus a firm center was founded at the beginning of the great dispersion. At different times schools flourished in Babylon, or Pumbeditha, in Tiberias, Nahardea, or Sera. Those of Babylon under their Rosh-Galutha (i. e. "head of the captivity") were the most influential. Thus it happened, that the commentaries of the Mishna and the Babylonian Talmud—emblematic of Judaism as the pagodas are of Buddhism—were compiled in the old Cushito-Semitic capital. It was the object of the Talmud to legalise the hatred of Christianity, which henceforth was to bind the dispersed Jews together. Another bond of union they have not. Another state the dispersed nation could never organise, since the authority of the RoshGalutha had dwindled away and the center dropped out. The written tradition was to hold the intriguing union together after the Jews, expelled from Persia, had taken refuge in Africa and Spain, where the disconnected congregations of the Synagogue dotted the Mediterranean basin. *Succession of the synagogue. Synhedrion.* *Origin of the Talmud in Babylon is ominous.* *Hatred of the cross religiously sanctioned by the Talmud, which therefore and henceforth is the single bond of union for the dispersed race.*

One of the most mysterious features of history comes out in the farthest-reaching influences ever exerted by these fragmentary parts of the house of Israel. In order to be just, due attention is to be given to the hidden cause of that universal prestige which Judaism knew how to maintain. We must investigate the religious philosophy affiliated and abetted by the Talmud as the source of Jewish propensities. *Phantasms of emanation intermixed with a corrupt monotheism. Kabbala.*

The post-Christian speculation of the Jews contained in the Kabbala, as much as the rabbis divulged of it in tracts and sermons, reveals corrupt Monotheism, subsequently adulterated by the oriental concepts of emanation. This part of the Jewish tradition which is held very secret, views the cosmos as a living body. By a clandestine relationship between the masculine and feminine principles all possible grades and spheres of the universe are brought under the conditions of attraction and repulsion.

Every thing and every event has its anti-type in heaven. A chain without end, reaching from thence down into the depths of nature, is so interlinked with all of the consolidary interests, that the highest purport is seen in the most insignificant event, and vice versa. Thus the chain, touched at the one side, transmits the vibration to the other, like the string of a cithara.This system of the "sephires" —the "hulls" —is altogether based upon the oriental phantasm of emanation. Only that the garments, into which the transcendentally conceived deity clothes itself, become less ethereal and are more tensely woven, the nearer they approach the material world. *Extent of this adulteration.*

Babylonian substitute for the Alexandrian synthesis of Philo. § 77, 93, 100, 108.

This in short is the Talmudistic attempt of the Babylonian calculation to bridge the chasm between the Infinite and the finite, which the Alexandrian speculation of a Philo found in the Logos. This calculation employs a world of ideas to render our synthesis and Philo's compromise superfluous. But on top of that compound of scholasticism, fatalism, and silliness, a superciliousness unheard of crowds up and foams out. A ridiculous haughtiness has put up its throne in this Talmud, the youngest child, the latest structure of BABEL.

Quotations showing the source of Jewish effrontery.

The rabbis are kings and patriarchs of the world. Whenever they betake themselves to their trumpets "and before the Holy One,—be He magnified,—blow them, then He rises in Heaven from His chair of judgment and takes His seat upon the throne of pardon". His figure' according to rabbi Ishmael's measurement, from his right arm to his hips is seventy times ten thousand miles broad; his beard is 11500 miles long. In the schools of the firmament debates go on before him for and against him. The rabbis, being eternal, ought to know what they are about; but they do not talk "out of school."

Israel is the Jacob of God. The seventy princes of the seventy nations are devils. Israel, therefore, is the lamb among seventy wolves. When the Messiah comes, then the Children of Israel will ride on the backs of the gentiles; each Israelite receives two thousand and eight hundred serfs from among their number for his private accommodation.

Statutes improving upon the Old Testament, reveal the roots of Jewish selfconceit and arrogancy.

From the aspect of such grotesque phantasms the light may be derived, by which to read and explain Jewish proclivities. In those statutes, engrafted so as to improve upon the Old Testament, lie the roots of Jewish selfconceit and effrontery. Every ideal which prompts the Aryan and Christian to ascend on the scale of moral progress is simply a thing of sarcasm to the admirers of the phantasmagories on the opposite pole.

System of casuistry and allowances.

What the infallible instructor says is to be obeyed; after rabbi N. N. has given his decision, private thought about the matter is indifferent. In and of itself no act is punishable; the question whether this or that is punishable or excusable is not thrown open. The question is: Am I allowed? And a permit is at hand for anything short of apostasy. Anything that had ever been held allowable by any rabbi, or which, under such and such circumstances in tenor with his other allowances, would most assuredly have been allowed by him, is justified.

Rabbi represents the conscience of the synagogue. § 130, 133.

The rabbis stand in proxy for the Jewish conscience at large. This is what they are paid for, and they are the tutors of private conscience—what is left of it.

Source of probabilism, indulgences, and Jesuitical ethics. § 163.

Here, therefore, we stand before the original font of indulgences, casuistic probabilism, and Jesuitical ethics. This system reveals an approximation to Christian thought, as embellished with second hand drapery. We shall have the opportunity to demonstrate how, by way of Spain, the outcroppings of allowances infected the Church. With this object in view we felt it a duty to uncover the sources and to

Outcroppings of Jewish syncretism to be reviewed later on. § 164, 200.

exhibit the principles of Jewish intermeddling with social and ethical problems as issues of this plagiarism. For Talmudistic religiousness is nothing but a shrewd imitation of the emanistic picture of the world as it was reflected in the oriental brain.

13000 traditional statutes of elders exclusive of the aditional sayings of Avicebron and Maimonides. § 180, 150.

The "Traditions of the Elders"—of which the Talmud already enumerates thirteen thousand, and to which at least those of Avicebron and Maimonides (not to speak of those of Rabbi N. N.) must be counted—is a system of crazy dreams about sublimity and servilism. This pomp for the sake of appearances, and this mystifying symbolism make the Talmud-Jew a sight to pity, if it did not create minds so unprincipled and obtrusive as to provoke indignation; and if Jewish cunning did not know how to utilise the effects of this indignation over the systematised pharisaism, how to turn its repulsion into martyrdom and to its credit.

The biblical element in Talmudistic Judaism does not amalgamate;

§ 130. The enormous fraud of Jewish dogmatism is a quodlibet accumulation of second-hand sophistry, old lumber, and Babylonian filth. In a loose way it has retained those shining jewels of truth once delivered to the fathers; but since the Old Testament refuses to be agglutinated to the heterogeneous elements of Babylonian origin, Talmudistic Judaism smarts under its incrimination. These jewels of the "Name", so burdensome, are rolled from shoulder to shoulder. They disarrange every

must be twisted to fit Talmudism by allegoric exegesis.

system. Because they can not be understood in their allegorical interpretation, rabbinical theology labors in vain to hide its vexation over the failure to fit in the prophecies somewhere. The old palladium mounted in the grotesque filigree-work of Babylon with its grave significance bears heavy upon the Jew as a standing reproach, a pending verdict against unrepented guilt. It ever haunts the perpetrators of the one great plot. Being too headstrong to retract, the blood of the Testament shadows them in their wanderings through the wide homeless world.

Some Jews are honest enough to give vent to that deep seated melancholy caused by the burdensome jewels, when each year on the tenth of August they pay the Turk for a permit to sigh and to cry aloud in the corner under the walls of Jerusalem. But otherwise second childhood prevails in the odd and mannered observances of the Synagogue, from which in comparatively recent times Isaiah 53, has finally been excluded. In all of that the shy, conscience-stricken features of old Ahasuerus are plain to the thoughtful observer.

The studies of the Moorish sciences tinctured with Talmudism, in which unwary and irenic scholastics once engaged themselves, helped to infuse oriental thoughts into Christianity after all. The Church just then showed many points of affinity for the Semitic compound of orientalism. With her ideas of the theocracy, of the high-priesthood, and the sacrifice, she was especially receptive for the Jewish ingredients.

Influence of Talmudism upon the Church at the time of Maimonides, Albertus Magnus, and Thomas Aquina. Frohschames, Michel, Baumann. § 122, 129, 129, 144, 147, 148, 150, 185.

Thus, despite the fear of Manichœism, Talmudistic elements were imbibed, additional to the Judaistic-Platonic doctrines of Augustine. We may merely allude to the influence of Maimonides upon Albertus Magnus and Thomas Aquina which is admitted by Frohschamer (Leipzig 1880); and by Michel (Fulda 1891) both of them catholics. (See also the Protestant Baumann-on Thomas Aquina.)

Maimonides, without betraying the secret of Talmudism, wished to show that Jewish Philosophy might be so interpreted as to conciliate Christian thought in favor of the persecuted Jews. He showed that Judaism was not Mohammedanism, and that it consisted of more than dreams and rearrangements of kabbalistic formulae, charms and ciphers.

At such signs of reform Christendom began to dream of a general conversion of the Jews, and made ready to meet them half way. But the old residue in Judaism refused to affiliate. Semitism does not give up itself; receptive as it is, it does not take what is against its nature. If given the choice it always takes to the crescent rather than to the cross. With the Church it was otherwise; unknowingly she adopted some of the Talmudistic peculiarities thus palmed off upon Christian scholasticism, even in the conception of a juridical, forensic justification. And more than that, we found sorcery, conjury, magic and necromancy underneath the old Akkadian and then Babylonian culture. It forms that stratum of most ancient cults, as found in the Shamanism and Fetishism of Ugro-Altaic and Mongolian nations. Thanks to the rabbis, these elements were peddled out in the Occident under the label of "black arts". The Aryans were not entirely disinclined to buy the secrets.

Christian theology contaminated, while Talmudism adopted nothing in exchange which was against its nature.

What Christendom imbibed from dealing with Jews.

Pico of Mirandula and Agrippa of Nettesheim in later times have taken the invoice of magic formulas, talismans, and amulettes, and of their uses, cataloguing them verbally and in a bona fide manner—for the trade. They are all written in Hebrew letters, these names and prescriptions by which spirits can be pressed into service. Sorcery belonged to the business of the rabbis. As "Lords of the Name" they were the proper persons to deal with.

Magic art, Babylonian faith, catalogued by Pico of Mirandola. and Agrippa of Nettesheim. § 26.

The Shemhamphoresh. the name of the "Unspeakable", is a chief means of magic in itself. It is able to accomplish anything. "Rabbi Chanina and Rab Oschaja used to study every Sabbath evening in the book of Jezirah, how to create a three years calf in a minute and a half, or something to that effect, so as to make a feast of it. This is in substance what the tract Sanhedrin tells us. Miracle working rabbis, as we find them today in Roumania and Russia, were in vogue all through the Middle-Ages. It was not only superstition and envy of benighted Christians that raised the "furor teutonicus" and caused several riots in which Jews were worsted. They were not persecuted from religious hatred. It was lynch-law, not to be palliated by any means, but it was provoked by the exacting practices of professional tricksters.

Magic art practiced, and peddled out by Jewish trickery.

Tract Sanhedrin on magic experiments. Chanina and Oschaja.

For Jews were the physicians, astrologers, sorcerers, possessors of secret Chaldean arts, from the Volga to the Ebro. . They were spies and governmental emissaries in keeping with the description of their characteristics previously given.

Cause of riots in the Middle-Ages in which Jews were worsted.

Before closing accounts, however, with Talmudistic Judaism we ought to keep in mind its probabilism for further reference, and by way of transition to the next chapter throw a glance upon their connection with the Arabs of Ishmaelitic and Edomitic extraction.

It cannot be denied, that these people were supported by the Jews in their conquest of Palestine, tho that Jewess, who is said to have been with the false prophet when he died just before he began his projected conquest, may be made an argument to prove the contrary. A Jew played the strong citadel of Cu-sarea into the hands of the Arabs. In Asia as well as in Ægypt, Islam was welcomed by the sympathising Jews. Most obvious was the intimacy between the Jews and the Moors in Spain. When at the defeat of Toledo the Christian Goths had taken refuge for prayer in a church, a Jew opened the gate of the city. Graetz has demonstrated how a pseudo-apocalypse celebrated the victory of Islam. Metatron answered Simeon ben Jochai: "God establishes the right of Ishmael in order to deliver you from malicious Edom", meaning the Christians.

Intimacy between Jews and Mohammedans.

Jews supporting the armies of Islam in their conquests.

Graetz.

Metotron's statement to Simeon ben Jochai as to God's favorites.

CH. IV. THE CHURCH AND ISLAM.

§ 131. Mohammedanism did not originate without Jewish intermediation, and it would not have spread so rapidly had it not been for Jewish instigations, and unmistakable signs of their sympathy. A Jewish gentry had settled among the Arabs ever since the times of the Maccabæans. In Yemen they held the controlling power. Some surmise that even the sanctuary at Mecca had been founded by them. However this may be, the country itself assisted in shaping the peculiar traits of the Southern Semites still more peculiar. Stony Arabia from Cape Ras el Hadd to Akaba, and from Aden to the Persian Gulf is as favorable for raising fanaticism as any region can be.

Jews of Arabia.

Sanctuary in Mecca.

Self-sufficiency of
Islam.

Islam will settle differences by a reasonable discussion with nobody.

Its rise is distinctly marked by a revival of oriental selfabnegation which accepts matters as settled by fate once and forever. What the Moslem needs to know of things and what he has to do with them, Islam reveals in detail; but on the whole it is sufficient to say Allah illa Allah. And Allah is great. What he did not command is not worth considering. He did not forbid much besides wine and pictures. The Alexandrian library was to be doomed to the flames because the books agreeing with the Koran were superfluous. Even if Omar did not command this act, the legend denotes the character of Islam. What does not submit to it **must** perish. Islam never

It requires no religious
conviction; only
political subjection and
external conformance.

demanded conviction, it simply required homage, nothing but external conformity. The giaur as such is a rebel, hence the scimetar for the infidel. As soon as Muhamed had forced Mecca to acknowledge him, he sent his menacing messages to the courts of Byzantium and Persia. As soon as the manifesto was ignored, those ferocious horsemen came storming along, who live in the shadow of their spears and cook their rice upon the firebrands of extirpated cities. This was perfectly in order, from an Arabian point of view.

Koran
on the calling of
Muhamed.
§ 124, 127.

The heart of Muhamed had been specially predestined and prepared for such exploits. He himself relates how: "Hereupon Gabriel commanded Michael to fetch a bowl of water from the sacred spring. Then he opened my breast, drew out my heart, and poured faith, wisdom and understanding into it, with the water of the spring."—Then came the ride to Jerusalem. Borak, the miraculous horse, waits for him. It had the body of a horse. but the face of a man, and the ears of an elephant; it had a camels neck, a mule's tail, and the hoofs of a steer. Its breast shone like a ruby. "Ascend, Muhamed!" Gabriel calls out. The ride begins. "Three times I was addressed on my way,'relates the "prophet','by two men and one woman, but I

Muhamed cautions not
to argue, because it
would have been fatal
to Allah's dominion.

gave no answer." "Thou hast done right," said Gabriel. Of course he did. Arguing would have been disastrous to Allah's campaign. Had Muhamed answered the first, the world would have become Jewish; if the second, it would have become Christian. Now it belongs to him. Finally they arrive at the heavenly tent. The angels sing: Muhamed is the prophet of God. The way leads through thousand spheres of light; he sees God! At a distance of two bow-shots he worships. God assures him that he once made the world for Muhamed's sake. Hence the world belongs to Islam. It is to be conquered and subjected to infallible Islam. This is the sum and substance of the Koran.

At the head of his veterans of ten years warfare, all in coats of mail made of fine iron chains, head covered with the conical steel helmet, armed with the round shield and the lance Caliph Omar gallops up his deploy on African soil. The collection of papyros manuscripts of Arch-Duke Rainer reveals the accoutrement of the Arabs, as Karabacek has shown from these documents. Now as far out as the Pamir is his, now Ægypt, also. Whilst the conquest of northern Africa gradually proceeds, the crescent is being established further north towards the Kurdish Alps.

We advanced fast in order to bring the situation under full view, from which the history of twelve centuries is to be understood. For the old polarity is thus restored in multiplied power between the Occident on one side, and the Orient, including the Equatorial-African deserts, on the other.

Sum and substance of
the world-theory of
the Koran.

Imagine a crescent shaped hemisphere, open side upward. The eastern horn may be Brussa, seat of the Anatolian Othmans at the time we now speak of, overtopped by the snowcapped Mt. Olympus. As the western terminal we may take Granada, the stronghold of the Andalusian caliphs, below the white summits of the Sierra Nevada. Between these two points the wide, broadening arc of the circle of the Ishmaelite culture is drawn far to the south. Later on this culture extended on the eastern side from Damascus to Samarkand, and down to the lowlands of India, and south from Mecca through the Soudan to Timbuctoo and the Senegal. This is the position which

Encouragement of the
Arabian warriors.
Rainer s collection.
KARABACEK.

Islam held opposite the occidental Indo-Germanic world.

What does this position signfy?

Concerning progress the Arabs seemed fit for nothing but to annihilate every culture save their own. But it happened here as in many other instances, that the conquerors were conquered by the cultures they could not destroy. Then the pens, if we may so call the stiles of the translators, proved mightier than the scimetars.

From the ruins the "classics" were recalled to life and made to speak once more to the oriental nations. In general, however, no more of literary merit can be ascribed to the Saracens. than to have transmitted certain impulses, and by their translations of the classics furnished a few crutches to the Occidentals. For, this is evident: as soon as the latter learned to read the originals again, they threw away the crutches.

The Semites here serve as intermediators, there in the desintegration of cultures. What the Arabs did in this direction ought not to be undervalued. The Mohammedan High-schools did very effective work in transmitting literature by their translations. In order to study medicine or algebra, to understand the meaning of the zenith or nadir, to learn astronomy and geography, the wealthy youths of Europe had to take lessons from the Arabs. They not only imported articles of trade from the far East, but brought with them also grammar and lexicography, just as the Elamite-Chaldeans had once been the factors of education in Assyria.

The Crescent.

Significance of the Saracenic translations of the classics for the culture of Europe in the Middle-Ages. § 139, 142, 145, 150, 156.

The caliphs of the West at the zenith of their Spanish rule called learned teachers from the borders of India to Zaragossa. Moorish castles contained large libraries. In the time of her prime the university of Cordova had four thousand students matriculated, who chief of all studied the natural philosophy of Aristotle and Pliny in translations. Personal originality or inventive ingenuity the translators never developed. Nevertheless, what Samarkand, the "cupola of the Islam" was for Asia, Cordova was in those times for Europe.

Transmitting science to Spain. § 150.

Universities at Zaragossa Cordova, and Samarkand. Translations of Aristotle and Pliny.

The Arabs were the founders of the medical art, A. v. Humboldt thought, who accredited them with originality at least with reference to this branch of human knowledge. We take exceptions, notwithstanding. They distilled alcohol to circumvent prohibition, and studied parts of medicine to meet certain requirements of polygamy, or to cure horses,—that is all. As regards the algebra of the Arabs, we simply adopt Humboldt's own conclusion: "It has developed from the confluence of two streams which for many ages had their separate courses independent of each other: one springing from India, the other taking its rise in Greece."

Arab culture not self-productive.

Al-cohol. Al-gebra. A. v. Humboldt.

Such is the case, in fact, with all the Arabian sciences, even with regard to the laboratory experiments based upon Aristotle's analytic inductions, and begun by Abu Jussuf in Basora, the contemporary of Scotus Erigena.

Least of all is Islam original as a religion. A piece of plagiarism throughout, the Koran is the type of its whole culture:—a pell-mell from beginning to end. Such syncretism merely copies or collects and selects what is suitable, its pretensions as to its revelations notwithstanding. Not a germ of spontaneous generation can be shown as inherent in it. Intermeddling, however, and overreaching as Semitism ever was, Islam carried a great deal of oriental thought even into the Church. We pointed out Maimonides, and now refer to Avicebrona also.

Islam as a religion is a plagiarism.

Koran the type of its culture. §§ 43, 47, 54, 56, 58, 71, 86, 125, 126, 132, 137, 136, 156, 175, 198.

Avicebrona. § 150.

It can not be proven that Gibbon misrepresented where he, on good authority quoted, "that the Latin Church has not disdained to borrow from the Koran (3, 29.) and the Sunnite traditions the immaculate conception of the virgin mother of Christ", a doctrine which, according to Fra Paolo in "Istoria de Concilia Trento" was condemned by St. Bernard as a presumptuous novelty.

Church allowed Moslem ideas to penetrate Roman dogmatics. Gibbon.

Idea of "the Immaculate" conception. derived from Islam. Fra Paolo, St. Bernard. §§ 55, 122, 124, 125, 126, 146, 149, 150.

It was from the valley of the Ganges by way of Delhi, that through the intermediation of the Arabs we received Mogul-Moorish architecture. That new cultural element took its rise among the western Ishmaelites and through them was brought to Spain. From thence it was soon thereafter communicated even to America, where we meet a predilection for that Moorish style in the synagogue and the Masonic "temple."

Moorish style of architecture copied from India. § 58.

This leads us to a brief review of Arabian, or rather Moorish art in general. Its renown was so great, that the Byzantine emperors hurried to get patterns from Bagdad for their summer-residences, altho that "dream in marble", the Taj Mahal in Agra may, according to Garbe, have been designed by a French architect. The art of Islam, with all its praise, was limited to mere constructive peculiarities for the purpose of keeping the female departments secluded, cool, and cozy. Sculpture and paintings are wanting.

Taj Mahal built by a French architect. Garbe.

In the first place the influence of this architecture reached not much further than Sicily and Spain. Afterwards it was transplanted to Mexico and Havana, There Moorish style is recognised in the scarcity of windows toward the street, and from whence that taste stole itself to New-Orleans and even to Baltimore. Where, however, Moorish architecture met with the Aryan-Gothic taste could not be corrupted by the Moorish plagiarism of Delhi's style of building.

Moorish style could nowhere compete with the Gothic.

The "Fairy-Tales" which poetical minds found reflected in the lines of the arabesque are in fact reducible to the Hindoos. Images having been forbidden by the Koran, these pleasing medleys of decorative profusion were adopted from the vegetative form of Hindoo existence. This happy application of patterns with natural and geometrical lines in order to break the monotony of large spaces on walls and ceilings, and to give corridors and verandas and kiosks the character of snugness and ease, is the only merit of Arabian imitative art. But even tho the imitation be not overdone, as we observe now and then in our surroundings, the style itself must be termed phantastic, like an unsuggestive dream.

Images forbidden; Arabesques for decorative purposes after Indian patterns.

This fairy-tale style dates back to Ninive, and without much modification extends to Granada. Everywhere, in the alternation of branches and foliage, of stucco and mosaic patterns, in the stalactite compositions of pillared arches there rules the geometrical principle which at last becomes as tiresome as our wall-papers copied after them. Hence this art with all its soothing effects becomes emblematic of the insipid and jejune life in a seraglio.

The single attempt in the Lion's court of the Alhambra of Phenician origin.

The beastlike figures under the lion-fountain of the Alhambra show a connection with monuments from Phenician tombs—certainly none with the lion of the occidental romance.

Symbolises that Islam culture could never come to an understanding with the Occident.

The oriental trend of mind, as reflected within the imaginary form of consciousness predominant in Islam, could in no way, not even in its imitations, come to an understanding with the Occident.

§ 132. In the light of history the states founded upon Islam are upshots of hot impulsiveness. After a short period of bloom they relapse into languishing torpidness which is always a symptom of hopeless decadence. The cause of such consumption of all higher vitality lies in the prophet's portentous gift of polygamy.

Polygamy the curse of the Turano-Semitic culture of Islam, and its national life.

Since we have given all the credit due to the promising features of Arabian culture, which suddenly subdued Bagdad and there came to full bloom with glowing colors as also in Cordova, be it in mathematics, poetry or philosophy, we are constrained to lay open that pestilent cancer which always consumes the vital sap of any nation contaminated by it. The real curse of Islam is the total defilement of domestic life. Carnal indulgence and cruelty, that is, sensuality intensely heated from both ends of a more than brutal depravity, have parched the life of those nations which fell victim to the crescent at a time when already they were in a sinking condition.

Pedigree of SIRE cannot displace MATRI-monial purity in ennobling the race.

No household in our sense, no fatherland, no sociability.

No Mohammedan throne or state under the fates of Islam was ever firmly joined, because that corner-stone of the state was missing which in Rome at one time was, and is in Berlin at present, called the domestic hearth-stone. Nothing less than that sacred tie can bind the state; no power and no law can substitute the purity of matrimonial love. Mere pedigree of sire may improve the blood of Arabian stock, but it cannot take the place of normal matrimonial relationship. Destitute of family attachment and home life the state has no patriotism at disposal. The Mohammedan does not keep house, nor can he carry on husbandry in our sense of the term. Knowing the gentler sex only in its most inhumane subjection, he has no idea of the nobility of womanhood, and is consequently barred from cultivating sociability.

Harem life makes reform simply impossible.

The degrading and ignominious institution of the harem is a nuisance which renders education, culture of humane sentiment, and even political reform simply impossible from Bokhara to Bornu, where today sultan Omar is enthroned upon an old family chair imported from a Westphalian farmer.

Products of Koran and Talmud: beggary, filth,

and periodical pestilence.

The Koran produces a state of affairs in which law does not warrant protection; where gossip, and intrigue, bribery and fraud prevail in the management of state and village; where an accumulation of beggary and filth upon the streets constitute all that is prolific exactly as is the case with the adherents of the Talmud, wherever they, huddled close together, are left to themselves. It is this condition of things which must be designated as the cause for the periodical spreading of the plague from Mecca to all parts of the world.

The Mohammedan will sit, eat, sleep, dwell, and dress today on the Bosporus and in Algiers exactly as he did in the Byzantine period. Tradition and law retard any advance toward humanitarianism, notwithstanding the admonitions of the European powers.

If one is tired of Europe and has a fancy for certain profligacies he may throw deceptive covers over the stagnant world under the rule of Islam, and make allowances from sheer sympathy. He may be an enthusiastic admirer of the hospitality of a Bedouin sheik, or of the unlocked booths of the bazaars. But he must admit the truth, that through its fatalism Islam has stiffened the tough varnish of Semitic culture into a hard coat of lacquer, by which any sign of growth into a semblance of civilised life is suffocated.

The Semitic culture of Islam a parasite upon decayed ethnical matter.

Islam is the parasite upon decayed ethnic matter. It either mummifies or murders the nations over which it holds sway.

Arabic onslaughts repulsed by the two Karls as before by the two Catos.

§ 60, 66. 71, 88, 137, 142.

Two futile attempts have been made by peoples of the Arab regions to get Europe under their control. Each time their impetuous onslaughts were twice repulsed, first by the persistency of the two Catos and again by the firm resistance of the two Karls.

Comparison between the principles of Christian and Semitic culture.

Selfconsecration in the interests of universal welfare.

But whether the wily spirit of the twins, Koran and Talmud, has been defeated with the same success is quite another question, remaining to be solved, when the Asiatics come again to contest the superiority and leadership of the Indo-Germans, and to set up blind fate against forethought as to the destiny of the human race. Christian consciousness conceives the pursuit of selfculture as an ideal duty, in the fulfillment of which alone personal life can prosper, through which the faculties of the mind are made to cooperate in so harmonising each other as the composition of human nature requires, and as the complex relations to environments permit. Hence the assiduity of idealists to improve the ethical and the æsthetical, the scientific and social forms of life, and hence the interestedness in universal welfare. The endeavors are concentrated not only upon one's own home or nation, but tend to ameliorate the condition of mankind throughout the world, in ever rejuvenating and indefatigable aspiration, with a cheerful and buoyant enthusiasm to the extent of selfsacrifice. Christianity is conscious of the fact that the highest gifts of this life can be preserved only by advancing evangelisation; and that resistance against the Bad is

Proper way to fight
the Bad is to extend good influence.

most properly and effectively accomplished by defending the good and by spreading its beneficial influences. A standstill in this missionary work means retrogression.

Of a morality in this sense the Semite has utterly disqualified himself to form a conception, be he a Jew, or as a Mussulman. Aside from an ardent devotion and ceremonious servility where the occasion requires it, he only knows of ritualistic performances with the object of gaining some sort of a paradise. Selfish and pharisaical morality of Islam.

An order of life under determinism is the only rational mode the Semite can conceive suitable to his nature. He wants to have the method and number of such observances as definitely prescribed as the taxes upon his brain and muscles are exacted. This all being objectively fixed he can subjectively engage in hypocritical contrivances to get around the laws or at least even with them, just so as to maintain a little balance due himself, at any rate. Tho he may groan under the burden imposed upon him, yet he cannot gather sufficient courage to emancipate himself, lest he might have to suffer and another would, perhaps, enjoy the benefit. Moreover it is pious to let fate have its course. Not to interfere with the decrees of fate, that is, sullenly to bear the unavoidable is the fixed form of a piety cold and hard, which spares one the annoying duty of sympathising with the hardships of another. Order of life under determinism. Cause of unsympathetic reserve.

Apparently very scrupulous, with studied ostentation, the external laws are satisfied by hook or crook in order to outwit the degree of fate and to gain the clear profits of eternal bliss none the less. Meanwhile the mind and character not only remain unchanged but are thus trained to an increase of cunning and dissemblance. Whatever is allowed to the most extreme limit of allowances is determined not by the Semite's conscience, but by the written conscience contained in some precedent decision on record, which may be similar to a present case given, and which therefore may be deemed fit to be advocated or legalised. Conscience by proxi the Imam. § 120.

Here, says the Imam, it stands written. All that is necessary is to settle with and idemnify that paper conscience embodied in the Imam. And from him an official indulgence can be procured for almost any case since a man versed in the sacred books can certainly appeal to some Imam's past decision in any emergency. Once more we stand face to face with the probabilism of ancient thought which attempted to reduce fate to natural necessity, and to bring it under the power of comprehension in the system of the zodiac, in the method of auspices. The Imam is nothing but that very fatalism personified, wherewith arbitrariness may play hide and seek. Probabilism. § 73, 129, 163, 164.

§ 133. At the close of our review of this period the two representative personages of the time appear before us, viz: the Bishop of Rome and the Caliph of Mecca. Retrospect and prospect.

Here Gregory, the Great, the "Vicar of God"; there Muhamed, the prophet of Allah: both representing types of two hierarchies, rising at the remarkable time of A. D. 600, corresponding with a former cycle of nearly the same date. This contrast affords one of the instances where extremes meet, from which the glare as from a search-light is thrown upon many, if not all the great conflicts of the Middle-Ages. The one representing the Orient, sends heavy armored riders around the great crescent line from Bagdad to Zaragossa, to Tours in France, to the parts where the Huns before were routed. The other, representing the Occident, props himself upon the sons of the dear Brunhilde, and upon noble Theudolinde, and upon Phocas, the vicious usurper; at the same time he makes England the fulcrum for his cross-shaped lever. This lever he sets in beneath the Germans, who cover the first expenses with the first "Peter's pence", and with the lives of three thousand monks at Bangor who refuse to become Romanised. Pope of Rome Caliph of Mecca, A. D. 600. at the close of the cyclical period. from 600-500 B. C. to 500-600 A. D. § 62, 76, 124, 127, 133, 136, 141, 144. 145, 172.

Both are highpriests, claiming, under mandates of the same nature, (tho essentially different) equal validity for their antagonistic decisions (altho of equal invalidness) which dispose of the fates of the nations. Whether they acted upon their commissions and built another story upon the structure of history, under forms and with means equally different, subsequent events will reveal. Mandates of Gregory and Muhamed essentially different. Question whether the modes of their execution are equally different. § 145, 164.

We have arrived at the rounding up of the great circle of cultures in the Roman basin, which began 600—500 B. C., and closes with 500—600 A. D.

The transition into that circle occurred during the time of that significant "reformatory" movement alluded to, which oscillated through the nations from India to Italy. And now we add that it is this very vibration which returns with the precision almost of a tide, in the same circuit encircling and closing this whole æon.

19

At about A. D. 600, the organisation of the Church culminates in the person of Gregory; and in the transformation of the Pantheon and Parthenon into Christian Churches. At the same time the reaction of Semitism comes to a point or two in the Talmud-Koran. For the Talmud is just at this time completed and in full bloom at Sora and Pumbeditha.

Emperor Justinian has compiled and abridged the law, having become aware of the legislative judiciousness of the "Barbarians" who put the "Salic law" into Latin; of Alaric's "Breviarium"; of Euric's "Leges Barbarum"; and of Gundobald's good Burgundian laws in Geneva.

In the far Northwest the bards sing of Kædmon.

From Babylon to Bangor the same oscillating waves of mental excitement.

This cyclical wave designates transition from a world of subsiding culture to the threshold of a world just emerging from blood.

We look back upon the history of the Mediterranean basin as upon a Middle-Age preceding Mediæval times; as a unit divided in the mean by the secreted moment of the nativity between I. B. C. and I. A. D.

The main feature on the surface of this period is Rome's position in the midst of the nations as the reservoir of all the results contributed by them towards the civilisation of the world. We witnessed how the essence of Semitism was emptied into the mixture, isolating or resolving and separating, as well as affiliating and uniting the leading minds of the world. We witnessed how, borne hither by the Semites, the great sign was raised in the midst of this nation, designating in the three leading languages of antiquity, the center of adoration and elevation of cultus and culture, of history and humanity, of the world and —its time. We finally saw, how the life, with its world-embracing and salutary principles radiated from this Mediator, in whose retinue at the hostelry a certain Augustus served; from the Mediator who, by virtue of the palpable blessings flowing from Him, is henceforth acknowledged as the ground and the crown of the new issue.

The external symbol of the mediation as historically manifested is the cross upon the Pantheon and St. Sophia; internally the word, as the instrument of the Holy Spirit, is agreed upon, as a matter of course, to be "the" book not in need of human sanction. In the meantime the crescent rises from the eastern horizon. Kaaba and Koran in conjunction with Kabbala and Talmud, engage to eclipse our emblem which resembles a star deprived of its rays,—and to give the lie to the Book. The polar stress is now shifted to the forms of life under these signs; history is agitated, and the nations are made to tremble in suspense because of their ignorance of what all these struggles mean. Are the people of modern times nearer understanding them sufficiently to know that they are still encountered by the last twins born of Babylon?

F. SIXTH DIVISION.—THE SECOND CIRCLE OF NATIONS.

INDO-GERMANS IN THE MEDIÆVAL TIMES.

SYLLABUS.

Re-entering our second of the ethnical circles we anticipate —seeing how the new historical coefficient, imparted to humanity in the midst of the nations at the middle of the times, is received and appropriated by the Europeans —the disposition of the ethnic groupings and of what metal the Germanic people are made. In the second chapter we will observe their labor under a sense of duty and equity, and elicit the importance of the German form of Government for the Occident. The third will acquaint us with the bearings of the great conflicts between Church and State. These contests for the supremacy we will learn to recognise as simply the form under which the struggle between Aryanism and Semitism is perpetuated. On the one side, the Aryans develop their fitness for comprehending and defending the Christian thought, becoming thereby the representatives of the Humanitarian ideas. On the other hand, the Semitic element concentrates itself into the same exclusive particularism and domineering attitude, and reveals the same world-consciousness and distorted Messianic desires, as has become obvious in the Sanhedrin—now blended with the Roman ideas of rule and unity.

CH. I.   GERMAN CHARACTERISTICS: KARL THE GREAT.

§ 134.   The Western Aryans under different names, but with traits of character distinctly similar, now present a picture of a new culture totally different from all the preceding cultures.

We first study the physiognomy of the Indo-Germans, if so we may call their ethno-psychological frame of mind. It is the more necessary, as in these features the Aryan qualification for the leadership in the work of civilising the world is at once recognisable.

When Cornelius Tacitus wanted to warn the Romans of his days, he cried out: "Not the Samnite, not the Punian, nor the Spanish and Gaulish tribes, not even the Parthians have so often administered warnings of danger to us; for a greater power than even that of the Parthian Kings is the liberty of the Germans."

With this quotation Giesebrecht leads over from Roman to German History. We may do the same.

In order that we may not be hampered in concentrating our attention upon the physiognomy of the Germans by reviewing the externals of the situation, we refer to the remarks on their migration to Europe.

Of the condition of the peoples North of the Alps before the time of Marius, historical data are almost entirely missing, so that only by way of conjecture it becomes probable, that it was the power of Celtic swarms accompanied by Cimmerians and Teutons, whom Brennus brought upon the Romans to teach them for the first time to keep their agreements.

The region of France between the Seine and Garonne seems to have been the first European home of the Celt-Iberians, from whence they settled the northern part of Spain, Britany and the Low Countries where they got somewhat mixed with the Germans. The Romans soon sized these "brothers" with their broad shoulders and high shields as very strong men. They seem to have assisted in reducing Syracuse and in the pillage of Carthage; to have roamed wrestling about the plaines of Troyes; from their midst the torch was thrown into the temple of Diana at Ephesus. Then Frankish horsemen in Roman service were encamped on the banks of the Euphrates, and Saxons were lying in the Arabian sands. When the Goths, following the Swedes or Swiss, left the Scandinavian peninsula, and landed in the delta of the Vistula and afterwards roved through the wide steppes of Sarmatia advancing toward the Danube, Dniepr, and Theiss, where their tall forms alarmed the Byzantine sentinels—a new element entered into History.

This is not to be understood as if the Northerners had not come in contact with other peoples heretofore. Proofs of this fact are lacking only because the back-lying countries from which they emerged, were perhaps not known to, at least not mentioned by, others. It is an acknowledged fact, however, that a thousand years previously Assyria had carried on a lively traffic with the Dakians, with the Getes, and with the Scythians still further North.

Objects of art and utensils of Semitic genre, weapons and tools were then brought up from Babylon to the Baltic upon routes still traceable. In return northern goods were taken back from the mouth of the Volga to the royal palaces of Assyria and Babylon. If we take it for granted that these objects discovered in Siebenbuergen (as represented by Thorma Broos in the "Archives" of Johannes Ranke) came in large quantities from the East to the Dakians and Gates along the Danube, as is affirmed by other things found and by many circumstances:—then these urns, amulets, images and decorative articles, or useful tools were imported from Akkad-Assyrian firms.

At about 530 A. D., as we adopt Ranke's statement, the Germans are settled, and govern themselves and the preceding occupants of the countries between Hungary and Helgoland, from the Tweed to the Atlas. Their reverses in Africa were compensated by the prosperity of the Lombards in the valley of the Po river.

In Rome the spoils of the whole world had been hoarded up. It is questionable whether the wealth of Europe today exceeds the value of the booty delivered at the capitol in the period from the triumphal entry of Scipio to that of Pompey. Even after the pillage by Alaric shiploads of treasures were still left for Geiseric, and for being swallowed up by the blue Tyrrhenian waters. Rome's monopoly had burst, the proud city broke beyond recovery. Every crevice in the huge structure of state was wide enough for the stout men from the Dniepr and the Weser to squeeze themselves through, and to take possession of one room after another in the crumbling palace. It is astonishing how quickly they accustom themselves to the novel scenes wherever throngs of them make themselves at home. They are discreet and conservative enough to let things continue which do not interfere with the immediate creation of a culture of their own. Turning up the subsoil, they prepare new ground, consisting of the weather-beaten and decomposing rubbish left from the old fabric—and of the fertilising new deposits of virgin soil, brought down from the forests with the avalanches in the last of the great migrations.

[Margin notes:]
Aryan Circle.
Struggles for supremacy between emperor and pope.
Rome under bans of the Semitic ideal of a world-theocracy.
Tacitus on liberty of the Germans, rendering them the peers of Romans, and a menace to their power. GIESEBRECHT. § 138, 139, 141, 175.
Romans taught for the first time to fulfill covenants.
Germans assisted in burning the temple of Ephesus; in the pillage of Carthage;
In Roman service on the Euphrates.
Trade between Getes (Goths) and Assyro-Babylon.
Siebenbuergen discoveries. THORMA BROOS.
Germans settle and govern themselves in all the territories between the Tweed and Mt. Atlas. RANKE.
The end of Rome, and entrance of the Germans.
The new principle planted into the upturned soil.

In their soil they carefully plant the principles, and build the foundations of their social life, viz: The feudal rights; their preference for rural life; their aristocratic sentiments of honor, fidelity, and liberty; their esteem of womanhood. Let us analyse these fine and far-reaching predispositions, and if possible, trace them back to their fatherland.

§ 135. The first scene of action of each, the Phenicians, the Hellenes and the Romans, had been limited. The talent of the Semites was their calculation.

The task of the Aryans in Rome was the establishment of law and the State, as it had been the cultivation of art and science in Greece. Each had to improve its part; one the intellect, the other the will; the one liberty, the other discipline. Now the Germans come in with their sentiment, the cultivation of which had been neglected hitherto by almost all the other nations. With this, their natural contribution to history, they introduced the fundamental principle for any thorough education of the mind. This peculiarity of the German mind is very old; it is traceable to the Iranian highlands. Its development went on slowly, but surely. It is designed to continue its steady growth in all combinations, and under all circumstances. The season of bloom arrives a little later in the North, and with the Germanic peoples it shall last a little longer. For, pervaded and permeated with Christianity, it shall spend its fragrance to not less prolific generations of the future, and to the world.

The continuance of stimulative attempts, the ever recurring dreams of men about the coming and going of things and events, testify to the inner promptings of human nature to master the environments and circumstances by thought, to take possession of the world through the mind. A person can find his position only in a well comprehended whole, in which he may assert himself and persist as a personality. Especially the Aryan form of consciousness reveals this tendency.

For disregarding the discussion of a comparison of the Aryan theories of cosmogony at this moment we deem ourselves excused. The Hindoo mind is filled with them; it wrought a variety of world-emanations and world-destructions. The changes are conceived as a perpetual play of rise and decay. The Chaldean, but not the Aryan, way of explanation was, to fix the changes to the stars. The Persian and the German Iranians harbor a hope, that in the three latter of the twelve millenniums Ahriman, the bad one, will be the victor. For, notwithstanding his victory, he will be overthrown in his last endeavor to destroy the world; whilst this destructive intent will be the very occasion for its glorious renovation. Alfadar brings it all about, he prevails over all rebellions, and of the happiness thus ensuing there is no end.

The philosophy of the Occident never slighted this belief in a final glorification. Heracleitos touched upon this thought, which was brought to notice still more by the Stoa. But in the German and Northern "Saga" it comes out most distinct and pronounced.

If the German mind was bent upon a bright future and on victory, it was not at variance with the Aryan method of constructing original tradition into myths full of deep meaning. The German simply keeps his future more vividly before his mind. He remembers more clearly that a deep and broad degradation cannot but cause the annihilation of the Old World.

He meditates on the shortening of the world's day; upon the fact that the dusk of the night sets in; that with the lengthening shadows the powers of darkness arise. Even the old gods, being implicated in the fight of men against the weird fiends,

are plunged into the universal conflagration. The Greeks and Romans conceived the crisis in the same light, except that in their opinion it had been overcome already in the contest with the Titanic nations.

The Germans preserve a deeper insight into the problem of the Bad, and they remain in the fight.

This is the profound and far-reaching significance of the world's drama in Teuton mythology, and of the conviction of it in the German character. This concept is, at the same time, a premonitory apprehension of the entire course of the world's history. It encourages the Germans to face the combat and to resist the Bad; it makes them interested in the studies of ethics and history.

The gods are imagined as having lived in a state of blissful innocence. As such beings the Ason are powerful joists in the structure of the universe. They are enthroned on high as the twelve judges in Asgard. There they perambulate upon green meadows. Their twelve chairs stand in the golden castle around the high seat of Odin. Such is the "golden age" of the Germans.

But with the arrival of the fiendish daughters of sin,stinginess, envy and thirst of gold,that gladsome innocence is lost to the gods. The evil women create the dwarfish gnomes to bring the glittering gold from the deep, black holes of the earth. And with the gold comes murder. The impassionate desires, the Wanen (the vain ones, the crazed) fall from the gods. Their ramparts are torn down and scattered. What shall, then, become of a world where the gods themselves fall in temptation? The answer is given by Igdrasil, the world ash-tree. Its roots drink from the deep grounds of that which is finite, altho the deep springs are the drippings which come down from the spheres of the infinite.

Mythologoy of the Edda.

Goblins dig gold.

Wanen.

World-ash-tree.

Up to Walhalla this ash-tree reaches; but "Transiency" is gnawing at its verdure. Eaten away by vermin from above and from below, the world-tree finally becomes rotten, and pines away. To fill the measure of sorrow, Iduna is ravished and carried off by the "Winter-storm;" the withered leaves all drop; every sign betokens that the world must succumb. Baldur, the luminous one, too, is overthrown, pierced by the mistletoe. This was, the Edda thinks, the saddest calamity which could have happened to the gods and to men. That was perpetrated by the gloomy, hateful Loki. Baldur can, of course, not be gotten back from hell; but how should he be revenged on Loki? How is this arch-fiend to be cast into fetters and in the bans of seclusion? With the intestines of his offspring it may be done.

Walhalla.

End of the old world.

Iduna.

Baldur.

Mistle-toe.

Loki must lie in bondage till the time of the gods dawns, when the moral bearers of the world vanish in the dusk, when all bonds of order and discipline are loosened, when the age of right and reason changes into an age of the sword, when the very sea roars up in rebellion. Thus arrives the day of final decisions, of the world-battle. Odin at the head of the Asen leads on to war, wearing his golden helmet. But he falls in the combat with Wulf, who is, in turn, felled by Widdar. The latter strikes down all the infamous wretches, and out of the world's conflagration rises the purified new world in glory.

Loki.

"Gœtterdæmmerung".

Asen—Odin.

Wulf—Widdar.

The pious and free men solemnise the victory. The renewed gods dwell upon Idafield, under the pleasure of the One who embraces the world, of whom an old hymn sings: "Once another One will come, more powerful than even he, whose name, however, I cannot as yet venture to tell." (Quoted from Sepp).

The world-embracing one to come.

This is the melancholy complaint of the nations, the marvelous tone of which dies away in the far north as a vision arching up above the blood-soaked earth like a wondrous rainbow, refracting the colors of truce which are hung out from Heaven after the catastrophe has been passed through, one end resting upon the Himalayas, the other upon Iceland.

From the world-conflagration rises the purified world in glory.

The horrible and unnatural massacres of the body-guards on the graves of princes by which servants were to be sent after them to the other world, remind us of the usage practiced from time immemorial by all the Aryans and Semites. The killing of the prisoners of war, of the domestic servants, of the retinue of attendants we find among the Germans, the Celts, the Scythians, and the Mongolians. It has been ascertained to have existed in the substrata of Greek and Roman culture. The account given by Leo Diaconus about the sacrificial obsequies at a Russian funeral in the year 921 A. D. is suggestive as to the ancient customs of the northern people in general. It was an act of humanism that the killing of captives was abandoned and they were rather sold as slaves.

Servants sacrificed among Aryans.
Leo Diaconus.

At Upsala in Denmark stood the temple described by Adam of Bremen. This edifice was gilded all over, and its glittering contours could be seen from quite distant plains. It contained the images of three gods: Thor, the most powerful, with his hammer thrones in the middle, for he reigns in the heavens creates the thunder-weather, and the fruitful seasons. Beside him sits Wodan carrying the arms; he instigates war and guides the battle. Fricco, the Fro, the mild god, is the third, vouchsafing to men peace and joy. Close to the temple stands a miraculous tree with many branches and ever green. From its roots a spring bubbles up in which they are accustomed to offer human sacrifices. If no trace reappears of those thrown in alive, it is considered the good sign of the gods accepting the offering and granting what has been prayed for. After this nine different animals are offered in their blood. The carcasses are hung up in the sacred park of the temple. Horses, dogs, men, are thus sacrificed, under the singing of elegies. One of the messengers of the Christian God has told us, that he saw there and counted on one of these occasions seventy corpses of men hanging upon the trees.

Thor's temple at Upsala.
§ 136. Adam of Bremen.

Wodan
Fricco.

Human sacrifices.
§ 41, 54, 110.

Such then, up to comparatively recent times were the usages of the Germans. They were no better than all the other heathenish peoples. The best which can be placed to their credit is their primitive force of body and mind, their sense of honor, and their decisiveness of character as revealed in all their usages, thoughts and songs.

In the scenes around Arthur's table and at the royal board where Adelgais, the Longobard, breaks horseshoes, bones of Buffaloes, of stags and bears as if they were hemp-stems, we see their unsophisticated honesty, bravery and sentimentality. With reference to religious consciousness there glimmers from a world of fairy-tales, myths, and legends (upon which we must dwell somewhat more fully later on) even the old snake-worship, precisely as it shines through the old Indian hymns. The queen of snakes with her dainty, precious crownlet, and the domestic pet snakes doubtless show a common source of religious remembrance in all nations.

Traces of snake-worship in the legends.
§ 43, 45, 48, 48, 54' 55, 86, 146.

Whether it can be said on such grounds that the Germans had been specially gifted or "predestined" for Christianity, as often has been alleged, or whether the idea should not be refuted as an exaggeration, we need not decide. But this is true, that as to truthfulness and chasteness they excelled others. And this also is obvious, that the prophecy of the concluding scene of the world's drama (as the Northerners conceived it according to their myths), meets the cordiality of the new doctrine almost

half way with German sincerity. The Germanic mind brings along a manly trust combined with a childlike and expectant hope. It is, furthermore, happily qualified for the reception of Christianity by its ardent yearning for the advent of a king of all nations whose authority extends through Heaven and over the whole world: "of rulers the greatest and richest, akin to all the kinsfolks in common kinship."   And

this new and noble prince is to lift up a new world out of the world's conflagration. To name Him they do not venture!

How they listened to and embraced the glad tidings, when communicated by the soldiers who with the legions of Treves had returned from the spot where it had happened; and when these fascinating stories—exactly answering their innermost but indistinct expectations—were in an enthusing manner and more clearly set forth

again in the speeches of the Culdeans (or Caledonians), and the Anglo-Saxon kinsmen, becomes evident from what followed.

§ 136. Pagan forms of cultus and pagan usages were retained a long time, and because of having been made subservient in part to symbolise Christian truths, were never thoroughly abolished.

Around the churches, former temples of gods, the heathen Christians would hold their common meals, camping under the trees or in linen tents. Upon the roasted steer they would feast as in the sacrificial meals of yore, excepting that in the places of former gods they would call upon the saints to go with them. When they rode to the massmeetings, religious or political, they would take along upon their floats the broad wagons drawn by oxen, in place of the images of their former gods those of the Merovingian Kings. And then one would have

heard across the meadows and along the peaceful valleys the sounds of the litanies coming out of yonder cloisters half hid by the dear old "hallowed" oaks and beaches and surrounded by fruit orchards. And among the crowd could have been heard at random the oaths of fidelity by St. Peter and all the other saints.

The suffering Redeemer of the world, however, was accepted rather reluctantly. What was their concept of the "Healing one"? In their "Heliand," that epic which

belongs to no particular tribe, the cognition held in common by all the Germans is succinctly mirrored. Outside of this they could agree in scarcely anything. The "German nation" always had to be taken as a mere abstract generalisation. The mark of its nationality is the predominance of envy which will allow preponderance to no tribe. That nationality consists of as many dialects and clan-interests as

would have been more than necessary to make the concentration of a fixed power utterly impossible. Federacies, however, are held together so much the firmer by the strong ties of fidelity; and the idea of the fatherland makes them terrible to any enemy. The German mind is prepossessed by a tendency to bias, partiality and queerness; singularities are cultivated to a detrimental degree. Inclinations of this sort are of doubtful value; and yet these defects alone account for the fact that no other nation has so many centers of culture, and enjoys such a diversity of excellent traits; and that no race equals the Germans in profundity of knowledge and scholarship. These national characteristics ever threaten political disruption, but they are

also favorable to a level brain and to the "balance of power;" they cause the cultivation of love for the fatherland and for the mother-tongue.

The development of a vigorous acorn which after being detached from its tree, sprouts and grows into an oak of its own, thus multiplying and differentiating the oak's organism into a profusion of foliage, acorns and so forth into an entire forest, may illustrate the mode in which the Germanic race became detached and developed into a variety of prolific nations. In this manner they formed a belt of minor political bodies from Cape North to Carthage. This belt everywhere stood the tests of strength as to its national connections as well as mutual protection.

In a special manner did the Germans constituting this belt preserve and nourish

a sense of liberty and independence. The belt of colonies with clear-cut German character formed a wall against new agglutinations of old ideas into a world-monarchy with its complement of deadening despotism, after which Romanism ever hankers, in determined opposition to Germanism.

It is worth while to examine more closely what it was that kept the fragments together, until they were able to come to an understanding as to the terms upon which all could stand shoulder to shoulder.

Let a scene be presented to our minds of those times when under the last convulsions of the dying culture and among its ruins a new culture like a fresh crop covered the deep-ploughed soil.

Do you see the old temple this side the cluster of dwelling houses, which once used to be a summer-resort of city folks who called themselves optimates? Its pillars still support a gorgeous cornice which holds back the dilapidated roof. The marble cubit at the base of the pillar is shoved aside; the heavy slab at the base of the other is cracked, both by the roots of a tree, the solitary remnant of the sacred grove. Thistles and wild roses ramify their roots into the cracks, helping to drive the foundations asunder. To the clefts in the wall and the cracks below a German veteran soldier has fastened a few beams for the support of the roof of his cottage thus being nestled under the classic portico. He has now become a settled farmer. His goats have climbed up to yonder mosaic floor of an old mansion, whose tottering portals still lean in the same position as they had once been forced open. The German has transformed the crumbling splendor of the atrium into his hay-mow.

Notice yonder aquaeduct of a thousand years standing, under the ruined and partly overhanging arches of which the beams of a temporary chapel are secured into the cleaving joints of the substructure. And in this chapel a home-carved picture of a saint is set up. Upon a spirited charger, a high functionary of the Church, in a white dalmatica with purple seam, rides through the wild field of mossy ruins, followed by a train of deacons, greeted with reverential bows by the blond peasants as well as by the black haired Jew and the dark complexioned fish-monger from Venice.

The settler's boys, lounging about the causeway which leads to town, look as tho they felt quite at home and would become soldiers first in order to see and to fight the world, and then become freeholders of the land of their father and of more, too. The Jew beside his curbstone-stand covered with cashmere shawls and silken textile goods, with weapons from Damask and jewels from Golconda and with coins to loan, leisurely instructs his boy how to become the future bondholder, since none but they are privileged to take interest on moneys lent.

Over the youthful activity in the fields and upon the markets, at the beginning of a new order of things, presides as yet, for instance in Soissons or in Lorch, the old Roman prefect, who in the distant, half submerged provinces still represents the rapidly changing government at the capitol. But in the great cities some Germans from the provinces are already foremost in attempting to form a new commonwealth. Imperial legislative and executive officers form the shell around the newly arrived masses of robust subjects.

Where the hollow shell of imperial government gave way, as was the case in Britany, Batavia, and Gaul, where people had to protect and learn to govern themselves, there they were guyed by the network of hierarchal government, knit together after the pattern of the by-gone civil authorities. So do the roots of the mountain fir hold together their part of the slope, after the rocks below have become burst and plunged down, the ground once supported by them following. At last the shadow of imperialism entirely vanishes from the Occident. Loose, single parts of official Rome here and there keep up some semblance of management until all personal authority becomes defunct, and only the regulative forms are left in the hands of a few patricians and the clergy. But the new inhabitants have become acquainted already with, and have accustomed themselves to, these forms of law and order upheld by ecclesiastical sanction and enforced by judicious leaders, in concert with bishops and abbots. The laws are collected and administered everywhere, so as to judge each according to the acknowledged rights of his own country.

Theodoric, the great Ostragoth, may serve to illustrate how the Germans planted their own civilisation in "adopted fatherlands." He is a prince of eminent wisdom and virtue, but not at all so exceptional a ruler as to be too good for a general example.

Filled with the veneration in which a youth of good breeding will look up to wise teachers of wide experience and high up in years, so Theodoric looked upon the college of senators. Nothing is more plain than his sincere regard for Christianity, and his prudent conservatism with respect to the customary civil institutions. As soon as he took the reigns of government he vowed to maintain justice above any private interest, This he conceived as the only duty and single prerogative of the imperial office; and he kept his vow to the perfect satisfaction of the different nationalities. Writing and brain work was left to those conversant with it. The sword and the plow were wielded by his own countrymen to whom this was no innovation. By his honesty of purpose to attend to the public welfare and by his assiduousness he won universal respect; in this consisted the secret of his success as a ruler. Only his tolerance against the catholics was abused by them. His efforts to protect persecuted Christians of his own, the Arian, persuasion were construed into a justification of intrigues against the rule of a foreign heretic of whose influence the domineering hierarchy became jealous, so that after his death from remorse his memory was made infamous.

Marginal notes:

Scene in Italy at the period of transition: illustrating the beginning of German culture with agriculture. § 63, 139, 222.

(agriculture rejected § 122, 149.)

Civil government passing into the hands of the clergy.

Petty states forming under adjustable laws of their own. § 133, 136, 141.

Roman imperialism vanishes from the Occident.

Theodoric the great Ostragoth.

His exemplary reign.

Ulfilas translates the Bible into the Gothic.

Next to Theodoric is Ulfilas, his elder contemporary and the first translator of the Bible into the Germanic idiom, the best type of the German mind in the early times of European reconstruction. Both show noble traits in their lives of which impulsiveness and hatred of duplicity ought not to be considered as destructive to their reputation.

History educates nations toward unity.
§ 78, 79, 142, 143, 144, 156, 171.

§ 137. The youthful nations were impressed with reverence for the unfortunate, tottering majesty of the old empire; and this sentiment was not at all unfavorable to their training for citizenship. They enwrapped themselves with the loose hanging cloak to which may be compared the mighty name of imperial Rome, whose splendor had reached into the dreams of their childhood.

Karl's coronation, desire of the nations to restore authority under an ideal representative.

When Karl the Great was crowned emperor in form and by right, the longstanding desire of the young nations was gratified. The attraction which a large unit exerts upon single parts, had drawn them across the Alps and educated them to the thought of forming a unitary social organism. The involuntary trend of public opinion now saw its ideal realised in the new German emperor.

Karl's cardinal idea: to be Constantine's successor.
§ 123, 132, 133, 137, 142, 145, 178.

When Karl took the crown from the ecclesiastical dignitary, he esteemed himself —we beg to keep this in mind—successor of Constantine and Theodosius.

"He is"—as Duemmler correctly observes—"both the most advanced man and influential restorer of the Latin sciences for the benefit of the Middle Ages, and at the same time the creator of the first German literature."

Patronising Latin science and German literature. **DUEMMLER.**

The palatinate of Aachen resembles a refractor focusing the old time and the new. Along with Byzantine embassadors the white Tunics of the Moors, and the turbans of the Saracens from Cordova glittering with precious stones, and the long linen gown of Saxon nobility appear before Karl in his firm, carved arm-chair. The purple toga of the Longobard sets off the contrast to the uncombed Avar. Then, again, Anglo-Saxon monks, Irish priests in long white cowls, and princes of the Church, like Hildebold of Cologne, receive a hearing. In Karl's state-hall, during his short stay at home, we observe teachers, students, and members of the chapel choir; pupils from the ranks of the poor, attending the new high school of the court; and men recognised as luminaries of their time by all the world, such as Alcuin Bishop of Tours, Theodulf from Orleans, Einhard, the emperor's son-in-law, and Agilbert, all in long cassocks trimmed with fur. The minutest details of everyday life are deemed significant enough to receive due attention, not always to the detriment of more weighty affairs of state.

Scene at Karl's palatinate at Aachen.
§ 142.

Fondness for the nimbus of Byzantium.
§ 142.

To Byzantium Karl looked, not only for acknowledgment of his right to the Roman insignia, but also for knowledge and for—courtly etiquette.

Intercourse with the western empire.

There was the monopoly of the fur-trade which imported the largest part from the forests of Karl's domains. There the Venetians exchanged occidental goods for oriental articles of luxury, which they sold at the mass in Pavia to Franconian nobles. All this was observed at the palatinates in Aachen and Ingelheim.

This Byzanz, however, appeared to Karl as more than an emporium of trade. It was, as we have seen, the museum of the classics. In the square stood the Pythian Apollo, the gigantic figure of Juno, brought from Croesus' temple at Samos. Here stood Heracles, chiseled by Lysipp for the Tarentines; there the metal cast of the snakes which once supported the Delphic tripod. Pillars of sea-green serpentine from the temple of Diana in Ephesus served now to carry the cupola of St. Sophia; and most renowned of all—the pillars from the Solomonic temple. All this aided in magnifying the eastern emperor in the eyes of Karl, who possessed nothing of the kind.

Constantinople the bridge over which Orientalism (as later on also corrective: classic culture) was conveyed to Europe. **HERDER.**

Antiquity is enchanting, and it served to uphold the glorious throne, glorious as seen from such a distance as Karl was from it. Herder called this throne the bridge over which the classic world would pass into the new. It was what Karl's throne was to the Germanic world.

It was not only in the time of Columbus' boyhood, when Constantinople fell and the scholars brought their books to Italy,—it was even as early as Karl's time—that Constantine's city served as a conductor of oriental ideas by way of the Latin nations. This city then already did not only send gobelin tapestry and fine embroidery, woolen stuffs of exquisite make and fashion, but above all the glitter of aristocratic vainglory.

We know nobility ever to cultivate a predilection for the nimbus of the Antique, and the Germans always thought much of what comes "from afar". Let us see what was imported from Byzanz on that score.

§ 127, at the end 142, 150.

Ambitious for appearances of dignity, Karl resorted to imitating oriental gravity, and managed to get possession of three silver tables. Upon one could be seen the picture of the whole known world; upon the other that of Rome; Constantinople sparkled upon the .third. This circumstance is very descriptive of the clever judgment which Karl had formed of the situation of the world. Throwing eager glances over to Constantinople and up to Rome, he perceives, as in a prophetic vision, all the complications which not only kept up Mediæval agitation, but also loomed up again before the imagination of Napoleon, and which down to our own days involve the touch-me-not of the eastern hemisphere.

Margin: Nobility always favors the nimbus of the antique. § 40, 67, 73, 78, 135, 137.

Karl must have had such a foreboding, when in his time he meditated upon this problem. For it was then that "the Holy Roman Empire of the German Nation" entered upon its duty of warding off oriental invasions, whilst at the same time plenty of portentous oriental influences were admitted unaware.

Margin: Karl's three silver tables, emblematic of the problems henceforth agitating the Germanic and Romanised nations up to the time of Napoleon. § 122, 125, 139, 178.

When Emperor Theodosius walked the streets of Constantinople, he used to please the people by wearing the shoulder-cape of Senuphius, the anchoret; and in this costume he also went to battle. The predecessors of Karl, the Franconian king, had long before adopted this pious fashion by wearing the mantle of St. Martin, when they started for the seat of war. Charles the Bald, long after Karl, continued this pious custom with his dalmatica trailing down from a silken cloth that was fastened beneath the diadem around his head. For,—so the annals of Fulda say—"he showed contempt of native Franconian manners, and held Greek glory to be the highest".

Margin: "Holy Roman empire of the German nation" opened its career by warding off oriental invasions. § 67, 78, 97, 125, 132.

The escutcheons of the European States today witness how the Byzantine taste for pomp and nimbus was perpetuated in order to cover up a wrong principle, and to amuse the people with something outlandish, with orientalism.

Margin: Yet admitting portentous oriental influences. §§ 20, 62, 67, 78, 81, 85, 95, 97, 122, 123, 121, 125, 126, 129, 130, 131, 139, 142, 146, 149, 150, 185, 188, 191.

Karl, after all, did not think quite as much of eastern pomp as his .weak descendants. He saw the ridiculous weakness over there. From this circumstance he concluded that he himself was destined to establish the true succession upon the throne of the Roman Empire. When he directed the collection of the old German "shield-songs", or when he forced the Saxons into subjection after eighteen expeditions, and when he ordered the statue of Theodoric to be brought down from Ravenna and to be set up before his castle in Aachen; he already posed as the personified continuance of the old monarchy.

Margin: Byzantine court-etiquette. The meaning of the Dalmatica, embellishing national escutcheons. Karl deemed himself the true successor upon the throne of the entire Roman empire. § 132, 133, 136, 139, 142.

This thought actually pervaded his whole policy; and he was encouraged in it by those who understood how to make his good qualities subservient to their own ultimate aims.

Margin: Sycophants: ¶ 71, 125, 126, 150.

"Hail to the Christ"—exclaims the Salian law—"who loves the Franks! May He protect their kingdom, for it is the nation which with the sword has shaken off the Roman yoke from its neck; the nation which, after having accepted of baptism, adorned the bodies of the martyrs with gold and precious stones, of the martyrs who once were burned, or decapitated with the ax by the Romans."

Margin: Conception of the Savior Byzantinised, § 125.

Evidently, this Christ is a copy of that conception of an awe-inspiring ruler, into which the Byzantine court-theology had disfigured the Savior. At the rear wall of the apsis in the Aachen cathedral, to which one ascends from the tenebrous church with its multitude of poorly arranged and clumsy galleries, there is enthroned a callous, gloomy figure upon the golden background of the painting—the Judge of the World. Emperor Karl was surrounded by objects wrought in such style wherever he turned his eye or his step. Textures which he imported, especially those for sacred use, golden decorations which he ordered from his goldsmiths; evangelaries which he made to be copied and bound, chapels which he built—everything breathes Byzantine taste. Even the suggestions intimated to him by the Eastern patriarch to take the part of the inconoclasts he did not altogether discourage, to the chagrin of the pope.

Margin: as is most obvious even at Aachen. Karl not adverse to Byzantine court-theology,

If the actions of Karl are scrutinised, we find in them all his guiding idea as to the important position of Constantinople. He was not averse to that attitude even, which the Byzantine court maintained with respect to theology. He himself assumed a somewhat similar position, so that it was just this Cesaro-papism which cautioned the hierarchy to look to its rights as against imperial infringments upon their own domain, at the proper occasion.

Margin: which cautioned the Roman hierarchy to look to its rights as against imperial infringements.

CH. II. DEVELOPING PRINCIPLES OF THE EUROPEAN CIVILISATION.

§ 138. The undercurrent of the ensuing history of the Aryans in New Europe we found in a great measure to be determined by the mythically biased form of consciousness, which they had brought along from their original home. Every group of this race is saturated with the elements of their common source. The modifications observed so far were produced by the various localities they severally occupied.

German peculiar ideas concerning freedom and right of possession.

Now let us consider, in the first place, to what concepts of freedom and to the right to possess the Germanic nations had advanced. In the preceding chapter we spoke, after all, merely of the Franconian part of the German empire.

The Pipins, Karl's ancestors, had all been of what we now would call Dutch descent; but the Franks had to a large extent become mixed with the Romanised Gauls. The pure Germans were subjugated to the idea of a Roman empire only after more than fifty fierce battles.

Germanic races not savages as misrepresented by Robinson and Guizot.

In short, we so far reviewed the interlappings of the vanishing Roman culture with the advancing Germanic civilisation. We perceived some of the commotion generated by the commingling upon the soil of a newly forming nation, where parts may appear comparatively uncultivated, but in no way as savage as Robinson and Guizot once misrepresented them.

Among the Franks the old pagan morality went to pieces. H. v. Leo.

The people of France came to view first, simply because they were just then the most prominent and pugnacious, sequent to many divisions of the empire among the Karolingian heirs. It was among the Franks, as H. v. Leo has proved, that the old pagan morality went to pieces. The ruins of that morality were the results of Roman dissipation and tribal jealousy between Celto-Romans and Germans, as became obvious in the wars between Brunhilde and Fredegunde.

Two sets of ethics externally enjoined. Wuttke, Dorner.

Among these ruins a very peculiar form of Christianity planted a rude code of manners and morals. We may even say with Wuttke and Dorner that two sets of ethics were elaborated: one for the worldly people or laity, the other for the orders, which enjoined the necessity of certain observances, especially of penances. In no other way could the heinous crimes of the Merovingian times be accounted for. In all the ferocious movements of that period there is only one feature helping us over the disgust. The thought of national unity was upheld under the unflinching resistance against tyrannical measures. The aspiration in this direction would have worked different results, if the fighters with their unsophisticated loyalty had been enlightened enough not to allow themselves to be made the tools of a hundred intrigues.

History must grope its way of progress, especially in matters of ethics. § 123, 127, 146

We know how history can only feel its way along the paths of progress, much more so on the narrow way of ethical improvement. As it was, the ethical conceptions had grown into a wilderness of underbrush.

Preservation of old German virtues under Culdean gospel-preaching notwithstanding the slanders of Boniface. Ebrard and Leo. § 135, 188, 139, 156, 158, 165.

The discrimination between the two sets of ethics alone explains how and why the new doctrines, brought by the unromanised Culdean missionaries into interior Germany, wrought so totally different results. Theirs was gospel preaching, falling into the minds of an unadulterated nation. Under their original usages and traditions, those noble Thuringians had preserved their natural virtues. When the missionaries met them, they found them a cordial and susceptible people, without casuistic reflection, but with naive sentiments grown from chaste habits, notwithstanding the slanders of Boniface.

Leo from his point of view could not appreciate this example of Bible-Christianity among the unmixed Germans, which Ebrard has elucidated and substantiated in a masterly manner from documentary sources.

We shall observe later on, how among the underbrush of Romanised ethics a tender root remained alive in this central and secluded region, which, figuratively speaking, we designate the heart of Germany.

The Roman nations had been the road-builders, in aid of distributing occidental culture in the same way as public highways are essential for the distribution of merchandise. They communicated the proceeds of ancient culture to the Aryans of the North, the good and the bad.

Later consequences of Thuringian aversion to being Romanised. § 127, 134, 132, 144, 156, 169.

The "Barbarians" could not discriminate if they were imposed upon in the transaction. The Southern Aryans communicated Christianity clothed with the forms of their old culture. It is not to be expected of the Goths and Franks that under so sparse preaching of the word of the cross, they should have been able to distinguish alloy or emballage from the genuine essence of religion. Christianity of that far less defiled quality, of the kind that Basilius and his Cappadocian friends had taught, which the Culdeans had preserved from patristic times, deeply touching the soul's chords, and which the Swiss and Thuringians had

Peculiarity of the Romanised form of Christianity.

accepted with the Gospel as preached by Willibrord, Gallus, Fridolin and other Anglo-Saxons, a century previous to Boniface,—such Scriptural subjective Christianity alone generates that spirituality, which sets men free and to thinking. This pristine piety, much like that of the Culdeans who had planted it in the heart of Germany,

Inner life of piety.

did not pay much attention to forms of cultus or church-government. Religion with them was treated as a matter of the inner life, and of conscientious selfdiscipline.

The Romanised Franks, on the other hand, furnished the objective factors for the external perpetuity of Christian culture. They were talented in organising, were learned in law, and fond of an Old Testament form of obeisance to an enjoined constitution. The essence of Christian piety with them was conformity to the institutional externals. As far as it goes, that was well enough; but the subjective assimilation of the essence and substance for which the Northern sense of liberty and personal dignity had a predilection, which had been nourished from Bangor and by the fraternities of St. Patrick, was in decidedly better tenor with the New Testament.

Subjective assimilation.

Fraternities of St. Patrick. Bangor.

The Franks organise, and enjoin conformity and obedience.

But Northern subjectivism, prone to sectarianism and separatistic selfconceit, like that of the Hellenes, had to learn that the organic connection with the body is necessary. The Saxons were bound to accustom themselves to exercise real membership in a churchly way. For in the progress of applied ethics, cooperation must go hand in hand with selfimprovement. Well, Boniface attended to the external requirement with an eye upon, and an ear for, Pipin's policy so perfectly coinciding with the aims of his own ambition. The interests of Rome and Paris, of St. Denis, St. Remi and Mayence, were intimately connected and identical.

Objective factors.

Difference between British missionary work among the Thuringians and the Swiss people § 127, 135. and the reconstruction of Boniface. § 139, 144, 156.

The process of social organisation and personal assimilation of Christianity, as thus initiated among the Latin and German nations in their close proximity, explains to some extent their contrast to the Eastern Aryans of Europe. The Slavs did not take hold upon the task of working out this problem in which we see the Romanised and Germanic nations becoming engaged. The Eastern nations were Byzantinised, and hence remained merely formal, less decisive and more pliable in consequence of their shallow religiousness. **The German disposition of mind required, and was assisted in, the reciprocity with Rome until the litigating parties arrived at a definite settlement.** The contrast between Latin and German nations being obvious from the beginning, it soon became clear, altho the nations were not sufficiently conscious thereof to formulate the discrepancies into a clear modus vivendi, that the one meant theocracy and law, the other personal piety, responsibility and Gospel. Tho polar strain was most vividly felt during that protracted procedure, wherein claims were to be adjusted between Christianity and ecclesiastical government, between Church and State, religion and diplomacy, dominion and "Service".

Difference between the eastern and western Aryans.

Slavs Byzantinised.

Germans had to sustain and to entertain reciprocity with Rome, until a definite settlement would be reached. § 135, 142, 145, 146, 150, 156, 171.

Tension between Roman and German peculiarities salutary; but final separation an intrinsic necessity from the beginning § 131, 132, 135, 145, 146, 150, 156, 171.

The Slavonic disposition of mind in its reciprocity with the Byzantine cast of religiousness did not require this settlement with the Greek form, or rather deformity, of Christianity. There an objective center of gravity and unity, or rather uniformity, existed. Nobody had a mind to inquire into subjectivity for assimilation or spiritual aspiration. The difference between the Slavs and the temper of the Greek Church was always enveloped in an oriental haze. For the Greek character had, unlike the Roman, passed away long ago. Hence there was no tension in the East, and no ethical improvement resulting.

Slavs in reciprocal relation with Byzantium no tension; no improvement. § 150, 189.

The Greek side of European culture we leave for further examination, because it was only since the variance between Othmanic, despot-ridden nations of Eastern Europe and the Germano-Romanised nations, under their constitutional or at least legal management, became so very pronounced, that a polarity has been rendered active which in its acuteness almost resembles that between the Ganges and the Tiber.

Greek Slavonic civilisations postponed. § 150, 189.

§ 139. We anticipate that in the west the princes were protectors of the rights of the people, and the wardens of governmental authority ever since Theodoric had made, and on the whole held, his vow in this respect conscientiously. In the eyes of the people their dignity consisted in being impartial judges by the nature of their office. Hence, as a general thing authority was respected by the masses, not so much the subjects of the princes as their retainers. The princes were obliged, under oath, to protect innumerable franchises and exemptions of hereditary personal rights, rights of cities, estates, and institutions.

German precedents congenial to Gospel truth. § 135.

Relations between princes and retainers based upon fidelity.

This was the case even in Spain despite the conglomeration of German, Franconian, Italian, Castilo-Catalonian, and Baskian elements. Every country having its own history, it was a sacred custom that each noble family was esteemed for some excellent service rendered to the commonwealth by one or more of its members. Distinction of that type deserved recognition which was not withheld, unless the privilege had been forfeited and withdrawn by tacit consent. This fact is reflected, as Ranke with fine insight pointed out, in the longwinded titles of sovereigns great and small still in vogue. For the history of civilisation they are of great weight, since in these tenures the rights and demands of the dignity and liberty of each baronage, of each county and free city are at least recognised, if no longer warranted. But in order to search deeper for these fixed rights and duties we go further back.

Princes the wardens of rights under oath.

Genesis of constitutional government.

The expected "world-embracer" had been preached to the Germans as a friend, just before the plaintive sounds of the "god-sagas" had died away on the Rhine, Weser, Main, and in the Thuringian forests. The great national epics composed from the hero-legends render these expectations evident.

"Heliand
not after Byzantine pattern
§ 125, 135, 136, 138, 159.

Upon the rainbow of peace, arching over the scenes of recent turmoil and grim battles, and in pensive meditation, those hopes arise which are plainly expressed in "The Heliand."

The "world's healer,"
§ 135, 159.

Relation to the Savior founded on vow of fidelity.
§ 134, 135, 138, 159.

The "World's Healer," as the Savior is so beautifully and originally conceived in the German "Heliand," is the good duke, a steadfast, trustworthy and mild leader, the cordial Lord of the Manor. He invites His kindred and retainers into His castle-hall and entertains them in the most bountiful manner. The description of such a "king of the common people" went to the hearts of vassal and serf alike, to whom nothing was more sacred than personal attachment to the prince under the vow of fidelity.

In this personal devotion (gilaubjan, that is, geloben, hence "to love" and "glauben") that relation of faith was founded in which the nations became Christians along with the princes.

Not the politico-Roman conception of the Savior attracted the Germans, but the Christ preached to them by the Culdeans and their Anglo-Saxon kinsfolks.
§ 135, 138, 142, 145, 146, 150, 156.

Peoples with the characteristic features of cordial and faithful adherence to customary relations between lord and retainers in troth and in deed were attracted by Christianity at the first instant. Previous to the times in which the policy of conquest and missionary efforts were intermixed, and the Byzantine picture of Christ was held out to them, they willingly embraced the glad tidings. The Christ of the Scottish and Anglo-Saxon gospel won the hearts of men, because it brought out the value of a person and entitled him to that freedom which is not at all inconsistent with proper relations of dependency.

Gospel attractive because of its being conducive to personal freedom first and foremost.
§ 134, 138, 141, 175.

A German of the average caliber is known for his preference of death to serfdom. He will maintain the right to personal freedom first and foremost, even if nice judgment and smooth conventionalism should be violated.

Principles requisite to constitutional government under elective kingship

To his principle of manliness he would adhere tho the nation should fall to pieces. He is shocked by an epithet like: I go with my country, right or wrong! His conception of a free man in the true sense is in no way marred, but on the contrary—according to his opinion—is favored and elevated by Christianity. The Germans frequently made themselves ridiculous when it seemed too hard a lesson for them to give up interests and ideas of subordinate import, yet this very love of independence, to the extent of clannishness, created the various leagues which continually compelled them to exercise that good faith upon which the confederacies were founded, and to practise that fellowship, by which their consciousness of common nationality was well enough cemented after all.

Love of independence, validity of man's parole of honor, practice of fellowship.

Thus the leagues, stimulating the practice of fidelity, honesty, and considerateness,—in a word the proverbial "Deutsche Treue"—were just as much, if not more, conducive to civilisation, than the governmental powers concentrated in dynasties. The Germanic peoples insisting upon the right of selfdetermination, prevented such concentration into "pure monarchy" as Guizot in the beginning of his political career taught to be the acme of civilisation. We are aware of the risk of provoking serious criticism as if our judgment was biased by national haughtiness, within a philosopher of another nation, within a man, perhaps, as good as Guizot. He is not to be vituperated, if he was not used to look upon the advantages of Germanic development in the light we do. We would therefore, by the way, beg leave to rather dispel the appearance of selfaggrandisement, and to retire into that modesty of the Germans to which other nations were accustomed. So far as the Germans are now known as the particular nation of late, they are simply attempting to promulgate true principles of ethics, and the world knows, that a few of them were set free by German conscientiousness. This motor-power of modern history, which it certainly ought to be, at least, showed its forebodings among the Germanic peoples throughout the Middle-Ages. Emphasising these facts in all honesty of purpose, the Germans themselves guard against a partial or artful interpretation of history, which in their own behalf they deem not necessary.

Criticism of the "pure monarchy" which Guizot mistook for the acme of civilisation.

Not celibacy (Guizot) was the reason that a priestly caste-rule could not be established, but the resistance of Germans based upon the oath of loyalty to princes
§ 143.

The staunch belief of the Germans in their rights, natural and divine, the pro-tection of which was made the duty of the ruler under oath, wrought out elective monarchies, created constitutions and charters. And the watchfulness as to personal rights was the cause—not celibacy as Guizot thought—that hierarchal assumption of supremacy and a perpetuating exclusiveness of priestly caste-rule was never agreed to! If it came to that, some parts of the Germans were ever ready to shed their blood for national independence from papal diplomacy. The free man, even when yet a heathen, had the feeling—tho he could not express it in so many words as did the poet:—

and upon the consciousness that God is on good terms with man regardless of officious intercessors.
§ 159.

that he may be on good terms with the gods, not on account of officious intercessors, but for his own sake. And now, with the loyalty of the cordial and benign but majestic prince of all the nations, on the natural basis of earlier and sound convictions, a new æra dawned upon the Germanic nations.

Concerning Boniface, the Saxons were fully aware of what was going on, when he drove away the married ministers of the Thuringians, or when he returned from the curia of Gregory and the court of Pipin. At last the Germans of the interior had to submit to the execution of Italian plans at Romanising, with the power of the state at command. They made the best of it, but never with all their heart. The way in which they had protested against the mode of their conversion was not forgotten in all the seven centuries following. A peculiar sympathy was kept up throughout this period with the remnants of the Culdeaus, with the Begghards and Lollards, Wycliffe's proteges, a matter over which Romanism ever betrayed fidgetiness, especially when the Bible was read in Anglo-Saxon at Lutterworth.

With Karl the preliminaries of a new European civilisation had attained to a fixed order of progression. To complete these transitory measures it had taken history four hundred years. Old memories of German mythology, which as yet had remained overlapping Christianity throughout this intervening period, just began to pass into extinction. The transition was precisely defined when emperor Ludwig the Pious took the precaution to make a memorandum of a few essential sentences of "Muspilli," the world-conflagration in his prayer-book, in order to save them from utter oblivion. This coincided with the composition of the epic on the "Heliand" which was the signal of advance upon the field of action in the new æra. Immediately the ethical results began to appear in the dawning of the new culture implied in the term "civilisation."

In the measure, as man's relation to God is clearing up, the relations to the environments also receive proper attention, and find their normal adjustment, so that even the earth will partake of the good effects. We come to see the connection between cultus and culture in a bright, new light; we perceive the conciliation of earthly existence with human destiny, which Greek culture in vain was striving at, which Christianity alone can fully realise. Will it not seem marvelous that the first domain of culture in general, which profits from reinstating proper ethical relations, is—agriculture? Wherever civilisation becomes visible we see it rooted in the occupation of farming, where it also will be consummated when swords shall be wrought into ploughshares.

The rapacious treatment of the soil to the extent of exhaustion, and felling the forests, cause destructive inundations here, and sterile plains there. Devastation of countries as fine as Mesopotamia or Spain has been, was and ever will be the consequence, if first occupants, heedless of the future and viciously inconsiderate of posterity, are greedy in appropriating what nature offers without doing anything towards its elevation in return.

Such people can take out of the soil as much as their haste permits and, hurrying to new fields, will abandon the wasted region in poverty. Even a settled nation like the Ægyptians have finally made their own country one vast grave of their own culture, by the neglect if not disdain of agriculture. And this aversion to rural pursuit will generally be found to correspond with the degree of religious decay, in porportion to the neglect of the cultus.

With Christianity there came a new kind of attachment to the soil and a most profitable pleasure in its cultivation. It seems as if man—reconciled to God, quitting the restless ways of Cain in the hunt for diversion or for luck, and obtaining that contentment which is not to be found in the attempt at dispelling the pains of remorse by excitement—learns to love the ground. His eye, when the heart is at peace and in love with God, finds a peculiar pleasure in nature, whilst in return nature seems to look up to man more amiably, and yields sweeter blessings. Mutual gratitude seems to take the place of former rebellion and toilsome recovery. The soil receives tender care and the surroundings seem to breath a paradisian serenity. Man now becomes conscious of his sacred right to say "My father made all of this; it belongs to me!"

In the beginning it is always pasture that the roaming cattle-owner is wanting. To obtain the best, he is ever ready to fight, until he makes fighting his pleasure. As soon as he has organised his forces, and yielded to the discipline which war peremtorily requires, he enters the borders of culture; but the state of civilisation does not begin, until he delights in cultivating a garden around his home.

It was the want of pasture that moved the German to cross the Alps and made him a terror to Rome and Byzanz. The Aryan was a farmer to the manor born; but to the establishment of husbandry and agrarian contentment and steadiness he did not accommodate himself until he could wander no further because the West was already possessed by others. The migrations had their cause and their end in these conditions; the altered circumstances made "farming off" to give way to "economy", that is, to rational and economical tilling of the fields.

The German began to love the ground for the possession of which his forefathers had suffered and for the improvement of which he himself had labored hard and continually. He became attached to his Hof or Hufe, that is, to real estate as measured by the number of oxen's or horses' hoofs it took to cultivate what by the casting of "lots" had become his allotment. It was marked out, and from these "marks" which religiously protected his rightful ownership, a thousand juridical regulations developed as the natural result.

With regulating the
"marks" i. e. boundary
lines, right develops into
jurisprudence.

Fundamental
conceptions of the
Germans as to
rights and duties.

Trials of cases in
daylight to "find" a
verdict.

§ 140. The German mode of thinking derived religion and right from the same source. The "Asega" or Assayers, with taciturn gravity and solemn deportment "scooped" the judgment of what was right—that is, dipped water from the sacred spring—so as to "find" a just verdict. They were servants of the "Asen," the gods of welfare. The free and public session of court "tagt", that is, always takes place in day-time, and "vertagt sich," i. e., adjourns at sunset, because the right can be found by daylight only, since it is the sun divine who brings out the crime. And never is corporeal punishment executed in the dark.

The Germans looked upon their rights as the highest treasure and guarded them with religious reverence. The "witan" and "wisdoms" (Weissthuemer), as the unwritten codes of the traditional rights of the people were called, in their plain-dealing tone, express a touching regardfulness as to what was ancestral custom or "Herkommen", what was "von Alters her".

It is a question, we repeat, whether such regard for unwritten laws is not a sign of higher morality than the "practice" of printed laws in the modern, so-called civilised world. The old-fashioned, singlehearted honesty with all its quaintness of judicial forms, was, to the German, duty pure and simple. The right is charged upon him by virtue of an ideal necessity. The demands of the law are of divine origin, hence its administration must keep aloof from subjective arbitrariness. Every single right is a bonus, a gift, a privilege; it entitles man to demand it as his own possession. But it implies, at the same time, a God-given charge to be attended to, hence, a right is a high privilege under obligation of faithful discharge of duty. For these reasons individual prerogatives carried along with them responsibilities in greater or lesser degree, which conditioned the respectability of those in service as well as those in authority.

Higher morality than
that yielded by modern
"practicing" law.

A right is a
divinely
warranted
privilege under
obligation of
faithful
discharge of
duty.

To insist upon personal liberty implies regard for the rights of others. Conflicts arise between personal freedom and social duties, which call for adjustment in a variety of judicial disquisitions. This was to be expected, especially in this instance where a state was in the slow course of its formation from elements so difficult to unite. Combinations multiplying, it required more prudence to adjust them, especially where the views and interests clashed with those of the Romanised opponents. It thus became obvious that the principles underlying the jurisprudence of both the Germanic and Romanic nationalities were at variance; and the dilemmas became aggravated by the circumstance that two modes of applying justice, one according to German rights and the other according to Roman laws, came into practice and demanded to be harmonised.

"German right"
coming in conflict with
"Roman law".

Difference between civil
and ecclesiastical
judicatories.

Canonics—"Schoeppen."

Interpretation of the Roman law was mostly in the hands of the clergy, the canonics; whilst German right relied upon the justice of the common-sense verdicts of free civilians, of the "Schoeppen" or Alderman, who from time immemorial, by force of "Herkommen", had "scooped" the right. Rome had the formulations of the right ready made in its laws so as to be applicable for any given case, its ultimate end being the state.

The German analysed the case (ur-theilte), and according to the merits thereof in its totality spoke the verdict; the right to be found together with the duty rested in the person.

Roman law
has the
state
for its object;
German right
remains in the
person.

Gradations of ranks.

Suzerain and vassal.

Serfdom.

Traits of humane
treatment of subjects.

Such were the fundamental differences between German right and Roman law, sufficiently heterogeneous in themselves to create the severest conflicts.

The gradations of ranks in the German organism of society had its natural development, so that even the relations between suzerainty and fealty were based on the concept of personal rights. The land and its inhabitants belonged to the lord of the manor, and his relations to his tenants occasioned rights and duties conditioned on both sides, tho usage had provided for special protective guaranties as to the rights of the weaker parties, of the freeholders "own people," which rights were always very circumstantially specified and enumerated in order to secure a humane treatment for the laboring class.

All drinks, for instance, and victuals to which the serf is entitled by right whenever he is on duty, that is, performs his part of the fealty upon the "Hof" or "Hufe", were minutely stipulated as to quantity and time, not by contract but by custom. Harsh as such serfdom may have been, its inhumaneness has certainly been exaggerated. The right to move somewhere else was always granted to the "villains" or retainers.

If we look at the life in a village or town, where the craftsmen, artisans and traders lived closer together, there was the right of the craft or guild to be invested with legal authority each according to its own rules. Free trade, which can only result from a highly diversified industry in larger factories, there was none. The purpose of the craft-usages was protection against unqualified or illegal competition. The rules of the guilds as well as the rights of the serfs show many traits of paternal care, intended for the amelioration of the poor man's lot, and for the adjustment of conflicting interests. Only think of the "right of sanctuary" or asylum, granted to monasteries and to "burroughs," where criminals could take refuge against lynch law. Think of the obligation of paying custom or duty, which originally means nothing but ground rent in the form of natural products. The tenth (or Zins) chicken is not to be exacted in case of a woman "lying in," since it is understood that she needs the strengthening soup. During the period of her "peculiar appetites" she may also go fishing, whatever the rights of the lord or the miller may be with reference to the use of the river.

In all cases of violation of rights the "Schulze," or village-mayor presides—the justice of the peace. He is appointed by either the judiciary of the district, or of the count's domain. He instantly attends to any grievance of a person wronged. For the deliberations of the "Witina Gemot" legislative measures are stipulated and administered. "Under den Linden" in the rear of the alderman's house he holds open court in proxi of the "Free Count", upon the "free chair", so that the right be decided free from fear or favor. He scoops the right in every case. From his decision there need no appeal be made, for his decision is supposed to be, as a matter of course, as it behooves the case. The rights of the peasantry everywhere are fostered with such benign earnestness and sacred respect for discipline and good order, with such cordiality and even good humor at t mes, and they are decided with such common sense and impartial justice, and generally with such public approval, that on the whole one may be tempted to compare that instinctive judiciousness with the intricate administration of justice in our civilised society much to the deterioration of the latter.

When feudalism had been fully established, the upholding of good order and general welfare on line with general humaneness through methods so simple and cheap, was rendered impossible. In these "romantic" times the cities and municipal franchises soon absorbed the rights of the country districts. None but the Celts had the right of conducting civil suits at law preserved for the clan: hence the preponderance of country nobility in France. There the landed knights or barons had no city aristocracy to contend with. When some of these barons agreed to take possession of the glen of an opposite clan, and to distribute ground-rents, fealties, and leases among themselves, there was no patrician either to curb their designs, or to deprive the petty tyrants of their usurped judicatory of which they had deprived the glen.

No further discussion in outlining the rudiments of German jurisprudence is necessary for the present. Not before other circumstances, leading to Christian monarchism, have been considered, can we inquire into the modifications of judicial principles as affecting the functions of the rulers, even those upon the principal thrones of Europe.

The traditional judicatories of the country districts were superseded by feudal rights. The descendants of the noble men, the athelinge of old, made it an honorable feat to restore the squandered fortunes by picking quarrels with others in order to seize their possession by coup de main. Fighting for spoils was their sole occupation.

Besides the secular we have now the "spiritual" lords. The laws of matrimony and of inheritances especially were under the control of the hierarchy, and they contrived to get as many legacies as possible for their cloisters and abbeys. The administrators of ecclesiastical estates, comprising fully one-third of Germany, for instance, stood equal in rank with the most powerful vassal of the king. Secular and spiritual lords coveted the possession of whole glens and counties, or they outrivaled each other to be entrusted with the management of a larger or smaller province according to rank, family connections, influence, or services rendered. The glens were divided, subdivided and dovetailed again in as many enclaves as the king had dukes, counts, barons, abbots, bishops, &c., for his vassals, which were to be rewarded or to be kept

Marginal notes:
Protection of handicraft.

Sacred adherence to humane usages.

"Judices" of the peace. ("Schulze".)

"Under den Linden."

Comparison between primitive and modern adjudication.

country-nobility of feudal times, especially in France, upsets the simple methods of justice.

Sword—law.

Ecclesiastic vassalage.

in good humor. The free peasantry, the middle class, almost entirely disappeared, except in Westphalia, Frisia, Scandinavia and Switzerland, where freeholders had been able to maintain their original rights. The farmer became a "Hintersasse," a settler in arrear to the "Freiherr," if not his subject. The lord aspired to become just as powerful and immediate a member of the national diet, or as independent a peer representing an estate in the king's council, as his duke or bishop. The duke on his part let no opportunity escape which might bring him nearer to his goal of changing his fealty into a hereditary principality.

Dukes, counts, palatines, and margrafen forgot that they were nothing but administrators and servants of the realm. Being vassals of the crown they claimed the right of giving away the crown to the one of their own number whom they would elect. Ambition, thirst of dominion, endeavor to fix an easy, rich, and permanent existence for posterity—these were the motives which set society into a turmoil lasting through four centuries. Everybody who could wield a sword and was knighted, was in some league and on the offensive; every city which could afford a moat and a strong wall, was in an intrigue or on the defensive.

In the measure as administrative fealty changed into ruling sovereignty, so feudal anarchy brought about changes in the military organisation of vassalage and gradually into all legislative and administrative functions.

Finally freedom remained the attribute only of the noblemen, the degraded descendants of the old "athelinge." But without a fief such mere titular freedom, into which the old ideal of manliness and freedom had become subverted, was rendered valueless as regards real rank and military occupation. Volunteered participation in the fate of the country in council or in the coat of arms had become utterly invalidated.

Independence from the landlords was now maintained through the common "freedom of the cities." It would have been impossible to save some selfconscious independence, some feeling of citizenship, and of personal security in the everlasting embroils of the fighting knights but for the opportunity to take refuge behind the moats and walls of the cities, by becoming "burghers." Thus the oldfashioned relation of dutiful fidelity between "Herren and Hoerigen" (lords and retainers), was abolished along with the old Germanic duty of all able men to take to arms and to follow the banner into the field of action.

§ 141. We hinted at the circumstance of a new element having entered German life, alluding to the formation of chartered municipalities, which dates from the German measures against the invasion of the Eastern savages, and was in Germany copied from the Romanised neighbors.

Whenever Franconian Knights had founded new states, cities were organised after the pattern of the old Roman municipalities in Italy, thus enjoying the same right of self-protection and selfgovernment as the castles of the princes around them on the hill tops. The cities utilised their opportunities by exacting grants, exemptions, and immunities from the crowns, charters from the empires, in recompense for services rendered to the king when he was embarrassed by the impudence of his secular or ecclesiastical vassals, if not rebels.

In Germany the people were averse to crowding behind walls, preferring a life in free air. When Henry the "townbuilder" wanted to fortify the borders against the Hungarian invaders, and in order to secure places of safety for the country people and their horses and herds, he had to coax them into these strongholds by granting many franchises. Otherwise the towns grew up from the clusters of dwellings around the castles and imperial palatinates, where the partisans and traders used to form small colonies. In most cases they nestled around the cathedral, the bishop's church. For there the best immunities were to be secured, as for instance the right of marketing. The "masses" were originally what we would call church fairs, one of the Roman contrivances to lift cash revenues for the church's benefit.

Originally the ground of townholders belonged either to the crown, to some member of the nobility, or to the "dead hand" of the church, that is, to the monastic order or to the seat of the bishop. The artisan or innkeeper would build his house upon the lord's ground and pay a cheap ground-rent, for which the tenant enjoyed the protection of the owner and his patronage. Unless the owner defended his ground he would certainly lose it, for under some pretense the victor would step into possession and succession of rights as if he had been the rightful owner by inheritance. Or the town itself would watch a chance to obtain the control of their own judicatories, and to drive out the descendant of a margraf who would still try to play lordship over the town.

Thus the old relation of attachment and fidelity was discarded. But contentment and prosperity reigned over the peaceful pursuits of city life, occasional riots notwithstanding. The spirit of independence was regained in these towns, and in lieu of fidelity to a lord, loyalty to the King was now cultivated. The burghers often yea, generally, were the most reliable supporters of the emperors in their bitter strifes with domineering hierarchs or obstreperous vassals. Then the supreme ruler would give his good cities new immunities and privileges until at last the cities were free states, indeed.

Their representatives ranked with the mighty princes in the national diets, and they combined their power in forming a "Bund," that is, a league or a confederacy, here and there. In proportion as the prestige of knighthood dwindled away during the period of the crusades, until their power was completely broken by the Swiss peasants, the cities grew in wealth and importance.

Prestige of nobility and knighthood dwindles away in the face of city-leagues.

Swiss peasantry.

These, then, are the three steps toward consolidation among the German nations, thanks to feudalism, and in spite of the perpetual dissensions. First a rabble of incohesive tribes, of which the Romans counted half a hundred; then their fusion into smaller units under popular leaders; until finally they felt themselves as one German nation under a duly elected bearer of the crown, in which all ideal authority was vested.

Three epochs in the construction of German civic polity toward unification.

We see the emblems of this ideal unity in the imperial banners floating over free and strong cities with direct representation in the "Reichstag", and with loyal, patriotic, and intelligent burghers.

Imperial banners floating over free cities, emblematic of ideal unity and independence.

During the transition the Pandects, the abridged code of Roman laws, was rediscovered in Italy. The thought was taken into consideration, whether it was not more rational to establish and maintain order by way of council instead of steel.

Effects of the recovery of the "Pandects." § 127, 141.

The first Hohenstauffen emperor held the first Council of Peace upon the Roncalian fields in order to agree upon a settlement with the obstinate Italian cities, and for the purpose of concluding a lasting peace and treaty upon the grounds of right and reason.

Restitution of legal methods in the settlement of combatant interests.

And sequent to the study of the original Roman law it was found, that its application would also check, to a great extent, the anomalies of the canonic law, which so far had predominated as it had been promulgated by the hierarchy. Roman legislation used to frame, to fix, to make the law; and the ecclesiastical continuation followed this practice, with this single aim to find the right, the Schoeppe still endeavoring to do justice to the person in whom the right was inherent in the particular case. To German intuition right existed as something subjective and yet objective at the same time. Everybody is born into that grade of rights and duties which belong to his rank. His individual rights belong to the rank in which a person is born. The dignity and grade of freedom correspond with the duties implied. By birth man is identified with both; privileges which are rights constituting a "noblesse oblige"; and duties, which are honorable privileges—to serve nobly!

1. First arbitration upon the Roncalian fields—"council of peace" on grounds of right and reason.

2. Amelioration of the anomalies caused by the canonic laws being at variance with German rights.

Comparison between Roman and German principles of justice:

Cognition of right into which a person is born—and the corresponding duty: "Noblesse oblige."

The right of the Roman rested on command. It grew from and with the unit of the "Urbs" and its orb, of the city with its annexations—a growth quite contrary to what we noticed among the Germans. The Roman law had been elaborated by deductive deliberation, and by a series of contracts between political parties, as agreed upon for reasons of state. This law was compact, practical, and well constructed. It was objective to persons and things, abstract so as to appear rational, authoritative and strictly impartial. According to its fundamental principle only the state had any rights, as if man actually existed for its sake. These principles through the canonical laws, had gained the upper hand in Germany, and they were at fault, if the German could neither see the justice of these Roman laws nor understand them at all. The peasants complained that "the right was more tightly concealed to the doctors than to the laymen, since none of them can find a key to it, whilst the layman keeps the key within himself". "The learned are but hired servants after all. They are not hereditary "Schœffen" of what is right. Yea, they are stepfathers and illegitimate heirs of the right."

Roman justice in the interest "Urbis orbique."

German mind not sufficiently sophisticated to comprehend the fundamental differences

Doctors of law unpopular.

In this forcible complaint German conscientiousness manifests itself against Romanism. The German Schultze had the confidence of the people by right; him they judged to be the hereditary servant of God, the only Lord of Judgment.

But Latin had become the language of the courts in Church and State. and of the schools, and the clerics had monopolised the art of writing. So Roman jurisprudence had prevailed wherever judicial views had to be compromised; Roman law soon mastered the situation in particular test-cases setting aside old opinions. In such test-cases even princes lost their right. True, many of them had perpetrated abuses of their highest prerogative of being the protectors of the people's rights. But on the whole the injustice of kings was scarcely as flagrant as seen from the aspects of that party in a litigation who could not carry his point. Henceforth OBEDIENCE was extolled and demanded as the fundamental virtue of a Christian, even at the expense of FIDELITY. The national capitularies, i. e., contracts, (nowadays called concordats) between princes and bishops or the curia; the old wisdom, i. e., regulations for

Ecclesiastics monopolised the administration of justice.

Princes lost their highest prerogative of protecting rights.

20

deciding the measure of retribution; the "reflectors of right" as the codes of the different nationalities were called (as for instance the Sachsenspiegel or Schwabenspiegel) which contained the sum and substance of the old upper-courts and the "Malstætten" or glen proceedings:—all were thrown aside.

In the eyes of new legislators these old "wisdoms" were disdained as mere childish attempts at justice.

Upon Germanic soil, "under den Linden" they had spoken in metaphors, and rhymed sentences full of sentiment; they had found verdicts against criminals according to proverbs. From Rome, mistress of the world and teacher of discipline, right came as a cognition. And cognition of right as such means a step forward in progress, and will be victorious. Rude power of might and sword could not come up to it. The recognition of lawfulness and legality was a necessity in times of feudalism. But an agricultural people will always be conservative; and a farmer's conservatism generally concurs with the degree of reluctance with which the ground he tills yields its harvest.

Most of the German soil is heavy, causing its owners to become a hard working people, not likely to give in to smooth-tongued dialecticians. They could not understand the intricacies of the doctors of "both rights"—as the Germans still say: "beider Rechte" instead of LL. D. —so they tried their best to abide them without going to law and suing at court.

The Germanic peoples—for circumstances essentially similar to those in the "Roman Empire of the German nation" wrought equal changes in all the other nations of Germanic origin—had cause for disgust with a duplex judicial administration of justice, since the Roman law revolutionised all matters pertaining to agrarian pursuits.

It is the peculiarity of Roman law, that it destroys the cognition of personality, by substituting for it only that which merely accidentally belongs to the person, namely, the value of his taxable private property. Real estate in the large family tenures had been protected by the German rights. Individually a person is not so much recognised as the proprietor, as the family, and ultimately the State. The distribution of the lands goes in lines of allodial holdings and dowries, of which one spendthrift shall not deprive the "house". Roman justice, starting with the state as a collective sum of possessors, does not care whether the individuals are impoverished by a continual diminution of the landed estates, which are thus permitted finally to be swallowed up by land-monopolists.

As in the case of agrarian "economy" (in the German sense of the term for husbandry) so the peculiar principle of Roman jurisprudence created also a new political economy, which altered the whole fabric of administrative functions. At the time of which we speak this change lay in the future. For the present the trouble was that most all of the legal business was managed by the economics with whom the interests of ecclesiastical government were paramount. For we repeat: canonical law regulated marriages, and questions of inheritance, and governed the schools.

§ 142. The manipulators of the ecclesiastical powers were cautious as yet in their advances on the line of secular pretensions. Henry I. was a Saxon, freely chosen,—which of course does not exclude the powerful influence of a bishop or two—by the two largest peoples of the "Holy Roman Empire of the German Nation." Not anointed by a bishop, he nevertheless called himself "King by the Grace of God." Tho not irreligious, he yet wore the crown without asking the sanction of a hierarch, because he did not want to be—according to his manly motto which Giesebrecht emphasises:—"a king of the clericals." This antagonism against the hierarchy in connection with the fact that Henry was a member of just that Saxon people who bore an old grudge against Rome ever since their forced conversion, is very descriptive of the undercurrent which once will break forth with effects more pregnant with consequences than all of Henry's noble deeds combined.

In the grand line of this Saxon house a strong family tree grew up like an oak, sound to the core, so that this stock of Thuringians seemed singled out to become the mainstay of the western Aryans. At the court of Otto the Great, those scenes repeated themselves which we witnessed in Aachen and Paderborn. Again there arrived the ambassadors from Paris and Byzanz, from Rome and London, Burgundian noblemen, chiefs of the Danes and Hungarians, even petitioners sent by the caliph of Cordova.

Upon this first summit of real Germanic kingship we will rest and take in the view.

At first sight we will be obliged to acknowledge a providential interposition. It was a powerful principle which we found in Roman law and in the Roman Church, this thought of objectivity as contrasted with German subjectivism. The nations of northern Europe had, and have to this day, to clear and to regulate the ideality, abstractness, and subjectivism of their thoughts by formative principles of practical Rome. The German mind is rather negligent as to the form into which thought is to be embodied; whilst it delights in soaring round about the heights of sentiment. This aversion to the practical representation of ideas in systematic shape and suitable organisms, associated with an aversion to authority and discipline, involves the peril of distraction, derangement and confusion. This danger to national existence could be avoided and checked only by adding to the purely Germanic culture the preservative and formative external institutes of right and religion from without. The pressure from outside which to the Germans was always a necessity, to remind them that the condition of their national existence lay in their organic unification, was supplied in due time.

Providence interposes to amalgamate German subjectiveness with Roman objectivity. § 137, 138, 139, 143, 146, 156, 171.

German sentimentality. § 93, 128, 134, 135, 141, 143.

———ooo———

With fullfledged European feudalism we stand at the ominous year 1000 A. D. In the East the fragments of Scythian material are scattered about from the Danube to the Gobi. The thrones of Asiatic despotism have been mastered by eunuchs and slaves of Turkish extraction. Into the western extensions of the eastern masses—which were ever on the alert to overflow the northeastern plains of the present Germany—Christianity is now slowly advancing. Into the woods of the Lithunians, between the lakes of the Prussians, across the marshes and heaths of the Vistula, Dniepr and Theiss, Christian culture moves forward to meet the missionaries coming from the south.

Situation of Europe at the ominous year A. D. 1000.

Still further south the Fatimides rule Africa, and blockade the waters of the Mediterranean, their corsairs ravishing the coasts. The Normans, a German tribe, have gained a foothold upon Sicily and in Apulia, wrestle with the sea-robbers, get a kingdom ready for themselves, and fight their way through, until they swarm about the old empire of the Sassanides.

Thus the stage is arranged and the roles are distributed for a new epoch. We see the Aryans of the Occident seized by the Asiatic torpidity which threatens to put them to sleep at the end of the world, which is supposed to draw near, as they march in processions to the tombs of the pioneers of Christian culture. But we observe also the rise of personages to whom the leadership is assigned through the period of transition. Notwithstanding the drowsiness preceding the new awakening, it soon becomes evident that the portion of the human race under discussion is of healthy stock, well qualified naturally, and swiftly advancing spiritually on the way to Christian civilisation; except that the way upon which this advance proceeds seems to be roundabout way. The Saxons are building city walls to provide strong shelter for occidental thought and against oriental barbarism; whilst at the same time they build domes in basilican style, and arrange marriages with Byzantine princesses, in line with the dreams of Karl about Constantinople.

Reappearance of Polar forces.

CH. III. CHURCH AND STATE; EMPEROR AND POPE.

§ 143. Europe had sustained the polar strain incessantly, but it is only now that its effects are rendered conspicuous enough to become plainly perceptible. The counteracting principles come to their issues. The same antitheses which always had caused the tension between Orient and Occident, begin to assume new shapes.

It becomes distinctly recognisable that all the struggle throughout the Middle-Ages is but the continuance of the heterogeneity of the eastern and western forms of consciousness. Before history passed into the first cycle of the new æra the extremes met in the Roman basin, where the effects of the polar tension were neutralised under high pressure. As the second circle extends before us, the opposite forces appear still more intrinsically interlocked in their array upon the European arena. From the Roman basin, the old conflict arises in a new form, in order to become definitely disposed of by the Aryans of the Occident. The thought of an ideal humanism, planted in the midst of the nations at the divide of times, must now persevere in its realisation, and maintain itself against the spirit of the most antique cultures agglutinated to, and peddled out by, Semitism.

Mongolians furnish the necessary pressure for unifying the Germans. § 52, 53, 55, 127, 140, end, 141, 145, 150, 152, 153, 156, 163, 171.

The history of the Germanic nations is the result of two currents of forces ever governing its course of events:—the one, generated from the powerful and instinctive inclination to preserve those peculiar characteristics of the mind, which may be subsumed under respect for personal selfhood, sentiment of honorable loyalty, and conscientious perseverance in accomplishing the ethical task; the other, the weak side,

Mongolians assist in the transition to a new æra.
§ 127, 140, 145, end 150.

Tho barred out one way, orientalism is allowed to encroach in another.
§ 67, 78, 81, 85, 87, 97, 100, 101, 122, 123, 125, 128, 130, 131, 137, 139, 142, 144, 146, 148, 149, 150.

Continuance of the old polar tension between the East and the West; opposite forces more intrinsically interlocked in their array upon the European arena, than formerly in the Roman crucible.

Two sets of forces propel German history toward political unification into a social organism.
§ 97, 137, 141, 142 156, 194.

A. Ethical convictions: 1. Feeling the necessity of unity, but unwilling to relinquish personal selfhood; and honorable loyalty; and unwilling to shirk the assigned task.

2. Admiring the organisatory talent of Rome, tho-it demanded subjection to its practice of unification; but unwilling to swerve from a natural growth of a unity of its own, under internal adjustments; and unwilling either to compromise with alien principles or to submit to diplomatic imposition of external uniformity.

Germans not disinclined to obey the demand of history, but contriving to establish a state after their own ideal.

B. Religious instinct made a Germanic union desirable, but no subjection of either church or state under the other.
§ 139, 146, 156, 171.

Persisting upon antagonistic ideas caused splits among the nations which were salutary in the end. § 139, 156

Profound interest taken in religion by the Germanic nations.

Influence of German piety upon the Middle-Ages.

Old forms of Church-government among Goths and Franks.

Eastern Franks formed the bridge for Roman encroachments upon German soil.

Clodwig (Clovis-Louis) at his baptism pocketed an insult.

of these ethnical excellencies was: insufficient cognizance of the necessity to work together, caused by a proneness to envy and separatism.

With equal instinct the German peoples felt, on the other hand, a compulsion to combine into a national brotherhood. Thanks to occasional family friction, immense heat was developed and their rough edges were smoothed off by grinding passions. They felt that they did not dare to swerve from the process of unification; but they felt most vividly, at the same time, that this process had to proceed in a way of natural growth and under internal adjustments. It was repulsive to the national spirit that artificial means should be applied, or a compromise should be arranged upon alien principles, and imposed upon them through the diplomacy of outside factors.

Tho the Germans resisted every attempt to force a union, they had ever since the time of their great leaders, Alaric and Theodoric, hovering before them that Roman or Celtic image of a state in resuscitated splendor, which once had been admired by their chiefs in imperial Rome. Hence, the petty tribal prejudices notwithstanding, the Germans were never disinclined to submit to unification as the demand of history, and to establish again such an exquisite state of their own. Both of these incitements were to effect the same end, namely the organisation of a state resting in selfcomposure upon the basis of political unity and personal liberty. The same impulses determine not only the history of Germanic culture but control the totality of occidental progressiveness. To Germanic history the new efficients are virtually what the spring is to a watch, the face of which plainly indicates the stage of the inner movement. The same set of motives revealed its significance in the phenomena of the religious sphere.

The wars raging to and fro all over western Europe between Germany and Italy, France and England, between Spaniards and Moors, all those wars of the crusades, and between Romanised and Germanic nations, between Welf and Waiblingen, emperors and popes:—they all originated from ethico-religious misunderstandings. And they all show the most singular and conspicuous trait of the German temper, in that the Teutonic sense of equity could never tolerate the subjection of the state under the church, and never would forbear the dominion of the state over the church.

It was chiefly for their watchfulness in these respects that the Germans were driven to political separations, whenever ecclesiastical problems demanded solution or settlement. Yet even in this spiritual condition and counterposition the German spirit remained true to itself. It produced so much a richer variety and riper fulness of cultural life. It is for reasons of just that course which history took with the Germanic nations, that they obtained the wealth and delicacy of their cognitions, and that by experimenting with them, they became the best qualified mediums for rendering civilisation the common property of humanity in general.

§ 144 Never upon Celtic territory were religious questions treated with such sincerity, and such profound and common interestedness, as among the Germans. It is in the nature of our problem that we examine the influence of German religiousness upon the history of the Middle-Ages.

Up to the times of the Merovingian kings the Church had been subordinate to the State. The Goths in Spain were on their guard against encroachments of hierarchal predominance. In France it was customary for the kings to call the councils or authorise their convocations, and to sanction their resolutions. They legitimised the election of bishops, and even appointed many of them themselves, regardless of higher ecclesiastical authorities. · Lay-delegates occupy seats and vote in the councils, and even the episcopal office is entrusted to lay-members.

But under Pipin matters changed. The eastern Franks have always shown it their chief object to adopt foreign practices, and thus adapted themselves to form a roughly constructed bridge over which the pretentious Roman culture in the search of power could march from the western Franks directly into the countries of the Germans.

On the occasion of Clodwig's baptism, when that proud Sigambrian bowed his strong neck before Remigius and, as the first German prince, conceded to Romish authority at the Roman font, he pocketed a hierarchal insult; and when, soon after, upon the ruins of the old Roman institutions, in which Christianity had housed itself, a Frankonian empire grew up, the plan of history as to the Franks grew clear. The subjugation of Germany under Rome was on the same occasion and in principle a decided fact.

The Church on its part took the new national royalty under its protection, were it only to spite the Greeks.

Upon a miniature copy of the mass-canon in the cathedral of Metz, made in the latter part of the ninth century, there is a picture. From some representation of clouds a hand stretches forth, holding a crown as if to put it on the head of the Frankonian prince. He stands between two bishops, straight and ghastly looking. Berengar and Luithard, both priests, had painted Charles the Bald sitting upon the throne, while a blessing hand reaches down from above (which latter picture is now in the state library of Munich, as an illustration of the golden code of St. Emmeran of Ratisbone).

Germanism came to its first bloom and found its necessary complement of unifying concomitants in the coronation of the greatest Frank on Christmas, A. D. 800. In this great event at Rome the idea of "a State of God to which the exhausted world betakes itself as for refuge" was brought to a semblance of realisation. State and Church are the two sides of the Kingdom of Heaven, being related in a manner analogous to that in which body and soul stand to the other. Both are considered as sacred and of mutual assistance. What Karl with powerful shoulders had lifted up from the quicksands of unsettled conditions which dated from the time of the migrations, he now laid down at the feet of that grand old idol, the one universal monarchy—the same old dream of the Sanhedrin, except that the Sanhedrin wanted the Messiah to erect it in order to cast down Rome.

The romantic part of the Middle Ages begins with an emperor and a pope, one of whom wields the protecting sword whilst the other represents the candlestick of Christendom. Romantic Mediæval age closes with their mutual denunciations; pope and emperor exchanging the epithet of antichrist. In proportion as the Karolingians had become too weak to support the weight of the crown, the popes had become strong enough to transfer it. They entrusted the protectorship of the Church—that is of their own interests whenever endangered by the princes in the neighborhood,—to the good swords of the German kings.

The German kings made it their highest point of honor to protect crucifix and brevier with their bodies. Ludwig wrote to emperor Basilius: "We call ourselves emperors of the Romans because the imperial dignity is derived from them, and because we are charged to protect the Roman people, their city, and their mother, the Church." This document was forwarded to Constantinople by Luitbrand.

This plaintive effusion clearly expresses what was said of the high conception of the Germans as to privilege and duty combined. But the more the representatives of this German sentiment acted accordingly in their reform of civil service, the more did the embodiment of the Roman will equip itself for government.

How Rome succeeded in fastening this idea deep into the Western Aryans—so that even modern statesmen of predominantly protestant states treat the representative of the Roman Church as a sovereign ruler—we can see in Guizot's "Civilisation of Europe", where the Church is conceived as the apparatus "of religious government." The highest colleges in these United States have inadvertently promulgated this French view for half a century.

The mixture of truth with the Plato-Augustine misconceptions resulted from virtually the same expectations as the Pharisees of old had fostered with respect to the Messianic kingdom. The consequences were an Old Testament form given to the New Covenant, and a political agitation pushing toward the supremacy of the theocratic thought. It is notorious how the contention came to a point in the conflict about the investiture into the episcopal office (renewed as late as 1874 in Prussia). It meant "Church government" and "state service." Who knows of these times will remember that Rome just then was very jealous in propagating "orders" for the purpose of having at disposal a standing army of political agitators under guise of humane benefactors. The strategic deploy of their lines determined the victory in advance.

Under Henry V. it was obvious that the great reformation of the Cluniacensians had been Hildebrand's skirmishing maneuvers. The king soon was made to feel the edge of St. Peter's sword. The fervent devotion to the Church, adoring her as the chaste and pure bride of the Lord, and the deification of the church-government at Rome, had become THE power.

At St. Rhemi four hundred prelates, bishops and abbots adjourned their session and rose from their seats with burning candles. These were extinguished in the order the names of the excommunicated were read. The first of those names was that of the emperor of Saxon extraction, the son-in-law of the English king. He was put under bans for the third time, tho he had rebelled against his father to please the pope.

Laity led by priests against the princes.

The reformation of the monkish orders began in Romanised countries which now had the benefit of the victory. Gathering around the popes,—whose agents used to look after properly matching princesses with princes—the nations now entered the scene, led by priests against the princes, whenever they refused to be used as checkerboard kings. Thus the popes had frequently had occasion to show how forgiving they were, for unfortunately the princes gave offence and chances to the pontiffs only too often.

Offending kings caused people to side with the pope, Henry Plantagenet.

Henry Plantagenet, for instance, made his private chapel a nursery from which he transplanted his creatures unto vacant dioceses, with as much impudence and unconcern as he would secularise the property of a rich abbey. Such reckless conduct was not, however, the rule.

The "two swords of Christendom" were now made the badges emblematic of the administration of ecclesiastical and civil government respectively. The relation between the two powers alternated in such manner, that through the period of the Saxon emperors, up to the middle of the XIth century the imperial power maintained its superiority.

Weak emperors and powerful popes alternate.

Counter-popes A. D. 1150.
Counter-emperors.

After the hierarchy,—in answer to the inauguration of a series of counter-popes by the father of Henry IV—had set up the first counter-emperor, the imperial power gradually lost so much of its prestige, that about the time of Philip of Suabia, the Roman curia held full sway over Christendom despite recreant or insubordinate princes. "The swords are given to the authorities upon earth for the protection of Christendom. To the pope God has given the spiritual sword, the worldly to the emperor. The pope, moreover, is privileged to ride upon a white horse on certain occasions, when the emperor shall hold the stirrups for him that the saddle may not turn".

Emperor to hold the pope's stirrups.
§ 45, 49, 122, 144, 145, 149.

This denotes that all opposition to the pope may be kept down by the "worldly" power of the emperor, who by "worldly" (we would now say civil) right is to enforce obedience to the pope.

Imperial power to enforce obedience to the pope.
"Saxenspiegel." amended.

This was the prevailing idea indoctrinated into the people and legalised by an amendment to the organic laws of the Saxons, the "SAXENSPIEGEL". It was this unconditional surrender of royal right for which the hierarchy had been striving methodically, until it was secured when the Guelphs acquiesced in the pope's pretensions to be the ruler of the universe by proxy. The spiritual sword of moral protection and defense was now surreptitiously changed into one of military aggressiveness.

Guelphs acquiesced in papal pretensions.

To quote Hauck, it was conceded to the pope "that the princes were deemed the servants of the 'Vicar of God'". They were to be the instruments of exalting the Roman church. They had to execute the pontifical mandates even in purely political matters, liable to be punished by the popes if they would demur against obedience or defy authority".

"Princes deemed to be servants to the "Vice-God."   HAUCK.

Pretensions of such wide scope were smuggled into the Germanic conceptions of right, and became effective as a matter of course as soon as feudal rights were applied to the relations of the emperor to the pope. For the pope was acknowledged as the supreme suzerain who distributed the countries as fiefs to the princes, his vassals. Whenever the pope saw fit to withdraw the fief, he only needed to "dispense", —release the subjects from their oath of allegiance.

Vassals of the Roman pontiff by application of feudal rights.

Simultaneous rise of popery and Mohammedanism
§ 124, 127, 133.

§ 145. In a previous chapter we found the rise of Gregory I synchronistic with that of Muhamed to be a significant coincident. Again we cannot but find it a very portentous fact, that a new stage in the development of theocratic aspirations appears in the East simultaneously with those under discussion: Seldjukkian princes paid homage to the caliphs just as the emperors paid homage to the popes.

Parallels of oriental and occidental development during the cyclical period up to A. D. 1250 as emperors paid homage to popes, so did sultans to caliphs.

Togrul Beg, ruling over the regions between the Yaxartes and Euphrates with a high hand, built a mosque in every city, before he would lay a foundation for his own residence. When he arrived at the caliph's seat of power at Bagdad, the latter sat behind black portieres, dressed in black. Togrul kissed the ground-floor and was led by a vizier into the interior of the palace. Ushered into the presence of the caliph he took his seat on the throne prepared for him opposite to that of the caliph. The document was read which created him vicar of the prophet, and then he was invested with seven ornates of state-regalia. Balsam was burned, as tho the incense could sanctify or disinfect his person; then he was girded with two swords and crowned with two crowns, signifying that the power of the Orient and the Occident was conferred upon him, antitypical of the procedures which transpired before his contemporary, Gregory VII, the vicar of Christ.

Another cyclical coincident
§ 62, 76, 124, 127, 133.

Scene at Bagdad:
reception of Togrul Beg.   § 144, 149, 172.

Collision of oriental and occidental aspirations to rule the world.
§ 81, 97, 147, 149, 150, 185.

The collision of the Togruls and Gregorys in the crusades was merely the contest for the dominion over the world. The offensive was skillfully taken by the Romans, and the battle opened at the expense of the Greek church. Boemund of Antioch defeated the Byzantine fleet, and then sneeringly sent a boat, freighted with noses and thumbs, which had been cut off from captured Greeks, to the emperor in Constantinople.

Inasmuch as the crusades were to some extent successfully utilised by the Roman See or papal curia, they must be accredited to the popes, altho for the first impulse given to the movement they were not responsible. Noblemen of all countries had made pilgrimages to the holy sepulchre prior to the XIth century; and to the Normans, after they had secured firm holds upon France, England and Italy, new adventures were a necessity. This is the reason why they extended their tournaments to the foot of Mount Carmel. Their more or less organised mass-expeditions were set in motion by the enthusiasm for deeds of valor, and this enthusiasm was sanctioned and utilised by the curia, and consecrated to her interests. Traits of intense piety and grand ideality are ostensible throughout the crusades. The numerous trains of people, according to the refrain of a crusade song, "forsook the world's good for the sake of the holy blood." *Crusades not instigated, but utilised by the "Holy See". New fields of adventure a necessity to the Norman.*

History does not deprecate the pious motives of a small fraction of the crusaders, but neither will she palliate the judgment, that the gross of them consisted of a disorderly element which was attracted to engage in the strange adventures for the wild enjoyment of licentiousness. *Selfish aims and outrages of the adventurers.*

Fondness for combat, animating the impoverished nobles, had been beset with restrictions at home. Feudalism declining in their native countries, they hailed the opportunity to go into frays abroad. *Results of the crusades.*

In the first place they made the regions of Greece their easy prey, and founded petty principalities there. Embarking in Venice and Constantinople, they made the Acropolis a Frankonian castle, whilst the Venitian traders took possession of the islands in the Levant. A multitude of Romanesque burgs with moats and portcullis, with ramparts and portholes dotted the classic country, and menaced its sparse occupants. Hellas and Peloponnesus were the bone of contention of Franconian barons and Norman pirates. Princes of Naples, of Burgundy and Hainault threw their iron dices for the possessions of the Ægides and Proclites of old—all under the pretense of doing honor to the sepulchre. *less favorable to hierarchal power than had been calculated upon.*

The Roman curia can be made responsible for such excesses no more than for the many other incidents which went against the hierarchical intentions.

The **palpable success of the crusades**, according to Ranke, was the consciousness gained by the occidental nations that they had to unite their forces against the Orient. But the issue of the exploits was to manifest itself in quite a different manner, in order to realise the value and permanent results which history intended for the enhancement of civilisation. As another direct result of the crusades the origin of new states deserves mention. The remains of the old ducal kingdoms, in which the king was but the foremost commander of the forces he was to lead into battle, furnish foundations for well organised and selfgoverning principalities; most all the smaller and many larger fiefs of Portugal and England secured independence; the orders of Knights Templars and of the Teutonic Knights founded their estates in Prussia and Livonia, upon Malta, Rhodes and Cyprus; Greece was filled with baronages. *Consciousness of the necessity of a unity against the oriental powers was forming. RANKE. New states organised. Small princes obtain power in proportion to the kings losing theirs. Militant orders. § 168.*

Excepting some subsequent effects, favorable to commerce, there was not much benefit to be drawn from the gigantic undertakings, least of all to the hierarchy. That the range of ideas and comparisons became widened was rather obnoxious to the curia. *Except the opportunities for comparison, the widening of the horizon and impulses given to commerce, little benefit was derived from the gigantic undertakings.*

The **direct gain for the church** consisted in the test of her influence in directing the pugnacious tendencies of the times, and especially of the Normans, against the schismatic East, and the impetuous and piratical Saracens. Through the agencies of the spiritual militant orders the popes gained new power over large districts and over princes. These results the church had realised; but others ensued which, tho invisible as yet, were destined to become evident at remote dates; results upon which the curia could lay no hold, because they were kept in reserve, were taken care of, and in due time disposed of, by a higher government. *Direct results in favor of ecclesiasticism. Satisfaction of having whipped the schismatic East. Additional suzerainty over large districts, over princes and politics, through the spiritual militant orders. § 168.*

Those really benefitted by the eastern expeditions were to be neither secular nor ecclesiastical princes, but the nations. The generation of new forces, disengaged during the long period of the crusades, was destined to arouse Asia in order to enjoin upon Europe the leadership in universal civilisation. *Other results as yet occult. Orientals returning the visits in due time. §§ 127, 134, 138, 142, 150, 163-166.*

So far the peoples had been lulled into the sleep of Roman generalness; the idea of the "Holy Roman Empire of the German Nation" had captivated almost every tribe of Europe. But to all of them the governing few meant "the state," and saints, monks and priests meant "the church". Now the enchanted nations awoke to a consciousness of their specific nationalities.

From across the Channel voices were heard, as that of John of Salisbury, saying: "Who made the Germans to dispose of the nations by setting one head-leader over all of them? Who gave these coarse people authority to act thus according to their own notions just as it pleases them?"

The English in arms had shown themselves equal, at least, to the Germans; the French, perhaps, superior. The nations had thus gained a **proper degree of national selfreliance**, which accrued to the advantage of the princes also, and most of all to the profit of the German emperor. Owing to his diplomatic negotiations with the Saracens, never forgiven him by the popes, he had become especially versatile in matters of this kind.

This emperor was Frederick II, the heir of the great Hohenstauffen Frederick Barbarossa. Universal monarchy seems to have appeared to him a notion of doubtful value. A glance upon the neighboring nations must have cautioned him to be reluctant in following the Karolingian polity. For, the symptoms of national consciousness and municipal independence increasing, growing civilisation rapidly spreading over the countries and differentiating the social organisms severally, made it obvious to him that the mirage of an occidental politico-theocratic monarchy must of necessity wane away.

When he found that there may be such a thing as a national form of worship adapted to the peculiarities of a people, as for instance in the case of the Arabs, he began to emphasise the value, dignity and characteristics of the various nations. He had made the acquaintance of Islam; and he pondered deeply over what the caliph of Cordova had intimated to his ambassador, John von Gorze: "With reference to one item your lord the emperor betrays a lack of wisdom, in that he does not retain full power in his own hands."

Frederick's wisdom did not allow him to become beguiled by the Asiatic insinuation. He was abreast with his period of cultural transition toward the dawn of humanistic studies, of enlightenment which sublimates power in order to disengage and liberate individual forces. In short, the two tallying halves of church and state, agglutinated by all means of cunning and power, fell completely apart. After Henry IV, the Thuringian's feud with Gregory VII, the great conflict between emperor and pope broke out again in unprecedented and most acrimonious animosities. What the Christian thought had been (as to civic government or state-power which once had superseded the Jewish church-state and pagan state-religion) the centuries had obliterated. Now the insignificance of the progress of this thought under the prevalence of repristinated orientalism was criticised. The impediments of the Christian thought were analysed—and it revived.

Thus the idea of theocracy and religious uniformity lost its enchantment when the fervor for crusading subsided. The energetic mind of the Occident took its position against the ancient paganism and Semitism which had smuggled itself into the Church. Frederick II consciously took the initiative in the direction of "enlightenment." The **thought of humanitarianism began to take the field.** The emancipating vehemency of freedom took hold of the task assigned to the Aryans, and found vent in that controversy which capped the climax when the pope called the emperor Anti-Christ, and the emperor, not daunted, returned the new title. It should be understood that, since we are compelled to outline the peculiar characteristics of the Roman theocracy as such, it is not intended to deprecate the blessings which Europe up to that time owes to it. Neither shall we ever forget those venerable persons who worked inside those palings with joyful selfdenial, men and women so rich in knowledge and so exalted by their piety.

CH. IV.   CHURCH-STATE AND LAMAISM.

§ 146. Ideas are destined to work themselves through antitheses and over the obstacles of opposition. The thought of humanism, imparted at the middle of the times, had to undergo the process. As the theme of a mystical composition submerges in the waves of modified variants, often seeming to disappear entirely under shrill discords, so the theme under discussion seemed to have become lost during the period of the crusades.

Nations in their juvenile exertions and aspirations have generally set at naught with a few powerful strokes the cool calculations of the diplomats. Frequently, however, superior statesmanship will regain the mastery, and they will succumb after all. We witnessed how, at the end of the Pre-Christian æra one nation after another, save the German, fell victim to Roman skill in politics. And the history of Rome after the middle of the times shows how every attempt at national emancipation found its master in the spiritual mistress of the world. Now, that certainty of success, that determination, which, with the hand at the sword's hilt, used to toss peace and war out of the folds of the toga; that cool calculation which taught the Romans to await their chances for dividing in order to dominate, and the circumspection of experienced politicians, was associated with inful and mitra.

Roman tactics superior to the vehement attempts at emancipation in juvenile nations.

Roman diplomacy biding its time for practicing its old "divide et impera."

Karl the Great had begun his career as a German; as a Roman ruler he closed it. In equal manner did every German "raising of shields," that is, every attempt at national emancipation from Rome, end with a more tightened inveiglement in the meshes of the Roman net spread through Europe. In the Romanised nations propensities ripened which Machiavelli designated as ruinous to humanity, and which finally obtained the victory in the absolutism of the courts and of the curia. Under such circumstances the strength of the Germans and their kings rapidly declined. The sentiments of magnanimity, courage, freedom, and dignity reigning in the castles, in the cities, and on the farms were made pliable to be subdued under Roman principles. Had it not been for the incessant moral coercion to agree to the establishment of a consistent view of life and a uniform world, this subordination of the German mind to Rome would not have been possible.

Machiavelli conspiring against Rome in the interest of another one-sided humanitarianism. § 182

Germans in search of a consistent view of political life were persuaded to agree and subordinate themselves under Rome. § 137, 138, 142, 143, 156, 171.

Let us see how German strongmindness and world-consciousness were remodeled: "It needs be represented to us in full view," says Waitz, "that the 12th and 13th centuries are marked by the intermingling of legendary elements into history. Even 'pious fraud' pushed into historiography." What caused this phenomenon just then?

Legendary elements infused to Christian theology corrupted even historiography. WAITZ.

In times long before the crusades we find elements of oriental world-consciousness in Europe in the form of fairy-tales. They are an heirloom of the Aryans, brought along from the common home, and held in veneration among the Germans not less than among the Hindoos. A very peculiar form of folk-lore lay concealed in their minds like indestructible seed deep in the soil of the woods.

Aryan folk-lore transmitted oriental views of life, § 150.

The queen of snakes with her golden crownlet speaks the same sentiments on the Rhine as on the Ganges. And new legends were added. Indian stories and fables, carried through the Mongolian world eastward to Tibet and China, were spread just as much through Persia, from whence the Arabs and Islam communicated them to Europe. "With reference to Europe," says Benfey, "the Byzantine empire, Italy and Spain served as ganglion centers for the transmission of these conceptions of the world." He substantiates this import of legendary contributions by quotations from the Panshatrantra.

(Queen of snakes) by way of Persia, Arabia and Spain, BENFEY.

Other channels of these influences opened through the crusades, in which the marveling, juvenile nations drew back the curtains so as to admire oriental life, the mysteries of which had ever hovered before their inquisitive minds. The occidentals had been charmed by the half opened view ever since the reports about the "Prester John" had traveled west, the memory of whose throne had attracted the first exploring expedition to the East, "deep into yonder regions where the barren tree stands before the temple in Tatary."

("Prester John"). § 125.

"That prince who succeeds in pushing through the lines of sentinels and through the armies which guard that distant temple of Prester John, so as to hang up his shield on the barren tree, will become lord over the entire country of the rising sun."

—Embellished with idea of world dominion. JOH V. HILDESHEIM.

So Johannes of Hildesheim once put the legend on record.

For a long period after the crusades it was the belief in the Occident that paradise existed in those regions, enclosed, as people imagined, by a fiery wall.

(Paradise).

A world of mysteries and of the miraculous opened itself.

(Bird of Simorg).

The bird of Simorg has its nest in the northern part of Bactria, the land of wonders, where, according to Ktesias, Herodot, and Strabo all the wondrous beasts, the dragons and the gold-producing ants have their home. Besides the bird Simorg there exists the bird Phœnix in this mysterious Orient, and the pelican, the griffin and the sun bird.

(Phœnix).

(The griffin).

There, the Wigalois relate, the cave exists which glows from an eternal fire; and in this fire the salamanders weave that costly texture full of lustre, the atlas, the incombustible phellel. From thence come silk, satin, and damask, and the heavy brocades, the acme of luxury in wearing apparel. People thought of the Orient as of a magic castle, filled with treasures of every description. The snake guarding hidden treasures, the virgins of the swan, the sprites of the fogs in the thickets of the mountainous woods; the goblins and the elves who come to help in the cellar and in the kitchen, have their homes in yonder land; Cinderella, the wish-bone, and the wish-tree, these are all objects whose memory is revived by new arrivals from India.

(Goblins, Elves).

(Cinderella).

(Wish-bone).

and made the Orient attractive to the Occidentals; during and after the crusades.

Magic night covers the countries of the setting sun.

It bears a certain historical interest to investigate the importation and trace the route of such tales as those alluded to; and to watch the approach of a moonshiny night drawing near from yonder eastern skies.

Buddha canonised as St. Jeioshaphat. Rudolph of Ems. § 59.

Reading the legend of Alexander in occidental dress, reading the poem of Anno, one can get a glimpse of the mystical sheen which illumines the magic night now covering the countries of the setting sun. Even Buddha immigrates, Rudolph von Ems has made him a Christian Saint in his "Balaam and Jehoshaphat". That is to say: the flight from real life into a world of dreams in pursuance of oriental ideas reached a terminus of extension unthought of before, when it appeared in full dress of occidental style.

In a dreamy twilight of this sort man does no longer maintain his fitness for life as it is. The real world is conceived as a poor abstract, existing apart from human life, as if moving according to different laws of its own. In the actual world, owing

Phantastic imagery supplants views of real life.

to the nominalistic and realistic controversies, men lose all their interest, and become unconcerned as to its continuity. Behind that phantom creation of the imagination, which is believed to be the real world of wonders and metamorphoses, our world of actual ʼreality disappears, whilst phantastic apperceptions throw their distracted images upon all relations of life in every particular. Christian doctrine of those times pictures this dream-world as Heaven, or—its opposite. And that fairy-

Metamorphoses. (a basis for ecclesiastical alleged miracles).

land with the Christian name overshadows the views of life so that strange figures and forces and miracles are imagined as playing into all human affairs and taking the place of the present prosaic form of existence.

Map of the world refracts the picture as reflected in the monkish brains of the 13th century.

A map of the world, painted by the monks of Ebsdorf in the beginning of the 13th century, but recently discovered, affords a significant view into the dreamy mode of thinking to which the occidentals had become inured in that peculiar period.

§ 147. Again, then, we meet with the world-consciousness of transcendentalism; for this is what we have before us in Romanticism. It is the reappearance of the

Chasm between real life and human destiny reappears. § 63, 123, 139, 158.

deep chasm between real life and human destiny, which the Greeks had endeavored to bridge. It is the same hiatus between the spirit and nature, which defied the speculation of the Hindoos with all their renunciation of the things of this world, and all their shirking of the ethical task required for living in it. Practically it is the

Practically a relapse into Hindooism.

eccentric asceticism caused by the desire to soar above the existence of probation, which renders it virtuous to condemn nature instead of redeeming its depressed life and transforming it into true relationship with personal life, and leading it up to the common glorious destiny. In order to justify this avoidance of the ethical duties, the world is denounced as the abode of seducing powers exclusively.

Perhorrescence of mundane conditions.

It is then imagined as a spacious gloomy castle with secret, subterranean gangways, trap-doors and dungeons, where countless uncanny perils are lurking. Everywhere snares are concealed in which the erring foot is caught; everywhere decoying voices are heard or

Compacts with Satan.

unearthly shrieks call for redemption and delivery from the powers of darkness. The enjoyment of earthly existence is denounced as a compact with the evil one. The impatience for enjoying heavenly bliss preposterously reaches out after artificial gratifications of Romantic

Indulging Romantic sensualities in Platonic reality.

sensualities in Platonic reality. Whatever decorates earthly existence is decried as Satanic; especially the appropriation of physical knowledge and critical science, and the aspiration to

Appropriation of scientific knowledge condemned.

prosperity are condemned, because all of this makes people too incredulous and independent to suit the miracle-mongers.

The Indo-Romanised form of consciousness despairs of and denies the permeation of the world with heavenly influences; according to Romanticism the ideal of humanism cannot be realised but by mystifying if not virtually annihilating the reality of mundane conditions. The true ideal of humanity remains transcendental and the dogma of transcendentalism prescribes contempt and renunciation of the world, selftorture and mortification of the flesh, the terms world and flesh taken in a materialistic instead of their biblical sense. This fleeing from the world corresponded with seeking refuge in the church, under equal misapplication of the term:

Monastic life the only refuge from the perils of worldliness.

Church. The monastery was the asylum paramount. The flight out of the world by vows of external renunciation was held forth by the church as the ideal of virtue, as perfect and even superabundant holiness; and a celestial world of saints made that degree of virtue glimmer down into earthly life. This sort of separation of the

Mischievous interpretation of Old Testament calls forth not only flight from the world, but also fight with the state.

Church from the world is strictly in accord with the Pharisæical interpretation of the Old Testament in which the difference of sacred from secular objects was of intentional necessity, whilst now it could get no further than to its last resort of a deadly conflict with the "world", that is, to an unmitigated fight with the state. This mode of separation could only run into that antagonism which ever renewed the ecclesiastical attempts to dominate over the state, whereby the church was rendered Church rendered worse than worldly. worse than worldly indeed. In the demand of mortifying the bodies according to the Deduction: The state should abandon itself to the Vicar of God. schematised rules or spiritual "councils", or advices how to die unto the "world", the command was included or deduced that the state should abandon itself to the "Vicar of God."

The faithful were instructed to seek the true contents of life in the "church" alone. Now, inasmuch as by the inversion of doctrine the people found their religious wants and the regulations as to conduct with their environments provided by the church, and as the church—meaning always the hierarchy in mediæval sense—frequently afforded protection to the weak and refuge from the tyrannical arbitrariness of the strong, there ensued a veritable emigra- Church usurped all things attributable to the Mediator alone. tion from the state into the church. As the church was then constituted, a state within the state, the people found satisfaction to a certain degree in ecclesiastical orders and offices and prescriptions; and such allegiance to the institution being identified with attachment to Christ, the power of the church became constantly extended and augmented. And in proportion to such church-extension the flight from the world became a fixed program of domineering over the world. Church government was esteemed as more authoritative than "worldly" government, i. e., the state. The state was doomed to humiliation, and degraded to the class of those things to which Christians must deaden themselves. The state with its ruler was tolerated only so far as it would subordinate its means of execution to the aims and interests of the hierarchical supremacy.

In accord with hierarchical views not only was matrimony desecrated, but the Matrimony degraded. whole order of life, public and private, in family and society, was perforated in the The whole order of life perforated interest of priestly rule, just as the order of nature was dissolved for the sake of for the sake of imitated miracles. ecclesiastical miracles. Possession of earthly goods was frowned at and decried as degrading the possessor to a second class Christianity, if the right of possession was Enrichment of the "mort-main". not waived in the interest of the church. The pious sons and daughters of the church were expected to donate at least parts of their inheritances to the "mort-main" Platonism as derived from Buddhism. the dead hand of the church: and the orders proclaimed the meritoriousness of communis- § 78, 81, 97, 103, 122, 124, 144, 149, 150, 185. tic in preference to private possession. This was nothing new, even in the Occident; for we have seen that Platonism had introduced and promulgated a view of life alien to Hellenic world-consciousness.

It was essentially from this oriental view that the European idea of communism originated. In fact the whole fabric of the mediæval hierarchal state is directly reducible to, and in line with, the Plato-Augustinian theory.

The hierarchy virtually contrives at indirectly rendering the state a Buddhistic-Platonic, fully developed as to views of the world and order of life, in furtherance of diplomatic schemes. as much as a Mosaic, theocracy. The entire visible universe is conceived as a pædagogical institute in which the head and master has authority over the pupils and minors in his charge and under his discipline. The philosophers must be without family cares and worldly connection, without possession. Such exactly is the "Church" with her priestcraft and monastic Communism after Platonic ideas. caste. That view of the world under the aspect of formalism, and asceticism, whether in § 68, 124, 160. Benares or in Rome, will produce the same effects: flight from the "world"; absorption of personality, of responsibility, rights, and duties, and contempt of nature, the realm of the relative good.

§ 148. Ancient Hindoo world-consciousness, however, could not have shaped Semitic legalism added to oriental contempt of natural life. such a cast of hierarchical malformation in the Christian Occident without the other ingredient of Semitic legalism. Had it not been for this addition of pharisæical self- Divine grace transformed into compulsion by law. conceit and statutory regulation of ritualistic observances, it would not have been possible to subvert the truth of Divine Grace, which moves and transforms life from within each person, into a force of law, which works compulsorily from the outside.

Gregory of Nazianz already had preached to the statesmen of his time: "The law of Heavenly things not to be ranked second to secular matters. GREGORY OF NAZIANZ. Christ subordinates you to our power and to our jurisdiction. For we also lord over things, and our diminion exceeds yours. Or do you think that the spirit should give way to the flesh, and that the heavenly things should rank behind the earthly?" That early, then, an aspect of Christianity had cropped out with the demand of political subjection, forgetful of the apostolic admonition to submit to the government even of a Nero.

The biblical passage: "compel them to come in", was made a criterion of the claim of the "Compel them to come in" made the criterion of the church rights in accord with Augustine's "State of God." "Tolerance is cruelty." AUGUSTINE. § 78' 122, 124. church upon the rights to apply the compulsory power of the state. Augustine already had designated tolerance as cruelty, a maxim enabling him to condemn the entire history of the Roman state as the pool of sin and Satan and as the house of Sardanapal, in order to put up his own THEOCRATIC church-state in its place.

Upon the ruins of the worldly state, once founded upon Roman lawfulness, Augustine built up the "State of God" filled with Mosaic legalism, high above this miserable world. Thus Semitic fanaticism had taken possession of the church in theory. Not much more than what the rigid thought of the church-father had projected was subsequently fashioned into the concrete.

In the Gregorian period, the latter half of the XIth century, the legalistic-theocratic ideas are firmly put together into a working mechanism; the massive building of the kingdom above the "world" is rendered complete. Hildebrandt, the Benedictine monk, made the entire church one vast cloister of which he was the absolute abbot and universal sole ruler. Giesebrecht has tersely expressed his observation of Gregory's (VII) activity: "He united religious devoutness with worldly circumspection and industrious management; monkish contempt of the world and an idealistic soaring up to spiritual life were associated with an air of imperious authority and with a very practical application of a tenacious, wary statecraft."

Descriptive of Gregory's character is his frequent repetition of Samuel's threat: "Rebellion (meaning disobedience) is equal to iniquity and idolatry". Not less frequently he used to quote Jeremiah: "Cursed be he that keepeth back his sword from blood."

Thus the Old Testament theocracy was taken up for continuance. Disobedience to Rome is idolatry and must be punished as such. It must be punished without mercy, for cursed is he who restrains the sword from blood!

This abuse of the sword of St. Peter may realise something like the compulsory conformance to external precepts which satisfies Islam,—conversion never. The world remains world under Rome as much as under Islam. Since then, under such methods, the success of Christianising the world was meagre enough, an excuse had to be constructed for the failure. The easiest way in that direction was to blame the world with being at fault. It was not explicitly stated that the state was Satan's dominion, but the state was harshly reprimanded throughout the Karlovingian method for its carelessness in not extending the territory of the church.

Thomas Aquinas taught that the state was nothing but a natural compact. If based upon a sort of "contract social" the state was of necessity deprived of all authority but that conceded to it by the popes. Without this concession its foundation must be considered profane, to say the least.

From this premise a doctrine of the state was deduced which renders it a socialistic organism without any objective right to claim for itself the character of an institution under orders from God. The State of God allowed the secular state no other prerogative than the right to make treaties, since in the eyes of the hierarchy the "worldly" state was nothing but a necessary evil.

"It was for this reason," says Frohschammer "that Thomas Aquina could in principle not be against slavery. Being doomed to slavery was, according to God's decree, the condition of a race in the way of punishment". This view seems to underlie the papal method of repeated abandonment of people to slavery, when under the ban of the church. The Venetians, for instance, under papal permit were to be made slaves by any one who had the power to do so. It was but the consistency of pontifical logic when it was held that natural man deserves no better treatment if he remains outside the supernatural sphere; and this supernatural sphere is under the exclusive administration of the functionaries and orders of the church.

Montecasino has been called the Athens of the Mediæval times. This monastery was built upon the spot where the old temple of Apollo once stood. Its heavy portals, cast by order of Desiderius in Constantinople, were opened to solemnise the entrance of Thomas Aquinas. Of all the messengers and legates which from thence were sent out on diplomatic errands to negotiate with the worldly powers, Thomas has become the most renowned. His scholasticism became, with many innovations, the theology of Rome. Asceticism increased in rigidity on the ascending scale from Montecasino to Premontre. The polity of the monastic hierarchism advanced in its crusades against the Albingensians and Stedingians under the stimulus of, and on a parallel line with, the inflammatory fanaticism of monkish fervency, utilised in completing the pontifical machinery. In times past the firm construction of ecclesiasticism was an European necessity, when rude masses were to be trained in discipline, or the weak had to be protected against the oppression of crowned persecutors. Without the hierarchal bulwarks it could not have been accomplished, that the culture achieved by the old world was rescued to become the natural vehicle for a new civilisation. Again the arts were cultivated and applied in creating works of incomparable beauty. But notwithstanding these merits. the hierarchal structure, with its pinnacles in the city upon the seven hills in form and methods, is to be designated as the veritable outgrowth of revived Semitism.

The oriental principles of state-theocracy furnished the material for the external unity and conformity (we may as well term it uniformity), whilst the growth of spirituality, the religious contents, the edification of the Romantic structure was entirely under the influence of the other forms of oriental world-consciousness, under transcendentalism with its contempt of natural life. Thus Mediæval **Catholicism was made up of pharisæical formalism, Israelitic legalism, and Ishmaelitic fanaticism; of old Roman energy animating a determined clergy; and of oriental apathy stupefying the laity.**

§ 149. Hindoo world-consciousness culminated in Buddhism. In spite of, or rather because of. teaching to disdain earthly existence, this orientalism created an hierarchal state in Europe equal to that in Asia.

·Of the latter Prschewalsky recently wrote: "The influence of the Lama is unlimited. It is considered the highest privilege to adore the priest and obtain his benediction, or at least to touch the hem of his garment."

The same deification of the representatives of the religious institution by the Mongolian highlanders thus described was utilised among the occidental nations in the accumulation of much wealth in the "mort-main", the "dead hand".

The same formative idea governs the Romanised, the Slavonian, and German nations of Europe and America, and takes the same advantages. By promulgating transcendentalism and world-sorrow the priests, in both instances alike, obtain their predominance, and know how to turn their prestige to account in enriching their organisation and the growth of its power.

The Buddhism of Tibet with its celibacy and torture, with its bells and incense, with holy water and rosaries, confessionals and legacies, amulets and pictures, and with its hundreds of thousands of monks and nuns, understands very well how to keep its adherents in the dull and dazed mood of semi-consciousness. In the gloomy temple, rendered more dusky by clouds of incense, the bald-headed priests in abundance and in luxurious vestments glide noiselessly over the costly carpets around the altar upon which is raised the shrine of the goddess. They light the sacred candles upon the precious, high candlestick under the murmuring of prayers and the tinkling of bells hanging around everywhere. So little does Buddhism differ from Romanism that even the relic-worship of Europe equals that of India. The similitude originates not alone from Nestorianism as referred to. Both Buddhism and Romanism result from the same principles of simulated contempt of natural life in order to dominate over the world, that is, the State.

The footprint of Buddha upon Adam's Peak in Ceylon, and his alleged·tooth, enveloped in rich wrappings, draw countless numbers of pilgrims. We notice in Europe that the saving power of miraculous places and pictures attracts the masses just as much as in India. Whenever in either case the pilgrimages increase, it is a sure sign that extraordinary measures must be resorted to in behalf of ecclesiastical diplomacy. This contrivance at times is deemed indispensable. The hierarchy then generally succeeds and the Buddhist especially never fails. Arranging pilgrimages for political ends are the only means of perpetuating, as by revivals, the philosophy of despondency and suggestion. The streams of pilgrims continually emptying at Hlassa and Urga afford as many opportunities for the increase of priestly power in Asia, as the Catholic demonstrations at Polish graves, or at the shrine of the holy coat in Treves, or at the well-spring in Lourdes.

The large cloister at Potala with its many annexes terminates in the gilt-decked palace of the Dalai-Lama. Occasionally he appears upon the high terrace and lifts up his arms to bless the masses of people who gather from the passes and crevices of the Himalayas and the Kuenlun.   In reverential awe they have been waiting for this greatest moment of their lives in order to go home and die in the assurance of perfection.

The Palatine hill where once the rulers of the world resided, was now a field of ruins. Between the huge, massive walls covered with ivy, sickly olives tried to prevail in the thickets of the wild shrubs. A few inner walls still show elegant frescoing, and blooming creepers have taken charge of the outside portals and pillars for their permanent decoration. In the quietude of this abandoned quarter pasturing sheep gave melancholy answer to each other until,after sun-set,the plaintive sounds of the cicade would give signs of life from among the sparse, dry bunches of grass. The splendor of the imperial city was gone forever. From among the cluster of broken marble palaces in Pallara the bell of the small chapel of St. Andrew sent its peals across the wilderness as over a large grave..

But from this grave of old Rome a new mistress of the world arose; and now the new pontifex maximus draws down upon their knees the swarms of pilgrims before him, when he raises his hands to the nations of the west, "urbem orbemque."

We have reached the summit upon which both in the Orient and in the Occident that view of the world tapers out, which we found petrified among the Hindoos and the Mongolians more than a thousand years ago, and which we find again as arrested or depressed life in the Middle Ages. By way of closing the retrospect of this period we add but one more remark.

The thought of true humanity had withdrawn into sacred recesses, away from the crowds of contending nations, away from the turmoil of feudalism, crusades, confederacies, and emancipation. Here and there this thought protrudes again when called forth by such philanthropists as the Saxon Meister Eckhart and, reappearing, substantiates itself in its holy beauty. It shines out of the features of Mysticism, from the works of the profound thinkers and great masters of Corvey and Canterbury, of Paris and Ratisbon.

Art frees itself from
Byzantinism.   § 125.
Cologne masters.
      Schœngauer
We observe now in the works of representative art this thought to be Germanised and the rigor of Byzantinism overcome and abolished.

In the paintings of Schœngauer and Meister Stephen of Cologne, the faces of praying men and adoring angels appear in childlike naturalness and touching beauty.

Like the flowers in the fore-ground of their pictures the painters of the age of transition themselves stand out like modest buds on the banks of the historic rivulet, full of promises of a new spring season. Our allegorical rivulet is the thought of true humanism; taking rise in the secluded and peaceful valley of Mysticism, and running through the wild underbrush of the church-polity in the dark ages.

G. SEVENTH DIVISION.—THE FIRST AND LARGEST CIRCLE OF NATIONS.

T U R A N O - M O N G O L I A N S.

SYLLABUS: THE AGE OF MISSIONS.

Syllabus.

History of civilisation
needs the disquisition
as to
Re-entering this widest sphere stretching abroad along the periphery of humanity an explanation is required for maintaining our former designation of the Mongolian world as the first circle of nations. For it might be objected that this caption is ill adapted to the topic under which the history of Europe is included and discussed. We rejoin that even after the revival of sciences the old background shines distinctly through to the extent of adumbrating that very world of nations which now stands in the foreground.

The period attracting attention virtually begins with the irritation of the West by the Mongolian invasions. As soon as the European nations come into contact with Mongolian elements after the discovery of new continents and the establishing of transmarine routes for international traffic, issues are joined and take definite contour. When this period closes, the prospect opens that those old Mongolian states will be permanently drawn into the progressive movements which tend to civilise the whole world.

Focusing this cultural advance our observations are directed to that extended domain under Mongolian dynasties which resembles vast fields of compact ice.

This domain, which, after the crusades, became affected by the progressive tendency, consists not of the East alone; for the Occident is only a large peninsula of the Orient.

Mongolian
bearings upon
European
progress.

Mongolian invasions
made
Too much have those relations been overlooked which secretly played between the two parts of the globe and connected Europe so intimately with Asia as its mainland. It seemed as tho the Aryan culture of Europe should unawares be absorbed again by the old culture of the countries from which the young nations had detached themselves. Buddhism not only continued to be a mental power but also a compact organism, and an attractive center of gravity exerting paralysing influences. It was Buddhism through which a copiousness of legends and fairy-tales had been transmitted to the Chinese. Turano-Mongolians in turn sent these reflexes of an imaginary world to Europe, where they became reunited with similar forms of consciousness at the time the power of Islam reached out over Byzantine and Cordova in order to grasp Europe.

Instrumental in the
establishment of
trans-oceanic relations
and international
intercourse, (as formerly
of city-life under
Henry I.) and showing
the Germans necessity
for uniting.
§ 140, 141, 142, 143, 145,
148, 156, 171.
In addition to these facts, which demand a more comprehensive retrospect than former cursory references, because of which the influence of Mongolian culture was undervalued, we wish to remind the reader that not our disposition of the material, but history itself thus drifts toward the periphery.

Turano-Mongolians
and Semites
transmit Buddhistic
views, to become an
ingredient of European
culture.
§ 74, 87, 97, 181, 142, 148,
147, 150, 185.
In this division we endeavor to demonstrate that the affairs of our race cease to be governed by the narrow circle of the Mediterranean, since the oceans are made the means of international communication. History again draws into its movements the great Pacific upon which the ends of the most pristine culture meet those of modern civilisation in order to render it universal.

CH. I.   TURANO-MONGOLIAN BEARINGS UPON EUROPEAN CIVILISATION.

§ 150. The political construction of Europe dates from the decomposition of its southern part. Provinces are rounding off into independent states, whilst other states crystalise under the formative principle of nationality. We have observed the mental strains regulating the formation of the social organisms. We witnessed how a new Roman dominion, then necessary and salutary, bound the nations together and tutored their cultivation. We exhibited the mediæval world-theory as the bond of unification. *Passing from Mediterranean to Oceanic dimensions of communication. World-theory of Mediæval ecclesiasticism bound the national units of Europe together*

The first opportunity for an emancipation from this bondage was, at the proper time, occasioned from without. The Christian thought with its cardinal principle of genuine humanitarianism had been lying sick in bed, as it were, most of the time, in the bed of Rome old and new, weakened and dormant, from its contact with and contest with the spirit of antiquity. It now arose to its gradual recovery. Pagan elements had encysted the systems of circulation and secretion in the ecclesiastical body which was to be the organism of the Christian spirit. Whatever the encrusting elements were, either oriental-Semitic or occidental-Roman, they were heathenish. Upon such grounds and into these directions Christendom had outwardly grown. Never had the soil been properly prepared, and the plant had assumed much of the nature of the sub-soil and of the building rubbish strewn over the fields of ruins. The Roman element predominated in the structural part, whilst in the functional,— in the movement of the vital sap and the work of assimilation, that is, in theology and philosophy always controlling historic progress—the effects of Hellenistic thought remained ineradicable. Above all stood Platonism in high esteem, and we have noticed how strongly it was infected with the pagan transcendentalism of the Orient, until the realistic and rather materialistic scepticism of Aristotle was intermediated and inoculated into Christian scholasticism through learned Jews and Arabs. They introduced another method of thinking, and contributed their pantheistic-emanatic and fatalistic modes of oriental thought toward the arrangement of Christian concepts. These ideas agreed so well with the Roman inclinations as to be utilised in an intellectualistic representation of the "faith", as doctrine was now called. *Pagan elements encysted the inner organs of the ecclesiastical organism. Græco-Roman paganism the structural—Semito-Buddhistic the functional part of the social organism of Christendom, at the dawn of the new æra. Mediums of transmitting Orientalism to the Occident. § 75, 81, 97, 122, 124, 126, 130, 131, 143, 146, 147, 149, 150, 185.*

The manner in which the alien elements were mixed into our religion is plainly observable, for instance, in the introduction to the writings of the pseudo-Areopagite, especially in his "Earthly and Heavenly Hierarchy." Equally evident is the influence which Alkendi at Basora had in this direction upon his contemporary, Scotus Erigena at the court of Charles the Bald. Most notorious is the influence of Maimonides, the Jew, as exerted upon Paris and Cologne; and not less obvious are the bearings of Salomo ben Gabirol, and of Avicebron with his new Platonism, upon the literary circles of the West. In short, we see how from many sources pantheistical gnosticism and oriental knowledge of nature—especially astrology, with which Jewish and Arabian disciples of Aristotle always loved to deal—were transmitted to, and imbibed by, the Scholasticism and Mysticism of the Occident. *Asceticism, (Plato). § 124, 147, 149. and worldly dominion (Augustine) Communism. § 66, 87, 97, 122, 138, 144, 147, 149, 160. Scepticism and intellectualism, ("faith'), through Aristotle as translated. Pantheistic gnosticism Kabbala. § 129.*

As in the patristic times the ear of the church had given a hearing to Plato, so the teachers of the mediæval church adopted Aristotle by way of Spanish Semitism. *Knowledge of nature. ALKENDI, AVICEBRON. § 130.*

To be sure, the universities and the theologians in the monastic seminaries alone engaged in the theories of the antique. Of the mental activity of the schools the people could not become aware; it was deemed rather dangerous that the "laos" should be made acquainted therewith. The laity was treated on the mental diet of fairy tales, legends and ghost stories. *Albertus Magnus. § 129. Probabilism. § 73, 129, 132, 133, 163, 164. Greek humanistics. § 127, 137, 142, 145.*

Man in mediæval times was practically kept under the norcotic influence of orientalism. In the first place people were hypnotised, figuratively speaking, into the dream life of Asiatic asceticism, which had come in across the Ægyptian desert. *Esoteric scholarship, sorcery. § 130.*

Then came the revival of legendary tradition which disclosed a world of phantastic and dreamy revery, whereby the belief in ecclesiastical miracles was fostered, the adoration of pictures and the trade in relics stimulated, and social and family-life perforated. *Immaculate conception. § 131. Phantastic legends. § 146. and relic-worship § 48, 124, 125, 127, 150, 151, 152.*

Few are the redeeming traits of mediæval piety as evinced in the heroism animating the chivalrous orders, and in the venerable features of Christian meditation and childlike pensiveness as expressed in the art of Fiesole and Schœngauer, or in the prayers of Bernard of Clairveaux. *Into the scholasticism of the Mediæval church.*

Two sets of
ethics
for two grades of
Romanised humanity.
§ 72.

The redeeming features of the Church of those times are scholasticism and mysticism, notwithstanding their splitting the world into a supernatural part of clerical and monastic ranks with ethics of their own, and a natural part of the "worldly," with a code of conduct deemed fit for the laity, made easy enough so as to secure their permanent subordination to the ecclesiastical authorities. Through such differentiation,

ersecution of heretics.

Aggressiveness of the
Turano-Mongolians
Indirect cause of
breaking up the
confounded views of
life

with the tribunals against heretics, and with the crusades against Katharians or Khazares, Waldensians and Stedingians, as the products of the double set of ethics, the cardinal principle of humanism had become entirely subverted and made irrecognisable.

Then that occurrence happened to which the onslaught of Turano-Mongolians had given the first impulse, and which thus indirectly caused the breaking up of those confounded views of human life in the castle, in the city, and in the country at large.

Fall of Athens
bewailed by
MICHAEL AKOMINATO

As bishop Hildebert of Tours had once sat upon the ruins of imperial Rome, so archbishop Michael bewailed the ultimate fall of Athens about the year 1200 A. D. Among the rubbish—all that was left of the Stoa Poikile—goats clambered around after a morsel of verdure or a bunch of grass. Michael Akominatos had concealed his fine collection of classic literature in the innermost sanctuary of the Parthenon church. He could scarcely find words to express his sorrow over the devastation of the city as compared with the splendor of yore: "The walls lying prostrate, the houses falling to pieces; across the places where once comfort dwelt now the plow is drawn."

Foreboding the
Fall of
Constantinople.
§ 137.

Then came the turn for Byzanz to become devastated and enslaved.

Look at the situation of the once powerful dominion of old and new (that is, of Latin and Greek) Rome. Upon the line Euphrates-Guadalquivir the remnant of the last of the ancient world-monarchies arose like a gigantic mountain with two cones. The contours of the solitary summits appear as if blended with heaven, while from their frozen slopes glaciers slide down; and as the icy region recedes it leaves bare yonder morains and fields of erratic boulders and fractured rocks of "the substratum."

What once had been West-Roman territory is now parcelled out to a medley of Frankonian, Gothic and Norman principalities and bishoprics. Now the East from the Halys to the Orontes is only enlivened by the masses of Scythian rudeness strewn in among the remnants of Greek culture. Palaces, propylæa, temples, cupolas stand amidst wildernesses of rubbish, serving as barracks or camping grounds for the nomades of the steppes. Upon the terraces of destroyed castles, in which kings had kept

Turcomans in sight.

house, stand now the black felt tents of the Turcomans. In this condition we find the new world at the dawn of enlightenment.

The new world in this condition reminds us of the old relations once existing between Orient and Occident.

Early communications
with Mongolia.
§ 52, 53, 55.

Ptolemy and Ammian knew of the road which led from the Yaxartes across the Musdag on the Altai mountains into Sera—that is, northern China—from whence Rome derived its silk. A sparse communication between the farthest ends of the historic world had been opened, tho a regular commercial connection was impossible on account of the desert regions of the Gobi and the high and sterile terraces of Iran. St. Louis once more sent a Franciscan monk to

French monks at the
Mongolian court.

the court of the Mongolian emperor, who took his route north around the Caspian Sea and found the court in camp in the Dsungary. Subsequently communications between the nations of uttermost antiquity were again interrupted for centuries.

Poetical legends revive
the old dread of
Mongolian invasions.
RAUMER.   § 44, 55, 60.

In the meantime the dread of the storms from the East, especially among the Greeks, had been poetically embellished in the Occident. Raumer directed our attention to these symptoms of the ethnical instinct. Alexander the Great had exiled a tribe of the Jews into the mountains of Mongolia. Upon these heights, it was said, he had fastened large trumpets. Whenever the wind was caught by, and went through, them they gave loud sounds, making the captive Jews believe that the hosts of the enemy as yet surrounded them. But after a while owls built their nests in the trumpets and the signals ceased to sound forth. Hence the captives, concluding that the king's armies had been withdrawn, made a break for freedom and stormed down upon Europe. They were the Mongolians. Against the terrible invasion none but the armies of Alexander could protect the countries of the setting sun. This was believed in Europe for many centuries. Now the great Alexander was gone, and the Mongolians came actually storming along through Tatary.

For the southern Asiatics these Tatars became what the Germans had been for the south of Europe. In either case the raids affected the civilised southerners in such manner as to alarm and stir them up, a result rather beneficial than damaging to the molested nations. At the period under discussion the northern semi-barbarians had to play this role once more.

First they inundated Hindoostan and Iran. By swift movements they pushed their swarms across Western Europe. When Bokhara had been taken, the Dgengis-Khan entered the grand mosque and exclaimed from the pulpit: "The field is mown, feed your horses!" The Korans were thrown under the horses' hoofs, and the sacred vessels of Islam were made their mangers. The city was plunged into blood. So was Persia tramped down by the million of Mongolian cavalry. Then Moscow fell like Bokhara, into the hands of Batu-Khan. Burning and killing, the train of the conqueror, which covered thousands of square miles, came wallowing along through Poland up to Liegnitz in Silesia. In this eastern part of Germany they arrived at the very instant that the pope caused the heretics to be slain in the countries of the Saxous and in the Provence.

Is it not remarkable that the season of blood for the hierarchy under Innocent III exactly coincides with that of the Mongolian power? In the person of the Dalai Lama the Grand Khan gave his countries a spiritual head whereby the immense empire came to have its religious backbone. This Dalai Lama in Hlassa is tantamount to what the pope and Rome are for Europe—representing the same principles under the same forms, however largely the contents may be at variance. For it is to be remembered that these Mongolians were no longer merely cruel conquerors.

The "golden tent" at Kiptshak had been stretched, figuratively speaking, over the countries of the Hoangho and the Ganges and as far as the Euphrates and the Volga; hence the appellation of "the golden hord." In the chancelry at Karakorum or Bokhara the imperial edicts were given in the seven chief languages of the realm, namely: Mongolian, Tibetian, Tungutian, Uighurian, Arabian, Persian and Chinese. Soon afterwards the missionaries, rather emissaries of the pope as well as of the caliph of Bagdad, and the ambassadors of Russia, Persia, Armenia, and France crowded the courts of the Khan, the son of Batu at Karakorum. In Bokhara the sciences received due attention, so that thousands of students sat at the feet of great teachers at the national academy. Thither the soldiers were attracted no less than those of the contemporaneous Thomas Aquinas at Paris.

But this rapid advance of Mongolian culture, notwithstanding forty virgins, richly adorned with precious jewels, were dispatched to the grave of Dgengis Khan. During the time of his death and funeral everybody was forbidden to shear sheep; the standards of the army were thrown down; for the dirge the drum was beaten. And to these Mongolian and Tatar hordes, rude in spite of their schools in Samarkand, the Byzantine emperors sent gold-glittering dalmaticæ and—their daughters.

Forty camel loads of Byzantine earth had been demanded by Timur, and Byzantium had delivered this tribute at Samarkand. Nevertheless, the mighty Timur knocked hard at the "high portals" of Byzantium and Trapezunt. At Ispahan he caused towers to be built from seventy thousand human skulls.

Finally the Mongolians drove before them a fugitive tribe of rebellious Turks. Sulaiman was persecuted from Khorassan into Armenia, and the grandson of Sulaiman now sent the Byzantine warriors behind their walls. His great successor completed the conquest. Constantinople fell.

With the overthrow of this East-Roman empire the formation of Europe and the condition of the whole world underwent a decisive change. We may ponder a little over the import of this catastrophe.

To Constantinople has been attributed the significance of being the museum and bridge of Hellenic culture. We remember how Byzantium since Karl and the Othons had actually served as the main conductor of Orientalism into Europe.

At first Greek thoughts had been carried from the libraries of Constantinople to Bagdad, from whence the Semites transmitted the translations of newly discovered writings to the Occident by way of Saracenic Spain. Byzantium possessed the advantage of being guardian and custodian of classic culture of which a mere shadow only reached the West in round about way to amuse and enthuse the people with the legendary stories of the Trojan war, and those of Alexander as given by Callisthenes. The monumental remnants of Hellenism had found refuge inside the city walls, and the literary fragments had been collected in the church archives and schools. It occurred now that these old, unappreciated treasures were directly transferred to Italy in order to stimulate the Orient for its task of opening a new æra—by the fugitives of 1453.

It had been the task of Byzantium to lead the Scythian and Slavonian parts of Europe into the by-ways of some sort of Christian culture; Byzantium alone was able to urge on the Bulgarians and Serbians to form states; and only through Byzantium were the Norman Warægians, and subsequently the people of the Russian empire, enabled to partake of the rudimentaries of culture.

21

Marginal notes:

Dgengis-Kahn and Batu-Khan in Southern Asia and Eastern Europe.

Just in time. § 127, 134, 138, 142, 145, 156,

Papal power in its prime simultaneous with the investiture of the Asiatic pope, the Dalai Lama. § 133, 145, 149.

Empire of Dgengis, Batu, and Timur. § 190.

Culture at Karakorum, Bagdad, Bokhara, and Samarkand.

Byzantine emperor sends gilded dalmaticas and—his daughter to Samarkand as tribute to Timur.

Constantinople surrenders, formerly the conductor of Orientalism to Karl, Otto, and Charles the Bald, now the bridge of Hellenic culture to Europe, just in time. § 12, 137, 142, 145, 156.

Greek ideas intermediated formerly by way of Bagdad and Cordova through Semites.

now directly brought to Italy by the fugitives of 1453.

When Byzantium had achieved the fulfillment of these appointments, this Eastern imitation of Rome had to sustain the fate of its original. The hand from on high disposed of the residue of Hellenism by striking down East-Rome at the proper moment.

The task of Byzantium transferred to Russia. § 138, 189.

In that Christianised continuation of Hellas, the Greek state-church, worldly power had been rendered hieratic and theological, if we do not want to say that it had become a spiritual power; whilst in West-Rome the spiritual power had usurped the civil government. Then the Greek part of Christendom went to the cloister, the asylum for enervated nations.

Cesaro-papal power in the East.

Papa-cesarism in the West.

Political problem: "Eastern question."

Idiotic sycophancy. § 71, 125, 126, 127.

The funeral-eulogy of Byzantinism.

The eastern church, always nourished by the controversies of court theologians, had engaged the thought and whim of the nation with the national dogma of the sending of the Holy Ghost by the Father alone. This dogma was made the political problem, beside which the usurpations of the throne and the palace-revolutions seemed insignificant. The fate of the dominion, diminishing to a mere district, was given into the hands of the monks. The patriarchal dioceses of Antioch, Jerusalem, and Alexandria had been abolished long since and had been turned into a sinecure for the court-confessor in the imperial metropolis; there those emperors sat enthroned who on account of the prestige of their orthodoxy posed in unparalleled idiotic superciliousness, withal their political insignificance.

When Luitbrand was German ambassador in Constantinople, he saw emperor Nicephorus enter St. Sophia. Instantly the choir intonated the anthem: "Behold the morning star is risen. He comes to darken the sun by his splendor; the deadly terror of the Saracens appears: Nicephorus, the ruler!"

§ 151. Byzantium had become Turkish.

The alleged head of St. Andrew delivered to the successor of his brother. Gazorovius

One of the princes of the dethroned dynasty, Thomas, the brother of the last Constantine, escaped from Morea over Corfu into Italy. He brought with him a precious relic which he had rescued—the head of the Apostle Andrew.

Relic-worship. § 25, 54, 55, 124, 125, 127, 156, 252.

In solemn procession the pope went out to meet the relic and to take charge of it. These are the words in which the head was addressed: "Thus you arrive at last, O, most holy and sweet flavoring apostolic head. Driven from your abode by Turkish rage, you come to your brother; as an exile you take refuge with the prince of the apostles"!

Italy prepared to receive the more valuable bequest, the humanistic thoughts of classic Hellas.

This alleged head of Andrew, transferred to his brother Peter in Rome, Gregorovius took as the symbol of the empire of Constantine and Justinian, except that the defunct empire left a still more valuable bequest to Italy and the Occident.

Cities had cultivated a spirit of resistance, selfreliance, selfgovernment.

To receive and to utilise this inheritance, which incited the students to study—the "humanistics", Italy was prepared best of all the western countries, on account of the high development of its municipal communities and its city life. During the conflict between Hohenstauffen emperors and popes, the citizens had attained to a high degree of freedom and selfreliance.

Owing to the Normans, moreover, a variety of new political formations had taken shape. Novel organisations in society were the natural results of the resistance which the cities had to offer, now to the pope, now to the emperor, now to the Saracens. The authority of a form of government similar to that of the tyrannies of Greece, was obliged to rely upon not only a money, but also a genuine aristocracy of intelligence and virtue. With that the vacancy caused by the disappearance of customary or feudal legitimacy was more than retrieved.

It is but necessary to a process of supplanting abolished authorities, that now and then a despotism of military leaders will ensue. Here and there an autocrat would make himself prince by a single coup de main, as Bernabo Visconti did, who made the subjected people feed his five thousand hounds. Such despotism knows no other means to rule, but fear and force.

Citizens took interest in politics.

Abuse of power as well as the power of "constructive" rule taught people to apply free criticism in the first place. For despotism creates a vivid personal interest in politics and calls forth general discussion of state affairs. Much was thus gained for the cause of human personality and freedom. "Constructive" princes gave positions to learned men, took poets into their houses, paid them salaries and created centers of enlightenment, education, and civilisation.

In the arrival of fugitives, and "revival of letters."

The Florentine Cosimo Medici patron of Georgius Gemisthos and of the study of "Humanistics."

Venice and Ferrara had opened correspondence with learned Greeks long before the fall of Constantinople. Georgius Gemisthos had then already come over from Byzantium and settled in Florence. Nobody could resist the amicable manner of that young and fervent rhetorician, who cared more for Plato than for dogmatics; least of all could Cosimo Medici, who founded for him the Platonic Academy. The old Aristotelian scholastics, led by George of Trapezunt, did not give up the field without a struggle, but Gemisthos and Platonism came out triumphant.

Petrarca himself, inspired by the products of Greek and Latin poets, had previously insisted upon the fresh and free activity of poetic circles; for the great catastrophe had cast its shadows long before its occurrence, and had occasioned a revival of search and thought before the exiles came over from Byzantium. After its fall a multitude of Greek scholars took refuge in Italy and brought many literary treasures and works of art with them, more than had been seen before. A craze for the classic antique was awakened; never had the meaning of ancient wisdom and art been better understood and appreciated. A great number of connoisers of art, and collectors of antiquities sprang up, who by their praises in verse and prose stimulated the studies of the "humanistics." Poets with idealistic ambition stepped forth in search of notoriety and preeminence.

> It is to be expected that the majority of poets were but poor plagiarists, who sang the glory of those paying them for their verses, such terms as esteem, glory, immortal fame, etc., play a conspicuous and very questionable role in these imitations of the classics. Even at the papal court Poggio and Cenci had organised a society in the merry meetings of which satirical epigrams were composed, sparing nobody.

> Most detestable is the role assigned to a good kitchen in that utilitarian poetry, in imitation of Horace, and the mockery of all that is sacred, in imitation of Aristophanes. Pulci, the humanist, proclaimed: "I believe in capons, in things cooked and roasted; sometimes in butter and beer. If I have no beer I take even hard cider; but of good wine I am exceedingly fond! I believe in cake and pastry, of which I esteem the one as the mother, the other as the son, whilst real pater noster is baked liver. Certain people expect snipe in the next world, fine wines and good beds, and in expectation of that they allow themselves to be stultified into obedience to the monks. We on our part prefer to enter the black valley where we do hear of Hallelujah-singing no more." This, according to Grupp's translation, was the new "faith."

Utterances of this sort are certainly characteristic of the manner in which humanistic studies were scandalised from Rome to Erfurt, by the kitchen-Latin of such sycophants, who, in search of the patronage of petty princes, popularised the Epicurean fashions.

As far as Italy is concerned the veil was drawn away which had been spread during the Middle-Ages. From the Italian cities the personality of man stepped forth to take possession of its birth-right. People of serious mind took it as their highest prerogative to obtain the most liberal education possible. Individually, one would without scruple sever his relations with state or church as it suited his case, and pose as a cosmopolitan. "In Florence"—said Burkhardt—"one was able to exist as an avowed infidel."

This is something entirely new in history, and equal in importance to the discoveries made just at that particular period. In fact it amounted to the greatest discovery, that man was discovered in his rights as a human being, in his value as to responsibility, and in his freedom to choose the means for his emancipation and cultivation. It is the man of modern times who thus makes his first appearance. It is no longer the man of barbarian times who prides himself with the honor of the rank into which he was born, but the man who asserts his selfrespect in the consciousness of his own dignity and freedom as a member of the human family.

§ 152. The progressive movement of the "revival of letters", also known as the period of the "renaissance", was not long confined to Italy alone. Soon the French court ratified the revolution in costumes and fashions.

> Francis I. would have it, that twelve silver statues of gods and goddesses should stand as candlesticks around the royal board; and Benvenuto was ordered to chisel them out. France was filling up with Italian artists. Rosso bought up one hundred and twenty five antique statues for the king and hauled them over from Italy. Titian painted Francis' portrait.

> The marvelous change of the times was demonstrated by those circles of humanists who gathered around Rabelais when he was either with the bishop or upon his parish at Meudon. In every possible form of persiflage he scoffed at "Romanticism" and then depicted his ideal of the future in his "Gargantua."

It is really astonishing how the old Hellenic thought of freedom, of which the renaissance talked so much, was made to agree so nicely with that despotism then perceptible in Italy and England as well as in France.

A little different we find the situation in Germany, where at the smaller and less luxurious courts the "humanists" were not pampered quite so much. Hutten was a free scholar; he rang out: "The spirits awaken; the studies are in bloom. It is a

Petrarca, pioneer of the "Renaissance." Humanistics scandalised by libertinism.

Pulci, translated by Gaupp.

The new discovery at Florence: an infidel. Burckhardt.

Truths to be recognised in the humanistics.

French court (Francis I.) and the renaissance.

Benvenuto, Rosso, Titian.

"Gargantua" a burlesque on Romanticism, Rabelais.

Compromise of liberty with absolutism.

Hutten on revival of letters.

pleasure to live!" The trouble was that he who led this free life was like many others of those heroic talkers about humanistics, a doubtful and rather objectionable representative of the new tendency.

Concerning German "humanistics" the names only need to be mentioned of such as Peurbach, Regiomontanus, Rudolph Agricola, Euridius Cordus, Crotus, Eobanus Hessus, which recall to memory their hilarious and literary societies at Nuernberg, Heidelberg and Erfurt. In illustration the remembrance also of the agile and illustrious Tritenheim may be freshened up. In his museum at Spanheim abbey stood Celtes' picture among rather heathenish surroundings, consisting of mottoes and books. The pity, however, was that the good natured monks were not in the least appreciative of Conrad Celtes' excellent Greek Grammar; nor did they feel the least inclination to adapt themselves to the classic tastes of their abbot.

Questionable phenomena of the era of humanistics less obnoxious in Germany than in Italy.

Eccentric. Tritenheim.

Agricola, Celtes.

The new æra of humanistic studies caused an enchantment under which many an eager student lost his balance. The humanistic zeal of Agricola and Celtes became so highly wrought, that these enthusiasts meant to render Germany more beautiful and more Latin than Latium itself. A certain Frischling desired that every mountain on German soil might be changed into a Parnassus or a Helicon, and every spring should become a Hippokrene. Mistress Venus had been banished into the Hœrselberg; now she was liberated, triumphantly raised upon the shield, and celebrated with loud dithyrambics in all poetical meters of the resurrected antique.

New formations in social life.

The "regeneration" of the Roman, under resuscitation of Greek world-consciousness—as which the "renaissance" is to be understood—transformed thoughts, and customs, and tastes, in short the entire range of the modes of life in every respect. Monkish theology considered women, for instance, as tools of Satan. Theoretically womanhood was completely ignored. It is true that chivalrous knighthood in a romantic manner rescued ladyship, but only to be rendered so abstract as to be restricted to the "kemnate" of the castle, there to become a "Frauenzimmer," or to be idolised in "notre dame." A cult of womanhood thus escorted the woman herself into seclusion and away into unapproachable transcendentalism. The renaissance reinstated woman into her ethical position in society. Whatever the economical progress of the modern world owes to statistics was initiated at Florence: there for the first time social theories were based upon facts thus ascertained.

Cause of womanhood better served than by chivalry.

Economic theories founded upon statistics of facts.

The Villani utilised statistical material even for historiography. They began to paint real pictures of the time when they wrote history, touching not only the political and administrative problems of the day, but taking the history of art, science and habits of life into their scope.

It is but natural that such a new life continued to grow in interest, and that its effects were spreading; that in contrast to the monastic flight from the world and contempt of earthly conditions, the value of real existence, love for the soil and its cultivation, and the duty of improving social relations and conditions all came to be recognised.

Architecture and renaissance. Schnaase.

Concerning architecture Schnaase admits, that the Gothic style is chiefly adapted to building churches. Wherever man feels himself as such and wants to feel at home, where the conveniences of light, pure air, and comfort become necessities in the dwellings of a free citizen, there the Gothic style (to say nothing of the Moorish), will gradually recede.

That bourgeoisie of a well situated middle class in the cities existed already when the renaissance set in. The new modes of life required new forms for the reconstruction of society as well as new designs for the structure of edifices. The style of the antique was borrowed. Doric and Corinthian columns, wreaths of flowers, and genii playing among them with amorettes, beside all the gods and goddesses of Greece, had to decorate the portals and window-casings up to the gable-ends of urban residences, as well as of princely palaces. The houses of the renaissance looked odd among the mediæval gables fronting the narrow streets in the gloomy cities of old. But they had come to stay and announced the dawn of a new æra. Now the world arose from sleep and rubbed its eyes. It was only through the contrast demonstrated by such object lessons that people could become conscious of the meaning of their time. "The study of the antique alone enables us to understand the Middle-Ages" we may say with Burckhardt.

Middle-Ages only to be understood from its contrast with the antique, in the study of this transitory period. Burckhardt.

Classic literature, taken as a standard in measuring the contrast of the two opposite modes of thought, enables the observer now as then, to distinguish their nature and the effects caused by the strain between them. The result of such comparison is similar to that understanding which one may gain of his own country and the character of his own nation by viewing it from the outside. One living in a foreign country and looking back with fond regard upon the scenes of his native home, is better enabled to compare and to appreciate the excellencies of both, his native land and the country of his adoption, than the other who cannot transfer his mind by the memory of his own experiences into different sceneries and situations. *Only from the position of the evangelical world-theory of the Gospel are the*

Educated people of the Occident were now in the position to apply the criterion by which since that period the world has become conscious of the failings of the classic period as well as of those of the Middle-Ages. The gospel of the secondary good, gleaming out of classic lore and art, assisted those who were able to compare it with the true Gospel of the Absolute Good, to understand the latter, and to appreciate it the better, since they obtained an insight into two æras. People had been surrounded by symbolism and forms of Christianity which were fully intelligible to a very few only. Now the old antitheses of the Aryan world-consciousness began to vie with each other, whereby man was set free to examine and to criticise. As the church had promulgated the idea of the transcendental, and had connived at the same time, at the classic conception of a world filled with affirmations of divine immanency, so man found out that he might choose between them, or—find the mode of mediation necessary to reconcile the truths contained in either cognition. *failings of the "Gospel of nature," § 64. i. e. of the secondary good, observable; there is no other criterion for distinguishing the chief opposite modes of thought and for judging the effects of the strain between them. Insight into two æras and thought upon the secondary good aided the students of the classics in appreciating the true Gospel. Humanistic studies set the mind free to criticise formalism and legalism, and enabled scholars to render conciliation of the truths contained in transcendentalism and immanency applicable.*

The most immediate effect, then, of the irritations caused by the Turano-Mongolian movements, was the infusion of Hellenistic ideas causing the revival of the "humanistics", which in turn resulted in the regeneration of the Aryan world-consciousness. For henceforth a new and consistent world-theory, respecting humanity and the conciliation of real existence with human destiny, was sought, substantiated, and practically inaugurated. *Infusion of humanistic thought was the direct effect of the Turano-Mongolian commotions. § 140, 150.*

We began to see the purport and significance of the new phenomenon originating in, or reducible to, Central-Asia. *This caused the "regeneration" of the occidental world-consciousness: § 127, 134, 138, 142, 143, 150, 155,*

The spirit of humanity, the humanism which upon its natural basis had been brought to its highest possible development in the Occident, which, however, had been adulterated and depressed by the intermixture of Semitic legalism, this spirit became now released from its despondency and hierarchal enchainment; it was gradually purified and restored to its full Christian meaning. *the conciliation of real life with human destiny. § 63, 92, 128, 139, 147, 158. Occidental world-consciousnes as to divine immanency emancipated itself from legalism and Buddhistic Semitic contempt of life.*

CH. II.   WIDENING OF THE HORIZON IN THE ÆRA OF DISCOVERIES.

§ 153.   The mental excitement which had agitated the minds of the western nations since the fall of Constantinople caused an almost radical change in the external forms and conditions of life throughout the world, in keeping with the spiritual advance now ensuing. On the whole, the world of antiquity had been entombed, like Herculanum and Pompeii, and forgotten. We witnessed its resurrection. Scholasticism and Romanism were critically tried and sentenced. More or less conscious of the circumstances, public life was drawn into the movement, and with more or less determination society underwent its alternation according to the verdict. *Sudden advance along the whole line of the newly animated nations of Mediæval Europe.*

In every direction the recovering mind apprehended a view of the world as it really is, different from all former views.

There is a mysterious law which prompts nations, rising after a long period of rest, to extend their relations. To such an impulse Europe now responded with a vehemency, as if something was to be made good that had been neglected for centuries. The entire organism of the European nations was set in motion at once. It had dreamt that the world revolved upon the Mediterranean Sea,—or the other "See", rather, near-by. As soon as the spell of this enchantment was broken, Europe arose with recuperated strength and undertook exploits into the wide world. *Man having discovered himself in the humanistics, made now for the discovery of his world.*

Man had been discovered; in the thought of humanity he came to himself; and he now went to discover the world, too.

We will take one more retrospective glance over the history of the Mediterranean before we leave it to its present historic insignificance, comparatively speaking. *Retrospect upon the history of the Mediterranean basin.*

The Mediterranean had become the domain of the Phenecians after they had pushed aside the trade of the Hittites and the Ægyptians. Even the Greeks were beaten by Carthage. But when the Numidian cavalry covered with the skins of leopards and lions, descended from the Alps to invade Italy,—on bare horseback, with bridles made of rush-grass, and waving shields made of elephants' ears—then the iron legions of Rome kept the field, and the dominion over the Occident was decided in favor of the Aryans against the Semites. The Mediterranean became the world's highway under the control of Roman boatswains. Most explicitly is the history of the Mediterranean shown in the alternate layers of cultural residue upon Cyprus. *Cyprus and Sicily represent in layers of cultural remnants the history of the cultured nations.   Cirvoca.*

Commercial relations established sequent to pilgrimages and crusades.

Deep below the other driftings Ægyptian and Phenecian remnants of sculpture are found; then some cuneiform inscriptions of the Persians, for the most powerful of the Darii had been in possession of the island. Then come the deposits of Greek and Roman culture, followed by Byzantine and Arabian remnants, which in turn are superseded by objects bearing decided marks of Genoese, Venetian, and Turkish improvements. According to Cesnola this island resembles a collective lens of all the vicissitudes experienced in the Roman basin.

Equal observations may be made around Syracuse, the other stapleplace of the Mediterranean, for the possession of which many a battle had been fought. Phenicians, Hellenes, Punians and Romans, Goths and Normans, Moors and French had spilled their blood upon this focus of covetous mariners. The searching archæologist may in one day travel from the Greek temple and Roman amphitheatre to the porphyry sarcophagi of the Hohenstauffen emperors.

Genesis of modern international commerce and trans-oceanic intercourse as connected with Turano-Mongolian movements.

During the Mediæval ages parts of the Roman basin, formerly of great importance, sank into oblivion. Other markets had not only compensated for the losses, but even extended the scenes of activity. Christian and Arabian civilisation combined, wrought peculiar industrial and commercial relations, through which goods were transported from the Baltic through the regions of the Oder and the Danube toward Constantinople and Asia. Fur from the Obi and ivory from the Senegal passed each other on the gulf of the three continents. Christian, Arabian, Buddhistic, and Mongolian caravans, pilgrimages, crusades and other martial exploits brought the nations into various forms of contact, which finally continued in the peaceable pursuits of commercial transactions. China exchanged its goods with the Venetians upon Malacca, where also the islands of the Indian archipelago brought their spices to market.

Moors blockade the Venetian line of commerce.
Columbus 1492.

Tur.-Mon. corsairs the direct cause of new maritime enterprises, as formerly of building of cities.   § 140.
and study of humanistics.   § 52.

But Venice commanded only an insecure overland route, so that whenever the Moors would block it up, its commerce would be captured. When this happened it caused Columbus to fit out his caravels at Palos. The coasts of Africa and Asia being completely at the mercy of Moorish corsairs, new roads had to be explored for navigation; the Rialto of Venice was deserted; the oriental lines held by the merchant princes suspended their traffic.

It is of great importance to take all this into consideration, in order to see in what very real manner the eastern incumbrance pushed the West into new channels of enterprise. On the very day that Ferdinand had driven the last vestige of Moorish rule from Spain and made his entrance into the Alhambra, Columbus received his commission from the king to go to Nipon in a western direction.

Columbus commissioned by Ferdinand at Alhambra on the day that Turkish rule was driven from Spain.

Mongolian visits returned by new routes.

When the new world was discovered, the old chain by which the "orbit" had been fettered to the "See" around the Mediterranean sank piecemeal to the bottom of the Atlantic Ocean. And at the time that the western exit was opened for Europe, the western gates of the Asiatics were also forced for Aryan culture to enter into the Turano-Mongolian countries by the eastern route.

Communication extended by water despite the corsairs.

Vasco de Gama doubles Cape of Good Hope.   § 76.

Modern world-traffic was then in its genesis. The two hemispheres began recognising each other and entered into reciprocal interaction. No sooner had the Atlantic Ocean been crossed, than the Pacific, too, was taken into embrace by the ships of the Aryans; in fact it was only then that ship-building commenced.

§ 154. In the quick succession of a few decades marine activity completely altered the condition of Europe.

Christians draw anchor at Calicut A. D. 1498.

For the first time earth was taken in full possession.

Albuquerque trades with the Chinese.

1517. Andrad in the South Sea.

1517. Turano-Mongolian circle disclosed at Yucatan.

1519. Cortez lands at Vera Cruz.

Conquest of Mexico preliminary to the storming of Peking.   § 54, 194.

Toltecian culture in Peru.   A. v. Humboldt.

When on the 28th of May A. D. 1498 the Christians for the first time drew anchor before Calicut, and with loud praises gave thanks to God for safe guidance around the Cape of Good Hope the greatest revolution in the history of culture had been accomplished. For the first time man had taken full possession of the earth. The Mediterranean was reduced to an inland lake. Only now had the East been made accessible, and the notion of Columbus realised.

That brigantine which noble d' Albuquerque had sent from Malacca to China returned with a full freight of silk; and in 1517 Andrad drew anchor upon the Southern coast of China. The world's commerce was inaugurated; the Augustinian and Franciscan monks were immediately following. In the same year, 1517, Hermandez de Cordoba disclosed the other side of the Turano-Mongolian circle of nations when he landed upon the strand of Yucatan. Buried since many centuries by the old forests the architectural works of the Maja were again beheld by the eyes of civilised man. The roads to Uxal, Copan, and Palenque with their gates of uncalculable age, and with their sculptured pictures were reopened.

Two years later Cortez landed at Vera Cruz. The graded towers and temple-pyramids of the Aztecs were seen swarming with worshipers in full action. The conquest of Mexico was only preliminary to the reduction of Peking, three centuries later. Then the empire of the Incas was laid open to the view of Europe. Toltecian life appeared in that shape in which it had taken a final rest from its wanderings from the North and along the Cordilleras to Peru. Transatlantic Mongolo-Malayan culture appeared at its acme, at its close. Agriculture had been remarkably developed. Streets had been built; and artificial constructions of high technique, up to heights of 12,440 feet, (according to Humboldt) covered the slopes of the mountains up to their crests.

The Incas worshiped the sun, a cult adopted from the Aymara, who most probably were Toltecs from the regions of Lake Titicaca. Upon one of its islands the ruins of an old palace of the Incas can be seen up to this day. Their daughters, the "sun-virgins", educated in strict seclusion, and also their ancestor-cult remind one of China. To the Inca-Indians Cuzco was the navel of the world, just as the Chinese considered their "Empire of the Middle" to be. The golden tiles of the Inca-palace near Cuzco glittered into the far distance. In the sun-temple of this metropolis, the mummies of the rulers were seated upon golden chairs, and these rulers used to handle the plough once a year, just as it ever has been the custom in China.

Similarity between Inca-culture and that of China.

The conquest and devastation of Peru will remain a stain upon the pages of the history of the Spaniards who so horribly abused their power during the century it took them to extirpate the Incas. By Spanish vandalism the voices were silenced which most likely would have testified to the fact that the pagan Incas were no worse barbarians than the Romanised Celts and Goths of the Iberian peninsula.

This world of Turano- and Malayo-Mongolian culture in the new Occident appeared to the astonished view of Europe for the first time. The marvel heightened when simultaneously with evidence of West-India's wealth specimens of an old, queer culture arrived from the extreme ends of the Orient. The Pacific with its two coasts was a surprise to the old nations around the Mediterranean, reminding them of the separation between Iran and Turan which had lasted 5000 years at the least. The transfer of a few sets of polar tension to the Atlantic Ocean in the first place brought to view the peculiar contrasts between ancient and modern history, which demarcate the old and new horizon in point of natural science and of world-consciousness.

News of Turano-Mongolian culture, arriving from the West and the East simultaneously, take Europe by surprise.

How limited had that horizon been previous to the renaissance.

The Iliad knew nothing of the world outside the Balkan peninsula and its archipelago; it scarcely alluded to some hordes of southern Scythia. The knowledge of the world ends with Paphlagonia toward the East, and with Thebes toward the South; this limited geography is enwrapped in nebulous mythical legends.

Comparison of the full horizon with the narrow views about the world in the dark ages.

Then came the church whose teachers adhered to a world-theory which comprised the Roman world-orbit. "On their map they located paradise and the center of the world at Jerusalem." We only need to glance over the old Catalonian chart of the world drawn A. D. 1375. A very slight attempt was made thereby to lift the world out of the fogs of the old legends. "The picture or figure referred to is as round as a ball the boys play with, only more like an egg; it is divided into four parts, representing the elements. For, as an egg is enclosed in the shell, and as the white of the egg again surrounds the yolk, so this world is on all sides surrounded by Heaven, corresponding to the shell of the egg. Heaven surrounds the pure air; the pure air surrounds the nebulous, as the white of the egg surrounds the yolk." On the uttermost end of the eastern side the locality is outlined where the anti-Christ dwells: "There is the figure of the great Prince of Gog and Magog, who at the advent of the anti-Christ will arrive with a large host." We also see the country of the cranes and the dwarfs. "And now, that these small people marry when they are only twelve years old, they defend themselves ably against the cranes, and take and eat them. Here ended the realm of the lord of China." In the monastery at Ebsdorf a map was discovered recently with date of 1260 A. D., which shows "the shining birds of the Hercynian woods and the miraculous fountain wherein bathing men are changed into women." Such is the derivation of our story of the storks fetching the babes from the land of wonders and fairies.

What geography owes to the embassies which came to the papal court, is not to be ignored. There was some correspondence with Armenia. Æthiopian emissaries came to Rome of whom Poggio made inquiry as to the rise of the Nile. This evinces the truth that since the age of Indicopleustes some advance had indeed been made in the knowledge of our earth. Yet how deficient was that knowledge, and how narrow the horizon in point of science when the æra of discoveries began to overthrow such childish perceptions, at the approach of the greatest epoch since the Middle of the times.

Papal court and geography.

Inquiry as to the Nile's sources. Poggio.

Progress since Indicopleustes.

§ 155. Modern geography dates from A. D. 1500, the year in which Brazil was discovered. From this year we may amply date also the present knowledge of the skies; for just then Copernicus was made professor of mathematics in Rome. Humanity began to explore earth and heaven at the same instant.

Changes wrought by the discovery.

Geography proper begins with the discovery of Brazil.

Copernicus, professor at Rome.

Through fourteen centuries Ptolemy's astronomy had held its sway. So long the earth had been imagined as the innermost core of a large onion, the diverse layers or skins of which were the planetary spheres. The church had fashioned her dogmas in conformity with such apperceptions; for somewhere between these spheroids the abodes of the blessed and the condemned were located, and above them all, far away, dogmatics had placed the ecclesiastical Heavens. It was not always an easy matter to figure out imaginary distances between spiritual objects.

Humanity at the same instant exploring the heavens and the oceans.

At last it was acknowledged an impossibil:ty; but just as impossible did it seem to purge the mind of the notion of mathematical measurements being applicable to the spiritual sphere. Unless the idea of space is subjected to philosophical treatment, an at least approximate cognition is out of the question, whilst at the same time the necessity is felt to form some adequate comprehension of these entities, the framework of all other realities.

When the scholastics argued about the number of angals which might find room on the point of a needle, they thought that the problem had been shifted upon the proper track; and it was with difficulty that the grave errors ensuing from such clumsy conceptions—as for instance agitating the doctrine of ubiquity of the Lord's body in the Lord's supper—could be overwhelmed.

The matter of locating spiritual objects, that is, forming the definition of the cognition of space, had been made plausible by some sort of an interpretation with which theologians and the laity had contented themselves. Then the shock came by which all these baseless tenets were overthrown.

In his tower of the Frauenburg cathedral, with the view over the roofs of the Ermelandish town toward the white dunes of the "haff" and the waters of the Baltic —Copernicus made his observations of the sky many a night. He took up the calculations of the ancients. He wrote to Pope Paul III that "for a long time he had pondered in his thoughts the uncertainty of every assertion made by astronomers concerning the several motions of the Heavenly spheres." After profound meditations upon the subject he found in Plutarch's writings that Heracleitos and Ekphantos, the Pythagoræan, had believed in the motion of the earth as a matter of course. This remark had fascinated Copernicus and stimulated his conjectures; it took him no great length of time to make an end of the uncertainties.

When Luther, sitting at dinner with some of his friends as usual, was apprised of the first rumors of this great scientific reform, he said to them: "This fool talks as tho he wanted to upturn the entire art of astronomy."

The Roman curia lacked the capacity to take cognizance of what was going on in Germany concerning the new views of Heaven and earth, so, at least, John of Kampen, wrote from Rome to Bishop Dantiscus. The progressive movement of the German spirit was thus ignored, and the process of emancipating the intellect went on without Rome, and—against it. Copernicus dedicated his book to the pope; but the Lutheran Andreas Osiander, then at Nuernberg, superintended the printing and wrote the preface.

The new theory was an audacious contradiction of sense-perception. With one stroke the earth was displaced from the dignity erroneously assigned to her, of occupying the spatial center of the universe. Scientifically the earth was relegated to a rather insignificant corner from the dominating position which had been assigned her by the shallow minds who had an interest to maintain; for since they had considered themselves centers of the universe, they dreamt of nothing but to rule upon this earth. Henceforth the Church, taken as the "government of religion", had to enure herself to the abrogation of her earthly and materialistic ambitions and allow herself to be led back to the figure of her Master, so insignificant in an earthly sense; to be led back to the invisible center and source of spiritual strength and dominion. Henceforth man was to learn that his concerns do not depend upon physical quantities and material forces, and political prerogatives, but that the standard of value is moral superiority and spiritual quality.

Since the earth ceased to be the spatial center and was no longer preponderating in weight, another measure was necessarily to be applied to earthly relations in general. The standard was difficult to be computed, since the search and the finding must, from necessity, involve a break with scholastic dogmatism; and since the application of the new norm must, from equal necessity, unsettle the whole social fabric. The discovery was made, however, and the inevitable consequences ensued.

Heaven as the habitation of nature divine and of the personal God needed to be conceived in a different relation to the earth. Heaven, in its true, that is, in the religious sense, was to be conceived as something else than the material sky; probably as a spiritual form of space, coexisting and coextensive with, and pervading and permeating the material form of our existence; at any rate as a spiritual sphere which in regard to space is not only not far from man, but even within him. The poor concept of Heaven and earth, of time and eternity—being imagined as realities beside each other, as concomitants intersected by distances—must of necessity be thoroughly modified if not entirely reconstructed.

Now intelligence became enabled to elaborate the truth, that both forms of existence are congruencies in a living, organic interrelation and immanency, without eliminating the aseity of either the divine, or the created, substantiality. The apperception of a local up or down, depending upon mathematical distances between spiritual and material concretes, could now be overcome by the insight into hyperphysical, but none the less real, correlation and coextension of things above and below.

As soon as such cognitions became successfully formulated and intelligible many superstitious ideas were set aside. The fears, for instance, of controlling influences from astral worlds, were abandoned, and with them sank the fetters by which the human mind had been bound down and subjected to the visible "spiritual" government. Shackle after shackle was broken, and man with his inner value was put into the position originally designed for him. It was the thought of humanity which loomed up with the discoveries upon earth and in the heavens.

Superstitious fears of astral influences abandoned.

CH. III. THE GERMANIC NORTH AND THE REFORMS.

§ 156. The new thought of humanism, which Italy had procured æsthetically, and which was rendered practical by France in matters of politics, was applied to philological research in Germany. Unless the ideal of man in his value and dignity could be founded upon, and secured by, the immanency of the Divine Being in reality, nothing would have been gained by the renaissance, by a "regeneration" of society originating in the revival of the classics. For, short of the form of God-consciousness alluded to, in its bearings upon the cardinal principles of humanism, nothing will avail as a basis upon which the life of a nation and its advance toward perfection may be perpetuated. Nothing but Evangelical God-consciousness will evince itself as the soil upon which true humanitarianism, that is, civilisation proper, can prosper.

Advance necessarily to be based on religious tenets.
§ 47, 54, 56, 58, 71, 86, 125, 126, 131, 132, 137, 139, 175, 199.

In the general development of the Occident two periods are patent in precise keeping with the ecclesiastical contingencies. The first manifests the tendency to externally fortify and preserve the efficacy of the civilising factors; whilst in the second period the energies are concentrated upon the work of internal edification. Northern piety strives for the purification of the religious constituents and for the harmonious improvement of the psychico-spiritual person in every respect. Thus Christianity appears first under the aspect of its objectivity and power, then of its subjectiveness and freedom. So far we have observed the activity of the first period.

Two periods of ecclesiastical activity.
The church to be externally fortified,
internally edified.

Without difficulty the Romanised nations were trained to the idea of a governmental unit and to the practices of concentrated power. They were servile and docile enough to cooperate in the efforts put forth to establish a universal monarchy. The polarity between the German and the Roman inclinations to flee and at the same time to seek each other as mutual complements, made the Germans to coincide at last with the tendencies of the times. Only externally, however, and for the sake of expediency did they allow themselves to be hitched to the Roman contrivances. To the hierarchal schemes of domineering supremacy the German peoples did inwardly and voluntarily never acquiesce. There existed no means on earth to enforce the demands of their mental submission except the innumerable forms of some "concordat" aiming at their final captivation; but even those maneuvres could not prevail tho they were resorted to almost to the point of exhaustion. No sooner had the curia thought to have found a modus vivendi than the Germans made it an occasion to assert their idea of personal rights and to emancipate themselves from the oppressive mediæval forms of social life.

Objectivity and power;
subjectivism and freedom.

Polarity between German and Roman inclinations to flee and yet seek each other.
§ 137, 133, 142, 143, 146, 171.
Germans never fully acquiesced to Roman supremacy.

For a long time a few thinkers and princes only gave occasional signs of that opposition in which the mind ceased to reduce everything to a spiritual relation or to that invisible world which ecclesiastical rule pretended to represent. Such minds addicted themselves rather to the idea of conquering the material world for themselves, than of going to put their lives at stake in fighting for the increase of papal power. The few of these summits—reaching out of the sea of humanity, upon which the ship of the fishers of men sailed—were by the men on board ever suspected as dangerous breakers.

So far only princes and bold thinkers had shown opposition.

Storms brewing for the crew in the ship of the church.

Those excellent and independent men indicate the increase of the conviction which they foreshadow, that hierarchal preponderance is contrary to the nature of things in general, and grows to become intolerable. In short, the signs are that a storm is brewing, accelerating the discharges of natural forces upon materialistic arrogancy under the garb of spiritual leadership. A great revolution is preparing which under selfsacrifice will transform the modes of thinking and the social forms of occidental life.

Spirit of opposition to priestly arrogancy and illiteracy is spreading—

popularised by men like Walther v. d. Vogelweide,

Wicleff,
Nicolaus v. d. Flue,
by Lollhards and "Friends of God,"
Moravians, Waldensians.
§ 130, 135, 139, 139.

Gradually the people in general became conscious of the trend of affairs. The inhabitants of the cities, especially those nearest to Rome, showed resistance to religious formalism and legalism, and became refractory against the political manipulators under the mitra or with the rosary. Everywhere voices were heard echoing the ominous sentences of Walther von der Vogelweide, who taught the Germans to sing songs in praise of the fidelity of old and songs of freedom. Then the opposition began to consolidate, the malcontents gathering themselves into retired sects so as to be more secure against secret persecutions and summary dealings.

Not in political defiance like the revolution attempted by Arnold of Brescia.

German opposition directed against pagan principles and conformity to the world.

Wycliff had taken the part of the Lollards; Nicolaus von der Flue inspired the Swiss folks, and on the lower Rhine the "Friends of God" drew nearer the Savior, to the detriment of priestly intercession. The opposition of the Waldensians and Moravians kept in respectful distance from ecclesiastical and civil power. They were all, by means of many aggressive tho unimpeachable methods, advocating the claim, that man's right of selfdetermination is to be respected. This claim, as embodied in writings of secret associations, badly disfigured in many cases, worked progressively in many ways. This opposition rarely broke out in open defiance of the worldly regime of the priesthood, as in the case of Arnold from Brescia. The parties of the opposition went to the root of the anomalies in protesting against the pagan principles by withdrawing from the heathenish exercises, which had been made requisites for testing obedience and orthodoxy, and had been invented to further the secular aims of the hierarchy. But the essence of Christianity had not as yet been distinguished from church and hierarchy, from faith and formalism, which all were considered identical. None as yet had dared publicly to apply the isolator which alone can effectuate the reduction of the Roman composition.

The church, once exceedingly venerable, great as the teacher, and trustworthy as the guardian, of the nations of Europe, had grown senile and pedantic in her ceremonials, and artificial in her sanctimoniousness, to say the least. She was no longer able to discipline the stretching of the young life in this world of ours with its cycles of nascency.

Attempted reforms as those of Clugny could not succeed tho the period of Henry II had offered most propituous opportunities. RANKE.

There had been a time when a reformation of the church, as to her "head" and members, might have been accomplished in peace and unity. This was when Olaf and Boleslaw planted the cross in Scandinavia and in Poland. The attempts at reform, initiated in Clugny, were just then gaining ground. But the reform was referred to the orders and the clergy, who thereby, instead of abandoning worldliness, were made the more efficient instruments of secularising the church, and became the standing army of papal autonomy. At that time Henry II (the Holy) went hand in hand with the pope. It seemed as tho the resolutions of the synod at Seligenstadt would create a national church in Germany (Ranke directs our attention to this promising feature in the reign of that emperor) equal to that which the French have enjoyed ever since Hinkmar of Rheims and Charles the Bald. The opportunity was allowed to pass by without being utilised. like so many other neglected opportunities of reform. But the fact is, after all, that they could not be utilised, simply because the proper point of time had not as yet been reached.

the proper time not as yet reached.

Political situation preparatory to the Reformation.

§ 157. Now, however, the Germanic North was thoroughly prepared for the reformation. The leagues of the cities, like that of the treaty-towns of the Hansa, had trained the citizens to a consciousness of independence, and had nourished the spirit of political freedom. The country-nobility, even more determined than the aristocrats in the cities, arose against overbearing, illiterate clericals. The lords of the Scottish clans, the barons of the German Gaue, the magnates with the mind of the old Vikings in the northern countries, were first in refusing further obedience to Rome. "Now was the time"—as Anton Guenther, the Catholic historian and philosopher used to emphasise—"when the process could begin, which was a necessity for the advance of occidental Christianity: the process of disquisition and liquidation". On many historical grounds an ecclesiastical renovation was a crying necessity, indeed. Whenever this evolutionary advance turned into a deplorable revolution the fault is, in a great measure, to be assigned to a well-intended but overstrained "zeal not according to knowledge". With the excited masses, bare of judgment, the friends of

Now was the time for necessary reforms.
ANTON GUENTHER.
§ 127, 134, 138, 142, 145, 150, 156.

progress could not argue. Neither was it of any avail to deliberate with conservatism, unless an honest basis for a compromise could possibly be found. The conservatives could not understand the necessity of recognising the just demands of the times. Thus the revolutionary renovation became a problem so gravely entangled as to be solved by no other than the radical means of force. Religious advance prejudiced by revolutionary commotions.

The stumbling block was lying beyond the Alps; it was "ultra-montane". In Rome the corruption had reached its highest degree, politically, about the year 1500. The Venetian ambassador wrote home under date of Rome: "Every night four or five are murdered: namely bishops, prelates and others, so that the whole city trembles for fear of being dispatched by the Cesar". In the citadel of St. Angelo the pope had always 700,000 ducats lying in reserve; but to maintain a force of police for public safety he does not seem to have deemed necessary. Still deeper, however, those nuisances were lying which provoked the Germanic subjects of the "church". Roman politics in their extreme corruption.
Report of the ambassador to Venice.

Mysticism had uttered loud protestations in which the beating conscience of the northerners knocked at the door of the Vatican—in vain. The humanists with their criticism, however, roused the sleepers. Only think of that dialogue on "the profession of the religionists". Altho monk and layman stand on equal footing, morally, yet the monk has certain higher privileges by virtue of his—profession (in the sense of business occupation). This was the point which Laurentius Valla attacked. It was owing to the comparisons which now the world began to draw and to circulate in print, that the depth and essence of Christianity broke forth in its seriousness from the rotten shells and hulls. Mysticism had protested for the sake of conscience.

Humanism attacks Romanism in its moral decay.
LAURENTIUS VALLA.

More than that. The abuse of German conscientiousness had caused them to engage in philological research and in   re-opening   the "Book of the Nations", as Gœthe calls it. It now as never before became evident that the literature contained in this book had not only been impregnated into the theocracy as an institution, but by way of inspiration it had been given to the prophets and apostles in the same manner, as the mother of the chosen people had by faith miraculously conceived life and seed, tho "past her age". This word, spoken by God into humanity, resumes its authoritative position, and vindicates itself in substantiating its primitive virtue. The Book of the Nations, so long withheld from them, is again given to the world. Printing in the service of reform.

"Book of the nations".
GOETHE.

regained for the world.

Upon this Book, and especially upon the exposition of its leading topic as elucidated by the great Apostle of the gentiles in the Epistle to the Romans, the loud protest, alluded to, is founded.

It here becomes necessary to reach back into the past in order to fetch up a few connecting thoughts concerning biblical and anti-biblical formations of Christianity. When the primitive church had triumphantly become the church of the empire, we deemed it sufficient to refer to Chrysostomos with a quotation descriptive of the beginning of aberrations. One somewhat acquainted with those church fathers—who, like Chrysostomos, had received a Greek education—will know that there exist good reasons for speaking of the "Platonism of the Fathers." He will know how powerfully this Platonism assisted in the introduction of the monkish asceticism of Buddhistic origin. Incipient deformations of Christianity examined. CHRYSOSTOM. § 124, 125, 137, 150

The sister of Basilius of Cæsarea and of Gregory of Nyssa was the chief director of the nunneries upon the mountains of Cappadocia. It was a circumstance of still greater significance, which did not go unpunished, that the teachers of the church imitated the bombastic rhetoric of paganism in the pulpit. Unobserved "the church had to a large extent molded her concept of Christian life and Christian graces after the ideals of the better heathenish circles; she had unawares built up her theology with material from Platonic philosophy, and she had in some degree conformed her cult even to the rites of the pagan mysteries." Platonism.

Worst of all, the church had allowed a heathenish construction of the sacrifice to be smuggled into the commemorative and communicative celebration of the Lord's Supper. A eucharist had been made out of it, an "unbloody offering" (such was that of Cain), a good work by which the worshiper seeks to receive something in return. Fatal deformations.

We quote the expression of a modern observer, that in the sacrificial rites the sincerity of religion reveals itself. And the sacrifice through which the Mediator really became our Savior, was now misrepresented to the extent of an adulteration. By the addition of heathenish embellishments the interpretation of the church had become so corrupted as to form the basis for priestly intercession or Talmudistic mediatorship and corresponding arrogancy. What had been accomplished by Christ for the sake of humanity in the giving of His body and the shedding of His blood in atonement, had essentially been withheld. The negative merit of the great sacrifice is the liberation from the "dead works" of legalism.

Through the erroneous Roman emphasising of the law, the Mosaic rituals remained in force, or rather regained it on the score of hierarchal commands. Positively, the fruit of the atonement was the offer of free grace; but the repristinated law barred the communicants from the assurance of pardon. For, what the Savior had merited to be appropriated as a gift

Asceticism.

Eucharist,

(Unbloody offering of the hostia).

Sincerity in matters of religion reveals itself in the sacrificial rites. Wuttke. § 108

Misapprehension of the facts of salvation and of the means of appropriating "Free Grace". § 148.

Meritorious works required.

Spirit of bondage cultivated.

Intercession of the "church" displacing the Savior. § 147, 148.

Fundamental significance of the sacraments reestablished by German profundity.

A world-theory, a view of human life in general, is implied in the ordinance of the Lord's Supper.

by trusting His grace and relying upon His ORDER OF SALVATION, had been made an equivalent for services rendered to the institution, which required meritorious works if one would obtain the vicarious merits of the Savior as augmented by the consecrated lives of monks and nuns and saints, as given into the administratorship of the priesthood. Under these circumstances a spirit of bondage had been cultivated, instead of educating humanity to evangelical cheerfulness. A society was raised which was permitted to live in unbridled worldliness on the one hand, and which on the other could never do justice to the requirements and penances of self-renunciation in order to earn Heaven.

Heaven had been opened to all who, heavy-laden, would come to the Son of God under the single ethical condition of renouncing sin in the order of repentance and of accepting forgiveness through faith. But now the church, that meant the hierarchy, interceded between the sinner and the Savior, and bartered out indulgencies for money.

Any catechism based upon the Bible fully expounds the leading truths as to the way of salvation and the order of its appropriation. Luther's tract on "The Freedom of a Christian" closes with the two axioms that he is "a free lord over all things, subject to no man, and yet a servant to everybody".

But not merely intellectually, nor even spiritually but also socially is the believer to become a follower of the Holy King to whom he has vowed fidelity. In the religious emancipation of the Germanic nations the significance of the most sacred institution, representing the one great sacrifice, was finally comprehended according to the definite expostulation of the Apostle with reference to the sacraments. By the proper participation in the sacraments, both exhibiting the fruits of the atoning death, the individual member becomes embodied in the organism of head and members. The faithful constitute a most intimate fellowship, since through love to their common friend, they are bodily connected with the crucified and glorified Mediator and only intercessor. In the biblical doctrine which intelligibly expounds the meaning of the sacred institutions, there is implied an entire world-theory, a view upon the relation between the Infinite and the finite. This is what concerns us here and now.

Not scientific advance, but, the "word of the cross" the fulcrum of the Reformation.

The the coincident facts were not accidental.

The sacrament is the touch-stone of sound theology—and the Keystone of the ecclesiastical organisation, and of religious edification, upon which the welfare of humanity hinges. § 76, 90, 221.

§ 158. In the preceding chapter we alluded to the great consequences following the overthrow of the Ptolemæic picture of the universe. To the Church this scientific reform seemed irrelevant; yet the religious reform, accomplished by means from her own resources and in accord with her own wants, was more than a mere analogy; and the synchronism of the coincidence cannot be considered as merely accidental;

Not that cross which Heraclius carried back to Jerusalem, and not the "mass" as an unbloody sacrifice, with a hierarchy built upon both, had been intended for pivots upon which the world was to hinge. The "Word of the Cross" and the living, personal testimony to the fact of the Resurrection, and the sacramental appropriation of the merits of the Savior and only Mediator through faith alone;—these form the fixed foundation upon which personal salvation, organic communication of the divine life, and edification of head and heart are to be reared. In the sacrament as the keystone to the Church organisation, and as the touch-stone of sound theology, Christian religiousness centers, and upon that the welfare of humanity is based.

Theology did not utilise the Copernican discovery. § 155.

as to the cognitions "space and time."

Cause of the discrepancies between Luther and Zwingli.

Deep conception of the sacrament representing the immanency of the divine nature and essence in nature and history. Calvin. Melanchthon.

"Unio mystica" of Bernard of Clairveaux and Meister Eckhardt.

We noticed what Luther thought of the reform of Copernicus. In an almost blindfolded faith he went to work, much afraid of the dialectics of natural, unguided reason, taking Heaven in the scholastic sense—much to the detriment of an understanding with Zwingli. Both the Swiss reformer and the Saxon stood firm upon the word, the one with more intellectual clearness, the other with a deep, intuitive feeling of the mystical import of "the" sacrament. Luther made it a virtue to obey the last will and testament of his Lord and Master. "With sovereign unconcern he went with his head through the wall", says the venerable Rocholl; "and against all expectations it became evident for once, that the head came out erect, and the wall broke down". It was at this point where the evangelised church, upon the height of the longstanding reformatory movement among the Germanic nations, broke down the ancient barriers between Heaven and earth: from the point of a more profound conception and true appreciation of the sacrament of holy communion. This is the truth which Luther felt deeper than he was able to philosophise upon and to formulate—upon which Melanchthon and Calvin agreed.

In the conception of the fact, that the immanency of the divine life in history and human nature is substantiated and so materialised as to remain immanent, the German Reformation culminates as the result of the search for the "Unio Mystica" from which the Germans, since Bernard of Clairveaux and Meister Eckhardt were not to be deviated.

In this aspect of the sacrament the contrast and seeming contradiction of spirit and body is conciliated. In the glorified body of the Risen Mediator the old opposites are actually united. What is earthly and natural is not estimated unworthy to be elevated or as unfit to be spiritually transmuted. Nourished with the glorified body the earthly bodies shall partake of the very substance of the life divine, in order to be fashioned and renewed "like unto Him;" and with the human bodies, thus partaking of the divine-human substance, the natural world—from which they were taken, and by the assimilation of which natural being attains to its purpose—becomes glorified also.

The unification of nature and spirit—intended ever since creation was thought of—is now apprehensively inaugurated and exhibited in the proper celebration of the Lord's Supper.

Previous to the Reformation a materialistic aspect, mixed with superstitious elements, preponderated in theory and practice. It is in the evangelical conception, in the simple biblical sense of the means of grace, that the truth of the unification comes to its right and ample presentation.

The laity previous to the Reformation, unenlightened by the living word and by the self-interpreting text and context, were by the formalism of the cultus ever misled into the superstitions of the natural religion of heathendom; and it cannot be denied that even protestantism was not entirely purged of these elements, up to our own time. Magic powers were attributed to dead works as well as to dead things. It was in opposition to this abuse of the sacrament and in order to prevent a relapse into destructive errors, that Zwingli, abhorring the deification of created things, was so reluctant to assent to the profound relation between natural and spiritual entities. Extolling the spiritual side at the expense of the natural elements—upon which the spirit works in order to appropriate, elevate, assimilate, transform and spiritualise nature—a large part of the church of the Reformation more or less undervalued the significance of the natural concomitant factors in the means of grace. The original intention, that man should be the sole instrumentality for this work of spiritualising nature: that man should set free and transform and, we might say, redeem the confined life of nature which became arrested on his account, wherein a large part of his ethical task consists; and the truth, that nature possesses sufficient aptitude to be spiritually affected so as to be elevated accordingly by way of human nature: these essential truths—bearing on the completeness of Christian hope and on the final perfection of the purpose of development—were not forgotten, indeed, by the Calvinistic wing, tho rather lost sight of in the Zwinglian doctrine of the sacrament, and were considered separately by the Reformed in the ethics which they were the first to cultivate.

The larger part of the German protestants took the glorified body of the Risen Lord as the major premise in the explanation of the sacramental elements and insisted upon the "communicatio idiomatum," i. e., on the unification of spirit and nature—not seldom tending to elevate the consubstantiated bread to the height of adoration, whilst neglecting the ethical discipline of the natural man and being satisfied with his dogmatical assent.

Under this polarity, which partly may be accounted for by slight differences of the national character, the two sister-churches of the Reformation not only equipoised and complemented each other in this central tenet, but also approached to harmonious cooperation in the measure as the dogmatical conception was elaborated and cogently formulated. Indifference on either side with respect to this union of the divine life with the human would not have been as salutary for the church in general, as the occasional controversies have proved.

Thanks to the controversies concerning the palladium of Christianity all hold now in common, that in the sacrament, as (in one respect) the memorial of "the" sacrifice, the contrast between Heaven and earth is overcome like that between body and mind. The chasm is bridged between the Infinite and the finite in the person of the Mediator Himself. In Him the Heavenly and the natural world blend and are unified. Where He is upon earth there is Heaven; and He is the head and center of the church militant as well as of the church triumphant.

Whenever the Mediator causes the announcement: "I am with you alway", this "I am" is concrete, not a sublimated abstraction; He is not merely representing the idea of divinity, or of spirit, but He is a historical person as which He continues to manifest Himself. His body is not dissolved into the spacelessness of eternity, but is and remains Deity Incarnate in humanity, and is glorified in the model human form which He deigned to assume to Himself. The King is thus present with His people at the appointed place in spiritual-corporeal reality. At the Lord's table Heaven reaches deep into the human world, even in the present form of existence. Earthly nature—along with the glorification of the human body in which it culminates and to which it pertains—is thus impressed with the divine mark of its final destiny. In the midst of the corruptible and solvable world we have the pledge of becoming incorruptible. Since we are assured that the eternal mode of existence enters into historic reality, the limits of space—which in our finite mode of thought seem to separate our world from the world up yonder—are made unessential and set aside in so far as to form no hindrance for the spirit to penetrate nature and to permeate personal life.

Close behind the thin veil of the visible surroundings, the Heavenly world co-exists, and tho overlapping it, blends with our own physical world. This Heavenly world does not, as mediæval scholasticism imagined, begin beyond the stars where space may have its limits. Thought issuing from the church itself has thrown down the Ptolomæic system to which formerly it had adapted itself. Theoretically, at least, the ancient form of world-consciousness is annihilated beyond reconstructibility.

Margin notes:

Superstitious perversion of the sacrament.

Differences between the two branches of the Evangelised Church:

both forming a salutary counterpoise

New perception held in common of the celestial form of existence concurrent with the historical reality. § 63, 64, 92, 119, 123, 147, 152.

Eternal form of existence realised inside the natural world of history.

Ancient forms of world-consciousness displaced for ever.

Ethical import of the reformed communion.

§ 159. As soon as the theological reform of the sacrament in theory and usuage became evident in its bearing upon the church as a visible organisation, the ethical effects of the dogmatical reconstruction in its bearings upon the social organism began to appear. It became historically manifest, that the whole fabric of the papal theocracy, the hierarchal "government of religion", must stand or fall with the papal mass; just as it had been universally felt, that "the freedom of a Christian" depended upon the reform of the Lord's Supper. In the sacrament freedom has its stronghold, and with the reformed administration of the sacrament the ideal of freedom was replaced upon its real basis. The willful arbitrariness of subjectivism found its corrective, after the formative thought of the "Holy Communion" insured the organical connection of the believers in Christ into a churchly corporation. Thus alone could free personal life be held together. In a normal manner, and quite sufficient for all churchly purposes of cooperation and reciprocal sympathy, the thought of humanism was thus realised in the maintenance of an organic whole, and in constituting a spiritual-corporeal community. The Kingdom of Heaven upon earth in the sense of the New Covenant became reestablished, in which the individual member trustingly submits his entire being to the government of one central will.

Personal freedom guarded against selfish separation by virtue of sacramental communion.

Church organism upheld.

Being embodied in the mystical body of the glorified Head the Christian finds the anticipations of his own destiny affirmed, just as it is impressed upon his entire nature and inherent in his innermost soul. Agreeing with this divine design, the will of the Christian becomes determined to conform the entire ego to this destiny, that is, to persist voluntarily in the course to perfection. Thus man becomes free indeed and in truth: whilst at the same time society is protected against the disintegration of which it is in peril from arbitrary and tyrannical subjectivism, and against libertinism, the caricature of freedom. In the Son of God, the "express image" of the Father's personality, the divine "likeness" of man became recognisable again to men.

Evangelical freedom not subjective arbitrariness.

From behind the host of saints—personifying the "thesaurus supererogationis," i. e. the treasury of meritorious works in proxy for those who pay cash for indulgences, —the personal God was brought near to man again; or rather man was personally brought back face to face with the sole Mediator, so as to regain the direct access to his Savior. Only thus the cognition of man's personal and immediate responsibility, the selfconsciousness of his value on account of his noble descent: in short his freedom was restored and fully warranted to him, notwithstanding his sinfulness. The most miserable outcast is precious in the sight of the Redeemer who shed His blood for the wretched; for such are especially invited, sought and reclaimed. Sunk ever so deep they are taken account of as divine descendants, and are welcomed at the feast of the King—whilst those ashamed of such company are rebuked for, and humiliated in, their pride. Indeed it is a marvelous community in which the idea of humanity is realised in such a manner, that kings and beggars stand equal at the baptismal font, around the Lord's table, and at the grave.

No human intercessions.
§ 139, 149,

Direct access to the Savior.

Value of personality on account of its noble descent,

One sunk ever so deep is welcome at the "Feast of the King".

True equality practically demonstrated.

To the Germanic people in the first place, again appeared the "King of the Common People" who at one time had been depicted to them in the "Heliand," to whom their ancestors had consecrated themselves and whom they had vowed to serve, not with fear and in a servile spirit, but with manliness and a cheerful heart—not to earn wages but in return of thanks. With Him they had entered into blood-kinship, hence they considered themselves to constitute a "Blutsfreundschaft."

Reappearance of the "King of the common people".
§ 135, 136, 137, 139.

In "Bloodrelationship" i. e. "Blutsfreundschaft".

In this practical way alone may the cardinal principle of general love to fellowmen be proclaimed in its full sense, and established in its binding force. One of the Apostles derives brotherly love from the love of God; the other demonstrates how from the love toward the Christian brother philanthropy in general wells up. To the poorest a task is apportioned which to accomplish is not beyond his ability: to assist in the happiness or in the rescue of some one, by doing which he will become cheered and himself enriched.

Love toward fellow-men.

In the institution of the sacrament and the order of its administration the error is provided against, as tho man could accomplish his task, the exercise of humanism, by the mere joining of church or societies, or by participating in solemn rites, or by the performance of patriotic acts. Such may all be considered as sacred, or as ethical at least in themselves, but they cannot make the actor holy. An act or work is not

Good works not meritorious; receive their value from personal character, not the character from performance ever so solemn.

to be severed henceforth from the person, from intention or sentiment. In order to have any merit or value whatever, good works must be products of organic-spiritual life and of unsophisticated thankfulness to the beloved Savior. As the fruits of the "tree" they afford no occasion for pride and ostentation,—for pharisæism.

The return to true Christian ethics, then, consisted in this: That personality was so highly estimated, that a "good work" because having no value in itself, received its value from the person. And that man can neither hide behind the generality of the church or the prevalence of general sinfulness, nor compensate for the neglect of duty by the enforcement of ritualistic performances or by the purchase of indulgencies catalogued in a scheduled tariff. But that, on the contrary, personal life requires a personal religiousness which is enjoined upon each one for himself, so that life itself will remind him of his duties, and of the fact that sin works out,—on the line of natural and ethical law in their correlation,—its own retribution: That each one is to examine for himself,—in the absence of a conscience by proxy in safe keeping of the church,—what the church offers without forcing it upon any one; and that each one is to work out his own obligations. That each member becomes a colaborer in the upbuilding of the church, for the purpose of which unity does not consist in uniformity, but in which edification the sacrament preserves this unity in diversity.

As it is with the relation of the individual to the church, so does personality, filled with the thought of selfdiscipline and responsibility, gradually adjust its relations to the state and to the complex conditions of the natural world. This world is not of a value so mean as to be avoided or to be disdainfully looked upon. It is to be overcome in its resistance to cultivation through mental activity and under selfdenial, so that by elevating the environment we develop our own nature. In the pursuit of this ethical purpose at the ethical apparatus each work receives its own dignity, because it assists in keeping order for the welfare of the whole and contributes to final glorification. No longer does contemplative quietism or a life evasive of the trials and troubles of this world receive higher esteem, than manual labor or an aspiring business occupation. Both contemplation and emulative activity, prayer and labor, are to pervade each other and become blended as in the case of spirit and body, Heaven and earth.

To be sure, the state is also promptly limited now to its particular domain of duty. The basis of all political economy, of public order and of justice is duly recognised,—tho noteverywhere adhered to. It is the rule: "Render unto Cesar the things that are Cesar's, and unto God the things that are God's." This word gives government its authority, especially as to the protection of freedom of conscience against every pretext of theocratic rule. By the spiritual discipline necessarily connected with the solemn act of communion the state-church is rendered as much an anomaly as a church-state. The experiences of a thousand years, in which the Christians under these forms of government had become persecutors where they formerly would rather suffer persecution themselves, had taught them the monstrosity of such inhuman practices in the name of God. Church and state will best serve each other for mutual benefit, if each remains independent of the other in carrying out the obligations appointed to either in its peculiar sphere. The protest of Spire as amended by the "Augsburg Confession" A. D. 1529, 1530, was the first charter of real selfgovernment.

The variety of denominations is not so great an evil as has been alleged. That was rather necessary to keep up energy for continuing in the great movement under self-criticism and emulative efforts. Under the circumstances as they are, resulting from historical conditions, each of these denominational sister-churches brings her peculiar charisms to full development to the enrichment of all the others. The keeping house of each by herself does not necessarily involve them in animosities, and in a near future may enhance the influence of their unanimity as to essentials. For the sake of SERVICE to the world in the way of its Christianisation the particularism in church-affairs is preferable to an artificial unification with a view to gain DOMINION and power.

This is not to say, however, that the tendency toward church-union was not to be hailed with satisfaction as a promising sign of the times. But that the most adequate and most effective means toward this end will be, partly pressure from outside, and partly cooperation in the work of evangelisation without pride and without envy. The highpriestly prayer offered in the night of the first communion, so closely related to the institution of the Lord's Supper, clearly indicates the direction in which the church is to proceed in order to comply with the last earthly wishes of our Lord.

§ 160. Equal with the bearing of the reform of the Lord's Supper upon ethics, tho not of the same importance, was the influence exerted upon æsthetics, upon the realm of the beautiful, and upon the arts and sciences. For also in this respect the natural was here rehabilitated in its proper position and valuation; since by the Reformation it was not made obligatory to piety identifying "lust of the eye" with the pleasure derived from the forms of beauty in nature. The gospel does not in this sense advise or prescribe a deadening of what is humane and beautiful in the realm of the secondary good. It is much more expected, that the natural shall be transfigured into the incorruptible splendor of the realm of glory. For, ethically understood, and under proper use, the natural is consecrated to become the vehicle of the spiritual. Thus from beginning to end Heaven and earth are brought into close relationship.

The Madonnas of Raphael belong essentially to the æra of the Reformation. When Duerer conceived his figure of Paul in the year 1526, he undoubtedly wanted to represent the knight of the New Covenant, who liberated the Christian from the shackles of Judaistic-Roman legalism, and in a valorous mood defended his freedom.

What a powerful impulse was given to the cause of humanism in the protestant choral. It was the trumpet sound for the German nation to rise. By this choral the fixed cadences of the Gregorian melodies soon became antiquated; in fact the whole liturgical order of worship prescribed by Rome was overthrown from Switzerland to Scotland. When a nation rises for liberty, it is not customary that it should march up as for parade; and the German temper was never accustomed to niceties, when issue had to be joined on questions of ideal import.

As to the spiritual warfare Luther least of all would advise the softness of indecision. Yet he displayed wisdom in guiding the Reformation into temperate methods of advance, as for instance when the iconoclasts went to extremes. Doellinger describes Luther as the genuine type of the German character; and in this capacity the great reformer was conservative in matters of fine arts.

Interest was awakened in the early history of the fatherland. The antiquities as witnesses of the remote past rose in esteem, whereby national consciousness became revived and the taste for venerable customs stimulated. As in Cambridge, where Whitaker had given similar impulse, so was national history made a special study in Wittenberg and Magdeburg. The treasures of old national songs and epics became thus unearthed and were turned to good account in the exercise of patriotism.

Of much greater importance, however, is the fact, that not only singing and studying were made attractive and useful, but that labor in all its branches was rendered honorable once more, since the double set of ethics—one for the "spiritual" profession (die Geistlichkeit) the other for the profane people—had been abolished. Opportunities were given to industry and the sciences to bud out in every direction. People grew bold enough to trust that the eternal truth needs no human props nor to be afraid of innovations, since in the end everything must be conducive to its triumph. The distribution of all that was worthy to be known had free course.

In Basil the Koran was printed. From the pulpits they preached against it. Luther praised the undertaking, saying that the wounds must be kept open in order to be healed from within.

With regard to the art of printing, new publications of smaller caliber were circulated rapidly enough to furnish a basis upon which the press was destined to grow into a powerful factor of civilisation. The value of personal property was rendered derisive by the Roman guides to holiness; in those ethics exhibited in the regulations of monastic life, the right to private possession was completely denied. The cloisters propagated a predilection for communistic living whereby the individual disappears in the order. This trait of orientalism was detrimental to labor, inasmuch as in such arrangements the stimulating impulse of enjoying the fruits of personal exertion does no longer animate the laborer under the imperative rule of a communistic oligarchy.

The socialistic enthusiasts of that time, in their endeavors and boisterous experiments to transplant communistic ideas into the domain of Protestantism, and to transform society accordingly, only protracted the old Asiatic-Roman world-theory, which holds the individual simply to be a tool in the fabric of the state, as a thing bare of any purpose except that of the communistic whole.

At the end of the 15th. and the beginning of the 16th. century, that is, prior to the relig- Peasants' wars.
ious rising, the white and blue flag with a picture of Christ was rebelliously raised in Alsace
and as by a storm carried from village to village. It was a recollection of the Jacquerie and
of the rise in Switzerland, where the peasants in similar forms demonstrated their grievances
—the same grievances which now infuriated the repressed and outlawed serfs and journeymen
in the country-districts. That flag was the storm-signal of a movement which had no other
connection with theReformation, than that it was caused by the exactions of those "spiritual"
superiors who held the tenures upon which those peasants were made to toil. A
social reconstruction was felt to be unavoidable. In Suabia the fraternity of "poor Cunrad" Necessity for "symbols of faith" to shelter true liberty.
constituted itself under the sign of the "Bund-schuh." The peasants' war terrorised Frankonia
and Thuringia; it spread from the Vosges to the Carpathian mountains. Up to 1525 A. D.
one hundred and sixty six castles were destroyed, and Thuringia alone counted three hundred
monasteries in ruins. Then came the Anabaptists, who made common cause with the desperate peasants, establishing such communistic municipalities as Nordhausen, Muenster etc·
To the right and to the left caricatures of freedom sprang up.

Safely through the tempests of such a season of history the treasure of true lib- General features of the Reformation.
erty could be carried only in the shrines of the confessions, those "Symbols of the
Faith" arranged by the reformers, adopted by the denominations, deliberated upon in
the diets, and laid before the world.

§ 161. Let us take a review of the whole movement in connection with its Protestantism vindicated as promulgating the chief requisites for political liberty. Vindication by De Laveleye.
starting points, and of the new developments ensuing, which so far have been out-
lined. Emil de Laveleye philosophised upon Catholicism and Protestantism as to
their bearings upon the liberty of the respective nations. He concedes the palm to
Protestantism, because of its preferable maxims having molded personal character
and selfreliance, personal responsibility and selfgovernment—the chief requisites
of political liberty.

Since this is acknowledged, Protestantism is expected not to go back on the Christianity has nothing to fear from isms.
principle of its origin; and the Protestants ought not to shrink from real religious
tolerance and liberty. They ought to manifest sufficient faith in Christianity, that
neither materialism, nor criticism, nor sectarianism can harm it in any way. It can
not hurt Christianity if her teachers are stirred up, or her denominations urged on to
continue in the process of purification. By force of the cardinal principle underly- Religious tolerance without indifference.
ing their own existence the Protestants are compelled to give room to as many in-
ternal schools and denominations at least as Catholicism grants to the tendencies of
widely differing orders. Protestantism can afford to be as undaunted against the Division of labor.
irreligious adversaries outside of its organism, as tolerant to the larger or smaller
sects inside its pales, which hold the fundamental tenets of Christianity in common.
The denominational diversity is not only a sign of progress but its condition.

Bodin, the advocate of the Huguenots, had already emphasised this in his colloqui with seven Differentiation a universal law.
representatives of religious parties, written in apology for tolerance. He argues that the
existence of different sects is conducive to peace in a State. With only two great parties a
State is ever in danger of a religious war, whilst many parties at variance hold each other in
check. In the interest of the Church itself such mutual recognition is wholesome, since the
developments take the same course in spiritual matters as in nature, where differentiation
goes on everywhere: the higher the functional capabilities advance in the scale of the organic
world, the more is labor divided.

In the evolution of nature one part after another became, most probably, detached from Solar system on analogy
a revolving globe because of the vehement swing of its revolutions. Left to its own whirling
course each part and subdivision rounded off itself, and joined the general concourse. Thus a
sun-system arranged itself, as we see it every night, moving upon the hinges of binding and
balancing forces, a wealth of forces which only lay dormant in the uniform mass of the original
ball. In an analogous manner the diverse denominations, now spread over the whole earth,
disengaged themselves from the Church of the Middle-Ages with its wealth of latent spiritual
incipiencies.

The analogy in respect to the development in the domain of the church corres- Church divisions conducive to civilisation as politically it was with colonial detachment.
ponds to the law of colonisation and emancipation, the workings of which are illus-
trated in the instance of Greece, recurring in church-history only on a higher scale.
When the mother-countries were unable to entertain the growing and crowding
constituents, they emigrated and started households of their own. It is when the
home-government, from fear of losing control, begins to become oppressive, that
colonies will declare themselves independent. Every separation causes distress.
Attempts made to frustrate the independency of new social formations generally
strengthen their establishment, if they are ripe for liberty. If the parent-society
22

understands the situation, it will not become weakened by releasing its offspring. On the contrary, every new departure will enhance the advantages gained by the variety of interrelations and the modifications caused thereby.

Good results from division of labor upon the field of Christian activity.

    Every healthy development of a nation will aid in the establishment of a system of coherent nationalities upon earth. So every one of the historically developed denominations, if energetically aspiring for the dignity of deserving recognition, will eventually serve the cause of the church in general. If every street of the New-Jerusalem, that is to say, each division of the Church universal, faithfully exercises the gifts peculiar to it, and elaborates a particular side of the truth, then each contributes to the realisation of a system of organically connected denominations upon earth. Then it will be generally apprehended that Christianity does not mean earthly dominion in any shape, but means service to the world without conformity to it. This is no strange idea. It is but the legitimate application of the thought of the Kingdom of God under which all are embraced, and from which to exclude another, no church has the power.

Narrow conceptions of the Kingdom of God.

The thought of this spiritual Kingdom of Heaven had become so narrow, that Rome as well as the Greek patriarchs each claimed to be entitled to represent it exclusively.

Relation of the denominations to one another and to the Kingdom of God.

This narrow view of the Kingdom of Heaven must become widened to the scope of humaneness. This Kingdom ought to be perceived as a thought so grand and prevailing as that each of the denominations upon earth will become magnanimous enough to waive its hegemony on grounds of priority, or higher purity, and to abandon the selfconceited opinion of its own infalliblity, and exclusive right to represent

Extent of the Kingdom of Heaven.

or establish this kingdom. Then each section will content itself with the consciousness of being an active member of the whole, subservient to the best interests of each and all, giving all honor to God alone. This was the motive of the Germanic people during the reformatory period.

The commotions bring to the surface filthy sediments with the pearls.

It is to be deplored that the movement, nevertheless, frequently took a course of rude violence. Inasmuch as Germany took the leading part the perturbations there threw up a mass of filthy residue along with the precious pearls.

    Even in Rome itself, however, it could not have been any better. Hence it is unnecessary to hesitate with our acknowledgment of the truth as presented in the "Historic-Political papers" or in Janssen's work. The kernel of development, from which we observed the rough hulls and crude dross to fall off, remains the sound core of advancing civilisation, nevertheless.

Deficiencies of Protestantism.

It is in the nature of development that the hulls can not be dispensed with until the fruits become ripe, just as every success upon earth is conditioned by wearing out, and working itself through, its enwrappings.

    § 162. Protestantism unravelled the intricacies of alien thoughts which had encrusted the gospel of salvation; it wrought out its clear apprehension, its proper appreciation, and pointed out the simple order of its appropriation.

Calvinism cultivated ethics for reasons of resistance to despotic persecutions; **pure morals.**

    It was unfortunate that in one section of the Protestant Church the applications of salvation in its practical and ethical bearings upon matters of political economy and social life were insufficiently considered. Politically Calvinism found conditions in the countries where it spread, far different from those of Germany. Under French duplicity and intrigues, and under Spanish despotism social problems had to be handled practically. Germany had to

Germany's failure to support Holland at the proper time cost it the "thirty years war". § 175.

suffer the "thirty years war" for leaving Holland in the lurch in its decisive struggle against "the council of blood," along with Metz it lost Alsace and Lothringia for going into league with the perpetrators of the "bloody marriage." The Reformed everywhere were forced into selfdefence and into practically working out ethics as well as dogmatics in order to demonstrate the legitimate cause of their strained relations to rulers who were tools of Rome.

Man's thoughts more influenced by his deeds, than his deeds by his theories. Fr. Jacobi.

What Fr. Jacobi wrote to Hamann is true: "that man's thoughts are more influenced by his deeds, than his deeds by his theories." Hence the Reformed nations were led to be more concerned about PURE MORALS and political liberty; whilst the Lutherans kept up

Lutheranism emphasises **purity of doctrine.**

dogmatical controversies and reared a church of theologians. They kept the laity out of representative Church-government, and being more concerned about PURE DOCTRINE, they cared little for participating in political affairs, and for personally aiding in the reform of

Ethical issues of the Reformation **vested with the crown,** § 175.

public life. The Lutheran Church of Germany has to blame herself for the retardation it had to sustain under an external embodiment of the ethical issues of the religious emancipation in the person of the "Landes-Vater" as the supreme overseer of the church. This fallacy not

whereby not only ecclesiastical vitality but even religious life was frequently stifled.

only checked the progress of political freedom and selfreliance, but also crippled the religious growth in many dry seasons. Notwithstanding the onesidedness and defect of Lutheranism, at first so reluctant to accommodate itself to the Calvinistic complement, Protestantism

The thought of humanism developing despite impediments.

on the whole represents the river bed in which the deep and broad thought of humanism was flowing through the nations, and, borne across the oceans, reached out a helping hand to humanity the world over.

The application of the thought of humanism in the practice of clear Christian ethics more than once had to rush through narrow canyons, and under the overhanging rocks of fanaticism; it has been thrown down many a rugged cataract. Many a liberal minded man mistrusted a church, in which the thought of apostolic love to fellow-men could again become concealed under hot, dogmatical conflicts not only on paper.

The churches engaged with dogmatics almost always neglect the exercise of broth- *Forebodings of the age of missions.* erly love. Lutheranism lost sight of it to such an extent, that it became unable to surmount its political bias. Instead of hurrying to the rescue of an outlawed sisterchurch, or a nation doomed to extirpation, it left brethren in perils like those which drove the non-conformists to extremes.

But notwithstanding such predicaments, perhaps even on account of them, the *Mutual recognition of evangelical denominations.* thought of humanism broke forth from the depths of the Germanic faithfulness to the "Captain of their salvation". As Hermann the Cheruskian of yore had broken the shackles of Roman despotism at the beginning of German history, so a Thuringian broke them again at the commencement of the new æra. The cause of Humanism is indestructible, irresistible: the thought of it developed under pressure a glow of prayer and spiritual valor the more intensified, inasmuch as it now more than ever contained the force, the experience, and the determination to transform the world in all its relations, and in its widest compass.

Centuries had been necessary for the thought of humanism, as compared to a stream, gathering up its small tributaries which from different and frequently opposite directions, came down the mountains of the Waldensians and Lollards along *Resume and prospect,* the quiet valleys of mysticism and separatism. The herterogeneous elements carried along by these rivulets became solidified by following their affinities, and sank to the bottom. Other elements in the same drift and working in the common ethical and final purpose of liberation, denied each other mutual recognition, nevertheless, but they became purged of their impurities in the process.

We have anticipated, and hence may have become somewhat unintelligible. For the present we sum up this as the result of our survey: The Renaissance and the Reformation evince the guidance by the hand from on high, which prepared the condition, and provided the opportunities, and utilised factors so remote, that the way in which they were directed towards and concentrated upon a definite scope remained *Swift advances under divine guidance* hidden until a long time post eventum. But it was just then and there—when the *Gervinus.* complications seemed to accumulate into an inextricable coil of confusion—that history advanced with one step so far as to defy comparison with all the progress made in the preceding thousand years and more. The gift vouchsafed and enveloped in these commotions is of such exquisite preciousness, that as Gervinus said, "it took humanity several additional centuries to accustom itself to the renovations".

Under high pressure and the old polar tension, humanism was wrought out anew, wrung from the most exorbitant measures of wild warfare and blood-thirsty fanaticism, and is now enjoyed by the protestant nations.

No more time should be lost for practical proof of the appreciation of that which had been given and regained under selfexertions to the extent of sacrificing all earthly goods for the sake of the Gospel.

Much less since it is in the nature of humaneness to multiply the enjoyment by sharing *Sharing Gospel-advantages with those at the other pole of the strains.* liberation, for instance, with others. Should not regained Christianity be shared with those who suffer none the less under depressing strains because of their living at the other pole of the tension?

We dare not ignore the law of culture, that life perpetuates tension under selfrenewal; *Law of selfmaintenance of cultural energies.* that the forces under polar constraint serve each other, to maintain themselves. *§ 21.*

CH. IV.   THE COUNTER-REFORMATION.

§ 163. The great movement among the Germanic nations from the Theiss to the Thames, from Geneva to Trondhjem and Reval was followed by a counter movement *Triangle Rome, Madrid, Paris.* from the Romanised parts of Europe in the triangle : Rome—Madrid—Paris. It was to be expected from causes alluded to. The attainment of religious liberty could scarcely have been possible without the timely intervention of the Turks. The horror caused by their menacing attitude weakened the power of the Habsburgs. This power, gained by a method of systematic political marriages was on the wane as *Counter-action to be expected,* *§ 135.* soon as the greatest feat of its characteristic diplomacy had been achieved; and when Spain-Austria had contracted the hatred of the Turk, it was completely unable to execute its menaces against the German protestants. The hordes of the crescent,

Habsburg's power, always un-German in its policy of marriages, and menacing the Reformation, was menaced by the Turks.

Protestantism at the mercy of the Habsburgians.

Islam curbs the designs of Habsburg.

Janizars similar to the employees of the counter-reformation. § 133, 145, 164.

Previous attempt to point out simultaneous factors and aims of a similar system of pretensions, tho they rested on essentially different religions. § 131, 145

Impress made upon the Latin (Romanised) nations during the conflicts with the Turks. L. v. Ranke. § 133, 145, 150.

Romanism tinctured with Othmanic culture.

Genesis of modern methods to demonstrate Rome's superiority.

Spanish temperament peculiarly qualified for being forged into weapons of the curia. § 133, 145, 150.

Scrutinising the secret of the success of the counter-reformation.

altho repulsed on the Danube and in Iran at the same time, yet approaching Vienna, evidently had to serve higher ends, otherwise the Reformation would have been crushed in its state of incipiency. For of an ally or support equal to the power of Habsburg the protestants could not avail themselves; because there was no such earthly power in existence just then.

Italy, despite its distraction and military incompetency, was still considered a great power by virtue of the intoxicating influences of latitudinarian popery and of its art. Spain had by the fall of Granada become a unit, but had fallen into the grasp of Habsburg by virtue of the diplomatic marriages ever coveted by this old dynasty, so that Austria had come under the control of the dusky cabinet in Madrid, and had to serve the "Church" in order to oblige the pope, that eventually he might, perhaps, arrange another marriage. In France a pack of courtiers had been raised, who cringed under the foot-kickings of a monarch just then and thus preparing the Olympic almightiness of the Bourbons. In England the bourgeoisie began, since the "War of the Roses", to raise their heads against the Tudors; but in respect to continental matters England was not at all formidable. The union of Kalmar was dissolved; Christian of Denmark could scarcely dispose of blood enough to glue it together again. Poland was under the permanent misrule of an anarchistic nobility. Russia as a power did not exist as yet. Hence there was no earthly succor for the German protestants, among whom Saxony and Hesse were weak enough tho being the strongest politically. They would have been lost had not the crescent curbed the designs of the house of Habsburg.

Like an ominous cloud Islam darkened the eastern horizon year in and year out. The corps of the Janizars had not yet been dissolved. From each victorious exploit multitudes of captured Christian boys were brought home to the "High Porte" and were drilled into blind obedience for special purposes. Living in barracks and in celibacy under cœnobial rules, they were trained half monks and half automatic fighters. Wearing long gowns, with the handshar in the belt, fanatical in whatever fate willed, they formed a gang ready for any act of trickery or violence. Young renegades of Christianity they were, molded into an elite troup of Islam, uniform in will and intellect, well qualified for any cruelty against the infidels.

Purposely we enlarge upon the Janizars, subsequent to and in connection with that which we attempted before by pointing out simultaneous factors and aims of a similar system of pretensions, tho based upon essentially different religions. Presently we shall offer in evidence other sequences of the same phenomenon, previously alluded to. The conflict with the Othmans originally fell to the lot of the Italians and Spaniards when the battle raged around Malta, Cyprus and Oran. The modes of warfare impressed those Romanised Christians so deeply, that they adopted a great deal of Turkish esprit de corps and discipline besides Arabian shrewdness. Ranke directs the attention to this curiosity on the score of affiliation. We may follow his tracks, altho he overlooked other circumstances connected with them.

Something very peculiar had come over these combatants during their engagements with the Turks: "a mixture of pride and perfidy, Romantic chivalry, treacherous diplomacy, and scheming strategy; of faith in the stars with consecrated devoutness to "our Lady". It is remarkable, almost incredible, what refinement the south of Europe owes to that contact with Islam. How far the really civilised element had been infected with the Turkish conversative accomplishments we cannot stop to investigate, not supposing that they resisted the charm of Turkish hightonedness. Our aim is simply to show the factors which of these elements the curia chose as suitable for imitation and adapted to Roman tactics. Our aim is to show the genesis of the modern methods applied by the "Holy See" in weaving new nets for the fishing of men. The Spanish brand of character is peculiarly qualified for being forged into tools strikingly similar to those manufactured by the Sultan for definite purposes. This becomes evident throughout the history ensuing immediately after the Reformation. For fully a century, at least, the workings of that half-cross-half-crescent-spirit tell on the reconstruction of Europe; and their efficacy continues much longer, only more on the sly.

The puzzle is, how the Christianised Germanic spirit, which ever insisted upon human rights and the dignity of personal life, could have become so obtuse, and its spreading so obstructed, as to enable the "counter-reformation" to succeed upon so large a territorial extent. Scrutinising this question it will be found that the Romanists practically had gained by the Reformation. Their tactics and even their tenets they learned so to modify as easily to be accommodated to altered conditions and expediencies, and at the same time to retain a certain intrinsic consistency with the hierarchical principle. It will be found that the order of Jesuits acquired admirable skill in utilising what could be obtained from the regenerated antique (the renaissance) for the purpose of imbuing accessible souls with an obedience and bigotry more slavish than any two sets of Roman ethics ever infused. For it was by means of just this order, and the use it made of the renaissance, that the catholic courts of the Habsburgers and the Valois now took to these Roman virtues. *Effects of the renaissance and the Reformation upon Catholicism.* *Spanish order of Jesuits, § 145.*

The order took its rise in Turkeyfied Spain with its odd mixture of Celtic, Gothic, Jewish and Moorish characteristics. Considering the form and work of the new order of the "Redemptorists" nobody can repress the remembrance of ancient orientalism. We cannot help extending the parallel which suggested itself to Ranke. We shall do so under the reservation, however, that when speaking of Buddhism, Romanism, or Protestantism, we must discuss the system as such only and as a whole. Upon persons and malformations which become parasitical to any system, we enlarge not. A system is to be judged by the influences which, in virtue of its principles, it exerts upon personal and social life wherever it obtains full and unchecked sway. *reminding one of Buddhist-Brahministic eclecticism, of Talmudism, and Ishmaëlitic fanaticism, pugnaciousness, and eternal subjection.*

§ 164. Be it far from us to belittle the merits of Jesuitism in regard to the polish it has laid upon rhetorical dialectics, and the smoothness to which the arts of diplomacy were trimmed down; or to underestimate the cultivation of prudent reserve which modern civilisation owes to these masters of pedagogical drill in reservedness and politeness. Our object in throwing the flash of history's search-light upon the order is to elicit certain ethical, or rather unethical principles on which it hinges, and to exhibit the effects realised through its instrumentality. *Merits of Jesuitism.* *Goal of Jesuitism is universal suzerainty of that which Guizot understands as the "church".*

An inspection of Jesuitism and its success demands the uncovering of its essence and temper, of the character manifest in its extreme high-churchism; it demands a clear understanding of the manner in which, ever since the origin of the order, Rome has improved every occasion, and utilised every opportunity to emphasise its pretensions of universal suzerainty, and to defy Protestantism; it demands an analysis of the cardinal motives inciting Jesuitical agility to persist in the futile attempts at obtaining the goal of universal secular dominion. *"Government of religion".*

Once before we quoted Mommsen's sentence, which seems to "hit the nail", when he said that morality with the Jews and the Romans, both experts in legalism, was nothing but "a catechism of allowances." We may add, that therein consisted the morality of the ancient nations in general. This, however, is not to be understood as a revocation of the truth, that, underlying all works and offerings, there existed an obscure impulse and prompting to compensate for guilt, or to expiate sins, or to offer or gain satisfaction as the cases might require. *Old Roman and Jewish legalism as a moral system of allowances: conscience by proxy contrived at. Mommsen. § 73, 127, 130.*

Furthermore we found, that the Semites developed the art of choosing that line of conduct which in a given case under such and such circumstances would "most probably" have been allowed, according to the collections of precedents established by the fathers, that is, in accord with the authoritative judgments of some imaum or rabbi, regardless of whatever authority that imaum or rabbi may have been. We observed how that casuistic morality had been palmed off upon the Church in aid of its promulgating two kinds of ethics; and how, with the affiliation of this theocratical and peculiarly fanatical Semitic ingredient, that impertinent tendency to probabilism obtained the means of firmly fastening itself upon the vital tissues of the ecclesiastical body. Here the obnoxious maxim, for instance, found its deep lodgment, that God had invested the church with the authority to extirpate the enemies of His Name. Under the presumption that the Kingdom of God was identical with the visible church, saints included, and with her exclusively, the treatment of every enemy of God was justified, who became suspected of insubordination to the edicts of his ecclesiastical superiors. In the figurative speech of Pope Gregory we found all these traits mirrored, which henceforth became the predominant features of a church whose noblest souls uttered moans like those described in the Apocalypse. *Degrees of Rabbis and imaums.* *Probabilism utilised in hierarchical interests. § 73, 129, 134, 163.* *Explicit traits of Semitism: oneness, rule, extirpation of opponents. Gascon VII. § 130, 147, 163.*

After a great organisation has tasted power, and has become determined as to the method of extending that power and maintaining its permanency, then every step advancing in this direction intimidates resistance, and every success increases the impossibility of retracting such a course. Hence persistency of method and consistent adherence to the maxims of theocracy is made the prime virtue and the mark *Charms of hierarchal power upon rulers and subjects.*

of Jesuitical faithfulness. The masses want to be governed thus, because they find their carnal indulgence as most safe and undisturbed and mental laziness best served under strict and accustomed methods. Hence they are soon captivated by such an easily comprehensible harangue. Especially nations of that stamp are charmed by the fanaticism thus generated as the most convenient surrogate or substitute for religiousness. It is the practical and consequential persistency, the unscrupulous sagacity combined with the indefatigable determination of fatalism wherein the order has its force and the secret of its success.

This sagacity, however, is but an improvement upon the shrewdness which the Spaniards had learned during their contact with the Arabs, with modern orientalism. Jesuitical morality is to be ascribed to this very method of pagan-Semitic probabilism which can easily be rendered subservient to hieratic aspirations towards theocratical rule.

Escobar's wisdom may illustrate our assertion as to the source of jesuitical casuistry. He presents an ambiguous question, such as may arise in the so-called "conflict of duties," an intricate case in which an ethical solution seems impossible. "Is it the duty of a person coming to the confessional to describe to his or her confessor the committing of such and such a sin?" Escobar rejoins: "Henriquez says, yes. Lessius says, no. And I myself? I agree with Lessius."

This dialogue at the same time illustrates how one in doubt as to his duty is not obliged to ask his own conscience. The theory of allowances has made it more convenient for him to choose any decision of somebody's else conscience which suits him best. He may follow the opinion of his adviser, who then must take the matter in question upon his own conscience. Escobar allows him to do so. But we have again the india-rubber conscience, in proxy and for money, which not only the Imaum supplies or the Rabbi, but also the Jesuit—at the confessional.

The doctrine of mental reservation, and the artifices of ambiguous words or construction of sentences, may be passed over under the concession that they may not be specific peculiarities of the order as such. But the more portentous is the introduction of the confessional as a substitute for the preaching of the Word of God, together with just such an abusive method of utilising the substitute as we observed in the above sample.

Probabilism owes its revival and ecclesiastical adoption to the innovation of the confession-box, inasmuch as this facilitates the application of ethical, or rather, judicial sophistry to each particular case. As soon as oral confession, after its elevation to sacramental dignity, had prepared the Roman domination to adopt the old method of probabilism, casuistry became its necessary complement. Moral philosophy was henceforth taken from the province of the conscience and transferred to intellectualism.

The church, requiring the submission of the intellect, substituted her decisions in place of the conscientiousness of its members; in other words, the priesthood took charge of the intellect of the laity, and took their actions upon its own conscience. It was this relinquishment of individual responsibility, which especially suited, among many other people, the courts of the Habsburgers and the Valois.

After the members of the church had been deprived of conscience, of their own, where was the church to derive conscience from? (It was this problem which prompted Kant to build up his theory of the categorical imperative.) Well, a system of generalising and analysing precedential cases and decisions similar to the requisite "law-brief" in legal practice was provided for.

Sins were externally classified regardless of motives. The measure of guilt was ascertained by the relation of actions—in their bearing upon hierarchal interests—to the CANONICAL RULES. The method of applying ecclesiastical jurisprudence was equal to that in which many criminal procedures are carried on, where the most subtle circumstances are investigated in order to fix the extent of punishment—if not to defeat justice by shrewdly resorting to legal technicalities. This moral system, if classification of sins and codification of fines deserves that name, was the work of a long lineage of casuists, strongly reminding one of the Roman "justice in private." It breathes, at any rate, the spirit of ancient Rome.

When alluding to the mode of Islam raising a body-guard for the secret purposes of the sultan, it will have been noticed that the highest merit of Turkish education consisted in its skill to drill human wills in the wiles of an insidious, deep, and burning hatred, and to bring them into obedience to a will not their own. The first exercises were calculated to alienate men from every affectionate relationship and then to enure them to blind submission, to absolute subjection.

Now the very same results were accomplished by the seminaries which the novices of the order of Jesuits had to enter. Subsequently they were subjected to the pedagogy in the houses of probation, which had to test the results of the preparatory

course and to lead the pupils, now puppets, over to the practical experimenting of Alienation from family affections.
the post-graduate course. The alienation from family affections and domestic habits
once completed, the usefulness of a Jesuit as a tool for the purposes of hierarchal supremacy straight and definite, is soon made perfect.

Then the Jesuit has every feature of his face under control so that his mien may not Thought moulded into a uniformity of scheming.
betray the inner workings of the mind. At the instant of being commanded by the superior
he renounces every trait of individuality, his own judgment, his personal ambition, his sense
of virtue. He can prove his disinterestedness to the extreme of selfsacrifice, yea, of prostitu-
ting his manliness. Thus Jesuitism is able to exceed even Turkish abnegation of personality. Dumb obedience.
To Jesuitism alone it is possible to cast thought into that mold of habitual simulation which
can maintain the uniformity of tendency, without donning an uniform like other orders; so
as neither to compromit nor deny the schemes of the order.

This obedience, considered as meritorious per se, is obtained under indispensable The world to be mystified as to the workings of the machinery and aims of either the curia or the order.
psychical exercises, called religious, of course. And it is practiced in such a manner,
that the object of the command and the effect of its execution by the agent, are to
him entirely irrelevant. Just as the individual member of the order has become
more of a dumb tool than a rational agent, so has the order surrendered itself to become the weapon in the hand of the curia. It may be, however, that vice versa, the
curia, dissembling independence, was used as the tool of the order, whenever an occasion demanded —which was frequently the case—that the world might be mystified
as to the workings of the machinery and the aims of either the curia or the order.

Gregory XIII founded the Roman institute of the "Propaganda" as the seminary for all "Propaganda" to curb Protestantism.
nations, with twenty class-rooms and three hundred and sixty cells for the scholars. Its true
designation, however, was the special drill requisite for leading the renegade Germanic
nations back to the fold. The accomplishments to be acquired there consisted in as much devout-
ness as readiness for any emergency. The Jesuit must have mastered the art of adjusting his Jesuitical training. L. v. Ranke, § 133, 145, 163.
measures to the spirit of the time. He must know how to cater to the popularity of those
nations without risking the loss of their respect, the command of which is to be upheld by all
means. A newspaper, for instance, is to be managed with such duplicity, that scarcely any-
body may surmise its being edited by members of the order in furtherance of its deep laid Intimacy between the Jesuits and the courts.
designs; that "leaders" may be composed in the language of modern infidelity, or in the tenor
of protestantism; that for an instance, in France, England and the United States simultaneously, articles may appear which clamor for the abrogation of the Upper House of parlia-
ment or of the Senate, in favor of certain hidden purposes of Romanism, wherewith to Jesuits the privileged educators of the wealthy youth.
amuse unwary politicians, and to belabor public opinion. This school of spiritual diplomacy
was "eminently qualified to instruct its emissaries in dignified and decorous deportment, in
the unfolding of pomp and ceremoniousness. In order to attract public attention and admiration. It perfectly understood how to instill a calculating, all-observing circumspection, an
indefatigable aspiration to victory by all means, and an unquenchable thirst of dominion".
This is what Ranke summed up as the result of his observation.

As from Damascus and Yemen to Tunis and Morocco the monkish orders of Islam
have their work assigned; so the order under discussion is charged with directing
the recapture of the Germanic nations and reduction of their countries by a sur-
reptitious warfare. In execution of this command the first efforts were directed Absolute monarchism appears for the first time in the Christian Orient.
towards securing the patronage of the courts. Once ingratiated in the favor of a
mighty ruler here and there, these were won for the scheme, and with them all the
means for making the pedagogy of the order the ideal of education in the national institutions of learning. For, by means of this education the courts gained nothing
less than absolute monarchism which now for the first time appears in the Christian
Occident.

§ 165. Precisely as during the period between Augustus and Diocletian the
power of ancient cæsarism gradually increased, so now, thanks to Jesuitism, the
Christian monarchies became encouraged to develop absolutism, as the history of the
Spanish-Habsburgian and French courts evinces, and of all the petty courts imitating
them.

Again human nature gravitates to the compact mass of a universal monarchy Humanity ever gravitates to compact units—in stagnant empires.
which bids fair to render individual existence secure—in a stagnant empire.

The Occident always contained a diversity of independent nationalities. Ever
since Wycliff taught the English to get along without a pope much better than with
even three; ever since the Germans had carried their point in the Council of Constanz National selfconsciousness gained through the Reformation,
to vote by nationalities, the political selfconsciousness of these nations slowly re-
turned. After the Reformation had rejected the rule of a hierarchal world-theory,

the Germanic nations had taken their several positions. Upon the strength and emulation of these very nationalities, upon their independence from, and decisive opposition to, Rome, the progress of humanity depended. To bind that diversity and to curb the symptoms of progress became now the aim of absolutism, which with Roscher we designate as **denominational absolutism**. For now the church, notwithstanding the claim of catholicity, became sectarian indeed, if it had not been so before.

On the whole this aspiration toward absolutism was, according to Roscher, quite harmless. Up to 500,000 ducats emperor Maximilian would have spent to become pope, if the cardinals had not charged more for it—whilst the same poor Austrian was refused admittance into his good town of Innspruck, because he had neglected to pay the hotel bill of his former visit. His bid was offered in the month of August 1511, when pope Julius II was lying sick. We see there was no method as yet in such bubbling up of absolutistic dreams.

Soon after this, however, the situation changed. The grandson of Ferdinand "the Catholic", and of Maximilian, "the last of the knights", occupied the throne of united Spain, held Naples and the Netherlands in his hands, and upon his head wore the crown even of Jerusalem. The imperial office was added. The victory of Pavia and the taking of Rome made the position of Charles V the most formidable the world as yet had seen, for he counted the Indians of both Americas his subjects. His preponderance might well have caused a feeling of embarrassment within a certain monk, when the young Dutch Spaniard presided over the German Reichstag. He terrifies Paris, stops the Othmans behind the Raab, and with a firm grasp holds them in Algiers. His armies conquer in Africa, subjugate Italy—they are victorious upon the heaths of Lochau over the Saxon elector! But notwithstanding this power Charles V's position was not as yet perilous to the cultural life of the world; it is after him that the Spanish monarchy becomes dangerous. Why? Not because it protects Europe against the Turk in the East with one arm, and carries European culture in the form of Romanism to the far West with the other. This Spanish monarch becomes a menace because he does it all with a purposive determination full of method under the direction of a Jesuit-General, in behalf of "the Church", in the interest of a largely modified "faith", to which his training enslaves him. The first absolute monarch in Christendom turns a criminal, and becomes one of the most heinous figures of history—whilst his father-in-law tries to play English absolutism to spite the pope.

To Roman Christianity Philip II is what the Sultan is to Islam. Silent in his seclusion he receives messages from a thousand secret agents. Whether the ciphered letters contain good news or dire disappointments, he perfectly controls his emotion if there is any left within him. From his cabinet, with the atmosphere of austere stiffness, he reaches deep into the course of human affairs, deep and direct into millions of horrified households. Too deep for any man to discern, his procedures move all in one direction. In conformity to his administration of justice which is executed with horrid mysteriousness, the whole mode of government is rendered terrible to the last resort. Sufficiently significant as to the nature of his deep and dark designs is what Prescott, his biographer, says of his "doing things quietly". The deadly stillness about his lair opposite the Escorial became exemplary to Spain. By the stakes of the auto da fe, which the king with his entire court used to attend from beginning to end, he made stillness reign from ocean to ocean. Just imagine the 988 nunneries in Spain alone, and his army of 32,000 Dominicans and Franciscan mendicants. In the two bishoprics of Pampeluna and Calahorra alone 20,000 clericals! A power hovered over the land certainly strong and cruel enough to frighten and to freeze all consciousness into one mold, all the fires of burning stakes notwithstanding.

Life in the Hofburg at Vienna exactly corresponds to that around the Escorial; and the effect of denominational absolutism upon the court and people was as palpable in Austria as in Spain. The monarchs were trained in early youth to build little altars for the saints, and were tutored to destroy the last vestiges of chivalry and constitutional liberties by persecuting the protestants.

At court blear-eyed bigotry and sheepish ennui sneak softly along under the livery of Spanish grandezza, black mandil and red stockings. Throughout the nation the same languor exists except that the rigor is mitigated by a licensed sensuality and frivolity as it is everywhere under the rule of Jesuitism. For, in a nation of well-behaving children, which in the sense of Jesuitism means punctilious observance of priestly prescriptions, the manners and amusements are scarcely censured, be they ever so worldly and vulgar. Under such liberality the Germans, to a large extent, and the French not less, befriended themselves with absolutism in proportion to their aversion to the discipline of Calvinism. The social habits required little decorum; but in official relations matters were taken very gravely and seriously, and a tone of refinement came into universal use, in which members of the estates even would most circumstantially (nothing short of a style of Chinese servility) declare "that after having reached the summit of happiness, in being permitted to dare to prostrate ourselves at the feet of your Majesty, we expire in most faithful submissiveness". To German ears such politeness was something new, but they had become educated, you know—recently. And if we take a glance at Polonia, poor Poland, we are compelled to admit Krasinsky's correctness, when he complains that "Polonia went down under this system". Those four hundred pupils of noble extraction, who received their education in the new university at Putulsk, were sufficient to inflate the entire nobility with a romantic but morose bigotry combined with corrupt morals.

It was the beginning of "Finis Poloniæ" when a king was vouchsafed to it who had been, and worse yet, who continued to be, a Jesuit. It was Johann Kasimir, that is, "Ja so mir"—(s. c. "Gott helfe"). .

§ 166. Having become acquainted with probabilism, with the confessional, and with denominational absolutism, we must for the sake of comparison also recognise the courtly absolutism in its elegancy. For this we go to France. *Courtly absolutism.*

During the period of the counter-reformation the difficult task devolved upon France to keep the polished and popular order of Jesuits in good humor, and at the same time to counter-balance the Spanish-Burgundian-Austrian combination. Rome never forgets its Latin: "Divide et impera!" The Jesuits instructed the French how to watch "the Balance of the European Powers." For a time, for almost a century, it seemed indeed as if the Habsburgian group should rule Europe. France resisted, successfully resisted that hegemony, but it furthered absolutism, courtly and denominational combined, nevertheless. France furthered it by obliging the hierarchy at the expense of the Huguenots. *French system of Jesuitism.* *Doctrine of the "Balance of Power" set up at the expense of the Huguenots. § 182.*

It was in the nightly consultation at Bayonne which Alba held with Catherine of Medici, and which William of Orange overheard, that Alba broke to her the plan which seven years later was executed. Bishop Perefixe's estimate is, that inside of six weeks 100,000 Hugenots had been killed in all parts of France. The death of 70,000 is proved by still more official authority. Gregory XIII had a memorial medal coined. By the repetition of such persecution, tho not in that wholesale manner, France was purged of the old Franconian and German chivalry; the Celtic element, more pliable and less true to principle, gained the upper hand. Richelieu utilised the thinned out and frightened populace for scaffoldings in the upbuilding of monarchical absolutism. Guizot, in his first period, took this for a triumph of civilisation. Buckle rehabilitated the shrewd cardinal on account of his success in the reconstruction of France and in curbing Spanish schemes. Mazarin, another ecclesiastical ruler, completed the work, and in Louis Quatorze the world witnessed the reign of an arbitrariness which paid as little regard to law as to public opinion. Christendom now perceived with admiration, if not with a shudder, a "Most Christian Majesty" under the caprices of his mistresses and flattered by his confessors—his conscience by proxy. And under the spell of such a sight the world, hypnotised as it were, by Jesuitism—made loyal allowances. The world's history met with a court which not only corrupted but literaly contaminated all the other courts of Europe. The smallest prince in Germany imitated—a new Sultan. Two cardinals of the curia assisted the court in this work, just for the chance to fan the fanaticism against the Reformation in Germany. They had succeeded even in hitching Habsburg and Bourbon together for this end in the "Peace of Mesdames" concluded at Cambray. *Gregor XIII and the "Night of Bartholomew". Perefixe.* *Richelieu, Mazarin, Polignac—cardinals. Buckle; Guizot.* *Damage done by the counter-reformation.* *Poisoning the morals of Europe.*

A third cardinal frankly confessed what he knew about Rome's partnership in the corruptive dealings of monarchical-denominational absolutism. "I hope," wrote Polignac on the 16th of March, A. D. 1709, "that posterity need not trouble itself with deciphering my dispatches in order to obtain testimony against the Roman curia. She shows by her deportment to have so deeply apostatised from the spirit of her testator, as to justify her desire that her enemies will never get an insight into the diary of those days. Today, when truth alone is the rampart affording protection against the impudence of the papal court, it would be iniquity to deny it, and abandon the truth." *Corruption of the papal court. Polignac.*

France was purged of its best elements. Its silk industry was ruined immediately and completely, by the weavers taking flight to England and Prussia. It took the government a century full of effort to restore the industry of the country to its former prosperity in order to reopen sources of revenue. Even after that lapse of time the government seems to have realised very meagre results. Marie Antoinette once had to deny herself the pleasure of a court-ballet because the minister of finance needed the money for importing glass-blowers from Venice. How France's losses became the gains of England and Germany becomes evident in the facts that Great Britain's textile industry dates from the very time when it gave quarters to the Reformed exiles; and that in consequence of its purgings France had the humiliating experience that a score of Prussian generals of French descent returned on a short visit to their ancestral homes in the year 1870. *The losses of the French became the gains of England and Prussia.*

Thus Jesuitism together with its projected absolutism was a failure after all, because it sacrificed the welfare of the nations and the cause of humanism to its intrigues and "fornication with the kings of the earth." When its prestige with the courts appeared to be on the wane, Jesuitism stooped to the lower experiment of making the subjects "drunk with the wine of her fornication." *"Fornication with the kings of the earth".* *Making the subjects "drunk with the wine of her fornications".*

For why did this order with "the abundance of her delicacies" finally fall into disgrace with the Bourbon courts in France, Spain, and Naples? Why did Pombal clean out the courts of Joseph I ?

Choiseul had demonstrated long before how profitable it would be to confiscate and secularise the property of such a wealthy and powerful state within the state, whilst in reality the ground of the disgust of the courts lay deeper. It was the same Choiseul whose first advice intending to cover the retreat of the traitors had been given in vain, who finally, because pious Maria Theresa did not heed the advice, had to convince her of the necessity and justice of harsh measures against the order, by laying before her the original documents, which dismantled the high treason of a Jesuitical conspiracy. Intentionally we desisted from enlarging upon such historical proofs of the Jesuitical tactics as came to light in the murders of princes. Motley adduced proofs sufficient in themselves, if there were not hundreds of similar cases, to stigmatise Jesuitism forever. The assassination of William of Nassau-Orange is not forgotten; and if it were, the verdict of history is not to be supposed as taking the place of final judgment against perpetrators of such crimes, for training such tools as the sneak of Delft.

Yet we adhere to our original intention simply to judge the system and to indict it by resulting facts, by the notorious effects in general, where it had a fair chance to realise its principles without impediment. This chance the Jesuits had in Brazil and Paraguay, where they held their subjects under unlimited dominion, and nobody disturbed them in establishing absolutism to their hearts' content. There the Jesuits commanded an army and cast cannons. They raised a nation which had no objection to kneeling before exquisitely wrought altars, which took delight in the numerous festivities, high and low, with which the patres amused them. But all that the Jesuits did, for Paraguay at least, was to raise several generations of errand boys.

It was the portentum of Roman casuistry, now as well as of yore, to disfigure the truth. True to this old inclination Rome, Christian in name, interpolated Roman Pre-Christian and Jewish Post-Christian misconceptions into those ethics, which are founded upon the high dignity and value of personal life. But that casuistry could obtain the degree of atrocities alluded to, is only reducible to probabilism and its method of indoctrinating the nations with its subterfuges. Probabilism was welcomed by the curia because of the convenience which it afforded to maintain its political predominance under largely altered conditions by inventing modes of accommodation to any vile practice. And because the Roman-Spanish method had proved so successful, it is hardly to be expected of the curia ever to open itself for the conviction of its error and to repent its wrongs. Contrarily, it is to be expected that Romanism will improve that method, and utilise the powers gained thereby in continuing its mode of training the nations in its ways. Of course we have in view such docile peoples only as prefer to be ruled by proxy-conscientiousness, or such as admire Semitic insolence and tenacity combined with Roman determination to either rule or ruin. But just on these grounds we anticipate that probabilism may estrange from earnest religiousness minds so noble as the American mind, minds biased to favor this system because it inwardly molests a person less than any other, minds easily captivated by apparent success.

Because of probabilism with its sophistry and delusive consequentialness the grand thought of "the kingdom"—that dome expanding wide enough to cover the peaceful reunion of those in all denominations which call upon the world's Savior—has at times been treated with indifference and neglect, if not contemptuously rejected. It goes without saying, that thereby the realisation of the final purpose of the King will not be frustrated, howsoever it may seemingly be obstructed. Hence Protestantism is justified in denying the attribute of catholicity, at the least, to the Roman church, in criticising its methods and tactics, in treating it like any other of the sects, may its organisation politically enjoy ever so much prestige.

An emblem of antagonism against the thought of universal Christian humaneness, a type of Roman narrowness and monarchical absolutism will ever remain the figure of yonder misanthropist in his chamber six by six feet amidst a confusion of rocks and sterile wastes on the slope of the Guadarrama, brooding over the consummation of a theocracy which might be covered by the dome arching over his brain. From his bed in the lonely, stony, and chilly cell, he had beside the view through the door no other than that upon the high altar below the cupola of the Escorial. The grate, upon which Laurentius had been roasted, outlines the groundplan of that immense edifice, built with the gold of Peru and, like the Tuilleries, with the confiscated property of ruined, if not extirpated, Reformed Christians. Over the main entrance stands to this day the image of the saint who was once made victim to the intolerance of blind heathen. State-religion with the "worldly" power at disposal had silenced the champion of religious freedom who yet bore testimony against irreligious bigotry. In vain, however, stood the stony picture of the martyr in its niche as a witness: no potentate would understand him, since votaries of martyrs seemed to have come into power in order to turn persecutors themselves. They burned, beheaded, and dispersed their own subjects, the brethren of him who once had been roasted. Hence silence reigns throughout Spain as over a large graveyard around the gigantic vault known as the Escorial.

CH. V. ENLIGHTENMENT AND ABSOLUTISM DISSECTING THE THOUGHT OF HUMANISM.

§ 167. We have attained to a position from which the course of events outlined in the four preceding chapters is to be reviewed under still another aspect.

Full contents of the cognition of humanism.

Engaged with the earnest labor of ecclesiastical reform, and under the pressure of persecutions outrivalling in fierceness and number of victims the so called ten persecutions of the patristic times, the spirit of investigation and discrimination had been awakened and now instituted another form of inquisition. The builders, at work in rearing a reconstructed church, had for their rule and compass the original charter of Christianity and that God-consciousness which had been regained by the perusal of the restituted gifts. Soon, however, the research penetrated into crevices where misunderstandings are possible, especially where eccentric investigators laid aside the rule and compass used by the reformers. The human mind had been outraged so long, that now, in striving after emancipation, it went far beyond the standard measure of freedom. Christianity had been identified with ecclesiasticism so long that many thought it more safe, in avoidance of a worse popery, to choose as a criterion of inquiry and research the opposite of religiousness: namely world-consciousness pure and simple.

Awakening of the spirit of inquiry.

Bible and God-consciousness set up by the Reformation.

Emancipation rejects the authority of the compass and rule of the Reformation; fear of another popery,

It was unavoidable, and, on the whole, it was harmless, that for some length of time the Christian thought was superseded by philosophical thinking.

and takes, for its sole criterion: world-consciousness.

What is called "enlightenment" was a great movement which pervaded every province of culture and all forms of earthly life—until it led to a crisis. Emperor Frederick II already had given some vent and impulse to criticism. Then came the study of the humanistics and the revival of letters which made the impulse irresistible and permanent. Both phases of reform beforeReformation became intoxicated by the new wine, and reeled from æsthetical dilettanteism to literary amateurishness, and staggered from antique verse-meter and rhetoric to mystical constructions of the universe. The results of these desultory and precocious attempts need not be put to derision, for in some respects they were of real import; and besides it is to be remembered always, that history must grope its way along through the enthusiasm and excitement of transitory periods.

"Enlightenment".

Cursory attempts to establish man upon concepts of humaneness which had been outraged by dogmatism.

History to grope its way.

Then came the religious reform, for which the profound study of Hebrew and Greek had done as much preparatory work as the contemplations of mysticism. Had it not been for this concentric synthesis of all preceding efforts towards a reform of the church, man could not have been fully reinstated into his true position, which includes his proper relations to the invisible realms of existence.

The Reformation alone restored the true idea of humanism in its full meaning: i. e. man to his true position.

Thanks to the Reformation man's destiny and his place in the complex organism of the visible universe—as set forth in the parables of the central revelation, but subsequently eclipsed again by one-sided and diverted world-consciousness—had been discovered anew. The true thought of humanism had been rendered formative once more in full accord with its contents, which are summarised (as has been demonstrated) in the conception of man as "the image," that is, representing the likeness of God and mirroring the universe. In the depths of personal life and in adequate proportions God and world-consciousness are to be inwrought one into the other.

1. Relation to his destiny for the higher world: Salvation. 2. Relation to nature: Selfculture.

Man is essentially a religious being as to his origin and destiny. He is also a free agent as to his development out of his own resources, that is, as far as for his own good selfculture is made obligatory.

This dual position not to be relinquished;

The cognition expressed in the term humanism implies both of these relations, the religio-ethical concerning his destiny for the higher world, and the ethico-cultural with respect to nature below him. He carries a purpose within him that ought to correspond with the design above him. He is appointed to become perfect in holiness as well as in the beauty of glory, both to begin with cultivating natural accomplishments and the susceptibility for spiritual gifts, and both to be consummated at their common goal. Men can not relinquish the one without prejudicing the other, without rendering the realisation of humanism in its genuine sense impossible. It has become obvious how profoundly the religious reform took both relations and obligations into its scope. The reformers conceived at one intuitive glance, that man in the midst of a dual relationship was to consecrate himself to the will of God, and that man, by virtue of the strength thus imparted, may devote himself to God's service as an instrument of the divine purposes in the world. Under the condition of non-resistance and cooperation man is to grow in sanctification so that of himself he may influence the natural world preparatory to its glorification along with himself.

none of this relation to be cultivated at the expense of the other.

Contents of the true concept of humanity as postulated in the Reformation.

Upon the basis of this double relationship humanity is to redeem the arrested and depressed life of nature in the process of reciprocal cultivation, to subdue the natural to the divine-human spirit, and, inasmuch as in his selfdedication nature in its entirety is implied, to consecrate all to God.

Man to appropriate the
divine life to himself, to
conduct this into the
life of the world; to
conduct the world
through and with
himself to the state of
glorious existence.
Thus man is to appropriate to himself the divine life extended to him for accept-ance in order to become qualified for service as its conductor into the life of the world; he is to conduct the natural world by the ethically elevating, spiritualising, and transforming process through and with himself into the state of divine glory. This, "in a nutshell" is **in substance, the world-theory of the Reformation,** the project and precept of civilisation, as expostulated by the evangelical denominations.

Precept and
project of
Evangelical
Christianity.

True monism of natural
and spiritual realities in
true humanism.

Proper blending of
sacred things with the
secular concerns,

the contrast between
sacred and profane in
church matters being
abrogated.

Christian and only true
and possible cognition of
humanity.

Onesided
theories
caricature either
religion or ethics.

Sum and substance of
the thought as
established by the
Reformation
unification of
God and man, of
spirit and nature
religion and
ethics.

Directions of the
thought of humanity.
This is the religio-ethical and none the less rational thought materialising itself in the acts and deeds of practical Christian life, properly blending the sacred with secular concerns, the earthly with the heavenly things. Herein is formulated the full cognition of what the concept humanity ought to contain, humanity as held together by the reality of the "image", as founded and fixed in the being of God, and as becoming realised in the concrete. Henceforth the old contrast between sacred and profane in church matters is abrogated, both being but different relations of the same reality. These two sides, conditioning and complementing one another, are in-separable; if they are separated, or taken as opposites or contrarieties, humanity itself is broken up and relapses into the ancient antitheses without humanism and without God. Whoever takes a position against this theory with its facts renders both religion and God-consciousness caricatures. Unless both are duly correlated by maintaining (1) the full cognition of the "likeness unto God", that is, of true humanity in unity and freedom as fixed in the prototype who is the image of the Father; and by thus (2) comprehending the intermediating position of man between the natural and spiritual worlds, as founded in, and revealed by, the person and work of the Mediator, neither of the above antitheses by itself will suffice to reduce the phenomena of history to a monistic theory of life, or to unlock the combination of the synthesis.

§ 168. A sad spectacle, to observe now, how flippantly and frivolously those themes were handled, which it took history and the ablest minds of humanity so many millenniums to elaborate, and which the Reformation under palpable divine guidance, and under the endurance of indescribable sufferings, had elucidated anew; how the freedom of inquiry, so conquerously obtained through, and maintained in hot and bloody contests after the religious Reformation, was now abused in unsettling all that had been given to, and accomplished by, the champions of the cause of humanism.

Radicalism
vivisecting the
thought under
pretense of
emancipation
from dogmatism.
Under pretense of evangelical freedom, and rampant under the field-cry of radical emancipation, emancipated minds undertook to dissect, we might say vivisect, that cognition of humanity which the Reformation had regained, had so cogently formu-lated, and so heroically defended. The concrete synthesis of fact and faith is now anatomised after the manner in which a scientist cuts up a human corpse, as tho the conception of humanism could be proved or disproved by the use of the scalpel.

Necessary restriction of
free thought by the
church which procured
freedom.

§ 119' 171, 177.
The reform of doctrine, discipline, usages, and form of organisation was compelled in several instances to refute, if not to repress, wild outgrowths, so as not to commit itself to the reproach of silent assent; for the enemies used to hold the reformers and the renovated doctrines responsible before the diets and courts for misdemeanors committed in the abuse of freedom. No sooner were the restrictions alleviated than that "enlightenment" tried to see what could be made of the evangelical thoughts of freedom and humanity in the interest of its onesided world-consciousness. Some of the heralds of enlightenment desired that the Church as such should be disestablished altogether, or at least become deprived of the right of manag-ing its own affairs, which they seemed ready to take under control themselves.

Enlightenment had
reasons to be afraid of
new ecclesiastical
suppression.
Those enlightened ones had reasons, perhaps, to fear lest a new persecuting church should arise. HENCE THEY SET UP THE PHYSICO-MORAL PART OF THE IDEA OF HUMANISM IN OPPOSITION TO THE RELIGIO-MORAL PART, as tho the latter were at variance with the former or irrelevant. The product was labeled "Natural Religion", from which "anthropomorphisms" were to be weeded out.

Humanity is to
become revealed
with all that
human nature
contains, hence
enmity to the
Christian
thought not to be
foiled by forced
restriction.
In short, it had the appearance as if a new antagonist had risen against the Christian thought. Yet it only seemed so. Experiences of the saddest nature may account for the anx-iety which the lovers of the Bible manifested during the controversies. Yet the controversies do not justify the loss of too much of that confidence to which the thought of true humanism in the concrete is entitled. Throughout history the intention is obvious, that humanity should come to know and to show itself in all its phases, and this intention never permits of being foiled by any forced restriction. Hence the church should be last in becoming faint-hearted concerning divine truth; and as far as sinners, unconverted and pardoned sinners make up her constituency, she ought to enure herself to the endurance of public criticism.

Let, therefore, the recovered, the reformed cognition of humanity be investigated and put to the test: to whatever is true and genuine in fact and sound in doctrine, no harm can be done thereby.   Antagonistic investigation will only urge on, and in the end, further those in the assurance of their faith who had weakened under the bold denials of a scepticism which from its nature must of necessity doubt its own assertions.   Let this fundamental bipolar cognition be analysed as to its different elements and interrelations; whenever mischief or misrepresentation is intended the procedure always accrues to the disgrace of the assailant.

Reason for allowing free criticism. §§ 60, 65, 81, 91, 128.

The concession here made to criticism and scepticism—so far as it waives the privileges of church-membership—should not be taken as a tolerance originating from indifference.   If it should seem strange to give so much license to free inquiry, then it is to be remembered that the Reformation owes its origin and success to this very principle; else it should seem strange, too, that astronomy, once enveloped in the church with all the other sciences, should have detached itself from the dogmas of that church and become independent, so as to enrich knowledge in general through unbiased research.   Instead of becoming confused by the division of mental labor, knowledge is rendered the more lucid and test-proof.   Hence there is no reason to be afraid of a onesided idea of humanism detaching itself to take an independent start upon a course of history of its own.   Such a separate movement can only tend to enrich the whole, tho it were but in the negative—and to enlarge our comprehension of what humanism implies and how that knowledge is to be applied.

No reason to be afraid of onesided treatment of the thought of humanity,

in attempting a new departure independent from church-dogmas toward a history of its own. §§ 2, 13, 38, 91, 110, 128, 168, 176, 185, 197, 205, 232.

As a general thing "enlightenment" was an anti-churchly movement that made it necessary to state the positive principle in counterposition.   But it is necessary also to state the well-founded reasons for opposing the ecclesiastical apperception of humanism, tho the statement may be taken almost as an excuse of the irreligionists.   That we do not advocate the workings of, and have no partiality for, the movement, will appear when we come to investigate it as to its own merits.

Irreligious humanitarianism had been called forth. Ecclesiasticism.

Even in the countries under Roman rule ecclesiastical diplomacy and despotic absolutism did not always succeed in suppressing free thought, critical examination and scepticism.

Romanism unable to quash free thought upon its own territories. Stachbreyer.

If Rome charges Protestantism with being responsible for radicalism, Bishop Strossmeyer has demonstrated to her, that she had to fight heretics, i. e., free thinkers, long before the Reformation and in her own strongholds.   The inquisition then in vogue was a judicature of the king, a measure of the worldly power, merely embellished with ecclesiastical pomp and sanctimoniousness, and, of course, highly approved of, if not explicitly sanctioned, by the pope.

Inquisition called forth the spirit of free inquiry,

When Conrad of Marburg attempted to introduce the inquisition into Germany as the first attempt at extending it, he was slain by Hessian peasants, because of his cruel treatment of Elizabeth of Thuringia.   Then followed the burghers of Naples and Milan in resisting the Spanish contrivance to ferret out secret Moors.   The people of Milan cried; "Long live the king!   Death to the inquisition!"   In Naples the bells rang the alarm, and nobles arm in arm with commoners cried; "The union shall live!"

which is not to be quenched by another inquisition.

In Rome Christine, the amazon daughter of Gustavus Adolphus, spent her Swedish fortune.   Said she to Burnet: "Of necessity the Church must be governed by the Holy Ghost, for since I am in Rome I have seen four popes, and I swear to you that none of them had any common sense".   To be sure, one may doubt whether she had much herself.   She had exchanged a crown for a free, lusty life, and now she covets a crown again, be it the Swedish or the Polish.   Her adventures are only referred to at this instance in illustration of the free and frivolous spirit of enlightenment, which ever since the reign of Leo X had seized Catholicism.   To illustrate the truth, on the other hand (which might be proven from numberless other instances of equal force) that onesided world-consciousness, or rather worldliness sprang not from the rigorism of the magistrate of Geneva.   Such reproach is ill becoming Rome in face of the fact that for the sake of contrast, Rome was not always very decided on the part of God-consciousness or godliness.

Christine, queen of Sweden, daughter of Gustavus Adolphus, criticising popery.

Rigorism of Genevus not responsible for onesided, worldly humanistics.

PHILIP'S BROODINGS IN THE ESCORIAL TURNED OUT TO BE OF REAL ADVANTAGE TO THE DUTCH AND THE ENGLISH, and to the Reformation together with the cause of humanism.

The Dutch opposed the introduction of the inquisition, as much as the deprivation of their constitutional rights, and the establishment of absolutism by military power.   Hollandish freedom had been reduced to the small town of Alkmaar, which fifty years previously had furnished the stake the first victims of the Reformation.   It was here that, in the days of the Bartholomew massacre, the freedom of Europe stood at bay, and fishermen, drowsy Dutch fishermen, withstood the veterans of Alva, the elite troops of the world.

Results of Philip's broodings to force the inquisition upon Holland.

The Leyden people dug out the last blades of grass which grew between the cobblestones on the streets, and cooked old shoes; but they held out until the waves drove off the Spaniards just at the hour when the battered wall broke down.   Those heroes of Leyden would eat the left arm in order to keep up strength for fighting with the right, until William's Geuses brought them bread, carried through the dams by the raging North-Sea.

Spanish wars against the Netherlands under William of Orange. §§ 166, 173, 174

Calvinistic nations become maritime and industrial powers.

It was Holland that broke the Spanish power; and it was God who scattered the Armada into the winds and waters. Holland and England and Brandenburg, all Calvinistic, rose at once to become and to remain the leading nations.

Hugo Grotius writes on international law.
§ 175.

The Dutch navy vanquished the Spanish everywhere and hoisted brooms to their mastheads, signifying that the sea was swept clean of absolutism. Their ships went out, bound for Japan around the northern coast, with evangelists on board; they hauled wool from Cyprus and silk from Naples. Amsterdam took the place of Venice. Leyden became a university; and Hugo Grotius wrote on international law. Upon the basis of Calvinistic ethics and energy, people of faithful and dutiful character rose to a religious world-consciousness never heard of before. Upon the basis of navigation and the maritime commerce of Reformed nations, upon the basis of industry which France had driven to London and Berlin, a general and very promising advance was made in all directions of ethico-cultural life, starting right in to build up a solid and genuine civilisation without artifices and without ceasing. And a party of Geuses, the Dutch water-beggars, laid the foundations for New York.

Water-beggars found New York.

Musings of a Dutch soldier.

A Dutch soldier sits behind the stove in his barracks, musing over the universe and its origin, over Heaven above and the affairs of mankind upon earth beneath. It is Descartes, the pupil of Spanish Jesuitism, seeking his way out of the labyrinth of probabilism. Laboring under the conviction that first of all it is necessary to doubt everything, he resolves to be a sceptic. Thinking, he breaks down the whole world-consciousness which has been imposed upon his thoughts. Only one thing he cannot argue away, his "cogito." From that simple point he levels the ground for a mental reconstruction of the entire "world-wisdom."

Descartes establishes another kind of inquisition—inquiry as to the "Ego".

Philosophy of Spinoza, Locke and Leibnitz initiated.

He initiates a new philosophy for Spinoza, Locke and Leibnitz wherewith to engage their meditations. The single thought left to certainty, above the possibility of a shadow of doubt, is that he who thinks is really himself. That the ego thinks proves its existence and selfconsciousness. This certainty becomes the foundation upon which the whole tower of conclusions is reared heavenward. In the ego lie the ideas, and the perceptions are formed. But from whence do they get there? Probably they are delusions which do not truly reflect things around one as they really are. Hence those perceptions and ideas and the process of their formation must be scrutinously examined. And one idea surpasses all the others which it is impossible that the ego should have produced of itself: the idea of an infinite being. Along with selfconsciousness the consciousness of God, then, the God-Idea, is to thought a necessity, since it cannot be thought away. Furthermore we find within ourselves the ideas of thought and of extension, over both of which we can think. This makes it necessary to presuppose subsisting existences; that is, substances conveying thought in their extensiveness. Thus Descartes penetrates deeper into, and advances higher, step by step, from his solitary "ego" because of its "ergo."

A new world-consciousness founded upon the ego, upon scepticism as to dogmatics.

Man, taken as the major premise, put into the central position.

It is plain that here a mode of ratiocination sets in, which is to hold sway over the new æra thus inaugurated.

Man, not God, is the major premise and stands in the center.

Significance of Descartes' speculation.

From within, man's aspirations reach out to construct his world, the new humanistics. Man is to appropriate to himself the objectivity of things, and to model them into conformance with thought. Man does not want the world to explain itself to him, because he must explain it to his own satisfaction. And the Master-builder of this world must be detectable under the given laws of thinking. That means, we must not accept anything as a matter of course, but are to reason out things ourselves,

"Aufklærung", enlightenment,

Then this new form of world-consciousness, which commenced with the protest of an autodidactic mind against all that is and was taught us to be so, the general "clearing up" (Aufklærung) ensued. Under the new aspects the fragmentary and illfitting parts of a sort of kaleidoscopic knowledge were removed in order to erect the new building upon the leveled ground of the ego. Soon the universities of Leyden and Utrecht were drawn into the Cartesian neology, and all the high schools of the German nations followed suit in the work which again made "man the measure of all things." This was the beginning of the "enlightenment" among the learned; its charm consisted in the facilities which it afforded for popularising this wisdom to the level of a jejune generalness and pretentious subjectivism.

In its scientific beginning.

§ 169. The Norman-French feudal lords had subjugated and trodden down the Anglo-Saxon element under papal sanction. But when the people of England arose in defense of their old church, the prime movers were discovered as coming from that

very Anglo-Saxon stock among whom Bangor and Lutterworth had not entirely been
forgotten. The people of England had become disgusted with the rule of cardinals.
The nation had become ripe for representative government after the pattern of the
Calvinistic synods. The supreme judicatory of Rome was abolished; neither Peter's
pence nor the money for a pallium should leave the country. The "spiritual" and
"worldly" estates were combined under the "crown". Queen Elizabeth resigned the
title of the "supreme head of the church", altho retaining the more resolutely "the
sovereign prerogative in all matters of state, ecclesiastical as well as secular."

> Thus the ground had been cleared in Reformed nations—to a certain extent: in the one
by application of ethical measures, whilst the Lutherans got mussed up a little through their
dogmatical controversies. Both courses were conducive to the accelerated development of
free mental activity, altho one anomaly continued, which at the bottom was as favorable to
absolutism as any world-theoretical heresy:—the state-church, reducible to the circumstances
created by Philip's filibusterings.

> "My crown," said Elizabeth, "is subject to the King of Kings and to nobody else". So much
had Philip's pressure accomplished, that the claims of church-dogma on one hand, and of
free criticism and public inquiry on the other, might be discriminated and liquidated.

What Descartes, the musing Dutchman, expostulated to the scholars, Shakespeare,
the practical Englishman, exhibited to the public. Irrelative of, and indifferent to,
the religious tenet of the state-church even, he analysed human nature in open view
of the nation, and popularised the result by the dramatic representations of characters in their bearings upon historical events. These realistic pictures called forth
a taste for both, anthropological and historical studies. In the grand descriptive
style of Daniel, in the language which Wycliff had fixed by his translation of the
Bible, and with an intuitive insight almost bordering on inspiration, Shakespeare
inadvertently pointed out the paths upon which, outside of the church and without
reference to her doctrines, the practical knowledge of man and the philosophy of history were to proceed.

In Hume, the subjectivistic historian, we see, bolder than anywhere else, that
side of philosophy preponderating, which considers human nature under the low
aspects of naturalism, not simply disregarding but even assaulting the spiritual, to
say nothing of the religious, elements of personal life. According to Hume the concept of humanity is an abstract generalisation; humanity itself is treated as a collection of individuals without the inner connection through any "center of cohesion."
Under pretext of close investigation analysis dissolves the race into atoms, detracting
the attention from the difficult problems (because of the inability to account for
them,) of the individualisation from the uniform bulk of natural generalness, or of
explaining personal life as to either its limitations or its independence, according to
its relations, adaption, and character. Hume estimated his work on "Human Nature"
as a stillborn child. But it was none. It grew up to become quite a selfwilled
and mischievous boy. It just suited the prevailing tendency of the time, which
moved in the direction of utilitarianism, and which pampered the physical appetites
of human nature. In Heaven and upon earth nothing was worth knowing, but what
might gratify wants of that kind, and these wants were much simplified by Rousseau.
On free English soil Hume thus wrought into system what had been hinted at by
Herbert of Cherbury and Hobbes. An abstract and rather hazy Deism was construed
into a sort of natural religion, which tried to bring under roof whatever remnants
retained from the God-consciousness, which could not be "cleared up" or cleaned
away. For a very indigent but so much the more pretentious "understanding" and
a very diverted and dissolute world-consciousness, this natural religion with natural
man as the center was sufficient, but not lasting.

Then came Voltaire, and—"after us the deluge." He was a pupil of the Jesuits
as were all the French enlighteners on the average. On his return from England
he made it his chief business to preach Hume and Deism.

Bitter rancor and malicious sneer was all that Voltaire, the plagiarist of Hume,
could add from his own understanding; and all that henceforth agglomerated around
Hume's wormy nucleus. We dismiss it as below our criticism; neither do we ascribe
much cultural import to the thirty thousand copies of the encyclopedia, through
which the unwarranted and unmitigated hatred against the Christian principle of

Marginal notes:

Saxon element of England, with its natural tendency to subjectivism. § 130, 135, 138, 139, 156, 175.

Representative government after the pattern of Calvinistic synods.

Another sequel of Philip's oppressive and destructive measures. Queen Elizabeth.

Shakespeare popularised what Descartes had expostulated to the scholars;

pointed out the paths upon which practical knowledge of human nature and the philosophy of history is to proceed.

Hume considers human nature under the low aspects of naturalism.

Rousseau showed how little religion was needed to make man happy.

English deism sufficed for a very much reduced understanding and a very dissipated world-consciousness;

rendered into French sensualism by

Voltaire, the plagiarist, the most malicious poet of fanatical infidelity.

humanism was spread among the nations. We decline to trace out just now the results of this conspiracy of godlessness. Samson's memoirs tell of them, and we need simply refer to Carlyle's very accessible sketch thereof.

We were compelled to take notice of the outcroppings of "enlightenment" in order to behold what had become of the problem of humanism under the onesided treatment regardless of its Christian concomitants. And we take notice of the fact, that the sale of the encyclopedia was as yet strictly prohibited by the French crown, when the protestant king feted its authors and made them courtiers at Berlin—just as he protected the Jesuits when they were driven out everywhere, in order to spite Maria Theresia. The English ambassador wrote home; "At this place nothing is seriously spoken of but Voltaire. He reads his tragedies to queens and princes until they weep, at the same time excelling the king in witticism and burlesque. In this town nobody is considered educated who does not carry the poet's work in his head or—in his pocket."

§ 170. This brings us face to face with the modern state. To Frederick, the Great, nothing was more repugnant than organised societies.

The circumstances during his reign, enlightenment in its free sweep, and his inclinations molded by training and experience, the bureaucratic machinery of government, which he regulated in avoidance of the star-chambers ruling in contemporaneous states, rendered the autocratic monarchy complete. His concept of the state was that it should keep aloof from religious entanglements; and that the king as its first servant should also stand neutral as to religious party strifes. On that score it was Frederick's maxim that every one of his subjects should believe and live according to individual preference—so long as his idea of the monarchy permitted. To decide what was in order this side the line of religious indifference, either Tersteegen's pietism or Wolf's rationalism, etc., was the office of the state-church. Of course, this rationalistic state-church just then served her first term as the first handmaid of the state; whose first servant was a kind of "acting bishop", within his country as in his diocese. In this enlightened despotism we recognise again the guarded indifference and tolerance found in various other places, where anything assuming a color of religiousness is tolerated, if only external conformity to the official religion of the state is observed for reasons of state, and where, therefore, the ideas of the subjects are cautiously watched, notwithstanding affected indifference and tolerance.

The Marshal of Saxony, for instance, dared to propose to the king to legalise marriages for periods of five years, whereby rich gains in the number of recruits for military service would surely be realised. "This king," said Hegel, who certainly ought to have fully understood him, "was the first reigning prince, who philosophically comprehended the aim of the state as a whole—who always acted in accord with the general idea before him, and who discountenanced special ties inconsistent with, or detrimental to, this general aim."

The king in his capacity as "bishop" decided what was against the general interests. Unless this is kept in view, it cannot be fully apprehended to what extent the religious side of the thought of humanity was kept in bondage. Notwithstanding the humane assurances of allowing everybody to go to Heaven sans facon, such a state has obviously no room for a free church. The predilection of Hegel for this sort of enlightened absolutism is explained by the same reasons enunciated at the instance of those ancient monarchies, where despotic governments abetted the cultures based upon indefinite ideas about the deities, and antagonised every manifestation of individual selfhood. To monarchical absolutism in its latest form the nations of Europe owe the establishment of modern state-machinery inclusive of standing armies; and also the system of arrondissements which required several territorial reconstructions.

To round off this or that province or state at the expense of third parties became the intermittent fever of the cabinets. Bruehl of Saxony had the house of Weissenfels dispatched inside of a few years. Eight granite coffins large and small witness that the court of Dresden must have been an expert in "doing it quietly." No humanistic enlightenment could hinder the partitions of Poland, or prevent several sequestrations—actions which signify that princes, in proportion to their forces and on the strength of their connections, dared to depart from the principle of nationality and from mutual recognition of legitimate possession. The answer to these cabinet cabals is the rise of secret societies and of antimonarchical clubs.

The Christian cognition of humanism and humanity being again rejected, it was felt that a substitue was necessary for the loss of unity. The North-European assertion of personality had degenerated into subjectivism which now began to question all authority even of the administration of justice. The idea of the Supreme Good had almost disappeared from the books of the searchers after truth, so that in consequence the objectivity of right and duty was more than questioned.

§ 171. An ideal conception of humanity became impossible under these circumstances. Disintegration of the bonds of common fellowship and sympathy on the one hand, and absolutism on the other should have taught the thinkers that abstract thinking leads to a mist; that the rough realities of life cannot be regulated by subjective thought and conflicting theories into which the facts, each taken by itself, will not fit. It ought to have become evident to moralisers that the inquiries as to personal life, since Descartes' propositions of scepticism, carry with them a despotic exclusiveness to the extent of denying the duality of the mind, and of aggravating its confusion about itself. What then, without the human "center of cohesion" or uniting factor, is to become of the tasks common to all and obligatory for each member of the human family, if on the basis of a onesided conception of personal life each one construes a world-theory for himself out of his own age under pretense of the right of private judgment, and if he then insists upon rendering his own view as binding upon others. If this is absurd, none can be made binding. Then either despotism, which is anarchism from above, or anarchism which is despotism from below, must be the natural sequence.

Any onesided explanation of the contents conveyed in the term of humanity can, in the last resort, found right and duty upon nothing but individual opinion, and can offer no uniting principle. The incompetency of erroneous doctrines as to the human soul and spirit shows itself practically in the severance of humanity, inasmuch as false theorising on that score will nourish hatred between the governing and the governed in the first place, until the peril threatening the social relations in general, the danger of disintegration, materialises. No statesmanship can save a nation from falling asunder under the auspices of a humanism severed from theism.

"The present mania for general legislation in the abstract is a menace to liberty in general", was that of which Mœser complained. "They contrive to adjudge every case by printed statutes, regardless of the variety of circumstances in each particular case, according to which justice is to be administered. Because Voltaire made it ridiculous, that one lost his case according to the laws of his village—which according to the laws of another village in the vicinity he would have won—the demand for general rules and for tolerating no others is vociferated. Proceeding in this course we would depart from the true plan of nature with its wealth of variety, and we would invite that despotism which presses everything into a few mechanical molds".

This dire complaint was made too late. It arose even from a miscomprehension of the necessity of progress in jurisprudence as indicated by Grotius' natural and national rights. As touching upon the leveling of justice to that equality before the law which sets up jurymen called from among the professional court-house bummers and ward-politicians, as if this would answer the principle of each to be judged by his peers, Mœser's warning will remain a reproach against the propensity of radicalism to degrade humanity to one common, low level. Radicalism makes it its business to trample under foot whatever stands out excellent from the broad stratum of general vulgarity—by the abuse of the old German jury-system and of the impartiality of law to which modern equality is no equivalent. But since we are on that level already, Mœser's protest came too late.

We have arrived at the age of enlightenment in full glare which, as Schiller described, becomes in crude hands a firebrand devastating countries and laying cities in ashes. According to Kant "enlightenment is man's outgrowing his selfinflicted dependency." Catholic as well as protestant theologians had understood this long before Kant; Lessing's "fragments" came not unexpectedly to the support of rationalism. Man with his reason has been made judge of all things. "Religion inside the limits of pure reason", and "education of the human race" were the catch-words of the time. They were the field-cries throughout the combat in which a shallow knowledge showed defiance against a deeper exposition of the true nature of the human mind. A few independent anthropologists were simply nicknamed for want of argument against their deeper solution of the problems growing from the duality of personal life.

Upon the whole, humanity as represented by the occidental Aryans had attained to the great opinion of itself, that it now had entered into the full possession of human rights and had achieved perfect selfknowledge. Under the spell of selfdelusion and selfsufficiency this humanity in partibus writes its history: histories of all nations spring up, histories of all sorts of poesy, of all religions.

23

Herder combined it all into his "ideas," trying to show forth the deeper relationship between nature and grace, or reason and revelation. He tried to supplant rationalistic moralism by the idea of humanity, which he made intelligible and popular in its full meaning by showing that: "Humanism is both at once, the religion and the goal of all men." Whatever, after Descartes, a subjectivistic investigation of human nature may possibly accomplish from below has certainly been obtained by Herder. But from the lack of means which his rationalistic state-churchism could not furnish, he failed to demonstrate the cardinal factor of his humanitarianism. That the uniting center of attraction was missing, was felt by Schleiermacher, who (like Kaftan and Ritschl at present) supposed that the default could be remedied by proving the connection existing between all things, and by emphasising the idea of the church.

It could avail but little to repristinate the dogma of the church in the place of the lost momentum from which the thought of humanism and the unity of humanity had taken its rise. Only where the contrasts resting in human nature are reconciled through the Mediator, and after they have been brought to full consciousness, these contrasts become practically modified and harmonised. In other words, to "enlightened" thinking He had become obsolete, in whom alone the measure and coherency of all things is to be found, in whom the ethical obligations and the eternal destiny of humanity are exhibited in the concrete.

The conflicts between Church and State, each representing one side of the problem to be worked out in coordinate methods of cooperation, have a still deeper significance than that referred to in § 159. These conflicts which have always agitated history result from the polarity between ecclesiastical and civil life treated of in § 119. Each of these spheres is animated by the energy to realise its conception of the ideal of what is purely and truly human, the one representing the natural, the other the spiritual pole of the synthesis: until the converging movements of history under higher guidance render their unification complete.

The necessity of discriminating between the antithetical constituents of human nature and of humanity in general, and the necessity of dividing the work among the spheres of religion and ethics through cultus and culture, could become evident in no other way but by the bearing of theories upon the course of events, or, as has been said, by the import of the historic undercurrents upon the transactions of history. As far as "enlightenment" is concerned, this necessary polarity between the two spheres entertaining each its side of the matter under discussion, had not been understood. In the "higher" grades of humanity, at least, the import of that part of humanism which the church is to cultivate, was considered immaterial and irrelevant. The polarity was paralysed by treating the spiritual side as contradictory to humanism.

Unfortunately the church, too, on the other hand, ignored this polarity. The ecclesiastical community falls into the error that the state is Christian, and that therefore every citizen is ipso facto a member of the church. The public had not become aware of the fact, that with the acceptance of the doctrine of the state being a "contrat sociale" the state ceased to be Christian; and that the church, by recognising any individual of the very promiscuous civil society as a church-member also, had allowed the opinion to prevail, as tho she had assumed the nature of the promiscuous public in her participation of progressiveness, and was therefore to be put on a level with other selfconstituted associations. The difference between the church and the world is removed because both apparently cover the same ground; the Church becomes humanistic and is considered to be of mere human origin; Christendom and Christianity are deemed as equivalent.

The ministry accommodates itself to this public opinion. Society on its part narrows the idea of the church to the circle of the theologians, or overstrains the idea of the general priesthood of all Christians, whilst the theologians on their part acquiesce in the common interpretation of humanism as sufficient for religion. External adherency to a confession, a "symbol of faith," now called "the faith," is deemed sufficient for being considered a Christian; it is held almost as meritorious if one still believes in a "higher being." Gradually the esteem in which the confession was held diminishes; and even in the church the recognition of orthodox doctrine becomes dim and is considered unessential. Those who were appointed guardians and defenders of the full and dual bearing of that which the term humanity contains, are the stewards of the divine mystery implied in it no longer. For by concert of opinion the Church, in order to remain popular with society and with the masses is determined as much as society upon the process of leveling. Flat superficiality on the part of ecclesiastical rhetoric—now called "sacred elocution"—is taken for profound prudence, since popularity is taken for success in enlarging the number of membership. In its method of keeping account of members joined and dollars collected, the church becomes "flatitudinarian" indeed; and by applying the methods through which moneys are made up, she becomes worldly in an alarming degree. *bearing of what the term humanity implies to become ignored; and are, each on his part, responsible for the leveling process lowering society, and for the worldliness degrading the church in an alarming degree.*

On the whole, enlightenment as a historical movement had to be instrumental, nevertheless, in the further development of the idea of humanity inasmuch as it applied this idea to all phases of practical life despite its onesided conception. Altho it was so onesided in its moralising that Christmas-sermons of that period are extant, in which "the utility of wintering cattle in stables" was made the topic, instead of the nativity of the Savior, The True Man:—yet that moralising of enlightened rationalism bore the good fruit of a thorough humiliation through a Napoleon. For it is questionable whether without this humiliation the sense of liberty and unity would have outlived "enlightenment", and whether the import of religion upon human life would have been so readily acknowledged again and so easily restored. *Enlightened rationalism humiliated by a historical chastisement.*

Enlightenment had to serve the purpose of ventilating the humanistic-cultural side in opposition to the domineering altho servile state-churchism. Through an entire century the state-churches had allowed the neglect of ethical studies withal the preaching of utilitarian morals; much less had these churches the courage to demand practical exercise of humaneness. *As against servile State-Churchism, enlightenment had thus served its purpose.*

Theology was at fault. For it was in consequence of the subtle controversies about the "communicatio idiomatum" that the doctrine of the true humanity of the Mediator had been rendered suspect of heresy in almost Byzantine fashion, that the secularised thinking of society found the church only too ready to go with it to the other extreme of ignoring the dogma of the deity of the Christ. The Church abetted enlightenment to such lengths, as that the great polar tension between the Church and society in general—which is necessary to preserve the religious side of the dualism manifest in human life, but requires selfdiscipline under auspices of an authoritative spiritual censorship—had become almost entirely neutralised. The Church had too much conformed herself to the "world"—and had thereby become degraded to a kind of spiritual police for maintaining order in the State. *State-churchism, charged to keep the public at p'used at any rate, had neglected to discriminate between utilitarian moralism and Christian ethics, and to demand the exercise of humaneness. After controversies of an almost Byzantine nature, the church becoming tired of them falls in with the reasoning of the unchurchly public, conforms itself to the "world".*

CH. VI. CIVILISATION RENDERED TRANS-OCEANIC, AND THE THOUGHT OF HUMANISM COSMOPOLITAN.

§ 172. After the severe chastisement contracted and sustained by the presumptuous and irreligious humanistics and by the insipid state-churchly rationalism, we hail the turn of the tide bearing upon its enlarging wave-circle the neglected religious side of humanism. This "reactionary" movement, as the "freethinkers" called it, affected, in the first place, those nations which on that account became now the influential nations of the Occident; not that their intellectualism just looked into created the new æra—at least not that alone. The new formations in course of preparation required the extension of transmarine relations in which a practical and free will got opportunities to manifest itself. The new formations ensuing furthermore caused the reaction which the extended relations were bound to call forth in the countries where that extension of civilising influences originated. *"Reactionary" movements and rationalistic state-churchism. Turn of the tide bearing upon its enlarging wave circles the neglected religious side of humanism. New æra not created by Intellectualism but by the extension of transmarine relations, requiring the energies of free will.*

The Hollanders under Philip had been first in pointing out the direction in which the cause of true humanism might ramify. The reaction alluded to was to come, first in order, from the United States. The European nations were thus and now brought into permanent contact with the ethnical substratum of the Ugro-Altaic and Mongolian nations east and west of Europe. *Contact with the Mongolian substratum rendered permanent by a new kind of colonisation.*

In the East, Europeans laid their hands upon Siberia, thereby freshening up certain old memories. We remember the slight acquaintances formerly made through Alexander, then some communication by way of the silk-road, then on the occasions when the Huns paid the Europeans a few visits, then at another call on the day that the popes disciplined some Saxons, and for the last time when, shortly after Marco Polo's return, Albuquerque, and again the Geuses. returned all those visits and knocked at the doors of China and Japan.

In the countries of the setting sun, whither Mongolians had migrated evidently the wrong way—for culture so far had ever taken the westward course—Mongolian empires had been founded and destroyed. Remnants of the Tshitshimekians were met with, who (most likely during the invasions of Dgengis-Khan's hordes), had at about 1200 A. D. left Asia by way of the Aleutes, and spread over the substratum of a preceding culture. A still higher culture was obtained under Toltecian and Aztecian dynasties which seem to have followed at the time of the new commotions caused by Kublai Khan.

Relations, then, are forming of which nobody had ever thought, not even those who just then were engaged in analysing and anatomising "humanity" with cuts of reason more or less dull. And with these new relations there rushed into Europe a flood of new thoughts. Remarkable rays of a light, kindled by old remembrances about going and teaching all nations, beckoned westward.

Those who had been waiting for the dawn of that light had experienced sore disappointments during the conquests and colonial exploits to which the Europeans at first betook themselves, attracted by rumors of gold.

The Roman nations inaugurated their colonial enterprises upon the ground that the pope had America portioned out to them for the purpose of "compelling" the aborigines to enter the Kingdom. It was for this reason that Spain and Portugal claimed sole control over the seas; and that Philip expected the influx of gold from Peru in support of Alva's attempt to extirpate heresy on Dutch territory.

Remarkable rays of light thrown upon old remembrances—which had been preserved in childish tales about fairy-lands, sought at first by the western route—had at the same time led a new generation of Europeans to the East.

On the 12th of March, 1514, the grand embassy of Portugal held its entree into Rome, bringing the news of the discovery of Malacca. It was made the occasion for the Orient to do homage to the Vice-God of Rome—for the extremes to meet. Marshaled by heralds, a rich donation was carried up to him, which consisted of the costliest vestments decked with precious stones, and golden vessels. Surrounded by these presents a Persian horse headed the procession. Gorgeously caparisoned it was led along under the jubilee of the spectators lining the streets, because on the back of this horse rode a leopard trained for the hunt. Then an elephant of largest size came waddling along. From the citadel of St. Angelo cannons thundered the salutes across the Tiber up to Peter's grave. Diego Pacheco delivered the grand oration and—thrice the elephant fell upon the knees before Leo X.

Pageants and anecdotes are instructive, inasmuch as they express the mode of thinking and the world-consciousness of a people prevailing at a given period of time. This thinking and going upon adventurous expeditions was accompanied with the inclination to lay the world at the feet of the father of the Christian household in filial obedience and devotion. This is one of the few traits which might reconcile one with such an arrangement for ruling the fates of humanity and with the disposition to submit to such paternal rule. This trait is similar to the single redeeming feature of Asiatic life pursuant to which the authority of the house-father is transferred to the ruler of the state. This patriarchal principle is ideal and amiable, even if subverted into oriental despotism. But admiring, perhaps in a sentimental mood, this ideal, as some of us have, it was forgotten that with the transfer of patriarchal authority to one who rules over a large territory, the childlike attachment and the parental love holding a family of good breeding together, cannot be transmitted to the sovereign of a multitude of diverse tribes, much less of a variety of nationalities. In spheres thus extended sentiments soon cease to reciprocate. Patriarchal rule and obedience to it then assume the nature of cold business transactions and despotic regulations. Under such government spiritual advance is out of the question; for nations treated as minors will never attain to manliness and selfhood.

And since this was the condition of the subjects of Rome just as much as in Peking, we are compelled to extend this conclusion to the Roman principle of colonisation, as implied in and illustrated by the display of patriarchal affection at the beginning of Rome's trans-oceanic connections.

§ 173.   The Germanic nations entered these connections in a different manner. First in order to extend the influence of the reformed religion were the water-beggars. These outlaws were virtually the founders of the second republic in the delta of the Rhine, after the pattern of the Swiss republican confederacy established at its head. The dashing daringness, with which "the Brill" was snatched from the clutches of Alva, encouraged the Hollanders in their gloomiest days and rekindled the fire of patriotism. The freebooters developed into a regular navy. Trade followed and created the Dutch East-India Company, whilst the England of Elizabeth as yet traded with Persia by way of Russian overland routes. The horizon continued to widen; such companies as the Russian, the African, the Turkish, and English East-Indian, started up in quick succession, all equipped with the privileges of great monopolies. The ports in

America were secured and French preoccupants pushed aside. On land and upon the waters Germanic mariners met and vanquished the Roman. The net result of the contest was destined to benefit mankind in general.   *Marines of Romanised countries assigned to secondary import.*

Finally the western Aryans met the eastern again for the first time since they had separated upon the terraces of Iran; one branch moving west, the other taking possession of the large peninsula between the Indus and the Ganges. Their meeting again at the opening of the new æra was of incalculable import.   *After long separation the western and eastern Aryans meet again. Fate of the Hindoos since that separation.*

After the Mongolian had set foot upon the neck of the peaceable Hindoo in the time of Babur, Grand-moguls held sway over the length and breadth of the Aryan country; after the death of Aureng-Zebs the downtrodden nation lay distracted. The satraps declared themselves independent; but the subjugated peoples rattled their chains in vain. England needed but little strategy to intervene in the internecine wars of the Indian rulers, and little effort to master and manage these nations by making the native rivals English vassals. Of course, in order to maintain English dominion, conquests became necessary. The wars with the Marattes were victoriously brought to a termination, and Pitt, by means of the famous East-India Bill prevented the East-India Company from becoming a state within the state, so that after the lapse of nearly a century D'Israeli was enabled to earn the glory of having added an empire to the crown of Victoria. England became, as Heeren judged, "a market for the products of English manufactories and a whirlpool in which the Indian treasures disappeared."   *Rivalry hegemony made Hindoo-princes vassals of the British crown. Cancellation of the charter of the East-India Company. Pitt. England swallowing up Indian wealth. Heeren.*

It may be that from the start the India-budget was a money speculation. Indeed, those hundred millions, which England received from Indian sources every year, amply covered the original cost. These millions upon millions prove the rich resources opened with cheap Indian labor, and prove the enormous advantages accruing from the new relations for both countries. English capital rendered the moist and fertile lowlands and the Alpine meadows profitable. Hence to the cause of humanity, which Providence, overruling history, has at heart, the fifty millions realised by Indian cotton-raising alone are of higher significance than the fact that British capital found its safest investment in Indian enterprises. These millions shall not lead us to ask whether we have merely to deal with mercenary schemes to mulct India systematically. We have a deeper interest in these results than the cash-balance sheet sets forth, inasmuch as they prove the permeation of the Hindoo nations with elements of European culture. Ignorant as to the bearing of these factors upon their future fate, the Hindoos could do nothing but submit to the unavoidable. The issues growing out of this mode of disseminating Christian world-consciousness will evince themselves as highly satisfactory to the Indian people, if the process continues in a tolerably humane way under just and judicious rule.   *Englands profitable investments. India's benefit.*

Concerning England this relation instantly became of far higher value than the financial profits. The best interest drawn from the Indian investments consisted in the stimulating reaction upon the religious life of the ruling nation. This blessing manifested itself immediately in the revival of the missionary zeal quickening the activity of the high-churchism of the state, which of yore had incited the English people to sympathise with their cousins on the continent.   *Higher than mercenary profits reverting to England. Revival of missionary zeal invigorates religious life at home.*

Since Alexander's expedition so little had been heard of India that Europe simply wondered at the legends about an oriental "Prester John" entwined with the rumors about the marvelous wealth of India. The great country of the East appeared to the mind of Europe as a distant mountain, inaccessible on account of the Turks. Now it was open for intercourse by way of doubling the Cape of Good Hope, the realities of the once mysterious regions surpassed the dreams of the European cousins. And for the realities of the present life the eastern Aryans were now reclaimed from their dreamy existence under the incubus of a selfconstructed invisible world, awakening when they became aware of the practical energy with which the western Aryan labored to overcome difficulties.   *Doubling Cape of Good Hope opened India to Europe, which on land had been obstructed by the Turks.*

The widely contrasting peculiarities of consciousness caused each branch of the same race to come again in contact one with the other, whereby the Hindoo frame of mind is to become elevated to its normal balance. For, in the midst of the times since their separation, the point of equipoise had been provided for, at which their estranging views of life might become reconciled; the synthesis of the polar antithesis had in the meantime become revealed, the "synthesis" of the seeming contradictory ideas which had always swayed both groups of the Aryans.   *The Anglo-Saxons entrusted with dividing the bequest of our common testator with the eastern relatives.*

It remains, for the present at least, the task of the Anglo-Saxons to divide the inheritance of Christianity with the Hindoos, as it behooves relatives. But in anticipating Asiatic prospects we have rather gone ahead of our theme.

§ 174. At the present stage of this disquisition it is our aim to show how the transmarine relations extended the horizon of the European nations, and how these new relations reacted upon their political economy and their social and religious life. No sooner had the Europeans taken a glance at the East, than that they slowly commenced to branch out to the new western continent also. Altho very little attention had so far been given to America, yet it was destined that from thence the greatest, most direct and most wholesome influences should be derived. The Dutch had taken the initiative in founding a North American colony, ever since William of Nassau-Orange had taken that step into consideration, when it seemed as tho Holland was to be sacrificed to Spanish fury, and abandoned to the sea from which it had been wrested.

Ten shirts, thirty pairs of stockings, ten shotguns with ammunition, thirty iron kettles and a copper pan they had paid for the land upon which New York stands today.

After this beginning the British began to look after their interests in the region of New Amsterdam, and to put in their claims. Upon this new soil colonial life thenceforth produced new ideas which in Europe had never been heard of before. Powerfully did these ideas react upon the mother country, its state-policy and its comfort.

Those forty-one men, who in the month of December A. D. 1620 stood around the table in the cabin of the Mayflower, were British Nonconformists. They stood waiting in solemn mood for their turn to subscribe the first constitution which was based upon the equality of the rights of each and all. It meant a simple social contract the like of which the world had as yet never witnessed. Based upon the freedom of conscience, political freedom was warranted. What would have been impossible in Europe was born upon the waves of the Atlantic ocean, to be carried out in the woods of the new world. This practical rise of an entirely new form of government,—after the pattern of the Calvinistic or rather biblical constitution of the church—the world owes as much to the English zealots, who sought religious and ecclesiastical unity in a ritualistic liturgy, as to these English and Caledonian dissenters, who cut loose from the anomalies of a state-church.

Huguenots and Culdean Presbyterians had taken refuge upon the Blue Mountains of North Carolina. When they met to organise themselves into a body politic, they called their home Mecklenburg in honor of the wife of George III. After the battle of Lexington they were foremost in raising their voice in favor of independence from the British crown.

This was the definite and decided motif of the counterbass intoned by the Mecklenburgian Americans, in harmony with which the melody of the Declaration of Independence was composed soon after: "We hereby declare. . . All laws and commissions confirmed and derived from the authority of the king or parliament are annulled and vacated; all commissions, civil and military, heretofore granted by the crown to be exercised in the colonies, are void. . . As all former laws are now suspended and the congress has not yet provided others, we judge it necessary for the better preservation of good order, to form certain rules and regulations for the government of this country, until laws shall be provided for us by the congress".

This declaration once put down in writing by Anglo-Saxons, "Orangemen" and French refuges, the thought of humanism was practically demonstrated to its full extent in the grand event of 1776—on the 4th of July.

The thought of humanity, then, is finally understood and takes the shape of a documentary instrument unequaled in the history of modern culture, of Christian civilisation, notwithstanding the erroneous deductions eventually drawn from it. Socially North America—with the exception, of course, of Roman Mexico, which is scarcely to be counted in as yet—is the offspring of England; but in such a manner that the mass of immigrants, incessantly flowing in from the "old country", is reduced to its elementary radicals, and is purged thereby of such old dross as, for instance, the primal ingredients of Norman feudalism, and of such repulsive residue as the refuse of Romanised nations brings along; whilst the Saxon traits are kept up and fostered, because of their principles of selfhood and honesty, and their sentiments of sympathy and fidelity. Springing up from forests and prairies under the canopy of the blue sky and the stars, state after state augments the power of the Union, which is built up like the primitive log-cabin, rough and ready, with a view to rapid improvement.

Marginal notes:

Benefits accruing to Europe from the reaction of America against false conceptions of the humanistic thought.

Dutch taking the initiative in colonising North America.
§ 166, 168, 173.

Price paid the Indians for the Manhattan peninsula.

The fortyone pilgrims on board the "Mayflower."

Simple and sincere social contract witnessed for the first time in history, different from that of Jesuitical invention.

Ideas of the human right to be independent.

Draft of the first constitution for normal selfgovernment at Mecklenburg, N C.

Grand instrument of modern civilisation 1776.

Norman traits discarded; Anglo-Saxon traits fostered.

David Crockett roams about in wildernesses so solitary, that herds of deer stare in amazement at the strange intruder, when one of their number is shot and drops down in their midst. From the scenes of the hunting grounds, from adventures with trappers and miners, with the bear and the buffalo, he comes to take his seat in congress. In the circus and at the presidential banquet he is always the same, "half horse, half alligator". As a matter of course he dies in his boots, a favorite of the people and hero of folk-lore.

Illustration of North American pioneer-life, generating a specific national character. Career of David Crockett.

Such is the stamp of the American nation as compared with others. In humble stations of life, under the pressure of the privations of pioneering the hearthstone is laid in the log-house; tender considerateness of mother, wife and sister becomes the stepping-stone to educational accomplishments, to virtue and honor, both becoming corner-stones of prosperity in a palace. Comfort is taken by storm and time by the forelock. Every muscle is strained, every force liberated and developed, utilised and improved upon, so as to increase and save human strength by subduing the powers dormant in nature. The most heterogeneous nationalities meet and mingle on foreign soil, and are pressed into service for mutual assistance. The people labor in the pursuit of common interests, and gradually amalgamate in the observance of the emphasised habits and customs of the country, until the antagonisms are either assimilated into, or disappear from, the establishment of a distinctly characterised nationality after all. Many prejudices must be thrown aside, many an old-fogyish form of conventionalism becomes ridiculous. For, in the forest, and on the frontier, even in the store or office, ceremonious circumstantiality ceases to be admired and becomes cumbersome; whilst true urbanity is not at all depreciated and vulgarity is ostracised. In a form of liberty entirely new in history, we witness how in a great nation, side by side with rude manners and bad characters, the excellencies of human nature also exist, and how both grow to proportions which in such close proximity would have seemed impossible. The world witnesses the successful experiment of testing which of the two, the Good or the Bad has the more attractive force, or gives the best satisfaction, and gains the most popularity.

Labor for common interests procures the true level of human dignity and equality.

Antiquated conventionalisms abolished.

Experiment to test whether the Good or the Bad is more attractive and gives the better satisfaction.

§ 175. We must return to the Rhine and its vicinity, where the thoughts were ushered into the world which rendered the wild West capable to respond to the demands of modern culture, and even to carry out the principles of Christian civilisation. For, said pope Æneas Silvius, "nowhere among the nations is found so much freedom as in the German cities, in comparison to which the populace of the Italian republics are mere serfs." Yet Germany had grown to be just as servile in the mean time. In consequence of the Reformation the power of princes had been largely enhanced. This result may be deplored, but since the German Reformation did slight the opportunity to create an ecclesiastical selfgovernment independent of the state, it was unavoidable. Under the denominational and monarchical absolutism, as facilitated by the errors of theologians and cultivated by the Jesuits, the political effects of the Reformation were crushed, and the unfolding of the thought of humanity and the happiness of the subjects was repressed. Keeping pace with the power of monarchical star-chambers, there grew up the intolerance of protestant as well as catholic state-churches with their procedures against witchcraft, at pillories and in chambers of torture. In the Thirty Years War, necessary for the preservation of the humanistic attainments and of religious freedom, these principles disappeared almost entirely under the selfish polity of conquest, and under disregard for nationalities, as practiced in the cabinets of both religious parties. The contest of intrigues ended "without an ideal," as Hegel designates the exhausted condition of Europe in the middle of the seventeenth century.

Retrospect upon European precedents, conditioning the success of this experiment.

Pope Æneas Silvius on German freedom. § 134, 141.

Effects of the Reformation frustrated by absolutism and State-churchism.

Thirty years war necessary to preserve religious and political freedom. § 162

Contest of intrigues ended without an "ideal". Hegel.

European culture appeared as if doomed to extinction; it was bare of an ideal since Germany, in addition to its impoverishment from being always the battlefield of the Europeans, had become isolated from the traffic of the world. Venetian commerce had founded and nourished the prosperity of the German cities. Now, with the oceans thrown open, the Venetian ships like those of the other Romanic powers rotted upon stagnant canals. Germany was switched off from international intercourse, and the great minsters dotting the routes of former munificence remained unfinished. Many other circumstances concurred to subject the empire to a deadening stagnation, and the nation, lacking the economical stimulus and hence growing indolent as to progress, entirely forgot to improve and complete its political and ecclesiastical arrangements. Previous beginnings, so full of promise of a glorious future, were abandoned under the general discouragement, and public life crept along as well as the policy of expediency allowed, whilst potentates great and small made themselves comfortable after the pattern of Versailles—and the wise heads wrote books.

Europe exhausted.

Germany, always the field of battle, impoverished also by the decline of Venice.

Germany paralysed

except in mental activity.

Germany had been able to break the fetters of a Roman world-monarchy, and to deliver the thought of universal humanism from its Roman bondage. But Germany proved unable to carry out, by practical and energetic measures, the great thoughts, which had been set free through its religious reform. Whilst the other Germanic nations busied themselves with naval exploits, and as fruits of their daring enterprises earned a large harvest of ideas and means, Germany had to commence anew with colonising and repopulating its own soil, and was compelled to stay at home. The circulation of its vital sap went on as in sleep. For the time being Germany consoled and contented itself with having its intentions and principles stored up in books and piled away in libraries—until the necessary awakening to its task in the world took place after a long and phlegmatic doze. Germany continued to argue upon the things of which it had full possession, about its cognition of the value and dignity of man, about the evangelical freedom of a Christian, about the state of spiritual childhood in the relation between God and man, etc. etc. Germany enjoyed the understanding of the true and illustrious idea of humanism; but its realisation it had to leave to other people.

Germanic nations pursue their task with practical energy—extensively:

The Germans write, argue, dream, build theories, in pursuance of their task—intensively.

Germany enjoyed the understanding of the illustrious idea of humanism.

Movement of liberating the "third estate,"

That great movement of liberating the "third estate"—beginning with Wycliff in England, having been taken up by the Taborites of Bohemia, and in the cause of which the Bundschuh-peasants had rung the alarm—had come to a dead stop.

reopened by Jesuitism in a negative manner.

State taught to be a mere human institution.

Power of princess undermined.

Laynez in Council of Trent.

The Jesuits saw fit to take up the popular cause to the advantage of their schemes. When they declared the state as of mere human origin, they had taken every precaution in advance, that matters of public interest were formulated according to their doctrine of the contrat sociale. Thus Jesuitism managed to get control over the course of events to the extent of dethroning any prince opposing this contract, the "head of the church" excepted. Such were the principles expressed by Laynez in the council of Trent, whose acceptance the protestants scorned, and which the Roman church never retracted.

Part taken by the German world-theories in neutralising political economies of Jesuitism.

Cause of liberation taken up positively.

Divine rights of humanity vested in civil representative government.
Hoffes, Grotius. § 188.
Seckendorf. Pufendorf.

Seckendorff wrote "the state of the Christians" in defiance of Jesuitical tenets; and Pufendorff, returning from Copenhagen and setting up natural law upon the principles of Grotius and Hobbes—still postulates duties to God in the first place, from which he deduces those to the ego and to fellowmen.

Small practical beginnings by the Puritans of Rhode Island.

Aside from those theoretical works scarcely any practical activity on the score of social development is perceptible. The prerequisite for the practical efficacy of the Christian thought would have been a reorganisation of political economy, such, for instance, as the Puritans had achieved in Rhode Island—but which in Europe under the sway of the Bourbons and Habsburgers seemed an impossibility. The occasion for this reorganisation was swiftly approaching, nevertheless. A storm was brewing in the West.

Why England escaped the destructive effects of the French Revolution.
Lecky.
§ 176, 177.

Lecky in his "History of England in the 18th century" has shown why this country escaped the destructive effects of the French revolution. Nothing but the revival of evangelical Christianity saved Great Britain from the contagion; for nothing less than personal religiousness and consecration to a life in obedience to the gospel enables people to comprehend the thought of humanism in its full and true sense. This was what Wesley preached, who had gone to Saxony in order to study the piety of the Moravians, and to ask Count Zinzendorf for advice. It was the preaching of the Wesleys and the Whitefields which generated that intense consciousness of personal responsibility and cooperation which alone is the preventive against the explosion of natural forces in riotous excesses. The world-theory implied in such sermonising, as based upon the genuine and restored God-consciousness, and as combined with the dual bearings of the thought of humanity: this alone makes people firmly adhere to true freedom, and assures a happy advance of civilisation and the prosperity of a nation.

Wesleyan Revivalism.
Zinzendorf.

Piety of the Moravians, furnish the first modern missionaries.
§ 130, 135, 138, 139, 156, 169.

Genuine religiousness alone assures national freedom and prosperity.
§ 28, 34, 44, 50, 55, 71, 86, 126, 131, 132, 137, 139, 156.

Justus Moser's fidelity to old German principles of jurisprudence in refutation of the "Vicar of Savoy."
Rousseau.

When the great Romanic revolution was in its state of incipiency the old Germanic conception of liberty revived, as if the salubrious breeze from the western woods and prairies reminded the Germanic mind of the days of its youth. The undaunted fidelity of Justus Moser alluded to, was patriotic enough to protest against the generalisation of laws and against the reduction of one's social standing to the common level of vulgarity.

He wrote against the "tyrannical fashion of composing codes of general laws", because they "estrange us from the nature of things which in its adaptedness for unfolding individuality demonstrates its wealth". Addressing the "Vicar of Savoy, in care of Monsieur Rousseau", he showed how dangerous the inclination to leveling legislation must of necessity become to freedom in general. Equally alarmed by the dream of a general form of legislation and jurisdiction was the pious and strict Karl von Moser. "Enwrapping a man in furs from head to heels in the month of May may be the proper thing for St. Petersburg, whilst in Naples such a dress would be unendurable". In Moser the FEELING of that which is humane to perfection, namely the consciousness of being a child of God, was active in the form of practical WISDOM.

Karl v. Moser exasperated by the tendency, to generalise "law-points" to individual cases.

Moser, a statesman, uniting piety of emotion with active bravery and practical wisdom.

———ooo———

The world stands wide open in the East and the West, prepared to receive the impartation of higher principles, awaiting new methods of cultivation. For the first time the surface of the earth in its entirety becomes historic ground. The expansive battle field is made a field of labor, and is made accessible by the amazingly rapid development of the means of traffic. Never before were the remotest corners of the world explored with more zeal than that manifest since the beginning of our own century. We may say that all preceding history in general, of which we have so far taken the philosophical retrospect, had simply been the preparation for the new æra of cosmopolitan and international relations of humanity, a history of preludes in their several departments. History proper, that is, the symphony of human affairs in concert, the description of the fugue-wise advances of humanity as a whole in its reciprocal interactions begins only now. All prior human activity resembles but a school where the lessons are inculcated in the class-room and the exercises for home work are prescribed; whereas now the common result of instruction is exhibited at the commencement exercises; that is to say, history is expected to demonstrate its education of humanity in the practical cooperation of the entire race. The familiar conversation of nations in narrow bounds must give way to international adjustment on a large scope, where the fates of widely separated nations and heterogeneous elements bear upon each other. The pursuits of life, formerly followed upon interior waters, are now going to be carried on upon the oceans. They are rendered places of exchange for the relative or secondary goods, and are virtually the message-bearers between the staple-markets of the world—the bearers of messages, too, from spheres above to spheres abroad.

Retrospect: For the first time is the entire world ready to receive higher: i. e. civilising principles of culture.

New æra of cosmopolitan relations.

It is now, that universal history proper begins.

Oceans bearing messages

also from spheres above to spheres abroad.

As many rivers send the waters of the continents into the great seas, so do the stories of the individual nations gradually run together into one universal history of mankind. This trend of history has become ever more conspicuous since the oceans have been girded and the earth is circumnavigated. In concurrence with these events the thought of universal humanism and the common rights of men were ever more elucidated—until they were at last acknowledged as being the cardinal principle of civilisation. In the face of this truth it is the more grievous to observe from the manner in which this cognition is distracted and caricatured, wherever it approaches practical realisation—how poorly mankind will stand the test of being humane.

Thought of humanism elucidated as the cardinal principle of civilisation.

CH. VII. THE COGNITION OF HUMANITY IN ITS DISTORTIONS.

§ 176. Historic development has arrived at that season in which the fruits ripen, at that age of maturity in which the features grow sharper and display the quality of the inner character. Recent events, which reveal the maxims underlying modern thinking, and in which modern culture culminates, are very descriptive of all the inner dispositions which humanity will follow in its pursuits as its history approaches the next summit. These events, furthermore, illustrate the mode in which history applies its means.

Grand prospects in view from the summit of present developments.

All inner dispositions of the human mind assuming shape in the concrete. § 2, 13, 17-19, 117, 119, 168, 185,

Europe and America pose upon an acme of civilisation from which the prospective view of a transition into the realm of true freedom and ethical progress takes in the full range of the ethnical horizon; but from which we also look down into an abyss yawning close by, into which the whole of modern culture is under dread of being thrown. Vigilance and circumspection may yet avert perils already casting their shadows ahead. Hence it is necessary to look beneath the surface of civilisation, and back upon the starting points of historical relapses, in order to understand the wild

The abyss yawning in close proximity to the summit.

Genesis of the great civilisation threatening relapse since the French revolution, which in comparison with the American is not even to be considered as its bad imitation.

excitement of the French upheavals and its still vibrating effects, which to all appearances are going to cause a repetition on so large a scope as to render the eruptions, which threw up a Napoleon, a mere local affair. With the same reference to the American revolution (by which radicalism has tried to justify the French, tho no such insurrection against the laws of history can take subterfuge under the American "Declaration of Independence") a general upsetting is now planned by the malcontents of all nations and zealously agitated.

Retrospect in order to discover the causes of retrogression underneath the surface of civilisation.

At the beginning of our disquisition we allegorised the going forth of the nations into all the world, their separation and dispersion, with the flowing of various rivers, from a common headland and a pure source. Considering the rapid increase of the bad ingredient, the general dispersion of the human family became evident as more than a mere guess for the sake of explanation.

Finally humanity was discovered to suffer under still worse conditions: In view of the sad effects of the first calamity we ascertained a state of aggravated dismay, caused by a still worse catastrophe, a wanton and sudden apostasy even from the mere natural principles of human existence.

We found the results of that sad departure from unity in the features scattered all over the face of the earth, those having fled in small groups to remote quarters resembling isolated and forsaken heaps of debris.

Evils as measures of preservation; § 58, 61, 74, 77.

But we observed also that the evils following, especially the stunned condition, the frightful flight, and the irksome work of wresting a livelihood from obstreperous nature were all made to serve as measures of preservation. For even on the downward course men are yet guided in their ways by the hand from on high.

Into their deepest descent the nations, even those abandoning themselves to the ravages of grossest depravity, took along within their innermost feeling some indestructible remnants of God-consciousness common to all in equal measure.

No people entirely deficient of culture § 50, 209.

Discussing in that connection the difference between cultured nations and uncultivated masses, we became convinced that people without any culture whatever never existed, because each and every cluster of human beings still has a direct or indirect bearing upon all other nations, and because not even the most shapeless ethnical rubbish in its apparent decay can be considered bare of specifically human forms of living.

as stimuli to individual exertion in developing various talents.

Providentially the fragments of lost humanity were so directed in their ways as that each part was thrown upon its own resources and its individual exertions, which were to stimulate the development of the various capabilities given and left to man to make the best thereof. The distribution over the globe under the various zones was to serve the definite purpose of filling the earth with men who were to cultivate it, and to develop thereby the resources of their own nature; with men who, under the pressure of this laborious process, should learn to seek the guiding hand. The susceptibility for such guidance, and the eye for its recognition, is given in the spiritual constituent of man's being, to be well taken care of and to be developed through selfculture into receptivity for increasingly better and higher

Salutary utilisation of evils under providential guidance to keep man susceptible for something better;

gifts. We take conscience in its immediateness as that prompting towards reunion which is nowhere entirely missing in the human soul. Corresponding with the promptings of conscience a system of mediatory and vicarious atonement was arranged for the purpose of conferring blessings upon the nations under conditions, of course, but ever under divine guidance. And this system, as little to be abolished as conscience is indestructible, conveyed the intention at the same time, to reveal the desire of the Savior to come to the rescue; and to call forth the desire on the part of men to seek after and find the uplifting hand again. This

by Prevenient Grace. § 120.

guidance and these arrangements we subsume under the phrase of universal revelation or Prevenient Grace.

But those multitudes which in deliberate defiance of this providence and grace mean to keep up a selfconstituted unity by force or strategy, will abruptly be put to confusion again and again.

What problems appear to be solved under this aspect, rendering further inquiry needless.

Unless the development of history is considered under this aspect, no correct view and no teleological appreciation of the life of individuals or of nations can be obtained. But taking this position we need no longer inquire as to the hulls, precipitates, and residue of traditional cults, nor into the political formations and deformations, social usages or artificial creations of culture in which life's currents sluggishly flow along as in old channels.

We are relieved of analytical guesses to be made from the heinous idolatries and abject subversions of the ideas of humanity in China and Japan, India and Ægypt, Africa and Australia, or in Germany or America. For, since by virtue of certain spiritual elements the compound of scums and dregs and settlings is cut, so that the obnoxious stuffs may be isolated and neutralised, we are enabled to reduce the distorted principles to their true value.

Cherishing traits of the excellency of human nature, even in people with deranged God-consciousness.

And we are enabled to discriminate—even in the labyrinthian courses of human life and thought under such inverted traditions and usages and abuses—the warm pulsations of the human heart, and the noble aspirations of human nature to purify itself from the effects of the deathly contagion.

Following that line of observation we find in the virtues of the gentiles more than "glistening vices". Be the God-consciousness, together with the world-consciousness depending upon it, ever so badly deranged, we still collect—like the bee collecting honey from wild flowers—hopeful and cherishing traits of human nature, from play and comedy, from lyric poetry and from acquaintance with the domestic life of those who dwell on the periphery. We may find even in the darkness of heathenism a noble sense of duty, of touching fidelity and unselfishness; we may there notice signs of benignity, acts of selfdenial and an admirable devotion to public welfare which may outshine the morality of the multitude of mere nominal Christians. A sense of real beauty and aspiration to true art are frequently met with. Looking at the attempts at carving, sculpturing, painting, and musical composition, in pottery, architecture, legends, proverbs and songs, we ought to become so interested in the poor wretched majority of the human family with its irreligious consciousness, as to learn to sympathise with it, because of the intensity and tenderness of sentiment thus revealed. Above all we shall have to acknowledge a spirit of reverence and devoutness towards the invisible deity, which puts to shame even the majority, perhaps, of modern churchmembership.

If we listen with sympathy to the scale of tones, from guileless merriment down to the melancholy and doleful complaint in elegies, we would find hearts worthy our friendship, hearts in search of peace and consolation. This yearning will have to be counted as valuable in proportion to vanquished selfishness, and will be adjudged with mercy by Him who hears the cries of the young ravens. When and by what means this mercy will manifest itself to nature-bound people in guiding and directing their preparation for the reception of pneumatic influences, does not here come in question. The noble traits of the natural man were pointed out simply to remind us of the fact, that even the nations farthest away from the divine-humane center of attraction do contribute, in certain respects, to human culture, tho that contribution may be visible to such only as stand very high above selfishness or very near the contributors,in the practice and cultivation of humaneness.

We come to consider some of the bearings of these facts, for we live in the age of Missions—altho the substance of this matter remains to be pondered in the closing part of this work.

The chapter now presenting itself, that is, the epoch now opening, demands of us that, in virtue of another enlightenment than that so far discussed, we may be able to form a true judgment as to character and the nature of events. Whatever conclusion is arrived at, depends upon the full insight into the moral essence of things and persons, and upon the discretionary ability to watch understandingly the historic undercurrent.

The value of our conclusions, yea, the correctness of our whole interpretation of history, depend upon the answer to the question whether we are justified in measuring world-theories by that rule, which was handed to the builders of history in the middle of the times.

§ 177. The mode in which Providence guides the movements of history concurrent with the lives of the nations is enshrouded in impenetrable mystery, notwithstanding the plan and the purposes being revealed. The reason why the ways and means for their fulfilment under divine overruling are veiled and incomputable consists but in the fact that the freedom of mankind comes into play. The work of restoring the "image" as revealed by the Mediator in a rich diversity of human beings continues through the times of the new dispensation, altho we can observe only half, at its best, of the fabric and the instrumentalities, and of the method of using the material. The way in which the renovation proceeds, we see in but one direction.

The ideal of man in his dignity as substantiated in the Mediator, and the problems to be solved, and the destiny to be realised by man, are revealed to him in the form of gifts intended for the happiness of mankind. These gifts are entrusted to Christians in their collective capacity for transmitting to humanity in historical order. And they convey with them the task of redeeming arrested life, i. e. nature-bound humanity. The administration of these irrevocably instituted ordinances is therefore not to be taken in the sense of a representative office apart from the congregation militant and triumphant. It is to be emphasised rather, that the gifts are to be husbanded by ministers and people conjointly. Whenever the church was understood to consist of the officers and theologians, history insisted upon the administration of the above gifts by hierarchy and society alternately if not in coordinate unison. For in the course of events it occurs now and then that the people,or society in its promiscuous generalness,sever the thought of humanity from its center of cohesion where alone it is safe from distortion—and that in an unjudicious zeal for a misunderstood liberty the cause of humanism is conceived in a vague and partial negative. In such cases the ecclesiastical organisation, the church-organism in its contrast to the civil authorities and to the "world," must throw the weight of its instruction into the scale.

Margin notes:

"Virtue of heathens" not glistening vices.

Involuntary longings for salvation. § 42, 43, 47, 53, 77, 81, 90, 96, 101, 120, 135, 157.

Influence of obscure nations upon culture in general. Syllab. Div. G. § 117.

Incitement to missionary activity.

Correctness of our interpretation of history depends upon our being justified in measuring world-theories by the rule handed to the builders of history in the middle of the times.

Plans and aims of history tho being revealed, as yet shrouded in mystery.

Mode of restoring the "image" through human agencies conditioned by faith—because freedom is to be maintained.

Significance of the Church administering the Means of Grace. GABEN—AUFGABEN. § 10.

Cause of humanism being distracted, now in the "church", then by the "world". § 119, 168, 171.

Whenever misinformed liberalism, often justifiable otherwise, conceives humanism in a vague negative, then the "church" must throw the weight of its instruction into the scale.

Or it happens, that, on the other hand, a domineering church—more or less streaked with hierarchical pretensions, be they catholic or protestant—obscures the precious gift of the humanistic thought, and abandons it to the political intrigues of parliamentary factions in order to make them tools of their rule. And in such cases the people at large, or Christian associations, rise to the rescue of humanism, and, on the strength of "public suasion" take the thought under protection and in cultivation. Whenever either of these cases comes to join issue, a revolution is imminent.

Or whenever hierarchal pretensions abandon the precious contents of the thought to political powers as tools of their rule, "public suasion" is to rise to the rescue of humanism.

Genesis of revolutions CHATEAUBRIAND. § 165, 166, 168, 175, 178, 179, 211, 222.

What was the aim of the most radical of great revolutions? Chateaubriand answers: "To found a society without a past and without a future upon doubtful reasons!" The old legitimist has precisely stated the character of this French movement. It was a very questionable reason upon which Rousseau had built his system of the nature of the wants, and the rights,of man. What was then the misnamed reason was but one of the wild outgrowths of carnal desire and moral indolence cut loose from the idea of God and from historical bonds. This world-theory presumptuously alleges that man by nature is a sociable creature, and that hence humanism is the creature of the social instincts. Upon the force, or rather absurdity, of this argumentation Rousseau pleads the rights of a commonality for which he invents the phrase, "contrat sociale," which in principle had been established much prior to his deduction.

Rousseau's efforts to rescue humanism from a system of outward and artificial conventionalism.

Natural sociability.

Return to the natural state. "Emile." BRIZARD. FAUCHETT.

That humanity, of which "Emile" is the blissful, because ignorant, representative, is of spontaneous growth, natural and radical in the extreme, fit to be raised by, and to associate with, the cave bear, and longing to return to its companions in order to become exceedingly and independently happy. "The human race had lost its rights, Jean Jacques has found them again," was the rejoicing ejaculation of Brizard. In the same strain Baudrillart praises it as the task of his age "to reinstate humanity into the possession of itself and its whole domain and all of its resources." Such was the purpose of the revolution, as Abbot Fauchett puts it in the vernacular of the rabble: "Man is born .to enjoy the good things of life. The earthly domain, common property of us all, has been forcibly appropriated by a few and withheld from us."

Return to the natural state was preached and—nearly accomplished. France was sufficiently qualified for the experiment.

English revolution as compared with the French. § 165, 166, 168, 175, 177, 178, 179, 211, 212.

The English revolution had been of a quite different character. Neither contrived at nor instigated by sophists, it was a national movement of patriotism upon the basis of an earnest necessity and religious maturity. It did not disintegrate society; merely changing the executive department of the political system to conform with the reformed concept of humanism, this revolution did not break up the social fabric. It was not brought about by Sansculottes but by Cromwell's army, the moral strictness of which was exemplary and stands unchallenged.

Cromwell's army. MACAULAY.

Macaulay describes it thus: "The most zealous royalists give testimony that in their camps alone no cursing was to be heard, that neither drunkenness nor gambling was to be seen, and that during the rule of the soldiery the property of the peaceable citizen was safe, and the honor of women kept sacred. The excesses occurring were of a quaint nature. A sermon suspicious of pelagianism,or a window exhibiting the picture of the Virgin with the child, would cause such excitement in the ranks of the Puritans, that the officers could scarcely by extreme measures control the troops." Such was the revolution in England, which the French have no right to claim as a precedent justifying their own.

German Reformation

In Germany the reformation had done away with those mediæval deformities which were allowed to continue in France and to oppress the nation. Celibacy, monastic mendicancy, monkish slothfulness, etc., had been gradually regulated by the state, and ameliorated if not abolished brevi manu, by the protestant thought. The thought of liberty had been modified by the religious conception of human dignity and responsibility, wherefore the political transformation took the normal course of an evolution, under the exercise of a little patience.

caused a normal evolution, not the French revolution.

France protests against hierarchal communities of feudal origin,

through Sophisms and sansculottes and Rousseau's children of nature,

after Port Royal, pronouncing the religious side of humanities, had been silenced.

In France the protest against the ecclesiasticism of the feudal times had been procrastinated and was entered first by sophists and then by Sansculottes. Human dignity and liberty were taken simply in their formal and egotistic aspect, because the formative, the religious principle had been exiled or suppressed, as in Port Royal. Hence the impossibility of a gradual reform when the revolution was provoked by governmental anomalies and unmitigated malpractices of the royal dynasty.

Precedents of the French Revolution.

France neglected its opportunities of normal development. Gerson, Andreæ. Beza in Poissy,

§ 178. The remnants of mediæval views and forms of life, especially the class-privileges, the immunities of the aristocracy scoffing the change procured by modern thought, scoffing reason itself, galled the common people. France, unlike Germany, particularly in this respect, had missed its opportunities, when Gerson, the great chancellor, and Peter d'Ailly by far surpassed the narrow Italian ideas; and again when August, the Saxon elector, sent the Formula Concordia to Francis I, and when

Jacob Beurlin with Andreæ upon the royal invitation appeared at court in Paris; and Huguenots not bent upon overthrow. when Beza vindicated the religious reform at Poissy. It was the last chance for France to adjust matters by way of an honest compromise, when under Henry Quatre 4000 noblemen took the part of the Huguenots who had enlisted 200 towns of surety for tolerance in the cause of reform.

The Huguenots were sincerely bent upon a normal evolution without any intent of a political overthrow. Their nocturnal meetings in the crevices of the mountains and their hymns of worship in the silent solitude of wildernesses were not heeded as the warnings, which indeed they were to serve to the Bourbons in foreboding the gathering storms of the revolution. The opportunities having been slighted, and the dragonades working effects opposite to those intended, the sequel was inevitable. For whenever that natural advance of a nation, wrought by its religious advancement, comes to be frustrated, anarchistic ideas will stir up the dregs of public opinion. If the pulse of spiritual life in the social organism beats slow and sluggish, it denotes religious and intellectual decline. But suppressing the normal evolution of true humanism results in anarchy. Wherever human nature is treated as a mere natural force a sudden explosion is to be expected at the slightest occasion. *Anarchy ensued from the suppression of religious reform.*

The first symptoms of the morbidity of French society cropped out in literature. Before it entered the stage of shameless frivolity, literature acted the role of Boethius, when he stood at the coffin of the Roman giant, figuratively speaking, soliciting sympathy. *First symptoms of the morbidity of France in literature.*

"His attitude toward positive religion, especially to Christianity is affecting that aristocratic suffisance which cautiously guards itself as much against uttering an offensive or aggressive word, as against giving any sign from which the open enemies of religion might draw the inference that one was in sympathy with it. Thus he kept distant from personal contact with Christianity in avoidance of compromising himself." The very same method of evading religious conviction, or if convinced of the truth, the same avoidance of decidedly avowing it, was the first fruit of this fashionable enlightenment. People were ashamed to incur the suspicion of being religious. *Comparison with the age of Boethius. § 65-66.*

This affected attitude of indifference in literature, which very much resembled silent contempt, indeed signified the transition of the spirit of the time from the proud and feigned nonchalance to fanaticism in the stage of sneer and sarcasm. As to sonnets, and the dissipation of belles-lettres in general, causing the giggles which were audible at night among the model-shorn shrubbery and trimmed boxtrees of Versailles, decency demands of us to observe silence. *Dissembling an aristocratic indifference to the religious base of humanism. § 67, 68, 188.* *Stage of sneer and sarcasm between feigned nonchalance and fanaticism.*

The system of such paternal rule of which the French complained, was no worse than that of all the other states, except that in France the straight-jacket of patronage-government was laced somewhat tighter. The tutelage under which the peoples were kept by the idea of the "legitimacy" (sc. of hereditary sovereignties) extended over the entire sphere of civil life, public and private. The state-craft of the seventeenth and eighteenth centuries made it its chief object to conceal the political realities under the judicial views of star-chambers and under the gravity of the periwig; and "legitimacy",—the fathership of the monarch over his subjects, the children who where not to question governmental measures—was the couched principle and secret of the jurisprudential wisdom of the cabinets. And that privacy of the cabinets was extended into the privacy of husbandry. Statial guardianship minutely defined all domestic, industrial and commercial relations down to the number of windows in each house, to matters of dress, and the courses at table. *Devices to conceal the perils.* *"Legitimism".*

The dissatisfaction with king and cabinet was only equaled by that with the oppression couched in their pretense of paternal care. The fifth part of French soil was in possession of the mort-main, i. e. the dead hand of the church, which not only received but also held fast and did not give, that is, paid no taxes. *Privacy of cabinets.* *Untaxed property in the "mort-main".*

The ecclesiastical tenures consisted of the most fertile lands throughout the kingdoms, the annuities derived from rents amounted to hundreds of millions, besides the 123 millions which the prelates, abbots, chapters and cloisters derived annually from the tithes. The number of Premonstratensian monks was not more than 399, but their income from these sources amounted to more than a million. Of the Benedictines of St. Maur there were 1672; who drew rents up to eight millions. Yet the clergy in general—we are pleased to state it, by the way—was not as worldly as might be expected; of the bishops only four submitted to the oath of allegiance to the constitution drawn up by radicalism. Notwithstanding the somewhat improved behavior of the priesthood it was impossible to uphold such a state of affairs. Necker demonstrated that with the antiquated system of taxation he could do absolutely nothing to restore the financial health of the realm. *Necker's financial difficulties.*

The trouble with that old system of finances and crown-revenues was that the "estates", the people of rank represented in the two divisions of the legislature, enjoyed among other immunities the exemption from taxation. Calonne demanded *Privileged classes exempt from taxation.*

that they should vote for a ground-tax upon their real estate. But since those wielding the money power, in their adherence to the old customs, would not yield an iota of their prerogatives, and since the aristocracy hesitated to grant the advantages of the modern ideas, advanced by themselves, to the oppressed classes, because the remnants of feudalism facilitated their policy of obstruction, France was compelled to fight them down.

The men of 1789: those belonging to the assembly constituent, the parties of the legitimists and of the convent, the Girondists and the members of the mountain—they all blasted away in quick succession one firm layer after another of petrified burdens and class-prerogatives, each party eager to advance over the scattered rival factions. The conservative champions of mediœvalism finally yielded to force; but it was now too late to waive a privilege here and there. Not yielding readily enough, they were doomed to annihilation. For on the score of rule the tables were suddenly and completely turned. To join in the cry of the new parole "liberty, equality, fraternity" would avail the aristocrats nothing. To don the tricolor, and to show himself to the patriots with the Phrygian cap of liberty" upon his head, in obedience to Lafayette's advice, could save the "legitimate" king no more.

Neither could the bawling on the streets, and the allegorical pageants, and the making of constitutions avail anything. It was the abolition of privileges, it was the establishment of equal rights and responsibilities for persons of all ranks, it was the deliverance of labor from serfdom, it was freedom of thought and speech, of association and of religious worship, which were to be achieved. It was the work of reconstruction by which the proclamation of human rights had to prove that it was more than phraseology. And to be sure, sincere in its persistency to obtain human rights, the revolution did not stop at vociferous demands.

The exasperated masses were in dead earnest, which earnestness substantiated itself in heaps of human flesh and streams of human blood. It need not be repeated that the establishment of humaneness by such methods was an undertaking demonstrating absurdity itself, because the humanity requisite for the reconstruction did not exist. Its proclamation turned into something like the silly masquerade of Clootz, the harlequin of the revolution.

It seems incomprehensible that the people in the act of realising their inborn rights did not shrink back horror-struck from the ruination caused by demolishing all historical rights.

The strange adventure of destroying reasonability, in order to build the right of reason upon the rubbish of hear-say radicalism, can only be comprehended as the result of a pestiferous condition of society in general.

On account of this decay the madness of the participants, who were seized and carried away by the raging torrent, or scared away under the reign of terror, may find excuse; tho the instigators deserve abhorrence rather than praise. Of these maladies of the times, however, we shall speak in the third book.

With Napoleon the sobering up, the reaction set in, though his own career denoted simply that critical stage of the sickness, when the febrile symptoms signify, that health sinks below the strength of resistance. This phenomenal figure represents, in a greater measure even than Karl the Great, the unification of Romano-Byzantine and German features of polity. The empire of the Carolingians leaned upon the powerful influence of popery, just then beginning to take the lead in politics. But Napoleon stood free upon the charred field of burnt-out ideas, opposite an exhausted popery, which, however, he deemed still useful enough as a prop to his personal aims at universal Cesaro-papism. For he intended nothing less than changing the curia together with the papal office into a charge d'affairs at his court.

The emperor had caused a catechism to be composed for the schools of the nation, in which religio-political text-book he commanded that a position be ascribed to him, which should be nothing short of deification but sacramental sanction. The emperor-god seemed to appear complete upon the column of Vendome; all that Napoleon thought necessary for his proper appearance in this attitude were the lessons he took from Talma, the comedian.

His program for the performance was ready. In the year 1813 there was to be held an œcumenical council. As the first thing on the program it was ordered that the pope presiding was to resign his worldly sovereignty. "From this moment on I would have made him the idol of the people, so that he should have neither missed his possessions, nor felt his degradation. I would have held my ecclesiastical convocations like my legislative sessions. My councils would have represented universal Christendom, of which the popes would have been the presidents, which I would have opened and closed, and the decrees of which I would have sanctioned and published, just as Constantine and Karl the Great used to manage ecclesiastical affairs."

The meaning of this reverie—which according to our principle of interpretation and method of comparison, was virtually nothing but a copy of Asiatico-Byzantine arrangements—would have been the fitting up of the pedestal upon which the emperor-god was to be enthroned; whilst of the freedom which Christianity vouchsafed to the nations when it separated the worldly kingdom from the spiritual, humanity would have been again forcibly and yet surreptitiously deprived. *(Meditation on the general overthrow, De Maistre, De Bonald.)*

Looking back upon the terrorism of the revolution, such thinkers as De Maistre and De Bonald recognise in this characteristic and instructive period a divine retribution and the prelude to the last judgment, a "shaking up of all human powers." In the vicissitudes of the revolution these sages conceived the rage of infernal powers let loose by the hand of the Most High as in other judgments, of which the one just experienced was but the continuation. Each divine visitation makes the infernal rage subservient to salvation. For it is to be remembered that the catena of chastisements and deliverances is interlinked with the first insurrection against the divine rule enacted on the banks of the Euphrates; and that the antagonism continues through all mundane æras to the end of the times. In the scenes witnessed upon quays along the Seine, the divine hand of discipline and deliverance was recognised as opening the ulcer on the social body, cutting deep and sharp into the putrid flesh emancipated, in order to cure the sore and save the organism. *(Infernal powers rendered subservient to true liberation. Series of insurrections from the banks on the Euphrates to those of the Seine. Lessons derived from the experiments to establish humanism without God.)*

§ 179. Our task of interpreting national paroxysms compels us to return to the axiom from which we set out. What significance of the great revolution, as taken in connection with other erratic and fitful experiments to establish humanism without God, did our disquisitions disclose? In the first place the revolution evinced the bankruptcy of the perversion and onesided treatment of the idea of humanity. A humanism severed from God-consciousness can never be made a success. That humanity—which, in order to spite God and religion, elevated the sample-product of an insane reason to the rank of a goddess—was by that usurper of divine prerogatives, treated with utter contempt, in a most inhumane manner. There is no power under heaven which, in such cases of disdain shown to the religious side of humanity, is able to prevent the transition from radical democracy to reckless and rank despotism. No earthly power is able to save such a humanity from sinking into the lowest condition of either servitude or brutality. *(Bankruptcy of a humanism based upon perverted ideas with disregard to God-consciousness. Absolute ignorance as to religion. Cognition of humanity totally emptied of its sacred contents. Hierarchy to be blamed. Responsibility of the instigators. Enthusiasm for bettering the condition of peoples, kindled not in France alone.)*

We see what good in the negative came out of the revolution through the self-revelation of human nature in all its capabilities. Now for the proper application of this knowledge. *(Disdain for the religious side of humanism does not prevent the transition from radical democracy to rank despotism.)*

The bitter truth contained in these empirical facts yields the criterion in the first place, by which Rousseau's theory of threadbare natural humanism ought to have been tested before its adherents put it into practice and thereby jeopardised true humanism. What Chateaubriand pointed out in his terse objection quoted above is correct; and what De Maistre said about judgment and deliverance is correct, also. *(Selfrevelation of human nature to the full extent of its capabilities. Rousseau's threadbare theory on humanism ought to have been examined, before putting it to practical test and jeopardising true humanism. Chateaubriand.)*

For, De Maistre, whose true patriotism and profound Christian Philosophy—matured in the heat and under the storms of the revolution—qualified him to form a correct judgment of it, made the following confession: "Rousseau was better than I am myself, as I have acknowledged unreservedly and without any reluctance. He strove after the Good with his heart, whilst I did it with the mind. His noble soul shuddered at the sight of those abominations to which the leading men of society and of politics stooped. And because he found the savages in the natural state less corrupt, he employed all his rhetoric to convince us that a mere negative condition was the sole aim which we should endeavor to reach and the only perfection which we could hope to acquire". *(Criticism of Rousseau by De Maistre. Savages less corrupt than leaders of society.)*

This was the trend of Rousseau's preaching and also the fallacy of the irenic opinion of his person manifest in Maistre's sentimental utterance.

But what other preaching was then to be heard of in France? Of sin and its consequences; of the "image" restored by the Mediator and to be renewed in Him and through the means of His grace; of human dignity and freedom: the children of that time knew absolutely nothing. The cognition "humanity" had been emptied of its essential and most sacred contents. The "negative" side simply remained, generating that spirit of negation which can tear down the fabric of a false culture and destroy much good with it, but which is unable to build up anything positive, unable to put anything better in its place.

Where is the fault to be lodged? The hierarchy had stopped up the rejuvenating well-spring of humanism. Bearing in mind the reign of Louis XIV, and keeping in view the complot entered into by absolute hierarchy and monarchy, in order to defeat the Huguenots together with their ideals of humanism, and in order to smother the moans of humanity, history charges the hierarchy with the greater guilt. Considering the audacity of the assaults upon humanity, it is to be admitted even, that the men of the revolution rescued parts of this ideal notwithstanding the wild measures employed. Owing to Jesuitism in league with absolutism the outraged nation conceived the thought of human dignity and human rights in the negative only; but it was well enough that so much of the idea was preserved. None of those men, however, to say nothing of the crimes committed by them or to be charged to their responsibility, is to be excused on that account. Excitement and allowing one's self to be allured into the risks of perilous enterprises will never suffice to receive the esteem of moral merit by the success resulting, if the way to reach it pass through deeds of horror.

Enthusiasm sobered down, disavowing fantastical procedures.

Epidemic nature of revolutionary paroxisms.

In the beginning of the movement the flame of enthusiasm for the improvement of the condition of the oppressed—vague and doubtful as it was conceived, and mad as to the method by which deliverance was contrived at—was comparatively pure. This flame was not kindled in France alone. We know of good men outside of it, who proved their philanthropy by large contributions to the sacrifice for the cause of humanity, embracing one another, regardless of rank, with tears of joy at the prospect of seeing their ideals realised. It was a grand spectacle to see the idealistic elation of the best men in all countries, who were aglow for the amelioration of suffering and the adjustment of rightful complaints. What soon thereafter made them turn their backs to the revolution in its progress—what filled the sober friends of the people with disgust and changed enthusiasm into abhorrence—were the excesses of that fickle temper which is the unfortunate heritage of Frenchmen. Nevertheless, the sluices were thus opened through which the stream of purification was let in. The dirt and pollution carried along with it decides nothing as to the quality of its source and the blessing left after the flood. An inflated national pharisæism often blames the reign of terror upon the rebellious people who went through the heat and chills of the inflammatory fever, and who suffered. Without palliating the moral responsibility of the actors, the epidemic nature of any revolutionary craze is to be brought into account. Close by the heights of ideal patriotism and genuine consecration to the cause of universal welfare, always yawns that abyss from which unreasonable demands arise, and wild frenzy, much similar to Shamanism, leaps forth. Whenever such paroxysms seize a nation, it is thrown down in an instant from the summit of artificial culture into the humiliating stages of its low beginning. The sensational details occurring under the general infuriation are usually described in full and painted in strong colors. But historiography is not to fall into the error of thinking that justice has been done to the subject with narrating the shocking circumstances.

Discretion necessary to judge actors and contemporary sufferers.

To form a true picture of the age, the quiet labor of the rural portion of a nation should always be brought into consideration together with the noise of the metropolis. Phenomena of ethical beauty may then be noticed, of sublime disinterestedness,of indefatigable labor and devotion to the common cause in the danger of hot riots. During the intervals of transition from one period to another, and under the tribulations incidental to the process of forced advance, and by the effects of great and long continuing worry, noble and sober characters are formed in all ranks and classes. At such times, in which entire nations glow like metals in a smelter, all phenomena in their sudden changes assume gigantic and spectre-like proportions. These circumstances are to be taken into account, lest we judge a generation only by the scums pushing themselves to the foreground or foaming out on top and swimming upon the surface. Be it ever remembered that in such times history rather unmakes that which seems to make history.

Performance of duty in the rural districts in offset to the noise of metropolitan cities.

Advantages apparent after stormy times,

In which history rather unmakes that which seems to make history.

For history is not to be pushed forward in jerks and by demonstrations of state or party. It owes its true progress to the unostentatious, noiseless, and faithful performance of duty; to the composure of mind which is only obtainable under the benign influences of the home circle; to the good tone of the family, and to the order of life and habits in well regulated domestic relations, which are the chief factors of rearing a generation of selfpossessed, honest and industrious citzens. Altho the operations of these coefficients of history are scarcely recognisable, yet they are not to be ignored; their effects will soon become visible in their neutralising, at least, the evils growing out of turbulent times.

Noble traits of character developed.

Upon the blessings ensuing from any revolution to the nation weathering it, we need to enlarge no further; they have never been questioned. "The Author of the world's history writes with Lightnings". Reading aright what is thus written by a hand unseen, we find it to convey grace, deliverance, salvation. Without this writ of

Overthrows humiliating to artificial culture.

fire, humanism would have to give up the ghost in the gloomy dungeons of its bastiles of sinfulness, slothfulness, and sullenness, into which it allows itself to be immured again and again.

CH. VIII.   COSMOPOLITAN WORLD-THEORIES – EUROPEAN SYSTEM OF STATES.

§ 180.   A reaction equivalent to that which had counteracted the previous attempts at emancipation is now to be encountered. It seems that the geographical position of Germany requires of its nation, that it should balance and adjust all the mental and spiritual contests agitating Christendom.   Hence it happened that the reaction against this latest phase of human precipitation set in on the German side of the Rhine.   The reaction began where once the movement of deliverance from Roman bondage had begun to refute a false liberty.   The deistical utilitarianism of England and the atheistic sensualism of France had rushed in over the ramparts of German conservatism.   Despotism, naturally following anarchy, had thereby been enabled to break the connections of historical development and for the duration of a few decades to change the boundary lines on the maps of Europe.   But through the same events the nations became also purged of corrupt customs, as grain is fanned upon the threshing floor.   The chaff of loose theories and anomalous practices was carried off by the storms.

The ideals of a very distorted humanity had succumbed to a rough, sometimes awfully rough reality.   Opportunity had again been given for becoming acquainted with the actual propensities of human nature, and to become reminded of that representative of humanity who alone should be taken as the model, who alone furnishes the rule and the tools for the reconstruction of the social organism.

There had been the cue and the coiffure a la Pompadour, symbolic of a culture of mere mannerism, when people, disgusted with the over-refinement of lap-dogery, played with Rousseau's "children of nature" and with savages.   The antagonists of modern conventional-ism and old cues were allowed to act the wild men to their heart's content as long as they only cried: "Look here, we savages are better men than you are!"   But ere long those savages jumped upon the smooth parquet of Europe and into the salons vacated by the refugees.   Then was the time, when the well bred European, too, tried his hand at what he might contribute to the swamping of the arena with blood.

In short, illusions and phantoms had been dispelled.   Society in its agonies almost involuntarily and instinctively ran for help to the principles of long, long ago, which in ancestral times had proved efficient in even worse emergencies.

The minds of Germany had gone through the disciplinary vicissitudes of a deep humiliation.   During the period, beginning with the Thirty Years War and continuing until the middle of the eighteenth century, Germans had to sustain the miseries of political apathy and literary destitution.   The poets imported their material from France in such abundance and of such taste, that the German mind withdrew from competition and took a rest.   Then came Klopstock who in the very strain of Milton and under circumstances of similar national distress, rallied his countrymen for a revival of the consciousness of their value.   His Christian epic in Greek hexameter became at once a barrier against flippant and flirting productions of enlightenment which in French ball costume and court livery had attracted a few rich clumsy Germans for quite a while.   Now it was shown how the grave and yet suave classic form may be appropriated to render the most tender and majestic ideals of the German Christian mind fit for presenting art at its acme.

The places of Rafael and Duerer in the period of the religious reform were filled by Milton and Klopstock at the dawn of the æra of cosmopolitan civilisation. Gœthe in his Iphigenia taught how a figure of the antique may be animated with warmth and emotion upon heights of cognition where form and essence, body and spirit conform themselves to each other. Is it not marvelous, how even the arts always mirror the epochs and illustrate the thought controlling them?

Here again it is to be noticed how the contrasts alternate between Hellenistic extolling of this world with its forms of beauty, and on the other hand, the Byzantine-Roman onesidedness of celebrating the next world, whilst treating the natural form and real life with contempt. This contrast is now reconciled. The restlessness and dissatisfaction called forth by the extremes of stiff transcendentalism and nude naturalism is harmonised by the intrinsic life propagated through Christian methods of civilisation, in which spiritual essence and natural forms as-

Side notes:

Germany, which had once concentrated the erroneous humanism of dogmatic ecclesiasticism, now successfully encounters the false humanism of freethinking worldliness.

Despotism, following anarchy, broke down the boundary lines on the European maps for a few decades only,

whilst the profound reforms procured were rendered permanent.

France slipped another opportunity to become reminded of that representative of humanity who alone furnishes the rule and the tools for reconstruction

The actual propensities of human nature

Return to humanism in the Christian sense.

Literary barrenness of the German mind during the period in which the French dictated in matters of taste,

until in Milton's strain the ideal of humanity is shown in the "Messias" of Klopstock.

Spiritual essence in natural form harmonised in the "Iphigenia" of Gœthe.

similate each other. In this blending of essence and appearance that form of existence is anticipated, which will be realised when the thought of humanity is apprehended in its full depth. Then even that delicacy of sentiment will come to be empiric which Fiesole. Schongauer and Meister Stephan once put into their paintings.

Understanding of classic measure, symmetry and appreciation of character and taste of the ancients assisted the Germans to appreciate also the excellencies of their own antiquities. They became incited to make themselves familiar with the features of the characteristic peculiarities of their ancestors. And a still deeper impulse led the modern mind back to Him, who in the primitive times had been by them embraced as the captain of salvation and king of the common people, in whose person alone the thought of humanism is definite and perfect, and the attainment of ideal humanity warranted.

Concerning the latter phase of the reaction as effected through literature the first beacon light gleamed up in Hamann's realism.

The conception of a spirituality in the concrete, which Oettinger expostulated as advantageous to religion—because according to him "corporeality was the end of all God's ways"— was also Hamann's conviction; only that his illustrious thoughts were given in such aphoristic utterances gliding over the entire field of contemporaneous literature like the zig-zag flashes of lightning, as to be poorly adapted to popularisation. Nevertheless, Hamann showed how the Savior of the world is to be perceived as the ruler of the universe, as which, after Hamann, He was exhibited in the writings of Lavater, Claudius, Joung-Stilling, Baader, J. F. von Meyer, Steffens and H. v. Schubert. Once more the Savior is acknowledged as the center of secular as well as sacred history. His person is not only adored as the Savior of men, but also conceived as the center of the visible universe which in and through Him is going to be

renewed and gloriously transmuted. In Him, as the Heavenly Head and center of the cosmos, the great process of the palingenesis originates and proceeds through the medium of humanity, and concludes with the redemption of the natural world. All of that which is human stands forth now under the aspect of a faithful covenant with Him who is the "center of equation", as it were, around whom in widening concentric circles even the visible universe moves, and in whose behalf a contest wages even in the spheres of the spiritual world. After this reaction of humanism against the "emancipation of the flesh," Romanticism revived, a school of literary dilettanteism which in song and music awakened long forgotten sentiments. The world of fairies and folklore was resurrected. The mysteries of the primitive forests, and the wondrous legend of the chapel in the woods with its sunken treasury vaults; the old castles with troubadour and tournament; the mountain caves with their elves and goblins; the enchanted virgins and the blue flowers with their miraculous power—they were presented

again to the imagination almost in their native vividness. Again the old knights rode out upon their adventures, and the rocks reechoed the bugle-call sounded among the dear old oaks yet standing in the familiar dale. Under the spells of the Antique, of the Renaissance, and of French robber stories, these legendary tales had been neglected and silenced, together with national history. Now the latter study especially revived once more and again exerted

its charming and educating influence over the academic youth. The Germanic nations seemed to remember the scenes of their common childhood; the educated at least opened themselves to the knowledge of past ages and of what once these times had been so full of promise. With Goethe they learned the significance of the Strassburg minister and to appreciate again the pious patriotism of Tauler, who had been among the first, if he was not the first one, to preach in German; and they learned to understand again his mystical contemplation. But venerable as the portals of stone were, love of the natural imagined to bear the springs of the fables murmur close beside them. Goethe's autobiography mingles "truth and fiction" like scenes under moonlight. The rambles of Romanticism in literature enchant the eager pursuers of

the loan-libraries, with dreams of convent gardens inclosed by high walls, and benumbs them with the temperature of the cross-passages in the cloisters. Partial loss of sober views of actual life, and disgust with its duties energetically to be practiced, was the consequence of nurturing the mind with such food.

The tendencies of Romanticism amounted to a retrogression from universalistic views as to humanism into national confines and narrow notions; to a relapse from Hellenistic realism to transcendental "Romance." Repeatedly we have noticed

plainly how the condition of culture depends upon the religious undercurrent and immediately shows itself in the "representative arts". Again the eye met the symptoms of the Byzantinism, couched under denominational absolutism: the lean and languid corpses of the Mediator and all the saints. Those paintings designate that æsthetics had been superseded by the reveries of asceticism; that the morbid mind craved to nourish itself upon the world-soreness in trying to satisfy the religious wants, as the pious had relied upon in bygone ages.

The professional propagators of the Roman world-theory availed themselves, furthermore, of a power of which no Roman ever had thought before.   The Germans with their great regard for everything in print were not aware that Jesuitism then already had learned how to manipulate the daily press in the dissemination of the Roman allurements just at the time when, more than ever, it would have been necessary to refrain from romantic intoxication. *(Jesuitism utilises the press to popularise its principles by cultivating Romanticism through enchanting descriptions of unreal life.)*

For just then Pope Pius had restored the order of Jesuits by reading mass at the altar of St. Ignatius (sc. Loyola), by the rehabilitation of the "holy" inquisition, and by the condemnation of the Germanic bible societies. For the first time again since James II, a cardinal appeared upon English soil in his official paraphernalia. While the victorious allies, constituting the "holy alliance," entered Paris, Catholics of Southern France made attacks upon the houses of protestants. Count De Maistre loudly proclaimed papal infallibility as the single means of safety, because of the pope being the umpire of the nations, and since therefore to him, as the common father of Christendom, all legitimate rulers were bound in obedience. In southern Germany the people were belabored to accept the same views. Haller, under episcopal permit, was secretly a catholic, tho as a magistrate of Berne he swore to protect the Reformed Church. Altho a citizen of a republic, he admonished the princes: "Beware of the term 'constitution'; it is poison to monarchism, because it presupposes and nourishes democracy." And the admonition lodged deeply with worried princes and loyal subjects, who were unsophisticated enough to forget that the Roman catholic countries were the hot-beds of revolutions. Politically the people were held in such ignorance of Metternich's popish coalition as to imbibe the hatred against the protestant north of Germany, administered in drop-wise doses by Roman newspaper correspondents in Munich and Vienna, Mainz and Treves. *(Reactionary steps conspired upon, against protestantism. Papal infallibity advised by De Maistre. as the basis for social order and for the reconstruction of Europe. Haller's intrigues. Secret catholic and monarchistic designs in republican and reformed disguise. Metternich's intrigues. § 184.)*

But as it had been contrived that the gradual ingratiation with Romanticism should prepare minds for Romanism, the tumults of the French, the Spanish, the Mexican and Italian overthrows chased terrified souls into the Catholic church, the only place on earth, where an inclination for Asiatic resignation and dream-life could find an asylum. In the turbid waters there was good fishing. *(Revolutions hatched out in Romanised countries.)*

§ 181. A reaction again altered the course of this under-current, as became manifest in all domains of science, foremost in the theories about state-rights. Before considering, however, the new experiments in this direction, it will be advisable first to examine another phenomenon.

The ancient, specifically oriental, form of consciousness persistently tends to obtrude itself upon the Occident. This manifests itself in the repeated attempts to establish an universal monarchy by means of a sort of spiritual monopoly. To succeed in the arrangement of such a world-wide empire the application of Asiatic views is indispensably necessary. This obtrusiveness cannot be taken as merely accidental concurrence. It is to be understood, rather, as a preappointed coefficient in the workings of history. *(Counter-action against Romanticism in the science of political economy. § 182.)*

It must not be regarded simply as the effect of a general law, according to which every thought takes place under the oscillations between contrasts. For if the formative cognitions proceeded after such lawfulness, the idea of humanity even would ever have to be conceived anew by each generation, and to be cleared up by going through opposite extremes. This mechanical and generalising aspect of history is insufficient to comprehend the changes as in any way conducive to human progress. The recurring symptoms of that obtrusive tendency of orientalism are not even explicable by the other observation that our race is more subject to the sway of feminine receptivity and passiveness—moving down glacier-like from the heights of Central-Asia upon Europe—in alternating advances and recedings, than to the impulses of masculine energy and aggressiveness. *(Examination of the persistent tendency to repristinate oriental views upon European forms of government—to establish a universal empire. Not explicable by referring to mechanical law of thought undulating between contrasts. § 22, 38, 39, 51.)*

Rather may the fact be argued that the tendency under discussion seems to be a part of the design underlying history. Most probably the idea of a massive materialisation of the Christian thought was intentionally permitted to remain among Christian nations as sedimentary remnants of nature-bound humanity. In our opinion Greek and Roman Catholicism is to be regarded as a sort of petrified layer, much like the ethnical substratum of pristine culture so often referred to. We deem it to be the necessary natural basis for spiritual culture. We conceive this formation as the transitory stage between the old and new dispensations, as the disciplinary state under the law preparatory to the state of free grace; as about the same that Mohammedanism is now to the Africans. If this should prove to be the case, then that compact organisation among Christians will have to be considered as designed and preserved not on its own account but in order to serve the whole. For this form of Christianity as a substratum holds undeveloped individualism in a firm and fixed position, preserving it against the perils of abortive and arbitrary subjectivism. *(The obtrusive tendency of orientalism not even explicable to the feminine receptivity of Asia and masculine energy of Europe. The motion between extremes of Catholicism, Greek and Latin, to be considered as sedimentary remnants of the culture of peoples in the nature-bound state, forming the natural basis for spiritual culture.)*

as men's "state under the law" transitory to the "state of free grace".

This system simply enjoins devoutness, selfrenunciation and ritualistic performances upon its adherents. Of the individual it requires neither the mental exercise which conditions the appropriation of the truth; nor does it enlist the individual member in the contest which ensues from the process of excreting alien elements.

Propædeutic significance of catholic legalism.

For this latter process of uninterrupted purification, Protestantism requires the judicious cooperation of every Christian, in order to make the government of the church the pattern for free self-government.

Minds to whom catholicism seems preferable.

Comparison between Catholicism and Protestantism:

Reliance upon church authority,

Hierarchism has made arrangments for preserving the unity, protecting the perpetuity, and augmenting the external power of the church, under which church-government can stipulate the easier terms of filial submission, reliance upon authority and childlike credulity. Hence to minds shunning the exercise of thought, the responsibility of personal sanctification, and the annoyances connected with the assurance of a vivid hope based upon a cheerful faith, this system of spiritual guardianship must appear preferable to Protestantism with its demand of manliness in the faith, and decisiveness in its good fight.

Catholicism lets individual life rest—undisturbed under the least possible selfculture, and unconcerned as to personal participation in affairs of ecclesiastical government—in the life of the genus, so to say, in the lap of the mother-church.

responsibility to God alone;

Protestantism is bent upon weaning individual life from the leading strings of human authority and from reliance upon it; bent upon educating people to answer for themselves, and to rely upon God alone.

obedient conformance,

voluntary acceptance.

Catholicism takes the responsibilities of the individual upon itself, and warrants his salvation under condition of his obedient conformity; whereas Protestantism charges every confessor with working out his own salvation, and with voluntary acceptance of the means of grace to this end.

Thought and external life under custody of priesthood and symbolism.

Piety made test proof in life's hand to hand warfare.

Catholicism keeps individual thought and external deportment under the spiritual guidance of the institution in its massive compactness—whilst Protestantism loosens the believer from the fetters of symbolism, and with a benediction dismisses him into the hand-to-hand warfare of life, so that he may gain therein a keen sense of personal responsibility, personal judgment, conviction, and experience.

Ecclesiastical indulgences; superabundant sanctity stored up from which lack of ethics may be cheaply replenished.

Catholicism binds and conceals individual piety, and absorbs meritorious works in its communistic chest of superabundant sanctity, from whence a lack of ethical integrity may cheaply be replenished. Under the impressive forms of the cult, and by the oppressive powers of external contrivances it fixes religiousness under the weight of symbolic surroundings, pretending thereby to shield Christian piety against profanation.

Caution in propagating the Kingdom of Heaven.

Protestantism endeavors to educate persons in clear, purely spiritual, and true cognitions, and is cautious as to the choice of external means of instruction, of discipline, and edification; cautious also as to the method of propagating the Kingdom of Heaven.

Relic-worship.

Critical sifting as to essentials and externals.

Afraid of progressiveness

Proper conduct in the world to cultivate character and to fulfill the ethical task.

Catholicism conserves, frequently more than conserves, the details of traditional tenets which have accumulated from the remotest times and obscurest corners of history. It preserves the old and outworn household goods and every piece of scaffolding once used in the upbuilding of the church, as relics, whose sacredness is said to grow with age, and to inhere in a most incredible manner in the most absurd objects. Protestantism, being inclined to critical investigation and sifting, cogently discriminates between encumbering and essential externals. Catholicism poses in the antiquity of its apparatus, and keeps the obedient children in the venerable father-house where progressiveness cannot taint the atmosphere, lest, by its being let in, the church would be contaminated with the airs of profaneness. The children of the "fathers" become drilled in the primitive method of picture-thinking in order to form apperceptions of a very materialistic supernatural world. Protestantism repudiates this combination of renouncing and at the same time domineering over the world. It teaches proper conduct in the world and cultivates firmness of character, which enables its members to take a hand in transforming the world, and in furtherance of fulfilling the common ethical task.

The past praised by Catholicism;

the future belongs to Protestantism.

Undervaluing the significance of religious forms and objectivity will not invalidate protestantism.

These are the curves which prescribe to Protestantism the direction for future advance, whilst Catholicism praises the past. Protestantism will sometimes depreciate the value of the Church as an institution to be strictly organised, and may undervalue the ethical significance of disciplinary functions, and concede little import to the educational influence of ritualistic forms of worship: the future will belong to it, nevertheless. For the task of the church is paramount to the ends of history. It consists in educating the children of men to true consciousness and elevating them to spiritual maturity; and it consists in the deliverance of nature from its state of confinement, in the advancement of the arrested culture of nature-bound people.

Hence mental labor and spiritual strife are what the future bears in its foldings, and for which Protestantism is to equip the faithful. In this coming contest many will be found wanting and will suffer shipwreck by steering under winds of misapplied freedom: yet this labor and strife for the maintenance of freedom in its true sense are the signature of the coming period regardless of such as may fall.

Coming contests for the maintenance of evangelical freedom,

implying the risk for many to suffer shipwreck;

Protestantism is charged with the administration of these guiding maxims. It ventures out upon the high waters, insisting upon the right of its disciples to take upon themselves the risk of leaving the father-house and to try their capabilities in a strange and stormy world, in order to become selfsupporting and weatherproof. Catholicism has faith in the safety of its children only so far as they stay inside the visible fold and remain in their natural simplicity;—whilst Protestantism, having faith in divine guidance and in humanity, lets its children roam through the open fields of thought with no less concern for their spiritual welfare.

will not induce Protestantism to retain its disciples under tutelage.

Catholicism, for the time being at least, forms the broad and massive basis for the idea of an organised corporation, if not of a permanent incarnation, in whatever proportions it may be mixed with the elements of the lowest substratum from which new personal life will ever detach itself. It forms the great store-house from which in successive ages, and under various circumstances forces may be secured which are yet to be rendered useful as historic coefficients. Should Protestanism ever become powerless against ecclesiastical anarchy, and allow the Christian thought to be dissolved through rank subjectivism, then Catholicism would form the necessary counterpoise.

By virtue of Roman organisatory skill, Catholicism affords a counterpoise to Protestant subjectivism.

For developing and realising the thought of true humanity in every individual, the history of the Christian world needs both protestant activity and advance as well as catholic conservation and patient perseverance. The perils, to which this cause of humanity is exposed on both sides, make it necessary that each in turn shall complement the other.

Thus it might be argued for the sake of irenics.

Of course, from the aspect of Catholicism this necessity of being complemented by Protestantism cannot be conceded, for Catholicism claims the realisation of the Kingdom of God exclusively for itself, consequently it insists upon its right of being intolerant, and persists in the wrong position once assumed.

Romanism will not acknowledge the necessity of being complemented by Protestantism, and will therefore persist in the wrong position once assumed.

Ecclesiastical measures of precaution—which on special occasions may become necessary, and which may become beneficial factors in preserving the cause of humanism in cases of emergency—were elaborated into a fixed yet flexible system with a definite purpose. It is on account of this flexibility that Rome is not altogether reliable as a depository of the thought of humanity, and as an administratrix of humaneness. The episcopal office was made less authoritative in order to establish a seat for the exaltation of one metropolitan; the complaints of nations during the strife for the supremacy of "spiritual power" were ignored; the possibility of reforms was forestalled by papal infallibility, and the danger may become palpable that a power arise in the Occident upon Asiatic principles, notwithstanding the staunch opposition which the efforts to that effect always had to encounter in the Germanic nations. Upon anticipations which hold the pliability and judaistic exclusiveness of Catholicism capable of still worse designs, we shall not meditate.

Flexibility of Roman principles renders Catholicism an unreliable ally of conservatism. § 136, 164, 165.

Possibility of modifying Catholicism—its reform—is forestalled by papal infallibility. § 180.

Reaction against Roman orientalism through the science of social polity. § 181.

§ 182. The German cognitions of the rights of monarchs and subjects were delineated when the development of freedom in young nations on new soil was put in contrast with the life and ideas of the ancient world.

German cognition of rights.

In the Orient monarchial absolutism is established as a matter of course, people submitting to it as to their fate. In yonder countries the pretentiousness of dominion knows no limit. Every kingdom is in perpetual animosity with all the adjacent kingdoms, each assuming the right to treat its neighbors as outlaws and the neighboring governments as rebels. The rulers like Cyrus and the Pharaohs are priests if not gods, concentrating all power in their persons.

Retrospect upon the differences between oriental and occidental forms of government

Absolutism of one person;

In opposition to the universal sway of formidable views Christianity, regardless of the enmity thus provoked, at once emphasised the freedom of every person. On entering Europe this Christian thought met a copious variety of nations with diverse formations, instead of oriental despotic massiveness and uniformity. After the Roman amalgamate of the heterogeneous is disintegrated, the Christian thought prevails, blesses labor, teaches to cultivate the homestead, makes people permanent settlers, and alters the autonomy of chiefs and war-kings into the elective kingship of the

Personal freedom of every Christian.

Rome—Byzantium intermediates oriental forms of rule.

Germans. This alleviated form of ideal, representative and responsible authority is preserved no longer, however, than to the time when the spirit of oriental monarchism, to which Rome and Byzantium in their weak old age had given themselves up, is slowly introduced and adopted by the Germanic nations in the measure they be-

Imposing them upon the Germanic nations under elective kingship.

Axiom of the oneness of state-power prevailed in the Romanised, and finally § 122.

come Romanised. The diversity and strength of single personages is supplanted by the units of states, developing their increase of power, as we have seen, under the dominant maxim of oneness. The Romanised monarchies were the first to shape themselves according to papal designs, and to occupy their place in that formation of politics which rested upon a somewhat screened world-consciousness, but open worldliness.

the Germanic nations.

The Germanic monarchies withstood the encroachment of orientalism for a very long period, until their very opposition caused the overthrow of German imperialism. Thus Germany arrived at the period of reaction which now engages our observation.

Genesis of the "European system of states".

It was in the extension of the Turanian power into Europe, the formation of the Turkish empire, which compelled Christendom to unite upon the defensive. And, besides, the discovery induced the nations to adjust the common interests sequent to maritime enterprises. This solidarity of interests promoted the formation of the European system of state-polity. The peculiarity of this order of things rested upon the mutual acknowledgment of the independence and sovereignty of each constituent part.

Conformity of political arrangements.

This was to history a new phenomenon, since no part of the world had ever enjoyed political relations of this kind, which in Asia, at any rate were impossible. The basis of this system was given in the essential unity of religion—of reformed religion which holds diversity in unity—as underlying the common cognitions of juridical principles which generated an approximate conformity of political arrangements.

The difficulty was that measures of this kind could be carried out in no other way than by the secret diplomacy of cabinets intriguing one against the other, ALSO A NEW PHENOMENON IN HISTORY. The reason that affairs were unmanageable otherwise, is simply because the members of the European organism were monarchical courts, mistrusting and at the same time emulating each other. To act in concert for the welfare of humanity was out of the question. Nevertheless all went well enough considering the circumstances. Altho a formal contract was never drawn up which would have bound the states to respect the rights of rival states; or by which the security of each was warranted and the mutual relations were regulated, yet the course of events itself procured the necessary equation, since a new thought struck Hugo Grotius.

International rights founded upon common consent.

"International Right" was the spontaneous product of progressive civilisation by which the governments were compelled to recognise and protect the historical legitimacy of the particular states. International right was repeatedly violated yet it always received the renewed sanction of common consent. Aside from that

Common recogisance of Christianised culture, i. e. civilisation.

equity agreed upon by public opinion, all states had eventually to submit to a general recognition of Christian morality as the basis of a good understanding in which minor difficulties were liquidated. Custom as fixed in a code of burdensome conventionalities generally becomes tyrannical on account of the cavil and censoriousness

New discoveries and colonisation

perpetuate different forms of government.

which it generates. Nevertheless, these conventionalities were on the whole not less conducive to the retention of selfrespect and considerateness as to the freedom of others, than to the cultivation of dignity and refinement.

European system the stronger for the lack of a written constitution.

Thus a group of states spontaneously organised itself—the more cohesive for the lack of a written constitution—which we may designate as the **European system.** On account of the continuance of new discoveries and colonial acquisitions the prestige of this system was soon recognised the world over in its universal importance. The power of the old Asiatic empires in their isolation—as for instance that of Persia un-

Obnoxious features:— the surveillance of cabinets,

der its sofis, of India under its moguls, of China, etc.—was completely overshadowed by the European system. The nature of its unity permitted the continuance of a great diversity of civil authorities: such as the hereditary monarchies, the aristocratic form of government in Venice, and the democratic in the Swiss cantons. This diversity did strengthen, rather than weaken, the European combination.

the necessary for maintaining "Balance of Power." § 160.

The secrecy of the cabinets was the only obnoxious feature of this system. But there was no other mode of managing the "balance of power" to be invented, especially since the Machiavellian doctrines had been promulgated, which, under pretense of being guaranties of general prosperity, had different ends in view. Richelieu planned the aggrandisement of the state in order to secure the perpetuity of absolute monarchism under the predominance of ecclesiastical unity. This plainly was the way he understood and tried to utilise Sully's humane idea.

It was well that Richelieu could not succeed. For after the Thirty Years War the shrewd devices to eternalise Roman supremacy were foiled through the polity of William II of Orange. Under the auspices of the Reformed nations of England and Holland, William organised the first league for the purpose of holding France and Spain in check. **The practice of balancing the powers of Europe was, therefore, not simply the invention of Machiavelli, but the outcome of protestant self-protection against Roman cunning.**

Machiavellian devices headed off by the reaction of Reformed nations. William II, of Orange.

Mercantile transactions demanded reconstruction of financial methods.

Cabinet polity could not succeed in baulking the destinies of Europe for the sake of small, mean ends. Many other factors in public life were to assist in shaping the character of the two succeeding centuries, and to shape it differently from that which the counter-reformation had tried to impose upon Europe.

Foremost of all the improved methods of balancing was the new financial system, the outgrowth of vastly increasing mercantile transactions. It seemed as if it had become the chief object of political economy to accumulate money. Factories were privileged to monopolise the industries; imports and exports were rendered difficult by tariffs which sometimes were almost prohibitory. Jealous of one another, the states tried to keep capital each within its own sphere of interest. Soon it became obvious how much of the strained relations was due to economic selfishness, and to what extent the luxury of standing armies and the preponderance of militarism was to be traced to cosmopolitan financeering. But under the circumstances all these developments conditioned upon each other were beneficial in their effects.

Militarism.

The nobility, for instance, had become degraded to parasitical existence at the courts. The "free lords" had lost their respectability to such a degree that the Spanish grandees took no longer any pride in being followed by large retinues of hidalgoes. The barons found that it did not pay to strut about in search of martial employment. The rulers—instead of bothering with enlisted volunteers, who would stand out on strike at the instant when delay was most precarious—drafted the recruits for military service from the youth of their nations, putting all ranks of citizenship under equal obligation in the defence of their own homes, and giving opportunities to the impoverished "notables" to enter courses of orderly life and regular habits in the pay and interest of monarchism. Thus an affluence of fighting propensities found engagement, much to the advantage of order and tranquillity. The new state, then, rested upon three well differentiated departments of administration;—the financial, judicial and military.

Different departments of governmental functions.

Standing armies giving employment to the declining nobility.

Christianity was to carry out the thought of an organised humanity.

§ 183. The ancient world consisted of unconnected nationalities. Christianity was to carry out the thought of an organised humanity. The Roman hierarchy deformed this thought by falling back upon the mechanical, world-embracing theocracy. The maintenance of national rights and peculiarities was thereby discouraged. Protestantism repristinates the natural and historical rights of the individual nations, and, upon ethical axioms, brings about organic interrelations in the interests of humanity as a whole, without forgetting that an accentuation of the principle of nationality is a remnant of barbarian clannishness.

Rome fell back upon a theocracy.

Protestantism gives new impulses to the nations to form ideal unions of individual states.

To the German empire, suffering most under this clannishness, another lease of prolonged existence had been granted, not, indeed, as a power, but from sheer political necessity; for the integrity of its geographical boundaries was to guarantee the common interests of the governments, if there were to be any concert in commerce, and hope for revenues. The parts of the German empire were so loosely connected, that despite the measures of Maximilian I in creating national judicatories intended to secure internal tranquility—a closer union and firmer legislation could not be established. Particularism and clannish jealousies obstructed the advance and order of the whole. The members of the German system were not kept together by common patriotism, so that in its external relations Germany had entirely lost its prestige. What kept the nation together was merely the ideal conviction that it must uphold a kind of union in behalf of the European system. Altho Scandinavia and France disregarded the import of this sentiment, it was instinctively felt by them as well. Hence the dismemberment of the German confederacy without a constitution was not insisted upon; the envious neighbors were satisfied with having humiliated the house of Habsburg-Lorraine into political insignificance.

German clannishness

Union of the German states foiled by the Habsburg dynasty.

Under such circumstances and in this manner Germany served in neutralising, or at least mitigating, all the contrasts entering its borders on every side. Occupied with this business of poising the polarities which agitated the incipient organism of Europe, Germany was in position to provide for itself a constant and profound, tho

Westphalian peace did not dismember German confederacy but curtailed the Austrian preponderance.

slow and unostentatious advance. Above all it worked out the postulate of a moral relationship between not only its own but all other states and all grades of culture. Just as the Christian thought had emancipated itself in this heart of Europe, so the demand for a general approach to genuine civilisation was ever and again held forth by the Germanic peoples. This demand was set up in the form of a counter-claim or

cross-action on the part of Protestantism, in the reaction against the last forcible attempt to establish a world-monarchy in Europe on the pagan principles of Asia. It

proclaimed the right of "the" true man to redeem the world of nature-bound humanity, and it announced a meeting under the Cross.

It was this cross-action which brought about not only the policy of balance of power, and the international law for the protection of weak states; which created not only a diplomacy of non-interference or neutrality; but which also brought to maturity something new in answer to the schemes of would-be founders of a modern world-empire.

The Congress of Vienna had raised the issue, that interstate relations can not be based merely upon the idea of the balance of power, but must rest upon principles of common justice and of equity. Still loftier maxims had been proposed by the three

allied emperors in their exchange of views at Paris. Henceforth the precepts of Christian ethics should animate the governments of the European system: righteousness and love should be applied in internal and external affairs of state. "The subjects of all Christian rulers should assist each other in all cases." Now the "Holy Alliance"

was formally resolved upon, not as an experiment of monarchical diplomacy, but as the result of grave experiences through which humanity had passed. It was solemnly recognised that Christian thought was to maintain public order and perpetuate national welfare; that the Savior of the world was the sole ruler of the peoples, and

that the princes as His vassals were appointed to conduct the secular administration of His Kingdom and of His right upon earth. **Not the pope but the princes advanced the thought of humanism** which thus entered into a new phase of practical realisation.

The secret source of the slurs heaped upon this "holy alliance" is easily to be discerned; its beneficent effects were palpable, nevertheless.

Treischke in speaking of Talleyrand says, that this politician gladdened the perplexed adherents of dynastic diplomacy by inventing the very opportune term of "legitimacy." This parole, notwithstanding the abuse to which monarchical absolutism may subject it, expresses a deep conviction of the necessity of rights as to their bearing upon historical evolution. If nothing but this general consciousness had resulted from the deliberations at Vienna in 1814, that much derided congress would be worthy of high esteem. For the acknowledgement of the hereditary rights of princes includes the old German view of the right into which every person is born, and the right of nations to claim their own princes against usurpers trying to subjugate them under foreign yokes. These rights alone pledge the security of normal development, whose great value will come to evidence in the stormy times approaching.

Be it granted that we are as yet engaged in gradually abolishing mediæval forms in order to make room for a rearrangement of social relations, of which, however, scarcely some dim outlines are conceivable; so much is certain, nevertheless, that Europe cannot as yet abandon its hereditary monarchies, constitutionally limited as they are. Least of all can they be dispensed with at present, in sight of the rapidly growing power of capital.

Nothing works with less mercy than cold cash. In its adhesiveness capital drifts to create oppressive rings and oligarchies, playing the role of the despot who puts the iron collar upon the weak protest of human emotions. The money-aristocracy will crown its syco-

phants, and put its puppets upon thrones—provided there are profits in it; bare of patriotism it will also dethrone them again, if thereby the courses at the bourses can be advanced. It will corrupt juries and "water" elections, buy up legislatures and senates "dirt-cheap," and make presidents—according to the prospects of increasing dividends and percentages. Future formations of this kind will of course resemble but alluviations of slippery loam, accumulations of drift-sand. The masses of the people will come to see that gold thus abused is poor

manure, after all, and will treat mammon as the debris of capsised fortunes and as the nuisance of civilisation.

When this money power subsides nothing will be more popular than the old legitimate dynasties, provided their scions have not forfeited the respect of the nations, and are equal to the occasion in stemming the tide of anarchism. They will then be esteemed as the reliable joists in the national structure, as the standards and safe-guards of law and order. They will represent the continuity of true historical development and will afford nuclei for the rational advance of civilised freedom for centuries to come.

Legitimate princes, as the last resort, cannot be supplanted by any system of radicalism; for they alone symbolise the community of interest. If at all conscious of the responsibilities resting upon them by virtue of their position, they will in an exemplary mode personify loyalty to the fundamental principles of their respective national constitutions and to their oaths of office: personify fidelity, merit, and public-mindedness. In case Europe—from misapprehending the value of such ideal and indispensable sureties of national prosperity, and discarding the moral and practical bearings of legitimate leadership—should sever the ties of the continuity of historical development, it may, nevertheless, indulge the prospect of enterprise and success; but future formations of social arrangements would assume the nature of the dunes on the ocean-shore, rendering public affairs fidgety and private life insecure under the changing hazards of arbitrary experimenting; causing that nervousness which is the most unpleasant feature of modern republics. Political organisms of that class can never be as satisfactory as national kingdoms built upon solid strata of moral granite.

§ 184. The ideal of the "holy alliance" had been formulated. The princes of the congress had in concert promised the European nations, their loyal subjects, to inaugurate a new order of things upon repristinated principles of objective justice and Christian sociology. But the august thought,revived under the appalling experiences of divine judgments, and underlying the good resolutions,soon had to encounter the reserve and resentment of cabinet diplomacy, the earthly alloy of the new instrument. It was only utilised in the prolongation of the accustomed routine of running the governmental machine. The Austrian school of statesmanship could conceive of no other pledge for the safety of throne and altar and for the proper order of political affairs in general.

Now the voice of patriotic journalism ventured to make itself heard, criticising the men of the "reaction" in their efforts to fustrate the fulfillment of the royal promises and stifle the clamor of the liberals who had been foremost in the enthusiasm against the Corsican tyrant. Mistrust, impatience, and preposterousness vitiated the just demands for constitutional reforms, whilst the governments on their part deemed themselves justified in falling back on retrogressive measures, lest Parisian radicalism might renew the turmoil on a still larger scale. The means for adjustment could indeed be derived only from the political situation in general, and this was made the subterfuge for a polity of procrastination, since the cabinets had cause to be alarmed, lest by granting liberties, they would lose their authority.

We cannot be astonished that such distrustful considerations caused to some extent, the misapprehensions of both, rulers and subjects, so that the lofty intentions of the emperors, suceered at by the hierarchy and mutilated by the agitators of discontent, could not be realised. The right of the peoples to corporate representation had been repressed by the Jesuitical absolutism of Louis XIV and Frederick the Great. It is notorious how Louis treated the representatives of the nation. The emperors were sincere in restoring these rights, but the councilors reminded them of the treatment which the daughter of Austria together with Louis XVI had received and the rights that had been grossly abused. Hence, whoever now reminded the men in power of the recent solemn vows, became suspect of being a rebel, and petitions to that effect were denied. The Germanic view of human rights and royal duties had passed into oblivion. Metternich's soliloquy characterises the onesided and stubborn adherence to a nugatory and evasive policy of state. He poses on his prognostic sagacity. "I look over a much broader domain of statesmanship than other diplomats do. I cannot refrain from saying to myself twenty times a day: Good God, how far am I in the right and how far have the others gone wrong! How very easy is it not tho, to find the plain, and simple, and natural right!"

This displays a marvelous talent indeed. It explains why not one of the deepest problems agitating humanity could attract or move him. The lever of his political wisdom, of his craftiness in forming treaties, and inventing police-measures, was nothing but the fear of the revolution, which he seemed to smell everywhere. His executive ability consisted in nothing but gagging public utterances, and in the routine of fettering liberalism hand and foot. He would not see that the promised reforms alone could alleviate the difficulties, and that a return to old Germanic royalism and to representative government alone could restore the faith in the good intentions recently formed under the pressure of the Napoleonic æra.

Thus the Holy Alliance had been lowered to the superintendency of the police and the gens d'armes. Mackintosh cried out in the English parliament that Croates and Kossacks would even invade and invest Hyde Park, if things going on in Troppau were to continue much longer.

safeguards against radicalism; (they alone representing the community of interests;;

and against factious contests which render existence insecure.

Nervousness of public life the most unpleasant feature of modern republics.

The reactionary "alloy in the Holy Alliance".

The good intentions issuing from humiliating chastisements revert into means to prolong cabinet rule.

Mistrust and impatience of the public temper.

Polity of procrastinating the fulfillment of royal promises.

Ideas of corporative representation of the people, once repressed by Jesuitical absolutism, is now again put to oblivion

by Metternich's regardlessness to royal promises and to the rights of subjects.

§ 180.

Police espionage, MACKINTOSH.

"Censure of the press" GENTZ.

"Censure of the press," said Gentz, "is the supreme law of European confederacy". Otherwise, he believed the revolution, like the shade of Banquo, would drive the living from their chairs. When Metternich heard of a publication containing the proceedings of representative citizens, called together by the crown in the capacity of a mere advisory "Landtag", he called it "the greatest of modern evils in their daily eruptions".

A few anecdotes of this sort sufficiently illustrate the spirit of the latest counteraction against reforms. Every new proposal of compromise was distorted at its birth by the obstinacy of the advisers of the "crowns", and by the acrimony, which the antagonism against such annoyances generated among the people, and which was food to the radicalism thus ensuing. Despite the caution observed by the spokesmen of liberalism in the communication of their arguments, they were branded as demagogues; and in order to curb their political agitation a system of passports and police-espionage was rigidly enforced. Instead of constitutions the countries received police ordinances, and the "subjects" (die Unterthanen) were commanded by every subaltern officer to wear loyal faces. Thus the people were intimidated into abject submission. In order to endure the vexatious feeling of being governed without a murmur, they were tantalised in general and in detail.

Even the smallest states protected their trade by different revenue tariffs. The farmers were as yet burdened with tithes, and with "Frohndienst".that is, a certain amount of manual labor for "his lordship"; and new taxes were laid upon rye, upon chickens, upon bees-wax! Now all this machinery to keep the subjects under awe of government was manipulated according to antiquated ideas of class-rule and rank prerogative, only aggravated now by the overbearance of a harsh and officious "bureaucracy".

Nevertheless, the high ideal of liberty, as defined by evangelical consciousness, had prospects of recovery. Some remnants of the old human rights and some ideas as to the old form of Germanic freedom had been practically preserved in the rural communities of Westphalia, where Freiherr von Stein studied up the matter; besides that which he had learned from von Moser.

"It grows darker upon earth, and people become more wild and radical—a. war of all against all has begun which can be terminated in no other way than by the thunderings from above and by quakings of the earth below". Gentz said this when for the safety of his own policy and that of others such utterances came much too late, even in Austria.

The academic youth of Germany prepared himself to regain what had been squandered: the unity of the nation against which the pope-ridden cabinet at Vienna had ever conspired. That aspiration grew and assumed the fervor and form of Hellenistic patriotism in its prime.

Whenever in ancient Greece nuclei of national unification formed themselves, they did not grow directly from political ambitions, observed Mommsen. They were the products of the national games, arts, and arenas. Upon the streets of Olympia there stood, as late as Nero's time, the statues of more than three hundred champions, every one of whom had contested for the crown of laurel, or for the distinction of being decorated with a twig of the pine tree. Historical anniversaries were celebrated on these occasions, by the representatives of every Greek village in the largest gatherings of this kind ever witnessed by history.

Nothing can be more descriptive of this phase of German development than a parallel with this feature of Hellenistic patriotism and ambition. The House of Habsburg had rid itself of imperial responsibility when it relinquished the crown of the "Holy Roman Empire of the German nation," without however giving up its pretensions to the control of affairs in modern Germany. In answer to this sumptuousness and with an enthusiasm tantamount to that of the Hellenes, the students of the universities agitated the regeneration of the fatherland. They were the men versed in the classics, who made the first attempts to unify the Germans into a national organism after the mediæval empire had gone to its final rest. The thought of unity in diversity sprouted in literary circles and took root in festive reunions of singers, turners, marksmen, etc., but it took a long time of yearning before fruits made their appearance. Tho slow and harmless, yet the movement went on with perseverance enough to disturb the statesmen of the old school in their sleep.

Many were the playful demonstrations of those enthusiastic and often fantastic social gatherings; but very small was the number of those who, like brave Moritz Arndt, possessed a clear view of genuine Germanic freedom, and who gave vent to the scorn against "French freedom" in which the youth of the historic school, and finally "Jung-Deutschland" in its entirety participated. "A person must be free. But if sticks and stones, meadows and mountains change hands as fast as feathers are driven by the wind, if that which ought to be most firm is rendered frail, then not real estate even will remain reliable security for a human-like existence; legislation should protect the possession of the ground as immutable a basis for a well-to-do middle class and a frugal living, as the old mountains which God made. The two classes of citizens which best preserve the stamina of a nation are the farmers in the country and the artisans in the towns. But these must of necessity lose their foothold and moral, conservative import, if the homesteads are lightly parted with, if the guilds are rashly dissolved, and if the industry in large factories is left without restriction to break up all the dignity and discipline of the guilds of old. An age like ours, seized with a delirium of liberalism, cannot be reminded emphatically enough of the truth that not all is freedom which assumes its name or its attitude."

Indignation over the decline of the middle classes, of agrarians, and artisans.

Thus Arndt poured out his indignation upon the Manchestrian theory of national economy. He prognosticated how, through the continual division of landed possessions into small parcels, the farming populace would be impoverished, and the middle-class destroyed, and the lands pass into the possession of jobbers and Jews. Arndt's exclamations implied remnants of the Romantic school, but it was the Romanticism "in the serene light of a good day's work" which acknowledges, as Arndt did, "how dangerous it is for manliness and virtue to grope about the daily walks of life in fantastic twilight of a fictitious world". His was not the romance in which the Brentanos and the Arnims delighted to roam.

Denouncing sham-liberalism, and Manchesterian economies.
ARNDT.
Arndt's Romanticism different from that of the Arnim-Brentanos.

In spite of patriots like Arndt, the superannuated wisdom, which the cabinets had inherited and copied from each other, remained incorrigible in its callous arbitrariness. Nevertheless, subsequent to the powerful declaration of God—as understood in the collapse of that universal monarchy reared up under wild ado—the keynote of reaction against perverted humanism had been touched by the "holy alliance" of the princes, which henceforth has the significance, at least of a prophecy.

Despite the invasion of the ideas underlying the "Holy Alliance", is retains at least the character of a prophecy.
§ 183.

CH. IX. THE THOUGHT OF HUMANISM PHILOSOPHICALLY CONCEIVED AND SOCIALLY APPLIED.

§ 185. Once more we are compelled to observe this thought in its bearing upon modern history. It is from a third aspect that we have to examine the invisible undercurrent of events, as far as, in the first place, the prominent nations are concerned. We see them remarkably agitated by the interpretations of man's being, and by the persistency in which each theory seeks to materialise itself in the complications of civilised life.

Idea of man formally reinstated through the renaissance.

traced to its essential source of the Reformation;
§ 109, 129, 169, 170.

The renaissance had formally reinstated the humanistics, and the Reformation had traced man's knowledge of himself to its real rootings. Then selfknowledge had been rendered superficial and profane to the extent of selfdelusion, since "enlightenment" had severed the thought of humanism from the correlative truths rediscovered and preserved through the Reformation, and had planted the earthly part thereof into a soil full of wild roots and seeds of weeds. For the purpose of obtaining a thorough cognition of human nature it was necessary that humanity should pass through the stage of its relative independence wherein, free from any constraint, human nature might reveal all its dispositions and propensities in every respect. The reality of what is contained in the term humanity came now to be expounded in this third phase of the development through scientific work and philosophical thought. The contents of the thought were to be generalised and reduced to a monism which might be understood by everybody. This was to be wrought out by the great systems of thought called forth by Romanticism, in the philosophy of identity—so called for reasons previously stated with respect to the common trend and the method of affiliated syllogising peculiar to these systems, which displaced one another in rapid succession. With the alternating theories of the ideal the attempts to reorganise social life kept pace. We shall see how, with equal swiftness, these constructions of humanitarian thought were caricatured by the materialistic world-theories.

severed from evangelical God-consciousness, it is rendered profane through "enlightenment"

Contents of humanity to reveal themselves in every respect, are to be free from all constraint.
§ 117. 118, 119, 168, 176, 197, 201, 205, 232.

Romanticism calls forth the philosophy of identity, in order to obtain a monistic view of life.
§ 180, 181.

In its endeavor to penetrate into the essence of things as to their origin, value and purpose, the philosophy of the Occident passed through three stages. The thinking of the ancients lost itself in the world, it was world-wisdom (Weltweisheit). Mediæval thinking formally followed in its steps, but exchanged the real for the transcendental world, and cultivating the monastic world-soreness, called itself "learnedness in divinity" (Gottesgelahrtheit). The philosophy of modern times, beginning in the sixteenth century, striving for a monistic comprehension of the human being, is trying to simplify man's dual connection with the physical and spiritual spheres of being. It sets out with man as the proper starting point for all knowledge.

Every student is fully aware how prominently man was placed in the center of every disquisition, hence we need not enlarge much more upon the uses and abuses made of this premise.

Three stages of occidental philosophy:
1. "World-wisdom". Classics.

2. Learnedness in divinity. Scholastics.

3. Search for a monistic conception of human nature: Metaphysians; Materialists.
§ 168.

To one fact, however, too much overlooked heretofore, our attention is again directed, namely that it was the oriental form of consciousness which vitiated modern occidental philosophy and sociology.

Evidently the polarity between Orient and Occident is still effective, as Ernst Curtius once very pointedly remarked: "The old contrast between the minds of Asia and Europe reaches over into modern times with a far greater import than we seem to be conscious of." The cause of our unconsciousness lies in the fact that this contrast is conditioned by ethical deviations.

On former occasions we pointed to Avicebron, the Arab, as one of the many conductors of oriental thought, and to Maimonides, the Jewish scholar. At that same time we might have also considered the influence of Platonism upon the renaissance, as formerly allusion had been made to the same influence upon the incipient scholasticism of the first state-church. We might have shown how, associated with this Platonism, Orientalism in general, that is, as a combination of Zoroasterianism with Pythagorœan and kabbalistic thoughts, was smuggled into Europe; we might have demonstrated this from the writings of Nicolaus Cusa and Giordano Bruno. Suffice it now to mention no one else but the Spanish Jew Spinoza, in whom all oriental pantheism is concentrated. Just as Giordano Bruno was the satellite of the Wittenberg movement, so stands a century later Spinoza in juxtaposition to the Protestantism of Geneva in the Netherlands. His one substance of all things in Heaven and upon earth can tolerate nothing but modifications. That God-substance is nothing but the oriental all-one-ness pure and simple, of whose shifting into and out of appearance the individual things are the mere modes; to which even personal life is related in no other way than drops are to the ocean.

It is but natural that with the increasing facilities for popularising ideas, Spinoza's conclusions, or rather Semitic translations of Brahmanism, were modified in various ways and were recast, until they could be rendered useful, in the first place, for the configurations in state-life. The simplicity of this form of thought is alluring, and seems sufficiently profound to afford a basis for the diplomatic indifference toward the religious side of humanism. Repeatedly have we noticed how natural it is for political absolutism to avail itself of the pantheistical theories advocating a general mechanism of things in public and private life. Pantheism invites despotism every time, whilst despotism in turn, for good reasons, patronises pantheism, makes it fashionable and respectable as the welcome agency for class-division and oppression—just as we witnessed the thralldom created by Brahma-Buddhism.

Spinoza became, in a clandestine way, the father of German Pantheism as construed by Schelling and Hegel. It has been shown that pantheism, whether it be scientifically arranged at Benares or Berlin, always subsides into materialism just when it seemed to have reached its loftiest climax of abstraction.

This vapid abstractness, resulting from the effete and dilating method of reasoning, exhausts thought until the entity of things, matters and facts, until being itself is rendered into nothing. Materialism, emphasising that which the senses perceive as something real, gives the lie to the pantheistic identity, by averring that, on the contrary, outside of this something there is really nothing.

One thing, however, we owe to the philosophy of identity, which ought not to be forgotten. It revived the old cognition of the uniqueness of man as to his capacity to represent cosmical being in its entirety.

"One who would write the history of his own life," says Schelling, "would certainly have to reduce thereby the history of the universe to its sum and substance". Schelling took man for the aim of creation, "since nature's ways do not radiate from narrowness into a wide compass, but concentrate from a large circumference to a center". In this sense "everything is for the sake of man". He included the starry worlds even which in his view form but the broad base of that pyramidal creation of which man is the apex. We know the bold flight of reason by which Hegel imagined the deity and the invisible world as coming to selfconsciousness in the human mind. Such extravagance cannot enchant us; but so much becomes evident even from Hegel's aberrations, that to him also man is the cosmical center, the blossom of the universe. Beyond this view of man everything else becomes to Hegel indistinct, and vanishes; for everything else is nothing but vague being in the abstract. Man alone is concrete reality, since the visible world comes to possess knowledge of self only within his mind. Others after him have corroborated this truth by the correct conclusion, that without man nothing can be conceived as being interrelated, and that without this conception of relationship existence is practically unthinkable, if not impossible. Our earth with all its reality is nothing if not part of man himself and not belonging to him; whilst the worlds of the firmament are not an unessential effervescence.

In the ground of such thoughts, especially as modified in Schelling, rooted the anthropological investigations of Steffens and Schubert, Ennemoser and Fichte, even the "microcosm" of Lotze, notwithstanding his intermixture of heterogeneous elements. Everywhere the "Ideas" of Herder reappear, that man is the consummation of earthly creation, and that transition to the invisible world of spiritual realities passes through the dual nature of the human being. *(margin: Anthropological investigations. Man the microcosm. Steffens, Schubert, Ennemoser, Fichte, Lotze, Herder)*

Steffens describes the prototype of man, in his capacity of representing the center of cosmical being, as the completion of an infinite past, as the cardinal pivotpoint of an unlimited present, encompassing the entire universe, and as the concealed outset of an infinite future. We thus find the ancient thought and mediæval speculation inadvertently coming to a synthesis again upon Christian grounds. Cosmosophy and theosophy coalescing in anthroposophy form so many steps of the ladder upon which the idea of humanity climbs up the ascent of theoretical selfcomprehension. *(margin: Transition of earthly creation into the form of spiritual reality passes through the dual nature of man. Man the completion of an infinite past; the turning point of an unlimited present; concealed starting point of an infinite future. Ancient thought and mediæval speculation come to a synthesis.)*

§ 186. At present this thought is being elaborated into a theory of sociology which is the concrete precipitate of its philosophical chemistry. Along with the theorising about human personality goes the practical work of a thorough reconstruction of society. A glance upon the proceedings, by which the interpretation of humanistic principles as manifesting themselves in the phenomena of the social world, is attempted, brings out a series of ideals according to which the humanity of the future is imagined to organise itself. *(margin: Genesis of modern socialism. Results of speculation applied in interpreting humanistic principles so far as they manifest themselves in the phenomena of social life.)*

How the ideals thus elicited were imagined to materialise, was anticipated in philosophical treatises, poetical declamations, in novels, and chiliastic expectations. Think of the state of Plato, translated into Latin by Augustine as "the State of God". Think of Rabelais' "Gargantua". The wild religio-political experiments of the anabaptists in Muenster had the same object in view. The "Looking Backward" of Bellamy, tho exposed as a clumsy plagiarism, goes in proof of our dogma, that every theory aims at substantiating itself in the social organism, tho it were but in the shape of an ulcer. The romantic novels in the interest of one or another tendency, or in uttterance of dissatisfaction with the political situation of their respective times, belong to this same genre of literature. *(margin: Experiments to materialise worldtheories in social reconstructions. "State" of Plato, shaping itself in the "State of God" of Augustine. "Gargantua" of Rabelais. "Kingdom of God" in Muenster. "Looking backward," Bellamy.)*

All of these, and many similar productions, betray the tendency to popularise the theories and to model society according to the form into which the humanistic idea was cast, that is, into which the prevailing public opinion of each period had been fashioned by leading minds. See for instance what an idyllic and inviting picture of life is painted by Thomas More upon his newly discovered "Island of Utopia."

The great chancellor depicts the social happiness of a million and a half of citizens, nicely grouped in companies of forty persons each. Everything breathes equality, liberty and peace. Fifty-four splendid cities, all laid out with geometrical precision and of equal magnitude offer fine homes for the dear folks. The houses are redistributed after each decade. Government conducts labor and is the wholesale merchant, monopolising industry and commerce. Government carefully prescribes emigration, fashion and every external form of life, private and public. Liberty is granted—on paper—in a few things, where its exercise can do no harm; for instance, religious liberty. Crimes are rare, because the allurements of gold are precluded, for even certain vessels, too vulgar to mention, are made of gold. In short, "Utopia" makes no exception from the rest of pet theories in lavishing a golden hue over everything— of which gilding also the thought of an "European republic" partakes. *(margin: "Utopia" of Thom. Morus.)*

Nobody will deny that this idea of an "European Republic" had already taken rise in the vision of Sully. Of course, it was but an idea, contrived, perhaps, to serve as a catapult against Spanish-Austrian schemes. At any rate, Ravaillac's dagger and a sudden thrust into the heart of Henry IV put an end to the whole matter. *(margin: "Republic of Europe", a visionary project of Sully. but sincerely thought of by William II, of Orange. § 116, 182.)*

Notwithstanding such encrossings of plans, unthought of in any Utopia, the thought of humanism continues in its purposive activity. The work of bringing all ranks down to a common level created the polity of equal rights in 1776 and 1789. *(margin: Onesided humanism promulgates "human rights". A. D. 1776.)*

It was during the prevalence of an abstract idea about human rights without mention of equivalent practical duties, that the foundations were laid for the Manchestrian school of free competition, in which a very onesided conception of humanity substantiated itself, for those doctrines to which socialism in its latest form is directly reducible. Bent on the leveling of social standings, France had dispersed the cliques and rings of the aristocracy, and England now broke up the guilds, once instituted for the protection of handicraft. The ground seemed to be leveled upon which society was to be reconstructed. *(margin: but slight common duties. A. D. 1789. Manchester sociology. abolishes guilds originates the steeplechase of industrial competition. Leveling social ranks.)*

The problem of organised labor began to engage the minds of the social builders at the same time that Ramsey organised Free-masonry. Reorganisation of society and of labor became one of the chief issues of the first revolution. It is thrilling to contemplate with what zeal Fourier applied himself to find methods and means for perfecting the welfare of the people by harmonising human passions with legitimate desires.

Every noon, precisely at 12 o'clock, the poor merchant goes home and waits for that capitalist who is to advance to him the million with which to erect the first phalang-stere, that is, the first communistic lodging-house for his ouvriers. Thus he expects him daily, but waits in vain for years—the rich patriot does not show up. Notwithstanding the disappointments the Fouriers addicted themselves to dreams of organising labor the world over; and this arrangement is firmly believed to render life happy for all in times to come. Social malformations, so it is syllogised, reflect the malformations of public life in general; consequently the whole system needs a radical transformation upon an entirely new basis. The contentment implied in a new world-consciousness will extend its blessing even to the animal, yea, to the inorganic world—as tho the brine of the ocean could be changed into lemonade. The wealthy patriot never came forth to assist in the work of reconstruction, but the idea stubbornly clung to its infatuated dupes, and socialism without the least reluctancy assumed its position among the sciences, and conquered seats of parliaments in growing numbers.

Thus socialism has become the science of that "equality, which is to be realised by state-governments upon the basis of the sovereignty of labor and the equal distribution of its products." This production is to be protected against the extortions of capital and of its taking advantage of its dependants, hence the necessity of trades unions. The catch-word "organised labor" was given out in the title of Louis Blanc's work wherein he denounces competition as a system of annihilating the rights of the common people and of the consuming public, of society in general. He succeeded in elucidating and popularising the demand that the socialistic state by its computation of interests must repress the competition of capital.

It was easier, however, for Louis Blanc to formulate the demand, than to experiment with his national workshops in the Palais Luxembourg.

On the whole we adopt the truism of Pierre Leroux: "While the German renders the abstractions of the mind a basis for cultural development, the Frenchman puts the whole man at stake. Thus the one arrives at logic, the other at sociology".

This sociology immediately sets out with atomising society. Adam Smith in his "Wealth of Nations" was certain in his mind, as to the admirable simplicity with which the interests of all would harmoniously adjust themselves, if only every individual were completely left to himself in the pursuit of his private happiness by way of emancipation and freedom to go where he pleased. A pity that of this anticipation the opposite immediately became apparent. Nevertheless, since every evolution and revolution stands or falls with the question whether or not social improvement is positively advanced thereby, it behooves humanity to take up the social problem, which means no more than to face the oldest and, at the same time, the latest problem of the world's history.

§ 187. This leads us to the observation of our own age.

The solution of the social problem pends on settling three questions, as L. Stein puts them: First comes the inquiry as to what society is, what its opposite, and its movement, that is: what is the constructive principle of social life. The true answer must be found, as to the form which society, as in reality it presents itself, is to assume, and wherein its progress consists; that is, how did society issue from history? Finally, what is the goal towards which society is to advance; how is the task of society to be accomplished? These propositions show, that the great problem of humanity is concentrating upon us in full orb, and that it can be solved only by the correct definition and adequate application of humanism in its dual aspect.

It is obvious that society as composed at present is in peril of being crushed by capital. Whence did this power derive its enormity? In keeping with the transmarine activity, developed by the nations concerned, labor had multiplied. From the prerequisites and the acquirements of this activity resulted, in the first place, the new policy of the cabinets and confederations of independent industrial states. Next in order there sprang up an acknowlegment of mutual interests with their contracting forces. By national treaties the forces of movable capital, in its enjoyment of security, for instance, were set free for competition and combination. Thus we find the power of money putting its stamp upon our age.

The phenomenon is not new. Our social condition pretty much resembles that of International treaties. Rome under the triumvirates, in the accumulation of wealth, at least, and with respect to cheap labor which destroys the middle class. That ominous hoarding of Capital movable, secure. wealth detrimental to the less wealthy, to say nothing of the unmitigated oppression of the poor, reappears everywhere in the national economy of the present time.

If, for instance, one of the ten rich dukes, or some one of the few other holders of England's tenures, is engaged in "rational farming", and comes to the conclusion that raising Present condition of the civilised world similar to that of Rome previous to its decline; large land possession left to hired hands with cheap wages. wool will pay better than raising grain, he will foreclose the leases of his tenants—whose ancestors tilled the ground as tenants of the ancestors of the lords of today—he will deprive droves of people of their homes, and will stock his lands with herds of sheep instead. Or if a German Jewish baron finds that investment in real estate is more secure and pays more interest, he will take advantage of financial embarrassments, and buy up all the small farms, upon which the hard-working and very frugal peasants can scarcely eke out a living, since land had been repeatedly subdivided, and since the competition of transmarine countries had spoiled the market for home-produce. The manager of the new land-complex, the "Herr England's large land tenures. Guts-Inspector", with a few hired journeymen and a few machines will then realise larger profits for the land-proprietor in the city, than could be expected from Northern Pacific stocks or Russian state-bonds.

These are no longer probabilities but facts resulting from the tendency of capital Farming on a small scale insufficient to support land-owners. to accumulate in the hands of a few privileged family coteries. It is true, capital stimulates industry and agriculture to some extent; but it pushes the middle-man to the wall, crowds him out of a settled existence, and crushes him down into the shiftless mass of the proletarians.

The same conditions enable capital to monopolise industry by setting up machines, for Manufacturing on a small scale detriment to new means of production in the hands of capitalists. the technical improvement of which the ingenious inventor was paid a comparatively paltry sum; whilst the dignified artisan of former times, the manufacturer on a small scale, with his couple of "Gesellen" and apprentices at his board and under his roof and discipline, becomes now a foreman, at best, or works by the piece, as long as the factory receives orders or as long as "the union" allows him to work and earn his bread from hand to mouth.

Since steam and electricity have become the motors of traffic and factory, we can Monopolies. speak of manufacture, that is, of handicraft, only in a very limited sense. The social partition lines of caste-like ranks are fortunately wiped away; but widening clefts are opened between the two very antagonistic classes. Movable, fidgety and cautious capital has become the chief factor in cultural movements. It enters into Capital's market-stand is the wide world. national relations and controls even international negotiations. It assumes the character of the great cosmopolitan—making the world its market-stand, and neglecting the true state of affairs at home, which should receive his undivided attention.

Of one circumstance, the "upper class," which is said to be ignorant of "how Class-antagonism. the other half lives," seems still to be ill-advised, namely: that the working people are making fast strides in the improvement of their intelligence. Labor follows suit in the social transformation, and here is where the parallel with Pompey's time will hold good no longer. The "fourth estate," organised labor in its opposition against the monopolising power of capital, has learned from its opponent Laborers' intelligence improved. how to combine and how to show distemper, and it has become selfish, too, in a method, as a class—as a majority. The impoverished class claims the right to work "Fourth estate." for a living, a living off the profits of labor's production, not from alms. These demands on the part of the "disinherited" are justifiable. Moreover, they learned from the higher class to disregard national boundary lines and patriotism and become international.

The "International" is actually but the reverse side and consequence of commercial and Labor learned from capital to combine financial combines. It is a specific growth of western Europe, and during the latter half of our century has been pressing, like an incubus, upon the European form of civilisation wherever this has spread its industrial establishments over the globe.

When France in its peculiar way entered its protest in the form of a just retri- and to discard patriotism for the "International federation of labor." bution to the debauchery carried on in high life, Germany and the United States could not be diverted from the normal method of working out their tasks. Both countries fought for their national existence, for those ideal liberties which the Ger- German "republic of letters". man "Republic of letters" had cultivated under the auspices of Klopstock, Herder, Fichte, Schleiermacher, Claudius, Perthes, Stein and their circles of staunch Christian and patriotic friends in north-western Germany. Industrial progress lingered behind until the last quarter of our century; for Germany had no chance to recover

German enterprise could
not revive before the
United States were
fully established in their
independence:

earlier from the ravages of the Thirty Years War: especially since the progress of development had been thwarted by the great stagnation of its traffic which had set in with the exclusion of Germany from the high seas in the period of the renaissance. **German enterprise could revive only after the United States had fully established their independence.** This made it possible for Germany to reenter transmarine relations, and to intermediate some wholesale exports. Moreover, the exclusion of the catholic in-

not before catholic
interference from the
Austrian side was
refuted and not before
the great unpleasantness
with France was
settled.

terference from the Austrian side, the consolidation of the North-German union, and the great unpleasantness with France had to be settled, before Germany could be rehabilitated, so as to claim recognition and its due share of the active and direct participation in the world's transactions.

Germany's growing
importance of
mercantile engagement
Sir Bartle Frere.

Sir Bartle Frere alone was aware of the increasing importance of Germany's mercantile circumspection in foreign ports. He warned the Londoners not to despise this modest rival, when he prognosticated that sudden advance which soon after vindicated the prediction and surprised the world.

Treaties of the United
States and of Prussia
with China and Japan.

Along with these outward signs of advance those changes occurred which were pointed out as partial causes for demanding the recognition of the "fourth estate," and the adjustment of matters concerning it. We mean the new part which Germany came to take in the transmarine relations. Full freedom of oceanic traffic was secured only after the United States and Prussia had concluded their treaties with China and Japan. And only now the power of capital had its free sweep and started upon its career, whereby the laborers in turn were provoked also to consolidate their interests, and to demand a settlement in full.

Capital sets out upon
its career of competition.
Michael Chevalier.

As yet the great war of free competition has scarcely begun. But already Michael Chevalier's apprehensions are becoming true, that" the small manufacturer is devoured by monopolies"; and we must now add, by those combinations called trusts, which explicitly make it their business to annihilate competitors by evading personal conscientiousness, to usurp the management of national treasuries, nunc pro tunc. A

Dodging personal
conscientiousness.

Trusts.

Selfsalvation expected
from the reorganisation
of the state.;

peculiar combat is preparing, indeed, along the whole line of industrial activity, international traffic and national finance. The illusion of winning it by dishonest strategy or by main force will be fatal to both combatant parties.

§ 188. But how may matters be compromised upon the basis of a peaceable adjustment, without jeopardising civilisation? How is the reckless freedom of competition to be checked or controlled? There is but one way to render the suicidal steeple-chase of industrial adventure innoxious, say Marx, Lasalle, Engel, and some others of their kin.

Part of the Germans'
again at theorising.

The state must be the employer; from one central directory the whole fabric of production is to be conducted. The clearances are to be distributed, according to a sliding scale of proportion, among all workers, being, as employes of the state, equal in rank. Marx & Co. provides that they shall not be paid their portion of the proceeds in coin, lest another formation of capitalism and competition should ensue from such a wage-system. To prevent this, the apportionment of the profits is to be equalised through a system of vouchers and orders by means of which every want may be gratified.

Jews in socialism:
Marx, Engel, Lasalle,
Singer.

Fallacies on account of
truths ignored.

Thus the ideal course of humanism is again switched off to run to the brink of the abyss. For that great mechanism of the socialistic state works like a machine set up for the purpose of crushing all ideals of humanity, which can prosper only under conditions of personal liberty. The truth that equality and fraternity can result from free and benign inclinations alone, and are to be practiced from motives of general love toward fellowmen, is totally ignored. Genuine fraternity, springing from the recognition of the divine image in every man, is explicitly disavowed in the socialistic state; freedom is denied point blank. But the bottom fact, the empirical truth is, that a machinery of selfsalvation from common sinfulness cannot be invented.

Vicissitudes of the
socialistic state of the
future.

If socialism should ever get an opportunity to be at the helm and control a state, its first job would have to be the creation of the requisite personages, that is, to overhaul the human components of the state so as to fit them for the new world. The educational institutions of the new state must certainly surpass anything undertaken so far in the line of instruction. For it is promised that with the disparity between rich and poor, also that between intelligent and stupid will disappear. It is conceded that, of course, it will take the training of a few generations, but that afterwards accommodation and hereditary law will accomplish the rest. Thus a herd of idiots would be raised, to which such a kind of development would be satisfactory, which takes bestiality as the standard of comparison. After that stage has been obtained, progress may consist in going a little further down the incline, to where the animal state of existence may be conceived as the most natural, and training would persist in making away with every trace of liberty and dignity, until nature were completely established in the rights which these "children of nature" claimed for her.

Now, since for the sake of argument it was conceded that the animal world evolved from a single typical protoplasm, it would follow in the practical wisdom of socialism, that the perfection of evolution would not have been reached, unless humanity was folded together again into the simple mouer of the first cell. That is, humanity would return to the old oriental doctrine of all-one-ness with its absorption of individual life. What Buddhism had been striving at, what Spinozism and Hegelianism syllogised, the people of the Occident would then have practically attained—as an opinion. Following out the high sounding premises, we arrive at the freezing-point of the misconception of man and his destiny.

The state built upon such premises cannot but fail, if such fundamental errors are adhered to, as for instance, that man's object in earthly life consists chiefly in the gratification of natural cravings, of sensual appetites. We do not impugn socialism with these false principles. For it is plainly stated that the collective and systematic production of the necessities and some commodities of life is arranged simply for this end: namely, to assign every equitable atom of the state to its place, and to let it have all the usufructuary enjoyment obtainable in the prescribed limits of production. But whilst the individual is, by this method, forced from his natural and organic relations of family and preferable affinities, and whilst the toiler is pressed into the mechanism of cooperation as a mere thing with no purpose in himself—the question whether this great machine or factory in which the state, or whether the great army into which humanity, is to be transformed, could possibly fulfil its promises, is simply dodged, or ignorance is pleaded, and absence of any aim on the scope of future formations is candidly admitted.

A socialistic state adequate to present ideas could be possible under such conditions only: "That one's occupation would agree with the capabilities and inclinations of the agent; that as a rule the management of the mechanism would be just and reliable, and that the productiveness and the profits would, on the whole, be satisfactory to everybody." Taken for granted that the socialistic state could meet all these requirements, then its success would prove nothing more than that its constituent members, that humanity had permitted itself to be rendered as stupid and impotent as a herd of dumb animals.

The humanity whose interest that state pretended to care for would exist no more.

The blame for such a degradation, the possibility of which is undeniable, would rest with those who allow the Germanic-Christian civilisation to decline. This civilisation considers the right of possessing property as connected with special duties appreciating property as a loan granted on conditions; as a fief which the possessor, holds in tenure from the Sovereign Lord; as the relative good—made good by its being related to the Supreme Giver through its proper use. The grave responsibility of a general overthrow would rest therefore with the possessing classes; and forced dispossession would be their punishment.

The people of wealth were under obligations first; it accrues to their misfortune that they forgot their duties. They ought to have been intelligent enough not to help in the disintegration of the social and economical institutions by means of a thoughtless, heartless, unprincipled and trifling class-legislation, according to a polity of go-as-you-please expediency. They should not have set an example of withdrawing from the influence of those civilising factors embodied in the Church, wherever she is true to the first principles of ethics.

As it is, that the privileged class to a great extent assumes the airs of aristocratic indifference, it practically denies what Christianity enjoins upon humanity, denies that the ideal good designed for every member of the human family alike has been given into the care of the church, which, by virtue of her first principle of reconciliation, is bound to discountenance every class-distinction and club-churchliness. As it is, the ruling class, altho unsuccessful in making the entire Church subservient to class-interests, has nevertheless brought the opprobrium upon her that she did not fulfil her "mission" among the "lower" classes. By transforming "their" church to a literary club-house and annexing to it a "mission-chapel" in a forsaken region of the city; or into an apparatus of "money-making" for church-purposes—and a little for humanitarian benevolence besides—a would-be aristocracy has done everything to estrange the "masses" from her missions; and the mass-meetings for evangelising the fashionable churches and the masses at the same time, cannot repair the division of the protestant denominations into social clubs. As long as the Church is separated from the world on lines of money-prestige, so long will the poor suspect "missions" as traps set for their subjection.

According to all indications a rearrangement of political economy in line with the altered conditions of industry and commerce is inevitable, is to be expected; the necessity of adjusting the disrupted concept of humanism is, therefore, a matter of historical sequel; and no other, no external contrivance at such adjustment can have the desired effect upon social reform.

Roman jurisprudence established the equality of every person before the law; the Roman Church to a certain degree maintained the equality of all sinners before the gospel. Practically, however, this equality of all men as to human rights was detained in the stage of mere possibility. That it may be realised will be the task of the social-political state; i. e. of that state which is permeated with the impulse that, paramount to all other obligations, the impartial care for the welfare of all its inhabitants must be the sole motive in all its functions.

The state based on "legitimacy" can afford to manage legislative and executive rule in accord with the straight lines of rank, to which it adapts its methods of public order, of taxation, and of military protection. This juridical state regards the subjects as existing for the sake of the nobility and its existence for the sake of the state; hence the state consists of well defined parts which submit to the rule of a fixed legalism for the sake of general security as the condition of peace and prosperity. Adaptation of the government to the demands of the time and to the interests of the "subject" has no place in this state.

In the social-political state the constituent persons group themselves into figures according to affiliating principles which they severally represent, and thereby render the government constitutional. The state now exists for the sake of the people and establishes a government of, for, and by the people. The groups and factions, representing diverse interests, must of necessity balance each other for the sake of the common welfare; and from all this results the differentiation of representative government into executive departments presided over by responsible men of merit, into upper and lower houses, etc.; and into a system of administrative agencies. Political science everywhere tends to that form of government; but its probation and universal introduction depends upon the repristination of the old Germanic and Christian maxim, that there exists no personal prerogative which is not connected with specific duties—that to rule means to serve. Experience teaches that even governments based upon direct election by majorities can remain satisfactory only under this condition. But whenever personal rights are accentuated at the expense of social duties; when the objectivity of law and duty is questioned by the arbitrariness of subjectivism, then human society is alternately threatened by anarchy and despotism; and the chances for the political advance of humanity on the line of true socialism diminish under retrogressive movements.

Our concern will be to watch the movement of the thought of humanism and to beware against its mutilations.

Pantheistic speculation—starting from above, and assigning a high position to man, as in German philosophy—cannot be accused of lacking ideality. Neither do the French social theories deserve such blame, inasmuch as the propositions of St. Simon, of Fourier and the "Travels to Icaria" by Cabet, are touchingly sentimental and idealistic.

It was materialism which dragged down these ideals from their high pedestals. Materialism as the reverse side of pantheistic philosophy, armed with its innumerable "irrefragable results of exact science", fell upon the Occident and took it by surprise. Man's world-consciousness completely severed from God-consciousness had been onesidedly cultivated: the ego in its loneliness had been taken under wrong treatment. Instead of its ego, which previously had been conceived as being invested with freedom, at least, and with the capability of reasoning, nothing was left after the evaporating process, but geological matter and motion with human nature as its product and its prey.

To materialism man is no longer a person standing in relation to God; the light of the thought divine is extinguished; the work of the thinking mind is mere phosphorescence of brain-shaped matter, closed up in its chest of universal darkness, i. e., nescience. The issues of this discovery of "the dynamic sociology", as propounded by Ward, would lead to an European chaos, America included.

In accord with the nature of things the oppressive atmosphere must develop tempests in the lower regions of humanity. The signs of the gathering hurricanes are now trifled with in the higher regions, as tho they were to be enjoyed as the fresh morning zephyrs of a new æra, in which finally man will delight in his sovereign self-sufficiency; whilst we have attended the idea of humanism up to its sublime heights, and on coming back find it, to our dismay, in its deep descent and radical profligacy, to a large extent.

CH. X.   THE ARYANS OF EASTERN EUROPE.   GREEK CATHOLICISM IN ITS ADAPTNESS TO PROCURE AN ASIATIC RENAISSANCE.

§ 189.   At last we now take the whole compass of the Christian nations of the Occident into one comprehensive view, under the aspect of being the bearers of the cardinal thought. *Prospectus.*

Never before was the horizon so widely extended; and these nations, altho not ruling the earth on the strength of political organisation, yet dominate over the world by the sway of their influence. Alongside and between the highways of communication, by means of which European culture took control of human development, there lie as yet the heaps of loose debris in the African negro states, and the solid mass of Islam and Buddhism. A panorama of ethnological history spreads out before our vision, such as man could never have imagined. The Christian nations have stepped out of their own narrow limits upon the breadth of the earth. At first they went out from their domiciles to go upon the market-place, as it were; and now they venture out to go to church with those whom they teach. By newly invented means of communication the mind has shortened the distances of space and time to such a degree, that only now a common activity, that is, historical life in a universal manner is rendered possible. The nations abandon their former exclusiveness; they literally flow together to converse with each other, and become conscious of the necessity to establish relations of reciprocal interaction. By the solidarity of interests humanity is induced to take modes of organic connection into consideration. Wherever one nation is set in commotion, the oscillations immediately spread through all of them. The whole earth, and even the air surrounding it, is made the theatre of history, so that only now universality can be spoken of as its chief attribute. All parts of the globe have been brought into comparatively close contact with each other, whereby all of its inhabitants are brought under the focus almost of one common biography. Gradually the purposes become perceptible, for which the great bulk of humanity has remained at rest during the past. We begin to see the purpose for which now the ethical task of delivering confined, and of redeeming arrested life by divine-human cooperation is unfolded; we learn intelligently to read the program of the coming æon. *Nominal Christian nations ruling the world, spreading culture.* *Ethnical debris of Africa.* *Solid masses of Islam and Buddhism.* *Only now universal history becomes possible.* *Purpose of the present unfolding of the ethical task to redeem arrested ethnical life.*

In order to notice how one part of our race after another is drawn into the common engagement, we must begin with a view of the Slavonic nations, which so far have attracted less attention than all the other Aryans. *Program of the new æra:* *Age of missions.*

The Romanic and Germanic nations also must pass in review once more so as to arrive at a full understanding of the work assigned to the Aryans, now as ever in the lead of historical development. At this time they will be considered under that aspect of the thought of humanity, which history in general, not merely in the Reformation and its counteractions has presented to us. Adhering to this cardinal thought we are compelled to follow the historic movements in the direction in which we meet again with the nations of the first circle. We thus return to the widest periphery to which the thought of humanism as proceding from the central source now radiates. *Nations upon the wide periphery of the first circle*

Upon the plains between the Black Sea and the White Sea, between the Bug and the Ural, in the low-lands of eastern Europe the Slavonic people had struck their camps. They have assimilated German, Finnish, and Tatar elements; they have allowed Turks and Mongolians to intermix with them. In the great steppes of Russia an ethnical mass is spread out which, altho nominally under the dome of Greek Catholicism, remains in a declining attitude toward western civilisation, if not against humanism in general. Those of the Slavs who are neighbors to the Germans, the Poles and the Bohemians, seem to have become conscious of the fact, that the individual person ought to be independent. It was on account of the appropriation of this alien element, that the social formations of Bohemia and Polonia have been called "caricatures of the Germanic principles," and that the Polish ship of state foundered. The Slavonic form of consciousness was in itself poorly qualified for emancipation. Gradually consolidating under the Russian scepter the Slavs relinquished selfhood, satisfied with having it represented by the Czar alone. *Slavonic peoples.* *under Greek catholicism.* *Bohemians tinctured with Germanic principles.* *Selfhood relinquished to the czar.*

It is difficult to define the peculiarity of the Russian character.

In their former home, the south-eastern régions of the empire, the Russians permitted themselves to be mixed with foreign ingredients. It is just there, says Nadeshdin, from whence "much of the Asiatic nature within the Russian is to be discriminated, which points to Altaic, rather than Caucasian origin". In addition there is to be considered the influence of Greek-Byzantine civilisation predominant at different periods; and above all the Latin-Polish as well as the German-Waroegian influences holding sway during the time when Russian culture was in its incipiency.

More satisfactory ethnic analysis than Nadeshdin's discrimination is yet to be made. Anutshin proposes to carry on the investigation of Russian characteristics under the aspect of natural selection and cross-breeding. But in order to understand the original character of Russia's nationality pure and simple we need not wait for an answer from analysis. It appears to us as the veritable task of Russia rather to accomplish an amalgamation than to reduce the composition to its radicals.

There are the ethnical types of the northern coast-regions, and of the bottom lands of the Volga: the Cossacks on the banks of the Don and on the slopes of the Ural. There are those Siberian tribes among whom prehistoric Shamanism lies bare upon the surface and may be studied to this day. And then the remnants of the Tsheremissians and Wotjakkians, etc.—all forming the nation which since recent times is known as that of all the Russians.

Russia, as the youngest member of the states organism of Europe, has brought these semi-barbarian and partly savage people under a single rule. We have found it a principle of history, to unify and balance peoples in whose behalf it is ever tending to gather them around an ideal center of gravity and attraction. A higher hand has prearranged and ordained these natural means to guide human affairs in an ethical way to their final purpose, the education of the children of men. To this intention is to be reduced the natural tendency of history towards universal hierarchies and world-monarchies, which furnish the objective rules and disciplinary factors for educating the masses. These formations, once existing, are made to serve, with their compulsory forces, the purpose of setting free subjective consciousness, so as to awaken it for refusing to bear this external compulsion any longer. Thus we may understand the purposes which Providence seems to have designed for the Russian state in these modern times.

Russia is made to be a task-master, and the Slavs are best adapted to constitute the apparatus through which Russia is to prepare the East for civilisation.

The national consciousness of the Russians dates its origin from the times of Wladimir the Great. What Arthur of the Round Table is to the Romanised Celts, what the Burgundian court and the heroes of the Amelungen and Nibelungen are to the Germans, St. Wladimir is to the Russians. At Kiev he holds court with song and in glory. The nobles of every Slavonic country ride thither to pay homage to their prince. Messengers sent to Constantinople return and report of the splendor of the Byzantine manner of worship. The mighty prince conquers the Chersonesus, demanding and receiving Anna of Byzantium for his consort, and allows himself by her to be converted to Christianity. Greek and Bulgarian priests are invited and arrive in great numbers.

Thus Russia is in fact made heir of Eastern Rome by virtue of her ecclesiastical inheritance. The consideration of the other, the political bequeathment, must be postponed until we have become acquainted with the contents of the religious testament, which in every case molds the character of an age—and of a nation permanently, if that influence is exerted upon it during its infancy.

§ 190. Once the people constituting the nucleus of the Russian nation had been commanded in droves to go down into the water of the Dniepr for baptism. Henceforth the Greek Church served as the backbone of "holy Russia" and is responsible for the condition in which today we find this uncouth giant of an empire.

The popes of that church perpetuate the most abject methods of religious performance, and the most despicable state of national existence is the result. The poor are considered to live for no other purpose than to keep up the practice of alms-giving; nobody thinks of educating them to selfrespect, or to become selfsupporting. They are not even spoken to as creatures possessing any claim to human treatment, whilst on the other hand the churches and the monastic institutions grow to enormous proportions. Agents peddling pictures of saints throughout the whole territory, from Novgorod to Missolonghi, clear between two hundred and a thousand per cent of profits. The cloisters are immensely rich, tho Peter the Great permitted them to possess no more than one inkstand, to be chained to the wall of the refectory. Perhaps they are allowed two by this time, tho the one would perfectly suffice their scholarly ambition.

The church is the avowed police-officer and taxgatherer of the state. Pobedonoszew was under the lately deceased emperor what Fouqué was to Napoleon—chief of the governmental force of detectives. It was altogether in keeping with Russian views and customs that once a colonel of the cavalry, Count Protassow, was appointed president of the "holy synod" of the czar. That state-church is nothing more nor less than a department of the administration, to the resort of which the collection of taxes belongs as its chief civil duty. The pope, low and raw, tho officiating in a church filled with costly shrines, pictures, incense and candles, with a wealth of jewels, relics, and old liturgies, is treated with disdain as soon as he steps out of his church. And yet this stupid priestcraft wields influence enough to keep the people in stolid devoutness and dumbfounded superstition. The Russian populace is as well drilled in kissing holy images as it is skilled in deception, theft and debauchery a moment after. And yet that people is highly endowed with excellent talents.

In the wide compass of this vast empire millions are therefore absolutely void of any trace of civilisation. The shamanistic Kirgees have their own way unmolested, while Lutheran pastors around the Baltic are put behind prison bars. The Tscherimissians worship today as they did five thousand years ago, with slaying a colt in the woods—with the difference only that now they do it in honor of the "Mother of God." Shamanism of the Kirgees unmolested; Lutheran ministers imprisoned.

In conformity with ecclesiasticism were fashioned the forms of government and life in general. Contemporaneously with Louis XIV Peter dared to say, I am the state —except that the absolutism of the French state with its estates of nobility and clergy was of historic growth, whilst in Russia the creation of rank was prompted by the caprices of a semi-Asiatic court, and the selection of persons to be elevated was made at random. The imperial favorites formed an unmanly, servile, and avaricious bureaucracy, which cringed before its superiors and oppressed the subjects who brought no bribes. The intelligence requisite for high positions was imparted into Russian life by foreigners;but this did not alleviate the obnoxiousness of the system. Peter the Great perfected the absolutism copied from Louis XIV. Raw material of Russian nobility.

Descriptive of the tyranny of the administration is the surveillance of pass-ports. They are not only a police-measure but also utilised in the collection of taxes. Taxation does not directly press upon the individual subject, because the community is held responsible for his taxes and must remit his apportionment to the revenue-department. The passport is the means by which the community may take hold of the tax-payer as a bail would of his principal. If he abscond, the community has to pay his assessment; it is the tax-payer and must make up the deficiency. "This method of raising the imperial revenue continues to this day" says von Falck. Probably those entrusted with collecting the communal tribute are, in cases of delinquency, no longer sent to Siberia minus their noses. It is probable, too, that the descendants of the old Tatar chiefs—privileged as a sort of nobility—and that the hierarchy, the priests of Lamaism and of Islam, and that the other holders of state offices are no longer entirely exempt from taxation, as they were up to recent times. But in whatever respect the ukases of the czar may have been affected by more humane meditations, even to the extent of abolishing serfdom, Russian absolutism has not abandoned any of its principles, and the oppression under which the starving peasants groan does not seem to become ameliorated, their loyalty notwithstanding. The extreme indigence of the Slavonian peasantry is of much earlier date than the famines of recent years may indicate. Measures were said to have been taken in order to meet the general destitution. But the effects are scarcely perceptible. In response to the shiploads of bread-stuffs, donated by the citizens of the United States, Russia put a higher tariff on grain imported from America. Attempts on the part of the government to introduce home-rule or selfgovernment to a certain extent have sadly failed. Passport system to serve purposes of revenue-collection and police-surveillance. Von Falck. Effects of gradual reforms. Abolition of serfdom. Enfranchised peasantry in starving condition.

In the regions of the Danube delta there are hundreds of thousands of enfranchised peasants loafing around, looking for work in vain. In an unspeakably miserable condition they return home to Great-Russia. On the lower Volga thousands crawl in and out of their dug-outs or reed-huts, or work for starvation wages on the shores of the Caspian Sea. Nevertheless, the most orthodox heir of Byzantium looks upon the "western corruption" with an amazing selfsufficiency. Hergenroether describes that supercilious Byzantine spirit which acts spitefully toward everything it cannot vanquish or which does not prostrate itself before the "Queen of the world". The work of the occidental church—under such an extravagant amount of freedom, as seen with the eye of New-Rome—seemed an impertinent innovation. With the same eye does the heir of New-Rome look upon western Europe today as upon apostates from his religion. For the secret of Russia's cohesion consists in nothing less, than this haughty attitude of superior orthodoxy. Russia's amazing superciliousness as to "Western corruption". Hergenroether. Occidental modifications of religious life considered as a sacrilegious innovation and apostacy.

Aksakow and Katkow asserted that Russia, to the detriment of completing her civilisation, had contracted from the West only a superficial coat of politeness and conventionalism. Every measure was therefore applied to wipe off that surcharge of foreign culture. Those Russian patriots may not have been much out of the way in their judgment. The only question is, what kind of culture could be brought forth without western incitements. The question is, in other words, what is the nature of the Russian thus covered with a mere coat of polish? Most likely, after it is rubbed off, the features of old Byzantium will reappear. Foreign culture rejected by patriots like Katkow.

From Byzantium Russia inherited all her tastes, even in regard to architecture. The Greek cross was taken for the groundplan, its outlines being marked by cupaloes. But behold how the original pattern was spoiled through the Sarmatian peculiarities, that is by retaining Byzantine vanity and pomp, minus its remnants of the Greek antique, and adding Asiatic barbarism and eccentricity instead.

The low and gloomy interior of the church edifices is not cheered with mosaic work or change of lines. Outside they appear as of despondent mind under the weight of disproportioned cupoloes, the inflated masses of which look like subverted balloons. Kugler compares them to "bundles of gigantic mushrooms". This style of architecture prevails in Moldavia, in Serbia, in Archangel—everywhere.

Just as the artistic pattern-book of Mt. Athos once for ever had to fix the forms under which the saints were to be represented, so the czar now prescribes to Russia the rules of art. Nothing is more emblematic of the stiff monotony and depressed mood of Russia than this ecclesiastical uniform thus stamped even upon the scenery of the land. Fioravanti was compelled to imitate the cathedral of Wladimir with its five onion-shaped steeples when he built the Kremlin. Hence it cannot be wondered at that Asiatic features prevail also in the designs of private buildings. Up to date we discern in the dwelling of the Bojar "the remnants of very ancient and traditionary habits symbolised, of habits which are traceable to the interior of Asia," as Von Reber avers.

In the shape given to environments, the mind is reflected as regards ethics as well as æsthetics.

It is worthy of recognition, that Russia has brought forth minds productive in all branches of science and literature; on the whole, however, they have lacked originality and depended on the impulses received from the West. It cannot be denied, that the state does much in furtherance of civilisation. The Arabian, Persian, and Turkish languages have been taught in all the state-universities. In Kasan and Crakow they have chairs for the languages of Tibet, Mongolia, and China. For many years past the government has granted stipends to students who devote themselves exclusively to Asiatic studies. Kasan is the book-emporium of the East, where all the Islam literature is printed which the publishers send to the Crimea, to Asia-Minor, and Turkestan.

§ 191. The endeavor to master Asiatic languages leads us to consider the other, the political part of the Byzantine inheritance. The intermediation between Orient and Occident, to which Constantinople owed its importance, was transferred to Russia, and made this empire one of the prominent factors in the history of the future. This task of intermediating devolved upon Russia when Constantinople and Trapezunt fell, and renders Russia the apparent continuation of New Rome in the East, and the counterpart to New Rome in the West. From the manner in which Russia has adhered to Byzantine conservatism and ecclesiasticism, it is to be inferred that she will even more tenaciously keep in mind the purport of her political legacy.

In Trapezunt stood the golden palace of the great Comnenians, with its view, the beautiful panorama of the Black Sea and its shores, among citadels and flower-gardens. Incomparable splendor garnished the state-halls of this summer residence, and the spacious libraries, described by Bessarion, were well stocked with rare manuscripts. Olive-groves, and orange orchards, and expansive vineyards surrounded the castle, rendering it an object fit for fairy-tales. In the bazars of the city below were piled up the goods of Asia: the gold-brocades of Bagdad, silks from China and Farther-India, honey from Migrelia, grain from Tauris. In exchange the ships of the Genoese brought broadcloth from Italy and Flanders, and steel ware from Germany. The wealth of the emperors exceeded all calculations. A sample of it can be seen today in the museum of Cincinnati, a wine bowl of exquisite workmanship, made of solid silver, weighing about a ton, and holding, I judge, at least thirty gallons. The fairy-tale of Trapezunt is not forgotten by the czars; and what once was an expedition from Sebastopol over to "Tarabison" is little more today than a pleasure trip of short duration.

The imagery of that ride leads over to Asia and to the observation of the political conjunctions in the crisis of "the eastern problem" now approaching. This "Oriental Question" is before the world not only since recent years. It concerns the great and portentous inheritance of which, according to the traditional polity of old, Russia feels now in duty bound to take possession.

Nine crowns, all kept in religious esteem, did history in its course bestow upon the head of the czar, and add to the jewelry-chamber of the empire. Above all glitters the crown which the sainted Basilius, the Byzantine emperor, presented to Wladimir, his son-in-law. Upon that first and most sacred crown followed those of Kasan, Astrachan, Siberia, Polonia, Tauris, etc., and finally that of Malta; all denoting the mode and direction in which that imperial polity is to proceed.

It was necessary to refer to Russia's genesis and present auspices in order to illustrate by a few strokes the significance of that country in the initial process of extending European culture into Asia. Russia's charge in the cultural movement of modern history may be compared to a break-water constructed to protect our cardinal thought, lest the force of the humanistic tide returning to the primitive home of the Aryans might through precipitation jeopardise the desirable result. The course of free thought towards the East needs to be slackened until the Asiatics gradually ripen to receive the idea of freedom without causing sudden explosions of the heavy and solid destructive masses. In the upheavals of the nihilistic turbulencies we have witnessed already, how dangérous advanced thought becomes to people unqualified as yet for applying it in the proper exercise of freedom. Deliverance from conditions which have arrested the progress of civilisation for thousands of years can only proceed cautiously and steadily. To the western Europeans it may seem as if Russia were absolutely retrogressive, when for good reasons, it simply shuts itself against a sudden inflation of alien elements. The world may be assured that Russia, notwithstanding the mixture of Asiatic-European world-consciousness, is wide awake, and not at all tardy in improving upon its present position. Russia is putting herself into condition to fill the appointment assigned to her in the near future. The latest movement by Russia of founding that gigantic banking system which virtually makes her the owner of China, goes far to vindicate this prediction.

Advance of free thought towards Asia needs to slackened.

Russia not at all stagnant.

For centuries Russia has kept an eye upon the Mediterranean in order to have an exit by water and to compete with the marines of other nations. It has kept its eye upon Asia and the Pacific, until of late; so soon as it seemed to the czar that the Pan-Slavonic sympathies were strong enough to secure and cover the western flank, from Prague to the mountains of Montenegro, it commenced operations there.

Slavonic folk-lore. § 61. SCHAFFARIK. PALACKY.

The expectations as to this Pan-Slavonic rally, seem to become sorely disappointed; the southern Slavs seem not to let themselves be captivated in the interest of Russia. Since Shaffarik and Palacky brought the rich literature of Slavonic folk-lore and heroism to light again, the Slavonic nations along the Danube seem to rise to the consciousness that they ought to keep independent of Russia. Whether they are mature for detaching themselves from Panslavism, and have become able to govern themselves in spite of the Russian agitations, may be questionable as yet; so much is unquestionable that Russia, whether it will control all the Slavonians of the south or not, will enter upon its inheritance—the old Mongolian territories.

revives pan-slavonic sympathies.

Political inheritance from the Mongolian empire.

In order to obtain a cogent judgment of the Russian giant it is necessary to make a brief abstract of title as to the Mongolian dominion, in its widest extent under Dgengis Khan. If it is understood how this conqueror wielded his power, then we know what to expect before long of the Russian management of Asia.

Mongolian designs since Dgengis-Khan. § 150.

In the year A. D. 1227 Dgengis died. China, the Caliphate of Bagdad, and Russia had been subjugated by him; the reins of government were managed in Karakorum and Samarkand. In front of his victorious armies from the slopes of the Altai Mountains the mighty Khan had proclaimed his laws. They were in force from Lake Kuku-noor, upon whose frozen surface king Tangut was vanquished, to the Dniepr, where the great prince of Kiew was reduced to vassalage. Millions of warriors were sacrificed in those incessant wars, yet the Dgengis Khan was no savage, if judged by his order of translating Uigurian, Thibetan, Persian, and Arabic books into the Mongolian language. One of the Mongolian princes wrote a history of the eastern Mongolians, Russia included.

His attempt at civilisation.

It was at the very time when the papal power under Innocent III stood in its zenith, daring to put England under interdict, that the Mongolian empire was put under the spiritual power of the Dalai-Lama. Khan Batu, grandson of Dgengis, foiled in his conquest of the world upon the Wahlstatt near Liegnitz, instituted the Asiatic pope at the head of all the Buddhistic Lamas, that his monarchy might secure its perpetuity through religious prestige, through the control over Buddhism by means of this pope as his tool. This was in the year 1260 A. D., the same year in which the western pope had to flee from Rome to Viterbo before Frederick's son Manfred. Khan Batu had done what the caliph of Cordova had advised Frederick II to do. But Frederick, Barbarossa's grandson, had sense enough to see that the Occident would not submit to the idea of the spiritual and secular powers being wielded by one hand. The Christian thought of freedom, not realisable unless the two powers are kept separate, was more powerful than the greatest conquerors. But the Orient submitted. What Frederick II had declined, the Mongolian Khan accomplished: the creation of a state-church for the sake of, and subservient to, the perpetuance of the policy of conquering all countries on earth. A part of this vast empire—encompassing China, Hindostan, Persia, etc., with its seats of culture in Karakorum and Samarkand, in Agra and Delphi, where the grand-moguls built their palaces and hoarded their jewels—was the province of Russia, a unit for the first time.

When popery was in its prime, the Dalai Lama was made the backbone of the Mongolian dominion. § 150.

Batu accomplished what a caliph had advised Frederick II, to do. § 145.

Thought of Germanic—Christian freedom stronger than the greatest conquerors: realisable only under separation of political from ecclesiastical power.

Nobody can successfully deny his ancestral lineage; much less can a state. European popery had planted itself upon the traditions, pretensions, and dreams of the old Roman Cæsarism. The soil upon which it grew transmitted its nature to the plant, gave it a firm hold, and communicated to its fruits a raw, earthly taste. In fulfilment of the dream the coat of mail was donned and a daring attitude assumed.

It is obvious, that Russian Cæsarism in like manner appropriated to itself the political traditions and dreams, the claims and aims of the mediæval Mongolians. Once there had grown up a church-state on the basis of western Rome; now there rises

before our eyes a state-church on the ecclesiastical basis of East-Rome, and upon the secular basis of Mongolianism. This state-church took possession of the Byzantine inheritance long ago; it will now put forth the claims of its political testament. Russia has commenced formidable litigations, demanding and laying its hands upon

the legacy of Dgengis Khan. The process will repeat itself, that a province becomes the empire, as it was in the cases of Persia, of France, of Prussia. In keeping with Asiatic custom it will most probably repeat itself, that secular and ecclesiastical power will be united in one man. Napoleon more than harbored this idea; foiled in its execution through the expedition to Russia, he as much as prognosticated that Russia would carry it out. The czars seem to have their hands at it, and skillfully to manipulate the fulfilment of the Mongolian dream.

§ 192. To be sure, Islam has as yet some power left to thwart such designs. The modern Othman dominion may be compared to the stony deposit of a moraine, gliding down from the heights of Central-Asia to the Danube and the Adriatic gulf. Turkey furnishes an example of slower migratory movements. In this case the masses are pushing, glacier-like, from the Gobi to Eastern Europe.

This Turanian moraine is interspersed to its whole extent with miracle-working graves, and dotted with sacred centers for pilgrimages. Mecca attracts the believers from Celebes to the Niger.

From Bokhara to Stambul, the strongholds of Ishmaelite sanctimoniousness, there issues forth wild fanaticism combined with that heinous superstition which uses Koran-passages for amulets and as fetishes. We find it thus in Delhi as in Morocco. A hierarchical priesthood with its agencies of monasteries and Fakeer villages is still influential enough to fan the fanaticism of olden times into the rage of an extensive conflagration. Even in Russia proper Mohammedanism holds its own. The Emir of Bokhara keeps the muftis and mollahs within his territories as strictly as ever in obeisance to the great prophet. Instruments of torture are still in use in his religious judicatories, altho Russia indeed now and then interferes with that custom. With firm step Mohammedanism advances among the hordes of the shamanistic Kirgheese, proceeding from Kasan and Ohrenburg in the North, and from Chiwa and Buchara in the South.

At all these places the Slavs under Russian rule stand face to face with a difficult task. The Byzantine legacy imposes the duty upon the heirs, to pay home the arrearages, during the process of which Byzantium had become insolvent when the Palæologi succumbed to the crescent.

Again Semitism, now in the form of Islam, had wedged itself between the Orient and the Occident, and had split the East-Rome empire in two. Prior to this event the occidental influence reached to the boundary line of China. The two circles of West Aryan and Mongolian cultures had almost touched each other at the period, when both China and Rome enjoyed the widest extent of their empires. As

far as Trapezunt Rome's dominion was unquestioned, and from thence its merchants spread Roman superiority to the Sererians in the Tarim-basin, who on their part stood under Chinese supremacy. Just then the crescent, the "half-moon," suddenly pushed itself between the countries of the rising and the setting sun.

The western world has ever since been shut off from the Orient as by an iron bar. Islam thus assisted materially in the consolidation of the Occident under the tapering power of Romanism. Islam, furthermore, in closing the roads to China and India, caused the Europeans to direct their attention to the oceans and their highways. Thus giving the impulse, it was directly instrumental in the disclosure of a new world, which in turn caused the rejuvenation of Europe, just at the time when it began to show the symptoms of old age, to weaken under its inertia.

When Islam subjugated Greece, the distribution of the classics occurred at the right moment, Europe being ready just then to take up the humanistic studies.

Islam carried its terrors to the gates of Vienna just in time to relieve the religious reformation of its perils, and to give it a chance to establish itself among the Germans.   It appears that Turano-Semitism in the form of Islam has served the ends for which it was appointed by the purposes of history under divine guidance.   And now it also appears that Russia is designed to push back the iron bar of Islam and to force an opening for direct railway connection with every part of Asia.   .   *(margin: Russia's task to push aside the bolt of Turano-Semitism.)*

The annexation of Siberia was of little avail in relieving Europe from the Turkish obstacle.   But now, since Russia has taken Gœk-Tepe it has a fulcrum in Central Asia, where it can rest the lever for prying open the rusty gate of Tatary.   It is but recently that with the occupation of Merv the Turkmenians were made Russian subjects, and already Merv and its vicinity up to Herat is completely Russified.   Just now the Tekkinzians have been vanquished.   One large district after another—filled with a warring, nomadic population, fluctuating hither and thither as aimlessly as the sand-driftings of their steppes—is drawn into the network of European culture, which Russia immediately spreads over its new possessions.   *(margin: Merv taken. Gœk Tepe upon the Pamir the fulcrum to force Mongolian exclusiveness. Russia's quiet and sure mode of advancing.)*

It is remarkable how Russia understands managing these Mongolians, and how little they resist the subjection to European forms of political organisation.   A new order of things has been pushed forward from the Aral and Caspian Sea to the Pamir regions of old without much ado.   Upon canals and railroads Russian cavalry and cannons and craftsmen are conveyed to the Orient.   In place of the felt-tents and earth-huts of Turkmenian auls, cities arise, built of brick and lined with asphalt pavements.   Where camels as yet carry the rolls of silk from Bokhara and Samarkand, electric cars will ere long take charge of the transport and will by express deliver Asiatic goods in western villages: carpets from China, shawls from Kashmeer, silk-plush and gold-embroidered brocades from Bokhara, across the Volga and Vistula.   In the meantime the project of the Siberian-Pacific-Sitka-Seattle railroad will approach its realisation without, perhaps, much ostentation.   *(margin: Railroad construction.)*

The XXth century will behold the opening of a grand view.   *(margin: Russia's prospects for the XXth century.)*

For when Samarkand with its golden cupolas, when the old seat of Tamerlane shall once have become the summer residence of the emperor of Central-Asia and Russia, then the partition wall of Islam, encumbering the relations between Europe and Asia, will be laid low.   And not before will the world have guaranty for the security of the overland route to the Pacific, for which the Russian outpost on the mouth of the Amur is not sufficient.   *(margin: Russia's qualification.)*

Where in bygone times the Turkish rulers sat reclining upon soft divans under golden canopies, at the foot of the rocky and high Altai-Mountains and on the Amu river, Russia has now taken command, and the sphere of her authority is continually widening.   Facts begin to verify our supposition, that only the Slavonic form of government, as embodied in the czar, is adapted to force the Mongolians into social order.   To spread Germanic culture it takes the colonising industry of many people; but the Slavs can best accomplish their mission in Asia under the direction of a single leader.   Where labor is undivided, and the organism is not differentiated as yet, the masses, resembling a unit of mere physical force, are set in motion by one single will; and to unorganised masses without a leader an attack from such a force is irresistible.   Hence our conclusion, that the mechanism of Russian autocratic rule is specially qualified for the task of compressing the Mongolian hordes.   And indeed it looks now as if the single will of the czar is engaged chiefly with the re-establishment of the old Mongolian empire under a new form.   His hand has taken a firm hold of China and Merv, of Kiachta on the Selenga river, of Nicolajewsk on the Amur, and of Pamir.   Resembling a pair of iron tongs with pinchers open towards the south, the Russian grip is silently extending, and we see no European power able to frustrate its designs.   The force at work in the triangle Moscow-Batoom-Samarkand is apt to change the map of Asia.   If Russia should be barred from capturing Constantinople, Bagdad would be bound to take its place.   *(margin: No European power can hinder Russia from carrying out her designs as to Asia. Romanic and Germanic nations as to their leadership in cultural advance.)*

Following the surview of the Slavonic power, which preponderates in the East by virtue of its national disposition, we are led from the Vistula back to the old home of the nations in Central-Asia, where the successor of the great khans recently planted his standard upon the "roof of the world" from whence we took our first survey.   It is evident that Russia conducts history back to the regions from whence history set out, if we witness how its influence already reaches into the "empire of the middle".

Here history calls us to return to the Romanic and Germanic nations in order to take a glance upon the "new world", and there to observe how the closing of the circle approaches completion.

France mentally arrested at the stage of culture in time of Louis XIV.

§ 193. It seems as tho we ought to be able now, to point out what countries in Africa or elsewhere are left to the Romanic nations for tutelage. But excepting the contribution of colonial products to the markets of the world, the value of their cultivation does not amount to much. How could it be otherwise, since even the Romanic people in Europe became arrested in their mental culture at that stage of spiritual development which had been reached by scholasticism and the mediæval troubadours, upon that stage which France occupied at the time of Louis XIV? We find the Italians to have fallen behind from where they stood in the period of the renaissance.

Italy fell behind the time of the renaissance.

It seems to us a plain fact that the initiative in cultural advance has passed from the Romanic to the Germanic nations.

Germany had always many centers of learning;

The Germans had their first period of literary productiveness under the Hohenstauffens, and afterwards had always numerous centers of learning where the mind was cultivated in its various functions. Never has any single city been able to represent or control the intellectual aspirations or achievements of the entire nation in such a measure, as is said of Paris, for instance, that it stands for France. After the Reformation first Holland, for a short season, and then England, took the lead, leaving Germany behind under its embarrassments of dogmatical controversies and political predicaments. After a long pause of mental stupor and literary inferiority Germany revived, however, and both countries carried mental and industrial energy and the sense of liberty across the ocean. There the "new world" evolved under trying hardships and mighty exertions.

but for ages was under political predicaments.

America outrivaling Europe in leading the march of civilisation.
HEGEL. PESCHEL.

Hegel, not Greeley was the first in saying: "History ever advances from east to west; as it began in Asia, so it ends in Europe". The idea that North-America is emulating, yea, outrivaling Europe's leadership in the march of civilisation did not strike Hegel. Only what he said of the westward movement was corroborated and amended by Peschel where he says in his ethnology that: "Europe is under the meridian of its civilisation, whilst over yonder in the United States the morning dawns". The cultural significance of Europe may eventually partake of the transiency which is the fate of all earthly objects of pride and plight. In such a general way this conclusion seems as reasonable as it flatters the Anglo-Saxon kinsfolks. But a parallel drawn to insinuate that the decline of Europe should accrue to the elevation of North America will sound a little preposterous to the Americans themselves.

Decline of Europe will not accrue to the elevation of North-America.

It has been said of North America that the magnitude of its coal fields surpasses that of Europe five times. This would indicate poor prospects for the future of Europe, since its industry necessarily would slacken, and it would become unable to keep up competition in the markets of the world. In the same way it has been argued, on the other side, that the irrational mode of farming and forestry would exhaust the resources of America in a comparatively much shorter time. But it is plain, in the first place, that other powers than coal-fires may be put into service in Europe by the time its coals give out—waterpower for instance being now transmitted over large distances. Moreover does the fate of nations not depend upon such calculations, for there are, after all, the ethical powers which decide questions as to the future.

Whimsical controversies as to future conditions.

Ethical powers decide future welfare.

In Europe the civilising movement originally went from the south to the north, from the Romanised to the German nations. But since the thought of humanism has prevailed among the western Aryans in that profundity to which the Reformation penetrated, the predominant influences drift in the reverse direction. This becomes especially manifest on the new continent, where the higher culture proceeds from the north to the south.

Since humanism prevailed in the Protestant North of either continent, higher culture proceeds from North to South from Germanic to Romanised nations.

It is possible that the culture even of the United States may suffer disaster on account of a superficial mode of thinking, and the selfsufficiency of wealth; or if the management of politics, through indifference toward religion and lack of vigilance, comes into the wiles of ecclesiastical diplomacy, with its Roman purposeness and its antagonism against this particular form of culture. But tho these dangers be imminent of which Josiah Strong has warned "Our country," yet a prophecy of the overthrow of the constitutional principles of the United States would certainly be put to shame; and an attempt at that would come to grief. The alarm has been given, and Roman craftiness will most likely be defeated, when the Americans of the north remember that their civilisation is not based upon technical progress and not upon the precedents of Mexican polity, but upon the ethical and at bottom religious propædeutics of the free nation.

Real dangers of American civilisation.
JOSIAH STRONG "Our Country."

Conditions under which the dangers may be averted.

In the new nation the successive stages of political development exist side by side from hunting and pastural pursuits to agricultural, industrial and commercial occupations, from nomandic life to one in a social organism. From the outset the country was covered

with a variety of colonial and municipal organisations; all forms of government were toler- *Components of North-American civilisation.*
ated except the monarchical, which was not to the taste of the Quakers and Puritans. Hence
the English and French cavaliers could not succeed in transplanting their accustomed social
forms upon these shores; neither could the Hollandish patricians. But otherwise all the
sociological phenomena ever promulgated in history appear in a process of mutual pervasion
and amalgamation. In jurisprudence we meet with axioms of the pandects, with traces of
the canonic laws of Rome, with feudal rights, with the principles of the Saxen-Spiegel, and
remnants of Spanish casuistry. Most obvious are the effects of the theocratic ideas of Geneva;
and of the democratic predilections of the Saxons. But neither the cosmopolitan republicanism of the Quakers, nor the aristocratic feudalism of Romanists and royalists has become
obsolete. Of lasting effect have become the municipal selfgovernment of the Dutch and
the subjectivism of the Germans; the slavery of Africa; the anarchism of French and Polish
radicalism, and the nomade-life of Italian and Chinese miners, not to speak of the Indians. *One great thought affiliating all these ethnical elements.*
On the whole the new nation forming itself was gradually permeated by one great thought,
which had composed the constitution, and on account of which that fundamental agreement
is held in universal esteem; which grants free play to every moral power, especially to that
of Gospel truth. To a stranger this composition of the national character of "the"
Americans appears as a perplexing medley, unpleasant for a mind accustomed to conservatism, unpleasant on account of the extremes meeting, and of the dark shadows thrown. Yet
the nation of the Union is an unit for all that, bearing a pronounced stamp of specific characteristics; assimilating foreign matters of preference through strong digestive organs—whilst
neutralising and ostracising unwelcome influxes. The United States as an unit is now *Aspirations to draw the South into line with the humanistic cause.*
getting ready to exert the molding influences of her peaceable policy upon the southern
republics in order to unify the new world socially, and to cultivate the cohesiveness which
conditions the prosperity of commercial enterprises.

In the new world the Germanic nations have stood the test of their superior abil-
ities for educating humanity. So far they have surpassed the efficiency of Romanis- *Moorish characteristics stamped upon Mexico.*
tic world-consciousness, altho on the whole America as yet needs to be guarded
against the Roman aspirations, and to prepare for a final contest with Roman
perseverance. In as far as the Andalusians occupied Mexico, we there find
Moorish characteristics predominant to this day. The traveler, whose experience
and acuteness of observation enables him to draw the comparison, is impressed with
everyday life on the streets of Mexican cities, as if he were transported back to
Damaskus or Tunis. Central and South America wait for the transforming influences
of the northern states.

§ 194. The effects of Romanism upon Africa demonstrate the dwindling away of *Effects of Romanism upon Africa.*
the historical significance of Spain and Portugal; for the future work of elevating
the inhabitants of their possessions, but faint hopes can be entertained. So do the
French disappoint the expectations of the people from Algiers and Madagascar to *Colonies labor under the same difficulties as their respective nations at home: they have not gone through the process of the religious reform.*
Tonquin, who were forced to accept their "protection". All the Romanised "colonies"
suffer the same deficiency as do the states ruling over them; they have not gone
through the process of religious reform; Africa, almost entirely without any history,
will be rendered historical only through the culture of the northern nations, through
the Germanic leaven, which England, the Netherlands and the Germans are now
endeavoring to mix into the masses of the dark continent.

The line Sansibar-Calcutta-Bangkok-Sidney is under the supervision of England. *Line Sansibar-Sidney under English sway.*
D'Israeli intended to make Queen Victoria not merely empress of India. He had
still greater projects in view. He was in hopes that Persia, Afghanistan, and Pales-
tiné might be added to the crown, by which acquisitions the basis for further operations in the Pacific was to be strengthened. The attention of all the maritime powers
of the Occident is now bent upon this basin over which the ethnical movement of history returns to its place of beginning.

When the English connected India with the Occident, the obstructions were almost over- *Obstructions of Islam cleared out of the way of humanistic progress on both sides.*
come with which Islam had impeded the communication between the Indo-Germanic rela-
tives. As the bulwarks of Mohammedanism are crumbling along the Slavonic inroad from
Moscow to Samarkand, so are the Turks retrenched along the English highway Cairo-Cal- *Line Moscow-Samarkand under Russian sway.*
cutta.

In the wondrous land of India the locomotive flings aside prejudices of most ancient *British influence upon India.*
standing. The Indian princes, whose dignity required that one seeking audience had to
wait hours and days for admittance, are enuring themselves to the punctuality of the clock in
the railroad depot. The rigid caste-ceremonials are gradually discarded; members of differ- *India's rapid transformation renders Britain's Asiatic success dubious.*
ent castes travel in the same cabins. Marquis Belhousie's plan to construct a railroad sys-
tem with 8000 miles of track is nearly carried out. Ninety-four per cent of the subaltern officers of the roads are natives. India thus undergoes a rapid transformation, which, however,
if continuing in the same rate of progression, will make it difficult for England to maintain
India as the basis of its eastern policy.

The final decision of the Eastern question lies in the dominion of the Eastern Mongolians. The die will be cast, where, in the harem of the "heavenly empire", filled with the daughters of the Mantchoos, the ruler over the fourth part of the earth's inhabitants sits enthroned upon the oldest seat of absolute monarchism.

China is a human reservoir whose dam is overflowing with the emigrants of that most prolific race. The danger of their submerging the Pacific coast has already been vividly felt in Washington.

As of yore, in repeated torrents, the Mongolians rushed forth over the western steppes until they were repulsed by the spiritual superiority of the Germans; so Chinese coolies are transported in swarms across the Pacific toward their East of old. Extremely cunning, and satisfied with the lowest and most meagre bill of fare, they contrive to push themselves into California; just as in ages past, Mongolian population had taken the same outlets when they inundated Peru as easily as Java. The present movement reminds us of the driftings of Aztecian-Toltecian influxes into America, but also demonstrates, how history closes its cyclical courses in the regions from whence it set out. Upon the strength of these facts our inference is justified, that the final issues may be determined in the same parts. For this reason we think, that the series of fire-signals and pillaged cities of Nineveh and Persepolis, Carthage and Corinth, Jerusalem and Alexandria, Rome and Byzantium, Moscow and Delhi, was completed by the storming of the imperial summer residence in Peking A. D. 1860.

In the center of the extensive gardens, dotted with hundreds of kiosks, stood the official pagoda which contained a gigantic statue of Buddha, decked with treasures of gold and precious stones. Images of demi-gods—or of the one altogether Bad represented by the emblem of the dragon, wrought from costly metals—stood in every nook and niche, encircled with flowers and colored candles. The stupefying vapors of narcotic incense ascended from the altars; the hanging lanterns shed their weird lustre through the gloomy hall—when the conquerors rushed in: a portentous event, When Europe thus penetrated into the center of proverbial seclusion, and desecrated the hitherto impregnable stronghold of religio-political mysteriousness and idolatry, it put its foot upon the neck of its oldest antagonist in his central lair.

Upon the most remote eastern shore, western civilisation planted the emblem of the new æra—designating, most probably, the beginning of the last cycle of historic movement, and the incipient consummation of universal history.

Slavs and Indo-Germans encircle Asia, one party arriving by the northern route of Siberia, the others by way of India: both meeting in the "Empire of the Middle". That China ever will play a prominent part, or become copartner in the work of universal civilisation is out of the question. The indications are, that China, notwithstanding its applying the technical skill of English engineers, and the military training of German instructors in the art of modern warfare, will be necessitated to enter into compromises with nations which, like that of Japan, it held in contempt.

China is compelled to adapt itself to European means of selfprotection, whilst most likely it will prove unfit to accommodate itself to the religious consciousness of the civilised nations. It will be compelled not so much by the "invasions of the red bristled barbarians," as by the steady approaches of Russia.

Of what little avail it was that China was busily engaged in constructing routes of quick transit for her armies, and in building fortifications at all the strategic points along the Mantchoorian boundaries, has become evident in her last defeat by the Japanese. The great empire of China must follow the example of the not less important empire of the Mikado, in engrafting modern culture directly upon its time-worn institutions. Russia has become expert in doing the same thing every day, in planting European civilisation directly upon the crudest barbarism. This proves that Russia, obtruding its rule upon the Baltic provinces in the same manner as upon Khiwa, that is, by means of its church—is well adapted for the subjection of Asia, since at bottom her rule is Asiatic, is Mongolian.

Whoever seizes the Pamir-regions possesses the key to Asia. From thence the nations descended into the countries below, and the power occupying these positions will have little difficulty in sallying forth from the same outlets, and in carrying its victories down the same valleys. Hence our belief, that the greater part of Asia will form the Russian empire of the future, that is, Asia will be itself again.

§ 195 We have been led back to the Uralo-Altaic and Mongolo-Malayan nations which we found to constitute the broadest and deepest layer of the ethnical strata at the beginning of history. And as these nations in prehistoric times covered the entire face of the earth, so does history now encircle the globe. The coasts of the Pacific upon which the great prehistoric migrations are traceable, are again drawn into the general concurrence of historical movements. China and the Farther Indias, severed from the other members of the human family through thousands of years, become reunited for participating in common blessings and in common work. China's literature, the most ancient of all literary productions, was founded—as we agree with Gabelentz—anterior to 3000 B. C. When the knowledge of this literature will have been made accessible, we will most likely obtain documentary proof of that original civilisation which the nations took along to their isolated abodes upon the isles and distant shores of the Pacific. What ancient relics have suggested to us respecting the first circle of nations and their degree of culture, will become verified when we come once more to view those localities under the light of historic purposiveness at the consummation of affairs in general. Let us review the indications of culture in the ethnical substratum enumerated, under the light of present ascertainments.

The Turanian, Ugro-Finnian, and the Mongolians in chief we called the ethnical substratum of historic humanity. We perceived them to constitute the largest and most peripheral circle of the nations. On returning to them the development of history—beginning in the Mediterranean basin and extending from thence to the Atlantic, and finally to the Pacific ocean—presents itself in the definite outlines of the compass. Undoubtedly the first commotions on a large scale took place upon the Pacific, the waters of which were up to the last century covered with the impenetrable darkness of prehistoric times. Still fewer traces of these can be expected in the countries where from earliest historic times onward culture after culture covered the nethermost layer. Foundations hidden in the depth of the earth are rendered less explorable, the more extensive and complete the structure becomes which is reared upon them. From these obscure depths but few and faint tokens have been brought to light. They are sufficient, nevertheless, to establish the truth of the primitive unity and continuity of historical beginnings in those parts of the world.

"The whole of America"—we say with Ratzel—"participates in the palæontological character of Polynesia and Northern Asia". America was the eastern part of the Mongolian domain "closely connected with all the nations around the Pacific". The Spanish discoveries in Mexico in 1517 A. D., are inexplicable unless viewed in relation to that palæontological unit of which they form the parts. In Honduras, Yucatan, and Guatemala the tall monolith figures of the Maja became objects of curiosity, and in Uxmal and Palenque entire edifices were found. The latter were recognised at first sight as witnesses of remotest antiquity, for forests thousands of years old had grown over and around them. Fra Lorenzo de Bienvenido wrote to his king that "they must be considered as having been existing before the time of Christ, since the trees covering the structures are as large as those in the countries below." The inhabitants at the times of the conquest, descendants, perhaps, of the builders, constructed their houses of wood, straw and earth. At the present stage of investigation we know to what epoch of culture those old sculptures belong; we find the frame into which the relics of the old Toltecian art had once been mounted, that culture which in turn was amended by the Aztecs. We find that Quetzcoatle, of tall stature and white color, was the priest of the Toltecs, and we find how he became their god. Embarking in a wondrous ship made of snake-skin he had taken leave of them, promising to return.

Meagre as these remnants of a vanished culture may be, they are rendered highly indicative by being placed into their correlations with the whole. That the remnants of this culture form a unit becomes evident from the ruins of ancient towns upon Eastern Ceylon; from the filled up channels of irrigation built by Singalesian kings; from the remnants of a high culture upon the Sunda Islands, and from the ruins of the ancient cities of Kambodsha.

Ferguson esteemed the discovery and comparison of these remnants the most important data for the history of oriental art. "They go far to assist in disclosing the knowledge of the most remote past. The stones of Farther-India speak to us of the antecedents of the known nations. Wieng-Shank, capitol of the Laos, reveals the story of the primeval pagodas in our own countries. The groups of ruins in Angkor, still more plainly the ruins of the cloister of Nakhor-Wat, "resemble the Aztec-Toltecian style of architecture." The tomb-pagodas of the old kings of Bangkok, altho of genuine Siamese character, are very much like the most ancient castles and temples of Kambodsha in their ruins. The figures in the outer court of the Siamese temple seem to look away over the distances of space and time toward their Central American colonies. They are the models of that vanished splendor which the old pyramids and terraces of Mexico indicate. Wienk-Shank contains terrace-buildings which date from pre-Christian times. "This method of building terrace-pyramids can be distinguished upon the island of Java, and can be traced from Tonga to Tahiti and the Easter Islands," said Bastian very recently.

The golden pagoda of Sangun shows two guarding griffins. From the aspect of Mongolo-Malayan culture as a unit the significance of the old golden throne of Burmah, standing under the eight-story pyramid of Mandelay, receives only now its explanation. It was reserved to modern research to interpret that old eastern culture covered up from time immemorial.

The ethnological investigations carried on upon the Easter Islands since the German admiralty received the reports of the Hyæna-expedition in '83, set out from the correct premise, that upon this solitary island of the Pacific "important indications are converging

Proofs for the axiomatic migrations of the Mongolians to be expected from Chinese literature reaching back to 3000 B. C. GABELENTZ.

Review of present ascertainments: § 44, 56, 57.

First commotions on a large scale took place upon the Pacific.

Palæontological character of America and Polynesia. RATZEL.

Discoveries in Mexico, Honduras, Yucatan, and Guatemala. LORENZO DE BIENVENIDO.

Pre-Toltecian edifices of Uxmal and Palenque.

Quetzcoatl Pre-Aztecian.

Relation of American remnants to those of Eastern Ceylon, Singalesia, Kambodsha. FERGUSON.

Buildings of Wiang-Shank (Pre-Christian) of Angkor, Naghor-Wat, Bangkor all resembling American vestiges of culture.

Terrace-pramids alike in Tonga, Java, Tahiti and Easter Island. BASTIAN.

Pagoda of Sangum with emblematic griffins.

Golden throne of Burmah in the pyramid of Mandelay.

German research upon Easter-Island.

Semblances of the
Ko-pito-pito.

Bird idol of Make-Make.

Quetzcoatl—from
Mungo-Capac to
Titicaca.   BASTIAN.

Animal masks of
Shamanism in Ceylon as
well as Tibet, Mexico,
Peru.   RATZEL.

which are apt to throw new light upon the problems of the prehistoric antecedents of the two continents." The colossal stone monuments, as for instance the idols upon the crater of Mt. Rana-Roraka are mostly broken and lie around in pieces; and the semblances of Ko-pito-pito are found not only in its vicinity but they are distributed over many distant islands. Altho disfigured and weather-worn they corroborate the symbolics of the bird idol Make-Make. Whether the most ancient and most colossal figures in the inside of the crater will afford definite solutions of the problem whether or not "those mysterious and colossal structures and sculptures will prove to be remnants of that bridge across which Quetz-coatle traveled to Mexico and from Mungo-Capac to Lake Titicaca" as Bastian concluded, will soon be decided by synthetical reconstruction of the essential facts.

In proof of the unity of the races in eastern Asia and western America, that is, of all those dwelling upon the coasts and islands throughout the Pacific, we also refer to the bestial masks mentioned before. "They formed a part of worship, as Ratzel conjectured, in Tibet, India and Ceylon as well as in Mexico and Peru." The Shamanes have the same masks of bird-heads as the Indians of North America.

We thus find the remnants indicative of "communication during the higher stage of Mongolian culture, remnants which plainly indicate a lively traffic among the nations over a vast portion of the earth's surface, the memory of which has vanished, and left only palæontological traces." These remnants, as now collected in archæological and ethnological museums, clearly and convincingly show, that the peoples of the Pacific basin partook of one and the same, and not a low stage of, culture.

Primeval culture of
America is Asiatic
beyond a doubt.

Every vestige of art, architecture and cultus bears the same original generic character. The grotesque arrangement of different animal forms in the sculptures and composite images of America is old-Asiatic beyond question.

At one glance we notice the similarity between the representations of snakes and fishes, and among the beavers and frogs, stretching out long tongues. The medley of monstrous visages and coiled snakes forms a confusing mass in one and the same picture, with marks of eyes added promiscuously. Human noses are embellished with fishes upon them. On top the symbolic figures thus crowded together, appear long-peaked birds. This Mongoloid taste pertains to the most ancient substratum of human history, now mostly covered by advanced forms, but partly lying open in its primitive shape.

Mongoloid elements
mixed everywhere in
the substratum lying
bare in places to which
access is yet to be
gained.

Purposive march
of civilisation
from the
Mediterranean to
the Atlantic and
across the Pacific
Ocean.

The countries, where these forms of oldest culture are visible upon the surface, are almost inaccessible as yet from the present centers of civilisation. The Slavonic nations are destined to bridge over the remaining hiatus in our knowledge between the primitive forms of life and the cultural attainments of modern Europe. When a few more barriers shall be removed, then history as a science will complete its record of advancing movements around the earth to the place from which history as such first set out, and where she will finish her endeavors to rehabilitate humanity.

It will come to notice
what purport history
conveyed in this mode
of completing its
cycles.   § 180, 218.

Facilities of intercourse
contract the Pacific
even to what the
Mediterranean was to
the Phœnicians,
Saracens, and Normans.

People arrested in their
development received
into the circle of
humanity.

§ 196. History took its way through the developments which transpired around three water-basins. Its first distinct curves swung around the Mediterranean; then across the Atlantic; and now the Pacific is again being linked into the chain of human affairs. The latter basin was the first over which migrations and colonial exploits of nations took place. The Mongolians went to the islands and became Malayans, shifting to America they became Toltecs, Aztecs and Indians. We have become persuaded of the historical significance of this broad Turano-Mongolian substratum, and we shall notice what purport history conveys in just this mode of completing its cycles in the region of its beginning. What once was the Mediterranean gulf, and what subsequently the Atlantic Ocean amounted to in the development of civilisation, that will be the significance of the Pacific Ocean at the approach of its completion. The facilities for quick transit contract the distances between Asia, America, and Australia into almost closer proximities than those were in the arena of Phenicians, Greeks and Romans, of the Normans and Saracens in their time. On the eastern shores of the Pacific we have the harbors of Seattle, San Francisco, Lima and Valparaiso; on the western side the great staple-places of Nikolajewsk, Wladivostock, Tokio, Canton, Singapore and Sidney have sprung up. They are all thriving seaports with a period of great influence before them, connected as they are by lines of geometrical precision, and so cosmopolitan in their nature, as that each of them already represents the interests of every nation. Thus people hitherto forgotten and arrested in their development are now being picked up and elevated to the historic rank of advanced nations; they are received into the circles of humanity, and invited to take part in circulating the blessings of civilisation.

Sea-ports of the Pacific
common property of all
nations.

This new phase of universal history is the most pronounced feature of our time and the near future. Most probably the rounding off of the line of progress as described will denote the disintegration of the Mongolian lump. So much is certain that history has run its race of extension since all waters and countries are opened and made stations of circuits with schedule time. Having taken up all earthly spaces, history will turn its attention from widening its spatial extent to intensifying its human contents.

Latest and last phase of universal history.

Disintegration of the Mongolian lump, § 18-24, 54-56, 59, 80, 119.

Allusion was made to three Mediterraneans, severally separating Asia, Europe and America each from its counterpart. The idea was then suggested, that these three continents might be destined to become three units of cultural variations. We may now conjecture somewhat upon the meaning of this supposition. It will be seen that it is only the Asiatic Mediterranean which separates Australia from its mainland. The connection between them is formed by the row of islands from Malacca over Timor. This makes Asia one geographical unit with Mongolian propensities. The American, the second unit, is unquestionable, the bridge still standing. And so may Europe be considered as the head of Africa, with the line Tiflis-Suez as the connecting joint of that body. This division, yielding three geographical units, seems to have been pre-arranged for the purpose of transferring the progress of history to the Pacific waters, the coasts of which seem to be the appointed localities where the final attainment of those aspirations is to be realised, which is underlying the indistinct and portentous commotions of the nations ever pressing towards the West. Again we are reminded that the smallest of these three units became the most valuable to the rest of the world. Ever since the great central point of the times Europe was the pivot point on which the history of the world hinged, because of its being the bearer of the highest and most profound thought and of its leadership in the advance of humanism.

History will turn from widening its extent to intensifying its human contents.

Significance of the three Mediterraneans. § 8

Three units of civilisation.

Asia-Australia.

Two Americas.

Europe-Africa.

Europe the smallest, yet most valuable continent.

Its missions, until recently in the attire of servants, have attained to imperial dignity. Its three prominent nations, the Romanic, Germanic, and Slavonian, have been successively and will be cooperatively, engaged in elaborating and substantiating the thought of Humanism in every direction. Hence the inference may promptly be drawn that these three nations will take possession of the three geographical units. That means the three continents will each be stamped with the cultural characteristics of its respective master-mind or protector. America will be governed by the Germanic, Asia by the Slavonian, and Europe-Africa by the German-Roman form of consciousness. As the Romans once guided the affairs upon the Mediterranean, Romanistic and Germanic nations upon the Atlantic, so will all insist upon the freedom of the Pacific as a public highway to a common market. Then history in its spatial extent will have gained its goal. Having settled its secular interests, the temporal career will then prepare for the great consummation of ethical ends.

Romanic, Germanic, Slavonic, each to work out a cultural unit.

America, Germanic.

Asia, Slavonic,

Africa, Roman-Germanic

Secular interests settled, ethical ends to consummated.

CH. XI. ETHICAL CHAOS RESULTING FROM CORRUPTING THE COGNITION "HUMANISM".

§ 197. Anticipating, as now, the final outcome of history, may seem preposterous. Hence the necessity of vindicating the inferences by a retrospect of the dangers to which the cause of humanism is exposed in extending its course towards the periphery. The one fact becomes manifest thereby that all movements of the nations are made subservient to this procedure, their defaults in the realisation of the thought notwithstanding.

Resume of the dangers to which the cause of true humanism is exposed upon its course of extension.

But to know only this much would afford no solace to the despair of humanity ever attaining a state of perfection. We can not rest satisfied until we conceive to what the final issue of development will amount. As a general thing subjected nations are forced to deliver whatever valuables they possess to the victors. This occurred at the time when the proceeds of humanity were taxed, when the ideas and the gods, loosened from their native soil, were flowing together into that chaotic compound in the Roman crucible. That "world-orbit" grasped after every new cult in order to stimulate its own fretful, enervated constitution. This may happen again when the great historic movements, after the race of progress around the globe has been run, shall come to a standstill. **The significance of this epoch will consist in the palpable revelation of all the contents of personal life, of human nature.**

Final issue of progress.

As once the nations were taxed as to their historic accomplishments—

so a final issue will reveal what use man has made of his capabilities and opportunities. § 10, 13, 15, 16, 25, 38, 117, 119, 166, 185, 197, 201, 205, 232.

At a final consummation of human affairs it must appear what man is and what he has made of himself in regard to both, the Good and the Bad. Because man is the theme of history, the great drama representing all the variations of personal life in its historical phases and individual experiences, must come to a close in the accords of an adequate finale. There is to be witnessed a rehearsal of all that man has earned from, or squandered of, his inherent potentialities; of the use made of his opportunities and of their neglect; of all the bright-shining results which his facilities yielded; and of his dark side, as well. These proceeds were successively formative in the make-up of man's history, unfolding in time and separated by space; they will then

Thought of human dignity quietly imparted to humanity at the time when the bankruptcy of selfculture was declared.

appear in their order and interrelations side by side, as in one grand panorama, now almost conceived to be contained in the cognition of Æon. The period of the great discoveries reminds us of the fact, that we are living already in the prelude to this great recapitulation and settlement of accounts.

The oldest stones speak to us of thoughts and acts of ancestral people in a manner unthought of a century ago. The speech uttered by Aztecian ruins, by Yenisei inscriptions; the meanings conveyed in Hittite, Assyro-Akkadian, and Ægyptian emblems of thought become ever more distinct and intelligible. In the usages and ideas of the most remote and almost forsaken peoples we hear voices, which more and more narrow down to a common language; voices which arouse our attention, and sympathetically affect us. This language mirrors to each of us his own image and teaches us to understand ourselves. We learn to compose the synopsis of our own being preparatory to the summons by which a higher voice convokes mankind to an act of summary adjudication.

It was the thought of human dignity, or rather individual value, which at a certain time when history heard man's bankruptcy announced, had quietly been sown into humanity, had rooted there, and grown to full consciousness. The sprout partook of the nature of its soil and of the atmosphere wherein it developed. Detachments going on among the worried peoples made contrasts appear, which in their turn were to assist in the further differentiation of individual characters and in the collective organisms being thus wrought out in life's contests. The idea, the great thought of humanism, thus passed through conditions which at times seem contradictory beyond reconciliation.

Now let us see what will have become of that idea at the termination of history's outspreading operations. At the threshold of early history we recognised, how without words the question was put, the old riddle of Œdipus: "What is man?" In the Son of Man we perceived the answer, not so much in words as in acts; in Him we see

whereof true humanity in its perfect realisation must consist; we learn to know humanity, personal life, as revealed in His sublimity, as exalted to and embraced by divinity. Human nature is rescued and under safe protection. It is redeemed even corporeally. For the bodily organism of the Savior, of earthly origin, had to be led up to glory, so that in the Risen One humanity in its entirety, through the ideal, man shines forth in the reality of perfect happiness and beautiful harmony. A truly

human being, ideal and essential is that person who lives in the safe state of communion with God, that is, whose self - and world-consciousness is, by way of free self-consecration, immersed into, and pervaded with God-consciousness. Both self—and world-consciousness are opened for the mysterious but empirically real influences upon the inner life; man unreservedly gives himself up to be illuminated and directed by God-consciousness. Only thus and now does man attain to the free and sublime position designed for him. That unique communion, that unifying blending

of the human with the divine nature as perfected in the God-man, is to be represented through, and manifests itself in, the innumerable individual instances constituting the various phases of historical development. That unity is to be reflected in the most manifold variety in those who become fashioned into Christlikeness. Independent of temporal considerations they dominate over the world whilst serving its best interests. They are to cultivate the earth, to cooperate in the redemption of arrested and the deliverance of confined life,—to spiritualise the world.

These outlines of historical advance, as given in the typical first man, are now clearly revealed and made easy to be comprehended and to be accepted. The ideal is

before the nations, the thought of humanity has become the great fact of history, and the exercise of humanism is acknowledged as the cardinal principle of civilisation.

But we have witnessed how this ideal, ever present, frequently seemed to have disappeared in history's stormy periods. We saw it disappear under the lingering adumbrations of gentile and Jewish conceptions of life. Subsequently the onesided

meditation upon the higher world, the retrogressive imitation of transcendental God-consciousness, fully obscured the consciousness of the reality, of the value, and the order of the present form of existence. This was characteristic of the period in which Romanism reigned supreme.

Then again was the right and relative good of this world accentuated in the time of the renaissance, during which the naturalistic argumentation went to the other extreme, of supplanting the ethical aspects of life by the æsthetical.

The religious reform finally expounded a deeper conception of the human potentialities and human destiny. Man is to harmonise transcendental cognitions with the thought of immanency; he is to cooperate in the elevation of the natural world into spiritual reality, he is to conciliate by acts his real existence with his not less real tho celestial destiny.

Again, however, the significance of the divine image, because of its bearing a religious significance, was carried into the vortex of mere world-consciousness by torrents of sceptical argumentation. The ideal of humanism was severed from God-consciousness and viewed through the spectacles of "enlightenment". The philosophy of identity had suddenly projected the idea into the dreamy and nebulous realms of pantheism, from which heights it was just as suddenly dragged down to the flats of materialism. In this humiliated condition, suffering from misapprehension, we find our model of genuine humanism comparatively neglected by some civilised nations of our century, when egoism was incited to press on in the progress of the natural and practical sciences under a pronounced worldliness.

It is this unqualified neglect which jeopardises the future welfare of humanity. The perils will not be alleviated by the arts and sciences in themselves, as some seem to fancy.

In times not far past a sceptic was treated with special respect, as if he were privileged to be an infidel, a "freethinker"; as if this or that individual had become more dignified by "advanced" views and was to be honored by marks of allowance and exception. Now scepticism is made the rule. Through the widening of the horizon, under attempts at democratising universal knowledge, and through the advantages held out to the masses by the sciences, scepticism became a power, without deepening the minds, much less taking care of the hearts.

We are now assaulted by a "monistic world-theory" dominant in the "liberally educated classes" especially, to whom man appears as a nature trained automaton, a brute evolved into civilisation. Human nature is defined as selfsufficient for the present, tho with still higher accomplishments on the scale of evolution, to be expected. It is considered as no more than a gradation of force-substance, which is alleged to come to its highest form in the secretions and functions of the brain.

This materialism is not a thing of that persuasion or intellectual conviction which was formerly made the criterion of ideas; it is a matter of the will, a matter of moral antipathy. It is the outspoken design of materialism to harmonise and formulate the social life of the future, by casting it into the mold of physical homogeneity. The harmony of forces is to be brought about by the abolition of common interests. Considered as the cause of all rivalry and contradiction, public-mindedness is to be supplanted by the unrestricted exercise of selfishness. It sounds absurd, that selfishness should be a general antidote for the rivalry of interests and mental dissent. But materialism argues, that labor would become so diversified that each individual would choose, in accord with its disposition and predilection, to pursue the work agreeable to it, and that thereby perfect harmony of interests would establish itself as the natural result.

The political economy growing from such naturalism talks so much of rights and the gratification of appetites, that duties are scarcely mentioned and selfrestrictions not at all. Since there are but individuals with equal rights, social distictions exist no longer. The social atoms aggregate into the socialistic state, that is—the association of the human world upon the basis and under the bonds of selfinterest.

Then, it is promised, that we shall have eternal peace, which trade dictates, because it has become the great power, and because it requires security, strict habits, and orderly management. Trade is expected to penetrate to the remotest countries, opening markets for all the products of labor, sources from which to derive the materials, and places of exchange—all with the exactness of the "drill-press". The electric spark, locomotives, steamers, agencies, and factories and branch-offices, are the great means of that universal commerce through which the oceans are bridged, and mountains are tunneled by day and by night, which incite stupefied nations, and set retarded cultures in motion. The products of the Ural and Siberia go to Girgenti and Avignon under schedule time and tariffs, which hold good along the entire line. The fruits of South German orchards, and the olives of the Provence are shipped to Scotland and to Baku under the same legal precepts and—free of duty. It is true, that in all this, international treaties have already succeeded to the extent of creating in most countries an approximate equality of legislation. But it is said, that the system as governed from one central office will become perfected more swiftly in every direction.

26

Marginal notes:

Natural side of the thought emphasised.

Worldliness of the renaissance.

Reformation conciliated real existence with Heavenly destiny. World-consciousness prevalent in the ages of the counter-reformation and of enlightenment. Identity philosophy projected the idea into dreamy and foggish realms of impersonality, and caused it to be dragged down to the flats of materialism. Religious side entirely discarded.

Even temporal prosperity jeopardised.

Infidelity a badge of respectability.

Scepticism the rule.

Neglect of cultivating the heart followed by shallowness of the brain.

Materialistic monism claiming first rank for its world-theory.

Irreligiousness no longer a matter of the intellect but of the will.

Homogeneity in unrestricted egoism.

Abolition of common interests.

Humanistic as practiced by materialism.

Prospects of socialism, regardless of the higher wants of the human soul.

We would not be understood as speaking in derision. To certain enthusiasts it seems as tho everything was going to facilitate the realisation of those projects through which the nations are to be conducted to a happy and peaceful union, which will render them a great industrial and brotherly association—one large "grange" of production and consumption. To every appearance a superficial, a quasi education inflates the coming generation with that pride which imagines itself to know everything. "Young America", the "young Czechians", the "young Socialists", know "it" a great deal better than their predecessors, and better than those who are in authority. It is an accomplishment too questionable to boast of, if by extolling the triumphs of "the XXth century", the toils and trials of bygone generations are deprecated. Such boasting cuts the continuity of history asunder, and men of such ingratitude are apt to squander inherited valuables for a song, and to turn savages.

Not everybody can be charmed by that alluring picture of earthly bliss in the near future. Lemontry already had his misgivings lest men would be degraded by which is poorly qualified
to unite men into one
great brotherhood. the gradual changes of modern economics. Perthes stated from his observations of the great factories in the first decade of our century, that man would become a machine and lose his ethical value. Marx was right when he signalised the perils of Marx
and
Sismondi
on changes of industrial
economy and
city-life. servitude and the oppressive power of capital. Sismondi predicted the dire results of concentrating moneys; he foresaw that by overproduction and free trade industry would transform its central places into battle-fields. Cherbuliez could not see progress towards general welfare in the predominance of industry in our civilisation. They all did not believe that a great system of production and consumption would unite men into one large human family.

§ 198. Let us take the liberty to ignore that dark apprehension previously disregarded, about the coal giving out. Even if electricity could not in every way supplant steam power, we are confident that man would discover and utilise resources of forces dormant in our planet and its atmosphere, which would prove inexhaustible. Neither will the dangers of the future lie in the direction to which Malthus pointed.

With the pathos of horror he lectured in 1798 upon the dreadful calamity of overpopulation. For he was sure that after a short time the earth would not yield the necessary food for the people. "At the great banquet of nature not all will find couvertes provided for them."

Malthus would think so no longer in the face of the accelerating ravages of death caused by suicide and industrial negligence, in addition to those caused by wars and natural calamities. Over-population is not to be feared as a universal misfortune, tho emigration and
immigration may become vexing problems of national legislatures. The Taiping insurrection is said to have cost thirty millions of lives.

Valuation of individual
life a sign of advancing
civilisation.
To be sure, new millions fill the places again and want to be fed; but is it true that they cannot find work, that the earth is so crowded as not to yield a living? Under certain circumstances, the growth of statistical numbers may become annoying. The valuation of individual life is a sign of advancing civilisation, and if the esteem
of it should decline, as for instance through a surplus of labor on the "market of labor," then man in general would sink to a lower grade. But never more will this become a universal phenomenon or a lasting condition.

Danger for the thought
of humanism not in the
wars of the future,—
which may be more
wholesome than
detrimental.
Where, then, would the dangers threatening future prosperity to be located? They cannot be assigned to the wars of the future; for, after human society would have been atomised into individuals, war would thus be the beneficial means of reuniting the centrifugal particles. Heretofore, every part of the long period of peace promoted the disintegration of feudal and ecclesiastical organisations, and not otherwise would it Times of peace promote
social disintegration:
territorial interests of
agrarians; sectional
division of
industrialism. be with projected social mechanism. Where the conservatism of an agrarian populace predominates, society as a whole would just as much be severed by territorial and class interests as by the sectional divisions of industry. As the world is constituted, the binding and stimulating effects of wars are indispensable. Mankind will have to Dangers lurk in the
moral decadence of
society. endure and overcome the relapse into barbarous conditions sequent to wars, until these become less frequent in the ratio as the demands of trade and the security of investment require indeed more considerateness on the part of those who would throw steel and explosives into the scale of settlement.

Danger lurks in the moral retrogression of society. If society at large should see its dream of a world-embracing association of production and consumption come true for a longer or shorter period, then humanity might, perhaps, be well enough provided
with means to satisfy natural wants. This is the conviction at least of socialistic doctrinarians. But in our opinion folks constituting the "association of production and consumption" would be far from being satisfied, and would have reason to

envy the polypi in their coral shelters, who have at least free tentacles. "In the human social organism the psychical constituents (that which concerns soul and spirit) attain such a high degree of development that the inner life of the individual person affects the whole of humanity in a similar manner, and has the same bearing upon the social organism, as the function of the single cell has upon the animate body." What Schæffle here calls development would be death to personal life in its psychical manifestations, the end of liberty. Individual originality would be rendered defunct in that system of evolution, whenever the "social organisation," in a worse than Roman conception of the state, should take the place and usurp the right of personality.

For in the last resort this social body (the commune ?) would become a jelly-like lump, which is fatally affected by the least unusual incitement. Such an undifferentiated mass of social corporation must of necessity become, after individuality and personal character are done away. The enthusiasts of ethnical psychology are trying to vindicate the doctrine of such an organism with the assertion that a sort of "national spirit" would animate this unit of humanity. This nervous lump with the nature of a swarm of bees would be rendered cohesive externally, perhaps, by telegraph wires; internally it would have to be held together by training an instinctive esprit de corps. Society thus equalised would arrive at that stage of cerebral irritability which is found among the Lapps and the Javanese, who are so sensitive as to imitate en masse the mimicry of any one addressing them or attracting their attention in a manner which amazes them.

Humanity in this shape of a socialistic commune, which assigns all individual selfhood to the state, would have to submit to the madest despotism ever experienced. If such a condition could become general the visionary associations, orders, Phalangsteres, etc., would be rejected as reactionary experiments and spurned as symptomatic of a chronic morbidity.

If it should become obvious that a projected conglomerate of undifferentiated society is infeasible, then the contrary method of free competition would retain the open field of the industrial chase for unscrupulous winners. True, competition sets free the energies of a nation and of each individual; but whilst it stimulates its rise, it also accelerates its decay. Sparing human strength, which is the redeeming feature of the industrial machinery, is impossible, where the "strife for existence" reigns after the ideal of Adam Smith.

If this international economy should become the condition of the future industrial society, then individual character would become the more sharply delineated, the more the whole of humanity would imbibe the spirit of progressiveness.

For society would owe its prosperity to the multiform and multiplying relations of the many constituent parts towards each other. But then another danger would threaten the highly differentiated social organism. For in proportion to its finer and higher development it becomes the more sensitive.

The wound of a worm heals easiest; to many creatures of the lower order nature restores entire members lost. Savage tribes show an aptitude for the healing process of nature which cultured nations lost long ago. The cause of this lies, to a great extent, in the progress of differentiation. As the organism unfolds itself, the organs correspondingly advance in their adaptability and capability to develop new differentiations. The further this development proceeds, the more tender and vulnerable are the specific organs, and consequently the entire organism. This holds true in society as well as in nature. Industry mechanically organised and highly differentiated is so much exposed to friction that to the individual, compelled to strain his intellectual powers to the last notch in order to succeed in the contest for existence, there is in the end left no other resource, but to be hurled over from insomnia into insanity, or to become a victim of despondency and to drop off by way of suicide. Taken as a whole this human fabric will perceive its diseased condition no more than a madman can be convinced of his insanity.

This single-handed contest with complex competition in the sense of the Manchestrian school of economics is as hazardous to ethics as dangerous to intellect. "For," says H. Fichte, "the higher the individual rises to a position of relative independence, so as to enjoy the achievements won by his own exertion with a certain degree of selfcomplacency and satisfaction, the greater is the probability and danger of his degeneracy." This aspect designates the position from which the growth of evil, as the dark shadow of modern civilisation, may be explained and is to be viewed.

By the transformation of society through the industrial changes the individual has become emancipated to a great extent from the guardianship of home-life and social custom. Freedom, the source of individual exertions, now also becomes the source of predicaments. In both cases, in tyrannical communism and Manchestrian freedom, the perils of our economics augment rather than diminish. Whether general interests have the predominant influence, so that personal advantages are made of small concern and are sacrificed to the selfhood of the state; or whether the con-

Materialistic sociology. Schæffle.

Social organisation displacing the rights of personality would be worse than the Roman concept of the state's supremacy.

Social body resembling a protoplasmic mass.

Ethnical psychology finds its ideal in the unit of the "national spirit".

Insane despotism of the socialistic commune.

Disadvantages of unrestricted freedom of competition.

"Strife for existence" would more than consume the human strength saved by machinery.

Highly differentiated organism liable to sudden collapse.

Victims of economical delusions:

Manchestrian doctrines as hazardous to the intellect as to ethics. H. Fichte.

Liberty the spur to exertion, also the source of social perils.

The dark shadow of modern culture.

Under Manchestrian liberty not less than under communistic tyranny the perils threatening economics rather augment than diminish.

Possibilities of averting disastrous experiments.

sideration of private prosperity prevails and subjective selfishness is insisted upon, from which society derives the nature of a contrat sociale, subject to abrogation at pleasure, the evils incumbent to the progress of civilised society will inevitably increase.

"Fourth estate" to be organised in order to purge itself of irredeemable elements.

It is possible, that the inorganic exudation of industry, called the proletariat, may be reabsorbed by the social organism, that the bourgeoisie may assimilate the laboring class by elevating it, by sympathising and candidly fraternising with it. In this case the "fourth estate" will either purge itself from irredeemable elements and form itself into differentiated units, or it will consolidate its interests with the intelligent classes and with productive capital. For the sake of such a more normal reconstruction by a method of organic membership, the laboring class will find it conducive to their welfare to uphold the present order of society which socialism is contriving to upset.

Present order of society to be upheld under increasing efforts of harmonising readjustment, by rational methods of economic reconstruction.

Peril to which the thought of humanism is exposed.

Such are the probabilities. Disastrous experiments and social perils,if not wilfully ignored, may yet be prevented by rational methods of reconstruction. There is room enough for improvement on earth. As America may become one large confederation of republics, so may Europe eventually constitute itself into a confederacy of free states, instead of remaining a system of armories and national debts. Nevertheless, success with the best of these possibilities, whilst enlarging the arena of turbulences, woud not abolish the peril to which the thought of humanism is exposed.

Real danger located.

Man does not become better, only more legalistic by more culture. Kant.

Viciousness of past ages only recast into modern molds.

Depravity despises to borrow respectability from hypocrisy.

§ 199. The dangers lie in materialism, as formulated in a world-theory. Man in general does not become better. It was Kant's opinion that he only becomes more legalistic. Individual morality—inasmuch as it rests upon personal conversion, upon a thorough-going change of the innermost mind in its center where all psychical and spiritual faculties are focusing—does not increase with cultural progress. It has been correctly stated, "that every vice of bygone ages, altho seeming to have disappeared, has only been recast into modern molds." Its present form may be more smooth and polished; under the guise of refinement it is more similar to a certain angel than to a beast. Iniquity in its present forms can avail itself of a great variety of masks and means, the analysis and exposure of which in special cases requires the closest scrutiny of chief-justices. But the sleekness of cloaked depravity notwithstanding, sin, ever on the advance, spurns to wear soft features; it despises to borrow respectability from hypocrisy, and boasts of its resolute character.

Crowding the cities a menace to morality.

We plainly observe this condition of things in the growth of the large cities. In the year 1860 Germany, for instance, contained but four cities with more than 100,000 inhabitants; now there are twenty-five. In the United States we had in the cities thirty years ago only one-eighth of the present population; now the fourth part of the nation crowds our one hundred and odd cities of over 50,000 inhabitants. It is an empirical fact that the Bad, like an epidemic is the more infective, the closer the masses live together, and that the means of mischief are multiplying in proportion to the measures taken for the suppression of crime.

Profligacy emboldened by decency retreating.

Growing indifference ad to resistance of wickedness.

Another feature becomes thus apparent. The bolder profligacy steps forth, the more will peaceable citizens—will decency retreat and give free sweep to rascality. The more viciousness makes it a study to circumvent the laws, and to dodge legal condemnation, and the more shrewd passion is concealed under the cloak of polite manners in order to break forth the more fervidly—the more callous and indifferent does society grow in resisting wickedness.

Old age prudent to avoid the annoyances connected with combating the bad. Lasaulx.

Increase of calculating trend of the mind. and of destructive forces;

"Old age gains more force of selfguarded prudency, than firmness and goodness of will-power." This verdict of Lasaulx may well be applied to humanity growing old. The more the spirit of the times develops a calculating and intellectual trend of mind, the more numerous the inventions and the distructive forces of science, the more will the way of progress be beset with dangers, if at the same time religious warmth and ethical energy correspondingly decrease. If humility of spirit is lost upon the height of industrial successes, then that haughtiness towers up, which defies heaven under the selfconceit of holding the earth in subjection.

Wherever physical life preponderates, as for instance in early childhood, the sensual appetites dominate, but guilelessness and good nature also are prevalent; anger is soon allayed, a conflict laid by as quick as it was provoked. A well-fed person is taken for a "hale fellow well met", whilst every artist will represent Mephistopheles by a lean bloodless figure. We conclude with almost unfailing certainty that both, the good as well as the bad features of human character assume more definite outlines, as natural simplicity gives way to selfconsciousness and mental control of the natural temper. With this increasing aptitude also grows the inner conflict shaping the character. In short, the real image of man develops under the lights and shades of inner conflicts and outward annoyances. The more spirited man becomes, the more he loses his pliability and gracefulness, the more apparent becomes his decisiveness and the more marked his inflexible determinateness. That vagueness of character is despised which covers contradictory elements by affecting an ever-compromising policy of expediency and allowances: whilst correspondingly more of that keenness of judgment will show itself, which possesses the courage of its convictions, acting upon principle regardless of fear or favor. The same development of characteristics we may with all propriety ascribe to highly developed nations as well as to individuals.

(margin: Cultivation of character the necessity for successful counteraction.)

(margin: Less vagueness of allowances and expediency.)

No doubt, the evils of the dark ages were more appalling than those of modern times. Violence, rudeness and lewdness were more visible at the courts and in the towns, with the shiftless rovers, as with the sedate monks. Dense was the smoke in the dwellings and deep the filth in the narrow streets breeding rapacious pestilences. Police and health-officers have diminished nuisances of that sort. Never was decency better supported by moral suasion and public opinion, bringing offenders to terms and ostracising vulgarity, than at present. Yet this does not suffice to annul our former judgment as to our highly polished civilisation. The malady does not come out perhaps, as hideous carbuncles as formerly; but it is festering upon the inner and most vital organs of the social body so much the worse.

(margin: Comparison between former and present forms of social life.)

(margin: Moral malady festering upon the inner organs of the social body.)

Darwin somewhere said, that in the progress of history phantasy was evaporating whilst reason was gaining strength. There is signalised just that danger of which we speak. In the Middle Ages piety was a powerful counterpoise against viciousness; of that power our time is deficient. Supercilious semi-culture, withal its acuteness of reasoning, cannot retrieve the defect. And it is doubtful whether the reckoning prudence spoken of is able to supersede piety, may it choose its means ever so rationally.

(margin: "Phantasy evaporating, reason gaining strength." Darwin.)

(margin: In the decline of piety, not to be superseded by rationalism, lies the danger.)

In the choice of means to counteract the dangerous outcroppings of modern civilisation nowhere is less discrimination exercised than in the international associations. Neither labor nor capital is scrupulous in its choice of international agencies. Nationality and patriotism form sacred ties for individual aspirations, since the truth of Guizot's definition of civilisation is acknowledged, according to which each contributes his best thoughts and acts to the welfare of his country and the nation is ready to accept and encourage such endeavor. To have in view the fair name of family and country is a most powerful regulator of social conduct and national prosperity. But this incitement to ethical reciprocity loses much of its force and salutary virtue, as soon as through enterprise, envy and dissatisfaction the ties are loosened which bind persons to their home and kindred.

(margin: Counter-acting dangerous outcroppings of modern civilisation by the "International.")

(margin: Proper incitement to work for the common welfare: Family ties and patriotism. Guizot.)

(margin: Guizot's good definition of civilisation. § 56.)

These circumstances bring us back face to face with the ancient boast of cosmopolitan virtues at large, which once inflated the Stoics, to whom social and home duties seemed nothing but encumbrances in attaining to their hazy ideal of humanism. In fact, for more than thirty years have people been nourished with the idea of supplanting the European system of states by one republic. This titanic structure stands so complete before the imagination of the "internationale" confederation of labor, that even a new common language for the entire brotherhood has been devised.

(margin: Virtue at random in cosmopolitanism. § 80)

(margin: Phantom of materialism as to a "European republic.")

Thus the portentous figure of an amalgamated unit rises in the distance of the times and throws its shadow ahead, a unit whose outlines are like those of the ghost of the ancient giant—Roman cosmopolitanism; a unit which in essence, according to the appearance which matters have assumed, is not altogether impossible.

(margin: Amalgamation of nations projected by the modern cosmopolitical "international federation of labor.")

§ 200. In the broad river of universal history which we have endeavored to explore along its whole course, we ever observed the well defined current of a certain form of world-consciousness carrying along a solid tendency to conform to the earliest traditions. This tendency took its shape for the first time in the Babylonian dominion, upon its Turano-Mongolian substructure. That very tendency continued its efforts to materialise itself in the Persian, Greek and Roman monarchies. When the Mediator entered history, it was this tendency which opposed His Kingdom by insisting upon its prepossessed idea of a messianic world-empire. Notwithstanding the disasters it has had to sustain, this very idea of worldly union and dominion uninterruptedly continues to flow down the river of time, always distinct, in the solid bundle (fasces) of Roman principles, no matter whether the stream changes its course

(margin: The arch type of the perverted cognition of human unity and dominion over nature.)

(margin: Origin of the tendency to erect a cosmopolitan world-empire in Babylon.)

(margin: Tendency perpetuated.)

from Byzanz to Aachen and Paris, or from Rome to Moscow. And this tendency will culminate, if indications do not deceive, in a worldly entity which will represent the clear-cut anti-type of the Babylonian proto-type, its broad platform included.

The memory of Babel calls forth in our combination of thoughts the symbolic figure of that titanic violence which persisted in the consummation of visible unity for the sake of cosmopolitan dominion, and in defiance of Heaven—despite its being pregnant with utter confusion, impotence, and dispersion. To the emblem of violence, defiance and confusion, exactly corresponds that anti-type which casts its shadow before. Minds with the necessary insight discern beneath the agitation for an international association how that anti-typical entity is assuming definite shape.

The investigation of that vast and dark-substratum spread over the face of the earth, we always judge to be an essential factor in the historical problem. Even the return of history to the regions of its beginning is evidence of their uninterrupted importance. With respect to both, time and space, history has slid over the compact Mongolo-Malayan strata without making an impression upon them. It is in respect to its design and intent that history returns to them by utilising the opportunities afforded by cosmopolitan culture, in order to throw out the Christian thought as a seed into the agitated chaotic world absorbed in selfishness under the guise of cosmopolitanism. These are the circumstances under which this thought will have to engage single-handed in the contest with the gigantic, hostile and grotesque world-consciousness of antiquity.

Why again in solitary contest? Because nations making cosmopolitanism their religion, may be incapable of embracing the thought, and will most probably withdraw from Christianity into the gloomy mass from whence, in their shattered condition, they emerged in the beginning. Ratzel finds, that in a mixture of nationalities a great anti-spiritual force is at work; nature gains preponderance over the spirit, the physical part of man triumphs over the psychical; natural impulses get the upper hand over the will and over justice.

Just imagine the condition of things if these observations should become verified by the great mixture of races which is now rapidly and on a large scale going on in America.

America, they say, is a revised and abridged edition of Europe. But the seven millions of negroes in conjunction with a motley crowd of Slavonic and Romanic "cheap labor" of base propensities—all upon a level of political rights without intellectual ripeness for selfgovernment—form a large interrogation point.

Since the disintegration of nations leading to this new mixture is also making rapid progress, it is obvious that the erratic elements deposited in America are not the most desirable material for building up a new nation. For the elements holding their own amidst the process of dissolution are not always the nobler for it.

Let us take a few instances to illustrate our allusions.

Of the Aryan element in its Indo-German purity France has purged herself, the Celtic stock remaining in sway. In Italy the Longobards and Goths had founded an influential nobility, but with the passing centuries nearly all the strength of that patrician element has dwindled away. Into Spain Semitic blood has been poured by the Phenicians, Arabs and Jews, so that the old Gothic aristocracy is simply disappearing. In Austria and Switzerland we see how a mixture of various nationalities is successfully engaged to curtail the supremacy of the Germans. England alone may be said to stand firm on Teutonic ground; and Scandinavia in her modest way. But through all these nations Semitic blood is spreading, which, since enfranchisement has been granted to the Jews, more than ever effectuates disintegration under pretense of cosmopolitanism—as a glance into the literature of the brand of the "Monist", edited by Carus, will demonstrate. "Amidst the ethnical chaos one state after another crystallises", said Droysen. But state after state may tumble back again into ethnical chaos. Political units with their preserving ingredients dissolve in the turpid fluids accumulating in the "international" pools. Already states accommodate themselves, more than they are ready to acknowledge, to international associations, to secret orders with their open exchange of encouragement.

This gradual dissolution designates national putrefaction. From the dark colored, chaotic flood—figuratively speaking—gigantic and awful forms may be seen to emerge, in juxtaposition to the remnants of sublime accomplishments, which will remind the educated—provided any of them are left to enjoy life—of the antediluvian sea-monsters.

Forerunners of the final appearance of personified wickedness arise.

These phenomena will rise from two different spheres, which according to our present terminology will correspond to the highest and the basest strata of society. They will correspond to past and present experience, and will substantiate our repeated judgment that grossest superstition from below always accompanies the airiest infidelity above. No state upon earth will then commit itself to the odium of bearing or protecting the Christian thought. And this thought in its original solitariness will then have to encounter twofold enmity. We must give the reasons upon which this presentiment is founded.

Grossest superstition always accompanying the most airy infidelity.

No state wants to contract upon itself the odium of bearing up or defending the Christian thought which then encounters twofold enmity.

§ 201. In the first place we refer to the situation preceding the advent of the Mediator upon the scene of universal history. Close beside the highest accomplishments of Roman society in regard to philosophy and æsthetics we have seen the ugly mantic cult of Akkado - Babylonian origin, the fright of ghosts, the oracle-business, and the belief in necromancy. Beside of the sublime heights of stoiçal affectation as to science and rhetoric, there yawned the steep abyss of wildest, superstitious frenzy. Nobody can imagine a Rome without its soothsaying from the entrails of birds and even of human sacrifices, without that stoicism which held its sway over the ranks of the educated, and which never denied its oriental extraction and Asiatic pantheism. These are the two phases of enmity to be encountered again by the Christian thought, of which we speak. At present this Pantheism is already the sole religion, rather intellectualism—and the only form of spiritual knowledge of the "liberally educated classes". Spinozism, as introduced by a plagiarist of oriental extraction—this becomes now remarkable—was the ground from which the great systems of quasi-religious speculation soared high up in our century. When it ascended into the thin regions, the gazers abandoned these systems to their inglorious descent, and returned to the solid monism of materialism altho it was discovered to be nothing but the substantial precipitate of pantheistical monism.

Combinations of infidelity and superstition at the time of Jesus repeated.

Stoical affectation and superstitious frenzy.

Soothsaying, necromancy.

Stoicism and pantheism.

Christianity again affronted by these two phases of enmity.

Since Lessing a laugh at the Heavenly world was deemed the counter-sign for entering the circles of respectability. The heroism of "pure reason" animated the chivalry of free thought—an aristocracy where a diploma was to be obtained tolerably cheap, "where the initiated took it for an insult, when," as Lotze said, "Heaven and eternal blessedness were offered as a reward". This heroism inflated people preparatory to an indoctrination of sheer selfadoration.

Spinozism is but oriental pantheism, under garb of Christian instead of Gnostic nomenclature; the ground from which the great systems of quasi-religious speculation soared high;

Then came that "crazy-quilt of Indian patches," stitched together artfully with German needles and thread," as Anton Guenther described Pantheism. Soon after, the Germans were upralded in English that Pantheism was the private religion of the fatherland. We must say that it was more: the secret religion of the literary classes, so far as they claimed education and exerted literary influence over the whole world. We must, moreover, confess that Pantheism was the secret of Schopenhauer's pessimism. And since that pessimism is so entirely a growth of the tropics, we confess in short, that—we approach Buddhism as a mode of thinking. History returns to its starting points.

and fell flat into the marshy monism of materialism.

Scepticism since Lessing.

The "Enlightened" ones indignant whenever Heaven was held out as a reward.   Lotze.

Not only have some writers glorified Buddhism as standing far above Christianity scientifically as well as numerically, but we see those associations forming already, in which the old Hindoo-philosophy is courted by the young monism of the Occident. As one of the signs of this betrothal we may only point to that Monthly "for the up-building of the metaphysical view of the world upon monistic grounds." American and English scientists are engaged in this enterprise in company with prominent Brahmins of Calcutta and Madras.

Pantheism compared to a "Crazy-quilt of Indian patches" stitched together with German needles.   Anton Guenther.

Pantheism the secret of Schopenhauer's pessimism,

Young occidental monism courting old Hindoo world-soreness.

The Theosophical Society of Madras prepares the unification of all Buddhistic sects into a sort of protestanism of the religious life of Asia. The result to be expected will be as nasty a mixture as Mormonism. The peculiar consummation of our diverting world-wisdom will flow together under the law of natural affinity. It is marked out as the religious syncretism which in the Apocalypse is termed pharmacopoia. For the same art of mixing denoted the consummation of ancient cultures, previous to the complete entrance of the supernatural into the world at the middle of the times.

"Monthly" for Buddhistic theosophy.

Syncretism the pharmacopola of the Apocalypse.

We turn to the reverse side of learned infidelity.

Reverse-side of learned infidelity.

Wundt defines the Spiritualists "as the pitiable victims of exodic Shamnism, having imported their hideous imagery about the human soul into Europe."—We are thus

Spiritualism akin to Shamanism.   Wundt.

transferred back to ancestor-worship, to the low sphere of a world of ghosts, from the fearful dreams of which the savage tribes could not save themselves. Again we stand before the feverish and fitful consciousness of the primitive, terror-stricken mass, fleeing from a curse which haunts them. But is it possible, indeed, that the old substratum of Mongolian Shamanism should be found an alloy of modern European culture? The sprouting of the old weedy seeds is not impossible on exhausted, barren ground, where the cultivation of the Heavenly plant has been willfully neglected, especially when history returns to its points of beginning. The flame of a deep-red gleam breaks forth everywhere from mysterious depths.

Periodically there went a hot wave of anguish over mediæval Europe. That anguish was caused by the monks admonishing people to repent. It was aggravated by the predictions of astrologers, by prophecies circulated through authors in Toledo and Paris, in Florence and Bologna. But its deepest source and incentive power was lying in the hidden depth of the human soul. In no other way is it explicable that the phantoms of religious visionaries, and the demoniac convulsions in hermitages and in the valleys of the Sevennes, down to the horrors of witchcraft, always kept pace with the spread-eagle attitude of highest worldly education and enlightenment. For never did infidelity extirpate superstition. This is more than evident from history. At the close of its career through barren heaths enlightenment may yet come to see, that the attempts to become as God in spite of Him will be put to grief. From the frying pan it will jump into the fire. The powers which infidelity has declared defunct a thousand times will then shake it like the ague. Kant, at least, believed the existence of an invisible world haunting us, after he had investigated Swedenborg's statements. The educated world of late denies faith in anything of the kind—consequently it will believe in the oracles of moving tables and knocking spirits. Nothing will be too weird in the line of old superstition, that infidels will not grasp after, in the heat of inner passions and in the cold shudderings of the feverish soul. This very scientific world will resort to pseudo-miracles altho hairs will stand on their ends from fright at the magical and occult phenomena. Despite, if not in consequence of having been mocked, the powers played with in sorcery will seize men as if they were their playthings; forces will fetter and fascinate them; visions of things and premonitious grasps of events near and far, heavenly and infernal, will touch human susceptibilities.

These phenomena are called magical because we are not as yet sufficiently acquainted with their inner nature as to systematically arrange and explain them. They were ever at work and will, yea, from the necessity in the matter, must make their appearance, because man is bound to appear in the completion of all his known and hidden potentialities, incipiencies, and proclivities.

It would be folly to predict the date of this completion, of the consummation of matters in prospect. But this much we venture to aver that the prerequisites for the occurrence of this revelation of man are at hand already, tho we may not be aware of them, or misapprehend the constellations of the signs of the times, if not altogether disregard them. We simply contend for the possibility that the collapse of our underminded world-civilisation may take us by surprise any day. More than that, we want to secure a position for our conviction, that more than one united counteraction of the preserving powers of civilisation may be expected, too, before the final crisis approaches. There is every reason to presume, that the power of capital may be checked once more; also that once more a healthy arrangement of political functions may be established, as, for instance, against the error of indiscriminate majority-rule; and that genuine liberty may have another lease of time. Nevertheless, the final catastrophe will come to pass, and illusions will come to grief.

§ 202. The approach of the end of the earthly form of existence is initiated. The contesting powers are putting themselves in definite array and decided opposition, taking the attitude of aggressive animosity on the one side, and of enduring resignation on the other, both rejecting every idea of a compromise for which no margin is left. The separation of all the nobler elements from the mass of vulgar dross, the draining off of the metal from the cinders is evidently going on. The key for understanding the struggle lies in the inciting motto: "Sicut deus eritis!"

The chasm between the sacred and the secular culture will come to full view only as we draw nearer to its edges. These two spheres of development become less congruous until they become extremely repulsive to each other.

The one is that of haughty world-consciousness attempting from its own resources to be as God so as to be under no religious obligations. People of that tendency flatten out upon the surface of things and spread into the broad periphery of worldly concerns and externalities; detaching themselves from the high and central fountain of pneumatic influences. *the one spreading out upon the periphery of worldly concerns, detached from the center,*

The other party of meek and humble God-consciousness concentrates itself in the direction of intensified personal life, and is anxious to sever itself from the views and propensities of the former. *the other concentrated into intensified personal life, severing itself from worldliness.*

Thus the chasm deepens and widens as the conflict proceeds and the crisis approaches.

There the nebulous outlines consolidate into the distinct figure representing all that is dark, base and bad. Here in the growing glory appears the holy "image" at the head of humanity, tho only in the refracted and many colored light of thousand-fold reflected rays. The bearers of His "image," purified under the care or in the fold of either catholic unity or protestant diversity, come to enjoy their blood-relationship in the realisation of a grand communion; they enjoy it altho it was brought about by the great pressure of common persecution and suffering. Among each other they are united by love, whilst the abhorrence of Godlessness—which all of them share in a measure equal to their love of their Savior—separates them from the lump of the abominable. For in the general pollution of carnal appetites the "emancipation of the flesh" in its nudity will be proclaimed, recognisible as the sediment of Greek naturalness; whilst the golden calf will receive due attention under popular round-dances. *Outlines of the figure representing all that is base and bad and consolidating.* *The bearers of the "image," reflectant from their being, come to enjoy the feast of the grand communion.* *Abhorrence of godlessness equal to the measure of love toward the Savior.* *"Emancipation of the flesh".*

Horrible nondescript bodies of pestilential gases, figuratively speaking in the sense of "physical analogies", will rise from that pool of putrefaction, into which all the refuse of worldly culture from Shanghai to Paris and San Francisco flows together. History never before witnessed a mixture of the Bad all in a lump, such as will then be animated by the infernal lust of destruction and by impotent defiance of God. Imagination shudders at the attempt of forming a conception thereof, or inventing a name or analogy for it. *Mixture of the bad all in one lump.*

We had occasion to look at the queer compound of man and beast in Turano-Mongolian art. This wild froth rising from certain fermentations in the human mind, was the expressive feature of those dark regions where we found the first sediments of history, that substratum covered up long ago, partly, however, lying open in wide tracts, to present view. In Asia we found it on the surface in primitive massiveness; upon the islands of the Pacific and in America it protruded in definite spots; in Africa we meet it broken up into debris. The weird forms of that low stratum reappear. Large parts of humanity will sink to that grade of consciousness, where the human eye will scarcely be recognisable, as it looks up from the repulsive medley of beastly convolutions. *Nature of the consolidated Bad as foreshadowed by Shamanism.* *Beastly features.*

Then the end of irreligious culture will return to the region of its beginning as history does. Then may come to full view what at the outset had only been typified. Once we found, merely guessing from the indications given by the broad substratum, and regardless of the historic cycles, that a collapse of culture was probable. Based upon this substratum we found universal history to commence its movements in definite curves, and to create a domain, in which now, since history presents to us its plain facts, we recognise the unfolding of that type of worldliness seen in the prophet's retrospective vista. As in a current this history moved through the broad ocean of nations, until it forms, in the consciousness of the Christian nations, a unit of experience comprising even people without a history in the usual sense. This movement is distinctly marked off as to its merely cultural or also civilising progress. *Worldliness of nature-bound consciousness hardening into the definite shape of the prophet's vision.*

Adopting Babylon in its symbolical import as the historic point of commencement, we distinguish the successive ancient monarchies down to the Roman empire, each fulfilling its specific part in preparing the scene upon which the world's Mediator took His position. In reverse order Rome then begins an ascending scale of monarchies, until at the close of the recurring cycles there looms up the ominous antitype of the figure seen at the beginning, resembling the Turano-Mongolian idea of power, and presenting even its materialisation. *Historic movements proceed in reverse order, correspond to the three first circles,—from Rome back to Babel.* *The ominous antitype of the figure seen at the beginning, becomes visible.*

If this figurative projecture of historical evolution could not make clear how the natural part of history is expected to wind up, then let us say, that we perceive at the close of history that confusion and maddening fray of which the name of Babel is proverbial and suggestive. Justified in taking Babel as the arche-type of *The natural part of history winds up with Babel-like confusion.*

Comparison between
present involutions of
worldly culture and the
problematic world-
monarcy of Babel.

worldly aspirations, which press on toward perverted ideals of unity, freedom and advance, we add, that the present anti-type reminds us of more than titanic defiance. But in order to understand the anti-type now revealing itself, we will have to go behind the typical event at Babel and to syllogise backward to where yonder dark chasm was widening when history emerged from chaos.

Advance of worldly
culture always
accompanied by the
decline of true
civilisation.
§ I 52, 11 40, 65-69, 78,
81, 104, 126, 127, 150,
169
To be further exhibited
in Book III
§ 213, 216, 218

The first foreshadowing of a worldly and organised consolidation—or rather the rebellious conspiracy against the divine sovereignty in the narrative of Babel—is instructive as to present developments. It reminds us of the fact that, altho the nations have made astonishing progress in mental culture, and are fitted out with technical facilities as never before, and stand upon heights of civilisation which afford much more relative security against the inimical powers of nature and social miseries: yet that, on the whole, these very nations of culture may rot and decay under their covers of safety and upon the very summits of civilisation, since they stand as distant from divine cultivation and discipline as never before. We will be reminded of such peculiar occurrences wherein the advance of worldly culture among the nations in general was always accompanied by the decline of spiritual culture, of true civilisation. Those phenomena, deserving special attention, will be further exhibited in the third book.

Man as a whole is to be
laid bare to the roots of
his being—before the
still deeper root of the
Bad back of him shall
come to view.
§ 117, 119, 168, 176, 185.
197, 201, 205, 232, 233.

For the present, it suffices to be reminded of the postulate that not only a part of human nature, but man as a whole, is to be laid bare to the roots of his being. Not before will the still deeper root of the Bad back of him come to view. No logic forbids the supposition that the gloomy mystery of the Bad is to be traced back to where it protruded from a personal center and source. When in the midst of the times we found this mystery dismantled, we acquiesced in the exposure of the instigator of deviltry. Difficulties not to be overcome in any other way received their solution,

The Bad not essential to
human nature.

to reject which would mean that the Bad is to be acknowledged as being essential to matter; that is, as being an original component of human nature.

The hearth upon which
passions are kept aglow
is to be sought outside
of man and what
belongs to him.

The hearth upon which the destructive heat of passion is kept aglow—which, baffling every precaution, repeatedly breaks forth in flames throughout all history— we remove to a realm outside of man and of what belongs to him. Inasmuch, however, as everything in the universe makes man the way and means of its revelation, sin and darkness take the same route.

Sin and darkness make
man the instrument, as
he is the way and
means of all revelation.

Effeminacy and cowardice would hide these facts from view, and trifle with things so stupendous. Humanity is the object upon which the horrible fiend fastens, in which he seeks to personify himself. Since the evil one is debarred from becoming incarnate, he will not cease to use human nature as his means, until he succeeds in taking possession of one as a vehicle of his ostentatious demonstrations and mystifica-

The Evil-one himself is
debarred from becoming
incarnate.

tions. Some person will attain to the requisite maturity and adaptness. The enemy of the Son of Man, so far tolerated under methods making him to destroy his own achievements, will then seize the opportunity to appear by his representative in

His final representative
"the man of sin".

order to arrange the final stroke. The "man of sin", the "son of perdition" will then discharge his assigned labors as the fruits of the infernal spirit, and throwing off all disguise, will reveal in bodily manifestation the substance of all iniquity.

Present
indications as to
his appearance.

In his nude immorality this product of modern times and infernal designs strips himself of every vestige of ideality of the True, the Beautiful, and the Good. He thus appears wherever modern man pushes away that upon which his dignity is founded: the principle of true humanism in Christianity. The ancient world did not have this foundation, hence these ideals

The ancient world
preserved the ideals of
the Good, the Beautiful
and the True, because it
did not possess the
ideal of humanity;
this therefore could not
then be attacked.

could not then be kicked away. In those times man constructed ideals of his own, enjoying them without being aware of the abyss beneath them and himself. These reflectent ideals were subsequently to become the bearing pillars of humanity upon the basis of the Christian view of life. Undermine this basis and the pillars tumble down; and along with the ideals man in his real value and significance falls from his position. Humanity is at once subverted to brutality. The animal in man, revealing itself more and more in the emancipation of the flesh, develops into the naked beast, fit to represent the personage which is aptly designated

The basis of ideal
humanity; being
undermined it becomes
degraded to brutality.

as "the beast risen out of the sea" (of nations).

The umbel fully
developed.   § 78, 77.

An awful metamorphosis takes place. Culture up to that height of evolution appeared as a beautiful flower, which now was thought to unfold into full bloom. Its roots ramified below the layers of all the historical strata—as the secret roots of all abomination. The broad, richly colored umbel bursts open and exhales its benumbing, poisonous fragrance: and being admired as culture, it utilises its deceitful attractiveness. But at the moment in

"Beast risen out of the
sea."

which the true nature of this deceptive secret appears, that very horror seizes mankind which is perceptible whenever one believes himself confronted with the world of ghosts and apparitions. Man gets into the habit of dissuading himself of the reality of the entities causing such momentary tremor, howsoever thoroughly it may have penetrated to the core of his frightened soul. But when at last the event occurs of which men ever felt premonitions, as of a monster "rising from the sea" of nations, men will no longer be able to persuade themselves of the scare being only imaginary. In opposition to the miracles from on high, which once were denounced as superstitions and impostures, miracles will come forth from below to mock the mockers. What of the evil eye, of black art, and sorcery ever and anon cropped out and scoffed at the world of enlightenment—whatever magnetism, somnambulism, or hypnotism, in fact or by way of delusion, were showing forth in faint and random phenomena, will then consolidate, intensify, and manifest itself as a personal, concrete power, hypnotising men by its very hideousness. The faces of the strong-minded even will then turn pale, and their bones will shake, when the man of sin will inaugurate his reign of terror. *[margin: Metamorphoses of the forms assumed by the antagonism to Christianity.]* *[margin: Miracles from below mocking the mockers.]*

§ 203.   It is postulated by history that the proto-type of all apparitions is to appear, inasmuch as man remains the theme of history under all circumstances. Hence man in both aspects, as to his faith in God or his enmity against Him, in what he loves or hates, must come to full and public view. The manifestation of either relation is possible in no other way than through a human being; just as humanism was revealed to the world from above through the Holy Person. Through Him ensued the work of rehabilitating mankind by regeneration. The issue was a new humanity in the form of a social organism, spread over the whole world and gathered from all nations. The work was accomplished through the instrumentality of the one, holy Church, which, tho hidden under many outward and visible organisations and malformations, forms essentially one community. That portion of humanity which in this historic connection is renewed into the likeness of the Man from above, expects with unfaltering certitude the appearance of Him through whom it came to exist, and with whom the mysterious inner life is to be rendered perfect and public. *[margin: Postulate of history.]* *[margin: Man in both aspects, in his love to God or hatred against Him and His children to be fully revealed in person. § 10, 35, 117, 119, 168, 176, 185, 191, 201, 202, 205, 206, 232, 233.]* *[margin: True humanism to culminate in a palingenesis and in the return of the Mediator in person.]* *[margin: Expectation of the church.]*

In an equal manner the opposite society in its organised form is awaiting its completion. Instinctively this organised "world" is bound to expect something nolens volens, and to turn its expectations athwart a leader—from below. The "world" demands that its life, long doomed to secrecy and ignominy by the power of Christian custom and law, must finally obtain the liberty to throw off its compulsory secrecy and to triumph over these restraints. It will thus publicly proclaim as its right, to be alone acknowledged worthy the name of human existence. *[margin: Expectation of the world.]* *[margin: Instinctively the organised enmity against God, the "world", too, is waiting for its leader.]* *[margin: Emancipated flesh claims to be alone worthy of existence.]*

Thus on both sides moral and historical consequences are coming to a head as a matter of necessity. That part of humanity perpetuating the nature-bound state of old obtains its full type and definite representation in the man of sin with his enchanting and demoniacal attractiveness. He comes with gifts for those who are enraptured with Hellenism, who revel in Buddhism, or stagger in Shamanistic frenzy. This representative of the merely natural humanism wields under alluring masks such a seductive power, and puts himself into such a broad attitude, and breathes forth such fumes of death, as to put the new humanity to its last test and to its hottest flame of purification. *[margin: Seductive influence of and intimidation through the "man of sin", who represents the mere natural irredeemable part of humanity.]* *[margin: Adherents of true humanism put to the last test in the crucible of purification.]*

In the ethical and mythological chaos the small band of the faithful, constituting the community of humanism revealed from above, will stand lonely and defenseless. The nominally Christian nations will, on the whole, have purged themselves of those elements which once served as their preservatives. The historical movement will then have flattened out so as to get along without the spiritual undercurrent, and will have finished its course from theocracy through Church-state and State-church-ism. Nations arrange their affairs according to "advanced principles," condemning Christianity to privacy as a political nuisance; tolerated on terms of time, it is then deprived of its historical rights. The crowds of profane people, detaching themselves from the ideals of their ancestors, and squandering their noblest inheritance, will not even suffer the silent admonition which the mere existence of that ostracised congregation exhibits to them. *[margin: Oppression and perseveration of the faithful.]* *[margin: The final fate of Christianity in the secularised world:]* *[margin: condemned to privacy, deprived of historic rights.]*

The strangest coincidence will be that the power of seduction and intimidation is wielded in no small measure by the very person, who, under the venerable vestments of historic dignity and the glimmer of three crowns, scandalises his position by abusing his former conservative influences in extirpating non-conformists on the one hand, and in selfdeification on the other. Since, as Goethe observed, the conflict between faith and infidelity generates the propelling force of historical development, it will hasten the final crisis. When systematic persecution grows hottest, when the arena and the catacombs again resound the wailings of the tortured and the perishing, then the great change shall occur which will take the "world" by surprise. The simplest drama drifts to a closing act which explains the plot, and redeems expectation from its many disappointments. A chain of intervening facts absorbs the attention, whilst the most interesting theme seems to be lost; until by a single accident the triumph of the good is ushered in, the spectator's suspense is relieved, his sympathy satisfied, his moral sense reconciled with the completion of the act. *[margin: The part which popery most likely is to take in the last appliance of oppressive measures.]* *[margin: Conflict between faith and infidelity had always generated a propelling force. Goethe.]*

A drama simply mirrors historic plottings and actions. During the developments of history the presumptive claims and the vain aims of the whole world dragged into the performance, conceal from man the leading theme of humanism under the suffering of the righteous. The nations gradually eliminate the limits once assigned to them, and identify themselves with the turbid mixture of the world's culture, having flowed together through the broken dams. The Christian thought seems to have been swamped, true humanism to be lost in the turmoil. History seems to have been derailed from its track and to end in a complete failure—all in the manner equal to the life of the Great Representative of humanity. But just at this instant the great change takes place. This climax is in itself the closing argument in refutation of the old assertion: Sicut deus eritis! The verdict now to be rendered settles the great historical litigation. The great truth implied in that promise—which in its falsification symbolises the subversion of the truth into the lie, and symbolises abuse of the truth for the purpose of distorting the divine purpose—is victorious after all. The formative thought, the constructive principle and motive purpose of history becomes visibly evident, and the motto in its true sense personified.

Christianity alone possesses the ties and the virtue to bind its adherents into spiritual unity, its ideas being realities and its facts being ideal. The church comprehended from the beginning, and in her first exhibition of the truth gave testimony, that in the God-man is given the proto-type and efficient factor, together with the pledge of the final perfection of a certain part of humanity. As the æsthetic sense of man demands from works of art, that the ideal sublimity and predominant thought animating the figure as a whole should be brought out by the finishing touches:—so the ethical sense, with still more forcible emphasis, demands final perfection and equity of justice as a matter of necessity. The Author of all has arranged from the beginning, and in the middle of the time has invisibly regulated that entire chain of development, interlinking freedom with necessity, which we call history. He, Himself, formulated the ethical and æsthetical demands and laws of the progressive movement in concurrence with the nature of things in general. He, Himself, in a conceivable manner, at the completion of the historical course, renders the final solution of the problems.

The decisive affirmation of the truth in the "sicut deus eritis" must consist in a public manifestation, through which unmistakable evidence is given to the eternal value of human ideals, of man's irrevocable destiny, and of the final earnings of his history. The palpable, visible appearance and reappearance of the Son of Man carries with itself a decisive and a separating effect. It is the last judgment. The touchstone or criterion of thoughts and acts—concealed throughout the historic evolution, so as to be known to faith only—becomes then disclosed to all. The effects of the leaven once added to the ethnical lump and causing it to ferment: the disintegrating and affiliating, the separating and organising, rejuvenating and preserving, the judging and adjusting effects are all rendered visible as in one grand cyclorama at the solemn second Advent of the Savior-Judge in His majesty. His presence throws light upon every relation, and makes it clear why everybody is judged according to the attitude of his own heart either towards or against Him.

That which ought not to have been is separated and banished from the world of true humanity. The dark spirits, who cannot bear to see the Son of Man and His cause triumphant, are expelled, and the effects of their influences along with them. The condemnation of the Bad, and of its instigator, and of those who by their acts identified themselves with both, is now manifest to the exclusion of all further controversy. The verdicts rendered long ago, are now simply confirmed and executed in such a manner that nobody dares to complain of injustice having been done him.

But for this final manifestation of justice history could not be considered as the sphere in which the spirit actuates itself; it would be natural history pure and simple. It would run in the spiral lines of an endless screw into the indefinite vagueness of the blue ether, never of any avail, a wearisome mismanagement, an unintelligible Vanity Fair. It would be unworthy of any cognisance; and we would have to despair of gaining wisdom from experience. Nowhere in the history of nature or in universal history would a purpose be conceivable; we would have to reckon with random quantities and the odds against us—a maddening, crushing aspect from which it would be best to turn away in hopelessness. But no; as it is, history has proved itself a well-arranged unit, a living organism with features the more expressive the finer it became differentiated; its constituent factors themselves determining its issues and serving to realise sublime intentions.

From the original chaos man emerged, uniting all the natural polarities in his own being; crowning the evolution of nature; containing within himself the type and theme of historical development. In that chaos at the middle of the times, when the fabric of ancient contrivances collapsed, the God-man and Mediator, center and source and model of a new humanity, took foothold upon man's rough earth. Again in the chaos of the latter days will He appear upon the scene, commanding peace, speaking the last verdict, and banishing the element of discord. Whosoever agreed with the mystical Head, and was attracted to Him as a center of homogeneity; whoever did not oppose being fashioned into His likeness; whoever was engaged in elevating earthly conditions and thereby cultivating the ego; whosoever and whatsoever is fit to be rescued and gathered from the collapse of worldly culture: He comes to take home to His own household. The members belonging to Him as their Head—analogous to the universe belonging to man—He will elevate into eternal fellowship with Himself. In the communion held at this reunion humanity in its fullness, perfection, and reality will be established. It will complete the reconstruction of the world of nations in the whole extent of its variety and differentiations as planned before the beginning. At the same time it will become evident that nations seemingly inactive, and that tribes paralysed from terror, deemed as having been forsaken and void of any culture whatever—were really not thus neglected by providence.

Whatever is fit to be rescued from the collapse, He comes to take home to His household.

His adherent members to partake in His own inheritance;

The system of nations in their gradation, and in their fractured condition all over the earth, reveals the thought according to which the roles for each to perform, were distributed. A rich variety of gifts and longings, aspirations and formations becomes known, none of which was entirely in vain. Refracted rays of the thought of humanity in many colors reflect the spiritual sphere of material or personal diversity under essential unity to which all pertain, each representing a part of that wealth of personal life which then becomes freed from raw hulls and mere external malformations.

each on his part reflecting the wealth of the world of unity under diversity; in their multiplicity resplendent with a part of Christ's perfect virtue; § § 14 end, see 117.

each man reflecting the wealth of personal life now freed from hulls and malformations.

CH. XII.   CONSUMMATION OF THE WORLD'S HISTORY.

§ 204.   Man being a combination of the natural and the spiritual world, it follows that history is partly natural history, running in the groves of physical law. The final crisis therefore not only concerns humanity or the moral world, but also the natural, the visible universe. Nature furnishing the corporeal part of man, it follows that with the revelation of man also the essential nature of the elementary world shall be completely revealed.

Part of history is natural history.

Nature participates in the history of man. The earth more than the mere stage for history to move upon.

At the commencement of our investigation we took our position upon the elevated region where the great mountain systems of Asia form their connection. There our imagination took a view over the mountain ranges, coast lines, and deserts of the earth. They all aided in determining the quarters for people to camp and dwell upon, and prescribed to historical sections their boundary lines.

Yet the earth is more than the mere stage for the historic movements. Man himself is fed by its elements. Iron and phosphor, salts and gases, etc., are the building materials of his body, and in large measure condition his moods and temperament. The human figure is a child of this earthly world, which nourishes man and carries him around. But "mother nature" is not above the nature of the child. Our body is subject to a state of permanent decomposition that is, is continually dying; and the earth will be overtaken by the same fate. The body is that by which man becomes visible, a transient composition of tangible matter. By the concurring decomposition man as well as matter is transmuted into something else, in a substance not visible to us. Hence the earth, too, is to partake of the same process.

As it supports man by virtue of its transmutability,

so it partakes of man's permanent decomposition, is continually dying.

Karl Ritter designates the earth as "a peculiarly organised cosmic individual, an entity sui generis with progressive development." Such the earth is indeed in its whole construction, in its substantiality, in the arrangement of its parts. On account of this form the earth in essence is subject to that form of decomposition which we call combustion; that is, designed for developing into a new or modified form of existence; the human body is the prophet of this transition.

The earth a cosmical individual, an entity sui generis. Carl Ritter.

What, then, will become of the earth? Viewing this question from the standpoint of the physicist, we would have to content ourselves with the negative results of either a very torrid, or a very frigid mode of destruction. That the earth shall once cease to be is admitted by every scientific observer. They only disagree as to the diagnosis of the malady causing the final demise.

Some think the earth will die of consumption, so to speak, that when all the carbon and nitrogen will be used up, organic life must vanish. Tyndall clung to the theory of a fiery end. "By a simple stop of its revolving motion the elements may easily attain to that degree of heat in which they must melt".

Dubois-Raymond is of the opinion, that the earth is doomed to glaciation. According to him the last great migration will rush from the poles to the equator; people will wander there to keep warm; and when the last inhabitant of the earth sinks down with chattering teeth, stark and stiff, then the last act of universal history will be accomplished. All scientists agree that as a matter of course the fate of man depends upon that of his dwelling place. The want of water would bring history to a standstill; lack of fuel would render history a thing of the past. Because of fire or ice enveloping the world, money would cease to be a power. "The earth will then as heretofore swing around the sun; but as waste a body as the moon now is".

In short, nature, not the spirit, is conceived as having to say the last word.

Why not reverse the matter? Why not concede the role of taking the initiative, at least, to the spirit upon essentially the same materialistic preambles? Let us take it for granted that moral ideas were indeed the products of nerve-action, equally dependent upon the action of the stomach, as the latter conditions the former. What, then, would hinder us from ascribing the determining part in the final catastrophe to the idea instead of the stomach? This has actually been tried. It has been said that the will power, underlying all that appears, must have accumulated sufficient strength first in the human will. For, only in this reservoir is gathered and contained that sum and substance of will, which surpasses the force of will in the abstract, which is conceived as actuating all earthly matter. As soon as personal will predominates over the blind natural will, the end may be brought about. That will-conveying substance which shall have been transformed into human thought may then determine to stop willing. The abstract remainder of will, marginal will at random, working merely as matter, must simply follow suit. Thus the end is at hand, the catastrophe sets in. Materialism, then, in either mode of apperception agrees with us at least in regard to the end of the world. Moreover the crisis is not tellurian but even cosmical. The sand of the dunes is as much concerned in the end of the world as the most remote astral nebulæ. For this universe constitutes an entirety; and as such it is of no more significance than that which the earth bears with reference to man. It is but the broad basis of the pyramid which we saw tapering up in man, its apex and crown; hence this whole mechanism of the universe must concur in his history and his destiny.

Inasmuch as in man the whole fabric of visible things related to him centers and makes him the microcosm, he, as the center, determines, in the reverse order, the fate of all his environments. It is astonishing, to be sure, that the incommensurable realms of the skies should be affected and their destiny determined by the issues of the comparatively small particles of humanity. The conclusion seems altogether preposterous. But the matter assumes a different aspect, if we consider that appearances as to quantity are delusive. This whole subject has been argued already. There we had extensive and quantitative preponderance in measureless spheres; here we have purview and qualitative weight in the smallest compass; there masses, here values; there immensities of distance, bound up in the mechanism of rigid lawfulness, of natural necessity, here in man the spirit looming up, surpassing and encompassing that mechanism by free thought; there the ponderous question, here the illumining answer.

By the way we may point to the notorious controversies respecting these problems, since Chalmers and Whewel, Zœckler and Peschel of late have written on the multiplicity of worlds. Pechel, in answer to those who insist upon the utility and purposeness of those worlds—because they find it unreasonable that so many stars should not be utilised for domiciles of reasonable creatures with a history of their own—rejoins: "They conceive of God as if he were a sort of real estate broker, whose practical instinct would certainly not have allowed him to build so many houses, being afraid of getting no tenants for them". According to our former conclusion we are inclined to agree with Schelling who said: "God has valued the man of earth so highly as to consider him sufficient for all His purposes. Man is the final aim of God, and in this sense everything is prearranged for his sake". Thus we conceive man as the epitome and aim of creation, on whose account its cycles through æons are focused from extension to intensity. The excellency of man is thereby exalted the higher, "as the basis upon which he stands erect, is the broader". The basis is the astral universe, "which none the less proclaims the glory and majesty of the Creator", as Schelling emphasises.

The decomposition to which man is subjected bears upon the transformation of his world with its entire heavenly periphery. Our bodies and the planet upon which we are flung through space, and the worlds of the universe are in substance all one and the same house falling to atoms.

Spectral analysis demonstrates this truth. It has helped us to abandon the illusion of an origin which sentimentally imagined the stars as clothed with the dignity of being angelic abodes. The whole great edifice made up of the same chemical and soluble elements must of necessity undergo the same crisis as that to which our bodies are assigned. Whether the process is called decomposition or combustion is immaterial.

This bulk of compressed and irredeemable life is that which "ought not to be". It is that which is irrational; embarrassing us whilst encircling us, fastening us between darkness and gravity; and torturing us with the anguish of opposing polarities.

§ 205. Repeatedly the different phases of human life have been enumerated which must develop the course of history, in order to verify the proposition that history means the complete unfolding of man. Often it has been attempted to show, how the progress of evolution would gradually abolish the cause of such abnormities as are undeniable, whenever the actual condition of humanity comes under consideration. But never has the demand been insisted upon that real progress must include the abrogation of those contrarieties into which man's dual being is divided. Concerning the strained relations, we refer to what has been said about "reflecting and unreflected consciousness." We desist from reviewing the mysterious capabilities concealed by the "night-side" of soul life which so seldom break through "day-consciousness." But we anticipate that in the end the separation of these two sides of the inner life shall cease. The strain between them is caused chiefly by the encumbrance of our personal life with our material corporeality, and is aggravated by a certain disintegration of our consciousness, by discrepancies among the faculties of the mind.

History means the complete unfolding of man.
§ 197, 201, 202, 232,

Real progress must include the abolition of the opposites into which the human dual being is distracted.
§ 96, 98, 175, 197.

Dual form of consciousness.
§ 15, 37, 111, 114.

Polarities to cease between corporeality and spirituality, causing the partition of consciousness.

From the depths of each human being conscience with its immediate feeling of value manifests itself as the representative of invisible, holy realities, whilst thought is captivated and molded by visions on the surface of this world and its laws. In the interior department of the mind faith holds sway; whilst in this province of the visible, piece-meal science insist upon its sole right to give explanations and to make its judgments binding. To harmonise the conflicts ensuing from the damaged condition and to bridge the chasm, is the demand implied in the concept of progress toward ideality. This conciliation is a postulate of reason as much as of moral sentiency.

But this liberation from an unnatural tension, this clearance of antitheses from the strains of antagonism can only be the sequel of the solution of another question and another tension.

Our environments in their present, which we call natural, form consist of nothing but matter. But we must remember that nature in its present condition is not natural in the sense of true reality and perfection. The materiality of nature, rendering it merely a catena of phenomenal appearances and veiling its essentiality is but the consequence of a thorough-going disturbance, because of which nature simply conceals the essence of things and the invisible world of our destiny, and distracts our attention from it.

Now these hulls will drop at the moment when, lightning-like from the sphere of the invisible, which blends with the visible except as to the usual concepts of spatial and temporal dimensions, our Redeemer will step over into our world of visible matters.

At the very moment of this appearance, when the personality of the Lord of creation shines forth, the veil falls and the cosmos undergoes the sudden metamorphosis into that form of existence which is nature essential and pure. A certain residue, consisting of the cinders separated by the smelting process, becomes purposeless. Of this we can speak metaphorically only, but the analogy holds good in describing the procedure.

Such a consummate perfection of the natural world is postulated even by the theory of "evolution". Progress essentially consists in gaining control over the phenomena of matter and over natural forces. All exertions of science have this end in view. Science searches in the heavens and upon earth for laws that will make forces and substances subservient in furthering the mastery of mind over matter. The obscure and incalculable domain of accidental happening is narrowed inch by inch.

Art pursues the same aim; for it does not content itself until the resistance of matter yields to thought, until it is made to represent the ideal. This being the motive of all progress, the goal of history can not be anything less. Subterranean and sidereal factors oppose the aspirations of man, as tho they had conspired to rebel against him. They try to absorb all his thoughts, to mystify them, and to dominate over them in their distraction; until finally they themselves shall be subjected to thought, and shall be made to obey its rule.

The subjection of elementary nature will not, however, be accomplished by hydraulics, screws, and nerve-reflex-action; and as little by chemistry as by mechanics. Dominion will not be attainable merely by inventing contrivances, as tho the mind had been given for no other purpose than to engage itself with nature; as tho the mind was to be but the means of overcoming it. The purpose intended by charging man with dominion over nature is not in the first place subjugation of creatures, but man's own spiritual freedom. No mind but that which is freed from its nature-bound state will surpass physical power with an authority approximate to that which was at the disposal of the Mediator.

This indicates and postulates a peculiar method of final consummation. All the power which the Mediator wielded over obdurate physical environments is made conducive to man's spiritual independence. This is to be inferred from the description of His deeds in the Book of the Nations. This dominion over nature can neither be wrought through physical arrangements nor by skill in any secret art. Tho miraculous, Christ's authority over, and command of, nature was natural, nevertheless; precisely as natural as the perfect unification of personal, that is, true physical and pure spiritual life within Him. Christ's command over nature was typical, and in its kind exemplary, altho as to its degree we must abstract from that nature which in our Savior was screened by our nature in its dependent state. In the glorified corporeality of the Risen One we observed the mode of that permeation of the corporeal by the spiritual substance which typifies and warrants the final transfiguration. This resurrected body, the first sample and pattern of a new kind of humanity, represents the unity of spirit and nature in its perfection. This modified and purified nature is no longer dead and obstinate matter. It is simply matter, or rather the essence of substance, in the form of entire subjection to the spirit; it is substance fashioned into the instrumentality of thought. Matter now solely serves to express thought in its willing and constructive capacity. Elementary substance, tho elevated into a higher state, becomes no more than pure nature, except that it is now visible in its true reality, as that essence of things which lies beyond the mere phenomena.

Those possessing the marks of membership in the mystical body of which the Mediator is the Head, view the material world in this sense. To them the stuff in nature has no more nor less significance. Their life's work consists in persevering to penetrate and permeate material nature with spiritual life, tending toward glorification. Thought pure and simple, the idea of development, and every analogy in nature postulate a glorification of their bodies.

Thought proposes or anticipates no more in this respect, than that which every noble creation of pure art indicates, upon which all works of sculpture, literature, painting and music inadvertently are bent: namely, the conciliation of mind and matter in real-ideal formations. Thought cannot rest satisfied, unless that final reconciliation is perfected in real forms, by way of the transformation of elements under the direction of thought into the state of their essential nature and purity, by vanquishing the antagonism between matter and mind, and by bringing both of them into full harmony.

Thus the Coming One is to be adored as the Great Artist, applying the finishing touch to what was invisibly prepared in His militant congregation upon the small earth. He is the Master-builder, projecting the restoration of the beautiful to its place in glory. With His appearance visible nature will be transformed from a concealing garment of the spiritual realities into a luminous environment of the new humanity in its glorified corporeality.

It is in the sphere of this unified personal and sublimated corporeal life that *The rupture of our dual consciousness healed.* the discords between matter and mind are overcome and harmoniousness prevails. Here, consequently,that rupture also is healed, by which our being in its present condition is distorted, so that we are crossed and recrossed by "reflecting and unreflected (or sub-) consciousness", by the seeming contradictions of faith and science, of divining and knowing. This conciliatory and redeeming consummation is pledged in the first and second advent of the Lord, our Mediator and Redeemer.

The return of Christ Jesus must not be imaged as tho He would need to travel *The Mediator's return not from sun distances.* hither from sun-distances into the present dimensions of space. For even now He stands in the center of all things and affairs ; embracing all, tho concealed and unapprehensible.

Unknown He dwells in His own Household. *The incognito of the Lord.*

His presence is analogous to that of the hero among the suitors of whom the myth speaks. These frivolous guests behave boisterously in his own halls, debauching his property, drinking his wine, courting his wife, not knowing that the master of the house is present. He observes them, not from afar. He moves among them in lowly garb, a stranger, whom the spendthrifts take for a beggar. But suddenly he makes himself known, throwing aside the concealing enclosures. The frivolous lips grow pale, for the debauchers stare at him with ghastly horror, seeing now what they alleged to be "Unknowable".

The mere dropping of the incognito amounts to a criterion, deciding the crisis of *Crisis at the "great day".* the last judgment. It transpires in a manner analogous to the discharge of the electric spark into a chemical composition, instantaneously separating the elements. Under the effects of this sudden reduction the most hidden ingredients become discernable. In separating the mixture   electrosis sets free the affinities. The *Illustrated by the discharge of an electric flux into a chemical composition. Electcosin.* appearance of the Mediator will produce the same effect. Thus that crisis comes to completion which began when "the word" was discharged into that sweltering *Completion of the reductive process begun when the "word" was discharged into the compound in the Roman crucible.* compound in the Roman crucible. The precipitate of the compound, falling away from the purpose-thought, will sink to the bottom as a caput mortuum.

§ 206. This crisis brings out still another sequel.

If the magnetic bar approaches a surface strewn with iron particles, they show *Communication of strength to Christ's adherents illustrated by the action of the magnet.* agitation as if animated with life from above; their susceptibility for the attractive force is awakened. They rise to meet that force attracting and governing them. As soon as nearness permits, the law of gravity, binding them down, is rendered powerless by the higher force of magnetic attraction. The loose particles give themselves up to the strong influence of affinity, adhering to it, and being held up and held together by it.

By virtue of the homogeneous efficient the dormant receptivity was quickened. *A higher force suspending the law of gravity.* We have the phenomenon of corresponding essentiality and polarity, in the approach of which the particles find their hold and their rest. The bar imparting its force bears them, with sufficient power to keep them safe, over the chasm which opens beneath, because of the suspension of the law of gravity.

This is a physical analogy of the process in which the Head of humanity attracts *So must Christians become agents of the attractive power.* to Himself all who throughout the course of history opened themselves to His influence, and who are drawn to Him through a sympathy mocking every law of natural necessity.

Furthermore; the persons thus attracted and held together by the Mediator become instruments themselves for the further communication of this attractive influence.

In a manner, equal to the spirit being the center and core of the human being in *Humanity proper is to the universe what the spirit-soul is to the human body.* the concrete, is humanity the center and essence of the natural world, the remotest spheres of the visible universe included. Inasmuch as this physical universe centers in the human body, it is also encompassed by the spirit. The human body is the locus and medium of unification, the organism in and through which the elevation of *The transition from natural life to its spiritualisation goes through the personal life of man.* the natural into the spiritual sphere is to be effected, the fabric where the assimilation is initiated. In the connection of the body and spirit the physical world as an entirety is apprehended, appropriated, and pervaded by the mind alone. By way of

27

personal life is nature conducted upward into new relations and functions, which were never thought of in the lower sphere of natural life left to its own helplessness.

Under the same rule of order the physico-psychico-pneumatic humanity is assumed, adopted, and conducted into higher relations, functions and beauty, by the God-man to whose likeness humanity is to be restored. When he took to Himself human nature and corporeality, even in its dilapidated condition, this restoration was His object. But because of the dilapidated condition, the elevation is of necessity conditioned by the ethical process prescribed in the order of salvation.

Jesus, by virtue of His own holy personality—having substantiated the union of corporeality and divine spirituality, and having glorified natural life as well as personal life—conducts in and through Himself the natural world back to its ideal and true form of being. At His final appearance He bodily transfigurates the members of the humanity belonging to Him as His body, into the state of glory—and Heaven and earth, belonging to them as their body, He transforms along with them. Thus the retardations and delinquencies of life in general, spoken of in the preliminaries, are finally also made good.

"Corporeality is the end of all the ways of God." First in order the Savior's dead body was lifted up in radiant glory; and in the end each member of His organically connected new humanity will be lifted up in its own spiritualised corporeality, fully conformed to the spiritual character contracted and built up during its preparatory state. And with that host of the redeemed made perfect, the visible cosmos, so intrinsically connected with humanity as to belong to it, will be transformed into the purity and beauty of a temple-like habitation.

Not before this has taken place can the full development and completion of history's course be realised. As creation in its entirety and whole compass was designed and planned for the appearance of man, so the New Heaven and the New Earth, and the labor of history with its weal and woe, is only complete with man made perfect. In the Son of Man and Mediator this completion of humanity was reached in the single specimen as its type. Not before human nature has reached perfection in its multiplicity, exhibiting the gifts and tasks as fully developed in all directions and relations, will the theme of history in its innumerable variations be

exhausted. That is, the august figure of man can only be expected to appear under the intonation of the closing accords, when with the glorification of man's personal life that main discord is solved, which divided his nature into body and spirit with two forms of consciousness. Corporeality, after being pervaded and permeated by the free spirit and rendered its instrument without any conditional reserve, is no longer an encumbrance. No longer is incipient potentiality bound up in occult mysteriousness and withheld from the use of its possessor. For personal man as a member of, and in connection and communion with, the universal Head of humanity,

then possesses and fully enjoys true freedom. Then he comprehends himself as the miracle and conundrum of the ages, as the seed ripe for the harvest, as the final aim of history. We may describe this fulness metaphorically, for that which Gœthe said is true: "Every thing transient is but a parable of transcendental reality."

A plant in its whole organism of cells and fissures, of roots, stems, and branches, up to its foliage and blossom, serves but one single purpose—the fruit. The fruit—tantamount to the seed, which was the ultimate source of its being and growth, and which is but reproduced in the fruit—was from the time of sprouting the final aim of the seed. And tantamount to

plant-life, only mirroring on a small scale the purpose of the entire universe, is the process of fruitbearing going on in humanity, for the sake of whose protective concealment this visible universe solely exists. This is the mystery which the universe preserves and silently matures hiding in its lap. Its secret is the seed unfolding and ripening. This is what the visible creation amounts to in relation to its secret—renewed humanity.

Pressing the parable a little further, we see at first the extensive green outlines of verdure. Then we look closer and admire the tender, richly colored, and fragrant calix of the flower, telling of plant-life intensified, of the bliss of nascency. It contains the mystery of the plant as in a sealed envelope: the new life germ seeming so insignificant as compared with the beautiful bloom. This cup contains the blessing: the pistil and ovary enclose the future life. The new seed in its receptacle is the aim of the whole fabric of plant-life: with its extensive crown of foliage, with its splendid child of the season—the blossom. When the seed is formed the beauty of the blossom may fade and wilt; the outward foliage may sink to decay; they all, even the old tree, having served their end. The seed ripens, absorbing all the interest and energy of the plant. And the seed alone contains the wealth of the harvest exceeding by far the value of that which is to perish.

The wide compass of the visible cosmos, the glittering garb of earthly and astral splendor is merely the enclosure of the next and narrower compass—the world of humanity. This in itself again contains the Church, bearing the seed, and with it the secret and life of the future. When the veilings of the visible church are dropped she will step forth in her beauty as the kingdom of Heaven in the triumphant state of perfection; and if we adopt the new humanity as the final product and fruit of history, then we have utilised in our way that concept by which Origen once pictured to himself the intricate arrangements of Providence for executing the plan of the world. *The visible cosmos merely the enclosure of the next and narrower compass, the world of humanity.* *And humanity again envelops the church, bearing the seed and the secret of future life.* *The church triumphant.*

We go even further. For, since the intensified center of creation has appeared in its perfection, there proceeds from this apparent mean or middle a reproductive and regenerative power affecting the most peripheral spheres. This widest environment rotates around man as its axis; it feeds him and becomes alive within him. And it is amidst the scenes of this widest sphere, that man is judged according to his ways of adjusting his relations to that environment, judged according to the manner in which he has treated the center and the periphery. Upon that scope man's actions forever remaining his own as witnessed by these scenes, give testimony in public for or against him; and there the completion of his renewal takes place: all in the face of the original Image in whose reappearance man recognises himself—a recognisance which reveals his secrets to the world, putting to shame all the denials of these secrets, too. It is then that man finds himself surrounded by a new world, in full possession of all his original gifts, in the free use of primitive incipiencies, all unfolded into a glory and majesty beyond all that ever could have been imagined. It is the radiance of what was formerly the secret of humanity, in which the wonder of the world is now rendered intelligible; which in throwing its light upon the great purpose of history—explains it all from the aspect of its consummation. *New humanity the final fruit and product of history.* *Origen.* *Amidst the scenes witnessing to his activity man is judged according to the manner in which he adjusted himself to the center and the periphery.* *Man is judged in the face of his deeds, in the face of the "Image".* *In the face of all the denials of these secrets.* *All the wonders of the world explained is the light of the final consummation.*

BOOK THIRD.

The

Problems of Historics.

RIDDLES AND RESULTS OF HISTORY.

SYLLABUS.

Should the closing part of this work contain merely a retrospective summary, Recurrence to postponed items. which the student might expect to find therein, it would be superfluous. The arrangement in two divisions of the material reserved, is to show certain groups of phenomena diagrammatically drawn and placed in proper light under the definite aspects suggested by the plan of history. This is done in order to answer with the utmost possible degree of correctness such questions as have forced themselves upon the observer's attention without finding satisfactory solution at the time, simply because it was during the previous considerations deemed better not to interrupt the connection.

The nature of the items thus postponed requires, that they be treated according General topics: I Purpose in finality. to their interrelations. Presented as thus classified the phenomena may be subsumed in the first division under the topic of purposive finality. The second is for the investigation of matters bearing upon the progressive and well planned movement of history toward the goal ascertained.

We are used to having attention called to the problems here involved by the inquiry, whether a steady and incessant progress could be proven, in what it consists II Progress after a plan. and where it is going to end.

We must refer to former passages pointing out where the real results of development are to be looked for. Anent thereto the desire for surity as to the goal grows more vivid. Hence, inductive investigation is called for, explicitly specifying the gradual degrees which designate the height of real attainment in the advance of civilisation.

This may properly be done in the conclusion, where once more the closing scenes of earthly history come to be contemplated. We shall not fail there to bring to notice a few circumstances in proof of the fact, that the essence of all things, affairs and thoughts must become manifest in the end.

A. FIRST DIVISION.—ENIGMATA OF HISTORY WITH RESPECT TO THE PURPOSE.

Never will history become to us more transparent than we are to ourselves. From Inductive investigation of the degrees of development towards its goal. unfathomable depths within us arise feelings and sentiments, thoughts and recollections and divinations apparently without connection and even contradictory—yet ever firmly cleaving to consciousness.

Doubtless, these phenomena occur according to certain laws, however enigmatical they may, for the time being, remain as to their sources and their bearings. This History no further elucidated than we have knowledge of ourselves. holds true with regard to nations as well as individuals. A few additional empiric truths, relevant to consciousness, will therefore engage our attention. We single out such questions as, if at all solvable, will afford stronger light upon the course of history as a whole. Conclusions on that score are to prepare us for considering the problem of the world's government on the line of inductive reasoning. To avoid much tarrying concerning a few minor points the remembrance of a few data already adduced is presupposed.

CH. I.   NATURE-BOUND PEOPLES AND MUMMIFIED NATIONS.

§ 207. With reference to former disquisitions some additional remarks are necessary concerning peoples who remained "children of nature" and others who appear as fragmentary remnants of primitive aboriginal culture.

The children of nature are found in those regions and in that condition always peculiar to them as far as history affords any knowledge of the ethnical fragments. For reason of their stationary existence they are to be considered as memorials of cultural relapses. They have been called "products of degeneracy." Many of them may more appropriately be designated as mummified nations.

The nocturnal heavens show, beside the stars with color and strength of light, nebulae with a faint and dusky gleam. These are heaped up around nuclei, or appear to be dust-like masses of exploded worlds. In fancy we witness a continual process of coming and passing away; we perceive therein at any rate transmutations of cosmical matter. Some astral elements are gathering and consolidating, whilst others dissolve and disperse into space—yet the region of those occurrences can ever be traced and pointed out.

Similar processes are observable among the ethnical elements, where equal transmutations are continually transpiring. Comparing this ethnical material to a tree with many branches spreading over the earth's entire surface, ever prolific in the production of new nations as its clusters of blossoms, we find most of the blossoms barren—nations which seem to lack every trace of culture, which show absolutely no progress.

Such nations with no historical record or import are designated savages.

How and why did they become arrested in their development? We may say that they were wanting in those requisites which cause differentiation—the polarity of personal, domestic and social life. But more than that is there missing the pressure of environments, which individualises and generates social peculiarities by prompting peoples to organise into separate vocations and classes.

Instead of those missing factors a great deal becomes evident of something which "ought not to be", as Schelling expressed it. This arrest of organic life on the scope of humanity ought to be no more than the excess of births and deaths in the physical world at large.

We are reminded of a factory of compressed yeast, producing five tons per day, so that the daily crop of incubated microscopic fungi amounts to 200,000 millions. Every large wave of the ocean carries with it innumerable jelly-fishes which are thrown ashore to dry up upon the sands. The houses of billions of the small scacalaicæ became their coffins; they had to die on the coasts of the Baltic or the Pacific that their cysts might form limestone and chalk. Those births and deaths in such masses involve riddles of historic import; for we meet a corresponding excess in the human world.

It seems strange that Christian culture should cause entire races to succumb because of being disqualified to adjust themselves to that which means death to barbarism. But the drift of history goes to unification.   Civilisation draws societies, and finally the remotest circles of nations ever closer together in the ratio of shortened distances, until the entire ethnical mass becomes one large body with many members for different functions. This embodiment of the civilising thought cannot, of course, assume its adequate shape, unless elements capable of improvement are assimilated, or others, proving unfit to accustom themselves to the civilising process, are expelled or perish. Just at present this latter part of ethnical refuse is swiftly diminishing. We hasten to shelter what may as yet be saved of the cultural vestiges of nature-bound nations, of their labors and languages, etc., in our ethnical museums.

Let us examine and classify some remnants of "natural" humanity. Organic formations of prehistoric u-ons are frequently found to be inclosed in rocks, where they were fastened secure as against the conditions of climate, or in order to be transported over the earth's surface. They belong to the stones which bear them under their bosoms, so to speak, where they moved and died. This analogy may illustrate the fate of nature-bound people arrested in the earliest stage of their progress. Such tribes and nations are imbedded, almost encysted in the customary rounds of their daily lives. In most cases every individual is enslaved by custom, to the rules of which every performance is tied down, and whose violation is held to be the same misdemeanor as, on religious grounds, it was held thousands of years ago. Such people are under constant anguish, not one step will they venture out at night without being afraid of evil spirits and spectres.

Then there are other peoples so little differentiated, so stiffened and immutable that with them there exists scarcely any possibility of further social disorganisation or degradation.

We think of the hordes roaming over the steppes of Central-Asia and through the western parts of the Sahara; which may represent the zero-point of receptivity and differentiation. They lead a stupid, vegetating existence, and, indeed, form no social strata. This lack of individualisation explains the unprogressiveness of nature-bound nations for thousands of years. These encysted lumps of humanity are no more organised than the protoplasmic mass of a mollusk. Even the bodily constitution of the individual is far less sensitive to surgical operations—which in these cases are scarcely accompanied by wound-fevers—than the constitution of civilised persons. *Lack of individualisation. Unorganised hordes even physically less sensitive.*

The susceptibility to nervous excitement in certain tribes of the Pacific islanders seems to contradict our observation, but rather corroborates it. Their staring at a foreigner and imitating every play of his facial muscles as if hypnotised by him proves that neither energy nor physiognomy is under control of selfconsciousness· They are so completely bound to the instinctive habits forming their second nature that they appear to possess in place of selfconsciousness nothing but an almost spontaneous and uniform habit of not only childish but embryonic life. *despite a certain nervousness. Neither physiognomy under the control of consciousness.*

Other peoples we find to be somewhat differentiated sociologically who, nevertheless remained in the lowest stages of social life, whilst nations of their kinship advanced to highwrought cultures. *Condition bordering on embryonic life.*

The use of human skulls for drinking cups is known to us from times as late as Alboin and Rosamunda; the inhabitants around Lake Albert in Australia have, up to date, advanced no further. Many tribes, like Tubi-nations, represent the "stone-age" at the present time. The Australian is, on the whole, the "diluvial man of our own age"; his feelings and intelligence are those "of a child of a civilised European", except that the Australian does not advance with his years. "The child of civilised nations bites, scratches, and rolls on the ground from spitefulness. The Australian draws pictures like those of the Hottentot artists, or like those made in the reindeer period". *Nations arrested in cultural development whose kindred races advanced. Australasians: "diluvial man of our own age."*

In civilised nations it takes a few years only to graduate through the stages of development from childhood to adult age; that is, through all the stages for which it took the nations, as such, scores of centuries. But the development of nature-bound peoples has, in the particular phases of their respective cultures, remained arrested up to date, leaving some as far back as they were in their childhood. *Children of civilised nations pass all the stages of cultural development in the few years between childhood and adult age.*

§ 208. We encounter an objection to this explanation of arrested social and cultural life from the lack of individualisation and social differentiation. "It can scarcely be admitted", says Herrmann Wolf, in his "Logic and Philological Philosophy," "that the development of the psychico-epistemological process should become stagnant in an entire nation and remain at that point." *whilst peoples of arrested development remained at the stage of their childhood. Objection against this conclusion of "arrested life", on the ground that intellectual development would not stop. WOLF.*

It may be rejoined, in the first place, why such arrest of progress should be rejected as improbable? We argue, that the limited terminology of isolated language was simply due to their becoming deprived of opportunities to converse with others· Flexibility of lingual symbols cannot be expected from people excluded from communication with strangers. The fixed position of simple terms could not be overcome when no new idea was to be conveyed; when the routine of everyday life, and simplicity of relations stopped the rudimentary syllables at a minimum, so that modifications of vowels and flexion of nouns and verbs were not required. Another than monotonous syntactic construction could not be expected from an isolated nation without "pressure from environment." Wolf's Logic simply underrated the paralysing effect of isolation. *Arrested logic accounted for by poverty of language. Paralysing effect of isolation not to be underrated.*

Recently Ehrenreich enumerated those nations in Brazil which are not to be catalogued among the other lingual families and thus stand "completely isolated". Nine of such came under his observation. We shall return to this circumstance, when we may, to some extent, agree with Wolf's objection on points which may surprise him. At present we maintain, that an arrest of cultural development, and a deficient capability for progress in general, is certainly thinkable in savage nations. We only state that, even accommodating ourselves to the above objection, there is left a possibility at least for progress in the downward direction to fossilisation. *Completely isolated people of Brazil. EHRENREICH. Granting Wolf's exception the possibility of a downward progress is not excluded.*

Motionless as regards cultural progress, almost petrified like wood at the seam of a coal-bed, do we find the superannuated debris of ancient nations. This fact induces those to agree with us, who take the nature-bound parts of humanity for mere products of nature—whereas we hold that they have degenerated into this state of bondage in consequence of a prehistoric dispersion. Even our opponents, then, know of "products of degeneracy", being cautious, however, to apply this term to a very limited cluster of phenomena. *"Products of degeneracy"*

Sœren Hanson, ten years ago, took the Esquimaux of Greenland for the remnant of a people, which, immigrating into South America from the Southern Pacific islands, at one time covered the entire continent. These Esquimaux, then, would be a sample of a tribe arrested or degraded in progress through isolation. Argyll takes the same view. Von Löhen finds "products of degradation" in the present inhabitants of the Canary Islands. The Weddu of Ceylon, according to Sarasin, are monumental remnants of a large nation of aborigines,

of whom no more than about 2000 lead a forsaken life in the interior forests. Ehrenreich has been mentioned. He seems to agree with Martius in taking the Karaya of Brazil as "dispersed fragments of a tribe of the Guayann", as also the tribes along Rio Aquiri and Madre de Dios. "They seem to have retained many features of the old Inca culture". This would go in proof of an arrested and afterwards degraded condition.

Recently report was made about the Aimara. Camping around Lake Titicaca they are, according to D'Orbigny and Mittendorf, the remnants of that nation which left the traces of the old Peruan culture of the Inca.

Upon the watershed between the Nile and the Congo rivers, Casati found such degraded remnants of Mande and Abisanga. Schweinfurth declares the African dwarf nations, as for instance the Acca, as a belt of inhabitants, stretching across the continent from ocean to ocean, who are related to the Bushmen. His conclusion is, that they are perishing remnants of the primitive Africans.

The Kassa nation in its separation from the Æthiopian empire shows, how Christianity decays under the preponderance of Mohammedanism; a repetition of a formula with the three holy names of the Trinity is all that is left of a forgotten past. The bearers of all such last remnants of cultures are in their last stages of decay.

As equally insufficient as the effects of isolation have, in our opinion, those influences been considered which conquering exerted upon vanquished nations, and vice versa. Take the spread of Islam for instance. It is no exaggeration to say that it affected peoples of an originally higher civilisation as a coat of lacquer would affect a blooming plant—they were suffocated. The same was the case at times with Mongolian domination, which had a mummifying effect upon Christian as well as upon Mohammedan nations.

§ 209. The condition of so-called uncultured nations has been pointed out sufficiently to prove their historic insignificance. The question returns, why were these valueless remnants of cultures like that of India, allowed to wither long ago, and to remain languishing in their arrested and degraded conditions through several millenniums? The fact of the slow process of decay affords not even the solace, that the cultures falling to pieces might serve as fertilizers for new ones. For, these remnants are like loose marl which neither decomposes nor permits anything to grow. Not even races, which remained without a history from the beginning, e. g., the Papua and the Esquimaux, crumble to pieces, and they seem to bear no other significance but to remain standing enigmata.

If progress was merely a matter of natural necessity, the decomposing mass ought to furnish humus, at least, upon which nature might raise new crops of cultures. As it is, the perishing ethnic element did not die, and we cannot see why they were kept alive.

But let us remember that people without any culture do not exist. Reasons for this assertion were laid down in §§ 37 and 176, to which we refer.

Just at this instant Lotze, the venerable scientist, comes to our assistance. "The hesitancy to estimate one part of the world as no more than a lifeless and blind agency for the purposes of the other part, and the desire to let all creatures participate in the rapturous embrace of animation, form series of inducements to seek the warmth of mental activity beneath the surface of matter and beyond rigid lawfulness of nature in its usual method of working. Another series of weightier arguments lies in objections preclusive of the idea, that no entity could exist without possession and enjoyment. Contradictory suppositions of that sort force the conviction upon us, that true being is attributed alone to entities with life of their own and that all entities can only be understood to have originated from conscious life, and that conscious life cannot be explained as originating from mere inanimate being."

The above author recapitulates: "Nothing hinders us from, and many circumstances enjoin upon us the supposition, that there is an inner life hidden in the simple elementary entities, tho in their compositions they may appear to us as inanimate matter; and enjoin upon us the further supposition that the lowest grades of our race participate in the inner life, by virtue of which all men are capable to enjoy under various modes of susceptibility, the peculiar circumstances they are placed in, or to make the best of their conditions."

Of the gist and import of this conception we have spoken already. We now apply this truth to those parts of the ethnical world which, as far as history and progress are concerned seem to lie prostrate as if they had become paralysed. Examining their condition more closely, we find these lowest of the historical strata to have once been animated by cultured life. An ability for varied work and enjoyment is manifest everywhere. Beside the psychical eclipse and in spite of it, we always find the lowest specimen of humanity to reflect that light of life which manifests itself in conscience making itself known by the feeling of gratification, whenever its dictates are obeyed.

Hence the work and enjoyment of uncultured, unhistoric nations is interesting enough to be worthy of recognition. "The value of civilised life, as against the existence of those who remained in nature-bound conditions, is not to be estimated by the accumulation of refinement or amount of pleasure," said Waitz. In proof of this truth even nations at the bottom of the cultural scale evince an unsophisticated, childlike appreciation of the Beautiful; we find dispersed rays of selfdevotion and its corresponding inner happiness; even traces of an ethical sense verified by acts of selfdenial. In the lowest stages of self-culture we find advances to the enjoyment of arts, be it in the melancholy modulation of the plaintive voice, or in the raillery of a love song, or in the pleasing forms of carved weapons and kitchen utensils. There is always some art contributing toward the ethnological museum of culture in general; and always a certain joy in recompense of artistic achievement.

Nations void of culture there are none, provided we measure them not by our own, but by their standards. Speaking of ethical and cultural cooperation in this sense, all people are found in some way to assist in the development of civilisation. If such, of course indirect, cooperation on their part could not be proven, it is to be presumed; since in this ethical realm the law of the preservation of energy is as valid as in the physical.

The remarkable instance that the two Akka boys in Verona in a comparatively short time learned to read, and to play the piano with ease, proves, in computation with innumerable facts of this kind, that in man everywhere the same potentialities lie dormant for acquiring equivalent accomplishments. Whatever Chinese and Japanese have done for representative art is all exceedingly childish, old as their cultures are, especially with regard to their perspective in drawing. And yet they understand the composition of colors to such a degree that an art-periodical in Munich spoke of an "actual symphony of colors." By way of comparison we put beside the Chinaman a raw savage, a Bushman, to whose drawing reference was made in some report of late. To all appearances these Africans, standing "in close proximity to the brute" seem to be skillful draughtsmen, nevertheless. Geometrical figures for decorative use executed by them were recently laid before the Anthropological Society in Berlin which were as correct as were their pictures of the human form; even "drawings of animals in motion were admired." Add to these testimonies those mentioned when the signs of the sun's generative effects were spoken of and the hook-and-eye shaped ankh-figures or "Mæander-crosses", investigated by Senf, who by this symbolism common to all nations proved the unity of the race and of religion—then we are vindicated in ascribing a sense of symmetry and beauty to every section of the human race.

We remember an expression made by Leo in his universal history: "History offers a chance to every human potentiality for acquiring universal importance." Leo speaks of national life from which no energy can come to naught. It may have become encysted, repressed, petrified, yet it remains, as the power of the sun lies preserved in coal-beds. The lack of a profound and vivid insight into the life of uncultured people, give us no right to deteriorate any of their merits.

In this respect we are like the wanderer who has never studied botany. Going through the heaths and over the mountain crest he scarcely notices the plants he sets his foot on, his eye being wearied by the monotony of the scene. Had he knowledge of, and love for, the flora, he would see more. The creepers beneath his feet would interest him in their variety and their peculiarities, and enable him to look into a world of unostentatious beauty. So are our eyes rather attracted by the mighty formations of advanced culture, whereby we acquire the habit of slighting that which is meek and lowly in the ethnic world. There is an eye, however, which does not lose sight of that which is despised on earth.

Universal history may be likened to an exquisite piece of textile work. The great patterns ingrained, the result of uncountable threads interwoven, which in themselves may seem irrelevant, we can only contemplate from a certain distance; if looked at too closely we can not enjoy the beauty of the picture, seeing but the single threads protruding and disappearing again and again in the intertwined whole. The threads in that artistic piece of tapestry become indiscernible, until at a proper point they reappear in order to perform their part in bringing out upon the picture this and that feature or tone of color, which to the experienced eye is indispensable if the whole is to produce the designed effect.

Thus individuals, tribes, and nations may disappear as tho they had been of no use, yet, on account of the part they played, insignificant as it may have seemed, they come to notice again, and become interesting. Yea, we find that for the whole they become, at some date, of real importance. If one or the other trace of their existence had not been preserved, the great system of cultural life could, perhaps, not be understood.

Taking one more glance upon these "uncultured" people so often designated as savages unworthy of our consideration, a general view will comprise a series of actions and reactions, of tension and equation running through the arrested life of ethnical strata and debris. Forsaken peoples have in their silent ways exerted influences not only like, but even in concert with, the imponderable forces stored up in the silent chambers of our planet. We found that the "dead" masses of people, those ethnical layers broadcast over large tracts of the globe,   that even single hordes have often made themselves very distinctly felt at critical moments of history. Frequently they have played most prominent parts in determining the shade of the gobelins or shape of the pattern woven and spread over them. Cases are not rare in which they imparted new impulses and gave different directions to historical movements, whether the civilised contemporaries were aware thereof or not. (Further consideration of this matter is to be deferred to the fifth chapter).

CH. II PAROXYSMAL MOVEMENTS IN NATIONAL LIFE.

§ 210. The river of history runs not smoothly, it has its rapids and cataracts. Now it runs faster or slower, now it seems to rest altogether between receding banks whilst at the next bend the waves dash against the rocky beach and the foam gathers among the rotting debris driven ashore.

When motion seems to stand still the smoothness of the surface is mostly deceptive.

It is as with the movements of our bodies. Respiration, circulation, the work of secretion and excretion, the whole process necessary to sustain the body by a sum of reflex-actions goes on without our being conscious thereof, or our will being consulted, or engaged in it. The operations of our organism quietly continue during sleep, and it is just then that internal activity is paramount. So is tranquillity most conducive to the inner growth and solid prosperity of a nation, to the adjustment of reconstructive measures, to the natural procedures of differentiation and division of labor. Rather in sleep than in storm are the organs invigorated or the forces stored up which are necessary in upbuilding or upholding the social fabric.

Philosophy has hitherto overlooked too much of the part which labor takes in national development. The salutary and normal beat of the pulse of social life is owing to labor, the fitful interruptions of which signify disorder, the stagnation of which causes cramps, inflammation, mortification. A tranquil and prosperous condition is not to be measured by gratification of appetites.

We agree with an English scientist stating "that every device intended to secure comfort and security without personal exertion and without exercise of the faculties of brain and limbs, works mischief."

Every mode of existence calculated to make a living without labor of some ethical import, must of necessity be prejudicial to the ends sought for. But the tendency in that direction is always predominating, especially in periods of high pretensions; and it always produces fatuity and stunt of organic development.

It creates effeminacy by turning victorious nations or successful speculators into powerful sponges absorbing the vital sap of their contemporaries. Such parasites rule classes or nations by pressing their exhausted inferiors into servitude, making them perform their own share of labor, and straining the prosperity and wealth of nations into their own money-vaults. Then they settle down with self-complacent satiety in the boastful and defiant attitude of oppressive power. Their end is putrefaction.

Applying again the metaphor of a current stream with its changing scenes and phases of utility to the course of history, we shall ever find that the quiet pursuits of industry and agriculture will best promote general normal welfare. Of course it does *Agricultural and industrial pursuits best promote general welfare.* not prevent an occasional overflow of a nation breaking through its narrow embankments, and consequently inundating nations upon comparatively lower levels of culture. Ordinarily such overflows are of benefit even to people overpowered thereby; for, in the end their productiveness is stimulated by the fertilising sediments of cultural surplus for which they seem to have been waiting in order to yield nobler fruits. *Laws of the reciprocal interaction, which regulates advance or disturbances, need to be formulated and fixed.* Of whatever nature the movements in national life may be, we have always to discriminate between upper currents and under-currents, the reciprocal interactions of which determine either the tranquil and steady course of history in its advancement, *Corrected sociology.* or the commotions and disturbances. Before the laws of interaction among such peoples (with, of course, more or less differentiated forms of civil life) can be fixed, a few general preconceptions need be re-examined.

Previous to the arrangement of geological science according to specific rules, computed from distinct alternative residues, etc., there was some talk of "catastrophism." *Law of coercion against the argument of unusualness:* This misleading notion disappeared, when inexplicable phenomena heretofore generalised into the term "catastrophism," were found to result from definite and corresponding causes. The observation of the silent and accumulative force of coercion yielded a better interpretation than jejune argument of unusualness.

In observing social catastrophes similar errors had been committed and allowed to stand uncorrected, until ethnical movements and formations were surmised to be caused by the collective work of individual exertions passing onward with a *The steadfastness of individual exertions and the coercive external circumstances governing men's actions, are fittingly to be subsumed under the historic law of pressure, § 9, 105, 142.* certain degree of quiet but irresistible steadfastness. As soon as ethnical changes were recognised as the effects of this historic law of pressure, historical movements were understood more cogently, and were found to work quite systematically. So long as a slowly shifting or expanding mass of people remains almost undifferentiated, the effects of its movements are explicable by the simplest causes. Equality of their conditions warrants the conformity of their movements. *Equality of conditions warrants conformity of effects.*

But whenever, on the other hand, as has been repeatedly observed, a national organism grows sensitive in proportion to its differentiation; then that stage is obtained in which a nation has learned to economise and preserve its achievements. It *In nations with differentiated society* thereby rises above uncultured neighbors, and immediately establishes various institutions and distinct spheres of rights and duties. Productive labor, protective measures, distribution of products—in short, division of labor is brought into system. This *with distinct spheres of rights and duties arise complications which continually require adjustments.* again at once causes complications requiring further adjustment; it causes class-interests and strain between different occupations. Under these altering circumstances *Personal ambition is set free and called to aggressive or defensive action.* an astonishing variety of personal ambition is set free and called forth into either aggressive or defensive action. In a populace bound by custom personal life is under durance, the individual soul of prince or beggar equally being hedged in *In custom-bound people, who submit to natural regulatives,* by fixed natural regulations according to birth, position, usages, social habits, etc. Then the mysterious but formative principle of mimicry molds the expression of the *the principle of mimicry moulds the physionomy of the social body,* social physiognomy, shapes the public mind, and prescribes the modes of action in the minutest details. Hereditary views and habits prevail throughout; and acquiescence in the natural causes of things binds up personal life in generalness as into swaddling clothes. On the whole, individual life moves in the tracks of the species and is carried along simply by the natural movements going on quietly under the broad, flat surface of generalness. The people appear as of one cast. The manifold character- *which moves upon the broad surface of generalness, in which the individual wears the stamp of the clan,* istics and social peculiarities of a nation receive the impress of the spirit of its time, which is even stamped upon its coins. And the individual bears the stamp of the clan. It partakes of the prejudices and obeys the impulses prompting the tribe. The individual mind is counted as of little consequence, and is indeed void of any selfhood and rather unconcerned about its being nullified. Unambitious, the mem- *and is no more than a vehicle of the life of its genus.* ber of that body politic is far from rising to make a public speech, from defending its right, from throwing its weight into the scales. It is no more than a vehicle of the life of the genus, circulating within it; and no more conscious of its dependent frame of mind than a child whose lips acquire the language of the country. Language, ad- *Clannishness of custom-bound nations.* age, song, public opinion, artistic tastes, judicial views, national games, social institutions, etc. are but outgrowths of the common life, the national **esprit de corps.**

Genesis of the distinct character of a nation

under the law of pressure and counteraction.

Reaction of personal life when treated as natural force.

Causes of wholesome commotions in highly organised nations.

Danger of ill-balanced growth of population ARISTOTLE.

Political eruptions.

Natural law governs history to the extent in which man is a part of nature.

Physical analogy as to volcanos and revolutions.

Stages in national upheavals.

Revolutions at first, private affairs of palaces; in nations answering our description of clannishness,

then local affairs of cities, leagues, etc.

Insurrections of heretics and peasants prepared the English Revolution.

French and American revolutions affected all civilised nations.

Hailing the outbreak. FICHTE.

Revolutionary excitement jeopardises progress and tends to relapse into barbarism.

Rousseau's "Emile".

§ 211. From mysterious depths rise the inclinations, sentiments and formative thoughts, which, working through millions of souls, fashion the character of the whole. The most minute features of this distinct nationality are represented in the individual. This continues until one class in a nation, or one nation on a continent assumes an arrogant attitude and claims more than its legitimate share of room and of right. The overbearing part presses upon the weaker and usually larger parties in the social fabric, and provokes counteraction. For, treating personal life as a natural force under high pressure, eventually causes the natural result—an explosion. The reaction ensuing is like a fever, the reaction of health against a disorder of the circulation or excretion. Hence the undulations of incitements by pressure and reaction will occur in no other but national organisms of a highly differentiated and sensitive constitution, in which they originate from the abnormal swelling of some organ at the expense of others, or by the lethargy of one of the functional systems obstructing and arresting the advance of the whole body politic.

Aristotle espied the danger of an ill balanced growth in numbers in which the stupidity of one class causes the consequent wealth and shrewdness of another to prevail. The customary means of legislation then avail no longer, since ignorance begets suspiciousness and everybody becomes suspected of partiality, until legal control and authority to rule are denied. As it causes an internecine revolution if one party presses upon the others, so war originates whenever one nation tries to overreach another. Thus national and international eruptions break forth with logical and almost geological necessity.

This is the most conspicuous experience of the truth that natural lawfulness governs history to the extent in which man is a part of nature.

An earthquake reveals a power which is caused by the planet's own heat. The eruption originates from some stoppage of circulation and ventilation in the veins of the earth. Compression forces the steam power to take vent through the crust above, whenever impediments are not overcome internally. A. v. Humboldt brought volcanic activity into the formula that it is "a reaction of interior forces of our planet against its crust". Analogous to these are the uproars in national life. We have the calm "andante" of habitual, firmly established and uneventful movement in the routine of every day life. This passes into the faster "allegro" whenever new ideas, brought out by the contest and by the tension of expectancy, incite an entire generation. Then the least mishap may turn the sensational masses into the temper of the "furioso", and attempts at reasoning about amelioration being futile, the uproar is apt to seize whole nations with the paroxysm of a raging "furore".

The history of revolutions evinces, that at first they were mere local affairs, palace-revolutions in nations answering our description of clannishness, as in Persia, Russia, and Constantinople. Then they took the shape of national excitements, and of general epidemics in our own times. Revolutions used to be city riots, until leagues took up the cause; finally they became events of universal import, in comparison with which the innumerable local symptoms of present dissatisfactions cease to be alarming. The insurrections of the heretics and the peasants prepared the transition to the great English revolution; the intrigues of cabinets and conspiracies of parties will lead to the disrupture of Turkey as it once conduced to the end of Byzanz, and in modern times to the revolutions of the United States and France. The latter two alone affected all civilised nations, because the principles at issue bear upon humanity in general and touch every one of all the modern problems. In both of them a universal thought worked itself through, a question in whose solution every human being is concerned.

Fichte in his "Contribution to correct some notions about the French Revolution," wrote: "Up to date mankind is far behind in the knowledge of what is wanting. But if I am not mistaken, we witness the dawn of a fresh spring-morning, and the zenith of day will be reached in due order of time." To be sure, that morning-dawn was of a bloody red. Thought has gone through blood ordeals ever since the beginning of the world.

There were always conservatives to oppose innovations and to foil precipitate advance, which marches double quick as if time was to be taken by storm. Those attacking and repelling in their rage and wrestle, act as if they were blind as to the merits of the issue, and in the frenzy of fanaticism tumble down a precipice.

As often as parts of society did attain a certain height of selfculture, society at large, always a heavy mass to elevate, relapsed for a time into the rude condition of barbarism sequent to series of common neglects and defaults; just like that ideal of Rousseau, the child of nature, which makes it his object to show his nudity and animal propensities, tho "Emile" may forget his role on occasions which require urbanity.

The deplorable commotions, reactions as they are, or rather suits at natural law in which social elements settle their conflicting interests—are historical necessities. The distress incident to such troubles is inevitable and as natural as the discharges of thunderstorms, since the physical and social atmosphere is what it is. They are like the destructive eruptions of the volcanoes, since the combination of the elements in the make-up of our earth are such as they are. To be sure, the moral liabilities of the individual are not suspended on account of these circumstances, and responsibility is not abated, tho the causes lying outside of the single person may alleviate his juridical guilt. At any rate, the paroxysms reveal human nature as it is. They explode at least every fantastical euphemism calculated to extol man—unregenerated man as Kant used to say—as a deity in miniature. The reality of human nature exposing itself in these natural paroxysms shows the absurdity of that haughty tendency of profane humanitarianism to deprive the thought of humanity of the fullness which is given in the Mediator. The grave responsibility of this one-sided humanitarian philosophy, preceding, for instance, the French revolution, consists in ignoring the truth of the Christian-humanistic ideal, whereby the essence of humanism was detached from its thought, and the thought put to derision: all in order to pettifog the self-conceit of man in his crude, unbridled state. Such seduction of contemporaries to false world-theories always ends in the destruction of man's dignity and liberty.

Commotions (suits at natural law) are historical necessities.

Individual liabilities not suspended,

tho the epidemic nature of the paroxysm may palliate judicial co-responsibility.

Paroxysmal fits explode the fantastical euphemism calculated to extol man in his "unregenerated" state. § 230, KANT.

They show the absurdity of profane humanitarianism in depriving the thought of humanity of the fullness given in the Mediator.

Seduction to false world-theories always ends in the destruction of human dignity and freedom. *§ 169, 177-179, 212.*

§ 212. Another circumstance needs to be considered in this connection.

The eruption of Mount Krakatau in the Sunda Straits caused an ocean wave to inundate a large tract of the island, and 37,000 human lives were swept away. Cannibalism is an ethno-psychological enigma; but the death of such a multitude of people at an instant is still more inexplicable.—In Australia recently ten and a half millions of rabbits were killed in one season—an enigma of natural history. Yet wholesale murder of men is a conundrum in the history of the human race surpassing both in its appalling effects. We shall recur to its consideration.

Excess of deaths

The paroxysms of nations, as we termed the rage of most revolutions, destroyed millions of human existences, each of which is more important and valuable than all the rabbits on earth.

aggravates the consistent solutions of certain problems.

The bloody upheavals of revolutionary civil wars we classify with insanity.

Insanity of most revolutions.

Stoll in his ethnology of the Indians of Guatemala points out, how mysterious phenomena among them may be reduced to the influence of the suggestive power of hypnotism. No doubt, nature-bound people are more susceptible to influences of this sort than cultivated people. But that does not exclude that nations of culture under the paroxysms discussed, relapse into the nature-bound state of people, in which all the symptoms of an epidemic are observable. The convulsions of the Camisards were as catching as the delirium of the Jacobines. As the depression of the social atmosphere before the storm of a revolution becomes general, so in any other case of public excitement the parole of the day, the terrible news, the catchwords carry an incendiary power. Whilst the excitement grows and lasts, enthusiasm and rage are subject to the same law of infection as epileptic fits and St. Vitus' dance. In such times of ecstatic passiveness a nation comes nearest to being a mere natural organism.

The epidemic-like phenomena of national paroxysms under conditions of ecstatic passiveness receive some light, through investigation of hypnotism. STOLL.

Convulsions of the Camisards.

Delirium of the Jacobines.

None, perhaps, has pictured the terrors of the revolution more fascinatingly than Taine, but not even this description can surprise those having insight into the depth of human nature as open to infernal instigations. In his collective capacity man is then a mere natural compound in which personal life is overwhelmed by the life of the species. The individual is, like a wave in a wild mountain stream, carried away by the general frenzy. Having lost the coolness of judgment and the force of resistance, the individual gives himself up to the blind public will as a mere instrument, under the spell of a strange enchantment. During such paroxysms personality seems to be emancipated, and high-minded spirits appear to be called forth, whilst in fact personal life is virtually thrown back into the generalness of the natural life of the genus.

Terrors of a revolution. TAINE.

Human nature open to infernal instigation. § 49, 58, 112, 202.

Coolness of judgment and energy of resistence lost under the general frenzy.

This rests upon the same law as that which Bastian found energetically active among certain tribes upon Java. Under a peculiar sensibility common to them, almost any nervous irritation was transferrable from person to person. The affected individual cannot help imitating every act of strangers rousing its wonderment. It is said to be a peculiar situation to find oneself in a sphere of general hypnotisation.

The law of mimicry active in Java, etc. (BASTIAN.)

is of little avail in explaining national paroxysms.

But even this comparison between natural phenomena and national paroxysms is of little avail.

We must adduce still another fact.

It is to be considered that in every man the propensity for insanity lies beneath the upper sphere of reason. Any specialist of mental diseases will testify to the almost indistinguishable transitions from sound sense to insanity. For, our reflecting consciousness, conditionally to be upheld day by day above the occult side of psychical life, is aptly to be compared to one of the two lenses constituting the meniscus. The least displacement in the set offers an entrance to sparks from the corresponding mysterious sphere of the spiritual realms. The soul may then be set in rapport with the celestial world—and with the world of evil spirits none the less. In the latter case the focus upon the views of life becomes seriously altered at the least. We

must stop short. It was only intended to bring out more plastic man and humanity in the tranquil walks of life during periods of uneventful times, in contrast to the convulsions and awful descents to which man is exposed individually and socially in the course of his history.

CH. III. UNDULATIONS OF ETHNICAL LIFE.

§ 213. The oscillations rhythmically recurring in the course of events must be reducible to the peculiarity of the human soul. The moods of the mind, now inclined to active enterprise, then again to passive resignation, change with the regularity of a pendulum. These emotions and passions chiefy determine the views men

take of things. Previously, allusion has been made to these conditions of the mind, and now we try to bring them under a common focus with other phenomena pertaining to the topic presently to be discussed.

Observing the intellectual grade of persons either by themselves or in society, there always presents itself a circle of unsophisticated ideas, matters of common sense, in the shape of a well defined tho modifiable world-consciousness predominant in a specific generation at a given period.

This mental horizon is ever widening by additional experiences, through comparison with which the old circle of ideas becomes disarranged. A readjustment of cogni-

tions is initiated in order to master the puzzling discrepancies. The new views must

always pass through the ordeal of conflicts and doubts, in the transition from untenable opinions to clearer comprehensibility, under the harmonising activity of the intellect, aiming at generalisation and unification of conceptions. A more correct world-consciousness is usually gained by the argumentation between the old tenets and the new experiences and conclusions. Mind becomes less clannish and more enriched.

This is the course of advance in a straight line. But this simple line of ratiocination already—abstracting as yet from the possibility of mixing in errors on the way from

perception to conclusion—shows perpetual oscillations between inner propensities and external preponderances, changes from intensification to superficiality, from musing contemplation to practical attention and application.

Not so easily understood, however, is the order and method of these alternations. Taking the line of cultural movement upon earth under one general aspect, we find one great descent, and one great ascent. The sinking begins with that appalling

subversion by which the unity of the human family was broken into the multiplicity of opinions and races. This subversion preceded the disaster, which was but its palpable, inevitable sequel; that disaster, which alone explains ethnological enigmas. Humanity, fallen into an abyss, falling to pieces, was conducted in all its affairs by an invisible hand, nevertheless.

The ascent begins with that great event—incomprehensible from the points of common reason—by virtue of which the fragmentary vestiges began to be gathered up, when those who had fallen into the dust, were lifted up again, when the unity of

humanity was manifest anew. The process of this elevation continued up to date.

That descent and this ascent, perversion there, and conversion here, scattering into diversion and gathering into unity, may each be taken as a movement commencing at the middle of the times made to distinguish either set of advance or relapse from the other.

Progress upward and wayward forms the diverging lines which center and cut one another in the "cross." This arrangement of historical material, on our part, is not artificial, but the precise description of the way in which the historical development of human culture actually moved, and is thus roughly outlined in its totality.

It is this double direction of the historic movements, from and around the center, which renders the great cyclical undulations observable and remarkable.

Lasaulx directed the attention to the fact that a series of great religious commotions occurred simultaneously. Abraham and Zoroaster were contemporaries, according to M. Mueller and Rawlinson. Both, Pentateuch and Rig-veda, date from the fifteenth century B. C. Israel's establishment in the promised land, and that of Hindooism in India belong together in point of time. Then we saw Confut-se in China, Buddha in India, and Jeremiah in Jerusalem. Along with prophecy among the Jews, theosophy rises among the Greeks; Hesiodos and Pythagoras, and the institutions generally ascribed to Numa and Servius Tullius:—all represent that wave of religio-philosophical reconstruction about the Sixth century B. C. Not less wonderful are the undulations conducted along that imaginary line (of the wireless telegraph, we are almost tempted to say), between Japan and Rome. The combination suggested by the names of Gregory, Procas, and Muhamed about 600 A. D.; and another at about 1200 A. D., with several Innocents to match the Dalai-Lama in Asia, afford sufficient evidence of the cyclical movements under discussion, making it almost necessary to speak of the wonderful harmony of coincidents at about 1500 A. D., marked by the names of Gutenberg, Constantine, Copernicus, Columbus, Charles V., Luther, Calvin, etc., marked also by a reform in Japan; not to speak of the wave of 1800.

For these phenomena we find no explanation in individual psychical life or in moods of the mind. To explain them in the way Schelling did, only multiplies the conundrums. The intermittant pulsation of ethnical life has other causes. For, as soon as it is conceded that humanity is really the organic totality of nations whose inner nature is apt to become incited to common passionateness, those polar fluxes are explicable, which so remarkably pass through contemporary nations of nearly equal delicacy of sentiency, sequent to higher culture.

In peoples of lowest cultural grades the effects are of course unnoticeable; we repeat that the participation in these extensive spheres of parallel coincidences cannot be shown everywhere. In parts of humanity lying as if petrified on the outskirts of the historic corporation they are hidden from our view. But that they were touched indeed by the same influences is not an illegitimate supposition.

As members of the great social organism they may even in their isolated condition have outgrown their childhood, and have their own ups and downs. It is a fact that insane people in their derangement still participate inwardly in the bereavements which during their confinement in an asylum, for instance, have befallen their families; and that when health returned they became perfectly conscious of it, tho their friends withheld from them what had happened. Idiots and deaf and dumb persons have made inner progress of mental life while outwardly scarcely any sign of it could be noticed; as soon as a cure was effected physically, they were in possession of mature powers of reason.

These psychological facts show individual natures—notwithstanding their being under bondage, isolated, and arrested in their development,—participating in the emotions pervading their relatives.

Hence the supposition is justified that the whole race is touched by the undulations which vibrate through ethnical life. It is by the most natural inference that human circles, bound up under abnormities of consciousness, are not excluded from the progressive movements of humanity as a whole, and that, unconsciously, under special guidance from above, they partake of the fluxes of polarisation and of general advancement.

All we contend for, is that cyclical motions of a spiritual nature may seize humanity in its totality and oscillate through the whole body. Hence we deem this supposition of a mysterious and involuntary sympathetical rapport among mankind, even unconscious thereof, as the only key fit to solve the problem of concursive advance, tho we should be able to trace the tidal waves of simultaneous commotions in the history of those nations of higher culture only, in which the effects of the flux come to the surface as plain facts.

Furthermore we observe the nations, and the present system of states especially, ever to waver between two poles. Just as energetic activity and phlegmatic lassitude alternate in the life of every individual, so do periods of social life change certain distinct features.

28

Marginal notes

Progress upward and progress wayward form the diverging lines, tangent to, cutting each other and centering in the cross.

This twofold direction of the historic rotations from and around the center, renders the great cyclical undulation conspicuous.

Religious commotions occurred simultaneously. Lasaulx. Abraham and Zoroaster. M. Mueller, Rawlinson.

Pentateuch—Rig-Veda. Buddha-Confu-tse. Jewish prophecy; Greek theosophy. Gregor, Procas, Muhamed. Innocent, Dalai Lama. Gutenberg, Constantinople, Copernicus, Columbus, Carl V., Calvin, Luther. Reform in Japan.

Schelling's explanation of such rhythms multiplies perplexities of histories.

Polar fluxes of passionateness explicable, if humanity is really conceived as an organic totality of nations.

Parallel coincidences hidden from view in nations lying petrified upon the periphery,

whose participation in the rhythms of history is to be presumed.

Illustrated by the rapport of insane persons with their families in serious bereavement.

Undulations of ethnical life.

The truth contended for is, that cyclical motions of a spiritual nature may seize humanity and scintillate through it as a body.

Sympathetical rapport may manifest itself involuntarily.

Subsequent to periods of war with their constraining circumstances, concentrative tendencies prevail for some length of time. National selfconsciousness is then most vivid. But soon after a relaxation usually sets in. During the times of renewed prosperity and rest, class-interests and selfassertion tend to loosen the inner connections formed under the pressure of common danger. Cooperative instincts, displeased with the obligations of fellowship, or discontent with the affairs of citizenship at home, seek to make common cause with corresponding causes in foreign countries. Tendencies become prevailingly international. When at first the determined energy of a definite nation rose in patriotism, it now sinks into promiscuous and vague cosmopolitanism. Such seemingly inconsistent alterna-

Nations and states waver between the two poles of energetic activity and phlegmatic lassitude.

tions have their common roots in the social oscillations, which in respect to both, the rise and decline of national selfconsciousness have their significance and assigned ends in the purpose of civilisation to become universal.

It has often been averred that the two great epochs of German literature coincide with the revival of cosmopolitan tendencies characteristic of that nation. This was at the close of the crusades, and again after the Prussian exertions about 1800 A. D.

Periods of war, national pride and patriotism alternate with times of recuperation, unconcern of common weal or woe, and vague cosmopolitanism.

From a mild sort of cosmopolitanism history derived much benefit in behalf of humanism. For, whenever national self-consciousness predominates, and nativism flourishes, a state becomes egoistical and proud, causing nations to separate in order to become powerful units in themselves. Problems and tasks enjoined upon humanity in general are partially considered under aspects of utility according to the selfish polity of a nation, a polity which depends upon national sentiment, or rather the caprice of a nativistic populace, or upon national superciliousness. The principle of national fellowship with other nations is then superseded by the expediency of selfishness, and subsides under national jealousies and animosities, under the weight of armament and the burden of militarism. Finally the thought of humanity is distorted and violated by secret agitation and international combinations of discontent and hatred.

The purpose of such alterations is to render civilisation universal.

From a moderate cosmopolitanism history derived much benefit.

Disadvantages of national egoism; Nativism Militarism.

More than once history has had to discipline nations inflated with national presumptuousness by interspersing foreigners among them, in order to teach them lessons of humility and to bring home to them the truth that no part of the human family is to be despised. So were the Mongolians instrumental in carrying the old legends of India to the occidental nations where the fairy-tales of their childhood reechoed in the faint home-recollections of the Germanic and Slavonic races. So had the Arabs to aid in spreading the forgotten thoughts of Greece over the West besides mixing in other Asiatic elements of cultural import. At the proper time those thoughts, at first utilised only in the interest of scholastic ecclesiasticism, came to assist in widening the views of life, and to liberate the mind.

Nations punished for selfishness by foreigners.

Especially noteworthy is the providential intermixture of the alien Jewish element. With respect to the Jews, it is obvious that the fragments of that nation were preserved for the purpose of counteracting the tendencies of nations to grow callous and ossify. We recognised the Semitic element as a dissolvent, as a decomposing ingredient wherever it is mixed into specific cultures of national growth.

Providential Intermixture of the Semitic element, which now as ever acts as a dissolvent.
§ 67, 78, 88, 128, 200, 201.

In a nation tainted with corruption exceeding the usual measure of depravity, the Jews provoke a salutary counteraction of fermentation, thus serving as a salt against decay. Besides their resembling a macerating fluid, which tests the purity of metals, the Jewish element tests the genuineness of patriotism. Against a narrow minded restriction of legitimate cosmopolitanism or nativistic tendencies it will insist upon toleration. After their own national particularism and theocratic bigotry had been eliminated from the Jews they became the staunchest advocates of cosmopolitanism and toleration, ever promulgating both with a dogged persistence as against the particularism of the nations which paid them back for their bigotry. Now and again they will cause Christian nations, growing indifferent as to their religious privileges, to appreciate the advantages of Christian civilisation. They ever serve as a standing admonition to Christendom, to beware of admiring external success on the score of mammonism, and to spurn the cultivation of sham and imitation. Their overbearing and ostentatious deportment teaches by object lessons the ugliness of these symtomatic traits of character; it teaches them to discountenance that pharisaical and abstract humanitarianism which, posing in selfcomplacency assumes the nil-admirari air under pretense of stoic cosmopolitanism.

Jews provoke salutary counteraction; resemble a salt against decay,

testing the genuineness of patriotism,

insisting upon toleration.

causing Christendom indifferent to religion

to appreciate the advantages of Christian civilisation;

to spurn mammonism sham culture, feigned humanitarianism.

and the selfcomplacency of stoic cosmopolitanism.

§ 214. This up and down, forward and backward movement of the thought of humanism, now to cosmopolitan platitude and then to national narrow-mindedness, is always in keeping with the fluctuations of the two chief modes of thinking ever manifest in the attempts to embody themselves in new social transformations and reforms. These oscillations also recur with the regularity of the pendulum. The extreme points of motion always clearly indicate the undercurrent of either the universalistic or the subjectivistic form of world-consciousness, each with a view to establish authoritative rule, which views alternate accordingly. The universalistic world-theory takes will in the abstract sense of generalness as the determining cause,

Undulations in the conception of Humanism, between cosmopolitan platitude and national narrowness, are in keeping with the two fluctuating modes of thinking;

and as that which is real in the realistic (Platonic) sense. Individual will is considered as being ruled by the will of the commonalty, which alone has any right. The right to have a will, attributed to the impersonal public, is conceived as the determining factor in human affairs, and requires obedience as the chief virtue, ecclesiastically and politically. Individual rights are valued and adjusted according to their subordination to the right of the social organism as a whole. "Concentration of governmental power" is made the catch-word as in the time of Guizot. After a longer or shorter time we find the tendency changing. The individual is taken for a determining factor and the sole reality. Individual will in company with other individual wills constitutes the will of the totality, at least of a majority. By free assent among themselves the individual wills represent a contract on terms, giving authority to will, that is, to the association of ideas—a social silent agreement separable at the pleasure of the arbitrating parties. This tendency reveals itself in every direction, even in the parcelling out of land; in the laying out of cities and in their petty jealousies; in the guarding against infringement upon state-rights; in the suspicion against the centralisation of governmental powers. Individual rights are made the regulator in the administration of justice, the common right being considered as the product of individual willingness.

There we have the ancient, here the modern state. The one held sway throughout the Middle-Ages, perpetuated by virtue of Platonism. The other developed from the philosophy of Meister Eckhardt, Descartes, Hobbes, and Rousseau. It is to be remembered, however, that generalising these movements of the nominalistic and realistic modes of thought as to their preponderance during the two periods referred to, does not exclude minor scintillations of both, universalistic and subjectivistic world-theories in each period.

That wavering alternation between the two principal conceptions of the origin and authority of the state, of the relations of right between the individual and the totality, rests upon the dualism of the given modes of thought. Feeling and passive selfabnegation prevailing, inclines to the oriental form of consciousness, where the individual is deemed to be but a particle of the all-oneness molding and conditioning his existence. Under the prevalence of practical energy and the sense of liberty the occidental forms of life arise, where personal ambitiousness asserts itself, whilst, perhaps, considerateness for the rights of others and the common welfare, and the maxim of equity is pushed to the background. Yonder, in the theocratic and despotic formations of society the individual is but a phenomenon of being in the abstract, being in general. Here the individual feels himself a person, as the essential part of being, whilst being in general, as far as it becomes an entity in the concrete form of existence is conceived as the fortuitous result which the person is bent upon to produce and to modify.

These two main forms of world-consciousness stand in relation to—yea, are connected with, the old polar tension. The preponderance of the one calls forth the counteraction of the other, whereby the oscillations originate which take place alternately in the formations of public opinion. A revolution, as considered from this point of view, is but a sudden transition in which the poles change places. These contrasting world-theories have always existed side by side, and in a general way fluctuated through the Orient as well, if not as often as they have excited the Occident. But scientifically conceived, and formulated, and purposely agitated they were not until the scholastic contests were enacted upon the occidental arena.

Realism represented universalistic tendency in which synthetical generalities were thought to condition the reality of being, the primary principal lying in the cognition of totality as preceding individual being and individuality.

Nominalism on the other hand, maintained the doctrine, that being in the abstract was real only in the things themselves, and outside of them did not exist at all.

As incapable as the schools were, to bring the contest to a satisfactory conclusion, as little could the contests accrue to the upbuilding of a harmonious society. The two world-theories, either of which ever rests on one of these two modes of thinking, the universalistic and the subjectivistic, seem destined to remain permanent in order to counterpoise each other.

Upon the happy accomplishment of this equation depends the salutary progress of family and national life, of political economy, and of civilising culture.

Marginal notes:

ever attempting to embody themselves in social transformations;

Indicating either universalistic or subjectivistic form of world-consciousness.

Discrepancies of modern sociology.

Alternations as to ideas of authoritative rule.

Universalistic world-theory takes will in the abstract sense of generalness,

so that the will of the commonalty alone has any right.

Individual rights to subordinate the organisation.

"Concentration of government".   Guizot.

Tendency changes to subjectivism.

By free arbitration individual wills are made the source of the general will.

"State a contract on terms"

separable at the pleasure of the parties. (SECESSION.)

Guard against infringements of state rights.

Common right the product of individual willingness.

The two theories represent the ancient and modern ideas about the state.

Both scintillate in each respective period, tho either one predominates.

These oscillations issue from the dualism of the given modes of thought.

Feeling and selfabnegation prevailing inclines to orientalism;

Energy and sense of liberty prevailing occidental forms of life take rise.

In pantheistic generalness lies the peril of theocratic despotism.

Here the concrete form of existence considered as the fortuitous result which the person is bent upon to produce or to modify.

Alternations of public opinion.

Scientifically formulated and agitated were these contrasting world-theories only since the scholastic contests upon the occidental arena.

Realism and Nominalism.

Schools reached no satisfactory conclusion and their contests could not accrue to the upbuilding of a harmonious society.

The process of detachment of individuals and classes from the commonalty, the reluctance of sharing the common obligations, and the desire to evade disagreeable duties result from false notions of freedom. It is the current of the tendency which characterises the left wings of parliaments, pretending to promulgate enlightenment, liberty and progress. The period of emancipation and separatistic subjectivism was followed by the reaction and relaxation, which found its utterance in the Spinozian world-theory. After Descartes the ego had reached its limits, emaciated individualism sank back into the generalness of universalism, with its abstract sublimate of substance from which everything could be made. Under the sway of the doctrine of generalised personality the states became absolute monarchies.

Frederick the Great hated the idea of municipal and corporative rights; and Napoleon said: "Fate? The state is the fate"! In our century the new reaction against universal generalness on the part of subjectivism is marked by the economic dogmas of Adam Smith's school running out into the Manchestrian theories. The formation of affairs is left to the will and energy of the individual under the catch-words "help yourself" and "free competition". The dangers of the dissolution of society becoming apparent, refuge is sought especially in Kantianism. Emphasis is given to obey the command; legalistic thought and authority of law are mistaken for the preservative forces of society; good times are expected from ballot and legislature. The right of forming commonalities, of organising any kind of associations is insisted upon, whilst, at the same time, protection for the individual and the association is demanded from the commonwealth. Coalescence of the rights to enjoy liberty and at the same time to rule is demanded by such wonderful coalitions as that formed by the hierarchy and the democracy. And another reaction will set in at the time, when it shall have become necessary that individual right must liberate humanity from the communistic state.

Thus the oscillation of world-consciousness will become noticeable in every relation of life. Even with respect to the public taste will we observe climatic changes as it were—seasons of fashion. For a period the Gothic style of architecture is dominant until the world gets tired of it, and the renaissance becomes the fashion; after which in turn a taste for the Romanesque or Rococo is cultivated for awhile. We witness continual efforts to rearrange the æsthetic expressions of the imagination on a parallel with the political and literary transitions. Every one of the æsthetic undulations is marked by intervenient shorter seasons of fashion, pertaining to things of everyday use, to household utensils, furniture and wearing apparel. But no more than the short seasons of fashions, can the more important alternations under discussion be explained by the law of nervous relaxation from monotony. For we know of entire centuries in which dresses were of the same cut.

These fluctuations are to be reduced to the prevailing world-consciousness governing the views as to the "Wealth of Nations" and luxury; to the desire to appear prominent and stately; to the prompting of demonstrating personal selfhood and distinction, or individual oddity; or to the uniformism of the state or the church.

When Charles the Bold went to the battle of Granson, he took a hundred gold-embroidered coats along. August of Saxony, trying to outrival the French court, spent 80,000 Thaler for a single play in his opera house. Count Bruehl, the Saxon minister, possessed seventy silken morning gowns. The desire of the lower classes to imitate such luxury was checked in those times of absolutism by special laws prescribing even the courses available for the various ranks. "We have seen well enough the ridicule of the old priggish ordinances; we have read from the statutes at large which fashioned men's gowns and womens' farthingales by acts of parliaments". That period was followed by the other, in which kings called themselves first servants of the states, dressing and living in the simplicity of the civilian. Plainness and equality in attire took the place of silly extravagance. And now the time is drawing near when in place of monarchs, the kings of railroads, and of the exchange will live in royal style. Luxury will not, perhaps, show itself in chests filled with fine linen or in the number of morning gowns, but it will display itself at any rate, in such a manner as to provoke the envy and wrath of the "proletarians", and induce them to jump from subjectivistic to communistic theories of life.

Our meditation comes near to an anticipation of the problem of advantages and reverses on the line of national and private prosperity, from the consideration of which we must desist as yet, however, until we have observed still more of the oscillations caused by the modifications of world-consciousness. So far we have reviewed the contrasts caused by the prevalence, periodically alternating, of either an universalistic or a subjectivistic world-theory. Both tendencies are necessary to poise the erroneous views of life, which, in their extremes, attempt to rule the true thought of humanity out of order. They are to keep each other in permanent mobility. Hence they never come to rest, like the perpendicle, fastened at one end, and oscillating from right to left and from left to right, until the finger stops the restlessness and regulates the movement. This finger is at hand.

CH. IV. HERO-WORSHIP; GENIUS AND TALENT. THE PRESS.

§ 215. Shall we have to examine the so-called "great men" with a view of accept- ing their agency as that finger which directs the perpetuum mobile of counter- poising world-theories? Much of their historic importance consists in their ability to unite opposing tendencies by finding the formula of the equation, or by mastering the contrasts; and in ameliorating the commotion and the strain of polarity—each for a certain length of time at least.

But let us put the question: Who creates, in whom originates historical move-ment? The literary master-minds, or those excelling in sciences and arts, or those leading on in battles? Do they not carry the masses along with them? Do not they start the series of new thoughts, or give the impulses for new discoveries and in-ventions? Are not they responsible for the wars? Are they not the founders of new states? The hero of hero-worship is Carlyle. Every one of his favorites he pre-sents as a representative and plenipotentiary of the Infinite One. But thereby he drags into mere terrestrial mutability what lies far above it. Others besides Carlyle have done this, who would bend to the bias of their views the select ones of Lange, for instance. But Carlyle assigns everything to the great instruments, and thereby deprives all their contemporaries of their merits as coefficients, and takes from his-tory the purpose animating it. He could not rise to the cognition that history per-forms anything; that it is, equal with nature, the incarnation of the all-controlling thought. In the last resort there is no history, for Heaven and the favorites of Heaven do everything.

Why did no one at the time of Alexander, we ask with Niebuhr, create a piece of art bearing the mark of perfection? Because the condition of men at that time afforded none of the requirements. And who creates those conditions? who causes the mood of an age? Men do that. Each period bears the peculiar impress of their character, formed according to their stage of consciousness. (Saying this, we ac-knowledge, of course, that a personality stands behind, beyond men.)

The biography of a particular personage unfolds before us the history of his age and generation. The first and lowest stage of individual life falls in the period of concealed vegetative formation, in which the spirit seems entirely absorbed in the work of rendering itself plastic, in the upbuilding of its apparatus. The absorption of an artist in shaping the creature of his imagination may illustrate this, except that the artist's mind cannot itself enter into his sculpture or painting, in the man-ner that the spirit animates soul and body.

For the spirit is, as an entity, dwelling within that individualised portion of life, within that soul, which was lying dormant in tellurian matter, which lives in the plant, and which in animal life approaches the manifestations of a will. What builds up the human body is the same life which builds up the palm-tree to conform to its inherent law; which moves the bird to leave for warmer climes; which teaches the beaver to construct its abode in the water; which the bee reveals to us when it forms its symmetrical cell. Why not call it the world-soul, which in its highest form of individualisation, and at the moment of its being embraced by the spirit, becomes psychical and begins to build the human body?

Into this physico-psychical frame, in accord with the psychical mode of forma-tive procedure, the spirit infuses the gift of language, its own form of communica-tion. The faculty of speech is built into that finely differentiated and henceforth loud-thinking organism. The soul becomes endowed with the ability to reflect the spirit, to become an object for its own self. This faculty of thinking aloud reveals its metaphysical nature, its systematic regularity the more distinct and mathemati-cal in proportion to its native naivety, being preserved more original and child-like and less sophisticated, preserved in that state wherein language comes from the heart, and in which the reflection of mind-life is least affected but most affectionate.

Thus the spirit, true to its nature of unity and communication, realises and man-ifests itself as the inspiration of the soul. And as the spirit personifies and charac-terises itself in the language of the individual soul, so it molds the art and poetry, the culture and character of an entire nation.

Evidently this vehicle of thought and apparatus of communication, through which personal life is to a certain extent, fashioned directly, is one of the data, which the "great men" find ready made. Upon mastering the language, and upon the use made of it, depends much of the success of their life-work. By means of it they appropriate to themselves the net earnings of preceding minds, and the advice of experienced contemporaries. Language designates the grade in the scale of progress, and the degree of the spiritual atmosphere forming the mental environments in which great minds find themselves. Above that they can rise only in proportion to their appropriation of the wealth of language, that it may be at their command for proper use. Hence their elevated pedestal is always formed by the achievements of the totality of their nation. If they are great they become conscious of the fact that they owe their position to the mental and moral atmosphere in which they were raised; and acknowledge that with and through this influence they had to acquire their talents; and that in the first place their receptivity had to be cultivated by others. All other cultural accomplishments depend upon this educational foundation; and only under this discipline will the spirit come to the maturity requisite to the yielding of fruits of the spirit; not otherwise is the ability obtainable to give in return and enrich civilisation. This reciprocal interaction between personality and totality, from which history ensues, is to continue and extend. Even the most insignificant or rather unostentatious life of any human being takes its share of imponderable nutrition from its mental atmosphere. The most humble member of the human family returns its contribution of mental-moral results to society—its bad influences too, frequently in the way of punishment for the negligence of society as to its duties towards individuals.

From this altitude of civilisation, a people in its enterprise and emulation appears as one large industrial establishment. The material is distributed among the individual workers, and the diverse products of toil, bearing the mark of more or less of their ingenuity and skill, is delivered into the storage. The wealth of the whole consists in the variety of talents displayed and results procured, in the promptness and agility of reciprocal interaction—all implying a high grade of organic differentiation. The prosperity of a nation therefore, consists in the sum of labor performed by the mass, and is enhanced in value proportionately to the variety, to the promptness of cooperation, and to the improvement of individual aptness. And upon the whole, this development of the functional part of the social organism transpires in the same unconscious process as that to which we alluded when speaking of the genesis, and again of the generative import of language. We also spoke of the recuperation of strength during sleep, when the vital organs of the body operate quietly but most energetically without our becoming conscious of it. In the same manner grows language, grow ideas, and grow up the men of fame.

§ 216. Notwithstanding this social, organic reciprocal interaction it is vitiating to speak of a national spirit, inasmuch as it causes an idea of a nation having a soul manifesting itself in the "voice" of the people. The spirit of a nation is nothing but what we designate by the vague phrase "spirit of the times," that is, the view of life or world-theory held in common by the mass of the people at a given period, and unconsciously governing them. The human spirit as such is not the product of the incidents of an age; it is not the square root of the sum of a column of added ciphers. As the personifying factor the spirit is an entity sui generis. It is this specific quality of the spirit which causes that proud delight, that just and ennobling selfesteem which may fill one with the consciousness of aspiring and attaining to a special branch of usefulness. True as it is that, with reference to the physico-psychical constitution and temperament, each individual is a child of his time: so false is it, to consider a person, a character, as being the result of circumstances. For, on the part of character, each is of a special value in himself, he is somebody in particular, the only one of his kind; he is an individ-able entity existing but in this one specimen.

There is a species of individual consciousness telling one in all modesty, but actually in excuse of a certain inertia, that he is a very small part of the human totality. It rather tarries in the esprit de corps instead of asserting itself as the personal will which consciously ought to disengage itself from that collective consciousness belonging to the people in common. True, this collective consciousness, tho but a matter of capricious opinion, wields a power from which emancipation is scarcely possible. It constitutes itself from traditional views and educational coefficients which come in an uninterrupted historical succession to be inherited by each generation severally. There arises the difficulty; for of whatever force that general consciousness may be, it can, on the one side, exert no other influence upon a person, but that to which, at the maturity of his mind, he is willing to submit; whilst at the same time for reasons of the relative dependency of the human being on its natural part, emancipation from common tenets of world-consciousness in its collective form and force can never be rendered complete. Tho it were possible for a person to soar above the world-consciousness predominant at his time in all other respects, **the language of his people would still bind him to participate in the views of life governing his contemporaries.** Thus the undeniable fact becomes evident that every individual temperament is the issue of two correlative factors. Man is endowed with relative independency designed for selfhood; whilst he is dependent at the same time upon environment, to which he is to adjust himself, and by means of which alone he is enabled to obtain his ethical culture. *[margin: Great minds are not developed of this regardless or the other flowing from the populace in a general way; yet, personality is not the result of circumstances. Person is to become disengaged from the vague "spirit of the times". Traditional views as educational coefficients too powerful to be discarded, to which even independent minds are tied through language. Man to adjust himself to environment forming the apparatus for his ethical culture.]*

Hence not the greatest of minds ever claimed the radiance of glory as His own. Excellency of mind is based upon the crystalline structure of a person's characteristics. The more surfaces and axes a crystal presents, the more receptive it is for the light penetrating them, and the more distinct and definite will be the magic play and brilliancy of the refracted rays. This is the secret of the influence which a symmetrical character exerts upon cultural advance in general. Our great lights would not shine forth in such lustre, if the texture and inner combination of their mental and moral incipiencies had been less receptive; if they had not consolidated under pressure or according to the laws of homogeneity and affinity by which impure elements were excluded, if they had been different from what they appeared to be. *[margin: Not the greatest of minds claimed His glory as due to himself. Crystalline structure of personal characteristics. Receptivity of mental and moral incipiencies, as consolidated under pressure, under exclusion of impurities—are the prerequisites to excellency.]*

Now in the measure as one of the correlatives exalting a mind preponderates, either adjustment to matters upon which we depend, or assertion of selfhood, the difficult distinction between persons of either' talents or genius will arrange itself. Here personal selfhood rises from the concealed spiritual spring to assert itself; here the texture of the inner life hidden beneath innumerable intrinsic relations, which remain mysterious despite the external manifestations of this individuality—the genius. There the environments chiefly furnish the lessons for ethical exercise, and serve as conductors of the light into a mind with refined receptivity building up its talents. *[margin: Talent: virtuosity of receptivity and of adjustment to externalities. Genius, hidden in the texture of the inner life. § 15.]*

Herder may serve as an example of a personality in which talent and genius were intimately blended, yet each conspicuously manifest. His greatness consisted, as Vilmar describes, the secret thereof, in "the grandeur of his universalistic culture". Besides of eminently noble ethical qualities, the caliber of his mental receptivity was capable of encompassing a wide range of erudition. In his clear mind, with the humane inclination of his emotional nature, there was room for the voices of all nations. His ethical delicacy and lingual versatility found the word for the touching utterances of grief and of mirth, the word which calls forth sympathy and conveys a solacing answer. The wide circle of humanity seems focussed in the center of his being, so sensitive for impressions and so able to echo them as the chords vibrating under the touch of the player when they reverberate in tones the mood of the soul.

The poet earns his renown by simply reflecting from his mind the life of his nation. The statesman and the conqueror cannot accomplish their work unless their individual gifts receive the cultivation necessary to qualify them to "take in" the details and tendencies of movements in a wide horizon, and to watch their chance for action. Thus talent controls the manner in which it allows itself to be influenced and in which it will exert influences in return, in which it inadvertently unites merit of sound judgment with celerity of action, and acts with tact. *[margin: Talent unites merit of judgement with celerity of practical and tactful application.]*

But the person of genius possesses, aside from and above his talent, an originality for which it is not so easy to give an account. Entirely distinct and exceptional in its peculiarity, it frequently fails to utilise those incitements of its surroundings for which every soul is disposed and for which it yearns. And more frequently it is not understood and misapprehended by inferior contemporaries, because of its aversion to adjust its conduct to the hollow phrases of the time, and to accommodate itself to the insipid affectations of culture. *[margin: Reasons for misapprehending the peculiarities of a genius. Genius declines to accommodate itself to the "spirit of the times".]*

Modern superficiousness unable to appreciate works of genius.   Seeck.

A tragedy of Shakespeare is rarely performed; the real opera is deserted while the "Variety Theatre" is crowded night after night. To use Seeck's criticism of modern superficiousness which is unable to appreciate genius, "modern taste will prefer a Thumann to a Duerer", a sensual Meyerbeer to a classical Bach or Schubert.

Genius proves the mind to be designed for independence;

partakes of the nature of the conscience.   Kæhler.

Genius and conscience phenomena of the same spiritual life, differing only according to its dual relations.

Genius is of that depth of acumen which abhors platitude. It acts under impulses of an incalculable singularity, which goes far to prove the selfhood and independence of the human mind. And this remaining balance, this margin of psychical life, which cannot be accounted for by the usual statistical squaring of accounts, partakes of the nature of conscience. Genius, like conscience is "a witness for that mysterious depth of our being beneath its earthly face and its everyday dress and working apparel, a witness for that profundity of the soul, from whence the lightnings arise which so frequently strike home into the 'reflecting consciousness' in a most bewildering manner." (Kœhler, Das Gewissen.)

In speaking of genius we meet again, as when we spoke of conscience, the occult rudiments of our being on that side of psychical life of which, unconscious and without control of it, as we are, we become reminded now and then. For genius and conscience are but different phenomena of the same principal part of our nature which only manifests itself in different directions according to its dual relations.

At this point, a hiatus for science, the "finger" procures the changes in the directions which human affairs are to take. ;

Here is the point where our anthropological system cannot be rounded off. Here is the gap at the bottom of which the open question remains. Here the nature of man also has the opening through which it receives influences from the spiritual world. And here it is that the Manager of History puts in His finger in order to procure the changes in the direction of human affairs. The undulations of ideas, resulting from earthly conditions, from the joint labor of the masses are merely accessory to this management, resembling the earth when it was bid to let plants grow. These incidentals are but erratic movements in concurrence with, or in antagonism to, the higher interferences.

Wilberforce, insisting upon the abolition of slavery,

It was of eminent import to universal history, that Wilberforce on the 24th day of March, A. D. 1807, after persevering in contest with Fox and Pitt for eighteen years, obtained the enactment of his "Bill to abolish Slavery". Is Wilberforce ranked among the great men? Altho not judging by success as does the world, which would have buried the originator's name under oblivion, we rank him among the champions of the cause of humanism. But he was only great in that he reflected upon, and persevered in agitating the measure for which the times were ripe; in that he assiduously challenged conservatism and became the mouthpiece of the humane principle of civilisation.

not a genius, but a champion of the cause of humanism.

Genius a failure if negligent in cultivating the receptivity of talent.

It is notorious that many a person of genius lacks sagacity and receptivity, celerity and pliability of mind, and trifles away the opportunities of making himself useful; while men without extraordinary talents enter the halls of renown, because of bestirring themselves to come to an understanding with their surroundings. Smoothness, like the polish which a jewel receives by grinding and rubbing, we may call that crystalline many-sidedness of a mind with a well cultivated receptivity, deficient of which the best endowed genius is a failure. The need of this aptitude for being molded and directed to a specific calling, profession or employment, is the more pressing, the more distinct and variegated the impressions become, which from a highly organised society are to be received and refracted, and the more complicated the problems which demand their practical solution by a genius. Hence we may understand, why in the normal course of historic advance the great ingenious minds become rare, in proportion as the many high qualities of contemporaneous society become more general. The higher the degree of general culture the more difficult will it be to become a leading man in the right track; for the reason that all around so many other talents and lights emulate to outshine each other—in some cases by crooked means. A genius without talent, tho a failure, is to be considered a genius nevertheless; whilst no quantity of talent per se can ever supersede genius. The secret of his prominency and of his strength lies in the creative power of the imagination, welling up from depths beyond the sphere of scientific research. But as the most genial artist cannot discard given forms, so can not the imagination of the genius dispense with the requisite erudition, nor dare to disregard externals, which prevent it from degenerating into empty, capricious phantasy. For even the imagination of the genius is the creative power in so far only, as it rearranges given forms into new combinations by new and appropriate methods. Its peculiar merit consists in this,

If the measure of mental advance becomes general excelling minds become rare.

No quantity of talent can supplant genius.

The secret of the genius lies in the "creative power of the mind", in the vivacity of the imagination.

It possesses ingenuity, i. e. the virtuosity to arrange given matters into new combinations by new and appropriate methods.

that it grasps at one intuitive and comprehensive glance the characteristic lines and
shades at hand, gently coercing them to express new conceptions of the essence of
things, or to represent the most delicate moods of the soul. Produced under these
conditions, a work of art calls forth or echoes at once the corresponding thought or
emotion in the beholder or the audience. Much like the genius of an artist or an or-
ator must be the ingenuity of him who governs a state or directs a battle. Even in
his, perhaps, uncouth designs, perpetrating cruelties with a high hand in order to reform or to transform, he needs an ideal to screen his disregard of human rights and
the destruction of cultures. He needs a new combination of ideas of which to make
himself the executioner. But in order to accomplish his plans of transformation or
of reform, a nation or more are necessary, which accede to his ideas because they have
already harbored them.

Genius enjoys the gift of the intuitive "grasp"; § 15.

Is necessary to pursue the realisation of some ideal.

To accomplish this realisation, a mass of people necessary who accede to the ideas of leading minds.

Most likely in ancient times, and surely in the dark Middle-Ages, when those
masses now claiming fanciful "associated ideas" as their own, did not yet exist, the
heroes of the mind were in fact of themselves and alone the originators of new ideas.
But to modern times this rule applies no longer. The truth is, that of late the masses
have become qualified to form "their own judgments," for the simple reason that they
have become conscious of their susceptibility and capacity to have ideas of their own.
Civilised nations are now deeply moved by public events. Down to the lower strata
of society the people are taking interest in affairs of state as well as in social problems. At present the many are engaged in what in earlier times were tasks incumbent upon single persons, and they therefore claim now also their part of glory and
hero-worship, eager at the least for mention in a paper. They know that they participate in the work of making heroes, or of unmaking individual fame. The difficulties
which obstruct the recognition of genius nowadays were formerly unknown;
especially as it is in the nature of highly wrought character to spurn excellency which
must be obtained by catering to popularity, and to avoid that newspaper notoriety
which provokes the envy of inferior minds to tear down the reputation of just that
character which is indifferent to frown or applause.

Participation of the masses in making or undoing "heroes".

Real excellency indifferent as to public frown or applause.

§ 217. In tranquil times and a normal run of affairs the mass forms a "public
opinion." With the growing condensation of the populace in large cities, with the
spread and increasing shallowness of intelligence, and with the widening of the
journalistic field, that "public opinion," manufactured and manipulated by the press,
becomes a menacing power. It is an irresponsible power, unreliable in every
respect, wielding a willful, fitful influence and working capriciously in any direction
it pleases, because bare of character and of any definite maxim.

Public opinion in its shallowness a menacing power.

Unawares public opinion becomes a tyrant, despite the many strong opinions uttered
against the nefarious practice of libeling by Supreme Courts, by its facilities to ostracise people of integrity at the instigation of the vilest, and to the satisfaction of a gossipy, clannish
populace. Methodically manufacturing "sensations" the press becomes, in the first place, the
formidable ally of such as are able to hire its assistance to carry out their wicked schemes;
whereby the press, in the second place, becomes a "paying business" whose success as such is
enough to command the admiration of the public which judges an establishment by the
money there is in it. Unawares, however, as if by way of retribution, this tool of public caprice with its delight in scandal, this tyrant allows itself to become the servant of a certain fac-
tion of the money power and to be led by it into a Babylonian captivity. For upon inquiry it
will be found, that not only in the offices of second-class newspapers the advertising agent
has as much to do with the tendency of a "leader", if not more, than the occupant of the edi-
tor's chair—and that this office fixture is generally a Jew. But tho the press is said to lose its
prestige at the rate of its venality,and despite its freedom to be impertinent, it is tyrannised as
much by the pennies of the "proletarian" as by capitalistic cliques—it still wields a greater
power than that which the commander of the German army possesses: a power with which
Governments even have to reckon. In order to utilise the press in molding public opinion
for certain ends, governmental agents must become silent partners of public enterprises.
Even those sitting upon thrones have to cultivate the friendship of journalism and to provide
for its pay, just as the military budget must be provided for.

Tyranny of the press.

Facility to defame and ostracise characters of integrity.

The press with all its liberty to be impertinent, is under the tyranny of certain influential factors.

Governments to become silent partners of journalistic enterprises.

Still more of an annoyance, an unprincipled servile tyrant, will common news-
paperdom become, when in times of excitement and turmoil resolute minds
make the press subservient to their designs. For in times of uproar and confusion
a leader is wanted by the vociferous multitude; and a leader is born up by the undercurrent, even if he should be "a dark horse". Any shrewd demagogue may of a

Press made a tool of schemers.

Short-lived renown
obtained by
demagoguery.

Napoleon's fraudulent
bulletins sent when
upon his "retirade".

sudden swing himself into the saddle of popularity until the delusion subsides and the public voice puts the rider to ridicule. The world sees many frauds of the brand of a Napoleon—writing his victorious bulletin to the "Moniteur" on Christmas-eve, 1812—not only among the French, and fortunately not always of his caliber. Our race, then will never be in want of heroes of some sort, even if it should be a balleteuse, or one hastily gotten up, either selfappointed or made to order in cases of emergency, since it seems destined that mankind is not always to enjoy a peaceful march of progress. Passions will seize the masses and forces burst their restraints.

True heroes
usually
recognised after
their weaknesses
are forgotten;
     Von Moser.

Thus the world will have heroes in which people see pet ideas personified, or fancy they see their own image. People will have them and glorify them, tho usually doing so too soon. A Wellington or Bismarck is, like hickory, of slower growth. The metal, of which a man must be forged whom history will acknowledge as a hero, will be assayed later on. As to true excellency our full recognition of deserts generally lingers behind, because, as Von Moser said, "the name of every great man must first have lost its cadaverous smell, the memory of his weaknesses." This must be so for the other reason that true superiority of mind and morals does not deem it necessary to defend itself against the calumnies of jealousy which only death shuts up. In short, an impartial verdict as to real merit can only be rendered by the peers of great minds; by the people at large, not before the issues of great deeds and the fruits of beneficient reforms have become palpable.

and the beneficient
results of their efforts
become palpable.

Hero-cult but a
sign of the
search after that
mind which
manages human
affairs through
human instru-
mentalities.

The radiance of
great lights
grows dim; only
surrogates of
the light of
Heaven until in
this light "the
finger" is
perceived which
makes use of the
earthly
candlesticks.

In order to conceive whether the rage of merely destructive forces—whether conquerors, who to all appearances had to serve as scourges of the nations—were really necessary; or in order to discern whether such visitations always occurred at the proper time: one would have to occupy a point of view above the process which tends towards completion. The cultus of heroes, of genius, of humanism are, after all, but modes and phases of the search after that mind which manages human affairs and rules in history through human instrumentalities. In reviewing the illustrious lives of the renowned, man simply follows the impulse to see in them his nobler self. Celebrating their memory and contemplating their virtues and merits, man rises above the prosaic routine and trivialities of every-day life, and in them objectivises his own views and experiences of life, until the rays of these lights and the haloes around their heads grow dim with the distance of time, and new lights arise. These must then again serve as surrogates for the Light of Heaven until men begin to see it and to perceive "the finger" which makes use of the earthly candlesticks.

CH. V. THE GOVERNMENT OF THE WORLD.

The divine
guidance

not to be inspected
while at work in the
minor details of history.

Lacordaire.

§ 218. The finger, which once was acknowledged by certain Ægyptians, or as we usually say, the guiding hand which leads to combinations and disentangles complications, which upturns the tables of the money-mongers and speculators and the boards of high councils in clearing the way for new æras; this finger cannot be looked upon while at work in the specialties and minor but momentous details in the general course of universal history. It can be looked for nowhere else than above the totality of events.

Purpose and plan of
history partly immanent
partly transcendental.
  § 5, 6, 60-62, 58, 101
       196, 208.

"As the master leads the chisel of his apprentice over the marble," says Lacordaire, "so the Divine Master architect circumspectly guides the hand of mankind, and teaches man with unceasing care and educational discipline to exercise all faculties in the work wherein he is to cooperate with Him."

Pure induction would
have had to come to the
same conclusion,

Speaking of the purpose and then of the plan of history we inferred, that both must underlie, and be implied in history; but must partly, in a certain sense, also lie above it. Since then the plan and the goal have been rendered intelligible. Something else, besides, led to postulates which found their answer only when "the Thought", hidden in things, made its appearance in person—with the entrance of the Mediator. In Him destiny and plan became disclosed.

Had this not been the case, we would, by the way of pure induction, still have had to arrive at the same conclusion, provided the single axiom is granted in the premise, that man as such possesses reason; i. e., that form of intellect which the Germans term Vernunft. Materialism avers this faculty of intelligence to be the final result of gradual civilisation, analogous to the accomplishments of domesticated animals. According to Schaeffler, reason, or let us rather say Vernunft, the higher form of the intellect in the human mind, "consists in the accumulative animation of man's social life and his capacity for acute apperception generated by the social adjustment of labor sequent to cultivation and continuity of social intercourse." This definition shows the reason why we deem it necessary at the present time to sue for an agreement with our axiom, as a common basis of operation. We assert that man has "Vernunft" previous to any mode or degree of erudition. *(margin: Materialistic concept of this intellectual faculty. Schaeffler.)* *(margin: Man endowed with intellect prior to erudition;)*

By empirics alone man does not obtain intelligence. Intellect (Vernunft) is designed to be developed by education, but is not thus to be acquired, nor can it be implanted by any training or hereditary law. Being the prerequisite for education, Vernunft is just the opposite of Schaeffler's product of socialistic evolution. *(margin: it being the prerequisite for education.)*

We claim no more than that which up to recent dates has ever been held as self-evident. This granted we need nothing else for our inductive proof of the government of the world by the Mediator.

The conclusiveness with which Goethe, from a ram's horn found upon the sands near Venice, syllogised the form of the entire skeleton, was found in the matter itself. As a matter of fact the explorer reconstructs from a part of a skeleton, found among a few other antediluvian bones in the interior of the cave, the whole stature of the megatherium. *(margin: Illustration; inductive reasoning of Goethe.)*

In all its workings reason follows this very same method of procedure, to persist in gaining an apperception of itself in the state of finiteness, to recognise its own significance in the relations with its own ego, and to construct out of itself an intelligible conception of the totality of perceptible and conceivable matters of which the individual knows itself to be a part. The attempts to such construction cannot but lead, with Platonism, to an unknown God, to an infinite personal mind. There is no other logic thinkable. This position we can not be induced to surrender. An impersonal reason in history, can, therefore, satisfy us no longer. "We are fully in earnest in acknowledging an inner leading principle, something which mysteriously overrules, overwhelms the arbitrariness of the historic current", said H. Fichte. "But this something is no weird, transcendental being, nothing which steals itself over man in order to impute to him consequences of actions for which he is not responsible. This factor neither blindfolds nor leads him as by magic. On the contrary, that which is to be chosen is rendered evident in his consciousness with such brightness that man cannot fail to choose the right thing, unless he refuses to accept the evidence. It is the actuation of ethical ideas in history which silently and ubiquitously works for definite historical ends; or to speak in less abstract terms, it is the willing, the craving after the Good, deeply and indestructibly implanted within us, which in truth and in the end always comes out triumphant, which punishes or rewards and ever maintains its right of final decision. Every act of humanity in its general work, politically or socially, is, as well as the individual agent, subject to its judgment". *(margin: In which method reason persists in gaining an apperception of itself in all its relations to its own ego and to the entire compass of perceptible and conceivable matters;)* *(margin: whereby it arrives at the conclusion of an unknown God. H. Fichte.)*

Were the management of universal history carried on according to Fichte's idea we should have an odd sort of government. This ethical volition evolving after the law of its own reason would as a selfgovernment prove a failure. Its always coming out victorious would happen under no other but those impulses which prompt nature's own nascency. It is plain how little that victorious good will corresponds with the real circumstances. Just as little does that reason, innate in history, answer the reasonable postulates of the human intellect. For, this reason of Fichte, outrunning itself in the intricate details of history, makes it quite inconceivable how it may outlast the conflict of intricacies, without supposing that a rather deranged reason or sheer irrationalness had seized the reigns of government. The essence of reason cannot be kept intact, if left pendent and envolved within history itself. Safe it is only as inherent in the nature of the divine person outside of history, as the wisdom of the living God, as His plan and purpose under a system of fixed laws. *(margin: Criticism of Fichte's idea of the government of the world.)* *(margin: Reason can remain intact only outside of history within the living God.)* *(margin: Laws imparted to history as its agencies did not satisfy W. v. Humboldt;)*

Wilhelm von Humboldt declared, as Dr. Rocholl was recently informed, that "imparted" laws as agencies of history could not satisfy him. The trend of his ideas has aided and corroborated our views more than once before. His "free working impulses" helped us out, in the first place, of a mechanical conception of history. In *(margin: who proposed "free working impulses".)*

Motion implies direction for which materialism has no explanation.
§ 3, 17, 18, 19, 21, 22, 23, 25, 101.

that connection Humboldt demanded more than the mere mechanical laws of nature; for history he demanded more than the rule of physiological principles or laws of life which only partly explain the historic motion, and scarcely half-way yields plausible reasons for periods of national bloom and decay, for the symptoms of health or disorder. As essential to an understanding of the human world he therefore demands more than the psychological laws of sensibilities and passive reflex-actions of the nerves. All of these laws are insufficient to explain history without doing it violence. Humboldt requires the historian to rise above the domain of palpable events and to begin the inquiry simply with a clear comprehension of motion, since the cognition of direction in motion is essential and cannot be accounted for by those laws.

To trace the control over human affairs back to an original cause not of a transient nature.

Where, then, asks Humboldt, is the historian to take his standpoint? "If we do not want to abandon the discovery of connection in the affairs of our race, we are compelled to go back to an original and independent cause not of a transient, phenomenal nature." Humboldt, in short, wants an adequate cognition of the world's government. "All knowledge is, at the last resort, attached to ideas which, if investigated as to their lineage and reduced to their original fountain-head, are found to center in a personal mind beyond this world of ours." With this postulate Humboldt pointed out that standpoint outside of mechanical, physical and psychical empiricism. Of course, if one could be justified in refusing upon grounds of empiricism to recognise the original, selfconscious power, which in the form of eternal existence, tho active outside the happenings of the finite world, yet keeps them under its control: then he might be excusable in denying that creative ingenuity which is able to overrule and to interfere with the mechanism of the universe.

All knowledge centers in a personal mind beyond our visible universe.

Denial of the selfconscious power outside of which and of its interference with the mechanism of the universe.

The higher "Thought" who evinces itself even to empiricism as a cause, takes a hand in the development of history, and cannot be conceived otherwise than that of the absolute personality.

But since, as empiricism even evinces, a higher thought, in the capacity of a cause, takes a hand in the development of history, then, most assuredly, it can be no other than that of a personality. For this interference must be preceded by a definite intent. This determination of the mind can only be thought of as proceeding from a certain act of an absolute and intelligent will with a certain object in view. Every experience and analogy indicates, yea verifies the correctness and legitimacy of our ratiocination. And where would be a deficiency or the least danger of acceding to the axiom, that a selfconscious absolute will stands above and regulates the connection in the developing process of history otherwise inexplicable?

Axiom: a selfconscious and absolute will controls the historic progress.

Problem: how to conceive the inframundane relation of this absolute mind to history.

§ 219. Another problem, however, is opened by the question how this personal absolute mind is to be conceived in its inframundane relation to history? The development of humanism—which history serves to envelop as much as it serves to reveal it, is not subject to necessity which conditions the development of nature. The historic process transpires, under the necessities at variance with those which nature has to obey, that is, under conditions of its own, which are ethical. Of course, as far as the externals of history are concerned, these ethical necessities coincide with the laws ever ruling the natural and temporal life of man.

The development of humanity not under natural but ethical necessity, under laws of its own.

Sphere in which ethical necessity nd natural laws coincide and are congruent.

But as far as man is pre-eminently a spiritual being, the nature of which spiritual part is unity, and hence the same in every human being and ever true to itself—so far is the historic development exempt from natural necessity. In the latter sphere the ethical law rules supreme, a law not at all opposed to, but even embracing the laws which reason construes from the natural phenomena. The laws of the inner life can be less adequately formulated into paragraphs than those of nature, since man's being is of unfathomable depth with a marvelous mass of interrelations. The most circumspect calculations of a probable course of history are, therefore, thrown out of gear by intervening events which arise in the obscurity of human nature. Now wild passions tear asunder the threads spread upon the loom of regular arrangements; then again the noble thoughts of men of genius cause unexpected turns in the affairs of the world.

Limits of natural necessity and selfdevelopment, § 20, 54.

Spiritual concerns pertaining to "essential unity" are exempt from natural necessity. § 6.

Laws of the inner life difficult to schematise, impossible to be calculated.

This leads us once more to consider the much argued doctrine of "free will."

It has been stated that will was not free to choose: that the ideas, claiming freedom of volition and at the same time to found this volition upon inciting motives which influence the choice, form an untenable contradiction. Here it is that the view upon the relation between Divine Providence and human freedom became

"Free will" under aspect of Divine rule. § 10, 11.

Freedom of volition in a theory an untenable contradiction.

Vitiated view upon the relation between Divine providence and human freedom.

vitiated in the premises. Willing and choosing are theoretically detached from man —from finite and dependent man, of whose mind the will is but one of the means of expression,—and then are made one abstract thing. Such a construction of abstract volition no one really demands, except those who intend to build upon it a false system of ethics.

Will and choosing identified in the abstract and then detached from man, made a foundation for a false system of ethics.

We are bold to demand and to maintain freedom, by virtue of which we are not chained to motives or methods of external influences from an abstract theoretical determinism. We state quite the opposite, namely that we often determine ourselves in the pursuit of, and contest for, higher interests of an ethical nature. The government of the world is not achieved in violation of freedom, but by means of it. "If providence," says Vico, "is the architect of nations, the judiciousness of men is the foreman of the builders."

No mechanical determinism.

With this conception the insight is gained, that we must not misconstrue the immutability of God. In the inner life of the divine nature we must not imagine a condition of inflexible constraint, but as regards the execution of purpose and plans we are compelled to attribute to God the freedom of changing His attitude toward the creature. Of this we are convinced because He is the living God of a single, a unique not a simple nature. Hence we may say with Lotze: "Any view acknowledging a life of God which does not stiffen into perpetual identity, will be able to conceive, His eternal interaction as a mutable coefficient or paracleitos. One may see how, at certain movements, this mode of cooperation and adaptation is rendered conspicuous by its modifying effects, and how it thus testifies to the incompleteness of the natural course of things." Here, after all, the circle-bound speculations are blasted; philosophy has found the right track for a new start in solving the problem of harmonising Divine Providence and human freedom. Dorner and Martensen agree with Lotze in their disquisitions on determinism and indeterminism.

Immutability of God not to be misconstrued as in deism.

Changeability of God's attitude toward man.

God of a unique but not a simple nature.

Divine interaction, Lotze.

testifies to the incompleteness of the natural course of things, Dorner; Martensen.

The incompleteness of the natural course of things "is witness to the interaction of Providence," of the living God. But as the natural world is an open system, not at all forestalling but requiring providential interference, much more is the world of history a system prearranged to give room to Divine interference and bent on completing its rounds under it.

Natural world a system not forestalling but requiring providential interference.

It will become apparent how the system is perfected.

Admitting that so far we have not surpassed the deistic conception, an objection might be raised from the other side of the house, which we may as well meet right here. We are accosted by the argument, that if individual happiness and the basis of social order, and the guaranty of its preservation were given solely in that revelation which the church claims to have in charge: then this revelation ought of necessity not to have been enveloped in hulls and shrouds. It should have been projected in a palpable awe-inspiring majesty, so that doubt could not have been able to bring forth probabilities for denying it, and denial would have been made impossible once and forever.

Exceptions taken on grounds of deism that the revelation which the church claims to have in charge, is necessarily occult.

Revelation of reason personified ought not to have been "incognito".

We are further told that if the cardinal center of this revelation were the eternal reason of the world, then this would have had to appear as the Lord and King and Shepherd of the nations, and to occupy its throne in open view of everybody. Then every possibility of vexatious scepticism would have been prevented.

If scepticism were prevented

Yes, and then all freedom would have been set aside, too.

freedom would have been nullified.

Long ago, Kant gave the necessary rejoinder. "Then," he said, "most of the legalistic actions would be performed under compulsion of fear, a few from hope, but none at all for the sake of duty. A moral value of deeds, upon which alone, in the eyes of the world and of Supreme Wisdom, the value of the person doing them depends, would not exist at all. So long as the nature of man remains what it is, man's conduct would also remain the same, that is it would be merely mechanical". This means, we would have no freedom. There would be no history. For history is the guide to liberty. The unhidden glory and majesty would have suppressed all opposition; but it would also have arrested the process of development before the world had attained to its state of maturity. As it is, the possibility must have been given to take offence at the mystery of Holiness and Love; to fall over "a stumbling-stone and rock of offence"; to become confused by the great paradox which consists in the peculiar mode and form of this revelation, and is set up in the midst of the world as an incitement to exercise the mental and moral incipiencies with which man is endowed. The possibility must be given to man to put himself into relation with revelation without compulsion; the possibility must remain even to go to perdition.

Kant.

There would be no moral value of deeds or in persons doing their duty,

and no history guiding on to liberty.

The will of God is effectuated in the course of things, because this will is the ideal aim of all occurrences, and is to be worked out through man under condition of his relative (not absolute) freedom. The Supreme Will, then, works under a system of limitation. It carries out its intentions in the play of interchanging influences of mind upon mind, in overcoming impediments through neutralising counteractions,

upon ways hidden or round-about. It effectuates itself under an exercise of long-suffering, through procrastination and retrogressive steps, even in instances where retrogression appears to be a defeat of the purpose. Since not all which is

real is at the same time rational, it follows not only that irrational facts must be possible, but also that it must be possible to make them subservient to the final real-isation of the rational. And all of this ensues, because the Absolute Will takes the

liberty to choose selflimitation instead of restricting the freedom of the finite will. This truth ventilates many questions. But even at this instant of our investigation, without having risen as yet above the standpoint of deism—answers are coming forth.

§ 220. There is a trace of providential traction, manifest in the desire for expansion seizing the nations from time to time, which is not explicable simply by a superabundance of cultural embarrassment necessitating an overflow.

At the period of the great migration in Europe, in the steps taken by the Spaniards and the Portuguese in matters of colonisation at the close of the Middle-Ages, we plainly see the providential arrangement; and we clearly notice a ruling hand in the order in which, since the time of the water-beggars, the European nations have spread themselves abroad.

Oppression and defeat were turned to most happy ends. It is marvelous how the circum-stances on those occasions, served in lifting the whole race upon the tracks of accelerated advancement.

Here virgin soil is broken, and new countries dotted with settlements; there people overripe with culture as in Tunis, Ægypt, Persia, and Japan, are stimulated afresh. Not so easy is it, however, to comprehend why entire peoples, torn away from their old ethnical connections, by arbitrary star-chamber proceedings, were hitched to alien nations. Charles V gives the Low-Countries to his son Philip; then blood is made to flow in rivers in order to dissolve the unnatural union which was not thus to be forced. What a clamor

has been raised over the partition of Poland; what an amount of injustice has been done in order first to form "United Kingdoms", and then to regain home-rule, as in the cases of Hungary and Ireland.

Yet in all these seeming anomalies deep plans are discernible.

We are shown up into council halls higher than those where the imperious wills of cabinets dispose of the weal and woe of nations; into the sphere from whence the Supreme Will guides the wisdom, or utilises the folly of, Prime-Ministers.

Explanations of such disposals of people, on grounds of natural science, may be precise and may seem sufficient to the analytic interpreter—in order to understand the fact, for instance, that the Ugro-Tatarian element was drawn to the neighborhood of the Germans, or that tribes like the old Prussian were welded together with other nations only to wrangle with them; in order to further dynastic interests. Examin-ing such plain facts a little closer, however, and taking again correlative bearings into considerations of a wider range, then causes and effects demonstrate the deeper intention which disposed of such people for cultural and ethical ends. For we find that whenever people, standing in the relations of a corresponding polarity to one an-

other, are thus joined together, a new force develops from just such a tension. That force will prove more effective than the forces working in the nations each by itself, which forces by the way of the combination will generate a new power superseding the former, and causing the amalgamated nation to take a new departure in prosper-

ity and prolificacy. This process is analogous to the genesis of individual life, where the offspring is of the more distinct quality and the less indifferent or common-place, the more marked the parental polarity. This single empirical fact throws sufficient light upon the higher guidance rendered obvious in the migrations and mergings of people.

Among the multitude of ethnical concomitants we found here "products of

degeneracy", and there a humus on top of the substratum formed by decaying masses. Now we find the key to unlock the secret of such deteriorations. We have become aware of the hand which has something to do with ethnical inundations and subju-gations. The dark substratum beneath this thin crust of cultural layer almost everywhere, was a standing conundrum. It remained an unsolved riddle, that the compressed strata of aboriginal tribes, after they had been covered by the new vegetation of cultivated and victorious nations, never became completely assimilated. This material, massive and marly, will never decompose. Neither is the humus, to continue the metaphor by which we designed the prevailing parties, ever absorbed by the crops of culture it yielded. Tho this humus may be "farmed out" in a manner forfeiting the name of cultivation, yet in quantity it does not diminish. The humus remains even under such circumstances, only that, in point of quality it becomes similar to the substratum. Not only does the humus not diminish, but it rather increases by the matter grown and decaying upon it. It was a great chemist who contended many years for establishing the truth which we here are free to apply in the cultivation of applied ethnology. For we found that in almost every case the subjugated strata of the social compound were always capable of being influenced by the peculiar qualities of the ethnical layer spreading out over them, and were benefited by the cultural growth springing up above and clothing them with verdure. They became incited to participate in the activity of their superiors and to enure themselves to the influences of their cultural work whereby they became elevated. In most of these cases the vanquished people derived the greatest benefit from the pressure occasioned by the subjugation.

Margin: Indestructibility of the ethnical substratum, which is never completely assimilated by higher culture.

Margin: whilst nations of higher culture are prone to sink down to the level of the lower strata.

Margin: Lowest strata adapted to partake of the qualities of their superiors,

Margin: and are benefitted even by the pressure of subjugation.

Never was any of the ethnical strata, or of the commotion going on about them, entirely void of the purpose; for never, neither in nature nor in history, is there anything lost. It is a weighty sentence which George Foster formulated long ago: "In any system where everything moves under mutual attraction nothing can be annihilated; the quantity of the constituent elements ever remains the same."

Margin: As little as in nature is there ever anything lost in history.

Margin: Nothing is annihilated of the constituent elements moving in a system of mutual attraction.   G. Foster.

Since that discovery the axiom of the preservation of forces has received the right of citisenship in the realm of natural science, and Helmholtz has written out the diploma. It only remains that the science of history also should recognise as an axiom: the indestructibility of cultural effects. This ought to be raised to the dignity of a cardinal dogma in historics. It should be acknowledged that the preservation of the total amount, the sum and substance of rational products yielded, as well-as the preservation of each individual energy and its agent, is guaranteed by the ordinances and arrangements of the Manager on high. For everything transpiring is included in the plan of final consummation, and everybody is concerned in the realisation of all purposes; hence, every thing, every person, every fact, will come to be unveiled in its ethical bearings. For above all does the unfurling of the moral standard belong to the Executive of the Government, which takes care that whatever was in harmony with the purpose, or what attempts had been made to foil it, must come to be publicly and universally known. It must become known that no willful arbitrariness can escape from justice which maintains the equipoise between the effects of man's acts and deeds. Hence the reverse side of the fatherly government of love, and the prerogative of the world's government are: administration of justice, retribution—a day of judgment.

Margin: "Preservation of forces". Helmholtz.

Margin: Indestructibility of cultural effects a historic dogma. § 4., 69.

Margin: Everything is included in the plan of final consummation—everybody concerned in the realisation of the purpose.

Margin: The day of judgment a prerogative of the executive of the world's government.

Let us take a glance at the interior of our hospitals. Immediately the impression will overwhelm us that if there were no God, nature at least would punish disobedience to its laws upon whomsoever made himself liable. Here we perceive the inexorable execution of a judgment given by a court in permanent session. The subdued demeanor of the culprits who have indulged in dissipation make the sombre, silent verdicts clearly legible. As nature deals out retribution for every form of excess, so every case of neglect is punished. Faculties not exercised will be crippled; of opportunities to improve them we shall become deprived if we repeatedly slight them. The eye of the cave-salamander becomes as a rudimentary organ, it dries up. The visionary power of the soul, the sense for things eternal must of necessity become stunted, if not made use of and improved.

Margin: Punishments under the laws of nature.

Margin: (Faculties not exercised).

How the abuse of the relations between man and the earth avenges itself, is shown not only by the condition of the countries where the ancient nations of culture disregarded that solidarity—tho recognising it very well in certain other respects. Reckless draining upon the sources of natural wealth is carried on to the serious detriment of posterity even in the most civilised nations of modern times. By the criminal destruction of forests, the mountains are made bald and barren, rivers are rendered shallow and made channels of periodical destruction, so that meadows become deserts. Such outrages committed upon nature have laid waste many regions of oriental culture, have rendered the country of Homer's time and the physiognomy of the "Promised Land" irrecognisable. They have created the "Sahara of the

Margin: (Destruction of forests).

If man turns nature's
blessings into curses,

Provence". In California, goldwashing was stopped by legislation in districts where fruitful valleys had been made inarable; the Volga low-lands are deluged by the sand washed down from mountains deprived of their vegetation. Thus nature takes her revenge if men turn her blessings into curses. By such object lessons nature imparts her teachings, but the teacher stands beyond her—it is He who speaks.

God is expected, for
reasons of personal life,
to render final
judgment.

For therein consists the object of the education of the children of men under divine guidance, that in the development of humanity a person, working at the apparatus of the environments, which are also in the hands of God, is taken out from the general life of the genus and lifted above the state of mere natural existence. Personal life is to be led up to self-consciousness and selfdecision. For this reason God must have the final word. The passive, natural condition of the individual does not postulate special verdicts of God.

Postulate: God is to
uphold the right by
declaring sentence
against the wrong.

This condition only appeals to sympathy and is not an object of special chastisement. But the guilt contracted in the state of personal life begets the expectation and postulates that God should speak. The more developed and intricate the concerns of personal life become, the more it becomes necessary that God should uphold the right by declaring sentence against the wrong.

Judgment not mere
balancing of laws.

Judgment then, involves more than that which is expressed in the phrase that "universal history executes the judgment of the world." People considering judgment to be no more than the balancing of laws—as the meaning of that sentence is understood—declare themselves to be satisfied with reducing this "balancing" to the law of "natural selection", whilst we are concerned with that judgment rendered upon the rational and moral conduct of men, in which personal relations are uncovered and made public. We are concerned with that judgment which holds the heedless or reckless person responsible, and condemns it to face the consequences of the fundamental, impartial, and unalterable principles of justice, as administered throughout the constitutional government of the whole realm presided over by God in person.

Point of view
above the
deistical. God
presides in person
at the world's
constitutional
government.

For, above all there is a point of view of the government of the world higher than the deistical, upon which we have thus far remained for the sake of argument. Since it is desirable that we should confide in the wisdom and love of the Divine Government with its mysterious ways and rulings, to trust even despite its permitting evil, and if we would learn to adore the self-inanition of the deity whereby God deigned to enter into our finite form of existence: then we ought to ascend to that view of the truth,

God's pleasure to
limit himself in
order to interfere
with, and enter
into, the finite
form of existence.

from which it is conceivable that God can and does limit Himself. To this position, however, we cannot rise by way of reasoning alone. The intellect does not constitute all of man's being anyway, much less at this new step where man in his entirety and inner essence is to stand forth in muster.

God's
condescension
§ 92, 101-104.

The conditions of and reasons for, a more adequate cognition in the matter of divine self-inanition have been stated previously.

not to be
understood by
way of thinking
alone.

§ 221. We may therefore now recapitulate the results of our inquiry. In one respect we perceive a state of affairs in which history seems to be abandoned to willful arbitrariness. The issue of history is incalculable. For, as Schelling puts it,

Recapitulation:
Issue of history
incalculable. Schelling.

"that which may be figured out, a priori, is not the object of history; and vice versa, what is to be taken for its object must not be calculable before hand." According to

A few more dilemmas of
thought as to divine
government,

this partially true statement we are challenged, it appears, to surrender everything which purports to be in accord with a rational plan and purpose.

originating from the
complication of human
affairs with
the Bad,

The wording of this opinion might be construed to imply that all of this plan and purpose was doomed to subside in the turmoil of subjectivistic liberty. Is there no surmise as to the source of the confusion which would point to the discovery? Yea, still more confounding is it that, with reference to the subject under discussion, other riddles present themselves which seem as if they could not be solved in the present condition

which modifies matters
§ 20, 40, 41, 110.

of our intellectual powers, and the solution of which could not be hoped for even from any future state. From the deistic standpoint we are unable to understand these riddes

The ignoring of which
leads to the disavowal
of the revealed, and
substitution of an
"unknowable" God,

for the simple reason that they originate in the complication of human affairs with the Bad, which indeed exists. The Bad is a mystery, and becomes the more mystifying in proportion as men are determined to ignore or to disregard it.

who is pressed into
service for arguments
sake.

In the last resort this attitude towards the problem brings man into the dilemma of disavowing the revealed, and to substitute an unknowable God, a God only to be accepted as a proposition necessary to that process of thinking which cannot arrive at desirable conclusions, unless the God-idea be pressed into service as a mere argumentative proof. Under this aspect, then, as a matter of course, the hypothetical God-idea is wrought accordingly. The consequence is, that man cannot be blamed for withholding his confidence from such a modifiable God, tho even so highly honored as to receive the attribute of "higher being", or of being the most sublime idea—and nothing more: being but an empty generalisation, the makeshift of human reason in its attempt to reduce wrong understanding and true sentiment to a synthesis. *The God of deism an attempt at combining true sentiments and wrong understanding.*

A less confused picture of history will become visible, and its more satisfactory understanding is obtainable upon no other than that stage of philosophy which requires the empty form of the postulated God-idea, the unknown God, to be filled with real contents. *The "God-idea" is to be filled with real contents*

This is the case in the Christian God-consciousness. Revelation imparts to thought the essence of fullness. Here the mind is relieved of the oppressive feeling caused by the erroneous apperception that the death of millions was a necessity for the purpose of serving the ambition of a single individual, as the stepping-stone to his greatness. *as in the Christian God-consciousness. No necessity to form many conclusions.*

There is no longer any necessity for generations to perish in order to raise a higher ethical life upon fields of ruins; no longer the necessity for the erroneous conception of the Good being the product or reverse side of the Bad. For in that Christian cognition alone the thought of freedom prevails over those necessities which cry to Heaven for a solution. *Christian cognition freedom prevails.*

This freedom is preserved and in safe keeping nowhere but in an invisible higher organism which gradually pervades that expanding visible organism of humanity, which is to cover the length and breadth of the earth's surface. Throughout the whole extent there are spreading out like threads in horizontal lines the billions of interrelations, binding together all nations, and hence indirectly, but not less firmly, all individuals as the many members of the one organism. This natural bond of humanity is thrown out like a net into the water with the connections out of sight, so that frequently the identity of the parts with the whole is rendered irrecognisable. *Freedom in safe keeping alone in an invisible organism framed into the visible organism of true humanity. Interrelations of this visible organism figure as binding threads running horizontally.*

Within this visible organism, broadcast over the globe, an invisible organism, centering in the Mediator, is to ramify and is to pervade and permeate and penetrate the former natural organism everywhere. The ways and relations radiating from this center and acting as threads which lead back to it, connecting and binding each member of the spiritual organism with the center, enter from above, vertically into the horizontal fabric of earthly history. Thus a new and higher organism is assuming shape under this process of pervasion. The threads of relationship with the center run to it from all directions of the compass of conscious activity. Every man born into this world partakes, by virtue of the spiritual part of human nature, of the light emanating from the Head and Universal Center of humanity. Every one is addressed as a personal being by a call setting free his selfhood. According to the eternal plan to be realised through free agents, every man is called to freedom by his participation in the light shining upon all. *The invisible organism centering in the Mediator is to pervade the expanding natural organism. Connecting and binding interrelations figure as threads issuing from the center of the spiritual sphere, which enter the horizontal fabric of earthly history in vertical lines. Selfhood is set free by a call to join the higher than natural organism of humanity.*

It would be folly to begin with enumerating the opportunities offered to each, individually, for entering into and carrying on the mysterious relations with Him by Whom each is created, and for the communion with Whom each one was destined. Such enumeration is almost impossible, especially since from the observation of others these relations are withdrawn. For they occur chiefly in that domain of psychical life which we call "unreflected (or sub-) consciousness", which is hidden from reflecting reason. We only insist upon the fact, that from this depth we receive impulses and impressions of which we become conscious and upon which we can meditate. We lay some stress upon this empirical fact because it affords a key to unlock other phenomena of equal bearing. *Opportunities offered for entering and carrying on the mysterious relations. Occurrences in the sphere of "unreflected (or sub-) consciousness. § 8, 15, 37, 112, 113.*

Enabled to form the apperception of an invisible kingdom built into the framework of the empiric mental cosmos, we discern that a unification of the visible with the invisible is rendered feasible indeed. The rearing of the spiritual kingdom is designed to include the whole of humanity in the broadest sense. The means of its construction are as veiled as the results of edification remain internal. It is quite sufficient to know that the gain for humanity consists in an organisation which holds it together in its spiritual consanguinity. A sphere is given in which it is *By the spiritual kingdom as built into the framework of the mental cosmos, the unification of the invisible with the visible is reserved. The means of construction are as veiled as the results remain internal.*

29

Privileges obtainable through the means of grace in the church.

made obligatory that the perfection of humanity be wrought out, in which each individual recognises its grand destiny and has extended to him the assurance of its attainment. It is the kingdom in which mankind becomes renewed by conformance with the original, essential and final destination; in which the human family regains its lost unity—where the necessity of the law is superseded by the new covenant of free grace.

The three inter-cohesive sphereoid, natural universe, human world, Kingdom of Heaven upon earth.

The innermost of the three concentric circles is now rendered distinct. The circle out on the periphery designates the natural universe. The human world forms the next, the mixed sphere of psychico-pneumatic life. The purely spiritual Kingdom of Heaven upon earth and in Heaven forms the central compass. This was always the goal toward which all rotating cycles of physical, mental, and ethical development were consigned from the beginning.

The confidential relations between sinner and Savior.

It was the result of a previous survey of this topic that we discerned the thought as having become a fact in the person of the Mediator at the fullness of time. The personal relation of each man to Him consists, as may be learned empirically, in the trusting devotedness and unreserved consecration to a love which embraces each individual created in the "image," even tho this may be blurred in the forlorn condition of the individual. The relation is founded upon confidence in a holy world-government conducted by love and justice, according to which gifts have been granted under the expectation of prompt returns; and signs of love have been communicated to a world of humanity wherein signs of appreciation rarely appear.

as regards the world's constitutional government and judgment.

It is confidence in a just government which uses discrimination as to the degree to which, considering indigent circumstances and giftedness, allowances can be made as to how far that could have been accomplished which had been commanded.

Most willingly do we agree with Droysen's sentence in his "Outlines of Historics": "History, too, teaches to understand God, and in God alone can we find its understanding." But we offer as an amendment that this understanding, since we can never obtain it otherwise than in parts, can satisfy no mind but such a one as knows itself to be understood, and trusts that that, which to us remains unknown, is properly provided for, nevertheless. This is possible only in the organism where Heaven and earth are in contact. With this organism the individual members do not, however, sustain rapport by reason alone; their feeling and will are likewise to be attached thereto. The individual must know and feel himself organically and historically connected with, and supported by, the Head. The member knows itself to be rescued and cleansed by, and safe only in the incessant and cordial relation with, the Head. In union with the Mediator the Christian partakes of the position in the midst of things. His vision therefore is rendered central as from the summit of a freestanding mountain.

In God alone is the understanding of history to be found. Droysen.
The conditions and experiences of faith.
Mind satisfied in knowing itself to be understood.
Organic connection of the members with the head; not merely on lines of intellectualism.
A Christian's central position, "central-vision".
Upon this scope mistrust, born of ignorance gives room to confidence.
Nothing happens perchance under auspices of blind fate.

Upon this scope the mistrust born of ignorance gives way to an assured confidence. Then such fortuitous events of history, as were designated the unaccountable margin of historics, and which people are quick to ascribe to fate—as an accidental matter, a chance or mishap—lose their embarrassing effects upon the faithful.

Hap-hazard seems to have great sway in the various predicaments which man has to endure, as well as in favorable contingencies of historic note. Quite a number of the most important discoveries and inventions are traceable to an occasion which seemed a matter of mere chance.

In the Cathedral of Pisa, Galilæo sees a lamp swinging from having just been refilled with oil, and is thereby led to find the pendular oscillations. An apple falling to the ground, leads Newton to discover the law of gravity and attraction. The flight of a swarm of pelicans towards the south prompts Columbus to steer in that direction, whereby North America is left to the Germanic nations and protestantism. Numerous are the "happenings" like finding gold in California, by which streams of emigration were directed to regions unknown or deemed inaccessible before. Is not then the coincidence of different and seemingly irrelevant circumstances to be exalted to the importance of a historic factor conditioning the progress of history? Should not that writer be correct, after all, who designates incidental happening as "the little finger" of the hand of God Almighty.

Instances of "fortuitous" events leading to great discoveries.

Experiences of providential care confirm us in the knowledge that "chance" exists not.

It is a psychological fact, founded upon experience, that people who recognise themselves as being incorporated into the center of things, are the more reluctant to acknowledge events as mere incidental, the more they experience the support of Providence. They see miracles everywhere, everywhere the "little finger" in occurrences which to others seem insignificant. On the strength of their own experience they see Small matters evince themselves as turning-points in our lives; furnish the measure for prudence and patience. the direct rulings of the Father in Heaven in small things by which they are confirmed of the providential care as a most indisputable fact, affording them an assured certitude, solace, security and encouragement. Facts occurring at just such a time make their pettiness, because of which otherwise they would remain unnoticed, the more remarkable, the plainer they evince themselves as turning points in our lives; by their bearing upon the sequences they become grounds of conviction from which · no one can dissuade us. Such facts furnish us the measure for our prudence and— patience.

By the repetition of striking experiences of that nature the thought is revived Providential care and guidance are veiled until their beneficial results are clearly perceived. within us of a providential guidance, howsoever veiled in mystery; and we are taught by it, to habitually give ourselves up to this guidance until we shall clearly see their beneficial effect upon the future. Drawn into the movement of a sacred history as if this were conducted for our private interests, we are gladdened to see more and more Selfknowledge derived and inferences of the future drawn from the personal experience of divine government. that our trusting hope does not deceive us, and that our patient waiting and childlike devotion were not in vain.

Thus the method of the divine rulings of the world becomes transparent to the attentive observer in such degree, as he sees the events of his own life being directed by Providence. Tho wrought out from raw material he knows himself to be guided upward and to be fashioned after the eternal proto-type, in order to become gloriously Only on these grounds the mystery of a government of the world for the benefit of Christ's adherents becomes lucid. transformed into His likeness. In the harmonious concord of all his inner potentialities man shows himself to be a living stone of the great temple which resounds with the anthems of praise. And from the methods in which his own affairs are governed, he has the indications for forming an appropriate conception of the manner in which all movements are to proceed in order to arrive at the consummation toward All in nature and history hinges upon the relation of the world to the Redeemer and those originally connected with Him even the glorification of the universe. which all creation is tending. It is only on these grounds that man may comprehend the world of nature and history and the government of both as one locked, complete system. In the mystical center of that system of the synthesis man, the miracle of the world, feels himself safe, knowing himself to be a component part of a redeemed humanity, around and for the benefit of which, as for its mystical seed, nature and history revolve. He feels himself safe as a member of that humanity which under a fatherly management is to be prepared for the final glorification, including the universe as belonging to humanity.

B. SECOND DIVISION.—RESULTS OF HISTORY.

Trusting and hoping, we must not, however, anticipate the glorious state of perfection to set in at once in compliance with our desires. The most difficult part of Pessimism as to real achievements. the way we have to climb is as yet before us. And before we can hasten to a close of our dissertation and exposition of thoughts upon the closing scenes of history, we can not evade the question as to the real issues of historic commotions. Inquiring as to real progress on the line of human happiness. What will it be, that has been accomplished by them? What proof of real progress on the line of human happiness can be adduced? Do the cultural establishments Helico-spiral yield a net gain, or are the profits required merely to keep them in running order?

We know that objections to our assertions of continual advancement come not alone from the adherents of Schopenhauer's world-theory. They say that every new phase of the rotary movements only plunges humanity into new distresses. Concerning real achievements even certain other seekers after truth, deserving still more consideration than the pessimists, have become sceptical.

With their spiral motion of culture we find no fault: we entertain a similar view. not circular motion of progress. Cultures were buried under ruins and have, at other times and places, been brought back to life. Thus reinstated they appeared enriched and moved forward on the ascendant plane. It has also been said that the historic motion was circular, meaning thereby that everything returns to the same level and that matters remain essentially what they always were. The culture of the Occident which arose after the great divide of the the times, would then represent a new, but scarcely improved, sphere above that oriental culture which went down with Rome.

This question of progress remains to be considered in order to satisfy the inquiry as to the specific and definite goal of civilisation in more than one respect. Investigating whether a real progress in economics can be vindicated, we must, in the first place, view the problem from its physical aspect. This will lead us to argue upon the topic of intellectual advance. Then questions as to æsthetical and finally ethical improvement will require our attention. To each of these disquisitions a chapter is to be dedicated. And then "the Theme" will resound in the great finale of the earthly drama. Its intonation will signalise the harvesting of the earnings of humanity into the garners, the transport of the fruits of the spirit, and of the essences extracted from the realm of the secondary good, into the state of permanency and beatitude.

CH. I. PROGRESS UNDER THE ASPECT OF PHYSICAL ACQUIREMENTS: ECONOMICS.

§ 222. A law of progress does not exist, since history is no mechanism. But progress there is, most assuredly. And it is perceptible if we only do not attempt to conceive it as moving in a single, straight line.

Progress is rather brought forth by a series of different, partly concurrent cultures running in parallel and intersecting waves. These wave-lines are not of equal length. Frequently they coalesce to run in one line until here and there they branch off again to the right or left, up or down. Most conspicuous is the sum of progress in physical results, in triumph over nature. "The human race becomes evermore liberated from the fetters of natural forces; man gradually becomes disengaged from the earthy lump that gave birth to him." This, in the words of Ritter, is the goal to be reached. In this physical emancipation great things have certainly been achieved, which we accredit to culture, provided we are not misunderstood as tho this acknowledgment included the waiving of our judgment as to the value of this freedom. We here discuss progress in respect to a very definite domain.

Every earthly development proceeds in a method common to all creatures. The young animal life as concealed in the egg, adheres as yet to its soft environment. It is covered and enveloped, and its parturition protected by the warmth of the brooding parent. It is a particular life already, but as yet tied up by and involved in the general life of its species. This evolutionary progress proceeds, under a series of detachments and separations during parturition. By loosening itself from enclosures life individualises itself, until finally the last decaying membrane or husk is thrown off and the new organism animated by its own internal impulses, and adapted to its surrounding, moves in the atmosphere of the external world.

In precisely the same manner personal life individualises itself in an ascending scale of progress toward self- and world-consciousness.

In a manner at least analogous does a nation develop from its state of being "nature-bound" by way of differentiation and organisation. We shall see the same mode of progress in the ever augmenting departments of social life. We subsume this development as the physical part of cultural progress in distinction from ethical advance.

At first nomade-tribes appropriate what the soil yields. When pasture is consumed the tents are taken down and the herds are driven to other fields. For the ground nothing is done. It yields but does not receive cultivation in return. Productiveness diminishing, the herd wanders away. Some bottom lands, perhaps, are plowed, if breaking up the soil, or rather scatching the surface deserves that name, and perhaps the shrubs are grubbed out to some extent. This primitive agriculture is carried on no longer than the productiveness of the virgin soil lasts. New lands are hunted up and farmed off. In the one instance as in the other, in the countries of the old Indo-Germans, as much as in Asia, the decline of such spontaneous harvest caused immigrations, whereby nations of culture, which once had begun career in the same way, are overpowered.

In the next state, the period of steadiness and settlements, a higher culture succeeds, founded upon more rational treatment of the soil, proving agriculture to be the first step toward culture. In the technical terms of agriculture lie "the etymological roots". The clod of ground becoming "an acre" which is fructified by intelligence and persevering energy, and designates the beginning of emancipation from the earthly clod. This is the usual way in which historical nations severally founded their existence.

But we repeat, that the soil most favorable to the founding of states is not that which requires the least exertion. The great valleys of Ægypt and Mesopotamia made persistent struggles necessary, in digging canals, in erecting dams, dikes and embankments. The high plateaus of Tenochtitlan and Mexico, and of Cuzco in Peru, show remnants of a high advance in culture, because they lie elevated to degrees of the moderate zone which necessitates the surmounting of many difficulties under mental exertions and manual toil.

Regions which necessitate mental exertions and manual toil.

This stage of progress affords the best opportunity for observing the transition from general forms of generic life to social differentiations. The mode of possessing the fields illustrates the gradual change. A certain area is at first the common property of the community. Only the improvements upon the land, house and garden, etc. are held by right of ownership, of labor. The land, subsequently, is parcelled out to freeholders who cultivate their "lots", whilst the woods and the meadows, the village greens and the river banks still belong to the commonalty, to which each of its members has the right of usufruct, pasturing his domestic animals upon the "commons". Sheep and geese are sent out with the herds of cattle under watch of a paid herdsman. The hogs fatten on acorn in the woods, which on that account enjoy the care of the public for their preservation. The more remote the time, the more we find Henry George's agrarian theories of common ownership of the soil in practice. Communistic possession precedes private ownership. All are in duty bound to the whole bound to the soil. Private titles are limited by the right of the community. Even after the partition of the fields the right of common pasture stood paramount, so that for the common good private real estate was taxed with pasture regulations and with the triplex system of farming, that is, parts of the whole "field" or as were in turns set aside to lay fallow; another part was designated for summer crops, and one third was sown with grain. Consequent to these regulations the individual owner was, for the sake of common pasture, limited to his certain share in the number of domestic animals. Agrarian conservatism did not allow progress to go on much more swiftly than the oxen yoked to the plough. Large tracts of land suffered under communal encumbrances, under the prohibition of taking them "under the plough." Common possession was protected at the expense of agricultural emulation, of progress and of private ownership. The right of possession remained subject to communal muncipal obligations, and the peasantry bound to that part of mother earth which was rendered sacred through long lines of ancestorship.

Transition from the life of the genus into the differentiation of social life.

Common property developing

Into right of private possession.

Henry George's theories valid in primitive stages of social life.

Private titles subject to communal rights.

Triplex system of farming.

Common ownership protected at the expense of private emulation.

Common possession, conditioned by natural advantages, is superseded by rational accommodations and legal adjustments.

From these stages of primitive order and ruling custom, social development takes new starts by way of detachment and division. Common possession, conditioned by natural advantages or by accommodation to natural environments, becomes superseded by rational and legal adjustments, and by the corresponding rise in the value of individual labor. The soil is divided, is made salable. Private proprietorship stimulates intensity of management, and the aspiration to independence is encouraged together with industriousness and a feeling of selfhood. Manual labor is honored; a decent living and frugal comfort anent to invigorating exercise is the reward. From the clod the factory hand is detached. Whether he is less nature-bound, is, however, another question—not solved by the nomade-life in the tenement houses of large cities.

Rise in the value of labor.

Free from the clod, nomade life of the "factory-hands".

§ 223. As the third stage of earthly progress we may consider, with Roscher, the preponderance of the money-power. True, it makes the soil more productive, by putting more and more instrumentalities, and finally machinery, into service. The modern age opens, the social dangers of our times take their origin. The worst of them is called forth by the profanation of agriculture.

Third stage of progress marked by preponderance of the money-power: Roscher.

of machinery;

Real estate is made an object of money speculation and with fancy prices put upon it, becomes a light-winged commodity, a disgust to heirs who hate field labor and the monotony of rural life. Real estate is abandoned to brokers, landsharks and capitalists. The uncultivated latifundia, of which the New England states, Maryland, etc., largely consist, are the result.

of depreciating rural life;

of real estate brokerage;

of incultivated latifundia;

all giving origin to the social dangers impending

Since the heedless parcellation of family-tenures has caused the depreciation of ancestral homesteads, the previous conditions, as for instance the private rights of possession, under regulations of common holdings in fiduciary trusts, are now almost everywhere abated.

Depreciation of the ancestral home-stead. Parcellation of land causes the abandonment of family holdings.

It is generally accredited to Christianity and to humanitarianism issuing from it, that serfdom and slavery are abolished. We aver, however, that this was the case only very indirectly. It has been rather procured by the modifying effects of the new relations between labor and capital.

Abolition of serfdom and slavery only indirectly caused by Christianity.

Where pastural and agricultural pursuits prevail, serfs and retainers upon the manor are still more profitable. And such social conditions would, in Russia for instance, be of good service for all concerned—in Russia, where twenty-five persons average the habitation of a square mile, or in the southern states of the Union. In Western Europe, however, where there are one hundred people on an average to the square mile, these conditions must change regardless of humanitarianism. For in crowded regions, a "labor-market", that is, the paid service of free men, is much more advantageous to the proprietor.

The fact has been pointed out that by the increasing and facilitated utilisation of men in productive labor, the slaves of ancient times became the serfs, "villains," and yeomen of the Middle-Ages, and those in turn became, through large manufacturing establishments and by the introduction of machinery, the journeymen, the day-laborers of modern times. We have lived to see the nobleman sink into poverty, as well as the farm-hand and the peasant whose ancestors were servants in fee to the ancestors of the former, and who himself had inherited the obligation to work two days of each and every week for the now dispossessed baron. Wherever population grows in density, where capital farms the land with the steam-plow, when time is money, where the distribution of products through the social organism is accelerated, there free labor is more conducive to personal welfare. We thus see in what high degree the development of political freedom is founded upon extending the productiveness of the soil and the mine, even upon ploughing the ocean.

Economic progress as a civilising factor, is largely due to the increasing density of population.

The first check of this growth since the reconstruction of Europe, after the fall of the West Roman empire and the storms of the migrations, occurred in the centuries of the crusades.

In the middle of the fourteenth century the diffusion of the people over Europe exhibits a marked change. The number of inhabitants has increased. Italy, France, and the Low Countries are the most crowded since the eastern parts had to suffer the Mongolian invasions and the central parts suffered under the ravages of the "black death" which took away 25,000,000 of people; under the wars with the Turks, and finally by the religious contests. The Thirty Years' War depopulated Germany from seventeen to four millions. Then came the civil wars raging in almost every one of the western states. Only after the Napoleonic war, throughout the first fifteen years of our century, a continual augmentation of people kept pace with the decades. Europe became rejuvenated. Adam Smith thought that England would need five centuries to double her population; but it took Europe only ninety years to double the number of inhabitants, and Germany only sixty years in spite of thousands upon thousands sacrificed to wars, and despite the largely increased emigration.

At bottom the sole reason for these attainments lies in the economical prosperity and the heightened consciousness of man's dignity, all resting upon the basis of rural husbandry.

The policy of monarchical absolutism was up to the middle of our century chiefly bent upon the "wealth of nations," upon "balance of power," upon increase of prestige, and somewhat upon law and order. Now we have to follow a social polity, governments have become civil, and legislatures are compelled to be deeply concerned in appeasing the demands of common welfare. Human rights and the pursuit of happiness are to be cared for first of all. This is the effect of the thought of humanism silently working through the study of humanistics on the basis of industriousness, and upon the basis, in the last resort, of agriculture.

See how much the condition of the third, now a fourth estate has been ameliorated, as illustrated by the contrast drawn by Roscher. "There is the South American, heaving under the burden of the heavy ores which he carries upon his back from the mines of the Andes to the smelters. Here the factory hand of Europe and North America, who is carried up and down the elevator plying between four and fourteen stories, in order to save the costly human strength for actual work. What freedom from drudgery, and what stages and times of advance lie between these two extremes. There slave-market and slave-raisers, here percentages of profit for the free laborer with all sorts of mutual insurances and free libraries".

The thought of humanism was active at great lengths, in the many institutions aiming at public health.

It is true, the ancients also paid some attention to sanitary measures. Every house of Antioch was, according to Mommsen, provided with running water, from the park at Daphne near by, dotted with well-springs. The oasis of Palmyra contained many exquisite water reservoirs properly emured and covered.

Not less was the Occident, even through the Middle-Ages, well supplied with baths, private and public. But the streets remained unpaved; the floors of the rooms were covered with straw and rush-grasses. Public cleanliness was never thought of, neither was it thought of to provide a city with good water. These cities with narrow streets, crowded between gigantic walls and moats, became the hot-beds of epidemic diseases.

The health offices of recent times carrying out sanitary regulations in the interest of laboring classes have much to do with the increase of population and public comforts.

§ 224. Civilisation is now at the point of conquering the distances of space and time, both of which impede human endeavor. Progress aims at freeing men from their restrictions as much as possible. In other words, it aims at the domination of the mind over circumstances hemming in the spirit. In the hurry of modern life natural restraints are more than ever felt to encumber communication and correspondence is already carried on upon a scope so extensive as never before had been imagined even as a mere possibility.

The history of the struggle against distances, in perfecting means of rapid transit may be divided into distinct periods.

At first we notice the old and unreliable means of communication with the great nations of Asia, depending upon opportunities of transport offered at points where goods were exchanged. Then the Phenician wholesale and colonial traffic brings about the first attempts at international intercourse, especially among the western Asiatics and the Hellenes. The third period of facilitated communication belongs to Rome in its central position, with its monopolies and its military roads to and from remote provinces and staple-places. The next step of advance upon connected routes and lines of navigation falls in mediæval times. The North and the East of Europe are drawn into the commerce of the world simultaneously with the rapid movements of Mohammedanism. It is only recently that Arabic books have unrolled a picture of the relations and routes between the Ishmaelites and the countries of the Volga and the Vistula. This period closes with the adventure of Columbus—for, strange to say, from the times of Themistocles until that of the doge Dandalo, comparatively very slow progress, if any at all, had been made in ship-building. The participation of the western hemisphere in the maritime commerce of the world will have to be designated as the fifth period.

Entirely new departures in the art of navigation have rendered it at last the most important factor in historic movement. Especially since, in our own day, steam and electricity have been hitched before advance on land and water, the world owes its greatest and fastest strides to their practical utilisation. With still larger promises ahead, concerning the communication to and from the former ends of the world, perfection seems so well nigh accomplished, that it may be said: In respect to rapid transit of thoughts, goods and passengers we live in the age best corresponding to the sixth period of the hexameron—in the age of surprises, of celerity.

A review of the stages in which so far man has tried to accelerate his travels is very instructive as to the degree in which peoples of arrested cultures still live under old restrictions of traffic.

Imagine those wagons covered with wicker-work and hides, of which Æschylos left us a description, and upon which the hordes of the Tatary dwelled and traveled along the Volga, as they still dwell and travel.

In India, ox-carts and elephants are the vehicles of travel, whilst the camel serves as the ship of the desert from the Niger to the Yantsekiang. Thus moves the Orient. China, of course, had its net of good roads, and Persia has its post-riders and runners, but traffic on the whole did not move any the faster for all that. Greece had been advanced as far as to have wheel-tracks, hewn into the rocks and meandering along every turn of the cliffs and abysses. But of any solid cause-way like the drive-road of Cyrus, from his residence to his fire temple, scarcely any trace is found. How slowly were the distances overcome. According to the Odysee the journey from Lesbos to Argos took three days. Xenophon praises it as a great feat, that a Milesian ship made the trip from Lampsakos to the Spartan landing in three days. Rome had its governmental postal routes through all the conquered provinces; proconsuls built their straight cause-ways even through deserts. But people upon journeys took their leisure. How cumbersome travel crept along during the Middle-Ages, we can compute from the records of the imperial expeditions to Rome, and of the rides from one palatinate to the other.

But in respect to technical appliances in conquering space and time our age stands unique. The first ocean steamer, the "Savanah" crossed the Atlantic in 1819. Since that time the earth has been rendered smaller to us through steam and telegraph. The Mediterranean in St. Paul's time was virtually more extensive than the Pacific is today to our missionaries to China.

The fact is, in short, that the earth is now more than ever before rendered subject to man's mind. Irrespective of the increase and density of population since traffic has been cleared from impediments, and communication by letter has been made almost free of expense; abstracting also from the results of chemical research, we marvel at the extent to which the mineral kingdom has been utilised in facilitating and contracting commercial relations.

Marginal notes:

Civilisation conquering the distances of space and time.

Dominion of mind over circumstances restricting the spirit.

History of the means of intercourse.

1. Period: Rare occasions of merchantile transactions.

2. Period: Phenicians make first attempt at international intercourse.

3. Period: Roman facilities, monopolies and military roads.

4. Period: Rapid movements of Mohammedanism.

From Themistocles to doge Dandalo and Columbus scarcely any progress in ship-building.

Latest and fastest strides of advance owing to navigation of modern times.

5. Period: Western hemisphere drawn into maritime engagements.

6. Period: Almost perfected celerity of communication.

Contrasts:

Moving-wagons, ("prairie-schooners") described by Æschylos,

India's vehicles: ox-carts and elephants.

The "ship of the desert".

China—net of roads.

Persia—post riders.

Greece—wheel tracks hewn into rocks.

Rome's governmental routes through African deserts.

First steamer crossed the Atlantic A. D. 1819.

1890 The Pacific less extensive than the Mediterranean in St. Paul's time.

Progress sufficient to surpass some of the ancient techniques has, perhaps, not been made. It is proven that the Ægyptians under the oldest dynasties used not only steel for chiseling hieroglyphs into granite and syenite, but worked even with circle-saw and with drill inside of tubes, the points and edges of the bores consisting of precious stones. On one of the granite sarcophagi in the great pyramid of Gizeh, a diamond saw had evidently been used. We need not doubt these accomplishments of the ancients.

The role which metals play has become of an import paramount to that of almost any other commodity. And what would become of our culture without coal? Wherever we may cast our eyes, metallic products present themselves, from a tiny needle to a cast-steel cylinder weighing ten thousand pounds, like the one which forty years ago a German firm exhibited in London. To such proportions has grown the manufacture and utilisation of iron. To be sure, it took a long course of development, reaching back to the time when the Calypians on the shores of the Black Sea brought iron products into trade, down to the consuming of such huge quantities as are required in the construction of suspension bridges and underground railroads.

Had it not been for the exactions imposed upon the earth, this development of the means of civilisation could not have become possible. But the great magazines were forced open in which the effects of the sun in the form of coal and petroleum were stored up in times of the remote past. In these magazines the warmth of the sun's rays was stored in a condensed state, in order to yield their wealth at the time needed. It was the time when that higher plane of civilisation was reached which of old never could have been expected.

Modern civilisation has thus been brought about by the cooperation of all parts of the globe in a world-embracing traffic; but not without its having been prepared by preceding cultures, however locally limited they may have been. Now the essence of each and all cultures in the totality of their subsumption and accumulated issues is put into circulation to be distributed everywhere for the benefit of all concerned. We are astonished to read the critical thoughts of Japanese and Hindoos upon the deepest topics agitating European nations, written in most excellent style.

For the first time in history we witness the lively interaction (sorry to say, almost blending) of all phases of culture, each claiming recognition as forming the first rank of civilisation, that is, of Christianised culture.

This seems to be the reason that the nations of culture contrive at arranging a universal measure of time, a standard time, upon the basis of common possession of space. Arago as early as 1819 directed the attention of his fellow citisens to the irregularity of the Parisian town-clocks. Since that date we have become far more punctual. The intense hurry of intercourse and the incessant increase of international transactions compel us to follow Herschel's advice. The annoyances caused by time-differences make themselves felt in every-day life. The result will be a normal chronometer for the entire world. And finally, the ever rising demands upon most accelerated communication will, perhaps, lead to the construction of that universal artificial language, which is now attempted in certain quarters.

These are some of the substantial results of progress as far as they pertain to the supremacy of the mind over nature. We do not here and now inquire as to the benefit accruing from these results for the cause of true humanism. Certain it is, however, that they can be rendered subservient thereto.

CH. II. INTELLECTUAL ACQUIREMENTS.

§ 225. Upon this topic, the results of intellectual progress, we need not enlarge very much. It may fittingly be restricted to the field of research and the modes of thinking.

In the ancient temples of Petra, hewn into the rocks, we notice the top-panels of the frontispiece to have been finished first. The propylæa crowned by these relief sculptures are kept out of view. In a similar manner, says H. v. Schubert, proceeds the development of scientific knowledge, not from below but from above.

The thinking mind does not set out from the wants of every-day life, it does not commence with what lies at our feet, it is called to action by what shines out from above our heads. Thought begins with the attention the starry worlds invite. Thinking, the work of the intellect principally, tends to the understanding of nature in order to master it. Even the wisdom of the temples consists in nothing but arrangements of natural knowledge. The deities thought out are essentially but personifications of physical phenomena, gods of nature who from their starry habitations above were supposed to direct forces and influences downward. The genesis of science lies in astrology. The Arabs, in pursuance of Ægyptian and Babylonian traditions on the whole line from Toledo, where they used to convene in astronomical congress, out to the observatory at Samarkand, affirm this statement.

Genesis of science in astrology.

The ancients nowhere promulgated the idea of an independent science. It was never emancipated from priestly tutelage in the precincts of the temples, not even among the Greeks. That is significant which Curtius said about their historiography. When they wrote history they meant apologetics of their deities—vindication of their oracles. The first advice which philosophy gave, was the acquisition of selfknowledge. But the error it contracted in the premises was the merging of gods and the world into one conception. This religio-philosophical religion was but guessing at nature. Upon Christian soil the "knowledge of the world" (Weltweisheit) donned the garb of "knowledge of Divinity" (Gottesgelahrtheit). The heaven of the stars and the gods broke to pieces. The supernatural nature of God shone forth and made men to recognise their own nature as supramundane. The church taught men to renounce worldly wisdom, tho fostering the same sciences which once had to vindicate oracles, in order to make them subservient to her own defense. Remnants of antique ideas were thus allowed to adhere to theology, to encumber Christian knowledge, and to mar the clearness of a Christian world-consciousness. It was in consequence of the religious reform that philosophy came to reconstruct herself upon the basis of selfconsciousness, of Descartes' "ego". Just as antiquity had been entangled in the mixture of God-and world-consciousness, and therefrom had derived abstruse views of earthly life, pure and simple; so were the Middle-Ages enraptured by a fanciful and distorted God-consciousness, by celestial visions.

Science of the ancients never emancipated from priestly tutelage.

Greek historiography. Vindication of oracles. Curtius.

Under the caption 'Learnedness of divinity'

the Church took "worldly wisdom" under its care, tho teaching the laity to renounce it.

Remnants of antique ideas allowed to adhere to theology, to mar the clearness of Christian world-consciousness.

The Reformation reinstated man into the liberty of expanding his mental capacities in the direction of both God- and world-consciousness.

Now man was posited in the mean, his import recognised. He was reinstated into the right to expand his thinking capacity in both directions. Thus light and air were gained for the liberty of scientific inquiry such as no age had ever enjoyed. In this fresh atmosphere Bacon wrote his "philosophia humana." But in vain was the toilsome effort to clean out the rubbish which vitiated the understanding, because the gentleman was himself wedged in between mediæval notions. It was the Dutch soldier behind the stove, who, determined to disengage himself from the traditional doctrines, threw aside the "idols, which Bacon could not conjure."

"Philosophia humana". Bacon.

Thanks to Cartesius we now practice investigation of doctrinal details unprejudiced; we have an exact science going to work by way of induction. The subsequent division of labor caused many auxiliaries of scientific research to become strong and fruit-bearing branches of the tree of knowledge.

Liberty of scientific inquiry. Descartes. Auxiliary branches of scientific research became specific sciences themselves. Division of scientific labor.

The joyful emulation and stimulation in the reciprocal interaction of scientific analysing has surpassed all expectations. The diver explores ocean bottoms; the microscopist measures the time of nerve activity; the astronomer figures out the velocity of stellar motion, and analyses the constituent elements of distant suns. One example may illustrate this division of scientific labor. France had been most inventive in the field of chemistry, whilst the Germans as yet had entirely neglected it up to the beginning of this century. Now, Germany possesses laboratories for the most specific investigations and experiments, built especially for their several purposes. Besides pharmaceutical, we have the metallurgical, the technological, chemico-physiological, hygienical, electrical, biological, and other laboratories.

"Chemistry of the heavens".

Chemical laboratories of Germany.

What we, however, would consider as no more than advanced intellectualism, Herbert Spencer calls "scientific progress." According to him it is "essentially a more skillful generalisation, which consists in uniting all homogeneous coexistencies and effects of phenomena into adequate groups of conception. One of the most significant compoundings of late has been accomplished among the formerly independent theories of electricty, magnetism and light."

H. Spencer's definition of scientific progress.

§ 226. As to the result and success of analytical research there is no controversy. And more than any set of facts do these results prove that science cannot dispense with the cognition of purpose. Each science by itself, as in the case of arts, aspires to dominion over matter. Whatever remains in the dark as yet, and resists the penetration and appropriation of the mind, is to become subject to human understanding. The more knowledge advances and expands, the more will the mere accidental phenomena vanish from our planet. Where the minds of humanity were formerly oppressed by inexplicable monstrosities, there we are enabled to observe

Science cannot dispense with "the purpose".

Accidental phenomena vanish in the light of inductive investigation.

Man finds within himself the affinities confirmed, which exist between the necessities inherent in things and the necessity of his logic.

system and lawful regularity. With the intelligent recognition of ruling laws inherent in realities and entities and corresponding with our own inner nature, grows the satisfaction of the observing mind. Man finds within himself the affinity affirmed, which exists between the intrinsic necessity of things and the necessity of his logic. It is harmony which makes it all clear to him. This gratification is one of the aims of the mind; it is mind manifesting its satisfaction at having found its object.

Aim of progressive civilisation; to displace imagination. Buckle.

Training of the intellect can forestall neither the play of the imagination nor superstition.

Imagination

Indispensible to carry out Spencer's "scientific progress".

Buckle's opinion is, that the aim of progressive civilisation consists in "investing the intellectual faculty with that authority which in the preceding stage of cultural development was claimed by the imagination". This bespeaks a favorable inclination towards the purposive development of intellectual culture. Upon earth, however, we may be compelled to reconcile ourselves with the impossibility of ever reaching that aim. For we experience that the most splendid training of the intellect can forestall neither the play of the imagination nor superstition. With all the stress put upon the intellect, superstition is on the increase even to an alarming degree. We furthermore know that without that despised imagination, all of our sciences would forever have to remain piece-meal in their specific researches. For not only would we lack the power to comprehensively arrange the specific results into homogeneous and generic groups, into compound cognitions; but even specific research itself would become enfeebled and discouraged, altho it is always urged on by incitements of a more or less clearly apprehended general view, which, without imagination, without the "creative power of the mind", is not obtainable.

As to progress in knowledge or rather epistemology, that much is sufficient which concerns mathematics and empirical sciences. Macaulay.

Concerning real progress we may agree with Macaulay. He seems to put knowledge into quarantine with the exception of mathematics and empiric sciences. And so much of progress in epistemology as Spencer's progress amounts to is sufficient for present use.

General interest taken in matters of scientific research is the greatest result of intellectual advance and its best evidence.

Unity of purpose manifest in all scientific quarters, to further the cause of

humanitarianism.

Specific studies endanger this unity of understanding through their dogmatising tendencies.

Common agreement upon one certain world-theory neither possible nor desirable.

And those aiding in that progress, are no longer only a few sparse individuals or select nations, as in former times. The entire mass of educated people on the face of the earth take a vivid interest in scientific research and experiments. This is the grandest result and the undeniable proof of intellectual progress. In international congresses we hear the presidents of geographical and other societies from every continent emphasise the unity of purpose into which all the sciences of all nations are bound together by the zeal to further the humanitarian cause. One may be afraid of the innumerable departments into which investigation of details splits science, lest the ideal blessings and the unity of human understanding may suffer from their selfcomplacent dogmatism and vociferous pretensions. But we keep in mind that a common agreement upon a world-theory is neither possible nor desirable. A world-theory which is not test-proof as to its consistency and truth when assailed, and which could not verify itself under cross-examination, deserves to succumb under the opposition of criticism. Hence we may agree with Bacon's saying that the human race cannot, despite the lack of an authoritative world-theory, or from fear of shifting world-theories, desist from claming its right to master nature, from taking possession intellectually of what has been bequeathed to it by divine legacy.

The human race cannot desert from claiming the right to master nature, despite shifting world-theories. Bacon.

CH. III. PROGRESS IN ÆSTHETICS.

§ 227. Concerning that which the fine arts have achieved in the line of advance we need not fear severe opposition. A brief review under two aspects only will suffice.

In three modes of consciousness and the world-theories fashioned after them,

mirrored in the arts:

We spoke of three principal modes of consciousness having become especially conspicuous throughout the course of history in shaping the world-theories governing the race in general. These three fundamental tendencies always distinctly express themselves in the realm of arts. We refer to the cognitions of immanency and transcendency, and the blending of both.

Immanency, transcendency, and blending of both.

Irrelevant are the monuments of bombastic style, of the nonsensical colossal; like some pieces found by Cesnola and Schliemann.

It is unnecessary to investigate again the rule of a taste for the senseless and the colossal. Oriental art, including the sculptures and buildings of the Siamese and of the Toltecs with their style of bombastic superabundance, needs no further consideration. Neither is it necessary to contemplate the unintelligible cameos brought from Cyprus by Cesnola, or the drawings of human figures found by Schliemann in Hissarlik and Mycenæ. They are on a level with the crude attempts to representative art made by the Bushmen upon the rocks of Africa; or with those "monuments" upon the island of Schonen. It is for the professional critics of art to entertain themselves with discoveries of that sort.

Marked character of Greek art.

The arts of the ancients in general present themselves in particular groups, severally marking their national characteristics. These circles, or schools of art, are classifiable according to customs, religions, languages. Mesopotamians, Ægyptians,

Hellenes maintain each their independence beside or opposite the others in all their works of art. Greece presents "the same principal ideas and forms in the Selinuntian and old Ionic temples as in the buildings of the Alexandrian æra", as Von Reber demonstrates. This art "announces the same traits of character in the Aeginetes which we admire in the sculptures of Pergamon."

Hellenic art proclaims the "gospel of nature".

The national character of each of the ancient nations of culture distinctly expressed in their respective monuments. Von Reber.

Art, of course, originates upon a national basis; but the proof and measure of true ideality consists in that perfection which is immediately understood by all, and commands universal and unsolicited acknowledgment.

The next great period of art is that of transcendency.

Art develops on national bases, conforms to religious tenets; the measure of its ideality and perfection,

Asceticism creates those distasteful, lean images of the saints, of which mention was made. The human body in its beauty of proportion is as badly vilified by the hand of the sculptor or the painter, as it is maltreated in monastic cells by self-inflicted tortures or under the hands of hangmen upon the rack in the municipal torture-chambers. We have shown, how the forms of consciousness call forth the adequate phenomena from the Ganges to the Orontes, and again from Byzantium to the Thames and the Ebro.

Art representing trancendentalism

Images of saints show the human form vilified, as the body was maltreated in monastic cells and upon racks in municipal torture-chambers.

The touching impressions of intense piety produced by mediæval art will not beguile us to excuse the deformities of consciouness which are of a far more serious nature, than even the castigations of the human body.

In the paintings of that period everything is figure and foreground; scenery, nature, projection are missing. In those of the next, nature is vindicated, as for instance in the minnesongs; but again nothing but foreground in which "red clover and green meadows" preponderate. Still there is progress. The variegated flowers upon the green sward, painted with tender considerateness call forth sentiments of child-like trustfulness. The delicacy of love toward moderate beauty conveys the secret of contentment which the works of Schœngauer and the Cologne masters impart. But even in their paintings scenic environment and background are missing. The landscape seems to have been considered too insignificant as to erase the abstractness of the views of life. Sacred history moves in a despised world. Earthly concretes are not worthy of mention. Comprehension of the secondary good in nature, landscapes which reflect human sentiments and moods of the mind, which awaken the echo of sympathy, are accomplishments of the humanistic art of modern times.

Paintings lack projection, and realistic background as the Chinese picture persons without standpoints.

Even the realistic art of the Cologne masters is base of scenic effects.

Art representing sentiments and calling forth corresponding words of the mind, by giving tones of color to landscapes in particular seasons and under peculiar atmospheric light,

Modern art has perfected the technique requisite to reproduce the effect of light and air which at last found recognition. Not even classic art thought of this element of psychical touch with which the tones of the atmosphere affect the inner life of man. A rapport of sentiment with nature may have existed, but the artistic ability to express it by shades of color was lacking. Much less was the susceptibility for such naturalness and refinement of emotion to be expected from the monkish artists with their Buddhistic contempt of nature-Earthly realism and delight in the beauty of nature was sacrificed to trancendental revery.

denotes the advance we owe to modern humanistics.

Third group of artistic schools.

Understanding the sentiment of a landscape and perfecting the means to express it, are merits of modern culture. Burkhardt in his "Renaissance" has convincingly shown, where this delight in, and refined susceptibility for, nature was resuscitated; and how, with their cultivation modern æstheticism was introduced.

Rapport between sentiment and nature resuscitated. Burkhardt.

The pervasion of natural with the spiritual life designates the third period of art growing from the Evangelical understanding of the dual life and its projected unification in this world. Rafael signalises the introduction of this new means to communicate feelings without words. In the beautiful picture of the Sistine Madonna the transcendental becomes immanent. The four Evangelists of Duerer show the same conception. Thus the new epoch was inaugurated.

Pervasion of natural life with the Evangelical theory of life, beginning with Rafael.

In the Sistine Madonna the Trancendental becomes immanent

Once worldliness had glorified the charms of nature; levity connived at the sinfulness with which the sensual is impregnated, and hypocritically identified nature with sin in order to palliate guilt and obtain indulgence. The world, outwardly converted through the law, had then entirely thrown away in fanatical asceticism what shortly before had been deified. The world, so recently intoxicated with an enchanted nature, was now enchained in a corresponding contempt of nature. Eager as ever to dominate externally, according to twisted ideas of dominion over nature, man, despite the chains and the assumed air of contempt, was filled with the lust of temporal possession and worldly rule.

The world assuming an air of contempt towards nature, was eager, nevertheless, to possess it and rule over it.

Sphere of the secondary pervaded with the Absolute Good; resulting

Thrown hither and thither by the unmitigated contrasts the world at last arrives at the true solution. The equilibrium is given in the formula: pervasion of the sphere of the secondary with the Absolute Good. The most unequivocal expression of the attempts to harmonise the opposite views of life, contained in the Evangelical thought of true humanity, is given in the paintings of Munkacsy.

from attempts to harmonise the opposite views of life implied in the thought of true humanity. Munkacsy.

§ 228. The history of music is unable to demarkate stages of development similar to those of the representative arts. From the mere rhythmical effect of drumming upon crude instruments, music gradually rose to express the ideal sentiment nurtured by the muses. Equal with sculpture, architecture, and painting with reference to their slow emancipation from temple-wall and tomb, music could but tardily sever itself from temple-ritual and funeral-rites, even after the first marked change wrought by the epics of Greek heroism.

The adventitious and abusive fates of this higher language of the soul may here be passed over. It was only after the enchanting and inspiring effects of tones were procurable by stringed instruments, that music could accomplish its greater feats. Music then advanced from rousing a rhythmical feeling to the enjoyment of the melody, and finally to the understanding of harmony. In no other but those nations which possessed the advantages of Christian civilisation were the powers of rhythm, melody, and harmony combined into that composite architecture of tones which prophesies the grandeur of the celestial symphony.

New appliances have facilitated the use of means for developing the educating and elevating power of music despite the fact, that with the invention of new instruments we are rather in the arrear. Notwithstanding this neglect music is enabled to create tone-pictures in which the souls of all men find their deepest and their common griefs and joys expressed in an unspeakable manner. It is the triumph of art, and

especially of this most abstract art, that it has become independent from world-theories and is able to represent them even in their conflicts; that it can make itself universally understood; that the human feelings stand under its direct command, in its finest details and in the grandest concert, whilst occupying in itself a position above passion and nationality.

We note, then, also in the sphere of æsthetical progress as the chief result, that among the fairly educated people of all civilised nations an understanding of the inner man was brought about on the basis of the humanistic thought, an understanding of which ancient æsthetics had not the faintest idea.

It is music principally, which, according to Kugler, together with art in general, "testifies to the power and independence of the mind as against the outward fate of nations."

The chapter on results of intellectual progress we closed with the probability of a universal language. And behold, this is beginning already to be realised in the fine arts. Whatever true art is endeavoring to express, is understood everywhere. It thus becomes instrumental in transmutating the diversity of nations taking delight in the fine arts, into the concrete of an ideal unity. It amounts to a presentiment of the future consummation of this reunion, yea, to even more than that. Until that consummation shall transpire art is justified in entertaining the hope of the grandest future; in the mean time it works for the benefit of true humanism.

CH. IV. PROGRESS IN RELIGIO-ETHICAL MATTERS.

§ 229. The most fascinating part of our disquisition now presents itself. The question is to be met, whether religious and moral life have advanced to the height of such results as have been gained on the scope of physico-psychical development. The solution of this enigma may be prefaced by finding the answer to the counterquestion: What was it that destroyed the ancient cultures? "Principally the fact," so answers Dubois-Reymond, "that the natural sciences were suffered to become arrested in their progressive march of cultural evolution. Had not the ancients neglected to exercise those faculties by which an absolute superiority of the mind over matter and crude force is to be obtained; had they not in religious strifes squandered their

opportunities to improve practical techniques by means of which natural forces are made to serve human interests, the German Norsemen and the Mongolian horsemen would both have been foiled in their attacks against the Roman empire."

Bernheim, in quoting this clever idiosyncrasy of the great scientist, marvels at

the "utter regardlessness as to the moral factors in history" manifest therein. This, however, was to be expected from the champion of the imperious dogmatism of science. With reference to the above quotation as a deterring example of onesidedness, we are the more justified in emphasising morality as the chief factor in history.

The progress of history must consist just in this, as Conrad Herrmann expresses it, that "man rises to an ever more perfect use of liberty." In this formula intellectual progress is combined with the conditions of ethical advance. Wherever this blending is not pursued progress is not permanent and is of mere relative value. It cannot then be said that the "story contains a moral."

Lord Acton says: "Unless the ethical sagacity of our race is subject to changes it remains unable to advance. What today is esteemed as a virtue may at one time have been deemed a vicious habit; defective jurisprudence, for instance, has changed with the latitudes. If King James had witches burned, and if Machiavelli taught regicide as an art, then we ought to keep in mind the age in which they lived and let them be judged by their contemporaries." Correct. Acton has in view social ethics, that nugatory moralism which results from changing world-theories as reflected in public opinion. Now, do we not find almost the same discrepancies inside the pale of Christian culture? Sybel points them out in saying: "Neither classic nor Christian antiquity, neither the Middle-Ages nor the Reformation, took any offense at the wild outrages of wars, at the tortures of cool criminal justice, at the extirpation of adversaries. In comparison with barbarities like these the horrors of our revolutions and reactions seem as child's play. The thought that the life of each man has a significance for, and is of consequence to, every other, has gained working force only in the latitudes." Upon the whole this judgment against ecclesiastical ethics is correct; for in the main they were but legalistic regulations of outward deportment. Whatever the church conserved in her dogmas had its reflex in public opinion, tantamount to the reflection of the tendencies of each age in the history of dogmatics. Public opinion of former times was in unison with what the doctrines of Christian theology imply, which, however, was generally either misunderstood or misconstrued, or kept out of sight by the administrators of the church on grounds of expediency. The application of the truth, as put up in general formulas, to special phases of thought and life, rested in the discretion of the church, rested there imbedded like a crystal in an old rock. After the right of private judgment had been established public opinion set this crystallised thought free, the generalness of legalism was dissolved. If not caricatured, the doctrinal precept becomes a vital maxim and serves society as a strengthening element. Its controlling influence being felt throughout the social organism, commotion and opposition are roused, and in the process ensuing "public morality" (that which the Americans call "moral suasion") is generated. It is that which a few moments ago, was called social morality in discrimination from Christian ethics. It must be clear that Christianity with its contents of truth cannot be held responsible for this rather shiftless morality which in palpable form is nothing but the product of social commotions, effecting, at its best, only an outward polish upon the manners of a people. That morality is legalistic. It takes its growth from custom and from disgust with custom.

A moral plant of this kind may succeed. The possibility cannot be denied that a system of moral philosophy may start out with personal right as a premise, and proceed through domestic relations and institutions of state or organised societies up to the common rights of humanity. Universal history in its continuance is essentially the gradual realisation of genuine manliness in all of man's social relations. "The continual approach to virtuosity in moral matters is tantamount to the growth of nature's nobleman, that is, the growth of history's ideal of a man bearing the features of the divine image," says Trendelenburg. "This growth towards perfection cannot thrive, however, unless the nations mutually complement each other in exchanging their best attainments, temporal and spiritual, and become willing to give and to receive".

Such progress in mere legalistic morality, however, affects not the inner motives of the multitude. Man may be better situated under the regime of such a social morality and urbanity, but this does not say that he has become better in himself.

Upon the scaffolding of a tower in course of construction, one or a few may stand higher than those working about its base. Up there not many have room; up there the view is wider, and the wages, perhaps, are higher, too. But that one, of those few above the rest of his fellow-laborers is not therefore the more virtuous. Such is exactly the case in the history of advancing civilisation.

In the face of this fact the question is decided already, whether with that kind of moral progress the happiness of man keeps pace. Again we may be reminded even of the dangers which necessarily become ever more menacing, of the dangers lurking beneath the thin, glittering surface of a public morality, that is, from beneath the good manners of refined training.

Because people are civilised, any sign of an upheaval of domestic society is frowned down, tho the same thing in a foreign country, in China, for instance, may be deemed justifiable because of being conducive, perhaps, to the Christianising of that empire. A revolution in Italy is encouraged, because it might weaken hierarchal supremacy. We reconcile ourselves to a war between two nations, or to an insurrection in Brazil or Cuba, because we expect our export to become stimulated thereby.

The hypocrisy of the social morality of utilitarianism and expediency has increased with the facilities to legalise shrewd acts of dishonesty by judicial technicalities. Nevertheless, there is no default or decline of moral progress, such as it is. It cannot be said that the seeming increase of crimes or the real increase of dissoluteness would in themselves prove retrogression. It might prove that the meshes of criminal justice are knitted somewhat looser. But the increase is explained by the fact that criminals are caught more easily than ever before, and that publication brings vicious actions speedily to general notice. Statistics are being perfected so as to counteract evils.

As a set-off against the increase of modern, legalistic wickedness we may point to many signs in proof of philanthropic enthusiasm, as for instance the greater care taken of the poor and fallen ones than in times past, or the contributions taken up to mitigate the miseries into which districts may be plunged at any moment.

The real impediments to progress, the dangers threatening public morality lie, as previously discussed, in the satiety with overdone social differentiation, in the moral unconcern, mental lassitude, and apathy of nations growing old.

Yet on the whole we repeat, taken collectively, that a certain progress, call it "public suasion," legalistic, civic or utilitarian morality is not only possible but a fact in evidence.

In Russia and Hungary the ten souls, averaging to a square mile, live in greater destitution than the hundreds in Belgium. This is equivalent to the fact that the farmer of today enjoys more comfort than the baron of A. D. 1500. And it is true that this external comfort, and security of person, protected by all kinds of insurance, is not on the decline; that good manners and social order are, on the whole, more respected; that the civilised nations under the sway of legalistic morality are unconsciously advancing from a state of natural bondage to more and more independence of mind. The improvement of state institutions is evidence of this advance and warrant its continuity. The state represents, as Dahlmann said, "the accumulated savings of human experiences and disposes of the power implied in that wealth, which ought to be applied in conducting the weaker majority of the race to higher stages of civilisation."

Notwithstanding this admission we deliberately assert that an ethical progress in the proper sense, correlative with religious progress seizing all the marching columns of mankind ought not to be expected, for progress after the manner in which mere morality advances is here impossible. Ethics roots in religion. The

symposium between Huxley, Manning, Salisbury, Gladstone, Tyndall, etc., published in 1876 has made this incontrovertible. And religion, which in reality must be Christocentric, cannot be trained into anybody, cannot be inherited. It needs to be generated anew in each person as pneumatic life. Nothing else will avail to subdue those pas-

sions which ever afresh threaten to subvert the progress of mere legalistic morality, which constantly endanger our modern sensitive state-organism based upon grounds easily shaken by partisan politics, underneath which uproarious intentions are aglow.

§ 230. Whilst we put the upward wave-lines of moral advance upon record, and give it due credit upon statistical tables, we dare not ignore the sinking waves of the religio-ethical movement. This is being run down because it does not run out into

generalities and into the masses, but goes soliciting person by person to move up- Duty of the modern state. DANHKAW.
wards. Laurent demonstrates "that the idea of progress ought to become manifest in Progress in respect to religiousness ought to become manifest as much as in sociology. LAUBERT.
respect to religiousness as well as in regard to morality and sociology."

Is then, this demand insisted upon, tho we found compliance to it impossible?
Does it not sound as if issuing from the desire to drag religion, too, into the service of The inner source and condition of the religious side of civilisation, cannot be said to develop.
mere utilitarianism? True civilisation can not be said to develop in the usual sense
of the term, as culture does. It always proceeds invisibly from the depth of consciousness, and is conditioned by the attitude this consciousness takes toward the
Supreme Good. It proceeds unconsciously inasmuch as thought is determined and
modified by the desire of.the will and according to the more or less intensity of the
feeling of quality.

Considering the religious problem in its bearing upon public, that is, social, Problem: religion as bearing upon moralism.
legalistic, utilitarian, or political morality, the first question to be met is, whether
religious improvement does not follow from the progress so far discussed and
acknowledged.

We are obliged to Kant for a sentence corroborating our view, which we may be "Man apt to be restored to true humanity by a sort of regeneration". KANT,   § 211.
allowed to put in evidence. In his "Religion inside the limits of pure reason," he
concedes that "man is apt to be restored to true humanity, to become a new man only by a
sort of regeneration, which is tantamount to a change of heart, equivalent to a renovation."
In this conclusion Kant crowns all that we have previously marked down concern- the specialist in moral philosophy.
ing this matter. It was clear to Kant, the specialist of the topic under discussion,
that a moral community in the proper sense could be conceived by thought in no other A moral community not conceivable unless as "a people under rule of divine law",
form than "as a people under rule of divine laws." These laws, he further argues, must
stand secure against arbitrariness, must stand above human authority. "Hence an
ethical commonwealth can not possibly be thought of, unless it be conceived as a
people governed and becoming civilised by divine laws, as a people of God." laws secure against arbitrariness, and above human authority.

"Properly," Kant adds, "this can only be initiated by God himself. To found a The postulates of Kant's reason in matters ethico-religious as concerning the "development" of civilisation.
moral people of God is a work whose accomplishment is to be expected from God
alone, not from man." This is what Kant's reason demands. We have seen previous
to this, that as members of this community new personalities are required, renewed
by "a kind of regeneration." What does this imply?

With reference to what has been said about the renewal of man we may thus Illustrative of the renewal of man.
further illustrate the matter: Standing before the show case of a jewelry store, we Utilitarian moralism and culture void of religion compared to dazzling but cold jewels.
admire the display of crystals and precious stones in all possible colors of the purest
dye. The collection reminds us of what our juvenile booklets contained about fairy
gardens. We perceive the mysteries of the mineral kingdom before us in palpable Lacking the cordiality of the inner life.
forms; formerly hidden in dark cavities they are now disclosed to us. Their glitter- Contrast illustrated by the difference between a precious crystal and a little wild flower.
ing splendor dazzles the eye, but warm our emotion they cannot. These cold stones
represent the most delicate phenomena of the largest kingdom of nature apart from
the exquisite art by which they were ground, polished and mounted. Yet they can Refutation of the identity of "ethics" and "morals", explanatory of the distinction of civilisation from culture.   § 8.
exert no higher influence than to excite cold curiosity and, perhaps, covetousness or
envy. They are all deficient in one thing, the inner life. In an analogous sense the same
thing is lacking in the realm of the political, legalistic morality of the natural unre-
generated man, sometime identified with "natural religion." That morality consists Natural or intellectualistic morality in all its glory of culture does not exceed the realm of the secondary good.
of the polish of the fashionable, the "accomplished" or the "cultured" people and is
artistically mounted upon calculating or affected politeness; notwithstanding certain
brilliancy or even natural bonhomie, at its best, it is bare of genuine cordiality, bare This culture would not have obtained its efficiency without the benign influence and patronage of Christianity.
of the pneumatic inner life. Legalistic and utilitarian humanitarianism cannot even
pass as an imitation of this inner life, much less take its place as a sort of surrogate.

As a matter of course this formative life from above proceeds in the diagonal to the effects being but products of natural development,
the processes under mere natural conditions. It begins with the ego becoming
reminded of its selfhood and destiny, being inwardly drawn, and feeling itself to be rising from below;
known by the personal God with whom the ego knows that He is on speaking terms. (up to the crown of queen Victoria).   § 17.
It grows into the comprehension of the perverted condition of things and
of the ego, and discovers that in consequence of this perversion, this very ego had The new life from above
haughtily raised itself to an imagined central position. For this reason the new life
under the renewal of selfconsciousness, begins with selfknowledge. The ego, breaking outlined in the changes it procures.
down under its presumptuous aspirations, allows itself to be transmitted to a higher

Position of the ego in a higher organism

in counter position to the organised opposition of "the world",

relinquishing selfglory, denying itself the glory of the world.

New cognitions as to the ego and the world,

prepare for the conception of Grace,

for a new form of God-consciousness always divined in the lowest state.

Experimental or rather empirical religion.

Man finds himself

assured of realising his destiny.

organism, disavowing its selfishness and wrong selfassertion. Thus the ego becomes an organ, a member. And from this new position it engages at once in a settlement with the wide world, that is, with the organised opposition to the spiritual counterpart, and its oppressive, degrading impositions. The ego breaks, as formerly with its selfglory, so now with the seductive glory of the world. It experiences a great change in its world-consciousness. And through both these new cognitions, after relinquishing selfishness in principle, there looms up and grows brighter and brighter the conception of Grace, that form of God-consciousness so different from all that had been thought of before, but which internally always had lain dormant as an unaccountable divination. It is now clearly recognised that it was this divination and Grace in which the process of regeneration commenced, illumining the soul in its totality like a solemn and silent sunrise, and shedding transparent light through the whole person now knowing itself to have been inwardly apprehended by God. This consciousness of God and Grace also closes the progress of renewal. Man finds himself to become ever more deeply attached to, and to be ever more vitally incorporated into, the Head and Mediator and Savior. Man virtually **finds himself** resting upon, and trusting in, and being supported by, Him—finds himself the more independent from the world and liberated from his own selfishness; finds himself safe and secure in the realisation of his destiny. Trying to describe the inner life of the "regenerated" person of man in the full sense of the word, we could only repeat ourselves without becoming any the better understood by those, who for reasons well known to themselves, have not as yet had those experiences. Suffice it to subsume that this new man, whilst serving out his time, already stands ruling above it in the sphere of eternity, until he is to be fully transmitted into the form of eternal existence. His inner life as concealed in the present state is supernatural, is peace and equanimity—it is glory, that is, beauty in its completion.

Moralism and ethics have to be distinguished from one another just as their respective products, culture and civilisation differ as to their origin, nature and success. In order to illustrate the contrast let us look down upon a simple wild flower decorating the borders between the woods and the heather. By a mystery, we call it life, material substance was here elevated to its highest glory, which, as compared with the splendor of the precious crystal or the star, is a miracle. It was life, mysteriously interceding and animating inorganic matter, which led the little wild flower up into its own wondrous world, into the company of most select associates.

That which causes the contrasting beauties of the crystal and the flora, also constitutes the difference between the fame of the natural-moral and the glory of the mystical new life. This intellectual morality is a utilitarian graduation of all which is good, and true, and beautiful in the realm of the secondary good. These natural ideas with all their influences upon the formation of public life in a general way would not have obtained their present recognisance if it had not been for the benign influences of Christianity. Altho shaped under religious patronage these ideals are but the result of a slow development from below, the products of long series of adjustments and traditional habits. Whilst on the contrary that which the Church understands and means by the "mystery of godliness" is a new life, the miracle of "regeneration", forming the soil which alone yields Christianised culture, i. e, civilisation.

Under the aspect of extensiveness the history of the new organism appears as a perpetual defeat,

seems, despite or because of its intensive power, so far as numbers go, to go down, retaining but a small minority, if it comes to sifting.

The spatial extent of the domain of true God-consciousness diminishes, always in the measure as politico-moral culture, under the assumed name of Christian civilisation, spreads out.

§ 231. No further than the community of the "Regenerated" lies potent within the present preparatory forms of social life, can it assume visible outlines. This is the reason why the history of this community as to its **extensiveness** appears as if it had sustained continual defeat and as being on the decline. The fact is, that in proportion to the expanse of cultural progress, to the spreading out of civilisation, the **intensive power** of religious spirituality is, as far as numbers go, taking a downward course, is at least restricted to a small minority. The extent of that domain in which the spirit under manifestations of true God-consciousness holds sway, visibly diminishes in comparison with the spread of intellectual and politico-moral culture, with the spread of modern world-consciousness now going under the **name** of Christian civilisation. Along the wave-line of this culture, commencing in the Orient and running over Athens to the present age, we observe the line of spiritual advance falling behind. The one sphere of **dominion** broadens in **extent**, whilst the other, the sphere of **service**, narrows down to invisible **intensity.**

The God-idea belongs to the original consciousness of man and is therefore common to all. This being the fact it seems to follow, that every **culture** should rest upon **cult**, that is, upon the cultivation of this consciousness. Indeed, the diversity of labor, education, and organisation, into which humanity has differentiated itself, ought to have been supported and illumined by this idea. For reasons of the inner difference between the moral and the religious sense, this was not the case, tho both are designed to approach toward one another and merge in final unification.

The ancient theocracies attempted to force unification of the two forms of consciousness, of the ethical and religious issues. The attempts at forced unification resulted in the religious life being rendered political and diplomatic, in its remaining interlocked with the thought of compressive uniformity. Very soon, however, symptoms of the separation of the ethico-political from the religious institutions became noticeable. The philosophical sects of India, the "mysteries," the Orphikans and Pythagoræns of Europe, the mode of keeping a priesthood and kingship apart in the mosaic theocracy not to be forgotten, are the signs that political formations and religious thought no longer covered each other. In the æras of Christianity the separation of the ecclesiastical from the political organisation was felt to be a necessity and was finally, tho only in principle, carried out.

That is to say, that religious ardor no longer warms up the political bodies of nations. Religiousness has withdrawn into closer quarters, so as to be able to retain its intensity. The extremities of the body politic become free, and have rather grown cold in regard to religion.

It is only for the sake of truth, not from pleasure in reproach, to be reiterated that the majority of the functionaries representing the cause of God-consciousness are in a great measure responsible for this state of things, which made the final separation of the church from the state a historic necessity. In its results this rejection of the "government of religion" accrued to the advantage of ethico-social progress; for thus alone could freedom in general be preserved. Deplorable as it is, the course of religiousness as an all pervading and solvent principle is, to outward observation, on the decline, the more the nations partake of the modern cultural progressiveness. As the metals oxidise when exposed to the air, so Christianity becomes indiscernible to the worldly-minded as soon as the breath of worldliness touches it. Natrium, the essence of salt of which Jesus spake more than parabolically, in illustration of the genuine congregation, is for this very reason visible scarcely for a moment.

And as corrosion proceeds toward the interior where the sterling quality of the core alone remains, in order to lend its strength to the whole, and to bear up the rotting crust: so is the invisible strength of the church to be protected by a certain appearance which is not intended to be attractive to the uninitiated mind, that ever allows itself to be misled by outward appearances. This observation leads us to find the true exegesis of Daniel's vision.

The primitive Church and the annal-writers of the Middle-Ages interpreted Daniel's image of the monarchies in their way correctly enough as inverted progress and increasing decay of worldly power—neglecting only the consideration as to the cause, the profanation of culture.

Once more we have traced the two lines into which the original unity of consciousness was split asunder. More than once we have shown how and why the parts had been intended to permeate and pervade each other and finally to reunite. The proto-type of this intent was manifest in a sufficiently clear manner.

When the Apostle upon the Areopagus adopted the word of the pagan poet "for we are also his offspring", he bent back the line of worldly culture pursuing the one-sided conception of the thought of humanity into line with the proper concept of the thought of true humanism. He showed that worldly morality ought to return to and unite with the religious affluence from the the common source, in order to attain to the state of real virtue, harmony, and peacefulness. He projected a future unification of culture and cultus, of the religious and the ethico-political (or social) issues and

30

institutes, pursuant to the preordained aims and ends of historic advance towards true civilisation. In this sense, which is also that of Dorner's Ethics, we work for the development of the moral sense in unison with the religious on separate, but converging lines. For Paul, and Herder, and Dorner agree, that "religion means the highest degree of humanism possible to be obtained by man."

CH. V. THE WORLD IN THE STATE OF PERFECTION.

§ 232. "Common sense and wit have indeed incarnated a great truth in the term of devil," says Montegazza. This exclamation he made at the sight of the wellfed apes in a Hindoo temple—in their bathing pond—and of the gilded image of a gigantic monkey which the sanctuary incloses. These remarks we mean to utilise in considering the consummation of the world's development after the manner in which we spoke of its judgment. In the transmutation of the world into the state of perfection, our concept of its government will become verified and all the causes pending in the highest court will show justice to come out triumphant at last. "Altho," says Carlyle, "the world in which we live does not belong to Satan, yet at bottom he always occupies room in it somehow, from whence to break forth now and then."

This is the unsophisticated and unphilosophical apperception of that basest factor in history, which has been tolerated for the time being to obtrude himself upon and to muffle himself in history.

It has been demonstrated, how at the final manifestation of the ideal proto-type of history, the principal factor of the Bad, that which "ought not to be," phosphorescing forth from the dark, will be ejected from the world of men.

We deemed it a demand of logic, that this principle is to be conceived as concentrated in a personal will. Only thus are we able to discriminate between the demoniac will and that of the human personality, and to charge the seductive instigation to an entity of the spiritual world, which finally is to be expelled from the realm of the secondary good at the time of its elevation into the realm of the Supreme Good.

"The aim of history cannot but lie in the realisation of that thought which is fully objectivised or projected in man, and is to be realised through man in every respect and to all those forms to which the finite is apt to conform itself, for being taken up by, and to be assimilated into, the ideal". In another place W. v. Humboldt adds, "that the diversified divulgation of the powers of the human mind must be the object which history aspires to render manifest". This conclusion is clothed in

somewhat misty language. But we have already become informed as to the essential truth contained in Humboldt's postulate, at the time when we demonstrated the complete revelation of every faculty and function of the human mind as the goal of history. One circumstance, however, remains to engage our attention for an hour.

The full realisation of the thought projected in man "in every respect, in all forms in which the finite is apt to conform itself", involves the equalisation of the real as a physical entity with the ideal, involves the merging of both. We keep in mind that, as regards the transformation of the physical world into the state of perfection, "the world of man" solely was under our focus. We have now only to go one step further, a step for which, at the previous contemplation of the final completion of the physical world, we were not quite prepared. In so much as the minds of philosophers had been engaged with a multiplicity of worlds, they lost themselves in

unveiling suppositions. This will be the case always, whenever human nature is not properly conceived in its sublimity—which fatal neglect consists in not recognising the entire visible universe as belonging to man in the manner as the pedestal belongs to the statue.

The cosmos is involved in the fate of man, who is appointed to be its lord and master. With his appearance nature's development was arrested; failing in his destination nature declined to respond to all his requests and desires, and became antagonistic to his pretensions. Man being restored, his environments rise with him. Man's redemption means nature's reconciliation. His calling upon earth preeminently includes the duty to redeem nature by improving and elevating it along with his own selfcultivation. This is almost entirely conditioned by close observation of its relations to him and of his duty towards it. It is entrusted to his care and becomes readjusted in its subservience to him until, sequent to the crisis of physical creation in its totality, it is bound to conform to his newly resurrected life. "The problem of human life is identical with the project of the universe," as Eucken corroborates the inferences here drawn from analogous facts.

In addition to the result of our former inquiry as to the destiny of the physical cosmos we now come to draw the final conclusion upon the subject.

We touched upon the existence of a created spiritual world. An objection to this doctrine or apperception cannot be raised on philosophical grounds. Whatever may be thought about the ranks of an angelic world is here irrelevant. Their's is a sphere of a spiritual existence. Of the physical, visible part of creation man is the final object and end. In him the physical meets the spiritual sphere for the purpose of their blending.

The celestial part of creation is included in this general unification in order to perfect the final consummation. It is included inasmuch as it, too, was intended to serve man's best interests. The celestial part must be included in the transit to perfection, else the reinstatement of man into the sovereignty over the universe would not be warranted, and the end of the fight for the possession of the world would be left undecided.

Abodes of angelic beings may exist in such plenitude that in comparison with them this visible cosmos, dispersed as it is into confusing heaps of stars, and in its constraint under mechanical laws, is to be taken as a very small part of creation in its totality, as no more than "a dark place." Conscious of the risk incurring in the transgression of our limit, we state this merely as a probability. But it does not invalidate our assertion that all of these realms would yet amount to no more than envelopings of man and his world. As this narrower, visible cosmos centers in man, so the cosmos encircling our universe is connected with, and related to him. All spheres take part in man's development and are awaiting his completion. When after the final crisis the ideality of man is rendered complete, then that consummation will ensue for which all spheres are preparing; and the thorough-going change of the entire universe will take place, in which the material and soluble substance will be fashioned into forms concrete and indissoluble and immaterial, yet no less material than the substantiality of which mind, in the present state even, may form a conception.

§ 233.   We remember from a previous discussion of this subject, that this visible world surrounding us in palpable shapes, is but the symbol or emblem of the world of true reality and permanency veiled by this coarse materiality.

Nature in its transciency and formations of stuff consists of more than mere phenomena of the material substance. It is just this matter as we call it, which is one of the world's unsolved riddles, because substance in its essentiality is more imperceptible than the essence of salt, the quickly oxidising natrium. It is indiscernible to scientific examination for good and very natural reasons. For matter in its present appearance in the visible form of nature is not what it ought to be, and must cease to be for any purpose whatever. It is, therefore, of no permanency. It is but disengaged force, which, instead of gravitating in life intrinsic, gravitates in its own center.

Recent conclusions of natural philosophy have corroborated this condition. Natural philosophy has, irrespective of Baader's views, repeatedly averred that visible matter can be accounted for in no other way than as having issued from immaterial principles. At the outset we conceded, for argument's sake, to the interpretation of Leibnitz, who tried to extricate matter from its confused, materialised condition by proposing the monads, in order to improve upon the view which had been entertained from times immemorial, namely, that nature pure and simple had become inverted into coarse materiality by a crisis prior to the creation of man. Fechner as well as Lotze knows nature to be an entity, imbued with psychical vitality and energy from its first beginning. The correctness of their inductions was acknowledged, and resulted in the axiom that mind is able to affect physical matter in the same mode as imponderable substance affects the ponderable.

Our object in stating these findings is simply to coax out the confession that matter—having protruded from an invisible nature, invisible at least to our eyes, and attempting to substantiate its possibility of becoming an abnormity—is also adapted to become reabsorbed or transmutated into the original state of invisible existence. Coarse sand is transformable into transparent crystal glass without any change of its essence. All we claim is that in a similar manner the earthly visible stuff, the lightless geological mass, is to be considered as reducible to its original condition, to its essential naturalness. Nature thus sublimated, as it were, will no longer be the veil concealing the spiritual world, or the mere semblance of the Beautiful and the Sublime, but will continue to be its most adequate expression without any further possibility of degradation.

Simultaneous with the final crisis pursuant to the reappearance of the True Man, the Mediator, and with the transfiguration of the cosmos into a state of different perceptibility, man will appear in the glory of his original destination. In the present state he is hemmed in and hampered by a corporeality which paralyses his most intense and normal aspirations. Our means of communication with our surroundings are insufficient; the unsatisfactory communication depends entirely upon a very feebly wrought, extremely sensitive and therefore most fragile nervous system of which our reflecting consciousness has scarcely a partial control.

The transactions necessary to report a sensation to our sensorium and to return the answer, requires a certain time. The most important actualisation of the will has to accommodate itself to the complicated apparatus of nerve-threads and ganglions, requiring time for the performance of its duties. Hence only one thought or act can be accomplished at a time, our day-consciousness can only proceed in the slow form of tedious intermediation. And yet we know of a different form of the mind's activity, not explicable by the most subtile observation and most elaborate doctrine of nerve-reaction. That form of consciousness which we call "unreflected", that part of the mind which is evidently free from the restraints of space and time, permits of our ratiocinative conclusion that the mind can work independent of the body and its functuary organs, and that certain states of mind are observable which border on disembodiment. It is agreed to, at any rate, that our knowledge and doings are under durance of a cumbersome technique, that thought and deeds are hindered by the temporary formation of the body in this respect is inadequate to the nature of the mind.

Along with the transmutation of the cosmos thus indicated, the mysteries will become disclosed which are as yet veiled by, but shine through, this temporary constitution of human nature. The dual form of consciousness becomes liberated from its polar strains. In a new form of corporeality the human being assumes and assimilates to itself new organs answering its new environments in the changed order of things. Now at last has man entered the state of perfection. For after the reappearance of the proto-type or image after whom man was created, his corporeality is to correspond with that of the glorified Mediator. The mystical temple edifice, representing the realisation of what was true in the thought of theocracy; the habitation

of the glorified Head with its glorified members, will be mystical no longer, but will stand forth complete as originally planned before creation began. Then at last man stands out conspicuously in the grandeur of his perfection. With this consummation history comes to a close. The fabric of the visible is then taken down, having fulfilled its purpose of serving as the scaffold in the upbuilding of that temple.

When the architect has completed the rearing of his monumental work, the auxiliaries of frames and scaffoldings must vanish with the building rubbish, and the contrivances and tools are put aside. Under the praises of the multitudes dedication is celebrated. Such an occasion forms a fitting analogy to that moment which inaugurates the course of the endless æons. The new family of mankind in holy community reveals the glorious realisation of man's being and destiny. The throngs of the spiritual realms, beholding it, unite in jubilant anthems of praise, and partake of the most intense raptures of blessedness.

"The Beautiful," says Gœthe, as related by Eckermann, "is an original phenomenon never making its full appearance as such, becoming visible, however, in thousands of modifications wrought by one creative spirit." This Beautiful is going to reveal itself in the harmony of man perfected. It will not consist so much in the sublime exhibition of human endowments hitherto hidden to the extent of fully one half of man's potentialities, as in the beauty and harmony of his internal qualities being displayed in their full glory, when the tattered, earthly attire falls away from the spiritualised body. This turning inside out will result from the convergence of the two lines of culture and cultus which hitherto ran in separate wave-lines repeatedly crossing one another in their several upward and downward courses. The majestic simplicity of the one has appropriated to itself the wealth of the other. Pious contemplation, childlike affection and gratitude, and ardency of consecration will no longer have to shun the seductive incitements of the manifold,ever diverting thought under the predominance of appetite and eccentric tendencies towards the periphery of externals.

It was the propensity of temporal nature toward eccentricity, which made it cycle through the diversity of cultural aims and educating elements, whereby world-consciousness abandoned itself to worldliness.

But after having been turned from its centrifugal tendency this world-conscious-ness will be embraced by God-consciousness into which it had become concentrated. Whosoever chose the attitude of affectionate child-likeness will come into posses-sion of the whole inheritance of culture without any boasting of achievements, with-out selfglorification.

Gradually the whole circumference of civilised life, generally speaking, had been drawn into the centripetal movement and into the emotion of intense attachment un-til it rests contented in the center. From this center, by way of numberless variations, will radiate the copiousness of all that which is virtuous and soulful, graceful and elegant, in youthful bouyancy and manly strength.

This beauty of the inner life will shine forth in external forms of beauty from man, the now universally recognised head of creation. The inner life of chivalrous fancy and delicacy, marking the ideal of the romance, will be reconciled by the grace-fulness elaborated in the antique. The plastic embodiment of the Beautiful will be the main feature expressing the virtuosity of the all pervading spirit. All the beati-tude of the spirit-soul will radiate from the new psychical body, which commenced its harmonising development amidst the shadowy forms of earthly beauty.

Then the great contrast between the higher and the lower world,between the celes-tial and terrestrial, which hitherto had caused the intermediate strains of polarity and all woeful departures and separations, will be abrogated by the Mediator, in Whom alone humanity finds its peace and rest.

§ 234. Man, being the theme of history, the realisation of the thought underly-ing his entire being, and its exposition in every respect, must be the goal of history. This realisation proceeds under methods of freedom. In freedom man had to affirm, and to conform himself to, his given position and incumbent destiny. In this rela-tive freedom, whose preservation or regaining was enjoined upon him by the nature of things, he was to make his potentialities evolve from their depths in a diversity of relations; in freedom he was to cultivate his gifts in the course of historic eventuali-ties. Without compulsion, under no other necessity but that of the Supreme Good he was to bring all the wealth of opportunities and accomplishments from the realm of the secondary good into subordination to himself and into relation with the com-mon center of all. In his capacity as the acme of all created being, he was to bend all which he represented into proper relation to himself as he is related to God. Ever free to maintain this concentrative tendency throughout all the ever renewing and changing conditions, he was to verify the saying that "we are kindred to the deity", to adjust his reality to his destiny. In free selfconsecration during his term of probation, with the tests and the contest rendered necessary for the very purpose of adjusting his conduct, that is,during the historical development, he was to divulge the mystery of his divine affiliation, the rich contents of his psychical and divine relations and obligations. Heretofore we symbolised ethical progress by con-current lines, each representing one particular phase of culture in competition with another through longer or shorter intervals. All the ups and downs formed a figure showing the modes of cooperation, reciprocity, and mutual stimulation in behalf of historical advance through civilisation to glorification. For the sake of still clearer exposition we may choose the metaphor of musical tones instead of geometrical signs.

Geometrical signs replaced by musical tones.

In the polyphonic composition termed a fugue, one voice gives the theme, and whilst it pursues the intonated air, another voice sets in and still another, each in a modified key answering the melody in its own manner. The theme continues its part as the melody, intertwining all voices into one complex and purposive whole, tho now and then the theme may seem to be lost—but we need not stretch the metaphor.

to illucidate the cultural development of history through civilisation to glorification.

The one theme conceived before the beginning, tho Son in Whom the thought of a world was conceived and projected, and through Whom it was realised, is now known and appreciated. In the first man this theme was intonated, and in a few distinct outlines the system of a developing world made its appearance. The theme, divined but not understood, was the basis of innumerable modifications ensuing. The inner wealth of the composition became unfolded, tho not comprehended; in a

What the theme is in a fugue, was the Son of God to history throughout its course as projected in Him before the beginning.

wild torrent of discords the flood of tones often seemed to rush over the banks. As the vociferous noise of roaring masses seems to drown the theme, so the thought underlying the world's composition underwent perversions in those ethnical factions which had broken loose from the unit of humanity. But the thought survives and revives, governs and gathers the medley of aberrations and opposing movements by strict contrapuntal rules; until at last the conflicting series are united

The theme drowned in the noise of discords,

again into majestic accords, until the harmony of unity rises from the perplexing confusion of diversity. So, speaking without metaphor, was the "Image" of the Mediator the theme of history, in the form of a gift and a task, contained in the prophesying figure of the first man at the beginning of history.

but emerges ever and again and leads on to the harmony of unity.

The "Image" bodily appeared, tho veiled, in the middle of the times, when in free selfconsecration and inanition the One, as a "sign of men", wrought out the image in a new departure of development. And finally it reappears and is reflected in a new humanity at the end of time.

The "Image" of the beginning, is the "sign of man" who wrought out a new departure of development in the middle of time, and who reappears at the end.

The work of history—the transition of the sublime Image of the Mediator, as proceeding from unity to diversity, and the impartation of that glory given in the Head to the many destined to glory—is now finished.

The key-note and the secret of the exceedingly wild and odd sounding polyphonic composition—emerging and submerging in thousands of inexplicable implications and intrinsic methods, developing many variegated groups and pitiable masses of detached humanity throughout times and climes far apart—exhibits, after all, a

The marvelous climax of the "concert".

marvelous climax of the concert. The plant has grown to a tree upon whose branches those of all nations, which represent the blooming crown of creation, assemble and form the congregation of renewed men, of a reunited human family: the children of God bringing forth their fruits.

The reunited human family, the children of God bringing their fruits.

The historic task of the nations being accomplished, history's secret becomes plain and conceivable. To that community, and through its instrumentality to the world, it is now rendered public and palpable why this image, impressed upon man, was to remain enigmatical until the riddles were solved; how they were solved

Among those who could appreciate the Son of God, and through them it becomes known why revelation remained veiled.

through the entering of the "Likeness of God" Himself and by His return in majesty into the midst of that new humanity in which He ever saw the reflection of Himself. This reappearance signalises the execution, is the affirmation, of judgment, and is at

In renewed humanity the Mediator ever saw the reflection of Himself.

the same time the absolute criterion of its justice. This appearance now as before, is to be faced by the Bad in its everlasting attempts at maintaining itself. It was destined to be driven out of the world of men where it was thought to have firmly estab-

His reappearance signalises the execution of judgment.

lished itself, but where it had lost its power in the realm of new life, because the "Word of His mouth" paralysed the tempter.

Tempter driven from the world.

Now the purified world is man's own. It now becomes a system open to his instantaneous insight and immediate influence, no more to be forced into subjection by screws, and sledges, and pulleys, and derricks, but being at his service voluntarily and joyfully. This new organism of the renovated world is now the place where un-

The purified world man's own.

bounded freedom dwells, in which the nature of things is adapted to mirror the glory of the royal race in every possible variation of the Beautiful.

Universal history is not the story of the earth alone. It is the memory of whatever event took place in the universe, that is, of whatever concerned humanity and pertained to its world.

The original "Type", entering time incognito as the "Word" incarnate calls forth the new race, and convenes the assembly of His Kingdom. *State of glory of the royal race.*

This earthly-Heavenly Kingdom always had been floating before the vision of humanity, was always the innermost of three concentric circles revolving upon the Mediator. Around this circle and in immediate proximity to it there revolves another, the circle of the historic world. It is the task appointed to those of the inner circle to pervade and to embrace the other in the same manner as the inner circle is attracted by its center. *History the memory of whatever took place in the universe concerning humanity.*

This second circle is again surrounded by a third, the world of nature, the cosmical organism. It was the task of the first circle to comprehend, yea, to surpass the emblematic glory of the third, and to elevate to its own source of glory this third circle by way of the second, through culture. These three circles perfectly correspond to the triad: spirit, soul and body. *Earthly-Heavenly kingdom had ever been floating before the vision of humanity always the innermost of three concentric circles.*

Now the work is done, as far as it could be done without abandoning or violating freedom. History having risen from its first insignificant premise, which contained the proto-type and motife of the whole, up to its fulfilled work, returns to its starting point in order to disappear. Spirit, soul and body are now translucent. What has caused all the torments in this world of man, relapses into nothingness. But whatever had been a formative concomitant of history looms up in the new sphere of permanency and unity, accompanied by the triumphant symphonies of all the spheres earthly and celestial, in Honor of Him who was their Creator and Liberator. *The next is the historic world, to be pervaded by the powers of the first in the manner as this was attracted by its center. The third circle is the natural world, the cosmical organism.*

RESULT AND CLOSING REMARKS.

Is there Any Possibility for an Adequate Construction of A Philosophy of History?

§ 235. Not unless we are permitted to avail ourselves of the aid of the deductive method. Unless we proceed from definite premises given in Christianity and preserved by the Church, a somewhat satisfactory purview of the life of nations cannot be gained. And such a philosophy will satisfy such only as grant the premises. This is to say: No system of philosophy, least of all of the Philosophy of History, can support itself on a base of pure thought—it must be borne out by data. Unless these are adduced in evidence and cross-examined, as to the competency of their testimony, it will be of no avail to arrange a system by interlinking all factors and effects pertaining to history into one locked syllogism. *Deductive method indispensable, which proceeds from definite premises given in Christianity. Pure thought cannot support a system of philosophy of history.*

We found it necessary to take our position outside of history. But the formulas proposed from which, for argument's sake, we set out, have become testproof by empiric facts inductively adduced and legitimately applied. "Hypotheses may find their affirmations in reality;" this was the result of Dr. Rocholl's critical review of former attempts at philosophising upon history, from which we set out with the result now before us. *"Hypothetical positions may find their affirmation in reality". Dr. Rocholl.*

A system of philosophy cannot be selfsupporting. What does that mean?

"Human knowledge on the whole," says Schelling, "has no character, no position unless supported by something which stands upon its own merits; and nothing is able to thus qualify itself and to be approved of, but what is real on the strength of freedom". Well said, if Schelling only had not thought it necessary to fix freedom upon metaphysical grounds. It was a rather slow process by which he came to adopt the great maxim, that "liberty is the Alpha and Omega of all philosophy". We have arrived at the same conclusion, but by way of induction, proving that which had deductively been reasoned out. Always keeping in sight of solid facts, we took ethnical material as we found it and as it still presents itself. *"Knowledge has no character unless supported by something which stands on its own merits". "Only what is real on the strength of freedom can qualify itself on such". Schelling. Criticism of Schelling's freedom on metaphysical grounds.*

Throughout the course of our procedure, we were coerced by the necessity to seek the key of interpretation in the matter itself, if phenomena were to be accounted for which otherwise baffle the understanding of the most conspicuous events of history. Once more the method of Leverier may illustrate and vindicate our mode of syllogising. Observation of disturbances in certain groups of stars, and the peculiar behavior of certain unknown bodies in their well known courses made it desirable to find out what caused these irregularities. Finally the savant believed that a certain hypothetical inference might set the matter clear. He surmised some undiscovered star to cause the trouble by its power of attraction. He demonstrated, how *"Liberty the A and O of all philosophy", but ever in sight of stern facts. The key to interpret history to be sought in its own material,*

Leverier's hypothesis leading to the discovery of the star and the disappearance of the irregularities.

all the irregularities indicating his supposition, made that supposition the only possible key to a satisfactory explanation. To him the presence of that obscure corpus delicti became sufficiently certain as to where at a certain astronomical spot its location in the immensity of space was to be computed. Galle, soon after, upon that very spot, detected the planet. This at once made all the irregularities disappear, and at the same time vindicated the legitimacy of hypothetical theorising.

Irrational phenomena, anomalies and disturbances reduced to a cause indicated but not intelligible

unless ascribable to a hidden malefactor,

In an equal manner have we been necessitated from the beginning to reduce a set of irrational phenomena—encountered at every step of historical advance amidst the cosmical environments of man—to reduce the anomalies and disturbances, interfering with the regular and rational course of things, to a cause indicated by the phenomena, tho not intelligible from the concurring, regular facts as far as they were known. We soon surmised a hidden factor which after its discernment would explain it all. And we became enabled to point out the spot in the background of the

problems which become explicable under the supposition that the irritating cause lay in the background of historical constellations,

and would be detected at the proper moment.

historical constellations where this malefactor is to be sought for, if the annoyances, pestering history, were ever to be accounted for. If an explanation and solution of the peculiar tension, apparent between opposite forms of consciousness by which the ancient world was rent in two, were to be discovered anywhere in history, it could be found at this conjunction alone. We also surmised that the grave questions with regard to fear, guilt and horrible sacrifices, the problems of the descent of peoples, and especially of the enigmatical phenomena originating in, and modifying, human con-

The healing of the disrupture by an efficient remedy

according to prescription

sciousness—every one of which problems agitated the nations because of their psychical bearings upon each individual life—must find their solution at a definitely appointed place and at the right moment. Furthermore, we made not light with the grave and premonitory apprehension, that the disrupture of all the forms of existence

to be administered by the church.

in this present life, which, notwithstanding their being lower by far as compared with its anti-types in the higher life of the future world of reality, would have to be brought to a logical and last actual equation. Since physical and ethical abnormities and logical dilemmas demanded the appearance of a factor efficient enough to

Sacred tradition put to empirical tests, and offered to free experimenting.

make amends for them, the advent could ensue nowhere else but at the hour and place designated, and in the manner foreshadowed.

For the appearance of the Savior the church recognised the expected creator of universal attractiveness.

We confided in the facts as represented by the Church. But we did not accept its testimony without putting the sacred tradition to the test of experience, not without offering the opportunity for freely experimenting upon the apparatus accessible to every one.

In the appearance of the Savior, as announced by the Church, we recognised the expected center of universal attractiveness, and the solution of all problems otherwise inexplicable. This Mediator we found to be the approved focus to which all those physical, ethical and mental demands pointed, yea, the one in Whom all the lines cut each other. His appearance is fitly to be compared to the keystone which supports the

Illustrated by the Keystone, and the stone reclining upon it.   § 35

ribs sprung from the depths and forming the grand, selfsupporting cupola of the expansive dome. Every stone in the cross-vault has its joints posited in the direction of the radii of the curve. The form of each is designed with reference to its leaning toward this fore-ordained keystone.

The world-theory discarding this body bearing up under the weight of all, leaves history a shapeless mass unfit to be joined together;

By this arrangement of transmitting horizontal pressure into vertical thruss, the open contrasts and tensions and problems were spanned, differing from the earthly edifice in that the pressure comes from below, and the center of gravity and attraction lies in the support from above as in the central sun—"the Center of Equation". A world-theory discarding this body bearing upon all relations and at the same time bearing the weight of all of them, would, instead of a well built dome, represent an indiscriminate mass of parts whose uncouth shapes forbade their jointure.

prevents a consistent theory of human life; and makes the much desired unification of the truths of dualism into a monistic world-theory impossible.

Disavow the central person and the matters of this world will lie about in heaps of desolation, lie in a dreary condition upon the periphery, distressful in a degree equal to the ratio of their distances from the center; lie about in heaps of a dead diversity without a purpose and deprived of any principle of holding them together, without holding out any hope of unity; that is: under Anti-Christian aspects matters can never be perceived in any other condition, but that which prevents a consistent theory of human life, and renders the much desired unification of the truths of dualism into a monistic world-theory impossible.

Leaving void the place of that center-piece inserted from above, history as a whole would not only resemble a palace in ruins, but would actually constitute an unintelligible relapse into Tohu Vabohu—into a world "without form and void."

World's history not a failure, but a reconstruction of fractured parts of humanity into unity, well planned.

We on our part have found the underlying plan. We found and followed the traces and threads of unity by which the parts of fractured humanity, even the debris of civilisation, are held together for an eventual reconstruction of things, and to pledge a higher insight into their finality.

In this plan we recognised the theme of history, and found the significance of man to consist in his being not only the bearer of this plan, but also commissioned to carry it out.

Man not only the bearer of this plan, but also commissioned to carry it out.

Thither we were guided by induction. But once in possession of the Synthesis, and knowing the secret of its combination, we were allowed to test and to verify our conclusion and comprehension thus gained, by deductive ratiocination.

Deduction confirms the correctness of the inferences derived from induction.

We were justified in pursuing our interpretation of history in the light of the plan thus discerned.

One of the fundamental questions was solved when to earthly history its sphere had once been assigned. Well says H. Fichte: "Present life is incomprehensible unless taken as a fractional part of future fulfilment. Neglecting this relationship of the part to the whole, life with reference to its beginning and end would be beset with voids, and our thirst for understanding would be mocked in a cruel manner. But our life resembles the projectional curve-line of a sectional cone whose upward direction, if profoundly figured out, necessarily points to an apex lying far beyond its hyperbola."

Present life incomprehensible if not taken as a fractional part of future fulfillment. H. Fichte.

Progress that reaches no goal. Illustrating historic life as the basal section of a cone.

This we found to be the case, as we went on our way. Something indefinite can never be clearly understood; but now, under the aspect of its totality, history was brought within a compass in which, and to a focus from which, we were able to survey this totality.

From that center, which in accord with definite premises and self-evident postulates, had become substantiated, we obtained a full view. The calculus of that projection of the conical section proved to be correct. Beginning and end were rendered ascertainable. From this point of view we gained our world-theory which claims scientific validity.

The world-theory herewith presented claims scientific validity.

In speaking thus of our part of human knowledge, we would like to be understood as meaning the knowledge of the plan, capacity, design, purpose and goal of history—not the specified knowledge of all the material, or rather immaterial and irrelevant, particles.

Positive knowledge of plan, purpose and goal of history.

The material of history is man; he is the substance of which history is made up. As little as "science" will ever be able to give the satisfactory explanation of matter or substance forming our palpable environment, so little will historical research ever be able to materially change our views of life, or expound to us how, or of what in essence, the human personality, the formative agent of history, is composed. And just as little will we be able to answer a series of minor questions, perhaps irrelevant to this composition.

As little as "science" will explain "substance" will detail of historical research alter the views of life thus gained, neither will it show of what or how personality is composed.

Understanding of history illustrated by the correspondence of the plan of an edifice with the building itself.

We claim to understand history, nevertheless. Holding up the ground-plans and designs of an edifice to our attention, knowing the purpose for which it is built—that is, possessing a conception of the whole—we come to understand the details in the design of the building.

It cannot be taken as boasting, if we deliberately state that certainly we comprehend the work of the architect and his artisans, notwithstanding the malformations, or æsthetic flaws, or application of defective material in the construction, and notwithstanding, perhaps, the faulty arrangement of the rooms inside as to their outfit and use.

Tho we may be ignorant as to the quality of building material, the chemistry of cement and the adaptness of window-glass or door-hinges, yet knowing the idea underlying the whole, we can judge as to the identity of the draft and picture with the work completed. In this sense we claim to have a correct view of history, to know for what it is to be taken.

We claim the knowledge of what history is to be, what finally becomes of it.

Our eyes can not follow the execution of minor details of historic life;

which would have been possible if freedom were to be included in the calculation.

This does not say that we should possess full knowledge of all the events, in all their bearings and knittings, and that, if we went so far in our pretensions, we were

The plan prejudiced because hid behind malformations, crowding themselves to the front and on top.

able to follow the execution of the plans with our eyes. But we claim that this even would have been possible, if our idea could include freedom into the calculable, that is, if the normal course of things had not been thrown out of gear by the abuse of liberty. Thought had to encounter this antagonism; and for this reason the plan, as far as its execution and details are concerned, was withdrawn from view behind the malformations which crowded themselves to the front and on top.

Hence we did not portion out the historical tasks to specific modern nations.

A lack of perspicuity will scarcely be charged against us. We took the advice of modesty not to engage in the mysteries of numbers, when the remarkable cycles of ages were alluded to, which might have induced us to imitate Pythagoræan adventures. For similar reasons we have not, as has been customary, portioned out the

No such classification of cultural advantages or defaults.

historical tasks to the modern nations. No predecessor in the domain of our knowledge could convince us of the propriety of discussing such a classification of cultural advantages or defaults. An aversion to all arbitrary treatment of history, well justified by experience, caused us to maintain our reserve on that score.

By conceiving the cardinal thought history becomes intelligible throughout.

And yet we say, that conceiving its cardinal thought, we have come to understand history thoroughly. Since this thought was represented in the Logos, we took the liberty to speak of a logic in history. Would we, however, be pressed to confine

Logic of history not in the sense of a methodology of reasoning.

the conception of logic to a mere methodology of reasoning, then, of course, we were far from speaking of a Logic of History in a sense so subordinate.

Not to be limited by the technique of epistemology.

Barrenness of modern logics.

Such limitation of logic to the techniques of epistemologists is no longer necessary. Reasoning must now have objective contents as it ever had them. But what today is termed Logics—a set of rules regulating the thinking process, a general theory on the technique of reasoning, applicable to any object of knowledge—simply sets up mental shelvings regardless of tenets and objects of thought. Against such a diminution of Logics to a sum of formulas and a classification of syllogisms we enter our protest, and mean to stand aloof, as we have done,

Logic as it ought to be will not content itself with teaching dialectics, but thinking for the sake of knowing.

from such cool indifference as to contents of thought, toward thought in the concrete. When modern logics will come to see the necessity of giving up such a position of impoverished aristocracy, it will not content itself with teaching dialectical thinking, but will teach thinking for the sake of knowing. It will then no more start from reason per se, either pure or uncritical, as the case may be, but from data of thought derived from outside. And with these contents the intellect will proceed from general cognitions—the universals for instance—in

Intellect will, in a matter of fact manner, proceed upon its way towards entering into relation with metaphysics.

a matter-of-fact manner upon its way towards entering into relation with metaphysics. Metaphysics sets out from the idea, or rather concept of purpose wherein alone rests the rationality of the thing per se.

"The appearance of the Logos comprises all that is real." Hegel.

The concept of that which is absolutely true, good, and beautiful, lies in the notion of finality. Or, let it be stated more definitely, and under the same right as Erdmann in his Logics, that the logically qualified condition of thought must have for its contents "the ultimate purpose to realise itself as the absolute reason, the "LOGOS".

But the bad appearing very real, we rather say: "all which is true."

It is the Logos "Whose appearance comprises all that is real". So said Hegel. We, however, who differ from him in this, that we hold the Bad to be something very real, must substitute another attribute to the Logos and say, "Whose appearance comprises all that is true and holy!"

Data of empirical reality all explained in the "Logos,"

When we firmly took our position in the middle of the times and with the personified universal reason of things, the Logos—we found in Him the empirical data of reality all explained. Issuing from Him the pervasion of the world with the Infinite goes on. In Him as the chief of sufferers we found the real condition of the

His suffering made it obvious that there is something "which ought not to be."

world to be such as to contain too much of that which "ought not to be". In Him as the Risen One we saw the world in its real condition, as that which is adapted to undergo a metamorphosis and is designed for perfection, with respect to both the

His resurrection shows the real condition of the world to consist in its adaptness to undergo a metamorphosis,

eternal-spiritual as well as the temporal-physical world. We found in the Logos the key which unlocked the mysteries, and solved the enigmata of the natural and the historical, that is, the moral world. In Him we found the plan, the theme, the purpose and goal of all the movements along the entire course of nature as well

In Him is revealed the goal of all movements in nature as well as in history.

as of history. In spite of the darknesses and malformations and caricatures of the thought, we found the theme and the plan to pervade the whole fabric of mundane transactions. Out of the contents of the thought thus revealed we may therefore be in a position to reconstruct the whole fabric, notwithstanding its being eclipsed.

Just this is the office of the Logic, or rather Metaphysics of History. "It has to furnish the principles of the inner connection and consistency of history, and has to define the character of those principles. By means of these it must become apparent what historical knowledge must be, that is, of what—according to the nature of things historical—knowledge ought to consist, so that the formations apt to ensue from the principles, "histories may be conceived in their inner necessity as a systematic unit." This is the formula circumscribing the scope of our science as given by Strodl. What the true idea is, namely, the consensus of principles underlying history, we believe to have convincingly set forth. Yet we may add in a closing remark, that:

Metaphysics of history.

Definition and scope of the metaphysics of history. Strodl.

Consensus of principles underlying history.

Inasmuch as the great design of the world is conceived in the Logos; and inasmuch as a development in freedom, answering the dignity of God and of man, was the necessary requisite even at the risk of intrusion on the part of the Bad and the evil:—we now can plainly see the inner consistency of this universal history, tho concealed under the mischief caused for the purpose of entangling and confusing the children of men.

The Great design of the world.

We observed the development from a germ to the new seed, under the aspect of a revelation of the eternal glory of the Logos, in the order of a gradual impartation of the Divine into the diversity of created life.

Gradual impartation of the Divine into the diversity of created life, reveals the eternal glory of the Logos.

This developing realisation is impossible without labor. It was designed and ordained from the outset that created life should actuate itself in concert with the Divine Will, even in that form which is inherent in the general order of things.

If the thought, the purpose of the world, had arranged matters so as to accomplish its designs without the resistance of a substance to be formed or worked upon with a view to its elevation—to accomplish its ends in a world of appearances and transient entities pure and simple without contrasts, the Beautiful could not have manifested its variety and ended in glory.

The developing realisation of glory impossible without the concurrent labor of created life, in concert with the Divine Will.

Where, without regard to the Bad, no concurring relations would have had to be adjusted, and where diverging and centripetal tendencies would not have had to be bent back and to be bound up in common interests: there could have been no exercise for the energies, no emulation, no vitality. Where the purpose of the world would have moved mechanically in its selfsufficiency, in rounds of everlasting repetition without impediment, without the conflict for maintaining selfhood against the multiplicity of distractions, there history would be inconceivable.

No exercise for the energies; and history would be inconceivable.

History as it is could not have been anything, if not the revelation of the glory of the Logos as the monistic unit, and as the intensum absolutum within the extensiveness of temporal and created multiplicity. Surely we are entitled, therefore, to speak of a Logic of History, which insists upon asserting its thought by facts—a Logic which, true to itself, persists in realising its ideality despite all the mischief and confusion wrought out by the lie.

A Logic of facts and truth despite the confusion wrought by the lie.

The thought which we found and dealt with under that name—so as not to confound it with the "idea" of Hegel, for instance—is not an indiscreet, capricious notion, but is—as the eternal and fundamental idea, necessary in itself and for its own sake—the truth. Hence it is not "a" Philosophy of History which is offered herewith.

Our "thought" (not to be confounded with the "idea" so much abused) is the idea necessary in itself and for its own sake, the truth.

In view of that idea—identical with and given in the ground-plan—any treatise of this kind is by virtue of the nature of its matter more than a philosophy. This book at least, despite its defects in diction and arrangement of detail, claims to contain more than that. If there be fallacies, they cannot invalidate the theme or underlying thought; the defects can only be charged against the mode of arguing, perhaps, and the legibility of the style.

Upon these premises is the treatise, here offered, more than a philosophy but The Philosophy of History.

Hence, its failings notwithstanding, the book is in essence

THE PHILOSOPHY OF HISTORY.